# AN INTRODUCTION TO
# PSYCHOLOGY

# AN INTRODUCTION TO
# PSYCHOLOGY
## THIRD EDITION

PATRICIA M. WALLACE ▲
University of Maryland

JEFFREY H. GOLDSTEIN
University of Utrecht
Netherlands

WCB Brown &
Benchmark
PUBLISHERS

Madison, Wisconsin • Dubuque, Iowa

**Book Team**

Associate Executive Editor  *Michael Lange*
Developmental Editor  *Sheralee Connors*
Production Editor  *Peggy Selle*
Designer  *Lu Ann Schrandt*
Art Editor  *Mary E. Powers*
Photo Editor  *Carol Judge*
Permissions Coordinator  *Gail I. Wheatley*
Visuals/Design Developmental Consultant  *Marilyn A. Phelps*
Visuals/Design Freelance Specialist  *Mary L. Christianson*
Marketing Manager  *Steven Yetter*
Advertising Manager  *Brett Apold*

## WCB Brown & Benchmark

A Division of Wm. C. Brown Communications, Inc.

Executive Vice President/General Manager  *Thomas E. Doran*
Vice President/Editor in Chief  *Edgar J. Laube*
Vice President/Sales and Marketing  *Eric Ziegler*
Director of Production  *Vickie Putman Caughron*
Director of Custom and Electronic Publishing  *Chris Rogers*

## Wm. C. Brown Communications, Inc.

President and Chief Executive Officer  *G. Franklin Lewis*
Corporate Senior Vice President and Chief Financial Officer  *Robert Chesterman*
Corporate Senior Vice President and President of Manufacturing  *Roger Meyer*

Cover credit © Santi Visalli/Image Bank

Copyedited by Barbara Day

The credits section for this book begins on page 543 and is considered an extension of the copyright page.

A Times Mirror Company

Library of Congress Catalog Card Number: 93–70402

ISBN 0–697–12757–5

Printed in the United States of America by Wm. C. Brown Communications, Inc., 2460 Kerper Boulevard, Dubuque, IA 52001

10  9  8  7  6  5  4  3  2  1

▼

BRIEF

# CONTENTS

# CONTENTS

# APPLYING PSYCHOLOGY

# CLOSE UP ON RESEARCH

# ▼ EXPLORING HUMAN DIVERSITY

# ▼

# PREFACE

About twelve years ago we began to develop a new textbook with a strikingly different approach for the introductory psychology course. Our goal was to create a comprehensive textbook that covered all the material for a solid introductory course, but did not become an encyclopedia in an effort to cover everything anyone might want included. We wanted the book to appeal to a broad range of students, from the eighteen-year-old fresh out of high school attending college full-time, to the person who combines career with college or the retired business person seeking enrichment. The examples used to illustrate psychological principles were chosen with this heterogeneous audience in mind. Problems at work, with children, with aging grandparents, with midlife, were all included along with discussions of the more common concerns of the traditional full-time college student.

We wanted to include excellent study aids for the students, and incorporate the study guide directly into the textbook to ensure that every student, not just those who could afford it, could take advantage of the kinds of structured review that psychologists know are critically important to subject mastery. Most professors, we've found, recommend the separate study guide if it is available, but do not require it. Students on tight budgets are likely to ignore the recommendation.

We knew that an affordable book was desperately needed. Shocked and dismayed by the skyrocketing cost of textbooks and their study guides, many students were slowly being priced out of education. Working with the publisher to eliminate unnecessary color and excessive white space; avoid expensive artwork, graphics, and photos; and rely on the paperback format, we found it was possible to offer a comprehensive textbook with an internal study guide at a very reasonable price. Many people are unaware of how much these features add to the cost of textbooks, and we knew that most of our colleagues and students would gladly forego them in the interest of saving money that could be better spent on reference works, journal subscriptions, on-line computer time, or next year's tuition.

That this textbook is now in its third edition testifies to the fact that thousands of students and professors agreed wholeheartedly with our approach. We haven't changed the basic approach for this edition, but we have done a great deal of updating and a certain amount of fine-tuning, based on very useful feedback from students and faculty who have been using it.

First, we broadened the nature of our examples and coverage still further by adding a much deeper exploration of human diversity. Your authors have spent a combined total of almost two decades living and working in foreign countries, and it was very natural for us to add to the book's cultural dimension. In addition to describing the research in the area, we've drawn from our personal experiences in different cultures and our professional relationships with psychologists around the world. We've also added more material about diversity within the United States, exploring the role of culture, gender, and ethnicity in behavior, and squarely addressing the nature and problems of a multicultural society. We developed a new box, one that highlights how the chapter's subject relates to human diversity. Examples include "Marketing to Ethnic Groups," "Sex Differences in the Brain," "Growing Old in America: Ethnic Minority Senior Citizens," "Ethnic Identity," and "Why Do Indochinese Students Excel in American Schools?"

Second, we made one change in the table of contents so that we could add a new chapter, Health Psychology, without increasing the total number of chapters. Social Psychology and Group Processes have now been combined into one chapter, Social Behavior, leaving room to examine some very timely issues concerning the relationship between psychology and health.

Third, we added a new section to each chapter's study guide, one that includes some open-ended questions about the subject to stimulate discussion and critical thinking. These questions are thought-provoking ones, encouraging students to examine how the material in the chapter relates to their own personal experiences, and how the material can be applied.

A complete instructional package also accompanies this text. An **Instructor's Manual** with **Test Item File** of over 2,000 test questions, prepared by R. Eric Landrum of Boise State University, Teresa Landrum and Steven A. Schneider of Pima Community College, is available. The Instructor's Manual includes chapter summaries, chapter outlines, key terms, discussion questions, essay questions, lecture suggestions, and film suggestions. The Test Item File includes more than 2,000 multiple-choice questions. Each multiple-choice item is page-referenced to the text and identified as factual, conceptual, or applied.

The questions in the test item file are available on *MicroTest III,* a powerful but easy-to-use test generating program by Chariot Software Group. MicroTest is available for DOS, Windows, and Macintosh personal computers. With MicroTest, an instructor can easily select the questions from the test item file and print a test and answer key. You can customize questions, headings, and instructions, you can add or import questions of your own, and you can print your test in a choice of fonts if your printer supports them. Instructors can obtain a copy of *MicroTest III* by contacting your local Brown & Benchmark sales representative or by phoning Educational Resources at 800-338-5371.

The *Brown & Benchmark Reference Disks,* created by Lester Sdorow of Beaver College, are available free to adopters. The disks include over 15,000 journal and book references arranged in files by introductory topics. The complete set of five disks is available in either IBM 5.25- or 3.5-inch size.

The *Brown & Benchmark Introductory Psychology Transparency or Slide Set* includes approximately 150 full-color acetates or slides specifically designed for classroom use.

*The Critical Thinker,* by Richard E. Mayer and Fiona M. Goodchild, both of the University of California, Santa Barbara, uses excerpts from introductory psychology textbooks to encourage critical thinking. This 80-page booklet is available free to adopters.

The *Instructor's Course Planning System* is a convenient and flexible housing unit for all of your print ancillaries. The *Course Planner* can be arranged by chapter in separate hanging file folders, along with an unbound copy of each text chapter, your own notes, the *Student Study Guide,* and the *Transparency Sets,* allowing you to keep all of your classroom materials organized and at your fingertips.

The *Brown & Benchmark Customized Reader* allows you to select over 100 journal or magazine articles from a menu provided by your sales representative. These readings will be custom-printed for your students and bound into an attractive 8 1/2 x 11 book, giving you the opportunity to tailor-make your own student reader.

Our *Custom Publishing Service* will also allow you to have your own notes, handouts, or other classroom materials printed and bound for your course use very inexpensively. See your Brown & Benchmark representative for details.

A *Customized Transparency Program* is available to adopters of our text based on the number of textbooks ordered. Consult your Brown & Benchmark representative for ordering policies.

A large selection of videotapes is also available to adopters based on the number of textbooks ordered directly from Brown & Benchmark by your bookstore.

*The Brain/Anatomy Software Program,* a four-level SuperCard™ program, teaches the basic neuroanatomy of a primate brain. Students can browse through the brain, organize structures into systems, and request anatomical or functional information about any specific structure or system. One copy is available on adoption or it can be shrink-wrapped with our text for a small addition cost.

*The Psychology Disk* is a set of 10 interactive simulations of psychology experiments designed for student use. The disk can be used with IBM and compatible hardware. Your bookstore can order *The Psychology Disk* directly from Brown & Benchmark.

*The Brain Modules on Videodisc,* created by WNET New York, Antenne 2 TV/France, the Annenberg/CPB Foundation, and Professor Frank J. Vattano of Colorado State University, is based on the Peabody Award-winning series "The Brain." Thirty segments, averaging 6 minutes each, vividly illustrate an array of psychology topics. Consult your Brown & Benchmark sales representative for details on this or any other of our textbook supplements.

# ACKNOWLEDGMENTS

We would like to thank the following psychologists, whose reviews of the three editions of *Introduction to Psychology* have helped improve its clarity, coherence, and accuracy:

Ivan R. Applebaum, Valencia Community College
Seymour H. Baron, Kent State University
Janet Belew, University of New Mexico
J.J. Berry, Oakland Community College
David Brodzinsky, Rutgers University
Jack I. Bushey, Harrisburg Area Community College
Frank Calabrese, Community College of Philadelphia
Kathryn Jennings Cooper, College of Redwoods
Virginia A. Diehl, Western Illinois University
William O. Dwyer, Memphis State University
Adeline E. Fain, Forsyth Technical Community College
Ira Fischler, University of Florida
Leslie E. Fisher, Cleveland State University
Robert Folger, Southern Methodist University
Lawrence Froman, Towson State University
Sara Gerling, Skidmore College
C. James Goodwin, Wheeling Jesuit College
Richard A. Griggs, University of Florida
John P. Hall, University of Houston-Downtown Campus
Bruce Hinrichs, Anoka-Ramsey Community College
Gordon K. Hodge, University of New Mexico
John H. Hummel, University of Houston-Downtown Campus
Doris Ivie, Pellissippi State Community College
Paul S. Kaplan, Suffolk County Community College
Patricia A. Kiernan, Bluefield State College
Alan R. King, Southern University in New Orleans
Stephen B. Klein, Old Dominion University

R. Eric Landrum, Boise State University
Gil Leary, Southern University at New Orleans
Timothy Lehmann, Valencia Community College
Charles R. Martin-Stanley, Central State University
Donald McBurney, University of Pittsburgh
Anna M. Nemec, Macon Junior College
Michael O'Hara, University of Iowa
Diana Oxley, Bank Street College, NYC
Michele A. Paludi, Kent State University
Frederick J. Parenté, Towson State University
Holly A. Pennock, Hudson Valley Community College
Norman J. Presse, Dalton College
Shirley Pritchett, North Eastern Texas Community College
Thomas M. Randall, Rhode Island College
Rebecca Reviere, Darton College
Steven A. Schneider, Pima Community College
E. Dean Schroeder, Laramie County Community College
John Turnbull, Connors State College
Michael G. Walraven, Jackson Community College
Leonard J. Williams, University of South Dakota
Herbert L. Ziegler, Chesapeake College
Elizabeth Zoltan-Ford, Towson State University

We thank Nicole Dresnin and Victor Perlman, students at Temple University, for helping to make *Introduction to Psychology,* Third Edition, even more user-friendly; Pawel Mlicki, for his thoughtful, helpful, and always grammatically correct comments; and John Floyd and colleagues at the University of Maryland European Division, who met with us in Heidelberg, Germany, for their many helpful ideas about teaching the introductory course with *Introduction to Psychology*.

▼

# HOW TO USE THIS (OR ANY) TEXTBOOK

## BECOME ACQUAINTED WITH THE BOOK

A textbook is a tool for learning and, like all good tools, has its proper uses. For whom was the book written? What are the authors hoping to accomplish? What are students expected to learn? This information can be found in the Preface.

Unlike a novel, a textbook is not necessarily to be read straight through from first page to last. Many people just begin reading a textbook on page one and continue until they finish, fall asleep, get bored, or find something better to do. This would not provide you with much of a framework for understanding the material.

Look at the *Table of Contents.* Notice that it is organized into topics, such as Biological Bases of Behavior, Sensation and Perception, Motivation and Emotion, Personality. These give you an idea of what psychology is about. A glance at the *Subject Index* provides a finer focus on the many areas included in *Introduction to Psychology,* Third Edition.

Pick a chapter, any chapter. Notice that it begins with a detailed *Chapter Outline.* This shows the chapter's overall organization. It will allow you to anticipate topics that are to follow as you read the chapter, it will permit you to locate desired material easily, and to see how it is related to other material. For example, in **Chapter 12, Abnormal Psychology,** Depression and Suicide are listed as Mood Disorders under the larger topic of Categories of Abnormal Behavior.

Using the *Chapter Outline,* form a map in your mind of the contents of the chapter. Then, as you read, you will be filling in the outline with details rather than charting unknown territory.

The Chapter Outline is followed by a numbered list of *Learning Objectives.* These are things we hope you will learn from the chapter, and the pages on which the material is introduced. The Learning Objectives will help you focus your study on selected questions and check your knowledge of the material. For example, after reading Chapter 12 you should be able to impress your friends by describing different kinds of conflict (Learning Objective 1), use the term "ego defense mechanisms" properly (Learning Objective 2), and talk intelligently about how

conflict and frustration relate to drug abuse and depression (Learning Objective 3).

As you thumb through the chapter, you will see key words in **boldface,** and definitions in *italics.* Following each major section is a fill-in-the-blank *Guided Review* geared to the Learning Objectives. A complete, page-referenced outline *Summary* is followed by a page-referenced *Action Glossary,* in which key terms are to be matched with their definitions.

About twenty multiple-choice questions appear in a *Self-Test.* These questions are referenced both to Learning Objectives and text pages. They allow you to check your learning and refer to chapter material that may require further study. They are also helpful in preparing for multiple-choice tests.

*Introduction to Psychology,* Third Edition can only deal with selected, even if the most important, aspects of psychology. A list of *Suggested Readings* at the end of each chapter will help you dig deeper into topics of interest.

In each chapter some material is highlighted by being set apart. Highlights include topics of special interest, material that does not fit easily within the body of the chapter, research, cultural variations, and applications.

Read a few of the sections that seem interesting to you. This will give you a better idea of a psychological approach to these topics.

## HOW TO STUDY

In Chapter 5 you will learn about learning. We don't think you should have to wait until midway through this course to learn how to study efficiently. So here is a preview of what you will find in Chapter 5.

### Develop a Personal Study Style

Try to create the best possible atmosphere for studying. Make sure you are in a situation where you can concentrate. Obviously, in order to learn something you must first pay attention to it. You will not learn what you've just read if you were singing along with the radio. Many people find that background music helps them concentrate by masking out occasional outside noises and creating a pleasant, predictable atmosphere. If you usually listen to music while studying, try studying without it for a few days and see whether you are able to concentrate better.

Create regular study habits. Block out study time in your daily schedule, perhaps early in the morning or after dinner. It is generally thought that you should study two hours for each hour of class time.

## Techniques for Learning from Textbooks

There is a lot of material to learn in the introductory psychology course—definitions, theories, research, important names, to say nothing of the stimulating and dynamic ideas you'll be expected to know.

Some of psychology's theories and research may strike you as frivolous or trivial. We think that many students find studies of laboratory rats uninteresting if not down-right silly. Yet thousands of researchers study laboratory animals. Regardless of what you may think, these are not stupid people—for one thing, nearly all of them have Ph.D.'s from respectable universities. How can intelligent people spend their professional lives studying rats? Don't stop merely by asking the question, try to answer it! How *can* intelligent people devote themselves to rodents in the lab? What assumptions and ideas justify this research? What have psychologists learned from it? Try to understand the phenomenon from their point of view. If you still do not find this research convincing, you will at least understand the rationale behind it. We could ask nothing more of students than that they try to understand psychology as psychologists understand it.

## Practice SQ3R

One method for helping you store textbook information is *SQ3R,* which stands for:

1. Survey
2. Question
3. Read
4. Recite
5. Review

*Survey* the chapter by looking at the Outline and leafing through it. Read the Learning Objectives and Summary.

*Question* yourself to make sure you have a clear idea of the chapter's contents, how they are arranged, and what the main points are going to be. You should be able to close the book and describe the main points of the chapter.

What do you already know about the subject? Relating new material to familiar ideas makes it easier to grasp.

The third step is to begin *Reading*. Don't try to read fifty pages at one time. It is better to stop and perform the other two "R's" after you have completed each major subheading. This is due to the effect of "spaced trials" on learning. Fifty pages of technical, information-packed prose is too much for most people to absorb at one sitting. So don't study everything at once. Break the material down into smaller units and study one chunk at a time. Once you've learned a chunk, go on to the next unit of material. By spacing your studies in this way, you'll be studying psychology several times per week, rather than say, just on Friday afternoons. "Cramming" for five hours the night before an exam is unlikely to produce as good results as studying for one hour on each of the five nights before an exam. The total amount of time you study will be the same, but the way you distribute that time will improve your grasp of the material.

Close the book and *Recite* **in your own words** the main points of the section you have just finished reading.

*Introduction to Psychology* is not a novel (for all we know, it may contain some fiction, but character development and plot are weak). It is a tool to help you meet specific learning objectives, such as understanding ego defense mechanisms. After reviewing a section, try to restate the important points in your own words. If you have difficulty doing this, review the material again. If you still cannot state its meaning, that should be the cue to ask your instructor for clarification. If you feel uncomfortable asking a question in a large class, ask it outside of class hours, or even put the question in writing and give it anonymously to your instructor. But do ask questions about material you don't fully understand. Trust us, they will be appreciated. Questions about the contents of the course are almost always welcome, particularly in contrast to the questions typically asked about tests, grades, and unexcused absences.

Use "mnemonic devices" to help you remember lists. Mnemonic devices are common tools in many professions, particularly those that require a great deal of memorization. Musicians all know "Every Good Boy Does Fine."

You can use the "method of loci" to remember lists: associate each item in a list with the parts of a well-known physical location, such as your house. Imagine a tour of your house. Make a mental association between the places on your tour and each item or idea you must remember. For example, imagine the front door blocked with apples, the living room floor covered with butter, the dining room table stinking of vinegar, and so on.

The final step is to *Review* the new material. Check on the information you were not able to recall in the "recite" step. By reviewing what you learn as you go along, you will find that your knowledge is cumulative, that ideas build upon and are related to one another. Occasionally, say while walking to class, riding the bus, doing dishes, before going to sleep, repeat to yourself the main points of a chapter or a lecture.

In *Introduction to Psychology,* Third Edition, we provide a **Guided Review** at the end of each section to help you with the "review" process. Read a single section of the chapter (about 10 pages), then recite and review it. As long as you have performed the "survey" step well, you will be able to integrate the material into the overall theme of the chapter. Stopping after shorter segments will also encourage learning to be spread out over time.

When studying a textbook or a report with no outlines, few subheadings, no key words or summaries, the SQ3R method will be valuable. You can use it for studying manuals on fixing a Volkswagen, reports on nuclear power plant accidents, articles in *Psychological Review,* and just about anything else.

We have designed each chapter with a built-in study system that will actively engage you in learning. No separate study guide is required. The text includes many devices designed to help you study, learn, and use the material.

## A Word on Social Studying

Social psychologists know the importance of group support and mutual give-and-take discussion. Law students, medical students, and other graduate students often study in small groups.

How does a group study? Everyone must read all the assigned material, of course. But each person is also responsible for learning a portion of the material especially well, becoming, at least as far as the group is concerned, a "specialist." Each member of the study group is to explain the important points of that material to the rest of the group, telling them the most important ideas, providing clear definitions of key terms, describing important research.

You might find this an enjoyable and effective way to study. Exchange names, telephone numbers, and available study times with your classmates. From three to five people can get together for an hour or so each week (more than five or six students have a tendency to erupt into a party). Study groups are no substitute for reading and studying each assignment thoroughly. But they are an additional way to learn the material, rehearse it in a coherent way, and practice using it.

## Reward Yourself for Learning

If you are like us, you'll treat yourself to something for finishing major tasks. After writing this introduction, for example, we're going out for coffee.

The rewards may even help your studies. Research on problem solving (discussed in Chapter 7) finds that putting a problem aside for a time, and engaging in an unrelated activity, can aid in finding a solution (a process known as "incubation"). So reward has its own virtues.

## Enjoy Your Studies

We love psychology enough to have made it our life's work. If you approach psychology with the proper attitude, you, too, will find it surprising, exciting, and at times infuriatingly difficult. That it is difficult is neither surprising nor exciting: People are complex, and cannot easily be studied scientifically. We hope you will come to appreciate the difficulties facing psychologists who try to understand the human animal.

# PART I

## INTRODUCTION TO PSYCHOLOGY

# CHAPTER 1

## PSYCHOLOGY: APPLICATIONS
### OUTLINE

▶ **Learning Objectives**

▶ **Psychology: A Subject for and about People**

- ■ Psychology: What Is It?
- ■ Who Are Psychologists?

▶ **Guided Review**

▶ **The Psychological Approach to Behavior**

- ■ Observing Behavior
  Levels of Analysis
  Hypotheses and Theories
- ■ Research Strategies
  Descriptive Research
  Experimental Studies
  Advanced Experimental
  Designs
  Experiments Using Animals

▶ **Guided Review**

▶ **Perspectives in Psychology**

- ■ Historical Schools of Thought
- ■ Behaviorism
- ■ Cognitive Psychology
- ■ Psychoanalysis
- ■ Humanistic Psychology
- ■ Sociocultural Perspective
- ■ Biological Perspective

▶ **Comparing the Perspectives**

▶ **Guided Review**

▶ **Applying Psychology**

- ■ Applied and Basic Research
- ■ Giving Psychology Away

▶ **Guided Review**

▶ **Summary**

▶ **Action Glossary**

▶ **Self-Test**

▶ **Thinking About Psychology**

▶ **Suggested Readings**

# PSYCHOLOGY: APPLICATIONS
## LEARNING OBJECTIVES

**After reading this chapter, you should be able to**

► **1.** define psychology and provide descriptive examples of the kind of subject matter psychologists investigate. *(p. 4)*

► **2.** provide examples of the kind of work psychologists do in educational institutions, government, business, and private practice. *(pp. 4-6)*

► **3.** explain the fundamental elements of the scientific approach to the study of behavior. *(pp. 7-10)*

► **4.** describe and provide examples of descriptive and experimental research in psychology and state the advantages and disadvantages of each. *(pp. 10-16)*

► **5.** describe historical approaches to the study of psychology and identify the founders of each school of thought. *(pp. 17-18)*

► **6.** describe six modern perspectives in psychology. *(pp. 18-22)*

► **7.** define and provide examples of applied and basic research in psychology. *(pp. 23-24)*

## PSYCHOLOGY: A SUBJECT FOR AND ABOUT PEOPLE

Thousands of babies were born today, starting out life gasping for their first breath, seeking comfort from human contact, eager to get nourishment to survive. Some were born in a hospital, many more were born at home. Their similarities are obvious; barring birth defects or injuries, they came into this world today sharing the standard issue of human equipment, the features that identify us all as members of the same species. But their differences, even from the first day of life, are also quite remarkable.

As they continue through their lives, many more differences will emerge. Some will be exposed to troubled, even devastating early environments, others will enjoy the nurturance of warm and caring homes. Each of them will experience a different world. Some will grow up in an industrialized country filled with computers, TVs, and spacecraft; others will experience much less of this, but perhaps more family, tradition, and sense of community.

What will happen to each of these infants? How will all the forces acting on them combine to affect how they think, what they do, and what they will become? How will their own goals and strivings add to their potential and counteract negative influences? Perhaps another Mozart was born today, whose enormous talents and hard work will leave us a gift to enjoy for many generations to come. Will any of them be like Anne Frank, whose optimism and kindness survived inside a culture filled with horrors most of us could never imagine? Will one of them have the determination, passion, and leadership of Martin Luther King, whose legacy continues to inspire the oppressed? Will one of them become a serial killer, apparently lacking any sense of guilt?

If you wonder about why people do what they do, you are in the right course. Welcome to psychology.

### Psychology: What Is It?

**Psychology** *is the scientific study of behavior and mental processes.* This is a straightforward definition and one easily italicized in a text and memorized for a midterm exam. In the last decade of the twentieth century, it is the one that most psychologists would endorse. Behind these words though, is a sprawling, multifaceted field that is growing and changing like the living organisms it studies. Virtually every word in this definition, with the possible exception of "the," has been the subject of heated debates and constant reevaluation. Is psychology a science?

Should we study only overt behavior? Should we include studies of mental processes and consciousness even though we usually can't observe them firsthand—at least not yet?

The answers to these questions have changed with psychology's growth of knowledge and methods, and the definition of psychology has changed with it. The issue of whether psychology involves the study of behavior, of mental processes, or both has been a particularly sticky one. Although early definitions of psychology emphasized mental states and consciousness, the field went through a long period in the twentieth century in which most psychologists, especially American ones, confined their attention to overt behavior only. They were reluctant to hypothesize about thoughts, dreams, or other internal states they could not easily measure or see with their own eyes. With the recent explosion of interest in how people think and what they think about, and especially with the invention of new technology to study brain activity, most psychologists now favor the inclusion of "mental processes" in the field's official definition.

### Who Are Psychologists?

If the woman sitting next to you on an airplane says she is a physician, you will probably make many assumptions about how she treats the sick, sees patients, and makes rounds in a hospital. You could be quite wrong—perhaps she is a researcher who spends most of her time analyzing blood samples. If the man on the other side says he is a psychologist, what assumptions would you make? From long experience, we know that most people would assume he deals with abnormal human behavior. Again, you could be quite wrong.

Given the enormous range of the field, it isn't surprising that the public is confused about who psychologists are and what they do. One specialty is clinical psychology, which involves the diagnosis and treatment of behavioral disorders. Another is physiological psychology, which is the study of the relationship between physiology and behavior. Social psychologists are interested in the way people behave in group settings. Other specialties are listed in table 1.1.

The kind of work psychologists do is equally diverse. You might have assumed that the man on the plane has a private practice and sees patients, but actually a minority of psychologists in the United States work in this kind of setting (see table 1.2). The largest proportion of doctoral-level psychologists work in academic settings, teaching psychology and doing research. An academic psychologist

## TABLE 1.1 Specialties in psychology

| Specialty | Description | Percent of Doctoral-level Psychologists |
|---|---|---|
| Clinical | Diagnosis and treatment of emotional and behavioral disorders. | 44 |
| Counseling and Guidance | Deals with personal problems not classified as illnesses, such as vocational and social problems of college students. | 11 |
| Developmental | Studies behavioral changes that occur during growth and development of an organism. | 4 |
| Educational | Studies ways to apply psychological principles to the educational setting. | 6 |
| School | Does testing, guidance, and research in the schools. | 5 |
| Experimental | Usually does research on topics such as perception, sensation, or memory, using either human or animal subjects. (Since many kinds of psychologists perform experiments, this category is not well named.) | 3 |
| Comparative | Studies the behavior of animals, often in natural settings. | 0.3 |
| Physiological | Studies the relationship between behavior and physiology. | 1 |
| Industrial/Organizational | Does research on human behavior in work settings, and applies psychological principles to business and management problems. | 6 |
| Personality | Studies the individual characteristics that account for each person's unique adjustments to the environment. | 0.8 |
| Psychometrics | Does research and development work on psychological tests and measurements, including IQ tests, vocational interest tests, and personality measures. | 0.8 |
| Social | Studies social interactions and the ways that human beings influence one another's behavior in group settings. | 3 |
| Psychology, General | | 2 |

From "Census of Psychological Personnel: 1983" by J. Stapp, A. M. Tucker, and G. R. VandenBos *American Psychologist*, Vol. 40, pp. 1317–1351. Copyright 1985 by the American Psychological Association. Reprinted by permission.

## TABLE 1.2 Employment settings of psychologists

| Setting | Percent |
|---|---|
| University settings | 18.3 |
| Four-year colleges | 4.7 |
| Other academic settings (two-year colleges, medical schools, etc.) | 6.3 |
| Schools and other educational settings | 14.9 |
| Independent practice | 17.5 |
| Hospitals | 8.9 |
| Clinics | 9.6 |
| Other human services (counseling centers, rape centers, child abuse centers, hot lines, etc.) | 8.1 |
| Business and government (consulting firms, government research organizations, criminal justice system, government agencies, private research, etc.) | 12.2 |

From "Census of Psychological Personnel: 1983" by J. Stapp, A. M. Tucker, and G. R. VandenBos. *American Psychologist*, Vol. 40, pp.1317–1351. Copyright 1985 by the American Psychological Association. Reprinted by permission.

whose specialty is physiological psychology might teach several courses, supervise a laboratory containing hundreds of rabbits in cages, do research on how the animal responds to an airpuff directed to the eye, publish the findings, and attend conferences. Some might say, but what do rabbits' eyelids have to do with psychology? As you will see as you continue your course, studies of animals have provided enormous insights about human behavior, and we've learned a great deal about what happens in the brain during learning from bunnies. We are not that interested in the rabbit's eyelid; we are very interested in how the brain changes with experience.

More and more psychologists are leaving the laboratory and entering business and government to apply psychological principles to real world problems. For example, someone with a background in comparative psychology might report to work at 5:30 every morning to a prairie-dog town, to observe the behavior of these very social

## CLOSE UP ON RESEARCH
### The Psychology of Psychology

One of the most interesting research topics in psychology is the field of psychology itself: how it is changing, who is entering it, who is succeeding, who is failing, why people choose it, and where it is going next.

Ray Over, for example, a psychologist at LaTrobe University in Australia, has conducted some interesting studies of the publications in psychological journals. In one study he found that since 1949, the number of papers published with more than one author has been growing considerably (Over, 1982a). This could mean that the pursuit of knowledge in psychology is becoming less and less a "lone-wolf" occupation. Research studies are more likely to involve teams of researchers with different specializations and complementary expertise. He also found that psychologists rarely list their names in alphabetical order on their published papers. Instead, they tend to list the authors according to how much each contributed to the research project. This is sometimes very difficult to do when more than two or three people are involved.

Several researchers have examined publication patterns to determine how men and women fare and whether there might be differences in either the productivity or recognition of men and women. One study measured research productivity by the number of papers published per year (Over, 1982b). Women published significantly fewer papers than men, but judging from the number of times each paper was cited in other articles, the quality of those papers appeared to be the same. Nevertheless, the top awards in most disciplines usually go to the prolific scientists, and psychology is no exception. The barriers and difficulties women face in a career in psychology seem to parallel those in other fields. They have more trouble finding jobs, they are promoted more slowly, and they are paid less than men with comparable qualifications.

Perhaps of more concern than the race or gender of the researcher is the nature of the subjects, which can affect the results and conclusions of research studies and limit the researchers' ability to make generalizations about their findings. Psychologists have historically studied people who were readily available, and most of them were young white middle-class men in college. Many are troubled by this lack of diversity, calling the field "womanless" or "raceless" (Graham, 1992). Fortunately, the problem is recognized and most psychologists are taking extra efforts to study a broader range of human beings.

rodents and gain insights about how industrial development might affect them. Studies of animal behavior are essential to protect our endangered species and prevent new construction from damaging our environment.

A social psychologist working for a government agency might be asked to study ways to control crowds at sports events, where numerous tragedies have occurred because of the intense excitement generated by close games and simmering antagonism. An educational psychologist working for a high school might be exploring ways to introduce computer-based instruction and provide training for the faculty. An experimental psychologist who performs research in cognitive psychology might be invited to appear as an expert witness at a murder trial to discuss how the key witness's recollection of events might be affected by the prosecutor's leading questions.

If the man on the plane is a clinical psychologist, his typical day could also be quite varied. He might be seeing patients in his own private practice, helping people overcome their fear of heights, their drug abuse, or their sexual problems. He might work in a hospital, holding group sessions for veterans who continue to have nightmares years after a war.

Outside the United States, the profile of psychologists is similar, although developing countries appear to have more people trained in the discipline working as health service providers, especially in clinical, counseling, and school psychology, rather than as researchers (Rosenzweig, 1992).

Psychologists specialize in behavior, but they are not the only ones interested in the subject. Partly because so many people believe psychologists are mainly interested in abnormal behavior, we are often confused with psychiatrists. In terms of education, psychologists usually have a bachelor's degree plus an advanced degree such as a Ph.D. (Doctor of Philosophy). Psychiatrists are medical doctors with an M.D. who specialize in behavioral disorders after attending medical school. Other professions that overlap psychology's interest include sociologists, who study groups and institutions within a society, and anthropologists, who are concerned with the physical and cultural origins and development of the human species.

Psychology's diverse origins and contemporary range of subjects is patently obvious in the library, and very frustrating to students (and authors) trying to locate books. Relevant materials are found in the psychology area, but also in sociology, anthropology, ethology, medicine, physiology, business, and even law. Students working on term papers trek up and down stairs and aisles carrying armloads of books from every floor. And why not? We have chosen for ourselves a subject that embraces every living thing on the planet, and understanding may come from many directions.

▶ **GUIDED REVIEW** *Learning Objectives 1 and 2*

1. Psychology is the study of _____, both of human beings and other animals. Many psychologists add the words "and mental processes" to the definition of psychology to emphasize that mental activities are also appropriate topics for psychological investigation.
2. The term _____ refers to specialists in psychology who have advanced graduate degrees in the field.
3. Psychologists usually specialize in subfields such as _____ (which deals with the relationship between biology and behavior), or _____ (which deals with the diagnosis and treatment of behavioral disorders). Other subfields include social psychology, developmental psychology, and comparative psychology.

*Answers*

1. behavior 2. psychologist 3. physiological psychology, clinical psychology

## THE PSYCHOLOGICAL APPROACH TO BEHAVIOR

The 200th anniversary issue of the Old Farmer's Almanac (1992) describes the Gemini, whose birthday falls between May 21 and June 20, as intellectual with a strong ability to communicate with others. Predictions are made for the coming year: September 23 through October 22 is a good time for love and recreation; January 20 through February 19 is optimal for travel, meeting new people, and having fun. Hungary, Kenya, and Kansas City are cited as places that offer new opportunities for the Gemini. Candidates for good mates are Libra, Aquarius, Aries, Leo, and Sagittarius all of whom, incidentally, are directed to quite different destinations for their travel enjoyment. (Gemini's new opportunities apparently don't include finding a suitable mate.)

The astrologer who writes these descriptions and predictions is no less interested in behavior than a psychologist. Indeed, many of our goals are the same. Both strive to describe, understand, predict, and control behavior. The element that sets the psychological approach apart from other means of knowing and understanding behavior

is the method. The astrologer looks for relationships between human behavior and the movement of celestial bodies, often ignoring evidence that contradicts the reliability of the technique. The psychologist relies on the scientific approach to find answers to the puzzles of behavior, with its strict rules of evidence and rigorous deduction.

The scientific approach carries a number of assumptions, and has several characteristics that distinguish it from other ways of finding truth and knowing about the world. Its most important assumption is **determinism.** *This means that events have causes and that scientists, at least, theoretically, can find out what those causes are.* Without this assumption it would be fruitless to try to determine why people behave as they do or to try to control or change their behavior.

One of the features that distinguishes the psychological approach from nonscientific approaches to behavior is that it emphasizes the use of empirical evidence collected by careful observation, experimentation, and measurement to demonstrate relationships between events. Much of what we think we know and understand about the world comes from anecdotal evidence, in which insights about behavior are derived from a single incident. A father who noticed that his week-old infant stuck out her tongue when he did might conclude that infants can mimic the facial expressions of their parents. This single observation would not satisfy the requirements of science; a scientist would need to conduct carefully controlled tests to gather empirical evidence in order to demonstrate that the infant's mimicry was reliable, predictable, and not just a pleasing coincidence.

Another important ingredient in the scientific approach is the requirement that findings should be openly published, and others should be able to replicate them if they set up the same conditions. Replication is particularly important. Since there is always variability in the way people behave, even when the conditions are identical, psychologists must draw conclusions from their data with great care. As we shall discuss again later, chance alone can affect the data, particularly in research studies involving small numbers of people. A single study cannot prove a hypothesis—it can only fail to reject it.

To illustrate some differences between the scientific approach and other approaches, consider a comparison among physics, psychology, and philosophy. Physicists might investigate the effects of gravity on the behavior of particles by carefully collecting data in different gravity environments, such as on the Earth, on the moon, or in space. They would use the empirical data to support or refute hypotheses, make predictions about what might happen on Venus, or on a space station with artificial gravity, and attempt to confirm or refute the predictions—all using empirical evidence and replication.

Although the subject matter is different, the approach in psychology is generally the same. Psychologists studying how children respond to different teaching methods in math would collect evidence by actually observing and testing children who were experiencing several different teaching methods, to gather data on their effectiveness. Replications would also be essential to ensure that the findings were not the result of chance—that, unknown to the researcher, one group of children contained a few "superstars" who were already studying calculus at home. Physicists, psychologists, and others who use the scientific approach are all forming hypotheses about relationships among variables, designing studies to test their hypotheses, collecting empirical evidence, drawing conclusions from the data about whether their hypothesis was confirmed or refuted, communicating their findings to others, and replicating their results.

In contrast, philosophers do not use the scientific approach to arrive at conclusions. A philosopher exploring the concept of justice might reflect on the nature of morality in humans, the use of punishment, or the concepts of good and evil. Although they might use examples to illustrate their ideas—and to counter rebuttals—they would not systematically collect empirical evidence to confirm or refute, and they would not set up experiments to test their hypotheses. They do not use a scientific approach because it isn't appropriate for the questions they explore. Consider the question of capital punishment. Although science can be used to determine whether it deters crime or saves money, it cannot help us decide whether it is moral or just.

## Observing Behavior

In India, cows adorned with garlands and tassels roam the streets, browse for food at marketplace stalls, break into private gardens, and cause traffic jams as they pause for a rest in busy intersections. The Hindi consider the cow to be sacred and have many laws protecting them; they even maintain special old age homes to care for beasts past their prime free of charge. Farmers who own cows regard them as members of the family and cow slaughter is prohibited. Hindi do not eat their cows, despite the frequency of

famine in their own human population. To beef-loving Westerners, the sight of starving people in the midst of millions of protected cows seems cruelly irrational and many experts hold the opinion that cow worship is the main cause of India's hunger and poverty.

The first step in the psychological approach is to describe behavior such as the cow worship in India. The most important tool we have to do it properly is objectivity. **Objectivity** *requires that events in the environment be observed as dispassionately as possible,* without usual human prejudices and emotional distortions.

This is not as easy as it seems. We have many expectations and preconceived ideas about how and why people do the things they do, and about what should be. Our ideas about the value of human life, for example, especially compared to the value of cows, make it very difficult to be objective in India. Rather than just describing the scene in the marketplace, we edge toward explaining and then attempting to control behavior. We seek a reason for what appears to a Westerner to be a suicidal religious doctrine, and then a method to change it.

Adhering to objectivity is obviously difficult in foreign cultures, but it is a challenge within one's own culture as well. The little girl in figure 1.1 has a forlorn expression but any inference about the context is hazardous. She might have lost her dog, she might be recovering from a temper tantrum, or she might be simply exhausted from a hike in the woods.

An objective description of an event should describe the people, their clothing, their postures and positions relative to one another, their facial expressions, their movements, their voices and words, and the environment. The description might offer hypotheses about the motives or emotions of the people, but it should make it clear that these are inferences and not objective observations. When information about an event is limited, the observer tends to draw inferences in order to complete the picture and put together a coherent and understandable happening. Often these inferences are inaccurate or biased due to faulty memory, prejudices, and stereotypes.

The inferences we might make about cow worship in the Hindu marketplace could be extremely wide of the mark, and our attempts to improve the situation based on them could be disastrous. Rather than being an irrational and suicidal cultural taboo, cow worship could be preserving Hindu small-scale farming and preventing even greater starvation and chaos that might result from trying to switch

**Figure 1.1** *An objective description of this photo would describe the child's clothes, position, and facial expression but would be cautious about inferring the causes or context.*

**Figure 1.2** *Behavior can be described on many levels, ranging from the physiological level to the social and political levels.*

# A NOTE ON NOTATION

Psychologists use a special method to identify references to specific articles, books, research studies, or monographs. Rather than including superscript numbers next to the material referenced in the text and footnotes on the bottom of each page, we put the name of the author (or authors) and the year of publication in parentheses right after the material it references in the text. If the author's name is mentioned in the text, the parentheses would usually only contain the year of publication. Sometimes the parentheses contain citations for more than one publication. You can locate the full citation in the reference list at the end of this book, which is arranged alphabetically by author.

to western-style agribusiness and the mass migration to the cities that accompanies it (Harris, 1974).

*Levels of Analysis*  The boys in figure 1.2 have their fists up and appear quite distressed. We might infer that a fight is going on, or about to start. While this description is accurate and objective, it is limited to one level of analysis. Behavior can be described on many levels, ranging from the physiological to the social and political.

On the physiological level, we might discuss the heart rate or blood pressure of the boys or the amount of hormones circulating in their bodies. Emotional behavior, including aggression, is related to a number of physiological changes, and we could easily have mentioned some of them in the description.

Any description and explanation of the boys' behaviors would be more complete if it included a discussion of previous experience. For instance, the boys' parents might have rewarded their sons for aggressive, dominating behavior from the time they started interacting with other children.

A social explanation of the incident might point to imitation: the boys may be copying behavior they see all the time in a TV detective series which is amply rewarded with stardom, high ratings, and letters from fans. On a political level of analysis, we might describe the scene in terms of the American culture and the nation's role in the world. Boys are often encouraged to be fairly aggressive in the United States. Collecting military weaponry is a common pastime for many children.

Which explanation is correct? They all are. Any human behavior can be described and explained on many levels; a complete explanation should include reference to several levels. Human behavior is so complex that it rarely has a single cause on a single level. When we try to predict a behavior like aggression, it becomes apparent that single-level explanations fall short. Aggression cannot be completely explained by hormones or particular kinds of brain activity. Nor can we explain it entirely in terms of upbringing, neighborhood experiences, or cultural expectations.

*Hypotheses and Theories*    Once scientists have made some objective observations of behavior on one or more levels of analysis, they might form a **hypothesis.** *A hypothesis is a tentative statement, not yet tested, about the relationship between two or more events.* For example, a scientist might formulate a hypothesis after watching several episodes in a restaurant in which patrons verbally attack waiters who took too long to serve them: "If people are frustrated by long waits, they behave aggressively toward the source of their frustration."

After testing this hypothesis, the scientist may form other related hypotheses: "If hungry people are frustrated by being denied access to food, they will behave aggressively toward the source of their frustration." "If people are frustrated by having to suddenly change their plans, they will behave aggressively toward the source of their frustration." After testing several related hypotheses, the scientists may formulate a **theory,** *a framework that attempts to tie together observations about a particular area of human behavior. A theory organizes previously unrelated facts and predicts new and untested relationships.* A theory not only states relationships, but attempts to explain why these relationships exist. The formulation of a theory generates further research. For example, scientists may propose a theory that links frustration of all kinds to aggressive behavior. This theory may stimulate people to deduce more new hypotheses, which, if tested and confirmed, would make the theory more convincing. If some hypotheses deduced from the theory cannot be confirmed, scientists may conclude that frustration only results in aggression in certain limited circumstances. The theory is then modified and refined to describe the conditions under which frustration can be expected to result either in aggression or some other behavior.

## Research Strategies

The rules that govern what evidence can be used to confirm or contradict a hypothesis are very strict. First, the evidence must be objective. Second, it must be public; it has to be there for everyone to see. For example, in a study of mental telepathy, a subject might describe a city park he has never been to but in which an experimenter is now sitting. Another experimenter, who knows the place, might write down the description and be amazed at how accurate it is: "It's grayish, with many people who seem very busy and anxious. There are a few plants nearby, and I hear the noises of the city in the background." At first this description might seem uncannily accurate. However, a person who doesn't know it is a city park could apply the description to hundreds of places. It might be a shopping plaza, a crowded office building, or a school yard. Finally, the evidence must be repeatable. Provided the sequence of causes really leads to the event, the experimenters should be able to set up the sequence a second, third, or fourth time and observe the same events.

Meeting these requirements means doing carefully controlled research. The two major kinds of research are descriptive and experimental.

*Descriptive Research*    Descriptive research is vital to the scientific approach. It consists basically of observation, but the kind of observations conducted can sometimes become very sophisticated. *In descriptive research, the scientist observes and describes what is happening in a situation without actually trying to control the forces that might be causing the individuals under observation to behave in certain ways.* There are many kinds of descriptive research: Three of them are field studies, case studies, and correlational studies.

A **field study** *is one in which the scientist goes to the environment in which the behavior of interest normally takes place.* Jane Goodall (1963) spent many years studying the behavior of wild chimpanzees near Lake Tanganyika in Africa. She actually lived on the site, taking notes and recording the day-to-day activities of the chimps.

In another example of a field study, a scientist spent a day observing children in a nursery school (Fawl, 1963). The investigator did not try to interfere with what the children were doing; he just observed their behavior in their natural environment. Among other things, he noted that the children experienced an average of sixteen frustrating events during the day. Although laboratory studies had shown that children often show aggression in response to frustration, the nursery-school children in this field study did not demonstrate the expected high levels of aggression. Thus, one important function of field studies is to confirm (or disconfirm) the findings that scientists obtain from the more controlled conditions of the laboratory.

A **case study** *involves repeated observations of the same individual over a long period of time.* For example, one might observe the progress of a woman trying to quit smoking. First, the individual might switch to low-tar cigarettes but find, after several days, that she smokes twice as many as her usual brand. Then she may try smoking only one cigarette per hour in an effort to maintain more conscious control over the habit. If this doesn't work, she might try stopping all at once. If the individual managed to not smoke for several months, we could conclude that "cold turkey" can be an effective way for some people to quit smoking.

The case study method is frequently used by clinical psychologists to provide detailed and precise descriptions of behavioral disorders. Consider, for example, the case of a person with multiple personalities (Ludwig, Brandsma, Wilbur, Bendfeldt, & Jameson, 1972). Jonah came to the hospital complaining of headaches followed by memory loss. The attendants at the hospital noticed that his personality changed quite dramatically. On one day he might be shy, retiring, passive, and very polite; on another day, he was cold and nasty. Although normal people show changes in mood from day to day, Jonah's switches were quite extreme. Psychiatrists found that Jonah had four distinct personalities: one primary one and three secondary ones. On tests of intelligence, all four "people" scored essentially alike, but on tests designed to measure emotionality, they were vastly different.

**Correlational studies** *observe and measure events, trying to find associations between them.* For example, one might measure personality traits in a group of children and find that those who tend to be more anxious also tend to bite their nails more. Or a researcher might find that people living in noisy environments are less likely to persist at a difficult task than people living in quiet areas. Associations between two **variables,** or *things that vary,* are often expressed in terms of a statistic called the **correlation coefficient,** *a measure of association that can range between –1 and +1.* High degrees of association are expressed in numbers approaching 1.00 (such as .80, .77, .95), or approaching –1.00 (such as –.85, –.90, or –.79). Low degrees of association are expressed in numbers approaching zero (such as .04, –.11, .15, or –.09). For example, if the relationship between nail biting and anxiety levels is very strong, the correlation might be high, perhaps around .75. If the relationship were very weak, the correlation coefficient would be near zero, perhaps .12. If the relationship between noise levels and persistence is also strong, the coefficient would be high. However, the value would be negative, perhaps –.81, because as one variable increases (noise), the other variable decreases (persistence). If the relationship were a weak one, the correlation between noise levels and persistence would be closer to zero, perhaps –.14. (See Appendix A for details.)

Descriptive research has a number of advantages and limitations. It provides a basis for forming hypotheses about behavior: A scientist must observe and describe behavior in order to obtain ideas about how people behave under certain conditions. Also, descriptive research provides a means to study behavior in the natural environment. The events in a laboratory experiment are carefully controlled. Sometimes people and animals behave differently in the real world. Field studies enable scientists to determine whether the conclusions they have drawn from their experimental studies apply in the uncontrolled real world.

An important limitation of descriptive research concerns the ability to draw conclusions about causes and effects. For example, one might be tempted to conclude that the association between anxiety and nail biting meant that high anxiety levels were *causing* children to bite their nails. However, this conclusion cannot be drawn from such a study. It could be that the children were noticing the terrible condition of their nails and became anxious because they were afraid their parents would notice too. Or perhaps some of the children were anxious and biting their nails more frequently because they were doing poorly in school.

Correlational studies, though they can point to associations among variables and suggest possibilities, cannot tell us anything conclusive about cause and effect. Drawing such conclusions from correlations is a very easy trap to fall into, and one of the most common mistakes people make when they read about psychological research. Suppose today's paper tells you that single people who have dogs are less likely to get sick, and generally live longer, than singles without pets. Does this mean that dogs run interference and block the incoming germs? Or that people without health problems in the first place are more likely to have a pet? Or that when people do become seriously ill, they can no longer take care of their pet and wisely give it away? The cause-and-effect relationship is especially important in this case because a hasty misinterpretation could lead you to do something that would have no effect on your health or longevity, or might even harm it. If you jump to the conclusion that a dog's presence will create a healthy atmosphere, you might invite a sickly stray home. The survey's results simply cannot tell us why the association exists. The best way to draw firm conclusions about causes and effects is to perform experimental research.

*Experimental Studies*    A great deal of psychological knowledge has been acquired from **experimental research** in laboratories and in the field (see figure 1.3). *In experimental research, the scientist seeks to control or manipulate some events to determine precise cause-and-effect relationships.*

A team of researchers noticed that people are able to remember what happened at an event much more accurately when they are aware of some common errors in observation. The researchers began to think that training might improve the accuracy of the observers, so they formulated the hypothesis that the more training a person receives in avoiding observational errors, the more accurate his or her observations will be.

In any experiment, the **independent variable** will be manipulated by researchers. *It is the variable that is the presumed cause of changes in the other variable.* In our example, the investigators hypothesized that an increase in the amount of training would produce an increase in observer accuracy. Thus the "amount of training to avoid observational errors" is the variable that will be manipulated. The other variable, observer accuracy, is called the **dependent variable:** *The researcher will measure this variable, and changes in it depend on changes in the independent variable.*

After formulating the hypothesis and identifying the independent and dependent variables, the researcher must create operational definitions for each. The **operational definitions** *state the procedures, or operations, that will be used to measure the dependent variable and experimentally manipulate the independent variable.* For example, if the researchers want to measure appetite

because they think some drug might affect it, they need to indicate how they intend to do it. Will they offer each subject a bowl of pretzels and count how many each eats? Will they ask each subject to rate himself or herself from one to ten on a "hunger scale"? Any psychological variable can be measured in a number of ways. Measurements of hunger, for example, might yield different results if different yardsticks are used because the phenomenon itself is multidimensional. A person who is rated as "very hungry" under one kind of measurement might score as only moderately hungry using a different operational definition of the variable "hunger." When we explore the concept of intelligence later in the textbook, you'll see that scientists have expended considerable effort on the measurement of this complex variable. Psychological variables like intelligence are more difficult to measure than physical ones like length or weight.

The researcher must also operationally define the independent variable by stating how it will be manipulated. If the study concerns drugs, the amount of drug might be manipulated by giving some subjects no drug and other subjects a specific quantity of drug. If researchers are studying how color affects learning in computer-based instruction, they might ask some subjects to use the color version of the program, and others to use the black-and-white version. If the researchers want to assess the effects of different levels of self-esteem on math performance, they must find some way to manipulate self-esteem without violating ethical principles and harming the subjects in any way. They might, for example, ask all the subjects to solve a few very difficult puzzles. They would tell each member of his experimental group that they did extraordinarily well to boost their self-esteem, regardless of whether or not their answers were correct. They might provide no feedback to the control group about their performance on the puzzles. After manipulating self-esteem in this way, they would give both groups the same math test to see whether the groups performed differently.

In the study on observer accuracy, the researchers wanted to manipulate "amount of training" and measure "the accuracy of the observer." The simplest way to manipulate the amount of training a person receives is to train some subjects and not the others. The subjects who receive training would be called the **experimental group.** *This group receives the independent variable treatment.* The subjects who do not receive training are the **control group.** In an experiment, *members of the control group do not receive the independent variable treatment.* To

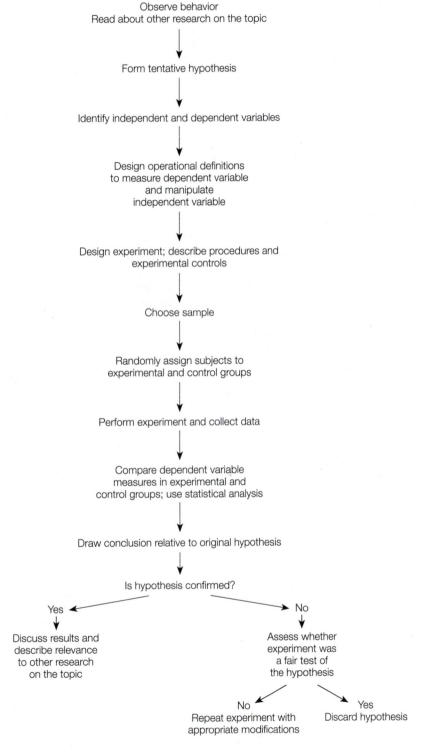

**Figure 1.3**  *Flow charting a simple experiment*

measure observer accuracy, the researchers could ask the subjects to relate as much as possible about the events that took place within the first hour after a lecture was over. They could also show all the subjects a slide, ask some questions about it, and score the answers. There are many possible operational definitions for psychological variables, each with advantages and limitations. For example, asking subjects to describe what happened after the lecture would be realistic to some extent, but the researchers would have a difficult time deciding whether the observations were accurate since each subject would have had different experiences.

The researchers in the study of observer accuracy chose to measure the dependent variable, observer accuracy, by showing all the subjects a videotape of a group discussion between several industrial managers. Afterwards, the subjects answered seventy-five objective questions concerning the videotape (Thornton & Zorich, 1980). The researchers manipulated the independent variable by giving different instructions to the different groups. Before the videotape, the subjects in the experimental group were lectured on observational skills. They learned about common mistakes observers make, such as losing detail through simplification, making "snap" judgments, allowing stereotypes to affect perceptions, and being influenced too strongly by a single characteristic of a person. The subjects in the control group did not receive this kind of training: they were simply told to watch the tape, take notes, and be prepared to answer questions on it later.

A critical feature of the design of any experiment is **experimental control:** *The experimental group and the control group should be as similar as possible in terms of how they are treated, their IQs, their goals, their interests, and their personalities.* The only systematic difference between the two groups should be in the amount of training they received in avoiding observational errors. Experimental controls ensure that the two groups do not differ in other ways. For example, all subjects should watch the same videotape under the same conditions. If the subjects who receive observational training watch a different tape, any difference between their test scores and the test scores of the subjects who receive no training might be related to the tapes rather than to the amount of training.

The choice of subjects for an experiment is also an important element. This **sample** should be *a representative subset of the group in whose behavior you are*

*interested.* For example, if you are interested in the effects of alcohol on teenagers, your sample should be representative of teenagers. In practice, psychologists have a very difficult time obtaining samples that are truly representative of the group to which they would like to generalize their findings, which is one of the reasons we are often so tentative about our conclusions. Reports of research usually include many qualifiers, such as "the data suggest that …" or "these findings indicate that under some circumstances …" (see box: Exploring Human Diversity).

The subjects in your sample must be **randomly assigned** to the two groups. *The experimenter should arbitrarily place subjects into the control group or the experimental group.* This ensures that one group will not have all the geniuses, most of the athletes, or all the females. Randomization is an important means of experimental control.

The final steps of an experimental study are to collect the data and analyze the results. Psychologists use statistics for data analysis, a mathematical tool that allows conclusions to be drawn from data that may not be clear-cut. (See Appendix A for more information.) In the experiment on observer accuracy, most of the experimental subjects had higher scores on the follow-up test than did the control subjects. The average number correct for the experimental subjects was fifty-two; for the control subjects, it was forty-five. However, some experimental subjects had lower scores than control subjects, perhaps because they did not watch the tape carefully despite their training. A statistical analysis demonstrated that even though some experimental subjects scored lower than some control subjects, the experimental group scored higher overall. The difference between their average scores was great enough that it was highly unlikely to have occurred by chance.

After the results are analyzed, the psychologist draws conclusions based on the hypothesis. If the data support the hypothesis, the experiment can contribute toward the development of a more general theory about human behavior, or help to confirm one that has already been advanced. If the data don't support the hypothesis, the researcher looks for the reasons. Was the independent variable manipulated in an effective way? For example, the subjects might not have paid much attention to the lectures on how to improve observer accuracy. In an experiment in which self-esteem is manipulated, perhaps the manipulation didn't work. Maybe the subjects who were "congratulated" on their brilliance knew they didn't know how to solve the problems, and that the feedback was fake. Researchers often do some checks after the experiment is over to make sure their independent variable was manipulated properly in the groups.

Another possible problem with an experiment involves the way the dependent variable is measured. Suppose every subject in the experimental and control groups answered all the questions accurately after the videotape. The test to measure observer accuracy would have been too easy and could not have detected any differences between the groups, even if there had been some.

If the experiment was a fair test of the hypothesis, then the researcher should discard the hypothesis and develop another one. You can see, however, why it is often difficult to disprove a hypothesis and confidently discard it. Experiments are not immune from Murphy's Law and much can go wrong. Also, the judgment about whether the experiment fairly tested the hypothesis is just that: a judgment. Human behavior is variable; and the statistics we use to compare the scores of one group to another and to decide whether a difference exists, depend on probabilities. In order to discard hypotheses, we have to replicate studies, and conduct several new ones with various modifications, such as different operational definitions, different samples, and slightly altered procedures.

*Advanced Experimental Designs*    Partly because of the cost of research, most experiments involve more than one dependent variable. A researcher investigating the effects of cocaine on mental processes would probably give the subjects a variety of tests to measure memory, problem solving, reaction time, and reasoning.

Many experiments also involve more than one independent variable. This gives the researcher an opportunity to learn the effects of two independent variables at the same time. For example, in addition to the effects of cocaine on cognitive processes, the researcher might want to learn more about the location in which the drug is taken. This experiment would then have two independent variables: amount of cocaine taken and location in which the drug is taken. For this study, at least four groups of subjects would be needed. Group 1 would sniff a substance that contained no cocaine in a laboratory setting. Group 2 would sniff the same control substance in a relaxed living room environment. Group 3 would sniff cocaine in a lab, and group 4 would sniff cocaine in a living room.

By comparing the responses of the four groups, it would be possible to determine the effects of cocaine on the dependent variables and also the effects of location. It would also be possible to determine if there is any **interaction** between the two independent variables, *suggesting that the effects of one independent variable depend on the level of the other.* For example, the researcher may find that the effects of cocaine are different depending upon where the subjects took the drug.

These complicated designs permit researchers to draw conclusions about several hypotheses without having to perform separate experiments. They also provide a means to determine the combined effects of variables, something not possible with simple designs.

*Experiments Using Animals*    Psychologists often use animal subjects in their research of human behavior. An important question is whether the behavior of animals is the same as the behavior of humans. The answer is "sometimes."

Depending on the problem, animal research can be very valuable. If researchers are investigating the activity of a single cell in the brain in response to the presence of a particular drug, it would be appropriate to use animal subjects. First, it would be unethical in most cases to place electrodes inside the brain of a human subject. Second, the effects of a drug on a single brain cell in the cat are likely to be very similar to the drug's effects on human brain cells. On the other hand, if the researchers are investigating a problem mainly confined to humans, it makes no sense to use animal subjects. For example, studies of love, panic in theaters, group decision making, or jury behavior require human volunteers.

There is a wide "gray" area in which animal behavior is similar but not identical to humans. The learning process is a good example. Are the principles that govern the way a rat learns to run a maze the same as the principles governing human learning? Researchers often use animal models to study learning and other psychological phenomena, but they are cautious about generalizing their conclusions to humans. They prefer to have some kind of corroboration from human studies to confirm their findings in animal subjects.

Psychologists who use animals in their experiments take care to safeguard their safety and welfare but the use of animals in psychological research, and research in general, is a controversial issue.

## PERSPECTIVES IN PSYCHOLOGY

Anything as complex as behavior requires breadth and imagination to study and psychologists have approached their subject from several different perspectives. Behavior doesn't have a single cause; we have already seen that it can be analyzed on several different levels. Our understanding can be enriched still further by looking at even a very simple behavior from several different points of view. This is what has happened in psychology, and is still happening. As we learn more about behavior, we find that old ways of looking at it are no longer adequate or no longer fit the findings, so some perspectives die out or are absorbed by new approaches. We also find that the views of our colleagues in ethology, sociology, microbiology, computer science, and many other fields add refreshing rays of light to our own way of looking at a particular phenomenon. No single perspective in psychology is wrong or right. Each contributes special insights and leads to a broader understanding of behavior.

In this section, we will examine two historical schools of thought that are now, for all practical purposes, dead. These are structuralism and functionalism, and though no one calls themselves by these terms anymore, the contribu-tions they made were substantial and many of their ideas have been incorporated into current theories. We will look also at the main perspectives that psychologists now, in the 1990s, find to be fruitful ways of viewing behavior.

## Historical Schools of Thought

The study of behavior has its roots in the writings of the Greek philosophers Plato and Aristotle, but most historians date the origin of modern scientific psychology to the middle of the nineteenth century. During that time, a German professor in Leipzig and an American professor in Cambridge were opening laboratories of psychology and beginning to train students in the science of human behavior.

The German, Wilhelm Wundt (figure 1.4), originally received a medical degree from the University of Heidelberg. At Leipzig, he was appointed to a chair in philosophy, but he pursued an experimental and physiologically oriented study of behavior. (His eclectic career illustrates the diverse origins of the science of psychology. The discipline has borrowed ideas and theories from medicine, physiology, philosophy, and many other subjects.)

Wundt's ideas and research methods were brought to America by Edward Titchener, one of his students. **Structuralism,** Titchener's school of thought (Lundin, 1987), *emphasized the basic elements of conscious experience: sensations, images, and feelings.* The structuralists used a variety of techniques to analyze conscious experience; the best known was **introspection,** *a rigorous and highly disciplined technique in which a trained observer analyzed his or her conscious experience in terms of elementary sensations and feelings.* For example, an observer might listen to a slow drip of water and report on the sounds he or she perceived. Not all students could master this technique; those who could not were encouraged to pursue careers in other disciplines (Fancher, 1979).

About the same time Wundt founded his laboratory in Leipzig, William James (figure 1.5) was opening one at Harvard University. James was a superb teacher, but his most important contribution to psychology was *Principles of Psychology,* a massive two-volume work published in 1894. It contained chapters on brain function, habit, sensation, perception, attention, memory, imagination, emotions, hypnotism, and many other topics familiar to modern psychologists. Throughout the work, James emphasized that which was practical and "functional,"

## APPLYING PSYCHOLOGY

### Ethical Principles of Psychologists

Any professional who conducts research or offers psychological services should be concerned with ethics. The practitioner has ethical responsibilities to clients such as protecting the client's confidentiality. The scientist has responsibilities such as insuring that human subjects give informed consent before participating in any experiments. The American Psychological Association has adopted a formal statement of ethical principles, revised in 1992, to guide the professional behavior of psychologists. The following is part of the preamble to the APA's guidelines.

> Psychologists work to develop a valid and reliable body of scientific knowledge based on research. They may apply that knowledge to human behavior in a variety of contexts. In doing so, they perform many roles, such as researcher, educator, diagnostician, therapist, and expert witness. Their goal is to broaden knowledge of behavior and, where appropriate, to apply it pragmatically to improve the condition of both the individual and society. Psychologists respect the central importance of freedom of inquiry and expression in research, teaching, and publication. They also strive to help the public in developing informed judgments and choices concerning human behavior. This Ethics Code provides a common set of values upon which psychologists build their professional and scientific work.

Recent surveys have asked practicing psychologists questions about their behavior in a variety of situations (Pope, Tabachnick, & Keith-Spiegel, 1987; Pope & Vetter, 1992) to learn more about how psychologists actually respond to ethical dilemmas. For example, the survey asked how often practitioners hugged a client, accepted gifts, broke confidentiality if a client was suicidal, used sexual surrogates with clients, or invited clients to a party; it also asked whether the respondents believed these behaviors were ethical. The researchers found that psychologists generally agreed about whether a particular behavior should be considered unethical and, in most cases, their behavior followed their ethical beliefs. Some "difficult" behaviors many respondents considered ethical included giving personal advice on radio or television, being sexually attracted to a client, and avoiding certain clients for fear of being sued. The researchers suggest that the profession may need more practical guidelines for practitioners in these areas.

*Source:* American Psychologist, 36(6):633, June 1981. Copyright © 1981 by the American Psychological Association.

partly as a reaction against Wundt's structural approach, an approach he perceived as excessively disjointed and mainly descriptive. The chapter on emotions in *Principles of Psychology* provides a good example of James's interest in the "how" and "why" of behavior. He points out that a person's actions have a significant effect on the emotions the person feels. (See chapter 8 for a detailed description of James's views on emotions.)

Whistling to keep up courage is no mere figure of speech. On the other hand, sit all day in a moping posture, sigh, and reply to everything with a dismal voice, and your melancholy lingers … (James, 1894).

The school of thought James inspired became known as **functionalism.** *It emphasized the function or purpose of behavior and how an organism's behavior helps it adapt to the environment.* The functionalists, influenced by Charles Darwin's research into the way organisms physically adapt to the environment over time, strove to learn more about behavioral adaptations. The functionalists followed an approach similar to a biologist's approach to an organism. A biologist attempts to learn the purpose or function of an organism. Similarly, functionalists broadened the scope of psychological investigations to include children, animals, and studies in natural environments; they did not limit themselves to a particular technique as the structuralists had done with introspection.

The structuralist school taught students to explore the mind, consciousness, awareness, and to do it as objectively as possible. Functionalism emphasized behavior and its

**Figure 1.4** *Wilhelm Wundt (1832–1920)*

**Figure 1.5** *William James (1842–1910)*

# EXPLORING HUMAN DIVERSITY
## Does Culture Affect the Discipline of Psychology?

We discuss the sociocultural perspective later in this chapter and call attention to the role of culture in human behavior. Psychological research is one form of human behavior, and we might ask an intriguing question about whether cultural factors influence the progress of psychological research itself. A number of writers argue that science in general, and psychology in particular, are embedded in a specific time and place and cannot escape their influence.

For example, the approach taken by Wilhelm Wundt, generally called the founding father of modern psychology, didn't last long. Leahy (1991) suggests that Wundt's views were very much influenced by the German culture in which he grew up. Like other German intellectuals of the time, Wundt took an "elitist" approach that valued synthesis and sought to describe an almost Platonic ideal of the human mind, rather than trying to understand individual differences.

The tide of events that led to World War I, the rise of the Nazis, and eventually World War II, completely overtook Wundt's way of thinking. The Nazis delivered the final blow as they destroyed much of the German intellectual community through fear, intimidation, or execution.

In the Europe of the period between the two wars, the climate favored the rapid rise of Freud's perspective, emphasizing as it did the unconscious, irrational, and often uncontrollable darker side of human nature. Freud was an outsider to the German intellectual group whose influence declined so dramatically in the early part of this century. He challenged authority and attracted many devoted apostles to his views. The Europeans found the horrors of World War I beyond comprehension and were attracted to a theory that offered some plausible explanation.

In America, where democracy and equality were cardinal values, Wundt's rational analysis of consciousness never took off. Instead, Watson's and eventually Skinner's behavioristic

approach dominated. This approach would naturally fit into the American way of thinking, one which stressed that people were fundamentally equal when they start out in life and that it is the environment that creates differences. The optimism of the behaviorist is clear and quintessentially American: utopia can be achieved if we manipulate the environment in just the right way.

In the larger scheme, psychology has planted its roots firmly in scientific ground even though there are other ways of learning about human behavior. Some argue that the West's scientific approach is culturally based. Psychology as we know it emerged when the nineteenth century western world was bursting with confidence about the marvels science could achieve, and awed by the progress that had already been made in medicine, physics, chemistry, and other natural sciences— all by using the scientific method. Applying the same method to ourselves and creating a "natural science of human behavior" was a logical next step, and it was one of Wundt's chief contributions. Some writers, who question whether the scientific method can be formally applied to much of human behavior, accuse psychologists of "physics-envy" and of engaging in Newtonian fantasies. They argue that the scientific method, though appropriate to study atoms, rocks, and blood cells, is not always the right tool to study ourselves. Certainly the study of human behavior in many non-Western countries does not rely heavily on the scientific method.

At the end of the twentieth century we stand committed to psychology as a science and scientific studies are the foundation for this text. Nevertheless, broadening the mind is a major goal of education and it is good practice to step outside the excitement of the field for a moment to try to see how our most fundamental ways of thinking developed, and how they might be influenced by our time and place in history.

relation to the environment. We know of no psychologists who call themselves structuralists or functionalists today, but the emphases of each school have been absorbed into how we approach the study of human behavior.

## Behaviorism

The school of thought known as **behaviorism** *proposed that only overt behavior be the subject matter of psychology and that the inner workings of the mind be ignored.* It developed during the early 1900s as a reaction against the technique of introspection. It has its roots in function-

alism, which also rejected introspection and emphasized objectivity. The American psychologist John B. Watson (figure 1.6) argued that Wundt's technique was a futile approach and that its results did not meet the criteria for scientific evidence. The data of psychology should be observable and measurable; hence the emphasis on overt behavior. As editor of the *Psychological Review,* Watson published an important paper describing the behaviorist position:

Psychology as the behaviorist views it is a purely objective natural science. Its theoretical goal is the prediction and

**Figure 1.6**  *John B. Watson (1878–1958)*

**Figure 1.7**  *B. F. Skinner (1904–1991)*

control of behavior. Introspection forms no essential part of its methods, nor is the scientific value of its data dependent upon the readiness with which they lend themselves to interpretation in terms of consciousness … (Watson, 1913).

The school of behaviorism had a large following in the United States and became associated with learning. B. F. Skinner (figure 1.7), a prominent American psychologist, developed theories about the role of reward and punishment in learning, excluding mental processes such as thought and imagery. An important tenet of the behaviorist viewpoint is that psychologists should be just as interested in the behavior of animals and children as they are in the behavior of adults. Thus, rat and pigeon cages became typical sights in the laboratories of psychologists; indeed, most of Skinner's theories of learning were based on studies of rats and pigeons (Skinner, 1987).

The behaviorist perspective is sometimes called "black box" psychology because it disregards what goes on inside the mind. It is only interested in the effects of the environment (input) on behavior (output). Mental processes take place inside the "black box" and are not considered appropriate for objective psychological analysis.

Behaviorism provided the impetus to change the definition of psychology and confine it to behavior alone (Chiesa, 1992). It has been a potent force in psychology and has contributed a great deal to our understanding of behavior, especially learning. As we pointed out earlier, though, most psychologists now prefer to expand psychology's definition to include "and mental processes," suggesting that the strict behavioristic viewpoint is no longer dominant.

## Cognitive Psychology

In contrast to the behaviorists, psychologists who favor the cognitive perspective emphasize the mental processes that take place inside the "black box." **Cognitive psychology** *focuses on reasoning and the mental processing of information, especially the processing involved in perception, memory, language, and problem solving.* According to this approach, explanations of behavior cannot be complete if they only include references to overt behavior and the effects of the environment. They should also include an analysis of mental activities.

During the early part of the twentieth century, cognitive psychology evolved from the work of a group of scientists in Germany known as the Gestalt psychologists (Mandler, 1985). **Gestalt** *means form, pattern, or integrated whole.* These researchers studied how the human mind receives information and interprets it. Perception was one of their favorite topics and they demonstrated how pieces of visual input are organized into meaningful wholes. The approach showed that the whole is more than the sum of the parts; a visual perception cannot be explained on the basis of sensory stimulus alone. Mental activities that interpret the input must also be analyzed.

The techniques of cognitive psychology are many and varied, including electrical recording of brain activity while a subject performs mental tasks and protocol analysis, a revised and updated version of introspection in which the subject "thinks out loud" and provides verbal reports on his or her mental activities while performing a task (Ericsson & Simon, 1984).

Cognitive psychology relies heavily on computer technology for its jargon and for many of its models. Many cognitive psychologists test their theories about the way the human brain works by developing computer simulations and artificial intelligence programs.

The cognitive perspective has attracted much attention and stimulated a great deal of research in the last two decades because it has expanded the boundaries of psychological investigation beyond the narrow strictures of behaviorism. Though it is criticized for being too mentalistic and for underrating the importance of emotions in behavior, it is one of the dominant approaches in contemporary psychology.

**Figure 1.8**    *Sigmund Freud (1856–1939)*

## Psychoanalysis

The ideas of Sigmund Freud (figure 1.8) are so pervasive in twentieth-century western thought that even students who have never had a course in psychology are familiar with terms like Oedipal complex, libido, and repression. **Psychoanalysis** *is both a school of thought and a system of therapy developed by Freud and expanded and modified by his students and followers. The approach emphasizes the importance of unconscious processes in personality development, especially unconscious memories of childhood events.* While Wundt was studying conscious processes, Freud was postulating the existence and influence of the unconscious mind, a realm unreachable through introspection. The well-known "Freudian slip" is an example of how unconscious thoughts can express themselves in overt behavior. A mother unconsciously worried over her young son's ability to cross streets might send him to the store saying, "Don't forget the blood" instead of "Don't forget the bread." These hidden concerns might also reveal themselves in dreams. Freud used a variety of techniques, including dream analysis and hypnosis, to reach and understand the workings of the unconscious mind.

In addition to its emphasis on the unconscious, the psychoanalytic approach also addresses the importance of instincts that compel people to behave in certain ways and the means that people use to control these instinctual pressures.

Attempts to control sexual instincts result in behaviors like repression, in which a motive is deliberately repressed or "forgotten."

Under Freud's guidance, psychoanalysis became an enormously influential school of psychology. Freud inspired a large number of students. Some students adhered strictly to his point of view; others proposed slight or sometimes drastic modifications to his theories about human behavior. Carl Jung, for example, believed that Freud overemphasized the importance of sexuality and underrated social and cultural factors. A number of psychologists argue that much of Freud's theory was based on the case histories of only a few Viennese patients. Much of it is also extremely difficult to test in the laboratory, making it a theory that no one can prove or disprove. Nevertheless, the influence of psychoanalytic thought in art and literature, and particularly in abnormal psychology and psychotherapy, is unmistakable.

## Humanistic Psychology

**Humanistic psychology** *emphasizes the uniqueness of human beings and focuses on human values and subjective experience* (Guilford, 1984). Psychologists who prefer this perspective consider the individual's interpretations of events as most important in the understanding of human behavior. They believe that other perspectives—behaviorism and psychoanalysis in particular—are excessively mechanistic because they view behavior as primarily controlled by the environment. Humanistic psychologists place greater importance on an individual's own will. Prominent psychologists who take the humanistic perspective include Abraham Maslow and Carl Rogers, whose work we'll learn more about in other chapters.

Humanistic psychology is more of a philosophical orientation toward human behavior. It relies not on the scientific method but on understanding the inner life of each person. It has been closely associated with a variety of consciousness-expanding techniques designed to reach this inner life, such as encounter groups, sensitivity sessions, and mystical experiences. Many humanistic theories propose that the major motivational force of human beings is **self-actualization,** *or developing the human potential to its fullest.*

The humanistic perspective reminds psychologists that one of their tasks is to help solve issues relating to human welfare. The cares and concerns of individual people sometimes become lost amidst the reaction-time experiments, the rats learning to run mazes, and the analysis of dreams.

## Sociocultural Perspective

The **sociocultural perspective** *focuses on the social and cultural factors that affect human behavior.* The science of psychology, founded as it was on the study of individual phenomena such as sensation, perception, and learning, was slow to begin a systematic investigation into the enormous impact of the social and cultural environment. Although Wilhelm Wundt was keenly interested in the subject and published a massive work called *Volkerspsychologie* (Folk Psychology) that attempted to apply psychological principles to the masses of data collected by anthropologists, his students focused their attention on his experimental laboratory work. While sociologists, anthropologists, and ethologists were exploring the social and cultural roots of behavior in field studies, many psychologists in America were embracing behaviorism, a perspective that stresses the universality of behavioral laws in humans and animals. In the last few decades, especially after World War II, psychologists have turned more attention to the social and cultural influences on behavior.

Humans are social beings and our behavior is very much affected by family, friends, co-workers, and even strangers. As psychologists began to investigate the social dimension they brought the scientific method with them, creating operational definitions and designing controlled experiments to investigate some very intricate behaviors. Based on this research we now know, for example, that an experiment itself is a social occasion and the characteristics of the researcher can affect how the subjects act in subtle ways.

Humans are also both the products and the producers of culture and our behavior always occurs in some cultural context. When we observe how people verbally attack waiters when their food order is delayed, we must be very careful to recognize that the pattern may not be universal at all. How people behave, especially in social situations, is partly a function of the rules and expectations absorbed from their culture. In a multicultural society like the United States, it is especially important to learn more about the role of culture in behavior.

## Biological Perspective

Taking a **biological perspective,** *psychologists explore the biological underpinnings of human behavior and draw inferences about the influence of evolution.* Humans are physical beings with hearts, lungs, brains, hands, feet, eyes, ears, and many other useful features. Many researchers approach the study of human behavior by considering the physical factors first, seeking to understand the biological underpinnings of our behavior. Progress in understanding behavior from this standpoint

has been very rapid over the past few decades as new technology has emerged to measure activity in the brain and relate it to mental processes and behavior. We have learned, for example, that some very interesting changes in the brain appear to be related to moods. It has also become clear that biology and behavior interact in complex ways. Behavior can affect biology, and biology can affect behavior.

The biological perspective also emphasizes the fact that we are physical beings who evolved over a long time and that this genetic heritage can predispose us to behave in certain ways. Just as we evolved eyebrows to protect our eyes, we may have evolved certain kinds of behavior patterns to protect our bodies and ensure the survival of our species. Because it is so widespread and "second nature," we hardly even remark upon the fact that everyone jumps when someone sneaks up from behind and shouts "boo!" The survival value of this behavior is obvious, and no one needs to learn it through experience. We may be predisposed to display even more subtle behaviors that can be attributed to our evolutionary past.

## COMPARING THE PERSPECTIVES

The major perspectives in psychology outlined here and in table 1.3 emphasize different aspects of behavior and approach the study of behavior in distinctive ways. In some cases, the perspectives may appear to conflict. For example, a scientist who approaches psychology from a behavioristic viewpoint is not likely to agree with the sexual instincts emphasized by someone from a psychoanalytic background. In other cases, scientists investigating behavior from different perspectives will find many areas of overlap and note that the findings complement rather than contradict one another.

Much research effort and theorizing has been devoted to behaviors such as aggression, learning, or perception. The information obtained from each perspective expands and enriches the understanding of these phenomena. It doesn't necessarily generate unresolvable controversy. There are no hard and fast lines drawn between the perspectives. Each offers special insights under different circumstances at different levels of analysis. Many psychologists do not cling to one perspective. They consider themselves "eclectic"—they appreciate the value of several perspectives.

## TABLE 1.3 The major perspectives in psychology

|  | Emphasis | Techniques of Study |
|---|---|---|
| Structuralism | The basic elements of conscious experience, especially sensations, images, and feelings. | Trained introspection |
| Functionalism | The function or purpose of behavior, and how an organism's behavior helps it to adapt to the environment. | Introspection<br>Experiments<br>Comparative studies of species |
| Behaviorism | The study of overt, observable behavior. | Experiments, especially using animals |
| Cognitive Psychology | The study of reasoning and mental processing of information, especially the processing involved in perception, memory, language, and problem solving. | Computer simulations<br>Protocol analysis<br>Experiments on memory, reaction time, problem solving, perception<br>Electrical brain recordings |
| Psychoanalysis | The importance of unconscious processes in personality, especially unconscious memories of childhood events. | Case studies |
| Humanistic Psychology | The uniqueness of human beings; human values and subjective experience. | Interview techniques, case studies |
| Sociocultural Perspective | The social and cultural influences on human behavior. | Experiments, cross-cultural studies, field studies |
| Biological Perspective | The biological underpinnings of behavior; the role of evolution | Experiments, animal studies |

▶ **GUIDED REVIEW** *Learning Objectives 5 and 6*

1. Historical perspectives that have been taken by psychologists include _____ and _____. Structuralism emphasized the basic elements of conscious experience through introspection. Functionalism, inspired by William James, focused on the purpose and utility of behavior, particularly as it permitted adaptation to the environment.

2. _____ founded by John B. Watson, stresses observation of overt behavior and the role of environmental factors, particularly rewards and punishments, in the control of behavior.

3. Cognitive psychology, with its origins in _____, investigates both overt behavior and private mental activities using a variety of techniques to make inferences about how we store and process information.

4. _____, proposed by Sigmund Freud, emphasizes the importance of unconscious processes, instincts, and early experience in behavior.

5. The more philosophical perspective, known as _____, emphasizes the inner conscious experiences of each individual person, using techniques such as encounter groups, sensitivity sessions, and mystical experiences. Humanistically oriented psychologists downplay the importance of the scientific method in the study of behavior.

6. The _____ perspective recognizes the influence of social and cultural factors on human behavior.

7. The _____ perspective explores the relationship between physical factors, such as brain activity and hormones, and behavior. It also considers the role that evolution has played in behavioral predispositions.

*Answers*

1. *structuralism, functionalism* 2. *Behaviorism* 3. *Gestalt psychology* 4. *Psychoanalysis* 5. *humanism* 6. *sociocultural* 7. *biological*

# APPLYING PSYCHOLOGY

Has psychology accumulated enough knowledge about behavior to help predict and control it in the real world? Can we apply psychological principles to some of our most difficult problems? We have no shortage of problems: racism, terrorism, drug abuse, senility, crime, violence, pollution, famine, poverty, war, recession, child abuse—the list goes on and on. But do we have good answers, and if we do should we offer them? Public interest in scientific solutions to the problems of humankind is intense and people are certainly willing to listen. In our scientific age, psychologists have in some ways become a source of authority on behavior that rivals and even surpasses that of religious leaders, parents, philosophers, and politicians. But before we try to answer these questions, let's look at the range of research in which psychologists are engaged from the standpoint of its relevance to problems.

## Applied and Basic Research

Psychological research varies along a continuum that ranges from the very basic kinds of research to the very applied. Basic research is not conducted because a social issue is in dire need of solutions; it is conducted because scientists are curious about the nature of human and animal behavior. For instance, the physiological psychologist studying the role of various vitamins in the brain development of rat fetuses is engaging in purely basic research to learn more about the world. No one is seeking to create "super-smart" rats.

The research on maternal nutrition, though, could have many practical applications and might offer information to community leaders trying to improve the diets of impoverished people. Based on the findings, the taxpayers might recognize the importance of the intrauterine environment to the baby's health and endorse prenatal nutrition programs.

At the other end of the continuum are the purely applied studies specifically designed to address a problem. A study of the behavior of hostages during a simulated kidnapping, an investigation of the relationship between behavior patterns and heart disease, or an experiment conducted for the highway department to determine human reaction times to different colors are all examples of applied research. (Applied research on the last topic, for example, led policymakers to use red for "stop" and green for "go"

in traffic lights.) Many applied studies are done for business to assess the effectiveness of advertising or help design user-friendly knobs and dials for videotape recorders and computer displays.

The distinction between basic and applied research is not always clear; they do not constitute two separate categories but rather are two ends of a continuum. Much research contains elements of both. When universities first began establishing departments of psychology in the late nineteenth and early twentieth centuries, most staff members concentrated almost exclusively on basic research. Such a young discipline did not have enough basic knowledge about behavior and mental processes to contribute much in the way of applications and specific answers to real world questions. Psychologists just beginning to learn how people developed prejudice could hardly be expected to design applied research studies to help create public policy or to suggest legislation that would eliminate prejudice.

As knowledge in the field of psychology grew, applications and applied research became much more common. Many psychologists are engaged in either applied research or in applying what has already been learned about behavior. Clinical psychologists, the largest proportion of psychologists, apply what has been learned about abnormal behavior to people in hospitals, outpatient clinics, community mental health centers, and many other settings. Psychologists working in business apply what has been learned about the psychology of large organizations. The ways in which our knowledge of psychology can be applied is almost endless.

A large number of psychologists engaged in research focus on applied issues rather than, or in addition to, basic ones. This applied research is carried out in government agencies, hospitals, universities, businesses, and just about anywhere psychologists are employed. Shifts in government funding policies have contributed to the trend toward more applied research. As money for research became scarce, government funding agencies like the National Institute of Mental Health and the National Science Foundation tended to emphasize investigations that might yield answers to important problems facing the American people. But part of the trend is also due to the maturation of psychology as a scientific discipline. We have the expertise and theoretical frameworks to perform intelligent applied research, and we can be confident in applying what we've learned about behavior thus far.

## Giving Psychology Away

George Miller gave a presidential address at the 1969 meeting of the American Psychological Association in which he encouraged "giving psychology away." It was time to offer whatever knowledge psychology had to solve the problems of society, and to assume the task as an obligation. Since then, psychologists have begun applying the principles of psychology to almost every area of human life. Some have argued that too much has been given away, much of it based on sketchy research. The psychology sections of the bookstores are overflowing with manuals that will help you lose weight, increase your self-esteem, improve your sex life, find a mate, increase productivity, give up smoking, influence people, and negotiate with your boss.

At the beginning of this chapter, we listed four goals of psychology: to describe, understand, predict, and control behavior. As psychology becomes more mature and its methods become more and more effective, the issue of control grows considerably. If we know powerful methods to control and change behavior, should we use them to solve some of society's problems? This may seem like a silly question, but think about the example of worshiping cows in India. We have the means to change that behavior, but do we really have the wisdom to decide whether the

behavior should be changed? Psychology is becoming a powerful tool but who should decide how to use it and for what ends?

We would argue that people have been trying to control, influence, manipulate, and change behavior from the earliest times, sometimes very effectively, sometimes poorly. Knowing better ways to do it through the scientific study of behavior won't make us any wiser or more ignorant than we are now. It will make us more efficient, but that very efficiency makes the question much more compelling. It will be up to us to decide what to do with the knowledge and how to make our world what we want it to be.

▶ **GUIDED REVIEW** *Learning Objective 7*

1. An important goal of psychology is solving the problems facing our world. Toward this end, psychologists conduct _____, which uses the scientific method to find answers to specific, practical questions. They also apply the knowledge they have gained from basic research to real world problems.
2. _____ is conducted primarily to learn more about the world; however, many psychological applications may arise from it.

*Answers*

1. applied research 2. Basic research

## SUMMARY

I.   Psychology is a subject for and about people. (p. 4)

    A.   Psychology is usually defined as the study of behavior; however, many psychologists add the phrase "and mental processes" to the definition to emphasize that psychology also includes the study of mental activity. (p. 4)

    B.   The subfields of psychology include clinical psychology, social psychology, physiological psychology, developmental psychology, comparative psychology, and many others. (p. 5)

    C.   Psychologists work in many settings, including academia, government, business, and private practice. (pp. 4-7)

II.  Psychology uses the scientific method in its approach to the study of behavior, an approach that assumes determinism and uses empirical evidence. Major ingredients in the scientific approach include formulating a hypothesis about the relationship between variables, designing a study, collecting empirical evidence, drawing conclusions from the

data, communicating the results, and replicating the findings. (p. 7)

    A.   The first step in studying behavior is to perform objective observations. (p. 8)

        1.   Behavior can be analyzed on many levels, from the physiological level to the social and political level. Most behaviors are influenced by factors operating at many levels. (p. 9)

        2.   After observing behavior, scientists formulate hypotheses and develop general theoretical frameworks to explain behavior. (p. 10)

    B.   Research strategies generally fall into two categories: descriptive research and experimental research. (p. 10)

        1.   Descriptive research relies on observation. Examples include field studies, case studies, and correlational studies. (pp. 10-11)

        2.   Experimental research involves the manipulation by the experimenter of the independent variable and observation of its effects on the dependent variable. Experimental controls are used to ensure

that the experimental and control groups are different only with respect to the independent variable. The independent and dependent variables in an experiment must have operational definitions. (pp. 12–15)

3. More advanced and complicated experimental studies may involve two or more independent variables operating simultaneously and the measure of several dependent variables. Complex experimental designs enable researchers to identify interactions between independent variables. (p. 16)

4. Field studies are important in psychology because they investigate the effects of variables in real settings. However, it is more difficult to control extraneous variables in the field. (pp. 14–16)

5. Experiments using animals are conducted to learn more about the behavior of animals and to acquire information that might generalize to human behavior. (p. 16)

III. Psychologists have emphasized different approaches in the study of behavior and have taken different perspectives. (p. 17)

A. Two historical perspectives, or schools of thought, were structuralism and functionalism. (pp. 17–18)

B. Behaviorism stresses the observation of overt behavior and the role of environmental factors, particularly rewards and punishments, in behavior. (pp. 18–19)

C. Cognitive psychology investigates overt behavior and private mental activities using techniques such as reaction time, electrical recordings of the brain, and protocol analysis to learn how the human being processes information. (p. 19)

D. Psychoanalysis emphasizes the importance of unconscious processes, instincts, and early childhood experiences. (p. 20)

E. The humanistic perspective emphasizes the inner conscious experiences of individuals, stressing the uniqueness of human beings and focusing on human values and subjective experience. (pp. 20–21)

F. The sociocultural perspective explores the social and cultural context of behavior, emphasizing how human behavior affects and is affected by social and cultural events. (p. 20)

G. The biological perspective focuses on the biological underpinnings of behavior, and also explores the evolutionary roots of human behavioral predispositions. (p. 21)

IV. The application of psychological knowledge to problems in the real world is an important goal of psychology. (p. 23)

A. Whereas basic psychological research is conducted to learn more about human behavior, applied psychological research usually involves using the scientific method to obtain answers to specific, practical questions. The two kinds of research overlap considerably. (p. 23)

B. As more basic psychological knowledge accumulates, more applications of psychological knowledge become possible. Psychology as a field has become mature enough to offer a great deal of useful information toward the solution of practical problems. (pp. 23–24)

## ACTION GLOSSARY

Match the terms in the left column with the definitions in the right column.

__ 1. **Psychology (p. 4)**
__ 2. **Determinism (p. 7)**
__ 3. **Objectivity (p. 8)**
__ 4. **Hypothesis (p. 10)**
__ 5. **Theory (p. 10)**
__ 6. **Descriptive research (p. 10)**
__ 7. **Field study (p. 10)**

A. *Descriptive research that usually takes place in a setting in which the behavior being observed normally occurs.*
B. *A tentative statement about the relationship between two or more variables that may be proved or disproved by the scientific method.*
C. *A type of research in which events are observed and described but not manipulated.*
D. *A set of statements or propositions that attempt to explain a body of facts.*
E. *The component of the scientific method in which scientists observe events without preconceived notions, prejudice, or bias.*
F. *Usually defined as the science of behavior; many psychologists prefer to broaden the definition by including the study of mental activity or processes.*
G. *One of the assumptions of the scientific method. Refers to the assumption that cause-and-effect relationships exist in the world.*

___ **8. Case study (p. 11)**
___ **9. Correlational study (p. 11)**
___ **10. Variable (p. 11)**
___ **11. Correlation coefficient (p. 11)**
___ **12. Experimental research (p. 12)**
___ **13. Independent variable (p. 12)**

A. *Descriptive research in which the characteristics and behavior of individuals are observed and measured, and attempts are made to find relationships between two or more variables.*

B. *A numerical value between -1 and +1 that indicates the degree of relationship between two variables in terms of both strength (the absolute value of the coefficient) and direction (the sign of the coefficient).*

C. *In an experiment, the variable that is actively manipulated and controlled by the scientist. Changes in this variable are presumed to cause changes in the other variable.*

D. *Anything that can vary, either in discrete steps or along some continuum.*

E. *Research designed to determine cause-and-effect relationships between variables by controlling the conditions under which observations are made. The independent variable(s) of the experiment are controlled and manipulated systematically in order to observe any resulting changes in the measurements of the dependent variable(s).*

F. *Descriptive research that involves repeated observations of the same individual over a long period of time.*

___ **14. Dependent variable (p. 12)**
___ **15. Operational definition (p. 12)**
___ **16. Experimental group (p. 12)**
___ **17. Control group (p. 12)**
___ **18. Experimental control (p. 14)**
___ **19. Sample (p. 14)**

A. *In an experiment, the group that receives the level of the independent variable that is not zero and the treatment under investigation.*

B. *In an experiment, the variable that will be measured by the scientist. Changes in this variable are hypothesized to depend on changes in the other variable.*

C. *In an experiment contrasting two or more groups, the group that is given no treatment, a placebo, or a zero level of the independent variable. Measurements on this group provide a means to assess the effects of a treatment given to a different group.*

D. *A subgroup of a population that is generally representative of that population. In research, conclusions drawn from the behavior of this subgroup can be generalized to the population from which the sample was drawn only if the subgroup is a representative one.*

E. *Refers to the experimenter's arrangement of extraneous variables, or those other than the independent and dependent variables. Ensures that all groups are affected equally by extraneous variables so that any changes in the dependent variable can be attributed to the independent variable.*

F. *Explains how a variable or phenomenon will be manipulated, produced, or measured for the purposes of research.*

___ **20. Randomly assigned (p. 14)**
___ **21. Interaction (p. 16)**
___ **22. Structuralism (p. 16)**
___ **23. Introspection (p. 16)**
___ **24. Functionalism (p. 17)**
___ **25. Psychoanalysis (p. 20)**

A. *A school of psychology associated with the ideas of William James. Emphasized the purpose and utility of behavior, particularly within the framework of evolution.*

B. *A technique in which trained individuals studied, analyzed, and reported on their own conscious experience in terms of elementary sensations and feelings, and in which the interpretation of experience and feeling were avoided.*

C. *A means of experimental control in which subjects are placed into groups by chance, such as by tossing a coin. Provided the sample is large, the technique ensures that the average characteristics of each group are approximately equal before the administration of the independent variable.*

D. *Occurs when the effects of one independent variable depend on the level of the other independent variable.*

E. *A school of psychology founded by Sigmund Freud. Emphasized the role of unconscious processes in behavior. Also refers to a body of techniques used to investigate the mind and to treat certain kinds of behavior disorders.*

F. *A school of psychology associated with the ideas of Wilhelm Wundt. Proposed that the major task of psychology was the study of the basic elements of conscious experience.*

___ **26. Behaviorism (p. 18)**
___ **27. Cognitive psychology (p. 19)**
___ **28. Gestalt (p. 19)**
___ **29. Humanistic psychology (p. 20)**
___ **30. Self-actualization (p. 20)**
___ **31. Sociocultural perspective (p. 20)**
___ **32. Biological perspective (p. 21)**

**A.** *An individual's motivation to develop his or her potential to its fullest.*
**B.** *Pattern, form, and integrated whole.*
**C.** *A perspective in psychology that stresses the role of reasoning and mental processing of information.*
**D.** *A school of psychology associated with the ideas of John B. Watson. Proposes that the only legitimate subject matter for psychology is overt behavior. One of the goals is to increase the objectivity of psychological inquiry.*
**E.** *An approach in psychology that emphasizes subjective experience and the uniqueness of human beings.*
**F.** *A perspective in psychology that emphasizes the social and cultural context of human behavior.*
**G.** *A perspective in psychology that emphasizes the biological and evolutionary roots of behavior.*

*ANSWERS*

*1. f, 2. g, 3. e, 4. b, 5. d, 6. c, 7. a; 8. f, 9. a, 10. d, 11. b, 12. e, 13. c; 14. b, 15. f, 16. a, 17. c, 18. e, 19. d, 20. c, 21. d, 22. f, 23. b, 24. a, 25. e; 26. d, 27. c, 28. b, 29. e, 30. a, 31. f, 32. g*

# SELF-TEST

1. The area or specialization in psychology that deals with the diagnosis and treatment of behavioral or mental disorders is
   (a) psychiatry.
   (b) clinical psychology.
   (c) social psychology.
   (d) personality.
   (LO1; p. 4)

2. The largest number of psychologists are employed by
   (a) mental hospitals and similar institutions.
   (b) colleges and universities.
   (c) federal and state agencies (other than *b*).
   (d) business and corporations.
   (LO2; p. 4)

3. Evidence collected by careful observation, experimentation, and measurement is
   (a) empirical.
   (b) anecdotal.
   (c) rational.
   (d) behavioristic.
   (LO3; p. 7)

4. The goals of psychology are
   (a) determinism, predictions, and treatment.
   (b) order, understanding, and control.
   (c) description, prediction, and control.
   (d) description, understanding, and prediction and control of behavior.
   (LO3; p. 7)

5. A tentative statement about the possible relationship among two events is a(n)
   (a) explanation.
   (b) hypothesis.
   (c) description.
   (d) correlation.
   (LO4; p. 10)

6. A theory is
   (a) a general organizing framework for previously unrelated facts.
   (b) a complex hypothesis.
   (c) proof about an explanation of behavior.
   (d) not related to hypotheses.
   (LO4; p. 10)

7. Scientific evidence must be
   (a) based on empirical evidence.
   (b) objective.
   (c) repeatable.
   (d) all of the above.
   (LO3; p. 8)

8. A professor found that the students in his or her class who were doing well had also done relatively well in high school and that those doing poorly had done less well in high school. This represents a
   (a) high negative correlation.
   (b) high positive correlation.
   (c) low correlation.
   (d) causal relationship.
   (LO4; p. 11)

9. In a study, a psychologist makes one group of animals hungry and leaves the other group well fed, which of the following is probably true?
    (a) Hunger is the dependent variable.
    (b) This is a case study.
    (c) Hunger is the independent variable.
    (d) This study is examining the effects of some variable on hunger.
    (LO4; p. 12)

10. A group of educational psychologists are interested in the effect of teaching technique on learning. They design an experiment in which they teach two nearly identical classes with different teaching methods and give the classes the same examination at the end of the semester.
    (a) The result on the examination is the independent variable.
    (b) The result on the examination is the dependent variable.
    (c) This is only a study of correlation.
    (d) This is a case study of educational practice.
    (LO4; p. 12)

11. An operational definition of intelligence might be
    (a) a person's score on an IQ test.
    (b) a person's problem-solving ability.
    (c) the amount of knowledge a person has.
    (d) the theoretical genetic basis of intelligence.
    (LO4; p. 12)

12. If the experimental and control groups are exactly the same (or as similar as possible) except with respect to the independent variable, which of the following is true?
    (a) No experiment is possible because there is no difference between the groups.
    (b) A case study is the study of choice.
    (c) Only a correlation would be appropriate.
    (d) Experimental control has been exercised.
    (LO4; p. 14)

13. Randomized assignment of subjects to groups in an experiment is
    (a) a way of assuring that the sample is representative of the population from which it was drawn.
    (b) a control procedure.
    (c) a way of operationally defining the independent variable.
    (d) necessary in a study looking at a correlational relationship.
    (LO4; p. 14)

14. A study investigating the effects of the level of hunger and fatigue on reaction time, measured in seconds, obtained the following average reaction times for four groups of subjects:

| *Level of hunger* | | *Level of fatigue* | |
|---|---|---|---|
| low | high | low | high |
| 1.0 | .5 | .5 | 1.0 |

These data suggest that
    (a) higher levels of fatigue result in shorter reaction times.
    (b) higher levels of hunger result in shorter reaction times.
    (c) neither hunger level nor fatigue level affect reaction time.
    (d) there may be an interaction between hunger and fatigue with respect to their influence on reaction time.
    (LO4; p. 16)

15. Why are lower animals sometimes used to study problems of interest of psychologists?
    (a) Animal psychological processes are all exactly the same as human psychological processes.
    (b) Some experiments are not ethically possible with human subjects.
    (c) Some studies are possible to do with animals, and the results are likely to be the same in the animal as in a human.
    (d) Both b and c are true.
    (LO4; p. 16)

16. The school of thought known as structuralism
    (a) was started by William James.
    (b) is associated with Edward Titchener.
    (c) is aimed at understanding the basic elements of consciousness or mental processes.
    (d) Both b and c are true.
    (LO5; p. 18)

17. A school of thought based upon the existence of an unconscious mind was
    (a) Freud's psychoanalysis.
    (b) James's functionalism.
    (c) cognitive psychology.
    (d) humanistic psychology.
    (LO5; p. 20)

18. A school of thought in psychology that admitted only to the importance of overt observable events and actions was
    (a) Freud's psychoanalysis.
    (b) James's functionalism.
    (c) Watson's behaviorism.
    (d) experimental psychology.
    (LO5; p. 18)

**19.** Cognitive psychology grew out of
   (a) psychoanalysis.
   (b) functionalism.
   (c) behaviorism.
   (d) Gestalt psychology.
   (LO6; p. 19)

**20.** A study aimed at finding out how to reduce the purchase of cola in vending machines, and increase the purchase of more nutritional juices would be an example of
   (a) pure basic research.
   (b) applied research.
   (c) experimental research.
   (d) correlational research.
   (LO7; p. 23)

*ANSWERS*

1. b, 2. b, 3. a, 4. d, 5. b, 6. a, 7. d, 8. b, 9. c, 10. b, 11. a, 12. d, 13. b, 14. d, 15. d, 16. d, 17. a, 18. c, 19. d, 20. b

# THINKING ABOUT PSYCHOLOGY

**1.** Some of the most interesting behaviors are very difficult to operationally define and can be measured in many ways. Design two different operational definitions for each of the following behavioral phenomena and speculate on whether the definitions are measuring precisely the same thing, or are measuring different aspects of complex phenomena: (a) aggression in adolescents, (b) shyness, (c) hunger.

**2.** A researcher proposes the hypothesis that physically attractive people are generally perceived to be warmer and more likable than physically unattractive ones. Design a study to test this hypothesis, mentioning your operational definitions, your independent and dependent variables, your sample, and your experimental controls.

**3.** A group of scientists is interested in studying why some people become alcoholics and others can drink just as much without ever developing an addiction. Compare how this team would approach the problem if they were using a (a) behavioristic perspective, (b) biological perspective, (c) sociocultural perspective, or (d) psychoanalytic perspective. How would their approach influence the questions they asked and the behaviors they choose to measure?

# SUGGESTED READINGS

American Psychological Association. (1987). Resolutions approved by the National Conference on Graduate Education in Psychology. *American Psychologist, 42*(12), 1070–1084. A look into the core curriculum for students planning to continue their studies in psychology.

Borchardt, D. H., & Francis, R. D. (1984). *How to find out in psychology: A guide to the literature and methods of research.* New York: Pergamon. An annotated guide that describes how to search published literature in psychology.

Corsini, R. J. (Ed.). (1984). *Encyclopedia of psychology.* New York: Wiley. A four-volume reference set summarizing a variety of issues and topics in psychology.

Leahy, T. H. (1991). *A history of modern psychology.* Englewood Cliffs, NJ: Prentice-Hall. An excellent review of psychology's recent past, covering behaviorism and cognitive science extremely well.

Martin, D. W. (1985). *Doing psychology experiments* (2nd ed.). Monterey, CA: Brooks/Cole. An easy-to-read introduction to research methodology that is very appropriate for lower-level students in psychology.

Martin, P., & Bateson, P. (1986). *Measuring behaviour: An introductory guide.* Cambridge, England: Cambridge University Press. An excellent beginner's book on the scientific method as it is used in social science.

Miller, S. (1984). *Experimental design and statistics* (2nd ed.). London: Methuen. This small handbook covers basic experimental design, descriptive statistics, and various kinds of inferential statistical techniques that can be used in simple experiments.

Segall, M. H., Dasen, P. R., Berry, J. W., and Poortinga, Y. H. (1990). *Human behavior in global perspective: An introduction to cross-cultural psychology.* New York: Pergamon Press. An exploration of the sociocultural perspective.

Skinner, B. F. (1953). *Science and human behavior.* New York: Macmillan. A classic on the subject of behaviorism.

Stanovich, K. E. (1986). *How to think straight about psychology.* Glenview, IL: Scott, Foresman. Explains how to evaluate psychological research.

Wertheimer, M. (1987). *A brief history of psychology* (3rd ed.). New York: Holt, Rinehart & Winston. A brief and clear primer on the history of psychology, beginning with Plato and proceeding to the major schools of the twentieth century.

# PART II

## BASICS OF BEHAVIOR

# CHAPTER 2

## BIOLOGICAL BASES OF BEHAVIOR
### OUTLINE

▶ Learning Objectives

▶ The Neuron: Building Block of the Nervous System

■ The Neuron's Structure
  The Dendrites
  The Cell Body
  The Axon
  The Axon Terminals
■ Moving Information Down the Axon
  The Resting Potential
  The Action Potential
■ Moving Information from One Neuron to Another
■ To Spike or Not to Spike

▶ Guided Review

▶ The Central Nervous System

■ Studying the Central Nervous System
  Anatomical Techniques
  Brain Imaging
  Electrical Recording
  Electrical Stimulation of the Brain (ESB)
  Brain Lesions and Brain Damage
■ The Brain's Structure
  The Cerebral Cortex
  The Lobes
  The Limbic System
  The Cerebellum
  The Medulla
■ The Spinal Cord

▶ Guided Review

▶ The Peripheral Nervous System

■ The Somatic Nervous System
■ The Autonomic Nervous System

▶ Guided Review

▶ The Endocrine System

■ Hormones and Glands
■ Hormones and Behavior

▶ Guided Review

▶ When Things Go Wrong: Malfunctions in the Nervous System

▶ Guided Review

▶ Hemispheric Asymmetry

■ The Split Brain
  The Left Hemisphere—Master of Language and Arithmetic
  The Right Hemisphere—Master of Space
  What about the Lefties?
■ Hemispheric Asymmetry: What Does It Mean?
■ Mind, Consciousness, and the Brain

▶ Guided Review

▶ Summary

▶ Action Glossary

▶ Self-Test

▶ Thinking About Psychology

▶ Suggested Readings

# BIOLOGICAL BASES OF BEHAVIOR
## LEARNING OBJECTIVES

**After reading this chapter, you should be able to**

▶ **1.** describe the neuron's structure. (p. 35–37)

▶ **2.** explain how the neuron moves information. (pp. 37–39)

▶ **3.** explain how neurons communicate with one another. (pp. 39–41)

▶ **4.** describe the methods used to study the nervous system. (pp. 41–45)

▶ **5.** outline the main structures of the brain and the spinal cord. (pp. 45–50)

▶ **6.** explain the role of the peripheral nervous system in the control of movement, the transmission of sensory signals, and the preparation of the body for an emergency. (pp. 51–54)

▶ **7.** describe the major endocrine glands and their hormones, and give examples of how some of them affect behavior. (pp. 54–56)

▶ **8.** define the neural disorders called epilepsy and Tourette's Syndrome, and stroke, and explain how studying these disorders can help scientists learn more about brain function. (pp. 56–58)

▶ **9.** explain the specializations of the right and left hemispheres of the brain. (pp. 59–64)

▶ **10.** describe how studies of split-brain patients have led to insights regarding the nature of the mind and consciousness in human beings. (p. 64)

On the afternoon of September 13, 1848, Phineas Gage was working with blasting powder and an iron bar, and an accidental spark caused an explosion that drove the bar through his head. The bar entered his left jaw, emerged near the midline of the top of his skull, and landed several feet away (figure 2.1)

Mr. Gage did not die from this wound. His fellow railroad workers drove him to his hotel in an oxcart, and he walked up the stairs to his room by himself. A physician dressed the wound, and within a few weeks Gage was back on his feet, apparently recovered.

He was not the same, however. Before the accident, Gage was well-liked and was very efficient at his foreman's job. After the accident, he became irresponsible, obstinate, and generally incapable of holding a job. He moved frequently and eventually became a circus exhibit. He lived for thirteen years drifting from job to job (Harlow, 1848; 1868).

The fact that Gage survived at all is amazing, but even more remarkable was his changed personality. His case, and many more like it, show that what we are—who we are—depends to a large extent on what is going on in the tissue we call the brain. Our thoughts, memories, rages, hopes, dreams, and longings all have some biological basis, and studying behavior without understanding something about biology is like describing a pencil as a stick of wood with a piece of rubber at the end. It is not a pencil, and it cannot write, without its hidden core of graphite. The human body, and especially its most astounding nervous system, is the foundation of human behavior and it is here that we begin our study of psychology.

Student protestations about the relevance of biology to an introductory course in psychology are not uncommon. In our years of teaching, we've heard students voice doubt about the importance of understanding how a nerve cell works, or about the role and location of various brain areas. The case of Phineas Gage is not so surprising—an iron bar went through his head. Of course it affected him. But what does Phineas's predicament have to do with biology's role in normal behavior?

One reason human beings may be reluctant to accept the role of biology in behavior is that they feel as though they don't have much control over this aspect of their being. While we can choose to try a new style of child rearing that avoids the use of punishment, we cannot easily choose to change the output of hormones from our glands or cause our neurons to operate differently. Our legal

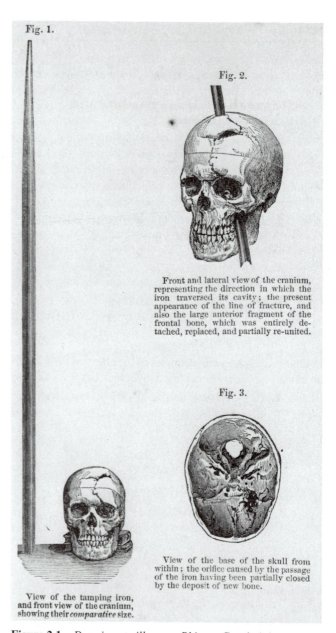

Fig. 1.

Fig. 2.

Front and lateral view of the cranium, representing the direction in which the iron traversed its cavity; the present appearance of the line of fracture, and also the large anterior fragment of the frontal bone, which was entirely detached, replaced, and partially re-united.

Fig. 3.

View of the base of the skull from within; the orifice caused by the passage of the iron having been partially closed by the deposit of new bone.

View of the tamping iron, and front view of the cranium, showing their *comparative* size.

**Figure 2.1**   *Drawings to illustrate Phineas Gage's injury.*

systems reaffirm the persistent belief that biology is destiny; if some biological basis for a person's crime can be found, that person is not responsible. The discovery that a serial killer has a brain tumor somehow "explains" the heinous crimes. The historical belief that women were biologically less able than men to control their emotions contributed to their lighter sentences for criminal behavior.

Our knowledge of the relationship between biology and behavior is still very primitive. Using animal models, we've learned a great deal about how an individual neuron works, but we know very little about how millions of them work together in the brain to produce thinking, feeling, striving, or dreaming. For this, we still rely heavily on cases in which something goes wrong—brain damage, epilepsy, surgical interventions. But new tools and new approaches are rapidly emerging. We now know, for example, that the delicately balanced chemistry of the brain is a critical ingredient in behavior, perhaps not such a startling discovery since humans have been using herbal concoctions to modify thought processes throughout history. But now we know much more about how those herbs and fungi can affect behavior and how drugs can mimic their effects.

We also know that behavior affects biology as much as the reverse, though we still have much to learn about this subject. Ingesting drugs is a behavioral act that has many biological consequences. Mood swings may alter a person's brain chemistry and even their immune systems in subtle ways. As more examples of the effects of behavior on biology surface, we may need to reevaluate some of our deeply rooted legal notions about responsibility.

The link between biology and behavior is a strong one. With each year that goes by and as new relationships are discovered, there is a richer, more detailed story to tell and we suspect that soon students will stop asking why their study of psychology begins with a diagram of the neuron, the building block of the nervous system.

## THE NEURON: BUILDING BLOCK OF THE NERVOUS SYSTEM

Living organisms are made up of cells, each with its own nucleus, cell membrane, and other structures. Some living things, such as the amoeba, consist of only one cell. Others, like algae, contain many cells very similar to one another. A living organism as complex as a human being contains an enormous number of cells organized into specialized groups to perform certain functions. Muscle cells are designed to contract, red blood cells to carry oxygen, and bone cells to provide a sturdy skeleton for the body.

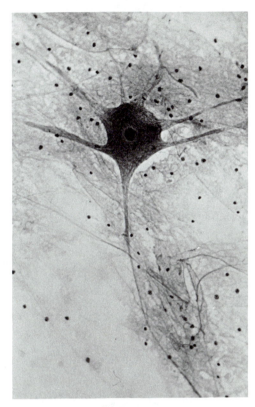

**Figure 2.2**   *The neuron is a cell that processes information.*

The **neuron** *is a cell that processes information. It moves information from place to place in the body and also collects input from other neurons, processes it, and passes the information to other neurons* (see figure 2.2).

### The Neuron's Structure

Although all living cells have many common features, they also show important differences that relate to their specialized functions. For example, a muscle cell is long and narrow, a shape that facilitates contraction. The neuron's structure enables it to process information. Neurons are not all alike; they perform somewhat different functions depending on their location in the nervous system. However, all neurons share a number of characteristics. Figure 2.3 shows the neuron's four main parts.

1. The *dendrites,* or input end.
2. The *cell body,* where the nucleus is located.
3. The *axon,* a long projection that carries information from the cell body to the axon terminals.
4. The *axon terminals,* or output end.

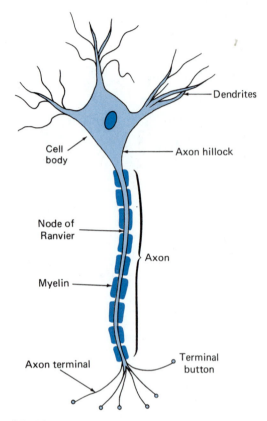

Figure 2.3   *The neuron*

*The Dendrites*    The **dendrites** *of a neuron look some-what like a tree, and, in fact, they are often called the "dendritic tree." They are the portion of the cell that receives most of the input.* Each of the tiny knobs on the tree receives a message from a nearby neuron. While some neurons in the nervous system receive input from only a few neurons, others have an enormous dendritic tree with thousands of knobs.

Dendritic trees, and the interneural links they represent, suggest an almost infinite complexity in the nervous system and a limitless potential for variation in messages. It is tempting to assume that the degree of branching is partly related to the degree of behavioral flexibility. Although this connection has not yet been clearly demonstrated, certain findings lead in that direction. For example, patients with **Alzheimer's disease,** *a condition involving progressive deterioration of cognitive skills,* show reduced branching in their dendritic trees, suggesting deterioration or elimination of some branches (Scheibel & Scheibel,

1975). Some classic experiments demonstrated that the environment in which a growing organism develops can affect many aspects of brain development (Bennett, Diamond, Krech, & Rosenzweig, 1964; Greenough, 1975; Rosenzweig, 1984), including dendritic branching.

In a set of classic experiments some rats were reared in standard laboratory cages by themselves, with only food, water, and nesting material. Others were reared in a more complex environment—one that might even be called "enriched." They lived with other rats in larger cages and were given many toys, such as dolls, tin cans, and blocks, to play with. When all the rats were grown, the researchers compared their brains and found, among many differences, that the brains of the enriched rats had larger dendritic trees. Neurons with more extensive dendritic trees receive more input and might make more connections with other neurons.

No one knows whether rats from an enriched environment are actually more intelligent than rats reared in impoverished laboratory cages, but they do have more flexible behavior. For example, they appear to be less emotional when psychologists test them in mazes, and they perform better on complex problems (Brown, 1968). The first time rats reared in standard cages are confronted with a new environment, they usually hide in the corner and lose control of their bladder and bowels.

It is clear that an enriched environment can have substantial effects on the brains of rats and other animals. Similar changes probably occur in growing children. Children reared in the relatively unstimulating environments characteristic of some institutions are often sluggish or retarded, suggesting possible brain abnormalities. Enriching intervention programs are known to be helpful (Hayden & Haring, 1985). Psychologists have known that the way infants are reared could affect their behavior. Now it seems possible that the way they are reared may affect their brain development as well.

*The Cell Body*    The **cell body** *is the part of the neuron that contains the nucleus, the structure containing the cell's genetic information, and many of the structures that maintain the life of the cell, manufacture proteins, dispose of waste, and produce energy.* It acts as the factory of the cell, receiving directions from the DNA in the nucleus to synthesize and assemble the required cellular components.

The size of the cell bodies of neurons varies considerably. Some are as tiny as four or five microns in diameter. (A micron is 1/1000 millimeter.) Others range up to 50 or 100 microns in diameter and are almost visible to the naked eye.

*The Axon    The long, thin tube that carries information from the cell body to the axon terminals is the* **axon.** Most axons in the human nervous system are surrounded by **myelin,** *a whitish fatty substance that provides insulation.* The membrane of the axon only comes into contact with the surrounding fluid at the **nodes of Ranvier,** *locations along the axon where myelin is absent.*

Most axons are surrounded by myelin because the substance acts like an electrical insulator and makes it possible for axons to transmit signals much faster. Ordinarily, the speed at which a message moves along an axon is proportional to the axon's diameter—the larger the diameter, the faster the transmission speed. Myelination makes it possible for messages to "skip" from one node of Ranvier to the next. In some myelinated neurons, the velocity of conduction is as high as 120 meters per second (268 mph).

**Multiple sclerosis,** *a disease that produces vision problems, muscle weakness, lack of coordination, and spastic motions, is caused by the loss of myelin in the nervous system.* This tragic disease affects one-quarter of a million people in the United States and usually is first diagnosed in young adults between the ages of twenty and forty.

*The Axon Terminals    When the axon reaches its destination, it branches. At the ends of all the branches are the output ends of the cell,* the axon terminals. These swollen endings contain **neurotransmitters,** *special chemicals that enable neurons to pass messages to one another.*

## Moving Information Down the Axon

*The process of moving messages from one end of the axon to the other is called* **axonal conduction.** It is basically an electrical process that involves the movement of charged particles, or ions, through pores in the axon's membrane. Sodium ($Na^+$), potassium ($K^+$), chloride ($Cl^-$),

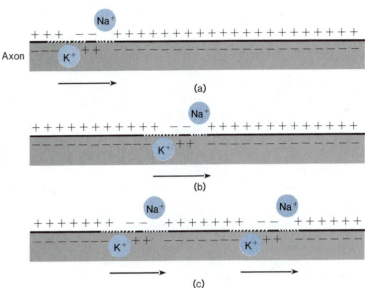

**Figure 2.4**   *Transmission of neural messages*

and large protein molecules with negative charges are the most important ions for understanding axonal conduction. These ions are not distributed evenly across the axon's membrane when the neuron is at rest, and their concentrations on either side of the membrane change dramatically when the neuron is moving a message. Most of the principles of axonal conduction were deduced from experiments on a surprisingly large axon in the giant squid (see Close Up on Research box: Studying the Squid's Axon).

*The Resting Potential    When the axon is at rest, there are more negative ions in the fluid inside the cell than in the fluid surrounding the cell because the membrane of the axon will not allow some of the larger ions, like sodium, to move back and forth freely. Sodium, which has a positive charge, is kept outside, and there is a buildup of negative charges inside. For most resting neurons, the difference between the charges on the outside and the inside of the axon is about −70 millivolts (1 millivolt=1/1000 volt). The charge difference across the axon's membrane is called the cell's* **resting potential.**

*The Action Potential    When the neuron is about to move a message, the resting potential changes drastically (figure 2.4). The membrane at the beginning of the axon suddenly becomes more permeable as certain channels in the

# CLOSE UP ON RESEARCH

## Studying the Squid's Axon

The details of axonal conduction were worked out many years ago in some classic experiments that took advantage of the enormous axon of the giant squid (Hodgkin & Katz, 1949; Hodgkin, 1964). Its unmyelinated axon is very durable and has become a favorite of neuroscientists. It can be removed from the animal, placed in a petri dish, and kept alive for long periods of time. Its diameter is about 500 times larger than unmyelinated fibers in the cat's nervous system. Thus, it is much easier to insert electrodes into the squid's axon. Finally, the neurons of the squid and the mammal work in very much the same way.

In an experiment designed to find which ions were most important in the axon's resting potential, the axon was placed in a bath, and an electrode inside the axon recorded its potential. When the concentration of sodium or chloride ions in the bath was changed, the resting potential of the axon did not change much. But if the concentration of potassium ions was altered, the resting potential changed considerably. This study demonstrated that the axon's resting potential is due to the different concentrations of potassium on the outside and inside of the axon, and to the fact that the membrane (at rest) is selectively permeable to potassium.

The squid's axon can even be squeezed, and the axoplasm inside can be pushed out with a roller. Then it can be filled with a fluid with specified ion concentrations to further investigate the electrical properties of the axon. When the inside of the axon and the bath in which it is floating have the same ion concentrations, the membrane potential is zero. But if the experimenters add potassium ions to the outside bath

and inject the axon with a solution that is low in potassium, then the recorded membrane potential is reversed. Instead of the usual –70 mv, the potential is +70mv. Studies like these show that the potassium level is an important factor in the resting potential.

The squid axon has also been important in studies of the action potential, especially in demonstrating that the axon's membrane opens up sodium channels and sodium ions rush into the cell. In one experiment, the axon was placed in different baths containing varying concentrations of sodium ions, and the size of the artificially generated action potentials was recorded. When the bath had a normal amount of sodium, the action potential was its usual size, reaching about +40 mv. But when the bath was diluted and contained a lower concentration of sodium, the action potentials' peaks were lower. This and other studies demonstrated that sodium is the key ion involved in generating an action potential.

The reason the squid's axon is so large is that the invertebrates do not have myelination in their nervous systems, and so the speed of conduction depends on the diameter of the axon. If information must be moved rapidly, the axon must be fairly large in diameter. The squid's axon conducts impulses at about twenty-five meters per second, a figure that compares well with myelinated axons in the mammalian nervous system (10 to 100 or 120 meters/second). This particular axon is wider in the squid because of its function. It controls the muscles that the squid uses to squirt a jet of water in order to suddenly change course and dart away.

membrane open rapidly. This allows the positively charged sodium ions to rush in. Just as abruptly, the membrane becomes almost impermeable to sodium, closes the channels, and the inrush of sodium stops. At the same time the membrane closes its doors to sodium, it opens its doors to potassium, a positively charged ion. The potassium ions are pushed out because the sodium ions have increased the concentration of positive ions inside the cell. Since positive charges repel one another, the potassium ions leak out toward the extracellular fluid where the concentration of positive ions is much lower. The loss of the positive potassium ions from inside the cell causes the axon to return to its original negative potential. *This*

*sudden burst of electrical activity inside the axon is the* **action potential,** *and constitutes the neural message carried by axonal conduction.* It is often called a "spike." The graph showing the changes in voltage (figure 2.5) makes the reason for the nickname clear.

Since some sodium ions enter and some potassium ions leave the cell each time the neuron fires, it would seem that the cell would eventually overflow with sodium ions and would not be able to produce any more spikes. However, a pump mechanism exists to prevent this from occurring. This **sodium potassium pump**, which requires about forty percent of the neuron's energy, *forces sodium out of the cell and potassium back in so that the neuron can continue to generate action potentials.*

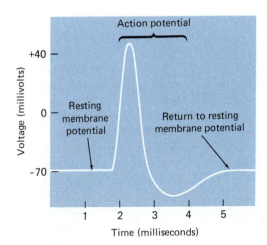

Figure 2.5    *The action potential, or spike*

Figure 2.6    *Example of a patterned sequence of spikes produced by a neuron within the span of one second*

The spike travels down the length of the axon as an action potential in one part of the membrane triggers another one in an adjoining membrane. In myelinated axons, the spike skips from one node of Ranvier to the next because the tight insulation prevents any movement of ions except at the exposed nodes. The action potential does not travel like a ripple in a pond; it does not fade away. When it reaches the axon terminals, it is the same size and strength as it was when it started. This is called the **all-or-none principle** or axonal conduction. *Either a full-sized spike is triggered and travels all the way down the axon, or it isn't; there is no such thing as a weak, half-sized spike.*

At any given time a single neuron's message is either an action potential or a resting potential. But the rate at which action potentials occur in a neuron can vary enormously; they can also appear in specific patterns, making it possible for a single neuron to move complicated messages. In one second, for example, one neuron might produce a patterned sequence of spikes like the one shown in figure 2.6. Even more important is the fact that the human brain contains billions of neurons arranged in specific structures and pathways. It is this vast network of cells and the ever-changing patterns of action potentials in different areas that provide the biological underpinnings of being human.

## Moving Information from One Neuron to Another

The role of the neuron is to transmit a message from one end to the other, and then pass a signal along to one or more neighbors. Conduction down the axon, especially myelinated ones, can be breathtakingly fast. Although the neuron uses an electrical process to move information down its own axon, it uses a chemical process to move it to the next neuron. *The process whereby information is passed from one neuron to the next is called* **synaptic transmission.** It occurs at *the junction between two neurons, the* **synapse** (figure 2.7).

The synapse between two neurons is usually located between the axon terminal of one neuron and the dendritic knob of another neuron. (A terminal is the output end of the neuron and the dendrite is the input end.) The information moves in one direction: from the terminal of the first neuron to the dendrite of the second neuron. In recent years, scientists have found that neurons are able to receive incoming information at many places besides the dendrites, such as along the cell body's membrane and even on the axon (Schmitt, Dev, & Smith, 1976); however, most synapses link one cell's axon terminal with another's dendrite.

*The axon terminal contains little pockets, or* **vesicles,** *filled with neurotransmitter.* Researchers have identified several kinds of neurotransmitters. A single neuron may use more than one neurotransmitter at its many terminals; it can also possess receptors for more than one neurotransmitter, creating quite a number of possibilities for communication between neurons (Nicoll, 1988).

The discovery of the neurotransmitters and their role in neural transmission started an avalanche of research into the biochemical basis of behavior. Botanists have known for some time that the organic structure of most plants used in religious ceremonies or witches' brews fall into a very small number of structural categories—the nitrogen-containing compounds known as alkaloids. Chemists observed that some of the most potent hallucinogenic plants bear an uncanny molecular resemblance to one or

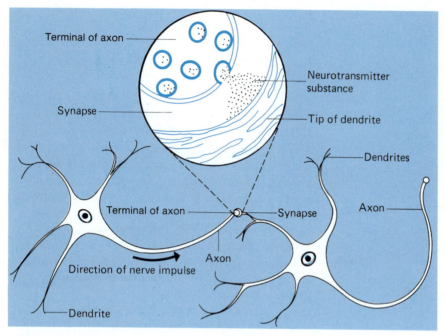

**Figure 2.7**   *The synapse*

more of the neurotransmitters, suggesting that their presence in the nervous system causes much confusion at receptor sites. Psilocybe, for example, is one species of mushroom used in Aztec religious rites to commune with the spirit world, and probably had been in use for at least 1700 years before the Spanish conquerors attempted to eradicate it. The active ingredient in this fungus, as in many hallucinogenic mushrooms, is psilocybin whose molecular structure is strikingly similar to serotonin, one of the neurotransmitters. Psychologists quickly began looking more closely at these neurotransmitters to learn how they affected the synapse, and how their actions affected behavior. We'll see some of this research in later chapters.

When a spike courses down the axon, it arrives very quickly at the neuron's axon terminals. This causes a vesicle of neurotransmitter to fuse with the terminal's membrane and release its chemical contents into the outside fluid (figure 2.7). When the molecules of neurotransmitter reach the dendrite of the next neuron, they attach to specific receptor sites on the membrane and produce a disturbance in the membrane's permeability to ions by opening or closing ion channels, either directly or

through the activation of intermediate proteins (Nicoll, 1988).

The distribution of positive and negative ions is uneven across the dendrite's membrane, just as it was across the axon's membrane. This means that any change in the permeability of the membrane will produce some movement of ions from one side to the other. The details concerning which ions move and why are rather complicated and not completely understood, but it is clear there is no sudden inrush of sodium ions as there is during a spike. Instead, the movement of ions is gradual, producing a less dramatic change in the potential at the dendrite. Nevertheless, this change is how the second neuron "knows" the first showed a spike.

Depending upon which ion channels are affected and whether the neurotransmitter caused an opening or closing of the channel, the neuron on the receiving end may become more or less likely to trigger its own action potential. Some synapses are excitatory because the ion channels are altered such that the inside of the neuron becomes more positive, making it more likely that the neuron will spike. Other synapses are inhibitory because the release of neurotransmitter into the synapse results in a decrease in the proportion of positive ions inside the cell. Thus, the neuron becomes more negative than usual and therefore less likely to spike. The neurotransmitter GABA is generally known as an inhibitory neurotransmitter; when it is released into a synapse, it causes inhibition in the next neuron (Dubinsky, Rothman, & Gottlieb, 1988).

The message that travels down the axon is in the form of an action potential, basically an electrical signal. When that message is moved to the next neuron, it is changed to a chemical signal through the release of neurotransmitter by the axon terminal. The message is transformed back into an electrical signal at the next neuron's dendrite. The nervous system is fluent in two languages: the electrical language is used for moving messages within a neuron, and the chemical language allows neurons to talk to one another.

## To Spike or Not to Spike

What makes a neuron spike? Is a neuron nothing more than a conduit that passes along anything that arrives as input? Or is it like a person playing the rumor game in which the message is subtly changed as it passes through the ears of each person in line? We mentioned earlier that a single neuron might be receiving input from hundreds or even thousands of its neighbors, and the brain would quickly become an explosion of spiking neurons if each one responded to every release of neurotransmitter. Instead, each neuron is capable of summarizing and integrating all of its incoming signals, creating a new message that it will pass along in its own pattern and tempo of spiking.

The neuron does its own summarizing electrically; it adds up all the electrical changes occurring in all its dendrites. If these changes are large enough and in the right direction, the neuron triggers its own action potential. If the changes continue to be large, the neuron triggers many spikes in rapid succession, up to one hundred per second. *The place at which incoming electrical activity from the dendrites is integrated and summarized is called the* **axon hillock;** *it is located in the cell body just at the point where the axon protrudes.*

The building block of the nervous system is thus much more than a simple, mechanical conduit. It is a tiny information processor that can summarize, integrate, and pass along an interpretation of its own environment. Scientists sometimes compare the human brain to a computer, but a better comparison would be between the neuron and a computer. Like present day computers, the neuron moves information down its length sequentially in digital fashion, transmitting signals of 0 (resting potential) and 1 (action potential). But even the tiny neuron is capable of more than most of today's computers: the neuron accepts constantly varying analog input in the rising and falling electrical patterns produced by the action of neurotransmitters at its many receptor sites. The computer needs a modem or other special device to translate analog signals into its restricted digital environment. The neuron can also sprout new axons, form new synapses, lose old ones, and develop incredibly elaborate dendritic trees.

The progress that has been made in understanding how a neuron works has been very great. But when they work together in the central nervous system, we move into terrain that is considerably less well charted.

▶ **GUIDED REVIEW** *Learning Objectives 1, 2, and 3*

1. The neuron is specialized to process information. Its four main parts are the _____, the _____, the _____, and the _____.
2. Axons are tubelike cables protruding from the cell body, usually surrounded by _____, a fatty insulating substance. Myelin is absent only at the _____. Myelination allows neural messages to skip from node to node. Loss of myelin is the primary cause of _____.
3. _____ is the electrical process by which a neural message moves from one end of the axon to the other. The _____ is the difference between the charges inside and outside of the axon when it is at rest. The _____ or spike is the neural message itself. It travels down the axon using the _____ principle of conduction.
4. The _____ is the junction between two neurons. _____ is a chemical process involving the release of _____ from the axon terminal when a spike courses down the axon. Neurotransmitter causes either an _____ or _____ electrical disturbance in the dendrite's membrane.
5. A neuron receives inputs from many neurons all over its dendritic tree. These are integrated and summarized at the _____, and the resulting summary determines whether the neuron will trigger its own spike.

*Answers*

1. dendrites, cell body, axon, axon terminals 2. myelin, nodes of Ranvier, multiple sclerosis 3. Axonal conduction, resting potential, action potential, all-or-none 4. synapse, Synaptic transmission, neurotransmitter, excitatory, inhibitory 5. axon hillock

## THE CENTRAL NERVOUS SYSTEM

One night, Mrs. O'C. had a dream about her childhood in Ireland and vividly heard the songs they danced to and sang in her youth. When she awoke the music was still playing. She checked the neighbors' radios but found none were left on. She considered the hypothesis that the fillings in her teeth were picking up radio signals, but dismissed it because she heard no commercials, no talking, no news. Mrs. O'C. concluded the music must be in her head.

The visits to the physician confirmed her suspicion; electrical recordings of her brain showed that she was having seizures in her right temporal lobe, an area involved in the processing of auditory messages. The seizures appeared every time she heard the music begin, and were apparently due to a stroke in the same part of the brain. Months later, the seizures—and the music—faded

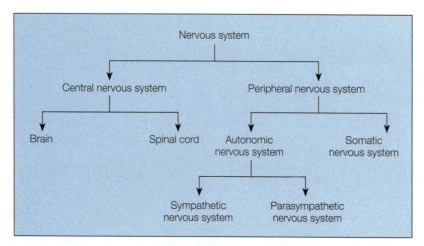

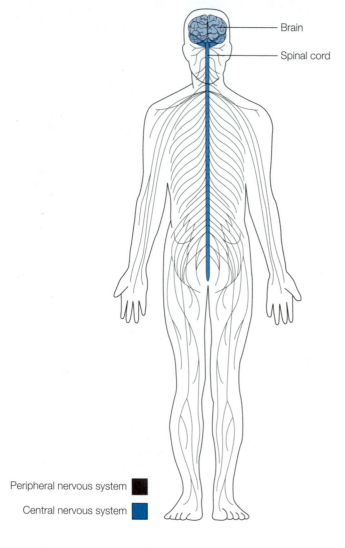

Brain

Spinal cord

Peripheral nervous system ▇

Central nervous system ▇

and Mrs. O'C.'s internal radio was silenced. The musical memories of her long forgotten childhood in Ireland, temporarily brought back to consciousness through a strange accident in the brain, were gone, and Mrs. O'C. missed them (Sacks, 1985).

The billions of neurons in the human body are part of the nervous system and together, they form the basis of our thoughts, actions, feelings, desires, and memories. They also give us the ability to move, breathe, digest food, pace our hearts, and store memories that may not be easily recalled, such as those of Mrs. O'C. The nervous system is never truly at rest until death; neurons continue to spike even during the deepest sleep.

The nervous system (figure 2.8) is usually divided into two main parts called the **central nervous system (CNS),** *which includes the brain and spinal cord,* and the **peripheral nervous system (PNS),** *which includes all the neurons that lie outside the brain and spinal cord.* Axons in the PNS regenerate if they are damaged; but for reasons not well understood, axons in the CNS generally do not regenerate. Much progress is being made to promote their growth and recovery of function (see Applying Psychology box: Brain Transplants). In this section we will explore the CNS, focusing on the activities of the human brain.

**Figure 2.8**  *The organization of the nervous system. The nervous system comprises the brain, spinal cord, and nerves.*

## APPLYING PSYCHOLOGY

### Brain Transplants

Damage to the brain, whether caused by disease, injury, genetic predisposition, aging, or other factors, has been extremely difficult to correct. The great majority of neurons are in place by the end of infancy; for humans, development of the nervous system is complete by puberty. Although axons in the peripheral nervous system can usually regrow and form new connections after damage, damaged axons in the central nervous system rarely re-form.

Despite this bleak pronouncement, scientists have found ways to promote the growth and return of function in damaged central nervous system tissue. For example, the application of electric fields to damaged spinal cord tissue appears to promote axonal regeneration and the recovery of function (Borgens, Blight, & McGinnis, 1987). Perhaps the most amazing line of research in this area involves transplantation of healthy tissue into the damaged area of the brain (Fine, 1986).

Some success using brain transplants has been reported for the degenerative disease known as Parkinsonism. This syndrome, one of the most common neurological diseases, affects more than one million people in the United States, most of whom are over the age of sixty. Symptoms include rigidity, tremors, speech impairment, and weakness, all of which grow increasingly worse as the disease progresses. Scientists agree that the disease is caused by the degeneration of cells in the substantia nigra, which produces dopamine, a neurotransmitter important in motor behavior.

The traditional treatment for Parkinsonism is L-dopa, a substance needed to synthesize dopamine and alleviate the deficit of the neurotransmitter. But after five or ten years, the drug seems to lose its effect. Recently, surgeons have attempted brain transplants in an effort to restore the capacity of this important brain area.

One approach involves transplanting substantia nigra tissue from healthy fetuses into the damaged brain. It has long been known that fetal neural tissue is more plastic than adult tissue, and grafts can often become fully incorporated into the host brain. Scientists have conducted many experiments with animals, using rats whose substantia nigra is damaged with a drug that selectively destroys neurons, fibers, and terminals that contain neurotransmitters like dopamine. These rats display Parkinson-like symptoms. When fragments of embryonic brain containing the precursor cells of the substantia are transplanted into the brain of the adult rat, the movement abnormalities are reduced.

This approach has been successfully demonstrated with animals, but there are potential problems for human beings. First, tissue grafts are notoriously vulnerable to rejection by the immune system when the donor is not genetically similar. Strangely, brain transplants are rarely rejected, even from donors of different species! The brain seems to be an "immunologically privileged" site, one to which the immune system has little access. A much greater problem is the ethical one. Aborted fetuses are the most likely source for fetal brain tissue.

Because of ethical and legal problems surrounding the use of human fetuses, scientists have studied other kinds of transplants for Parkinsonism that might also provide the needed dopamine. Recently, surgeons in Mexico successfully transplanted cells from a part of the patient's adrenal gland to his brain and found significant improvement in the patient's condition. Part of the adrenal gland also produces dopamine, and it appears that the transplanted cells help to alleviate the patient's dopamine deficit. Since the patient is serving as his own donor, there are no immunological or ethical problems (Lewin, 1987). Surgeons in this country are eager to begin clinical trials to determine whether these brain transplants will help patients with Parkinsonism.

Although these results are promising, they make it clear that there is much that we don't know about the brain. For example, some patients with adrenal transplants show unusual and unexpected behavioral changes after the surgery, such as delusions, strange sleep patterns, and lowered sensitivity to pain. The adrenal gland produces a great deal more than just dopamine, and its transplantation to the brain seems to be causing unpredictable effects (Lewin, 1988).

## Studying the Central Nervous System

Studying the CNS may sound like a pursuit only possible with the sophisticated equipment and high technology found in large research centers. In fact, much of what we know about the brain was learned with little more than keen observation. A sharp knife and a microscope were the first important research tools, and once the electrical nature of the brain was understood, voltmeters and microelectrodes were added to the tool box.

The most common methods used to study the relationship between brain function and behavior are (1) anatomical techniques, (2) brain imaging, (3) electrical recording, (4) electrical stimulation of the brain (ESB), and (5) brain lesions. Each has advantages and disadvantages; it is usually necessary to use more than one method to definitely relate brain function to a particular behavior.

*Anatomical Techniques*    In anatomical studies, neuroanatomists examine brain tissue and pathways, and note correlations between the appearance of the tissue and the behavior of the animal or human. The experiment that found increased dendritic branching in enriched rats is a good example of an anatomical study. Specific changes in the anatomy of the rats' brains were related to the characteristics of the rearing environment and to later changes in behavior.

Anatomical methods do not just consist of sectioning the tissue and looking at its structure. Neuroanatomists make extensive use of stains and dyes to highlight different parts of the neuron; they may also inject radioactive substances and follow their course. For example, one very powerful technique involves the injection of radioactively labeled glucose. Since active neurons need nutrition, they pick up the glucose from the bloodstream before the less active ones do. Later examination of the brain tissue reveals which areas were most active at the time; they will have the highest concentrations of radioactivity.

*Brain Imaging*    In recent years, a variety of techniques have become available in the general category of brain imaging. One of the earliest is **computerized axial tomography,** *or a* **CAT** *scan; it uses a computer and multiple X-rays to obtain detailed pictures of the brain and other organs* (figure 2.9). Because the pictures are clearer than normal X-rays, exact locations of tumors or other structural abnormalities can be identified. **Magnetic resonance imaging (MRI)** *shows more detailed images of the brain compared to CAT scans, using magnetic fields and radio waves rather than X-rays.*

An important group of brain imaging techniques provides information not just about anatomical structures but about the brain at work. Using **positron emission tomography,** *or PET, the patient is injected with radioactive versions of substances used by the brain, and the location and decay of the substances is tracked. The high-resolution images show where the chemical is taken up.* Early PET scan studies used radioactively labeled glucose to assess metabolic activity in different areas of the brain. More recently, radioactive forms of oxygen, neurotransmitters, and psychoactive drugs have been used

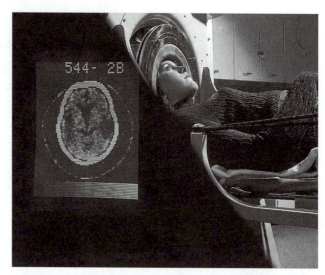

**Figure 2.9**    *An example of a CAT scan*

to determine where these substances are taken up and where the receptor sites are located. Although PET scans require an on-site cyclotron and a team of experts, they are extremely promising for studies of brain function.

Brain imaging detects differences in the structure and function of the brains of normal people and of people with behavioral disorders (Andreason, 1988). For example, studies of people suffering from schizophrenia, a severe mental disorder, show various differences in neurotransmitter function and brain structure as measured by CAT and PET scans. These differences may lead scientists to learn more about the nature of the disease and its possible cures.

*Electrical Recording*    The fact that neurons transmit messages using action and resting potentials means that a great deal of brain activity is electrical. An **electroencephalograph,** *or EEG, measures the electrical activity of the brain and records it. Electrodes placed on the scalp record the rapidly changing electrical events occurring between them as waves on moving chart paper.* Computer-assisted statistical analysis of large numbers of EEGs from people of all ages show that the wave patterns are different depending on age, location of the electrodes, state of consciousness, presence of certain behavioral disorders, and other variables (John, Prichep, Fridman, & Easton, 1988). Chapter 3 will explore the relationship between the EEG and consciousness in more detail.

In medicine, the EEG is used to monitor patients with epilepsy, stroke, head injuries, or infections that might affect the nervous system. Using multiple electrodes placed over the skull, neurologists can determine the general location of abnormal brain activity. For Mrs. O'C., the EEG patterns emanating from her right temporal lobe were abnormal, confirming the diagnosis that the auditory sensations she was experiencing were due to damage in the part of the brain that processes memories for sounds. In her case, the neurologist asked her to raise her finger slightly each time the music began while her brain waves were being recorded. Each time she raised her finger, the pens recording the EEG from the temporal lobe showed unusual spikes and sharp waves. As the weeks passed and the music faded, so did the abnormal patterns on her EEG.

Most states also use the signals on the EEG to determine whether a person is legally dead. We used to consider a person legally dead when his or her heart stopped. Now, with advances in technology, a patient can be maintained on life-support equipment even though he or she may have no hope of ever regaining consciousness. The concept of brain death emerged as a result of many legal battles over whether it was moral, ethical, and legal to disconnect a patient's life-support equipment.

While the EEG is used to record a kind of summarized electrical activity in large parts of the brain, microelectrodes can be used to record activity in small groups of neurons and in individual cells. A tiny hole is drilled through the skull. The microelectrode is then inserted into the brain and placed next to or into the axon of a neuron, where it detects the changes in voltage that accompany spikes.

Fascinating findings that relate the activity of particular neurons to specialized behaviors or complex perceptions have emerged from this technique (McGinty & Szymusiak, 1988). For example, one area of the brain contains "place cells," that respond only when the animal is in a particular part of its cage (O'Keefe, 1979). Another kind of cell, found in the monkey brain, responds only when the animal is looking at a familiar face (Leonard, Rolls, Wilson, & Baylis, 1985). Perhaps neurons like these, and thousands more that respond to other important stimuli in the environment, form the basis of what we understand as perception and recognition.

*Electrical Stimulation of the Brain (ESB)*    Electrical stimulation of the brain (ESB) is a technique used to relate activity in particular brain regions to behavior. An elec-

trode is inserted into a specific brain region, and then current is passed through it. This causes rapid spiking in the surrounding neurons. During some kinds of brain surgery in which this technique is used, the patient is wide awake. The surgeon electrically stimulates some brain area and notes any reactions in the patient. (The patient does not experience any pain from the electric current since the brain feels no pain. This operation requires only a local anesthetic on the scalp.) The use of this technique has revealed a great deal about the functions of various brain areas.

*Brain Lesions and Brain Damage*    Though the changes in behavior that people undergo after brain damage can often be tragic, they provide scientists with insights into how particular areas of the brain are involved in specific behaviors. Our understanding of the brain processes, especially those underlying language, has advanced considerably because of studies of patients with brain damage. In animal experiments, portions of the brain are destroyed by a lesion, produced either by cutting away sections of the brain tissue or by administering large jolts of electrical current. Then the behavior of the animal is observed. Any changes might be due to the damage in that brain area.

Brain damage in some areas of the brain occasionally produces rather remarkable changes. In one of the most studied cases in psychology, the patient H. M. underwent an operation designed to relieve severe epilepsy. Surgeons removed a small part of the brain. After surgery, H. M. had fewer epileptic seizures, but he also showed an astounding memory deficit. Minutes after reading a magazine article, he could read it again as though he had never seen it before. Apparently, his ability to remember new information for more that a few seconds was completely lost (Milner, 1970). H. M.'s case and others like it (Zola-Morgan et al., 1986) suggested that the area that was removed, a structure called the **hippocampus,** might be *an area of the brain that has some role in long-term memory.*

## The Brain's Structure

The human brain is actually very large, but it is folded and convoluted inside the skull. The working parts of the brain are the neurons, but the brain also contains **glial cells.** *These cells perform chores, such as filtering substances from the bloodstream, preventing important chemicals from leaving the brain, providing the myelin sheath, and forming a supporting matrix.*

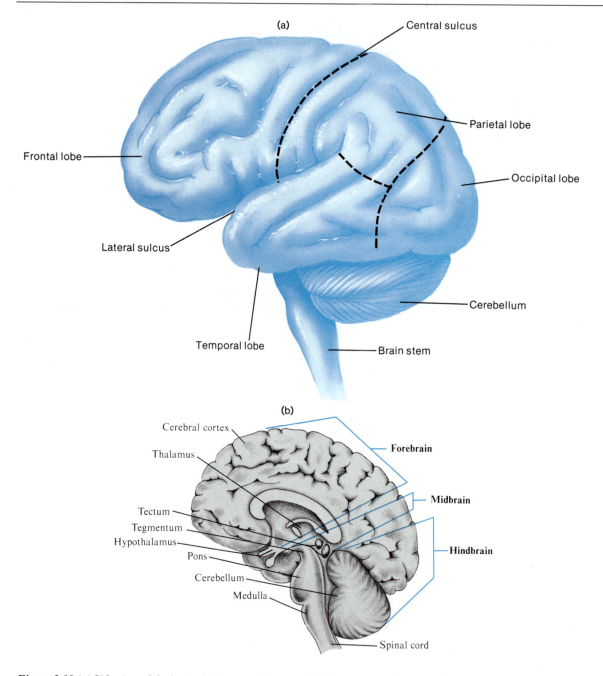

**Figure 2.10** *(a) Side view of the brain (b) Cross section of the brain*

The brain is shaped like a mushroom (figure 2.10). The stem contains the structures that take care of basic and somewhat mechanical functions like breathing and heart action. ***The huge overhanging top part of the brain is "newer"; it evolved later, and its structures and pathways perform the functions related to human intelligence. This brain area is the massive* cerebral hemispheres.** The left hemisphere controls activities on the right side of the body, and the right hemisphere controls activities on the left side of the body. The **corpus callosum** *is a bundle of fibers that links the two hemispheres.* (Usually, the left hand does indeed know what the right hand is doing. In a special case we discuss at the end of this chapter, the communication between the two hemispheres is broken, and the person has "two brains in one.")

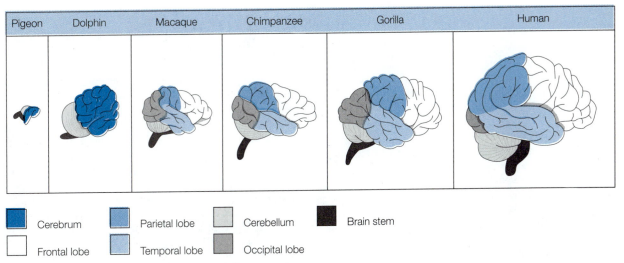

| Pigeon | Dolphin | Macaque | Chimpanzee | Gorilla | Human |

■ Cerebrum     ■ Parietal lobe     ▢ Cerebellum     ■ Brain stem

▢ Frontal lobe     ■ Temporal lobe     ▨ Occipital lobe

**Figure 2.11**     *The relative size of brain areas in different species*

During the Middle Ages, the idea arose that different areas of the brain were involved in different behaviors. This concept was carried to an extreme during the eighteenth and nineteenth centuries by a group called the **phrenologists.** *They believed you could understand a person's behavior by feeling for bumps and depressions on the skull.* Some phrenologists even tried to mold the behavior of children by putting caps on their head to produce bumps in certain places.

Today, most people would agree that the phrenologists carried things a bit far. Their initial idea did have merit; it is clear that certain brain areas are indeed involved in particular behaviors. However, brain areas are usually involved in more than one behavior, and each behavior involves many brain areas. Pathways in the brain that span several structures seem to be more related to particular behaviors than individual structures or discrete areas. Nevertheless, it is important to keep in mind how quaint and naive scientific ideas may sound 100 years after they have been proposed. We can only wonder which of our ideas will sound absurd to people in the twenty-first century.

Anatomists mapped the brain and named its structures long before anyone was able to relate activity in particular areas to brain function. They named brain areas based on how they looked rather than on what they did. Although hundreds of structures have been identified, named, and renamed, we will only examine a few of the major ones.

*The Cerebral Cortex*     **The outer layer of the cerebral hemispheres, with all the folds and crevices, is the cerebral cortex.** The word "cortex" comes from the Latin word meaning "bark"; the cerebral cortex is literally the bark of the brain. The huge size of the cerebral hemispheres in humans and in other primates is due partly to the enormous development of cortical tissue. This tissue does most of the higher-order information processing; you are using it right now to read and understand this sentence.

The most obvious difference between animal brains and the human brain is the amount of cortex in proportion to body size (figure 2.11). The lower mammals have less cortex than humans but much more cortex than birds, reptiles, or fish. The amount of cortex an animal has is a rough index of its capacity for learning. Animals such as reptiles and fish have less need for a large cortex because they can find food and take care of themselves soon after birth.

*The Lobes*     The cerebral hemispheres include four major subareas called lobes: the frontal lobe, the parietal lobe, the temporal lobe, and the occipital lobe. The **frontal lobe,** *very large in human beings, is involved in memory, reasoning, thinking, and movement.* The **occipital lobe,** *located in the back of the brain, processes visual information.*

Across the top of the brain is the **parietal lobe,** *an area that processes sensory information from the skin.* The amount of brain tissue devoted to each body part is not

# EXPLORING HUMAN DIVERSITY
## Sex Differences in the Brain

Are the brains of men different from the brains of women? One way scientists have attempted to answer this question is by studying the brains of patients after autopsy. In a study of 100 men and women, the corpus callosum was found to be generally larger in women even though the overall average size of the men's brains were larger because of their bigger body size (Allen and Gorski, 1991). Studies of living humans using magnetic resonance imaging have been ambiguous on the subject of sex differences in the corpus callosum. Some find a difference, others find none, and a recent one found small and complex interactions among gender, handedness, and the size of the corpus callosum (Allen et al., 1987; Bleier et al., 1986; Habib et al., 1991). A study of fetal brains suggests that the right hemisphere of males grows more rapidly than the left, but that the growth pattern for the two hemispheres of females are more even (de Lacoste et al., 1991).

Despite the ambiguity of the findings thus far, much speculation has emerged about how they might relate to differences between men and women in cognitive skills, particularly those that appear to be handled in an asymmetric fashion by the right and left hemispheres. The hypothesis emerged that women's brains are less lateralized than men's because their hemispheres communicate more efficiently thanks to their larger corpus callosum. One researcher, in a rather astounding leap of logic, concluded that the "inference is that women tend to use both hemispheres and men only one. This has important educational and work-deployment implications" (Ames, 1991).

Linking the gross size of the corpus callosum to interhemispheric communication is still premature, given our lack of knowledge about how the hemispheres communicate. The corpus callosum certainly serves as a pathway over which messages can travel, but it also might inhibit communication. Just as having a larger brain does not necessarily mean a more efficient one, a larger corpus callosum may not indicate more efficient interhemispheric communication.

Linking brain structure to sex differences in behavior is even more speculative, especially since there appear to be no reliable sex differences in performance on most cognitive tasks in the first place. Numerous studies have been done but when differences are found, the results are inconsistent. Although women have often been found to achieve higher scores than men on various tests of verbal abilities, the difference has been getting smaller and smaller over the last few years. Studies also have found the men outperform women on certain tests of spatial abilities but again, the difference is small and appears to be limited to tests that involve only one particular kind of skill: the ability to rotate an object mentally (Resnick, 1993). It is clear that performance on cognitive tests varies widely from person to person, but knowing a person's gender is of little use in predicting that person's performance on any of the tests.

Unfortunately, the subject of sex differences in the brain and their link to behavior is a political hot potato because it is so easy for the public to leap to unwarranted conclusions. People who hold stereotypes about cultural, ethnic, or religious groups, or about men and women, are eager to read about biological "explanations" that appear to support their views. Speculation and inference can easily turn into proven "fact" that reinforces stereotypical views about the behavior and capabilities of blacks, whites, Hispanics, Asians, or men and women. Most people also mistakenly believe that biology is destiny, and are not aware of two very important facts about the relationship between biology and behavior. First, biological factors (such as hormones or genes) vary considerably from person to person, and second, behavior affects biology.

News reports of scientific studies can easily distort actual findings, partly by oversimplifying, but also by emphasizing the sensational and leading people to believe that one study proves a hypothesis. (As we saw in chapter 1, the process of science requires much more replication and confirmation than that.) A few years ago reporters from the *L.A. Times* picked up a research paper read at a meeting of the Society for Neuroscience by Doreen Kimura, dealing with hormonal fluctuations in women and performance on cognitive tests. The story wound up on the front page and the *New York Times* picked it up the next day. They put it on their front page as well, with the headline "Female Sex Hormone Is Tied to Ability to Perform Tasks." The reporters missed the actual point of the study, but what is more interesting is that out of the hundreds of papers presented, they chose this one as the single major scientific breakthrough, worthy of front-page status.

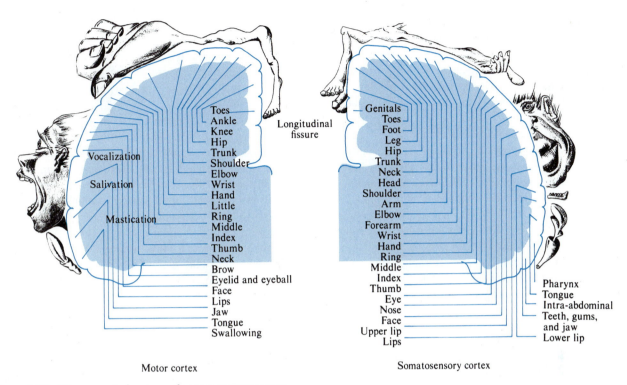

**Figure 2.12** *The amount of motor and somatosensory cortex that serves each area of the body is proportional to the sensitivity of the area.*

proportional to the size of that part. Those body parts that perform fine movements and are more sensitive are the ones that have the largest brain area devoted to them, both in the parietal lobe and in the areas of the frontal lobe that control movement. Figure 2.12 shows a drawing of the body parts in proportion to the amount of brain tissue. The fingers, mouth, and tongue need a lot of brain area. But the huge torso really requires very little.

The **temporal lobes** *process auditory information and, apparently, auditory memories as well.* Electrical stimulation of this area in a person sometimes provokes a vivid memory, and damage can cause surprising effects as well, as it did for Mrs. O'C. Following are two examples of what patients have said when stimulated in various places on the temporal cortex during neurosurgery (Penfield, 1975).

I think I heard a mother calling her little boy somewhere. It seemed to be something that happened years ago. … It was somebody in the neighborhood where I live.

Yes … I heard voices down along the river somewhere … a man's voice and a woman's calling … I think I saw the river.

In animals, the lobes of the cortex often function differently. One lobe may be extremely well developed during evolution because of the particular niche filled by the species. For example, a large amount of the human parietal lobe is devoted to processing information from the fingers. This arrangement would not be very useful to a cat; instead, a large portion of a cat's parietal tissue processes input from the whiskers. In a pig, a large section of the cortex is devoted to the snout.

*The Limbic System* **Below the cortex is a group of structures that form the limbic system. These brain areas appear to be involved in emotional behavior.** Brain damage in one section can cause a peaceful, calm animal to become extremely aggressive and dangerous. Damage in another part might cause an animal to show no fear at all. For example, a monkey might pick up a live snake, showing no emotion other than curiosity.

The **hypothalamus** *is an important part of the limbic system. Despite its tiny size, this structure and the pathways that run through it play major roles in some of* *our most fascinating behaviors, including sex, aggression, eating (and overeating), drinking, and control of body temperature.* It is not surprising that damage in this area can have many different effects, depending on where the damage occurs. A lesion in the central portion, for example, causes a rat to overeat and become grossly obese within a few weeks.

In the early days of electrical-stimulation experiments, a group of psychologists was studying the effects of tiny electrical stimulations in the brains of rats (Olds & Milner, 1954). When they inserted an electrode into a rat's brain, their aim was not always very good. They were aiming for a lower region of the brain, but they accidentally hit the hypothalamus. When the rat recovered from the operation, they turned on the current. Strangely, the rat did not eat, fight, or look frightened. It just kept returning to the corner of the box where it had received the shock. James Olds and his colleagues were intrigued and later learned that the rat would press a lever until it dropped from exhaustion to stimulate its brain in this way. Running through the hypothalamus are pathways that are involved in reward, and these researchers accidentally hit them with their microelectrodes (Olds & Fobes, 1981). Humans, incidentally, also find this kind of stimulation quite pleasurable.

*The Cerebellum*    *Located behind and partly underneath the cerebral hemispheres is the* cerebellum, *a large structure involved in coordination and movement.* This brain area regulates the rate, force, and coordination of every move, working with both the spinal cord and the areas of the frontal lobes involved in the control of movement.

*The Medulla*  *LLA large area of the lower part of the brain, called the* medulla, *controls many of the maintenance functions of the body such as heart action, breathing, and digestion.* Part of it also plays an important role in waking and sleeping.

## The Spinal Cord

The spinal cord, *a long mass of nervous tissue, carries sensory information from the arms, legs, internal organs, and trunk to the brain. It also contains neurons that carry information in the opposite direction, from the brain to the body.* These neurons carry signals that produce contraction or relaxation in the muscles of the body. If you damage your spinal cord, you might lose all feeling in the parts of your body located below the damaged area; sensations would not be able to pass by the injury and reach your brain. Your brain would not be able to send signals to your muscles to make them contract; consequently, the parts of your body below the injury would be paralyzed.

Although the brain is the master information processor, the spinal cord does some simple processing. Some reflexes occur without any help from the motor areas of the brain. The knee jerk is a good example. When you strike the hollow of your knee, your leg kicks. The information travels from the tendon in your knee to your spinal cord. Neurons traveling from the cord to the muscles in your leg are then excited, causing your leg to jerk. The information from your knee also travels to your brain, and you feel the sensations; however, the jerk would have occurred even if it had not reached the brain.

Another example shows the importance of spinal reflexes (figure 2.13). If you touch your finger to a hotplate, you pull it away *before* you ever feel the pain. The reason is that the action potentials from your finger travel first to your spinal cord and then immediately back to the muscles in your finger without going to the brain first. You only feel the pain when the messages finally reach the brain. Fortunately, the route from your finger to your spinal cord and back is much shorter than the route from your finger to your brain.

---

► **GUIDED REVIEW** *Learning Objectives 4 and 5*

1. The two parts of the nervous system are the _____ and the _____.
2. Five methods of studying the relationship between brain and behavior are _____, _____, _____, _____, and _____.
3. Major brain areas include the _____, divided into left and right _____, and also into lobes called _____, _____, _____, and _____.
4. The _____ performs some simple information processing and controls certain reflexes, such as the knee jerk.
5. One way that animal brains differ from human brains is in the size of particular brain areas, especially the _____. The amount of cortex is a rough index of the importance of behavioral flexibility in the species.

*Answers*

*1. central nervous system, peripheral nervous system 2. anatomical techniques, brain imaging, electrical recording, electrical stimulation of the brain, brain lesions 3. cerebral cortex, hemispheres, frontal, temporal, parietal, occipital 4. spinal cord 5. cerebral cortex*

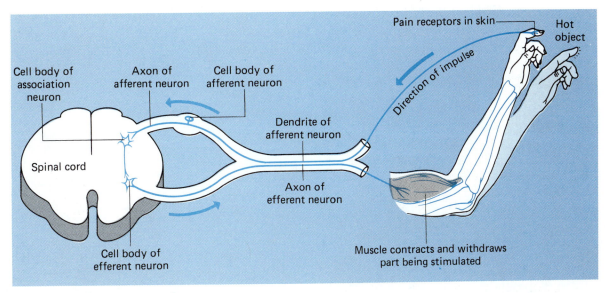

**Figure 2.13**  *An example of a spinal reflex*

# THE PERIPHERAL NERVOUS SYSTEM

All the neurons that lie outside the brain and spinal cord belong to the peripheral nervous system (PNS). The PNS includes two major divisions: the somatic nervous system and the autonomic nervous system.

## The Somatic Nervous System

The **somatic nervous system** *is the part of the PNS that carries information to the spinal cord from the body, and sends messages back to the body to produce overt behavior in the form of movement.* Sensory neurons bring information from all over the body to the spinal cord where it is relayed to the parietal lobe of the brain. *Neurons carrying information toward the central nervous system are called* **afferent.** In your leg, for example, these sensory neurons receive input from muscle fibers, tendons, joints, and special structures in the skin. They carry messages about the position of your knee joint, the location of a mosquito on your thigh, or the discomfort of a tight-fitting shoe.

When your want to initiate a movement of the big toe the signal originates in the cortex (although no one understands quite how). It is relayed back down through the spinal cord to the motor neurons in the leg through **efferent** *pathways, which carry information away from the central nervous system.* The message is then passed along these neurons, whose axon terminals synapse onto

muscle fibers in the toe, rather than onto dendrites of other neurons. When the message reaches the axon terminals, the neurons release neurotransmitter that causes the muscle cells to contract, moving your big toe. The whole process takes only a fraction of a second.

Spinal cord reflexes involve neurons in the somatic nervous system. In the knee-jerk reflex, a sensory neuron in the knee joint triggers action potentials in response to a blow on the knee, and sends a message to the spinal cord, where the axon terminals of the sensory neuron are located. The terminals transfer the message through a synapse to the dendrites of a motor neuron, which then pass the information along its axon back to the muscles of the leg.

## The Autonomic Nervous System

*Another set of neurons, most of which lie in the PNS, is the* **autonomic nervous system (ANS).** *It connects the brain and spinal cord to the stomach, intestines, heart, blood vessels, bladder, lungs, and other body organs.* This network was named "autonomic" because at one time everyone believed it operated automatically without any voluntary control. Recently, though, scientists have found that some people are able to learn some control over its functions if they receive the proper training. This special kind of learning will be discussed further in chapter 5.

One function of the ANS is to help the body cope with emergencies and then help it relax when the crisis has

SYMPATHETIC DIVISION

PARASYMPATHETIC DIVISION

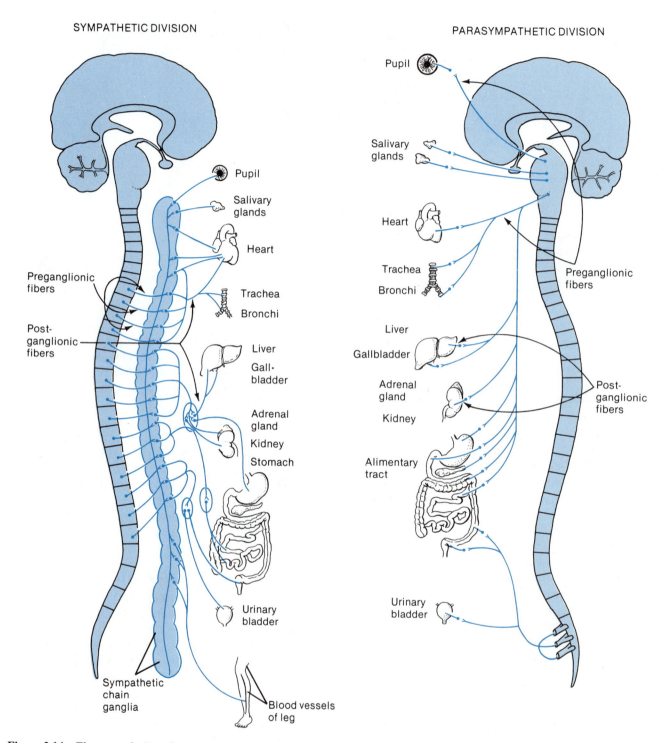

Pupil

Salivary
glands

Heart

Trachea

Bronchi

Liver

Gall-
bladder

Adrenal
gland

Kidney

Stomach

Urinary
bladder

Preganglionic
fibers

Post-
ganglionic
fibers

Sympathetic
chain
ganglia

Blood vessels
of leg

Pupil

Salivary
glands

Heart

Trachea
Bronchi

Liver

Gallbladder

Adrenal
gland

Kidney

Alimentary
tract

Urinary
bladder

Preganglionic
fibers

Post-
ganglionic
fibers

**Figure 2.14**    *The sympathetic and parasympathetic divisions of
the nervous system*

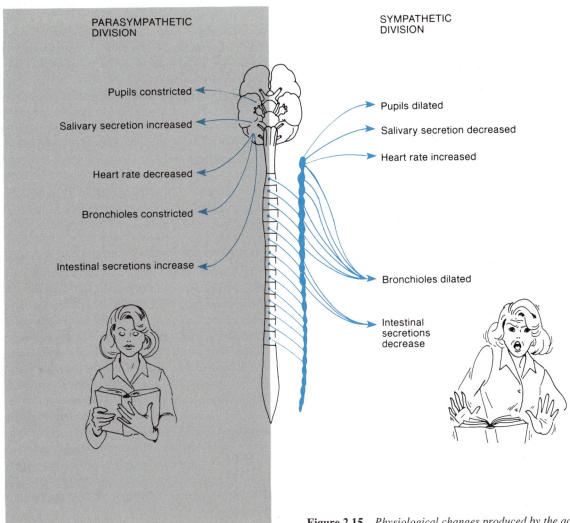

**PARASYMPATHETIC DIVISION**

Pupils constricted

Salivary secretion increased

Heart rate decreased

Bronchioles constricted

Intestinal secretions increase

**SYMPATHETIC DIVISION**

Pupils dilated

Salivary secretion decreased

Heart rate increased

Bronchioles dilated

Intestinal secretions decrease

**Figure 2.15** *Physiological changes produced by the activation of the sympathetic division of the nervous system*

passed. To perform these two activities, the ANS has two parts: the sympathetic division and the parasympathetic division (figure 2.14).

Suppose you are sitting calmly in a hotel room in Mexico reading a travel guide. Out of the corner of your eye you spot a fist-sized dark shape on the floor. You get up to move a little closer and discover it is a tarantula. Your heart races, your blood pressure rises, you breathe faster, your mouth gets dry, and you desperately try to remember the Spanish word for "help." ***The activation of the* sympathetic division *produces physiological changes such as increased heart rate, blood pressure, and respira-***

***tion to help your body cope with an emergency*** (figure 2.15).

These changes slow down bodily processes that are not terribly important during an emergency (such as digestion) and speed up those that will help you to run faster or fight harder. For example, the increase in blood pressure brings more oxygen to the muscles so they can contract very tightly. The sympathetic nervous system also triggers hormonal reactions that assist in putting the body on "emergency status." ***The entire spectrum of changes produced by sympathetic activation is called the* fright-fight-flight response.**

You have probably read stories in the newspapers about people able to perform amazing feats of strength and endurance during a crisis. A woman can lift a car off an injured child after an accident. A seriously wounded soldier can carry an unconscious friend away from the battle. Soldiers often say they can't even feel the pain of their wounds until they get back to the medical aid station. Boxers sometimes say the same thing about the injuries they suffer in a boxing match. These types of responses are made possible by the sympathetic division of the ANS.

The **parasympathetic division** *returns the body to normal when the emergency is over. These neurons slow the heart rate and breathing and decrease the blood pressure. Generally, the neurons of the parasympathetic division reach the same body organs as do those of the sympathetic division, but they have the opposite effect.* These two subsystems, the parasympathetic and the sympathetic, act in concert and help to create a balance of neural and hormonal activation.

There does not need to be a tarantula in your room for your sympathetic division to activate. This system is active throughout the day: when the phone rings, when the boss calls you into the office, when you are worrying about the children playing in the street, and when it is examination time. The long-term effects of chronic sympathetic activation can have serious consequences. Some people have high blood pressure, others develop ulcers, and still others find they suffer from insomnia, nervous tics, depression, or a drinking problem.

▶ **GUIDED REVIEW** *Learning Objective 6*

1. The _____ includes all the neurons outside the brain and spinal cord.
2. The PNS has two major divisions: _____ and _____.
3. The _____ includes the _____, which prepares the body for emergencies by increasing heart rate, breathing rate, and blood pressure, and by decreasing responses such as digestion, and the _____, which helps return the body to normal.
4. Sympathetic activation produces a spectrum of changes called the _____.

*Answers*

*1. peripheral nervous system (PNS) 2. somatic nervous system and autonomic nervous system 3. autonomic nervous system (ANS), sympathetic division, parasympathetic division 4. fright-fight-flight response*

# THE ENDOCRINE SYSTEM

The **endocrine system** *includes a number of glands that release important substances near capillaries carrying blood so the substances reach all parts of the body through the circulatory system.* These substances, or **hormones,** *are special chemical messengers that regulate physiological processes in the body.* Most are designed to affect a specific target organ some distance away; but some have more general effects throughout the body.

The endocrine system is extremely well integrated and interactive in the sense that activity in one area of the system affects and is affected by activity in another area. The way a person behaves is part of a loop—hormones can affect behavior and behavior can affect hormone levels.

## Hormones and Glands

Figure 2.16 shows the major endocrine glands in the body. Table 2.1 lists some of the glands, the hormones produced by them, and their chief functions. The glands vary both in the hormones they produce and in their functions. *The ovary, for example, produces the hormones* estrogen and progesterone, *which affect female sex characteristics such as breast development and the arrangement of fat in the body.* Part of the adrenal gland produces the hormone norepinephrine, which acts as a neurotransmitter in the nervous system. Norepinephrine is important in the fright-fight-flight response. The sympathetic nervous system triggers its release when the body is under stress, and many of its effects on the body duplicate the effects of sympathetic activation. For example, the hormone causes blood pressure to rise and heart and respiration rates to increase.

*The* **pituitary gland,** *located at the base of the brain just under the hypothalamus, is called the master gland. It produces several different hormones, most of which act on other endocrine glands* (table 2.1). One of its products is a hormone that stimulates the thyroid gland and triggers the production of the thyroid's hormone. The pituitary also produces adrenocorticotrophic hormone (ACTH). When this substance is released by the pituitary, it triggers the adrenal gland to release some of its hormones.

Another reason the pituitary is called the master gland is that it acts as the intermediary between the brain and the endocrine system. The hypothalamus, the structure located just above the gland, controls the activity of the pituitary. *Neurons in the hypothalamus produce* **releasing factors,**

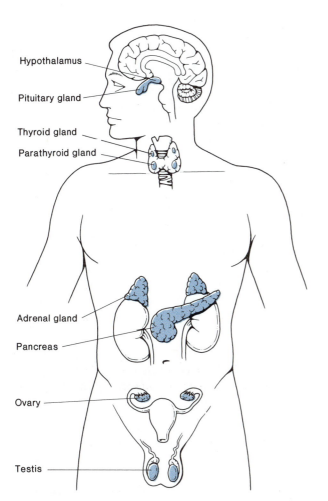

**Figure 2.16**  *The major endocrine glands. The ovaries are found only in females and the testes are found only in males.*

*substances that trigger hormone release by the pituitary gland.* For example, when a person is under great stress, the hypothalamus will release corticotropin releasing factor, which then stimulates the pituitary to release ACTH. This is a complicated system but one that permits a finely tuned integration of the two major physiological systems involved in behavior.

## Hormones and Behavior

Hormones have important effects on a great deal of behavior in animals, including aggression, courtship and sexual behavior, learning and memory, maternal behavior, hoarding (in rodents), scent making (in several species of mammals), and migration (in fish and birds). Maternal behavior in rodents is a good illustration of how hormones influence behavior. Nonpregnant female mice will build nests if they receive small doses of the ovarian hormone progesterone (Lisk, Pretlow, & Friedman, 1969). Several hormones in rats, especially ones from the ovaries, influence behavior like retrieving and caring for pups after they are born (Moltz, Lubin, Leon, & Numan, 1970). Injections of these hormones in a sequence that mimics the hormonal events of pregnancy caused virgin female rats to begin caring for a strange female's pups.

In human beings, the link between hormones and behavior is less direct. For example, adoptive parents can provide wonderful care for babies without receiving hormone therapy. Nevertheless, hormones do seem to have important effects on several behaviors in human beings. In men, *the sex hormone* testosterone, *released from the testes, is involved in sex drive.* Large reductions of this hormone, especially if they occur before puberty, usually

| Gland | Principal hormones | Chief functions |
|---|---|---|
| Pituitary gland | Thyroid stimulating (TSH, thyrotropin) | Stimulates thyroid |
| | Adrenocorticotrophic (ACTH) | Stimulates adrenal gland |
| | Follicle stimulating (FSH) | Reproductive functions |
| | Luteinizing (LH) | |
| | Prolactin | Milk production |
| | Growth (GH) | Growth |
| | Antidiuretic (ADH, vasopressin) | Water retention by kidneys |
| | Oxytocin | Uterine contraction |
| Thyroid | Thyroxin | Increases metabolic rate |
| Adrenal gland | Cortisol | Formation of glucose |
| | Mineralocorticoids | Sodium retention; potassium excretion by kidneys |
| | Norepinephrine | Fright-fight-flight |
| Testes | Androgens (testosterone) | Secondary male characteristics |
| Ovary | Estrogen | Secondary female characteristics |
| | Progesterone | |

**TABLE 2.1 The principal endocrine glands and their hormones**

result in lowered sex drive and lowered aggressiveness (Rubin, Reinisch, & Haskett, 1981). The effects of castration on prepubertal boys have been known for two thousand years. Such boys, called eunuchs, had little sexual appetite and were therefore employed to attend the harems of wealthy men in ancient Rome.

The connection between hormones and behavior is not one-way. Behavior can affect the endocrine system just as hormones can affect behavior. For example, as an individual begins to worry, get angry, or become emotionally excited, several events happen. First, the sympathetic nervous system is activated. This triggers the fright-fight-flight response and the release of certain hormones from the adrenal gland. At the same time, the hypothalamus directs the pituitary to release ACTH, which then triggers the release of different hormones, like cortisol, from another part of the adrenals. **Cortisol, *an adrenal hormone, helps the body return to normal when a stressful experience is over and supplies the cells with nutrients that are vital in repairing injured tissues.*** Thus, the hormonal response to stress is quite complex, involving responses that help the body cope with the emergency and help it resist the harmful effects of stress.

▶ **GUIDED REVIEW** *Learning Objective 7*

1. The endocrine system includes glands that release _____, special chemical messengers that regulate bodily processes.
2. Most hormones are released into the _____ by a gland and trigger activity in a target organ some distance away.
3. The _____ is the master gland because it releases hormones that control the activities of other endocrine glands and provides the link between the brain and the endocrine system.
4. The brain controls the endocrine system through the hypothalamus. Neurons produce _____ that affect the release of hormones by the pituitary.
5. Hormones affect a variety of behaviors in mammals, including sex, aggression, migration, and emotional behavior. Maternal behavior in rodents is under the control of several hormones, including _____ and _____. In humans, the effects of hormones on behavior are less direct.
6. Behavior also affects the endocrine system. Emotional behavior, for example, triggers the hormonal events associated with stress, including the release of hormones by the _____ glands.

*Answers*

1. *hormones* 2. *bloodstream* 3. *pituitary gland* 4. *releasing factors* 5. *estrogen, progesterone* 6. *adrenal*

## WHEN THINGS GO WRONG: MALFUNCTIONS IN THE NERVOUS SYSTEM

At about the same time the iron bar was flying through the air heading for Phineas Gage's jaw in the nineteenth century, scientists were beginning to look closely at the relationship between brain and behavior, relying heavily on the behavioral changes that occur when a part of the nervous system is damaged. In France, Broca was suggesting that specific damage in certain parts of the left hemisphere were related to disorders of speech. As we've discussed, identifying a link between brain and behavior by observing the effects of neural damage is a risky business. The link can only serve as a hypothesis and further study involving other approaches is always needed. Even with the caveats, though, scientists have gathered a tremendous compendium of information by investigating the behavior of people who have suffered some form of damage to their nervous systems.

The human brain is well protected but it can still be harmed by a wide range of environmental and internal insults. Damage can occur from ruptured blood vessels, lack of oxygen, traumatic head injury, poisons, and fevers. It could also be due to genetic abnormalities or an unfavorable prenatal environment. The range of behavioral problems that can accompany nervous system damage is equally wide.

One of the most frightening and misunderstood disorders of the brain is **epilepsy, *defined by its major symptom: seizures caused by abnormal firing patterns in the brain.*** For reasons we still don't clearly understand, a local burst in neural firing spreads to other parts of the brain and can trigger a major seizure (Dichter & Ayala, 1987; Hauser & Hesdorffer, 1990; McLin, 1992; Seidenberg & Berent, 1992). If you were walking with an epileptic, you might not even notice a very short seizure (petit mal). The longer grand mal seizures can involve serious convulsions that are unforgettable to a bystander who has never seen them; usually the epileptic does not remember the episode.

In some people, epileptic seizures begin soon after a head injury or stroke. The abnormal firing bursts in Mrs. O'C's temporal lobes appeared to be a kind of musical epilepsy precipitated by a mild stroke. Other risk factors include central nervous system infections, cerebral palsy, mental retardation, Alzheimer's disease, and alcohol. Some kinds of epilepsy appear to be inherited. Studies of twins, for example, have shown that a child with an epileptic identical twin is more likely to develop the disorder than one with an epileptic nonidentical twin. There have been studies on a few large families in which epilepsy is very common, and scientists have been able to trace the genetic pattern through the generations. For most cases of epilepsy, though, the cause is simply unknown and we can only speculate.

Historically, treatments for epilepsy have included visits to hot springs resorts, diets of barley water and porridge, and even electric shocks. Now, epileptics are treated with anticonvulsant drugs, which are remarkably effective in most cases. In very severe cases, the patient may become a candidate for surgery in which the damaged brain tissue is removed, or sections of the brain tissue are cut to prevent the localized bursts of firing from spreading.

The involuntary bursts of neuronal firing in the brain that begin an epileptic seizure are sometimes quite mysterious and strangely personal to the epileptic, and also probably dependent on the location of the abnormal brain tissue where the bursts begin. Mrs. O'C., for example, declined to take drug therapy. She said, "I need these memories, I need what's going on. And it'll end by itself soon enough."

Despite the effectiveness of the treatments, epileptics are often the victims of outdated laws and suspicions. Until recently, some states permitted epileptics to be sterilized and had strict rules about marriage. The McCarran-Walter Immigration Act grouped epileptics with lepers, alcoholics, paupers, and prostitutes. Though most of these laws have been repealed, many of the misunderstandings about epilepsy remain.

Another brain malfunction that has serious behavioral consequences is a **stroke**—*a rupture or blockage of a blood vessel in the brain.* The onset of a stroke is usually sudden, and the behavioral changes that follow can be dramatic. Some people might be unable to speak, even though they know what they want to say. Others might find they are unable to move their left leg. Still others might find themselves totally unable to understand what people are saying even though they can hear quite well.

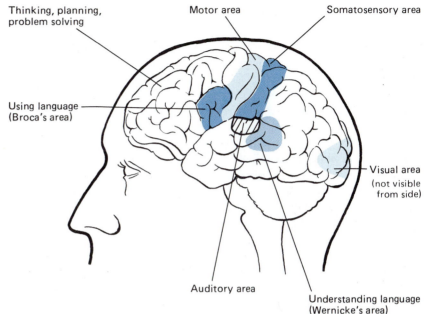

**Figure 2.17** *The main areas involved in language processing in the left cerebral hemisphere*

The results of a stroke depend not only on how much brain tissue is damaged by the loss of blood supply and oxygen but also on where the brain damage occurs. As we discussed earlier, the left side of the body is controlled by the right side of the brain, and vice versa. Therefore, a stroke on the left side of the brain will usually result in weakness or paralysis of some of the muscles on the right side of the body.

Figure 2.17 shows the locations of several major brain areas important for language. **Broca's area** *is a region of the frontal cortex involved in speech production.* The region was named for Paul Broca who was one of the first to identify the link between the left hemisphere and language abilities. One of Broca's patients was unable to speak although he appeared normal in other ways. After the patient died, Broca did an autopsy and found a lesion in the area of the brain that now bears his name. Further study showed that damage to this area usually results in a condition in which the person appears to know what to say and what words to use, but has difficulty producing speech. (The first one to guess the link between the left brain and speech, incidentally, was apparently an obscure country physician named Marc Dax. He read his one and only scientific paper on the subject at a conference in 1836 in France, but the medical community ignored it.)

Language is an incredibly complex human behavior, however, and like most behaviors, it is not localized to a single brain area. **Wernicke's area,** *part of the auditory cortex, appears to be involved with understanding of and memory for meanings of words.* Damage to this area does not impair patients' ability to articulate words, but what patients say does not make sense. In addition, the patients have great difficulty understanding the meaning of other people's speech (Kertesz, Lau, & Polk, 1993).

Broca's area and Wernicke's area appear to work together. In general terms, Wernicke's area deals with the generation of language and the memory of what words mean; Broca's area is involved with the memories of what movements of the tongue, lips, and larynx go with each word. These critical language areas are closely integrated with motor areas that control the movements of the mouth and tongue and with visual areas that receive and process input from written language.

Recovering from a stroke is a long and arduous process involving many months of hard work and therapy. Often the help of a specialist is needed. The functions previously performed by the damaged neurons must be assumed by healthy ones. It is like going back to school and relearning things. Sometimes the relearning is not complete, perhaps because the damage was too extensive. We can learn and form new synapses at any age, but it is easiest while we are young and growing.

Tourette's syndrome, named for Gilles de la Tourette who first identified it in 1885, is another example of what can go wrong in the nervous system. No two cases are identical, and at this stage of our understanding it may be that we're trying to isolate a single disorder when we're looking at a myriad of them. *The symptoms of* **Tourette's syndrome** *can include excessive nervousness, hyperactivity, attention problems, tics, jerks, impulsiveness, extravagant mannerisms and facial expressions, explosive uncontrollable cursing, and obsessive or compulsive behavior.* Tourette himself thought the disorder was a sort of possession of primitive impulses and urges, and even now, no one is quite sure what it is although scientists agree it has some organic basis in the brain (Cohen et al., 1988).

In some people with Tourette's, the symptoms are mild enough so that the person appears ebullient, energetic, witty, and inventive, characteristics more likely to be envied than treated. But the person usually also shows tics, impulsiveness, and impatience. One patient called Ray had such a case of Tourette's. He suffered from volleys of extremely violent tics coming every few seconds since the age of four, and had been teased by his friends throughout school because of them. Highly intelligent, Ray graduated from high school but failed to keep a job for very long because his employers objected to his tics, not because they thought he was incompetent. Fortunately Ray was a gifted jazz drummer who played on weekends, earning some repute for his wild improvisations and bursts of musical creativity. His quick reflexes, also a symptom of Tourette's, made him a talented ping pong player as well (Sacks, 1985).

Although identified more than a century ago, Tourette's syndrome is only recently receiving attention (Cohen et al., 1988; Shapiro et al., 1988). The syndrome may be partly due to disturbances in dopamine activity, the same neurotransmitter involved in Parkinsonism (see "Brain Transplants" and "The Dancing Mania"). Some link would not be surprising given the role that the chemical plays in motor activity, but Tourette's is clearly a complicated condition that involves more than just abnormal movements and tics, and its causes are not likely to be uncovered easily. Nevertheless, drugs that reduce dopamine activity can also reduce Tourette symptoms, but because some of the symptoms are desirable they may become an important part of the person's personality and life-style. Losing the quick sense of humor and lightning fast reflexes may be a high price to pay for eliminating tics. Ray, for example, chose to take the drugs during the week when he was working at his regular job, but not on the weekend when he could "let fly."

► **GUIDED REVIEW** *Learning Objective 8*

1. The major symptom of _____ is the occurrence of seizures. The cause is often unknown, and treatment usually involves anticonvulsant drugs.
2. _____ is due to a ruptured or blocked blood vessel in the brain. If it occurs on the left side, it usually results in some type of language problem. In most people the major language areas of the brain, called _____ and _____, are on the left side of the brain.
3. _____ can include excessive nervousness, hyperactivity, attention problems, tics, jerks, and other behavioral problems, uncontrollable cursing, and obsessive or compulsive behavior.

*Answers*

*1. epilepsy 2. A stroke, Wernicke's area, Broca's area 3. Tourette's syndrome*

## EXPLORING HUMAN DIVERSITY

### The Dancing Mania

The European continent was afflicted by a rage of plagues in the Middle Ages and certainly the Bubonic Plague or Black Death is the most widely known. Less publicized was the "Dancing Mania" that spread on its heels, which no one has yet ever been able to explain satisfactorily.

In 1374, a band of people coming from Germany arrived in the streets of Aix-la-Chappelle. They formed a circle and began to dance wildly, foam pouring from their mouths, all control over their bodies apparently gone. The contagion spread as the spectators joined in the dancing until all the participants dropped to the ground from exhaustion. As the months passed, neighboring villages "caught" the disease and wild dancing could be seen all over Europe, accompanied by street musicians.

People of the time held varied beliefs about the cause of the disease. Many assumed the dancing mania was caused by supernatural force and those who were consumed by it sought treatment by making a pilgrimage to the tomb of Saint Vitus in southern France. The pilgrims spread their contagion as they travelled. Others believed it to be due to the bite of a tarantula, and the style of music played to the dancer's gyrations became known as the tarantella. Paracelsus, a noted physician of the time, tried to debunk the value of the pilgrimage and promoted his own cures: immersion in cold water, fasting, and solitary confinement.

Strangely, both the pilgrimages and Paracelsus's approach were effective though the reasons for their success are not clear. Many scientists in our century believe that the disease was a true case of mass hysteria that simply wore itself out. Others, however, intrigued by the recent findings on the role of dopamine in motor disorders suggest that the dancing mania could have been caused by contamination of the grain supply by fungi that contained chemicals resembling dopamine, one of the neurotransmitters important in motor

activity. (The box called "Brain Transplants" describes dopamine's role in Parkinsonism, a movement disorder caused by destruction of the cells that manufacture dopamine in the brain.) Any treatment that caused the dancers to switch to an uncontaminated food source free of the dopamine-like chemicals would therefore be effective since the victims' brain activity would begin to return to normal.

A modern case study of the dancing mania involved Josette, a woman in her twenties who was being treated for Huntington's chorea. This tragic disease causes increasing nervousness, agitation, abnormal movements, and sometimes paranoia. The neurologist was treating her with drugs that affect dopamine levels when she began complaining of "dancing all night." The neighbors called the police because of the incessantly blaring radio. Even in the doctor's examining room, Josette maintained her pacing and waltzing, and the neurologist quickly decided that her dancing was due to the increasing dosage of medications, not to her Huntington's chorea. After a few weeks in which the dose was lowered, Josette finally was able to get a peaceful night's rest (Klawans, 1990).

Research into the chemical basis of brain activity has opened up a new window on our understanding of human behavior. As we learn more about how some of the neurotransmitter substances have natural mimics in the vegetable kingdom, we reevaluate the role that herbs and fungi play in a cultural context. The plants grow naturally almost everywhere on the globe and people in many cultures, both present and past, have used them for religious reasons, medicine, witchcraft, rites of passage, and to commune with ancestors or spirits. In an age of science, the consequences of ingesting a "magic mushroom" would no doubt be called a motor disturbance, or a hallucination. In Europe of the Middle Ages, the same event might have been called a vision.

## HEMISPHERIC ASYMMETRY

Like most living things, human beings are not symmetrical creatures. Most prefer a particular hand for writing, drawing, throwing a ball, or reaching for a can of spinach on a high shelf. Most also favor one or the other foot for kicking, pushing, or stepping off a diving board. Truly ambidextrous humans are very rare. The symmetry that is obvious in hands and feet was seen in the brain as well, when physicians noticed the relationship between the

language problems in stroke victims and the conditions of their brains on autopsy.

Broca's observations captured the imaginations of current and future neurologists intrigued by the possibility that the brain contained some localization of function. Before Broca, a widely accepted belief in medicine was that the brain functioned as a unitary whole, even though anatomists had observed for some time that there were a number of structural and morphological differences between the left and the right side of the brain. The connection between the autopsy results and the behavioral problems challenged the assumption of functional unity, and eventually tore it down. Although "localization of function" is far too strong to describe the role of specific brain areas in particular behaviors, the studies of left–right brain asymmetries have demonstrated clearly that the human brain is not a democratic blob whose neurons voice their views equally in all things.

Since the nineteenth century, neurologists have been collecting evidence to determine what kind of brain damage on which side of the brain affects which behaviors. Case studies on left brain damage proliferated quickly. Besides language, damage to the left side of the brain might result in problems in arithmetic, naming, and memory. Although damage on the right side usually resulted in paralysis or weakness on the left side of the body, behavioral problems were difficult to describe and were rarely seen in the medical journals. The left brain came to be known as the "major" hemisphere, and the right the "minor."

Although speculations abounded about the role of the right hemisphere, the limitations of studies of brain damage prevented the emergence of any definitive answers. For example, damage to one part of the brain could easily affect other areas, even far from the site of the injury. Also, just because a patient with a specific kind of damage shows no obvious behavioral impairment does not mean that area of the brain was just "sitting it out" as a worthless freeloader. Other brain regions may have picked up the slack. Interpretations of the role of a particular brain area that depend on what happens when that region is damaged are very problematic. They are like the explanation of the function of a lamppost by a man who is leaning on it: since he falls when the post is knocked over, the post was obviously there to hold him up.

A remarkable opportunity arose that allowed scientists to bypass the pitfalls of most clinical case studies and investigate the asymmetry of the brain's functions more directly, as we shall see in the next section.

## The Split Brain

In some very rare cases of severe epilepsy, drugs do not help, and the damaged brain tissue cannot be safely removed. One treatment, however, involves cutting the corpus callosum, the bundle of fibers connecting the right and left hemispheres. Severing this structure prevents a seizure that originates on one side of the brain from

spreading to the other, so the patients who undergo it often show a reduction in the severity of their seizures. On first inspection, the patients with a split brain show no behavioral changes. They don't have a "split personality," and they read, speak, do arithmetic problems, and generally function normally. Yet despite the apparent normalcy of these people, some researchers such as Roger Sperry (who was awarded a Nobel prize for his work) were convinced that a person with a split brain must be different in some way. Eventually they developed tests that showed some remarkable differences (Sperry, 1974, 1982; Gazzaniga, 1967).

If you are blindfolded and an object is placed in your left hand, the messages from your fingers will tell your brain what the object is. These messages will reach the right side of your brain first, but they would quickly travel along the corpus callosum to the left side. In a person with a split brain, the messages from the left hand only reach the right side of the brain. The left brain literally has no idea what the left hand is doing.

In addition, these patients can receive visual signals only on one side of the brain. If we show a picture in the left side of a person's visual field for a brief moment, that information would only reach the person's right brain. Pictures or words flashed to the right visual field only reach the left brain provided the subject focuses on a central point (figure 2.18).

Normally, of course, a person with a split brain does not walk around blindfolded. It is also simple to move the eyes so that both sides of the brain can "see" the picture. But by using tests that send messages to only one side of the brain, scientists have found that the human brain is not only anatomically asymmetric—it is functionally asymmetric as well (Hellige, 1990; Bradshaw, 1989).

*The Left Hemisphere—Master of Language and Arithmetic* LLWhenever the researchers flashed a written word to the left brain, the person could read it easily. But when they showed a word to the right brain, the person said there was nothing there. It looked as though the left hemisphere did all the reading. Actually, it does most of the reading, but it does *all* the talking.

When arithmetic problems were presented to the left hemisphere, the person could solve them. The same problems presented to the right hemisphere elicited only blank stares unless the problems were simple additions with sums of less than twenty. This led many people to think that the left hemisphere used a kind of analytical

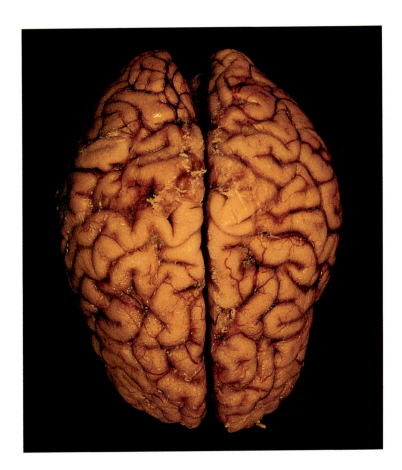

**Plate 1.A** *The two halves of the human brain, called hemispheres, are clearly seen in this photograph.*

**Plate 1.B** *This photograph shows neurons in a midregion of the brain. Notice the large number of dendritic branches that extend from each cell body.*

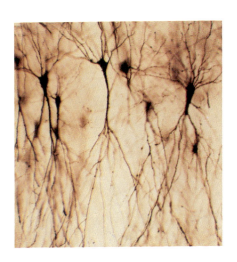

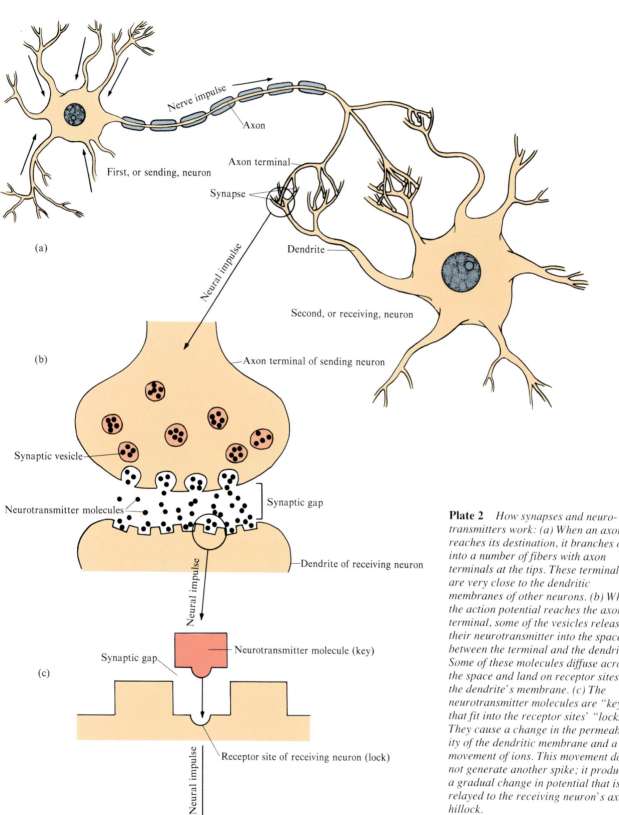

(a)

Nerve impulse

Axon

First, or sending, neuron

Axon terminal

Synapse

Neural impulse

Dendrite

Second, or receiving, neuron

(b)

Axon terminal of sending neuron

Synaptic vesicle

Neurotransmitter molecules

Synaptic gap

Dendrite of receiving neuron

Neural impulse

Synaptic gap

Neurotransmitter molecule (key)

(c)

Receptor site of receiving neuron (lock)

Neural impulse

**Plate 2** *How synapses and neuro-transmitters work: (a) When an axon reaches its destination, it branches out into a number of fibers with axon terminals at the tips. These terminals are very close to the dendritic membranes of other neurons. (b) When the action potential reaches the axon terminal, some of the vesicles release their neurotransmitter into the space between the terminal and the dendrite. Some of these molecules diffuse across the space and land on receptor sites on the dendrite's membrane. (c) The neurotransmitter molecules are "keys" that fit into the receptor sites' "locks." They cause a change in the permeabil-ity of the dendritic membrane and a movement of ions. This movement does not generate another spike; it produces a gradual change in potential that is relayed to the receiving neuron's axon hillock.*

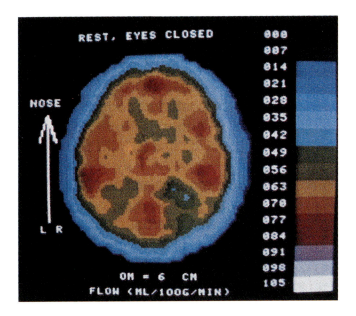

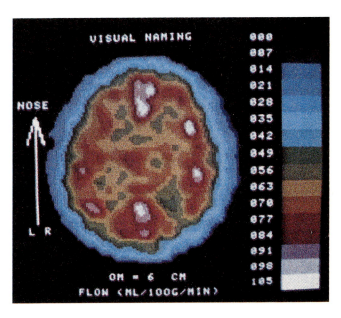

**Plate 3.A** *These images are created by computer interpretation of multiple X rays. The image on the left is of an individual resting with eyes closed. The image on the right is of an individual looking at objects and naming them.*

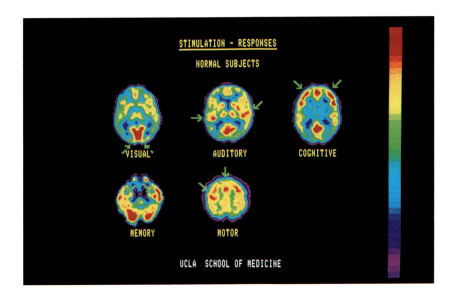

**Plate 3.B** *The PET Scan.   The red areas of these PET scans reveal the regions of the brain that are the most active during the performance of particular tasks.*

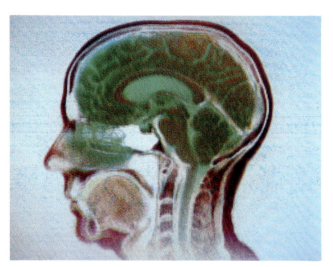

(a)

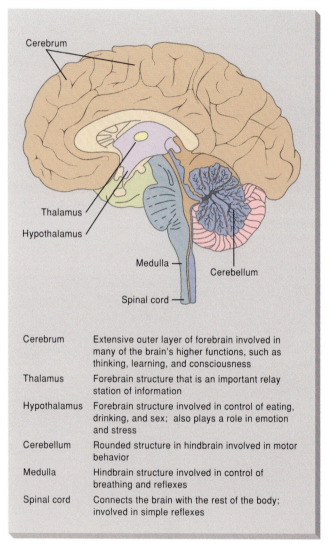

Cerebrum

Thalamus

Hypothalamus

Medulla

Cerebellum

Spinal cord

| | |
|---|---|
| Cerebrum | Extensive outer layer of forebrain involved in many of the brain's higher functions, such as thinking, learning, and consciousness |
| Thalamus | Forebrain structure that is an important relay station of information |
| Hypothalamus | Forebrain structure involved in control of eating, drinking, and sex; also plays a role in emotion and stress |
| Cerebellum | Rounded structure in hindbrain involved in motor behavior |
| Medulla | Hindbrain structure involved in control of breathing and reflexes |
| Spinal cord | Connects the brain with the rest of the body; involved in simple reflexes |

(b)

**Plate 4** *Structure and regions in the human brain. (a) This image of a cross-section of the brain includes some of the brain's most important structures. (b) This drawing reproduces some of the brain's main structures from the image of the brain shown in (a) and describes some of their main functions.*

approach to the world. It controlled everything the person said, it could understand written words, and it could do arithmetic.

Since the right hemisphere did not control verbal skills, scientists were initially unable to determine its function. Eventually, however, techniques were designed to allow the right hemisphere to be heard; scientists discovered that although the right hemisphere did not control speech, it did control the left hand. Instead of asking for a verbal answer, they asked a person to point to answers, using the left hand. They found that the right hemisphere had some strengths that the left hemisphere lacked.

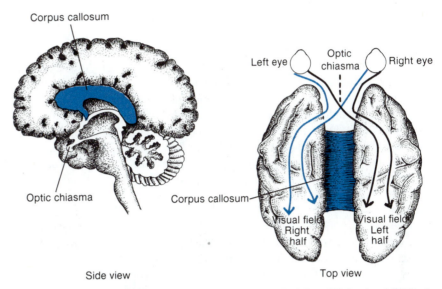

Side view    Top view

**Figure 2.18** *The pathways traveled by information from the left and right visual fields of the eyes to the left and right hemispheres*

*The Right Hemisphere—Master of Space*    When the researchers showed the word "fork" to a person's right hemisphere, the person had no trouble pointing to a fork with the left hand. The right side can "read" simple nouns like "fork" or "brush" reasonably well, but it cannot read verbs or long sentences or "talk about" what it reads.

The right brain also seems to need to look at words for a longer period of time before demonstrating its linguistic abilities. In one experiment, split-brain patients wore a patch over one eye and a special contact lens over the other. This allowed visual input to reach only one side of the brain, regardless of how much the patient moved the eye. The experimenters could then present the same visual stimulus for as long as half an hour, giving the patient a chance to ponder the words (Zaidel, 1975). Using their right hemispheres, the patients were able to read nouns and verbs much better, and on one test, they demonstrated a mental age only two years lower than when they were using their left hemispheres. However, the patients were still unable to read and comprehend sentences when using the right hemisphere.

Although the right side doesn't seem to read as well as the left, it seems to be involved in a very important component of language processing. Evidence suggests that information about the nonlinguistic components of communication, such as tempo, inflection, emotion, and tone, are processed there (Code, 1987; Pimental & Kingbury, 1989).

The right brain deals with space and patterns extremely well. When researchers asked patients to copy some simple drawings, the patients could do it much better with the left hand even though they were right handed. People are also much better at copying a pattern of shapes with colored blocks when using the left hand (right hemisphere). On one test, a patient was to use his right hand for this task, but he performed poorly. He kept trying to use his left hand to "help." He finally had to sit on his left hand to keep it from interfering (Gazzaniga, 1967).

The superiority of the right brain in dealing with space has been demonstrated in other ways as well. In one study, subjects were shown a group of geometric forms and were asked to pick out the matching one from among several forms hidden from view behind a screen (Franco & Sperry, 1977). The patients were consistently able to do better on this task using their left hands, showing that their right brains were more adept at dealing with shapes and patterns, both visually and by touch. Other studies have suggested that the right brain is also superior at recognizing faces and voices and at musical perception (Sidtis, 1984; Van Lancker, 1987), supporting the view that the right brain takes a more holistic approach, and the left brain takes a more analytical approach.

The way the two hemispheres seem to handle visual space and patterns is intriguing. When patients are asked to copy a complicated figure, the ones with left hemisphere damage get many of the details right but miss the overall shape. The ones with right hemisphere damage get the general pattern, but miss the details (Robertson & Lamb, 1991).

The right brain has a sense of humor and may be more emotional than the left brain. On one occasion a psychologist presented a picture of a nude to a patient's right brain.

She started to laugh, and the testers asked why. Her left hemisphere had not "seen" the picture and did not know why she was laughing. She said, "Oh, I don't know … nothing … oh that funny machine."

Although most of our information about hemispheric asymmetry comes from studies of brain-damaged or split-brain patients, studies of normal people have added some enriching detail. Inventive methods have been devised to present stimuli to one side of the brain or the other. Although the information can obviously travel across the corpus callosum in a few milliseconds, psychologists can use that split second to detect slight preferences or advantages.

One experimental strategy relies on the neural routes that visual images travel from the eyes to the brain. Images presented to the left visual field, which reach the right sides of both eyes, follow a path to the right hemisphere. The reverse is true for images presented to the right visual field (see figure 2.18). Word recognition generally shows a right visual field advantage, again supporting the idea that the left hemisphere is dominant for the verbal aspects of language.

The existence of visual field advantages has been used to study the way the two hemispheres analyze different components of the visual environment. One hypothesis, consistent with the notion that the right hemisphere may be analyzing the more "global" aspects of the scene, suggests that the right brain processes the lower spatial frequencies in patterns while the left processes the higher spatial frequencies (Christman, 1989; Christman, Kitterle, & Hellige, 1991). Spatial frequency measures the level of detail in a visual image. For example, wide stripes would show low spatial frequency, but thin stripes spaced close together would have high spatial frequency. In a more natural visual image with both high and low spatial frequencies, the low spatial frequencies would give information about the global pattern, and the high frequencies would reveal elements of detail. (In a pyramid of Coke cans, the pyramid shape outline would represent the lower spatial frequency, and the individual Coke cans the higher spatial frequency.) Generally, subjects respond faster to lower spatial images presented to their right hemisphere, and higher spatial images presented to their left. Perhaps the right brain analyzes the forest, and the left analyzes the trees.

Another technique used to investigate brain asymmetries in both normal and brain-damaged people is called **dichotic listening,** *in which different auditory stimuli are simultaneously presented to each ear* (Kimura, 1961). Information coming into each ear is competing for the person's attention and most right-handed people pay a little closer attention to what their right ear hears, if it is speech. Since messages from the right ear reach the left hemisphere first, these studies support the view that speech is decoded mainly by the left hemisphere. When the stimulus is music, or sounds like laughing, crying, sighing, airplane takeoffs, or a flushing toilet, the left ear has a slight advantage (Hugdahl, 1988; Bartholomeus, 1974; Gordon, 1980; Curry, 1967). Although dichotic listening studies are difficult to interpret they provide general support for the kinds of asymmetries that have been detected using other methods (Niccum & Speaks, 1991; Efron, 1990).

*What about the Lefties?*    Right handers comprise about ninety percent of the current world's population. A preference for the right hand was also present in most of our ancestors. Drawings in caves and on most walls of Egyptian tombs suggest such a preference, and most drawings of hands from prehistoric times are of the left hand—the artists were probably using their right hand to trace their left. Studies of paleolithic tools and weapons show they were generally made to be used by the right hand. And studies of some fossilized baboon skulls suggest that the fatal blow was probably administered by an early human wielding a club with the right hand.

In terms of hemispheric asymmetry, left-handed people are considerably more variable that right-handed ones; they are clearly a mixed group with respect to brain organization. For example, about ninety-five percent of right handers show dominance in the left hemisphere for speech production. One might suppose that left-handed people show dominance in the right hemisphere for speech, but in fact, about sixty-two percent show left hemisphere dominance. Nineteen percent of the lefties are right hemisphere dominant for speech, and the remainder appear to rely on both hemispheres equally.

A particularly intriguing finding about left handers is that their corpus callosum is about eleven percent larger than their right-handed counterparts (Witelson, 1987). A larger neural bridge between the hemispheres could mean a great many things, including more efficient interhemispheric communication. One of the fascinating characteristics of left-handed people is that they tend to do quite well on the Scholastic Aptitude Test. Of the children who score highest, more than twenty percent are left-handed or ambidextrous, a rate twice as high as that found in the general population (Benbow, 1985). Whether their performance has anything to do with their brain organization or their larger corpus callosum is unknown.

The cause of hand preference is still very much a mystery, although scientists suspect that genetic factors or prenatal hormones might be involved (Carter-Saltzman, 1980; Geschwind & Galaburda, 1987; Hellige, 1990). Some evidence is emerging that gender, handedness, and performance on tests that generally show hemispheric differences interact in complex ways. In one study left-handed males outperformed right-handed males on tests involving verbal or sequential tasks. But for females, the reverse was true (Gordon & Kravetz, 1991). Also, magnetic resonance imaging studies in humans have shown that the differences in the corpus callosum depend both on sex and on handedness (Habib et al., 1991).

Hand preference, like many behaviors, is a complex phenomenon that probably is influenced by biological factors, but is also affected by environmental events. The incidence of left-handedness dropped considerably during the early twentieth century because John B. Watson recommended that children should be taught to use their right hands only. Schools followed his advice and left-handedness declined. Unfortunately, the attempt to change hand preference was carried a bit far, and some children began to stutter or suck their thumbs. Now, psychologists advise allowing children to use whatever hand they choose.

Such a decided species preference is quite uncommon in the animal kingdom. Although animals generally show a tendency to use one paw or the other (for pressing levers in laboratories, for example), the overwhelming popularity of one side in a whole species is rare. Perhaps we should be asking why more people are not left handed, not why some are. No one has yet advanced a completely plausible explanation for this, but one recent suggestion relates the dominance of right-handedness in humans to the evolution of rock-throwing and the calming influence of a mother's heartbeat on babies (Calvin, 1991). Human physiology is such that the heartbeat is more easily heard from the left side of the chest and the sound of a heartbeat is known to quiet babies. Suppose our primitive female ancestors tended to carry their infants with the left arm, much the way modern mothers usually do, because the baby seemed more relaxed on that side. The mother would then use her right hand for other tasks and one of these might well have been rock throwing. The ability to bring down an unsus-

pecting rabbit from a distance with a quiet baby in tow would have conferred quite an advantage on our ancestral mothers, and any genetic predispositions toward right-handedness may have been passed along to both male and female children. Even if right-handedness offered no particular advantage to men they may have been moved in that direction because the ability to throw rocks while carrying an infant contributed so much to the fitness of the women.

## Hemispheric Asymmetry: What Does It Mean?

The excitement that followed in the wake of Sperry's initial discoveries created a tidal wave of research looking for more differences between the right and left hemispheres. Many were found and some researchers expressed concern that there may be too many. It's likely that the methods used generated some misleading results (Efron, 1990). For example, people tend to scan a scene in the same direction and some of the visual field advantages may have been due to scanning preferences, rather than hemispheric asymmetries.

The split-brain studies generated much philosophizing about the way human beings think. One proposal was that humans have two modes of thought: one rational, logical, and sequential (left brain), the other emotional, creative, and holistic (right brain) (Bogen, 1969). This notion was picked up by Madison Avenue to enliven its sales pitches. We recently saw an advertisement for a diamond ring that featured a vertically split screen. On the left was a man with glasses, dressed in a suit, discussing the benefits of the ring in terms of investment and durability, and touting the deep discount offered by the merchant. On the right, the same man in jeans and a sweatshirt, relaxing on a sofa, was poetically admiring the ring's beauty and imagining his wife's joy. The two argued back and forth about why they should make the purchase, each accusing the other of being too "left brained" or too "right brained."

Another even loftier proposal was that people from different cultures emphasize one or the other mode of thought, and thus might have evolved brains with different organizations. For example, Eastern cultures and philosophy might have more advanced development in "right-brain abilities," while Westerners might be more comfortable with left-brain activities. The speed with which these ideas penetrated pop culture was astounding and our concern with the neglected right hemisphere was a focal point. Courses popped up to help people develop their right brain. Books on the self-help shelves offered to improve "right-brain thinking" in ourselves, our children, or our management style. Perhaps we are all eager for a simple solution that begins like the old joke: there are two kinds of people in this world …

Though the popularized version of the left–right distinction in the brain went beyond what has been demonstrated, there is clearly some hemispheric asymmetry for function in the human brain. Most of the data from a wide range of studies lead to the conclusion that there are several ways in which the right brain operates rather differently from the left. Though there doesn't appear to be any absolute specializations of function, there is certainly asymmetry. For many behaviors, both sides are capable but one may be more capable than the other, or may approach the task in a somewhat different and complementary way.

The studies of hemispheric asymmetry of function shed light on a very important problem in psychology. Are behavioral functions localized in particular brain areas much like the phrenologists believed? Is there a "left-brain ability" or a "pleasure center"? Is there a small set of neurons somewhere in your frontal lobes where the memory for the key words in this chapter will be stored? Or are the neurons and structures in the brain so closely integrated, so dependent on one another, that most or all of them are involved in one way or another in complex behavior?

The answer to the question of whether or not functions are localized in the brain appears to lie somewhere in the middle. The brain appears to contain identifiable subsystems, or modules, that we are beginning to understand but these are not the "centers" the phrenologists conceptualized. Their notion of centers reflected the everyday language of behavior—aggression, kindheartedness, egocentrism, envy. The picture that is starting to emerge of the brain's subsystems hints that they are much more difficult to pigeonhole. In processing a visual scene, for example, one subsystem might be working on the global aspects of the image, another the detail, as we discussed earlier (Christman, Kitterle & Hellige, 1991); both are doing their jobs simultaneously, or in parallel. We are just beginning to invent parallel processing as the next breakthrough in computers; it appears that our brains may be using it routinely.

## Mind, Consciousness, and the Brain

People with a split brain seem to have two separate minds, or different consciousnesses. They can do two tasks as quickly and easily as normal people can do one. The two minds learn clever ways of communicating with one another but do not always agree. Remember the patient who had to sit on his left hand to keep it from interfering while he worked on a block problem with his right hand.

Perhaps these studies, more than any others on the brain, show that what we call "mind" or "consciousness" is really brain. They shed light on an age-old controversy called the **mind–body problem;** *it debates the question of whether the mind is nonphysical and the body physical, or whether both are physical.* Throughout history many scientists and philosophers have argued that mind and body are separate elements and that the mind that thinks, feels, decides, remembers, and understands, is something nonphysical. Psychologists and other scientists have not taken a unified stand on this issue; there is still no clear-cut answer to it. However, studies like those on the split-brain patients, and other more recent experiments exploring the biological basis of consciousness, are leading many scientists to the conclusion that mind and body are one and the same. When the brain is split in half, the mind is also split in half, creating two minds in one. Mind does not appear to be something separate and apart from the neurons and chemicals that make up the brain. When a person's brain is damaged, his or her mind will be altered. If the brain is damaged too much, as in the case of Phineas T. Gage, the person may change so much that we can no longer recognize him or her.

Not all scientists agree with this idea but it will have far reaching implications if human beings gradually come to accept it. If mind is an emergent property of the organization of our brains, rather than a separate entity, then we would have a radically different view of ourselves.

It is humbling to think of the billions of neurons and chemicals in our brains—and then to realize that *they* are doing the thinking. What else can think about its own workings? What else can invent ways to improve and repair itself? What else lasts for seventy-five years or more, operating on a huge assortment of fuel and requiring little or no maintenance? As little as we may know about the brain, we know enough to appreciate how remarkable it is.

▶ **GUIDED REVIEW** *Learning Objectives 9 and 10*

1. In the split-brain operation, the _____ is severed, dividing the brain into right and left halves.
2. For most right-handed people, the _____ is specialized for language, arithmetic, and analytical skills. The _____ is superior in spatial abilities.
3. The brains of _____ people show variable hemispheric specializations. In some, the right brain is specialized for language, and in others, language abilities are more symmetrical.

4. A person with a split brain has two "minds," suggesting that the mind is the same as the brain and is made up of chemicals and neurons. The question of whether the mind is nonphysical whereas the body is physical, or whether they are both physical is the _____.

*Answers*

1. corpus callosum 2. left hemisphere, right hemisphere 3. left-handed 4. mind–body problem

# SUMMARY

I. The neuron is the building block of the nervous system. It is specialized to process information. (p. 35)

   A. The four main parts of the neuron are the dendrites, the cell body, the axon, and the axon terminals. (p. 35)
      1. The dendrites are the input portion of the neuron. (p. 36)
      2. The cell body contains the nucleus and other structures that help to maintain the life of the neuron. (p. 36)
      3. The axon is the long thin tube that carries information from the cell body to the axon terminals. (p. 37)
      4. The axon terminals are the output ends of the cell. (p. 37)

   B. Axonal conduction is the electrical process whereby information is moved from one end of the axon to the other. (p. 37)
      1. At rest, a neuron shows a resting potential, the difference in charge across the axon's membrane. (p. 37)
      2. When a neural impulse is generated, an action potential is produced. The action potential travels down the axon using the all-or-none principle of axonal conduction. (pp. 37–39)

   C. Synaptic transmission is the process whereby information is moved from one neuron to another. It is a chemical process involving the release of neurotransmitter from the axon terminals as a result of the arrival of an action potential. The neurotransmitters affect the electrical properties of the next neuron's dendrites. The neurotransmitter produces either an excitatory or an inhibitory disturbance in the dendrite's membrane. (p. 39)

   D. A neuron receives inputs from other neurons all over its dendritic tree. The incoming messages are summarized and integrated at the axon hillock. If the resulting summary is large enough, the neuron will trigger an action potential. (p. 41)

II. The human nervous system is divided into the central nervous system and the peripheral nervous system. The central nervous system consists of the brain and spinal cord; the peripheral nervous system includes all the neurons lying outside the brain and spinal cord. (p. 42)

   A. There are five methods commonly used to investigate the relationship between the brain and behavior. (pp. 43–44)
      1. Anatomical studies compare the appearance of brain tissue and note correlations between its appearance and the behavior of the organism. (p. 44)
      2. Brain imaging techniques, such as PET, use radioactive tracers or X rays to view brain structures and assess changes in metabolic activity. (p. 44)
      3. Electrical recording techniques can record the activity of groups of brain cells, as in the EEG, or the activity of individual brain cells. (p. 44)
      4. Electrical stimulation of the brain is used to activate specific neural pathways or areas and to observe any changes in behavior. (p. 45)
      5. Studies of animals or people with brain lesions or brain damage can lead to some insights about the possible role of the damaged portions of the brain. (p. 45)

   B. The human brain is shaped like a mushroom, with the older, more primitive areas in the "stem" part and the more recently evolved areas in the "cap." (p. 46)
      1. The cerebral cortex is the outer layer of the cerebral hemispheres. (p. 47)
      2. The cerebral hemispheres include four major subareas called lobes. (p. 47)
      3. The limbic system, a group of structures lying below the cortex, seem to be involved in emotional behavior. (p. 49)
      4. The cerebellum is located behind and partly underneath the cerebral hemispheres; it is involved in coordination and movement. (p. 50)

5. The medulla is a large area in the lower part of the brain that controls maintenance activities such as breathing, heart rate, and digestion. (p. 50)

C. The spinal cord performs simple information processing and controls certain reflexes, such as the knee jerk. (p. 50)

III. The peripheral nervous system (PNS) is divided into the somatic nervous system and the autonomic nervous system. (p. 51)

A. The somatic nervous system includes sensory and motor neurons that carry information from the body to the spinal cord, and vice versa. (p. 51)

B. The autonomic nervous system, most of which lies in the PNS, includes the sympathetic division, which prepares the body for emergencies by raising the heart rate, breathing rate, and blood pressure and by moderating other physiological responses. The autonomic nervous system also includes the parasympathetic division, which helps return the body to normal after sympathetic activation. The entire spectrum of physiological responses produced by sympathetic activation is the fright-fight-flight response. (p. 51, 53)

IV. The endocrine system includes several glands that release hormones. (p. 54)

A. Hormones are special chemical messengers that can regulate bodily processes in distant target organs. They are released into the bloodstream by endocrine glands. The pituitary gland is the master endocrine gland; it provides a link between the brain and the endocrine system. The hypothalamus controls the activity of the pituitary gland; it releases substances called releasing factors, which affect the release of hormones by the pituitary. (pp. 54–55)

B. Hormones affect a variety of behaviors in many mammals, including sex, aggression, migration, emotional behavior, and maternal behavior. In human beings, the effects of hormones are less direct than in other mammals. The relationship between hormones and behavior is complex. Hormones can affect behavior, and behavior can affect the activity of the endocrine system. (pp. 55–56)

V. Studies of brain disorders can help researchers better understand brain function. (pp. 56)

A. Epilepsy is a disease that involves the occurrence of seizures. The causes of the disease are varied, and treatment usually involves the administration of anticonvulsant drugs. (pp. 56–57)

B. Stroke is a rupture or blockage of a blood vessel in the brain. The behavioral changes that follow a stroke are varied and depend on where the brain damage occurred and how much brain tissue was damaged. Stroke victims sometimes suffer some type of language deficit. (p. 57)

C. Tourette's syndrome involves excessive nervousness, hyperactivity, attention problems, tics, jerks, impulsiveness, extravagant mannerisms and facial expressions, explosive uncontrollable cursing, and obsessive or compulsive behavior. (p. 58)

VI. Studies of people with brain damage or a split brain suggest that the right and left hemispheres have somewhat different specializations. (pp. 59–60)

A. An operation called the "split-brain" technique severs the corpus callosum and is performed only in cases of extreme epilepsy. The split-brain patients have been tested to determine hemispheric specializations. (p. 60)
1. In right-handed people, the left side of the brain is superior in the performance of language, arithmetic, and analytical tasks. (pp. 60–61)
2. The right hemisphere appears to be superior at tasks involving spatial abilities. (p. 61)

B. The hemispheric specializations of left-handed people are more varied than those of right-handed people. The causes of hand preference are unknown, although some studies implicate genetic or hormonal factors. (pp. 62–63)

C. The mind–body problem debates whether the mind is nonphysical whereas the body is physical or whether they are both physical. (p. 64)

# ACTION GLOSSARY

Match the terms in the left column with the definitions in the right column.

___ 1. **Neuron** (p. 35)
___ 2. **Dendrite** (p. 36)
___ 3. **Alzheimer's disease** (p. 36)
___ 4. **Cell body** (p. 36)
___ 5. **Axon** (p. 37)
___ 6. **Myelin** (p. 37)
___ 7. **Multiple sclerosis** (p. 37)
___ 8. **Axon terminal** (p. 37)
___ 9. **Neurotransmitter** (p. 37)

A. *The whitish fatty substance that provides insulation along the length of the axon.*
B. *Progressive deterioration of cognitive skills caused by neural degeneration.*
C. *The basic structural and functional unit of the nervous system that processes information.*
D. *Chemicals contained in the vesicles of the axon terminal and involved in synaptic transmission between neurons.*
E. *The input end of the neuron that receives messages from other neurons. It is usually shaped like a tree, with branches covered with knobs.*
F. *The long, thin part of the neuron that carries information from the cell body to the axon terminals.*
G. *The output ends of the neuron, located on the tips of the branches of the axon.*
H. *The part of the neuron containing the nucleus and other structures responsible for maintaining the life of the cell.*
I. *A disease caused by the loss of myelin in the nervous system. Symptoms include vision problems, muscle weakness, lack of coordination, and spastic motions.*

___ 10. **Axonal conduction** (p. 37)
___ 11. **Resting potential** (p. 37)
___ 12. **Action potential** (p. 38)
___ 13. **Sodium-potassium pump** (p. 38)
___ 14. **All-or-none principle** (p. 39)
___ 15. **Synaptic transmission** (p. 39)
___ 16. **Synapse** (p. 39)
___ 17. **Vesicle** (p. 39)

A. *The difference in charge across the axon's membrane when the neuron is at rest.*
B. *The process by which a neural message is moved from one neuron to another at the junction between the two neurons.*
C. *The process by which neural messages are moved from one end of the axon to the other by means of the movement of ions across the axon's membrane.*
D. *Refers to the property of axonal conduction in which an action potential is conducted along the axon without a reduction in its size.*
E. *A transient change in the potential across the membrane of an axon. It is the neural message traveling down the axon and is sometimes called a "spike."*
F. *A saclike structure in the axon terminal that contains neurotransmitter.*
G. *A metabolic mechanism that forces sodium ions out of the cell and potassium ions back in to prevent the eventual loss of the potential across the axon's membrane as the positive sodium ions accumulate with each action potential.*
H. *The junction between two neurons, usually between the axon terminal of one neuron and the dendrite of the next.*

___ 18. **Nodes of Ranvier** (p. 37)
___ 19. **Positron emission tomography (PET)** (p. 44)
___ 20. **Axon hillock** (p. 41)
___ 21. **Central nervous system (CNS)** (p. 42)
___ 22. **Peripheral nervous system (PNS)** (p. 42)
___ 23. **Computerized axial tomography (CAT scan)** (p. 44)
___ 24. **Electroencephalograph (EEG)** (p. 44)
___ 25. **Hippocampus** (p. 45)
___ 26. **Glial cells** (p. 45)

A. *The area of the cell body where the axon protrudes. It is involved in the summarization of the incoming electrical messages from all the neuron's dendrites.*
B. *A device used to measure and record the electrical activity of the brain by means of electrodes placed on the scalp.*
C. *A part of the limbic system of the brain that may play a role in long-term memory.*
D. *A technique that utilizes the computer and multiple X rays to visualize the brain.*
E. *The part of the nervous system that includes the brain and spinal cord.*
F. *Locations along the axon where myelin is absent.*
G. *A brain imaging technique that uses radioactive substances to identify brain areas with high metabolic activity.*
H. *Supporting cells within the brain.*
I. *All the neurons that lie outside the brain and the spinal cord.*

___ 27. **Cerebral hemispheres (p. 46)**
___ 28. **Corpus callosum (p. 46)**
___ 29. **Phrenologist (p. 47)**
___ 30. **Cerebral cortex (p. 47)**
___ 31. **Frontal lobe (p. 47)**
___ 32. **Parietal lobe (p. 47)**
___ 33. **Temporal lobe (p. 49)**
___ 34. **Limbic system (p. 49)**
___ 35. **Hypothalamus (p. 49)**

A. *A group of brain structures that appear to be involved in emotional behavior. Located below the cerebral cortex.*
B. *A bundle of fibers that connects the left and right cerebral hemispheres.*
C. *The large outer layer of brain tissue of the cerebral hemispheres.*
D. *A person who believed in the now obsolete theory that attempted to link behavioral traits to bumps and depressions on the skull.*
E. *A brain structure involved in sex, aggression, hunger, thirst, and other motivated behaviors, as well as autonomic and endocrine functions. Located just above the pituitary gland near the base of the brain.*
F. *The lobe of the cerebral cortex involved in the processing of sensory information from the skin. Located between the occipital and frontal lobes.*
G. *A lobe of the cerebral cortex involved in memory, reasoning, thinking, and movement.*
H. *A lobe of the cerebral cortex involved in processing auditory information. Located on the sides of the brain.*
I. *The two symmetrical halves of the top part of the brain connected by a bundle of fibers.*

___ 36. **Cerebellum (p. 50)**
___ 37. **Medulla (p. 50)**
___ 38. **Spinal cord (p. 50)**
___ 39. **Occipital lobe (p. 47)**
___ 40. **Afferent pathway (p. 51)**
___ 41. **Efferent pathway (p. 51)**
___ 42. **Autonomic nervous system (p. 51)**
___ 43. **Sympathetic division (p. 53)**
___ 44. **Fright-fight-flight response (p. 53)**

A. *The entire spectrum of physiological changes that prepares an organism for an emergency. Produced by activation of the sympathetic division of the autonomic nervous system.*
B. *Pathway that carries information toward the central nervous system.*
C. *The large spherical brain structure involved in motor coordination. Located beneath the occipital lobe.*
D. *A component of the autonomic nervous system whose activation during stressful situations results in such effects as increased heart rate, blood pressure, and respiration, and inhibition of digestive activities.*
E. *The part of the nervous system that connects the brain and spinal cord to body organs such as the stomach, intestines, and heart.*
F. *A subarea of the cerebral hemispheres that processes visual information.*
G. *The mass of nervous tissue carrying information between parts of the body—such as the arms, legs, and trunk—and the brain.*
H. *Pathway that carries information away from the central nervous system.*
I. *A lower part of the brain involved in maintenance functions of the body, such as heart action, sleeping and waking, breathing and digestion.*

___ 45. **Parasympathetic division (p. 54)**
___ 46. **Endocrine system (p. 54)**
___ 47. **Hormone (p. 54)**
___ 48. **Estrogen and progesterone (p. 54)**
___ 49. **Pituitary gland (p. 54)**
___ 50. **Releasing factors (p. 54)**
___ 51. **Somatic nervous system. (p. 51)**
___ 52. **Testosterone (p. 55)**

A. *A substance released by an endocrine gland into the bloodstream or body fluids that acts as a special chemical messenger to regulate physiological processes in the body.*
B. *A component of the autonomic nervous system that returns the body to normal after a stressful situation. Its activation decreases heart rate, blood pressure, and respiration rate.*
C. *Substances released from the neurons of the hypothalamus that control and direct the activity of the pituitary gland.*
D. *A system of glands that releases hormones into the bloodstream.*
E. *One of the two divisions of the peripheral nervous system, which includes sensory and motor neuron carrying information from the spinal cord to the body and from the body to the spinal cord.*
F. *Hormones secreted by the ovaries.*
G. *Male sex hormone released from the testes.*
H. *The master endocrine gland located at the base of the brain beneath the hypothalamus. Produces several hormones, most of which stimulate other endocrine glands to release their own hormones.*

| | | |
|---|---|---|
| ___53. | **Cortisol (p. 56)** | *A.  Areas of the brain important for language.* |
| ___54. | **Epilepsy (p. 56)** | *B.  A rupture or blockage of a blood vessel in the brain.* |
| ___55. | **Stroke (p. 57)** | *C.  A controversy that debates whether the mind is separate and distinct from, or a part of* |

___53. **Cortisol (p. 56)**

___54. **Epilepsy (p. 56)**

___55. **Stroke (p. 57)**

___56. **Wernicke's area and Broca's area (pp. 57–58)**

___57. **Dichotic listening (p. 62)**

___58. **Mind–body problem (p. 64)**

___59. **Tourette's syndrome (p. 58)**

*A.  Areas of the brain important for language.*

*B.  A rupture or blockage of a blood vessel in the brain.*

*C.  A controversy that debates whether the mind is separate and distinct from, or a part of the body.*

*D.  A hormone released by the outer part of the adrenal gland that participates in the body's response to stress.*

*E.  A disorder associated with changes in the electrical activity of the brain. The major symptom is the occurrence of major or minor seizures.*

*F.  An experimental technique in which separate messages are presented to each ear simultaneously through headphones. The technique is useful in studies of functional lateralization of the brain.*

*G.  Symptoms include excessive nervousness, hyperactivity, attention problems, tics, jerks, and other behavioral problems.*

*ANSWERS*

54. e, 55. b, 56. a, 57. f, 58. c, 59. g

37. i, 38. g, 39. f, 40. b, 41. h, 42. e, 43. d, 44. a, 45. b, 46. d, 47. a, 48. f, 49. e, 50. c, 51. e, 52. g, 53. d,

20. a, 21. e, 22. i, 23. d, 24. b, 25. c, 26. h, 27. i, 28. b, 29. d, 30. c, 31. g, 32. f, 33. h, 34. a, 35. e, 36. c,

1. c, 2. e, 3. b, 4. h, 5. f, 6. a, 7. i, 8. g, 9. d, 10. c, 11. a, 12. e, 13. g, 14. d, 15. b, 16. h, 17. f, 18. f, 19. g,

## SELF-TEST

**1.** The cell in the human body that contains an axon, dendrite, and cell body is called a

    **(a)** nerve.

    **(b)** neuron.

    **(c)** synapse.

    **(d)** vesicle.

    (LO1; p. 35)

**2.** Dendritic trees

    **(a)** carry neuronal information toward the cell body.

    **(b)** carry neuronal information away from the cell body.

    **(c)** are only structurally important.

    **(d)** contain neurotransmitters.

    (LO1; p. 36)

**3.** The frequently myelinated part of the neuron is called the

    **(a)** axonal terminal.

    **(b)** cell body.

    **(c)** dendrite.

    **(d)** axon.

    (LO1; p. 37)

**4.** An axon that has a higher concentration of negative ions inside rather than outside of its membranes

    **(a)** is displaying an action potential.

    **(b)** is displaying a dendritic potential.

    **(c)** is displaying a resting potential.

    **(d)** has an excess of sodium ions inside the cell.

    (LO2; p. 37)

**5.** The low concentration of sodium ions inside the axon is maintained in the face of continued axonal firing or action potentials. The mechanism

    **(a)** depends upon the existence of myelin.

    **(b)** depends upon the existence of potassium ions.

    **(c)** is entirely passive (i.e., requires no energy).

    **(d)** is the sodium-potassium pump.

    (LO2; p. 38)

**6.** Synaptic transmission

    **(a)** is mediated by the release of a chemical messenger.

    **(b)** produces a spike on the receiving dendrite.

    **(c)** depends upon actual contact between neurons.

    **(d)** occurs only in the central nervous system.

    (LO3; p. 39)

**7.** The place in the cell at which electrical activity (neuronal information) is integrated and summarized is

    **(a)** the node of Ranvier.

    **(b)** the synapse.

    **(c)** the point at which the axon connects to the cell body.

    **(d)** the point at which the dendrite connects to the cell body.

    (LO3; p. 37)

**8.** The electroencephalograph (EEG)

    **(a)** is an electrical recording technique.

    **(b)** is an electrical stimulation technique.

    **(c)** is an anatomical technique.

    **(d)** must be used to declare a patient legally dead.

    (LO4; p. 44)

9. During an experiment on brain function, a part of the hypothalamus of a rat is painlessly destroyed with a small lesion. The rat is allowed to recover and is observed for three months. The rat is observed to become obese during this time, whereas other rats without brain lesions in other areas of the brain do not. A reasonable interpretation of this result is that

   (a) the lesion stimulated the rat's appetite.
   (b) the hypothalamus affected eating behavior in some way, although the precise mechanism is unknown.
   (c) the hypothalamus is involved in taste.
   (d) rats usually get obese if allowed access to sufficient food.
   (LO4; pp. 45, 60)

10. The parts of the cerebral cortex that have visual functions are the

   (a) frontal lobes.
   (b) parietal lobes.
   (c) temporal lobes.
   (d) occipital lobes.
   (LO5; p. 47)

11. The part of the brain that seems to be involved in the processing of emotional information is the

   (a) cerebral cortex.
   (b) medulla.
   (c) limbic system.
   (d) cerebellum.
   (LO5; p. 49)

12. The part of the brain that appears to play major roles in behaviors such as sex and aggression is the

   (a) hypothalamus.
   (b) cerebral cortex.
   (c) medulla.
   (d) corpus callosum.
   (LO5; p. 49)

13. The spinal cord, usually thought of as only carrying information between the brain and the body, actually processes neuronal information. The specific behaviors involved are called

   (a) motivations.
   (b) feelings.
   (c) reflexes.
   (d) sensations.
   (LO5; p. 50)

14. A sensory neuron carrying information from the toe to the spinal cord is part of the _____.

   (a) autonomic nervous system
   (b) somatic nervous system
   (c) brain
   (d) limbic system
   (LO6; p. 51)

15. Sympathetic nervous system activity involves

   (a) a decrease in blood pressure.
   (b) an increase in the activity of the stomach and intestine.
   (c) an increase in heart rate and respiration.
   (d) salivation.
   (LO6; p. 53)

16. The pituitary gland controls the _____ and is in turn controlled by the _____.

   (a) stress response; ACTH
   (b) hypothalamus; endocrine glands
   (c) endocrine glands; master gland
   (d) endocrine glands; hypothalamus
   (LO7; pp. 54–55)

17. The dominant male sex hormone is

   (a) estrogen.
   (b) testosterone.
   (c) cortisol.
   (d) progesterone.
   (LO7; p. 55)

18. A brain disorder that results in seizures is called

   (a) Alzheimer's disease.
   (b) epilepsy.
   (c) multiple sclerosis.
   (d) Wernicke's disorder.
   (LO8; p. 56)

19. A stroke that damages Broca's area in the left frontal lobe may result in a condition known as

   (a) speech difficulties.
   (b) obesity.
   (c) multiple sclerosis.
   (d) epilepsy.
   (LO9; p. 57)

20. Some psychologists have suggested that the split-brain operation

   (a) can cause epilepsy.
   (b) causes too much brain damage to be used as a treatment for anything.
   (c) decreases intelligence.
   (d) creates two minds in the same person.
   (LO10; p. 60)

*ANSWERS*

1. b, 2. a, 3. d, 4. c, 5. d, 6. a, 7. c, 8. a, 9. b, 10. d, 11. c, 12. a, 13. c, 14. b, 15. c, 16. d, 17. b, 18. b, 19. a, 20. d

# THINKING ABOUT PSYCHOLOGY

1. The text contains a detailed diagram of only two neurons, but explains that communication among neurons is much more elaborate. Neurons receive inputs from several neighbors and synapse onto several more, sometimes even back on themselves or the neighbors that sent them the input. Diagram a hypothetical subsystem containing eight neurons, showing some of these more complicated interconnections. Identify whether each synapse is inhibitory or excitatory.

2. Assume that one neuron in your diagram begins spiking because a scientist stimulated it with a microelectrode for a brief moment. Trace the pattern of activity that might occur in the others because of this interference. What factors would affect how the other neurons behave?

3. You are driving down a dark highway and a deer runs out in front of the car. You swerve to miss the animal and safely stop the car, in the mud off the road. Using your knowledge of the nervous and endocrine systems, identify some of the physiological events that would occur during these few seconds.

# SUGGESTED READINGS

Bloom, F. E., Lazerson, A., & Hofstadter, L. (1985). *Brain, mind, and behavior*. New York: W. H. Freeman. An introductory textbook dealing with the neurosciences; is coordinated with the PBS series called "The Brain."

Bradshaw, J. L. (1989). *Hemispheric specialization and psychological function*. New York: John Wiley and Sons. A scholarly review of research on hemispheric asymmetry.

Churchland, P. M. (1984). *Matter and consciousness*. Cambridge, MA: MIT Press. A fascinating discussion of the mind–body problem, behaviorism, and other topics that affect our understanding of ourselves.

Eccles, Sir John, & Robinson D. N. (1984). *The wonder of being human: Our brain and our mind*. New York: Free Press. A short book that describes the humanistic approach of these two neuroscientists.

Hellige, J. B. (1990). Hemispheric asymmetry. *Annual Review of Psychology, 41,* 55–80. A review of asymmetry in animals and humans and their implication for behavior.

Kolb, B., & Whishaw, I. Q. (1985). *Fundamentals of human neuropsychology* (2nd ed.). New York: Freeman. An advanced text on neuropsychology that also includes thought-provoking essays on the nature of the mind.

Reinvang, I. (1985). *Aphasia and brain organization*. New York: Plenum. Examines the relationship between language disorders and brain organization in human beings.

Zivin, J. A., & Choi, D. W. (1991). Stroke therapy. *Scientific American,* July. A review of some of the recent and promising treatments for stroke.

# CHAPTER 3

## THE PSYCHOLOGY OF CONSCIOUSNESS
## OUTLINE

# THE PSYCHOLOGY OF CONSCIOUSNESS
## LEARNING OBJECTIVES

**After reading this chapter, you should be able to**

▶ **1.** define the term *consciousness* and trace the history of the study of the phenomenon within psychology. (pp. 74–75)

▶ **2.** describe how researchers use the EEG and evoke potentials to explore conscious activity. (pp. 75–76)

▶ **3.** describe the physiological and behavioral changes associated with the circadian rhythms and their disruption. (pp. 77–80)

▶ **4.** identify the stages of sleep. (pp. 80–81)

▶ **5.** explain what happens when a person is dreaming, and describe how a researcher might interpret the content of a dream. (pp. 81–84)

▶ **6.** describe the possible functions of sleep and dreaming. (pp. 84–85)

▶ **7.** trace the history of hypnosis, and define the hypnotic state of consciousness. (pp. 85–86)

▶ **8.** explain what is meant by posthypnotic suggestions, posthypnotic amnesia, and age regression. (p. 86)

▶ **9.** explain how the social aspects of hypnosis affect a person's hypnotizability. (p. 87)

▶ **10.** describe how hypnosis is used in law enforcement, and explain why this practice may present significant problems. (pp. 87–88)

▶ **11.** list the major categories of psychoactive drugs. (p. 89)

▶ **12.** explain several of the factors that determine how drugs affect the body and behavior. (pp. 90–93)

▶ **13.** list two examples of drugs in the general depressant category, and explain how they affect behavior. (pp. 93–95)

A woman in Arkansas shot and killed her husband and was convicted in circuit court of manslaughter. She recalled, and testified, that she and her husband had argued and that she had wanted to leave the house but her husband wouldn't allow it. She also remembered picking up his loaded gun. Under hypnosis, she further recalled that her husband grabbed her from behind, that they wrestled until the gun went off, and that her finger was outside the trigger guard—information that would have helped her case for self-defense. Unfortunately, the state courts refused to admit her "hypnotically refreshed" recollections.

Why would this defendant's memories of that night be more vivid under hypnosis? And why is the American system of justice reluctant to find such memories credible? The answers lie in the elusive concept of consciousness, an awareness of one's internal and external environments. Consciousness is not something either present or absent. Consciousness is a shifting state, one that alters because of sleep, dreams, drugs, meditation, and treatments such as hypnosis. The reluctance of the courts to accept hypnotically refreshed memories is due to lack of knowledge about altered states of consciousness, especially hypnosis.

Consciousness is a shifty, slippery concept, and psychologists have a difficult time defining it. Our English language seems to conspire to increase the fuzziness of the term. We say, "She is conscious of her musical talents," meaning she is aware of having musical ability, even unduly proud of them. If we say she is "unconscious of her musical talents" we imply modesty, not coma. We also use the word alone, as in "he is conscious," meaning he is awake, aware of his environment, perhaps recovering from a head injury. When a person is unconscious with no hope of ever regaining consciousness, he may soon be declared brain dead and taken off life support even though he might live many more months with the help of respirators and feeding tubes. To us, though, his permanent loss of consciousness reflects the loss of life itself.

The notion that there are "altered" states of consciousness, such as the one the hypnotized or drugged person is in, suggests that there is a normal state. We start with that one. It has provided more than enough mysteries for psychologists to investigate.

# THE STUDY OF NORMAL CONSCIOUSNESS

Your state of consciousness as you are reading this sentence is probably the one that is normal for you. You are alert, awake, thinking, and aware of your surroundings. If you start to daydream, your state of consciousness will change slightly. No longer will you be aware of the meaning of the words on this page. In fact, you may find yourself reading a whole paragraph without understanding a single word. Instead of focusing your consciousness on the book, you may be daydreaming about last night's party, tomorrow's meeting with the boss, or your psychology class.

## What Is Consciousness?

**Consciousness** *is your state of awareness of external and internal events.* This definition incorporates a wide range of mental activity that can be categorized in many different ways. For example, mental activity might be passive or active (Deikman, 1971). In a passive state, you simply "take in" your environment rather than plan or make decisions. You might listen to music, look at a landscape, or lie on a beach feeling the sun warm your skin. In a more active mode, you might plan tomorrow's picnic, solve a crossword puzzle, or decide whether to open your own restaurant.

The normal state of consciousness can be distinguished from several alternate states. This distinction usually refers to a qualitatively different state of awareness. For example, during a dream you are aware of events, but not the same ones that you would be aware of if you were awake. Nevertheless, even though the awareness is of a different nature, you are still aware.

Some processes are characterized by a much lower level of awareness than the ones that take place during your normal state. Much of the neural activity that takes place in your brain has very little to do with consciousness. The neural activity might be controlling heart rate, body temperature, or the secretion of hormones. The nervous system is responsible for coordinating and controlling many activities, most of which never reach awareness.

The most useful definition of consciousness, the awareness of internal and external events, covers a broad range of mental phenomena, including sensation. This is the process by which information in the environment is translated into neural messages through activity in the sense organs: the eye, ear, nose, taste buds, or skin.

Information about the external world cannot reach a person's consciousness without first being experienced through the senses. This involves the process of perception, in which information from the senses is integrated and understood, the process of attention, which controls what we focus on, and the processes of learning, memory, motivation, and emotion.

Psychologists ordinarily study each of these processes separately even though they are not separate at all. To avoid the illusion of separateness, many psychologists adopt the term "information processing" and use it as a theoretical framework to investigate human behavior. **The information-processing approach** *studies how people attend to, select, and integrate information and how they use it to make decisions and guide their behavior* (Kantowitz, 1984). The approach emphasizes the analogy of the movement of information through a computer, using terms borrowed from computer science (such as input, output, and processing) to describe behavior.

The many terms used in the study of consciousness can be very confusing because they are not clearly defined. Some terms include references to a particular aspect of the theory of one psychologist and a slightly different feature in the theory of another. One reason for this confusion is that the study of consciousness has a turbulent history.

## The History of Consciousness in Psychology

Early definitions of psychology emphasized consciousness and "mental life." For example, in 1890, the American psychologist William James defined psychology as "the science of mental life, both of its phenomena and their conditions." Another early definition (Ladd, 1887) called psychology "the description and explanation of states of consciousness as such."

Perhaps the most important tool of the early psychologists studying consciousness was introspection, the technique developed by Wilhelm Wundt. Introspection involved trained observers who noted their own thoughts and feelings and avoided the intrusion of any meaning. An observer might perceive the color red and report reactions without reference to the possible meaning of red (in stop lights, in blood, in a flag). These introspectionists were trying to be objective; they wanted their descriptions of experiences to be free of personal biases. But there was no way to validate or replicate the observations since independent observers could not share the introspectionist's experience. The technique could not pass the critical test of objectivity.

Trends in the other sciences during the late nineteenth century were further emphasizing the importance of objectivity. This emphasis on objectivity was not lost on psychologists, particularly John B. Watson at the University of Chicago. He and many of his contemporaries were frustrated with introspection because it limited psychology. For example, you could not obtain or rely on introspection reports from infants, animals, or emotionally disturbed people. Watson urged psychologists to focus their attention on objective observations of behavior. Most psychologists were receptive to this view and consequently abandoned the study of consciousness. The objective observation of behavior very soon developed into "behaviorism," an approach to psychology that accepted only observable behavior as its subject matter.

The behaviorist approach was dominant in psychology for many years, espoused by several very famous researchers, most notably B. F. Skinner (Skinner, 1938, 1953, 1974). However, during the seventies and eighties psychologists began turning once again to the study of consciousness, often over the vehement protests of many behaviorists (Hilgard, 1980; Skinner, 1984). Studying private mental experience objectively is difficult, to be sure, but not impossible. Psychologists concluded that they could not ignore such an important component of human life just because it was a tough nut to crack using the scientific approach. The development of the EEG and other methods to observe brain activity was eagerly applied to the study of consciousness. The click and clatter of pens tracing patterns across an endless roll of chart paper offered a reassuring way to objectively observe aspects of consciousness, without having to rely on the self-reports of introspection.

## Electrical Signs of Consciousness

The brain is a complex organ that generates electric currents based on biochemical activity, as we discussed in chapter 2. The Austrian scientist Anton Berger first demonstrated that these signals could be monitored by placing electrodes on the surface of the scalp in 1924 and since then, psychologists have used the brain's electrical signals to study many aspects of brain function.

*The EEG*    The electroencephalograph, or EEG, is one of the most important tools used by scientists studying consciousness. Electrodes placed on the scalp can detect

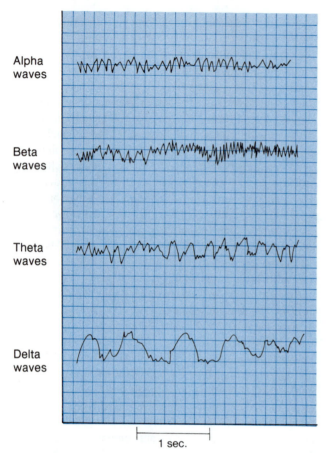

Alpha
waves

Beta
waves

Theta
waves

Delta
waves

1 sec.

**Figure 3.1** *EEG brain waves*

very slight changes in the electrical activity of the brain. Because the movement of charged particles plays such an important role in the neuron's messages, the electrical charge in any brain area is constantly changing, depending on the activity of the neurons in that area. At one moment, the charge over the visual area of the brain might be slightly negative relative to the charge over another part of the brain. The EEG records these differences in charges for parts of the brain, producing a chart of their changes over time. Most researchers agree that what contributes the most to the EEG record (figure 3.1) is the excitatory and inhibitory potentials originating from the dendrites of cells within the range of the recording electrodes.

An individual's EEG is extremely complex, and the waveforms vary depending upon the part of the brain from which they originate, the task the individual is performing, and the person's emotional state. For example, activity in the parietal lobes shows distinct patterns when a subject is performing tasks that vary in attentional demands. A task that requires the person to pay attention to visual cues is associated with

different waveforms compared to one that involves internal information processing, such as mental arithmetic. Emotional factors also appear to influence the EEG. The patterns are distinguishable depending on whether a subject is viewing scenes evoking positive or negative feelings (Ray & Cole, 1985).

Computers have made the EEG even more useful for studying conscious processes. When a stimulus, such as a loud noise, is repeatedly presented to a person, the EEG appears to show little change because there is activity in the brain in addition to any special response to the noise. But by averaging the brain's response to many noises, a computer can filter out the electrical activity that "drowns out" the brain's response to the noise. What remains is a waveform pattern that shows the brain's reaction to the noise. The waveform is called the **evoked potential;** *it is the neural response to a stimulus, such as a sound, obtained by averaging many EEG patterns during repeated presentations of the stimulus* (see figure 3.2).

The evoked potential is still a crude measure of events in the enormously complex brain, but a number of studies have found that the waveforms vary depending on what kind of mental activity is occurring. For example, a particular waveform appears while a person is making a decision about what to do in a simple button-pressing task, and then changes again when the person makes the muscle movements (Begleiter & Porjesz, 1975). Recordings of evoked potentials are not exactly the same as mind reading, but they are observable signs of conscious processes, events that were previously private.

▶ **GUIDED REVIEW** *Learning Objectives 1 and 2*

1. _____ is the awareness of internal and external events.
2. The term _____ is frequently used to refer to many of the events collectively involved in consciousness, such as sensation, perception, and cognition, to avoid the illusion that the events are separate processes.
3. Consciousness was first studied using _____, but many felt the technique was not objective enough. _____ emphasized the observation of behavior rather than studies of private mental activity. Now the study of consciousness is an important part of psychology.
4. Advances in electronics have permitted scientists to study consciousness more directly, using the _____. The _____, which averages many EEG records obtained during repeated stimulus presentations, is another important tool in the study of consciousness.

*Answers*

1. *Consciousness 2. information processing 3. introspection, Behaviorism 4. EEG, evoked potential*

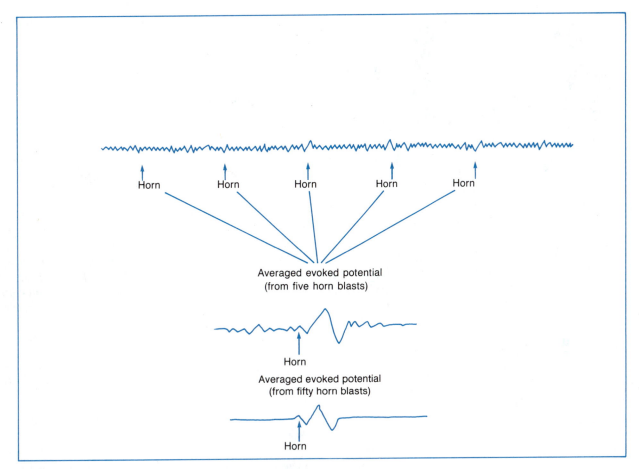

**Figure 3.2**  *The evoked potential. The top line shows an EEG record during a period of time in which a horn was blasted five times. The neural response to each blast is drowned out by other neural activities. Averaging the brain's response to many blasts produces an evoked potential that shows the response to the sound without background noise.*

## BIOLOGICAL RHYTHMS, SLEEP, AND DREAMS

*"To everything, there is a season and a time for every purpose."* These words from the Book of Ecclesiastes describe one of the most fundamental characteristics of living things. Like virtually every species with which we share our planet, and probably because we happen to live on a mass that rotates in space with extraordinary regularity, we have rhythm. All of the rhythms are associated with biological changes, and some with drastic changes that result in what could only be called altered states of consciousness.

## Biological Rhythms

Humans try to insulate themselves from the cycle of daylight and darkness and the changing of the seasons using electric lights, air conditioning, and central heating. But we evolved on this planet and we respond to its characteristic rhythms with synchronous rhythms of our own.

The best understood cycle is the **circadian rhythm,** *the twenty-four-hour rhythm that corresponds to the earth's daily rotation* (figure 3.3). For most people on regular schedules, body temperature usually peaks around 2:00 P.M. and is at its lowest point between 2:00 and 4:00 A.M.

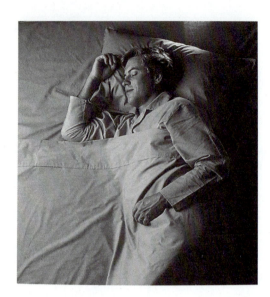

**Figure 3.3**    *The circadian cycle, the most pronounced biological rhythm, moves in synchrony with the day/night cycle.*

Weight shows a circadian rhythm as well, peaking in the late afternoon or early evening. Heart rate peaks in the early afternoon and blood pressure in the early evening. Some systems peak in the middle of the night, such as the content of sodium in the plasma. Practically every physiological system shows a circadian rhythm, although they don't all necessarily peak at the same time of day (Luce, 1970). The Research Box: The Biological Clock describes hypotheses about the mechanisms underlying the circadian rhythm.

The pronounced rhythmicity of these physiological systems has some important implications. People are more susceptible to the effects of drugs at different times of day. One study of cancer patients found marked differences in the response to chemotherapy depending on the time of day at which the drugs were administered (Hrushesky, 1985).

Behavior is also affected by the day/night cycle. People usually perform best in the early afternoon and worst in the early morning hours (Akerstedt & Froberg, 1976). But there is considerable human diversity in this kind of rhythmicity. Some of us are "early birds" and others "night owls," both in behavior and in our physiological rhythms (Horne & Ostberg, 1977).

The circadian rhythm in behavior affects the performance of people who work at night. Even if they have a chance to sleep during the day, they make more mistakes at night. A group of researchers in Sweden determined the accuracy of three shifts of gas-meter readers responsible for recording number entries in a factory ledger (Bjerner, Holm, & Swensson, 1955). The factory operated twenty-four hours a day. The researchers were able to determine the number of errors made each hour of every day between the years 1912 and 1931. The workers showed the worst performance around 2:00 in the morning.

*Shift Work and Jet Lag*    A growing number of businesses and factories are operating around the clock, and many are resorting to shift work to staff their operations. Some companies ask their workers to change to a new shift every seven days, moving from the day shift to the evening shift to the "graveyard" shift. A strategy favored in Europe is to move workers to a new shift every day or two. Regardless of the actual schedule, shift workers have difficulty establishing a regular twenty-four-hour biological rhythm.

Scientists at the Civil Aeromedical Institute conducted a study on the effects of a twelve-hour shift rotation (Higgins et al., 1975). They measured a variety of physiological and behavioral activities in fifteen men, first during their normal waking hours and then after a "shift" when they began sleeping between 10:30 A.M. and 6:00 P.M. Some men adjusted easily to the new working hours, and their physiological systems began peaking around 4:00 A.M. instead of 4:00 P.M. A few never adjusted at all. It took most of the men several days to modify their cycles in accordance with the new day/night cycle. The subjects took an average of five days to begin showing a peak body temperature at the right time of "day." For most subjects, several physiological systems were "out of synch" for a few days.

The subjects' performance on the behavioral test after the shift was dismal, and it was still not quite normal even nine days after the shift. Again, some subjects adapted better than others, but it is clear that shift rotations can present a serious problem to workers' health and to performance on the job.

Apparently, some shift-work schedules are less taxing than others. Studies of humans living under conditions without time cues show that humans tend to adopt a longer "day," usually about twenty-five hours, suggesting that our natural rhythm is slightly longer than an earth day. Researchers assisting the managers of a chemical plant in Utah experimented with a new shift schedule that took advantage of the longer human rhythms and also respected the length of time most people take to resynchronize after a phase shift. The workers, who formerly changed shifts weekly, were asked to change every twenty-one days to a new shift that required staying up later rather than going to bed earlier. Staying up later is easier for humans because of our longer natural "day." These workers were very pleased with the new schedule; turnover dropped and production rose (Czeisler, Moore-Ede, & Coleman, 1985).

Switching to a new shift is very much like taking a plane across several time zones, an event that can result in jet lag. During the first few days at the new location, people have difficulties adjusting to the new schedule. They wake up during the night looking for twenty-four-hour restaurants, and they can't concentrate during important morning meetings. The strategies that help people adjust to shift work can help with jet lag. If you arrive at your destination at 11 P.M. your time, but it is only 5 P.M. local time, stay up. Take advantage of the fact that your natural rhythm is probably longer than twenty-four hours to help you adjust to the new time schedule.

*Longer-Term Rhythms*     Even while watching birds migrate, salmon swim upstream, and squirrels hibernate, it is easy to ignore or dismiss the possibility that people may be affected by the annual cycle in which the earth moves around the sun. Perhaps the arrogance that comes from control over the environment through modern conveniences has led people in industrialized countries to believe that the seasons no longer affect them. Yet scientists are finding that the seasons do affect us in surprising ways.

Seasonal rhythms exist in quite a number of human behaviors, including conception, mortality, and suicide (Aschoff, 1981), though the changes are rather small. Seasonal variation on Scholastic Aptitude Test scores has also been reported (Kimura, 1991), but for men only. A group of seventy-two Canadian men and women were tested in May and October, and though the performance of the women was about the same both times, the performance of the men on the problems measuring spatial ability was twenty-five percent better in the spring.

One seasonal rhythm that has received much recent attention is called SAD, for seasonal affective disorder (Nelson et al., 1990), whose symptoms include depression, lethargy, increased sleeping, weight gain, and cravings for carbohydrates. The immune system is also negatively affected making sickness more likely (Kasper et al., 1991). For people who have it, SAD comes in late autumn or in winter. When summer comes, patients either return to

normal or flip-flop to a state of energy, elation, and even mania. Like clockwork, the symptoms return the next year when the seasons change again.

The causes of SAD, or any seasonal change in behavior, are difficult to determine. Throughout each year, a number of events occur that may contribute to behavioral changes. Many of them are linked to culture: school starts in a specific season (September for Americans, April for Japanese), and Christmas and Hannukah come in December. Others are more closely related to the characteristics of the seasons, but they might have psychological effects of their own that have nothing to do with the effects of the seasons themselves. Examples include spring planting time, the fall harvest, or the start of deer hunting season. It is difficult to separate the potential causes of seasonal changes in human behavior.

In the case of SAD, though, it is clear that the disorder is not simply due to the holiday blues or other cultural events tied to the seasons. People in the Southern Hemisphere who have SAD are six months out of phase: their winter starts around May, which is when their SAD symptoms begin appearing (Terman, 1988). A very interesting hypothesis for the cause of SAD suggests that patients with the disorder are especially sensitive to the length of the day and the amount of light; the shortened days of winter generate chemical changes in the body that may result in SAD symptoms. Light has important influences on chemical events in the brain, particularly those involving the neurotransmitter serotonin, which is linked in circuitous ways to carbohydrate metabolism, sleep onset, mood and circadian rhythms. SAD patients may have faulty serotonin metabolism that may be especially affected by the changing amount of light over a year's cycle.

Although the links between SAD, brain chemistry, and light are still tenuous, physicians have begun treating the disorder with light, often with remarkable success (Rosenthal et al., 1988; Lewy et al., 1988; Wurtman & Wurtman, 1989). Huge fluorescent panels emitting very bright light can be installed in the home so that the person who has SAD can sit in front of them for several hours a day reading, knitting, relaxing, and soaking up the rays. Recovery is often very fast after phototherapy begins, often within just a few days. We should add that the lighting level needs to be very, very bright to have any effect on the brain's biochemistry, in case you were thinking of using the technique to cure your own winter blues. Outdoor lighting is at least twenty-five times brighter than what exists in most indoor settings, although

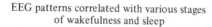

EEG patterns correlated with various stages of wakefulness and sleep

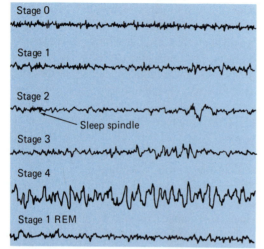

EEG patterns corresponding to various behavioral states

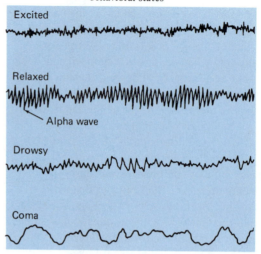

**Figure 3.4**   *EEG patterns typical of wakefulness (Stage 0) and various stages of sleep. Source:* A Manual of Standardized Terminology, Techniques, and Scoring System for Sleep Stages

of Human Subjects, *by A. Rechtschaffen and A. Kales, National Institutes of Health, No. 204, 1968.*

we don't usually notice such a difference due to the adaptation of our visual systems.

Is SAD a qualititatively distinct disorder limited to a few people with abnormal brain chemistry, or is it an exaggerated version of an annual rhythm that evolved for good reason and that we all have? Many scientists hypothesize that a milder form of SAD could be quite normal and could have evolved to provide for seasonal energy savings in winter. The increased food intake, longer sleep time, craving for carbohydrates, and general lethargy would all be advantageous to conserve energy and put on fat for the long winter when food supplies were low. Budgeting our annual energy expenditure according to the seasons may be a useful survival strategy.

## The Stages of Sleep

The alternate state of consciousness known as sleep has rhythms of its own that exist within the twenty-four-hour circadian rhythm. The seven or eight hours a person sleeps are actually very active ones. A person goes through several stages of deeper and deeper sleep, then into a dream, then back again to lighter sleep, repeating this cycle four or five times per night. The EEG has always been a favorite tool of sleep researchers because the patterns for each stage are distinguishable.

As the person drifts off to sleep, the patterns on the EEG gradually show fewer and fewer **beta waves,** *high frequency, low amplitude waveforms characteristic of the alert state* (figure 3.4). **Alpha waves,** *lower frequency and higher amplitude waves occurring about eight to twelve per second, are characteristic of the relaxed state.* **Delta waves,** *very low frequency (one to four per second) and high amplitude waves, are characteristic of the EEG pattern of people in the deeper stages of sleep, especially Stages 3 and 4,* as shown in figure 3.4. **Slow-wave sleep** *describes the four stages of sleep.*

About every ninety minutes or so, and after a person has drifted to Stage 4, then back to a lighter sleep stage, the EEG shows some unusual patterns. Very rapid beta waves begin appearing even though the person seems to be quite asleep. The person has entered **REM,** *a period of sleep associated with dreaming and characterized by rapid eye movements, beta waves on the EEG, and a loss of tonus in the muscles of the neck.*

As the night continues, the person goes through about four or five episodes of REM sleep that grow longer and longer. These REM episodes are very intriguing, as we shall see in the next section. Figure 3.5 shows the cycles of sleep during a typical night.

## CLOSE UP ON RESEARCH

### Night Work

A night's sleep can be a restful and enjoyable experience; it can also be filled with troubling, amusing, or just puzzling events. Most people, for example, talk in their sleep at least once in a while. Talking can occur in either REM or slow-wave sleep, and can be a single word, a grunt, or what seems to be one half of an entire conversation—complete with pauses that suggest the sleep talker is listening to another party speak. Sleep-talking is not abnormal and does not appear to be associated with any mental disturbances, although young children with behavior problems and frequent nightmares are more likely to talk in their sleep (Arkin, 1978; Hawkins & Williams, 1992).

Dreaming is also quite normal, but some dreams can be very terrifying. Psychologists have been able to identify two different kinds of dreams that cause people great anxiety: nightmares and night terrors. Both are very difficult to study in the laboratory because they are not very common, at least in most people (Murray, 1991).

A nightmare is a terrified awakening from sleep without any obvious external cause, such as a car backfire or a siren. People wake up with intense anxiety, sweating, dilated pupils and sometimes difficulty in breathing. They can often describe the frightening experience with vivid detail, recalling being chased, being threatened, and sometimes being killed. Sometimes the plot of the dream is very explicit with easily recalled characters and action sequences.

Nightmares seem to mainly occur in the second half of the sleep period, and they are mostly associated with REM sleep, particularly those that are especially vivid. They seem to be a function of daytime anxiety, since people who are under more stress experience more of them. For example, soldiers who have been in combat report a higher rate of nightmares compared to soldiers who have never seen battle. People who experience frequent and recurring nightmares often show a profile of disturbance on psychological tests, but they can also be more creative, artistic, and open.

Night terrors are quite different from nightmares and appear to be related to development. These events are episodes of extreme terror and panic that occur early in the sleep cycle, usually within slow-wave sleep. They last only a few minutes and the person usually has no recall of the episode. People who experience night terrors are more difficult to arouse and can't explain why they are so frightened. Children are more likely to suffer from night terrors than adults but fortunately they seem to outgrow them by their teen years.

Some people experience both night terrors and sleepwalking. Again, children are more likely to walk in their sleep than adults, and boys are more likely to sleepwalk than girls. In children, sleepwalking usually begins around the age of seven and disappears by the time the children reach their teens. Like night terrors, episodes of sleepwalking usually occur during periods of slow-wave sleep and last only a few minutes. Sleep walkers rarely recall the episode. Sleepwalking appears to run in families. One Japanese study found that children whose parents were sleepwalkers as children were more likely to walk in their sleep (Abe, Amatoni, & Oda, 1984).

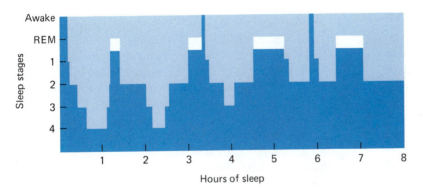

**Figure 3.5**  *The sleep cycles during a typical night*

## Dreaming

What is a dream? What do the characters and plots of our dreams tell us about ourselves, our past, or our future? The very private events we call dreams go on night after night, some terrifying, some illuminating, some boring, and some simply puzzling. Most are quickly forgotten but the memorable ones can remain with us throughout our lives.

Interest in dreams is as old as human history, and one of the first books about dreams is an Egyptian papyrus dating back to 1350 B.C. The Egyptians believed that dreams were messages from the gods who might be demanding greater piety or warning the dreamer of some impending event. The gods might also choose to answer a particular question through a dream, though special dream interpreters would be required to help the dreamer sort through the images. Religious writings contain many references to dreams and their use in foretelling the future. The birth of Jesus Christ was announced to Joseph this way by an angel of the Lord who came to him in a dream.

In the 1950s, some exciting things were happening in psychological laboratories that enabled researchers to learn much more about dreams from an objective standpoint. First, researchers who were watching sleeping subjects noticed the rapid eye movements and wondered whether they might be related to dreaming (Aserinsky & Kleitman, 1953). They started waking people up at different times during the night and found that most of the time, people who were exhibiting the rapid eye movements would report a dream. This serendipitous observation was very significant and started a tidal wave of research on dreaming. Now there was an observable indicator for an alternate state of consciousness. Scientists no longer needed to rely on people's recollection of dreams in the morning—they could wake them up during REM and the chances were very good that the person would report a dream.

By watching for REMs, and later by watching the EEG, researchers could collect enormous amounts of information on patterns of dreaming. It became clear, for example, that everyone dreams. Although some people say they never dream, everyone shows the typical brain patterns in the night and will report a dream if they are awakened at the right time. Further research also demonstrated that dreams are not completely confined to REM sleep, so the indicator is not completely reliable. Dreams that occur in slow-wave sleep are somewhat different in character though. The typical REM dream is movie-like with a sequence of events, but the slow-wave dream often is about a single sensation, such as suffocating or falling.

The content of dreams is a fascinating subject that has received much attention, especially within the psychoanalytic framework. Sigmund Freud became interested in dreams as a source of information on the unconscious. After studying both his own dreams and the dreams of his patients, Freud proposed that they contained a great deal of symbolism, especially about troubling events that happened in the person's early childhood. The story and characters of a dream were its manifest content, but these should be used to disclose the dream's latent, or hidden content, which often included unresolved sexual desires

from childhood. Freud believed that dreams represented wishes that were repressed out of normal waking consciousness because they were too painful or socially unacceptable to think about. In sleep, people have less control and the wishes will be expressed, often through symbols. Rather than feature a penis in a dream, for example, the person might substitute an object like a cigar or fountain pen. It was the task of psychoanalysts to uncover the hidden meanings of the symbols in the dream and help the patient resolve unconscious and repressed desires.

Students of Freud expanded the scope of a dream's latent content to include other kinds of repressed wishes such as aggression. But the hypothesis that dreams contain many hidden symbols is not easy to test. Saying a person's dream image of a canoe is the manifest content for a more hidden meaning of the female sexual organs is difficult to contradict.

Studies in the laboratory have found that most dreams are rather ordinary and appear to reflect a person's present concerns and anxieties rather than deeply repressed desires from childhood. People who volunteer to sleep in a laboratory, for example, might dream about electrodes. Nevertheless, childhood traumas can certainly haunt some people's dreams. For instance, victims of childhood sexual abuse may have troubling dreams in adulthood with themes of aggression or child abuse. Many dreams appear to contain symbols that are very personal to the dreamer, but often their meaning is not hidden. For example, one woman who was sexually abused in childhood dreamed about standing helplessly by as her father opened fire on a crowd of children, crippling one little girl. The dreamer can identify the meaning or at least offer a plausible interpretation. Nevertheless, it appears some dreams are very obscure and may contain deeply hidden meanings; psychotherapy can often be very helpful in these cases.

The content of people's dreams is affected by many things, but it may be possible to influence that content under some circumstances. In a recent study, women who were very afraid of snakes were asked to sleep in a laboratory for several nights to find out whether pre-sleep suggestions could influence their dreams about something that truly made them nervous—snakes. They were all asked to stand next to a live boa constrictor in a cage, and different women were given different kinds of suggestions. For example, one suggestion featured the woman walking in a park on a sunny afternoon in a very pleasant state of mind. While walking, she encounters a snake but remains

## EXPLORING HUMAN DIVERSITY
### Dreaming Across Cultures

Consider a boy who has a dream in which he and his father are traveling together on a bus. The pavement is wet from rain and the bus swerves to avoid hitting an oncoming tractor-trailer. The vehicles crash. The boy, unharmed by the accident, searches through the wreckage for his father. He finally finds him in a hideous pile of blood and crushed flesh, dead.

The Freudian interpretation of this terrifying dream would probably rest heavily on the existence of unconscious, repressed wishes from childhood (Segall et al., 1990). Based on observations of his Viennese patients, Freud hypothesized that young boys in puberty felt strong sexual desires for their mothers. But since their fathers are their mothers' appropriate sexual partners, the boys feel jealousy and hostility toward their fathers. The boy's sexual attraction to his mother and hostility toward his father are both unacceptable and cause him great distress. Consciously, the feelings are repressed, but they find expression in the boy's dream.

A central argument against much of Freudian interpretations was that Freud's proposals were based on a very limited sample of patients—upper class Viennese. As a result, Freud was quite limited in his ability to sort out various alternative hypotheses and many of his conclusions could not be reliably tested. For example, the boys might have felt hostility toward their fathers not because of sexual feelings toward the mother, but because the father was the one (in Viennese society) who disciplined the children.

In an early study of adolescent boys in the Trobriand Islands in Papua New Guinea, Malinowski (1927) found boys dreaming about ill fates befalling their uncles rather than their fathers. Following a Freudian line of reasoning, that the dreams' latent content revealed an unconscious wish, the boys must have felt hostility toward their uncles. But why?

In the culture of the Trobriand Islanders, the role of disciplinarian in a family is assumed by the uncle. It is possible that Freud picked the wrong variable. He could not perform any tests to eliminate either the "mother's lover" role or the "disciplinarian" role because in Vienna, the father played both roles. Perhaps the target of the boys' hostility is the disciplinarian of the family, the one who punishes the children, rather than the one who is the mother's lover (Campbell & Naroll, 1972).

Malinowski's study on the Trobriand Islanders is not enough to confirm or refute anyone's hypothesis about the source of boys' hostility, or even confirm that it universally exists. Much debate still exists about his observations and conclusions (Spiro, 1982; Brown, 1991). Rather the study highlights the value of cross-cultural research in helping scientists sift through alternative hypotheses about human behavior and provides a cogent warning about generalizing from limited single-culture samples.

calm and relaxed, and stops to observe it. A much less pleasant suggestion described the woman in a strange place, in a tense mood, and very anxious. A snake darts near her feet and she feels a sense of panic. Other suggestions were similar except that a squirrel was substituted for the snake.

The dreams of the women who had the pleasant pre-sleep suggestions showed more positive emotion in their dreams compared to those who had the unpleasant suggestions. Whether the suggestion contained a snake or a squirrel did not make any difference. It seems that the emotional content of dreams can be manipulated to become positive, even after a rather stressful experience (De Koninck & Brunette, 1991).

An intriguing and controversial phenomenon that has attracted attention is the "lucid dream," in which the person knows at the time that he or she is dreaming. Surveys suggest that a great many people have had this experience at least once but, like many phenomena dealing with con-

sciousness, it is extremely difficult to demonstrate and study in the lab. Researchers have been experimenting with methods in which the dreamer is trained to signal the onset of a dream to the observers by a prearranged sequence of eye movements. Studies using this technique suggest that physical actions in a dream are correlated with tiny, but corresponding muscle movements. Tiny movements in the leg might occur when the person dreams about kicking an object. Some people claim to be able to engage in lucid dreaming at will and control the content of their own dreams. Researchers are exploring ways to increase the frequency of lucid dreaming, such as flashing a light whenever the person enters REM sleep. Whether people can achieve more conscious control over their dreams through training is a question that requires more research (LaBerge, 1985; Gackenbach & LaBerge, 1988; Gackenbach, 1991; Tholey, 1983; Blackmore, 1991).

If you don't recall your dreams most of the time you're not alone. With four or five every night, it is not surprising that we only recall the most vivid or bizarre. Light sleepers tend to recall dreams better than heavy sleepers, and the dreams that occur close to morning are more easily recalled.

## The Functions of Sleep and Dreaming

Anyone who has had to stay awake all night knows how insistent the urge to sleep can be. The incredible strength of the urge suggests that sleep serves some very important function. But what is it? Why do we sleep? The intuitive answer is "to rest." Perhaps our nervous systems become worn down during the day and need time to recuperate.

The trouble with that hypothesis is that neurons do not rest at night. In fact, during REM sleep, they are at least as active as they are during the waking hours. One way to determine why we sleep is to conduct sleep deprivation experiments in which subjects are deprived of all or parts of their sleep for long periods of time. If, for example, people who are deprived of sleep for two or three days begin to lose their memories, we might suppose that sleep is important for some process involved in memory. In some ways, however, the approach has the same flaws as the lesion experiments discussed in chapter 2. Even if a certain behavior is affected when a process (or brain area) is eliminated, it does not necessarily mean that that process (or brain area) is directly involved in the behavior under normal conditions. Combined with other kinds of experiments though, the sleep deprivation study can be a useful tool to learn more about why we sleep and dream.

It is not easy to keep people awake for two or three days straight. In one series of experiments (Webb, 1975), the subjects became very grouchy, grim, and apathetic, as well as very sleepy. They also showed slight hand tremors, difficulty in focusing their eyes, drooping eyelids, and an increased sensitivity to pain. They were especially sleepy at night when their biological rhythms moved to a phase normally associated with sleep. After three days of sleep deprivation, many showed moments of confusion, although they could still manage to perform a task if they wanted to. In a very few instances, and only after prolonged sleep loss, a subject may show some extreme abnormal behavior. In this particular experiment, one subject had hallucinations about a gorilla and fell to the floor screaming in terror during one of the psychological tests. Instances like these are quite rare, however. Wilse

Webb and Rosalind Cartwright (1978) summarized the sleep deprivation literature by saying that the main effect of sleep loss is simply sleepiness.

Based partly on these studies, Webb (1975) proposed that sleep evolved as a way of keeping humans out of danger for part of the day, especially that part when they would be most vulnerable to predators. If this were the main function of sleep, then it really would have very little function anymore.

Scientists who focus on the significance of dreaming, however, do not agree that deprivation has so little effect or that dreaming is as obsolete as the appendix. Deprivation of REM sleep appears to have some important, though subtle, effects on memory. In one study, subjects, wearing EEG recording electrodes, were asked to memorize a ghost story before they went to sleep. Some subjects were then deprived of Stage 4 slow-wave sleep by being awakened each time their EEG indicated Stage 4. The others were deprived of REM sleep by the same technique. The REM-deprived subjects were much less able to recall the story in the morning (Tilley & Empson, 1978). Studies like this suggest that REM sleep is somehow involved in the storage of memories, particularly of emotionally charged events that took place during the day. Dreams may in some sense function as "safety valves," allowing the gratification of wishes that could not be fulfilled during the day.

Another theory about the role of dreaming suggests that it gives our nervous systems a chance to practice coordinated motor sequences while we are not moving. Young animals and humans spend considerable time in REM sleep. Perhaps this provides their nervous systems with stimulation during a period of life when stimulation from the environment is not abundant (Roffwarg et al., 1966). The REM sleep may also allow key sensory and motor areas of the nervous system to "practice" during this important period of maturation.

One kind of practice that REM sleep may be providing involves the ability to coordinate the eye movements necessary to see depth in the visual field (Berger, 1969). The rapid eye movements may be stimulating the motor system responsible for the coordination of the two eyes. In fact, one study found that depth perception is better immediately following REM sleep than it is right before it (Lewis, Sloan, & Jones, 1978).

Sleep and dreaming may serve more than one function. It is quite possible that several of these hypotheses are correct.

▶ **GUIDED REVIEW** *Learning Objectives 3, 4, 5, and 6*

1. The most pronounced biological rhythm is the _____, which repeats every twenty-four hours. Human beings show dramatic physiological and behavioral changes within this cycle.
2. Sleep constitutes a large part of the circadian cycle, and it has rhythms of its own. Periods of _____, in which the EEG records show increasingly slower and larger _____ waves, alternate with periods of _____ sleep, in which rapid eye movements appear and the brain shows _____ waves, patterns characteristic of waking.
3. _____ sleep is associated with dreaming. Dream content usually reflects a person's anxieties and concerns, although the symbols may not be obvious.
4. Since the nervous system is as active during sleep as it is during waking, resting is not the main reason we sleep. Studies involving _____ have found that two or three days of sleep loss is not very damaging, although some people may show marked behavioral changes. REM sleep may be the most important component of sleep. It appears to be important in _____, particularly of emotional events.

*Answers*

*1. circadian rhythm 2. slow-wave sleep, delta, REM, beta 3. REM 4. sleep deprivation, memory storage*

# HYPNOSIS

The word "hypnotism" was not used until the middle of the nineteenth century, but hypnotic phenomena have been observed since ancient times. Few topics in psychology are surrounded by as many misunderstandings, myths, mysteries, or rumors, perhaps because much of what the public knows about hypnosis comes from watching stage acts. It is likely that much of the behavior of the contemporary hypnotized subject is strongly influenced by those stage acts, since that is what the subject expects will happen. The modern study of hypnosis developed from **mesmerism,** *a body of knowledge and superstition named after one of its eighteenth century proponents, Anton Mesmer.*

Mesmer was an Austrian physician who used what he thought was magnetism to treat his wealthy Parisian patients. The patients sat around a large tub of water filled with iron filings and held onto metal rods through which the "magnetic fluid" was supposed to flow. Making a theatrical appearance in flowing silk robes, Mesmer made passes over each patient with his hands and muttered impressive-sounding jargon to aid the magnetic transfer. Mesmer's unorthodox treatments received a less-than-friendly reception from the medical community, and the treatments were eventually discredited by a team sent by the French king to investigate mesmerism. This group of scientists, which included Benjamin Franklin, attributed the cures that Mesmer and his followers achieved not to the power of magnetism but to the power of the imagination.

Mesmer's flamboyant technique did not intentionally include hypnosis. But as his followers dropped the more bizarre elements of the treatments, they began to focus on the production of "magnetic somnambulism" (sleeplike state), still insisting that magnetism rather than imagination was of primary importance. Eventually, some physicians discovered they could use mesmerism to relieve pain, even during surgery. Dr. William Curtis wrote "On Tuesday, Feb. 4th (1837), before a numerous company assembled to witness the operation, I extracted a large molar tooth without the knowledge of the patient whilst in a magnetic sleep. The patient is a girl ... only mesmerized a few times ..." (from Gibson, 1977).

The medical community did not welcome this novel approach to surgery despite the fact that chemical anesthetics were still unknown and many surgical patients died from the shock of the pain. Mesmerism was still linked too closely to magic and superstition for people to take it seriously. It did not acquire any scientific respectability until the middle of the nineteenth century when James Braid, a Scottish physician, (figure 3.6) renamed it "hypnotism" and attributed the phenomenon to mechanical changes in the nervous system rather than to "magnetic fluids." Braid's physiological notions were still quite inaccurate, but he provided enough plausibility so that serious researchers began looking into it more closely.

Hypnosis became a popular tool of psychiatrists during the late nineteenth century, particularly those treating patients with physical symptoms that had no apparent organic cause. A patient who was paralyzed for no obvious physical reason and who probably became that way because of a psychological trauma would be a prime candidate for therapy with hypnosis. Yet despite the new

**Figure 3.6** *James Braid, a Scottish physician who studied hypnotism*

scientific credibility of the technique, it again fell out of favor. This time physicians probably lost interest because it was unreliable. The degree to which people can be hypnotized varies considerably, and it is impossible to predict in advance who can be hypnotized. A physician who tried to hypnotize a patient and failed miserably would certainly lose some prestige and might hesitate to use the technique again. In the United States, psychologists lost interest in hypnosis because of the rise of behaviorism and the general tendency toward studying only observable behavior. Today, however, there is renewed interest in the phenomenon, interest that has accompanied the resurgence of investigations into consciousness.

## What Is Hypnosis?

Hypnosis is another psychological term defined differently by different psychologists. One group sees hypnosis as a state of heightened suggestibility, not anything unusual and not very different from an ordinary state of consciousness (Barber, 1969). Others, particularly Ernest Hilgard (1977), view the phenomenon as an example of divided consciousness. These psychologists use the metaphor of a "hidden observer" to explain how part of a person can be aware of some things while another part seems unaware of the same things. For example, when a person is told that she or he will not be able to hear anything, part of the person responds as if she or he were indeed deaf. But under appropriate circumstances she or he may be able to report the sounds that were present in the room. The person's "hidden observer" was listening.

Perhaps the best way to define **hypnosis** *is as a state of consciousness in which an individual typically displays the following characteristics:*

1. *Attention is highly focused.* Most people pay very close attention to the hypnotist's voice and may ignore other voices or noises in the room.
2. *The subject is more suggestible and prefers to let the hypnotist tell him or her what to do.* For example, when the hypnotist says "Your body feels very relaxed," the subject readily relaxes.
3. *The subject willingly and uncritically accepts many illogical situations,* and might, for example, pet an imaginary rabbit.

The suggestibility of the subject during hypnosis can be extended beyond the session itself by means of **posthypnotic suggestions.** *Hypnotized people are told that they will perform in a certain way, often in response to a certain signal, when no longer hypnotized.* Often people will comply with the suggestion even though they are unaware of its origin. Subjects might be told that after they wake up, they will not be able to find their keys. Later, they will absentmindedly search for the keys.

*A special posthypnotic suggestion is* **posthypnotic amnesia,** *in which the subject appears to forget everything that transpired during the hypnosis session because the hypnotist suggested that the event be forgotten.* These memories are not lost forever; they can be retrieved at a signal from the hypnotist.

A rather controversial aspect of hypnosis is **age regression:** *when a hypnotized person is told to relive an experience of childhood, he or she sometimes seems to do it with remarkable vividness.* One subject who had a very refined British accent began speaking in the Cockney accent she had used as a youngster (Gibson, 1977). Another began speaking fluent Japanese, which he had not used since childhood and had almost completely forgotten (Fromm, 1970).

In an early experiment to test the accuracy of subjects' recollections during age regression, fifty college students were hypnotized and told to regress back to their birthdays and to Christmas Day at the ages of four, seven, and ten (True, 1949). At each age, the subject was asked "What day of the week is it?" The reply was checked against a calendar. Their accuracy was truly amazing—eighty-one percent were correct. Unfortunately, attempts to repeat this experiment have met with failure, increasing the controversy over age regression under hypnosis. Many scientists suspect that age regression is simply the result of the person's increased suggestibility and increased willingness to act out a role. Whether long-forgotten memories or childhood abilities can be retrieved in this way is still a matter of dispute.

## Who Can Be Hypnotized?

The fact that not everyone can be hypnotized is one of the most perplexing characteristics of hypnosis. Hypnotic susceptibility does not seem to be related in any straightforward way to personality traits, and so far, it is not easy to predict who can be hypnotized and who cannot. One promising lead deals with how much a person fantasizes (Lynn & Rhue, 1988). People who fantasize much of the time, have vivid mental imagery of events, have occasional difficulty discriminating between real and imagined events, and display other characteristics related to fantasy and absorption, are called high "fantasizers"; they appear to be more susceptible to hypnosis than nonfantasizers.

Standard procedures for testing hypnotic susceptibility have been developed by Hilgard and his associates (Hilgard & Hilgard, 1975). First the hypnotist tells the subject to relax and to listen carefully to the hypnotist's voice. Then the hypnotist counts backward from twenty, telling the subject to relax more deeply and to accept whatever instructions the hypnotist offers. This first part of the session is called **hypnotic induction;** *it is a series of suggestions designed to put the person into a light hypnotic trance if the subject is susceptible and willing.* In the second part, the subject is scored on five items, all designed to determine how imaginative the subject is and how willing he or she is to accept the suggestions of the hypnotist (see table 3.1).

## Hypnosis as a Social Occasion

Hypnosis, at least the way it is generally done, is very much a social event and researchers are investigating how the characteristics of the hypnotist and his or her relationship to the subject influence the outcome. People who are easily hypnotized often show some commitment to the hypnotist and are prepared to follow suggestions based on a feeling of closeness and trust. When this dynamic social relationship doesn't exist, perhaps because the subject is opposing the hypnotist or lacks trust, hypnosis may not occur.

The importance of this social ingredient was demonstrated in a study in which subjects were prescreened on a hypnotizability scale and categorized as low or high on hypnotizability. Half of each group was then introduced to a rather detached hypnotist who used last names only and turned on a cassette recorder to provide instructions. The other half met a warm, engaging hypnotist who tried to establish a strong interpersonal bond with the subject. In fact, the hypnotists were the same people who were trained to create interpersonal situations that varied dramatically in their intensity.

The results showed that people who were highly hypnotizable to begin with remained that way, even with a detached hypnotist. But the ones who originally were categorized as low on hypnotizability were much more affected by the social aspects of the situation. They were more likely to be hypnotized by the hypnotist who worked hard to establish a positive interpersonal bond (Lynn et al., 1991).

### TABLE 3.1 A portion of the stanford hypnotic clinical scale (SHCS)

| Item | Score |
|------|-------|
| 1. Moving hands together (or 1a. Hand lowering). Describe movement: (At end of session, probe for type of experience if movement is very fast:) Score (+) if movement is slow and hands are not more than six inches apart by end of 10 seconds. | (1) _____ |

\*   \*   \*

3. Age regression (school)
   Selected grade: _____
     Where are you? _____
     What are you doing? _____
     Who is your teacher? _____
     How old are you? _____
     What are you wearing? _____
     Who is with you? _____
   a. Hypnotist's rating:

_____ : _____ : _____
No        Good     Fair
regression

*Source:* "Hypnosis in the Relief of Pain," *by E. R. Hilgard and J. R. Hilgard. Copyright © 1975, 1983 by William Kaufmann, Inc., Los Altos, CA 94022.*

## Hypnosis and Law Enforcement

The use of hypnosis by police has created a great deal of controversy. Scientists who work with hypnosis are fully aware that hypnotized people can exaggerate, make up stories, and even deliberately lie. They wonder whether police should rely on any information obtained by this technique.

The courts are not wholeheartedly endorsing the practice either. As we saw in the case of Vickie Rock, the woman convicted of manslaughter, the courts refused to admit her hypnotically refreshed testimony that would have bolstered her defense.

The police are more enthusiastic about using hypnosis as a means to help witnesses retrieve memories that might otherwise be deeply buried, thereby helping them solve cases. They view the memories more as "tips" than as testimony under sworn oath.

Some laboratory simulations of crimes provide some support for using hypnosis to help eyewitnesses remember. In one experiment, the investigator let sixty-five subjects watch movies of crimes and later compared their memories about details while under hypnosis and while in an ordinary state of consciousness (Griffin, 1980). Most subjects were able to relate more details under hypnosis, provided they were susceptible to the procedure in the first place.

However, other studies have found that hypnosis actually hinders accurate recall (Sanders & Simmons, 1983). A large group of college students were shown a twenty-second videotape depicting a pickpocket stealing a wallet. A week later, all the subjects returned to the lab. Half were hypnotized, and the other half were simply given instructions to "replay" the incident on an internal, mental television screen. Then all subjects viewed a videotaped lineup that included the perpetrator, and they answered ten specific questions about the theft.

Only seventeen percent of the hypnotized subjects correctly identified the pickpocket in the lineup, compared to forty percent of control subjects. The hypnotized subjects also made more errors on the questions. They were particularly susceptible to so-called "leading" questions. For example, one question was "Did you notice it when the victim looked at his pocket-watch?" The question implied that the victim actually did look at his watch when in fact he did not. The researchers concluded that hypnosis is a hindrance to accurate recall because it makes the person too susceptible to suggestions.

Perhaps of even more concern in a legal context is the finding that "pseudomemories" can be implanted rather easily in very susceptible subjects. A pseudomemory exists when a subject reports events consistent with a posthypnotic suggestion but not consistent with the subject's initial, waking description of the same event. For example, McCann and Sheehan (1988) attempted to implant in hypnotized subjects the suggestion that they had heard a car backfiring or had heard shots during a night of sleep the previous week. Later, when they were asked about the night's sleep while not hypnotized, nearly half were sure they had heard the noises or were confused about it.

In studies in which the event to be remembered is more tightly controlled, pseudomemories are less likely. McCann and Sheehan (1988) showed a group of highly hypnotizable subjects a videotape of a bank robbery by unmasked men. One week later the subjects were hypno-tized and the experimenters attempted to implant pseudomemories:

> Look carefully now and tell me whether you can see the robber's mask. He has a stocking over his face and appears to have a moustache. Tell me when you can see him clearly. ...

Afterwards only twenty-three percent of the subjects showed pseudomemory effects, substantially lower than under less controlled circumstances. Nevertheless, the phenomenon of pseudomemory has been clearly demonstrated, making any testimony provided by previously hypnotized subjects open to question unless the hypnosis session is controlled very carefully.

Despite the controversies, the number of police departments that use hypnosis is rapidly growing. More than ten thousand police officers have received training in hypnosis, and many police departments have behavioral science units that routinely use hypnosis.

▶ **GUIDED REVIEW** *Learning Objectives 7, 8, 9, and 10*

1. Hypnosis developed from a body of knowledge and superstition called _____. It was particularly useful in treating patients with sensory or motor difficulties produced by psychological traumas rather than organic damage.
2. The state of consciousness an individual is in during hypnosis is still controversial. Some view it simply as a state of _____. Others see it as a state of _____. Characteristics of the hypnotized subject include highly focused attention, increased suggestibility, willingness to act out roles, and uncritical acceptance of illogical situations.
3. A hypnotized subject may also be susceptible to _____, which means that the subject carries out a suggestion after awakening. _____ is a special kind of posthypnotic suggestion in which the subject forgets what happened during the session. Some hypnotized subjects can show _____, in which they appear to relive past events.
4. Susceptibility to hypnosis varies considerably between people and can be measured by a _____.
5. Hypnosis is a _____ occasion and the relationship between the hypnotist and the person being hypnotized can affect the outcome.

*Answers*

1. *mesmerism* 2. *heightened suggestibility, divided consciousness* 3. *posthypnotic suggestions, Posthypnotic amnesia, age regression* 4. *hypnotic susceptibility test* 5. *social*

# CHEMICAL ALTERATIONS IN CONSCIOUSNESS

If the cocaine business were legal and listed on the stock exchange, it would rank very near the top of the Fortune 500 in domestic sales volume. According to a survey in 1991, 1.9 million Americans used the substance at least once a month. Cocaine sales comprise only a small part of the total drug business in the U.S., which also includes traffic in heroin, marijuana, psychedelic drugs, tranquilizers, and a bewildering array of other mind altering substances, as well as legal trade in alcohol, barbiturates, tobacco, caffeine, and prescribed mood elevators, tranquilizers, and antidepressants.

The range of drugs capable of producing changes in behavior and in consciousness is very wide. Even aspirin might be included since it relieves pain. **Psychoactive drugs** *are those whose main effect is supposed to be an alteration in consciousness.* These drugs can be grouped into several categories, as shown in table 3.2. Some scientists group marijuana under hallucinogenic drugs, but because its effects are not quite like those of the others in the category, many prefer to group it separately.

The United States has carried on a love affair with drugs that waxes and wanes with extreme vehemence (Musto, 1991). Crude opium, for example, was brought to the New World by European explorers and settlers who used it to relieve pain. Laudanum, opium in an alcohol extract, was a common medical treatment and Benjamin Franklin used it to alleviate the pain of kidney stones. Toward the end of the nineteenth century, cocaine became one of America's favorites. The Coca-Cola company introduced a drink in 1886 offering the advantages of coca (the plant from which cocaine is derived), but none of the dangers of alcohol. The drug companies offered cocaine in numerous forms to please a wide range of customers, including teething babies.

By the 1890s, the public became increasingly aware of the dangers of addiction, at least some of which was caused by physicians who overprescribed medication. Strict laws were passed to regulate traffic in dangerous

## TABLE 3.2 Classification of psychoactive drugs

| Classification | Description | Examples |
|---|---|---|
| General depressants | Act in various ways to reduce activity in the nervous system. At lower doses, produce slowed reaction time, poor coordination, relief from anxiety, mild euphoria, and drowsiness. At higher doses, produce sleep, general anesthesia, coma, and death. All produce tolerance and dependence. Withdrawal can result in anxiety, insomnia, tremors, and convulsions. | Alcohol<br>Barbiturates (e.g., pentobarbital, secobarbital)<br>Nonbarbiturate sedatives (Quaalude)<br>Antianxiety agents (Valium, Librium, Miltown, Equanil) |
| Stimulants | Produce an excitatory effect on the central nervous system. Behavioral effects vary depending on type of drug and dose. Can result in wakefulness, alertness, raised metabolism, elevated mood, suppressed appetite, euphoria, nervousness, paranoia, and convulsions. | Amphetamines (Benzedrine, Dexedrine)<br>Cocaine<br>Crack (prepared from cocaine)<br>Caffeine<br>Nicotine |
| Opiates | Includes natural and synthetic substances that relieve pain and are chemically related to morphine. Effects include strong euphoria, loss of appetite, nausea, and constipation. Severe withdrawal symptoms. | Opium<br>Morphine<br>Heroin<br>Codeine |
| Hallucinogenics | A heterogeneous group of compounds that can produce visual, auditory, or other hallucinations and can separate the individual from reality by inducing distortions in cognition and perception. | LSD<br>PCP (Angel Dust)<br>Mescaline<br>Psilocybin |
| Marijuana | Although sometimes classified as a hallucinogenic or psychedelic drug, marijuana might also be classified as a depressant. Effects vary and may include dry mouth, dizziness, nausea, mood changes, daydreaming, sleepiness, and mild sensory distortions. | Cannabis<br>Marijuana<br>Hashish<br>THC |

drugs. The public's mood was such that alcohol was also eventually banned in 1920 with the start of the temperance movement. But by the 1960s, the mood changed again. Although opium and its synthetic relative heroin were still shunned, attitudes toward cocaine, marijuana, and psychedelic drugs softened. Marijuana and the psychedelic drugs became shortcuts to the higher levels of consciousness sought by Eastern religions. Cocaine penetrated upper-middle class America as a fashionable drug for fast lane high achievers, and it reached the poor in the inner cities. Profits from drug dealing became very, very big business.

In the 1990s, much like the 1890s, the American public has swung back to the view that mind altering drugs are dangerous and rather than expanding consciousness, they interfere with our ability to reach our full potential. People are seeking natural methods to reach health and fulfillment, through the foods they eat, their exercise regimens, their attitudes toward life, their religions. Yves St. Laurent was widely criticized when he named a new perfume "Opium." The time had passed when the word elicited a sense of mystery. Yet despite the changing attitudes, America has a deeply rooted drug problem that is more persistent than ever. What is it about the mind altering chemicals that attracts so many people despite the risks? The answers lie both in the drugs and in ourselves.

## How Do Drugs Work?

Despite the widespread use of drugs and the intensive research into their mechanisms of action, it is still not clear how most drugs produce their behavioral effects. Furthermore, even though two drugs produce similar behavioral changes, they might do it in different ways. For example, both marijuana and alcohol can cause a person to feel euphoric but the two drugs work very differently.

The effect of a drug depends on a number of factors, including the way the drug is taken, how much is taken, how rapidly the drug reaches the bloodstream, how much of the drug reaches the nervous system, and how quickly the drug is broken down and excreted from the body. Drugs injected into a vein affect a person much more rapidly than those taken orally. The injected drug enters the bloodstream immediately and reaches all parts of the body within minutes; the drug taken by mouth must be broken down by digestive enzymes in the stomach before it is absorbed into the bloodstream. Because the effects of an injected drug are so rapid, there is usually no time for anyone to counteract an overdose.

The dose of a drug also helps determine its effects. Sometimes there is a simple relationship between dose and response: the greater the dose, the greater the behavioral change. But very often a larger dose of a drug produces

## APPLYING PSYCHOLOGY

### Pumping Iron ... With Help

The invention of new forms of drug abuse has been so fast in the past decades that scientists barely have time to begin collecting information on one drug before another one takes its place. An example is the widespread abuse of anabolic-androgenic steroids, which apparently was inspired by Olympic and professional athletes who used them to maximize their physical performance.

These substances are derivatives of the male sex hormone testosterone. They are legitimately prescribed for a variety of ailments, but increasingly they are being sold illicitly to enhance muscular development and improve athletic performance. One study found that nearly seven percent of male high school seniors admitted to taking steroids, and that most of the drug takers were not athletic competitors; they simply wanted to improve their appearance (Buckley et al., 1988).

As more and more young men began taking steroids, the reports of adverse effects have grown. Mood disorders, suicidal tendencies, and marked aggression have all been

reported, along with various health consequences such as hypertension, heart problems, sterility, acne, and reductions in the size of the testes. There is mounting evidence that these steroids are addictive, as well. Many users show tolerance and need increasing doses to continue to achieve the desired effect, and many also experience withdrawal symptoms when they stop using the drug. During withdrawal, the person first experiences hyperactivity which is then followed by depression, fatigue, insomnia, and decreased sex drive (Brower et al., 1991).

Many people who take steroids for body building also take other drugs, especially other hormones to counteract the potential side effects of the steroids. Although major sports organizations now routinely require urine tests for steroids and disqualify anyone who tests positively, the tests are both difficult to do and controversial because of concern over civil liberties. This is yet another drug craze that is having tragic consequences.

completely different responses. For example, low doses of cocaine usually produce euphoria and a sense of well being in the user, but higher doses can lead to extreme anxiety and suspiciousness.

Even if we know exactly how a drug was taken, how much of it was taken, and all the other factors surrounding the use of the drug, we still might not be able to predict how that drug will affect a specific person. Different people respond very differently to the same drug. For example, several cups of coffee produce nervousness in most people, but it can produce severe panic in certain susceptible people (Charney, Heninger, & Jatlow, 1985).

*Tolerance and Dependence*    Some psychoactive drugs produce a phenomenon called **tolerance,** *a term that refers to the fact that after taking repeated doses of a drug, the person requires a larger dose to achieve the same behavioral or physiological effect.* A person's tolerance to a drug is a very complicated matter. It depends only partly on how often and how much of a drug has been used. It also depends on psychological factors, such as where the drug is taken. In a study that demonstrated the importance of psychological factors in the development of tolerance, rats were injected with glucose and increasing doses of heroin on alternate days for one month. Some rats were injected with heroin while they were next to their home cage and injected with glucose in a separate room. Others were given the glucose near their home and the heroin in a strange room. Then all the rats were injected with very large doses of heroin, either in the same environment in which they had been receiving their heroin injections or in the other room. This large dose was lethal to many rats, but particularly to those that were injected in the room where they had been getting only glucose. In other words, they were more vulnerable to the large dose if they were in a room where they were not "expecting" heroin. The researchers speculate that many deaths due to "overdoses" may really be due to a temporary drop in tolerance because of psychological factors. The user dies even though the dose is the same as one injected only days earlier (Siegel, Hinson, Krank, & McCully, 1982).

Because psychoactive drugs within the same class are often chemically very similar, they sometimes produce **cross-tolerance,** *a phenomenon in which tolerance to one drug has the effect of causing tolerance to another, even when the other drug had never been used.* For example, a person who has developed tolerance to alcohol

will also show tolerance to other drugs in the general depressant category.

Several of the psychoactive drugs also have the ability to produce **physical dependence.** *By the usual definition, a person has become dependent upon a drug if tolerance has developed, if the drug is needed for the person to function normally, and if continued doses are required to prevent the onset of withdrawal symptoms.* By this definition, virtually all of the drugs in the depressant category may result in dependence. In fact, a person who has developed a tolerance for the barbiturates and suddenly stops taking the drug might die from convulsions. All of the opiates can produce physical dependence as well.

Many of the psychoactive drugs produce psychological dependence even if they do not produce physical dependence. **Psychological dependence** *occurs when a person learns to use a drug habitually to relieve stress or to relax. This is true even if little or no physical dependence has developed and no physical withdrawal symptoms would appear if the person stopped taking the drug.* Psychological dependence on a drug can be an extremely powerful force. For example, people who smoke cocaine (rather than "snort" it) often show a pattern of behavior that is clearly self-destructive; they may spend most of their waking hours taking the drug or finding means to obtain it (see Applying Psychology box: Cocaine).

*Psychosocial Drug Effects*    The fact that people react differently to the same drug is partly due to personality and to social factors surrounding the use of the drug. For instance, people who take the hallucinogen PCP, or "angel dust," sometimes show violent and self-destructive behavior; but some suspect that these reactions are more common in people with a latent mental disorder. The social environment in which a user takes a drug can also have an important influence on the drug's effects. A person who smokes marijuana while alone may experience drowsiness and daydreaming. In the company of other people and with the same drug dose, the same person might show garrulousness and hilarity.

A fascinating study that examined muscle tension after withdrawal from caffeine (White et al., 1980) demonstrated how complex drug effects can be. Two groups of subjects—one that rarely drank coffee and one consisting of heavy coffee drinkers—avoided caffeine for three hours. The researchers then measured muscle tension in

# APPLYING PSYCHOLOGY

## Cocaine

I felt like I could handle just about anything that came up. ... I never felt so confident.

What's the big deal? I couldn't notice much of a difference.

You really feel like you're flying. ... It tickles my nose though.

According to the reports of cocaine users, this very popular drug produces quite a range of experiences. Most users feel euphoria, elation, and a sense of clear and powerful thinking. These sensations usually disappear within an hour, and some users become depressed and begin to crave more cocaine.

The use of cocaine dates back at least five thousand years, according to archaeological evidence in Ecuador. To the Incas, the coca plant, from which cocaine is derived, was divine and was treated as a symbol of high social and political rank. The Inca leaders controlled the use of coca, confining it mostly to the ruling classes. Unauthorized chewing of the coca leaves was considered a sacrilege.

Today, the cocaine in use in the United States is usually finely chopped cocaine hydrochloride. The powdery substance is placed in a mound on a smooth surface, such as a mirror, and inhaled through a rolled dollar bill or a straw. It is easily absorbed into the bloodstream through the mucous membranes in the nose. "Crack" is a much more potent form of cocaine prepared from cocaine hydrochloride. The white crystal slivers are smoked and the vapors inhaled.

Cocaine acts like a local anesthetic when applied topically. A local anesthetic blocks axonal conduction. Internally, the drug acts as a stimulant rather than an anesthetic. It raises heart rate, blood pressure, and if taken in large doses, body temperature. It is called "sympathomimetic" because it mimics many of the effects of activation of the sympathetic nervous system. It interferes with synaptic transmission, especially of cells that use dopamine or norepinephrine. These transmitters are involved in mood and emotions, hence the dramatic effects on behavior. Overdoses can produce agitation, hallucinations, convulsions, and death. Long-term use may result in permanent damage to the brain areas that use the neurotransmitters affected by cocaine.

Cocaine produces tolerance and dependence very quickly, and the habit is extremely difficult to break. At one cocaine hotline in a private clinic in Washington, D.C., half the people who call to make an appointment never show up. Ronald Wynne, the clinical psychologist who runs the program, says that "anything is easier to deal with than crack addicts ... they make you feel so impotent." Cocaine deaths were up 500 percent in the District of Columbia in 1987. The Omnibus Drug Act of 1988 called for a major expansion of treatment and education programs to help the millions of people who abuse drugs, but the treatment process is clearly an uphill battle.

Although most cocaine users are male, the use of the drug by women has risen steadily. Children born to mothers who used cocaine during pregnancy often show a number of symptoms, including irritability, incessant crying, and an aversion to being touched by other human beings. Their dislike of human contact may make it more difficult for them to form a strong bond with their caregiver, since touch is an important component of that bond. As the children grow older, many of them have very difficult problems in school.

Cocaine, once a chic drug for the rich, is now a national epidemic that causes incredible tragedy.

their forearms using **electromyography (EMG),** *a technique that records electrical signals from muscle tissue.* Half of each group then drank straight grapefruit juice whereas the other half drank juice laced with a heavy dose of caffeine. Both groups believed they were drinking juice with caffeine, but neither could tell for sure. The EMG measurements showed that the heavy caffeine users had more muscle tension after caffeine withdrawal than did the light users, showing the importance of tolerance and dependence on the effects of a drug. However, heavy caffeine users all showed a decrease in muscle tension after drinking their grapefruit juice, regardless of whether the juice contained any caffeine. Low caffeine users showed a slight increase in tension. This study suggests that both the light and heavy coffee drinkers all behaved in accordance with their expectations of how caffeine would affect them after a long abstinence. And their expectations affected their behavior even if their drink contained no caffeine.

*The Effects of Drugs on the Brain*    Most of the psychoactive drugs seem to produce alternate states of consciousness by acting on the brain, particularly at the synapse. They appear to change the way neurons in the brain communicate with one another.

The hallucinogenic drug mescaline, for example, is structurally very similar to one of the neurotransmitters used in the brain to pass messages from one neuron to the next. Scientists hypothesize that the receptor sites in the brain that normally respond to the neurotransmitter probably respond to mescaline just as well.

Cocaine molecules act on the synapse in a different way. Normally, the neurotransmitter molecules are released by one neuron, diffuse across a tiny gap between the neurons, and attach to receptor sites on the membrane of the next neuron. The neurotransmitter must be removed from this gap quickly to make room for the next release of neurotransmitter. One way the neurons accomplish this rapid removal is by taking the neurotransmitter molecules back up. This is an efficient process since the same molecule can be used again when the neuron sends another chemical signal to its neighbor. Cocaine seems to interfere with this process by preventing the reuptake of the neurotransmitter. Too much neurotransmitter is left in the gap, confusing the neuron that is receiving the chemical signal (Van Dyke & Byck, 1982).

*Two neurotransmitters,* called **dopamine** and **norepinephrine,** are particularly involved in the behavioral effects of cocaine. Both play important roles in mood, emotions, and reward. As a person uses more and more cocaine, tolerance develops because the neurotransmitters, lacking a reuptake mechanism, become depleted. Compounding the problem, the receptors on the membranes of the receiving neurons become overstimulated and eventually grow less sensitive to the transmitters. Thus, more and more cocaine must be taken in order to take advantage of an ever smaller neurotransmitter supply.

Chronic use of certain psychoactive drugs that manipulate neurotransmitter activity may produce serious and possibly permanent damage in the brain. Cocaine may permanently eliminate the ability of the nerve cells that use the transmitters to transmit nerve impulses. A newer drug, "ecstasy," produces widespread destruction in neurons that use a neurotransmitter involved in sleep. Animals given ecstasy stay awake nearly all the time and their damaged neurotransmitter system takes more than a year to recover.

A long-term goal of the studies linking drugs to brain activity is the development of treatments, especially new drugs that treat acute withdrawal or block craving (Holloway, 1991). Methadone is one example. This substance interferes with the action of heroin on brain cells and helps relieve the addict's intense craving. Drugs are available that stimulate dopamine secretion, and these may

| TABLE 3.3 **The behavioral effects of depressant drugs** |
|---|
| Normal behavior |
| Relief from anxiety |
| Disinhibition, euphoria |
| Drowsiness |
| Sleep |
| General anesthesia |
| Coma |
| Death |

be helpful in treating cocaine withdrawal. Clinical trials are now underway for a large number of substances that scientists hope will make drug cravings more bearable. Unfortunately, drug addiction is a very complex problem, not confined to the chemicals in the brain. Although treating drug abuse with more drugs may help, behavioral treatment and educational programs are also necessary.

## Close-up of the General Depressants

General depressants represent the largest drug problem in the United States. More than nine million people are alcoholics, and millions more are physically dependent on other drugs in this category, such as sleeping pills and tranquilizers. These drugs produce tolerance (some very quickly), and all are capable of producing physical dependence.

Barbiturates, the nonbarbiturate hypnotics, and a variety of antianxiety agents, as well as structurally unrelated chemicals such as alcohol and drugs used for anesthesia, are all examples of general depressants. These substances, as shown in table 3.3, produce a similar sequence of behavioral effects with increasing dose. In fact, any general depressant might be called a tranquilizer, a sleeping pill, or even an anesthetic depending on the dose given.

*Alcohol*    The most widely used general depressant is ethyl alcohol. For the light social drinker, alcohol provides an occasional pleasure, but for many people alcohol is the cause of behavior and health problems. For instance, about one in four mental patients is an alcoholic. Drunken driving either directly causes or contributes to twenty-five

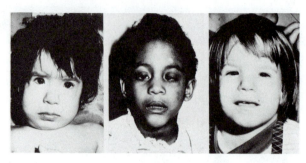

**Figure 3.7**  *Children afflicted with fetal alcohol syndrome*

thousand deaths every year. Alcohol is the root cause of cirrhosis of the liver, the sixth leading cause of death. Some researchers estimate that in more than sixty percent of violent homicides, the killer had been drinking. Alcohol is also an important factor in sex crimes.

Another hazard associated with alcohol is **fetal alcohol syndrome (FAS),** *a condition that affects some babies born to mothers who drank during their pregnancies. Symptoms include mental retardation, growth deficiencies, hyperactivity, poor attention span, and unusual facial characteristics such as drooping eyelids and crossed eyes.* The photographs in figure 3.7 show children afflicted with the disorder (Streissguth, Landesman-Dwyer, Martin, & Smith, 1980). Because so little is known about FAS and how much alcohol can cause it, obstetricians are recommending that pregnant patients avoid alcohol altogether.

The effects of alcohol on the brain are not well understood, but researchers have found that alcohol depresses activity in brain cells in several areas, particularly the cerebellum, the structure involved in coordination and fine motor control (Bloom, 1985).

Alcohol produces the range of behavioral changes shown in table 3.3. In the body, alcohol dilates the blood vessels of the skin, producing a warm flush. Using alcohol to keep warm in winter is pointless, since the initial warm flush is followed by a decrease in body temperature; the peripheral dilation of the vessels causes a loss of body heat.

Why one individual becomes an alcoholic and another, who drinks just as much, does not, is one of the most perplexing problems in drug research. Clearly, the causes are diverse. Rather than focusing exclusively on a single cause, many psychologists are adopting the biopsychosocial approach to understanding this kind of addictive behavior, emphasizing the multiple and interacting causes (Marlatt & Baer, 1988).

Various studies have examined developmental, personality, and environmental variables such as anxiety levels, family environment, parent-child relationships, parental discipline, and impulsive behavior in childhood. Some studies find significant relationships.

One of the most consistent findings is that people who abuse alcohol or show other addictive behaviors have a history of nonconformity, impulsive behavior, depression, and low self-esteem. On the other hand, many people show behavior like this and never become alcoholic. In addition, it is not always easy to tell which comes first—the behavior or the alcoholism.

Variables relating to the family include genetic or prenatal factors, not just environmental factors that start after birth. Several studies have found that children, especially boys, born to alcoholic fathers are more likely to become alcoholic later in life even if adopted by nonalcoholic parents when very young and not exposed to a home life with an alcoholic parent (see Loehlin et al., 1988 for review). One possible explanation for this is that certain genes affect proteins involved in alcohol metabolism.

To learn more about this suspected predisposition, scientists have compared the responses to alcohol of people with or without an alcoholic parent (Schuckit, Gold, & Risch, 1987a, 1987b). In general, the offspring of alcoholics respond less intensely to moderate doses, a response that may be related to differences in the way their endocrine systems operate.

*Other General Depressants*    Insomnia is a common complaint for which general depressants may be prescribed as an adjunct therapy since the drugs appear to act on specific pathways in the brain involved in wakefulness (Kales & Kales, 1984). Barbiturates were once frequently used for this purpose, but all of the general depressants can induce sleep if given in an appropriate dose. Although they may be helpful for a short time, they quickly begin to cause more problems than they solve.

After a person takes certain kinds of sleeping pills (Feinberg et al., 1977), the amount of REM drops dramatically while the amount of Stage 2 sleep increases. The person may be sleeping more but dreaming less. REM sleep is probably the most critical portion of the night's sleep, so this loss reduces the quality of the person's sleep time. When the drug is withdrawn, the amount of REM sleep increases dramatically. In severely dependent users, this may cause nightmares, vivid dreaming, and very disturbed sleep. Many people believe that they can't sleep without their pills; in fact, the pills are causing their insomnia.

When the so-called "minor tranquilizers" were first introduced, physicians thought they could safely prescribe them to relieve anxiety and to aid sleep. But research eventually revealed that drugs such as Valium, Librium, and Quaalude posed as many dangers as the barbiturates. They also induce tolerance and physical dependence. General depressants have a variety of names: sleeping pills, sedatives, barbiturates, minor tranquilizers, and antianxiety agents. Each category differs chemically, but the human brain seems to react similarly to all of them.

Our survey of consciousness led us down some paths in psychology on which there are still many unsolved mysteries. We still have much to learn about sleep and dreaming, about hypnosis, about the world of the drug addict, and probably about states of consciousness that haven't even been studied yet. Exploring these private mental events is very rewarding, but more than a little frustrating; clear-cut answers continue to elude us. Each new study seems to raise more questions than it answers, but finding the right questions is the first critical step.

---

▶ **GUIDED REVIEW** *Learning Objectives 11, 12, and 13*

1. Drugs whose main effect is to produce an alteration in consciousness are called _____.
2. Psychoactive drugs can be grouped into several categories, including: _____, _____, _____, _____, and _____.
3. Some psychoactive drugs produce _____, which means that the dose of drug must be increased in order to achieve the same effect. Some also produce _____ or addiction. Because the effects of some of the drugs are so pleasurable, they can also produce _____.
4. The effects of a drug depend in part on _____ factors, such as the personality or expectations of the user and the social circumstances in which the drug is ingested.
5. Many psychoactive drugs produce their effects on behavior and consciousness by acting on the brain, particularly at the _____.

6. _____ produce a sequence of changes, including relief from anxiety and euphoria; sleep; coma; and eventually death. Sleeping pills are a widely used depressant; however they produce more problems for insomniacs than they solve because they interfere with REM sleep. Alcohol is another depressant drug. It is dangerous to pregnant women because it may produce the _____ in babies. The causes of alcoholism are unclear, but they may include genetic factors, family history, childhood problems, and personality disorders.

*Answers*

*1. psychoactive 2. depressants, stimulants, opiates, hallucinogens, marijuana 3. tolerance, physical dependence, psychological dependence 4. psychosocial 5. synapse 6. Depressants, fetal alcohol syndrome*

---

# SUMMARY

I. Consciousness is the state of mind that shifts slightly from moment to moment. (p. 74)

   A. A working definition of consciousness is the awareness of internal and external events. (p. 74)

   B. Early studies of conscious processes used introspection; behaviorists rejected this tool and instead favored the study of overt behavior. Recently, conscious processes have become an important focus of many psychological studies. (p. 75)

   C. Your state of consciousness is related to the activity of neurons in your brain. This activity can be measured in various ways. (p. 75)

      1. The EEG records electrical activity in large areas of the brain. Certain waveforms are known to be related to particular states of consciousness. (pp. 75–76)

      2. The responses of brain cells to specific stimuli can be measured using evoked potentials, which average EEG patterns recorded after repeated presentations of the same stimulus. (p. 76)

II. Sleep and dreaming constitute alternate states of consciousness. (p. 77)

   A. Sleeping is part of a twenty-four-hour circadian rhythm during which people show cyclic physiological and behavioral changes. (p. 77)

      1. Disruptions in the circadian rhythm, produced by shift work, cause the physiological cycles to become desynchronized; resynchronization can take several days. (pp. 78–79)

   B. Sleep can be divided into two stages. In slow-wave sleep, the EEG patterns show alpha and delta waves; in REM, the patterns show faster beta waves. (p. 80)

C. REM appears to be associated with dreaming although dreaming also occurs in slow-wave sleep; the content of dreams often reflects a person's anxieties and concerns. (pp. 80–84)

D. The functions of sleep are not well understood, but REM appears to be important in memory storage, particularly for emotional events. (p. 84)

III. The modern study of hypnosis developed from mesmerism, a body of knowledge and superstition popular in the eighteenth century. (p. 85)

A. The exact nature of hypnosis is controversial. It appears to be a state of consciousness characterized by highly focused attention, increased suggestibility, willingness to act out roles, and uncritical acceptance of illogical situations. Some view it as simply a state of increased suggestibility; others view it as a state of "divided consciousness." (p. 86)

B. For reasons that are not well understood, people vary dramatically in their susceptibility to hypnosis. (pp. 86–87)

C. Hypnosis is a social occasion and the characteristics of the hypnotist can affect the hypnotizability of the subject. (p. 87)

D. The use of hypnosis to help eyewitnesses recall events concerning crimes is growing, but many psychologists are concerned about the practice because of studies showing that hypnosis does not necessarily produce accurate recall. (pp. 87–88)

IV. Chemical alterations in consciousness can be produced by a wide range of psychoactive drugs, including general depressants, stimulants, opiates, hallucinogens, and antipsychotic agents. (pp. 89–90)

A. The effects of a drug depend on a variety of factors, including the dose, the route of administration, the amount that reaches the bloodstream, and the rate of excretion. (pp. 90–91)
1. Some drugs, such as depressants, can produce tolerance and physical dependence and/or psychological dependence. (p. 91)
2. Psychosocial factors are important influences on the behavioral effects of psychoactive drugs. (pp. 91–92)
3. Psychoactive drugs generally produce their effects on behavior by altering the activity in certain synapses in the brain. (pp. 92–93)

B. Depressants produce a wide range of behavioral effects, such as relief from anxiety, euphoria, and coma or death, depending on the dose that reaches the brain. Drugs in this category produce tolerance and dependence. (p. 93)
1. The most widely used general depressant is alcohol. (pp. 93–94)
2. Sleeping pills are another example of general depressants. (pp. 94–95)

## ACTION GLOSSARY

Match the terms in the left column with the definitions in the right column.

___ 1. **Consciousness** (p. 74)
___ 2. **Information processing** (p. 75)
___ 3. **Evoked potential** (p. 76)
___ 4. **Circadian rhythms** (p. 77)
___ 5. **Alpha waves** (p. 80)
___ 6. **Delta waves** (p. 80)
___ 7. **Slow-wave sleep** (p. 80)
___ 8. **REM** (p. 80)
___ 9. **Beta waves** (p. 80)

A. *High amplitude, low frequency brain-wave patterns of one to four cycles per second recorded by means of an EEG. The appearance of these patterns in the EEG usually signifies slow-wave sleep.*

B. *Regular brain-wave patterns from eight to twelve cycles per second recorded by means of an EEG. Usually accompanies behavioral relaxation.*

C. *A state of awareness of internal and external events; includes perceptions, private thoughts, dreams, and other mental activities accessible to others only through verbal report.*

D. *The stage of sleep characterized by high amplitude, low frequency wave patterns on the EEG, including delta waves. Can be divided into four stages depending on its depth.*

E. *A waveform obtained by averaging many EEG patterns recorded during a series of repeated presentations of a sensory stimulus.*

F. *The stage of sleep characterized by rapid eye movements and high frequency, low amplitude beta waves on the EEG. Most dreaming appears to occur during this stage.*

G. *An approach to the study of human behavior that emphasizes the integration of sensation, perception, cognition, memory, and other processes. The approach uses many analogies from computer science, such as the concept of the flow of information through a system.*

H. *Changes in physiology or behavior that go through a complete cycle in twenty-four hours.*

I. *High frequency, low amplitude waves characteristic of the alert state.*

___ **10. Mesmerism (p. 85)**
___ **11. Hypnosis (p. 86)**
___ **12. Posthypnotic suggestion (p. 86)**
___ **13. Posthypnotic amnesia (p. 86)**
___ **14. Age regression (p. 86)**
___ **15. Hypnotic induction (p. 87)**
___ **16. Psychoactive drug (p. 89)**

A. *The subject appears to forget what happened during the hypnosis session until signaled to remember.*
B. *An altered state of consciousness in which the person seems very suggestible.*
C. *A technique in which the hypnotist suggests that a hypnotized subject relive, through fantasy, earlier experiences and memories.*
D. *A hypnotized subject is told that he or she will perform some activity after the hypnotic trance is ended, perhaps on some signal from the hypnotist. The subject is often unaware of the suggestion or of the reason for his or her activity.*
E. *A drug whose main effect is designed to be an alteration in consciousness.*
F. *A procedure used to produce a hypnotic trance in a susceptible person, usually involving relaxation and suggestions.*
G. *An early version of hypnotism named after one of its eighteenth-century proponents. The technique was thought to operate through "magnetic fluids."*

___ **17. Tolerance (p. 91)**
___ **18. Cross-tolerance (p. 91)**
___ **19. Physical dependence (p. 91)**

A. *A state in which an individual has developed tolerance to a particular drug, needs it to function normally, and experiences withdrawal symptoms when it is no longer administered.*
B. *A phenomenon produced by certain drugs in which increasing doses are required to achieve the same behavioral or physiological effect of the drug the longer the drug is used.*
C. *A phenomenon in which tolerance to one drug develops because of continued use of another chemically similar drug, even though the first drug was never used.*

___ **20. Psychological dependence (p. 91)**
___ **21. Electromyograph (EMG) (p. 92)**
___ **22. Norepinephrine and dopamine (p. 93)**
___ **23. Fetal alcohol syndrome (FAS) (p. 94)**

A. *An apparatus that records electrical signals from muscle tissue.*
B. *A group of symptoms characteristic of some babies born to women who drink a great deal of alcohol during pregnancy. Symptoms include drooping eyelids, crossed eyes, growth deficiencies, hyperactivity, and mental retardation.*
C. *Neurotransmitters used by the nervous system, especially in pathways of the brain involved in mood.*
D. *A state in which a person comes to rely on a drug habitually for the relief of stress, for euphoria, or for other effects.*

*ANSWERS*

20. d, 21. a, 22. c, 23. b
1. c, 2. g, 3. e, 4. h, 5. b, 6. a, 7. d, 8. f, 9. i, 10. g, 11. b, 12. d, 13. a, 14. c, 15. f, 16. e, 17. f, 18. g, 19. e,

## SELF-TEST

1. The focusing of consciousness is called
   (a) attention.
   (b) perception.
   (c) sensation.
   (d) thinking.
   (LO 1; p. 75)

2. Wundt studied consciousness using
   (a) psychoanalysis.
   (b) introspection.
   (c) hypnosis.
   (d) mesmerism.
   (LO 1; p. 75)

3. An electrical recordin technique that averages the brain's response to many presentations of a specific stimulus is called the
   (a) electroencephalograph.
   (b) electromyograph.
   (c) evoked potential.
   (d) CAT scan.
   (LO 2; p. 76)

4. A circadian rhythm is based upon a cycle of about
   (a) an hour.
   (b) a day.
   (c) a lunar month.
   (d) a year.
   (LO 3; p. 77)

5. The timing of the circadian rhythm is synchronized by
   (a) the lunar cycle.
   (b) prenatal factors.
   (c) the changes in noise usually found in the day and at night.
   (d) the day-and-night light cycle.
   (LO 3; pp. 77–78)

6. If locked away in a deep cave or other continuously dark place, a person's sleep/waking cycle generally
   (a) runs freely and averages about 25 hours.
   (b) stays the same as it was above ground.
   (c) becomes shorter so that the person awakes at midnight.
   (d) breaks down so that the person does not have long periods of sleep and waking.
   (LO 3; p. 78)

7. In one study of the distribution of people's errors during the circadian cycle, the worst performance was
   (a) at about 8 A.M.
   (b) at about 10 P.M.
   (c) at mealtime.
   (d) at about 2 A.M.
   (LO 3; p. 78)

8. During slow-wave sleep, the predominant wave form of the EEG
   (a) shifts from the delta wave to the beta wave.
   (b) shifts from the beta wave to the alpha wave.
   (c) shifts from the beta wave to the alpha wave to a predominance of delta waves.
   (d) is the alpha wave.
   (LO 4; p. 80)

9. The stage of sleep during which most dreaming is thought to take place is
   (a) the stage of REM sleep.
   (b) the stage of alpha waves.
   (c) slow-wave sleep.
   (d) when delta waves predominate.
   (LO 5; p. 82)

10. The main result of a single night of sleep loss appears to be
    (a) hallucinations.
    (b) paranoia.
    (c) sleepiness.
    (d) heart problems.
    (LO 6; p. 84)

11. Hypnotism grew out of a body of knowledge and superstition whose eighteenth century proponent was
    (a) Benjamin Franklin.
    (b) Anton Mesmer.
    (c) Sigmund Freud.
    (d) William Curtis.
    (LO 7; p. 85)

12. Hypnotism involves
    (a) attention and suggestibility.
    (b) a kind of magnetism.
    (c) an involuntary compulsion.
    (d) age regression.
    (LO 7; p. 86)

13. Testimony received under hypnosis
    (a) is widely used by the police and welcomed in court.
    (b) is rarely used by police, but welcomed in court when it is.
    (c) is absolutely prohibited for court use.
    (d) is controversial.
    (LO 10; pp. 87–88)

14. General depressants
    (a) include alcohol.
    (b) reduce activity in the nervous system.
    (c) are not addictive.
    (d) both a and b.
    (LO 11; p. 89)

15. Sondra was addicted to heroin. After a car accident in which she broke her arm, she was taken to a hospital, and a physician gave her the standard-size injection of morphine to relieve the pain. It did not relieve her pain, and she requested a higher dose. This illustrates
    (a) tolerance.
    (b) cross-tolerance.
    (c) dependence.
    (d) addiction.
    (LO 12; p. 91)

16. The development of tolerance is usually associated with the use of
    (a) alcohol.
    (b) opiates.
    (c) barbiturates.
    (d) all of the above.
    (LO 12; pp. 89–91)

17. Cocaine
    (a) causes more neurotransmitter to be released at the synapse.
    (b) stimulates the dendrites that cause euphoria.
    (c) acts as a mild depressant.
    (d) blocks reuptake of neurotransmitter at the synapse.
    (LO 12; p. 93)

18. The fetal alcohol syndrome
    (a) is a major cause of alcoholism.
    (b) is found only in the babies of very heavy drinkers.
    (c) may result from relatively modest drinking in susceptible fetuses.
    (d) is actually a drug interaction between alcohol and other general depressants.
    (LO 13; p. 94)

**19.** The general depressants prescribed for insomnia
- **(a)** provide natural and restful sleep if not used more than a couple of times a week.
- **(b)** stimulate REM and provide good relief from insomnia.
- **(c)** cannot result in dependence if used only for inducing sleep.
- **(d)** depress the amount of REM sleep and reduce the quality of the person's sleep time.
(LO 13; p. 94)

**20.** The most serious drug problem in the United States from the perspective of the number of people affected (and damaged) is from
- **(a)** the opiates.
- **(b)** cocaine.
- **(c)** alcohol.
- **(d)** hallucinogens.
(LO 13; pp. 93–94)

ANSWERS

1.a, 2.b, 3. c, 4. b, 5. d, 6. a, 7. d, 8. c, 9. a, 10. c, 11. b, 12. a, 13. d, 14. d, 15. b, 16. d, 17. d, 18. c, 19. c, 20. c

# THINKING ABOUT PSYCHOLOGY

1. Using your knowledge of the EEG, draw a diagram that shows samples of what your own hypothetical patterns might have shown over the past twenty-four hours, identifying the different waves. Make notes next to the changes in rhythms that explain what might have caused them.

2. Tim S., a reporter for a major news service covering a recent airline crash, described one of his dreams. He was wandering through a grocery store and the cans on the top shelves were shaking and wobbling. When he tried to hurry through the narrow aisles the cans started crashing down on his head. The store's manager laughed while he watched the scene through video cameras. How would you interpret Tim's dream? What limits your ability to provide an accurate interpretation?

3. At the end of the nineteenth century in Paris, hypnotism was a major issue in medical and legal circles. In one particularly spectacular case covered in all the papers a woman was accused of conspiring to murder a Parisian bailiff; in her defense, she said she had been hypnotized by her lover. She was acting under his instructions and was not responsible. Many societies provide lighter sentences or even "not guilty" verdicts when there is some reason to believe the person was not entirely responsible. Should hypnotism be considered in this category? Describe the features of hypnotism that support your conclusion.

# SUGGESTED READINGS

Hilgard, E. R. (1980). Consciousness in contemporary psychology. *Annual Review of Psychology 31:* 1–26. An excellent article that explains the history of the study of consciousness in psychology and portends future trends.

Moore-Ede, M. C., Sulzman, F. M., & Fuller, C. A. (1982). *The clocks that time us: Physiology of the circadian timing system.* Cambridge, MA: Harvard University Press. An introduction to the role of circadian rhythms in physiology and behavior.

Nelson, R. J., Badura, L. L., and Goldman, B. D. (1990). Mechanisms of seasonal cycles of behavior. *Annual Review of Psychology, 41,* 81–108. An article that describes recent research on biological rhythms and the behavioral changes that accompany them.

Rosett, H. L., & Weiner, L. (1984). *Alcohol and the fetus: A clinical perspective.* New York: Oxford University Press. A readable book that covers the problem of fetal alcohol syndrome.

Spanos, N. P., and Chaves, J. F. (1989). *Hypnosis: The cognitive-behavioral perspective.* Buffalo, NY: Prometheus Books. The book of articles that explores the competing theories that attempt to explain hypnosis and emphasizes the role of social factors between the hypnotist and the hypnotized.

Udolf, R. (1983). *Forensic hypnosis: Psychological and legal aspects.* Lexington, MA: Lexington Books. The author, trained in both psychology and law, presents his view of the use of hypnosis to memory enhancements in criminal cases.

Ward, C. A. (Ed.) (1989). *Altered states of consciousness and mental health: A cross-cultural perspective.* Newbury Park, CA: Sage. An intriguing book of articles that explores various aspects of consciousness studied in both the laboratory and in natural settings.

Webb, W. B. (1975). *Sleep: The gentle tyrant.* Englewood Cliffs, NJ: Prentice-Hall. An old but still very readable and interesting popular account of sleep.

# CHAPTER 4

## SENSATION AND PERCEPTION
### OUTLINE

# SENSATION AND PERCEPTION
## LEARNING OBJECTIVES

**After reading this chapter, you should be able to**

▶ 1. define sensation and perception, and explain why they are difficult to differentiate. (p. 102)

▶ 2. describe the main components of a sensory system, and explain how scientists investigate the properties of each component. (pp. 102–103)

▶ 3. diagram the structure of the eye, and label its main parts. (pp. 104–105)

▶ 4. explain how the visual system processes information about color, pattern, and the distance of objects. (pp. 105–109)

▶ 5. describe the three main parts of the human ear. (pp. 110–111)

▶ 6. explain the nature of sound and how the human ear is able to transform sound information into neural messages. (pp. 111–112)

▶ 7. name and describe two types of deafness. (pp. 112–114)

▶ 8. describe how the vestibular system provides information that helps to maintain balance. (p. 114)

▶ 9. describe the nature of the skin, and explain what kind of information the receptors in the skin are able to process. (p. 115)

▶ 10. explain factors that influence our perception of pain and treatments used to control pain. (pp. 115–118)

▶ 11. describe the chemical senses, and explain why they are important in communication and in the choice of food. (pp. 118–121)

▶ 12. describe the general principles of perception first recognized by Gestalt psychologists. (pp. 121–124)

▶ 13. explain how individual factors, such as previous experience and culture, can influence perceptions. (pp. 124–126)

▶ 14. show how the processes of perception and attention are related.      (pp. 126–127)

▶ 15. define ESP, and list several different categories of the phenomenon. (p. 127)

▶ 16. explain a study that appears to demonstrate the existence of ESP. (pp. 128–129)

▶ 17. discuss reasons why scientists are skeptical about the existence of ESP. (p. 129)

Christina, an intelligent, cultivated computer programmer and mother of two, needed a gallbladder operation. On the day before her surgery, she had a very distressing dream in which she was swaying wildly, unsteady on her feet, and couldn't feel the ground beneath her. Later that day, her dream came true. She no longer had any "sense" of her own body.

At first, the doctors assumed she was simply anxious because of the impending surgery but her unusual symptoms persisted. She couldn't stand up unless she looked at and concentrated on her feet. Her face, with its slack jaw, held little expression despite the turmoil she felt inside. She described her terrifying state as being "disembodied." Soon the medical staff discovered she had a severe infection that affected one of her sensory systems, one most people don't even know they have. It is the one that send the brain signals about the location, orientation, and movement of the body. A normal person knows exactly where her foot or hand is, but Christina didn't know unless she looked (Sacks, 1985). She lost her sense of her own body, even her own self, and had to relearn how to walk, sit, and talk, all without the internal sensory signals we all take for granted.

The sensory systems receive information about external and internal environments, but they are not cameras or tape recorders. They interpret, filter, and sometimes deceive. They evolved over thousands of years to provide humans with information they need to survive. The human species has five basic senses: vision, audition, touch, smell, and taste. We also have others that are less widely known, especially ones that transmit information about our internal environment. Other species have senses that we cannot even imagine. Some snakes can detect infrared radiation and frogs can sense seismic vibrations (Lewis & Narens, 1985). In this chapter, we explore how we sense and perceive the world around us, relying on the powers of our sensory systems.

## VISION

Humans are remarkably trusting creatures when it comes to seeing. Despite the sage's advice, we believe considerably more than none of what we read and half of what we see. Juries place great faith in an eyewitness who swears "That's the man, I'd know him anywhere," despite the fact that inaccurate identifications are common.

The visual system is the means by which we receive information about the patterns of light in our environment.

Vision is the sensory system we know the most about, but it shares many features in common with the other sensory systems.

## Common Features of the Visual System and Other Sensory Systems

**Sensation** *refers to the transmission of information about the environment to the brain.* All sensory systems are designed to perform this function. Most psychologists view sensation as the events taking place in the eyes, the ears, or the other structures that receive environmental information. Once the information arrives in the brain, sensation begins to blend with **perception,** *a process that involves the interpretation and integration of incoming sensory information.* Sensation and perception are very closely related events, and there is only an arbitrary distinction between them. For example, when a black cat crosses the road, the visual system senses a dark object of a certain shape moving in the distance. The sensory system processes the incoming information, but that information quickly merges with memories of bad luck and traffic accidents in the process of perception.

The structures of sensory systems all have certain basic features. Each has a **sense organ,** *such as the eye or the ear, that performs the first steps in transforming environmental energy into neural activity.* One of the functions of the ear, for example, is to collect sound waves in the air. All the sensory systems have **receptors,** *or specialized neurons that actually perform the transformation of physical energy into neural messages.* **Transduction** *refers to the process by which physical energy originating in the environment is converted to neural signals.* This differs from one sensory system to the next because the nature of the stimulus varies. In vision, the stimulus is light; in the skin, the stimulus might be pressure on the skin. Each system also has an afferent pathway of neurons that leads to the appropriate brain areas.

## The Sensitivity of Sensory Systems

One characteristic of all sensory systems is sensitivity. This property can be measured by **absolute threshold,** *the least amount of energy necessary in order for a sensory system to detect it.* At what point does a light, twenty feet away, become too dim for a person to see it? Or, when is a sound too quiet for a bat's ears to detect it? Table 4.1 gives some approximate absolute thresholds for human sensory systems, though they vary from person to person.

**TABLE 4.1 Some approximate values for absolute thresholds**

| Sense | Threshold |
|---|---|
| Vision | A candle flame seen at 30 miles on a dark, clear night |
| Hearing | The tick of a watch under quiet conditions at 20 feet |
| Taste | One teaspoon of sugar in two gallons of water |
| Smell | One drop of perfume diffused into the entire volume of a six-room apartment |
| Touch | The wing of a fly falling on your cheek from a distance of one centimeter |

From Eugene Galanter, "Contemporary Psychophysics," in New Directions in Psychology, by R. Brown, et al. Copyright 1962 CBS Publishing. Reprinted by permission of the author.

In theory, it may seem easy to determine when a person stops seeing a dim light at twenty feet and thus determine the absolute threshold. The experimenter would simply turn on a light, making it dimmer and dimmer for each trial, and ask the subjects whether they saw it. In practice, though, there is a range of light intensities of which people are not really sure. People who don't mind ambiguity will say that they did see the light even when it is extremely dim. Others want to be very sure, so they will say they didn't see any light even when they thought they might have. The former would seem to have a much more sensitive visual system than the latter. The difference between the two, however, is not in visual sensitivity; it is in personality, judgment, or other nonsensory variables. A technique called **signal detection** *circumvents the problem of individual differences in "willingness to guess" in studies of absolute thresholds.* The experimenter occasionally includes a trial in which no signal is presented. Frequent "false alarms," in which the subject says "Yes, I saw the light" when no light appeared, are taken into account in the calculation of sensitivity (Egan, 1975; Ludel, 1978).

Another measure of sensitivity in a sensory system is the **just noticeable difference, or j.n.d.** *This represents how finely tuned a system is. How much of a change in the environment is required for the system to detect it?* For example, can a person detect the difference between one and two teaspoons of sugar in a gallon of water? Between a spot of light at 450 nanometers and one at 460 nanometers? Between a 100-gram weight in one hand and a 120-gram weight in the other hand?

A remarkable feature of the j.n.d. is that it follows **Weber's Law.** *This principle states that the j.n.d. is a constant fraction of stimulus intensity, at least within the intermediate range of intensities for the sensory system.* For example, the j.n.d. for a 100-gram weight might be 2 grams, meaning that a subject holding a 100-gram weight could not reliably distinguish it from weights of 99 grams, 101 grams, or even 101.5 grams. The comparison weight must differ by at least 2 grams. A subject holding a 200-gram weight would have a j.n.d. of 4 grams, and a person holding an 800-gram weight would have a j.n.d. of 16 grams. The constant fraction for weight lifting is 1/50. Other sensory abilities, such as detecting changes in the pitch of a sound, the taste of a sugar solution, the loudness of a tone, or the brightness of a light, have their own fractions.

In practice, Weber's Law means it is easy to feel the difference when someone adds a can of soda to your day pack but not to your big backpack. Further, on a three-way light bulb, the change from 50 to 100 watts is much more noticeable than the change from 100 to 150 watts.

## The Visual Stimulus—Light

Light waves are thought to be a form of electromagnetic radiation, but even physicists do not completely understand them. They travel at a speed of 186,000 miles per second (300,000 km/sec) and exist in an enormous range of **wavelengths,** *the distance from the peak of one wave to the peak of the next.* Human beings can see only a very small fraction of the electromagnetic radiation present in the environment (figure 4.1). The **visible spectrum** *is the tiny portion of the electromagnetic spectrum visible to the human visual system;* it ranges from 380 nanometers (one-billionth of a meter) to 760 nanometers. Babies and many animals can see almost the same range of wavelengths as adult humans. The visible spectra vary for different organisms. A bee, for example, cannot see red, but it can see ultraviolet wavelengths. And the pit viper has a special sensory system that can detect infrared radiation.

Within the visible spectrum, different wavelengths of light are seen as different colors by animals that have color vision. The shorter light waves appear purple or blue to us, and the longer ones appear red. We can only guess what the bee "sees" when it looks at ultraviolet light.

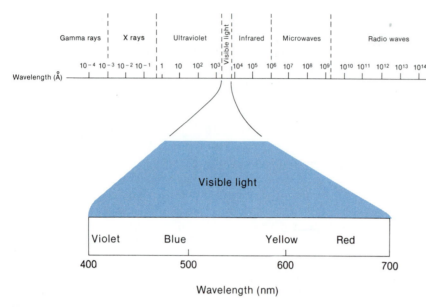

**Figure 4.1**   *The electromagnetic energy spectrum, with enlargement of visible portion*

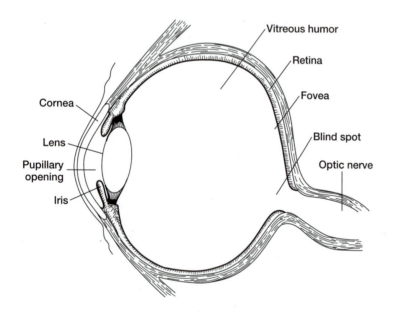

**Figure 4.2**   *A side view of the eye*

## The Structure of the Eye

The eye is the sense organ for vision (figure 4.2). Most of the structures shown in figure 4.2 are designed to focus or modify the light waves coming into the eye before they reach the receptors in the back of the eyeball. The **cornea** *is the transparent protective covering on the front of the eye; it helps to focus the light.* The **iris** *is the part of the eye that has color, and it is a muscle that opens wide or contracts around the pupil, thereby regulating the amount of light that reaches the inside.* The **lens,** *the transparent elastic tissue located behind the iris, refracts light rays so they are properly focused on the receptors in the back of the eyeball.* The lens can become thicker or thinner and thus "fine tune" the focusing process. Using the process called **accommodation,** *the shape of the elastic lens is adjusted by surrounding muscles in order to focus on nearby distant objects.* As you get older, lens tissue becomes more brittle and less able to thicken, making it more difficult for you to focus on nearby objects. It gets harder to read the fine print without glasses. The lens also has a yellow tint to screen out some of the blue and ultraviolet light, a tint which becomes more dense with age.

Changes in the lens are usually responsible for **cataracts,** *a condition in which the lens tissue becomes cloudy, eventually resulting in blindness.* Cataracts are caused by ultraviolet light, X rays, and even heat. Glassblowers sometimes suffer from cataracts because of their frequent exposure to bright light and heat. Modern surgical techniques can now remove cataracts; before these techniques were developed, people with cataracts became permanently blind.

*The Retina*   The center of the eyeball is filled with a jellylike substance that is usually clear, but may sometimes contain shreds of debris that create moving shadows in the field of vision. At the back of the eyeball is the **retina,** *the paper-thin layer of receptors and other cells covering the inside back of the eyeball.* You can see the retina by shining a flashlight on a person's pupil. Although the pupil looks dark, it is actually almost transparent and only appears dark because there is no source of light inside the eye. Since the retina contains many blood vessels, it will look reddish-pink under the light. If you have ever taken a photograph with a flash camera and found that your subjects had red eyes, you have taken a picture of their retinas. Sometimes the flash attachment on a camera is right next to the camera lens. When you photograph people who are looking directly at the camera, you light up the portion of the retina that is directly in line with the lens. To avoid this problem, buy an extension that moves the flash a few inches further from the lens. Then the flash still goes through the pupil and lights up part of the reddish retina, but not the same part you are photographing.

*Rods and Cones*    The retina contains two types of receptors: the rods and the cones (figure 4.3). At first glance, the diagram may seem odd because the rods and cones appear to be facing away from the direction in which the light is coming. The receptors are inverted because of their heavy requirement for oxygen. They must be close to the bloodstream; the blood vessels would block some of the light if the retina were turned over.

The **rods** *are receptor cells, most of which are located on the periphery of the retina; they respond at very low light intensities though they cannot discriminate between the different wavelengths (colors).* The cones are concentrated in the **fovea,** *or the center of the retina.* **Cones** *are receptor cells that process color information and information about very fine-grained patterns.* When you look at this sentence, you are using the cones in your fovea to see the print. Despite its enormous importance to the human visual system, foveal vision covers only a very small part of the visual field—about the diameter of a quarter held at arm's length.

In accordance with their different functions, rods and cones differ in their quantity and distribution in the human eye. There are many more rods than cones in the eye even though rods are totally absent in the fovea. As you leave the foveal region, the density of rods increases rapidly, reaching a peak about twenty degrees from the foveal central point. Thereafter, the density of rods diminishes gradually (Osterberg, 1935).

Cones can resolve finely detailed patterns better than rods because of the way each receptor passes its messages to the brain (figure 4.3). Through their connections with several kinds of intermediate neurons in the retina, information from the 130 million rods and cones eventually converges onto one of the approximately one million

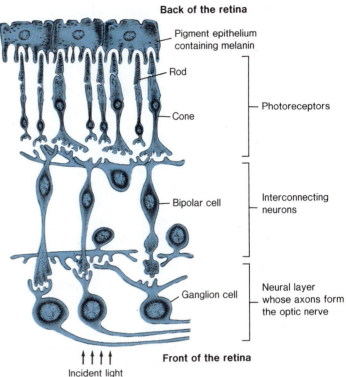

**Figure 4.3**    *A schematic diagram of the human retina*

ganglion cells, *neurons which lead out of the retina toward the brain.* The input from a great many rods converges onto a single ganglion cell. This means that the brain receives only a summary about the activity of individual rods, so the picture it gets is "grainy." In contrast, the brain receives much more detailed information from the cones. One ganglion cell might receive input from only a few cones. In addition, there are clustered in the fovea a small number of cones (perhaps 50,000) that have their very own ganglion cell "pipeline" to the brain.

## Transduction in the Receptors

Each time light strikes a rod or a cone, chemical changes take place that result in the release of neurotransmitter by the receptor cell. These events are the most important part of the transduction process in the visual system.

The chemical reactions were first observed by Franz Boll in 1876 when he isolated a brilliant red substance inside the receptor of a frog. This substance was **photopigment,** *a remarkable light-sensitive chemical that loses its color in the light but regains it in the dark because the chemical changes are reversed.* It is the chemical breakdown of photopigment molecules exposed to light that causes electrical disturbances in the membrane of the receptor, and triggers a change in the neuron's release of neurotransmitter. Light energy is thus transformed into a neural message. In the dark, the photopigment molecules are resynthesized from their components.

*Dark Adaptation*    **Dark adaptation** *refers to the phenomenon in which a person's sensitivity to light increases as he or she spends more time in the dark because the receptors are resynthesizing their photopigments.* You have probably experienced this in movie theaters; when you first enter, you cannot see any seats. But after a few minutes, your eyes become more sensitive.

Although the change in sensitivity is obvious, it is not so obvious that the change actually occurs in two stages; the process occurs at different rates for rods and cones (figure 4.4). During the first three to four minutes in the dark, a person's sensitivity increases and then levels off; after seven to ten minutes, sensitivity increases again and continues to do so for another twenty to thirty minutes. Sensitivity after dark adaptation increases about one hundred thousand fold.

## Organizing Visual Information

As the information from the rods and cones travels from the receptors to the ganglion cells and then to the brain, it is summarized, modified, enhanced, exaggerated, and deleted. Interestingly, recent work suggests that different kinds of information from the visual environment may be processed independently by different visual pathways (Livingstone, 1988). One pathway appears to process shape and pattern information; another processes color information; and a third processes movement, location, and spatial organization, including depth. We perceive a whole picture only after information about its color, contrast, movement, shape, and other attributes are separately processed and finally integrated. This is another example of our brains' ability to process information in parallel.

## Seeing Patterns

Seeing patterns, such as the words on this page, involves the activity of neurons all along the visual pathway to the brain. Because of all the changes, what you actually perceive is not quite the same as what was originally

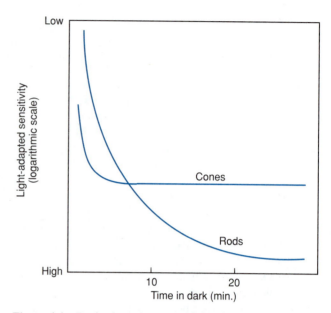

**Figure 4.4**    *Dark adaptation curves for rods and cones*

sensed at the level of the receptor. Information at the receptor level is organized around receptive fields.

*Receptive Fields*    The **receptive field** *of a cell in a sensory pathway is the area in the environment in which the presentation of a stimulus will cause a change in the cell's firing rate.* For example, the receptive field of a ganglion cell is a specific area in the visual field. When a light stimulus appears in that area, the ganglion cell will change its firing rate. Since a ganglion cell receives input from a great many receptors, it acts as a clearinghouse for information from a particular zone in the retina.

Some pioneering studies on cats (Kuffler, 1953) demonstrated how the receptive field organization leads to an enhancement of contrast. An electrode was inserted directly into the ganglion cell of an anesthetized cat, and records of that cell's firing pattern were made as the cat's eye was stimulated with light. When a tiny spot of light appeared in most places on a screen in front of the cat, the ganglion cell did not change its firing rate. But when the light appeared in a small area where the spot was hitting the ganglion cell's receptive field, the cell made three different kinds of responses.

When the light appeared directly in the center of the field, the response was an immediate burst of spikes followed by a return to normal when the light was turned off. When the light appeared in the outer portion of the field, or surround, the cell showed no response until the light was turned off; then it showed a rapid burst of firing. In a small ring between the center of the field and the outer portion, both the onset and the offset of a light caused a short burst of firing. This pattern of response became known as "center-on, surround-off." Later studies found that if a light appeared in the center and the surround at the same time, the cell showed no response (Rodieck & Stone, 1965). This kind of organization demonstrates that the ganglion cell is comparing the brightness of the center spot to the brightness of the surround. When the contrast between the two is maximal, the cell will give the greatest response.

*Identifying Features*    Studies of the way the visual pathways process information about patterns and shapes began with the Nobel prizewinning work of David Hubel and Torsten Wiesel. Using single-cell recordings, they demonstrated that certain cells in the cortex appeared to respond selectively to particular stimuli. They used the term **feature detector** to describe these cells; it refers to *cells in the visual cortex that change their firing rates in response to specific stimuli located in their receptive fields* (Hubel & Wiesel, 1959, 1962, 1965). One group of cells, which they called "simple cells," increased its firing rate most vigorously when a straight line or bar was shown in its receptive field. As the bar was turned, the cells' response diminished. Hubel and Wiesel hypothesized that simple cells were receiving input from groups of cells in the brain that had overlapping circular receptive fields arranged in a line.

Complex cells comprised another group of feature detectors; these visual cortical cells responded best when the stimulus was a line turned in a certain orientation and moving in a specific direction. Some cells even showed "preferences" for bars of a specific length.

Feature detectors are sensitive to specific and very basic features in the environment. It is tempting to speculate on how they contribute to perception, how they develop, or whether everyone has the same set. We know that they can be modified by the environment: kittens that grow up wearing goggles that let them see only horizontal lines have a shortage of feature detectors sensitive to vertical lines (Hirsch & Spinelli, 1971). The capabilities of our visual systems, even at a basic level, are partly determined by what we see during development. What would we be able to see if we grew up in a very foggy climate where we could never see more than five meters ahead? Or if our ancestral architects had shunned the rectangular building design in favor of graceful curves?

## Seeing in Color

Humans and many other animals share the ability to see in color, relying on one means or another to discriminate between different wavelengths of light. The process by which humans see color was a matter of some debate with two competing theories: the trichromatic theory and the opponent process theory. As it turned out, both were correct but each was used in a different part of the sensory system.

*Trichromatic Theory*    Cones come in three different types, each of which is most sensitive to a particular range of wavelengths. There are cones that are most sensitive to light in the blue range, in the green range, and in the red range (Marks, Dobelle, & MacNichol, 1964). For example, when blue light reaches the retina, the blue-sensitive cones react the most and produce changes in the firing rates of the neurons to which they are connected. The **trichromatic theory** *predicted the existence of three classes of cones in the retina and their selective activation by red, blue, and green as a means to transform color information in the environment into neural signals.* Other colors were thought to be produced by mixtures of those three and by activity in more than one kind of cone. Purple, for example, produces a response in both blue and red sensitive cones.

This very elegant system of color vision was first proposed in 1802 by Thomas Young and later modified by Hermann von Helmholtz. But its verification had to wait for the invention of **microspectrophotometry,** *a technique that could measure light absorption in individual cones.* A tiny beam of light is shone on a single cone, and the amount of light reflected back is measured. Whatever wavelengths are not reflected back are absorbed. Tests of many cones demonstrated that they tended to fall into one of three categories, each most sensitive to a different color (Marks et al., 1964).

More recently, scientists have obtained electrical recordings from single cones in primates and human beings. These studies also confirm the existence of three different kinds of cones, called L, M, and S. They respond to long, medium and short wavelengths (Schnapf, Kraft, & Baylor, 1987; Boynton, 1988).

*Opponent Process Theory*    Single-cell recordings from visual areas of the monkey brain shed light on the way color is processed beyond the receptor stage. In an early study (DeValois, Abramov, & Jacobs, 1966), four different kinds of cells were found that responded to not one, but to two colors by changing their firing rate.

One kind increased its firing rate when the animal was looking at green but slowed down its rate when it was looking at red. Another increased for red but slowed down for green. The third and fourth kinds responded to blue and yellow by speeding up or slowing down. The **opponent process theory** *had originally predicted that individual cells could code information about two separate colors by slowing their firing rates for one color and accelerating their fire rates for the other color.* Both the trichromatic and the opponent process theories were correct for different parts of the visual system.

The opponent process theory explains the occurrence of **negative afterimages,** *which are sensory images that appear a different color than the original stimulus.* If you looked at a red square for about thirty seconds and then looked at a white space, you would see a green square about the same size. The green square, of course, would not be on the paper but in your brain. It is produced by the sudden increase (or decrease) in the firing rate of those brain cells that had changed their firing rate for red. The sudden change in the opposite direction signals green, so you "see" a green square.

The way the visual system moves from a trichromatic coding system to an opponent process system is complicated. One theory proposes a special kind of neural wiring diagram in which an opponent process cell in the brain receives input from all three kinds of cones; some of the input is inhibitory and some is excitatory (Hurvich & Jameson, 1974). For example, a red-green opponent process cell might receive excitatory input from blue and red cones and inhibitory input from green cones.

The engineers who designed color television used a similar wiring diagram (Coren, Porac, & Ward, 1979). The color in the television studio is broken down into three components (red, green, and blue) by the camera. Then it is transformed into two "opponent process" signals instead of three. When it reaches your television set, it is transformed back into the red, green, and blue signals.

Most people who are color-blind see some color, but they have difficulty distinguishing certain colors. The most common form results from absence of normal red-sensitive cones. People with this disorder have trouble distinguishing red from green. A much rarer variety of color blindness occurs when only one type of cone functions; these

people see the world entirely in black, white, and shades of gray.

In the movie version of *The Wizard of Oz,* Dorothy's world was magically transformed from drab black and white to brilliant color when the tornado set her house down in a Munchkin village. Understanding the sensory mechanics underlying color vision could never fully describe the perceptual experience and the way in which color enriches our lives and affects our emotions, but it provides the necessary groundwork.

## Seeing Depth and Distance

Although the retina has only two dimensions, human beings process information in three. We use two different kinds of cues to see depth: **monocular cues,** *based on the cues available to one eye,* and **binocular cues,** *which take advantage of the fact that we have two eyes spaced slightly apart.*

The monocular cues are based primarily on experience. For example, we learn that people are larger than house cats; when we see them together we judge their distance by making unconscious calculations. If the image of the cat is very large on the retina relative to the image of the person, we assume the cat is closer. Another monocular cue involves the perception of detail. Objects we perceive as clear and detailed are probably closer than objects that seem fuzzy. If you are nearsighted perhaps you can recall your first day wearing glasses and the problems you had judging distance. Everything seemed so clear—and therefore much closer than it really was.

The most important cues for depth, however, come from the use of two eyes. Aircraft pilots are medically grounded if they lose sight in one eye, even temporarily, because of their urgent need for extremely precise depth perception. Monocular cues are simply not enough.

**Convergence** *is a kind of binocular cue for depth that uses information supplied by the muscles that move the eyes.* When you look at an object close to the end of your nose, you can feel the contraction of the muscles that pull your eyes toward the nose. The muscles that pull your eyes outward, toward the temples, are contracted when you view an object in the distance. These muscles send signals to the brain that help identify the distance of the object, even when the movement is so slight that you cannot consciously detect it.

The most important cue for judging distance comes from **stereoscopic vision,** *the fact that the two eyes see* *overlapping but slightly different views of the world.* The closer the object is, the more different are the views the two eyes see. If you hold your finger about a hand's length from your nose and then alternately close one eye and then the other, you will appreciate stereoscopic vision. Although the cue is processed unconsciously, it is vital for judging distance.

The 3-D viewers children play with create stereoscopic vision artificially. Special cameras are used to take simultaneous pictures of the same scene, from two slightly different angles. The picture displaced to the left appears only to the left eye in the viewer, and the right eye sees only the one displaced to the right. The visual cortex fuses the two images, creating the illusion of depth. Thus, it is just as though the person were really seeing the image with his or her own two (slightly separated) eyes.

The visual cortex appears to contain cells designed to process stereoscopic information coming in from the two eyes. Most of the simple cells that Hubel and Wiesel investigated in monkeys responded only to a stimulus in one eye. The complex cells showed more preference. Some responded to input from one eye only, others to the other eye, and some to both, although most showed a preference for one eye or the other. There are also, however, some cells that apparently play an important role in depth perception. These are strictly binocular; they will only respond when both eyes are stimulated simultaneously (Clarke & Whitteridge, 1978). Significantly, they tend to respond best when a stimulus is almost, but not quite, in the same location of the visual field of both eyes, a feature that suggests they are responding to stereoscopic information. Various studies have demonstrated that such cells exist in humans as well (Hitchcock & Hickey, 1980; Sloane & Blake, 1984).

## Visual Problems

Even the federal government recognizes the importance of vision; blindness is the only sensory handicap that earns an extra tax exemption. Although total blindness is not very common, more than six percent of the people in the United States have a visual impairment that limits their activities in some way.

One of the most common visual disorders is nearsightedness. People who are nearsighted cannot focus properly on objects in the distance because their eyeballs are elongated. The image is focused just in front of the retina. Farsightedness in young people is usually caused by the opposite problem—short eyeballs. In older people it may be caused by changes in the lens. Eyeglasses correct both problems.

Glassblower's cataract is not the only occupational hazard related to vision. Staring at computer terminals can cause various visual disorders. Complaints about terminals have increased steadily over the past few years, and government agencies are studying the possible health risks. People who work with computer displays report more visual fatigue, headaches, blurry vision, eye strain, and burning sensations in the eyes than do other people (Dainoff, Happ, & Crane, 1981), and some say their color vision is affected after watching the screen for long periods of time. No one is quite certain why these visual problems occur, but it may be partly due to the dot matrix letters. The eye may continually try to focus the letters better in a futile attempt to produce a clear image.

▶ **GUIDED REVIEW** *Learning Objectives 1, 2, 3, and 4*

1. Sensory systems are the means by which information about the environment is transmitted to the brain, a process called _____. Sensory systems include _____, the specialized cells that change physical energy into changes in neural firing rates; a _____, which modifies the physical energy before it reaches the receptors; and a pathway of neurons that lead from the sense organ to the brain.
2. The sensitivity of a sensory system can be measured by _____, a value that refers to the least amount of energy that can be detected. Absolute thresholds are not single numbers but a range in which the subject is not sure that the stimulus has been presented.
3. _____ is a technique used to measure sensitivity. It takes into account the fact that people vary in their willingness to guess about the presence of a stimulus.
4. Sensitivity of sensory systems is also characterized by the _____, the amount of change in the environmental stimulus required for the individual to notice a change. _____ states that the j.n.d. is a constant fraction of stimulus intensity.
5. The stimulus for the visual system is light. Light waves have different _____, and human beings can only see certain wavelengths of light, called the _____. Different wavelengths of light are seen as different colors.
6. The eye is the sense organ for vision; some important structures include the _____, the _____, the _____, and the _____.
7. The _____ is the layer of receptor cells in the back of the eyeball. There are two types of receptors: the _____, which are specialized for night vision, and the _____, which see color and finely detailed patterns.
8. The receptors are connected to the _____, which lead out of the optic nerve to the brain.

9. The process of transduction in the rods involves the chemical breakdown of _____ on exposure to light.

10. The process of _____ involves the recovery of the photopigment molecules.

11. The _____ organization of cells in the visual system enhances contour and contrast by special sensitivity to light onsets and offsets and to differences in brightness between adjacent areas on the retina. Receptive fields of ganglion cells are circular, with a center region and a surround.

12. Cells in the cortex, sometimes called _____, have preferred stimuli, such as bars, moving bars, or lines in specific orientations.

13. Color vision in human beings is explained by two different theories: the _____ and the _____ theory. The trichromatic theory predicts that there are three types of receptors, each sensitive to a different wavelength of light. The opponent process theory predicts that each cell is responsive to a pair of colors (red-green, blue-yellow). The trichromatic theory is correct for the retina, and the opponent process theory is correct for cells in the brain that process color.

14. The ability of humans to perceive depth and distance is due to _____ and _____ cues, which involve the use of one eye and both eyes, respectively. Monocular cues include the use of knowledge about the size of objects. Binocular cues include _____, in which the brain receives signals from the eye muscles. Organisms with two eyes having overlapping fields of vision have _____, and the disparity between the two views provides an important cue to distance.

15. Some common visual problems include color blindness, usually caused by an absence of functional red-sensitive cones; nearsightedness and farsightedness, caused by eyeballs that are too long or too short, respectively; and _____, or clouding of the lens tissue. Frequent use of video display terminals (VDTs) may also produce visual problems.

*Answers*

1. sensation, receptors, sense organ 2. absolute thresholds 3. Signal detection 4. just noticeable difference (j.n.d.), Weber's Law 5. wavelengths, visible spectrum 6. cornea, iris, pupil, lens 7. retina, rods, cones 8. ganglion cells 9. photopigment 10. dark adaptation 11. receptive field 12. feature detectors 13. trichromatic theory, opponent process 14. monocular, binocular, convergence, stereoscopic vision 15. cataracts

## AUDITION

**Audition** *is the sense of hearing.* The human auditory system is very efficient at some tasks and less so at others. Human ears are able to detect rapid changes in sounds, though the range of sounds they can hear is limited compared to animals like dogs or bats. To understand language, we need to be able to hear rapid changes, so our hearing abilities are just right for us. Our ears are good at detecting the location of sound sources, but other animals have far superior capabilities in this area (Knudsen, 1981). Imagine a barn owl hunting for mice at night and then diving for its prey. You can see why it needs a keen ability to locate sound sources. A small error in judgment could mean simply a missed meal, or it could mean a suicidal dive into the ground at top speed.

## Sound

**Sound** *is the physical energy in the environment that is transformed by the auditory system.* Sound waves are produced when things vibrate in air or water (for example, vocal cords, gongs, or clarinet reeds). When something vibrates, it causes the molecules around it to collide with one another, pushing molecules forward in wavelike motions. Sound waves consist of alternate **compressions,** *in which the air molecules are pushed closer together,* followed by **rarefactions,** *in which the molecules spread out.* Just as waves move through water for long distances without actually moving the molecules of water themselves more than a few centimeters, sound waves travel through air or other media. The air molecules themselves move back and forth over very short distances, but the alternations of compressions and rarefactions may travel for a long way.

The **frequency of a simple sound wave** *represents the number of alternating compressions and rarefactions passing through a given point over a period of time.* It is usually measured in **Hertz (Hz),** *or cycles per second.* **Pitch** *refers to the way the physical stimulus is experienced by human beings, and it roughly equates to the sound's frequency.* High pitches are associated with rapid vibrations, and lower base notes are associated with slower vibrations. The spoken voice is usually around 1,000 Hz. If you think that a 20,000 Hz tone is high, imagine what the bat hears when it is listening to a sound at 150,000 Hz. Although the barn owl can locate sounds very well, it can only hear sounds ranging from about 100 to 12,000 Hz. Superior abilities in one area are usually offset by inferior abilities in another.

Most of the sounds we hear are complex mixtures of many sound waves. The sound of speech, for example, is not a single sound wave at 1,000 Hz; it is an intricate blend of many sound waves.

## The Ear

The sense organ for hearing is the ear, shown in figure 4.5. The ear has three main parts: (a) the **outer ear,** *the exterior part that collects sound waves;* (b) the **middle**

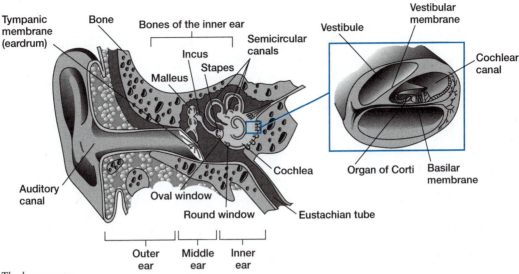

**Figure 4.5**   *The human ear*

**ear,** *which contains several important bones that amplify and transmit sound waves;* and (c) **the inner ear,** *which contains the sensory receptors for audition.*

Sound waves follow a path from the outer ear through the **auditory canal,** *which connects the outer ear to the middle ear.* Here, the waves set the eardrum and three tiny bones of the middle ear into vibratory motion. The vibrations of the bones set the fluid of the inner ear into motion. The snail-shaped **cochlea** *is the inner ear; it contains the receptors for hearing.* The *sensory receptor cells for hearing, called* **hair cells,** are located along the **basilar membrane,** *the membrane inside the cochlea that follows its curvature* (figure 4.6).

When you have a cold, you may have trouble hearing because the tissue in the middle ear becomes inflamed from the infection and blocks the passage of air. For the eardrum to vibrate normally, the pressure of the air on both sides of the drum must be equal. Since the inflamed tissue interferes with the movement of air in this area, it also prevents the eardrum from vibrating properly. The hearing difficulty that most people experience when they are flying on an airplane is also due to pressure differences on either side of the eardrum.

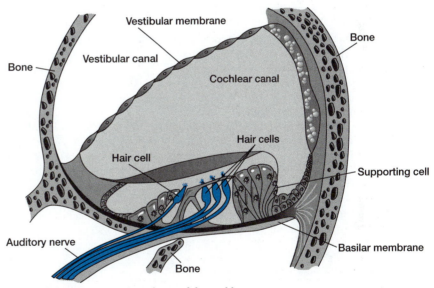

**Figure 4.6**   *A cross section of part of the cochlea*

## The Coding of Sound

Nobel prize winner Georg von Békésy worked out the details of how the basilar membrane responds to sounds of different frequencies (von Békésy, 1949). He discovered a fairly close relationship between the frequency of a sound and the place on the basilar membrane that was most deformed in response to that sound. High-frequency sounds produce the most deformation of the membrane near the stapes (one of the bones of the middle ear),

# APPLYING PSYCHOLOGY

## Space Motion Sickness

On December 21, 1968, the Apollo 8 spacecraft was launched from Cape Canaveral on a Saturn V. It was the first time human beings tried to orbit the moon, and the three man crew successfully reached lunar orbit on Christmas Eve. The historic mission was commanded by Frank Borman. One of the first things he did after the spacecraft left earth was vomit.

This embarrassing malady was not limited to the Apollo 8 commander. Space motion sickness has afflicted almost half of the astronauts and cosmonauts in one form or another. The Russians have had as much trouble with this problem as the Americans. Titov experienced nausea and vomiting on the Soviet Vostok mission in 1962. Symptoms usually begin the first day in space and sometimes last as long as a week. Although the condition does not seem to be serious, it can be disabling to an astronaut who has important work to accomplish.

On longer missions, such as those of Skylab or Soyuz, when the astronauts and cosmonauts stay in space for months at a time, space motion sickness does not present too much of a problem. Missing two or three days of work at the beginning of the mission is inefficient, but it doesn't threaten the success of the entire mission. For the crews of the space shuttles, however, space motion sickness is a much more serious hazard. These spaceships were designed to make short, busy missions. If half the crew is debilitated by nausea and vomiting for two or three days, the mission's goals will be in jeopardy. NASA is focusing considerable attention on learning more about the disorder, especially on finding ways to predict it, treat it, and prevent it.

This kind of motion sickness appears to be only remotely related to seasickness. Astronauts who are totally immune to motion sickness in normal gravity sometimes show extreme susceptibility to space sickness in zero gravity, making it extremely difficult to predict who the next victim will be. Therefore, NASA can't easily solve the problem by testing astronauts on the ground and eliminating those susceptible to motion sickness in boats, cars, or airplanes.

Treating space-sick astronauts has not been very successful. The remedy that has been used is called ScopeDex, a combination of scopolamine and Dexedrine. Scopolamine helps eliminate the nausea, and Dexedrine counteracts the drowsiness and lethargy that are side effects of the scopolamine. Unfortunately, this drug helps only some of the astronauts.

Another promising technique is biofeedback, a procedure that has been successful in treating motion sickness in air crews. Subjects learn to control their autonomic responses, including stomach queasiness, as they are gradually exposed to more and more provocative stimulation. While sitting in a rotating chair, they receive feedback about some of their ongoing biological processes and attempt to voluntarily modify them. (See chapter 5 for a more complete description of biofeedback.)

Much of NASA's interest is very practical; the agency would like to have either effective countermeasures for the disorder or successful predictive tests. But some of their research is devoted to understanding the basic nature of the phenomenon. Many scientists now think that the problem is due to the unusual barrage of sensory signals the brain receives in a weightless environment. Two sensory systems seem to be involved—the visual system, which normally receives input in a "head up" orientation but which receives input in all directions in space, and the vestibular system in the inner ear, the sense organ that detects gravity on earth and tells the brain which way is up. In the weightless environment of space, both of these systems are receiving strange and unfamiliar information, and probably more important, their signals conflict with one another. The result, for reasons no one understands, is uncomfortable feelings in the stomach, nausea, and vomiting.

whereas low-frequency sounds deform the membrane further away. Thus, the frequency of a sound is coded at the level of the receptors; different hair cell receptors respond to sounds of different frequencies.

The way people determine where a sound in the horizontal plane is coming from involves the distance between the two ears (Middlebrooks & Green, 1991). If someone snaps his or her fingers while standing at your left side, the sound wave will reach the left ear first. If the finger snapper is standing in front of you, the sound wave will reach both ears at the same time. If the sound comes from the right, the wave will reach your right ear first. The brain relies on these time differences to determine where the sound originated. In fact, the human brain can detect differences down to a fraction of a millisecond, making it possible to identify with incredible accuracy the direction from which the sound wave is coming. Not surprisingly, it is harder to tell where sounds are coming from if they vary in the vertical dimension.

## Hearing Problems

You can get some idea what it might be like to be blind by covering your eyes. To understand what a profound hearing loss might be like, imagine sitting in on a conversation with friends and being able to see their lips move but being unable to hear them.

There are two general kinds of deafness. **Conduction deafness** *results when the receptor cells for audition are intact, but there is a problem somewhere along the route from the eardrum to the cochlea.* A person with this kind of deafness would not be able to hear sounds conducted in air but would be able to hear a tuning fork vibrating against his or her skull. The sound waves can be transmitted through the bones of the skull and can set the cochlear fluid in motion. The hearing difficulty associated with a common cold falls into this category. **Nerve deafness** *is due to damage to the receptors in the cochlea or to the auditory nerve.* The sound waves arrive at the cochlea, but the hair cells of the basilar membrane fail to send messages to the brain. The progressive degeneration of the hair cells would cause nerve deafness. Usually, the receptors responsive to the higher frequency sounds are the first to begin degenerating.

The isolation of deafness is severe and sometimes leads to personality problems. When people start to lose their hearing later in life and are not aware of it, they may begin to think others are deliberately whispering to prevent them from hearing. Symptoms of paranoia may result. Their misperceptions may make them more hostile and suspicious.

Philip Zimbardo and his colleagues experimentally demonstrated a relationship between hearing loss and paranoia (Zimbardo, Andersen, & Kabat, 1981). Three groups of college men with normal hearing were hypnotized and given posthypnotic suggestions. One group (the control group) was told they would have itchy ears. A second group (the experimental group) was told they would have a partial hearing loss. Hearing loss was also suggested to the third group, but they were aware of the suggestion.

The subjects in the experimental group became more irritated, hostile, and unfriendly compared to the subjects in either control group, demonstrating that hearing loss can very quickly produce personality problems, particularly if people are unaware of the sensory deficit.

Loss of hearing in older adults is a serious handicap and may cause personality problems. In children, hearing problems are even more tragic because they interfere with language development. Psychologists know very little about what the best methods are for training deaf children to communicate. Some believe that deaf children should not learn sign language because it might lessen their

**Figure 4.7**  *Communicating via sign language*

motivation for the incredibly difficult task of learning to speak. They argue that learning to speak offers the deaf child the best hope of becoming part of normal society. Others believe that deaf children should learn "total communication," both sign language and oral speech (figure 4.7). They feel that sign language allows a child to communicate better at home and at an earlier age. Because it becomes more and more difficult to learn language as a child gets older, the ability to communicate early is crucial. Unfortunately, factual information on the success of each method is scarce (Benderly, 1980).

The structures of the ear can be damaged by a staggering variety of microbes, mishaps, and mistreatments. Genetic defects account for a large number of hearing losses. Infections in a pregnant woman are a leading cause of deafness in infants. From 1963 to 1965, there was an epidemic of German measles in the United States; the number of deaf children born during those years doubled. Furthermore, certain drugs, such as streptomycin, taken during pregnancy may produce nerve deafness by causing degeneration of the hair-cell receptors. After birth, children and young adults can suffer hearing loss from meningitis, from drugs such as streptomycin, and even from the common cold.

Noise pollution is another leading cause of hearing loss. Soldiers, police officers, riveters, rock stars, airplane mechanics, and those who work with frequent loud noise usually have some hearing loss. Once it became clear that noise could damage the receptor cells in the ear, Congress passed the Walsh-Healey Public Contracts Act in 1970. This law specifies how loud the noise in factories, offices, and apartment buildings can be in **decibels (dB),** *the unit*

| TABLE 4.2 The decibel levels for some common sounds | | |
| --- | --- | --- |
| Decibel | Type of Sound | Times as Loud as 0 dB |
| 0 | The least sound heard by a normal human ear | — |
| 10 | The rustle of leaves in a light breeze | 10 |
| 20 | An average whisper four feet away from hearer | 100 |
| 50 | Average residence | 100,000 |
| 60 | Normal conversation at three feet | 1,000,000 |
| 90 | A moderate discotheque | 1,000,000,000 |
| 110 | A pneumatic drill | 100,000,000,000 |
| 120 | A jet engine | 1,000,000,000,000 |

Source: Data from B. Tannenbaum and M. Stillman, *Understanding Sound,* p. 31, McGraw-Hill, New York. . *Copyright © 1973 by Beulah Tannenbaum and Myra Stillman.*

*used to measure noise levels.* Table 4.2 gives some examples of how loud various noises are.

No law can prevent people from willingly exposing themselves to loud noises, though, and amplified music is one of the major causes of noise-induced hearing loss. It is probably not an exaggeration to say that many twenty-year-olds who listen to rock music have hearing equivalent to that of a person who is fifty years old. The Walsh-Healey Act allows exposure to 110 dB for no longer than thirty minutes per day, but rock music fans often expose themselves to louder noises for much longer periods. Once the receptor cells for hearing are destroyed, they cannot be replaced. The hearing losses produced by noise are permanent.

## Keeping Your Balance

The inner ear contains the receptors for another sensory system besides audition: the **vestibular system.** *The main functions of this system are to provide information about head orientation and movement, which is useful in maintaining upright posture and in controlling eye movements.* The system is not well known because the sensations arising from it rarely reach the level of consciousness, although they do appear to cause motion sickness in some circumstances. The astronauts have become painfully aware of this sensory system since they sometimes suffer from the disorder described in the Applied Psychology box: Space Motion Sickness.

The **semicircular canals** and the **vestibule** *are the two main components of the vestibular system* (figure 4.5). The canals are oriented in three different planes; when you rotate your head in one of the planes, such as by shaking your head "no," you cause movement in the fluid of the canal oriented in that direction. The fluid movement

stimulates the receptor cells located inside the canals. The sacs inside the vestibule have receptors that are embedded in a gelatinous mass. When the orientation of the head shifts, the mass shifts with it and stimulates the receptors.

▶ **GUIDED REVIEW** *Learning Objectives 5, 6, 7, and 8*

1. The auditory system transforms _____ in the environment into neural messages. Frequency of sound waves is measured in _____ and roughly equates to our sensation of _____.
2. The sense organ for hearing is the ear. Sound waves set the _____ into motion, and the vibrating membrane sets the bones of the middle ear into motion. These bones produce wavelike motion in the fluid in the _____.
3. The receptor cells for hearing are located on the _____ membrane. Movement of the membrane and of the fluid in the cochlea causes the receptor cells to release neurotransmitter, thereby changing the sound waves into neural messages.
4. Deafness is classified into two types: _____, in which sound waves do not reach the receptors, and _____, in which the abnormality is in the receptors or auditory nerve.
5. Hearing loss may be caused by genetic problems, prenatal infections, reactions to drugs, and noise pollution. Noise levels are measured in _____.
6. The _____ is another sensory system located in the inner ear that provides information about head orientation and movement, and helps to maintain upright posture and control eye movements.

*Answers*

*1. sound waves, Hertz, pitch 2. eardrum, cochlea 3. basilar 4. conduction deafness, nerve deafness 5. decibels 6. vestibular system*

## TOUCH, SMELL, AND TASTE

We receive what appear to be very vivid images of our world from our ears and eyes, filled with rich and precise

# CLOSE UP ON RESEARCH

## Body Awareness

The woman we described at the beginning of this chapter lost her sense of her own body because of an infection that damaged neural pathways in her spinal cord. She no longer was receiving messages from her muscles, tendons, and joints, telling her brain where they were or what they were doing. Without those messages, she could no longer feel her body and make the countless adjustments needed to gracefully and effortlessly move about. She learned to use her eyes and watch what she was doing, but they were always a very poor substitute for the real thing, normally provided by a sensory system we call proprioception. It is a hidden sense we take for granted, using it continually to adjust and monitor our body posture. Without it, Christina felt disembodied. Her body had become blind and deaf.

Receptors located throughout the body send information about their location, orientation, and movement to the parietal lobes of the brain. Experiments in monkeys have shown that neurons in the parietal lobes are responsive to different kinds of body posture and limb movements, reminding us of the way feature detectors work in the visual system. Some neurons respond only when a limb is moved in a particular direction, and they fire more rapidly when the limb is moved quickly. Others respond best when multiple joints are moved simultaneously, especially when the joints are in a single limb. For example, one neuron might show the fastest firing rates when the wrist and fingers of the same hand are flexed at the same time.

Knowing the location of a single foot is not much use if you are trying to walk, run, dance or traverse a balance beam. We must have a single, integrated picture of the entire body in space, of all the joint positions and movements relative to one another. Proprioception is not a favorite research topic in psychology, perhaps because vision and audition seem so much more relevant to human behavior; no one has yet learned very much about how information from these receptors combine to provide a coherent sense of body awareness. Yet this small corner of sensory psychology shows how much activity is going on "behind the scenes" in the brain to make life both possible and utterly enjoyable.

detail. But the images we receive from the other senses are more diffuse and vague. Our olfactory environment, for example, is hard to describe. Odors can be overwhelming but they can also drift into and out of consciousness. Psychologists know less about these other senses, perhaps because the stimuli are harder to control in a laboratory.

## The Skin Senses

The part of the skin you can feel on the outside of your body is only a fraction of your skin. The **epidermis,** *or outer layer of skin,* covers the **dermis,** *the inner layer of skin that contains most of the receptors for touch, temperature, and pain* (figure 4.8).

Skin contains an enormous variety of structures, and many of these are receptors. It would be convenient if touch, temperature, and pain information were each handled by a different receptor, but that is not the case. *One kind of receptor in the skin,* the **Pacinian corpuscle,** *seems to transform changes in mechanical pressure on the skin into neural information.* But the other receptors do not appear to be related to a single kind of sensation; they seem to respond to more than one kind of stimulation.

Information from the skin receptors is organized very logically by the nervous system. For instance, sensations from the right leg are kept separate from those coming from the left leg, and those are kept separate from information coming from the right arm. The brain receives the information according to where it comes from on the body and processes it in the parietal lobes. Even in the brain, the information from different parts of the body is kept together. As we saw in chapter 2, the amount of brain tissue devoted to processing sensations from a particular body area is related to the sensitivity of that area, not to its size. For example, the amount of parietal lobe tissue that processes information from the fingers is proportionately quite large compared to the amount devoted to processing information from the torso.

## The Special Sense of Pain

A young woman in Canada could take a bath in ice water or in water that was almost boiling. Electric shocks didn't bother her. Pinches, punches, burns, needles, and dental drills produced little response from her. For as long as she could remember, she had never felt any pain. If that sounds like a desirable state of affairs, read on.

As a child, she bit off the tip of her tongue; she also suffered third-degree burns on her legs when she knelt on a radiator to gaze out a window. She had severe problems

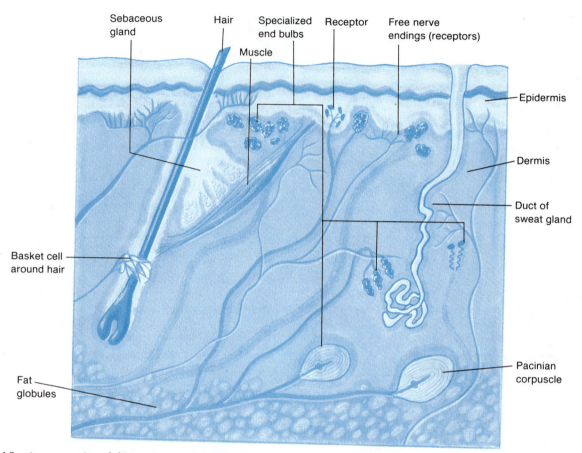

**Figure 4.8**    *A cross section of skin*

in her joints because she rarely shifted her weight from one foot to another. She only lived to the age of twenty-nine (Melzack & Wall, 1965).

Pain is the body's way of telling us something is wrong. It is an extremely important warning system that helps to prevent further damage. For example, when you feel pain in your joints, you shift your position; this action prevents you from stressing those joints to the point of permanent damage.

Although it is clear we need pain to survive, it is not clear what pain is. The sensation of pain depends in part on the nature of the stimulus. Damage to the tissues apparently activates pain receptors; but pain is not always proportional to the extent of tissue damage. The same stimulus can produce very different reactions in different people and also in the same person at different times.

*Theories of Pain*    Although we know we need pain to survive, understanding how we perceive pain has been a

remarkably difficult challenge. One early hypothesis, called the **gate control theory of pain,** *proposed that a gate exists in the spinal cord that controls whether information about painful stimulation will reach the brain* (Melzack & Wall, 1965). The intensity of pain messages carried by the very thin nerve fibers leading to the spinal cord would be compared to the messages about touch, carried by the larger nerve fibers. If the pain messages were stronger, the gate would open and the signals about pain would reach the brain. If they were weaker, the gate would remain closed. This notion helps explain why rubbing your leg reduces feelings of pain from an injured foot.

Different kinds of pain messages appear to take different paths to the brain (Melzack, 1990). When you burn your hand, for example, your sense of pain rapidly rises and then falls in intensity. After a few minutes the sharp pain is replaced by a dull throb that might continue for days. The sharp pain appears to follow lateral pathways up the spinal cord, but the throbbing variety follows more medial pathways and sends messages to parts of the brain involved in emotion.

Some recent research using PET scans has shown the brain areas that are activated during painful stimulation (Talbot et al., 1991). Men between the ages of twenty-five and thirty-one volunteered for an experiment in which researchers administered heat pain on their right forearms while brain activity was measured through the injection of radioactive isotopes. The areas of the brain that had the highest activity were on the left side (since the pain was on the right forearm), in the somatosensory area of the cortex, and in one of the brain areas involved in emotion. This study points to a significant role for emotion in our perception of pain.

An important contribution of the gate control theory was the proposal that the brain could send messages back down the spinal cord to control the gate. Although the existence of this gate is hypothetical, it is clear that pain signals are not simply traveling up a one-way street. Events in the brain, conscious or unconscious, can clearly control how much pain a person feels, as we shall see in the next section.

## Treatments for Pain

Three methods used to treat pain include morphine, electrical stimulation, and acupuncture. These are not the only treatments, but they are particularly interesting because they all seem to relieve pain by a common underlying mechanism.

*Morphine*    This extremely potent pain-relieving drug is the active ingredient in opium. Opium has been used for medicinal purposes since at least 300 B.C., and references to the drug date back thousands of years. In addition to its well-known use as a pain reliever, it has been employed to treat coughing, diarrhea, insomnia, snake bite, asthma, epilepsy, and even deafness. It does cause constipation, inhibit coughing, and promote sleepiness, but it probably is not useful for asthma, epilepsy, or deafness. The drug also produces tolerance and physical dependence.

Why morphine is so effective at relieving pain was a complete mystery until a series of startling scientific discoveries were made in the 1970s. Researchers reasoned that if morphine controls pain, it must be acting on the nervous system, probably the brain. They concluded that the brain must contain receptors for the drug. Experiments using radioactively labeled opiates proved that the brain

does indeed contain such receptors. When radioactively labeled opiates were injected, they became particularly concentrated in the pituitary gland, the hypothalamus, and the limbic system, apparently because these brain areas have specific receptor sites for opiate molecules. But the researchers did not know why the human brain would contain receptors for a plant.

Finding the answer did not take long. If the brain contained opiate receptors, it probably also contained its *own* opiatelike substance. Brain tissue from the areas where the receptors were found was tested, and a chemical that acted like morphine was discovered (Hughes, et al., 1975). Therefore, the human brain's opiate receptors are really not designed for the plant. They are designed to work with the brain's own pain relievers, endorphins. **Endorphins** *are a group of opiatelike substances released by the lower part of the brain.* The fact that the opium plant's molecules fit the receptors is just a curious coincidence.

Since these original discoveries, scientists have found that the brain contains not just one opiatelike compound but a "whole zoo" of them, as one pain researcher put it. Although the discoveries solved one mystery, they created many more. Endorphins are not just involved in pain; they are implicated in mental illness, memory, temperature regulation, and motivation, and they appear to be partly responsible for stress-induced analgesia. Indeed, they appear to be released during a wide range of experiences and to be related to many behavioral systems (Bolles & Fanselow, 1982; Koob & Bloom, 1983; Martinez, Weinberger, & Schultees, 1988).

Morphine is widely accepted as a treatment for pain but is used very sparingly because of the danger of addiction. Some scientists argue that morphine's addictive potential is strongest when it is used for sharp and intense pain, but very weak when it is used to treat the chronic and excruciating pain typical of surgery or cancer patients. The typical experiments that measure morphine's addictive potential have generally used sharp pain, but ones that use chronic kinds of pain find little tolerance or dependence potential (Melzack, 1990). As we learn more about pain and how morphine affects it, it may be possible to make important changes in treatment to provide greater relief to patients.

*Electrical Stimulation*    Another way to relieve pain is through electrical stimulation of the brain. Electrodes are implanted in specific brain sites, and a tiny current is passed through. Usually the patient controls the stimulation, and most find it remarkably effective in relieving pain. This procedure does have its drawbacks; it requires surgery, and if the patient uses it too much it seems to lose its effectiveness. Apparently it produces tolerance and dependence, as do many drugs (Hosobuchi, Adams, & Linchitz, 1977).

The brain sites most effectively stimulated are near the hypothalamus; these are the same ones that are most responsive to endorphins. In addition, drugs that interfere with the brain's response to endorphins also inhibit the pain-relieving effects of brain stimulation. These drugs probably "lock up" the receptor sites to which the endorphin molecules attach themselves. It is possible that brain stimulation works by activating the patient's own endorphin system (Liebeskind & Paul, 1977).

*Acupuncture*    One of the most controversial topics in American medicine is acupuncture, a system of pain control developed by the Chinese. Long thin needles are inserted into the skin at specific sites, and (in modern acupuncture) an electric current is passed through the needles for about twenty minutes (see figure 4.9). The sites vary, depending on the location of the pain, but the needles are usually inserted in a location quite distant from the injury. For example, a man undergoing surgery for stomach ulcers had acupuncture needles inserted in his ears (Dimond, 1971).

There appears to be no doubt that acupuncture works; it clearly relieves pain in many people. The acupuncture procedure is used for as many as ninety percent of the surgery patients in China. *Why* it works is still a mystery. The Chinese, relying on the oldest healing tradition in the world, believe the procedure improves the internal balance between yin and yang, the two opposing elements in the universe. Western scientists, though, prefer a more scientific explanation.

One hypothesis involves the gate control theory. The needles stimulate the larger touch fibers rather than the pain fibers, and when these signals reach the gate in the spinal cord, they cancel out the pain messages arriving by way of the thinner nerve fibers, closing the gate. Another hypothesis is that the needles somehow activate the patient's endorphins, and these substances relieve pain all over the body.

A third explanation of the potent effects of this ancient tradition is that it acts as a **placebo,** *an inert or innocuous (harmless) medication given to satisfy the patient.* (The familiar "sugar pill" is the classic example.) If the patient

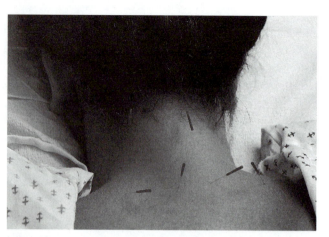

**Figure 4.9**    *A woman undergoing acupuncture*

believes the placebo will help, it often does. Scientists estimate that at least one-third of the patients suffering from pain will report relief if treated with a placebo. In a study comparing the effects of placebos to those of morphine, the innocuous placebo was able to relieve pain in dental patients about as well as 8 mg of morphine (Levine & Gordon, 1984). How placebos work is still unclear, but many scientists think they enable the patient to activate the brain's endorphin system.

Acupuncture may prove to be useful in studying placebo effects. In China, the procedure is being used in a culture in which everyone believes in its usefulness. Even if the placebo effect plays a substantial role in acupuncture, the procedure might also affect the patient's perception of pain in other ways as well, such as through endorphin release.

## Smell and Taste: The Chemical Senses

**Olfaction,** *or the sense of smell,* and **gustation,** *the sense of taste,* are usually grouped together as the chemical senses because they respond to a physical stimulus rather than a light wave, sound wave, or pressure.

The receptors for smell (figure 4.10) and taste (figure 4.11) are able to transform information about a molecule, either in the air or in a liquid, into neural messages. Most scientists agree that the tiny hairlike projections of the receptors have sites that can interact with molecules. Presumably, the shape of the molecule affects *how* it interacts with the receptor, and it perhaps affects to which receptors it adheres.

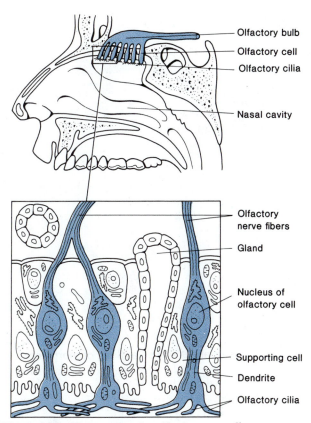

Olfactory bulb
Olfactory cell
Olfactory cilia
Nasal cavity
Olfactory nerve fibers
Gland
Nucleus of olfactory cell
Supporting cell
Dendrite
Olfactory cilia

**Figure 4.10**    *The receptors for olfaction, or smell*

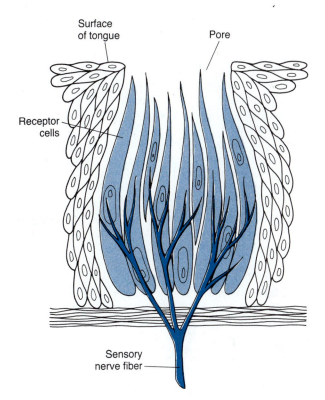

Surface of tongue
Pore
Receptor cells
Sensory nerve fiber

**Figure 4.11**    *The receptors for gustation, or taste*

Tastes are generally divided into four basic categories: salty, sweet, bitter, and sour. Odors are harder to classify and we tend to use quite a number of adjectives for them, such as musky, floral, or minty. Although some studies have found that receptors on the tongue or in the nose are responsive to only a particular category of chemicals, the specializations are far from perfect. The same receptors respond to several different tastes or smells, although with different firing patterns (Pfaffman, 1955; Pfaff, 1985).

If particular receptors don't signal the presence of a particular smell or taste, how do we know what the chemical is? Some fascinating studies on cats suggest that the brain uses patterns of collective activity in millions of neurons to identify particular substances in the chemical senses (Freeman, 1991). In these studies, sixty electrodes were used to record EEG activity all over the olfactory bulbs while the cat sniffed various odors. Each time the cat inhaled, bursts of activity were triggered everywhere in the bulb but the amplitude of the bursts varied in different locations depending on the odorant. It was possible to draw a kind of topographic contour map for each odor that

showed the spatial EEG patterns over the bulb. This shows that perception of a particular odor is related to the pattern of activity across the whole olfactory bulb rather than to the activation of a particular class of receptors. It was especially interesting that the topographic map for a particular odor was stable—unless the animal learned something new about the odor. Again, we see that environmental events can modify how our sensory systems work.

*The Importance of the Chemical Senses*    It is easy to see how humans rely on their senses of sight, hearing, or touch. But why do we need smell or taste? What do they have to do with our survival?

The answer to that question is better understood if we look at smell and taste from an evolutionary perspective, comparing our abilities and preferences with those of other animals. The chemical senses are crucial in the choice of foods and in communication.

The sense of taste and taste preferences of a species are closely connected to the species' eating habits. For example, humans can taste, and usually prefer, sweet foods. This is not accidental; it is because we have relied

# EXPLORING HUMAN DIVERSITY

## The Worst Smell in the World

Western travelers to Asia would probably agree that it is the odor of the big, ugly durian fruit which grows throughout Southeast Asia. Described most graphically by an English teacher as "the smell of someone eating onions in a public lavatory," the durian is banned on the Malaysian railroads, Singapore Airlines, and many other organizations concerned about the effects the fruit has on the quality of the environment their customers must share. Yet millions of people perceive the durian's aroma as enticing.

"The worst smell in the world" has a strong cultural dimension; there is no agreement among the world's noses on what it is, and no universal yardstick we can use to measure. Many Asians, for example, would nominate certain dairy products popular in the West, particularly the stronger smelling cheeses, as truly disgusting. A derogatory slang term for Westerners in Japan is "butter eater."

Diane Ackerman in *A Natural History of the Senses* describes an English custom of the Elizabethan Age which would repel modern Britons and many others. This was the exchange of love apples in which lovers would place small, peeled apples in their armpits and when the apples had absorbed their sweat give them as erotic gifts.

The best smell in the world is equally debatable with culture again playing a key role in how smells are perceived. In something as mundane as cleaning agents, the world's markets have quite different tastes, demonstrated by sales figures. French people prefer flowery scents while Germans go for pine. Americans, North and South, seem to prefer stronger scents in their soaps and cleaners with Venezuelans coming out on top. Top selling brands contain ten times the pine scent common in the United States. The Japanese prefer a much more delicate scent. Europeans complain that North Americans smell like soap.

The perfume industry derives only twenty percent of its income from perfumes. The lion's share comes from such items as new car spray, cake-baking aromas (used by real estate agents to make a house on the market seem more like a home), and numerous other scents.

---

heavily on ripe fruits for food during our evolution. It was also important to avoid rotten fruits, so we developed a dislike for and an ability to detect sour and bitter flavors. The flavors themselves are not in the foods. They exist on our tongues and in our brains, and they have evolved differently in other animals. Animals that rely on rotten fruit (e.g., insects) probably find them to be quite sweet. And the cat does not prefer the same foods we do. It does not eat fruits, has never relied on them, and has consequently not developed the same sense of "sweet." Instead, it prefers salty tastes like those of fresh meat.

Airborne odors also play an important role in communication between animals. Much research has gone into learning more about how airborne odors influence insect behavior; this knowledge is very useful in controlling infestations in agriculture.

Odors are also known to be important in communication between mammals. A mouse gets much biographical data about another mouse from a single sniff. It can tell whether the newcomer is male or female, whether it is a member of the group or a stranger, whether it is in heat (if it is female), whether it is a dominant or subordinate male, and whether it is frightened. **Pheromones** *are the odors that mice and other animals use in communication* (Whitten & Bronson, 1970). These pheromones can have

intriguing effects. Urine from male mice, for example, will accelerate the onset of puberty in young females, but urine from females will delay puberty (Drickamer, 1988). The urine from males can also influence the biology of a pregnant female. If a recently impregnated female smells the urine from a strange male, she will abort her fetus, come into heat again, and mate with the stranger. From the male stranger's point of view, the chemical is quite useful.

A pheromone appears to be the reason pigs are so enthusiastic about their search for truffles. The French have always used the animal to find the highly prized delicacy, a fungus that smells like a combination of musk, nuts, and ozone. Truffles contain a substance also present in the testes of the boar, one that plays a role in the animal's mating behavior.

Whether odors are also used in human communication is not known, but our sense of smell is certainly refined. For example, human beings can tell two people apart by smell unless the two people are identical twins on the same diet (Wallace, 1977). There are also several studies that suggest that odors play a role in our sex lives. For instance, the substance in truffles that attracts the pig is also produced by the testes of men. Students at the University of Birmingham in England were shown pictures of normally dressed women and were asked to score the pictures for beauty. Some of the subjects had been exposed to the chemical during the viewing, and these subjects rated the pictures as more beautiful than did the other subjects (Kirk-Smith et al., 1978). Considering how much money we spend on perfumes, deodorants, scented candles, and other artificial stimulation for our chemical senses, it would not be too outlandish to suppose that odors play a much larger role in our lives than we suspect.

(a)

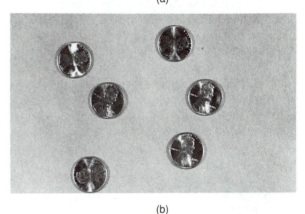

(b)

*Figure 4.12    Because of perspective, these coins seem to be different sizes*

▶ **GUIDED REVIEW**    *Learning Objectives 9, 10, and 11*

1. The skin senses are made up of a collection of overlapping senses that detect touch, temperature changes, and painful stimulation on the skin. The skin has an outer layer, or _____, and an inner layer, or _____.
2. Our experience of pain is determined not only by the actual stimulation but also by personality and emotional and cultural factors. Stress reduces sensitivity to pain, a phenomenon called _____.
3. The _____ of pain predicts the existence of a "gate" in the spinal cord that controls whether information about pain reaches the brain. The gate is affected by the relative amount of stimulation from large and small fibers and by messages coming from the brain.
4. Three treatments for pain include morphine, electrical stimulation of the brain, and acupuncture. The effectiveness of all three treatments may be related to the brain's own opiatelike substances, called _____. Placebos may also be effective in relieving pain in some cases for the same reason.
5. The chemical senses, which include _____ (smell) and _____ (taste), can detect the presence of certain molecules in the air or on the tongue. The receptors in the nose and on the tongue probably have sites that interact with the molecules that produce taste or odor sensations.
6. The sense of taste is important in the choice of food. Different animals have different taste preferences depending on their eating habits. Smell is important for communication in mammals. Communication odors are called _____.

*Answers*
*1. epidermis, dermis 2. stress-induced analgesia 3. gate control theory 4. endorphins 5. olfaction, gustation 6. pheromones*

## PERCEPTION

With a basic knowledge of how the sensory systems operate, and some understanding of how the process of sensation merges and interacts with perceptual phenomena, we move on to explore the nature of perception. Perception of the environment is influenced by many things, some completely unrelated to the physical world.

An important ingredient that affects the way we perceive the world is our need to make order out of it. The physical world is an overwhelmingly complicated mixture of wavelengths, patterns, movements, sound waves, and airborne molecules. It is a barrage of stimulation that requires some sorting and organizing.

The importance of pattern and organization as perceptual principles was first recognized during the early twentieth century by the proponents of Gestalt psychology. The word "gestalt" means "pattern" or "form" in German; these scientists emphasized that perception involved more than the mere addition of the total number of sensations impinging on the sensory systems. In other words, the whole (perception) is more than the sum of its parts (sensations).

## General Principles of Perception

The image in figure 4.12a is extremely complicated. Because of the way our brains are organized and because of our experiences, we can look at such complex images and easily sort them out. We use several methods to accomplish this: (1) perceptual constancies, (2) figure-ground relationships, and (3) perceptual organizing principles.

*Perceptual Constancies*   Is the coin in the foreground much larger than the one in the background? Its image on your retina would tell you that it is, and a ruler would tell you the same thing. But your perception of the two coins tells you they are the same size, the same circular shape, and about the same color. (Check figure 4.12b to see the actual characteristics of the images.)

   **Perceptual constancy** refers to *the ability to perceive an object as constant, despite changes at the retina in size, color, or shape.* It probably develops from infancy as our experience with objects grows. Colin Turnbull, an anthropologist, described a case in which an African pygmy, who had lived in the forest all his life, had no chance to see objects at a long

distance. The pygmy had not developed some aspects of perceptual constancy of size.

> . . . Kenge looked over the plains and down to where a herd of about a hundred buffalo were grazing some miles away. He asked me what kind of insects they were, and I told him they were buffalo, twice as big as the forest buffalo known to him. He laughed loudly and told me not to tell such stupid stories.... We got into the car and drove down to where the animals were grazing. He watched them getting larger and larger, and though he was as courageous as any pygmy, he moved over and sat close to me and muttered that it was witchcraft.... Finally, when he realized that they were real buffalo he was no longer afraid, but what puzzled him was why they had been so small, and whether they really had been small and suddenly grown larger, or whether it had been some kind of trickery (Turnbull, 1961).

Perceptual constancy has been proposed as a possible explanation for an intriguing phenomenon called the Müller-Lyer illusion. In figure 4.13a, the vertical line on the right appears noticeably longer than the one on the left

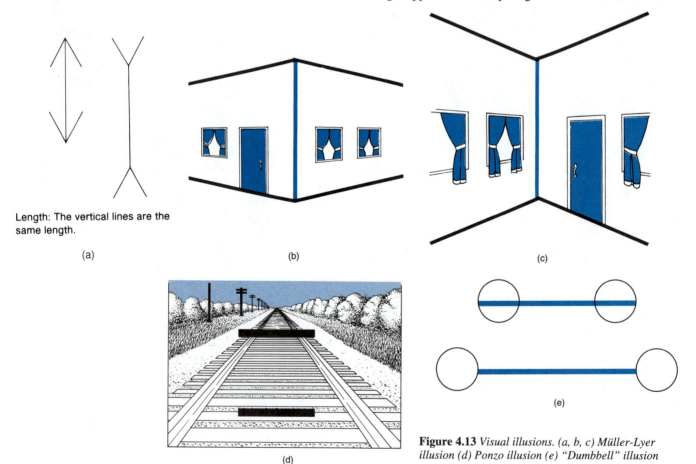

Length: The vertical lines are the same length.

(a)

(b)

(c)

(d)

(e)

**Figure 4.13** *Visual illusions. (a, b, c) Müller-Lyer illusion (d) Ponzo illusion (e) "Dumbbell" illusion*

although both are exactly the same length. Gregory (1966) explained this phenomenon on the basis of what he called "misapplied size constancy." He suggested that the "fins" on the ends of the lines make us see depth in the pictures; the left line looks like part of the outside corner of a building (figure 4.13b) and the right line looks like part of an inside corner of a room (figure 4.13c). Since an inside corner seems further away than an outside corner, we infer that the left line is closer. Since it produces the same-sized retinal image as the line on the right, it must be shorter. Gregory further suggested that it doesn't matter whether you consciously perceive distance and three-dimensional structures; your perceptual system takes them into account anyway.

a. Reversible figure-ground

b. Principle of similarity

c. Principle of proximity

d. Principle of closure

e. Principle of good continuation

**Figure 4.15** *The organizing principles of perception*

The notion of "misapplied size constancy" might also be used to explain the Ponzo illusion in figure 4.13d, which also contains some suggestion of depth and distance. But many investigators point out that it does not explain the illusion in figure 4.13e, called the "dumbbell illusion." Here, there are no obvious perspective or distance cues, but the line on the bottom still appears to be longer than the one on the top. Although explanations can be suggested for some illusions, many are still puzzles given our current understanding of perception.

*Figure-Ground Relationships*    Another general principle of visual perception is that we tend to perceive some images as figures and others as grounds. Figures usually have certain properties that grounds do not. Figures are

**Figure 4.14** *Reversible figure-ground illusion*

closer, more like "things," more easily remembered, and seem to have a shape. If they are moving, their parts are moving together relative to the background. In contrast, grounds are relatively formless, further away, and stationary. Figures stand out in our perception; this may be due to the way our visual system is organized. We mentioned earlier that our visual systems are good at detecting contrast, a feature that is important in picking out a figure against a ground.

Figures 4.14 and 4.15a show visual illusions with reversible figures and grounds. At first, most people perceive the black shapes as the figures and the white shapes as the formless background, probably because the black shapes have more contour and are more "thing" like. But keep looking at them and the figure-ground relationships will shift in a startling way. The suddenness of the figure-ground shift demonstrates how dependent we are on our principles of perception to help us interpret the external world. It is difficult to see these figures *without* the perceptual anchor of a figure-ground relationship, so there is usually a very sharp switch from one view to the other.

*Organizing Principles*    We bring order to the complex visual patterns striking the retina by using the organizing principles shown in figure 4.15.

Using the **principle of similarity,** *we perceive images that resemble one another as being part of a group, even though they may be apart.* On a data entry terminal, for example, the system designer might design the screen so that related items are in the same color. Computer screens at airports take advantage of the principle of similarity. If a user pressed a key for restaurants, all the restaurants would be highlighted in red on a graphic map of the airport terminal. Because of the principle of similarity, you see figure 4.15b as columns of similar figures, rather than as rows of alternating circles and squares.

The **principle of proximity** *predicts that we will perceive objects that are close together as a group.* People describe figure 4.15c as three columns of three circles each. Interior designers suggest grouping pictures on a wall or knick-knacks in a cabinet rather than spacing them evenly across the space allowed. This approach takes advantage of the principle of proximity.

Another important means of organizing the visual world is the **principle of closure.** *The brain tends to fill in the gaps in an incomplete picture in order to perceive a complete form.* This is especially true if it is a familiar shape, such as the face in figure 4.15d. You can see how familiarity with different shapes might bias a person's perception of incomplete forms.

The last set of drawings in figure 4.15e demonstrates the **principle of good continuation.** *Images that appear to follow in the same direction will be perceived as part of the same figure.* The outline of the baby is easily perceived even though the vertical bars break up the image, because the lines in the outline follow in the same direction. The image behind the bars need not be a familiar one. If the shape was an irregular rock, we would still perceive the rock as an image behind bars because the outline of the rock would appear to follow in the same direction.

Another organizational scheme has to do with movement. If objects move together in the visual scene, we tend to see them as a group. In the absence of any other organizing features, synchronous motion will create the perception of a group. For example, a computer screen filled with evenly placed dots will not easily generate any groupings. But as soon as some of the dots begin to move synchronously, they will immediately appear as a group regardless of where they are on the screen, or how close together.

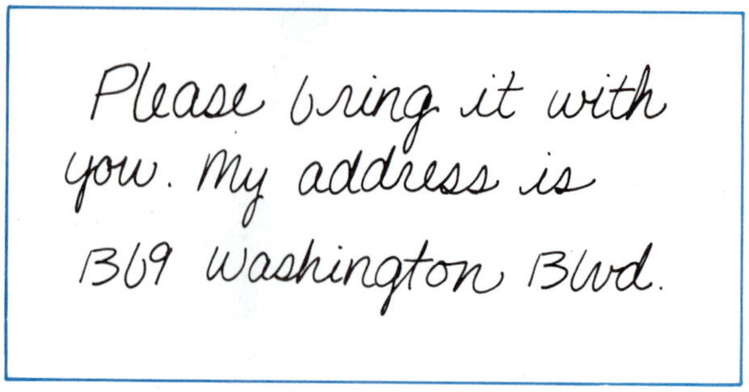

**Figure 4.16**   *Perceptual set*

## Individual Factors in Perception

The process of perception is similar in all of us, but that does not mean we all see the same event in exactly the same way. The images on the retina are modified, reorganized, distorted, ignored, and given meaning at all levels of processing. Perception is a process in which we draw inferences about the cues in the environment and even when the stimulus is the same the inferences we draw from them may be rather different. Some factors that can affect perception include previous experience, personality and interests, prejudice and culture.

*Previous Experience*    Read the message in figure 4.16. You probably had no problem reading the 13, the B (in Blvd.), the b in bring, or the 6 in 1369 despite the fact that the image on your retina was identical in both cases. The words that preceded the ambiguous images established a context and created a **perceptual set** *or expectation about what you would see.* This set, made up of your recent experience, influenced how you perceived the image. Another example of seeing what you expect to see is the fact that you probably did not notice the typographical error in the previous sentence.

Some intriguing studies have been done to learn how previous experience and expectations influence perceptions of pain (Rachman & Arntz, 1991). Generally, people tend to overpredict pain and then make adjustments later according to how painful the experience actually was. But the ones who underpredict, dismissing the oncoming surgery or dental procedure as trivial, report the actual pain as much more unpleasant than those who either correctly or overpredicted it in the first place. After an underprediction, the person will magnify pending painful

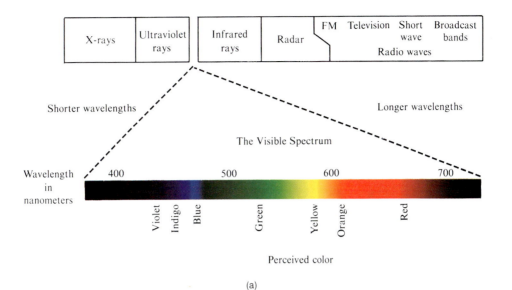

| X-rays | Ultraviolet rays | | Infrared rays | Radar | FM | Television | Short wave | Broadcast bands |
| --- | --- | --- | --- | --- | --- | --- | --- | --- |
| | | | | | | Radio waves | | |

Shorter wavelengths

Longer wavelengths

The Visible Spectrum

Wavelength in nanometers

400    500    600    700

Violet  Indigo  Blue    Green    Yellow  Orange    Red

Perceived color

(a)

(b)

(c)

(d)

(e)

**Plate 5**   *(a) The electromagnetic spectrum and visible light. Visible light is a narrow band in the electromagnetic spectrum. Visible light's wavelengths range from 400 to 700 nanometers; X rays are much shorter and radio waves are much longer. (b) Ultraviolet rays. Most ultraviolet rays are absorbed by the ozone in the earth's upper atmosphere. The small fraction of ultraviolet rays that reaches the earth is the ingredient in sunlight that tans the skin and can cause skin cancer. (c) Infrared rays. The electromagnetic radiation just beyond red in the spectrum is felt as heat by receptors in the skin. (d) Additive color mixtures occur when lights are mixed. For example, when red and green lights are combined, they yield yellow. The three colors together give white. (e) Subtractive color mixtures occur when pigments are mixed or light is shown through colored filters placed over one another. Most of the time blue-green and yellow mixed together will give green, and complementary colors produce black.*

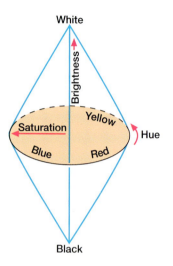

**Plate 6.A** *A color solid. The qualities of hue, brightness, and saturation can be represented three-dimensionally. Hue is represented by points along the circumference of the color solid; brightness is represented by points on the vertical axis; and saturation is represented by points along the horizontal axis.*

**Plate 6.B** *The eye's blind spot. There is a normal blind spot in your eye, a small area where the optic nerve leads to the brain. To find your blind spot, hold this book at arm's length, cover your left eye, and stare at the red pepper with your right eye. Move the book slowly toward you until the yellow pepper disappears. To find the blind spot in your left eye, cover your right eye, concentrate on the yellow pepper, and adjust the distance of the book until the red pepper disappears.*

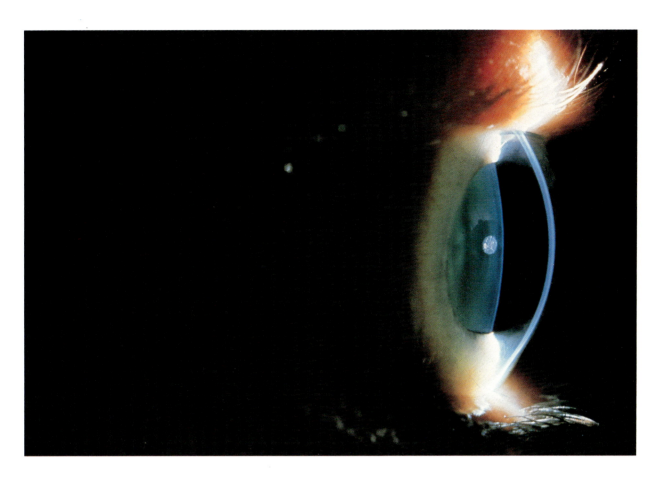

**Plate 7.A** *The iris, the pupil, and the cornea can be seen in this photograph.*

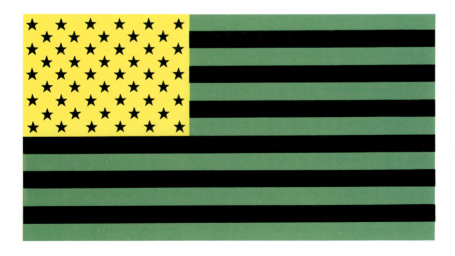

**Plate 7.B** *Negative afterimage. If you stare at the center of the flag for approximately thirty seconds and then look at a white wall or piece of paper, you should see a negative afterimage in colors opposite those in the flag.*

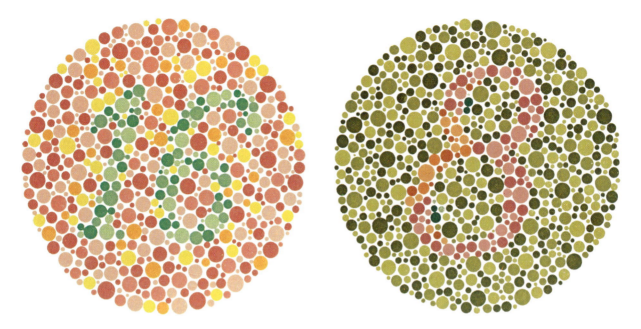

**Plate 8.A** *Examples of stimuli used to test for color blindness. In the left circle, people with normal vision see the number sixteen, but people with red-green color blindness do not. In the right circle, people with normal vision detect the number eight, but those with red-green color blindness see the number three or none. A complete color blindness assessment involves the use of fifteen stimuli.*

The above has been reproduced from *Ishihara's Tests for Colour Blindness* published by KANEHARA & CO., LTD., Tokyo, Japan, but the tests for color blindness cannot be conducted with this material. For accurate testing, the original plates should be used. Reprinted by permission.

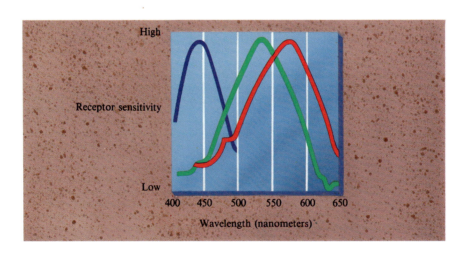

**Plate 8.B** *Relative sensitivity of the cones.   The three kinds of cones (blue, green, and red) each respond to a wide range of wavelengths of light. But each is maximally sensitive to particular wavelengths. The blue cones are maximally sensitive to short wavelengths, the green cones to medium wavelengths, and the red cones to long wavelengths. According to the trichromatic theory, the perceived color of a light depends on the relative amount of activity in each of the three kinds of cones.*

**Figure 4.17**   *The perception of a scene depends partly on the interests of the perceiver. A politician might perceive the messages on the signs; a pickpocket might focus on the location of accessible wallets*

experiences and be very reluctant to adjust even when they are proven wrong. Although exaggerated and routine overprediction is not very useful since it makes people fearful, underprediction may be equally troublesome. It may be adaptive to err on the side of caution by slightly overpredicting pain; the body can prepare for the experience, perhaps by triggering endorphin release. We've noticed that many physicians avoid the word "pain" and use "discomfort" instead to try to alter people's perceptions of pain. These studies suggest that the strategy may backfire.

Previous experience seems to affect perception even when the person is not aware of the previous experience

(Merikle, 1992). Perception without awareness is a controversial subject in psychology because most of the studies rely on reports from the subjects about awareness rather than objective data. For example, a person might be shown a target word such as "glass" so quickly they say they didn't see what it was. But when they are later asked to choose the target word from a group that doesn't contain the target, they tend to pick one that is similar in meaning, such as "cup." Apparently they perceived something, even though they say they weren't aware of it. Some psychologists argue that this kind of nonconscious acquisition of information plays a large role in our behavior (Lewicki, Hill, & Czyzewska, 1992).

*Personality and Interests*    The personality and interests of the individual perceiver are other factors that can influence the focus of a person's attention. One person in figure 4.17 would probably pay attention to the signs. A pickpocket might attend to where the wallets are.

In one attempt to link perception to personality traits, people were classified as extroverts or introverts based on their answers to a questionnaire (Eysenck, 1967). Several experiments found that the outgoing and sociable extroverts tended to have less sensitive sensory systems than did the more withdrawn introverts. For example, one study found that introverts have lower average thresholds for vision (Siddle, Morrish, White, & Mangen, 1969), hearing (Stelmack & Campbell, 1974), and touch (Coles, Gale, & Kline, 1971). It is possible that extroverts have a neural system that is slower to respond and more weakly aroused. These studies were particularly interesting because the extroverts were more likely to say they saw a stimulus when they were not sure. The introverts just preferred to say they saw the stimulus only when they were certain.

Interests also affect how we perceive the world around us. The dieter, for example, sees food in any ambiguous shape. The famous inkblot tests that we'll discuss again later in this text rely on the notion that people project their own interests or desires into their perception of an ambiguous picture.

*Culture*    The pygmy's experience with the buffalo is a good example of how culture can influence the way a person perceives. Other examples come from research on the cultural factors that influence susceptibility to optical illusions (Segall et al., 1990). The underlying hypothesis to this kind of research is that people learn how to draw inferences from visual cues based on their experience with their own environment. If their environments are different, the inferences people draw might be different as well.

When people are misled by an optical illusion, they are essentially making an inference that works well in their environment most of the time, but which misleads in a two-dimensional drawing.

For example, most people in industrialized countries grow up in a "carpentered world," exposed to squares, boxes, rectangles, doors, and right angles from the moment of birth. Could this exposure make us more susceptible to visual illusions that trick us by leading us to perceive depth when none exists? One explanation for the Müller-Lyer illusion is that we see inside and outside corners, and the depth cues influence our judgment of size. But if we grew up in a culture with few carpentered angles, would we be so susceptible to this illusion?

When psychologists tested Zulus, who live in rounded huts and have less experience with carpentered right angles, they found that they were indeed less susceptible to certain kinds of visual illusions compared to Europeans (Segall, Campbell, & Herskovitz, 1966). An even more convincing study compared the susceptibility of black and white children from Illinois to the susceptibility of children in Zambia. Some of the Zambian children were from rural areas and others were from the city. The American children were most susceptible to the illusions, and there was no difference between black and white children. In Zambia, the rural children with little schooling were the least susceptible (Stewart, 1973), a finding that fits well with the hypothesis that we become more susceptible to these illusions as our experience with a carpentered world grows.

The perception of pain is also subject to cultural influences, roles, and expectations. On a hiking trip in the Himalayas, the responses of the Nepalese porters to electric shocks was compared to the responses of the Western hikers (Clark & Clark, 1980). The abilities of the Nepalese and the Westerners to detect the low-current shocks did not differ, but it took much higher voltage levels for the Nepalese to describe the shocks as "faint pain" or "very painful." The Nepalese interpreted the sensations differently, perhaps because they lived under harsher conditions.

## Perception and Attention

The process of perception is very much affected by **attention,** *a phenomenon that involves filtering of incoming stimuli.* Human beings do not pay attention to everything in their environments; nor do they attend to all the stimuli impinging on their sense organs. Rather than become overwhelmed by the enormous complexity of the physical world, we attend to some stimuli and do not notice others. William James (1894) recognized the importance of attention very early: "A thing may be presented to a man a hundred times, but if he persistently fails to notice it, it cannot be said to enter his experience."

*Selective Attention*    Human beings have a great deal of control over which stimuli they attend to and which they do not. The process of attention is a selective one. At a cocktail party, a person might pay strict attention to a conversation with the boss while "tuning out" nearby chatter. Yet even though the person's attention is given to a certain category of incoming information he or she can still monitor other events, such as the arrival of new refreshments at the bar, the entrance of new guests, or the music on the stereo. The person's attention can also shift very suddenly because of this monitoring process. For example, if another guest mentions the person's name, the person's attention is likely to shift from the current conversation to the dialogue in which his or her name was mentioned.

Studies of attention have found that people have a limited ability to process incoming information. If they are not attending to it, they usually cannot recall very much of it. In an experimental technique called **shadowing,** *subjects listen to one set of stimuli through one sensory channel and another set of stimuli through a different channel. They try to repeat aloud, or shadow, the messages coming in through one of the two channels* (Cherry, 1953). Typically, they recall very little or nothing of the message coming in through the other channel, even if the same stimuli are repeated over and over to the unattended sensory channel. For example, subjects who shadow a set of words entering one ear, while another set is presented dichotically to the other ear, usually cannot recall anything from the unattended list of words (Moray, 1959).

It might seem as though the person became functionally deaf in one ear. But apparently the words are heard; they just do not remain very long in the person's memory. If the experimenter interrupts the shadowing task and quickly asks the subject to recall as many words as possible from the unattended channel, the person can often remember the last five or six words (Glucksberg & Cowen, 1970; Norman, 1969).

The fact that a person can choose what to attend to, what to perceive, and how to filter incoming sensory information, leads to the inevitable conclusion that perception is not at all mechanical. In addition to the individual factors affecting perception that we discussed earlier, there are also cognitive factors. Look at the Necker cube in figure 4.18. Your perception of the box's orientation may change suddenly and spontaneously, but if you practice with it you will be able to control the switch. Your cognitive processes can alter the way you perceive that image just as they determine what you will attend to.

An intriguing theory that attempts to bring together all the elements involved in perception, from the feature detectors in the visual cortex to the role of cognition in perception, and that fits in with our growing interest in parallel processing in the brain, is called **observer theory** (Bennett et al., 1989; Banks & Krajicek, 1991). *It proposes that perception is performed by "observers" whose job is to make inferences.* The observer defines the relationship between a certain kind of input, say a straight line in the visual field, and a particular perceptual conclusion that it will pass along to other observers. The observers operate on different perceptual tasks, such as color perception or form perception, and also at different levels of analysis. For example, a primitive observer might be one that analyzes a single edge in the visual field.

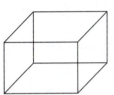

**Figure 4.18**   *Necker cube*

Observer theory offers a way to understand how you can switch orientations in the Necker cube. Observers would not be linked in a chain but would probably form complex networks; sometimes higher level observers could provide input to lower level ones. When you switch the cube, your higher level observers would be providing some input to lower level ones that detect lines, edges, and depth cues, and would bias their output.

Observer theory is beginning to attract attention because it may provide a conceptual link between the findings about subsystems in the brain that are known to process particular perceptual features, and the processes that affect perception at higher levels, such as cognition, personality, or culture. We can think of them all as observers at different levels of the process.

▶ **GUIDED REVIEW** *Learning Objectives 12, 13, and 14*

1. The process of perception is influenced by general principles that operate in everyone and by individual factors. It is closely related to the process of _____, in which incoming stimuli are filtered.
2. _____ refers to the tendency to perceive objects as constant, despite changes on the retina in size, shape, or color. Some images are perceived as figures, usually those that are closer and have shape.
3. Several organizing principles predict how we will sort images into groups or patterns. The _____ states that objects that are closer together will be seen as part of a group.
4. Previous experience affects perception by establishing a _____. The context of a particular image creates a set of expectations and therefore influences the way we perceive the image.
5. The _____ proposes that perception is accomplished by observers whose job is to make inferences that relate sensory input to perceptual conclusions, and pass their information on to other observers.

*Answers*

1. attention 2. Perceptual constancy 3. principle of proximity 4. perceptual set 5. observer theory

# EXTRASENSORY PERCEPTION

What I'm looking at is a little boat jetty or little boat dock along the bay. It is in a direction about like that from here. Yeah, I see the little boats, some motor launches, some little sailing ships, sails all furled, some with the masts stepped and others are up. Little jetty or little dock there.... Funny thing— this flashed in kinda looks like a Chinese or Japanese pagoda effect....

Pat Price was describing the Redwood City Marina. He had never been to the marina, and he was not there when he described it, although an experimenter was. Price was in a laboratory at the Stanford Research Institute, miles away, participating in an experiment on remote viewing.

## What is ESP?

**Extrasensory perception (ESP)** *is perception that does not require stimulation of a sense organ.* Researchers usually break it down into three main categories:

1. **telepathy**—*the transfer of one person's thoughts to another, as in remote viewing;*
2. **clairvoyance**—*the ability to perceive objects or events not present or affecting the person's senses; and*
3. **precognition**—*the ability to perceive future events.*

# EXPLORING HUMAN DIVERSITY

## The Rise of Antiscience

One of the fallouts from the breakup of the Soviet Union and the decline of communism appears to be a startling rise in mysticism, belief in the occult, and reports of paranormal phenomena. Faith healers are appearing on Russian television, UFO sightings are growing, and people are seeking the advice of astrologers in record numbers. Reports of these phenomena are not confined to the tabloids, but appear in reputable and sometimes scholarly publications and broadcasts. The official news agency Tass carried a report of a ten-year-old from Soviet Georgia who can attract metal objects. The back cover of a scholarly journal published by the Academy of Sciences of the former U.S.S.R. carries a strange message, titled "Voice from Space." It reads, "I am not an executor of fate. . . . I come from nowhere and there is nowhere I can go. I am beyond time and space . . . but I am always, at all times, with you as a small particle of the great thinking matter."

The effects of dramatic cultural and historical events appear to be a major cause for these accelerating antiscientific trends. The former Soviet Union is facing enormous challenges following its breakup. The economy is in dreadful condition, and people feel little security for their future. The social system they believed in and worked under for seventy years has crumbled and failed. This kind of social unrest and chaos creates the kind of environment in which belief in paranormal phenomena flourishes. Russian intellectuals are alarmed by these trends, concerned that these irrational beliefs are spreading a distrust for science and its methods.

Unlike the people of the Soviet Union, Americans are not experiencing a surge in antiscientific sentiment. Nevertheless, according to a survey conducted by the Gallup organization, belief in supernatural and paranormal phenomena is remarkably high. One in four people said they believe in ghosts, and one in six say they have communicated with the dead. Twenty-five percent say they have experienced telepathic contact and ten percent said they have been in the presence of a ghost. About half of the sample said they believe in extrasensory perception.

Our emphasis on science and its methods in this textbook has been constant, but it is important to recognize that science does not rule out the existence of various phenomena, even ones that current thinking would consider bizarre or ridiculous. It merely takes the Missourians' point of view: "Show me."

---

Another phenomenon usually grouped with ESP is **psychokinesis,** *the ability to move objects without touching them in any way.* The field of psychology called parapsychology investigates ESP and psychokinesis using the scientific method.

## Does ESP Exist?

Although a great many people in the world believe that extrasensory perception exists, and many claim to have had their own psychic experiences, the subject is tremendously controversial in scientific circles. Most scientists are skeptical, partly because ESP experiences usually do not take place in a laboratory. They are usually the anecdotal reports of people who are involved in some major life crisis; very often the psychic experience is about a close family member.

For example, the sinking of the ocean liner *Titanic* in 1912 elicited many reports of psychic experiences. On the night of the disaster, a woman in New York had a dream in which she saw her mother in a small boat tossing about on the waves. The woman did not even know her mother was on the ill-fated ship until she saw her mother's name on the passenger list in the newspaper. The mother survived and later confirmed the accuracy of her daughter's dream (Pratt, 1973).

Stories like this one are not difficult to find. They are anecdotes that are very susceptible to the rules of chance. For instance, Titanic passengers' relatives numbered in hundreds of thousands and on any particular night a few of them would be dreaming of oceans, boats, or swimming. Those that had such a dream on the fateful night, however, might think they had a psychic experience; it may only have been coincidence. Anecdotes do not satisfy the scientist's strict criteria for demonstrating the existence of a phenomenon. Repeatable and carefully controlled experiments, conducted under the critical eyes of unbiased observers, are required.

*Experiments in Parapsychology*    Research in parapsychology has been going on for more than fifty years in this country. Courses in the subject are offered at major universities, doctorate degrees are awarded, and the United States government provides money for research. There is a division of parapsychology in the American Psychological Association and also in the American Association for the Advancement of Science. One of the most convincing of the hundreds of experiments that have been conducted is the study on "remote viewing," with ex-police commissioner Pat Price.

Price was invited to participate as a subject because he told the experimenters he used parapsychology all the time in his everyday life. During an experiment, Price remained in the laboratory with one experimenter, while another went to a locked safe, picked up a randomly selected set of "traveling orders" that told him where to go, and then followed the orders. After the experimenter had time to reach the site, Price, still in the lab, began to describe the "view" into a tape recorder (Targ & Puthoff, 1977).

This procedure was used nine times, and the traveling experimenter went to an arts-and-crafts plaza, a swimming pool, a nature preserve, and other visually distinct places. A judge compared the taped descriptions to the actual sites and was able to match seven to the correct locations. This is a remarkable number of "hits," if Price were merely guessing, the judges may have matched only one site to the taped description.

## Skepticism

The experiments appeared to be well controlled, and there did not seem to be any way for the subject to cheat. However, a short time after the results were published, two scientists found a very significant flaw (Marks & Kammann, 1978). Pat's taped descriptions contained important cues that could reveal to the judges which site was being described. For example, the experimenter with Price said, "Nothing like having three successes behind you." This statement, and others like it, gave away the *order* in which Price was describing the sites. Since the judge already knew the order in which the travelers visited the sites, the job of matching the site to the description became much easier. One of the scientists criticizing the study was able to match the five sites to five taped descriptions without even visiting the sites! When those little cues were deleted from the transcript, judges could not match the sites to the descriptions.

Flaws like this one, and even outright trickery, have been found in many supposedly "conclusive" experiments on ESP (Hansel, 1980). Most scientists question whether parapsychologists have come up with even a single reliable result, one that can withstand rigorous experimental conditions and that can be repeated. People on both sides of the controversy have strong feelings. Parapsychologists compare themselves to stoned prophets and burned witches, blaming the priggishness of contemporary science for their lack of acceptance. On the other hand, many scientists feel they have "bent over backwards" in giving parapsychologists a chance to demonstrate their claims.

We have much to learn about how human beings sense and perceive their environment. The results of many experiments remain unexplained, and the history of science is filled with examples of how yesterday's impossibility became today's fact. Certainly, no scientists want to look ridiculous one hundred years from now because they scoffed at parapsychology. Yet as each new and "incontrovertible" finding in the field is disputed—invalidated as outright trickery or flawed by sloppy experimental procedures—one begins to wonder whether ESP exists or whether we simply want it to exist. The only answer we have right now is that we just don't know.

▶ **GUIDED REVIEW** *Learning Objectives 15 and 16*

1. Three types of extrasensory perception, or ESP, are _____, _____, and _____. _____, which refers to the ability to move objects without touching them, is also usually grouped with ESP. The scientific investigation of ESP is called _____.

2. Recent experimental results suggesting that some form of ESP exists includes studies demonstrating _____ _____, a type of telepathy. The subject remains in the laboratory and describes a scene, perhaps miles away, visited by an experimenter. Most experimental demonstrations of ESP phenomena, including remote viewing, have been shown to involve trickery or to have serious experimental flaws. This would suggest that either ESP does not exist or that it is a very elusive phenomenon that is extremely difficult to demonstrate under laboratory conditions.

*Answers*

1. *telepathy, clairvoyance, precognition, Psychokinesis, parapsychology* 2. *remote viewing*

# SUMMARY

I. The visual system is the means by which we receive information about the patterns of light in the environment. (p. 102)

    A. All sensory systems share many characteristics, including their involvement in the tasks of sensation and perception, their general structures, and their ability to transduce physical energy to neural signals. (p. 102)

        1. The sensitivity of sensory systems can be described by their absolute thresholds or by their j.n.d. (pp. 102–103)

    B. Light is the environmental stimulus for the visual system. (p. 103)

    C. The eye is the sense organ for vision, and it consists of several specialized structures, such as the cornea, the iris, the lens, and the retina. (p. 104)

        1. The receptors for vision are located in the retina. (p. 104)

        2. The retina contains two types of receptors: rods and cones. Rods are specialized for vision in low-light intensities, and cones process color and pattern information. (p. 105)

    D. The transduction process involves the breakdown of photopigment in the presence of light. This causes electrical disturbances in the membrane of the receptors. (pp. 105–106)

        1. The process of dark adaptation involves the recovery of the photopigment molecules. (p. 106)

    E. Seeing patterns in the visual field requires the activity of neurons all along the visual pathway to the brain. (p. 106)

        1. The visual system organizes patterns in the visual field using receptive fields. (p. 106)

        2. Single-cell recordings in the cat visual cortex led to the discovery of feature detectors, cells that respond only to certain stimuli in their receptive fields. (p. 107)

    F. Two theories have been proposed to explain how humans process color information. (p. 107)

        1. The trichromatic theory proposes the existence of three kinds of cells with sensitivities to different ranges of wavelengths. (p. 107)

        2. The opponent process theory suggests that individual cells are sensitive to pairs of colors and that they respond to each member of the pair by increasing or decreasing their firing rates. (pp. 107–108)

    G. The visual system processes depth information using both monocular and binocular cues. (pp. 108–109)

    H. Visual problems include color blindness, nearsighted-ness, farsightedness, and cataracts. (p. 109)

II. Audition is the sense of hearing. (p. 110)

    A. Sound is the physical stimulus in the environment that stimulates the auditory system and is transformed into neural energy. (p. 110)

    B. The ear is the sense organ for audition; it consists of the outer ear, the middle ear, and the inner ear. The receptors for audition are on the basilar membrane of the cochlea. (pp. 110–111)

    C. Sound waves of different frequencies cause different parts of the basilar membrane to vibrate in resonance, thereby providing a mechanism for the coding of sound. (pp. 111–112)

    D. Two types of deafness are conduction deafness and nerve deafness. Deafness can cause personality problems and is particularly detrimental in young children who have not yet acquired language. (pp. 112–114)

    E. The inner ear contains receptors for another sensory system: the vestibulars system which provides informa-tion about head orientation and movement required for posture and balance. (p. 114)

III. The senses of touch, smell, and taste play important roles in our lives. (pp. 114–115)

    A. The skin senses include a group of overlapping senses that detect touch, temperature changes, and painful stimulation on the skin. (p. 115)

    B. The experience of pain is partly determined by the actual stimulation and partly by other factors, including personality, emotions, culture, and stress. (pp. 115–116)

        1. The gate control theory of pain predicts the existence of a "gate" in the spinal cord that controls whether neural messages carrying information about pain will reach the brain. (pp. 116-117)

    C. Several treatments are available for pain; some of them seem to share common underlying mechanisms. (p. 117)

        1. Morphine appears to relieve pain by mimicking the activity of natural opiatelike chemicals produced by the brain, called endorphins. (p. 117)

        2. Electrical stimulation of the brain may relieve pain by activating areas that produce endorphins. (pp. 117–118)

        3. Acupuncture is a controversial technique that relieves pain in some patients. (p. 118)

    D. The chemical senses, which include olfaction and gustation, detect the presence of certain molecules in the air or on the tongue. (pp. 118–119)

        1. In some animals, chemical senses play important roles in communication and in the choice of food. (pp. 119–121)

IV. Perception is not easily distinguished from sensation; it involves the integration and interpretation of sensory information. (p. 121)

**A.** A number of general principles of perception help human beings organize their perceptual worlds. (pp. 121–122)

    **1.** Perceptual constancies refer to the ability to perceive an object as constant, despite changes at the retina in size, color, or shape. (p. 122)

    **2.** "Figures" are perceptually distinct from "grounds" because of their contrast and contours, their form, and their nearness. (p. 123)

    **3.** Organizing principles of perception include the principle of proximity, the principle of similarity, the principle of good continuation, and the principle of closure. Synchronous movement also affects perception of a scene. (pp. 123–124)

**B.** Individual factors affect the perception of objects and events. (p. 124)

    **1.** Previous experience affects perception because of the effects of perceptual sets. (pp. 124–125)

    **2.** Personality and interests affect what people pay attention to and thus what they perceive. (p. 125)

    **3.** Culture influences perception by controlling people's perceptual experiences. (pp. 125–126)

**C.** The process of perception is affected by attention, in which incoming information is filtered. (p. 126)

    **1.** People demonstrate selective attention, in which the filtering process is under the control of the individual. (p.126)

    **2.** The observer theory proposes that perception is accomplished by brain subsystems called observers whose job is to make inferences that relate sensory input to perceptual conclusions, and pass their information on to other observers. (p. 127)

**V.** Extrasensory perception (ESP) refers to perception that does not require stimulation of a sense organ. (p. 127)

**A.** Categories of ESP include telepathy, clairvoyance, and precognition. Psychokinesis is also considered a form of ESP. (pp. 127–128)

**B.** The question of whether ESP exists is controversial. (p. 128)

    **1.** Some experiments, such as those on "remote viewing," appear to demonstrate the existence of some forms of ESP. (pp. 128–129)

**C.** Many scientists are skeptical of the existence of ESP because the experiments on them are usually flawed in some way. (p. 129)

---

## ACTION GLOSSARY

Match the terms in the left column with the definitions in the right column.

___ **1. Sensation** (p. 102)
___ **2. Perception** (p. 102)
___ **3. Sense organ** (p. 102)
___ **4. Receptors** (p. 102)
___ **5. Transduction** (p. 102)
___ **6. Absolute threshold** (p. 102)
___ **7. Signal detection** (p. 103)
___ **8. Just noticeable difference (j.n.d.)** (p. 103)
___ **9. Weber's Law** (p. 103)
___ **10. Wavelength** (p. 103)

*A. Specialized neurons located in sense organs that transduce parts of the physical energy in the environment, such as visible light into neural messages.*

*B. The j.n.d. of a particular characteristic of a sensory system is a constant fraction of the stimulus intensity.*

*C. A technique to measure absolute thresholds. Takes into account the fact that threshold measurements depend on the sensitivity of the individual's sensory system and on the person's willingness to say he or she sensed a stimulus when he or she was not quite sure.*

*D. The process by which incoming sensory information is integrated and interpreted by the brain.*

*E. The point at which a stimulus becomes too weak for an individual's sensory system to detect.*

*F. The process by which information in the form of physical energy in the environment is transmitted to the brain through the sensory systems.*

*G. The distance from the peak of one light wave to the peak of the next.*

*H. A measure of sensory-system sensitivity that represents how well an individual can detect a very slight change in a stimulus in one characteristic, such as weight, intensity, or color. The measure indicates how "finely tuned" the sensory system is.*

*I. A structure designed to receive environmental energy, such as light or sound, and perform the first steps in transforming the energy into neural messages.*

*J. The process by which receptors in the sense organs transform parts of the physical energy in the environment into neural messages.*

___ **11. Visible spectrum** (p. 103)
___ **12. Cornea** (p. 104)
___ **13. Iris** (p. 104)
___ **14. Lens** (p. 104)
___ **15. Accommodation** (p. 104)
___ **16. Cataract** (p. 104)
___ **17. Retina** (p. 104)
___ **18. Rods** (p. 105)
___ **19. Fovea** (p. 105)

A. *A type of receptor primarily located in the periphery of the retina. Is responsive in dim light but does not discriminate between different colors.*
B. *The process by which the lens of the eye changes shape in order to focus light images on the retina.*
C. *The portion of the electromagnetic spectrum that humans can see.*
D. *A small depression in the center of the retina with a high density of cones and very clear pattern and color vision.*
E. *The transparent protective covering over the front of the eye.*
F. *The tissue behind the iris that can change shape, or accommodate, in order to focus the images of objects on the retina.*
G. *Colored muscular portion of the eye that surrounds the pupil and regulates the amount of light that enters it.*
H. *The layer of receptors and other cells in the back of the eyeball.*
I. *Clouding of the lens tissue that can eventually result in blindness.*

___ **20. Cones** (p. 105)
___ **21. Ganglion cells** (p. 105)
___ **22. Photopigment** (p. 105)
___ **23. Dark adaptation** (p. 106)
___ **24. Receptive field** (p. 106)
___ **25. Feature detectors** (p. 107)

A. *The substance in the receptors of the retina that undergoes a chemical transformation when struck by light. The chemical change causes the receptor to adjust its release of neurotransmitter, thereby transducing light energy into neural energy.*
B. *A type of receptor located mainly in the center of the retina. Transmits detailed pattern and color information.*
C. *Cells in the brain designed to detect specific features of the environment, such as a dark bar that is oriented vertically.*
D. *Neurons in the retina in the afferent visual pathway.*
E. *That portion of the visual field in which the presentation of a visual stimulus will produce an alteration in the firing rate of a neuron.*
F. *The process by which the eye becomes sensitive to images in dim light, dependent on the resynthesis of photopigment in the receptors.*

___ **26. Auditory canal** (p. 111)
___ **27. Trichromatic theory** (p. 107)
___ **28. Microspectrophotometry** (p. 107)
___ **29. Opponent process theory** (p. 108)
___ **30. Negative afterimage** (p. 108)
___ **31. Monocular cue** (p. 108)
___ **32. Binocular cue** (p. 108)
___ **33. Convergence** (p. 108)
___ **34. Stereoscopic vision** (p. 108)

A. *A theory that proposes that color vision is based on the operation of three different kinds of cells, each sensitive to a different range of wavelengths. The theory is correct for the processing of color vision by cones.*
B. *The situation in which an organism has two eyes with overlapping fields of vision so that the images received by each eye are slightly different and become more disparate as the object moves closer; an important cue for judging distance.*
C. *The long passageway leading from the outer ear to the middle ear.*
D. *The process used to verify the trichromatic theory of color vision in which a tiny beam of light is shone on a single cone and the amount of light reflected back is measured.*
E. *A binocular cue for depth perception involving signals from the muscles surrounding the eyes.*
F. *An illusion of seeing an image of one color, such as green, after staring at the same image in another color, such as red, apparently produced by the sudden change of firing in opponent process cells.*
G. *A cue for depth perception based on the cues available to one eye.*
H. *A theory that proposes that color vision is based on the operation of cells, each of which responds to two different colors. The cells fire fast for one color and slow for the other.*
I. *A cue for depth perception requiring simultaneous messages from both eyes.*

| | | |
|---|---|---|
| __ 35. | Audition (p. 110) | A. The part of the ear that transduces sound into neural messages. Includes the cochlea, the basilar membrane, and the hair cells. |
| __ 36. | Sound (p. 110) | B. Cycles of a sound wave per second. |
| __ 37. | Compressions (p. 110) | C. One part of a sound wave in which the molecules of air are spread out. |
| __ 38. | Rarefaction (p. 110) | D. The sense of hearing. |
| __ 39. | Frequency (of a sound wave) (p. 110) | E. The outer fleshy part of the ear, the auditory canal, and the eardrum. |
| __ 40. | Hertz (p. 110) | F. The physical energy transformed into neural messages by the auditory system, produced by the vibration of things in a medium such as air or water. |
| __ 41. | Pitch (p. 110) | G. Contains the tiny bones located in the ear (the malleus, incus, and stapes) that transmit vibratory motion from the eardrum to the inner ear. |
| __ 42. | Outer ear (p. 110) | H. One part of a sound wave in which the molecules of air are pushed closer together. |
| __ 43. | Middle ear (pp. 110–111) | I. The number of waves passing through a point per unit of time, usually one second. |
| __ 44. | Inner ear (p. 111) | J. The experience by humans of a sound along a continuum from high to low. |

| | | |
|---|---|---|
| __ 45. | Cochlea (p. 111) | A. The long membrane inside the cochlea that follows its curvature and vibrates in response to sound. |
| __ 46. | Basilar membrane (p. 111) | B. A part of the vestibular system in the inner ear that functions in the detection of head orientation. |
| __ 47. | Hair cells (p. 111) | C. A sensory system that provides unconscious information needed to maintain posture and head orientation and to control eye movements; the sense organ is part of the inner ear. |
| __ 48. | Vestibular system (p. 114) | D. A type of deafness caused by damage to the receptor cells for hearing or to the auditory nerve. |
| __ 49. | Semicircular canals (p. 114) | E. The snail-shaped inner ear that contains the receptors for hearing. |
| __ 50. | Vestibule (p. 114) | F. Unit used for measuring noise intensity levels. |
| __ 51. | Conduction deafness (p. 113) | G. Part of the inner ear that functions in the vestibular sensory system, particularly to detect rotary motion. |
| __ 52. | Nerve deafness (p. 113) | H. A type of deafness caused by a problem along the route from the eardrum to the cochlea. |
| __ 53. | Decibel (pp. 113–114) | I. The receptors for hearing located along the basilar membrane. |

| | | |
|---|---|---|
| __ 54. | Epidermis (p. 115) | A. Proposes that a mechanism in the spinal cord controls whether information about painful stimulation will reach the brain. The mechanism's actions are determined by the proportion of painful stimulation to other kinds of stimulation and by efferent messages from the brain. |
| __ 55. | Dermis (p. 115) | B. An inert substance given to a patient who is told that the treatment is a drug with powerful healing properties; a "sugar pill." |
| __ 56. | Pacinian corpuscle (p. 115) | C. The inner layer of skin; contains most of the receptors for the skin senses. |
| __ 57. | Gate control theory (p. 116) | D. The sense of taste. |
| __ 58. | Endorphins (p. 117) | E. A group of chemicals produced by the brain that acts like opiates and relieves pain. |
| __ 59. | Placebo (p. 118) | F. A receptor in the skin that seems to transform mechanical pressure on the skin into neural information. |
| __ 60. | Olfaction (p. 118) | G. The sense of smell. |
| __ 61. | Gustation (p. 118) | H. The outer layer of skin. |

__ **62. Pheromone (p. 120)**
__ **63. Perceptual constancy (p. 122)**
__ **64. Principle of similarity (p. 124)**
__ **65. Principle of proximity (p. 124)**
__ **66. Principle of closure (p. 124)**
__ **67. Principle of good continuation (p. 124)**
__ **68. Perceptual set (p. 124)**
__ **69. Attention (p. 126)**
__ **70. Shadowing (p. 126)**
__ **71. Observer theory (p. 127)**

A. *Proposes that brain subsystems make inferences and draw perceptual conclusions, and pass their conclusions onto other observers.*
B. *The expectancies or predispositions that affect the perceptions of an individual.*
C. *Filtering of incoming stimuli.*
D. *When a space is enclosed by lines, it tends to be perceived as a figure.*
E. *Similar objects are seen as members of the same group.*
F. *An experimental technique in which the subject listens to different messages in each ear and tries to repeat aloud one of the messages; used in studies of selective attention.*
G. *A biological odor that is used in communication between members of the same species.*
H. *The ability to perceive an object as constant, despite changes at the retina in size, color, or shape.*
I. *Objects that are closer to one another are seen as part of a group.*
J. *Images that appear to follow in the same direction are perceived as part of a group.*

__ **72. Extrasensory perception (ESP) (p. 127)**
__ **73. Telepathy (p. 127)**
__ **74. Clairvoyance (p. 127)**
__ **75. Precognition (p. 127)**
__ **76. Psychokinesis (p. 128)**

A. *The ability to perceive future events.*
B. *The transference of one person's thoughts to another person.*
C. *Perception that does not require stimulation of a sense organ.*
D. *The ability to move objects without touching them.*
E. *The ability to perceive objects or events not present or affecting the person's senses.*

*ANSWERS*

71. a, 72. c, 73. b, 74. e, 75. a, 76. d.
54. h, 55. f, 56. f, 57. a, 58. e, 59. b, 60. g, 61. d, 62. g, 63. h, 64. e, 65. i, 66. d, 67. j, 68. b, 69. c, 70. f,
37. h, 38. i, 39. i, 40. b, 41. j, 42. e, 43. g, 44. a, 45. e, 46. a, 47. i, 48. c, 49. g, 50. b, 51. h, 52. d, 53. f,
20. b, 21. d, 22. a, 23. f, 24. e, 25. c, 26. c, 27. a, 28. d, 29. h, 30. f, 31. g, 32. i, 33. e, 34. i, 35. d, 36. f,
1. f, 2. d, 3. j, 4. a, 5. j, 6. e, 7. c, 8. h, 9. b, 10. g, 11. c, 12. e, 13. g, 14. f, 15. b, 16. i, 17. h, 18. a, 19. d,

## SELF-TEST

1. Sensation involves
   (a) the interpretation by the brain of information about the environment.
   (b) the transmission of information about the environment to the brain.
   (c) events that take place in the sensory receptors and the pathways to the brain.
   (d) both b and c.
   (LO 1; p. 102)

2. A measure of the sensitivity of a sensory system is the
   (a) absolute threshold.
   (b) just noticeable difference.
   (c) measurement of individual difference in judgment about stimuli.
   (d) both a and b.
   (LO 2; pp. 102–103)

3. In vision, the process of transduction occurs in
   (a) the rods and the cones.
   (b) the lens and the retina.
   (c) the vitreous humor.
   (d) the pupil.
   (LO 3; p. 105)

4. A receptive field of a cell
   (a) is a receptor cell such as an individual rod or cone.
   (b) can be a part of the focusing mechanism.
   (c) is an area in the environment in which the presentation of a stimulus will cause a change in the cell's firing rate.
   (d) is part of the nervous system.
   (LO 4; p. 106)

5. The trichromatic and opponent process theories of color vision
   (a) appear to be useful ways to understand processes in the brain and the retina, respectively.
   (b) appear to be useful ways to understand the processing of color information in the retina and the brain, respectively.
   (c) have been replaced with a more recent and technologically sophisticated theory.
   (d) are part of an unresolved controversy.
   (LO 4; pp. 107–108)

6. Stereoscopic vision
 (a) is produced by convergence.
 (b) results from the two eyes seeing the world from slightly different perspectives.
 (c) is the most important monocular cue for distance and depth perception.
 (d) is not as important for distance perception as a sure knowledge of the actual distance from an object.
 (LO 4; pp. 108–109)

7. The stimulus for hearing is
 (a) composed of alternating compressions and rarefactions in the air.
 (b) frequency.
 (c) amplitude.
 (d) loudness.
 (LO 6; p. 110)

8. The actual receptor cells for the sense of hearing are
 (a) located in the middle ear.
 (b) located in the inner ear along the basilar membrane.
 (c) located along the outside of the cochlea.
 (d) directly stimulated by the eardrum.
 (LO 5; p. 111)

9. Space motion sickness that involves nausea is most likely the result of some sort of stimulation of the
 (a) middle ear.
 (b) cochlea.
 (c) vestibular system.
 (d) stomach or intestines.
 (LO 8; p. 114)

10. The brain's interpretation of the sensory information coming from the ear's receptor cells
 (a) depends upon where in the cochlea the stimulated cells are located.
 (b) depends upon the frequency of the sound stimulus.
 (c) depends upon which of the three bones of the middle ear are stimulated.
 (d) both a and b.
 (LO 6; pp. 111–112)

11. Nerve deafness
 (a) is presently irreversible.
 (b) can be caused by loud noises.
 (c) can be treated with a hearing aid or can be surgically repaired.
 (d) both a and b.
 (LO 7; pp. 112–114)

12. Painful sensations
 (a) require a stimulus that actually damages tissue.
 (b) are due to activation of the Pacinian corpuscle.
 (c) have been hypothesized to be partly under the control of a "gate" in the spinal cord.
 (d) are always the result of tissue damage.
 (LO 10; pp. 115–117)

13. Endorphins are
 (a) opiatelike substances found in the brain.
 (b) modern drugs, based upon the chemical model of the opiates, that have been developed to treat pain and that have fewer side effects than morphine.
 (c) found in the skin.
 (d) found in the pain receptors.
 (LO 10; p. 117)

14. The basic taste categories are
 (a) sweet, sour, salty, and bitter.
 (b) sweet, sour, and salty.
 (c) mint, musk, sweet, and salt.
 (d) carbohydrates, proteins, and fats.
 (LO 11; p. 119)

15. Perceptual constancy
 (a) refers to an inability to adjust for difference in viewing conditions.
 (b) refers to the ability to perceive objects as unchanging despite changes in the characteristics of the retinal image.
 (c) is inborn.
 (d) holds for size and distance perception but not for color perception.
 (LO 12; p. 122)

16. Most people see the following display as four groups of five dots: "..... ..... ..... ....." This is an example of the perceptual organizing principle called
 (a) closure.
 (b) proximity.
 (c) figure.
 (d) familiarity.
 (LO 12; p. 124)

17. One way in which experience influences the way in which the world is perceived is through the formation of
 (a) figure-ground relationships.
 (b) new brain cells.
 (c) perceptual sets.
 (d) culture.
 (LO 13; p. 124)

18. The selective focusing or filtering of perception is called
    (a) attention.
    (b) perceptual constancy.
    (c) habituation.
    (d) perceptual organization.
    (LO 14; p. 126)

19. Extrasensory perception is a phenomenon
    (a) that is alleged to take place via the stimulation of an as yet undiscovered sense organ.
    (b) that is disbelieved by a majority of people.
    (c) that has had several important and clear experimental confirmations.
    (d) whose existence is supported largely by anecdotal evidence.
    (LO 15; p. 127)

20. The experimental procedures and controls of studies demonstrating ESP are usually
    (a) found to be sound.
    (b) designed by sophisticated scientists.
    (c) found to be flawed.
    (d) unfairly attacked as unsound.
    (LO 16; pp. 128–129)

*ANSWERS*

1. d, 2. d, 3. a, 4. c, 5. b, 6. b, 7. a, 8. b, 9. c, 10. d, 11. d, 12. c, 13. a, 14. a, 15. b, 16. b, 17. c, 18. a, 19. d, 20. c

# THINKING ABOUT PSYCHOLOGY

1. Science fiction stories sometimes feature a "cyclops," which technically refers to a race of giants in Greek mythology that has one eye in the middle of the forehead. Using your knowledge of the visual system, how would someone with just one eye be different from a normal human being? What visual capacities would be missing?

2. You're cooking a meal at home and you smell something burning. You race to the kitchen, see the fat in the frying pan on fire and grab the handle. You drop it because of the intense heat, and then reach for the fire extinguisher. Combining what you learned in earlier chapters with the information in this chapter on the sensory systems, describe the events that are happening in the body and brain.

3. Although the examples used to explain the organizing principles of perception were visual ones, such principles should also apply to audition in the other senses. What organizing principles might apply to ordering sounds in our environment?

# SUGGESTED READINGS

Ackerman, D. (1990). *A natural history of the senses*. New York: Vintage Books. A charming and well-written popular book on the role sensation and perception play in our lives.

Freeman, W. J. (1991). The physiology of perception. *Scientific American,* December, 78–85. A discussion of how the brain transforms sensory messages into conscious perceptions.

Gordon, I. E. (1989). *Theories of visual perception*. Chichester, England: Wiley. An overview of the major theories of visual perception for the advanced undergraduate.

Hubel, D. H., and Wiesel, T. N. (1979). Brain mechanisms of vision. *Scientific American*, September. A description by the two Nobel prize winners of their research on the activity of cells in the visual cortex.

Irwin, H. J. (1989). *An introduction to parapsychology*. Jefferson, NC: McFarland. A reasonably balanced discussion of the field of parapsychology.

Melzack, R. (1973). *The puzzle of pain*. New York: Basic Books. An introduction to the nature of pain and a description of Melzack and Wall's gate control theory.

Weale, R. A. (1982). *Focus on vision*. Cambridge, MA: Harvard University Press. A closer look at some of the properties of the visual system, including chapters on developmental changes and visual perception.

Wilding, J. M. (1983). *Perception: From sense to object*. New York: St. Martin's Press. A well-written book that emphasizes the active nature of the perception of events.

# CHAPTER 5
## LEARNING
## OUTLINE

▶ Learning Objectives

▶ What Is Learning?

■ Learning, Maturation, and
Genetic Influences
Learning and Performance

▶ Guided Review

▶ Classical Conditioning

■ Pavlov's Dogs
■ Properties of Classical
Conditioning
The Rate of Conditioning
The Conditioned Stimulus—
Stimulus Generalization
The Conditioned Stimulus—
Stimulus Discrimination
The Pairing Procedure
Extinction
Second-Order Conditioning
■ Classical Conditioning and
Learning Relations

▶ Guided Review

▶ Operant Conditioning

■ Learning by Consequences
■ Thorndike's Cats and Skinner's
Rats
■ Characteristics of Operant
Conditioning
Shaping
Superstition
Extinction
■ Reinforcement
Positive Reinforcement,
Negative Reinforcement,
and Punishment
Schedules of Reinforcement
The Nature of Reinforcement
■ Biofeedback

▶ Guided Review

▶ Learning and Cognition

■ Insight Learning
■ Cognitive Maps
■ Observational Learning

▶ Guided Review

▶ The Limits of Learning

■ Flavor Aversions
■ Biological Predispositions
and Learning

▶ Guided Review

▶ Summary

▶ Action Glossary

▶ Self-Test

▶ Thinking About Psychology

▶ Suggested Readings

# LEARNING
## LEARNING OBJECTIVES

**After reading this chapter, you should be able to**

▶ **1.** define *learning.* (pp. 140–141)

▶ **2.** explain some problems associated with distinguishing learning from behavioral changes. (pp. 140–141)

▶ **3.** describe classical conditioning, and identify several factors that influence the rate of conditioning. (pp. 141–143)

▶ **4.** explain *stimulus generalization, stimulus discrimination,* and *extinction.* (pp. 143–145)

▶ **5.** define second-order conditioning, and show how it might affect the reward value of previously neutral stimuli. (pp. 145–146)

▶ **6.** show how classical conditioning might affect a person's tolerance to drugs. (pp. 146–147)

▶ **7.** define operant conditioning, and describe some of its properties, such as shaping, superstition, and extinction. (pp. 147–151)

▶ **8.** describe the concept of reinforcement. (pp. 151–153)

▶ **9.** define biofeedback, and show why it is an example of instrumental conditioning. (pp. 153–155)

▶ **10.** define insight learning, and provide an example of its occurrence. (pp. 156–157)

▶ **11.** define a cognitive map, and describe a study demonstrating that such a map exists. (p. 157)

▶ **12.** define observational learning, and explain some of the studies that suggest children can acquire aggressive responses through this form of learning. (pp. 157–159)

▶ **13.** describe a study dealing with flavor aversions, and explain its implications for general principles of learning. (p. 161)

Ten years after the Vietnam War, a veteran who had seen much combat was sitting at his desk in a Chicago bank building. In the men's room next door, a maintenance worker was replacing the mirror and accidentally dropped it on the floor. The veteran heard the shattering glass and froze. Sweat poured down his chalky white face and his heart raced.

A colleague who was passing by the door saw the veteran's face and rushed into his office. She quickly scanned the room for an attacker. There was no one else. She got a glass of water for the man, and slowly he began to loosen his grip from the desk. He muttered something about broken glass and grenades.

Both of these bank employees heard the sound of the breaking mirror in the bathroom, but only the veteran reacted strangely. The two people behaved differently in the face of the same event because of learning. One had learned to associate the sound of breaking glass with an exploding grenade because he had been in a hotel in Saigon when a guerrilla tossed a grenade through a window. The other had certainly heard glass breaking before, but she had never associated it with anything so traumatic.

## WHAT IS LEARNING?

Like any complex psychological phenomenon, learning is difficult to define. A good starting point is to define it as the relatively permanent changes in behavior that occur because of prior experience. Prior experience refers to virtually any event in the environment and even includes internal events such as an upset stomach. After one experience of eating rotten strawberries, for example, you learn to avoid them in the future. In many cases, the effects of the prior experience never even reach the level of consciousness.

The previous definition of learning is a very useful one, but it has certain deficiencies. In particular, it does not clearly make distinctions between learning and other things that affect behavior, such as maturation, genetic influences, motivation, and injury.

### Learning, Maturation, and Genetic Influences

The behavior of any organism changes from moment to moment; not all of these changes are due to learning. For example, a human baby begins to walk at about the age of one. We usually refer to this as "learning to walk," but

**Figure 5.1**   *Hopi woman holding child on a cradleboard*

evidence supports the view that maturation of the nervous system and the muscles is more important than prior experiences. Babies who never receive any training or encouragement to walk still learn at about the same age. For example, infants of the Hopi tribe, a group of Pueblo Indians living in northeastern Arizona, spend most of their first year in cradleboards; they get little chance to practice walking or to learn any of the motions (figure 5.1). Nevertheless, Hopi babies begin walking at about the same age as other babies.

Even though walking occurs primarily because of the maturation of the nervous system and the muscles, it is still affected by learning. Depending on the culture, people might learn to point their toes a little more inward, outward, or straight ahead.

Behavioral changes may also be more closely related to the messages contained in the genes than they are to learning. Song sparrows, for example, begin to sing their own songs even if they are raised by a canary (Marler & Hamilton, 1966). They do not need to learn the song from any model. A great many behavioral changes, however, contain elements of learning as well as genetic control. Human smiling, for example, might appear to be primarily under genetic control since even congenitally blind and deaf babies perform the response. But smiling is obviously influenced by learning, too. In most cases, it is usually too simple to say that a behavior is either "genetic" or "learned." Genes and environment often interact in complex ways to produce behavioral change.

*Learning and Performance*    We ordinarily cannot measure learning; it is an inferred phenomenon. All we usually do is measure behavioral changes as they are reflected in performance. But performance may not always be an accurate measure of learning.

Suppose you work very hard to learn the names of all the people who will attend an important business meeting. Then the meeting is called off, so you never use the information. You learned the names, but you never say them; the learning has not changed your behavior. However, the learning has produced the potential for a change in behavior, one that might be transformed into an actual change at another time. For such reasons, many psychologists like to include the notion of potentiality in their definition of learning.

Your performance may not reflect what you have learned for other reasons; motivation, fatigue, injury, and emotional state may affect how you perform. A cat might have learned to associate the sound of a bell with dinnertime, but it may pay no attention because it isn't hungry, it's busy playing, or it's too tired to eat. And anxiety-ridden test-takers have trouble showing what they learned because of emotional factors.

In practice, it is not always possible to distinguish between changes in behavior due to learning and those due to maturation, genetic influences, motivational shifts, fatigue, or other factors. Nevertheless, it is best to define **learning** as *the relatively permanent changes in behavior, or potential for those changes, that occur because of prior experience, excluding behavioral changes due to maturation, genetic factors, motivational shifts, fatigue, or injury.*

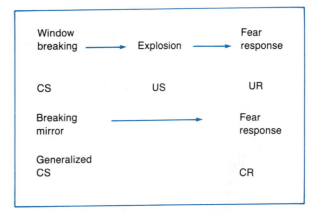

**Figure 5.2**    *An example of classical conditioning*

sented to an organism in a specific sequence and the organism forms an association or connection between them. One of the stimuli must automatically elicit some response from the organism; the other can be a neutral stimulus, one that has no meaning prior to the conditioning experience.*

This simple form of learning is extremely common. It allows organisms to identify those events in the environment that are particularly relevant. The veteran had been conditioned to associate the sound of breaking glass with an explosion. Essentially, classical conditioning is a method used to predict events, although the "prediction" is not usually a conscious one. The veteran certainly did not consciously predict a terrorist attack on the bank.

There are many stimuli in the world that will automatically elicit some response from an organism. A puff of air that touches your eye will cause you to blink. A hot probe on the finger will make you withdraw your hand and feel pain. An explosion, or any sudden loud noise, will cause activation of the sympathetic nervous system. In classical conditioning, an **unconditioned stimulus (US)** *is an event that elicits an automatic response from an organism, one that is not learned.* The first component of classical conditioning is the presentation of a US which elicits the **unconditioned response (UR),** *the automatic response to a US.* In the case of the veteran, the US was the explosion, and the UR was the fear response (figure 5.2).

The **conditioned stimulus (CS)** *is a neutral stimulus that precedes the US during classical conditioning;* it acts as a warning signal that the US is coming next. After many pairings, the organism begins to associate the CS with the US, and the CS, when presented by itself, will elicit a

# CLASSICAL CONDITIONING

The Vietnam veteran's experience was an example of **classical conditioning,** *in which two stimuli are pre-*

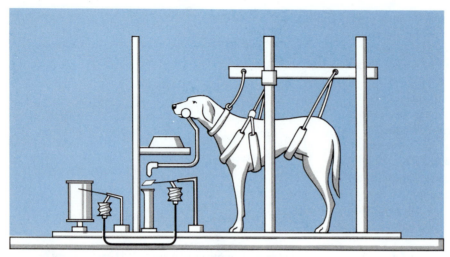

**Figure 5.3** *An apparatus for studying classical conditioning. Once a dog was strapped into a stand as shown, an experimenter could begin testing the effects of various stimuli on the salivary response. Saliva could be collected in a glass funnel.*

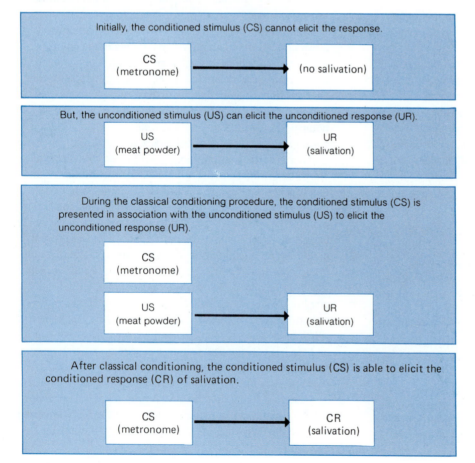

Initially, the conditioned stimulus (CS) cannot elicit the response.

| CS (metronome) | → | (no salivation) |

But, the unconditioned stimulus (US) can elicit the unconditioned response (UR).

| US (meat powder) | → | UR (salivation) |

During the classical conditioning procedure, the conditioned stimulus (CS) is presented in association with the unconditioned stimulus (US) to elicit the unconditioned response (UR).

| CS (metronome) |
| US (meat powder) | → | UR (salivation) |

After classical conditioning, the conditioned stimulus (CS) is able to elicit the conditioned response (CR) of salivation.

| CS (metronome) | → | CR (salivation) |

response. The **conditioned response (CR)** *refers to the organism's response to a previously neutral CS after it has been paired with a US.* For the veteran, the sound of shattering glass was the CS, and the fear response was the CR.

## Pavlov's Dogs

The Russian physiologist Ivan Pavlov performed the first experiments on classical conditioning. As a young man, Pavlov had incredible energy, and he directed almost all of it toward science. His indifference to earthly concerns was legendary. At one time he and his wife were living in poverty, unable to pay their bills. To help him out, his students took up a collection and asked him to give a lecture series. He gave the speeches but used the money to buy lab animals instead of necessities for the family.

When Pavlov began working with dogs, he was not studying behavior; he was investigating digestion. By putting meat powder in a dog's mouth, he could elicit salivation and collect the saliva in a tube (figure 5.3). Pavlov soon noticed, however, that the dog started to salivate before he offered it the meat powder, first when the dog saw the bowl, then when he heard Pavlov open the door. To learn more about this strange phenomenon, Pavlov began using a clicking metronome as a CS. Immediately following this sound, he placed food in the dog's mouth. After doing this several times, he noticed that the dog began to salivate as soon as it heard the metronome (figure 5.4).

**Figure 5.4** *A diagram of classical conditioning*

These observations led Pavlov to a turning point in his career. He did not know whether to continue his studies of digestion or to begin investigating how the dog's salivary gland "learns." Fortunately for psychology, Pavlov chose to study conditioning.

## Properties of Classical Conditioning

The basic model of classical conditioning is deceptively simple. A US that elicits an automatic UR is paired with a CS. Eventually, the CS itself can elicit a response from the organism. This response is the CR. Pavlov, and many later researchers, investigated variations of this model to determine the properties of classical conditioning. Research on this topic is still very active; all of its properties are not yet entirely clear (Rescorla & Holland, 1982). Some questions about classical conditioning include:

1. How fast does conditioning occur?
2. What characteristics of the CS affect conditioning?
3. How does the pairing procedure affect conditioning?
4. How does an organism forget a conditioning experience?
5. Can a CS that elicits a response be used as a US and paired with a new CS?

*The Rate of Conditioning*    Pavlov found that the more times the metronome was paired with the food, the more quickly the dog would salivate to the sound of the metronome alone. This observation is very logical and suggests that the association became stronger each time the two stimuli were paired. However, the first few pairings are the most important in classical conditioning. After this, the CR usually does not get much stronger (figure 5.5). Under some conditions, even a single pairing can be powerful enough to produce conditioning. This can happen if the US is particularly traumatic, as it was for the Vietnam veteran.

The usefulness of the CS as a predictor, and hence the rate of conditioning, are also affected by how consistently the CS is followed by the US. If the CS sometimes occurs alone, it will not be a completely reliable predictor, and learning will be slower. The fastest learning takes place if the two events are consistently paired and neither one occurs by itself. This means that certain CSs will work better than others: novel, unusual, and intense CSs are usually more effective than familiar ones.

*The Conditioned Stimulus—Stimulus Generalization*
Once the organism has made an association between the US and the CS, it will begin to respond to the CS alone. It will continue to respond even if you change the CS

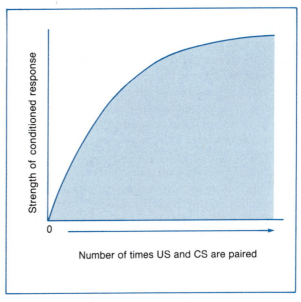

**Figure 5.5**    *A graph showing the theoretical relationship between the number of times the US and CS are paired and the strength of the CR when the CS is presented alone. Actual data will depend on many factors, such as the delay between the US and the CS and the emotional impact of the US.*

slightly. For example, the veteran originally learned to respond with fear to the sound of a grenade breaking a window. But a breaking mirror on a bathroom floor produced almost as much fear. And the dog that responded to the metronome by salivating will probably also respond to a bell or buzzer. This phenomenon is called **stimulus generalization.** *The more similar a stimulus is to the original CS, the more likely it is that the organism will demonstrate a CR.*

Stimulus generalization often involves similarities in sound, sight, or other physical characteristics. In humans, though, a stimulus generalization can be much more abstract. In an early study, a researcher found that generalizations could even be based on similarities in meanings of words (Razran, 1939). He classically conditioned human subjects to salivate to the sight of certain words, such as style, urn, freeze, and surf. Then he presented some words that were similar in sound (stile, earn, frieze, serf) and others that were similar in meaning (fashion, vase, chill, wave). The subjects showed much more significant responses to the words that were similar in meaning.

*The Conditioned Stimulus—Stimulus Discrimination*
**Stimulus discrimination** *refers to the fact that an organism can learn to distinguish between a CS that reliably precedes a US and similar stimuli that are not paired with the US.* For example, dogs trained to salivate at the sound of a metronome can learn to ignore a buzzer if the buzzer is presented alone several times. Pavlov found that dogs could make very subtle distinctions between sounds. This technique is frequently used to assess the sensitivity of sensory systems in animals. In one of Pavlov's studies, dogs were able to discriminate between a metronome ticking at ninety-eight beats per minute, and another at one hundred beats per minute.

Pavlov and his colleagues wondered what would happen if the dog's ability to discriminate were pushed to its limits. He conditioned the dog to salivate when it saw a circle and to ignore an ellipse. Then he slowly began to make the ellipse more like a circle and the circle more elliptical. Pavlov's description of the dog's behavior is fascinating.

> The hitherto quiet dog began to squeal in its stand, wriggling about… and bit through the tubes connecting the animal's room with the observer…. In short, it presented all the symptoms of a condition of acute neurosis (Pavlov, 1927, p. 291).

Pavlov called this behavior experimental neurosis; it consists of severe agitation and aggressive behavior in an organism when a previously established learned response is disrupted in some way. Pavlov hypothesized that some forms of mental illness might be due to similar disruptive conditioning experiences.

*The Pairing Procedure*    The manner in which the US is paired with the CS has turned out to be an interesting and controversial issue. First, conditioning does not seem to occur unless the neutral CS comes first. If it comes after the US, even very soon after, the organism never learns to make the CR to the CS alone. This kind of backward conditioning, in which the US precedes the CS, probably is ineffective because the CS cannot be used to predict the occurrence of the US. If the sound of breaking glass followed the explosion, the veteran would pay little attention to it and would certainly not become fearful each time he heard it. (In this case, he probably wouldn't even hear it.) By the same token, simultaneous conditioning, in which the CS and the US occur at the same time, is also not very effective. Again, the sound of breaking glass

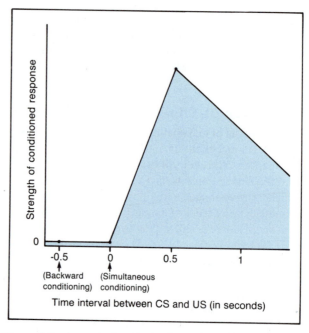

**Figure 5.6**    *A graph showing the theoretical relationship of the CR and the time interval between the CS and the US. When the US comes before the CS (backward conditioning) or at the same time as the CS (simultaneous conditioning), learning does not occur. The best conditioning occurs when the time interval is about one-half second.*

cannot be used as a predictor if it occurs at the same time as the explosion.

Under most circumstances, the most successful conditioning occurs when the CS begins just a fraction of a second before the US. For example, the dog would learn fastest if the metronome sounded about one-half second before the food was put in its mouth. Shorter or longer intervals usually produce slower learning (figure 5.6). There are some exceptions to this general rule, however.

*Extinction*    **Extinction** *occurs when the CS is repeatedly presented without the US, causing the response to the CS to gradually diminish.* The dog's salivation response to the metronome, for example, could be extinguished by making the sound over and over without following it with food.

Extinction may seem to be like forgetting, but the two are not quite the same. If a response is extinguished, it is not forgotten in the sense that it will never happen again. Responses that are extinguished often show **spontaneous recovery,** *the sudden reappearance of a CR after its apparent extinction.* For example, if time is allowed to

# CLOSE UP ON RESEARCH
## Phobias and Fetishes

Two psychological disorders that appear to have their roots in classical conditioning experiences are phobias and fetishes. A phobia is an intense and irrational fear of something such as furry animals, heights, or closed-in spaces. Although most people who have them do not know how or why they were acquired, many psychologists believe that a classical conditioning experience is the key ingredient.

The first study in which a phobia was experimentally created in the laboratory, one which was unethical and never should have been conducted, involved Little Albert. John Watson and Rosalie Rayner (1920) gave Albert white rats to play with; initially the 11-month-old showed no fear and played with them happily. But then Watson and Rayner began to strike a steel bar every time Albert reached for a rat. While Albert wasn't afraid of rats, he showed a strong startle and fear response to the loud noise. Soon he began to show the same fear response to the rat, crying whenever he saw one. Albert had been classically conditioned: the loud noise was the US, the rat the CS, and fear was the response.

A fetish exists when someone is sexually aroused by or attached to an inanimate object or situation. Again, many psychologists believe that early classical conditioning experiences play a key role. A teenage boy, for example, might visit a pornography shop located next to an ice cream parlor and begin to associate the sexual arousal he feels at the shop with the ice cream advertising. He might develop a fetish about ice cream in this way. Fetishes can be surprisingly diverse. One particularly obscure case involved a man who was sexually aroused by watching other people sneeze (King, 1990).

Fetishes have been experimentally induced in the laboratory, as well. In one study, young men were shown color slides of women's boots and then slides of attractive, nude women. Sexual arousal was measured with a device that recorded changes in penis size. After several pairings, the men began to show sexual arousal to the presentation of the slides showing the boots alone. They also showed some stimulus generalization since they responded to pictures of women's shoes (Rachman & Hodgson, 1968).

Based on the hypothesis that most phobias and fetishes are acquired through classical conditioning, many therapists use extinction procedures combined with other techniques, such as relaxation therapy, to try to reduce or eliminate them, often quite successfully. The therapists do not have to know precisely what was involved in the original classical conditioning in order to use extinction. As we learned in the text, though, extinction is not forgetting and any classical conditioning situation is very complex. Classically conditioned responses are very stubborn and they may reappear.

---

pass after the dog has stopped salivating to the sound of the metronome, the dog will show spontaneous recovery and start salivating again.

Recent studies of extinction, particularly of fear responses to a particular CS, show that the phenomenon is incredibly complex (Bouton & Swartzentruber, 1991). When an organism learns a particular association between two events designed by the experimenter, such as a bell and a shock, it is hardly surprising that the animal begins to show fear responses to the bell. But the animal is learning much more than what the experimenter thinks. It is using every sensory system at its command to make valid predictions and associating the whole context of the situation with the shock, including the smells, sights, noises, feel of the floor, and the state of its own body. Any or all of these could be the CS. Even if the experimenter extinguishes the fear response to the bell, any of the contextual cues could trigger the fear response again. Fear responses, once conditioned, are notoriously difficult to extinguish and relapse is common. The complexity of the extinction process is especially relevant to its use in therapy for people who have conditioned fear responses, such as the veteran.

*Second-Order Conditioning*   One of the most important features of classical conditioning is the way in which one conditioning experience can lay the groundwork for another. After many pairings of the CS and the US, the CS begins to elicit a response from the animal when presented alone. This CS can then be paired with another neutral stimulus; after many pairings, the organism will respond to the new stimulus. In effect, the CS can now act as a US. This phenomenon is called **second-order conditioning;** *it occurs when a previously established CS is used as a US in a new conditioning experience.*

In the example of the salivating dog, the dog first is conditioned to respond to the original CS, the metronome, by salivating. In the next phase a new stimulus, perhaps a light, is presented immediately before the metronome, and the original US, the meat, is omitted. In the first few trials the dog responds to the metronome by salivating. After several pairings of the light and the metronome, the dog begins to salivate in response to the light presented alone.

If the circumstances are right, the light can then be paired with another new stimulus, which can then be paired with another one, and so on. But if the first CS, the metronome, is repeatedly presented without pairing it with the original US (the meat), the metronome will eventually lose its ability to elicit a response.

The response will undergo extinction. For second- and higher-order conditioning to occur, the original CS must occasionally be paired with the original US to ensure that extinction does not occur. In general, the further away the CS is from the original CS in higher-order conditioning, the weaker the response and the more easily it is extinguished.

Second- and higher-order conditioning are important because they help explain how certain stimuli can acquire the ability to elicit responses even when they never seem to have been paired with any obvious US. A check in the mail, for example, might have been paired with money, which was paired with packages of food, which is paired with satisfaction of hunger.

## Classical Conditioning and Learning Relations

Recent work on classical conditioning shows that it cannot be fully understood in terms of a mechanical event in which there is a simple pairing of a CS and a US (Rescorla, 1988). It appears to be a much richer phenomenon in which the key ingredient is the learning of relations between events important in the animal's survival. The animal is acquiring a warning signal that a significant event is about to occur. The value of the information in the warning signal is critical.

All CSs are not created equal. The animal comes to any learning situation with a history of previous learning, and it would be nearly impossible to present a stimulus that was truly neutral. Furthermore, some stimuli appear to have special meaning because of the evolutionary history of the animal. Also, conditioning does not occur in a vacuum with only the presumed CS and US present. It occurs in a rich context of stimuli bombarding all the senses, external and internal; the organism already has learned relations among many of them, and is learning more as conditioning or extinction proceeds.

All CRs are not created equal, either. The choice of what to measure as the response can make a difference when the researcher tries to draw conclusions about the nature of conditioning. Measuring a fear response by recording heart-rate changes can show a different pattern compared to other possible measures of fear, such as freezing or pupil dilation (Spear, Miler & Jagielo, 1990).

In most cases, conditioning will result in a CR that very closely resembles the UR. But in some, the CR is rather different. It appears to represent a preparation for the upcoming US rather than an early response to it. The appearance of a rival male in the territory of certain species of fish acts as a US that produces a typical UR of aggressive behavior. If a warning signal, such as a red light, reliably precedes the appearance of the rival, the fish will learn a conditioned response. It approaches the site of the signal and the place where the intruder will appear, all fins erect and ready for battle. In a sense, the fish is preparing for the contest. And this preparation helps it win. Conditioned fish show considerably more aggression in these contests (Hollis, 1984).

Another example in which the CS may be helping the organism to prepare for the upcoming US is in the development of tolerance to psychoactive drugs, a phenomenon discussed in chapter 3. The development of tolerance appears partly due to physiological changes in the body, especially in the brain and the liver. Tolerance also appears to be a function of conditioning (Siegel, 1975).

In one experiment, rats received fairly large doses of alcohol every other day for eighteen days. The experimenters removed them from their home cages, took them into another room that had dim lights and a blaring radio, measured their rectal temperatures, and then injected the alcohol. The rats' temperatures were taken again after forty-five, sixty, and seventy-five minutes (Le, Poulos, & Cappell, 1979).

Rats get drunk when they consume alcohol. One of the symptoms of their intoxication is a drop in body temperature, perhaps by two degrees Centigrade. But they show tolerance after they have received several injections, and their body temperatures might drop less than one degree. As expected, the same dose of alcohol produced a smaller effect on their bodies after they had used the drug for a while.

All of these tests were conducted in a strange noisy room with dim lights. But what would happen if the animals were tested in their home room where they had never received any alcohol and where they were not expecting any? If tolerance is purely a physiological phenomenon, the results should be the same. The experimenters injected these same rats in their home rooms. They suddenly lost much of their tolerance to the drug. But when they were injected again the next day in the noisy room, their tolerance seemed to come right back.

This study shows that tolerance is not just a physiological phenomenon; it is also related to classical conditioning. The drug injection is the US, and the UR is the drop in body temperature (and probably all the other effects of alcohol as well). The CS is the noisy room the rats had come to associate with the coming injection. The nervous systems of the rats produced a CR to the noisy room, and this CR was an *increase* in body temperature that helped their bodies prepare and compensate for the imminent alcohol injection. Because of this preparation, the alcohol only produced a very slight drop in body temperature (less than one degree). Since the rats had not formed any association between their own home rooms and the alcohol injection, they did not exhibit any CR in their home rooms.

We mentioned in chapter 3 that a large proportion of deaths attributed to drug overdoses may not really be due to overdoses since many of the victims did not seem to be injecting, sniffing, or swallowing particularly large quantities relative to their usual doses. The studies on classically conditioned responses to drugs lead to the conclusion that this simple form of learning plays an important role in a person's tolerance to a drug at any particular time. Tolerance is a physiological phenomenon that varies from moment to moment depending on psychological factors.

Classical conditioning is a very basic form of learning and researchers continue to be surprised by how often its principles help explain puzzling behavior. If you suffer from allergies, you might be interested to hear that allergic reactions can be classically conditioned. For example, pollen may cause you to sneeze but you may come to associate the sight of flowers with pollen. If you become classically conditioned to sneeze at the sight of flowers, even a vase of artificial flowers could set off an attack.

▶ **GUIDED REVIEW** *Learning Objectives 3, 4, 5, and 6*

1. During classical conditioning, an _____ (US) that automatically elicits an _____ (UR) is paired with a _____ (CS). After many pairings, the animal learns the association between the US and the CS and begins to respond to the CS presented alone. This response to the CS is called the _____ (CR).
2. _____ performed the first studies of classical conditioning, using dogs. The US was meat in the dog's mouth, and the UR was salivation. He taught the dogs to associate a sound

(CS) with the meat, and after many pairings, the sound elicited a CR when it was presented alone.
3. The _____ depends on several factors, including how many times the US is paired with the CS and how novel the CS is to the animal.
4. The CS must precede the US for conditioning to occur; the most rapid conditioning takes place when the CS-US interval is about _____.
5. After conditioning, the animal will generalize its learning to stimuli that are similar to the CS, a phenomenon called _____. If similar stimuli are presented without the US, the animal will come to discriminate between the CS and other, similar stimuli in a phenomenon called _____.
6. _____ may occur when a previously established learned response is disrupted by presenting two similar stimuli between which the organism cannot discriminate and by following only one stimulus with the US.
7. A CR can be inhibited through _____. The CS is presented repeatedly without the US until the animal stops responding to the CS.
8. After conditioning, a CS can be used as a US in a new conditioning procedure with a new, neutral stimulus serving as the CS. This phenomenon is called _____.
9. The development of _____ to drugs appears to be partly a physiological phenomenon and partly due to classical conditioning experiences. Rats conditioned to associate a particular room with a drug injection began to make physiological preparations to compensate for the coming injection as a CR to the special room.

*Answers*

1. *unconditioned stimulus, unconditioned response, conditioned stimulus, conditioned response* 2. *Ivan Pavlov* 3. *rate of conditioning* 4. *one-half second* 5. *stimulus generalization, stimulus discrimination* 6. *Experimental neurosis* 7. *extinction* 8. *second-order conditioning* 9. *tolerance*

# OPERANT CONDITIONING

In classical conditioning, the organism is learning to associate two events in the environment because one can be used to predict the onset of the other. In **operant conditioning,** *the organism is learning to associate its own behavior with events in the environment. It is learning the consequences of its actions.*

A woman whose children had just become old enough to enter school went on her first job interview in seven years. She was very nervous and anxious to please the personnel officer at the insurance company where she was applying for an assistant manager position. Instead of asking a series of questions, the interviewer made one simple request: "Tell me about yourself." The woman began talking about her home, family, volunteer activities, and education. Most of the time, the interviewer remained passive and looked down at her papers on the desk. But whenever the woman mentioned anything about organizational skills, the interviewer glanced up, looked her in the eye, and encouragingly said, "mmmm." By the end of the interview, the applicant was only discussing her skills at organizing volunteer work. She didn't get the job, but at her next interview she skipped any discussion of home and family and concentrated on her volunteer work.

## Learning by Consequences

Operant conditioning is the way organisms learn to modify their behavior by learning the consequences of that behavior. Although she may not have been aware of it, the applicant for the assistant manager position was learning which topics were followed by rewards and which were not. When she discussed her volunteer activities, the interviewer showed interest, clearly a rewarding event. As she continued talking, she began to speak more and more of her organizational skills rather than her home and family, topics not followed by any rewards. The general principle of operant conditioning is simple: If a behavior is rewarded, repeat it.

There are three important components in operant conditioning: the stimulus, the response, and the reinforcer. In the preceding example, the general environment of the job interview is the stimulus, and the woman's verbal behavior is the response. The reinforcer is the interest of the interviewer as shown by eye contact and verbal approval. A reinforcer is anything that tends to strengthen the response that immediately preceded it.

## Thorndike's Cats and Skinner's Rats

At the same time Pavlov was unraveling the puzzles of classical conditioning, an American graduate student, Edward L. Thorndike, was studying animal intelligence. Unlike most of his contemporaries, Thorndike was convinced that most people were overimpressed with the intelligence of animals. Anecdotes of dogs or cats that traveled cross-country in a successful search for their owners were common, but stories of animals who got lost in their own neighborhoods were never reported. In fact, he thought the topic of his research should be animal stupidity rather than animal intelligence.

**Figure 5.7**   *Thorndike's puzzle box for cats*

Thorndike's most promising line of investigation dealt with how cats solve problems. He put a hungry cat in a puzzle box (figure 5.7) and placed some food just out of its reach. A wire loop hanging from the inside top of the box would open the door if the cat pulled it. At first the cat tried to squeeze through the bars or reach its paw toward the food. Eventually, it accidentally pulled the wire, and the door opened. The next time it was placed in the box, the cat performed unsuccessful escape routines for a shorter period of time and then pulled the loop. After several experiences in the box, the cat went directly to the loop, pulled it, and got out of the box immediately. Thorndike timed the cat's escape performance on each trial, and it gradually decreased (figure 5.8).

Thorndike did not see much "animal intelligence" in the cat's behavior. Instead, he saw the cat performing a great deal of random behavior that eventually included the correct response. This response was followed by a reward (escape and food), and the cat then began performing the behavior more frequently whenever it was placed into the puzzle box. It was as if the cat intended to stop performing responses that were followed by nothing and to continue to perform those that were followed by a reward (figure 5.9). Thorndike called this phenomenon the **Law of Effect;** *it states that the probability of a response depends upon that response's effect on the environment. Responses followed by a reward tend to be repeated.*

Thorndike used the term " instrumental conditioning" rather than operant conditioning to refer to the process whereby an organism learns the association between behavior and its consequences. The term "operant conditioning" was introduced by B. F. Skinner, who began studying the phenomenon in the 1930s, developing techniques that eventually became standard for investigations of this kind of learning. Much of what we know about operant conditioning was learned in his laboratories and those of his students. He placed a rat into a **Skinner box,** *a special cage, equipped with a lever and a food bin, used for investigating operant conditioning.* Each time the rat pressed the lever, a pellet of food was released into the bin. Some boxes were also equipped with lights and buzzers, and some had grid floors for delivering shock. The lever was usually wired to a **cumulative recorder,** *an instrument with moving chart paper on which a pen moves a notch each time the organism makes a response, in this case, pressing a lever* (figure 5.10). (The term "Skinner Box" was not invented by Skinner; he detested the nickname.)

Skinner's focus was on **operants,** *responses such as lever pressing that occur in the absence of any particular stimuli, or at least any stimuli that are immediately obvious.* Before conditioning, the person or animal spontaneously emits these responses at some baseline rate. In his learning theories, Skinner used the term *operant conditioning* rather than *instrumental conditioning* to emphasize the way in which the conditioning procedure affects the frequency with which a response, or operant, is emitted. In his research he usually obtained a baseline rate of spontaneous responding, say of lever pressing, using the cumulative recorder. Since rats will rarely press the lever unless they receive training, the baseline for this response would be close to zero. Then he introduced an operant learning scheme, and observed the change in the frequency of lever pressing.

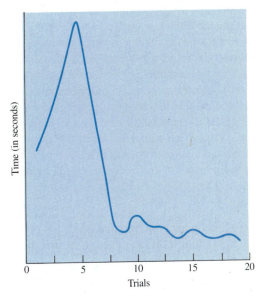

**Figure 5.8**    *A learning curve showing how the time a cat took to escape from the puzzle box decreased*

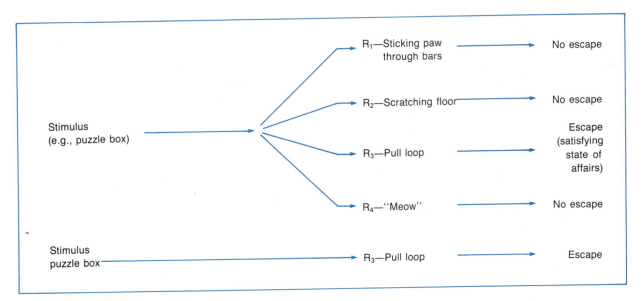

**Figure 5.9**    *Thorndike's Law of Effect*

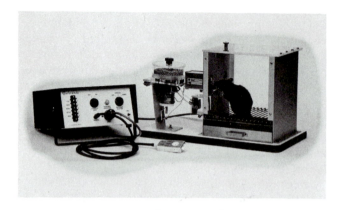

**Figure 5.10** *(a) A Skinner box and (b) cumulative recorder.*

Instead of the term *"classical conditioning,"* Skinner prefers *"respondent conditioning"* to emphasize that the response in the situation is not freely emitted. The **respondent** *is equivalent to the UR.*

## Characteristics of Operant Conditioning

Some of the properties of operant conditioning and classical conditioning are quite similar; others are very different or at least not applicable to the classical conditioning situation. For example, if the time between the behavior and the reinforcement is very short, about one-half second, learning proceeds very quickly. Giving a dog a bone for a trick it performed an hour ago is useless. The

short time interval between the CS and the US is important in classical conditioning also. It seems that organisms need predictors that predict something is going to happen very soon, rather than minutes or hours later, although there are some exceptions.

Other characteristics of operant conditioning that bear some resemblance to classical conditioning are stimulus generalization and discrimination. For instance, the woman at the job interview would probably generalize what she had learned to other stimulus situations, such as other job interviews in banks, retail stores, or factories. Just as in classical conditioning, however, the amount of generalization decreases as the stimulus becomes less and less similar to the one in which the learning occurred. She probably would not generalize what she had learned to an afternoon conversation with a neighbor. The process of stimulus discrimination in operant conditioning involves learning that a response produces a reward in one context but not in another.

*Shaping*    One of the characteristics of operant conditioning not present in classical conditioning is shaping. Suppose you are trying to train your dog to lie down, and you are using dog biscuits as rewards. The dog is too excited to lie down, so you never reward him. The solution to this problem is **shaping,** *a technique in which you reward successively closer approximations of the desired response.* For example, you first reward the dog when he crouches slightly; then you only reward him when he crouches almost to the ground. Finally, you only reward him when he touches the ground with his belly and actually lies down. Professional dog trainers use shaping extensively.

A manager might use shaping techniques with a new employee. Suppose the employee's job is to write summaries of scientific articles, and she does a very poor job in the beginning. The manager might wait a few days and finally give her a reward, perhaps a smile and a positive comment, for a summary that is at least grammatically correct. Before another reward is forthcoming, however, the summaries must be improved, at least in the manager's eyes.

The advantage of shaping is that it permits operant conditioning of responses that do not occur. If a parent has a son whose room is always a mess, it is difficult to reward him for cleaning up the room. But the parents can still use shaping by rewarding the boy for cleaning up a little corner or perhaps for putting up a poster. The parents would then raise the criterion for the next reward.

*Superstition*    The conditions under which operant conditioning occurs require that the response be followed by a reward. They do not necessarily require that the response must *cause* the reward. What would happen if a reward happened to accidentally follow a response?

Skinner (1948) answered this question by delivering food into the bin of a pigeon's Skinner box every fifteen seconds. Just before the food arrived, the pigeon was doing something, perhaps scratching the floor, turning in circles, or pecking the wall. Even though the reward arrived regardless of what the pigeon did or did not do, the particular behavior the pigeon was performing just before the reward increased in frequency. Skinner called this behavior **superstitious**; *it involves the formation of a false association between a response and a reinforcer when there is no cause-and-effect relationship between the two.*

Superstitious behavior is not restricted to pigeons; human beings show similar behavior. For example, a man gets in an elevator and presses the button for the floor to which he wants to go. The elevator is programmed to delay closing the door for several seconds after a button is pushed, but the man does not know this. Since the elevator does not move, he is not rewarded, so he presses the floor button again. The door closes and the elevator rises. The next time the man gets in the elevator he immediately presses the button *twice*, as if he must do this before the elevator will move. Since the elevator will always move after he presses a button twice, he will continue to receive rewards for his superstitious behavior.

Some people have a strong belief that they can control chance events, and these seem to be the ones who are quick to acquire superstitions. In one study, researchers tested this hypothesis on the putting green by giving their subjects a chance to choose the color of their golf ball, and recording whether they tended to choose the same color after a successful putt. Those who scored high on a test designed to measure their belief in whether they could control chance events were more likely to use a "lucky ball" of the same color (Van Raalte, Brewer, Nemeroff, & Linder, 1991).

*Extinction*    The problem of getting rid of undesirable behavior can usually be solved by extinction. In classical conditioning, extinction involves presentation of the CS alone, without pairing it with the US. In operant conditioning, extinction involves withholding the reward for a response. For example, if a rat has learned to press a lever for a pellet of food, withholding the reward will eventually result in the extinction of the lever-pressing response.

Extinction procedures can be used in many situations to get rid of an undesirable response, but it requires withdrawing the reward. Suppose a one-year-old baby won't go to sleep unless her mother walks with her every night. Assuming that the baby's crying is reinforced by the walking, the mother could put the baby on an extinction schedule and withhold the reward for bedtime crying. On the first night, the baby might cry for an hour; on the second, maybe only thirty minutes. By the third or fourth night, the baby should go straight to sleep. As we mentioned earlier in conjunction with classical conditioning, though, extinction is not forgetting and a response thought to be extinguished might come back.

## Reinforcement

The concept of reinforcement is central in operant conditioning. Most psychologists maintain that during operant conditioning, the organism is learning an association between its own response and the reinforcer. It is called a "reinforcer" because it reinforces, or strengthens, the response that precedes it.

*Positive Reinforcement, Negative Reinforcement, and Punishment*    Psychologists usually distinguish between positive and negative reinforcers. A **positive reinforcer** *is a reward for performing some response that tends to strengthen that response.* The food pellet in the Skinner box, for example, provides positive reinforcement for the rat's lever pressing. A **negative reinforcer** *is a stimulus, such as a loud noise or a shock, that is removed following the performance of some response, thereby strengthening that response.* For example, suppose you walk into a room with a dreadful buzz that seems to be coming from one of the fluorescent lights. You make several responses, such as pulling out one or two plugs or flipping some unidentified switches on the wall. Finally, the buzzing stops. The response that immediately preceded the silence is the one rewarded with negative reinforcement.

**Punishment** *is not reinforcement because it does not strengthen a response. It is a stimulus that tends to decrease the probability of the response that immediately preceded it.* If a personnel officer made a gruff "hmph" each time a job applicant said something about her family during an interview, the applicant would quickly decrease that response because it was followed by a punishing stimulus.

Although punishment is an effective way of suppressing undesirable behavior, it has several problems. First, it teaches people what behavior they should *not* do, but it does not teach what they *should* do. Using positive reinforcement for desirable behavior and punishment for undesirable behavior is much more effective than using punishment alone. Another problem with punishment is that it elicits an emotional reaction, such as fear or anger. The more severe the punishment, the more intense the reaction. This automatic reaction is very important in classical conditioning. The person doing the punishing and the context of the punishment comprise the CS, the punishment is the US, and the emotional reaction, perhaps fear, is the response. Eventually, the person being punished shows a classically conditioned fear reaction to the person who does the punishing. Parents might easily become a CS for a fear reaction if they use too much punishment on their children.

*Schedules of Reinforcement*    **Continuous reinforcement** *involves reinforcing a response every time it occurs.* This method of reinforcement is best during the first stages of conditioning when the person or animal is just learning the response. It produces the fastest learning. Although it may seem that this method would be the most effective way to maintain some behavior, Skinner and his students found that **partial reinforcement,** *in which a response is rewarded intermittently,* is actually more effective.

A response maintained through partial reinforcement is very resistant to extinction. Under a continuous reinforcement schedule, the person or animal comes to expect a reward every time, so when the reward stops, the behavior extinguishes rather quickly. But under a partial reinforcement schedule, the organism does not expect a reward every time. If you try to extinguish the response by not rewarding it anymore, the organism will continue to respond for some time.

One of the major hazards in any extinction schedule is the chance that the response will receive a reward and the organism will be moved from a continuous reinforcement schedule to a partial schedule. For example, the parent who is trying to extinguish the baby's crying behavior at bedtime may feel so desperate by the second or third night that he or she goes in to comfort the baby. Now the baby learns that bedtime crying is rewarded some of the time, so the crying will be much more persistent. Maintaining the

extinction schedule under these conditions takes nerves of steel, but it is the fastest way to a more peaceful bedtime for both baby and parents. The slowest way is to let the baby cry on some nights and to comfort him or her on other nights.

There are four different kinds of partial reinforcement schedules: fixed ratio, variable ratio, fixed interval, and variable interval. The **fixed ratio schedule** *reinforces a response after it occurs a certain number of times.* For example, a supervisor might reward an assembly-line worker on a piece rate arrangement, awarding $10 for every five completed toasters. In the laboratory, a rat that received a food pellet for every fifteen lever presses would be on a fixed ratio reinforcement schedule.

The **variable ratio schedule** *rewards a response after it occurs a variable number of times.* Sometimes, perhaps because a few toasters were sent back with defects, the worker might have to produce eight of them to get the reward. At other times, five would be enough. A slot machine works on a variable ratio schedule. It is programmed to deliver rewards after a variable number of lever presses. Gamblers bet that the next winning lever press will come after fewer rather than more tries.

In the interval schedules, a reinforcement is provided for the first response that occurs after an interval of time, usually measured from the last reinforcement. It does not make any difference how often the subject responds during the interval. No reinforcement will be forthcoming until the interval is over and the organism makes one more response.

A **fixed interval schedule** *provides a reward for any correct response that occurs after a specific time interval passes since the last reinforcement.* For example, a rat might have to wait exactly thirty seconds after each reinforcement before a lever press will result in another pellet of food. A paycheck is a reward offered on a fixed interval schedule, usually every two weeks or every month. Another example of a fixed interval schedule is a child who is fed at specific intervals, despite the fact that he or she complains of hunger between meals. Regardless of the child's requests for food, the parent only feeds the child after the specific interval is over.

An interesting behavior pattern appears in fixed interval schedules of reinforcement. The animal or human begins to estimate the time interval rather well, showing a "scalloped" pattern of responding. For example, immediately after a reinforcement, the organism shows very little response, but the rate of responding increases dramatically toward the end of the time period until the next reinforcement is given. The rat does not begin pressing the lever immediately after eating a pellet. It begins to press the lever after twenty or twenty-five seconds have passed.

A **variable interval schedule** *provides a reward for any correct response that occurs after a variable time interval passes since the last reward.* For the rat, sometimes the interval might be twenty-two seconds; at other times it might be thirty-seven seconds. The average interval would be thirty seconds. Real estate salespeople are familiar with the variable interval schedule. Their paychecks, in the form of commissions for a house they sold, arrive at varying intervals.

*The Nature of Reinforcement*    Determining what will and what will not act as a reinforcer is a difficult problem. The reinforcing nature of some things, such as food to a hungry animal, has a certain intuitive reasonableness. The term **primary reinforcer** *refers to events that aid biological survival.* Other examples include water to a thirsty animal or warmth to a cold one.

The vast majority of reinforcing events, however, are not so obviously reinforcing. The slot machine delivers shiny circular pieces of metal to the person who is persistent at pulling its lever. These pieces of metal have no intrinsically rewarding qualities. They do not quench thirst, satisfy hunger, warm cold hands, or provide gratification for sexual urges. Yet they act as a very potent reinforcer since they maintain "lever pressing" (or pulling) at an incredibly high rate. **Secondary reinforcers** *are events that tend to strengthen responses but do not aid biological survival directly.* Whether an event will have secondary reinforcing properties depends on the learning history of the organism rather than on biological survival needs. For instance, the first time a person walks into a candy store with a nickel to exchange for a piece of chocolate, he or she learns to associate money with primary reinforcements. Using classical conditioning, the money has become the CS and the candy the US. Second- or higher-order classical conditioning experiences would lay the foundation for other things that have been paired with money becoming potent reinforcers.

Social events are an important category of secondary reinforcers. A smile from the boss, a pat on the back, or praise from a parent are all powerful reinforcers that can produce dramatic changes in the frequency of responses. They are so powerful and widespread that many scientists wonder whether they are "secondary." Perhaps the need for social approval is almost as important for biological survival as food or water.

The Close Up on Research box: Human Verbal Learning discusses how a psychologist rewarded himself for memorizing boring lists; his secondary reward may have been acclaim from colleagues.

A reinforcer is something that strengthens a response. But this only defines reinforcement after the fact. For example, you won't know whether marbles will act as reinforcers for Johnny until you offer them as rewards for finishing homework. The definition of a reinforcer is not entirely circular; if marbles work in one context, they are likely to work in another. Thus, once you know that something is a reinforcer for a person, you can use it to modify many different kinds of behavior (Meehl, 1950).

David Premack developed another approach to the definition and prediction of reinforcement (1959, 1965). He saw reinforcement as the opportunity to participate in some activity, such as eating, rather than as the thing itself, in this case, food. The reward value of these different activities depends on how frequently the animal normally participates in it. The **Premack principle** *states that activities that are more common or probable in the animal's life will act as reinforcers for activities that are less probable.*

For example, lever pressing is a much less probable activity than eating, so eating will reinforce lever pressing. In instrumental conditioning, then, it is possible to use the eating response as a reinforcement for lever pressing, but it is not possible to use lever pressing as a reward for eating. If playing with marbles is a highly probable activity in Johnny's life, then the opportunity to do it will serve as a reinforcement for doing his homework, an activity that is less probable. On the other hand, if Johnny is working on a fascinating science project related to his beetle collection and has never played marbles in his life, the opportunity to play marbles will not reinforce doing his homework. Instead, the reverse would be true. Allowing him to work on his homework would serve as a reinforcement for playing with marbles. The Premack principle provides a theoretical basis with which to predict whether something will be reinforcing without actually testing it.

## Biofeedback

One example of how operant conditioning can be applied is **biofeedback,** *a technique in which a person learns to gain control over some physiological response by having access to information about the ongoing state of the*

# CLOSE UP ON RESEARCH
## Human Verbal Learning

Whereas many of the early psychologists interested in learning were using rats in mazes or Skinner boxes for studying the details of reward and motivation, Herman Ebbinghaus was studying the way humans learn verbal material (Ebbinghaus, 1964). He acted as his own subject, collecting data about his performance in learning and remembering lists of verbal stimuli.

Ebbinghaus chose to use consonant-vowel-consonant "nonsense syllables" like caj, cik, or gej. He reasoned that words or phrases would be too complex and that any investigations using them would not reveal very much about the elemental associations being formed during a learning experience. Ebbinghaus argued that his 2300 nonsense syllables represented a pool of minimal verbal units free of previous associations. (Later experiments demonstrated that these so-called nonsense syllables are not always nonsensical to people and often have strong associations. For example, a syllable such as "bal" has a much higher association value than one like "cij." The higher the association value of the syllable, the easier it is for subjects to learn and remember it.)

A typical experiment for Ebbinghaus involved serial learning. He made up a list of syllables and read through it at a rapid and uniform rate. Occasionally he would stop and test himself to see if he could remember the next syllable before seeing it. He continued this way until he could recite the entire list in the correct order without any errors. He usually scored his performance by noting either the amount of time or the number of trials required to learn the list perfectly. After an interval of time, Ebbinghaus would use the "savings method" to measure how much of the material he had retained. He relearned the list and compared his performance to his original learning performance. Generally, it took a much shorter period of time and fewer trials to relearn a list; the difference was the amount "saved." The saving score is usually expressed as a percentage of the original learning score.

Using this technique, Ebbinghaus and his followers were able to demonstrate many things about the learning and retention of nonsense syllables. For example, longer lists take longer to learn. This is not only because there are more items on the list; the learner seems to devote more time to each item. Also, the more meaningful the nonsense syllables, the easier they are to learn. Studies using nonsense syllables found the serial position effect, which means that the subject makes more errors on items in the middle of the list than on items in the beginning or end.

Ebbinghaus's data contributed considerably to our understanding of retention. The amount of savings on a relearning task drops dramatically during the first hours after the learning task. Thereafter, the percent saved hardly drops at all.

Most psychologists no longer use Ebbinghaus's methods of studying human verbal learning because the serial learning technique is fraught with complications. Also, many now prefer to use material rich in meaning in order to learn more about how humans process larger units of information. Nevertheless, Ebbinghaus's contributions to the field were enormous, and his studies provided a solid groundwork for future research.

*response.* Until the late 1960s, most scientists thought it would be impossible to gain any voluntary control over internal physiological functions. But the development of biofeedback made everyone question this assumption. For example, people can learn to reduce their heart rate simply by watching a monitor that provides feedback about tiny changes in heart rate. Each time it decreases, they are rewarded by their success and repeat the behavior that immediately preceded the slight drop. This causes the heart rate to decrease still further, providing another rewarding success. Eventually, responses that do not reduce heart rate extinguish, and responses that do become more frequent.

When you ask subjects what behavior they are performing in order to reduce their heart rates, they are usually quite vague. They might say, "Oh, I just try to relax," or "I think about a very calm day I had last week when I was in the mountains." They rarely say they are moving certain muscles or concentrating on their hearts. No one is quite sure *what* response is being rewarded in heart rate biofeedback, except that whatever it is, it results in the drop in heart rate. It most likely involves activation of the parasympathetic nervous system, a division of the autonomic nervous system discussed in chapter 2. This system helps restore the body to normal after a stressful event. Activation of it would produce lowered blood pressure, slower respiration, and decreased heart rate.

Biofeedback has become a useful tool in some areas of medicine (Olton & Noonberg, 1980; Drucko, 1991), particularly in treating tension and migraine headaches, ulcers, asthma, high blood pressure, and circulatory problems. A study conducted on patients with stomach

## APPLYING PSYCHOLOGY
### Invisible Walls

If you jog in suburban neighborhoods, you may have had an unnerving experience in which an angry dog comes racing after you but stops abruptly just before it reaches the end of the property. The owners may have installed an "invisible fence" to keep the dog on the property, another intriguing application of operant conditioning in the real world.

A cable is installed all around the property and linked to a radio transmitter in the house. The dog wears a special collar with a radio receiver. When the animal comes within a few feet of the invisible fence, it hears a beep and has one second to move away from it before it gets a shock from the collar.

The operant conditioning occurs during the first week after the fence is installed. The fence line is staked with white flags and the owner walks the pet around the property, shaking each flag and shouting "NO!". When the dog wanders into the activated field, it hears the beep but the signal has no significance yet. The dog then gets the shock and moves quickly out of the field. The owner rewards the dog with pets and smiles for moving away from the field.

Using a judicious combination of punishment (shock), negative reinforcement (the termination of the shock), and positive reinforcement (praise from the owner), the dog learns to avoid the invisible barrier and to move quickly away from it when it hears the beep. After a few weeks, the owners can take the flags down.

Can you trust an invisible fence? Even if the dog is a pitbull? The fence is only as reliable as the operant conditioning the dog received. If the dog was not trained properly, it might also have learned that the shock stops quickly if it races across the activated field at top speed.

ulcers demonstrates how biofeedback is used (Welgan, 1974). One of the symptoms of ulcers is excess stomach acid, so the five men who participated in the study used biofeedback to learn to control the acidity in their stomachs. Tubes were placed into their stomachs so samples of the contents could be obtained and information about its acidity relayed to each subject. After baseline acidity levels were obtained, the men received feedback about any changes in acidity. At the end of the sessions, these patients' stomach acidity was reduced to about twenty percent of its original level.

Biofeedback, however, does not always produce such reliable results, and there is much controversy about the results it does produce. In particular, scientists wonder whether biofeedback is any more effective than simple relaxation training. Although biofeedback has not turned out to be the great breakthrough in medicine that many hoped for, at least with respect to the treatment of stress-related illnesses, it seems to offer some advantages in the treatment of severe muscular disorders. Patients with cerebral palsy or spinal cord injuries use computers and electrodes attached to muscle groups to obtain feedback about any tiny muscular changes. The electrodes detect muscular activity invisible to the naked eye, and the computer patiently provides rewards for increasing the intensity or duration of muscular activity. Children with cerebral palsy who showed no improvement in motor function over a five-year period learned to use their hands well enough to drink from a glass or dress themselves.

Although the techniques are experimental and need much refinement, they are promising.

▶ **GUIDED REVIEW** *Learning Objectives 7, 8, and 9*

1. Operant conditioning occurs when an organism learns the consequences of its actions in particular contexts. The three principal components of operant conditioning are the _____, the _____, and the _____.
2. Thorndike developed his _____ by observing cats in puzzle boxes. Responses followed by reward (escape and food) were repeated the next time the cat was placed in the box. Responses not followed by reward became less frequent.
3. B. F. Skinner studied _____ conditioning in rats, using lever pressing in the _____ as the response, food as the reward, and a _____ to chart the animal's behavior.
4. Operant conditioning proceeds most quickly if the time interval between the response and reinforcement is short. Other properties of operant conditioning include stimulus generalization and discrimination; _____, in which the organism is rewarded for successively closer approximations of the desired behavior; and _____, in which the organism learns an association between a response and its consequence by accident since that response did not actually cause the consequence to occur.
5. A _____ reinforcement refers to a reward that increases the frequency of the behavior that preceded it. A _____ reinforcement also increases the frequency of the behavior that preceded it, but it is rewarding because it terminates an annoying state of affairs. A _____ decreases the frequency of the response that precedes it.

6. A major problem with the use of _____ as a means of behavioral control is that it produces an emotional reaction in the subject, and the punisher may elicit a classically conditioned fear reaction.

7. Schedules of reinforcement include _____ and _____. Four types of partial reinforcement schedules are _____, _____, _____, and _____.

8. Reinforcement increases the strength of the response that precedes it. _____ satisfy biological needs, whereas the reinforcement value of _____ comes from learning. _____ suggests that the more probable activities in an organism's life can reinforce less probable activities.

9. _____ is an application of the principles of operant conditioning. Patients learn to voluntarily control ongoing physiological processes, such as heart rate, by receiving feedback about the activity of those processes.

*Answers*

*1. stimulus, response, reinforcer 2. Law of Effect 3. operant, Skinner box, cumulative recorder 4. shaping, superstition 5. positive, negative, punishment 6. punishment 7. continuous, partial, fixed interval, variable ratio, variable interval 8. Primary reinforcers, secondary reinforcers, Premack's principle 9. Biofeedback*

# LEARNING AND COGNITION

The principles underlying operant and classical conditioning can explain a great deal about the learning accomplished by both animals and humans. By emphasizing the important role of stimuli and rewards in the environment, conditioning theory can explain some very complicated behaviors. In fact, it almost seems possible to explain *all* behavior in terms of stimuli, responses, and rewards without ever having to talk about cognition, or what is happening inside the head.

However, there are many instances of learning that cannot be fully understood by referring to the principles outlined in operant or classical conditioning. As psychologists began to study these instances more thoroughly, they learned that cognition plays an important role in learning, particularly in the higher primates and in human beings. The thoughts and mental activities that take place during the learning process are as important as the time delay between the CS and US, the strength of the reinforcement, or the schedule of rewards.

The contribution of cognitive psychology has been significant, and it certainly is not limited to the psychology of learning. We have already examined some of these contributions in the discussion of consciousness in chapter 3. The cognitive approach to understanding human behavior has also provided important new insights to studies of perception and memory. In terms of learning,

though, this approach has been of primary importance because it has offered more complete explanations of some instances of learning than have conditioning theories. Explanations of more complicated learning processes such as insight learning, cognitive maps, and observational learning, would be incomplete when they are restricted only to stimuli, responses, and reinforcements. Complicated learning processes can be better understood if we also describe the cognitive process.

## Insight Learning

Unscramble the letters in "OTAPI." One way to do it is to write down the letters in slightly different sequences until you recognize a word. Another way is to simply look at "OTAPI" and try to visualize different sequences until you come up with the answer. If you did it the second way, you probably pondered for a minute or so and then "saw" the solution very suddenly. You had an insight. Now try to unscramble "OREEHCI."

The original studies on insight learning were conducted with chimpanzees. Wolfgang Kohler, a psychologist working at the University of Berlin's primate colony in the Canary Islands during World War I, was studying their problem-solving abilities. Kohler maintained that learning is a cognitive phenomenon, particularly in apes and human beings. The animal studies the problem, trying out different solutions in its head, and finally "comes to see" the solution. When the insight finally comes, it is sudden, and it allows the animal to perform the solution without any errors.

Kohler invented all sorts of problems for the chimps to solve. In one experiment, he placed a banana outside the cage of the smartest chimp, Sultan. Inside the cage were some boxes and two hollow sticks, one slightly thinner than the other. Both sticks were too short for Sultan to use to reach the fruit. But one could be placed inside the other to form a longer double stick. After an hour of unsuccessful attempts to reach the fruit with his arm, one of the sticks, or even the box, Sultan seemed to have given up—but not quite:

> Sultan first of all squats indifferently on the box… then he gets up, picks up the two sticks, sits down again on the box and plays carelessly with them. While doing this, it happens that he finds himself holding one rod in either hand in such a way that they lie in a straight line; he pushes the thinner one a little way into the opening of the thicker, jumps up and is already on the run towards the railings, to which he has up to now turned his back, and begins to draw a banana towards him with the double stick (Kohler, 1925).

The chimp's solution to the problem of reaching the banana is an example of insight learning. Although we can never know what was going through Sultan's mind, we can guess that *something* was happening. He acted as though he had solved the problem in his head, because as soon as he put the sticks together, he ran over and got the banana.

Based on studies like this, **insight learning** *can be defined as follows:*

1. The learning appears to be sudden and complete.
2. The first time the solution is performed, it is usually done with no errors.
3. The solution is remembered very well.
4. The principle underlying the solution is easily applied to other situations.

The characteristics of insight learning cannot be fully explained using the principles of operant or classical conditioning. The animals don't show many successive approximations of the solution that can be rewarded. In insight learning, the animal seems to know the correct solution to the problem even though it has never been rewarded for it, or anything like it, before.

## Cognitive Maps

The way an organism learns about its territory seems to involve more than simple stimulus-response connections. For example, you know a direct route from home to work, but even though you have never taken a longer route, you would probably be able to without making any mistakes because you have a cognitive map of the area "in your head."

A **cognitive map** *is a hypothetical representation of a situation stored in memory or a kind of mental picture of a situation or learning event.* Much of the research on cognitive maps deals with how people and animals acquire and use representations of space, but the term refers to mental pictures of any kind of learning situation. Humans and many animals seem to acquire these maps without ever having been rewarded for making a long series of stimulus-response connections.

Early studies of animals demonstrated that rats, for example, appeared to develop cognitive maps of mazes (Tolman & Honzik, 1930). In one series of studies, the animals were allowed to explore for ten days a maze without food in it. On the eleventh day, they were given a food reward in the goal box. The next time they were placed in the maze, they ran directly to the goal box, making almost no mistakes, just as though they had been receiving a reward there for the past ten days. They did not

have to slowly learn the correct path by trial and error, requiring a reward for each successive approximation of the correct solution. They had a cognitive map and could use it.

Animals more intelligent than rats are even better at learning the spatial layout of their environment. One experiment with chimpanzees showed that they acquire remarkable maps of their terrain (Menzel, 1973, 1978). The chimps were kept in a one-acre enclosure containing trees, fences, and other landmarks. An experimenter would take out the chimps, one at a time, and hide eighteen pieces of food in different places, allowing the chimp to watch. Then the chimp would be set free to find the food.

As soon as they were let loose, the chimps scrambled from one hiding place to another, finding and eating the food. However, consistent with the theory of cognitive maps, they did not retrace the experimenter's steps and get the food in the same order in which it was hidden. They used a much more efficient route, collecting all the food in one area before moving on to the next.

How does a representation of the environment develop? At first, people appear to acquire a representation of an area based on sequential routes they have taken (Smyth, Morris, Levy, & Ellis, 1987), perhaps using stimulus-response connections. For example, people who have lived in a city for a short time tend to draw sketchy maps that emphasize familiar routes. After a few years, their maps show boundaries of areas and landmarks. Once they have developed an integrated cognitive map, they can easily find their way to various landmarks even when their usual routes are blocked.

## Observational Learning

Learning how to drive a car by yourself, without ever having watched someone else do it, would be perilous. You might accidentally step on the accelerator and learn that it makes the car move. But what about stopping? There is precious little time to randomly try several different responses before you hit the brick wall. You would not have time to learn that turning on the lights, setting the clock, or pushing the automatic gearshift into D2 were all unrewarded responses.

Fortunately, humans and some of the other higher animals do not need to learn everything by direct experience with responses and rewards. They can learn through **observational learning**, *in which an organism acquires a response by imitating a model.*

**Figure 5.11** *Children imitating an aggressive model*

An interesting example of observational learning occurs in monkeys. Rhesus monkeys that grow up in the wild usually show intense fear of both live and toy snakes; monkeys reared in the laboratory do not. It is possible that the wild monkeys developed their fears from classical conditioning, but some researchers wondered whether they were simply passing the fears from one generation to the next through observational learning. Mineka and her colleagues (Mineka, 1985; Cook & Mineka, 1987) trained the wild monkeys to reach across a clear plastic box to get a food treat. The wild monkeys reached across readily when the clear box contained a block or other neutral object, but when it contained a live snake, the monkeys showed intense fear. Laboratory monkeys that watched their behavior quickly acquired a fear of snakes that lasted for months, demonstrating that observational learning could indeed play an important role in the development of such fears. Studies like these also provide an example of the value of contemporary research on animal learning (Domjan, 1987).

A series of experiments by Albert Bandura and his colleagues investigated observational learning in children (Bandura, 1977). In a typical experiment, children sit and watch a model performing some action on television, and then they are given an opportunity to imitate the model (figure 5.11). One study examined children's responses to an aggressive model (Bandura, 1965a). The child actress on television walked into a room in which there was a large, inflatable Bobo doll and shouted, "Clear the way!" When the Bobo doll did not respond, the actress knocked it down, screaming, "Pow, right in the nose, boom, boom." Then she struck the doll with a mallet, saying, "Sockeroo, stay down." In one version of the television program, the model was rewarded for behaving so aggressively. An adult came in and gave the child candy and soft drinks. In another version, she was punished with a spanking and several verbal admonishments: "Hey there, you big bully, you quit picking on that clown." In a third version, the model was neither rewarded nor punished.

After watching the program, each child was taken into a room with many toys, including a Bobo doll, and the experimenters observed whether the child imitated the aggressive model in any way. Some children were offered incentives for imitating the model, including juice treats and praise, while others were not.

Boys were very likely to imitate the actress, even if they saw the actress punished. They were even more likely to imitate the actress if they were offered some incentive for doing so. Girls, who showed less aggression toward the Bobo doll in most cases, were nearly as aggressive as the boys if they were offered some incentive. Clearly, both the boys and girls had learned something from observing the model on television. The girls, though, were more likely to show what they had learned if they knew they would receive some reward.

Whether a person will imitate a model depends on many factors, including the model's status, the model's similarity to the person in age and sex, whether the model's behavior is rewarded or punished, and whether the model's behavior is unfamiliar to the observer. Why a person will imitate a model, in the absence of direct rewards and punishments, is still a matter of some controversy. Albert Bandura (1965a) proposes that when observers pay attention to something going on around them, they form mental pictures, or cognitive representations, of what they observe. What they have learned, therefore, is not so much a response but a cognitive representation of a response.

The capacity of humans to learn through observation is a powerful one that saves us from making costly mistakes. In school, a child will observe many examples of both rewarded and punished behavior, and will learn a great deal from them. At work, we learn something every time someone else gets promoted or fired. In some cultures, the models that are available for children are mainly family or group members. But in industrialized countries, the media offers an abundance of models that create opportunities for observational learning. Many American children spend more time watching models on TV than they do with their own parents. The ability to learn through observation gives humans a shortcut over trial and error, but what is learned depends on the model.

▶ **GUIDED REVIEW** *Learning Objectives 10, 11, and 12*

1. More complicated instances of learning, particularly by higher primates, require an understanding of _____. These instances cannot be entirely explained by simple associations between stimuli, responses, and rewards.
2. _____, sometimes observed in higher animals, occurs when the organism seems to reason out a problem and then perform the solution. The principle features of the phenomenon include a learning curve that is sudden and complete (or "scalloped") rather than slow and arduous, an error-free performance of the solution the first time it is attempted, a good memory of the solution, and the ability to transfer the principle learned to other, similar situations.

3. Learning about the layout of the environment involves the acquisition of _____. Using these maps, animals and humans can reach goals despite complicated detours that require them to use paths and motor actions they have never used and for which they have never been rewarded.
4. The ability of some animals, particularly human beings, to learn through observation demonstrates the importance of cognition in some types of learning. Subjects will mimic the actions of a model even though the subjects have never been rewarded for performing the action. In general, the principles of _____ are similar to those of operant conditioning except that the subject is not being rewarded directly. For example, subjects imitate a model who is being rewarded for a particular action more than they imitate a model who is not being rewarded.

*Answers*

1. cognition 2. Insight learning 3. cognitive maps 4. observational learning

## THE LIMITS OF LEARNING

Two animal trainers, Keller and Marian Breland, were trying to teach a cow to perform a lively act on stage.

> It was a hilarious script… it required the cow to perpetrate various outrages on the poor old miner—kick over his bucket, chase him around the campfire, knock down his tent, and finally stage a wild bullfight with him.… we put a considerable amount of money into developing and selling this show before we had even trained the cows… however, when we started into production of the behavior, interesting but painful problems began to develop. Aside from the matter of kicking the bucket, which we could not condition with food reinforcement at all, we were able to condition all the required behavior in the cow… but all in lugubrious slow motion no matter how hungry she became. The whole slowed down performance looked quite ridiculous (Breland & Breland, 1966).

Apparently, cows can learn only some things through operant conditioning and food rewards, and then they learn slowly. There are some things they have a great deal of trouble learning and some things they may not be able to learn at all.

Animal trainers have known this for years, but it came as something of a surprise to psychologists. Traditional learning theory had always maintained that it made no difference what response was paired with what reward. The animal should learn to associate the two as long as they occurred close together in time and as long as the beast was physically capable of the response. But as the Brelands discovered, they simply could not teach the cow

# EXPLORING HUMAN DIVERSITY
## Becoming a Criminal

In Youngstown, Ohio, two teenage girls were arguing about a boyfriend when one of them picked up a handgun and fatally shot the other. In the District of Columbia, a 15-year-old boy driving a stolen car got impatient with a slow-moving pedestrian and allegedly gunned him down with a semiautomatic pistol. A 16-year-old boy who had been shot five different times goes to the emergency room full of pride, not fear. An epidemic of violence plagues this country and no city, county, or rural backwoods is immune.

Why do some people become criminals? Psychologists, sociologists, anthropologists and many more have attempted to answer this gnawing question, one that desperately needs an answer. Over the years, two major theories evolved: biological theories, which hold that criminal behavior was innate, that some people were just "born criminals," and social or environmental theories, which emphasize the critical role of learning.

Taking a biological approach, researchers looked for differences in the brains, hormone levels, or other characteristics in hardened criminals. One of the more famous cases involving a biological theory featured Richard Speck, who was convicted of killing eight nurses in Chicago. Speck had an XYY chromosome configuration. The extra Y chromosome was thought by some to cause violent behavior. Although some obvious biological malfunction is found in a few cases, the vast majority of people who commit violent crimes do not show any consistent biological pattern that would support the "born criminal" point of view.

Although biological factors may be involved, the social environment and learning must play major roles. The definition of "crime" is socially determined, and what counts as crime in one state or country may not be defined that way in another. People learn what is or is not lawful behavior. Too, research has shown that not all people are treated the same by the criminal justice system. It is clear that the poor and minorities, in particular, are more likely to be defined as being "criminal" by the legal system. It is not only behavior, but how society responds to it that determines whether or not one is labelled a criminal.

People learn the kind of criminal behavior that is consistent with their social and cultural situation (Kornhauser, 1978). An office worker might observe coworkers improving their lot by faking travel vouchers, and learn fraud as a means to solve financial problems. A street gang member might have quite different models, ones that used firearms to obtain money. Through observational learning, the social and cultural situation can provide models that affect what kind of crime a person commits.

While there is much we do not understand about why certain individuals commit crimes, research on crime rates between particular demographic groups have shown clearly that the kinds of crimes people learn to commit, as well as the rates of crime within a given group, are greatly explained by social context (Cloward & Ohlin, 1960). Some children grow up in a subculture of violence, the kind that offers rewards for criminal behavior. What we do not yet understand is why, when similar people are raised in a particular social and cultural setting, some learn to commit crimes while others do not.

Since patterns of criminal behavior usually begin in early teenage years, social scientists have tried to determine what accounts for learning such behavior. Studies have found a relationship between crime and employment (Votey, 1991). Once people are employed, they are less likely to commit crimes, suggesting that the environment in which the employed person lives is less likely to provide criminal models compared to the environment of the unemployed person. Employment also provides a means to make ends meet. A major problem is that the opportunity to learn delinquent behavior almost always occurs before the opportunity to learn work skills (Votey, 1991).

Age, social class, race, and education level are also related to rates of crime and delinquency (Tonry, 1991). Blacks are disproportionately represented among the more poorly educated, single-parent families, and lower socioeconomic status, and they account for higher rates of criminal behavior (Champion, 1990). Significantly, when factors such as work experience, family status, and education are controlled, rates of crime and delinquency between races are quite similar (Votey, 1991).

The highest rates of crime are found among the urban poor, the poorly educated, and the unemployed. Though these people may have high aspirations for success, they have few models who have reached them using legitimate means. Instead, their models might be rich drug traffickers. The strain in their lives created by poverty might lead them to choose the most accessible path they see to achieve goals they view as unattainable in any other way (Agnew, 1992; Mickelson, 1990).

Learning theory suggests that criminal behavior, like any human behavior, is subject to the rules of reward and punishment. If people are rewarded for violent crimes, they will continue; if they are punished, they will stop provided they have alternatives. Yet the setting for crime seems to conspire against any effective use of these learning principles. Crime provides instant and fairly consistent rewards, but punishment, if it occurs at all, is long after the act. And to make things worse, the people who are most likely to become criminals are those who have the fewest alternatives for reaching their goals.

to kick the bucket with its rear leg. Futhermore, they could not teach the cow to do anything quickly; she did all her tricks at her own bovine pace.

Why should it be so difficult to teach the cow to kick the bucket and so easy to teach it to chase (or at least follow) the miner? Studies on animals have shown that the principles of learning derived from conditioning studies are not quite as universal as once believed. Organisms seem to have many built-in biological predispositions that make it easy for them to learn some associations but make it almost impossible for them to learn others, regardless of how much reward or punishment is used. These predispositions appear to have evolved, and they are connected with the animal's life-style and habitat. The Brelands think that it is extremely difficult to teach a cow to move quickly for a food reward because in the cow's environment there is no need to rush for food. Grass doesn't get up and run away. A dog might easily learn to perform some trick quickly for a food reward because it is a hunting species that must move fast to get its food.

## Flavor Aversions

Some of the best studies on these predispositions deal with **flavor aversions,** *the avoidance of specific tastes.* A team of researchers demonstrated that it is easier to teach a rat an association between the taste of food and an illness than between the taste of food and a shock (Garcia & Koelling, 1966). In part of this experiment, they offered one group of rats some flavored water and another group some "bright and noisy" water, water that appeared to flash lights and make clicking sounds each time the animal took a sip. Then half of each group was made sick by exposure to X rays, and the other half was given a shock.

According to traditional learning theory, the rats that had been punished for drinking flavored water should have avoided flavored water; those that were punished for drinking the bright noisy water should have avoided that kind of water. As it turned out, their avoidance behavior depended on what *kind* of punishment they received. If they became sick, they avoided only the flavored water. The rats that had drunk the bright and noisy water did not associate it with the sickness. Also, the rats that were shocked did not associate the shock with the flavored water—only with the bright and noisy water.

This and other studies show that there are particular associations that are very easy to make and some that are very difficult. Which ones are easy to make depends on the species of animal. Birds, for example, do not easily associate the taste of food with illness, but they readily associate illness with the color of the food. Perhaps this is because visual cues play a large role in the bird's normal food-getting behavior. In humans, tastes are paired with illness. A person who gets the flu after trying Szechuan stir-fry pork for lunch may form an association between the Chinese food and the sickness. He or she may never want to taste the food again, claiming that the food tastes bad. This occurs even when the person knows that the onset of the flu had nothing to do with the novel food.

Flavor aversion techniques are being used to manage wildlife populations so that they can be better protected. For instance, coyotes are sometimes shot by ranchers because they prey on domestic livestock such as sheep. In a study in California, sheep carcasses laced with a mild poison were scattered across an open range (Garcia, Rusiniak, & Brett, 1977). The wild coyotes took a few bites, became sick, and began avoiding live sheep. The same technique is being used to alter the hunting habits of wild cougars and hawks that prey on sheep.

State biologists in Alaska are using the technique to convince bears to avoid campsites. The biologists are placing lumps of beef fat containing lithium chloride and wrapped in cloth soaked in Pinesol disinfectant along bear trails. The bears love the beef fat, but the lithium chloride gives them an upset stomach. After one or two experiences with the fat, the bears associate the scent with sickness and avoid the Pinesol-cleaned trash cans at the campsites.

In humans, the principle underlying flavor aversions is used to treat alcoholism in what is called "emetic therapy." Alcohol is paired with substances that cause the person to feel nauseated and vomit, and an aversion to the taste of alcohol develops. The treatment is a new one but some reports suggest that it may be promising. In one study, sixty percent of patients who underwent emetic therapy remained abstinent for one year (Elkins, 1991).

## Biological Predispositions and Learning

The flavor aversion studies made it clear that animals, and probably humans as well, have biological predispositions that make it easier to form some associations and make it more difficult to form others. They also challenged another assumption about learning: that the reward (or punishment) must immediately follow the response. Under some circumstances, animals can learn to avoid a particular food even if the sickness comes hours later.

After much research on flavor aversions and other phenomena that show the limits of learning, most psychologists agree that we do not have to develop new laws of learning for each species. The principles of conditioning may need to be slightly modified, but they need not be discarded (Rescorla & Holland, 1982). For example, although an animal does learn to avoid a taste even if the sickness comes hours later, the learning is stronger if the delay is short. Nevertheless, the phenomenon is a fascinating one that calls into question many of the fundamental assumptions of behaviorism and created tremendous controversy and much heated debate. When John Garcia and his colleagues first tried to publish a study demonstrating it, one reviewer reportedly said, "this phenomenon is about as likely as bird droppings in a cuckoo clock."

While flavor aversion research was showing that general principles of operant conditioning didn't always apply and that we should consider the evolutionary history of an animal, scientists taking the cognitive approach were showing that there are many examples of learning that also

didn't fit neatly into the behaviorist's theory. These studies also generated much controversy and criticism from behaviorists. B.F. Skinner, whose entire life was devoted to behaviorism and the experimental analysis of behavior, was vehement in accusing cognitive scientists of illogically speculating about internal processes which they could not observe. Progress in psychology is not just built on patient, painstaking, and dispassionate research; the human element of conflict plays an important role.

▶ **GUIDED REVIEW** *Learning Objective 13*

1. Animals and humans possess biological _____ that allow them to learn some associations very easily but that make it very difficult to learn others.
2. _____ studies show how associations between taste and illness occur in rats and other mammals.

*Answers*

1. *predispositions 2. Flavor aversion*

## SUMMARY

I. Learning represents changes in behavior as a result of experience. (p. 140)

A. It is very difficult to separate learning from changes in behavior due to maturation or genetic influences. (pp. 140–141)

B. Learning cannot be observed directly; performance is observed. Despite the difficulty of separating learning from other variables, learning should be defined as the relatively permanent changes in behavior, or potential for those changes, that occur because of prior experience, excluding behavioral changes due to maturation, genetic factors, changes in motivation, fatigue, or injury. (p. 141)

II. Classical conditioning involves the formation of an association between two stimuli, one of which (US) automatically elicits a response (UR), the other of which (CS) reliably precedes the US and after many pairings will produce a response (CR) when presented alone. (pp. 141–142)

A. Ivan Pavlov first demonstrated the principles of classical conditioning using a dog's salivation response to meat powder. (p. 142)

B. Classical conditioning has a number of properties. (p. 143)

1. The rate of conditioning depends on factors such as how many times the US is paired with the CS and whether the CS is a novel or familiar stimulus. (p. 143)

2. Organisms exhibit stimulus generalization, in which they will respond to stimuli that are similar to the CS. (p. 143)

3. After training, organisms also exhibit stimulus discrimination. An organism trying to perform a very difficult discrimination may show experimental neurosis. (p. 144)

4. The best pairing procedure involves presenting the CS about one-half second before presenting the US. (p. 144)

5. A CR can be inhibited by an extinction procedure. (p. 144)

6. Second-order conditioning involves using a previously neutral CS that reliably elicits a CR as a US in a new conditioning experience. (p. 145)

C. The CR may or may not be similar to the UR; in some cases, the CR is a preparation for the US. Tolerance to drugs may be affected by classical conditioning because of physiological preparation. (pp. 146–147)

III. Operant conditioning involves the formation of an association between a particular response and the consequences of that response. (p. 147)

A. The three important components of operant conditioning are the stimulus, the response, and the reinforcer. (p. 148)

B. Early researchers who investigated the properties of operant conditioning include Thorndike, who formulated the Law of Effect, and Skinner, whose theories of behaviorism are based on the fundamental properties of operant conditioning. (pp. 148–149)

C. Some of the characteristics of operant conditioning are similar to those of classical conditioning. Others, such as the following, are somewhat different. (pp. 150–151)

   1. Shaping is a technique in which successively closer approximations to the desired response are rewarded. (p. 150)

   2. Superstition involves the formation of spurious associations between a response and a reinforcer. (p. 151)

   3. Extinction in operant conditioning involves withholding the reward for a previously rewarded response. (p. 151)

D. A reinforcement strengthens the response that preceded it. (p. 151)

   1. Both positive and negative reinforcement strengthen the preceding response. Punishment tends to decrease the probability that the preceding response will occur again. Punishment may produce a classically conditioned fear reaction. (pp. 151–152)

   2. Schedules of reinforcement include continuous, partial, and various kinds of partial reinforcement schedules including fixed ratio, variable ratio, fixed interval, and variable interval. (pp. 152–153)

   3. Primary reinforcers satisfy biological needs; secondary reinforcers acquire their rewarding properties through learning experiences. (p. 153)

E. Biofeedback is an example of operant conditioning in which a person learns to control a physiological response by having access to information about its activity. (pp. 153–155)

IV. Some examples of learning are not easily explained by the principles of conditioning. These examples involve cognition. (p. 156)

A. Insight learning appears in some problem-solving situations; the organism seems to learn the correct solution suddenly, performs the solution with no mistakes the first time, remembers the solution, and applies it in other situations. (pp. 156–157)

B. Cognitive maps are hypothetical representations of a situation stored in memory. (p. 157)

C. Observational learning occurs when an organism acquires a response by imitating a model. (pp. 157–159)

V. Learning is limited partly because of biological predispositions. (pp. 159–161)

A. Flavor aversion research demonstrates that for certain animals it is easier to form associations between taste and illness than between other stimuli, such as visual cues and illness. (p. 161)

B. Studies on flavor aversion suggest that biological predispositions exist for each species that make it easier to form certain associations and difficult or impossible to form others. (pp. 161–162)

## ACTION GLOSSARY

Match the terms in the left column with the definitions in the right column.

___ **1. Learning (p. 141)**
___ **2. Classical conditioning (p. 141)**
___ **3. Unconditioned stimulus (US) (p. 141)**
___ **4. Unconditioned response (UR) (p. 141)**
___ **5. Conditioned stimulus (CS) (p. 141)**
___ **6. Conditioned response (CR) (p. 142)**

A. *In classical conditioning, the stimulus that automatically elicits a response from an organism.*

B. *A stimulus which, through classical conditioning, comes to elicit a conditioned response because it was paired with an unconditioned stimulus that automatically elicited an unconditioned response.*

C. *A response elicited by a conditioned stimulus after classical conditioning.*

D. *Relatively permanent changes in behavior that occur because of prior experience. Can be theoretically discriminated from changes in behavior primarily due to maturation, genetic influences, fatigue, injury, disease, or drugs.*

E. *The process by which an organism forms an association between two stimuli in the environment. One stimulus is neutral; it has no particular meaning prior to the conditioning process. The other automatically elicits some response from the organism. When the neutral stimulus reliably precedes the stimulus that automatically elicits a response, the previously neutral stimulus elicits a conditioned response.*

F. *In classical conditioning, the response automatically elicited by the unconditioned stimulus.*

___ 7. **Stimulus generalization** (p. 143)

___ 8. **Stimulus discrimination** (p. 144)

___ 9. **Extinction** (p. 144)

___ 10. **Second-order conditioning** (p. 145)

___ 11. **Spontaneous recovery** (p. 144)

___ 12. **Law of Effect** (p. 148)

___ 13. **Operant conditioning** (p. 147)

A. *The sudden reappearance of a CR after its apparent extinction.*

B. *A type of classical conditioning in which the original conditioned stimulus is used as an unconditioned stimulus in a new conditioning procedure with a new conditioned stimulus.*

C. *In classical conditioning, the process in which the organism learns that a particular stimulus is associated with an unconditioned stimulus whereas another stimulus is not. The organism learns to make a conditioned response to only one of the two stimuli. In instrumental conditioning, the organism learns that a response is followed by reinforcement under some circumstances but not under others.*

D. *The probability of a response depends upon that response's effect on the environment; responses followed by a reward tend to be repeated.*

E. *In classical conditioning, a procedure in which the conditioned stimulus is presented repeatedly without pairing it with the unconditioned stimulus. Diminishes the size of and gradually eliminates the conditioned response. In instrumental conditioning, it refers to the withholding of reinforcement following a response.*

F. *In classical conditioning, once a conditioned response has been established to a particular stimulus, similar stimuli will also evoke the response. In instrumental conditioning, an organism tends to repeat a response in circumstances similar to the ones in which the response was originally learned.*

G. *The process by which an organism comes to associate a response with the consequences of that response.*

___ 14. **Skinner box** (p. 149)

___ 15. **Cumulative recorder** (p. 149)

___ 16. **Operant** (p. 149)

___ 17. **Respondent** (p. 150)

___ 18. **Shaping** (p. 150)

___ 19. **Superstition** (p. 151)

A. *An instrument with moving chart paper on which a pen moves up a notch each time an organism makes a particular response. It is used to show changes in the rate of response.*

B. *In operant conditioning, organisms come to repeat responses followed by rewards even though those responses did not cause the reward and their pairing was only coincidental.*

C. *The unconditioned response in classical conditioning. The term, used by B. F. Skinner, emphasizes the fact that the response is not freely emitted.*

D. *The process by which unusual or difficult responses are conditioned. Successive approximations that come closer and closer to the desired response are rewarded.*

E. *The experimental apparatus used to study operant conditioning in animals. Contains some means to provide rewards and some task for the animal to learn.*

F. *A response that is spontaneously emitted; it occurs in the absence of any particular or obvious stimuli.*

___ 20. **Positive reinforcement** (p. 151)

___ 21. **Negative reinforcement** (p. 151)

___ 22. **Punishment** (p. 151)

___ 23. **Continuous reinforcement** (p. 152)

___ 24. **Partial reinforcement** (p. 152)

___ 25. **Fixed ratio schedule of reinforcement** (p. 152)

___ 26. **Variable ratio schedule of reinforcement** (p. 152)

___ 27. **Fixed interval schedule of reinforcement** (p. 152)

A. *A partial reinforcement schedule in which a response is rewarded after it occurs a fixed number of times.*

B. *Any rewarding stimulus that increases the probability of the response that immediately preceded it.*

C. *A method of reinforcement in which a reward is supplied after every response.*

D. *A partial reinforcement schedule in which the first response that occurs after a fixed time interval is rewarded, but all other responses are ignored.*

E. *A procedure used to decrease the probability that a response will occur by presenting an aversive stimulus whenever the response occurs.*

F. *A partial reinforcement schedule in which a response is rewarded after it occurs a certain number of times. The number of times varies from trial to trial.*

G. *Removal of a stimulus, such as a loud noise or shock, following the performance of some response, thereby strengthening that response.*

H. *A method of reinforcement in which a response is rewarded intermittently.*

____ **28. Variable interval schedule of reinforcement (p. 153)**

____ **29. Primary reinforcer (p. 153)**

____ **30. Secondary reinforcer (p. 153)**

____ **31. Premack principle (p. 153)**

____ **32. Biofeedback (p. 153)**

____ **33. Insight learning (p. 157)**

____ **34. Cognitive map (p. 157)**

____ **35. Observational learning (p. 157)**

____ **36. Flavor aversions (p. 161)**

A.  *A type of learning in which the learner acquires a response through observation of the consequences of the actions of a model.*

B.  *An advanced form of learning seen in primates in which the organism seems to grasp the solution to a problem suddenly and perform the required responses completely and without error the first time.*

C.  *A perceptual representation of an area that an organism develops through experience in the area.*

D.  *A partial reinforcement schedule in which the first response that occurs after an interval of time is rewarded, whereas all others are ignored. The interval of time varies from trial to trial.*

E.  *Activities that are common function as reinforcers for activities that are less probable.*

F.  *An application of operant conditioning in which an individual learns to gain control over some physiological response by receiving feedback about the ongoing state of the system.*

G.  *A reinforcer that does not obviously aid biological survival but which probably acquired its reinforcing value through classical conditioning.*

H.  *Events that aid biological survival.*

I.  *The avoidance of specific tastes.*

*ANSWERS*

20. b, 21. g, 22. e, 23. c, 24. h, 25. a, 26. f, 27. d, 28. d, 29. h, 30. g, 31. e, 32. f, 33. b, 34. c, 35. a, 36. i

1. d, 2. e, 3. a, 4. f, 5. b, 6. c, 7. f, 8. c, 9. e, 10. b, 11. a, 12. d, 13. g, 14. e, 15. a, 16. f, 17. c, 18. d, 19. b,

# SELF-TEST

**1.** Since learning itself cannot easily be measured, most researchers demonstrate that learning has occurred by measuring changes in

   **(a)** a potential to act.

   **(b)** the actual performance of some behavior.

   **(c)** the presentation of the conditions for learning.

   **(d)** both a and c.
     (LO 2; pp. 140–141)

**2.** The procedure for classical conditioning involves pairing

   **(a)** two previously neutral stimuli, with the same one always coming second.

   **(b)** a neutral stimulus with an unconditioned stimulus, the neutral one coming second.

   **(c)** a neutral stimulus with an unconditioned stimulus, presenting only the unconditioned stimulus if the subject makes the response (e.g., salivation).

   **(d)** a neutral stimulus with an unconditioned stimulus, with the neutral stimulus coming first.
     (LO 3; p. 141)

**3.** The unconditioned stimulus

   **(a)** is neutral before the conditioning session.

   **(b)** produces the conditioned response as a consequence of the training session.

   **(c)** elicits an automatic and unlearned response from the subject before the training session.

   **(d)** is a cue for learning.
     (LO 3; p. 141)

**4.** Stimulus generalization is

   **(a)** the tendency for stimuli (CSs) similar to the original CS to elicit the CR.

   **(b)** the ability to reliably distinguish between the original CS and similar stimuli.

   **(c)** the tendency to make similar (to the CR) responses to the original CS.

   **(d)** a characteristic of operant conditioning but not of classical conditioning.
     (LO 4; p. 143)

**5.** Stimulus discrimination

   **(a)** involves the CR appearing after some stimuli but not after others.

   **(b)** involves the tendency to make a variety of conditioned responses to the original CS.

   **(c)** is a characteristic of classical conditioning but not of operant conditioning.

   **(d)** involves the same stimulus eliciting different behaviors.
     (LO 4; p. 144)

**6.** Presenting the CS by itself, without the US, produces

   **(a)** extinction.

   **(b)** observational learning.

   **(c)** generalization.

   **(d)** discrimination.
     (LO 4; p. 144)

7. Second-order conditioning
   (a) involves the same stimulus (CS) eliciting two responses (CRs).
   (b) involves relearning after extinction.
   (c) involves the distinction between classical conditioning and operant conditioning.
   (d) is a classical conditioning procedure in which a CS becomes a US in a new learning session.
   (LO 5; p. 145)

8. The key element in operant conditioning is
   (a) the type of stimulus used.
   (b) the age of the subject.
   (c) the consequence of the behavior.
   (d) whether the response is elicited or emitted.
   (LO 7; pp. 147–148)

9. A reinforcer is
   (a) the same as motivation.
   (b) a stimulus that strengthens the preceding response.
   (c) the same as an unconditioned stimulus.
   (d) learned.
   (LO 8; p. 151)

10. A mouse is put into a box and observed. In the first five minutes, the mouse grooms, sniffs, and walks around the box picking up bits of dust. These behaviors are
    (a) operants.
    (b) respondents.
    (c) reinforcers.
    (d) artificial.
    (LO 7; p. 149)

11. The reinforcement of successive approximations of the desired terminal behavior is called
    (a) classical conditioning.
    (b) discrimination.
    (c) generalization.
    (d) shaping.
    (LO 7; p. 150)

12. If the relationship between emitted behavior and the reward is accidental and coincidental, the behaviors resulting are called
    (a) generalized.
    (b) operants.
    (c) superstitious.
    (d) random.
    (LO 7; p. 151)

13. The procedure called extinction is performed in operant conditioning
    (a) by not following the to-be-extinguished behavior with a reinforcer.
    (b) by presenting the CS without the US.
    (c) by following the to-be-extinguished behavior with an aversive stimulus.
    (d) by terminating conditioning trials and allowing the subject time to forget the behavior.
    (LO 7; p. 151)

14. The reinforcement of the first response that occurs after a set time interval
    (a) is called a fixed ratio schedule.
    (b) is called a fixed interval schedule.
    (c) is called continuous reinforcement.
    (d) is an application of classical procedures to operant conditioning.
    (LO 8; p. 152)

15. Biofeedback is a
    (a) technique in which brain stimulation and other physiological techniques are used with learning.
    (b) technique in which classical conditioning is used by physicians to control body responses.
    (c) technique in which an individual uses operant conditioning to learn to control body responses using only information for the reinforcer.
    (d) generally accepted technique in which a person learns control over body responses, even to the point of reversing the effects of epilepsy and curing heart disease.
    (LO 9; pp. 153–155)

16. A cognitive map is
    (a) an example of insight learning.
    (b) the result of classical conditioning.
    (c) characteristic of human learning but not of animal learning.
    (d) a mental picture or diagram of a situation.
    (LO 11; p. 157)

17. Observational learning is
    (a) the result of classical conditioning that goes on unconsciously.
    (b) the result of operant conditioning that goes on unconsciously.
    (c) imitation of a model.
    (d) only possible in human subjects.
    (LO 12; pp. 157–159)

18. Observing violent episodes on television
    (a) results in increased aggression by children.
    (b) results in decreased violence because the subjects "get it out of their systems" by watching.
    (c) has no effect on violent or aggressive behavior.
    (d) increases aggression in girls but decreases it in boys.
    (LO 12; pp. 158–159)

19. An interesting and important observation about learning is that
    (a) any response can be trained in any subject if the reinforcer is chosen correctly.
    (b) there are biological limits on what responses can be learned effectively by which subjects.
    (c) classical conditioning is only possible with mammals.

    (d) operant conditioning will not work at all with animals more primitive than the mouse.
    (LO 13; pp. 159–162)

20. The relationship between a particular taste and a subsequent illness
    (a) cannot be learned effectively.
    (b) is learned effectively by some animals but not by humans
    (c) is innate.
    (d) is easier for the rat to learn than the relationship between a particular taste and a subsequent shock.
    (LO 13; p. 161)

*ANSWERS*

1. b, 2. d, 3. c, 4. a, 5. a, 6. a, 7. d, 8. c, 9. b, 10. a, 11. d, 12. c, 13. a, 14. b, 15. c, 16. d, 17. c, 18. a, 19. b, 20. d

# THINKING ABOUT PSYCHOLOGY

1. The managers of a manufacturing plant producing various chemical substances want to be sure the workers will notice a particular smell because leaks would be very hazardous. The smell is a faint one that resembles chlorine bleach. They decide to try a classical conditioning program with volunteers, in which the smell will be the CS and a loud siren the UCS. Using figures 5.2 and 5.4 as models, diagram the classical conditioning procedure and explain how the training program might proceed.

2. A number of fast-food companies began marketing campaigns that invited customers to scratch a small section of a card with a penny to uncover one of several hidden images. If the patron scratched the correct square and the image matched a target on the card, a free hamburger was the reward. In the beginning, patrons eagerly scratched their cards. But after a month or so most of the cards were tossed in the trash unscratched and management decided the campaign was useless. Explain how this game demonstrates several principles of operant conditioning, including the effectiveness of various schedules of reinforcement. What might they do to revive customer scratching behavior?

3. In Japan, bowing to someone to show respect is commonplace and expected. During a conversation one person might bow slightly several times to the other to show agreement or acknowledgment. Some Japanese also bow while talking on the phone even though the other person can't see. How might the principles of stimulus generalization apply?

4. Imagine you are the president of a new manufacturing company that will make children's clothing, with two facilities. For one line of coats, made in one facility, you want to offer the lowest price possible so you need to keep production costs low and volume high. For another line of shirts made in the other facility you want to emphasize very high quality and charge higher prices. What kind of reward structures might you set up for the staff at each facility in order to achieve your goals? What problems would you predict would be associated with each facility?

## SUGGESTED READINGS

Bandura, A. (1977). *Social learning theory*. Englewood Cliffs, NJ: Prentice-Hall. A description of Bandura's theories concerning children's social development and observational learning.

Glaser, R. (1982). Instructional psychology: Past, present, and future. *American Psychologist,* 37, 292-305. An article discussing psychology applied to instruction.

Hellige, J.B. (1990). Hemisphere asymmetry. *Annual Review of Psychology,* 41, 55-80. A review of the research on hemispheric asymmetry.

Kohler, W. (1925). *The mentality of apes*. New York: Harcourt Brace. A classic in cognitive psychology that describes the experiments conducted with chimpanzees and insight learning.

Skinner, B.F. (1938). *The behavior of organisms*. New York: Appleton Century Crofts. The classic work describing the principles of operant conditioning.

Spear, N.E., Miller, J.S., and Jagielo, J.A. (1990). Animal memory and learning. *Annual Review of Psychology,* 41, 169-212. A summary of research on classical and instrumental conditioning in animals.

# CHAPTER 6

## REMEMBERING AND FORGETTING
## OUTLINE

▶ **Learning Objectives**

▶ **The Three Storage Systems**

- Sensory Store
- Short-Term Memory
  The Capacity of Short-Term
  Memory
  Losing Information from
  Short-Term Memory
  Transfer to Long-Term
  Memory
- Long-Term Memory
  How Is Information Stored in
  Long-Term Memory?
  Forgetting from Long-Term
  Memory

▶ **Guided Review**

▶ **Retrieving Information**

- Search Strategies
  Retrieval Cues
  State-Dependent Memory
- Memory Reconstruction
  Eyewitness Testimony
- Recognition Memory
  "It's on the Tip of My Tongue"
  Recognizing Familiar Faces

▶ **Guided Review**

▶ **Biological Basis of Learning and Memory**

- Changes in the Brain during
  Learning
  Learning in *Aplysia*
  Classical Conditioning in the
  Rabbit

- Making a Memory
  Where Is the Engram?
  What Is the Engram?
- Modifying Memory
  Memory Disruptors
  Stress and Memory
  Memory Improvement Drugs

▶ **Guided Review**

▶ **Improving Your Memory**

- Improving the Storage Process
  Paying Attention
  Rehearsal
  Organizational Strategies
  Efficient Learning
- Improving Retrieval

▶ **Guided Review**

▶ **Summary**

▶ **Action Glossary**

▶ **Self-Test**

▶ **Thinking About Psychology**

▶ **Suggested Readings**

# REMEMBERING AND FORGETTING
## LEARNING OBJECTIVES

**After reading this chapter, you should be able to**

▶ **1.** describe the nature of the sensory store. *(p. 173)*

▶ **2.** describe short-term memory, and explain how information is maintained in STM, transferred to long-term memory, or lost from short-term memory. *(pp. 174–176)*

▶ **3.** describe long-term memory, and explain how information is stored in and lost from it. *(pp. 177–181)*

▶ **4.** identify and describe two strategies for searching long-term memory. *(pp. 181–184)*

▶ **5.** explain some of the processes involved in memory reconstruction. *(pp. 184–186)*

▶ **6.** compare "recall" and "recognition," showing how the two kinds of retrieval are different. *(pp. 186–187)*

▶ **7.** explain some of the changes that occur in the brain during learning, relying on evidence from studies of animals. *(pp. 187–188)*

▶ **8.** define the "engram," and describe several studies that attempted to find its location and identify its properties. *(pp. 188–189)*

▶ **9.** describe several ways memories can be modified. *(pp. 189–191)*

▶ **10.** list and describe several methods that can be used to improve the storage process. *(pp. 191–193)*

▶ **11.** explain how memory can be improved by improving retrieval. *(p. 194–195)*

A psychology professor tells the story of how she tried to reduce the use of traditional gender-biased language in her psychology lectures by using "he" half the time and "she" the other half, instead of always using "he." At the end of the semester, she told her students what she had been doing. They had definitely noticed, but told her she went way overboard. They said she always used "she" and never used "he." Recalling that she taped her lectures, she asked a student to count the pronouns. The objective count revealed they all had faulty memories. She used "he" eighty percent of the time (Mandler, 1979; 1990).

How we remember, misremember, and forget the events in our lives has always been an important topic in psychology. In recent years, psychologists have taken a very cognitive approach to memory. In contrast to the last chapter, where we focused mainly on the simpler forms of learning, this chapter will explore how we store and recall rather complicated material.

## THE THREE STORAGE SYSTEMS

Human memory consists of three different but interacting storage systems: the *sensory store, short-term memory* (STM), and *long-term memory* (LTM). Each system has its own functions, and information can be transferred from one to another (Atkinson & Shiffrin, 1968).

A simple model of how these three storage systems operate together will help you to better understand human memory (figure 6.1). Suppose your spouse writes the grocery list containing three items and puts it on the bulletin board. The information first is received by one of your sense organs, your eyes. Then it is deposited into the sensory store for vision. This storage system holds everything that the eyes see, but it can only hold it for a very brief moment. If you are going to remember the grocery list long enough to buy the items at the supermarket, you must store the items in STM.

STM can only hold a limited number of items, and it can only hold them for about fifteen seconds (Brown, 1958; Peterson & Peterson, 1959). Unless you rehearse the grocery list, you will forget it by the time you get to the market; if you keep rehearsing it to yourself, the information can remain in STM indefinitely. Unfortunately, if a dog runs out in front of your car while you are on your way to the store and your rehearsal is disrupted, you will probably forget the list.

When we say we want to remember something, to commit it to memory, or learn it "by heart," we want to store it in LTM. If you rehearse the grocery list, organize it, and integrate it with information already present in your LTM, some of it will be stored in LTM. Once there, it can be stored indefinitely. Furthermore, there appears to be no limit to the amount of information we can place into this remarkable storage compartment. LTM also seems to store information that we can't consciously retrieve; we know it is in there somewhere because it can affect our behavior in subtle ways.

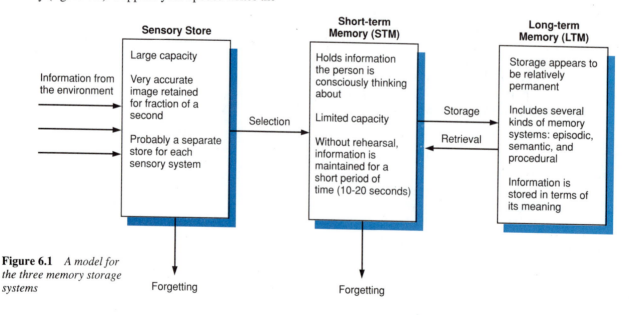

**Figure 6.1**  *A model for the three memory storage systems*

## Sensory Store

The **sensory store** *is the component of the memory system that receives information from the environment. This storage system can maintain a very accurate and complete representation of the environment as it is received by each sensory system, but it can only maintain it for a fraction of a second.* Although there is probably a sensory store for each of the five senses, practically everything we know about the sensory store comes from studies using visual or auditory input. The **iconic store** *is the sensory store for visual information,* coming from the Greek word "eikon," which means "image." The **echoic store** *is the auditory sensory store.*

The existence of a sensory store for visual input was first demonstrated in some classic experiments by George Sperling (1960). He presented letters on a screen for 1/20 of a second and asked the subject to write them down. When there were only four or five letters on the screen, the subject could usually recall all of them, but when there were more than that, the subject usually could still recall only four or five items.

It would seem that the subject could see only four or five of the letters. But the subjects in the experiment said that was not so. They could see them all, but they began forgetting them after they had written only four or five items.

Sperling devised a very clever means of proving that what his subjects said was true. He presented the subjects with a slide containing twelve letters arranged in three rows. Just after the slide was turned off, he sounded a high, medium, or low tone that was a signal for the subject to report the top, middle, or bottom row. The subjects were able to repeat any row, even though the screen was blank. This study made it clear that people can store a great deal more than just four or five items at a time, even if only for a brief moment.

There are some people, usually young ones, who seem to be able to hold a visual sensory image for much longer than a brief moment, sometimes as long as several minutes, although they don't necessarily have conscious control over their ability. These people demonstrate the phenomenon of **eidetic imagery**, *which refers to an especially clear, vivid, and detailed visual image of something previously seen.* A child who is playing from sheet music at the piano might turn the page, but replay the same music from the previous page because he is reading the eidetic image, rather than the new page. One study found that about five to ten percent of elementary children show some elements of the phenomenon (Haber, 1974), but the ability seems to fade as people grow older (Kunzendorf, 1989). Nevertheless, a study of Japanese college students found fifteen out of 327 who demonstrated eidetic imagery (Matsuoka et al., 1987).

One way in which scientists measure eidetic imagery is to display a patternless array of dots, and then what appears to be another patternless array minutes later (Miller & Peacock, 1982). If the first pattern is superimposed on the second a picture or word appears, but only people who can visualize a very detailed and precise image of the first pattern can identify the combined picture or word. One particularly remarkable subject was able to perform well at this kind of test even when the second array was shown to her the next day (Strohmeyer, 1970). To test yourself at this task, turn to figures 6.2, 6.6, and 6.9.

Some researchers propose that eidetic imagery is mainly due to the immaturity of the sensory system, and that the sensory store for visual input is holding the image for an unusually long time. But the phenomenon is controversial, and no completely satisfactory explanation has yet been advanced for it.

The echoic store for auditory information shares some common features with the iconic store (Moray, Bates, & Barnett, 1965; Darwin, Turvey, & Crowder, 1972). The main difference between the iconic and echoic stores seems to be the length of time it takes information in them to decay. Information in the iconic store decays in less than a second; decay in the echoic store takes several seconds.

Some of the information held in sensory store is transferred to STM, where it can be remembered for longer than a few milliseconds. Attention is one important determinant of which information is transferred. Whenever you view a scene and place images into your iconic store, you can transfer some of those images to your STM simply by paying attention to them.

**Figure 6.2** *Look at these dots for a moment, then look away for about 30 seconds. Turn to page 176.*

城     CASTLE

**Figure 6.3** *Recognition and meaning are determinants in the transfer of information storage systems.*

Another important element in the transfer process is the meaning of images. Look at the Japanese kanji in figure 6.3 for a very brief moment, and then look away. In your mind's eye, or iconic store, you can see the image. However, if you wait a few more seconds and then try to write the symbol, you will not be able to. Now look at the word next to the kanji for a brief moment; then look away. It is a very simple matter to wait a few seconds and then write the word, even though the word contains more lines. The English word has meaning to you; but unless you can read Japanese or Chinese characters, the kanji character for the word does not. You are able to recognize patterns in the English word, but the kanji seems to be random lines. Transferring an item from iconic store to STM means that you must analyze the item for meaning and recognize the visual pattern that makes up the image. We will see that attaching meaning to patterns is a critical factor in the transfer of information from STM to LTM.

## Short-Term Memory

If you have looked up a telephone number in a directory, you already know a great deal about STM. You repeat the number to yourself until you dial, and then you forget it. If the number is busy, you may have to look it up again. **Short-term memory** *is the component of the memory system that holds information the individual is consciously thinking about at the moment. Its capacity appears to be limited to about seven items, and unless the information is rehearsed, it will be lost from STM in about fifteen seconds.*

Evidence proving the existence of STM comes from studies of the **serial position effect,** *a phenomenon in which a person's ability to recall items from a list depends on the item's position in the list* (figure 6.4). The **primacy effect** *occurs when items in the beginning of the list are recalled well;* the **recency effect** *occurs when the items toward the end of the list are recalled well.* Those words that come in the middle of the list are usually not recalled very well, unless they are highlighted in some way, perhaps by using boldface or a yellow marker. The

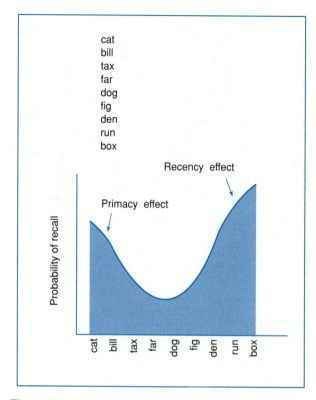

**Figure 6.4** *The serial position effect*

reason for these serial position effects is that words in the beginning of the list have been committed to LTM, and words near the end are still in STM. If the subject is distracted, those items at the end of the list that had been in STM will be forgotten. Under these circumstances, there will be no recency effect at all. Studies like these make it clear that human beings do have a short-term memory.

*The Capacity of Short-Term Memory*     The amount of information that can be held in STM is an intriguing question. Your own experience should tell you that STM's capacity is limited, perhaps to the amount of information in a seven-digit telephone number. Experiments that test a subject's ability to recall a series of items usually report similar results.

This finding created quite a puzzle for psychologists because it was difficult to define the abstract term "item." People could remember seven numbers, seven proper names, seven letters, seven faces, seven Shakespearean verses, or seven proverbs. Clearly, the amount of information in each of these "items" is very different. One psychologist addressed this problem in 1956 in a paper

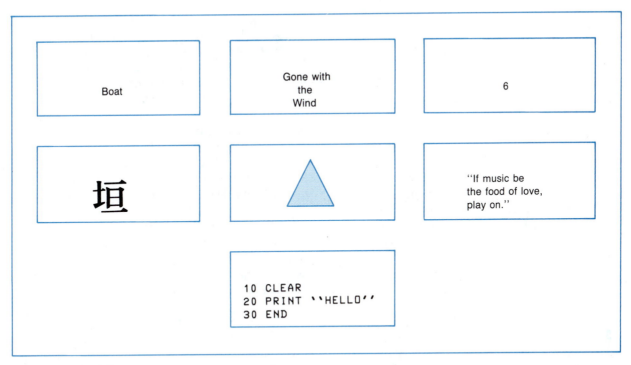

**Figure 6.5**    *"Chunks"*

called "The Magical Number Seven, Plus or Minus Two" (Miller, 1956). He suggested that STM could hold about seven chunks of information. **A chunk** *refers to anything that is represented in long-term memory as a single unit.* Look at the boxes in figure 6.5. Most of them will be chunks to you. A few of them might only be chunks to a student of Shakespeare, a computer programmer, or a person who reads kanji.

A chunk can contain a great deal of information, but STM can only hold about seven chunks at a time. The capacity of STM cannot be increased by trying to remember more than seven or eight chunks, but it can be dramatically increased by reorganizing information into larger chunks. One student with an average memory tried to improve his ability to repeat a sequence of digits read to him (Ericsson, Chase, & Faloon, 1980). At first he could only correctly repeat seven or eight digits, but after twenty months of practice, he was able to correctly repeat almost eighty digits.

The researchers found that the student's improved skill was entirely due to the reorganization of information into increasingly larger chunks. For example, if the sequence 3492 appeared, it was recorded from four chunks into one as "3 minutes and 49.2 seconds, near world-record time"

(for the mile). Most of his larger chunks were running times for races, but he also recoded strings of numbers into dates or ages. His remarkable ability could only be demonstrated on number strings, however. When they read him a list of letters, his memory span dropped to six. This shows conclusively that the capacity of his STM had not changed—only the size of his number chunks.

Besides a limited capacity, the STM also has a limited ability to hold items for any length of time. In one classic experiment, subjects tried to remember three letters of the alphabet. After eighteen seconds, they could not remember the letters (Peterson & Peterson, 1959). These people were not slow-witted; they were simply not allowed to rehearse because they were counting backward by threes during those eighteen seconds. Unless the chunks in STM are rehearsed, they are forgotten fairly rapidly.

These limitations on STM are very puzzling considering how much work it must do. For example, with a STM that can only hold seven items at a time, how can we read so quickly and comprehend what we are reading? The answer appears to lie in the idea that STM is not just a passive storehouse for a limited amount of information. It is a dynamic information processor, one that performs computations, screens information, and interacts constantly

**Figure 6.6**  *Try to superimpose figure 6.2 on this one. Can you see a recognizable image? Turn to page 182.*

with LTM. Many psychologists prefer to call STM "working memory" to emphasize its information processing role (Waldrop, 1987). To show how this might work, and how STM must interact with LTM, read the sentence below once. Then look up and try to recall the sentence.

"In the failing days of the Roman Empire, the emperors were increasingly protected by German troops recruited or enslaved through military conquests."

When you tried to recall the sentence you were probably unable to repeat it word for word—too many chunks. But your STM was working with your LTM's storehouse of information on the Roman Empire so you could reproduce much of the meaning. Perhaps some of the information in your LTM even leaked into your recollection even though it wasn't in the original sentence. In contrast, people who have little or no knowledge of the Roman Empire would have a much harder time trying to recall this sentence since there would be little in their LTM related to it. This is one of the reasons why it is so difficult to design tests of reading comprehension that are valid measures for people who grow up in difficult cultures. A person reared in China might know the Chinese emperors very well but know nothing about the Roman ones. The less information you have in your LTM about a subject, the smaller will be your chunks and the more trouble you will have recalling the details of a paragraph.

*Losing Information from Short-Term Memory*    A long running controversy exists over how information is lost from STM. The **decay theory of forgetting** *maintains that information simply decays or fades over time, usually within fifteen seconds, unless it is constantly rehearsed.* The **interference theory of forgetting** *proposes that information remain in STM until new information interferes with or replaces it.*

Attempts to confirm one of these theories and discard the other have been frequent but unsuccessful. For

example, the study (Peterson & Peterson, 1959) in which the subjects forgot three letters after just eighteen seconds because they could not rehearse would suggest the decay theory is correct. They were not trying to add new information, but they forgot the letters anyway. Another study, however, found that subjects could recall three words quite easily after a fifteen-second delay if the task used to prevent rehearsal involved detection of an auditory stimulus rather than counting (Reitman, 1971). Perhaps the counting task provided some interference and the auditory task provided none.

If STM is really doing a great deal of its own information processing, then information is lost purposefully, not simply because it decays or is replaced. This means that the loss of information would depend partly on its interest and value and would not be uniform.

*Transfer to Long-Term Memory*    The manner in which information in STM is rehearsed is important to whether it will eventually be transferred to LTM. If you simply want to remember a phone number for a short period of time, perhaps until you dial it, you use **maintenance rehearsal;** *using this technique, a person maintains information in STM by continually repeating it. When the person stops repeating the information, it is lost.* **Elaborative rehearsal** *facilitates the transfer of information from STM to LTM. This process involves organizing the information and integrating it with the knowledge that already exists in LTM* (Craik & Lockhart, 1972).

A fascinating study demonstrates how important the integration process is in the transfer of information from STM to LTM (Bransford & Johnson, 1973). A group of people read the story in figure 6.7 under the title "Watching a Peace March from the 40th Floor." Another group read the same story under the title "A Space Trip to an Inhabited Planet." Each group performed a distracting task for a short time afterward, and then each group was asked to recall the story.

The researchers were very interested in how well each group was able to recall the underlined sentence about the gentle landing. This sentence did not fit in well with the "Peace March" story, but it was an important element if the story was about a space trip. Only eighteen percent of the group that read the "Peace March" story recalled anything about this sentence. But fifty-three percent of the

Watching a Peace March from the 40th Floor

The view was breathtaking. From the window one could see the crowd below. Everything looked extremely small from such a distance, but the colorful costumes could still be seen. Everyone seemed to be moving in one direction in an orderly fashion and there seemed to be little children as well as adults. The landing was gentle, and luckily the atmosphere was such that no special suits had to be worn. At first there was a great deal of activity. Later, when the speeches started, the crowd quieted down. The man with the television camera took many shots of the setting and the crowd. Everyone was very friendly and seemed glad when the music started.

**Figure 6.7** *The importance of organizational framework in the transfer of information from short-term memory to long-term memory*

people who read the story with a space trip title recalled something from this key sentence. This simple experiment demonstrates how people use an organizational framework when they transfer information from STM to LTM.

The distinction between maintenance and elaborative rehearsal shows the importance of the level of processing you use to encode the information in the first place. A shallow level of processing might only involve noting some visual features of textual material, such as the font or the capitalization. A deeper level would involve processing the meaning of the information, and relating it to ideas or concepts that already exist in LTM. The deeper the level, the more it involves LTM, the more likely the new information will be transferred and stored. For example, if you view a sequence of word pairs, such as "lobster-shorts," and are asked to count the vowels, your level of processing will be shallow and you'll do poorly on a test that asks you to recall the second word when only "lobster" is presented. If instead you're asked to create a sentence using the two words, your level of processing will be deeper because the task requires you to analyze meaning and relate the meanings of the two words to one another. You'll do better on a later recall test even though you were exposed to each word pair for the same amount of time. Clearly, the way you study is at least as important as the amount of time you devote to it.

## Long-Term Memory

**Long-term memory** *is the relatively permanent memory storage system that holds information indefinitely.* In it we store last year's Superbowl score, the image of a tiger, and how to ride a bicycle. We also appear to be storing information that we can't consciously retrieve, but which still affects our behavior.

LTM appears to contain several different kinds of memories. For example, **episodic memories** *record life experiences* (Tulving, 1972). Your memory of your first day of school, the events at last week's company meeting, or the birth of your first child are all examples of episodic memories. Retrieval of these memories usually involves associations with particular times or places. **Semantic memories** *store information about the world independent of time, place, or other contexts. They store facts, rules, and concepts.* Semantic memories include all organized knowledge we have about words, their meanings, and how we manipulate them. We all have semantic memories about the word "tiger" although we might not recall where or how we acquired them.

**Procedural memories** *are memories for performing particular types of actions.* They consist of internal representations of stimulus-response connections that store the procedures we use for doing things. Many of the behaviors we acquire through operant conditioning create procedural memories.

Memories can also be categorized by whether they are implicit or explicit. An explicit memory is one that we can consciously recall. An implicit memory is one that has been stored in LTM but which does not have to be recalled to consciousness in order to affect our behavior and demonstrate that the memory exists. Most procedural memories, for example, appear to be implicit. Another example of implicit memory is when prior exposure to a particular stimulus affects your later response to that stimulus, even if you aren't consciously aware that you ever saw it before.

*How Is Information Stored in Long-Term Memory?*
Researchers have been approaching the question of how information is stored in long-term memory from a number of different angles. One very active area of research involves how people store and organize semantic information. Given our extreme dependence on language, it is important to understand how we organize our knowledge of words.

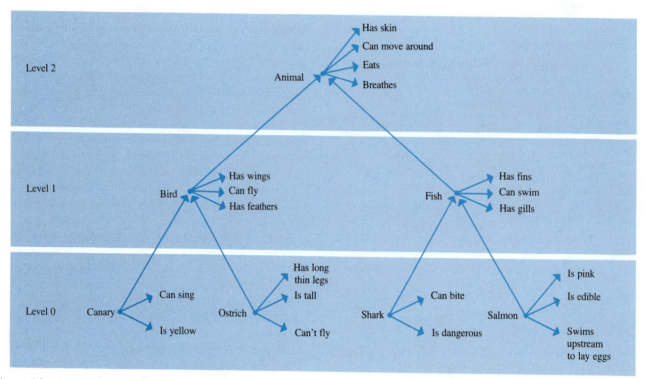

**Figure 6.8**    *A semantic network*

LTM and STM appear to handle semantic information somewhat differently. For example, suppose you were shown a list of words: car, lamp, chair, plane. If you tried to recall them fifteen seconds later, using STM, you might confuse car with char or lamp with lamb. But if you stored the words in LTM and tried to recall them twenty-four hours later, you would be more likely to confuse car with auto. LTM seems to contain concepts arranged in terms of the meanings and relationships of those concepts.

Cognitive psychologists are very interested in how those meanings and relationships are organized at even higher levels. How, for example, do we answer the question, "Is a robin a bird?" We need a very elaborate categorization and organizational system in our memories, one that permits access to the properties of things, their relationships, examples of instances of the thing, and probably counterexamples as well (such as "bat is not bird").

One theory proposes that our knowledge is organized in **semantic networks,** *hypothetical hierarchical structures for semantic memories* (Collins & Quillian, 1969). Figure 6.8 shows how a semantic network might be arranged.

Each node, or concept in a semantic network, such as bird, animal, or canary, is organized into a hierarchy in which one node is a subordinate of another. Characteristics of the general class of "animal" are stored with the node "animal" but not with subordinate nodes such as "bird."

One way to test this model is to ask subjects to answer questions such as, "Does a canary have wings?" and measure how long it takes them to respond (Collins & Quillian, 1969). The model predicts that subjects would take longer to answer questions that contain nodes more distant from one another in the network. For example, it should take longer to answer the question "Does a canary have skin?" than "Does a canary sing?" The results of studies like this confirmed the hypothesis. It did indeed take longer to answer a question about a canary's skin.

Deciding whether a canary has wings requires you to consciously call up information from LTM, to retrieve explicit memories. Recent studies on memory are leading to the conclusion that LTM may not be a single, unitary storehouse to hold all kinds of information. There may be multiple memory subsystems (Zola-Morgan & Squire, 1990; Schachter, 1987; 1990). In particular, researchers are concentrating on the different subsystems that appear to underlie explicit memories and implicit memories.

Implicit memories are not easy to investigate, but one popular experimental technique is called priming. Priming occurs when previous exposure to a stimulus affects your later response to it in some way even though conscious recollection of the stimulus is not required and may not occur. For example, suppose you are shown a sequence of words, one at a time, for a very brief period (50 msec). Later you see another sequence of words, some of which came from the original group, and are asked to identify each one. Priming occurs when you are able to identify the words that were in the original list more quickly. Strangely, priming occurs even though people can't even recognize that they've seen the words on the original list before.

Priming is known to affect many kinds of behaviors, often without the person being aware of it. Sometimes priming occurs even though we consciously try to prevent it. In a study of gymnastic judging, researchers found some troubling priming effects that could easily bias judges' scores in international competition. Judges were shown videotapes of various gymnastic moves, some perfectly executed and some with form errors, such as toes not pointed. When a judge saw the same move performed in the same way twice, the judge's accuracy was excellent. But when the same move was performed differently in two separate sequences, the judge's scoring of the second sequence was affected by the way the move was performed the first time. If the first move was perfect, the judges gave the second move a higher score even if it had defects. But the reverse was also true. If the first move was flawed, the judges noticed imaginary errors in a perfect second move. The researchers repeated the experiment, but this time they warned the judges about the priming. They still showed the priming effects. Gymnasts who do their warmups in front of the judges should take heed (Ste-Marie & Lee, 1991).

Much of the evidence that implicit and explicit memory are handled by two different subsystems comes from studies of amnesia victims (Zola-Morgan & Squire, 1990; Squire & McKee, 1992). People who have amnesia because of brain damage, stroke, alcoholism, or other reason, have severe problems with memories they consciously try to recall. If you ask them what happened yesterday or even just a few minutes ago, they often can give no answer. On tests of explicit memory, they do equally poorly. If they study a list of words and then try to recall or even recognize them later, they often cannot. But strangely, many amnesiacs do as well as normal people on tests designed to tap implicit memory.

In one study, amnesia patients and normal controls were shown pairs of pictures of faces and asked whether the pair showed two different people or two different views of the same person. Their reaction times were recorded. Some of the picture pairs were repeated after a ten-minute delay, and not surprisingly, the normal controls showed faster reaction times for the repeated pictures. But very surprisingly, the amnesiacs did, too. Even though the amnesiacs couldn't consciously remember having seen any of the faces before, they still showed priming effects (Paller et al., 1992). This kind of study suggests that implicit and explicit memory systems are separate since one can be damaged or destroyed without affecting the other.

*Forgetting from Long-Term Memory* Can you remember the name of your first grade teacher? Certainly the information was stored at one time—the teacher was a central figure in your life for nearly a year. If you can't recall the name, is it still somewhere in your LTM?

Many psychologists propose that the LTM has almost limitless capacity and though we forget, it is not because the memory itself is gone. We just can no longer retrieve it.

The work of Wilder Penfield (1975), a brain surgeon who used electrical stimulation to learn more about the function of parts of the human cortex, led scientists to suspect that some memories might be permanent and forgetting simply a failure in retrieval. (His main motivation was to perform needed brain surgery, and he was electrically stimulating the patient's brain to make sure the operation would not destroy critical brain tissue.) Sometimes he would stimulate the patient in the frontal or temporal lobe, and the current would cause the patient to remember some event in vivid detail. During one operation, for example, the patient appeared to relive a long-forgotten childhood experience. During another, the patient heard Christmas songs in her church at home in Holland.

Why are some, perhaps most, memories so hard to retrieve? One possibility is that by constantly adding information to our LTM storehouse we create interference among the memories. ***One kind of interference is called retroactive: the learning of new material blocks the***

# CLOSE UP ON RESEARCH
## Infantile Amnesia

Can you recall what happened on your first birthday? Your second? Can you remember anything at all about what happened the day you were born? A peculiar thing about human memory is that it suffers almost complete amnesia for events that occurred during the first few years of life. Even though infants are learning a great deal about language, object permanence, smells, tastes, the behavior of Mom and Dad, and many other things, they will not be able to recall events that occurred during this time. Their episodic memory for the first few years of life is strangely deficient (White & Pillemer, 1979).

An early study of infantile amnesia investigated the childhood memories of college students (Waldfogel, 1948). The subjects recorded all their memories for events that occurred before their eighth birthdays. No one recalled anything that happened before the age of three and a half, and most of the events occurred much later (figure 6A). It appears that adults are much better at recalling events that happened after the age of four or five.

The amnesia is not simply due to the fact that more time has passed. For example, a person who is fifty-years-old can remember many events that occurred thirty years ago (when he or she was twenty years old), but someone who is thirty-two can remember nothing about events that occurred thirty years ago. The amnesia is also not due to the fact that language has not developed completely; even animals show the phenomenon. They, too, show a puzzling inability to recall events that occurred during infancy (Spear, 1979; Miller & Spear, 1989). Researchers have proposed a variety of factors that might account for this phenomenon.

Freud suggested that the amnesia was due to repression of sexually unacceptable thoughts and desires. He proposed that the memories were not forgotten but were rendered inaccessible to consciousness. Freud's theory postulates that the child's first few years are filled with erotic fantasies about the parents, and since the fantasies cannot be fulfilled and cause great anxiety, they are pushed out of consciousness and repressed.

Another hypothesis suggests that infantile amnesia is not so much due to guilt or anxiety as to our changing category systems. In order to remember a birthday cake, you must have certain storage categories containing general information about cakes, birthdays, and candles, as well as associations between these categories. You must store the information about the cake in these categories. When you retrieve the memory later, you retrieve it based on the same category system. A candle will remind you of the cake at your tenth birthday party. An infant, however, must have quite different category systems from the adult, partly because he or she does not use language yet. As the child grows, the category system becomes more and more adultlike, and events are more easily recalled. The candle will probably not bring forth the retrieval of a memory about your first birthday cake because when you stored the information about that cake, you had a very different category system.

Infantile amnesia may also be related to the drastic changes in the sensory world. The images associated with an event must seem very different to a one-year-old, and the same images seen by the twenty-year-old are simply incapable of acting as retrieval cues. To an adult, a table looks like a flat surface about waist high; to an infant it looks like a massive overhead structure.

Many researchers think that some of the physiological changes in the developing brain play an important role in infantile amnesia (Bachevalier, 1990). It is possible that the brain stores episodic memories inefficiently during the first few years of life while brain structures are still maturing. Maturation of the hippocampus, a structure very much involved in memory, is not complete until a child is four- or five-years-old. Perhaps the ability to retrieve memories about events coincides with the maturation of this important brain area.

None of these explanations for infantile amnesia is mutually exclusive. Physiological changes in the brain may be occurring at the same time the child's category system shifts. Or the child may be experiencing changing sensory experiences along with social pressures not to discuss certain embarrassing events. The phenomenon is an intriguing one that is likely to have multiple causes.

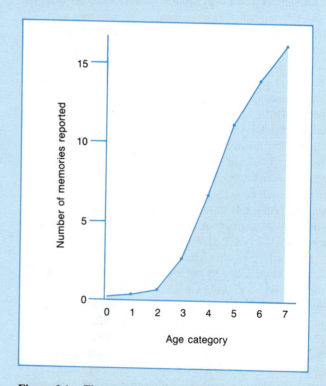

**Figure 6.A**    *The average number of infant and early childhood events recalled by college students*

*Source:* S. Waldfogel, *"The Frequency and Affective Character of Childhood Memories," in Psychological Monographs 62 (Whole No. 291), p. 62, 1948. Copyright © 1948 American Psychological Association.*

*retrieval of old material.* A person who learns French and years later studies Japanese might try to recall the French word for cat. Instead of *chat,* the Japanese word *neko* comes to mind. Another form of interference, **proactive interference,** *occurs when previously learned material interferes with the retrieval of new information.* The linguist, for example, might be speaking to a Japanese waiter in Tokyo and say "Sukiyaki, s'il vous plait." His old memory for the French *please* interfered with his new memory for the Japanese phrase for please. (You'll read about a strategy for remembering the meanings of these two easily confused terms later in the chapter.)

Interference can be thought of as retrieval failure in the sense that the original memories don't seem to be erased. They just become more difficult to retrieve. For example, a study of interference demonstrated that well-learned items on a list would interfere with the recall of items that were less well-learned. But the subjects could still recognize the weaker items, so the memories for them were still there (Murnane & Shiffrin, 1991).

The retrieval process, then, is critically important. How we retrieve information, and why we often fail miserably, is the subject of the next section.

---

▶ **GUIDED REVIEW** *Learning Objectives 1, 2, and 3*

1. Human memory consists of three interacting storage compartments called _____ , _____ (STM), and _____ (LTM).
2. Information is first processed through the sensory store, which receives a great deal of information from the external environment. There is probably a separate store for each sensory system, although research has focused on the _____ for vision and the _____ for audition. _____ refers to a special ability in which a person holds particularly clear and vivid visual images of things previously seen.
3. The _____, in which the recall of items from a list depends on the item's position in the list, demonstrates the existence of STM. The beginning items benefit from the _____ and have been stored in LTM. The last items on a list benefit from the _____ and are held in STM until the subject has to recall them.
4. The capacity of STM is about seven _____, a term meaning anything that is represented in LTM as a single unit. Additional information can be held in STM by increasing the size of the chunk, not by holding more of them.
5. Information is lost from STM either through _____, from incoming information, or (probably) both.
6. Information in STM will be lost within about fifteen seconds unless it is rehearsed using _____. Transferring STM's information to LTM, however, requires _____. This involves organizing the information and integrating it with knowledge already existing in LTM.
7. Three kinds of memories in LTM are _____, _____, and _____.
8. Forgetting from LTM appears to involve retrieval failure, which can be partly due to interference caused by newly acquired information. In _____, the learning of new material blocks the retrieval of old material; in _____, previously learned information interferes with the retrieval of more recent memories.

*ANSWERS*

*1. sensory store, short-term memory, long-term memory 2. iconic store, echoic store, Eidetic imagery 3. serial position effect, primacy effect, recency effect 4. chunks 5. decay, interference 6. maintenance rehearsal, elaborative rehearsal 7. episodic, semantic, procedural 8. retroactive interference, proactive interference*

## RETRIEVING INFORMATION

What is the capital of New York?
Where were you on September 3, 1980?
Who wrote *The Grapes of Wrath?*

To answer these questions, you must retrieve information from your LTM. This is no easy matter, considering that it contains millions of bits of information. However, much of the time we have no trouble at all. In this section, we will discuss how we search our LTM for information, how we recognize information that already exists, and how we elaborate on and reconstruct a memory using bits and pieces of information we are able to retrieve.

### Search Strategies

One way to find a particular item of information in LTM is to use a **sequential search,** *a retrieval strategy that searches every piece of information, one at a time, until the desired item is found.* If you used a sequential search to find a book in a library's collection, beginning with the first book on the first shelf, it would be very time-consuming; the process is time-consuming for searching LTM as well.

A sequential search, however, is used to examine the contents of STM. In a series of very clever experiments, subjects looked over a list of a few numbers or letters until they felt they had stored the whole list in STM. Then various test items were presented, and the subjects simply identified whether each had been in the original set

**Figure 6.9** *When the two dot patterns are combined, they look like this.*

(Sternberg, 1966, 1967, 1969). The more items that were in the original set, the longer it took for the subjects to respond to each of the test items. This suggested that the subjects searched their STMs sequentially to decide whether the test item matched any of those in the original set. (Longer lists required longer sequential searches.) Surprisingly, the response times for no and yes answers were about the same. This meant that the sequential search was exhaustive; it continued through all the items contained in STM even though the subject might have found a match early in the search. An exhaustive sequential search of LTM would take years; however, the search strategy is quite efficient for STM. Another kind of search, one that appears to be used for a search of LTM, narrows down the search set. Using **retrieval cues,** *pieces of information used to help locate related items of information in memory,* a much more efficient search of LTM can be conducted.

*Retrieval Cues*     Retrieval cues are absolutely essential in any search of LTM. In one experiment, subjects were given a list of categories, such as fruits, animals, or crimes and were then shown instances of each category (plum, horse, murder) and asked to memorize them (Tulving & Pearlstone, 1966). The next day, some subjects were given the category titles (fruit, for example) and were asked to recall the instances within that category. They could recall about thirty instances. Other subjects tried to recall the instances without the category titles; they could only recall about twenty instances. Later they were given the category titles, and they were able to recall about twenty-eight instances. Giving the subjects the category title as a retrieval cue was clearly very useful in helping them remember.

No one really knows exactly how long-term memory is searched, but figure 6.10 shows one plausible strategy that relies on semantic networks to recall a semantic memory: the capital of New York. The retrieval cue "New York" causes the node labeled "New York" to be activated. The

activation spreads out from there, moving from node to node until it reaches the one labeled "Albany," which has as one of its characteristics "state capital."

Trying to recall episodic memories, such as where you were on September 3, 1980, really taxes the retrieval system of your brain, and retrieval cues become even more important. One answer might go like this:

> I have no idea . . . wait, I must have been living in D.C., working for NASA. That fall I was going back and forth to Cocoa Beach, since the shuttle was about to go up. . . . Let's see . . . we had a bad hurricane that season. Was that around September? Yes, I remember I was trying to call my mother on her birthday, which is Sept. 4, from the motel in Florida, and the lines were down. I had to spend the whole weekend in that fleabag . . .

Although most of our knowledge about information retrieval comes from laboratory studies, some field work on the subject has been conducted. In one study, college students were asked to keep two diaries during a semester which were collected weekly (Skowronski et al., 1991). In one diary, the students entered information about themselves and in the other they made entries of events that happened to another person, usually a friend. For each entry, the person rated its memorability, its pleasantness, and also how typical it was for the person. For example, if the person always got A's in math tests, a C on a test would be rated as atypical.

After the semester was over, the researchers gave each person a memory test by reading entries from the diaries and asking them to rate how well they remembered each one. Pleasant events were recalled better than unpleasant ones, although unpleasant ones were better recalled than neutral ones. This pattern was observed for the typicality judgements also. Events that were very atypical for a person were recalled best, but very typical ones were recalled better than neutral ones. Clearly, we do not just recall events that fit in with our existing ideas about ourselves or other people. These findings give us clues about the factors that affect retrieval in the real world for information that is relevant to our lives.

*State-Dependent Memory*     Retrieval cues can be sights, sounds, smells, tastes, or anything that helps you find information. They can also include your state when you learned the material in the first place. A phenomenon called **state-dependent memory** *occurs when a person who learns material in a particular state, such as when*

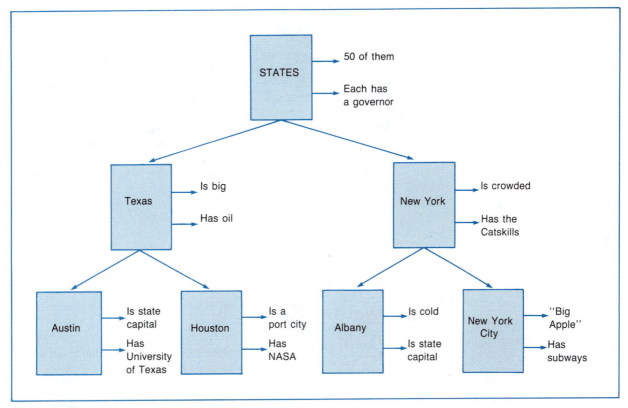

**Figure 6.10**  *A semantic network strategy for searching long-term*

**he or she has been drinking alcohol, is able to recall it better when in the same state again.** The phenomenon applies to alcohol intoxication, other drugged states, and possibly even mood (Overton, 1964; Swanson & Kinsbourne, 1976; Siegel, 1988).

In conditioning, for example, the effects of drugs become part of the context, and thus part of the conditioned stimulus. This appears to be why the drugged state serves as a retrieval cue for the conditioned response. As a practical matter, this phenomenon could have some relevance to therapists who treat phobias. For example, suppose a person is being treated for fear of heights. In order to proceed with extinction, he has to be exposed to heights, little ones at first, without any fear reaction. But some people can't go near even the tiniest step without feeling fear. To get the process going, the person might be prescribed tranquilizers so he can be exposed to the steps without fear. But then the tranquilizers become part of the context for the extinction. When the person stops taking

the tranquilizers, the progress might be lost because the context in which the extinction was occurring had been changed (Bouton & Swarzentruber, 1991).

The importance of mood states in retrieval is controversial, but some experiments have found a tendency for people to recall events better when they are in the same mood as when they first experienced the event. In one experiment, subjects wrote all their emotional experiences for a week in a diary. At the end of the week, each person was hypnotized and put into either a happy or sad mood (Bower, 1981). While in the trance, the subjects tried to recall the incidents they had written in their diaries. Those in a sad mood tended to recall many more unhappy incidents, whereas those in a happy mood recalled the pleasant experiences. The mood the person was in during the recall test was an important retrieval cue that helped locate memories formed when the person was in a similar mood.

The existence of state-dependent memory effects shows how students might improve their scores on tests: study

# APPLYING PSYCHOLOGY

## Judging the Accuracy of Eyewitness Testimony

In the 1972 case of *Neil* v. *Biggers,* the U.S. Supreme Court made it clear that they are aware of the problems with eyewitness testimony. The annals of criminal justice include a number of case histories detailing the miscarriage of justice because of mistaken eyewitness identifications. In *Neil* v. *Biggers,* the Court was concerned with the factors that should be considered in determining whether an eyewitness's identification is accurate. The Court decided that the following five factors should be considered in judging the accuracy of an identification:

1. the opportunity of the witness to view the criminal at the time of the crime,

2. the witness's degree of attention,

3. the accuracy of the witness's prior description of the criminal,

4. the level of certainty demonstrated by the witness at the time of the confrontation, and

5. the length of time between the crime and the confrontation.

These criteria were established with very little input from psychologists, primarily because they had little to give at the time. The subject of eyewitness identification attracted very little research interest until the mid-1970s. Now psychologists have some information about the usefulness of the Court's criteria and can make suggestions for criteria that might be added.

For example, a witness's certainty about an identification is a very convincing element in trials, so it is not surprising that the Court included this criterion. When a witness says, "That's the woman. I'd know her anywhere!" judges and juries are very likely to believe the witness regardless of evidence to the contrary. However, study after study has found that there is little or no relationship between an

eyewitness's certainty and his or her accuracy in making an identification.

In one study, unsuspecting subjects witnessed a staged crime—an act of vandalism. Later they were asked to pick out the perpetrator from a live lineup and to state how certain they were that their choices were correct. (Sometimes the perpetrator was in the lineup and sometimes he was not, a circumstance typical of actual lineups.) The correlation between the subjects' accuracy and their certainty was zero. Subjects were just as likely to be dead sure they were right when they were wrong as they were to be accurate but rather unsure of themselves. Most of the people who were certain but wrong had chosen someone out of the lineup in which the perpetrator did not appear. The ones who made no choice in the lineup without the perpetrator seemed much less sure of themselves. The researchers hypothesize that a person's certainty about an identification comes more from making a choice in the first place; if they make one, then they are sure (Malpass & Devine, 1981).

A criterion that probably should be added to the Court's list is *the conditions under which the witness makes the identification.* Some conditions, because of their suggestiveness, seem to provoke witnesses into making inaccurate judgments. In an experiment, for example, some subjects who were trying to pick out the vandal from the lineup were given the suggestion that the vandal was present, even though sometimes he was not. The error rate for these subjects was extremely high—51.5 percent compared to 25 percent for subjects who did not hear the suggestion.

If and when the United States Supreme Court reassesses the issue of the accuracy of eyewitness identification, psychologists will have learned a great deal more about the phenomenon and will be able to offer useful advice.

under conditions that are as similar as possible to those that will be present during the test.

## Memory Reconstruction

Once a memory has been located in LTM, it would seem to be a simple matter to recall it exactly as it happened. But recall is not so simple. Even memories that seem very vivid may be partly reconstructions. For example, people often make mistakes trying to date events. In one study, subjects were asked to recall the dates of events like the assassination attempt on Ronald Reagan by John Hinckley

(March, 1981) or the shooting of Pope John Paul II (May, 1981). Probably because the Reagan shooting was more accessible and they recalled more details about it, most people thought it occurred more recently. It may seem logical to assume that vividly recalled events are more recent, but that is not always so (Brown, Rips, & Shevell, 1985). A librarian friend of ours has a general rule to help his patrons find articles. When they say, "I saw it in the last six months or so," he mentally doubles the time frame and looks back at least one year.

People also seem to perform reconstructions based on an attempt to make an event more realistic or plausible. Sometimes the reconstruction is correct, but sometimes it turns into an almost incredible distortion.

The distortions that usually occur in the "rumor game" show how reconstructions occur. In one game, the first person in line heard the following story:

> Five men on a subway in New York held up a black man on his way to a business meeting. They all had knives, and none of the three other people on the train offered any help. The victim handed over his wallet, saying 'Shalom to all of you, brothers.' The muggers got off the train at the next stop.

Each person who heard the story was able to recall only one or two critical incidents and reconstructed the rest, and their reconstructions usually filled in the gaps imperfectly. One person mentioned that the muggers held up some Jewish person. Someone later in line said, "Three guys held up a rabbi." The last person heard that a black guy mugged a priest on a train. Each person filled in gaps using information and assumptions that already existed in his or her LTM.

People are most likely to make reconstructive mistakes and distortions when they learned something after the event that contradicted what they originally saw. The new information seems to get incorporated into the original memory, and when we retrieve the original memory, it has been subtly changed. American courts are very concerned about this kind of mistake. (See Applying Psychology: Judging the Accuracy of Eyewitness Testimony.)

*Eyewitness Testimony*    Laboratory studies of eyewitness testimony confirm the view that our reconstructions can be distorted by new information. In one study, college students were shown a series of thirty color slides of the events at a staged traffic accident (Loftus, Miller, & Burns, 1978). Half the subjects saw a red Datsun traveling along a side street approaching a stop sign, and the other half saw the Datsun approaching a yield sign. In both cases, the Datsun turned right and hit a pedestrian in a crosswalk.

After viewing the slides, the subjects were asked many questions about the accident, including one very critical one: "Did another car pass the red Datsun while it was stopped at the stop sign?" In legal jargon, this is a leading question because it implies that a stop sign was there. Half the subjects from each group heard this question, while the other half heard an identical question except that the stop sign was called a yield sign. Thus, half the observers were being given correct information about the version of the

**Figure 6.11**    *Studies of memory show that eyewitness testimony is subject to a great deal of error, because of the process of memory reconstruction.*

accident they witnessed. The other half were given false information.

Later on, the subjects saw a pair of slides—one showing the Datsun at a yield sign and the other showing the Datsun at a stop sign—and were asked to indicate the one they originally witnessed (figure 6.11). Nearly all the subjects who were given correct information in the questionnaire chose the correct slide. On the other hand, more than eighty percent of those who received misleading information picked the wrong slide—the one they had never seen. They did this even though the one they actually had seen was being shown at the same time. The leading question had apparently caused a change in the subjects' memories, or at least in the way they reconstructed their memories of the event.

New information can have powerful effects on memory of faces as well, a point extremely worrisome to legal professionals who must rely on eyewitness testimony for identification of suspects. In a series of three experiments, subjects saw a person's face in a photo, in a film, and live. Later they were exposed to a description of that person, ostensibly given by another witness. When the other witness's description included an incorrect feature, such as a moustache that didn't exist, the subjects were much more likely to incorporate the mistaken feature into their own idea of what the person looked like. When they tried to pick out the correct person from a lineup of twelve people, seventy percent of the subjects identified someone who had the mistaken feature. Only thirteen percent of the control subjects, those who had not heard the misleading "evidence" from another witness, picked a person with the wrong feature (Loftus & Greene, 1980).

In real life, mistaken eyewitness identifications are not uncommon and they can cause grief and tragedy. People have been arrested, charged, and convicted solely on the strength of eyewitness testimony even when supporting evidence is weak or nonexistent. In one well-publicized case, a man was identified as a rapist and convicted by a jury, despite a great deal of material evidence showing that he could not have been at the scene (Loftus & Ketcham, 1991).

Studies of eyewitness testimony demonstrate that memories are malleable things that can be subtly changed after they are stored. When we try to remember some event, we retrieve some accurate bits of information about it and fill in gaps to round out the story. Memory reconstructions are especially affected by new information, some of which may be wrong.

## Recognition Memory

Recognizing something you have seen before is quite different from recalling it. The difference is obvious on college tests, for instance. Multiple-choice questions ask you only to recognize the correct answer when you see it; essay questions require that you recall the answer. Students generally agree that essay questions are more difficult; they must know the material better in order to do well. The essay question gives few retrieval cues to help students remember information; the multiple-choice test gives the ultimate in retrieval cues—the answer itself.

Recognition memory is spectacularly good for visual information. In one experiment, subjects were given a chance to study 612 pictures of common scenes at their own pace, usually a few seconds per picture (Shepard, 1967). On the recognition test, they averaged ninety-seven percent.

*"It's on the Tip of My Tongue"*    The **tip-of-the-tongue phenomenon** *refers to the failure to recall information when you are certain the information is contained in*

> *Albert Camus; John Steinbeck;*
> *Herman Melville; O. Henry*

*your LTM.* Suppose you are trying to think of the author of *The Grapes of Wrath.* You are fairly sure you know the answer—it is on the tip of your tongue—but you just cannot recall it. You know that if you saw it, you would recognize it instantly. (If this description fits you, look at the bottom of the page and try to recognize the author's name.)

People are usually very accurate in their predictions about whether they can really recognize a correct answer. It seems that they know what is in their LTM, even though they cannot always retrieve it easily. An important ingredient in the tip-of-the-tongue phenomenon, though, is how well you integrated the information into your LTM in the first place. If you used a deeper level of processing your feeling about whether you know the answer, and could recognize it if you saw it, will be stronger and more accurate (Lupker, Harbluk & Patrick, 1991).

Some studies suggest that the subsystems involved in recognition memory may be different from those involved in recall memory. For example, when subjects are asked to memorize a list of words and then later are asked to recall them, they tend to recall the more common words first. (Shepard, 1967; Gorman, 1961). If the list contained names like Bob, David, Wentworth, Jim, and Humperdinck, they would tend to recall Bob, David, and Jim more often than Wentworth or Humperdinck. If their memory is tested using recognition, however, perhaps by showing them a long list of names and asking them to pick out the ones they saw earlier, they tend to recognize the odd names better than the common names.

*Recognizing Familiar Faces*    We mentioned earlier that researchers are being drawn to the conclusion that memory appears to be a collection of subsystems that handle separate kinds of tasks, rather than a single, unitary whole that processes and stores all kinds of information in the same fashion. Our ability to recognize the faces of familiar people seems to be one of these subsystems, distinguishable from other memory subsystems. Although tentative, the evidence for this viewpoint comes from studies of brain damage.

Three weeks after giving birth to her baby, a woman was admitted to the hospital because of severe headaches and occasional grand mal seizures. Her EEG was abnormal. After a few days in the hospital, she began to improve, but it became clear that she was having trouble with her memory. She could speak and understand language normally, perform arithmetic problems, and repeat back sequences of digits. Her vision was normal, and she could remember most things quite well. She could even easily discriminate the faces of strangers. But when her husband or her mother came to visit, she didn't recognize them until they began to speak. When she looked at pictures of her children, she said, "They don't look like they should."

Ordinarily, when people suffer brain damage from disease or injury, they show a wide range of behavioral changes, some slight, some more severe. But occasionally a person shows a disability in a single function. The woman in the above example simply could not recognize familiar faces. Studies of patients like this one lead researchers to believe that the underlying brain mechanisms for facial recognition are different from those for other memory skills or for other visual abilities. Perhaps the ability to recognize familiar faces is so important to human beings that we have evolved special biological underpinnings for it. As the next section will show, psychologists have learned a great deal about the biological events that take place when a person learns and remembers; however, many mysteries remain.

---

▶ **GUIDED REVIEW** *Learning Objectives 4, 5, and 6*

1. Retrieving information from STM might be accomplished through an exhaustive _____, in which you search items one by one; this kind of search of LTM is very time-consuming. _____ narrow down the search set; they include anything that helps you find the correct location in LTM. They might also include your state of mind when you learned the material. Memories are _____ for states like intoxication or mood.

2. The retrieval process is partly an accurate "reading off" of information contained in LTM and partly _____. The reconstruction process is vulnerable to distortion, particularly when you receive new information that contradicts what you had learned first.

3. _____ is easier than recall because a person simply has to identify that an item is in his or her LTM but not retrieve it. The _____ phenomenon refers to the failure to recall information when the person knows the information is contained in LTM.

4. Recognition of _____ seems to be based on different underlying biological mechanisms. People with brain damage in a particular area of the brain sometimes have trouble with this ability but not with other memory skills.

*ANSWERS*

1. *sequential search. Retrieval cues, state dependent* 2. *reconstruction* 3. *Recognition, tip-of-the-tongue* 4. *familiar faces*

---

# BIOLOGICAL BASIS OF LEARNING AND MEMORY

The human brain, a four-and-a-half-pound mass of tissue, can hold all the memories you are able to store in it. It can process the information, decide which information to ignore and which information to attend to, put some of it into short-term memory, and place some of it into long-term storage where it could last almost a century. Nevertheless, the chemical and electrical events that accomplish all of this are still poorly understood.

A very old but still workable theory of how the brain accomplishes learning and memory was proposed by D. O. Hebb (1949). He suggested that information processing begins with changes in the firing patterns of particular neural networks in the brain. The transfer of information to permanent storage, however, probably involves physical changes in the brain, most likely in the synaptic connections between neurons.

## Changes in the Brain during Learning

Tracing what happens in the brain during a learning experience is a formidable task. The brain contains billions of neurons, and changes in firing patterns might be limited to a very small network. Simply recording the activity of one or two neurons in the hope that they might show some changes during learning is like hunting for the proverbial needle in the haystack. However, there are more efficient ways to approach the problem (Farley & Alkon, 1985). One way involves using an animal with very few neurons, and the other approach involves tracing the activity in groups of neurons rather than in individual cells.

*Learning in Aplysia*    A snail-like creature rapidly becoming a favorite of some researchers studying learning and memory is *Aplysia* (Kandel, 1976; Marcus & Carew, 1990). The attraction of this unassuming beast is its tiny nervous system. Unfortunately, a creature this simple cannot study nonsense syllables or press levers, but it does show some plasticity in its behavior. If someone squirts water on *Aplysia's* siphon, the animal will withdraw its gill. If its siphon is repeatedly stimulated, the gill withdrawal response habituates, growing weaker and weaker. Some psychologists argue whether **habituation,** *the gradual diminishing of a response after repeated presentations of the stimulus,* is a form of learning. But most psychologists consider it related to learning in the sense that the animal is making a behavioral change with experience.

All the neurons involved in the habituation of the gill withdrawal reflex have been mapped, and researchers have been able to follow the activity in each one while the animal "learns." By eliminating one neuron after another, they finally concluded that most of the change in the nervous system accompanying this kind of habituation occurs at the synapse between the sensory neuron and the motor neuron. The sensory neuron releases less and less neurotransmitter as habituation proceeds, and the motor neuron's response predictably becomes weaker and weaker.

The patience required to perform a study like this has paid off. It is clear that changes in the synapse can and do occur during habituation, at least in the gastropod. The change is not a permanent one, and the synapse returns to normal a short time after the experimenters stop stimulating the siphon. Most researchers had tacitly agreed that plastic changes in the nervous system must involve some kind of change at the synapse. But proving it in a live animal, even one as simple as *Aplysia,* was a very difficult challenge.

*Classical Conditioning in the Rabbit*     Following the course of neuronal events during a learning experience in a mammal is a daunting task, but several groups of researchers are making the attempt. One group is focusing on the events that take place during a motor learning task in a rabbit (Swain et al., 1992; Thompson, 1986, 1987; Thompson, Patterson, & Berger, 1978; Weisz & LoTurco, 1988). A puff of air directed toward the rabbit's eye (US) automatically elicits a blinking response (UR). If the rabbit always hears a tone (CS) just before the puff of air, it will eventually begin to blink in response to the tone by itself (CR).

The hunt for the circuitry involved in learning this response led first to the hippocampus. People with damage in this area often have problems with memory. H.M., for example, whose hippocampus was damaged during surgery, was never again able to transfer information from STM to LTM.

Hippocampal neurons show changes in firing rates that correspond to the events taking place while the animal is learning. For example, in early learning trails, these neurons showed a significant increase in firing just after the puff of air and before the eyelid response. After learning, the hippocampal neurons increased their firing rate after the tone and before the puff of air. This means that the hippocampal neurons were anticipating the puff of air.

The precise role of the hippocampus in learning is still unclear, but many scientists suspect it is very much involved in STM and in the transfer of information from STM to LTM. The weight of the evidence suggests that permanent long-term memories are not stored there but in other areas of the brain.

The study of the conditioned eye-blink response is leading to the conclusion that two brain circuits operate at the same time during this kind of learning. One is "informational" in the sense that it links the specific stimulus to the response. For the eye-blink response, this brain circuit includes the cerebellum, which is apparently the place where the link between the stimulus and response is stored. For example, removal of the cerebellum permanently abolishes the response. The other brain circuit seems to have more to do with the motivation required to learn a response to an aversive stimulus in the first place and involves higher brain regions. The second circuit probably has much to do with all kinds of learning experiences that trigger emotional reactions. The hippocampus, whose role has always puzzled scientists, may play a key role in the interaction between the two circuits.

As we have seen, behavioral studies suggest that memory appears to be made up of several subsystems. These studies of conditioning in the rabbit are providing tantalizing clues about the neural circuitry that may underlie some of them and about how they might interconnect.

## Making a Memory

Although all the neurons you will ever have already exist by the time you are two-years-old, they do not remain the same throughout your life. They form new synapses, lose old ones, strengthen or weaken the ones they have, and grow new branches all the time. Scientists hypothesize that the formation of a memory requires just such changes in the brain. The **engram** *refers to the memory trace, the hypothetical neuronal changes that occur when an organism learns something.*

*Where Is the Engram?*     Hunting for the location of a stored memory may seem rather simple. One approach is to teach an animal a task and then lesion part of its brain. If the animal cannot remember what it had learned, the part of the brain that was lesioned contained the memory.

Karl Lashley performed experiments like this and obtained very confusing results. He found that despite some very extensive lesions, a rat would continue to perform a task it had learned. It would only forget the task, which involved learning the difference between a light and a dark alley in a maze, if the visual cortex were completely removed. Lashley wondered whether the rat "forgot" simply because it could no longer see. After many such experiments, he concluded that lesion studies, by themselves, cannot identify the location of the engram. When part of the animal's brain is damaged and the animal no longer performs, it is difficult to tell whether the engram or some other function required for performance, such as vision, hearing, pattern discrimination, or motivation has been damaged.

Using electrical and pharmacological microstimulation of neurons, anatomical studies, and electrophysiological recording in addition to lesion studies, scientists are now better able to locate the neural circuitry that is both necessary and sufficient for a learned response. This circuitry appears to be localized to particular brain areas, although it may be stored in multiple sites within the brain area. The studies we discussed earlier, such as those on the rabbit's eye-blink response, all provide clues to the location and characteristics of the neural circuitry involved in particular kinds of learning.

*What Is the Engram?*    Most scientists agree that the formation of the memory trace must involve changes in neural activity, especially changes in synaptic connections. Examples of such changes might include the formation of new synapses, the alteration or deletion of existing ones, or the modification of transmitter activity. A logical assumption is that the pattern of communication between neurons is altered because of experience. But just what those biochemical and physiological changes are has been a subject of much debate.

Neurons show relatively permanent changes in their firing patterns through experience, as we have seen in *Aplysia* and also in the rabbit's brain. The phenomenon of long-term potentiation (LTP) might help explain how this occurs. When a brief train of electrical stimulation is applied to a specific neural pathway, the strength of the synaptic connections increases and remains high for days or even weeks. The implication is that a synapse will become stronger when the presynaptic neuron fires repeatedly and causes increased firing in the next neuron (Thompson, 1986). LTP is under intense investigation; it represents a relatively permanent change in neural connections as a result of a short experience. Scientists can study how LTP might affect ion channels, neurotransmitters,

membrane permeabilities, and other features of the synapse.

Early studies that attempted to analyze the biochemical changes that occur during learning compared the brains of animals that had learned a task to ones that had not. For example, one group of rats learned to avoid a shock by jumping onto a platform whenever a buzzer sounded (Rees et al., 1974). A second group heard the buzzer but could not avoid the shock, and a third simply remained in the home cage. The animals were injected with a radioactive tracer and their brains were examined.

The most common finding in studies like this one is that an animal that learns something shows greater synthesis of proteins and RNA, a substance produced by DNA that directs the manufacture of proteins. Furthermore, the changes in synthetic activity are larger in certain parts of the brain, such as the hippocampus. Recent studies on brain tissue in vitro also implicate specific kinds of RNA in information storage, and even identify the enzymes being produced (Black et al., 1987).

It is tempting to conclude that the formation of a memory trace is initiated by the altered neuronal firing patterns associated with the learning experience. These, in turn, trigger biochemical events that produce relatively permanent changes in synaptic connections. The biochemical events might include the production of key enzymes that affect neurotransmitter activity, receptor sites, or membrane permeability. Work on simple nervous systems strongly suggests that memory traces are created this way. Whether the same pattern will hold for humans is unknown.

Although the basic process may be the same at the micro level, learning and remembering even a very simple list of words is much more complicated than what *Aplysia* does. Our biological models of the process must also be more complicated. Learning and remembering a list of groceries apparently involves several subsystems in the brain, not just a few neurons that can be mapped.

*A recent approach that some scientists are taking to develop models of the interactions between the subsystems in the brain is called* **connectionism.** It relies heavily on complex computer models that hypothesize brain subsystems acting in parallel, each analyzing and dissecting a particular portion of a task. The models propose various ways the subsystems can interact with one another in network fashion, strengthening some connections and weakening others. If the model can "learn" a list of words like a human does, making the same kinds of mistakes and showing the same degree of success, then the features that were programmed into the model might be similar to those in the human brain. Most of the time, of course, the models fail miserably but each failure tells us how something about how the brain does *not* operate. Our biological tools are still too primitive to fully grasp the complexity of events in the human brain; these computer models offer a means to learn how the brain works by analogy (Hintzman, 1990).

## Modifying Memory

The attempt to describe the nature of the engram has been so difficult that many scientists have turned their attention to learning about events that can modify memory. Most of these studies have used "memory disruptors"; however, a few have discovered means to improve the process of memory formation.

*Memory Disruptors*    A variety of substances and events can disrupt memory. Drugs that inhibit protein synthesis are remarkably effective, supporting the view that the formation of an engram requires protein synthesis. Another disruptor is **electroconvulsive shock (ECS)**, *a treatment in which electric current is passed through the brain until convulsions occur.* It has been used as a treatment for various mental disorders, especially depression, since the 1930s. One reason the use of ECS has decreased is that it produces amnesia. A patient might be unable to recall very much about the twenty-four hours preceding the treatment. This characteristic of ECS, however, interested memory researchers.

Whether ECS interferes with the consolidation of memories or their later retrieval is not certain. At first, the research suggested that memories take some time to form, and that during the early stages, they are very vulnerable to disruption by the drastic changes in neuronal firing patterns produced by ECS. If memories are allowed to consolidate for a period of time, they seem to become more and more resistant (Duncan, 1949; Gold, Macri, & McGaugh, 1973). Other work, however, suggests that ECS may affect retrieval more than memory consolidation. For example, memories whose consolidation was disrupted by ECS are sometimes retrievable through "reminders," such as electric shocks. Also, memories that should have been well-consolidated have been disrupted by ECS days after the event (Ribbons & Meyer, 1970). Some scientists propose that memories are formed within moments after a

learning experience and that ECS disrupts the hypothetical cataloging process by which a stored memory is retrieved (Miller & Springer, 1973).

*Stress and Memory*    Freud proposed that stress, particularly traumatic events in childhood, would have very specific effects on memory. The person would repress the conscious memory of the stressful event although the event would spill into dreams in disguised forms. Given the existence of state-dependent memory, it would not be surprising if stress, and all the biological changes that accompany it, would have important effects on memory, much like alcohol or other drugs. But stress has a special place in learning. It acts as much more than just another feature of the context. It is one of the driving forces that tells us what is important to learn and remember and what isn't.

**Epinephrine** *is a potent hormone released by the adrenal glands during stress.* In a study to assess its effects on memory, rats, who ordinarily prefer the dark, were given a mild foot shock when they tried to enter the dark compartment of two-chambered box. One group received an injection of saline after training, while five other groups received increasing doses of the hormone. Later they were all tested to see whether they remembered to avoid the dark side of the box.

The rats that received high doses of this stress hormone did poorly on their memory test, suggesting that there may be some truth in Freud's proposal about the effects of stress. Strangely, the rats that received no hormone, or low doses of it, also did poorly. It was the rats that had received medium doses that remembered the task the best (Gold & VanBuskirk, 1975).

This study shows that the hormones involved in stress can have important influences on memory. If the learning experience is too stressful or not stressful enough, the memory for it will be weak. Memory for a task seems to be best when the stress levels are somewhere in the middle. This finding can help explain a widely known phenomenon called the Yerkes-Dodson law (1908), which relates arousal level to performance and which we'll discuss again in chapter 8. An individual who is extremely aroused or under a great deal of stress rarely performs very well on any task, whether it involves learning and remembering, driving a car, or running a footrace. Very low levels of arousal also result in poor performance. The best performance comes when arousal levels are somewhere in the middle.

*Memory Improvement Drugs*    Although there is no magic pill that will suddenly make you a memory expert, there are some drugs that mildly improve memory. One such drug is **arecholine,** *a substance that increases activity at synapses in the brain that use the neurotransmitter acetylcholine* (Sitaram, Weingartner, & Gillin, 1978). Volunteers received injections of arecholine and then were shown a list of ten words. The subjects receiving the drug recalled slightly more words than did the controls, especially toward the end of the testing session. The drug hardly made the people into "memory experts," but it did produce a noticeable improvement in the subjects' ability to recall their list.

An important factor in senility appears to be a disruption in the network of neurons using acetylcholine (Bartus, Dean, Beer, & Lippa, 1982). Studies of aging animals have found changes in this network, and similar changes have been seen in the brains of people who were senile. Drugs like arecholine are sometime effective in improving the memories of aged people. Again, these drugs do not work miracles, and they do have side effects, but this important clue is leading to a better understanding not only of aging and senility but of the biology of memory.

▶ **GUIDED REVIEW** *Learning Objectives 7, 8, and 9*

1. One hypothesis about the biology of learning and memory states that _____ involves changes in the firing patterns of neural networks in the brain and _____ requires physical changes in neurons.
2. Studies of *Aplysia* have identified the neural changes occurring during _____ , a phenomenon in which the response to a stimulus diminishes as the stimulus is repeatedly presented.
3. Brain activity during _____ in the rabbit has been monitored. During the conditioning process, neurons in the hippocampus and cerebellum appear to be involved.
4. Finding the location of the _____ , or memory trace, for a particular memory has been very difficult, especially when using only lesion studies.
5. The nature of the engram has been equally evasive. However, most studies show that the formation of a memory requires the synthesis of _____ and _____ .
6. A recent approach that some scientists are taking to develop models of the interactions between the subsystems in the brain is called _____ .

7. Memory formation or retrieval can be disrupted by several procedures, including _____ , a treatment in which electric current is passed through the brain until convulsions occur.
8. Too much or too little _____ , one of the hormones released during stress, retards memory formation. However, injection of an intermediate amount of this hormone can improve memory formation.

*ANSWERS*

1. STM, LTM 2. habituation 3. classical conditioning 4. engram 5. protein, RNA 6. connectionism 7. electroconvulsive shock (ECS) 8. epinephrine

# IMPROVING YOUR MEMORY

An old joke states, "The two worse things about growing old are first, that you begin to lose your memory, and second . . . I can't remember." Research on memory has been intense, and out of it has grown a number of practical ways to improve memory. We just mentioned some promising chemical approaches; this section explores behavioral techniques to improve memory.

## Improving the Storage Process

Storing information in LTM can be improved in several ways. First, you can pay more attention to what it is you want to store. Second, you can begin the storage process by actively rehearsing information you want to remember. Third, you can organize the information better and integrate it into the information that already exists in your LTM. Finally, you can learn more efficiently by applying some of the principles of learning discussed in the last chapter.

*Paying Attention*    You have probably had the experience of reading a paragraph and then not being able to recall a single idea or message. Your mind wandered. You were thinking about the dog barking or the noisy air conditioner. You were daydreaming. In other words, you were not paying attention to the words in the paragraph. The only information in sensory store that is transferred to STM is that to which you are paying attention. It does not even have a chance to be stored in LTM unless you give it your attention.

*John:* Hi there, Joe. I want you to meet Sara Armo.

*Joe:* Glad to meet you. I'm Joe Downing.

*Sara:* So you're a friend of John's. What did you say your name was?

If you have ever been introduced to someone and almost immediately forgot the person's name, you are not alone. The reason people do this is that they are not paying attention. The information never got out of sensory store, let alone transferred to LTM.

*Rehearsal*    Holding Joe's name in STM for longer than a few seconds requires a rehearsal:

> *Joe:* It's Joe Downing.
>
> *Sara:* Well, I'm very happy to meet you, Joe.
>
> *Joe:* And I'm glad to meet you. John has told me a lot about you.
>
> *Sara:* Nothing bad, I hope. Do you also work for National Industries, Joe?

Rehearsal by itself, however, does not transfer information from STM into LTM. If you really want to remember a person's name the next time you see him or her, you must store it in LTM. You need to perform a deeper level of processing using elaborative rehearsal, not just mainte-nance rehearsal. Organizing the material and integrating it into your present network of knowledge are the keys to elaborative rehearsal.

*Organizational Strategies*    Organizing and integrating a new piece of information can be accomplished in many ways. Two of the most effective ways are using a mne-monic device and chunking.

> *Joe:* Yes, I sure do.
>
> *Sara:* Downing, Downing ... like 10 Downing Street. Are you British?
>
> *Joe:* That's right, mate!

Sara's technique for remembering Joe's name was first to rehearse it. Then she performed an elaborative rehearsal using a **mnemonic device,** *a system that helps integrate new information with information already existing in LTM.* She associated the name with an image that already existed in her memory, and she made the connection between Joe, the name, and the image. The strategy of using old knowledge as a framework for storing new pieces of information, especially relying on mental imagery, is the mnemonic device.

A very effective mnemonic device for remembering grocery lists, speeches, or anything that must be recalled in a specific order is the **method of loci.** *This memory improvement technique associates each item in a list with the parts of a well-known physical location, such as your house.* Imagine a tour of your house. First you enter the foyer, then the living room, the dining room, the kitchen, the staircase, and so on. Make a mental association between the places on your tour and each item or idea you must remember. For example, with the grocery list, imagine the front door blocked with apples, the living room floor covered with butter, the dining room table stinking of vinegar, and so on.

Mnemonic devices are common tools in many profes-sions, particularly those that require a great deal of memorization. Every musician knows about "*Every Good Boy Does Fine.*"

While mnemonic devices are certainly useful for remembering grocery lists and musical notes, they also can help you remember more difficult material. Suppose you want to give a presentation on business computer systems to a group of potential customers, and you want to discuss several main applications, including inventory, accounting, and communications. You can use the loci system, imagining stacks of boxes blocking the entrance to your home, adding machines and calculators piled on your coffee table with their paper spilling onto the floor, and an old-fashioned telephone attached to the wall in your dining room. This method will ensure that you don't leave out any major points. Mnemonic devices are also fre-quently used to make computer software more "user-friendly." To help you remember what retroactive and proactive interference mean, try using the first two letters of each word: REcent material interferes with the recall of previously learned information, and PRevious material interferes with the recall of recently acquired information.

Another strategy to help you organize and integrate new information is chunking. We saw how this method could be used to remember incredibly long strings of digits. You can use chunking to help you store more useful informa-tion as well. Suppose you are trying to remember the ten most important companies that do business with your law office: National Employment Bureau, Standard Coin Company, Delta Freight, Energy and Gas, Inc., Keller Cash Registers, Charley's Carburetors, Reliable Tempo-rary Employment Counselors, New York Executive Search Company, New Jersey Money Markets, and BST Motor-cycles. Trying to recall each item individually would tax your retrieval system, but you could chunk them into

# EXPLORING HUMAN DIVERSITY

## The Educated Chinese

Definitions of an "educated person" depend heavily on culture, but they all reflect a people's shared assumptions about what information educated people should have in their long-term memories. The Chinese defined an educated person as one who could read and write Mandarin Chinese well. The famous Chinese imperial civil service examinations sought to discriminate among applicants on the basis of how many of the thousands of complicated ideographs they could remember. In order to succeed on these tests and be considered an educated person ready for government service, Chinese students had to emphasize rote memory skills. Endless drills, practice, and repetition were their main strategies.

In the United States, entrance examinations such as for the Foreign Service stress analysis, judgment, and critical thinking much more than the Chinese tests did. Questions might ask the test-takers to analyze how two words are related to one another and choose another pair of words that are related in the same way. The words themselves may not be difficult or obscure so the test is not really measuring the breadth of vocabulary which might be acquired through rote memorization. Instead, it is attempting to measure the test-taker's analytical ability, something that is not acquired through repetitive drills. This kind of emphasis is partly due to what we, as a culture, consider important. Americans value independent thinking and analytic reasoning. We always ask even very young students, "But what do YOU think about it?" Chinese students are raised in a Confucian society in which the elders were venerated as a source of authority and wisdom. They were not expected to form their own opinions in school, only to memorize the teachings of their elders.

America's emphasis on analytical ability and reasoning, rather than rote memory of terms, concepts, definitions, and dates, fits in well with our own multiculturalism. If we wanted our students to memorize a body of facts we would have to agree on what that body should be. In the past, there was some agreement; while students weren't expected to memorize any Chinese characters, they were expected to recite, for example, particular dates and their historical significance (1066, 1492, 1776). But in recent years, scholars have pointed out the content students were expected to learn was very culturally bound. Our decisions about what is important and what isn't depend very much on our culture, and our definition of the educated person reflected those decisions. But is the French Revolution more important than the Boxer Rebellion? Maybe to Americans of European descent, but not to Chinese-Americans.

Unlike Japan, where the central government dictates what books will be used in all prefectural schools, America allows considerable autonomy in school districts. Communities can choose texts that reflect a much broader choice of information. The texts themselves are increasingly multicultural, drawing examples from many races, cultures, and ethnic groups. In higher education, the requirements for a bachelor's degree have become much broader also so that, for example, students can take courses in Indian or Spanish literature in place of the previously required course on English authors. In practice, this means that America does not have a single, shared definition of an "educated person" the way the Chinese did.

There is considerable debate about whether America's definition of the educated person has become too loose. Some authors argue that the lack of shared knowledge makes it harder to communicate with one another (Hirsch, 1987). They also suggest that some schools deemphasize the accumulation of knowledge by rote memory altogether, and that this hinders the students' ability to do well on entrance examinations, even those that are supposed to be measuring thinking skills rather than content. As we discussed in this chapter, storing information in LTM depends to a considerable extent on what is already stored there about the subject. If a person has stored only very sketchy information about hearts or blood, can they draw any analogy to batteries, gasoline pumps, or engines, even though they know the meanings of all these words? Perhaps there is a middle road; one that acknowledges the role of culture in choosing the definition of the "educated person," but still encourages some consensus about shared knowledge.

categories. One chunking system might group the companies according to their general purpose: transportation, money, and jobs. Then, all you have to do is recall the categories.

**Transportation**
Delta Freight
Energy and Gas, Inc.
Charley's Carburetors
BST Motorcycles

**Money**
Standard Coin Company
Keller Cash Registers
New Jersey Money Markets
**Jobs**
National Employment Bureau
Reliable Temporary Employment Counselors
New York Executive Search Company

*Efficient Learning*    Although much of the material in the last chapter dealt with very simple forms of learning, it included some useful strategies that can aid the storage of more complicated information. In particular, make liberal use of rewards and space your learning experiences.

Suppose you must study a report and give a presentation about it the next morning. Tell yourself that as soon as you have learned the report to your satisfaction, you will reward yourself with a movie, a new shirt, a trip to the ice cream store, or a swim in the pool. The reward will help you more if you get it very soon after the learning experience. Delaying the reinforcement too long will make learning less effective.

Studies of conditioning find that learning is much more efficient if the trials are spaced some time apart rather than one after another. If you want to learn a list of foreign words, for example, you could do so more easily by studying it a short time each day for several days rather than a long time on a single day. The effects of spaced trials on learning explain why students who "cram" the night before an exam usually do not perform very well. The same amount of study time can be used more effectively if it is broken into shorter segments.

## Improving Retrieval

One way to improve retrieval is to use better retrieval cues. Finding your lost car keys is much easier if you focus on retrieval cues rather than hunt throughout your house. First, imagine when you had them last. What were you wearing? Did you have a purse or briefcase with you? Which room of the house did you enter first? Second? Did you open the trunk of the car? Using each of these retrieval cues in succession will help you remember where you put the car keys.

In one experiment, subjects were asked to recall the names of their high school classmates years after they had

graduated (Williams, 1976). The people explored one retrieval cue after another, and sometimes they recalled hundreds of names:

> Now, people I knew through my sister—hm—I didn't know them very well, they were just acquaintances, there's Leanne, and don't even remember his name . . . wow, OK, I just located a storehouse of people. There was an afterschool thing where I used to go all the time, and there was lots of people there, and I have a whole building full of people, but I can't remember a lot of those names. There's Ruth Bower, Susan Younger, Sue Cairns—oh, wow, Jeff Andrews, Bill Jacobsen, I just located a whole another group of people, whew (laugh) wow-um.

When subjects tried to recall the names of high school classmates, they also included the names of people who were not in their class at all but whom they knew in different settings. Retrieval is a process of reconstruction, and incorrect information will often be included in the retrieval.

An important retrieval cue can be your state when you learned the information. Memories can be state-dependent and thus more easily remembered in the same state. For example, if you were drinking when you lost your address book, perhaps having a drink will help you remember where you put it. Or, if you were extremely happy when you lost it, getting into another happy mood may also help you find it.

Long-forgotten memories are sometimes successfully retrieved using special techniques, such as hypnosis. For instance, subjects recall the happenings at their fifth birthday party, the events at their mother's second wedding, a foreign language they haven't spoken for years, and even license-plate numbers on a van (see chapter 3). However, hypnotized subjects can also fabricate information quite convincingly. In one experiment, subjects confidently recalled information not only from their past but from their future (Barber, 1965).

Other special retrieval techniques include brain stimulation and psychoanalysis. We don't recommend that you try the former, but the latter can have interesting results. Under certain circumstances, a person will forget a particularly traumatic experience because remembering it is just too painful. In psychoanalytic terms, this is "motivated forgetting," or repression. The memory may not be completely lost; it may make its presence known in dreams or in free associations. A person who saw a friend drown, for example, may seem to have forgotten the whole experience, but bad dreams about water may persist.

Improving retrieval should also involve a solid understanding of the factors that bias your memory. Recall the example at the beginning of this chapter of the psychology lecturer who tried to reduce her gender-biased language, and how both she and her students had very faulty memories of what happened. Also recall the way memory works to reconstruct events by using bits and pieces of memory and filling in the gaps with plausible fictions.

As a student, you should have an effective strategy for remembering information that appears in textbooks. This information is usually arranged in chapters, each thirty to fifty pages long. The chapters are usually broken down into subheadings, and sometimes these subheadings are subdivided still further. A single assignment might involve reading one or two chapters. If you haven't already done so, you should read the material in the beginning of this text. It offers many helpful hints about how to study based on sound psychological principles.

▶ **GUIDED REVIEW** *Learning Objectives 10 and 11*

1. Improving your memory can be accomplished by first improving the storage process. Important elements of this process include paying attention, rehearsing, and using an organization strategy to integrate the information into your LTM. A _____, for example, uses old information as an anchor for storing new data. The _____ links items or concepts to places on a tour of a well-known location, and it helps you remember those items in order. _____ organizes material into ever-larger units so they can be stored in LTM as single entities. Rewarding yourself and spacing your learning trials will help you improve the storage process.
2. The retrieval process can be improved by using better _____, including your state of mind when you originally stored the material. It might also be improved by special retrieval techniques, such as hypnosis or psychoanalysis.

*ANSWERS*

1. mnemonic device, method of loci, Chunking 2. retrieval cues

# SUMMARY

I. The three storage systems of human memory are the sensory store, short-term memory (STM), and long-term memory (LTM). (p. 172)

   A. The sensory store initially processes information from the environment and appears to hold virtually all the information impinging on the sensory systems. (p. 173)

   1. Eidetic imagery refers to the ability to hold a clear, detailed, and vivid image of things previously seen. (p. 173)

   B. Short-term memory holds information about what the individual is consciously thinking. (p. 174)

   1. The capacity of STM is about seven chunks of information. (pp. 174–176)

   2. Unless the information is rehearsed, it is lost from STM within about fifteen seconds through decay, interference, or both. (p. 176)

   3. Information in STM can be transferred to LTM using elaborative rehearsal. (pp. 176–177)

   C. LTM is the relatively permanent storage system with an unlimited capacity. (p. 177)

   1. Information in LTM is stored in terms of its meaning rather than in terms of its sound. The semantic network theory proposes that semantic memories are organized in nodes arranged in hierarchical structures. (pp. 177–179)

   2. Forgetting from LTM may be due to an inability to retrieve stored memories or due to the effects of interference. (pp. 179–181)

II. Retrieving information from LTM requires a search of its contents. (p. 181)

   A. Search strategies include sequential search and the use of retrieval cues. (p. 181)

   1. Rapid searches of LTM rely on retrieval cues. (p. 182)

   2. State-dependent memory involves the facilitation of recall when a person is in the same biological state during learning and retrieval. The person's biological state acts as a retrieval cue. (pp. 182–183)

   B. The retrieval of memories from LTM often involves some reconstruction and distortion, apparently in an attempt to make vaguely recalled memories more realistic and plausible. (pp. 184–185)

   1. Studies of eyewitness testimony demonstrate some of the processes involved in memory reconstruction. (pp. 185–186)

   C. Recognition differs from recall because a person has more retrieval cues available during a recognition test. (p. 186)

1. The tip-of-the-tongue phenomenon occurs when a person fails to recall information he or she knows is contained in LTM but is able to recognize the information. (p. 186)

2. The ability to recognize familiar faces appears to be separate from other memory skills. (p. 186)

III. Learning and the formation of memories involve changes in neuronal activity and in synaptic connections in the brain. (p. 187)

A. Scientists have attempted to trace the changes that occur during learning by studying simple animals and systems. (p. 187)

1. Studies of *Aplysia* show synaptic changes correlated with simple forms of learning. (pp. 187–188)

2. Studies of the activity of neural pathways in the rabbit brain show changes associated with classical conditioning. (p. 188)

B. Research on the engram, or memory trace, has not clearly demonstrated its location or nature. (p. 188)

1. Memories appear to be stored in localized areas involving definite neural circuits. (p. 189)

2. The physiological changes that occur during learning include increases in protein and RNA synthesis. These events may be related to the changes that probably occur in synapses. (p. 189)

3. Connectionism emphasizes the role of brain subsystems acting in parallel, each of which analyzes a particular portion of a task. (p. 189)

C. Researchers are examining events that modify the formation of memories in an attempt to learn more about the process. (p. 190)

1. The formation of a memory can be disrupted by electroconvulsive shock and by protein synthesis inhibitors. (p. 190)

2. Stress can either facilitate or inhibit the formation of a memory, probably through the action of epinephrine. (p. 190)

3. Certain drugs improve the formation of memories. (p. 191)

IV. Improving your memory can be accomplished in several ways. (p. 191)

A. The storage process can be improved by

1. paying closer attention, (p. 191)

2. rehearsing important information, (p. 192)

3. using organizational strategies to improve elaborative rehearsal, (pp. 192–193) and

4. using more efficient learning strategies. (p. 194)

B. Retrieval can be improved by using better retrieval cues, including the state in which you learned the material initially. (p. 194)

---

# ACTION GLOSSARY

Match the terms in the left column with the definitions in the right column.

___ 1. **Sensory store (p. 173)**

___ 2. **Iconic store (p. 173)**

___ 3. **Eidetic imagery (p. 173)**

___ 4. **Echoic store (p. 173)**

___ 5. **Short-term memory (STM) (p. 174)**

___ 6. **Serial position effect (p. 174)**

___ 7. **Recency effect (p. 174)**

___ 8. **Chunk (p. 175)**

___ 9. **Decay theory of forgetting (p. 176)**

___ 10. **Interference theory of forgetting (p. 176)**

___ 11. **Maintenance rehearsal (p. 176)**

___ 12. **Primacy effect (p. 174)**

A. *Anything represented in LTM as a single unit, such as digit, a word, or a well-known quote.*

B. *The sensory store for auditory information.*

C. *A method by which information can be kept in STM by repeating it over and over.*

D. *A theory that attempts to explain the loss of information from STM by stating that the information gradually fades as time passes.*

E. *One of the three storage systems for memory. Information is received from the environment through the sense organs and is maintained in this system for a very short time.*

F. *The storage system for memory that includes the information an individual is consciously thinking about at the moment. Its capacity is limited to about seven items; unless the information is rehearsed, it is lost from this system in less than a minute.*

G. *A theory that attempts to explain forgetting from STM. It states that the information is lost when new information intrudes or replaces it.*

H. *The sensory store for visual information.*

I. *Items at the end of a list are recalled more accurately than are items in the middle of a list.*

J. *A phenomenon in which a person's ability to recall items from a list depends on the item's position in the list.*

K. *Clear, detailed, and vivid image of something previously seen.*

L. *A phenomenon in which items at the beginning of a list are recalled well.*

___ 13. **Elaborative rehearsal**
        **(p. 176)**

___ 14. **Long-term memory (LTM)**
        **(p. 177)**

___ 15. **Episodic memory (p. 177)**

___ 16. **Semantic memory (p. 177)**

___ 17. **Semantic network (p. 178)**

___ 18. **Retroactive interference**
        **(p. 179)**

___ 19. **Proactive interference**
        **(p. 181)**

___ 20. **Sequential search (p. 181)**

___ 21. **Retrieval cue (p. 182)**

___ 22. **State-dependent memory**
        **(p. 182)**

___ 23. **Procedural memories**
        **(p. 177)**

A. *Information contained in LTM that has no association to a particular time or place. It includes memories of facts, rules, and concepts.*

B. *A piece of information used to help locate another related item of information in memory.*

C. *The relatively permanent memory storage system in which information can be stored for an indefinite period of time.*

D. *The phenomenon in which previously learned material blocks or interferes with the retrieval of material learned more recently.*

E. *The phenomenon in which the retrieval of information is facilitated when the person is in the same biological state as when the information was learned. The biological state acts as a retrieval cue.*

F. *The record of personal life experiences contained in LTM.*

G. *A retrieval strategy in which items of information in memory are examined one at a time in a search for a particular item of information.*

H. *A proposed type of hierarchical organization for semantic memory.*

I. *A method that permits transfer of information from STM to LTM. The information is integrated with knowledge already existing in LTM.*

J. *The learning of new material blocks the retrieval of old material.*

K. *Memories for performing particular types of action; made of internal representations of stimulus-response connections.*

___ 24. **Tip-of-the-tongue**
        **phenomenon (p. 186)**

___ 25. **Habituation (p. 187)**

___ 26. **Engram (p. 188)**

___ 27. **Connectionism (p. 189)**

___ 28. **Electroconvulsive shock**
        **(ECS) (p. 190)**

___ 29. **Arecoline (p. 191)**

___ 30. **Epinephrine (p. 190)**

___ 31. **Mnemonic device (p. 192)**

___ 32. **Method of loci (p. 192)**

A. *A hormone released by part of the adrenal glands during stress; also, a neurotransmitter.*

B. *The memory trace; the hypothesized neuronal changes that occur when an item of information is stored.*

C. *A system for improving memory in which the items of information are associated with the parts of a well-known physical location, such as a house.*

D. *Failure to recall a piece of information when the person is certain the information is contained in his or her LTM.*

E. *The gradual diminishing of a response as a result of continuous exposure to the stimulus which evoked the response.*

F. *A system for improving memory that helps integrate new information with information already existing in LTM.*

G. *A technique sometimes used to treat depressed patients; involves delivering an electrical current to the brain that is intense enough to produce convulsions.*

H. *A drug that increases activity at acetylcholine synapses.*

I. *An approach that emphasizes the role of brain subsystems acting in parallel.*

*ANSWERS*

*1. e, 2. h, 3. k, 4. b, 5. f, 6. j, 7. i, 8. a, 9. d, 10. g, 11. c, 12. i, 13. i, 14. c, 15. f, 16. a, 17. h, 18. i, 19. d, 20. g, 21. b, 22. e, 23. k, 24. d, 25. e, 26. b, 27. j, 28. g, 29. h, 30. a, 31. f, 32. c*

# SELF-TEST

1. Echoic memory is a part of which storage system?

    (a) sensory store
    (b) short-term memory
    (c) long-term memory
    (d) semantic memory
       (LO 1; p. 173)

2. The time limit on iconic store is approximately

    (a) less than one second.
    (b) several seconds.
    (c) fifteen seconds.
    (d) one minute.
       (LO 1; p. 173)

3. Rehearsal is a technique that maintains information in which storage system?
   (a) iconic store
   (b) echoic store
   (c) short-term memory
   (d) long-term memory
   (LO 2; p. 176)

4. The capacity limit on short-term memory is about _____ chunks of information.
   (a) one or two
   (b) seven or eight
   (c) twelve or thirteen
   (d) unlimited
   (LO 2; pp. 174–176)

5. Remembering what you ate for dinner last night is an instance of
   (a) sensory store.
   (b) short-term memory.
   (c) semantic memory.
   (d) episodic memory.
   (LO 3; p. 177)

6. An exhaustive sequential search is a strategy used more often to retrieve information from _____ rather than from _____.
   (a) sensory store; long-term memory
   (b) long-term memory; short-term memory
   (c) short-term memory; long-term memory
   (d) short-term memory; sensory store
   (LO 4; p. 181)

7. You learn a list of definitions for words after drinking two cups of coffee. Later you discover that you recall the definitions better after drinking two cups of coffee than after no coffee. This illustrates which of the following?
   (a) episodic memory
   (b) semantic memory
   (c) the use of retrieval cues
   (d) state-dependent memory
   (LO 4; pp. 182–183)

8. _____ refers to the fact that memory can be distorted when new information that contradicts what is originally seen is learned after the event.
   (a) Recognition
   (b) Reconstruction
   (c) Chunking
   (d) Habituation
   (LO 5; p. 184)

9. In retrieving information from memory, _____ tasks are easier than _____ tasks.
   (a) recall; recognition
   (b) reconstructive; recall
   (c) recognition; recall
   (d) reconstructive; recognition
   (LO 6; p. 186)

10. The ability to recognize _____ appears to be controlled by brain mechanisms different from those involved in other memory functions.
    (a) faces
    (b) words
    (c) numbers
    (d) places
    (LO 6; p. 186)

11. The kind of learning studied in the snail-like creature *Aplysia* is
    (a) classical conditioning.
    (b) operant conditioning.
    (c) habituation.
    (d) orientation.
    (LO 7; p. 187)

12. Training a rabbit to blink its eye to a tone instead of to a puff of air (which originally accompanied the tone), appears to involve
    (a) the sensory neuron releasing less neurotransmitter into the synapse.
    (b) neural circuits in the cerebellum and hippocampus.
    (c) the frontal lobes increasing their firing after the tone and before the puff of air.
    (d) operant conditioning.
    (LO 7; p. 188)

13. Research by Karl Lashley, designed to determine the location of a stored memory, led him to believe that
    (a) a memory for a particular event is concentrated in the hippocampus.
    (b) a memory for a particular event is located in the cerebellum.
    (c) lesion studies provide a clear-cut method for locating the engram for particular tasks.
    (d) a memory for a particular event is stored in multiple locations in the brain.
    (LO 8; p. 189)

14. Studies of rats have found that rats that have learned something show greater amounts of both _____ and _____ than do rats that have not learned.
    (a) RNA; proteins
    (b) RNA; DNA
    (c) DNA; proteins
    (d) neurotransmitters; RNA
    (LO 8; p. 189)

15. Which of the following enhances memory by affecting acetylcholine synapses?
    (a) electroconvulsive shock
    (b) stress
    (c) epinephrine
    (d) arecoline
    (LO 9; p. 191)

**16.** The first step in improving one's memory is
 - **(a)** rehearsal.
 - **(b)** attention.
 - **(c)** organizing information.
 - **(d)** elaborating information.
   (LO 10; p. 191)

**17.** Which of the following is most likely to transfer information from STM into LTM?
 - **(a)** attention
 - **(b)** maintenance rehearsal
 - **(c)** organizing information
 - **(d)** repetition
   (LO 10; p. 192)

**18.** Which of the following processes might produce an apparent, but not actual, increase in the size of STM?
 - **(a)** attention
 - **(b)** maintenance rehearsal
 - **(c)** elaborative rehearsal
 - **(d)** chunking
   (LO 10; p. 192)

**19.** Which of the following is not a technique that specifically improves retrieval from LTM?
 - **(a)** maintenance rehearsal
 - **(b)** retrieval cues
 - **(c)** hypnosis
 - **(d)** brain stimulation
   (LO 11; p. 192)

**20.** A person who wants to remember to describe five different insects in a specific order for a speech in biology class might best use
 - **(a)** eidetic imagery.
 - **(b)** the method of loci.
 - **(c)** classical conditioning.
 - **(d)** maintenance rehearsal.
   (LO 12; p. 192)

*ANSWERS*

1.a, 2.a, 3.c, 4.b, 5.d, 6.c, 7.d, 8.b, 9.c, 10.a, 11.c, 12.b, 13.d, 14.a, 15.d, 16.b, 17.c, 18.d, 19.a, 20.b

---

# THINKING ABOUT PSYCHOLOGY

**1.** A woman confounded everyone at a party by reciting a list that was read to her only once containing over 60 digits. She had actually prepared the list in advance but even so, it took her only a couple of minutes to prepare and memorize it. Using what you have learned about the organization of long-term memory, explain how she could have done this, and try it yourself.

**2.** Identify each of the following as episodic, semantic, or procedural memories: (a) how to tie a knot, (b) your first day at school, (c) the names of the countries of Europe, (d) how to type, (e) the word for "cat" in French, (f) the taxes you paid in 1993.

**3.** Suppose your child is studying Columbus's voyage to America in 1492 on the Nina, the Pinta and the Santa Maria. You'd like to help him remember all the significant facts. Explain how you might use mnemonics, elaborative rehearsal, repetition, stress, or other techniques to ensure he gets questions on Columbus correct.

---

# SUGGESTED READINGS

Allport, S. (1986). *Explorers of the black box: The search for the cellular basis of memory*. New York: Norton. A book covering the work of scientists, such as Eric Kandel, who investigate the biological basis of memory.

Ellis, H. C., & Hunt, R. R. (1989). *Fundamentals of human memory and cognition* (4th ed.). Dubuque, IA: Wm. C. Brown Publishers. An introduction to the field of memory and cognition; emphasizes practical examples.

Hintzman, D. L. (1990). Human learning and memory: Connections and dissociations. *Annual Review of Psychology, 41,* 109–139. Excellent review of newer approaches in memory research.

Loftus, E., & Ketcham, K. (1991). *Witness for the Defense*. New York: St. Martin's Press. A personal account of the authors' experiences eyewitness memory research and applications.

Renner, M. J., & Rosenzweig, M. R. (1987). *Enriched and impoverished environments: Effects on brain and behavior*. New York: Springer-Verlag. A comprehensive review of the effects of enriched environments.

Rosenzweig, M. R. (1984). Experience, memory, and the brain. *American Psychologist, 39,* 365–376. An article that reviews some of the research on the brain mechanisms underlying learning and memory.

Solomon, P. R., Goethals, G. R., Kelley, C. M., & Stephens, B. R. (1988). *Memory: Interdisciplinary approaches.* New York: Springer-Verlag. An advanced book that explores memory from the viewpoints of neuroscience, cognitive psychology, developmental psychology, and social psychology.

# CHAPTER 7

## COMMUNICATION AND COGNITION
## OUTLINE

▶ **Learning Objectives**

▶ **Communication**

- The Nature of Language
  The Structure of Language
  Communicating through
  Language
- The Acquisition of Language
  Language Development
  Theories of Language
  Learning
- Nonverbal Communication
- Animal Communication
  Can Animals Use Language?
  Teaching a Language to
  Primates

▶ **Guided Review**

▶ **Cognition**

- The Cognitive Revolution
- Can Computers Think?
- Language and Thought
- The Structure of Thought
  The Nature of Concepts
  Learning Concepts

▶ **Guided Review**

▶ **Problem Solving**

- Steps of Problem Solving
  Analyzing the Problem
  Search Strategies
  Deciding When to Stop
- Creative Problem Solving
- Group Decision Making

▶ **Guided Review**

▶ **Intelligence**

- Measuring Intelligence
  The Concept of Mental Age
  The Development of the
  Stanford-Binet Test
  The Wechsler Adult Intelligence
  Scale
  Refining the Intelligence Test
  with Computer Technology
  Attempts to Measure Different
  Components of Intelligence
- Practical Issues Involved in
  Testing
  Reliability
  Validity
- Ethical and Legal Issues
  Surrounding IQ Testing
- The Nature of Intelligence
- Factors Influencing Intelligence

▶ **Guided Review**

▶ **Summary**

▶ **Action Glossary**

▶ **Self-Test**

▶ **Thinking About Psychology**

▶ **Suggested Readings**

# COMMUNICATION AND COGNITION
## LEARNING OBJECTIVES

**After reading this chapter, you should be able to**

▶ 1. describe the nature of language, its structure, and the way people use language to communicate and comprehend meaning. *(pp. 202–204)*

▶ 2. outline the steps children go through during the acquisition of language, and discuss the theories proposed to account for language learning. *(pp. 202–207)*

▶ 3. understand that communication occurs through channels other than spoken language, such as body posture, gestures, eye contact. *(pp. 207–209)*

▶ 4. explain the progress and the conclusions of research that attempts to teach a language to apes. *(pp. 209–212)*

▶ 5. recognize cognitive science as the combined efforts of psychology, linguistics, computer science, and other disciplines. *(pp. 212–214)*

▶ 6. describe the relationship between language and thought. *(p. 214)*

▶ 7. explain the nature of concepts as they relate to the structure of thought. *(pp. 215–217)*

▶ 8. explain how concepts are learned. *(p. 216)*

▶ 9. list the three steps involved in solving a problem. *(pp. 218–221)*

▶ 10. identify several factors that influence how a problem is initially analyzed and whether the analysis will be successful. *(p. 215)*

▶ 11. explain and provide examples of the two general types of search strategies used by problem solvers. *(pp. 219–220)*

▶ 12. describe the nature of creative problem solving, and describe how incubation can facilitate the process. *(pp. 221–222)*

▶ 13. identify the attempts scientists have made to measure intelligence, and describe the tests that are currently used. *(pp. 223–225)*

▶ 14. discuss some of the practical and ethical issues involved in intelligence testing, including the issues of the reliability and validity of the tests. *(pp. 226–228)*

▶ 15. describe three theories of the nature of intelligence. *(pp. 228–229)*

▶ 16. describe the studies that attempt to analyze the factors that influence intelligence. *(pp. 227–228)*

When the child was found hiding in the woods, he was nearly eight-years-old. He had long straggly hair, was covered with dirt, bruises, and scars, and could not stand erect for more than a few minutes. Medical and psychological tests showed him to be basically healthy, though he could not speak, walk on two legs, or use eating utensils. Doctors concluded that he had been abandoned as an infant and raised by wolves.

Three years of intensive training enabled the "wild boy of Aveyron" to master some basic skills, such as eating with a knife and fork, walking erect, sleeping in a bed, and bathing and dressing himself. At the age of eleven, he still behaved more like a two-year-old than a boy nearing puberty. His speech consisted of grunts and a few badly formed words. Despite years of effort to teach him speech, he never fully learned the language, remaining at the level of a three- or four-year-old. He never seemed to acquire the ability to reason or solve problems, and he tended to rely heavily on the trial-and-error method of performing complex tasks (Curtiss, 1977).

The wild boy of Aveyron may have been mentally retarded, but the fact that he survived argues against that hypothesis. It is more likely that he had difficulty developing the cognitive abilities typical of any normal adult because he had been without the benefit of human contact during an important phase of development, one in which human children acquire language at an astounding pace. Although the boy was able to perform some of the basic cognitive processes, such as perceiving and remembering, he was tragically deficient in some of the cognitive abilities so critical to humans. Because he never acquired much language, he was unable to think, reason, or solve problems like a normal adult.

Speaking, thinking, reasoning, and problem solving are all important mental processes that fall under the general heading of "cognition." They are of tremendous interest to psychologists because they are characteristic of human beings and uncharacteristic of most animals. Although scientists certainly agree that animals are capable of solving problems, and some suggest that the higher primates may even be able to learn a human language, no one would deny that human beings have elevated these cognitive processes to a fine art. It is hardly surprising that psychologists spend a great deal of time studying these characteristically human behaviors.

# COMMUNICATION

**Language** *is the system of sounds and symbols by which we communicate meaning.* It is a universal trait of human beings; all people speak and understand a language unless physical or mental handicaps prevent them from doing so. (In fact, tests of language abilities are used to diagnose neurological impairment. See Applying Psychology: Diagnoses of Speech Disorders.) The ability to use language is such an important trait that it helps to define "being human"; it enables us to think extremely complex thoughts and to imagine and represent ideas or objects not physically present in space or time. It also enables us to communicate our thoughts to one another, albeit imperfectly at times. And perhaps most important, it permits us to have a culture: a tradition of beliefs, rules, and artifacts we can pass on to future generations.

What is a language? How do we use it to express our thoughts? How can we acquire such a complex vocabulary and system of rules long before we start kindergarten? This section will consider these questions and will examine the various systems of communication used by other members of the animal kingdom.

## The Nature of Language

There are approximately 2,800 different languages in the world. Each one communicates meaning through its own vocabulary and phrasing, a fact that creates great problems for diplomats. Yet despite their enormous differences, all human languages have three important characteristics in common. They all are creative, they are governed by rules, and they use arbitrary symbols that represent objects and events.

Languages are creative because the number of ways words can be combined into sentences is theoretically infinite. Although you repeat certain sentences several times each day, most sentences are new. With a limited number of sounds and words, human beings are capable of creating novel sentences throughout their lifetimes.

A second important property of natural languages is that they all involve **grammar,** *a set of rules that governs the use of words, their functions, and their relations in a sentence.* The creation of a sentence must follow certain rules about using words as verbs, nouns, adjectives, and other parts of speech; the arrangement of the word order; and even the inflections. Utterances that do not follow

## APPLYING PSYCHOLOGY
### Diagnoses of Speech Disorders

Knowing whether there is a problem with a person's language and speech is often crucial. The following two cases demonstrate that knowing when to intervene and when not to may have critical effects on people's lives.

Jimmy was an alert two-year-old who understood directions and conversations but who was speechless. His mother was concerned, but not to the point of seeking help until Jimmy passed his third birthday without emitting a single meaningful word. The family physician calmly acknowledged all the information offered by Jimmy's mother and then offered his professional opinion: "Jimmy will grow out of it." As the child approached his fourth birthday, he spoke his first words, his first phrase, and his first sentence all at the same time. "Mamma, kitty's got a robin!" came the shriek from the backyard. She knew at once that the voice was that of her son and that the doctor's advice was correct. By the time he was five, Jimmy's language was completely normal.

In contrast is the case of Vernon N., a forty-three-year-old former teamster and self-educated amateur archeologist. Following a stroke almost one year earlier, his relatives insisted upon admitting him to a nursing home, claiming that he was senile and incapable of handling his affairs. Like many aphasics (those without speech), Mr. N. did seem infantile. He lacked expressive language except for some automatic speech, which he generally used inappropriately. He cried easily and appeared apathetic and withdrawn. He used the phrase "I can't think" over and over, and he too was convinced of his mental incapacity.

On testing, it was found that indeed he could think; he scored at the ninetieth percentile on a test of recognition vocabulary and showed good auditory comprehension for short, simple messages. It took a great deal of supportive counseling and therapy before he agreed to enter treatment; but once he did, Mr. N. made excellent progress. He later took a seasonal position as a receptionist in a local museum that featured an extensive collection of American Indian lore.

It is sobering to speculate how many untested and untreated aphasic individuals are languishing in nursing homes or occupying some dim corner in private residences on the mistaken premise that they are mentally defective.

---

these rules are difficult for others to understand and may even be unintelligible. Although some schools stress the study of grammar through a variety of mechanical means, such as sentence diagramming, they are really reinforcing what most people learned when they were two- or three-years-old. By the time children are five, the vast majority of their sentences are easily understood by others because they follow the rules of grammar (for their language) quite well.

*The Structure of Language* Although language involves both sounds and symbols, we will focus primarily on the spoken component. The basic unit of oral language is the **phoneme,** *a single sound element from which spoken words are formed.* In the English language, there are approximately forty-five phonemes. The phonemes /p/ and /b/, for example, help us distinguish between the words "pill" and "bill." Many of the phonemes in other languages are similar or identical to those in the English language; some may be quite different. For instance, English has two separate phonemes for /f/ and /h/, but Japanese has only one phoneme somewhere between the two sounds. The Japanese language also has only one phoneme that falls somewhere between the English /r/ and /l/. This feature of the Japanese language helps explain why a Japanese speaker sounds as if he is saying "herro" for "hello." Anyone who tries to imitate accents has to pay special attention to the phonemes in each language.

The **morpheme** *is the smallest unit of meaning in a spoken language.* Morphemes consist of one or more phonemes. Some morphemes are words, but any syllable or group of syllables that conveys meaning and indicates functions or relationships is a morpheme. The "ing" at the end of verbs and the "s" at the end of plural nouns are both morphemes. The English language contains about fifty thousand morphemes.

One or more morphemes constitute a word, and words combine into phrases and finally sentences. The sentence is the normal unit of conversation, and a great deal of study and research has gone into how people produce and comprehend sentences.

*Communicating through Language* Any sentence, even the simplest one, contains information at two different levels. One level is called the **surface structure** *and represents the organization of words in a spoken sentence.* The second level is called the **underlying representation;** *it is the meaning that the speaker is actually trying to convey.* In many cases, the surface structure and the underlying representation are the same: for example, "Mary loves John." But in some ambiguous sentences, the underlying representation may not be so obvious. Consider the following examples:

Nothing is better than Brand X.
He shot off his mouth.
The shooting of the hunters was terrible.

For each of the examples, the underlying representation is not entirely clear. The first sentence might mean that no other brand is better than Brand X, or it could mean that having nothing is better than having Brand X. Alternate representations for the second and third examples are too ghastly to describe.

A distinction between the surface structure and the underlying representation can also be seen in cases in which the surface structure varies but the underlying representation remains essentially the same. The sentences, "Psychology is an interesting subject," "I find psychology interesting," and "Among all the interesting subjects I know, psychology is number one," all have essentially the same underlying representations, but their surface structures are different.

Before speaking, we must establish the nature of the underlying representation and then choose a surface structure that conforms to our language's grammatical rules. The mental operations that accompany this feat are obscure. Furthermore, the method we use to interpret the surface structure of the utterances of others is also poorly understood.

The **semantic approach,** *a method used to explain the relationship between surface structure and underlying representation, emphasizes the sentence's division into propositions* (Clark & Clark, 1977). The **proposition** *is a unit of meaning or an idea that consists of a verbal unit and one or more nouns.* A sentence consists of one or more propositions. For example, the sentence, "Jake sold some shoes to Bob today" contains a series of three propositions combined into one sentence (figure 7.1). The greater the number of propositions in a sentence, the longer the time it will take to comprehend it (Anderson & Bower, 1973).

Jake sold some shoes to Bob today.

Propositions:

1. Jake sold some shoes.

2. The shoes were sold to Bob.

3. The shoes were sold today.

**Figure 7.1**    *A sentence contains one or more propositions, each expressing a unitary idea.*

Whereas speakers have to transform underlying representation into a surface structure, listeners have the opposite task. They must listen to the surface structure and somehow determine the underlying representation. Most psycholinguists believe that listeners automatically divide spoken speech into **constituents,** or *phrases and subphrases.* "The furry mouse ran into the garage" has two major constituents: "The furry mouse" and "ran into the garage." Each of these constituents could be divided into smaller units, but people seem to make a special effort to preserve the integrity of each constituent. For example, subjects who listened to sentences through one earphone were occasionally interrupted by a click in the other ear. They tended to recall that the click occurred very near or at the boundaries between the constituents of sentences, even though the click actually occurred right in the middle of some constituents (Fodor, Bever, & Garrett, 1974). The listener apparently analyzes the meaning of these constituents rather than the individual words they contain.

## The Acquisition of Language

Perhaps the most remarkable achievement of childhood is the development of the ability to understand and speak a language by the age of two. If you have tried to learn a second language as an adult, you probably recognize how extraordinary the child's linguistic accomplishments are. On their way to fluency, children pass through identifiable stages of language development.

*Language Development*    **Cooing** *refers to the vocalizations of the very young infant.* These sounds are often vowel-like vocalizations in which the phoneme /u/ appears frequently, although the phoneme may occasionally be preceded by a single consonant, resulting in sounds like "moo" or "coo." *The infant begins* babbling *around six or seven months of age; these vocalizations include strings of consonants and vowel phonemes.* During the babbling phase, the babies utter the phonemes from languages all over the globe but eventually come to use those in their own language more and more frequently.

In addition to the sounds of the language, the baby is learning a great deal about communication and conversation during these early months (Rosenthal, 1973). The conversations that take place between the mother and the baby show particular temporal arrangements that set the stage for later verbal communication. For example, some interactions show reciprocal turn-taking (Bruner, 1977).

One study investigated the interactions between newborns and their mothers in the hospital during breast-feeding. The researchers watched the mothers from the moment they took their babies out of the crib to breast-feed until they returned them. Every five seconds the researcher recorded the activities of the mother and baby. They observed that there were large individual differences in the way the mothers and babies interacted. Some babies almost never gazed at their mothers, and some mothers spent almost the entire time vocalizing. The largest proportion of the babies' vocalizations occurred when the mother was already vocalizing. The babies tended to "join in" when the mother was speaking or cooing (Rosenthal, 1982).

By the end of the first year, the child is making holophrases, *single-word utterances that carry a great deal of meaning, usually using only a few phonemes.* Children typically utter words like mama, dada, baby, milk, or kitty. Although they are only using holophrases and their vocabulary is quite small, they are able to communicate quite a range of meanings through inflections, pitch, and other devices. Imagine the difference in the word "Mama" when uttered by a child who sees his mother come home from work and one who is demanding candy. Children also use the same word to communicate different meanings in different contexts. For example, the word "bye-bye" might mean "Good-bye," "He went bye-bye," or "I want to go bye-bye."

Telegraphic speech *refers to the utterances of children who are beginning to use two-word sentences such as "Daddy come" or "Cookie gone."* The tiny sentences are called telegraphic (Brown, 1973) because they omit small words such as the, to, for, and be, thereby making the informational yield somewhat like that of a telegram. But even though children are using only about two words per sentence, their speech is amazingly complex. Several researchers hypothesize that this stage is characterized by a system of rules for sentence construction (McNeill, 1970; Bowerman, 1973; Nelson, 1978).

When children begin speaking four- and five-word sentences, another new development occurs. They begin to master certain inflections, like the plural "s" and the present-progressive verb form ending in "ing." According to research on the topic (Brown, 1973), most children seem to acquire these morphemes in a specified order. The "ing" is learned first, followed by the prepositions "in" and "on," followed by the plurals, and so forth. The ones acquired earlier seem to be grammatically simpler.

Watching children master these rules is a fascinating experience. When they first acquire a rule, they are likely to apply it incorrectly. Although they had previously been saying "feet" as the plural of "foot," they may start saying "foots" when they acquire the rule for plural "s." As they learn more about how the "s" is used, they may say "footses" or "feetses" before finally returning to "feet." The application of the general rule of adding "s" to make a noun plural is *over-generalized* by the child. Overgeneralization indicates that the child is constructing language by applying rules, even though the rule may not be applicable. The manner in which children learn these rules is a controversial subject in theories of language learning.

*Theories of Language Learning*    The way in which psychologists have viewed the process of language development has changed dramatically over the last fifty years. John B. Watson, the father of American behaviorism, argued in 1924 that language is a complex behavior learned primarily through the laws of classical conditioning and stimulus-response associations. Later behaviorists stressed the importance of operant conditioning and imitation (Skinner, 1957; Staats, 1971; Bandura, 1971). An infant utters meaningless sounds, imitating some of the sounds around him, and is selectively rewarded for those sounds that duplicate or approximate the morphemes in the parents' language. When a babbling infant says "da da," his or her father picks the infant up, smiles, and says, "Yes, I'm dada." In this way, children's verbal behavior is shaped and rewarded, and they gradually come to speak the language of their parents.

The effects of operant conditioning and imitation are apparent in the way children learn the phonemes associated with the language spoken in their homes. Babies babble all kinds of sounds, but soon their babbling begins to "sound" more like the parents' speech in the sense that the phonemes are more recognizable and typical of the parents' language.

Nevertheless, the behavioristic view of language learning seems to fall short for a variety of reasons. For example, Noam Chomsky (1959), a psycholinguist, pointed out that children's language acquisition is anything but slow and gradual. Instead, it is breathtakingly fast. And rather than merely duplicating sounds, words, and sentences that have been reinforced, children say many things that have not been reinforced and that they may not even have heard before. Two-year-olds, for example, might begin saying, "I dooed it!" after they have already been using the correct form of the past tense verb. They are overgeneralizing the rule about using "ed" for the past tense.

Recent research on language acquisition stresses that the process is essentially one in which children actively attempt to induce rule systems from the speech they hear everyday. Their progress suggests that they are generating hypotheses based on certain operating principles and that they are testing their hypotheses. For example, children learning to use "ed" to change a verb to the past tense seem to be formulating a hypothesis about the nature of the language. They might then test that hypothesis by using "ed" on verbs, such as "Baby cried" or "I walked." Finally, they might overgeneralize and extend their hypothesis to "I falled down" or "Daddy goed."

In order to efficiently develop hypotheses like this one, some scientists have suggested that children use certain operating principles, such as paying attention to the ends of words, avoiding exceptions, looking for prefixes or suffixes that change the meaning of the word, and looking for systematic changes in the forms of words (Ferguson & Slobin, 1971; Slobin, 1979).

The question of how children come to induce these rule systems so well, and why they do it in the first place, seems to require the interplay of three main forces. First, all human beings appear to have a genetically endowed predisposition that enables them to acquire a language and discover the grammar that underlies the speech to which they are exposed. Second, children hear a steady barrage of speech, appropriate to their level of development, that

further enables them to grasp the essentials of their own language and provides feedback for their learning. And finally, children seem to have an incredibly strong motivation to learn language. All of these forces combine to enable children to actively induce rule systems from the speech they hear everyday and to become fluent in their native tongue before they enter kindergarten.

That a genetic predisposition for language learning exists is supported by many arguments. For example, recall the studies on the specializations of the left and right hemispheres in human beings discussed in chapter 2. For most people, language functions are lateralized on the left side of the brain. The brain contains areas crucial for language development, and if these areas are damaged in some way, language abilities are affected.

There appears to be a critical period for language development, a fact that adds further weight to the argument that a genetic predisposition exists. The term **critical period** *refers to a period of development during which the organism is particularly vulnerable or susceptible to certain environmental influences.* During the first few years of life, children acquire language at an astounding rate. However, if they are not exposed to language during those years, as in the case of the wild boy of Aveyron, their ability to acquire language is limited. It is as if there is a period of life during which the individual's brain is particularly sensitive to environmental factors that encourage language development. During other periods of life, the person can still learn a language, but the process is much more tortuous. A child who grows up in a bilingual home, for example, acquires both languages and usually becomes fluent in both. The person who tries to learn Russian in college may spend years on the task, but the person rarely becomes completely fluent and usually speaks the second language with an accent. It is very difficult for most people to correctly pronounce phonemes that are not typical of their own native language and that they had no opportunity to acquire during the first few years of life.

Although many psychologists agree that a critical period for language does exist, most would prefer to call it a "sensitive" period. It is still possible for a person to acquire a second language after childhood, and there has been at least one case of a severely isolated and abused youngster who acquired her first language in her teens (Curtiss, 1977). Genie was reared in the attic of her parents' home, away from nearly all human contact, during

A. Between the mother and the one-year-old.

Mom: (pointing to a picture of an elephant)
What's that?

Daughter: Doggie

Mom: I think it's an...elephant.

Daughter: Efant?

Mom: Yes! It's a big elephant!

B. Between the mother and the two-year-old.

Mom: What is this animal called?

Daughter: Elephant?

Mom: Yes! That's very good. It's a big gray
elephant with big ears.

Daughter: What's he doing?

Mom: What do you think he's doing?

Daughter: Taking a baf?

Mom: Yes, he's taking a bath in an
enooormous bathtub.

**Figure 7.2**  *Conversations with a growing child*

Infants two- to three-months-old are able to discriminate words spoken with motherese intonations better than words spoken in a flat tone of voice (Cross, 1978; Grieser & Kuhl, 1988; Hirsch-Pasek et al., in press). A conversation between one of the authors and her one-year-old child is shown in figure 7.2A. As the child grew, the complexity of the mother's sentences increased. The same conversation about an elephant was repeated when the child was two-years-old and is shown in figure 7.2B.

These exchanges provide the child with important feedback about the language and about her progress. First, the parent prompts the child, encouraging her to talk. Second, the mother repeats what the child says, using correct pronunciation and grammar, often giving an expanded version of the primitive utterance of the child (Cazden, 1972).

Children seem strongly motivated to learn language. They are not simply a passive recipient of genetically programmed predispositions or environmental forces surrounding them. Some psycholinguists argue that children's repeated attempts to induce rule systems, even in very difficult circumstances, is a part of the genetic inheritance associated with language. Others are not so sure. However, it is certain that children try very hard to learn to communicate even in the most inauspicious circumstances. Sometimes, for example, the normal, hearing parents of deaf children will choose not to teach them sign language based on the theory that it will be easier for the children to learn to speak and read lips. An investigation of some of these children found that they often used a system of gestures that began to acquire some of the properties of language, even before they learned anything at all about English. The "language development" of these children was surprisingly similar in pattern to that of hearing children in the sense that it began with single signs and progressed to two- and three-sign sentences (Feldman, Goldin-Meadow, & Gleitman, 1978).

## Nonverbal Communication

A smile, a gift of a box of chocolates, the clothes you wear, and footprints at the scene of a crime are all forms of **nonverbal communication,** *the transmission of information, whether intended or not, by means other than words.* We send messages to others not only by what we say, but by how, where, and when we say it. Facial expressions, gestures, body movements, and tone of voice are forms of nonverbal communication increasingly

the first thirteen years of her life. When she was discovered by the authorities, her behavior was about like that of a one-year-old. Despite her tragic isolation, she was able to learn language after several years of intensive therapy, although she is still not proficient. Most psycholinguists agree that the environment is extremely important for language development, although not as important as the behaviorists had argued.

Parents and other adults use "motherese" with children, a simpler version of the language that has shorter sentences, higher pitch, slower tempo, and stronger intonation. Studies have shown that mothers in several cultures use motherese and that it has both linguistic and social benefits. For example, infants are sensitive to and prefer speech in which the pauses are placed at the boundaries of clauses rather than in the middle of clauses.

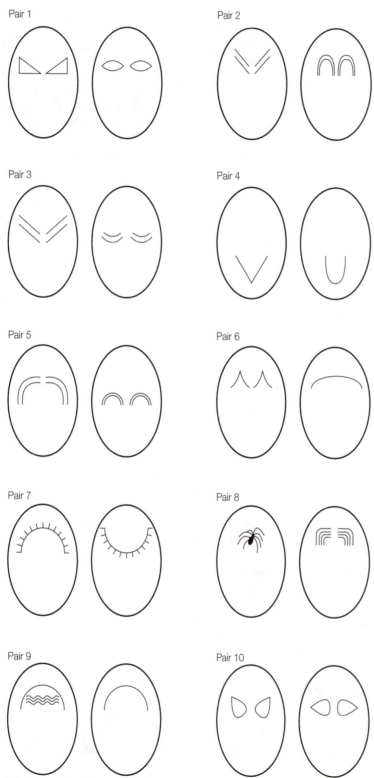

**Figure 7.3**  *Identifying Threatening Faces*

studied by psychologists and social scientists (e.g., Ekman, 1982; Leonard, Voeller & Kuldau, 1991). The sociologist Erving Goffman (1959) and psychologists Michael Argyle (1975), Gregory Bateson (Bateson & Ruesch, 1951), and Robert Sommer (1969) were among the first to study nonverbal communication.

There are wide cultural and individual differences in the meaning and interpretation of nonverbal information. But there are consistencies, also. For example, Aronoff, Barclay, and Stevenson (1988) showed subjects pictures of masks that were worn by different cultural groups in their religious and battle ceremonies (see figure 7.3). Across all cultures, threatening masks had a similar underlying pattern that distinguished them from masks that were not designed to portray threat. The threatening masks contained more triangles and diagonal lines, whereas nonthreatening masks had more rounded forms.

The tendency to allow silent pauses between words varies enormously from one place and one group to another. New Yorkers and Californians, for example, tend to be "high-involvement" speakers, who frequently interrupt or enter a conversation before another speaker has clearly finished speaking. In contrast, in Japan verbosity is frowned upon, and the proverb "silence is golden" is still used favorably. From early childhood on, Japanese children are inducted into the practice of *omoiyari* ("empathy"), and should try to understand others' wants silently. The Japanese value "implicit, nonverbal, intuitive communication" above an "explicit, verbal exchange of information" (Minami & McCabe, 1991). These differences may give rise to the stereotypes of New Yorkers and Californians as aggressive or "pushy", and the Japanese as "inscrutable" and mysterious.

Men and women also have different ways of communicating that can lead to misunderstanding. A couple are in their car on a long-distance journey. The woman asks her husband, "Would you like to stop for a drink?" "No," he says, and they do not stop. He was later upset to learn that his wife was annoyed because she had wanted to stop for a drink. He asked, "Why didn't you just say what you wanted? Why did you play this game with me?" She explained that she was upset not because she did not get her way, but because her preference had not even been considered. From her point of view, she had shown concern for her husband's wishes, but he had shown no concern for her's. Deborah Tannen (1990) compares such differences in the communication styles of men and women to a "cross-cultural" difference. It is not so much that men want to dominate women as that they simply have different ways of communicating. Women, Tannen writes, "speak and hear a language of connection and intimacy, while men speak and hear a language of status and independence."

Misunderstandings and stereotypes may be reduced if we can learn to recognize and appreciate these different styles of communication.

## Animal Communication

It has been said that language is the trait that clearly separates humans from other species (Descartes, 1637). In recent years, this has been questioned, and psycholinguists now agree that many species of animal have extremely complex systems of communication, using visual cues, sounds, touch, odors, and tastes. Although no species has been demonstrated to use language with the richness and variety that humans do, some researchers believe that a few species either possess a communication system that qualifies as a very primitive language or can be trained to use one.

Some animal communication systems based on sound are truly remarkable. Termites signal one another by drumming their heads against the floor, resonating corridors in their nests. To the human ear, the sound is like that of sand falling on paper, but an analysis of these drumming sounds reveals a high degree of organization and complexity. The beats occur in regular, rhythmic phrases that differ in duration and signal important messages to members of the species. Lewis Thomas (1974) eloquently describes the termite's signal:

> From time to time, certain termites make a convulsive movement of their mandibles to produce a loud, high-pitched clicking sound, audible ten meters off. So much effort goes

into this one note that it must have urgent meaning, at least to the sender. He cannot make it without such a wrench that he is flung one or two centimeters into the air by the recoil (p. 21).

Animals produce sounds by many different means. Prairie hens, rabbits, and mice tap their feet; woodpeckers bang with their heads; fish make sounds by clicking their teeth, blowing air, or drumming with special muscles against inflated air bladders. The proboscis of the death's-head hawk moth is used as a kind of reed instrument; the insect blows through it to produce high-pitched notes. Gorillas beat their chests. Turtles, alligators, crocodiles, snakes, and earthworms make vocal sounds.

Birds have a whole glossary of warning calls, mating signals, territorial pronouncements, calls for assistance, and demands for dispersal. The recorded songs of the humpback whale sound like music to many humans, but no one knows what the sounds mean to the whale. They may be simple statements about navigation, the location of food sources, or territorial signals; or perhaps they are music.

*Can Animals Use Language?*    There is no doubt that these various forms of signaling among animals constitute methods of communication, but do they constitute language? To be considered language, a communication must meet the criteria listed earlier, including creativity, the use of a grammar, and the use of arbitrary symbols for objects or events. Animal communication systems often show one or more of these characteristics.

One approach places the communication systems of animals along a continuum, with simple, primitive communication systems existing at one end and human language at the opposite end (figure 7.4). Many species are able to respond only to dramatic changes in their environments; the chirping of the cricket, for example, is related to temperature. Birds and bees communicate a much wider variety of messages. The communication systems of primates are quite complex, incorporating vocalizations, facial expressions, body gestures, and even odors. The communication system of humans reaches quite another level of sophistication, employing its enormously complex grammar, vocabulary, and symbolic written messages to convey information.

*Teaching a Language to Primates*    Since the 1930s, psychologists have attempted to teach human language to chimpanzees, our closest animal relatives (Kellogg & Kellogg, 1933: Hayes & Hayes, 1951). They raised chimps

**Figure 7.4** *The communication systems used by certain animals can be extremely complex.*

in their homes and treated them like children in an effort to encourage language development, but they were not successful. Although the chimps could understand a great many words, they were never able to speak more than a very few simple words.

Recently, teams of psychologists reasoned that the chimps did not learn to speak because they lacked the proper vocal apparatus (Gardner & Gardner, 1971; Premack, 1971; Premack & Premack, 1982). They decided to teach chimpanzees communication systems that did not include speaking. One group focused on American Sign Language; another group used "Yerkish," an artificial language involving a large number of computer-generated symbols developed at Yerkes Primate Laboratory in Georgia; and a third team invented a language that employed colored plastic symbols.

Sarah, a chimpanzee, was one of the pupils who learned to read and write with variously shaped and colored pieces of plastic (Premack, 1971; Premack & Premack, 1982). The teaching process with Sarah began with simple conditioning procedures: She was shown an object, such as a banana, and the symbol for banana, a pink plastic square. To obtain the banana she had to place the plastic square on a magnetic board. In the first phase of the project, Sarah was required to place only one word on the board, for instance, the name of the fruit she wanted. After she learned the symbols for some verbs, she had to place two words in the appropriate sequence to receive what she wanted, for example, "Give apple." When she had learned the name of her trainers, three-word sentences were required, such as "Give apple Gussie." Finally, Sarah had to use four-word sentences: "Gussie give banana Sarah."

One of the essential features of language is **displacement,** *the ability to talk about things not actually present.* When Sarah was given a piece of fruit and two plastic words, she was required to select the correct word for the fruit before being allowed to eat it. Often, however, she selected the wrong word. In many cases, these "errors" seemed to reflect her preferences in fruit rather than any mistake in selection. She tended to choose the symbol for the fruit that she liked best, even though the other fruit was present. This behavior suggested that Sarah could generate the meaning of the fruit names from the plastic symbols alone (Premack & Premack, 1982).

Sarah also learned to use conditional "if . . . then" sentences. For example, if she wished to receive a piece of chocolate, she had to follow closely the meaning of a sentence like "Sarah take banana *if then* Mary no give chocolate Sarah."

Sarah's accomplishments were astounding. She eventually developed a vocabulary of over 125 words that she used with a reliability of over seventy-five percent. The achievements of the chimps in the other "language" programs were equally impressive. Washoe, the first chimp to learn American Sign Language, made up several words. For example, she combined the signs for "water" and "bird" to identify a duck.

Although the chimpanzee language training programs all broke new ground and the remarkable pupils continue to surprise their trainers, some scientists question whether the chimps have actually learned to use a human language. Detailed analyses of some videotapes taken of Nim Chimsky (a chimp named after Noam Chomsky), who acquired American Sign Language, raise serious questions about whether the chimp was truly using a language the way human children do (Terrace, Petitto, Sanders, & Bever, 1979; Wellman, in press). As the French linguist Ferdinand de Saussure pointed out, a parrot may speak words but it does not know the system of language.

**Figure 7.5**  *Scientists are attempting to teach human languages, such as American Sign Language, to chimpanzees.*

Herbert Terrace raised Nim like a human infant, with bottle feedings, diaperings, and much cuddling. (Figure 7.5 is a photo of Nim.) When Nim was less than a year old, he became the first chimp to take classes at Columbia University. On at least one occasion, Nim's ability with sign language saved his life.

Someone spotted him about to drink some cleaning fluid in the kitchen and frantically signed, "No! Stop! Don't eat!" Nim moved the jar away from his mouth and put it down (Glass, Holyoak, & Santa, 1979).

Despite Nim's remarkable progress, Terrace noted that nearly ninety percent of Nim's signs were responses to his teachers' signs and that about half of his signs repeated some or all of what the teacher had just signed. Nim was mainly reproducing language, not producing it. Nim also frequently interrupted the trainer while she was signing.

Based on the tapes, Terrace wondered whether very much two-way communication was taking place.

Other scientists involved in the training programs have also begun to question the reliability of some of the original and spontaneous phrases sometimes used by the chimps. Researchers working with Lana, a chimp that learned "Yerkish," noted that she first called a cucumber "a banana which is green." They question, however, whether such performance is reliable (Rumbaugh, Gill, & VonGlasersfeld, 1973). Although the achievements of the apes have been remarkable, the evidence that they use language in a creative way is not compelling.

Since language abilities are based partly on the existence of genetic predispositions, they are a product of evolution. Yet the evolution of those abilities may have occurred rather recently (Chomsky 1972, 1979;

Lenneberg, 1967). Although apes may have evolved some of the abilities essential to the development of language, particularly the ability to apply arbitrary symbols to name objects (Terrace, 1985), they may not have evolved the ability to generate creative sentences the way humans do.

Scientists will undoubtedly continue to design language training programs for apes, to learn more about language in humans and to learn more about the thought processes of animals and how humans might communicate with some of the other species sharing the earth.

▶ **GUIDED REVIEW** *Learning Objectives 1, 2, 3, and 4*

1. Language is the system by which we communicate meaning through sounds and symbols. All natural human languages have three important characteristics: They are creative, they use arbitrary symbols to represent objects and events, and they are governed by a set of rules, called _____.

2. The basic unit of oral language is the _____, a single sound such as /p/ or /b/. The smallest unit of meaning in a language is the _____, consisting of one or more phonemes.

3. A sentence possesses a _____, which consists of the words and their organization, and an _____, which is the meaning the speaker is trying to convey.

4. The _____ suggests that the underlying representation of a sentence consists of one or more _____, or unitary ideas.

5. The speaker must transform the underlying representation into a surface structure, and the listener must listen to the surface structure and grasp the underlying representation. The listener divides speech into _____, or phrases, to aid in this task.

6. Children go through stages during language acquisition, including _____ and _____, single-word utterances called _____, and two-word sentences. The two-word sentences are called _____ because they omit the small articles, verbs, and prepositions.

7. The most widely accepted theory of how children learn language argues that language is only partly acquired through _____ and _____. Other factors include a _____ that lays the groundwork for language learning during the early childhood years, and a strong motivation to acquire language. Some call these years a _____ for language acquisition, but they are best thought of as sensitive years since it is still possible to acquire language outside of this age range.

8. People transmit information both intentionally and unintentionally by means other than speech, a field of study called _____. Differences in _____ can give rise to misunderstandings and stereotypes.

9. Although animals have complex communication systems, there is much controversy over whether any of the communication systems meet the criteria of a _____. Several attempts have been made to teach language to primates, using American Sign Language, plastic symbols, or a computer-operated keyboard containing symbols. Most of the subjects in these experiments performed extremely well, acquiring hundreds of symbols and learning complex relationships and word orderings. Despite their accomplishments, however, the apes do not seem to be able to use language _____ in the same way as humans.

*ANSWERS*

*1. grammar 2. phoneme, morpheme 3. surface structure, underlying representation 4. semantic approach, propositions 5. constituents 6. cooing, babbling, holophrases, telegraphic 7. imitation, reinforcement, genetic predisposition, critical period 8. nonverbal communication, communication styles 9. language, creatively*

# COGNITION

The study of human thought or "cognition" is one of the most difficult tasks in all of psychology. Although everyone thinks during practically every waking minute, thought processes are not easy to examine in an objective, scientific way. Thinking is a private event.

During the early part of this century, psychologists explored the nature of human thought with the technique called introspection, discussed in chapter 3. The method required people to analyze their own thought processes as objectively as possible. The technique had many drawbacks, not the least of which was its reliance on subjective information, and many psychologists lost interest in it. The behaviorists of the early twentieth century emphasized the use of strictly observable and measurable behavior, and the introspection method fell out of favor. As a result, scientists did not attempt to systematically study thinking or consciousness until recently (Crick & Koch, 1992).

## The Cognitive Revolution

The growth of cognitive psychology began in earnest in the 1960s, and signaled renewed interest in the study of human thought. Psychologists had begun to develop remarkably inventive tools to study thought processes; some even used modified versions of introspection. A

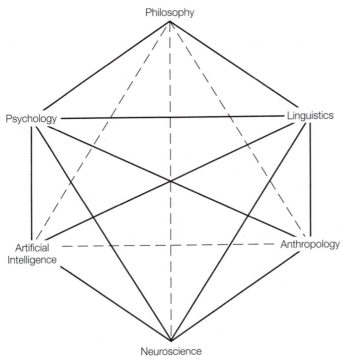

**Figure 7.6**  *Connections among the cognitive sciences*

psychologist might ask a subject to work on a geometry problem, for example, and to "think out loud," tracing the steps he or she goes through to reach the solution (Newell & Simon, 1972). Many studies used reaction-time measures. Subjects are asked to process some information, usually presented visually; computerized displays and digital timing devices enable researchers to examine the most minute differences in processing time for various tasks. The computer provided not only a new means for analyzing research data, but itself became the focus of cognitive research. In some respects, the computer is the laboratory rat of the cognitive psychologist.

While psychologists were engaged in these developments, others were becoming interested in the nature of thought, particularly in the fields of linguistics, anthropology, philosophy, computer science, and the neurosciences (see figure 7.6). The situation was ideal for individuals from these different disciplines to collaborate in studies of computers and human cognition. The last 20 years have seen rapid growth in interdisciplinary centers of "cognitive science," and many journals and other publications are now devoted to the subject (Gardner, 1987).

To study human thought and consciousness, cognitive scientists must first clearly define thought. One of the controversies within cognitive science touches directly upon this definition, namely whether computers can be said to think.

## Can Computers Think?

Modern cognitive psychologists have focused increasingly on **artificial intelligence,** *the attempt to simulate human thought processes with computers.* Computers can solve certain types of problems much faster and with greater accuracy than humans. They can be programmed to profit by their mistakes, to program themselves. But can computers be said to think?

One criterion for determining whether a computer can think is to compare its answers with those of humans. According to the "Turing test," proposed by the British mathematician Alan Turing, if an observer cannot distinguish the answers of a programmed machine from those of a human being, the machine can be said to think. This suggests that an appropriately programmed computer isn't just imitating thought, it really *is* thinking. According to one commentator, "The programs are not merely tools that enable us to test psychological explanations; rather the programs are themselves the explanations" (Searle, 1980). As you may imagine, the view that computers actually think is controversial. Is it thinking merely to produce the same answers as a human? Not everyone thinks so. For example, Margaret Boden (1977) asks, "What hope could be more self-defeating, or less authentic than that of illuminating human science by reference to machine research?" Indeed, computers are programmed so that we will interpret their behavior as thought. Nobel Prize laureate Francis Crick has warned of the "pernicious influence" of using the computer as a model for the brain.

The current approach to modeling the brain involves computers that process and store information not serially, in one location at a time, but in parallel at many locations, as the brain is thought to do (Bechtel & Abrahamson, 1991; Horgan, 1992; Pribram, 1982). This approach, called **parallel distributed processing (PDP)** *or connectionism, views thinking as a set of connections among cognitions,* rather than the cognitions themselves. PDP is able to simulate such complex cognitive events as typing, reaching smoothly for a glass of water, and memory (Kosslyn & Hatfield, 1984). PDP may be a more successful model for perception, that does not involve abstract symbols, than for symbolic thinking, such as problem-solving and creativity (Gardner, 1987).

Cognition is a very broad subject, encompassing many topics we have already covered or will cover in other chapters. It includes consciousness, memory, perception, attention, problem-solving, decision-making, planning, meditating, daydreaming, and imagination. Thinking relies heavily on language. After considering the relationship between thought and language, we explore some of the fundamentals of the thinking process, including the structure of thought and the concepts that comprise it.

## Language and Thought

As adults we do most of our thinking with language, and it is difficult to imagine how, as young children, we were ever able to think without it. (Recall the stroke victim who had almost no language abilities; he kept repeating, "I can't think!" over and over.) To early behaviorists, thought itself was seen as a form of speech—speech that was inaudible, internal, and subvocal. But psychologists generally agree that speech is not necessary for thought. Mathematicians and musicians certainly seem able to think about their subjects without using language. And very young children and animals demonstrate some remarkable problem-solving abilities without the aid of language.

One view of the relationship between language and thought, proposed by some early cognitive psychologists such as Jean Piaget, argues that language and thought have separate origins. This theory suggests that language develops from interaction and communication with other people. Thinking develops from interaction with objects in the environment. As the child grows to adulthood, the systems underlying language and thought become inter-dependent, and language comes to function as the servant of thought.

Another view of the connection between language and thought states that thinking is determined to a considerable extent by language. First proposed by Benjamin Lee Whorf (1956), the **linguistic relativity hypothesis** *states that an individual's perceptions, thinking, and view of the world depend on the particular language he or she speaks.* As Edward Sapir wrote, "No two languages are ever sufficiently similar to be considered as representing the same social reality. The worlds in which different societies live are distinct worlds, not merely the same

worlds with different labels attached" (quoted in Gardner, 1987).

Language, according to the linguistic relativity hypothesis, sets limits on what we can experience and think (Fishman, 1982). If we do not have a term or phrase to describe a concept, the linguistic relativity position is that we would have great difficulty thinking about the concept. An example might be the word for "give." In English, the word is used whether one gives something to friends, strangers, children, bosses, or the President. The Japanese, however, have several words for "give," and the use of each one depends on the status of the giver relative to the receiver. One verb is appropriate when the speaker is higher in status than the receiver, another when the speaker is lower in status than the receiver. Whether or not the receiver is a member of the speaker's family or circle of friends is also significant in choosing the correct verb. According to the linguistic relativity hypothesis, these fine distinctions in the Japanese language would enable people to perceive subtle differences in status and group member-ship. In contrast, the nature of the English language would make it much more difficult for native speakers to perceive such distinctions.

Critics of this hypothesis point out, among other things, that people can use long strings of words to describe and communicate concepts in any language (Au, 1983, 1984). Even though English speakers do not have a range of words for "give" that are appropriate in different contexts, English speakers can add words that make the phrasing distinctive in each case: "I'm giving you this book" (to an equal); "I would very much like to give you this book as a token of my great appreciation" (to royalty).

Thinking is not completely dependent on language and culture. There seem to be universals in human cognition. Berlin and Kay (1969) showed that, despite wide cultural variations in the *words* for colors, *perceptions* of colors were universal. Of course, some aspects of intellectual development are determined by culture (Ross, 1992). For example, Melissa Bowerman found that Korean children as young as eighteen months understand complex distinc-tions made in their language. Perhaps a modified view of the relationship between thought and language is the best conclusion we can reach at the moment. Language makes it easier to experience events for which we have an adequate vocabulary (Cole & Scribner, 1974; Slobin, 1971).

It is easier to recognize and recall objects or events that can be linguistically coded.

## The Structure of Thought

Randy: A penny for your thoughts.

Tim: Oh . . . I was just wondering whether that collie intends to run across the street.

In order for a person to have thoughts about "collies," "running," and "streets," he must have concepts. **Concepts are the mental constructs that enable us to make classifications; they are categories that represent classes of things with shared characteristics.** The world consists of an enormous number of objects, actions, and abstractions, and to make sense of the world, human beings must somehow order and classify these into some meaningful arrangement. Concepts are hierarchically arranged (Collins & Quillian, 1969). A collie is an instance of a dog, running is an instance of movement, and street is an instance of roadway.

*The Nature of Concepts*    A concept is defined by one or more **attributes,** or *features of an object or event used to identify it as a member of a particular class.* For example, possession of wings constitutes one of the attributes for the concept "bird." Members of a class will have many attributes, but only some of them will be relevant to the concept itself. Somebody's pet bird might be yellow, for example, but this attribute is irrelevant to the concept "bird." The concept "voter" might have the following relevant attributes: age eighteen or older, United States citizen, registered to vote. Attributes such as sex, race, religion, and occupation are irrelevant to the concept "voter" but may be relevant to other concepts.

The assignment of attributes to a concept is not always clear-cut. For example, it is difficult to come up with appropriate attributes for the concept "furniture" (figure 7.7). Sometimes, attributes are connected by some kind of rule, such as "either-or." An attribute of furniture might be that it is either something to sit on or something to put objects on. Judging from the examples in figure 7.7, however, the attributes of furniture are more complex than this.

One approach to the nature of concepts divides the attributes of a concept into defining features and characteristic features. The **defining features of a concept** *are*

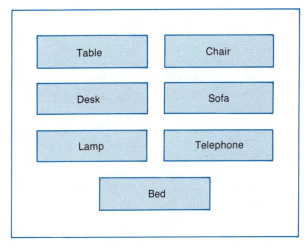

**Figure 7.7**    *Choose the best examples of the concept "furniture." What attributes do they share?*

*those attributes that are essential for category membership.* A bird, for example, must have wings and feathers. **Characteristic features of a concept** *are those attributes that many, but not all, members of a class possess.* The ability to fly would be a characteristic feature of the concept "bird" because there are many birds, such as penguins and ostriches, that do not fly (Smith, Shoben, & Rips, 1974). An instance of a category with all the defining features and all the characteristic features of the concept would be a "better" instance than one that had only a few of the characteristic features. A robin, for example, is probably a "better" example of a bird than a penguin because the robin has more characteristic features. When speaking about penguins, people might use a kind of verbal hedge before placing it into a specific category (Lakoff, 1972). They might say, *"Technically speaking,* a penguin is a bird." This tells the listener that the instance is lacking many of the characteristic features of the category.

Another approach to understanding concepts involves the notion of the **prototype,** *the best example of an object or event within a particular category* (Rosch, 1973; 1975). This approach suggests that the boundaries of a concept are not clearly delineated and that some members of a class are "better" than others because they are closer to the prototype. For example, a table might be considered an excellent example of furniture, but a telephone or lamp would be further away from the prototype.

The concepts we hold for colors seem to fit well into the notion of prototypes. People seem to organize their understanding and perception of colors into a limited number of **focal,** or *basic,* colors (Berlin & Kay, 1969). The English names for these focal colors are black, white, red, green, yellow, blue, pink, orange, brown, and purple. Although people from various cultures may place different boundaries between two focal colors, they tend to agree on the color that best represents red or blue, for example. Some scientists argue that the focal colors, or prototypes, for these colors are physiologically based.

Eleanor Rosch (1973) investigated the nature of color concepts in the Dani, a group of people in New Guinea. Their language has only two color terms: *mili,* which means dark, and *mola,* which means light. Rosch selected eight sets of three colors each. Each set contained one focal color, such as green, and two colors slightly above or below it on the color spectrum (slightly yellowish-green and slightly bluish-green). Rosch asked the Dani subjects to learn eight different names; each name applied to one focal color and its two surrounding colors. In a second series, she asked them to learn names for another eight sets of colors; however, this time each set contained a focal color and two colors on the same side of the spectrum. The green set, for example, might contain the focal color green, a slightly yellowish-green, and a very yellowish-green.

Rosch found that the Dani learned the names for the focal colors faster than the names for nonfocal colors, even when the focal color was not at the center of the set in terms of the color spectrum. However, the Dani learned the name of the focal color fastest in the first experiment, when it was in the center. It seems that a focal color represents a prototype for a color category and that the category is most easily learned when the instances of it are organized around the prototype.

*Learning Concepts*    A time-traveller visiting a modern office for the first time might approach an IBM PC and hear that it is a microcomputer. Having never seen or touched any computers, the visitor might begin to form a concept for the term "microcomputer," including tentative attributes like "many labeled keys," and "a greyish color." On another desk, the visitor might see an Apple II, notice the keys and the color, and guess that it, too, is a micro-computer. On the next desk, however, is a manual type-writer. The visitor, using his tentative attributes, might incorrectly guess that the typewriter is a microcomputer but hear that it is not. Now the visitor must search more critically for common features of the Apple and the IBM

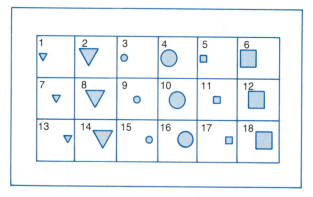

**Figure 7.8**    *Cards presented to a subject in a hypothetical concept-learning experiment.*

PC and also for features that those two machines do not share with the typewriter. In this way, the visitor uses both positive and negative examples of a concept to identify the concept's relevant attributes. Two of the major tasks in learning a new concept are to separate relevant and irrelevant attributes and to determine which ones might be defining and which ones are characteristic.

Early research on this topic has led to the conclusion that many people use trial and error to grasp the nature of new concepts; however, many use more efficient and sophisticated hypothesis-testing strategies (Bruner, Goodnow, & Austin, 1956).

One method that researchers use to study concept learning strategies involves a series of cards with a single geometric shape on each: the kind of shape, the size of the shape, and the position of the figure differ on each card (figure 7.8). The concept to be acquired is chosen by the experimenter. The subject's job is to determine the attributes of the concept.

In the experiment, the subject picks one card after another, and the experimenter simply says whether the card is a positive or negative instance of the concept. If the concept for figure 7.8 were "small figure," all the odd-numbered cards would represent positive instances.

A strategy a subject might use to acquire a concept in a problem like that in figure 7.8 is the **conservative focus-ing strategy.** *A learner uses one positive instance of the concept as the focus and then tests individual hypotheses, one at a time, to ascertain the nature of the concept.* For example, the subject might choose #1 in figure 7.8, hear "positive" from the experimenter, and then use this as the focus card. The subject might then choose #3, which differs in shape but not size or position. The experimenter would also say this a positive instance, and the subject would conclude that shape was irrelevant to the concept. The subject might then choose #2 to test whether size is relevant to the concept.

Concepts, and the language underlying them, are the building blocks of knowledge and thought. From very early childhood, adding one block at a time, each of us constructs an enormous edifice of interlocked ideas, and no two of them are exactly alike. What you believe to be the defining and characteristic features of a concept like "collie" may be very similar to those of another person who is familiar with dogs. But what about the concept "husband"? Some parts of our knowledge structure may be relatively stable; others, particularly those acquired recently, may be volatile.

# PROBLEM SOLVING

The study of problem solving and decision making is among the fastest-growing areas of psychology (Kahneman, 1991). One of the most fascinating aspects of thinking is that it includes the ability to solve problems like the ones in figure 7.9. We are capable of thinking abstractly, of mentally testing hypotheses, and of trying out various solutions in almost unlimited ways. By using

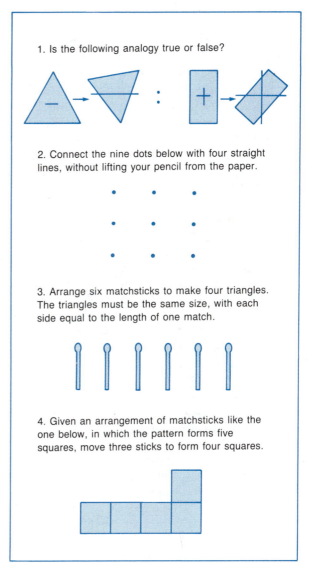

**Figure 7.9** *These problems require creative solutions. The answers to these and other problems presented in the text are at the end of this chapter.*

concepts and the relationships between them, we are able to solve problems in geometry, semantics, algebra, business, politics, and even art.

At the same time that computers are being programmed to simulate human problem solving, research by cognitive psychologists raises questions about how rational humans are when solving problems. Even the "framing" of a problem influences its solution: people are more likely to opt for a medical procedure that ensures a "90% survival rate" than one that has a "10% mortality rate," even though these two are identical (Gilovich, 1991).

Any problem contains three main parts: a **given state,** *the state one is currently in,* a **goal state,** *the place where one wants to be,* and a **path,** *the route from the given state to the goal state.* The job of the solver is to find a path through the "problem space," space composed of all the possible knowledge and operations that can apply to the problem.

## Steps of Problem Solving

Regardless of what kind of problem a person is trying to solve, there is usually a series of steps involved: (1) analyzing the problem, (2) searching for a solution, and (3) deciding that a solution has been discovered.

*Analyzing the Problem*    Analyzing the problem is essentially the job of gaining an understanding of and encoding the "givens." In some problems, the givens are all provided to the solver, but in most problems, the solver is expected to provide some information from his or her own experience and knowledge. For example, a question that might appear on a college entrance exam may ask you to apply principles of geometry.

Not surprisingly, familiarity with the elements of the problem, and with the information that might be needed to fill in the gaps of the givens is useful to a solver. Research suggests that people do their best problem solving when the problem is concrete rather than abstract, apparently because people are more familiar with the ideas in the problem and can form a kind of mental model to manipulate (Johnson-Laird, 1983).

Although familiarity is useful most of the time, it can sometimes be a hindrance to problem solving. People may prematurely define the problem space too narrowly and close their minds to useful information. The example of the nine dots shown in problem #2 (figure 7.9) shows how this can happen. If you defined the problem space by thinking that you should not move your pencil outside the

imaginary square delineated by the outer dots, you will never reach a solution. Your previous experience with squares and with playing "connect the dots" may have led you to define the problem space too narrowly.

What people refer to as a "mental set" and psychologists call a **cognitive set** *refers to the tendency to cling to a certain interpretation of the problem, an interpretation that is familiar and that led to correct solutions on previous occasions.* A classic demonstration of the effects of a cognitive set on problem solving was demonstrated in early research on the "water-jar problem" (Luchins, 1942). Subjects were shown pictures of three water jars with different volume capacities and were told they had an unlimited supply of water. In the first problem, Jar A could hold 21 quarts, Jar B could hold 127 quarts, and Jar C could hold 3 quarts. The task was to use the jars to obtain 100 quarts of water.

A simple solution is to fill Jar B, pour out enough water to fill Jar A, leaving 106 quarts in Jar B. Then Jar C could be filled twice from Jar B, thereby leaving 100 quarts in Jar B. The mathematical solution is $B - A - 2C$.

A group of subjects were given one problem after another, like those in figure 7.10, which could be solved using $B - A - 2C$. The last problem, however, could be solved simply by filling up Jar C (8 quarts) from Jar A (14 quarts) to arrive at 6 quarts. But most of the subjects who had done the earlier problems relied on the more complex, but tried and true, $B - A - 2C$ formula. They had developed a cognitive set.

Sets can exist because an experimenter induces them or because of previous experiences and expectations. In another classic experiment, subjects were given the objects in figure 7.11 and told to mount the candle on the wall in such a way that it would burn without dripping wax on the floor. The solution (figure 7.12) is to tack the box to the wall and use it as a ledge for the candle. Most subjects, however, were unable to discover this solution because of **functional fixity,** *the tendency for people to have difficulty imagining new uses for familiar objects.* They saw the box as a container rather than a ledge. When people were given the boxes separately, without the tacks in them, their functional fixity was reduced, and they were better able to solve the problem.

The initial analysis of the problem often has an important impact on how easily and quickly a solution is reached. Some research suggests that people who take longer to analyze and encode the information solve the problem more quickly than people who breeze through that

| GIVEN JARS OF THE FOLLOWING SIZES | | | OBTAIN THE AMOUNT |
|---|---|---|---|
| A | B | C | |
| 21 | 127 | 3 | 100 |
| 14 | 163 | 25 | 99 |
| 18 | 43 | 10 | 5 |
| 9 | 42 | 6 | 21 |
| 20 | 59 | 4 | 31 |
| 14 | 36 | 8 | 6 |

**Figure 7.10**  *Luchin's water-jar problem*

Source: "Mechanization in Problem-solving: The Effect of Einstellung" by A. S. Luchins, *Psychological Monographs, 242* p. 54 (6 Whole No. 248). Copyright 1942 American Psychological Association.

**Figure 7.11**  *The candle problem. The figure contains a candle, matches, and a box of tacks. Think of a way to get the candle on the wall so that it will burn properly. Use only the objects illustrated in the figure.*
From Bourne/Ekstrand/Dominowski, *The Psychology of Thinking.* ¨ 1971, p. 52. Reprinted by permission of Prentice-Hall, Englewood Cliffs, New Jersey.

step. Consider problem #1 in figure 7.9. This is an analogy problem requiring **inductive reasoning,** *the ability to take specific experiences and form general rules, ideas, or concepts.* People who do well at this kind of task are quick to make inferences and apply them, but they often take longer to analyze and encode the initial information. In this problem, superior reasoners might carefully encode the nature of the relationship between the figures on the left of the colon before going on to analyze the set of figures on the right. They might verbalize the relationship mentally, perhaps by describing it as "the outer figure is rotated about 45 degrees to the right, and the inner figure is enlarged."

*Search Strategies*    I forgot the combination for my bicycle lock. Fortunately, the lock only has three numbers, and I remember that all three of them were 7 or higher.

Once a problem has been understood, the solver must attempt to find a solution. One way might be to use trial and error; however, this method is rather inefficient. The bicyclist might, for example, simply try 789, then 998, then 777, and so on, hoping to come upon the solution by chance. For most problems, some kind of strategy would be much more efficient. Psychologists have identified quite a number of strategies typically used by problem solvers, including algorithms and heuristics.

An **algorithm** *is a general procedure that guarantees a solution to a problem.* For example, if you were asked to find the length of the hypotenuse of a right triangle whose legs were two inches and five inches long, you could use the

algorithm $a^2 + b^2 = c^2$. For most problems, there are no mathematical algorithms available, and the only method of guaranteed solution is an exhaustive search of all possibilities. The person who forgot her lock combination might try a "tree" like the one in figure 7.13.

One of the disadvantages of algorithms is that the number of possible choices is often extremely large. In the eight letter anagram TERALBAY, for example, there are 40,320 possible letter combinations. Using the algorithm approach to checkers would involve the consideration of $10^{40}$ possible moves. Even at three choices per millisecond, a move would take $10^{21}$ centuries to consider (Samuel, 1963).

A more commonly used technique in problem solving is the employment of a **heuristic,** or *rule of thumb.* The heuristic is a general principle that can be used to solve the problem, although its use does not necessarily guarantee a solution. The heuristic is actually a selective search through the possible solutions. When the number of possible solutions is very large, the heuristic reduces the cost of the search by considering only some likely solutions, but at the risk of not solving the problem.

One commonly used heuristic is called **means-end analysis.** *This approach to problem solving examines the difference between the present state*

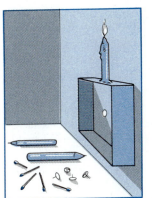

**Figure 7.12**  *The solution to Duncker's candle problem*

From Bourne/Ekstrand/Dominowski, *The Psychology of Thinking.* ¨ 1971, p. 52. Reprinted by permission of Prentice-Hall, Englewood Cliffs, New Jersey.

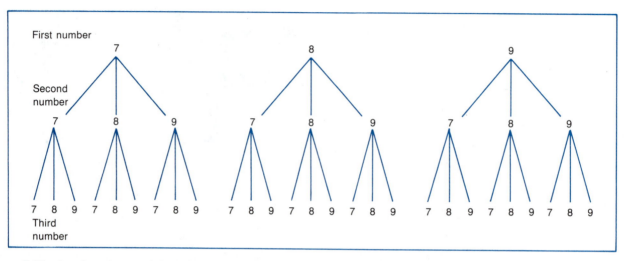

**Figure 7.13**    *An exhaustive search for a three-digit combination in which all digits are seven or higher*

*of affairs and the final goal state, and it tries to reduce that difference by setting up sub-problems.* Consider a simplified version of the problem of the hobbits and the orcs:

> Two hobbits and two orcs are sitting on the west bank of a river. They have access to a boat that will hold no more than two creatures at a time, and they all want to get across. Orcs are nasty creatures, however, and if at any time they outnumber the hobbits on either side of the river, the hobbits will be eaten. How can you get them all across to the other side of the river?

Using means-end analysis, we would first examine the difference between the given state, with all the creatures on one side, and the goal state, with all the creatures on the other side. We would begin moving creatures two at a time, perhaps one hobbit and one orc, to the other side of the bank. Then we would have to bring the boat back, so we would have to decide whether to let the orc or the hobbit take it. If we let the orc take it, the hobbit on the west bank would be eaten. So we send the hobbit. Solving each subproblem brings us closer to the final goal.

People generally rely on heuristics that worked for them in the past. An anagram solver may have had some luck solving anagrams with a T and H in them by first placing those two consonants together in the beginning of the word. The anagram RTIEH would be quickly solved with this heuristic. The anagram GHIETH would not. It is not uncommon for people to develop a cognitive set about certain heuristics and to continue to rely on them when they clearly no longer work or when much simpler

solutions are possible. The people trying to solve the water-jar problem were victims of such a set.

The focusing strategy we discussed in connection with concept learning is another kind of heuristic. It is a very useful one to use in the game Mastermind, in which a codebreaker has to try to guess the codemaker's color scheme in a row of four pegs. There are six possible colors, so there are a total of ($6^4$) or 1,296 possible codes. The codebreaker makes a guess on the first trial, and the codemaker tells him how many pegs of the right colors were in the right positions and how many correct colors were in the wrong positions (figure 7.14).

A study of strategies used in a simpler version of the game, containing four pegs and only three colors, found that the most successful players used a focusing strategy (Laughlin, Lange, & Adamopoulos, 1982). Thirty-six percent of the players began with a guess that contained only one color, such as red, red, red, and red. This focusing strategy would tell the player how many red pegs were in the answer. The second guess might be blue, blue, blue, and blue, thereby telling the player how many blue pegs were in the final answer. The number of yellow pegs could be deduced by subtraction. Thereafter, the player would choose only sequences that contained the correctly colored pegs, thus reducing the size of the problem space considerably.

A theoretically even more efficient strategy was used by thirty-one percent of the players. This "tactical" approach requires that the player collect hypotheses into two approximately equal subsets so that feedback will

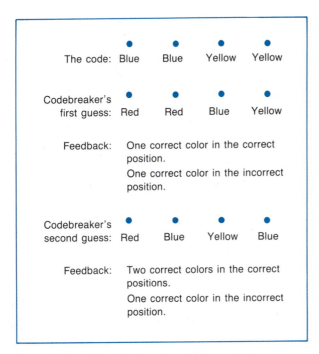

The code: Blue  Blue  Yellow  Yellow

Codebreaker's
first guess: Red  Red  Blue  Yellow

Feedback: One correct color in the correct position.
One correct color in the incorrect position.

Codebreaker's
second guess: Red  Blue  Yellow  Blue

Feedback: Two correct colors in the correct positions.
One correct color in the incorrect position.

**Figure 7.14**    *A simplified version of Mastermind*

allow him to reject one set of hypotheses on each guess (Johnson, 1971, 1978).

It requires rather deep insight into the game and a great deal of memory and information processing, probably much more than most people have. A tactical first guess of blue, blue, red, yellow, for example, would divide the hypotheses into two sets that are more nearly equal than a first guess of red, red, red, red. But the information from the feedback would overload most people and place too many demands on their short-term memories. In practice, the people who used the focusing strategy solved the problem in the average of 5.27 guesses; those who used the theoretically more efficient tactical strategy solved the problem in 5.98 guesses.

*Deciding When to Stop*    A **well-defined problem** *provides the necessary information, either directly or indirectly, for a single possible correct solution.* Deciding when to stop is an easy matter when solving these problems. A person solving an anagram, for example, knows to stop when she has made a word out of a string of letters. In contrast, an **ill-defined problem** *is one in which all the needed information is not given and for which there may be more than one solution; however, some solutions may be better than other solutions.* Most problems in life fall

into this category. Deciding when to stop trying to solve ill-defined problems is much more difficult. It may involve weighing the benefits of an optimal solution against the drawbacks of the amount of time and the increased cost that a better solution might require. For example, say a chemist developing a new insecticide is faced with deadlines and budget constraints. The decision about whether the problem is solved may be based more on these factors than on an evaluation of the new poison.

## Creative Problem Solving

Many of the problems discussed earlier can only be solved by a "creative" approach. The subject of creativity is one that has interested psychologists for many years, and there is much controversy over what it is, who has it, and how it can be encouraged.

The type of problem like that of the lost bicycle combination is best solved by using **convergent thinking,** *thinking in which a person applies his knowledge and the rules of logic.* Many problems, however, such as the ones involving the arrangement of matchsticks (figure 7.9, problems 2 and 3), are best approached with **divergent thinking.** *This mode of thought involves stretching the imagination to conceive of new possibilities.* Divergent thinking appears to be the most important ingredient in the creativity required for certain kinds of problems. Creative people are able to free themselves from the limitations of cognitive sets and other obstacles and can examine potential solutions and possibilities that are unusual and often unique.

Creative approaches to problems generally can be fostered by two techniques. First, problem solvers should not attempt to define the problem too quickly. They should look for new relations between the elements of the problem, new ways to conceive the problem, or new "givens" implied by the stated facts. If the solvers are first relying on a means-end analysis, they might try to work backward from the goal state to obtain a fresh look at the problem. The solution to the following problem is facilitated by this approach:

> A man had four chains, each with three links. He wanted to join the four chains into a single closed chain. Having a link opened cost two cents, and having a link closed cost three cents. The man had his four chains joined into a closed chain for 15 cents. How did he do it?

Another technique that appears to aid problem solving is **incubation,** *in which the person sets a problem aside after a series of unsuccessful attempts at a solution.* The solver should engage in other pursuits, although his or her mind may still be devoting a limited amount of processing capacity to the problem. Upon returning to the problem, the person's approach may be freed from previous cognitive sets.

An experiment involving the above problem about the chains demonstrated that incubation can help people find solutions (Silveira, 1971). A control group of subjects worked continuously on the problem for about half an hour, and about half found the correct solution. Several experimental groups spent a limited amount of time in their initial attempts and then took a break. The experimental groups, especially those taking the longest break (four hours), were more successful in solving the chain problem than the control group, even though the amount of total time spent on the problem was the same. The incubation period appeared to facilitate the problem-solving process.

Sometimes the incubation period ends with an "insight" like the kind described in chapter 5. The story of how Archimedes helped determine whether his King's crown contained the correct amount of gold illustrates this process. The King of Syracuse had given a goldsmith a certain amount of gold to use in the crown. When the crown was constructed, the King suspected that the gold in it was not pure. Perhaps the goldsmith had mixed the gold with another metal and had stolen the leftover gold. He asked the famous mathematician, Archimedes, to find out if the crown contained the right amount of gold without damaging the crown.

Archimedes studied the problem and examined all the ways he knew to analyze the metal. He could not think of any method without damaging the crown, so he set the problem aside, allowing it to incubate. One day he stepped into his bath and noticed the water displacement, and the solution came to him. He ran (naked) through the streets shouting "Eureka! Eureka!" He knew that different metals displaced differing amounts of water. All he had to do was compare the displacement of the crown to an amount of pure gold equal to what the King had given the goldsmith.

## Group Decision Making

When groups rather than individuals make decisions, they fall prey to particular difficulties, which Irving Janis (1982, 1989) labelled **groupthink**, *the tendency to make irrational and uncritical group decisions.* Janis analyzed a number of American foreign-policy decisions that were

unsuccessful, for example, the Bay of Pigs invasion of Cuba in the 1960s, and the escalation of the war in Vietnam. He found that members of government policy-making groups overestimate the importance of the group, are not open to contradictory information, and feel pressure toward uniformity and consensus within the group (Hart, 1991).

Some means to overcome groupthink have been offered (Callaway, Marriott & Esser, 1985; Janis & Mann, 1977; McCauley & Segal, 1989). Group leaders should encourage the voicing of all positions on an issue. Long-standing beliefs of the group should be challenged so that new or innovative ideas might be expressed. Once a group decision seems reasonable, the group should analyze all the possible consequences of the decision. The group should encourage expert opinions from people outside the group.

---

▶ **GUIDED REVIEW** *Learning Objectives 9, 10, 11, and 12*

1. Any problem consists of the following: _____, _____, _____ and _____.
2. The three steps in problem solving are (1) _____, (2) _____, and (3) deciding that a solution has been discovered.
3. The analysis of a problem involves acquiring an understanding of the _____. Familiarity with the elements of the problem can facilitate problem solving since people do better with concrete, familiar problems than with abstract problems. Familiarity can hinder problem solving when a _____ or _____ develops.
4. Two common search strategies in problem solving are the use of an _____ and the use of a _____. One example of a heuristic, or rule of thumb, is _____.
5. Deciding when a solution has been discovered is simple when the problem is well defined. For _____ problems, this decision is often based on factors other than whether the solution is optimal.
6. Group processes that may interfere with the quality of decisions are referred to as _____.
7. Creative problem solving requires _____ thinking rather than convergent thinking. Creativity can be encouraged by incubation.

*ANSWERS*

1. *given state, goal state, path, problem space* 2. *analyzing the problem, searching for solutions* 3. *given state, cognitive set, functional fixity* 4. *algorithm, heuristic, means-end analysis* 5. *ill-defined* 6. *groupthink* 7. *divergent*

# INTELLIGENCE

It probably will surprise no one that people differ in the degree to which they are able to learn, solve problems, think logically, use language eloquently and precisely, understand and acquire concepts, deal with abstractions, integrate ideas, attain goals, and perform many other intellectual tasks. Most people believe that these skills, as well as other cognitive abilities,

**Figure 7.15**   *Alfred Binet (1857–1911)*

make up a person's intelligence (Anderson, 1992; Sternberg, 1985). Yet the concept of intelligence is very abstract, and there is a tremendous amount of controversy over what it is, how it should be measured, and even whether it should be measured at all.

Intelligence is not easy to define. A working definition of **intelligence** is *a combination of abilities that enable a person to learn from experience, to think abstractly, and to adapt successfully to the environment.* A survey of psychologists and educators showed that most agreed that intelligence should include abstract thinking or reasoning, capacity to acquire knowledge, and problem-solving ability (Snyderman & Rothman, 1987). A majority of those surveyed included adapting to one's environment, creativity, general knowledge, linguistic and mathematical competence, memory and mental speed. Very few thought that achievement motivation, goal-directedness, or sensory acuity should be considered important elements of intelligence.

Our notions about the concept of intelligence have been closely linked to attempts to measure it in different people, and many lay people believe that the word intelligence is synonymous with the scores people achieve on various tests of mental ability. In order to fully understand the nature of intelligence, it is first necessary to understand how scientists and educators have tried to measure the phenomenon.

## Measuring Intelligence

Early philosophers and scientists did not allude to intelligence as a separate trait and did not appear to try to measure it in any way. Instead, intellectual activity was seen as a part of sensation and perception, soul, and consciousness. It was not until modern times, particularly during the late nineteenth and early twentieth centuries, that scientists became interested in intelligence as a separate entity and wondered how to measure it.

Sir Francis Galton, a naturalist, mathematician and cousin of Charles Darwin, developed the first set of tests designed to measure intelligence. Galton was convinced that intelligence ran in families (his, in particular) and that the trait probably had some biological basis. He measured a number of anthropometric and sensory-motor traits (such as head size, strength of hand grip, breathing capacity, and reaction time) and separated out those that were capable of distinguishing eminent British scientists from people he considered less intelligent. He examined thousands of people, but none of the traits he measured correlated with his concept of intelligence. (He did, however, invent and use the correlation coefficient.)

*The Concept of Mental Age*    In the early twentieth century, Alfred Binet made a breakthrough in the attempt to measure intelligence (figure 7.15). The French government commissioned Binet to develop techniques for identifying schoolchildren who would be too slow to benefit from the regular elementary school program. He had done extensive research on the subject of cognitive abilities and had studied the growth in intelligence of his own two daughters. His earlier work had led him to conclude that intelligence was a global process and that individuals differed widely in this global capacity.

In his initial research, Binet and his colleague Theodore Simon collected a series of short tasks related to everyday problems. Trained examiners administered the tests to individual students. Binet hoped that by using a wide range of test items, he would tap enough different abilities to be able to assess each child's general potential. The items sampled a wide range of functions including judgment, comprehension, and reasoning—functions Binet felt were the most important factors in intelligence.

After several years of refining the scale, Binet and Simon suggested the notion of **mental age,** *a child's score on a test compared to the scores of a large, representative group of children the same age.* A child who scored the same as the average group of six-year-olds would have a mental age of six regardless of the child's actual age in years.

A few years later, the German psychologist William Stern argued that children's mental age should be divided

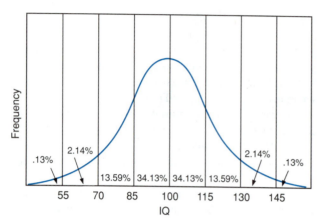

**Figure 7.16** *The distribution of IQ scores is a normal bell-shaped curve*

by their chronological age to yield an **intelligence quotient**, or **IQ**. *The IQ was expressed as*

$$IQ = \frac{MA}{CA} \times 100$$

*where MA = mental age as determined by the standardized tests of intelligence and CA = chronological age.* If a ten-year-old child successfully completes the tasks that a majority of twelve-year-olds are able to complete, the child's IQ is

$$\frac{12}{10} \times 100 = 120.$$

Although IQ is commonly used to express levels of intelligence, it is not what Binet believed intelligence to be. He thought intelligence was too complex to be expressed by a single number and that it could not be measured along a linear scale.

*The Development of the Stanford-Binet Test* **The Stanford-Binet test of intelligence** *is a widely used modification of Binet's original test; in this revision, there are several test items for each age group, and each successfully completed item earns the child a "score" of two months of mental age.* The Stanford-Binet test considers the fact that some children will fail one or more items at one age level but then pass several for an older age level.

An important modification in the contemporary version of the Stanford-Binet test of intelligence is the use of tables rather than the formula MA/CA to ascertain the IQ. In this method, the average score for all children of a particular age is assigned the value of 100 with a standard deviation of 15 (or 16 on more recent tests). Figure 7.16 shows the theoretical distribution of IQ. This distribution shows that IQs follow the normal bell-shaped curve; most children of a certain age tend to cluster around the mean with fewer and fewer children attaining scores on either the extreme lower end or the extreme upper end. Fifty percent of the age group fall above the average of 100, and fifty percent falls below it. Scores tend to cluster around the mean, so that about sixty-eight percent of the scores fall within one standard deviation of the mean (85 to 115). Although in any small sample of children, the distribution may deviate somewhat from the theoretical bell-shape, the normal curve is used to provide an estimate of where each child falls in relation to age mates.

With respect to IQ, the following terms describe various scores:

| IQ Score | Descriptive Label | Percent of Population |
|---|---|---|
| Above 130 | Very superior | 2.2% |
| 120–130 | Superior | 6.7% |
| 110–119 | Bright normal | 16.1% |
| 90–109 | Average | 50.0% |
| 80–89 | Dull normal | 16.1% |
| 70–79 | Borderline | 6.7% |
| Below 70 | Mentally retarded | 2.2% |

*The Wechsler Adult Intelligence Scale* David Wechsler (1939) pointed out that the Binet tests of intelligence were primarily designed for children and that there were no useful tests to measure intelligence in adults. Although more difficult items could be included on the Binet tests, the items were not really relevant to the lives of adults. They were designed to determine the abilities and interests of the school-child; adults found them boring. Another problem with the Binet tests was that they emphasized speed and the routine manipulation of words, factors that might handicap the older person. Furthermore, the tables for ascertaining scores were based on scores from young people.

Wechsler devised the **Wechsler Adult Intelligence Scale,** or **WAIS,** *to measure the mental abilities of adults.* It is divided into eleven subtests that are grouped into a verbal scale and a performance scale. Each subtest is designed to measure specific components of intelligence, and the scales permit an overall assessment of verbal and performance abilities.

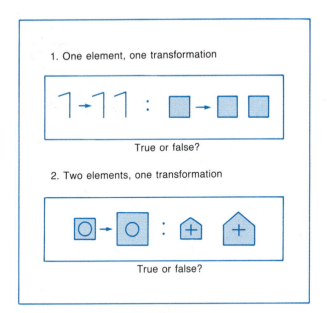

**Figure 7.17** *Two analogy problems that differ in the number of elements that must be encoded*

*Refining the Intelligence Test with Computer Technology* The breakthroughs that have been made in cognitive psychology have led to proposals for improving mental abilities tests to enable us to better understand the meaning of the test scores. With the aid of computer technology it would be possible to record not only whether an answer was correct, but how long the test-taker took to respond. By constructing tests that include problems that vary in specific dimensions, it is possible to obtain a great deal more than just an overall performance score; the computer could record and compute the test-taker's encoding speed, inference speed, and accuracy as well as other measures.

For example, the two analogy problems shown in figure 7.17 each require only one transformation. In the first, the number of figures is doubled; in the second, the outer figure is enlarged. They differ in the number of elements the test-taker has to encode: in the first problem there is only one, but in the second there are two. If we can assume that the amount of time to perform a single transformation remains the same for both problems, then subtracting the time the person takes to solve the second problem from the time it takes to solve the first results in an estimate of the time it takes the person to encode a single element.

One recent theory integrates neurophysiology and intellectual abilities. According to this view, general intelligence is related to the speed of neural transmission. People whose brains work faster tend to be more efficient at a variety of tasks (Anderson, 1992).

*Attempts to Measure Different Components of Intelligence* Most scientists view standard IQ tests as limited in the range of intellectual abilities they are capable of measuring. In a recent survey of psychologists and educators, most thought the tests failed to adequately measure creativity and adaptation to one's environment (Snyderman & Rothman, 1987). Both of these traits are important in most people's definition of intelligence, yet they are both difficult to measure.

For example, questions that might tap creative thinking or problem solving are not generally included on any IQ test. The skills measured on the printed tests of intelligence are almost all academic skills. The test problems are well-defined rather than ill-defined. They are clearly stated, all the information needed to solve each problem is provided (or at least in the head of the test-taker), and there is only one correct answer. Many researchers have attempted to devise ways to present ill-defined problems where more than one answer is possible in order to measure creativity (see Close Up on Research: Measuring Creativity).

Measuring how well a person can adapt to the environment is also not typical of a printed IQ test. In order to measure the ability to adapt, one must collect information about how a person responds to problems outside the testing room. One person might display very adaptive behavior in a corporation, another in a hospital, and a third on the police force.

Frederiksen (1986) has used simulations of real world problems to broaden understanding of people's ability to adapt to real world problems. In one simulation, subjects are presented with a real psychological investigation, a graph or table depicting the results of the investigation, and a statement of the major finding. The test-takers are asked to write hypotheses that might explain the finding. The responses are scored in terms of quality, quantity, and originality.

Interestingly, the quality measure correlated fairly well with the subjects' GRE test scores, a measure known to

# CLOSE UP ON RESEARCH

## Measuring Creativity

Researchers have as much difficulty defining and measuring creativity as they have with intelligence. The term is one that suggests a wide range of abilities, interests, and accomplishments. Definitions of the term vary widely. Some definitions emphasize the production of socially valued products, such as inventions or works of art. Others describe creativity more as an ability than as a set of extraordinary accomplishments, and some subjects might be called "highly creative" even though they have never produced anything. Almost all scientists who study creativity agree that it is not the same as intelligence, although the two overlap slightly (Getzels, 1975; Richards, 1976; Barron & Harrington, 1981; Sternberg, 1985).

The most widely used measures of creativity are tests of divergent thinking, based on the work of J. P. Guilford (1967). These tests include items, such as those shown in figure 7.A, that assess the subject's ability to provide many answers to a single question. They differ from the items on most intelligence tests that measure convergent thinking, items that usually have only one correct solution.

Guilford believed that the major components of creative thinking included fluency, flexibility, elaboration, and originality. Fluency, for example, might be measured by asking the subject to think of as many words as possible that contain the letter z. The subject's originality might be assessed by asking him to name a variety of unusual uses for a familiar object, such as a brick.

Another widely used test of creativity that also emphasizes divergent thinking is the *Torrance Tests of Creative Thinking* devised by Paul Torrance. The test is appropriate for school-age children. In the "Just Suppose" component of the test, for example, the child is shown a strange picture, such as clouds linked to the ground with strings. The child is asked to think of things that might have caused this situation.

The question of how valid these tests are is controversial. Do scores on these tests of creative ability actually relate to the number or quality of an individual's creative accomplishments? A survey of the many studies that attempted to correlate scores on creativity tests to assessments of a person's creative accomplishments suggests that the tests are valid to some degree (Barron & Harrington, 1981); however, the correlations are usually low.

Newer tests of creativity, such as the Lifetime Creativity Scales (LCS) (Richards, Kinney, Benet, & Merzel, 1988) attempt to assess original activity at work and leisure by using interviews that discuss the person's whole life. The responses are scored in terms of levels for peak creative output and levels for extent of creative involvement, either in the person's work setting or avocation. For example, an optician who spent four years selling optical items, then acquired an optical shop, and now grinds lenses to prescription while managing the retailing of standard optical products would be given a "moderate" score for peak creativity. High-peak creativity is shown by an entrepreneur who advanced from apprentice to independent researcher of new products before starting a major paint manufacturing company. The value of this kind of test is that it accesses a lifetime of work and play in any field, not just a thirty-minute sample of behavior using pencil and paper.

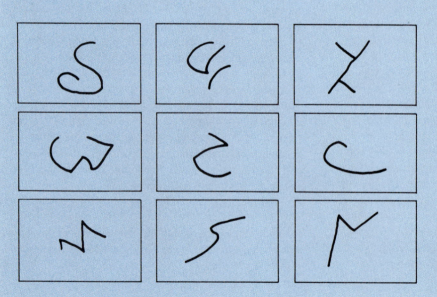

*Figure 7.A Sample items from creativity tests*

Sample Items from Creativity Tests

1. **Name** as many objects as you can that weigh less than one pound.

2. **Write** as many sentences as you can that have four words, each word starting with these letters; t,a,s,a. (One sentence might be Tomorrow a salesman arrives.)

3. **Write** as many meanings as you can for the following words:
   a. duck
   b. sack
   c. pitch
   d. fair

4. **Name** as many uses as you can think of for:
   a. a toothpick.
   b. a brick.
   c. a paper clip.

5. The child is shown pictures like those in figure 7.A and is asked to make meaningful drawings and to label them.

predict first-year grades in graduate school. The quantity and originality measures did not correlate with GRE test scores at all, but they did predict later accomplishments of the subjects, such as doing independent research, being an author or coauthor of a paper, or designing laboratory equipment. Thus the simulations appeared to predict behavior in the real world somewhat better than conventional aptitude tests.

## Practical Issues Involved in Testing

The use of intelligence tests is a very controversial subject for practical and ethical reasons. Two practical issues involve the reliability and validity of the tests.

*Reliability*    In psychological testing, the term **reliability** *refers to the consistency of scores obtained by the same subjects when they are reexamined on the same test on different occasions.* It does not refer to whether the test is accurate or a useful measure of a particular trait; it refers to whether people tend to get the same scores the second time they take the test. This concept is important because it provides some information about the error of measurement. If the test has a great deal of error in it because of factors irrelevant to the test's purpose, then the test is not reliable. Your IQ score on one day might be very low because of irrelevant factors such as fatigue, depression, or unclear instructions. On another day, your IQ score might be much higher because these factors all combined in

some favorable way. If your score on the test is affected by these factors to any great degree, the test is not reliable.

The most common means of providing information about the reliability of any test is the correlation coefficient. The reliability of a test can be determined in several ways. In the **test-retest method**, *a group of people are given a test twice, on two different occasions usually separated by a time interval of less than six months, and the correlation between their two scores is calculated to obtain an estimate of reliability.* In the **alternate-form method**, *a group of people take one form of the test on one occasion and another, comparable form on another occasion; their scores are correlated to obtain an estimate of reliability.* This latter method is more appropriate when the scores of the people taking the test might be changed simply by the practice they gained during the first administration.

Studies of the reliability of the Stanford-Binet show that it is quite high; most of the correlations between scores on one form and scores on another are around .9 (McNemar, 1942). When the scores of a group of seven-year-olds who took two different forms of the test were compared, the children tended to receive approximately the same score on both tests. It is interesting that the reliability of the test was not as high in the upper IQ ranges, a common finding on studies of the reliability of IQ tests.

*Validity*    The **validity** *of a test reflects whether the test measures what it is supposed to measure.* The validity gives some indication of what can be inferred from test scores and what conclusions might be drawn. Although the names of most IQ tests suggest that they are measuring "intelligence" or "abilities," the actual traits being measured are probably much narrower.

Validity is ordinarily determined by analyzing the relationship between performance on the test and performance on some independent indication of the trait. For example, one validity measure of the IQ test might relate the scores of a group of subjects to their grades in school. Or, the test scores might be correlated to teachers' ratings of students' abilities. Correlations of this kind for the Stanford-Binet are usually in the range of .4 to .75. These measures of validity would not necessarily indicate that the test is a valid measure of intelligence; that question would have to depend on how intelligence is defined. They only suggest that it is reasonable to use the test as a valid predictor of performance in school.

## Ethical and Legal Issues Surrounding IQ Testing

The use of intelligence or ability tests is extremely controversial. A person's score on these tests can influence many events in life, including admission to college, advanced placement in high school, assignment to special education programs, and acceptance in particular career fields. The usefulness of these tests and the wisdom of using them as predictors are subjects of increasing concern to psychologists, the public, and the courts (Glasser, 1981; Gould, 1981; Jensen, 1968; Kaplan, 1982; Linn, 1982; London & Bray, 1980; Messick, 1980).

In the California case of *Larry P.* v. *Wilson Riles,* the plaintiff argued that minority children were over-represented in classes for the mentally retarded because the decision to place children in these classes was based on their IQ test. According to the plaintiff, these tests did not fairly assess the abilities of black children and should not have been used as assessment instruments. The state supreme court agreed and imposed a moratorium on the use of intelligence tests in the placement of students in special education programs for the mildly mentally retarded (Lambert, 1981). Although evidence was presented in favor of the validity of these tests for this purpose, particularly when they are used in conjunction with other assessment tools, the judge decided that being placed in a special program might stigmatize children for life. The court concluded:

> . . . to remedy the harm to black children who have been misidentified as EMR (educably mentally retarded) pupils and to prevent these discriminatory practices from recurring . . . the defendants shall direct each school district to reevaluate every black child . . . without including in the psychological evaluation a standardized intelligence or ability test that has not been approved by the court. . . . (*Larry P.* v. *Wilson Riles,* 1979.)

A report by a committee of the National Academy of Science addressed the controversy over intelligence and ability tests (Holden, 1982). The committee reviewed all the literature and court cases on the subject and decided that these tests are valid and useful in predicting an individual's academic performance, for minority groups as well as whites. The tests are biased in that the items in them depend heavily on experience in mainstream American culture, but according to the committee, there is no way to produce a test that is not culture-dependent.

The committee cautioned that the tests are of limited use and should not be the sole criterion for making any decision. They also argued that testing should be conducted in an ethical manner and that the testing program and any classifications of children must have instructional validity—it must be useful for the child. For example, a test designed to assess ability in young children should lead to opportunities to improve weak areas. If the test finds that a particular child has very poor reading skills, the information should be used to provide the child with required instruction rather than to label the child as a nonreader.

The report emphasized that a procedure that used tests to select people for various programs is more equitable than a procedure that did not use such tests. Abolishing tests would not alter the fact that test scores of blacks and Hispanics are usually lower than those of whites or the fact that minority children are more likely to be included in special education programs. As long as some groups have more members with less education and fewer advantages than other groups, the disadvantaged groups are likely to be overrepresented in remedial programs.

## The Nature of Intelligence

The nature of intelligence can easily become lost amid all the controversies and debates about the measurement of intelligence and the use of IQ test scores. The term "intelligence" is commonly used to refer to a combination of abilities that enable an individual to survive and adapt to the environment. These abilities vary depending on the nature of the culture, the historical period, and the kind of career a person chooses. For example, the skills and abilities that lead to successful adaptation in rural Asia are different from the skills needed in contemporary urban America. Most people use the word "intelligence" to refer to the kinds of skills required for their own contemporary culture.

Although the word "intelligence" is used very broadly, IQ tests measure only a limited number of abilities. They stress verbal reasoning and the ability to deal with numerical and abstract symbols, but they ignore other abilities that might reasonably be included in any definition of intelligence, such as mechanical skills, motor skills, musical abilities, artistic talents, creativity, and adaption to the environment. In addition, IQ tests do not measure the kind of practical knowledge required for success in particular areas (Wagner & Sternberg, 1985) or assess motivation and attitudes. IQ tests sample only some of the traits thought to be included in a definition of intelligence.

Based solely on the results of studies using the IQ tests, and therefore limited to the kinds of behaviors sampled by these tests, two main hypotheses have emerged about the nature of intelligence. The **two-factor theory of intelligence,** *proposed by the English psychologist Charles Spearman, suggests that intelligence is made up of two principal components:* (1) the g-factor, the general component of intelligence and the major determinant of performance on cognitive tests; and s-factors, special factors that contribute to an individual's performance in specific cognitive areas, such as verbal reasoning or spatial relations.

Both Binet and Wechsler assumed that intelligence was a general and fundamental trait. Even though their tests sampled many different abilities, there were few children who performed extremely well on some abilities and very poorly on other abilities. For the most part, children with high scores in one area tended to have high scores in most of the others as well.

A second theory of intelligence, proposed by L. L. Thurstone (1938), argued that intelligence consists of seven separate and independent abilities, not the single undifferentiated general factor that Spearman suggested. Thurstone referred to **primary mental abilities,** *independent abilities including verbal comprehension, word fluency, number, memory, space, perceptual speed, and reasoning.* According to this theory, individuals differ in each of these mental abilities, some showing greater capacity in one area and others in another area. This theory has received only limited support, partly because the determination of the "primary abilities" depends on which items are included in the test. Some researchers have argued that there are twenty different factors, and others suggest that there may be more than a hundred (Ekstrom, French, Harman, & Derman, 1976). In addition, test scores on each primary ability are correlated, indicating that children who do well in one area tend to do well in others. This provides support for the g-factor theory.

Robert Sternberg has recently described a promising new approach to the nature of intelligence that does not rely heavily on IQ test scores (Sternberg, 1980, 1985). His **triarchic theory of intelligence** *emphasizes how people solve problems, not whether they get the right answers.* The theory proposes that we examine the mental activities people engage in when they are trying to solve problems. Much research in cognitive psychology is moving in this direction (Pellegrino, 1984; Smith, Morris, Levy & Ellis, 1987).

The triarchic theory is a complicated one that attempts to weave together many aspects of intelligence not addressed extensively by earlier theorists. In addition to exploring how people solve problems, the theory emphasizes the context of behavior, proposing that we should pay more attention to intelligent behavior in real-world settings. This is clearly a welcome suggestion to psychologists who have criticized IQ tests for failing to measure adaptive behavior in the real world. The theory also examines how intelligence is applied to totally novel problems and how it is seen in situations where the person's response is "automatic" because of previous experience with similar problems.

Important ingredients in the triarchic theory are **meta-components,** *higher-order mental activities used in planning, monitoring, and making decisions in the performance of a task.* For example, when people try to solve the analogy problem in figure 7.17–2, they must first decide on a strategy. Some people have great difficulty devising a strategy for solving a problem like this; others quickly see that the best strategy is to determine how the first figure is changed into the second figure (the outer box increases in size), and then generate an abstract statement (the outer figure is enlarged). Tests are being devised that will assess a test-taker's encoding processes and provide some information about the person's meta-components.

People use meta-components when they decipher the meaning of an unknown word. People who can encode words into known prefixes, suffixes, or other word parts have a strategy that will help them make a good guess about a new word. Those who don't know how to use the strategy or lack knowledge about the meanings of word parts will be less efficient (Kaye, Sternberg, & Fonseca, 1987).

Sternberg's theory is fascinating because it emphasizes how to increase intelligence in people, not just how to assess the behavior. He argues that people with learning disabilities might be deficient in their use of strategies to solve certain kinds of problems and limited in their knowledge of the context of these problems. Both of these might be taught more explicitly than they are now (Kolligian & Sternberg, 1987a; 1987b).

## Factors Influencing Intelligence

Because efforts to determine what factors influence intelligence have relied on IQ tests as measures of intelligence, this section might more appropriately be titled "Factors Influencing Performance on IQ Tests." The research on this topic has been extraordinarily controversial and has caused some of the most heated debates in the

**TABLE 7.1   Correlations of scores on IQ tests between people who are related genetically in varying degrees and who also vary in the degree to which their environments are similar**

| Relationship | Correlation on IQ Test Scores* |
|---|---|
| Monozygotic twins reared together | .86 |
| Monozygotic twins reared apart | .72 |
| Average of parents correlated with child reared in parents' home | .50 |
| Dizygotic twins reared together | .60 |
| Siblings reared together | .47 |
| Siblings reared apart | .24 |
| Cousins | .15 |
| Adopting parent and adopted child | .19 |

*Correlations represent a weighted average of the values obtained in several studies.

From Thomas J. Bouchard and M. McGue, "Familial Studies of Intelligence: A Review" in *Science* 212:1055–1058, 1981. Copyright© 1981 by the American Association for the Advancement of Science. Reprinted by permission.

history of psychology (Gould, 1981). The debate centers around the relative contributions of environmental influences and genetic factors.

The general approach is to collect IQ scores from people genetically related in varying degrees, especially from **monozygotic twins,** *who are identical and have 100 percent of their genes in common,* and **dizygotic twins,** *who are fraternal and as genetically related as regular siblings.* Studies like these generally find that people who are closely related tend to perform similarly on tests of IQ, a fact that is not very surprising considering that they share many common genes and many of the same environmental influences. A large number of studies on monozygotic twins have found high correlations between their IQ test scores, ranging around .85 (table 7.1) (Bouchard and McGue, 1981; Loehlin, Willerman & Horn, 1988).

What is surprising is that the correlations between the test scores of related people tend to follow a pattern. The closer the genetic relationship, the higher the correlation. Of particular interest is the comparison between the correlations for monozygotic twins reared together and dizygotic twins reared together. Although both kinds of twins are reared in the same home at the same time by the same parents, the similarity in IQ scores is much higher for monozygotic twins. One possible reason for this is that genetic factors play an important role in performance on IQ tests. Thus, the monozygotic twins are more similar to one another because they share all of their genes, while dizygotic twins only share about half of their genes.

Perhaps even more surprising is that individuals who are closely related genetically but who are reared apart in different homes still perform similarly on IQ tests, although not as similarly as if they had been reared together. The correlation between the IQ test scores of monozygotic twins reared apart is around .72, not very much lower than the .85 found for monozygotic twins reared together.

Another approach to assessing the contribution of genes is to study the similarity of adopted children to their biological and adoptive parents. If genes play an important role, the adopted children should show some similarity to their biological parents.

The Colorado Adoption Project has been following 182 adopted infants and has been comparing their behavior to the behavior of their natural and adoptive parents (Plomin, Loehlin & Defries, 1985; Loehlin, Willerman & Horn, 1988; Thompson, Detterman & Plomin, 1991). The scores of the children on intellectual tests resemble those of their natural parents more than their adopted parents.

Data like these are enormously difficult to interpret. Monozygotic twins look identical, so the parents may treat them more similarly than do the parents of dizygotic twins. Thus, the difference in the correlations between monozygotic and dizygotic twins may not be entirely due to genetic factors. Also, monozygotic twins separated at an early age are not necessarily placed randomly by adoption agencies; many agencies try to find a home that is similar to the one from which the twin came. Therefore, just because members of a twin pair are reared apart does not necessarily mean they do not share common environmental influences.

Nevertheless, the studies generally conclude that genetic factors have a role in the development of intellectual abilities, although the precise nature of that role is not clearly understood. As we discuss in chapter 9, the behavior of any organism is the result of the interactions between its genes and its environment. Performance on IQ tests, and probably intelligence itself, is made up of behaviors influenced by both genes and environmental factors. Genetic factors appear to determine a range within which the environment can then modify behavior. Some people might inherit genes that would enable them to have average to superior intelligence, provided they received at least some physical and emotional care. Whether their ultimate IQs are average, above average, or superior would depend on the environment to which they are subsequently exposed (Thompson, Detterman & Plomin, 1991). The environmental influences that might affect their ultimate

# EXPLORING HUMAN DIVERSITY

## Why Do Indochinese Students Excel in American Schools?

Why do the children of Southeast Asian "boat people" excel in the American school system? In part because of family support and cultural values that support learning and teaching.

These conclusions are based on a study of 1400 refugee families with children in low-income school districts. Nathan Caplan, Marcella Choy, and John Whitmore, psychologists at the University of Michigan, studied the school achievement of a random sample of 200 of these Indochinese families and their 536 school-age children. These young refugees had been in the United States for an average of three and a half years. All the children attended schools in low-income, metropolitan areas.

In terms of both grades and scores on standardized achievement tests, the refugee children scored well above average, particularly in areas such as science and mathematics, that do not depend so heavily on English language skills. Four out of five students received either As or Bs in mathematics. And eighty-two percent of them had an A or B grade-point average.

One finding from this study was particularly unexpected. Caplan and his colleagues found that the more brothers and sisters an Asian child had, the higher the child's grades. This is not usually found. Instead, studies in the United States and Europe report a negative correlation between family size and grades: the more siblings a student has, the lower the student's grades tend to be (Zajonc, 1976). On average, there is a fifteen percent decline in grade-point average and other

achievement measures with each additional child in the family (see figure 7.B). Why would there be a positive relationship between family size and grades among the Asian refugee families and a negative relationship among American families?

For these Indochinese students, the apparent disadvantage of additional siblings was somehow turned into an advantage. According to the researchers, cultural values from the Confucian and Buddhist traditions of East and Southeast Asia played an important role in the educational achievement of the children. In these traditions, respect, cooperation, and harmony within the family are central. These values are translated into practice by family support for education. After dinner, the table is cleared and homework begins. The older children, both male and female, help their younger siblings. "Indeed, they seem to learn as much from teaching as from being taught. . . . The younger children, in particular, are taught not only subject matter but how to learn."*

Children whose parents read aloud to them had higher grades than other children. Caplan and his colleagues conclude that "Reading at home obscures the boundary between home and school. In this context, learning is perceived as normal, valuable and fun." (p. 22).

Other recent studies emphasize the importance of parental practices and values in school performance (e.g., Steinberg, Dornbusch & Brown, 1992).

*See! We told you way back in the How To Study section that you would learn a lot by teaching your classmates as you went along. But did you take our advice? No-oo. Here we are halfway through the semester, and finally you see evidence that teaching is a form of learning.

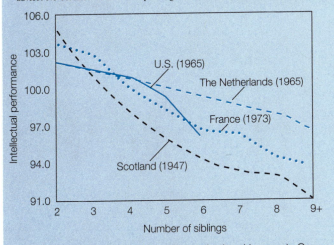

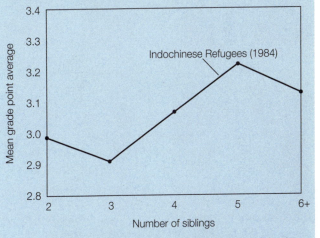

Family size corresponds with academic achievement. On the left, intellectual performance — as measured by IQ and by standardized achievement test scores — falls as the number of siblings rises. In contrast, on the right, the grade point average of Indochinese students increases for the most part with the number of siblings.

**Figure 7.B** *Family size and academic achievement.*

performance would include prenatal and postnatal nutrition, the stimulation they receive in infancy, the encouragement and rewards they receive from their parents and teachers, the quality of the academic training they receive, and the attitudes of their peers toward intellectual pursuits.

Fortunately, the debate over the relative contributions of genes and environment to performance on IQ tests has abated somewhat, and many scientists have become more concerned with the steps we need to take to raise intelligence-test scores and encourage the development of intelligence in general.

There is no doubt that a person's performance on tests of intellectual ability is also influenced by environmental factors. Malnutrition and exposure to toxins during fetal life produce deficits in intellectual development. The amount of stimulation during development alters the structure of the brain and presumably enhances intelligence as well. The size of the family appears to be related to IQ scores: in general, the more children in a

family, the lower the IQ scores (see Exploring Human Diversity). Also, first-born children have higher scores on IQ tests than later born children.

Adoption studies have also demonstrated environmental effects on IQ scores and scholastic performance. Children born to parents with low socioeconomic status and then adopted into families with parents of middle or high socioeconomic status generally show higher IQs and fewer school failures than would be expected (Dumaret, 1985; Duyme, 1985).

The environment can cause dramatic changes in IQ test scores. In one study of California school children, fifty-nine percent showed changes of fifteen points or more between the ages of six and eighteen. Another thirty-seven percent showed changes of twenty points or more, and nine percent showed changes of more than thirty points (Honzik, MacFarlane & Allen, 1948). Some approaches being used to encourage the cognitive development of children will be explained in the discussion of infancy and childhood in chapter 9.

---

▶ **GUIDED REVIEW** *Learning Objectives 13, 14, 15, and 16*

1. _____ is a combination of abilities that enables a person to learn from experience, think abstractly, and adapt to the environment. It often includes a span of cognitive abilities, such as problem solving, language comprehension, concept formation, and many others. Different theorists emphasize different cognitive abilities.

2. _____ designed one of the first instruments to measure intelligence. The test consisted of a series of items related to everyday problems, and established the items that could be passed by a majority of children at each age level. The child's IQ score was his _____ divided by his _____, multiplied by 100.

3. One of the most widely used IQ tests today is the. _____, a modified version of Binet's test. Another widely used test is the _____, which includes items appropriate for adults.

4. Techniques used in cognitive psychology, especially _____, offer ways to obtain information about how a person solves problems on IQ tests, measures that may be more useful than overall performance scores.

5. The _____ of a test refers to the consistency of scores obtained by the same subjects when they are reexamined on the same test on different occasions. Two methods used to assess this are the _____ and the _____.

6. _____ of an IQ test reflects whether the test measures what it is designed to measure.

7. Since intelligence refers to the ability to adapt to the environment, any measure of intelligence will depend

on the _____ to which the individual is adapting. IQ tests developed in the United States measure a narrow range of abilities that might be included in intelligence, and they are specifically biased toward adaptation to contemporary American culture.

8. The _____, proposed by Spearman, suggests that intelligence consists of a general g-factor and a number of special s-factors, each of which contributes to a specific cognitive area. A proposal by Thurstone suggests that intelligence consists of separate and independent _____.

9. A new theory of intelligence, called the _____, incorporates research in cognitive psychology and emphasizes how people solve problems.

10. Studies of the correlations between the IQ test scores of individuals who are genetically related in varying degrees suggest that genetic factors contribute to performance on IQ tests. However, these studies are difficult to interpret. The safest conclusions are that both genes and environment _____ in their effects on behavior and that genetic factors determine a range of intelligence within which the environment is able to modify the behavior.

*ANSWERS*

1. Intelligence 2. Alfred Binet, mental age, chronological age 3. Stanford-Binet, Wechsler Adult Intelligence Scale 4. computer-assisted testing 5. reliability, test-retest method, alternate form method 6. Validity 7. culture 8. two-factor theory of intelligence, primary mental abilities 9. triarchic theory 10. interact

1. True

2. Start

3.

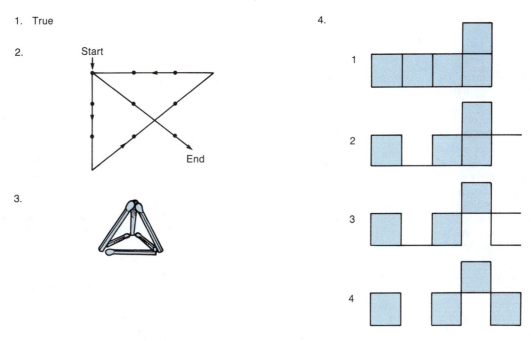

4.

**Figure 7.18** *Solutions to problems from figure 7.9.*

The Hobbits and the Orcs (page 220)

Send over one hobbit and one orc. Have the hobbit bring the boat back, pick up another hobbit, and take him to the other bank. Have the hobbit bring the boat back again and pick up the orc.

Anagrams: (page 220)

RTIEH = THEIR          GHIETH = HEIGHT

The Chain Links Problem   (page 221)

Take one of the four chains, and open all the links (3 X 2 cents = 6 cents). Connect two of the four chains with one link (3 cents), use another to link the third three-link chain to the chain that now contains seven links (3 cents), and use the third opened link to connect one end of the chain that now contains eleven links to the other end (3 cents). The total cost is 15 cents.

Analogy Problems   (page 225)

1. True          2. True

SEND HELP IMMEDIATELY

# SUMMARY

I. Language is the system by which we communicate meaning through sounds and symbols. (p. 202)

  A. All natural languages share three characteristics: creativity, the use of arbitrary symbols to represent objects and events, and rules of grammar. (p. 202)

    1. The structure of oral language includes a number of elements: the phoneme, the morpheme, the word, the phrase, and the sentence. (p. 203)

    2. To communicate, a speaker transforms the underlying representation of a sentence into a surface structure. To understand, the listener grasps the underlying representation from the surface structure by dividing the speech into constituents. (pp. 203–204)

  B. Language acquisition is one of the most remarkable achievements of the child. (p. 204)

    1. The development of language involves several stages, including cooing, babbling, holophrases, and telegraphic speech. (pp. 204–205)

    2. The most widely accepted theory of language learning proposes that several factors are important, including imitation and reinforcement, genetic predisposition for language learning, and the child's strong motivation to acquire language by inducing the rule systems underlying the language. (pp. 205–206)

  C. Not all communication involves words. (pp. 207–209)

  D. Many animals have very complex communication systems. (p. 209)

    1. Animal communication systems do not meet the criteria for human language. (pp. 209–212)

    2. Attempts to teach language to apes have met with much success, although the apes do not appear to use the language creatively. (pp. 209–212)

II. Cognitive psychology includes the study of human thought. (pp. 212–222)

  A. Cognitive science involves the combined efforts of psychology, linguistics, anthropology, the neurosciences, and computer sciences. (pp. 212–213)

  B. In humans, language and thought are closely related. The linguistic relativity hypothesis proposed a very close relationship between the two. (p. 214)

  C. The structure of thought is arranged as a hierarchy of concepts. (p. 215)

    1. Each concept has one or more attributes used to place objects or events into classes. (p. 215)

    2. People acquire concepts through trial and error or through more efficient strategies, such as the conservative-focusing approach. (p. 216)

III. Any problem consists of a given state, a goal state, a path from the given state to the goal state, and a problem space. (p. 218)

A. There are three major steps in problem solving. (pp. 218–221)

    1. The analysis of the problem involves acquiring an understanding of the givens. Familiarity with the elements of the problem can either facilitate or hinder this step. (p. 215)

    2. The search for a solution might involve one of several strategies, including the use of an algorithm or a heuristic. (p. 219)

    3. The decision that a solution has been reached is simple for well-defined problems but much more difficult for ill-defined problems. (p. 221)

B. Creative problem solving requires divergent thinking. Creativity can be encouraged by incubation. (pp. 221–222)

IV. Intelligence is a combination of abilities that enable a person to learn from experience, think abstractly, and adapt successfully to the environment. (p. 223)

A. Alfred Binet designed the first intelligence test for children. (p. 223)

    1. Stern used the formula of mental age/chronological age to obtain an intelligence quotient. (p. 224)

    2. The Stanford-Binet test of intelligence is a modification of Binet's test. (p. 224)

    3. The Wechsler Adult Intelligence Scale (WAIS) is a test designed to measure mental abilities in adults. (p. 224)

    4. Further refinements in the intelligence test may involve the use of the computer to assess the speed of responses. (p. 225)

B. There are several practical issues involved in intelligence testing. (pp. 226–227)

    1. Reliability of a test refers to the consistency of scores obtained by the same subjects when they are reexamined on the same test on different occasions. (p. 226)

    2. The validity of a test reflects whether the test is measuring what it is supposed to measure. (p. 227)

C. IQ testing has raised many ethical and legal issues because some children of minority groups tend to score poorly and their test scores are used to place them in special education programs. (p. 228)

D. Theories have been proposed to explain the nature of intelligence, including the two-factor theory of intelligence and the theory that emphasizes separate and independent primary mental abilities. The newer triarchic theory incorporates cognitive psychology research and emphasizes how people solve problems rather than whether they get the correct answers. It also stresses the context of behavior in the real world. (pp. 228–229)

E. Both genes and the environment influence intelligence test scores. (pp. 229–232)

# ACTION GLOSSARY

Match the terms in the left column with the definitions in the right column.

___ 1. Language (p. 202)
___ 2. Grammar (p. 202)
___ 3. Phoneme (p. 203)
___ 4. Morpheme (p. 203)
___ 5. Surface structure (p. 204)
___ 6. Underlying representation (p. 204)
___ 7. Semantic approach (p. 204)

A. A single sound element from which spoken words are formed; the basic unit of oral language.
B. The organization of words in a spoken sentence.
C. The system of sounds and symbols by which we communicate meaning.
D. The smallest unit of meaning in a spoken language. Can be either a single word, such as "run," or any syllable that conveys meaning, such as "ing" at the end of a verb.
E. A method of explaining a sentence's underlying representation; emphasizes a sentence's division into propositions.
F. A set of rules that governs the use of words, their functions, and their relations in a sentence.
G. The meaning the speaker is trying to convey in a sentence.

___ 8. Proposition (p. 204)
___ 9. Constituents (p. 204)
___ 10. Cooing (p. 204)
___ 11. Babbling (p. 205)
___ 12. Holophrase (p. 205)
___ 13. Telegraphic speech (p. 205)
___ 14. Critical period (p. 206)

A. A period of development during which the organism is particularly vulnerable or susceptible to certain environmental influences, such as exposure to language.
B. Vowel-like sounds or sounds beginning with a single consonant; characterizes the vocal behavior of the very young infant.
C. The speech patterns characteristic of children beginning to use two-word sentences.
D. The phrases or subphrases of a sentence.
E. A unit of meaning or an idea that consists of a verbal unit and one or more nouns.
F. Single-word utterances, which often carry a great deal of meaning, produced by a child just learning to talk.
G. The vocal behavior of infants at age six months or older; includes strings of consonants and vowel phonemes.

___ 15. Displacement (p. 210)
___ 16. Artificial intelligence (p. 213)
___ 17. Linguistic relativity hypothesis (p. 214)
___ 18. Concepts (p. 215)
___ 19. Attribute (p. 215)
___ 20. Defining feature (p. 215)
___ 21. Characteristic feature (p. 215)
___ 22. Prototype (p. 215)
___ 23. Parallel distributed processing (PDP) (p. 213)

A. An attribute present in all members of a particular class or concept.
B. That which is the best example of an object or event within a particular category and which is matched to a greater or lesser degree by other examples of the category.
C. A feature of an object or event used to identify it as a member of a particular class or concept.
D. The ability to talk about things not actually present.
E. An attribute that is present in many, but not all, members of a particular class or concept.
F. Simulation of human thought with computers.
G. Suggests that an individual's perceptions, thought patterns, and view of the world are dependent upon the particular language he or she speaks.
H. The mental constructs that enable us to make classifications based on shared characteristics.
I. Connectionism, or the view that thinking is a set of connections among cognitions.

___ 24. Conservative focusing strategy (p. 216)
___ 25. Given state (p. 218)
___ 26. Goal state (p. 218)
___ 27. Path (p. 218)
___ 28. Cognitive set (p. 218)
___ 29. Functional fixity (p. 218)
___ 30. Inductive reasoning (p. 219)
___ 31. Nonverbal communication (p. 207)

A. The ability to take specific experiences and form general rules, ideas, or concepts.
B. A method of learning concepts in which the learner uses one positive instance of the concept as the focus and then tests individual hypotheses, one at a time, to determine the nature of the concept.
C. The strategy one uses to move from the given state to the goal state in problem solving.
D. The tendency for people to have difficulty imagining new and unusual uses for familiar objects.
E. The solution to the problem or the place where one would like to be.
F. The state one is currently in.
G. The transmission of information by means other than words.
H. The tendency to cling to certain interpretations of the requirements of a problem, especially ones that have been successful in finding a solution to a similar problem.

___ 32. **Algorithm (p. 219)**
___ 33. **Heuristic (p. 219)**
___ 34. **Means-end analysis (p. 219)**
___ 35. **Well-defined problems (p. 221)**
___ 36. **Ill-defined problems (p. 221)**
___ 37. **Convergent thinking (p. 221)**
___ 38. **Divergent thinking (p. 221)**

A. *A person who is solving a problem applies the rules of logic to arrive at a single correct solution.*
B. *Problems that provide the necessary information for a solution and for which there is only one correct solution.*
C. *A rule of thumb, or general principle, that involves a selective search through the possible solutions to a problem.*
D. *Problems for which all the needed information is not given and for which there may be more than one correct solution.*
E. *A general procedure or operation that guarantees a solution to the problem.*
F. *An approach to solving problems in which the solver tries to reduce the difference between the given state and the goal state by setting up and solving subproblems.*
G. *A person solving a problem stretches his or her imagination to conceive of a variety of possible solutions to a particular problem.*

___ 39. **Incubation (p. 222)**
___ 40. **Intelligence (p. 223)**
___ 41. **Mental age (p. 223)**
___ 42. **Intelligence quotient (IQ) (p. 224)**
___ 43. **Stanford-Binet (p. 224)**
___ 44. **Wechsler Adult Intelligence Scale (WAIS) (p. 224)**
___ 45. **Reliability (p. 227)**

A. *The abilities that enable a person to learn from experiences, to think abstractly, and to adapt successfully to the environment.*
B. *A term used in psychological testing that refers to the consistency of scores obtained by the same subjects when they are reexamined on different occasions.*
C. *The most widely used revision of the early Binet test of intelligence.*
D. *A measure that expresses a person's mental attainment in terms of his or her test scores relative to the scores of a large representative group of people of the same age.*
E. *A test that measures the mental abilities of adults.*
F. *A technique used to aid the problem-solving process; a difficult problem is set aside after a series of initial unsuccessful attempts at solving the problem.*
G. *A number used to express a person's intelligence; determined by dividing mental age (as measured by Binet's early intelligence test) by chronological age and multiplying times one hundred.*

___ 46. **Test-retest method (p. 227)**
___ 47. **Alternate form method (p. 227)**
___ 48. **Validity (p. 227)**
___ 49. **Two-factor theory of intelligence (p. 229)**
___ 50. **Primary mental abilities (p. 229)**
___ 51. **Triarchic theory (p. 229)**
___ 52. **Metacomponents (p. 229)**
___ 53. **Monozygotic twins (p. 230)**
___ 54. **Dizygotic twins (p. 230)**

A. *Independent abilities such as verbal comprehension, word fluency, and perceptual speed.*
B. *A method of assessing reliability in which subjects are given different forms of the same test on two different occasions, and their scores are correlated.*
C. *Fraternal twins.*
D. *Identical twins.*
E. *Suggests that intelligence consists of a general g-factor, which affects performance on all kinds of cognitive ability tests, and several specific s-factors, which affect performance in specific cognitive areas.*
F. *Reflects whether a test actually measures what it is supposed to measure; gives some indication about what conclusions can be drawn from test scores.*
G. *A method of assessing reliability. Subjects are given the same test on two different occasions, and the scores are correlated.*
H. *A theory of intelligence, couched in cognitive psychology, that stresses how people solve problems rather than whether they get the right answers.*
I. *The higher order mental activities used in planning, monitoring, and decision making.*

ANSWERS

*1. c, 2. f, 3. a, 4. d, 5. b, 6. g, 7. e, 8. e, 9. d, 10. b, 11. g, 12. f, 13. c, 14. a, 15. d, 16. f, 17. g, 18. h, 19. c,
20. a, 21. e, 22. b, 23. i, 24. b, 25. f, 26. e, 27. c, 28. h, 29. b, 30. a, 31. g, 32. e, 33. c, 34. f, 35. b, 36. d,
37. a, 38. g, 39. f, 40. a, 41. d, 42. g, 43. c, 44. e, 45. b, 46. g, 47. b, 48. f, 49. e, 50. a, 51. h, 52. i, 53. d,
54. c*

# SELF-TEST

1. Which of the following characteristics is *not* a universal characteristic of all languages?
   (a) creativity
   (b) rule governed
   (c) standard tenses for verbs
   (d) use of arbitrary symbols to represent objects and events
   (LO 1; p. 202)

2. The unit that is a sound element from which spoken words are formed is called a
   (a) phoneme.
   (b) morpheme.
   (c) word.
   (d) semantic approach.
   (LO 1; p. 203)

3. The sentence, "They are eating apples," has two
   (a) surface structures.
   (b) underlying representations.
   (c) morphemes.
   (d) inflections.
   (LO 1; p. 204)

4. The stage of single-word utterances appears at about the age of
   (a) two to three months.
   (b) two and one-half years.
   (c) twelve months.
   (d) four years.
   (LO 2; p. 205)

5. Eye contact, posture, gestures, and intonation
   (a) convey information to other people.
   (b) are means of nonverbal communication.
   (c) can be considered different channels of communication.
   (d) all of these are true.
   (LO 3; p. 207)

6. The linguistic relativity hypothesis claims that
   (a) language determines thought.
   (b) thought determines language.
   (c) thought and language are completely independent.
   (d) thought and language are initially independent, but language eventually comes into the service of thought.
   (LO 5; p. 214)

7. As a result of her research with the Dani, Rosch reported that the Dani learned the names for color categories best when
   (a) focal colors were the center of the category.
   (b) focal colors were not the center of the category.
   (c) a focal color was not in the category.
   (d) They were unable to learn color names under any circumstances.
   (LO 5; p. 216)

8. The defining feature of a concept is one that is true for
   (a) some members.
   (b) most members.
   (c) few members.
   (d) all members.
   (LO 7; p. 215)

9. The best example of a category is called a
   (a) focal color.
   (b) prototype.
   (c) defining feature.
   (d) characteristic feature.
   (LO 8; p. 215)

10. Learning new concepts requires
    (a) identifying relevant attributes.
    (b) determining which attributes are defining and which attributes are characteristic.
    (c) developing a conservative focusing strategy.
    (d) both a and b.
    (LO 8; p. 215)

11. The three steps in problem solving in order are
    (a) searching for a solution, analyzing the problem, and deciding that a solution has been discovered.
    (b) analyzing the problem, searching for a solution, and deciding that a solution has been discovered.
    (c) analyzing the problem, deciding that a solution has been discovered, and searching for a solution.
    (d) searching for a solution, deciding that a solution has been discovered, and analyzing the problem.
    (LO 9; pp. 218–221)

12. A person who solves a problem in a more complicated way than necessary because of prior experience in solving similar problems may be demonstrating
    (a) functional fixity.
    (b) inattention to the problem.
    (c) a set.
    (d) lack of familiarity with the material.
    (LO 10; p. 218)

13. A person who cannot solve a problem because he or she cannot imagine new uses for a familiar object is demonstrating
    (a) functional fixity.
    (b) inattention to the problem.
    (c) a response set.
    (d) lack of familiarity with the material.
    (LO 10; p. 218)

14. A general procedure that guarantees a solution to a problem is called a(n)
    (a) heuristic.
    (b) response set.
    (c) algorithm.
    (d) means-end analysis.
    (LO 11; p. 219)

15. Creative problem solving of ill-defined problems is best approached with _____ rather than with _____.
    (a) convergent thinking; incubation
    (b) incubation; divergent thinking
    (c) convergent thinking; divergent thinking
    (d) divergent thinking; convergent thinking
    (LO 12; p. 221)

16. The intelligence test developed by Binet was designed to
    (a) support his theory of intelligence.
    (b) examine racial differences in intelligence.
    (c) identify children who would not benefit from the regular elementary school program.
    (d) compare mental age with chronological age.
    (LO 13; p. 223)

17. Elizabeth is seven-years-old and has a mental age of nine. Elizabeth's IQ, according to the Stern's formula for calculating IQ, is
    (a) 135.
    (b) 129.
    (c) 78.
    (d) 108.
    (LO 13; p. 224)

18. The extent to which a test measures what it is supposed to measure refers to the concept of
    (a) validity.
    (b) reliability.
    (c) legality.
    (d) culture dependence.
    (LO 14; p. 227)

19. Spearman argued that intelligence is made up of
    (a) primary mental abilities.
    (b) a general factor.
    (c) both a general factor and specific factors.
    (d) independent abilities, such as divergent and convergent thinking.
    (LO 15; p. 229)

20. Correlations of scores on IQ tests are highest for which of the following?
    (a) siblings reared together
    (b) parents and their children
    (c) dizygotic twins reared together
    (d) monozygotic twins reared together
    (LO 16; pp. 230–232)

*ANSWERS*

1. c, 2. a, 3. b, 4. c, 5. d, 6. a, 7. a, 8. d, 9. b, 10. d, 11. b, 12. c, 13. a, 14. c, 15. d, 16. c, 17. b, 18. a, 19. c, 20. d

# THINKING ABOUT PSYCHOLOGY

1. Can computers think? If so, what do you mean by thinking? If you do not believe that computers think, can you envision a machine that does think? What would be some of the implications of a thinking machine?

2. Why has the concept of intelligence and its measurement proven to be so emotional and controversial in psychology? Would it be possible to develop a test that is completely uninfluenced by learning and culture?

# SUGGESTED READINGS

Adler, R. B., & Rodman, G. (1988). *Understanding human communication* (3rd ed.). New York: Holt, Rinehart & Winston. An undergraduate textbook on communication that covers perception, language, listening, nonverbal behavior, and other topics in communication.

Angoff, W. H. (1988). The nature-nurture debate, aptitudes, and group differences. *American Psychologist, 43* (9), 713–720. A discussion of the genetic and environmental contributions to intelligence; stresses that the debate on this issue is not relevant to the important matter of whether intelligence can be changed.

Fancher, R. E. (1985). *The intelligence men: Makers of the IQ controversy*. New York: Norton. An unusual discussion of the nature-nurture controversy and its relevance to intelligence.

Gardner, H. (1985). *The mind's new science: A history of the cognitive revolution*. New York: Basic Books. A book that covers the history and the emergence of cognitive science from its interdisciplinary origins.

Gilovich, T. (1991). *How we know what isn't so: The fallibility of human reasoning in everyday life*. New York: Free Press. How biases interfere with personal judgments and decisions.

Matlin, M. (1983). *Cognition*. New York: Holt, Rinehart & Winston. A comprehensive introductory text on cognition; includes chapters on language, concept learning, and problem solving.

Miller, G. A. (1981). *Language and speech*. San Francisco: W. H. Freeman. An introductory text on the topic of language.

Scientific American. (1992). Mind and Brain. *Scientific American,* September. Articles on the relationship between the brain and thought, language, consciousness, and learning.

Simon, H. A. (1992). *Models of life*. New York: Basic Books. The autobiography of one of the few psychologists to receive a Nobel Prize. Simon's life runs parallel with the development of cognitive psychology.

Smith, M. M., Morris, P. E., Levy, P., & Ellis, A. W. (1987). *Cognition in action*. London: Lawrence Erlbaum Associates. Shows the importance of cognition in everyday events, including reading a book, recognizing faces, reaching for a glass of beer, being an eyewitness, and the logic of Sherlock Holmes.

Sternberg, R. J. (1985). *Beyond IQ: A triarchic theory of human intelligence*. New York: Cambridge University Press. A seminal book that introduces the new theories of intelligence; emphasizes the "how" of problem solving and the context of intelligent behavior.

Trehub, Arnold. (1991). *The cognitive brain*. Cambridge, MA: MIT Press. A technical book on the relation between the brain and language, concept formation and problem solving.

# CHAPTER 8

## MOTIVATION AND EMOTION

## OUTLINE

▶ **Learning Objectives**

▶ **Motivation—A Description**

■ Theories of Motivation
Drive Reduction Theory
Optimum Level of Arousal
Theory
Expectancy Theory
Opponent Process Theory
■ Classification of Motives
■ Motivation and the Brain

▶ **Guided Review**

▶ **Human Motives: Four Examples**

■ Hunger
Peripheral Controls
The Brain's Role in Hunger
Obesity
■ Sex
Biological Influences
Psychological Influences on
Sex Behavior and Sex Roles
Cultural Influences on Sexual
Behavior
■ Sensation Seeking
Low- and High-Sensation
Seekers
Why Seek Sensation?
■ The Need for Achievement
Measuring n Ach
High and Low n Ach

▶ **Guided Review**

▶ **Emotions**

■ Describing Emotions
■ Expressing Emotions
Managing Emotional Expression
Measuring Emotional
Expression
■ Theories of Emotion
The James-Lange Theory
Emotions and the Brain
Emotion and Cognition
Emotions and Culture
Emotions and Evolution

▶ **Guided Review**

▶ **Summary**

▶ **Action Glossary**

▶ **Self-Test**

▶ **Thinking About Psychology**

▶ **Suggested Readings**

# MOTIVATION AND EMOTION
## LEARNING OBJECTIVES

**After reading this chapter, you should be able to**

▶ **1.** define the term "motivation," and describe four theories that have attempted to explain it. *(pp. 242–245)*

▶ **2.** describe one system that attempts to classify motives. *(pp. 245–246)*

▶ **3.** discuss the brain mechanisms underlying motivation. *(p. 246)*

▶ **4.** describe some of the biological and psychological factors underlying hunger. *(pp. 247–250)*

▶ **5.** describe some of the biological and psychological factors that affect the human sex drive and human sexual behavior. *(pp. 250–252)*

▶ **6.** define the term "sensation-seeking," and discuss the theories that attempt to explain the existence of this motive. *(pp. 252–254)*

▶ **7.** define the motive called "need for achievement," explain how it is measured, and discuss the characteristics of people who score high or low on this motive. *(pp. 254–257)*

▶ **8.** define the term "emotion," and explain how researchers have attempted to categorize emotions. *(p. 257)*

▶ **9.** discuss how human beings express emotions. *(pp. 258–260)*

▶ **10.** identify and describe several different theories of emotion. *(pp. 260–267)*

We try to begin each chapter in this text with a case study, an anecdote, or some examples of how the discussions that follow relate to life. Our motivation is clear: psychology is a field that embraces many fascinating subjects, ones that are very dear to all humans. We want you to see that what psychologists have learned about behavior can enlighten us and help us all understand ourselves and others better. We also want to point out what is not well understood—what we don't know—and ask you to think about the unresolved issues in the field. The "opener" for a chapter, just like the "teaser" at the beginning of a movie or the cover photo on a magazine at the newsstand, can heighten interest and motivate people to learn more. Part of our motivation is to influence your motivation.

Human motivation and emotion are complex mixtures of biology, cognition, and culture. Whether you continue to read this chapter now will be determined by a maze of interacting forces, beginning with your biological state and extending all the way to your feelings about how your psychology course will help you reach your goals.

## MOTIVATION—A DESCRIPTION

The term "motivation" comes from the Latin word meaning "to move." A **motive** *is something that moves an organism to act.* It is *why* we do things rather than what we do or how we do it. **Motivation** *refers to a presumed internal state of an organism that causes it to move toward some goal.* The state may exist partly because of internal factors, such as insufficient food. It might also develop from external factors.

### Theories of Motivation

"Why did I do that?" Why did I enroll in that sky-diving course, or say something so stupid at the committee meeting? Why do I keep buying lottery tickets? Why do I find it impossible to pass a donut shop without indulging, even though I'm determined to lose weight? All of these questions are asking about motives, and theories to explain them abound. You may have developed a theory of your own: perhaps you believe you are self-destructive, and your patterns of behavior conform to that view.

Psychological theorizing about motivation emphasizes that sometimes a person is "pushed" forward; something inside us is driving us to eat, achieve, or quit our jobs. But we also can be "pulled" toward something, a goal that we're striving toward or a particularly desirable state.

Several of the major theories of motivation have something to say about "push" and "pull."

*Drive Reduction Theory*    One of the earlier theories of motivation, the **drive reduction theory,** *proposed that organisms experience the arousal of a drive when an important need is not satisfied, and they engage in behavior to reduce the arousal and satisfy the need.* **Primary drives** *are those that motivate the organism to fulfill some basic need necessary for its survival (or the survival of the species), such as hunger, thirst, or sex.* One of the early proponents of this theory was Clark Hull (1943, 1952).

An important component of the drive reduction theory is **homeostasis.** *This term refers to a state of balance necessary in many physiological systems.* For example, temperature control requires a balance between hot and cold stimulation, and the control of body weight requires a balance between food intake and energy expenditure. Organisms are motivated to maintain homeostasis in their physiological systems, and their drives help them accomplish this.

Primary drives are biological ones necessary for personal and species survival. **Acquired drives** *develop through learning.* For example, children learn that they never get to eat unless they wash their hands first. They will probably develop an acquired drive to keep clean, based on this learning experience. Or a teenager who learns that possessing money attracts more members of the opposite sex may develop an acquired drive for money.

The drive is the force that motivates an organism to action; it is the "push" that drives us to action. Which action the organism finally performs depends on the strength of the organism's **habit.** *A habit is a response to some stimulus; the strength of the habit depends on the connection between the stimulus and the response that influences what kind of behavior the drive will energize.* For example, hunger might be the drive that pushes you toward the kitchen. But what you do when you open the refrigerator will depend not only on what's in it, but on habit. If your previous learning experiences taught you that carbohydrates reduce hunger quickly, you will probably choose the leftover spaghetti rather than the chicken or the pickles.

The drive reduction theory is simple and straightforward, but there are some human behaviors it cannot explain. For instance, the theory assumes that human beings, and other animals as well, are always driven to

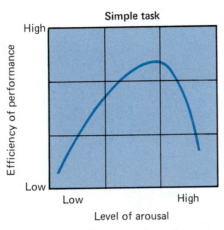
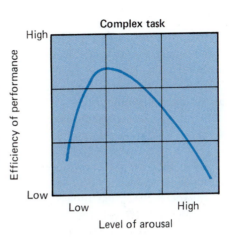

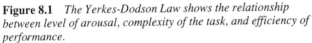

**Figure 8.1** *The Yerkes-Dodson Law shows the relationship between level of arousal, complexity of the task, and efficiency of performance.*

reduce their arousal levels (by seeking food, water, shelter, etc.). It would seem logical to conclude, then, that we are happiest when we are stuffed with food and drink, sexually satiated, and lazing around doing nothing. However, for human beings this state would rapidly lead to boredom. Humans are curious creatures who seek arousal; they are not always motivated to reduce it. If they were, why would they climb mountains, skydive, or go to a movie? In addition, human beings do not always behave in accordance with their biological self-interest. They diet until they are extremely thin, sit in unbearably hot sauna baths, and occasionally even sacrifice their own lives for an important cause.

*Optimum Level of Arousal Theory*    Drive reduction theory was revised to better explain why people sometimes seek to increase their arousal levels. The new version, the **optimum level of arousal theory,** *states that drives do not necessarily motivate an organism to seek the lowest level of arousal. Instead, they provide motivation to seek an optimum level of arousal. What the optimum level is depends on the circumstances and on the person.* For example, a person deprived of stimulation for most of the day might seek a high level of arousal that evening by going to an exciting football game. Another person, home from a hard day of selling encyclopedias to reluctant parents, might seek a lower arousal level by sitting in an easy chair and watching a television show.

As early as 1908, comparative psychologists Robert Yerkes and J. D. Dodson were emphasizing the effects that different arousal levels had on learning (Yerkes & Dodson,

1908). They varied arousal levels in mice by changing the intensity of electric shocks and by observing how well the animals performed in simple and complex mazes. The mice performed best in difficult mazes when the shock level was intermediate. This finding can be presented in a graph as an inverted, U-shaped function (figure 8.1). The **Yerkes-Dodson Law** *states that performance on a learning task is related to arousal; the best performance results from intermediate levels of arousal.* Performance is also related to the difficulty of the task. Yerkes and Dodson found that the mice performed simple tasks better when the stimulation was more intense. For complex tasks, low to intermediate arousal was best. The Yerkes-Dodson Law shows how the optimum level of arousal theory can be applied to performance on a task.

If you are trying to influence motivation and performance in others, the Yerkes-Dodson Law is good to remember. Imagine a swimming coach whose team members are ready to start the big meet. She wants her swimmers to be highly motivated but knows that too much arousal could hinder performance, and too little could hurt it. If she gathers them together in a group and gives an all-purpose "this is the most important day of your life" speech, she will probably create too much arousal in some of the swimmers and their performance would suffer. Some swimmers might do their best under these circumstances, but others might freeze up. If she says, "don't worry about this one—we have many meets ahead of us," she may not create enough arousal in some swimmers. If she knows her swimmers well, she could talk to each one individually, modulating her motivating message in accord with the arousal level of each person. Marketing execs designing ad campaigns must be on guard for this effect. An ad featuring a twisted car wreck might motivate some to buy a safer, heavier car; it might motivate others to take the bus.

The drive reduction theory and optimum level of arousal theory both emphasize the states within a person that push them to action. But what about the "pull"?

*Expectancy Theory*    If you just bought a lottery ticket, you might spend considerable time deciding how you would spend the money if you won and find the activity quite pleasing—at least until the drawing. If you are attending college, you might be thinking about longer term goals and take specific courses to help you reach them. To understand the motives for these kinds of behavior, we must look beyond the forces that "push" us, and into those that "pull." **Expectancy theory** (or theories, since there are many versions) *emphasizes the importance of rewards or goals as well as how a person's expectations of consequences can influence his behavior.*

According to expectancy theory, the hunger drive is only part of the reason a hungry rat is motivated to find its way through a maze. It is also motivated because of previous learning experiences in which it had come to expect a bit of food at the end. Its motivation is composed of two major features: the **valence**, or *attractiveness of the goal*, and the **expectancy**, or *the likelihood that its behavior will lead to the goal.* A simple way of explaining the expectancy theory is to say that motivation = valence × expectancy.

The actions that hungry people take to satisfy their hunger depend very much on valence and expectancy. Let's say there is a deli that sells foot-long hot dogs on the corner of a person's block. This person loves to eat these dogs, so the valence is high. But what about expectancy? How does the person evaluate whether his or her actions will lead to the desired reward? If money is lacking, the person will not go to the deli even though he or she is hungry and the valence of the hot dogs is high. The person's motivation to walk down to the deli is tempered by (1) the valence of the hot dogs and (2) the expectancy that walking down there will lead to eating one.

*Opponent Process Theory*    The **opponent process theory** *proposes an explanation for the way in which acquired drives are gained* (Solomon & Corbit, 1974; Solomon, 1980). *It suggests that a stimulus is followed by*

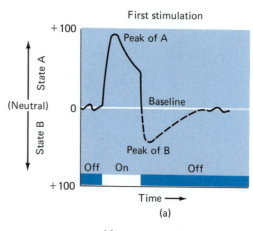

First stimulation

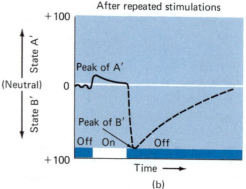

After repeated stimulations

**Figure 8.2**    *Response to a US (a) the first few times it occurs and (b) after many stimulations*

*a particular response and that this initial response is followed by an opposite reaction. After repeated stimulus presentations, the first response diminishes, but the opposite reaction that occurs after it grows in strength.* The **a-process** *is the initial reaction to the stimulus,* and the **b-process** *refers to the opposite reaction that occurs after the initial reaction* (figure 8.2).

When a person is injected with heroin, the initial response is euphoria. This lasts for a few hours and is followed by discomfort until the person returns to the resting state. After repeated injections, the a-process, the euphoria, diminishes and is replaced by a weaker kind of contentment. The b-process, or discomfort, grows into the agony of withdrawal. Thus, the user continues to inject the drug primarily to avoid the painful b-process.

Another example concerns how a sauna bather comes to seek the seemingly painful heat of the sauna. The first time the person enters the sauna, the experience is a painful, burning sensation. Afterwards, relief is experienced

| | |
|---|---|
| Abasement (to comply and accept punishment) | Infavoidance (to avoid humiliation) |
| Achievement (to strive and reach goals quickly and well) | Nurturance (to aid or protect the helpless) |
| Affiliation (to form friendships) | Order (to achieve order and cleanliness) |
| Aggression (to hurt another) | Play (to relax) |
| Autonomy (to strive for independence) | Rejection (to reject disliked others) |
| Counteraction (to overcome defeat) | Seclusion (to be distant from others) |
| Deference (to serve gladly) | Sentience (to obtain sensual gratification) |
| Defendance (to defend and justify oneself) | Sex (to form an erotic relationship) |
| Dominance (to control or influence others) | Succorance (to ask for nourishment, love, aid) |
| Exhibition (to excite, shock, self-dramatize) | Superiority (to overcome obstacles) |
| Harmavoidance (to avoid pain and injury) | Understanding (to question and think) |

**Figure 8.3** *Some hypothesized nonphysiological human needs*
Source: Data from H.A. Murray, *Explorations in Personality.* Copyright © 1938, Oxford University Press.

followed by a slow return to normal. After several exposures to the sauna, the pain (a-process) diminishes and the relief (b-process) grows into very pleasurable deep relaxation. The opponent process theory is a useful one because it helps explain why something that would seem to be painful, like sauna bathing, can come to be a powerful acquired motivation.

## Classification of Motives

The list of motives is almost as long as the list of different kinds of human behavior. In early theories of motivation, psychologists equated motives with instincts, and they began making lists that included the obvious ones, such as hunger, thirst, and sex, as well as more exotic ones, such as pugnacity and curiosity. By the 1920s, psychologists had added so many instincts that the list totaled nearly 6,000! (One rather curious one was "the instinct to avoid eating apples in one's own orchard.")

H.A. Murray (1938) attempted to develop a kind of catalog of human motives, in which motives could be classified as either primary or secondary. The primary needs were the physiological ones, such as hunger or thirst, while the secondary ones were more complex, involving higher cognitive functions and social behavior. Figure 8.3 shows some of Murray's list of secondary needs.

Although Murray believed that these needs were present in everyone, he proposed that they varied from one person to another. Some people, for example, might have a very strong need for order and this need would motivate them to organize events, household affairs, even other people's lives. Others might show a strong need for counteraction, which means they are motivated to get even when they feel unjustly accused or harmed.

One of Murray's most important contributions was the development of a means to assess these different needs in people. The **Thematic Apperception Test, or TAT,** *is one of the more common tests used to measure motivation.* The theory behind this test is that an individual's fantasies and imagination in response to ambiguous stimuli can reveal a person's motives. An experimenter shows a subject a series of pictures containing ambiguous figures and the subject makes up an imaginative story about what is happening. The researcher then attempts to draw conclusions about the strength of each motive based on the stories and descriptions.

For example, one of the ambiguous pictures might show a person standing next to someone lying on a bed. A person who has a strong need for "nurturance" would be motivated to take care of others, especially those who were weak or ill, and would seek opportunities in which this need might be expressed. This person might make up a story for this picture that reflects and dramatizes the nurturant motive. Someone with a strong need for achievement might describe the picture very differently, perhaps by emphasizing the extraordinary skill of the caregiver in causing rapid recovery.

Some of Murray's proposed needs have been the subject of much research in psychology, and we'll explore one of them (need for achievement) later in this chapter, as one of our four examples of human motives. Others, such as the need for affiliation, have also captured the attention of researchers. People who score high on this motive prefer to be with other people, to cooperate and to form close attachments. They like writing letters to other people, keeping in touch, and are eager to share experiences and secrets. They try to meet other people and form friendships, and they consider social skills to be important.

In American culture, women tend to score higher than men on the need for affiliation, but the differences are surprisingly small given the persistent stereotypes about women and their stronger emotional ties to others (Helgeson & Sharpsteen, 1987).

Someone who scores high on need for affiliation is not likely to score high on another of Murray's motives: the need for power. People who score high on this motive tend to seek positions of authority, assume leadership roles, and generally seek to dominate other people in social situations.

As you might imagine, scoring stories for their emphasis on various needs is a difficult challenge and raters often disagree about what motive is being expressed. Nevertheless, the TAT is an enormously rich source of information about the variety of human motivation and has been a favorite tool in this kind of research.

## Motivation and the Brain

Research on the biological basis of motivation began when James Olds and his colleagues made some startling discoveries about the rewarding properties of electrical stimulation of the brain (ESB) (Olds, 1958). As discussed in chapter 2, tiny electrical shocks to certain parts of the brain, the areas around the hypothalamus in particular, can be very rewarding. Rats will press levers thousands of times per hour to receive these shocks and will sometimes ignore food (Routtenberg & Lindy, 1965). In some cases, rats will even neglect their own newborn pups (Sonderegger, 1970). The studies on ESB suggest that the brain contains an integrated "reward system" not specifically tied to a particular motive, such as hunger, but involved in all kinds of motivated behavior.

Since Olds' original discovery, the studies on ESB have uncovered many interesting facts about the phenomenon (Olds & Fobes, 1981). For one thing, stimulation of the hypothalamus is very rewarding, but the hypothalamus is not the only rewarding site. Rewarding sites have been found in many brain regions, including the cortex, the hippocampus, the thalamus, and the olfactory bulbs. The reward system seems to be widespread, a finding that is not surprising considering how important it is to our behavior and survival.

In human beings, electrical stimulation of rewarding brain areas evokes quite a variety of sensations. One patient reported, "I have a glowing feeling . . . I feel good" (Heath, 1964). Another kept pressing a button to stimulate his own brain because each shot of ESB produced a vague

memory. He wanted to know more about the memory and bring it into clearer focus. There is still much to learn about this important brain system, particularly the way it might operate in human beings.

A number of studies have also begun tracking the biochemical events that are involved in reward, tracing the neurotransmitters that are released along the pathways that respond to electrical stimulation. Dopamine, for example, seems to play a prominent role in the brain substrates that underlie reward and reinforcement. It is intriguing that dopamine also is affected by the psychoactive drugs that influence mood. As we discussed in chapter 3, cocaine's effects are partly due to its influence on dopamine synapses; the drug interferes with the reuptake of the neurotransmitter. The evidence is leading to the hypothesis that the release of dopamine in the brain is a key ingredient in reward across all kinds of situations. Perhaps drugs like cocaine cause biochemical events that mimic the brain's natural reward system, and thus provide the necessary reinforcement to lead people to continue taking them.

▶ **GUIDED REVIEW** *Learning Objectives 1, 2, and 3*

1. The study of motivation explores the _____ of behavior rather than the "what" or "how."
2. The _____ of motivation proposes that organisms have certain needs, such as the need for food or water. When the organism is hungry, it enters a _____ in which it is motivated to action that will reduce the hunger drive. Motivation is the striving to maintain _____ , or balance, in the organism by reducing drives. The behavior that the organism finally performs depends on the organism's _____ strengths, developed through learning.
3. The _____ theory of motivation takes into account the fact that people do not always seek to reduce their drives to the lowest possible level. They sometimes seek to _____ drive rather than reduce it.
4. The _____ points out the relationship between performance, arousal, and the difficulty of the task. For a task, a moderate level of arousal produces the best performance; high and low levels of arousal hinder performance. For easier tasks, _____ levels of arousal facilitate performance.
5. The _____ theory of motivation emphasizes the "pull" of goals rather than the "push" of drives. Motivation is a function of both the attractiveness, or _____ , of the reward and the _____ , or the likelihood that some behavior on the part of the organism will lead to the reward.

6. The _____ theory of motivation explains how motives are acquired. A stimulus triggers an _____ that diminishes with repeated presentations and a delayed and opposite _____ that strengthens over time.

7. The variety of human motives have been named and classified in many ways. An early scheme, devised by Murray, measured human motives by using the _____.

8. The brain contains a _____ that functions in all kinds of motivated behaviors. Electrical brain stimulation of sites along the system is rewarding. The neurotransmitter _____ appears to play a prominent role in reward mechanisms.

*ANSWERS*

*1. "why" 2. drive reduction theory, drive state, homeostasis, habit 3. optimum level of arousal, increase 4. Yerkes-Dodson Law, difficult, higher 5. expectancy, valence, expectancy, opponent process, a-process, b-process 7. Thematic Apperception Test (TAT) 8. reward system, dopamine*

# HUMAN MOTIVES: FOUR EXAMPLES

The number of human motives is almost equal to the number of humans. Psychologists have attempted to classify these motives, using one scheme or another. Most scientists distinguish between primary and acquired motives, a distinction that separates motives based on biological needs from those based on learning. However, this separation is not always clear and, in some cases, is quite arbitrary.

The motive to quench thirst, for example, would seem to fall into the category of primary drive; humans need water to survive and the body contains several controls to ensure that the drive for fluids is activated when supplies are low. But learning and culture play important roles in everyone's drinking behavior. Passing a cola vending machine might easily arouse one's drive for fluids well before any physiological regulatory mechanisms were activated. We share a cultural expectation to offer a beverage to visitors and the phrase, "let's have coffee" carries a more social than physiological meaning. The motive to eat also is affected by biological, social, and cultural factors. Humans need food to live, but eating disorders such as anorexia nervosa, discussed in later chapters, are not uncommon. Although some motives are primary and others acquired, most seem to have elements of both and fall between the two extremes. In choosing the examples of motives for this section, we selected ones that covered this range.

## Hunger

If you were to fast for a day, your mind would be obsessed with thoughts of food by dinnertime. It might be difficult to concentrate on reading the newspaper because you would keep noticing the ads for a new Greek restaurant, a cake sale at the local church, and the twelve-cents-off coupon for steak. You would experience how compelling the motive to eat can be.

Human beings have a fail-safe mechanism for survival— if they do not get enough to eat, they begin to focus all their attention on food until their hunger is satisfied. The way this mechanism works, how it arouses the hunger drive, how it usually prevents overeating, and how it occasionally fails, has been the subject of a great deal of research. Scientists have been searching for this mechanism to find out why it fails and why so many people become overweight. They have actually been successful in finding not one mechanism, but many; and they keep finding more.

*Peripheral Controls*    If you asked people how they knew they were hungry, they would probably say that their stomach was growling. If you asked them why they stopped eating, they might say that it was because their stomach felt full. The stomach and its contractions certainly provide signals that tell you to start and stop eating, but they do not provide the only signals. Messages about the need for food must come from other places as well.

Another signal seems to come from the intestinal tract. **CCK,** *a hormone released from the intestinal tract when the contents of the stomach pass into the small intestine, appears to provide one of the signals that says you have had enough to eat.* When animals are injected with CCK, they stop eating (Smith & Gibbs, 1976). CCK appears to suppress intake by making the animal reject substances that have a perceived caloric value (Fedorchak & Bolles, 1988). Unfortunately, CCK only inhibits eating for a short period of time; animals that continue to receive injections go back to eating normally after a few days. Apparently there are multiple controls over hunger and satiety; if you fool one, another steps in and overrides it.

The liver also plays an important role in hunger by monitoring and filtering the blood so that it always contains the correct amount of nutrients, including glucose and proteins. To accomplish this vital task, the liver has **glucoreceptors** *that monitor glucose levels in the blood.*

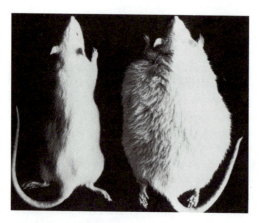

**Figure 8.4**  *A normal rat and a rat made obese by lesions in the ventromedial hypothalamus*

If the blood contains too much, perhaps because you have just finished a meal and the circulatory system has absorbed many nutrients, the liver stores the excess. Glucoreceptors were first discovered in experiments on dogs. An injection of glucose directly into the vein that carries blood from the intestines to the liver caused a hungry dog to stop eating for quite a while (Russek, 1975). Thus, the liver's main role is to monitor the body's fuel supply and to signal satiety.

*The Brain's Role in Hunger*    Figure 8.4 shows an obese rat. In slightly more than one month, this rat nearly doubled its body weight, going from a slim 200 grams to almost 400 grams. In human terms, this would be equivalent to a normal-sized person gaining 150 pounds in four weeks. What happened to make this rat so fat?

The rat became a voracious eater about one week after its **ventromedial hypothalamus (VMH)** had been destroyed. *A lesion in this tiny part of the brain results in a dramatic increase in food consumption.* Without this brain area, rats simply could not stop eating (Brobeck, Tepperman, & Long, 1943). This suggests that neural activity in the VMH is involved in satiety.

If the VMH might be involved in satiety, then the **lateral hypothalamus (LH)** might be involved in hunger. *Lesions in this brain area, which is right next to the VMH, cause an animal to hardly eat at all.* In fact, it must be force-fed to survive. Perhaps brain activity in the LH triggers hunger, and without the LH, the animal simply never feels hungry.

Further support for the complementary roles of the LH and VMH came from electrical stimulation studies.

Stimulation of the LH led to feeding in rats, whereas stimulation of the VMH caused animals to stop eating.

The discovery of the effects of lesions in the VMH and LH was an important breakthrough in psychology. As is usually the case, however, the more we learned about these two syndromes, the more confused the story became. For example, animals with VMH lesions overeat if food is easily available, but they will lose weight if they have to do anything too strenuous to obtain their huge portions. Normal rats, on the other hand, will work quite hard to obtain a reasonable number of calories for the day. VMH lesioned rats are also very finicky about the taste of their food. They readily eat chocolate cookies but refuse any food that tastes a little bitter. A hungry rat works very hard to get food and will eat foul-tasting rat food to maintain its body weight. These findings were puzzling and suggested that the whole story was not yet told.

Other hypotheses have been proposed in addition to the hypothesis that lesions in the VMH produce obesity by destroying the "satiety" center. One suggests that the lesions damaged parts of the animal's reward system, the brain mechanism that underlies all different kinds of motivation (Powley, 1977). The damage might enhance the rewarding value of food, causing the animal to overeat. This explanation might also help us understand why the animal with a lesion in the LH refuses food. Certainly many of the same neurotransmitters involved in reward are also involved in eating disorders, suggesting a relationship between the two systems (Morley & Blundell, 1988).

*Obesity*    According to the *Guinness Book of World Records,* Robert Earl Hughes weighed 1,041 pounds when he died at the early age of thirty-two. Clearly, whatever signals the brain or the body uses to stop eating were not working in his case. Despite our progress in understanding these signals, we know very little about how to control obesity. If we did, Americans would not be spending billions of dollars each year on diet books, low-calorie foods, weight-loss programs, and diet drugs.

Attempts to find a single cause of obesity have met with failure. Obesity is not a single disorder, and it is not likely to have a single cause. The chubby baby, the woman who fails to return to normal weight after pregnancy, the overweight executive, and the sumo wrestler all have overweight in common, but the causes are probably quite different.

Some of the factors that explain why people get fat include genetic predisposition, metabolic rate, hormonal imbalance, too many fat cells in the body, improper eating habits, boredom, and even viral infections (Lyons et al., 1982). One proposal, the **emotional arousal theory (EAT),** *suggests that overeating is an instrumentally conditioned behavior that serves to reduce anxiety in the obese* (Leon & Roth, 1977). Some studies of obese people under stress have supported this hypothesis (e.g., Pine, 1985; McKenna, 1972). Animals, too, seem to react to stress by overeating. Rats stressed every day by mild pinches on the tail increased their food intake considerably (Rowland & Antelman, 1976).

Why stress should produce overeating in some people is not clear, but there is evidence that the effect is mediated by endorphin, the opiate-like substance released by the brain that relieves pain (Morley & Blundell, 1988). Injections of endorphin, or opiates, increase food intake in animals. Of great interest are the effects of naloxone, which blocks the effects of endorphin. In one study, obese subjects were injected with either naloxone or a placebo before breakfast. The naloxone-treated subjects ate considerably less and said they felt quite full and thought less about food (Wolkowitz et al., 1988).

Another popular theory maintains that people who become obese rely too heavily on external cues, such as the taste of food or the time of day, to decide when and how much to eat. In contrast, people who can maintain a normal weight rely more on internal cues, such as stomach pangs, to regulate food intake.

In one study, overweight and normal-weight subjects were brought into the laboratory near the dinner hour, ostensibly to participate in an experiment on personality. While they were filling out some bogus questionnaires, they were offered crackers. For half the obese and half the normal subjects, there was a clock in the testing room deliberately set to run fast. For these subjects, the dinner hour approached more quickly than normal. When it was actually around 5:30, the subjects' clock read 6:00. For the other half of each group, the clock was set to run very slowly, so 6:00 came and went while the clock was still reading around 5:30. The experiment was designed to find out how many crackers each group of subjects would consume (Schachter & Gross, 1968; Schachter, 1971). The obese subjects ate more crackers when they thought it was the dinner hour. The subjects of normal weight, however, ate more crackers when it actually was the dinner hour. The obese subjects seemed to be relying on the clock to trigger eating, while those of normal weight were probably relying on internal cues.

The reliance on external cues seems to be at least one cause of overeating. At the beginning of a summer camp, a group of normal-weight girls was tested to see how responsive they were to external and internal cues (Rodin & Slochower, 1976). Candy, cakes, and other treats were easily available at the camp. At the end of eight weeks, the girls were weighed. Those girls most responsive to external cues at the beginning of the summer were the ones who gained the most weight.

Unfortunately, no one knows why some of these children were more responsive to external cues. Perhaps there is some genetic predisposition involved, or perhaps they learned it at an early age. A baby fed on a rigid four-hour schedule might learn to ignore hunger cues that come at other times and instead rely on external cues, such as the sight of the bottle, to trigger hunger and feeding. A baby fed on demand might learn to rely more on internal cues.

Obesity is not a simple problem, and studies trying to find differences between overweight and normal-weight subjects in their responses to external cues have not always been successful (Rodin, 1981). There are some obese people who rely very much on internal cues, and there are some thin people who rely completely on the taste of food or the time of day. Clearly, obesity has many causes, and an overreliance on external eating cues may be just one of them.

Although it is not always clear why people become overweight, it is a little clearer why they stay overweight. First, the larger a fat cell becomes, the more easily it can store more and more fat. Thus overweight people, who already have more fat cells, can put on weight more easily than thin people. Second, obese people usually have higher levels of insulin, a hormone from the pancreas needed to allow glucose to enter cells. This means that the storage of fat is more efficient in the overweight person. Higher insulin levels also produce a higher level of hunger, so the overweight person feels hungrier most of the time.

A third reason overweight people stay overweight is that whenever they try to diet, they are fighting their own **setpoint,** *the weight that a person can maintain effortlessly without dieting* (Bennett & Gurin, 1982). The body automatically feels hungry when weight drops below this setpoint. When weight surpasses the setpoint, the person feels less hungry and eats less, and his or her weight drops back. Unfortunately, a person's setpoint may not equal ideal weight.

Going on a diet is really an attempt to get below the setpoint, and the body responds as though it were in a state of starvation. Metabolism drops to conserve energy, hunger increases, and physical exercise is avoided. The person may lose weight rapidly during the first few days of a diet, but as soon as these mechanisms to counteract starvation are activated, it becomes more and more difficult to lose each pound. Even though the person may consume only a few hundred calories a day, the weight loss may be very small. The feeling of hunger will persist, not only as long as the diet lasts, but until the person's weight goes back up to its setpoint. This may explain why so many people lose weight but so few keep it off. The most effective way to lose weight permanently is to change the setpoint. Unfortunately, no one knows how to do that.

This may be gloomy news for people who want to be thinner, but the picture may not be entirely dark. Fatness, if not obesity, has certain advantages. Recent research shows that the female must store a certain amount of body fat in order to begin and maintain normal menstrual cycles (Frisch, 1988). Women whose fat levels drop below a certain point, because of excessive dieting or strenuous exercise, often experience reproductive abnormalities, including infertility.

Treatments for obesity are also being developed. Frequent physical exercise seems to be a promising way to change the body's setpoint. Also, receptors related to appetite and clearly affected by amphetamine, a drug that depresses appetite, have been found in the brain (Paul, Hulihan-Giblin, & Skolnick, 1982). There is hope that scientists will be able to produce drugs that block these receptors as amphetamines do but that do not produce the same hazardous side effects as amphetamines, especially tolerance.

People's attitudes also seem to be a key ingredient in whether or not they will lose weight. In one study, people's answers to a question about the likelihood that they would lose weight over the next six weeks turned out to be the best predictor of their success (Schifter & Ajzen, 1985).

Psychologists may have an overpessimistic view of weight-loss programs, according to one scientist (Schachter, 1982). Clinicians tend to see only those obese people who seek treatment, not the ones who succeeded on their own. Also, clinical psychologists often only see the patient make a single attempt. Interviews with a wide range of people revealed that around sixty percent of those who had been obese at one time in their lives were now at a normal weight, due to their own persistent attempts at weight loss.

## Sex

The human sex drive is one of the most complicated motives we have. It is influenced by biological, psychological, sociological, and cultural factors. It is usually called a primary drive because the species would die out if it did not exist. As far as we know, however, an individual suffers no physical problems from abstention.

*Biological Influences*    In the lower animals, hormones are the most important factor regulating sexual behavior. Estrogen and progesterone are the sex hormones released by the female's ovaries, and androgens are the sex hormones released by the male's testes. The mating behavior of animals like the rat or the mouse, for example, is very closely tied to the levels of these hormones circulating in the blood. If the male rat's testes are removed so that no androgens are released, the animal will stop mating within a few weeks (Davidson, 1966). If the animal is later given injections of testosterone, one of the important androgens, its sexual behavior will return.

The sex behavior of some animals with normal levels of circulating androgen can be increased by adding hormones. Normal male rats given testosterone show more intense sex behavior than usual (Beach, 1942; Cheng & Casida, 1949).

In female animals, the role of hormones is equally important. Unlike humans, female rats are sexually receptive only at the time at which mating would most likely result in pregnancy. The fluctuation in the female's receptivity is controlled by the changing levels of estrogen and progesterone in the female's bloodstream. Removal of the source of these hormones eventually causes the animal to lose interest in sex behavior. Replacement of the hormones through an appropriate sequence of injections will result in the reappearance of typical mating responses.

In human males, the relationship between hormones, sex behavior, and sex drive is similar but less direct. When men lose their testes for one reason or another, perhaps through accident or disease, some lose their potency almost immediately and others show a gradual decline over a period of years. Once they begin hormone replacement therapy, their sex drive and sex behavior return (Money & Ehrhardt, 1972). Thus, the presence or absence of the hormone is related to the presence or absence of sex drive and sex behavior in men.

Whether smaller fluctuations in testosterone level have any influence on the sex behavior of a man from day to day is a very difficult question to answer. Testosterone levels do vary from one day to the next, often in response to stressful situations. For example, the stress of war seems to lower testosterone levels in troops (Rose et al., 1969). Testosterone levels also appear to be affected by the anticipation of sex. Men who know they are about to leave an isolated Arctic military base sometimes report that their beards start growing faster, a sign of increased testosterone production. In monkeys, testosterone levels appear to be related to dominance level in the group. One study found that the monkeys that became dominant in a newly formed group showed remarkable increases—as much as 238 percent—in their testosterone levels (Rose, Bernstein, & Gordon, 1975). The testosterone levels decreased in the monkeys that became subordinate.

Despite these fluctuations in hormone levels, investigators have not been able to find any clear relationship between the amount of hormone circulating in a human male's bloodstream and the intensity of his sex drive or the amount of his sex behavior. It seems that men require a minimum amount of male sex hormone for normal sex behavior; once the man has this amount, fluctuations in his sex drive or behavior are due more to psychological factors than to biological factors.

The role of hormones in the sex behavior of women is even less direct. Women show sex drive and sexual behavior throughout their entire menstrual cycle, demonstrating that the link between the levels of circulating estrogen and progesterone and sex behavior is very weak or nonexistent. Nevertheless, some scientists have reported survey data showing that women report more frequent sex behavior around the middle of their cycles—about the time when they would be ovulating (Hart, 1960; Udry & Morris, 1968). Others, however, have found evidence that there is a peak of sexual behavior around the time of menstruation rather than at midcycle (James, 1971; Spitz, Gold, & Adams, 1975).

When a woman loses her ovaries through surgery, she ordinarily experiences little or no change in sex drive. Although the loss of estrogen and progesterone probably will cause vaginal dryness and other physiological changes that may indirectly affect sexual behavior, she usually reports that her sex drive is just as strong as it was before the surgery. The loss of ovarian function after menopause also seems to have little or no effect on sex drive in women (Kinsey, Pomeroy, Martin, & Gebhard, 1953). The studies that attempt to establish some relationship between sex drive and ovarian hormones in women find either no

effect or very small ones, suggesting that if there is a link it is not a strong one.

Some research suggests that sex drive in women is related to the presence of low levels of androgen, probably released by the adrenal glands. Injections of testosterone increase sexual interest in some women (Salmon & Geist, 1943; Bancroft and Skakkebaek, 1978). This treatment, however, has to be conducted very cautiously because of its masculinizing side effects.

*Psychological Influences on Sex Behavior and Sex Roles*    Individuals are treated differently from the day they are born based on whether they are male or female. They learn their **sex roles,** *the attitudes and behaviors believed by their culture to be appropriate for each sex.* Even children as young as eighteen months begin to show a great deal of interest in play considered appropriate for their own sex. Researchers observing toddlers in their homes note that girls are more likely to play with soft toys, dolls, and dress-up clothes, and boys are more likely to play with blocks, trucks and cars, and toys that require some form of manipulation (Fagot, 1974).

By the time people reach adulthood, they have developed clear pictures of what it means to be a man or a woman as defined by their society, and these images have important effects on their sex behavior. Our culture's definition of a man usually includes traits like aggressiveness, ambition, and willingness to take risks. Adjectives like emotional, passive, dependent, and affectionate are usually applied more frequently to women. These expectations about the behavior of men and women can have effects on attitudes toward sexuality.

Attitudes about sex are rather different in men and women. Women tend to be more conservative about sex compared to men, and are less likely to have casual affairs. Young women are more concerned than young men about damaging their reputation. In fact, many young men see casual sex as a way to enhance their reputations as masculine. Parents are also less likely to approve of casual sex by their daughters. America went through a period in the 1960s and 1970s in which attitudes toward sexual behavior in men and women changed, but the two sexes still have different expectations for themselves regarding their sexual lives, and report different behavior as well (Hendrick & Hendrick, 1987).

The turbulent sixties and seventies created so many changes in American sexual attitudes and beliefs that it is not surprising that men and women continue to read each other's signals incorrectly. Teenage boys, conscious of liberalized attitudes on the part of the girls, tend to view many of their outward behaviors as being sexually motivated even when the girls say they are not. Skimpy clothing is a good example. Girls are likely to interpret it as a sign of comfortable dressing rather than sexy dressing, but boys tend to see it as a "come on." Although changes in attitudes about sex may be inevitable, they create an atmosphere in which people have difficulty knowing how to interpret signals; bad feelings and sometimes tragedies result. Some surveys have found that more than half of college women said they had been pressured into unwanted sex, either by physical force or by psychological pressure. College men also report engaging in unwanted sex, mainly because they felt pressure from peers, or were afraid to be thought "unmasculine" (Christopher, 1988; Muehlenhard & Cook, 1988).

*Cultural Influences on Sexual Behavior*   There are cultures in which nearly every form of what Americans would consider sexual excess or deviance is accepted and may even be expected. Among the Gusii of southwestern Kenya, for example, hostility and humiliation are normal features of sexual activity. A Gusii man believes that he must overcome the woman's natural resistance and cause her some form of physical pain and humiliation (Davenport, 1977). In other cultures, sex is clearly associated with pleasure. In Mangaia, one of the Cook Islands of Polynesia, premarital intercourse is strongly encouraged for both sexes. Men are expected to express their virility by experiencing many successive orgasms. Even though sexuality is assumed to be stronger in men than in women, women are expected to be eager and active sex partners. Romantic love is not seen as a necessary part of a youthful heterosexual relationship. Affection is thought to develop out of satisfactory sexual relations; love is expected to grow as sexual appetite declines.

One of the major generalizations that emerges from studies of sex behavior in different cultures is that all societies regulate sexuality in some way. The nature of the rules varies from culture to culture, but apparently sex is so important to the survival of the species that all societies have developed regulatory mechanisms. In a classic survey of sexual attitudes and practices in different cultures, Clellan Ford and Frank Beach (1951) concluded that the American culture was one of the more restrictive ones. However, the changes that have taken place during the

years since they conducted their survey probably have made the United States one of the more permissive societies in terms of sexual attitudes and practices.

## Sensation Seeking

Climbing mountains, taking drugs, and trying new sexual experiences are all characteristic of people seeking sensations. This motive is part curiosity, part thrill-seeking, and part adventure. **Sensation seeking *refers to the need for varied, novel, and intense forms of stimulation and experience.*** Studies on this motive are trying to explain why human beings do things that sometimes conflict with the motive for personal survival.

*Low- and High-Sensation Seekers*   Not everyone finds rappelling off a mountain an exhilarating experience. People differ considerably in the extent to which the sensation-seeking motive drives their behavior. Marvin Zuckerman and his colleagues (Zuckerman, 1979) devised the **Sensation Seeking Scale,** *a test used to measure how important sensation seeking is in a person's life.* Some of the items on the scale are shown in table 8.1. The test measures four different aspects of the sensation-seeking motive: thrill and adventure seeking, experience seeking, disinhibition, and susceptibility to boredom. Questions in the first two categories try to determine how much the person needs risky adventures or novel experiences. Questions relating to disinhibition refer to an individual's motive to behave in an uninhibited way and to seek experiences that break or bend social rules. For example, one item states, "I often like to get high (drinking liquor or smoking marijuana)." The last group of questions tries to determine how easily the person is bored and how upset the person gets by boredom.

People who score high on this scale are quite different from those who score low. High scorers are more likely to be male and in their late teens. As people get older, the motive to seek sensations becomes less compelling. Not surprisingly, high-sensation seekers differ from low-sensation seekers in their behavior as well; high-sensation seekers tend to engage in riskier sports like parachuting and scuba diving, and they like the idea of traveling to exotic places. They are drawn to gambling, prefer higher odds, and make bigger bets. They are more likely to volunteer for psychology experiments, particularly those that promise a little excitement. For example, they volunteer more readily for experiments involving hypnosis, sensory deprivation, and drug-taking than for experiments that require subjects to learn lists of nonsense syllables. This finding is particularly unnerving to psychologists who seek volunteers for their research because it may mean that they are testing a biased sample.

---

**TABLE 8.1 A portion of the sensation seeking scale**

**Sensation Seeking Scale—Form I**

*Interest and Preference Test Form I*

*Directions:* Each of the items below contains two choices, A and B. Please indicate *on your answer sheet* which of the choices most describes *your likes* or the way *you feel.* In some cases you may find items in which both choices describe your likes or the way you feel. Please choose the one which better describes your likes or feelings. In some cases you may find items in which you do not like either choice. In these cases mark the choice you dislike *least.*

It is important you respond to *all items* with only *one choice,* A or B. We are interested only in *your likes or feelings,* not in how others feel about these things or how one is supposed to feel. There are no right or wrong answers as in other kinds of tests. Be frank and give your honest appraisal of yourself.

1. A. I like the tumult of sounds in a busy city.
   B. I prefer the peace and quiet of the country.
2. A. I prefer my meals at regular times.
   B. I like to eat when the mood strikes me.
3. A. I dislike the sensations one gets when flying.
   B. I enjoy many of the rides in amusement parks.
4. A. I would like a job that would require a lot of traveling.
   B. I would prefer a job in one location.
5. A. I do not find gambling worth the risk.
   B. I like to gamble for money.
6. A. I am invigorated by a brisk, cold day.
   B. I can't wait to get into the indoors on a cold day.
7. A. I like a lively party with a lot of people and noise.
   B. I prefer a quiet party where I can relax and converse with a few friends.
8. A. I find a certain pleasure in routine kinds of work.
   B. Although it is sometimes necessary, I usually dislike routine kinds of work.
9. A. I often wish I could be a mountain climber.
   B. I can't understand people who risk their necks climbing mountains.
10. A. I dislike all body odors.
    B. I like some of the earthy body smells.
11. A. I get bored seeing the same old faces.
    B. I like the comfortable familiarity of everyday friends.
12. A. Society should maximize the individual's freedom and opportunity for the "pursuit of happiness."
    B. Society should protect mankind from all extremes of hunger, fear and insecurity.

---

From *Sensation Seeking: Beyond the Optimal Level of Arousal* by Marvin Zuckerman, 1979. Copyright 1979 by Lawrence Erlbaum Associates, Inc. Reprinted by permission of the author.

*Why Seek Sensation?* It is not difficult to see why curiosity in an animal could be necessary for its survival. Acquiring information about the environment in which one lives is not an idle and worthless pastime; it is one that might easily be considered a primary motive. An animal's curiosity can help it to find out about hiding places, food sources, shelter, and the location of prey. Such information may become vital in the animal's future. Sensation seeking goes beyond mere curiosity; it is a search for novel, varied, and exciting experiences. The sensation-seeking motive is so strong in some humans that it sometimes conflicts with the motive to stay alive.

One way to understand the motive of sensation seeking is to use the opponent process theory of acquired motivation. For example, how can we explain why a person skydives? During the first free-fall, parachutists may experience terror: their eyes may bulge, their lips may retract, and they may even experience involuntary urination. After landing, the jumpers may look stunned and dazed for a few minutes, but then they may begin lively chatter with the other jumpers. After several jumps, the a-process of terror diminishes while the b-process of relief grows. Now the parachutists experience a thrill during the jump and extreme exhilaration afterwards. Some parachutists claim this "high" last as long as eight hours (Epstein, 1967; Solomon, 1980). The increase in strength of the opponent b-process is the key to the acquired motivation. It offers a good explanation for why a person might come to exhibit some rather dangerous acquired motives.

Another approach that may help us understand the sensation-seeking motive is to look at it in terms of the optimal level of arousal theory. This theory predicts that a person will not necessarily strive to reduce arousal by satisfying drives but will seek the optimum level of arousal. For high-sensation seekers, that level might be quite high.

A test of this hypothesis examined people's physiological responses to a novel stimulus (Neary & Zuckerman, 1976). Both high- and low-sensation seekers wore earphones while a tone was presented over and over for ten trials. On the eleventh trial, a different sound was presented to test the subjects' reactions to a novel auditory stimulus. During all the trials, the experimenters recorded the subjects' **galvanic skin response (GSR),** *a measure of activity in the autonomic nervous system. When the sympathetic division of the autonomic nervous system is activated by some stressor, one of the responses is increased sweating in the hands and feet. The GSR is a measure of changes in sweat gland secretion.*

The high-sensation seekers tended to show a large GSR the first time they heard the tone and also when they heard the novel tone in the eleventh trial. They reacted more strongly to novelty than did the low-sensation seekers; however, after hearing the first tone once, their autonomic arousal dropped down to about the same level as that of the low-sensation seekers. This study shows that the high-sensation seekers are more easily aroused by novelty but do not necessarily have a higher baseline level of arousal.

This finding presents a problem with respect to the optimum level of arousal theory. Perhaps the term "arousal" is too general, and the sensation seekers are not seeking an overall higher level. They seem instead to be seeking new sensations that are pleasurable, not annoying or irritating. Zuckerman's (1979) revised theory takes this into account. He proposes that high-sensation seekers have a more active and more efficient general reward system in their brains, made so partly by greater activity at norepinephrine synapses. As a result of the greater activity in the reward pathways, the person is peculiarly responsive and especially alert to novel stimulation. Zuckerman supposes that whether a person is high or low on the sensation-seeking motive depends to a considerable extent on such biological factors, some of which may have a genetic component.

## The Need for Achievement

When John Opel began doing well in business, he did very well. In 1981, he became the chief executive officer of IBM. When a hometown reporter asked Opel's father what he thought of John's success, he replied, "I always knew Johnny was a good boy" (Stacks, 1983).

The **need for achievement** or **n Ach** *involves the desire to independently master objects, ideas, and other people and to increase one's self-esteem through the exercise of one's talent.* Opel's father equated John's remarkable achievements in the business world with being "good." Other cultures might not agree with the career path he labeled this way.

Research on the need for achievement has focused on many different aspects of the motive. Early research investigated and measured individual differences in both the strength and the characteristics of the motive.

*Measuring n Ach*    The Thematic Apperception Test (TAT), discussed earlier, is one of the more common tests used to measure motivation, including the need for achievement (Murray, 1938). Below is a story about a

picture showing a boy with a vague operation scene in the background. The story was scored high in n Ach. Notice that it contains imagery relating to achievement, especially long-term involvements.

> The boy is thinking about a career as a doctor. He sees himself as a great surgeon performing an operation. He has been doing minor first aid work on his injured dog, and discovers he is suited for this profession and sets it as an ultimate goal in life at this moment. He has not weighed the pros and cons of his own ability and has let his goal blind him of his own inability. An adjustment which will injure him will have to be made. (McClelland, Atkinson, Clark, & Lowell, 1953)

In contrast, the following is a story scored low in n Ach because it contains little achievement-oriented imagery:

> Young fellow is showing anxiety toward impending operation.
>    Some malady has been diagnosed.
>    The doctor has prescribed an operation to remove the source of illness and the boy wonders about the advisability of such a plan.
>    The operation will be performed and successfully. (McClelland et al., 1953)

*High and Low n Ach*    People who score high in n Ach on the TAT and other tests behave differently compared to those who score low. High n Ach scorers are more likely to become entrepreneurs or to do well in business. They usually prefer to work with capable people who can help them succeed. They focus on the future and make long-range plans to achieve their goals (Raynor, 1982).

The choice of tasks in an experimental situation is also related to a person's n Ach score. In a well-known experimental game, subjects are asked to toss rings at a vertical post for money (Atkinson & Litwin, 1960). They can choose how far they wish to stand from the post, and their choice affects the monetary payoffs for each successful toss. If they stand very close to the post, their chance for success is very high, but the payoff is low. If they stand far away, the chance for success is very low, but the reward is much greater. High n Ach people tend to choose an intermediate spot; people lower in n Ach tend to choose locations either close to the post or very far away. In one study (Hamilton, 1974), the high n Ach subjects chose distances that made their likelihood for success about 4 out of 10. Low and moderate n Ach subjects chose distances that resulted in success probabilities that were either very high or very low.

# APPLYING PSYCHOLOGY

## Battle Fatigue

A very extreme form of emotional reaction sometimes occurs in individuals involved in combat, usually after they have just completed a difficult mission. The military calls this reaction "battle fatigue." Initial symptoms include emotionality, irritability, sleep disturbances, and exaggerated startle responses. In some cases, soldiers show severe tremors, muteness, hallucinations, hysterical blindness, stupor, and uncontrollable panic (Chermol, 1983).

The causes of battle fatigue are not well understood, although most agree it is the inevitable result of continual combat rather than isolated cases of "nerves" in a few soldiers with previous personality problems. Statistics on the incidence of the problem show some interesting trends that indicate potential causes. For example, during World War II, armored divisions had the highest incidence of battle fatigue, and air crews had the lowest incidence. The air crews, however, sustained higher battle casualty rates. Soldiers in armored divisions were probably more vulnerable to battle fatigue for a number of reasons, including their long confinements inside tanks, their almost continual mobility, and their inability to take any personal action against threats in hazardous situations. Soldiers in armored divisions may develop greater feelings of helplessness than do air crews, thus increasing the risk of battle fatigue.

The air crews may have had fewer cases of battle fatigue for other reasons as well. They had more regular sleeping schedules, better nutrition, and more opportunities for recreation and rest between missions. Even though their casualty rates were higher, they felt themselves to be members of an elite group and had high morale and esprit de corps. The importance of morale is also demonstrated by the fact that volunteer infantry units, such as the paratroopers, had lower battle fatigue rates than nonvolunteer units, even though the former may have had higher casualty rates.

The treatment for battle fatigue varies, though the military generally tries to return the victim to his or her unit as quickly as possible. Those in the infantry who suffer battle fatigue, for example, might be treated right at the brigade clearing station. In severe cases, the victim might be returned to the division rear and treated by mental-health officers or trained NCOs. About eighty or ninety percent of these people can be returned to their units within a few days. Those who do not recover may be evacuated to corps-level medical facilities, but this option is not a desirable one. At least some of these patients exhibit long-term psychological problems partly *because* their symptoms caused them to be removed from combat. They apparently feel overwhelming guilt at having deserted their unit, and they try to justify their removal by unconsciously perpetuating their symptoms. Studies of motivation in combat usually point strongly to the importance of group loyalty in combat. It is not unusual for soldiers wounded in battle to return to their unit before they have recovered so they won't "let their buddies down."

Preventing battle fatigue is an issue of great concern to the military. Some recommended countermeasures include the following (Chermol, 1983):

1. Ensure that individuals involved in combat operations get adequate sleep.

2. Train soldiers to function in an NBC (nuclear, biological, chemical) warfare environment. Lack of knowledge about and confidence in safety equipment can be a major contributor to stress during combat.

3. Provide rigorous physical training programs during peacetime; physically fit soldiers tolerate stress better.

4. Provide accurate and timely information to troops; rumors and dishonesty create more stress.

5. Establish the "buddy system" to help build cohesion; have squad members observe one another for signs of battle fatigue.

Studies like the ones using the ring-toss game suggest that people high in n Ach are not gamblers. They focus their attention on tasks that are challenging but that allow a fair chance of success based on the subject's abilities. They seem to be driven more by a motive to seek success rather than one to avoid failure. They are more persistent on difficult tasks (Feather, 1962).

As research on achievement motivation progressed, it became clear that the motive was a very dynamic one.

People high in n Ach behave differently in different situations, and low n Ach people sometimes show remarkable needs for achievement. The interaction between the situation and the personality of the person in determining how much achievement motivation might be demonstrated has received a great deal of attention. According to earlier theorists (McClelland et al., 1953; Atkinson & Feather, 1966) the expression of the achievement motive in any particular situation depends on several factors, including (1) the person's expectation of success in the situation, (2) the value the individual places on the reward being offered, and (3) the individual's perception of how instrumental his or her own behavior will be in bringing about success. (You may notice that there is a certain similarity between these three factors and the concepts of valence and expectancy.)

The theory is not without critics. Many scientists question the reliability of the TAT testing method. The tests may be good at assessing n Ach in white American middle-class males, but they seem to be much less useful for other groups, such as women and blacks. One study, for example, found that women whose stories about pictures of men were scored high in n Ach and whose stories about pictures of women were scored low in n Ach tended to be underachievers (Lesser, Krawitz, & Packard, 1963). Also, critics argue that achievement-motivation

theory has focused too heavily on personality and not enough on the situation (Maehr & Nicholls, 1980).

The need to achieve is a complex motive and researchers are trying to do more than simply list the many differences between people with high and low n Ach. They are dissecting it both psychologically and culturally, asking why people have a high need to achieve (Heyman & Dweck, 1992; Dweck, 1992). Do they want to show off their success to others? Do they enjoy learning and mastering new challenges for the sheer enjoyment of it? Are they insecure and trying to prove something? If you have a high need to achieve, the answers to these questions are important. If your need derives from a desire for recognition, failure would be frustrating and embarrassing. But if you're intrigued by mastery of a task, failure would be viewed as valuable feedback.

Culturally, our definition of achievement motivation and much of the research that has been done on the topic seems to suggest a bias toward an American version of

▶ **GUIDED REVIEW** *Learning Objectives 4, 5, 6, and 7*

1. The motivation to eat is controlled by multiple biological and psychological factors. Signals from the stomach signal both hunger and satiety, and a hormone from the digestive tract, called _____ , also signals satiety. The liver contains _____ , which monitor glucose levels.

2. Lesions of the _____ produce overeating and obesity; lesions in the nearby _____ cause an animal to stop eating altogether. These brain areas are involved in hunger and satiety, but they cannot be called "feeding" or "satiety centers." Damage to these brain areas may interfere with food intake by damaging the brain's reward system.

3. Obesity has multiple causes, one of which may be stress. Another cause may be an overreliance on _____ _____ to trigger eating, such as the time of day, rather than internal cues, such as stomach contractions. Once a person becomes obese, it is very difficult for that person to lose weight because the body's weight _____ is set at a higher level.

4. The human sex drive is influenced by a combination of biological, psychological, and cultural factors. In lower animals, biological factors are most important, especially the ovarian hormones _____ and _____ in females and the testicular hormones called _____ in the male.

5. A minimum amount of male sex hormone is required for normal sexual behavior in men. Loss of the _____ will result in the loss of sex drive and sex behavior. However, day-to-day fluctuations in the level

of circulating _____ are not related to changes in sex drive or sex behavior.

6. In women, changes in the level of _____ hormones do not appreciably affect sex drive or sex behavior. Sex drive in women is affected by _____ , probably from the woman's adrenal gland.

7. One of the main psychological influences on sex behavior involves the acquisition of _____ , the expectations and behaviors an individual's culture believed to be appropriate for each sex.

8. _____ refers to a motive in which a person seeks novel, varied, and intense forms of stimulation and experience. Low- and high-sensation seekers score very differently on the _____ .

9. Attempts to explain the sensation-seeking motive include the _____ theory of motivation and the _____ theory. Another hypothesis suggests that the motive may be related to the activity of the _____ in the brain.

10. The need to achieve (n Ach) is sometimes measured by the _____ . People who score _____ on n Ach tend to be persistent and seek challenges of intermediate difficulty in which their chance of success is fair and in which their own behavior is instrumental in obtaining the reward.

*ANSWERS*

*1. CCK, glucoreceptors 2. ventromedial hypothalamus, lateral hypothalamus 3. external cues, setpoint 4. estrogen, progesterone, androgens 5. testes, testosterone 6. ovarian, androgens 7. sex roles 8. Sensation seeking, Sensation Seeking Scale 9. opponent process, optimum level of arousal, reward system 10. Thematic Apperception Test, high*

| | |
|---|---|
| abase | affectation |
| abash | affection |
| abhor | affinity |
| abysmal | afflict |
| acclaim | affright |
| accursed | affront |
| acerbity | afficionado |
| acquisitive | afoul |
| acrid | afraid |
| admire | agape |
| admonish | aggravate |
| adorable | aggress |
| adulate | aggrieve |
| adulterate | aghast |
| adventurer | agitate |
| adversary | agreeable |
| adversity | alack |
| aesthetic | alacrity |
| afeared | alarm |
| affect | alert |

**Figure 8.5**  *A partial list of words with emotional overtones*

"achievement." To achieve in America means to take risks, assume challenges, set reachable goals, work hard, persist, delay gratification, and eventually succeed. People in other cultures may also have needs for achievement but they may be expressed differently and be affected by different environmental influences. A German manager of a large plantation in Thailand once gave his Thai workers a bonus equal to one day's pay to reward them for their successful harvest and encourage them to work even harder for the next phase. They were all delighted about the bonus but to his amazement, they all took the next day off. For them, economic gain was less important than spending time with their families.

# EMOTIONS

Emotions may be the most potent motivators of all. We get into fights because we are angry, risk our lives because of love, and stop eating because of grief. Emotions can also be the goal of motivated behavior. We might carefully plan a vacation to experience happiness and relaxation or go to a horror movie to experience fear. Avoiding emotions, particularly very severe and unpleasant ones, might also be a goal. According to the Food and Drug Administration, Americans take about five billion tranquilizers every year in an attempt to avoid anxiety, depression, or

pain. And the United States military took special steps during the Korean and Vietnam Wars to help people avoid the severe emotional reaction called battle fatigue (see Applying Psychology box: Battle Fatigue).

Finally, emotions may just accompany motivated behavior. Pleasure, for example, is not just a goal of sexual arousal. It accompanies it. The relationship between motivation and emotion is a very complex one that is not well understood. Nevertheless, no one would deny that emotions are extremely important to human beings.

## Describing Emotions

**Emotion** *is a complex reaction with two main components. One component involves a series of physiological changes; the other involves a subjective experience or "feeling," that is influenced by cognitive, social, and cultural factors.*

The dictionary lists literally thousands of words that have some emotional content (figure 8.5). In different languages, there are words to describe complex emotions that don't have any counterpart in English. For example, the Germans use the word "Schadenfreude" to refer to the tendency to feel happy when someone else suffers a misfortune. But are there thousands of different emotions? Many psychologists argue that there are only a few primary emotions, perhaps six to twelve. Silvan Tomkins (1981a), for example, maintains that there are nine primary emotions: interest, enjoyment, surprise, fear, anger, distress, shame, contempt, and disgust. Each of these emotions has its own underlying biological accompaniments in the form of facial expression, voice patterns, muscular changes, and brain activity.

Other psychologists see human emotions not as independent categories but as states that are more or less related to one another. Figure 8.6 shows a "circle of emotions" that depicts how different emotions are related. States opposite from one another on the wheel are opposite emotions. Happy, for example, is the opposite of miserable but is very closely related to delighted, pleased, and glad (Russell, 1980). This circle was designed by asking subjects to sort twenty-eight emotion-laden words into groups of four, seven, ten, and thirteen, based on similarity.

The two most important dimensions on which emotions seem to be categorized are the pleasantness of the emotion and the intensity of the arousal. These two dimensions are represented by the axes in figure 8.6. Alarmed and bored, for instance, have about the same degree of moderate unpleasantness, but they are very different in arousal.

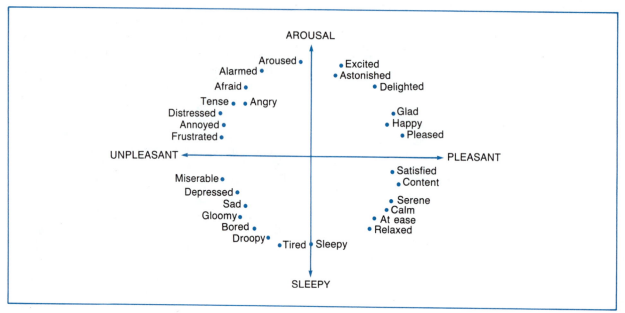

**Figure 8.6**    *A circle of emotions*

Serene and miserable are about equal in their arousal but are very different along the pleasantness dimension.

## Expressing Emotions

An emotion is not just a private event; it is a means of communication (Oatley & Jenkins, 1992). Emotions are expressed in many ways: by what we say and how we say it, by our gestures and postures, by our facial expressions and by our body movements. The facial expression of many primary emotions is remarkably similar in people from different cultures (figure 8.7). All people smile when they are happy and frown when they are sad. People from widely different cultures usually have no trouble identifying the emotions expressed in photographs. Even people from remote tribes in New Guinea, who have never had an opportunity to see the facial expressions of westerners in context by watching movies, are able to identify the basic expressions of Westerners. It is not just the smile that is similar in many peoples; contempt, with downcast gaze, arched eyebrow, and tilted head, appears to be recognizable across cultures (Izard & Haynes, 1988; Ekman & Friesen, 1975, 1986, 1988).

Humans appear to be able to make distinctions between facial expressions by five months of age (Schwartz, Izard, & Ansul, 1985), and perhaps even earlier. One study found that ten-week-old babies responded differently to their mothers' expressions of happiness, sadness, and anger (Havliland & Lelwica, 1987). By one-year-old, it is clear that infants can interpret their parents' facial expressions quite well and take cues from them. For example, on the visual cliff apparatus, discussed in chapter 4, seventy-four percent of babies crossed when their mothers showed a happy expression, but none did when she looked fearful (Sorce et al., 1985).

Adults do quite well at identifying the emotional expressions of infants, especially for expressions of joy, interest, distress, and surprise (Emde, 1985). All this evidence supports the view that many human facial expressions of emotion are universal and the abilities to display and interpret them begin quite early in life. This adds weight to the hypothesis that only a few primary emotions exist, and that these emotions have some biological basis.

Emotions are also communicated especially well through nonverbal aspects of speech. Arousal is associated with increases in pitch, loudness, and rate of speech, whereas anger appears to be communicated by even speech with occasional sharp increases in pitch and loudness. These cues are recognizable and are used by people of different cultures (Trick, 1985).

The survival value of the ability to accurately communicate and interpret basic emotions across cultures with

**Figure 8.7** *The facial expressions of many emotions are similar and can be easily identified in different people.*

different languages is obvious. It would be very helpful to be able to identify a friendly stranger from a hostile one, and the universality of the way these two emotions are expressed by the face makes it possible. It is possible that the need for this basic form of cross-cultural communication was one of the reasons that facial expressions evolved in the first place, and why at least some of them became standardized in the human species.

*Managing Emotional Expression*    Emotional expression, however, is not simply a genetically controlled event that is common to all humans, and over which we have no control. We all are able to manage our emotional expressions to some extent. Cognitive, social, and cultural factors play important roles in determining how we express our emotions.

In managing our emotional expressions, we follow "display rules" as best we can, and as we learn them within our culture. Though you aren't taught this as a subject in school, you have learned a great deal about "emotional etiquette" and what is appropriate to display in various situations within your culture. For example, in Western cultures, a visible display of positive emotion over a victory is not considered good form. Athletes learn that being a "good sport" means smiling when you lose, and being modest when you win. The winners are expected to conceal joy and happiness about their triumphs to avoid making the losers feel bad.

An intriguing study demonstrated how people manage their emotions in a winning situation, at least when the losers are there to watch. Subjects were asked to work on some computer-generated problems that were quite difficult, either alone or with two other people. The other two people were not actually other subjects, but were confederates who knew the purpose of the study and were trained to argue for answers other than what the subject chose, regardless of what that was. After each problem, the subject entered his or her own answer into the computer and a message appeared to provide feedback. Regardless of whether or not the subject answered correctly, the message was very rewarding. One message, for example, said "Right! Fewer than 10% of college students typically answer this question correctly." Video cameras recorded the subjects' facial expressions and gestures during the experiment and judges rated the tapes afterward for intensity of emotional expression, amount of smiling, number of "victory gestures," and other indicators of emotion.

Everyone found the experiment very believable, and they all showed positive emotional expressions when they were told they answered problems correctly. But the expressions were considerably stronger when subjects thought they were alone compared to when the other people were present. As expected, the subjects were following the display rules of the culture for this circumstance: winners should be modest in front of losers (Friedman & Miller-Herringer, 1991).

Interestingly, there were marked individual differences in the ability to manage emotional expression in this experiment. Men were less able to control their expressiveness in public than women, but it seemed as though some people, male or female, appear to wear their hearts on their sleeves, despite their attempts to follow the display rules for the situation. Others can more effectively conceal whatever emotion they are feeling.

*Measuring Emotional Expression*    Facial expressions are a reasonably reliable indicator of emotion so it is not surprising to find that different facial muscles are used in each of the emotions. Paul Ekman and his colleagues developed a scoring system to analyze facial muscular actions that produce expressions, focusing on the muscles around the mouth and the eyes. For example, they have identified specific muscular movements that produce a genuine smile produced in happiness and on the basis of specific muscle changes have been able to distinguish that smile from one that is really masking negative emotions, or one that is produced while lying (Ekman and Friesen, 1982; Ekman et al., 1991).

Since different emotions produce such remarkably different feelings, one might suppose that the physiological events that underlie each one could be distinguished. In fact, it is very hard to tell whether a person is feeling sad, angry, happy, or disgusted by recording physiological events such as heart rate, blood pressure, pupil dilation, or sweat gland responses. Although changes in these variables are usually associated with emotions, the pattern of responses doesn't seem to bear any clear relationship to specific emotional states.

The anatomical arrangement of the sympathetic nervous system explains why the physiological changes during an emotion are so global. A single signal from the brain sends messages through the sympathetic division to all the organs and glands. The signal is designed to prepare the body for an emergency. It does not single out individual organs or glands.

Even though a person's different emotions may be accompanied by similar physiological changes, individual differences show up in the global patterns. In some early work on emotions, subjects were exposed to several different events that produced arousal, such as a painful stimulus, some mental arithmetic, and a word fluency test (Lacey, 1959). The researchers measured several physiological variables during the session, such as sweat gland activity on the palms, heart rate, and blood pressure. For each person, all the tasks that produced arousal tended to produce the same kind of pattern. For example, one person showed large changes in sweat gland activity but little change in heart rate. Another showed large blood pressure changes, but no sweat gland activity. Individuals seemed to react in their own way to all the arousal-producing stimuli in this experiment; also, some react more strongly overall, some more weakly.

A recent suggestion is that each of the physiological systems that are active in emotional response, including facial expressiveness, has its own operating characteristics in each of us. Some of us have a cardiovascular system with high gain: heart rate rises rapidly during emotion. Others have mostly calm systems that react slowly but take longer to recover (Cacioppo et al., 1992).

The finding that people seem to have their own individual emotional "fingerprint" may help us understand why people react differently to long-term stress. Disorders that are aggravated or caused by stress can be quite varied and can affect most physiological systems. Perhaps someone whose usual emotional reaction features highly variable heart rate will be the one whose circulatory system suffers the most, and who ultimately gets a cardiovascular disorder.

The fact that different emotional states, such as fear, anger, or shame, are not clearly associated with particular physiological patterns is one of the main reasons scientists are concerned about polygraphy, the technique that is supposed to determine whether a person is deceitful by observing physiological reactions to interrogation. The Close Up on Research box: Detecting Deceit explores this issue in more detail.

## Theories of Emotion

Theories of emotion have offered a range of ideas to frame our thinking about why we feel happy, sad, afraid, or disgusted. We know, intuitively and through many experiments, that emotion is a complex phenomenon related to events taking place in our bodies and the thoughts going on in our heads. An early question was, "Which comes first?" If you ask the proverbial man on the street why he is crying, he might say, "My dog died," indicating that this person believes that emotions start in the head—with an appraisal of a situation that then triggers a physiological reaction. Yet an early theory of emotion questioned this intuitively appealing sequence of events. This theory was proposed in 1890 by William James, the pioneering American psychologist, and at about the same

# CLOSE UP ON RESEARCH
## Detecting Deceit

Is there any way to tell whether a person is lying? Much research has been devoted to this question, partly because of its importance in criminal investigations. Most people know about the polygraph test, for example, which is one of the methods police use to try to distinguish between truthful and deceptive individuals.

The polygraph technique attempts to use the physiological measures of heart rate, blood pressure, sweat gland activity, and respiration to detect deception. One kind of polygraph session begins with a lengthy interview (Reid & Inbau, 1977). The polygrapher asks many questions, trying to learn something about the subject's background, attitudes, and personality. Then the examiner reviews the questions that will be asked during the actual test. Most examiners use three types of questions: irrelevant questions that have nothing to do with the crime, relevant questions that pertain directly to the crime, and control questions designed to stimulate the innocent person to tell a lie. The examiner might ask, "Other than what you have told me, have you ever stolen anything?" This polygraph technique relies on the assumption that most people will not be able to recall everything they have ever stolen or will not have told the examiner about every single theft. There are many small thefts that people might forget about—taking money from their mothers' purses, "borrowing" pens from the office, or remaining silent when a cashier hands back too much change.

During the test, the examiner will observe the responses, especially to the relevant and control questions. Presumably, innocent subjects will show greater responses to control questions; deceptive subjects will respond more to relevant questions.

Many psychologists have strongly criticized the traditional polygraph technique (Bashore & Rapp, 1993). Studies to assess its accuracy have had very mixed results, but most have found that examiners differ considerably in their judgments when they rely solely on the chart paper. Both in the laboratory and in the field, there are many "false hits" where innocent people are declared guilty. In the real world, it is often like a game of cat and mouse between the examiner and the subject (Kleinmuntz & Szucko, 1984b). The technique relies on very shaky assumptions, one of which suggests that an innocent person will be more nervous while telling a small white lie than while telling an extremely consequential truth. Another assumption is that lying is a simple response that results in a certain pattern of physiological changes. As discussed in the text, specific emotions do not generate specific physiological profiles in all people.

Another approach to detecting deception relies on facial expressions which are better indicators of emotional feeling than are internal physiological changes (Ekman et al., 1991). In one study, student nurses were videotaped while they watched short films, the last of which contained unpleasant scenes of amputations and burns. The nurses were interviewed after each film and told to try as best they could to conceal their negative feelings after the third film, since they would need to be able to control their outward display of emotions throughout their careers. Raters scored the videotapes of the nurses for facial expression, vocal responses, and hand and body movements. They also guessed whether each nurse was telling the truth about her feelings for each film.

Women who were trying to conceal their true feelings had different behavior patterns in several respects. The muscles they used to generate a smile were slightly different, and the pitch of their voice was higher. Also, they tended to use slightly fewer hand and body movements. Overall, the raters had a very good "hit rate" in guessing truth or deception in this setting (86.4 percent).

Behavior patterns that are displayed during deceit are likely to be affected by culture. A study in Amsterdam illustrates this (Vrij & Winkel, 1991). Two cultural groups were asked to participate in a study to assess the ability of police officers to detect lying about a theft. One group included whites with Dutch ancestry, and the other group had a Surinam background. Half of each cultural group was given a pair of headphones to hide in their pockets. No one stole any headphones, of course, but the subjects that were told to lie about having them in their pockets were also told to pretend that they had shoplifted them.

The deceptive Dutch and Surinam subjects displayed rather different behaviors compared to the truthful ones. They vocalized more "ahs," their speech was faster, and they tended to hold their hands and arms more rigidly. Regardless of whether they were truthful or deceptive, the behavior patterns of the Dutch and Surinam subjects showed several differences. The Surinam subjects looked at the interviewer less frequently, smiled and laughed more, spoke more slowly, and made higher pitched exclamatory remarks. They also were livelier in the sense that they moved their hands and bodies more often.

One conclusion from this research is that in a cross-cultural interaction, people can make many mistakes about deception. The Surinam subjects' normal emotional expression included several behaviors that white subjects might associate with their notions of lying, such as averted gaze and high pitched voice. Although people are good at judging the basic emotions across cultures from facial expressions and other nonverbal cues, they can easily be misled when they try to judge something as complex as guilt, shame, or an attempt to deceive. The complexity of emotions, and its interaction with cognition and culture, makes any attempt to detect deceit fraught with error.

time by Carl Lange, a Danish psychologist. They suggested that the physiological events come first, and only later do we interpret those events as a particular emotion and assign a name to it.

*The James-Lange Theory*    This theory proposes that the emotional state we feel is the result of the physiological changes occurring in the viscera and muscles. For instance, people feel afraid because their hearts are racing; their hearts do not race because they are afraid. Thus, the **James-Lange theory** *suggests that the physiological changes in the body come before the subjective experience of emotion; feedback from the viscera and muscles then result in the emotion.*

Studies of patients with spinal-cord damage have generally supported the James-Lange theory. These patients have no feedback from their muscles or viscera below the injury, and many of them say that their feelings of emotion changed considerably after the injury. They say that their emotions have become rather "cold" and "mental."

> Seems I get thinking mad, not shaking mad, and that's a lot different.

> I say I am afraid, like when I'm going into a real stiff exam at school, but I don't really feel afraid, not all tense and shaky, with that hollow feeling in my stomach, like I used to.

Thus, people who get no messages from their bodies and who don't know when their heart is racing or their stomach is tightening up, have qualitatively different emotional experiences. This suggests that bodily cues are very important in judging the intensity and possibly even the nature of the emotion. A problem with this theory is that scientists have not been able to establish specific physiological patterns associated with each emotion. As we saw earlier, the physiological events are rather global, though they differ from one person to the next. If your heart races when you are happy *or* frightened, how would you know the difference?

More recently, an interesting twist has been added to the original James-Lange theory. **The facial feedback hypothesis** *proposes that feedback from the facial muscles and the viscera contribute to the experience of emotion.* In his book *The Expression of Emotion in Man and Animals*, Darwin first pointed out how important facial expressions are. He suggested that outwardly expressing emotion in the face intensifies the emotion. The

appeal of this hypothesis is that facial expressions of emotion, unlike visceral changes, are very rapid and they are different for each emotional experience.

In one study designed to test the role of facial feedback, subjects watched six videotaped scenes: two pleasant comedy skits, two unpleasant scenes of traffic accidents and a ritual suicide, and two neutral sequences about the use of computers in the apple harvest. Some subjects were told to pose the appropriate facial expression for each scene so that judges observing their faces could tell what scene they were watching. Other subjects were told to suppress their facial expressions so that judges would not be able to tell which scene they were watching. A third group was given no instructions (Zuckerman, Klorman, Larrance, & Spiegel, 1981). During the scenes, the experimenters recorded heart rate, GSR, and blood pressure. Afterwards, the subjects filled out questionnaires asking about their actual emotions during the scenes.

The subjects who exaggerated their facial expressions showed the largest changes in autonomic activity, whereas those who suppressed their facial expressions showed the smallest autonomic reactions. Although the results appear to provide evidence for the role of facial feedback in emotion, they are controversial (Tomkins, 1981a; Buck, 1984; Tourangeau & Ellsworth, 1979). Critics wonder whether subjects who voluntarily control their facial expressions in accordance with the experimenter's directions can really provide valid evidence about whether feedback from natural expressions can affect the experience of emotion. It may be that the easiest way to change your natural facial expression is to use some emotion-management technique that affects all physiological responding. We saw earlier that many people do a fairly good job of controlling their facial expressions when the cultural display rules require it.

*Emotions and the Brain*    Walter B. Cannon objected to the James-Lange theory, pointing out the fact that visceral changes are similar in many states of arousal, and also that emotions occur too fast for us to patiently wait to observe and then interpret the physiological events. Instead, he argued for the important role played by the lower brain areas in mediating emotional experience. **Cannon's theory of emotions** *suggested that emotion originates in lower brain areas, whose circuits then activate both the cortex and the viscera.* Findings from people who are injected with substances that create sympathetic activation support Cannon's hypothesis. Most of the time, when a drug causes a person's heart to race they simply say, "My heart is racing," not "I feel angry."

The brain's role in motivation and emotion is certainly a central one. As we saw earlier, studies on electrical stimulation of the brain show that pathways exist that mediate reward, presumably a pleasurable state. Much of what we know about brain activity and human emotions comes from studies of patients with either behavioral disorders that affect emotions, or brain damage.

For example, people with mood swings who move back and forth between extreme mania and depression over a period of weeks or months, sometimes show patterns of activity in particular neurotransmitters that fluctuate with their swings in mood. This suggests that changes in certain brain chemicals may be affecting their emotional behavior, but the evidence is still circumstantial; it is not at all clear why their neurotransmitter activity might be rising and falling (Schildkraut, 1978; Maas, 1989; Conte, Vita, and Sacchetti, 1988). Nevertheless, given what is known about the role of certain neurotransmitters in reward systems, and the effects of mood-altering drugs on emotions, the likelihood of links between brain chemistry and emotional behavior is high.

Studies of brain damaged patients have not identified any particular "brain centers" that are responsible for emotions such as anger, shame, happiness, or fear, although areas of the limbic system are likely to be involved. As we mentioned in chapter 1, damage to some parts of the limbic system in animals can result in high levels of aggression, while damage in other parts might eliminate behavior normally associated with fear.

In humans, damage on the left or right side of the brain has different effects on emotion, indicating that the processing of emotion may be asymmetric. People with damage in the left hemisphere often show hostility, sadness, and depression. But if the damage is on the right, the patients are often strangely calm about their condition, and continue to make plans that fail to take account of their condition. They also show less emotional expression in their faces (Blonder et al., 1993). The right side of the brain may play a special role in processing emotions (Davidson, 1984; Tucker, 1989).

*Emotion and Cognition*     Neither the James-Lange theory nor Cannon's theory give much attention to cognition. Another theory of emotions proposed in the 1960s, sometimes called the **cognitive-physiological theory of emotions,** *emphasized the interaction between a person's thoughts and his or her physiological arousal* (Schachter & Singer, 1962; Lazarus, 1984). *This theory suggested that whenever people are emotionally aroused, they decide which emotion they are feeling by cognitively evaluating and appraising situational cues.*

Suppose you are walking down a dark alley and a mugger appears from the shadows, brandishing a handgun. Your sympathetic nervous system will be activated. You will cognitively appraise the situation, noting the gun, the dark alley, the mugger's snarl, and feel fear, rather than joy, sadness, or disgust.

In an early experiment, subjects were given injections of epinephrine, a drug that mimics sympathetic activation. Some subjects were told about the drug's effects; others were either misinformed or given no information. Then all subjects were placed into one of two situations: an anger-producing one or a euphoria-producing one. In the "anger" situation, subjects were supposed to fill out a very insulting questionnaire. One item, for example, asked "With how many men (other than your father) has your mother had extramarital relationships? 4 and under——; 5-9——; 10 and over——." The situation that was supposed to encourage euphoria included a confederate who laughed a lot, flew paper airplanes, and sometimes asked the subjects to join in the fun.

The subjects who were either misinformed or not informed about epinephrine's effects were more likely to join in if they were placed in the "euphoria" situation or to feel angry if they were filling out the questionnaire. These people did not expect to feel emotionally aroused, and when they did, they appraised their emotion in terms of the situation in which they were placed. In contrast, those who knew about the side effects of epinephrine already had a cognitive "excuse" for their bodies' reactions. They did not need to attribute their sympathetic activation to the situation.

Although this study was criticized on many grounds, and some labs have failed to replicate it, it did call attention to the relationship between emotions and cognitions. For example, college students were divided into two groups and given harmless placebos. One group was told to expect that the pill would make them yawn and make their eyes tired; the other was told the pill would produce heart rate increases, flushed face, and other symptoms of sympathetic activation. Then all the subjects were tempted to cheat on a test. The subjects who thought

| Pleasantness | How enjoyable is the experience? How pleasant or unpleasant? |
|---|---|
| Attention | Are you devoting all your attention to the event? Are you trying to think about something else? |
| Certainty | Are you certain how the event is going to turn out? Do you understand what is happening during the event? |
| Coping ability | Can you cope with the event? |
| Control | Do you have control over this situation? Is someone else in control of it? |
| Responsibility | Are you responsible for causing what is happening? Is someone else responsible? |
| Goal/need conduciveness | How important are the events that are going on to you? Are there obstacles standing between you and what you want in this situation? |
| Legitimacy | Do you think that what is happening in this event is fair? |
| Norm/self-compatibility | What do you think are the appropriate feelings in this situation? What would others think is the appropriate emotion? |
| Anticipated effort | How much effort do you need to cope with the situation? |

**Figure 8.8**  *Dimensions of cognitive appraisal*

the pill was causing their high arousal levels were more likely to cheat than were those who were expecting only tired eyes. The people all felt sympathetic arousal; one group had a "logical" explanation for it (the pill) and therefore did not interpret the feeling as guilt. Perhaps it was easier for them to cheat because they interpreted their arousal as a drug side effect rather than as guilt. The other group cognitively appraised their arousal as guilt and were thus inhibited from cheating (Dienstbier & Munter, 1971). Cognitions and emotions are undoubtedly connected in complex ways, and these studies show some intriguing ways in which they interact.

If we are appraising situations, what dimensions do we use to evaluate them? What characteristics of the situation are critical in helping us evaluate it for an emotional response? Several psychologists have explored this issue, suggesting that people tend to use certain yardsticks to cognitively evaluate situations (figure 8.8) (Smith and Ellsworth, 1985; Scherer, 1984). For example, we tend to use some measure of our ability to cope with a situation to help evaluate it. If we think we're up against something that's too much for us to deal with, we're more likely to experience fright. Another dimension has to do with our feeling of responsibility for a particular situation. If we feel responsible, we're more likely to feel intense emotion compared to situations in which someone else was responsible.

*Emotions and Culture*    A twenty-seven-year-old assistant manager in a medium-sized advertising company was having trouble getting up on time and was frequently late for work. His coworkers didn't say anything most of the time, but occasionally they would subtly mention that a client was trying to reach him or the phone on his desk was ringing. One morning he came to work late, again, and over eighty of his fellow workers, including the CEO, were waiting in a large group by the door. Everyone bowed very low and the CEO made a short speech: "We are very sorry for the inconvenience our hours of operation make to you. We understand how difficult they are and regret all of the trouble they cause you." The man turned bright red, mumbled his apologies, and was never late again.

The assistant manager felt intense shame and no doubt the CEO knew he would. The CEO quite correctly predicted that the emotion of shame, and the assistant manager's aversion to it, would be a very potent method of getting him to come to work on time. This true story took place in Japan; in that culture, inconveniencing others is viewed very negatively. In America, the CEO might have threatened to dock the assistant manager's pay or fire him. But the CEO probably wouldn't have thought to trigger shame in quite this way.

The emphasis on the role of cognitions leads us naturally into a discussion of how culture interacts with our emotions. We've seen that people tend to express the basic emotions in quite similar ways, so that we all can understand a smile or frown, and people around the world agree on the meaning of a core group of facial expressions. But culture plays a key role in moderating our expression of emotion, and in helping us cognitively appraise situations in appropriate ways.

Our cultures teach us display rules that tell us when, where, and how much we should show emotions. For example, blacks display emotion with more liveliness than whites, showing more changes in facial expression, voice pitch, and body movements. Within America, the display rules for women appear to be somewhat different from those for men. Women generally display more emotional expression, and smile more than men.

Americans, in general, are known around the world as "smilers." Germans, in contrast, are taught to display a more stoic look. It's not surprising that the differences in our display rules can lead to problems in communication across cultures. Americans are likely to think that Germans are aloof and unfriendly. Whites may think the emotional expressiveness of blacks is inappropriate.

We saw some startling cultural contrasts in display rules during the opening parade ceremonies of the 1988 Olympic games held in Seoul. Wearing cowboy hats and costumes, the American athletes haphazardly paraded around the stadium track waving and smiling to the people in the stands. Germans marched in orderly rows with serious and determined expressions. Many newscasters in Seoul criticized the Americans' frivolous attitude, but the athletes were simply following their culture's display rules, which happen to have a great tolerance for youthful enthusiasm in a competitive situation.

Culture also provides guidance in how we cognitively appraise different situations. Clearly, the same event can cause different emotions in people depending on the person's culture. If you see someone eating a hamburger, you're not likely to respond emotionally—unless you're in India where cows are sacred.

Although events might trigger different emotions in various cultures, are people around the world using similar dimensions to cognitively appraise situations? We mentioned earlier that a number of dimensions seem to be evaluated during the appraisal process (figure 8.8). Even if the answers to the questions about each dimension are different, are the questions the same?

One study explored this issue by asking people from the United States, Hong Kong, Japan, and China to think about an emotional event that they had experienced as vividly as possible (Mauro, Sato, & Tucker, 1992). Once they had the event and its emotion in mind, they were asked to answer questions about how they were appraising the situation. For example, they were asked, "How certain

were you that you would or would not be able to cope with what was happening?" Another question was, "To what extent did you feel that you could influence what was happening in this situation?" Each of the questions were designed to ask about the dimensions that people use to appraise a situation.

The people from these cultures showed remarkable similarities with respect to the questions they were asking, and in how their answers related to the emotion they felt. This was particularly true of the simpler and more basic questions, such as those about the pleasantness of the situation, its certainty, the person's coping ability, and a few others. These dimensions of appraisal may represent common elements that people from many cultures use to appraise a situation. There were some cultural differences on a few of the cognitively more complex dimensions, such as control and responsibility, but they were small. These findings suggest that people from these cultures are asking many of the same questions when they cognitively appraise a situation; the aspects of the situation that are important to appraise in an emotional context are similar.

*Emotions and Evolution*    We can get a broader view of the nature of emotions if we look at how they may have evolved, and what their contribution to survival and fitness may have been. The brain areas important in emotions, particularly in the limbic system, do not exist only in human beings. They are very primitive structures. They were the first parts of the brain to evolve and they can be found in creatures as far removed from humans as alligators, birds, fish, and frogs. Whether these animals feel emotions the same way we do is a question that is not easy to answer. These animals certainly behave emotionally. A frightened bird shows rapid heart beat, increased blood pressure, heightened activity, squawking, and many of the same signs of fear that human beings show. This kind of emotional behavior appears to be important in the bird's survival. A bird that faces a large predator with no emotional behavior would quickly become the main course for dinner and would probably not leave very many offspring. Thus, the importance of emotions in helping organisms survive may explain why they evolved and, indeed, why they exist now.

It is easy to see how the emotion of fear is important for survival. Without fear and all the physiological changes accompanying it, an animal might not move quickly enough to escape from a predator. Other emotions might also have an evolutionary basis. Disgust, for

# EXPLORING HUMAN DIVERSITY

## Marketing to Ethnic Groups

American business has been slow to develop marketing strategies aimed at specific cultural groups. Believing that most human motivations were universal characteristics that transcended cultural distinctions, major corporations avoided the extra expense of developing products or launching ad campaigns tailored to minorities. Navigating right down the mainstream, many companies chose the white middle-class family with approximately two children to extoll their products' virtues. This image of the American dream was expected to appeal to everyone. But as America grew increasingly multicultural, the "mainstream" shrank and corporations took a closer look at their segmented markets.

Early attempts to market to minorities were not always effective. In one case, a telephone company tried to add a Latin flavor to its ads by hiring Puerto Rican actors. The wife in the ad said to her husband, "Run downstairs and phone Mary. Tell her we'll be a little late." Culturally, this ad contained two errors: (1) Hispanic wives generally don't order their husbands around, and (2) the caller probably wouldn't bother to call since tardiness is not a serious social gaffe. Despite such rocky starts, corporations are now learning the basics of multicultural marketing.

Consumer products corporations, for example, are recognizing that culture affects what kinds of products people prefer. There was a time in the United States when cosmetic companies produced none or only a very few shades of darker liquid makeup for blacks, but the range of choices has increased considerably. Gerber introduced tropical fruit flavors in its baby foods to appeal to Hispanics. Frito Lay developed "Plantinos" for the same cultural group. Interest in Hispanics is particularly strong because of their growing population. By the year 2000, Hispanics should number over 30 million. Many major companies already deliver advertising in Spanish.

Corporations are also investigating how different motivational messages appeal to America's cultural groups, even when they are trying to sell them all the same product. Some companies found that ads directed toward Hispanics were more successful if they featured evocative and aspirational messages about lifetime goals rather than informational themes about safety or convenience. Pepsi had a very successful "Casa de Sus Suenos" (house of your dreams) campaign that appealed to Hispanics in this way. Companies are also learning that the Hispanic market is segmented; the higher income families of Puerto Rican descent living in Florida are a different market compared to the Mexican-Americans of Texas.

In the global marketplace, corporations have learned a great many lessons about marketing across cultures through embarrassing blunders. The automobile called "Nova" caused great amusement in Puerto Rico because the word sounds like "no va," which means "it doesn't go." "Pinto" was a poor choice for a car in Brazil: it's a slang word meaning "small male appendage." When Coca-Cola first tried to market its soft drink in China, they chose Chinese characters that when pronounced, sounded like the name. The meaning was unfortunate, however. The characters symbolized "bite the wax tadpole."

A great many mistakes have also been made because corporations failed to learn about cultural taboos, norms, or preferences. A telecommunications company designed an ad featuring an executive with his feet propped up on the desk, a posture that was highly offensive to people in the Middle East. A company promoting mouthwash showed a young couple holding hands, a public display of affection that was unacceptable in Thailand. The Marlboro man had to be overhauled in Hong Kong. The Chinese just couldn't identify with a man on a horse looking over thousands of acres of empty land, though they did like the cowboy hat (Ricks, 1983).

Marketing to cultural groups is enormously challenging. Exxon spent millions of dollars choosing its name so it would create the right image around the globe and not carry an offensive or obscene meaning. To be successful in the twenty-first century, companies will have to be very canny about the role of culture in motivation and consumer behavior.

example, might be the emotional reaction that helps prevent organisms from eating poisonous foods. When you put something in your mouth that has a foul taste, you show disgust and spit it out. The reason a particular food tastes bad to us is that it is poisonous, and we have evolved taste buds that react to the substance. But the emotion of disgust that accompanies the taste adds urgency to the situation. The food doesn't just drop out of your mouth. You actively and urgently spit it out.

The ability to interpret emotions in others is also important to our survival, and may have a biological basis as well. We saw earlier that babies begin to interpret facial expressions of their parents quite early, and react appropriately to them. In the same way that we appear biologically wired to send certain emotional signals, we may be biologically predisposed to detect and interpret them in particular ways. For example, much like we are predisposed to associate a novel taste with an illness, we may be biologically prepared to associate a particular emotional expression such as anger with danger or harm (Dimberg, 1990). The smiling assassin is especially confusing.

The importance of emotions in our survival and their existence in animals with little or no cortex suggest that although cognition may affect emotions, cognitive activity may not be necessary for an emotion to occur (Zajonc, 1984). One theorist maintains that emotions are a primary and independent system that combines with other systems (such as cognition or perception) (Tomkins, 1981a).

An experiment that supports this point of view shows that a person can feel an emotion about something without really ever analyzing it cognitively. Many different polygons were presented one at a time to a group of subjects for a very brief moment, 1/1,000 second. Later, the subjects were shown more polygons, some of which they had already seen. They rated each one for "liking," and they also reported whether or not they recognized the polygon from the first series. Their chances of being able to identify which polygons they had seen before were no better than simply guessing. However, when they rated the shapes for liking, they tended to like those they had seen before better. Cognitively, the subjects could not tell the old shapes from the new, but emotionally they could. This suggests that a person can form an emotional attachment very quickly, with little or no cognitive appraisal (Zajonc, 1980).

Studies like this one lead to the conclusion that emotions can operate independently of cognition, something we might expect given their early evolutionary development and their dependence on lower areas of the brain. But it is also very clear that emotions in humans can involve a strong cognitive component, and a sociocultural one as well. Cognitions can both cause the physical components of emotions to flair, and can affect them once they are underway. They can even make them vanish. Determining whether the cognitive component comes before or after the physiological one may be a chicken-and-egg problem. They interact very closely. Cognitions are needed to evaluate situations, and culture provides the context in which emotions are expressed and events evaluated for their significance.

## ▶ GUIDED REVIEW  *Learning Objectives 8, 9, and 10*

1. Emotions are complex reactions involving two components: a _____ component and a _____ . There appear to be a limited number of _____ emotions. The two most important dimensions on which emotions can be discriminated are _____ and _____ .

2. Emotions are expressed by facial expressions, verbal and nonverbal aspects of speech, gestures, and body movements. Facial expressions of _____ appear to be universal in human beings.

3. People manage emotional expression by following _____ appropriate for the situation in their culture.

4. Activity in the _____ is similar for intense emotions. However, facial expression can distinguish one emotion from another, and brain activity and chemistry may also be able to do so.

5. The _____ theory of emotions suggests that emotions are the result of visceral and muscular changes. A newer hypothesis includes feedback from the _____ as being important in the experience of emotions.

6. _____ states that activity in the lower brain areas is critical in emotions.

7. A _____ of emotion suggests that bodily changes are interpreted as a particular emotional experience after a cognitive appraisal of the situation.

8. _____ affects the display rules that people use to manage their emotional expressions. Some groups are more expressive in public than others in particular kinds of situations.

9. An _____ approach to emotion suggests that emotions have evolved because they help organisms to survive. This approach suggests that organisms can feel emotions without any cognitive appraisal.

*ANSWERS*

*1. physiological, subjective experience, primary, pleasantness, arousal level 2. primary emotions 3. display rules 4. autonomic nervous system 5. James-Lange, facial muscles 6. Cannon's theory 7. cognitive-physiological theory 8. Culture 9. evolutionary*

# SUMMARY

I. The study of motivation attempts to explain the "why" of behavior. (p. 242)

   A. Several theories of motivation have been proposed. (p. 242)

      1. The drive reduction theory proposes that organisms experience the arousal of a drive when an important need is not satisfied, and they engage in behavior to reduce the arousal. (p. 242)

      2. The optimum level of arousal theory of motivation suggests that organisms do not always seek the lowest level of arousal; they seek an optimum level, which depends on the circumstances and the organism. (pp. 243–244)

      3. Expectancy theory emphasizes the role of rewards in motivation. (p. 244)

      4. The opponent process theory attempts to explain how drives are acquired. (pp. 244–245)

   B. One scheme used to classify motives is Murray's, which categorized motives as either secondary or primary. (p. 245)

   C. Brain mechanisms underlying motivation appear to involve a pathway in the lower brain areas that mediates reward for all kinds of motivation. (p. 246)

II. Four examples of human motives are hunger, sex, sensation seeking, and the need for achievement. (p. 247)

   A. Both biological and psychological mechanisms control eating behavior. (p. 247)

      1. Peripheral controls include signals from the intestines and the liver. (p. 247)

      2. The brain, especially the hypothalamus, plays an important role in hunger. (p. 248)

      3. Obesity appears to have multiple causes. (pp. 248–250)

   B. Sex behavior is affected by biological, psychological, and cultural factors. (p. 250)

      1. The major biological influences on sex behavior involve sex hormones. (p. 250)

      2. Psychological factors affect the development of sex roles in human beings. (pp. 251–252)

      3. Cultures differ considerably in their regulations and traditions regarding appropriate sexual behavior. (p. 252)

   C. Sensation seeking refers to the need for varied, novel, or intense forms of stimulation or experience. (p. 252)

      1. People who score high on the Sensation Seeking Scale behave differently from those who score low. (p. 252)

      2. Various theories of motivation have been used to explain sensation seeking, including the optimum level of arousal theory and the opponent process theory. (pp. 253–254)

   D. The need for achievement (n Ach) involves the desire to independently master objects, ideas, and other people and to increase one's self-esteem through the exercise of one's talent. (p. 254)

      1. n Ach is often measured with the Thematic Apperception Test. (p. 254)

      2. People who score low or high on tests that measure n Ach behave differently. (p. 254)

III. Emotion consists of two components: a physiological component and a subjective experience. (p. 257)

   A. There appears to be a limited number of primary emotions; these emotions appear to differ along the dimensions of pleasantness and arousal. (p. 257)

   B. Emotions are expressed by facial expression, the verbal and nonverbal aspects of speech, gestures, and body movements. Facial expressions of primary emotions appear to be universal in humans. (pp. 258–260)

   C. Emotions are accompanied by activity in the autonomic nervous system, although different emotions produce very similar patterns of response. (p. 260)

      1. Activity in various brain regions and changes in brain chemistry are associated with different emotions. (p. 260)

      2. An individual's response to many different intense emotions seems to be similar, although the autonomic "fingerprint" of different individuals varies. (p. 260)

   D. Various theories of emotion have been proposed: (p. 260)

      1. The James-Lange theory suggested that emotions are the result of visceral and muscular changes. (p. 262)

      2. Cannon's theory of emotion emphasized the importance of brain activity in emotions. (pp. 262–263)

      3. According to cognitive-physiological theory, after a cognitive appraisal of the situation, bodily changes are interpreted as a particular emotion. (p. 263)

      4. Emotions, and especially emotional display rules, are affected by culture. (p. 264)

      5. An evolutionary approach to emotion suggests that emotions have evolved because they help organisms to survive. (p. 265)

# ACTION GLOSSARY

Match the terms in the left column with the definitions in the right column.

___  1. **Motive** (p. 242)
___  2. **Motivation** (p. 242)
___  3. **Drive reduction theory** (p. 242)
___  4. **Primary drive** (p. 242)
___  5. **Homeostasis** (p. 242)
___  6. **Acquired drive** (p. 242)
___  7. **Habit** (p. 242)
___  8. **Optimum level of arousal theory** (p. 243)
___  9. **Yerkes-Dodson Law** (p. 243)
___ 10. **Expectancy theory** (p. 244)

A. *A revision of the drive reduction theory that takes into account the fact that people do not always seek a lower level of arousal.*
B. *That which motivates an organism to satisfy some basic biological need, such as hunger or thirst.*
C. *Organisms are driven to reduce their state of arousal and achieve homeostasis.*
D. *A drive that develops through learning.*
E. *Performance on a difficult learning task is related to arousal; the best performance results from intermediate levels of arousal.*
F. *Something that moves an organism to act.*
G. *Stresses the importance of rewards and goals and how people's expectations of consequences can influence their behavior.*
H. *A connection between a stimulus and response.*
I. *A presumed internal state of an organism that causes it to move toward some goal.*
J. *A state of balance necessary in many physiological systems.*

___ 11. **Valence** (p. 244)
___ 12. **Expectancy** (p. 244)
___ 13. **Opponent process theory of motivation** (p. 244)
___ 14. **a-process** (p. 244)
___ 15. **b-process** (p. 244)
___ 16. **Thematic Apperception Test (TAT)** (p. 245)
___ 17. **CCK** (p. 247)

A. *In the opponent process theory of motivation, the reaction that follows the initial response to a stimulus.*
B. *The attractiveness of the goal.*
C. *Attempts to explain how acquired drives are acquired. Proposes that a stimulus is followed by a particular response, and that the response is followed by an opposite reaction. After repeated stimulus presentations, the first response diminishes in strength and the reaction increases.*
D. *A hormone released from the intestinal tract that acts as a signal for satiation of hunger.*
E. *A psychological test used to measure motivation, based on the theory that fantasies and dreams can reveal a great deal about a person's motives.*
F. *The likelihood that an individual's behavior will lead to a particular goal.*
G. *In the opponent process theory of motivation, the response that occurs immediately after the presentation of a stimulus.*

___ 18. **Glucoreceptors** (p. 247)
___ 19. **Ventromedial hypothalamus** (p. 248)
___ 20. **Lateral hypothalamus** (p. 248)
___ 21. **Emotional arousal theory (EAT)** (p. 249)
___ 22. **Setpoint** (p. 249)

A. *Proposes that overeating is instrumentally conditioned behavior that serves to reduce anxiety in the obese.*
B. *Lesions of this area of the brain produce overeating and obesity in experimental animals.*
C. *The particular weight that an individual can maintain effortlessly.*
D. *Monitor the levels of glucose, a form of sugar, in the bloodstream or other body compartment.*
E. *Lesions in this area of the brain inhibit eating in experimental animals.*

___ 23. **Sex roles** (p. 251)
___ 24. **Sensation seeking** (p. 252)
___ 25. **Sensation Seeking Scale** (p. 252)
___ 26. **Galvanic skin response (GSR)** (p. 253)
___ 27. **Need for achievement (n Ach)** (p. 254)
___ 28. **Emotion** (p. 257)

A. *A measure of activity in the autonomic nervous system; used as an indicator of emotional arousal.*
B. *The attitudes and behaviors a society believes to be appropriate for males and females.*
C. *The need for varied, novel, and intense forms of stimulation and experience.*
D. *A psychological test designed to measure individual differences in sensation seeking.*
E. *A complex reaction involving two components: a series of physiological changes and a subjective experience or "feeling."*
F. *The motive to achieve success, to independently master objects, events, and other persons, and to increase self-esteem through the development of talent.*

___ **29. James-Lange theory**
    **(p. 262)**

___ **30. Cannon's theory of**
    **emotions (p. 262)**

___ **31. Cognitive-physiological**
    **theory of emotions (p. 263)**

___ **32. Facial feedback hypothesis**
    **(p. 262)**

A. *Suggests that facial expressions contribute to the experience of emotion.*
B. *Proposed that the physiological changes occurring in the viscera and muscles were the cause, rather than the result, of the emotion.*
C. *Suggests that emotions originate in the activity in lower brain areas rather than activity in the viscera.*
D. *Emphasizes the role of cognitive appraisal of a situation in a person's subjective experience of emotion.*

ANSWERS

19. b, 20. e, 21. a, 22. c, 23. b, 24. c, 25. d, 26. a, 27. f, 28. e, 29. b, 30. c, 31. d, 32. a,
1. f, 2. i, 3. c, 4. b, 5. j, 6. d, 7. h, 8. a, 9. e, 10. g, 11. b, 12. f, 13. c, 14. g, 15. a, 16. e, 17. d, 18. d,

# SELF-TEST

**1.** The theory of motivation that proposes that the purpose of behavior is to reduce arousal is called the
    **(a)** drive reduction theory.
    **(b)** optimum level of arousal theory.
    **(c)** expectancy theory.
    **(d)** opponent process theory.
    (LO 1; p. 242)

**2.** The motivation of a housewife who is home alone all day and who wants to go out to dinner and to a movie in the evening could best be explained by which of the following theories?
    **(a)** drive reduction theory
    **(b)** optimum level of arousal theory
    **(c)** expectancy theory
    **(d)** opponent process theory
    (LO 1; p. 243)

**3.** In expectancy theory, the attractiveness of the goal is termed
    **(a)** homeostasis.
    **(b)** acquired drive.
    **(c)** expectancy.
    **(d)** valence.
    (LO 1; p. 244)

**4.** In opponent process theory, the first response _____ over time, and the second response _____ .
    **(a)** is stable; increases
    **(b)** increases; decreases
    **(c)** decreases; increases
    **(d)** decreases; is stable
    (LO 1; pp. 244–245)

**5.** Murray's method of assessing motives in people involved
    **(a)** a multiple-choice test that asked people to choose from different options.
    **(b)** interviews with a therapist.
    **(c)** asking people to make up stories about ambiguous pictures.
    **(d)** an analysis of dream content.
    (LO 2; p. 245)

**6.** Which of the following brain areas appears to have pathways most intimately involved in reward?
    **(a)** hypothalamus
    **(b)** medulla
    **(c)** cerebellum
    **(d)** temporal lobe
    (LO 3; p. 246)

**7.** Which of the following substances, when injected into the liver of a dog during feeding, will cause a hungry dog to stop eating?
    **(a)** CCK
    **(b)** insulin
    **(c)** glucose
    **(d)** caffeine
    (LO 4; p. 247)

**8.** A lesion in what part of the brain will prevent a rat from ceasing to eat when it is full and eventually will lead to obesity?
    **(a)** lateral hypothalamus
    **(b)** ventromedial hypothalamus
    **(c)** hippocampus
    **(d)** lateral thalamus
    (LO 4; p. 248)

9. If a male rat has its testes removed, what hormone will cause its sexual behavior to return?
   (a) testosterone
   (b) ACTH
   (c) estradiol
   (d) progesterone
   (LO 5; p. 250)

10. Sex roles refer to
    (a) a person's sexual behavior.
    (b) the attitudes and behaviors believed by a person's culture to be appropriate for each sex.
    (c) the sexual attitudes a person adopts during adolescence.
    (d) alternate life-styles.
    (LO 5; p. 251)

11. Which theory of motivation seems best able to explain high sensation-seeking behavior?
    (a) drive reduction theory
    (b) classical conditioning
    (c) expectancy theory
    (d) opponent process theory
    (LO 6; p. 253)

12. People who are high-sensation seekers show _____ galvanic skin response to a novel stimulus than do people who are low-sensation seekers.
    (a) much weaker
    (b) slightly weaker
    (c) similar
    (d) stronger
    (LO 6; pp. 253–254)

13. In a ring-tossing game, people with high n Ach scores tended to stand _____ the post while people with low n Ach scores tended to stand _____ the post.
    (a) close to/far from
    (b) far from/close to
    (c) at an intermediate distance/close to or far from
    (d) close to or far from /at an intermediate distance from
    (LO 7; p. 254)

14. In the "circle of emotions," the two dimensions for describing emotions are
    (a) pleasantness and arousal level.
    (b) pleasantness and physiological.
    (c) intensity and physiological.
    (d) physiological and expressive.
    (LO 8; p. 257)

15. The facial expression of emotions has been found to be
    (a) completely culturally specific.
    (b) universal for some basic emotions.
    (c) universal for all emotions.
    (d) difficult to interpret across cultures.
    (LO 9; p. 258)

16. Few Germans walk along a main street with a big smile. This suggests that
    (a) biological factors are important in emotional behavior.
    (b) the culture's display rules discourage the behavior.
    (c) climate affects culture, and therefore emotional behavior.
    (d) evolutionary factors have influenced the display of emotions.
    (LO 9; pp. 264–265)

17. In the James-Lange theory of emotion, what is the sequence of events in emotional response?
    (a) physical arousal followed by subjective feelings of emotion
    (b) emotion followed by physical arousal
    (c) only physical arousal
    (d) cognitive appraisal followed by emotion and then physical arousal
    (LO 10; p. 262)

18. According to Cannon, emotion originated in the _____ rather than in the viscera.
    (a) heart
    (b) cortex
    (c) lower brain stem
    (d) hypothalamus
    (LO 10; p. 262)

19. In an experiment by Schachter and Singer, subjects were given injections of epinephrine and were then put in different situations. Which subjects were most likely to show anger in this situation?
    (a) People who were misinformed about the effects of the injection and were not exposed to any emotion-stimulating event.
    (b) People who were correctly informed about the effects of the drug and were not exposed to any emotion-stimulating event.
    (c) People who were given an insulting test to fill out.
    (d) People who were misinformed about the effects of the injection and were given an insulting test to fill out.
    (LO 10; pp. 263–264)

20. The evolutionary perspective on emotion suggests that although _____ may affect emotions, it may not be necessary for emotions to occur.
    (a) physiological arousal
    (b) feeling
    (c) expression
    (d) cognitive activity
    (LO 10; p. 267)

*ANSWERS*

1. a, 2. b, 3. d, 4. c, 5. c, 6. a, 7. c, 8. b, 9. a, 10. b, 11. d, 12. d, 13. c, 14. a, 15. b, 16. b, 17. a, 18. c, 19. d, 20. d

# THINKING ABOUT PSYCHOLOGY

1. A woman from the United States was taking her one-year-old child for a walk in a stroller in Heidelberg, Germany. The weather was brisk and three different German women, strangers to the American, stopped the American on the sidewalk, sharply admonishing her to put warmer clothes on the child or take her back home. The American, who was accustomed to cold weather and often took her child out back home, was incensed by their behavior. Hypothesize about how this experience demonstrates ways in which culture and emotion interact.

2. Bungee jumping is an unusual pastime that gained popularity in the late 1980s. The jumper is fitted with a harness attached to one end of a long chain or rope; the other end is secured to a high platform such as a bridge or the top of a crane. The length of the rope is carefully measured so that when the person jumps off the platform into a free fall, he or she will be jolted to a stop or swing in midair, just before reaching the river or ground. Jumpers express great fear before jumping, followed by exuberance afterward. What might motivate people to do this? Use the theories of motivation discussed in this chapter to frame your answer.

3. In chapter 3, we discussed how some people show seasonal changes in mood, becoming more depressed and lethargic in the winter and more energetic and happy in the spring and summer. Relying on your understanding of evolution, hypothesize about why such seasonal cycles in human emotion might have evolved.

# SUGGESTED READINGS

Ben-Shakhar, G., & Furedy, J.J. (1990). *Theories and applications in the detection of deception: A psychophysiological and international perspective*. New York: Springer-Verlag. A detailed examination of the validity and accuracy of the polygraph technique.

Deci, E. L., & Ryan, R. M. (1985). *Intrinsic motivation and self-determination in human behavior*. New York: Plenum. An advanced text covering research on human motivation, especially as it relates to human performance.

Ekman, P. (1982). *Emotion in the human face* (2nd ed.). New York: Cambridge University Press. A book on facial expressions that display emotions in various cultures.

Logue, A. W. (1987). *The psychology of eating and drinking*. San Francisco: W. H. Freeman. A text that explores many behaviors related to eating and drinking, including obesity, anorexia, and bulimia.

Oatley, K., & Jenkins, J. M. (1992). Human emotions: Function and dysfunction. *Annual Review of Psychology, 43*, 55–85. A review of research on human emotions, including those involved in behavioral disorders.

Plutchik, R. (1980). *Emotion: A psychoevolutionary synthesis*. New York: Harper & Row. A presentation of the theory that emphasizes the role of evolution in emotion.

Thompson, R. A. (Ed.) (1990). *Nebraska symposium on motivation, Volume 36: Socioemotional development*. Lincoln: University of Nebraska Press. This annual series contains articles by noted researchers in motivation and emotion. Volume 36 reviews emotional development in infants and young children.

Thomson, J. G. (1988). *The psychobiology of emotions*. New York: Plenum. Describes theories of emotions, emphasizing the complex interactions between body and behavior.

White, G. L., & Mullen, P. E. (1989). *Jealousy: Theory, research, and clinical strategies*. New York: Guilford Press. An unusual book exploring the roots of the emotion of jealousy.

# PART III

## DEVELOPMENT

# CHAPTER 9

## LIFE-SPAN DEVELOPMENT: INFANCY AND CHILDHOOD
### OUTLINE

▶ **Learning Objectives**

▶ **The Study of Human Development**
- ■ Cross-Sectional and Longitudinal Studies
- ■ Perspectives in Human Development

▶ **Guided Review**

▶ **The Forces That Shape Development**
- ■ Genetic Forces
  - The Gene
  - Genes and Behavior
- ■ Environmental Forces
  - The Prenatal Environment
  - Nutrition and the Internal Environment
  - Shaping Your Own Environment
- ■ The Interaction between Genes and Environment in Development

▶ **Guided Review**

▶ **Birth and Infancy**
- ■ The Abilities of the Newborn
  - Motor Behavior
  - The Sensory World
  - The Newborn's Speech
- ■ Emotional Development
  - Temperament
- ■ Social Development
  - Mother Love in Monkeys
  - Personality Development and Attachment

▶ **Guided Review**

▶ **Childhood**
- ■ Cognitive Development
  - Sensorimotor Stage
  - Preoperational Stage
  - Concrete Operational Stage
  - Formal Operational Stage
  - Evaluating Piaget's Theory
- ■ Social and Emotional Development
  - The Family
  - The Influence of Peers
  - The Cultural Context
- ■ Moral Development
  - Moral Reasoning and Piaget's Stages
  - Kohlberg's Six Stages of Moral Development
  - Evaluating Theories of Moral Development
- ■ Resilience

▶ **Guided Review**

▶ **Summary**

▶ **Action Glossary**

▶ **Self-Test**

▶ **Thinking About Psychology**

▶ **Suggested Readings**

# LIFE-SPAN DEVELOPMENT: INFANCY AND CHILDHOOD
## LEARNING OBJECTIVES

**After reading this chapter, you should be able to**

▶ **1.** describe the two major types of studies conducted to explore human development. *(pp. 276–277)*

▶ **2.** describe three major perspectives used to approach the study of human development. *(pp. 277–278)*

▶ **3.** explain how genes can affect behavior, and describe the kind of study scientists use to learn more about the role of genetics in behavior. *(pp. 279–282)*

▶ **4.** provide examples of how the environment affects development, including the prenatal environment, nutrition, and an individual's capacity to shape his or her own environment. *(pp. 282–283)*

▶ **5.** discuss the nature-nurture issue, and explain how genes and environment interact. *(p. 283)*

▶ **6.** explain some of the recent trends in childbirth in the United States. *(pp. 284–286)*

▶ **7.** describe the sensorimotor abilities of the newborn. *(pp. 286–288)*

▶ **8.** explain what is meant by the term "temperament," and discuss genetic and environmental effects. *(pp. 288–290)*

▶ **9.** describe the phenomenon of attachment, including the role it plays in social development. *(pp. 290–293)*

▶ **10.** describe Piaget's theory concerning cognitive development. *(pp. 293–296)*

▶ **11.** give examples of the influence of family, peers, and culture in social and emotional development during childhood. *(pp. 297–300)*

▶ **12.** describe and evaluate Piaget's and Kohlberg's theories of moral development. *(pp. 300–303)*

▶ **13.** define the concept of resilience. *(p. 303)*

A human life begins as a mere pin-head-sized speck, the union of a sperm from a man and an egg from a woman. Within a few short weeks the speck becomes recognizably human; a few months after that it emerges as an air-breathing, squalling, wriggling infant. In the months and years that follow, the human grows and develops, learning to communicate, walk, count, read and write, tell right from wrong, make friends, go through puberty, find a mate, have children, raise children, grow old, and die.

Within that broad framework of development, human lives take very different courses. We all start out with different genes, and we're all born into different family environments and cultures. Our parents and culture adhere to different child-rearing philosophies. Our period of history differs, as well, and this can have dramatic effects on our development. Children growing up in wartime who face a daily threat to their survival have a very different childhood from their siblings born just a few years later. People born at the beginning of this century gathered around the fireplace for evening games and conversation, and watched horse-drawn carriages pass their doors. Children born today will gather around the TV to watch astronauts living and working aboard Space Station Freedom.

## THE STUDY OF HUMAN DEVELOPMENT

The discussion of development in this chapter and the next is different from all of the other chapters. Rather than focusing on how and why people behave in particular contexts, these chapters look at patterns of change and continuity in a human life. In this context, **development** *refers to patterns of forward movement or change beginning at conception and continuing through the entire life span.* Obviously changes do not just occur in one area of a person's life; they occur in cognition, social behavior, physical attributes, sexuality, and in just about everything else.

### Cross-Sectional and Longitudinal Studies

Because developmental psychologists are interested in changes over time—sometimes very long periods of time—their approach to their subject is slightly different from that of other psychologists. They follow all the usual rules of science discussed in the first chapter and they take advantage of experimental and correlational methods.

However, they must consider the aspect of change across time. There are two basic ways to do this: the cross-sectional study and the longitudinal study.

The **cross-sectional study** *compares the characteristics of groups of individuals of different ages on a behavior.* For example, ultrasound examinations of women at different stages of pregnancy have found that fetuses show different kinds of eye movements related to age. Rapid eye movement seems to begin around twenty-three weeks (Birnholz, 1981). Another cross-sectional study compared the way children, aged three, four, or five, appraised emotional expressions in other children, and the way they drew conclusions about why the child was displaying a particular emotion. All the children were reasonably accurate in identifying an emotional expression (such as happy, sad, angry, and so on). But the older children were better than the younger ones at identifying the cause (Fabes, Eisenberg, Nyman, & Michealieu, 1991).

The **longitudinal study** *follows the same group (or groups) of people through time, observing the changes in behavior that occur at different ages.* Another study on eye-movement patterns monitored rapid eye movements in a group of infants during the first month of life, then again at three months, six months, and one year of age. The year-old infants were given a test of mental development, and their scores were compared to their previous rapid eye movement patterns. Babies who had frequent rapid eye movement storms at six months of age were more likely to have lower mental development scores (Becker & Thoman, 1981).

Both types of studies have advantages and disadvantages. In the cross-sectional method, for instance, the age groups might be different because of factors other than age, including age of parents, quality of schools, and historical factors. People in their eighties probably have a vivid memory of the Depression and might behave differently from fifty-year-olds because of that memory, not because of age differences. The longitudinal method also has disadvantages; it can be very time consuming and expensive, and subjects may move to other parts of the world without telling the researchers.

A more comprehensive approach is to combine the cross-sectional and longitudinal methods, often in complex ways. In the first testing session, groups of different ages are compared and then followed at later ages. For instance, one group of researchers found that the expression of emotion during learning was consistent during the first year of life (Sullivan & Lewis, 1989). Bands were attached

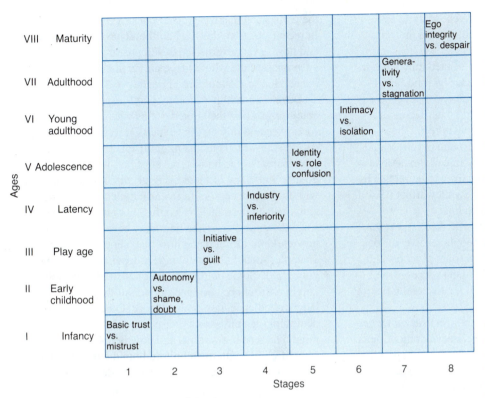

Figure 9.1   *Erikson's eight stages of development*

to the babies' wrists with velcro and a string from the band led to a circuit that activated a slide projector and tape recorder. Each time the infant waved her arm, a slide showing a smiling baby appeared for 3 seconds, along with a recording of children's voices singing "Sesame Street." Most infants doubled their rate of arm-pulling when it was followed by the slide and singing, and they tended to show expressions of joy or interest. During extinction (when arm-pulling no longer activated the circuit) the babies showed different emotions, usually anger, sadness, or fear. The researchers first did a cross-sectional study by comparing the reactions of infants two, four, or six months of age. Adding a longitudinal measure, all the babies were tested again two months later, when they were four, six and eight months of age. The babies tended to show the same emotional expressions to each phase of the experiment as they had earlier. For example, babies who displayed anger during extinction tended to display it again two months later. These results suggest that an infant's emotional responses to a learning event are reasonably stable, at least across two months (Sullivan, Lewis, & Alessandri, 1992).

## Perspectives in Human Development

Throughout the world, people hold views about human development, although they may not be able to express them very clearly. Consider, for example, how people from different cultures weigh the relative influence of inborn traits, environmental events, and individual effort. Researchers posed this question to people from various parts of the world with different religious and cultural traditions (Thomas, 1988):

This girl gets the highest marks in her class in mathematics. Which of these three reasons do you think is the cause for her doing better than the other students? First, because she was born with more ability in math? Or second, because she has had more teaching in math? Or third, because she tries harder than the others—she studies very hard?

Many people said the girl's success was due to a combination of these factors, but the interviewees differed on how important they thought each one was. Over three-fourths of the Muslim respondents in Sudan thought that the girl's success was mainly because she tried harder than the others. Thai Buddhists also generally credited hard work and willpower. Chinese in Taiwan, who come from a Confucian cultural tradition that emphasizes the importance of personal willpower and individual effort, were split on how they answered this question. Those that were enrolled in a university tended to strongly favor individual effort; the general public sample favored heredity. Surprisingly, the United States respondents also favored innate ability (fifty-four percent). It was interesting that very few of the respondents from any of the cultures thought that the amount or quality of teaching was the critical ingredient. (How would you answer the question?)

Developmental psychologists in the western world have looked at development from many angles as well, focusing on different aspects of development and emphasizing different influences. Three perspectives that have been particularly prominent include the psychoanalytic approach, the cognitive-structural approach, and the behavioristic approach.

Psychoanalytic thinkers have contributed much to our understanding of human development. Sigmund Freud emphasized the notion that early childhood events have important influences on an individual's later behavior, even when the person cannot consciously recall these events. Much of his work revolved around psychosexual development and focused on the role of early experiences and the child's developing relationships with parents. His theory of psychosexual stages and how they affect personality is examined in more detail in chapter 11.

Erik Erikson, another psychoanalytic theorist, explored personality development and how people resolve various conflicts that arise at each stage. Erikson's psychosocial conflicts span the entire life development process from infancy to old age (figure 9.1). We'll be discussing them in the context of each age period.

The **cognitive-structural approach** *focuses on stages of development,* especially intellectual development. Jean Piaget is the towering figure and most influential proponent of a stage theory. He was a Swiss psychologist who explored cognitive development by careful observation of his own and others' children. His work led him to the conclusion that children go through a progression of stages in the way that they tackle cognitive tasks, each qualitatively distinct from the previous one. The notion of stages of development has been applied to other areas as well, especially moral development.

Behavioristic thinking has also affected theories of human development and constitutes a third significant perspective in the field. The important role that reinforcement plays in learning is a key issue in this approach. Behaviorism stresses the fact that the process of development involves the accumulation of learning experiences and that each individual's learning history is unique. For example, a psychologist taking a behavioristic approach would look closely at a child's reinforcements to try to learn why that child does poorly in math. Are parents or teachers rewarding the child in some way that leads to the poor performance, perhaps without even realizing it? Are they failing to reward behaviors that would lead to better performance?

Developmental psychology has done considerable growing on its own in the last hundred years and much has been learned about how people change across time. One important "development" in developmental psychology is the realization that the process doesn't stop at adolescence. In recent years, studies on adulthood have mushroomed and now psychologists see development as a process that encompasses the whole life span, from the moment of conception to the moment of death.

Developmental psychology plays a special role in countries such as the United States where parents are eager for advice and rely on the "experts" more than in other cultures, in which parents might listen more carefully to grandparents. The bookstores are filled with child-rearing guides, and many of them disagree with one another and with their predecessors from earlier generations. The situation can become very confusing to parents, especially since the guides cross the boundary between explaining how children develop and how they should develop. For example, should you encourage independent thinking in your child? Some cultural or religious traditions hold that children should be seen and not heard; they should be taught obedience, not independence. Others value independent thinking, and assertiveness about "speaking your own mind." Describing what is, and how people develop is a scientific issue. Giving advice about how they should develop goes beyond what science can do.

▶ **GUIDED REVIEW** *Learning Objectives 1 and 2*

1. Studies of development involve all the experimental and correlational approaches discussed in earlier chapters. They also involve _____ designs, in which groups of people of different ages are compared, and _____ designs, in which the same people are observed as they develop over time.

2. Three major perspectives in human development include the psychoanalytic approach, the cognitive-structural approach, and the behavioristic approach. The _____ approach stresses the effects of early development experiences on later behavior, particularly personality development. _____ , for example, proposed eight stages of development, each of which involves the resolution of a psychosocial conflict. The _____ approach focuses on stages through which individuals move during development. The cognitive developmental theory of _____ is a good example. The _____ approach features the importance of reinforcement in development and the unique learning history of each individual.

*ANSWERS*

1. *cross-sectional, longitudinal* 2. *psychoanalytic, Erik Erikson, cognitive-structural, Jean Piaget, behavioristic*

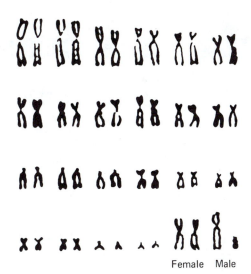

Female    Male

**Figure 9.2**  *Human chromosomes*

# THE FORCES THAT SHAPE DEVELOPMENT

The two major forces that shape development are genes and environment. These two forces always work together in their effects on the developing organism. Even at the very first, when a sperm cell and an egg join, the organism is more than just the genetic information contained in the two cells. The egg cell, in particular, contains an enormous quantity of nutrients and is already providing an environment that will interact with the genetic instructions.

## Genetic Forces

Jim Springer and Jim Lewis are identical twin brothers who were adopted into separate families at four weeks of age. They had no contact until they were thirty-nine-years-old. Nevertheless, the similarities between the twins are uncanny. Both were named Jim, and both had first married women named Linda, were divorced, and then remarried women named Betty. They each had a dog named Toy and a son called James Allen or James Alan. They both liked math and hated spelling. In adulthood, they both enjoy mechanical drawing and carpentry. They smoke and drink about the same amount, and they both bite their fingernails. They have the same pulse, blood pressure, sleep patterns, and hemorrhoid and headache problems, and they both gained ten pounds at about the same time of life. Many of these similarities, such as a fondness for "Lindas and Bettys," are simply remarkable coincidences. But investigators who study twins reared apart notice that such

coincidences are frequent in their subjects; some of the similarities must surely be due to the effects of genes on behavior (Bouchard, cited by Holden, 1980). The role that genes play in the development of the human being is not limited to eye color or bone structure. The effects of the genes go far beyond physical characteristics.

*The Gene*    Almost every cell of the human body has forty-six **chromosomes,** *long chains of genetic material located in the nucleus of the cell* (figure 9.2). Each chain consists of **DNA,** *the substance that contains genetic information.* DNA molecules are made up of three elements arranged more or less like a ladder: sugar, phosphates, and bases. Figure 9.3 shows an example of a very small segment of the DNA making up a chromosome. **Adenine, thymine, guanine,** and **cytosine** *are the four bases that make up DNA; it is the sequence of these bases arranged along the chromosome that comprise the genetic code.*

A **gene** *is a very short length of DNA consisting of only a few hundred bases; it is the basic unit of heredity.* Some genes give instructions to other genes. Other genes code for specific proteins used in physiological processes in the body. For example, a gene on a particular chromosome might code for an enzyme used in the metabolism of norepinephrine, an important neurotransmitter. Another gene might be the clock for its neighbors, sending instructions to turn them on or off. The chromosomes contain thousands of genes and each has its own function in the body.

The complex interactions of these proteins and the metabolic activities that they direct are what goes into the making of a human being. In different cells, different genes are active; this is why some genes become kidney cells and others become neurons. Genes do not code continuously for proteins throughout a person's life; they function on and off, and some remain dormant for years.

The forty-six chromosomes in the cell are arranged in pairs. You inherit one chromosome in each pair from your mother and the other from your father. Thus, you have twenty-three chromosomes from your mother and twenty-three chromosomes from your father.

The terms **heterozygous** and **homozygous** *refer to whether the complementary genes on a pair of chromosomes are identical; "hetero" means they are different, and "homo" means they are the same.* For example, people who have type AB blood have a gene for type A on one chromosome and a gene for type B on the other

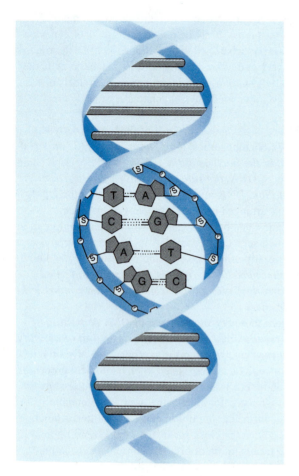

**Figure 9.3** *A schematic diagram of the double-helix structure of DNA. T = thymine, A = adenine, C = cytosine, G = guanine, S = sugar, and P = phosphate*

| TABLE 9.1 Examples of dominant and recessive genes in humans | |
|---|---|
| **Dominant** | **Recessive** |
| Ability to roll the tongue | Inability to roll the tongue |
| Freckles | No freckles |
| Free earlobes | Attached earlobes |
| Inability to fold tongue | Ability to fold tongue |
| Huntington's chorea | Tay-Sachs disease |
| Achondroplastic dwarfism | Hemophilia (located on the X chromosome) |
| Nail-patella syndrome | Color blindness (located on the X chromosome) |
| | Sickle-cell anemia |
| | Albinism |
| | Phenylketonuria (PKU) |

chromosome. They are heterozygous for this trait because the two genes are different. People who have type O blood have a gene for type O on both chromosomes. They are homozygous for this trait.

The blood groups can illustrate the phenomena of dominance and recessiveness as well. A **dominant gene** *is one that will be expressed regardless of which gene is on the paired chromosome.* A **recessive gene** *is one that is expressed only if it is paired with another recessive gene.* For example, people with type A blood have at least one gene for type A—a dominant gene—on one of their chromosomes. But the other chromosome might have either another gene for type A or perhaps a gene for type O blood, which is recessive. The only people who have type O blood are those with the genes for type O on *both*

chromosomes. Both the gene for A and the gene for B are dominant over the gene for O. But A and B are **codominant** with one another, *meaning both genes are expressed.* This is why a person with a gene for A and one for B has type AB blood rather than type A or type B. Recessive genes are not rare. In the United States, more people have type O blood than any other type of blood.

Many genes that affect proteins in the blood can now be detected. Tests are sometimes used to determine whether it is possible that a man is the father of a child. A type O man who believes that a type A baby of a type O mother is his child is mistaken. The father would have to be either type A or type AB. Examples of other genes that act as dominant or recessive in humans are listed in table 9.1.

*Genes and Behavior*    Genes cannot directly affect behavior; they can only code for specific proteins or direct the activities of other genes. But to the extent that these different proteins can affect behavior differently, genes can affect behavior. In a hypothetical example, suppose a person has genes that code for a very efficient enzyme that breaks down alcohol, and this individual consumes an average of two drinks per night for fifteen years. Since this person had the physiological ability to break down the alcohol rapidly, he or she would probably never get drunk. Another person, however, who had genes coding for a less efficient version of the same enzyme, might feel woozy for a couple of hours each evening after having two drinks. This person may, because of his or her genes, be more predisposed to becoming alcoholic, given a similar pattern of social drinking and environmental stresses.

Scientists have proposed specific genes that affect susceptibility to alcoholism, but the findings have been controversial (Bolos et al., 1990). It is probably too simple to suppose that single genes confer this kind of susceptibility and our example is merely hypothetical. The role of genes is undoubtedly very complex, involving tens or hundreds of genes that affect many biological functions (Lykken et al., 1992). The effects of various combinations of genes may predispose people to behave in certain ways; it may not be possible to isolate a single "alcoholism susceptibility" gene.

It is possible to learn more about the role genes play in the development of complex behaviors by comparing the similarity of people who share environments, to those who share only genes (Loehlin, Willerman, & Horn, 1988). For example, in the **adoption study,** *the similarity between an adopted child and the adoptive parents on a particular behavior is compared to the similarity between the child and the biological parents.* In theory, the biological parents contribute only genes to the child, but the prenatal environment, and perhaps the postnatal environment as well, come from the biological parents. For some traits, such as eye color, one would expect the adopted child to closely resemble the biological parents rather than the adoptive parents. For other traits, the child would resemble the adoptive parents much more than the biological parents. The language the child learns is a good example: a Japanese child reared from birth by English-speaking American parents won't speak Japanese.

Most behavioral traits, however, seem to fall somewhere between these two extremes. Studies of temperament in infants, for example, suggest a genetic contribution. As anyone who has worked in a nursery knows, some babies seem calmer than others and are more easily soothed when they are in distress. Others seem more irritable. In a variation of the adoption study, the temperament of adopted and nonadopted one- and 2-year-olds were compared to the other children in the family in which they were being reared. Adopted babies share none of the genes of their siblings, while biological siblings share fifty percent of their genes, on the average. If genes have some influence on temperament, genetically related siblings should be more alike than unrelated children even though the pairs are all growing up in the same family. In this study, the biological siblings were much more similar to one another than the sibling pairs that came into being through adoption (Braungart et al., 1992).

There are many common misconceptions about the role of genes in behavior. One is that genes predetermine a particular behavior rather than predispose an individual toward the behavior. Thus, people with an alcoholic parent might mistakenly assume that they are destined to the same problem. This is not true. It only means that they may be more vulnerable. For example, social class appears to influence the development of alcoholism in children born to a father with some history of alcohol abuse. Sons adopted by fathers in skilled occupations were less likely to become alcoholic than were sons adopted by fathers in unskilled occupations (Sigvardsson, Cloninger, Bohman, & von Knorring, 1985). Genes do not predestine, they only predispose.

Another myth about genes is that if something is genetic, meaning that genes are involved, then it must be universal. Hair color, for example, varies considerably among people but it still is influenced by genes. People often claim that human aggression cannot have any genetic basis since some cultures are not aggressive at all. Unfortunately, this line of reasoning is not valid. The most important characteristic about genes is that they vary among people. If a genetic predisposition exists for a particular trait, that trait will be expressed differently for different people, even if they are reared in the same environments, simply because their genes differ. The environmental influences contributed by culture clearly affect aggression in different societies, but the behavior may also be affected by genetic factors.

A third misconception is that if a behavior is genetic, it cannot be changed. Any predispositions produced by genetic factors can often be mitigated or changed completely by environmental influences. As we shall see later, temperament in babies may have a genetic component, but it can also change during the first year of life—for better or worse—by environmental forces. The parents' behavior seems to be critical. Another example of this genetic-environmental interaction involves **phenylketonuria (PKU),** *a disease transmitted through two recessive genes that causes a lack in the enzyme needed for metabolizing one of the amino acids, phenylalanine. Toxic by-products build up in the individual's body, resulting in severe retardation and light skin and hair.* If the trait is detected early, a baby can be placed on a diet low in phenylalanine. Fewer toxic by-products accumulate, and the child is much less affected. Babies are generally tested for this hereditary problem soon after birth. Modifying the environment, in this case the nutritional environment, alters the way the genes are expressed.

As evidence about the genetic contributions to more complex human behavior mounts, it becomes even more important to dispel this myth about the immutability of genetic effects. Scores on intelligence tests, temperament, susceptibility to alcoholism, and other behaviors may have genetic components, but they can also be influenced by environmental factors. Fatalism about how "an apple never falls far from the tree" is not warranted. Genes and environments operate together, constantly interacting in their effects on the developmental process.

## Environmental Forces

The effects of the environment on human development begin at the moment of conception. The environment, as we discuss it in psychology, includes a great deal more than the child's room and family life. It includes the prenatal, hormonal, and nutritional environments. In fact, it includes everything outside of the DNA, including the womb, the body, the family, the school, and the culture. In this section, we give examples of just a few environmental forces, ones that are easily overlooked when thinking about the factors that affect development.

*The Prenatal Environment*    While the genes are direct-ing some cells to specialize, the environment in which they are acting is having important effects. The hormones present are particularly critical. If the fetus is a male, it begins to release a male sex hormone that causes the fetus to develop male sex organs. If the fetus is a female, no male sex hormone is released; the fetus develops female sex organs. These prenatal hormones affect the brain as well. Many scientists are convinced that the sexual behavior of adults is partly dependent on the presence of these hormones in prenatal life, as we shall see in the next chapter.

Another important component of the prenatal envi-ronment is the drugs the mother is taking. During the 1960s, some pregnant women were prescribed a minor tranquilizer, thalidomide, to help relieve morning sickness. The babies of many of the women who took the drug during the first few weeks of pregnancy were born with tragic limb deformities.

As more research is conducted on the problem, it is becoming clear that many otherwise safe drugs are not safe for pregnant women. Alcohol, for example, can produce the fetal alcohol syndrome in babies. Babies born to mothers who drink a great deal during pregnancy can have a variety of problems, including weak sucking abilities, hyperactivity, delayed development, and mental retarda-tion (Streissguth et al., 1980). Problems persist into adulthood: the victims have trouble living independently, holding down jobs, and continue to have problems concentrating.

Drugs are not the only things that can affect prenatal development. The mother's emotions can affect the growing fetus. Severe stress results in the release of hormones in the mother that can cross the placental barrier and increase activity levels in the fetus, an effect that may extend until after birth (Yang, Zweig, Douthitt, & Federman, 1976).

With biological changes occurring so rapidly, the prenatal environment seems to be a very vulnerable one. The DNA does not unfold in a vacuum and the characteris-tics of the human's first home can have important effects on development, many of which we do not yet fully understand.

*Nutrition and the Internal Environment*    Food is a basic requirement of development—without it, the infant will die. But even if infants get enough calories, the kind of calories they consume can have subtle effects on development.

Eating too little protein is particularly harmful if it occurs during the early part of life when the brain cells are still dividing (Winick & Rosso, 1975). The effects of malnutrition on the brain usually are reversible if they occur later. If they occur while the brain cells are still dividing, however, the person will be left with fewer brain cells and will probably suffer some mental impairment. In animals, early malnutrition can have devastating effects, including reduced brain weight, loss of myelin, delayed brain development, delayed physical and motor develop-ment, and increased aggression. In humans, early malnutri-tion may have similar effects.

The role of nutrition in development can sometimes be quite subtle. Some scientists believe, for example, that synthetic food colorings can result in hyperactivity in certain responsive children (Weiss, 1981). Others maintain that aggressive behavior in children can be part of a "junk-food syndrome" (Bland, 1982). Eating too many empty calories deficient in key vitamins and minerals may alter biochemical activity in the brain, and may result in aggression, bad dreams, fatigue, and stomach pains. Eating too many calories, even if they are nutritionally sound and don't result in obesity, may hasten the aging process.

*Shaping Your Own Environment*    A growing number of researchers in psychology are beginning to emphasize the way that individuals, even young infants, shape their own environments (e.g., Scarr, 1992). Infants can influence the way their caretakers behave and respond to them, and babies begin making choices about their environments very early. Babies are active, influential partners in their interactions with other people. As children grow older, their behavior influences the other members of their family, their friends, and their teachers. Their early choices will influence the availability of opportunities later. For example, active, sports-minded children might choose soccer, while others choose board games, books, or bingo. The soccer player will acquire a great deal of information about team work and rules that the bingo player may not learn. By the end of junior high school, the soccer players are acquiring a set of values and attitudes that will influence both their later opportunities and choices. The ones who choose to read will, after a few years, have read a great many more books than the others and will have been exposed to a much wider range of knowledge. They, too, will have had a dramatic effect on the range of opportunities.

From the beginning, small individual differences in behavior can become magnified as the child's behavior affects the people and things in the surroundings. Even within a family, where many of the environmental forces acting on development would appear to be similar, children develop differently. As any parent who has more than one child knows, each child is unique. One might have an affectionate and loving temperament, another might be more withdrawn and unresponsive to the affection of others. One of the most surprising findings of many of the studies that look at genetic influences on behavior is that unrelated children who share the same family are so dissimilar. It seems that within families, children grow up in "microenvironments" that they help to shape themselves. A new mother demonstrates this in her conversation with a therapist:

> Therapist: Do you think your infant interacts differently with you when you are feeling depressed?
>
> Caregiver: Yes.
>
> Therapist: Can you describe how his interactions change at those times?
>
> Caregiver: (Smiling) He just laughs as if to make me laugh and come out of my depression. He's got those noises and sounds.

> Therapist: Do these interactions snap you out of the depression?
>
> Caregiver: (Nods, smiling broadly) Yes.
>
> Therapist: Do you think he does it intentionally, to pull you out, or do you think it's by accident?
>
> Caregiver: It seems like it's on purpose, like he calls me, laughing instead of whining (Trad, 1992).

## The Interaction between Genes and Environment in Development

A very old debate in psychology deals with the **nature-nurture issue.** *This issue revolves around the question of the relative importance of genetic factors (nature) and environmental factors (nurture) in shaping the characteristics of the developing human.* The argument has surfaced in many forms over the years. Behaviorists were closely aligned with "nurture" because of their emphasis on the environment. Scientists interested in evolution and with biological training usually emphasize the important role of genes in development and behavior.

Neither extreme point of view is correct. Since genes and environment cannot operate independently, they both must contribute to development and behavior by interacting. Some behaviors seem to have more genetic predisposition than others; deciding just how much genetic predisposition each one has is another topic for debate.

One very good example of the way in which genes and environment interact involves critical periods. Some environmental influences, such as malnutrition, are particularly devastating if they occur within a certain age range. Although the environment can usually have a good deal of impact outside of this age range, the critical period is especially sensitive and vulnerable. Malnutrition will affect the organism outside the critical period but its effects may not be so great. The genes dictate when that critical period will be, and the characteristics of the environment combined with the timing of the genes determine how development will proceed.

Critical periods exist for many environmental effects. Thalidomide had negative effects only on children whose mothers took the drug during the first few weeks of pregnancy. There also appear to be critical periods for attachment to the mother and for language learning as well. Nevertheless, human beings are remarkably adaptive. It would be much too rigid to suggest that a baby who did not develop a close relationship with a caregiver would forever be deficient in intimacy.

The nature-nurture debate continues; it is not a trivial issue. The outcome of the debate has implications for the way we choose to intervene in social problems. For example, if you support the theory that alcoholism has a strong genetic predisposition, you might support programs that attempt to prevent alcoholism in the siblings of known alcoholics. If you believe that environmental factors are the dominant influence in the disorder, you would attempt to remove alcoholics from environmental stressors. Because genes and environment interact, however, it is quite possible that *both* strategies might help alleviate the problem of alcoholism.

▶ **GUIDED REVIEW** *Learning Objectives 3, 4, and 5*

1. _____ and _____ are the two major forces that shape development.
2. Most body cells contain forty-six _____, or long chains of _____, the material that contains the genetic code. The code is the sequence of the bases _____, _____, _____, and _____ along the DNA. A _____ is a short sequence of bases, and each chromosome contains thousands of genes.
3. Genes can affect behavior indirectly by altering body chemistry and physiological functions. The _____ is one method used to determine whether genetic factors influence the development of complex behavioral traits.
4. Environmental factors begin affecting development from the moment of _____. The prenatal environment, for example, is critical in development. Drugs such as thalidomide and alcohol can be quite harmful to the developing fetus.
5. Nutrition is an important environmental variable that affects development throughout life. Malnutrition is particularly harmful to the developing brain if it occurs when brain cells are still _____.
6. Babies can shape their own environments, altering the way members of their family behave toward them through their own behavior. Within a family, babies develop within _____ that they partly shape themselves.
7. The _____ issue argues about the relative importance of genes and environment in human development. Most scientists agree that genes and environment must always _____ in their effects on development.

*ANWSERS*

1. Genes, environment 2. chromosomes, DNA, adenine, thymine, guanine, cytosine, gene 3. adoption study 4. conception 5. dividing 6. microenvironments 7. nature-nurture, interact

# BIRTH AND INFANCY

The most rapid developmental changes in a person's life, particularly biological ones, occur during the nine months preceding birth and the year after birth. From the microscopic fertilized egg, the developing human being's weight is multiplied about 11 million times by the time of birth (figure 9.4). Fortunately, during the baby's first year, weight gain slows down considerably, but it still usually triples by the first birthday. Never again in the life of a human being will biological changes proceed at such breakneck speed.

The process of childbirth is truly magnificent and often ranks among the most memorable experiences of parents' lives. The experience varies in different cultures, with some highlighting the role of the home and family, others the hospital and medical staff. Even in the United States, ideas about childbirth have changed many times. During the twentieth century, advances in medical science have been able to reduce the rate of birth injuries and infant mortality during the birth process. The result, however, has been to take childbirth out of the home and into the sterile environment of the hospital. Giving birth came to be seen as a condition of sickness, requiring medication and medical intervention, rather than a normal developmental process. At the peak of this trend, mothers were receiving many kinds of drugs to relieve the pain of childbirth, to speed up labor, and even to make them forget the entire experience.

Recently, however, people in the United States have begun to view childbirth as a very normal process that requires little or no medication and that can even take place at home. One part of this trend is the Lamaze method of childbirth. In this method, both the father and the mother attend classes prior to the birth of their child that cover prenatal development, labor, and delivery. Relaxation, neuromuscular control, and breathing techniques are taught during the classes to aid the mother during labor and delivery. The method is partly based on the sound psychological principle of conditioning. The mother is conditioned to begin breathing exercises with each contraction and to relax between contractions, thereby learning to control her pain and reduce her fear. The Lamaze method also emphasizes the father's role in childbirth; he is a "coach" for the mother, helping her through all the stages of labor, timing her contractions, pacing her breathing, and giving her moral support and encouragement. He is present in the delivery room and usually holds the newborn baby immediately after birth.

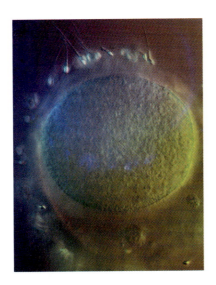

**Plate 9.A** *Sperm swarming about an ovum (egg) prior to fertilization.*

**Plate 9.B** *The mass of cells resulting from the repeated division of the fertilized egg after conception.*

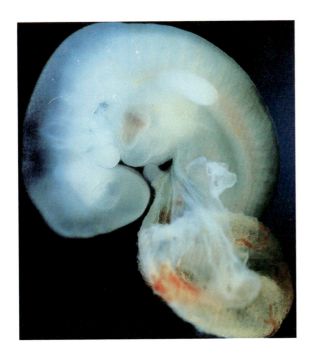

**Plate 9.C** *At 4 weeks, the embryo is about .2 inches long, and the head, eyes, and ears begin to show. The head and neck are half the body length; the shoulders will be located where the whitish arm buds are attached.*

**Plate 10.A**  *Fetus at 8 weeks, the beginning of the fetal period.*

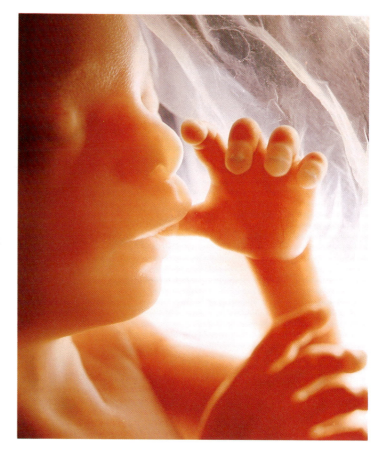

**Plate 10.B**  *At 4 1/2 months, the fetus is about 18 cm long (just over 7 inches). When the thumb comes close to the mouth, the head may turn and lips and tongue begin their sucking motions—a reflex for survival.*

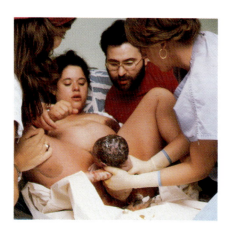

**Plate 10.C**  *Birth is a time of dramatic transition for a fetus; the baby is on a threshold between two worlds.*

*Babinski reflex*

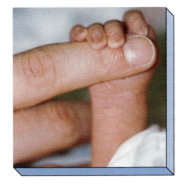

*Grasping reflex*

*Moro reflex*

| Reflex | Stimulation | Infant's response | Developmental pattern |
|---|---|---|---|
| Blinking | Flash of light, puff of air | Closes both eyes | Permanent |
| Babinski | Sole of foot stroked | Fans out toes, twists foot in | Disappears 9 months to 1 year |
| Grasping | Palms touched | Grasps tightly | Weakens after 3 months, disappears after 1 year |
| Moro (startle) | Sudden stimulation, such as hearing a loud noise or being dropped | Startles, arches back, throws head back, flings out arms and legs and then rapidly closes them to center of body | Disappears 3 to 4 months |
| Rooting | Cheek stroked or side of mouth touched | Turns head, opens mouth, begins sucking | Disappears 3 to 4 months |
| Stepping | Infant held above surface and feet lowered to touch surface | Moves feet as if to walk | Disappears 3 to 4 months |
| Sucking | Object touching mouth | Sucks automatically | Disappears 3 to 4 months |
| Swimming | Infant put face down in water | Makes coordinated swimming movements | Disappears 6 to 7 months |
| Tonic neck | Infant placed on back | Forms fists with both hands and usually turns head to the right (sometimes called the "fencer's pose" because the infant looks like it is assuming a fencer's position) | Disappears 2 months |

*Rooting reflex*

*Stepping reflex*

*Tonic neck reflex*

**Plate 11**   *Infant reflexes.*

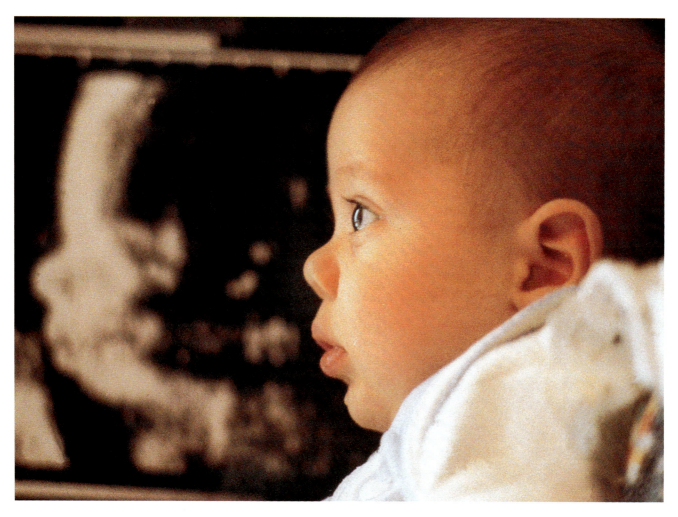

**Plate 12.A**    *A 6-month-old infant poses with the ultrasound sonography record taken 4 months into the baby's prenatal development.*

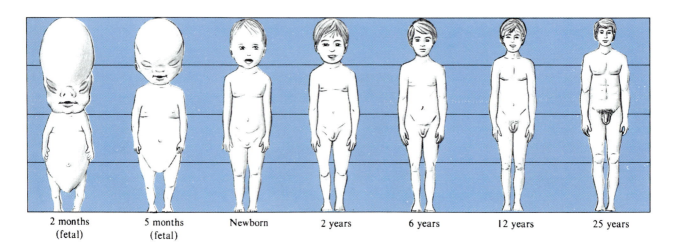

| 2 months (fetal) | 5 months (fetal) | Newborn | 2 years | 6 years | 12 years | 25 years |

**Plate 12.B**    *Changes in body form and proportion during prenatal and postnatal growth.*
*Note the changes in body proportions from 2 months into fetal development to 25 years of age.*

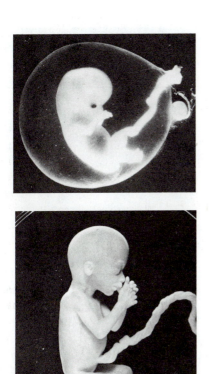

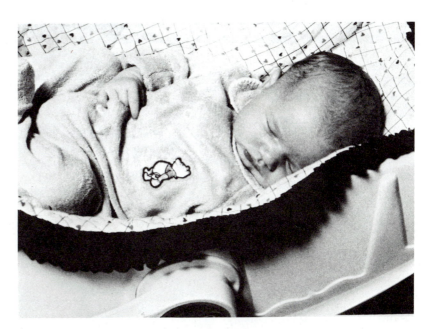

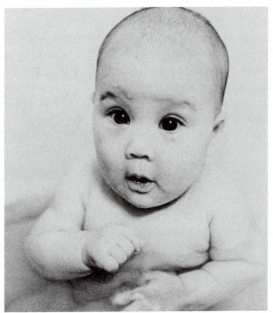

**Figure 9.4** *Tremendous changes occur in a human being from the moment of conception to the first year after birth.*

Emotional support during childbirth is a key ingredient, and the Lamaze method relies heavily on the father. At one United States hospital, specially trained women called "doulas" offered this kind of support, from admission through delivery, to a group of new mothers in labor. "Doula" is the Greek word for an experienced mother who guides a new mother in infant care. Compared to a control group of new mothers, the ones who had their own doula needed fewer cesarean sections and less pain medication.

Other new trends in childbirth include rooming-in, in which the baby stays in a bassinet in the mother's hospital room rather than in the nursery with all the other babies, and birthing rooms, where the furnishings are more homelike. The number of mothers breast-feeding their infants is also increasing rapidly.

| TABLE 9.2 Milestones of motor development in three areas | | | |
| --- | --- | --- | --- |
| Age in Months | Head | Control of Trunk and Arms | Legs |
| Birth | | | |
| 1 | Side-to-side movement | | Limited-support stepping reflex |
| 2 | Hold head and chin up | | |
| 3 | | Hold chest up in face-down position | |
| 4 | | Reach for objects in sight (without success) | |
| 5 | Head erect in sitting position | | |
| 6 | | Sit up with some support | |
| 7 | | Roll over in prone position | |
| 8 | | | Walk with assistance |
| 9 | | | |
| 10 | | | Support self alone |
| 11 | | | Pull self up in standing position |
| 12 | | | |
| 13 | | | Walk alone |
| 14 | | | |

From John W. Santrock and Steven R. Yussen, *Child Development,* 3d ed. Copyright © 1987 Wm. C. Brown Communications, Inc., Dubuque, Iowa. All Rights Reserved. Reprinted by permission.

These trends are also beneficial for the baby. Babies born to mothers who receive heavy medication during labor often are sluggish for at least three days after birth. Reducing the amount of medication helps the baby adjust to the outside world more quickly. Although the experience of birth is a very stressful one for the baby and the mother, the hormones produced during this stress appear to be critical in helping the infant survive during delivery and outside the womb. Babies born through a planned cesarean section lack this surge of hormones and are more likely to have breathing difficulties (Lagercrantz & Slotkin, 1986).

Encouraging the mother to keep the baby in her room has advantages as well. In addition to reducing the number of infections that spread rapidly in the crowded nursery, rooming-in encourages the growth of love and attachment between the two.

## The Abilities of the Newborn

Unlike many newborns in the animal kingdom, the human newborn seems very dependent and vulnerable. It can't survive alone and seems to be able to do little more than cry, sleep, and suck. But researchers have created many inventive ways to find out more about what a newborn can do. They've learned to record subtle changes in babies' heartbeats, arm waving, sucking patterns, leg kicking, and eye movements, and they have found that newborns are astonishingly capable individuals.

*Motor Behavior* Infants are born with a group of reflexes, some of which are critical to survival. Sucking is an example. The **rooting reflex** is *another reflex present at birth; when infants are stroked near the mouth, they will open their mouths and turn their heads in the direction of the stimulation.* Other reflexes are less obviously connected with important biological functions. The **Babinski reflex** *results in bending of the toes when the sole of the foot is stroked; normal infants curl their toes upward; older children and adults curl them downward.*

The motor areas of the cortex are not well myelinated at birth, so infants' voluntary motor coordination is not yet developed. However, as the months go by, infants gain more and more control over the large muscle groups (table 9.2). Control first appears in the head and extends downward as they grow older. For example, at two months babies can hold their heads and chins up; at three months they can raise their chest as well.

*The Sensory World* The newborn can sort out the sensory environment very early. In one study, three-day-old babies listened to tape recordings of either their mothers or female strangers reading a story. During the readings, the babies sucked on a pacifier containing electronic equipment that controlled the tape recorder. The baby could control which voice came on by changing the sucking pattern. To everyone's surprise, these tiny infants changed their sucking patterns in order to hear more of their

**ONE-MONTH-OLD**

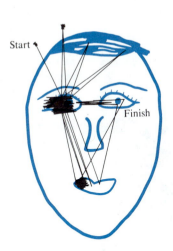

**TWO-MONTH-OLD**

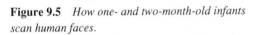

**Figure 9.5**  *How one- and two-month-old infants scan human faces.*

mothers' voices. Not only could they discriminate between the two voices, they clearly preferred their mothers' voices and would work to hear them (DeCasper & Fifer, 1980).

The world of sound is obviously not a big confusing jumble to newborns. Besides being able to discriminate their mothers' voices, they can identify their own vocalizations. Calm babies begin to cry when they hear the tape-recorded crying of other babies, but they cry very little if they hear a recording of their own crying. Listening to their own crying on tape often stops babies from crying, even when they are only eighteen-hours-old (Martin & Clark, 1982; Simner, 1971; Sagi & Hoffman, 1976). Some psychologists maintain that this represents the earliest glimmerings of empathy, a clear sign of social behavior. Empathy in this sense is only a very primitive ability to detect the emotional state of another being and to respond in kind.

During the 1960s, experts in child care believed that babies could see little more than light or dark patterns during the first weeks of life. Today psychologists know that newborns see shapes very well, although their color vision takes longer to develop. Classic studies of infant perception have been conducted by Robert Fantz and his coworkers (Fantz, 1961; Fantz, Fagan, & Miranda, 1975a, b). These researchers presented two images to infants and observed how long they looked at each. Using this technique, they found that babies prefer facelike figures to bull's eyes, and bull's eyes to solid circles. Infants also

spend more time looking at novel images rather than familiar ones.

Studying what infants prefer to look at or listen to has provided some fascinating insights about babies. One particularly intriguing, and puzzling, finding is that babies spend more time looking at attractive faces compared to unattractive ones (Langlois et al., 1991). Photos of men, women, and infants were judged on their attractiveness by undergraduate students, and then collected into pairs of stimuli. Each pair contained photos showing people of the same sex, same race, and same age, but one of the pair had been judged high on attractiveness while the other had been judged low. Six-month-old babies were then shown the slide pairs and their looking patterns were recorded. The infants spent more time looking at the attractive faces, regardless of the race, sex, or age of the people in the photos.

This finding comes as a surprise to most people who believe that "beauty is in the eye of the beholder," and that judgments of attractiveness are gradually learned through cultural transmission. Most of the babies had little experience with the faces of other infants, and since most were white they also had little experience with the faces of black women. Yet the infants "agreed" with the judgments of adults about their attractiveness. These researchers suggest that judgments of "attractiveness" may be less a culturally distinct judgment than we thought. They might have evolutionary roots, or they might be related to the best example of the prototype of "face." People with average features, for example, are generally not judged average in attractiveness at all. They are usually judged highly attractive.

Although we don't know why infants prefer attractive faces over unattractive ones, we do know how they visually scan faces, and what features they concentrate on (Salapatek, 1975; Banks & Salapatek, 1981; Maurer & Salapatek, 1976). When infants are shown pictures, their eye movements can be recorded photographically, and their scanning patterns can be correlated with the contents of the images. Figure 9.5 shows how one- and two-month-old infants scan the faces of people (not drawings or photographs) through a mirror arrangement. The scanning patterns of the two-month-old babies were somewhat

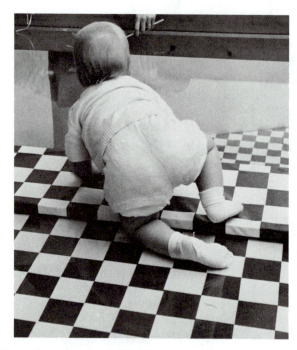

**Figure 9.6**  *The visual cliff. The side with the pattern several feet below the glass looks like a sharp cliff to the infant.*

different from those of the younger babies. The older infants scanned more of the faces, focusing their attention on the eyes and mouth. The one-month-old babies paid more attention to certain areas on the head and the chin.

The visual abilities of infants develop rapidly enough to provide some measure of protection against dangers. Some classic studies were performed by Richard Walk and Eleanor Gibson (1961), who used the visual cliff apparatus to study depth perception (figure 9.6). The "cliff" is a solid glass tabletop suspended over a checkerboard-covered "shallow" side and "deep" side. Infants refuse to crawl across the deep side despite coaxing by the parents; they are relying more on the messages they receive from their eyes about depth, than on those from their hands, which tell them the floor is solid. Even before they can crawl, infants show an increase in heart rate when they are placed face down on the deep side, suggesting that depth perception appears very early.

*The Newborn's Speech*    The rudiments of speech communication seem to be present in infants as well. They engage in various kinds of "vocal dialogues" with their mothers. In one experiment, researchers recorded the vocalizations of three-day-old infants and their mothers

during breast-feeding (Rosenthal, 1982). The infants were more likely to start cooing and gurgling when the mother was vocalizing than when she was silent; the babies seemed to "join in." In other experiments, older babies developed patterns of vocalization in which they alternated with their mothers, much like the normal pattern of conversation.

## Emotional Development

Human infants have a great deal of growing to do in the first year of life and much of it revolves around emotional development. Babies have their own emotions and can affect other people with them in subtle ways.

*Temperament*    Infants show some remarkable individual differences during their first year of life. Some are quickly soothed by a warm caress, others seem much fussier and are difficult to calm when they become distressed. Some react strongly to a sudden noise by crying and rapid heart beat; others seem barely to notice such disturbances. Some infants seem eager to play little games, show more smiling and are generally more socially responsive than others. In other words, babies seem to have different temperaments, beginning very early in life (Rothbart, 1991; Collins & Gunnar, 1990).

Measuring these differences in temperament has been a difficult task. Researchers have used many yardsticks, such as general activity levels, how often a baby cries, laughs, or smiles during a one-hour test period, questionnaires filled in by the parents, observations of the baby's interactions with others, or records of heart rate responses. Using these and other measures, babies can be scored on their level of both positive and negative emotionality. Some babies are high on both, some on neither. Many are high on one kind of emotionality but low on the other.

Interest in babies' temperament is very keen because researchers believe it may form the foundation of later personality development. As we mentioned earlier, babies begin to shape their own environments, and a baby's temperament may be one of the important ways to do it. Differences in temperament appear to be partly due to genetic variation, judging from the findings from adoption studies (Braungart et al., 1992) and from the fact that the differences appear so early. Yet, as is true with most behaviors that have some genetic component, it can change. Temperament is only moderately stable in the early months—a fussy, irritable baby can become calmer and more social, and vice versa.

# APPLYING PSYCHOLOGY

## The Challenge of Child Care

With more and more women with young children joining the labor force, the question, "Who takes care of the kids?" has become a critical one. Parents agonize over the choices they must make when their infant arrives. Should the mother return to work? Should she work part-time? Should the father stay home? Should they enroll the child in a day-care center, seek the help of grandparents or other relatives, or hire a babysitter? Their choices are affected by their economic situation, the policies of their employers, the culture, and their concern for the healthy development of their new baby.

Research on the effects of maternal employment and different kinds of child-care arrangements is generating a great deal of heated debate. Studies of children whose mothers work and who receive nonmaternal care for at least part of the day have found both positive and negative effects. For example, children ages three to six who attend preschool generally benefit from the experience. Developmentally-oriented preschools can make a substantial contribution to children's cognitive and social skills, and help prepare the child for an easier transition to kindergarten. This is particularly true for children from disadvantaged environments.

For younger children, though, the effects of maternal employment, and the alternate child-care arrangements that go with it, are not clear. Some researchers find that children whose mothers return to work during the first year of life may not fare as well as children whose mothers reenter the work force a year or two later (Baydar & Brooks-Gunn, 1991; Vandell and Corasaniti, 1990). Boys, in particular, may show more insecure attachments though the long-term effects of these findings are unknown (Belsky & Rovine, 1988). Other researchers question these findings and suggest that infants who receive high-quality nonmaternal care suffer no ill effects, and may even benefit from the experience of having more than one supportive caregiver (Fox & Fein, 1990).

Parents of older school-age children also have difficult choices to make about after-school care. Some parents choose after-hours care at the school if it is available, some hire babysitters or ask relatives and neighbors for help, and others let their "latchkey" children come home to an empty house. Surprisingly, a recent study found that children whose mothers were home to take care of them had more behavior problems compared to latchkey children or children who attended school programs. But the differences disappeared when family income and emotional environment were controlled, since many of the mother-care children were in difficult homes with single, unemployed mothers (Vandell & Ramanan, 1991).

This study and others like it point to the importance of the quality of the child's care, whether it is from the mother, the grandmother, a relative, a babysitter, or a day-care center. Although we often assume that mother-care is best—especially for babies— this may not be true if the mother is in poverty, single, and under a great deal of stress. Day-care centers in the United States vary enormously in quality, though parents are not always very good at discriminating the good ones from the bad. In some, the reality of life at an overcrowded center with inattentive, poorly trained and underpaid child-care workers is very different from the descriptions in the glossy brochures (Fallows, 1985).

Among industrialized countries, the laws, policies, and customs for new parents vary considerably. In the United States, new mothers might receive six weeks off, often without pay. Many European countries offer more generous benefits to make it economically possible for the mother, father, or both to spend more time at home with their infants. Swedish mothers, for example, can stay home for most of the first year with ninety percent of their salary paid by the social insurance system. By the end of the third year, most Swedish children are in some form of alternate child-care arrangements, usually state supported day-care centers that double as preschools. Studies of children who enroll show that the centers have many positive effects on cognitive, emotional, and social behavior, even for those who started day care in infancy (Andersson, 1992).

The controversies and questions surrounding child care can only be partly resolved through psychological research. While the Swedish model is an attractive one and seems to provide a positive environment for child development in a country where most mothers work outside the home, it is costly and would mean higher taxes or loss of other benefits. As the debate over child care continues, parents will be wrestling with these difficult issues.

One group of researchers was interested in learning more about infants whose temperaments change in the first year of life (Belsky et al., 1991). They took multiple measures of temperament at three and nine months of age, and also many measures of family interactions before and after the baby was born. One of their findings was that some infants who started out as difficult babies, with high levels of fussiness and negative emotions, became more agreeable later. The mother's behavior was an important ingredient. Mothers with happier marriages and high self-esteem, and who had harmonious interactions with their babies, were more likely to see this shift. Some babies, however, showed temperament shifts in the other direction and the results suggested that the father played a role in this unfortunate development. Fathers who were insensitive, dissatisfied with their marriages, and generally uninvolved with their infants, were most likely to see their baby go from a pleasant 3-month-old to a negative and irritable 9-month-old.

## Social Development

During the first year of life the infant begins to develop socially as well as emotionally, forming relationships with the family that may last a lifetime. In particular, an attachment develops between the child and the caregiver, whether it is the mother, the father, both, or some other person. Attachment is not simply a matter of finding a person who will take care of a baby's physical needs. It is an important part of emotional and social growth, and it is vital to the development of a healthy personality (Sroufe, 1985; Collins & Gunnar, 1990).

*Mother Love in Monkeys*    Classic studies of monkeys reared without their mothers show how important the attachment process is (Harlow, 1962). Infant monkeys were taken away from their mothers soon after birth and kept in cages with two artificial substitute mothers. Both artificial mothers were wire models with heads, and one had a terrycloth covering. The infant monkeys became quite attached to the cloth-covered "monkey," running to it in times of stress and spending a great deal of time holding on to it. The monkeys preferred this cloth surrogate even when the wire surrogate was the one that always provided the food (figure 9.7).

Formerly, many psychologists believed that infants became attached to their mothers through classical conditioning—the mother became associated with food. But the attachment of these monkeys to the cloth surrogate was not based on food rewards; it was based on other factors, one of which seemed to be the softness of body contact with the terrycloth. Later studies showed that infant monkeys prefer cloth surrogates that move gently to those that are stationary. No one would conclude that the essence of mother love is soft skin or a swaying motion, but body contact and the normal motion accompanying the carrying of a baby seem to contribute to the phenomenon.

The monkeys reared with the lifeless surrogate mothers, even cloth surrogates, did not develop normally. They

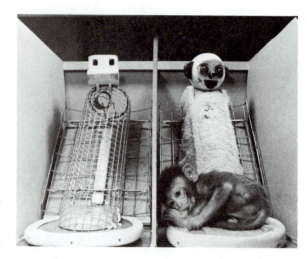

**Figure 9.7**    *A "wire surrogate mother" (left) and a "cloth surrogate mother" (right) for an infant monkey (Courtesy Harlow Primate Lab, University of Wisconsin)*

became very fearful and aggressive, and the females made poor mothers when they reached adulthood. Monkeys, it seems, need a live, affectionate caretaker to develop normally. Although similar studies have never been conducted on human beings, there is good reason to believe that the attachment process is as important to humans as it is to monkeys. Infants reared in institutional settings, where they get adequate physical care but are unable to develop an attachment with one individual, develop abnormally. They become socially apathetic and usually have poor cognitive development as well.

One aspect of mother love that may be especially important is body contact. In studies on rats, pups reared without maternal contact fail to synthesize certain proteins essential for growth. The deprived pups are not suffering from poor nutrition; their brains appear to be releasing an endorphin (described in chapter 4) that interferes with the synthesis of proteins needed during early life. If the rats are once again returned to their mothers or given an artificial substitute, such as frequent stroking with a wet paintbrush, their development resumes normally (Schanberg, Bartholome, & Kuhn, 1987). In human babies, touching also seems to be important to development. Premature infants given frequent back massages and other body contact experiences showed a fifty percent increase in body weight over a twelve-day period (Schanberg & Field, 1987).

*Personality Development and Attachment*    From the first day of life, babies begin to develop personalities and form relationships. Erik Erikson's theory (1972) of human development, which covers the entire life span, stresses the idea that human beings are both the products and the shapers of their histories, and that each human being faces a series of psychosocial conflicts at each stage of development. These conflicts represent opportunities for growth, rather than tests of character that, if failed, will damage the developmental process irreversibly. Born in Germany in 1902, Erikson's life was spent in periods of tremendous political upheaval in Europe, when wars disrupted families and bombs destroyed entire cities. Not surprisingly, his ideas about human development stressed the importance of a person's time and place in history.

Erikson's theories emphasize attachment and the developing relationship between the child and the caregiver during the first year of life. **Trust versus mistrust** *is the first psychosocial task the human faces. This conflict revolves around whether the baby can successfully form a trusting attachment with his or her caregiver.* If such an attachment is formed, the baby develops a sense of trust and learns that it is possible to depend on adults to provide reliable and loving care. If the baby fails to develop this sense of trust, personality development will be affected.

A British study illustrates what can happen to children who do not develop an attachment during the early part of life (Tizard, 1975). The subjects were babies reared in residential nurseries run by British voluntary societies. Although they had wonderful physical care and received a fair amount of attention from adults, they could not form lasting attachments to specific people. Turnover among the staff was high because the institutions were used to train student nurses. As the children grew up, they were much more clinging and dependent on the nurses than were children reared in normal families. They cried and whined more, they were less willing to share their belongings with other children, and many were unusually aggressive. In addition their mental development was slightly retarded, and they generally became toilet trained at a later age than children reared in their own homes. Whether these personality disturbances continued into later childhood depended on whether the children were adopted, restored to their natural mothers, or left in the institution. The adopted children fared quite well; the adopting parents were carefully screened, loving people who probably provided an environment in which the child could form a normal attachment. The children restored to their own mothers, however, often continued to show personality disturbances. Several natural mothers had ambivalent feelings toward the youngsters, and some did not want the child home.

In the extreme case of institutional rearing, a baby might not form an attachment to one particular person, but even in normal families, babies can form different kinds of attachments. Mary Ainsworth and her colleagues developed the **Strange Situations Test,** *designed to assess the nature of the attachment between an infant and mother or other caregiver.* It consists of a sequence of episodes in which the mother and a stranger leave the room and return while researchers carefully observe the child's behavior. (The Close Up on Research: Measuring Attachment describes this test in more detail.)

Some babies show **secure attachments** *to their caregivers; they show a healthy balance between dependence and exploration, using the mother as a secure base for exploration of a new environment but decreasing their explorations when she leaves the room.* They actively greet the mother when she returns. Other babies show **insecure attachments;** *they show several different reactions to the mother's departure and return, including avoidance, resistance, and ambivalent emotional responses* (Ainsworth, Blehar, Waters, & Wall, 1978).

Attachment classifications for infants are relatively stable over time, unless some major changes or stresses occur in the family. For example, maltreated toddlers do not behave in a consistent way on these tests so their attachment classifications change more than children who are not abused (Schneider-Rosen et al., 1985).

The Strange Situations Test has been used to assess attachment patterns in different cultures, though the results are difficult to interpret. In the United States, about seventy percent of the children fall into the secure classification, twenty percent in the avoidant group, and ten percent in the resistant group. Higher proportions of avoidant and resistant classifications have been found in tests conducted in Israel, Japan, and West Germany. Interpreting this kind of research in different cultures is particularly tricky because the situation itself may mean quite different things. In Japan, for example, babysitting is not a widely known form of child care so leaving a child in a room with a stranger is not common. The entire situation may cause more fear than it would to a baby in the United States (Sagi et al., 1991).

# CLOSE UP ON RESEARCH

## Measuring Attachment

The way a child becomes attached to the primary caregiver has been a topic of considerable interest to psychologists and parents alike. However, studying attachment behavior and measuring it in real-life situations has been extremely difficult. A great deal of information has been accumulated through interviews with parents, but this technique has many drawbacks. Parents' memories are notoriously selective when they are discussing their children and the way they interact with them. Many parents tend to report that they used whichever childrearing practices were endorsed by the experts of the era.

Researchers in child development are now depending more heavily on actual observations of interactions between the caregiver and the child. Videotape recordings are especially useful because researchers can play the tapes over and over to different people, making sure their judgments of the events are reliable.

One very popular strategy for assessing attachment behavior is the Ainsworth Strange Situations Test (Ainsworth & Bell, 1970). It consists of a sequence of episodes designed to determine how the child behaves in a series of introductions, separations, and reunions with the child's mother and a stranger. Some of the episodes are described below:

Episode 1: Mother, accompanied by an observer, carried the baby into the room. Then the observer left.

Episode 2: Mother put the baby down in the specified place and then sat quietly in her chair, participating only if the baby sought her attention. (Duration: three minutes.)

Episode 3: A stranger entered, sat quietly for one minute, conversed with the mother for one minute, and then gradually approached the baby, showing the baby a toy. At the end of the third minute, the mother quietly left the room.

Episode 4: If the baby was happily engaged in play, the stranger was nonparticipant. If the baby was inactive, the stranger tried to interest the baby in the toys. If the baby was distressed, the stranger tried to distract or comfort him or her. If the baby could not be comforted, the episode was curtailed; otherwise it lasted 3 minutes.

Episode 5: The mother entered and paused in the doorway to give the baby an opportunity to respond spontaneously to her. The stranger then left unobtrusively. What the mother did next was not specified except that she was told that after the baby was again settled in play with the toys, she was to leave again after pausing to say "bye-bye." (Duration of episode undetermined.)

Although the Strange Situations Test provides much richer and more meaningful information about attachment than interviews, it has been criticized. In particular, the sequences are very fluid, and experimental controls are lacking. For example, if the baby begins to cry in the middle of episode 4, can we assume it is because the mother is gone? Or should we attribute the baby's distress to an inability to relax in the presence of a stranger? Despite these difficulties in interpretation, most researchers agree that direct observation of this kind is very informative.

Why do some children form secure attachments and others insecure ones? Interactions with the caregiver seem to play an important role. Parents who are anxious themselves about separations are more likely to have children who show anxiety on these occasions. Insecure attachments are also more common in children of mothers with major depression, compared to mothers with minor or no depression. A parent's idea of what a relationship with an infant should be like may also play a role. A mother, for example, may develop her thinking about the proper relationship with an infant through her own childhood experiences. If she experienced rejection or was pushed toward independence early, she may follow that pattern with her own child (Crowell & Feldman, 1991). A baby's early temperament may also affect the development of attachment patterns. A baby who smiles a great deal and obviously enjoys peekaboo games or "this little piggy"

may easily become securely attached, and also elicit the kind of behavior patterns from her parents that reinforce secure attachment.

Attachment patterns in infancy seem to be related in complex ways to later development. For example, researchers observed the behavior of preschool children whose attachment behavior had been measured in infancy. The children who had developed secure attachments during infancy, especially the girls, tended to be more socially adept and competent with their peers, participated more, and generally attained higher social status when compared to those with insecure attachments in infancy (La Freniere & Sroufe, 1985). In contrast, children with insecure attachments at 12-months-old are more likely to show excessive dependency and behavior problems in preschool and later.

The nature of the attachment an infant forms early in life may have wide-ranging effects during the child's later development; more research is needed to understand these effects (Sroufe, 1985).

▶ **GUIDED REVIEW** *Learning Objectives 6, 7, 8, and 9*

1. _____ is an important developmental transition for both infant and mother. New trends in the United States include the use of the _____ method of prepared childbirth, rooming-in, and birthing rooms. The trends make childbirth less a medical event and more a personal one that involves less medication and more opportunity for _____ between mother and baby.

2. Motor abilities of the newborn primarily consist of reflexes, such as sucking, _____, and the _____. The infant's motor skills develop from the head downward. Tests of sensory abilities show that the baby can discriminate sounds and visual stimuli at a very early age.

3. Infants show differences in _____ very early, and these may form part of the basis for later personality differences. The behavior of the mother and the father is associated with changes in temperament during the first year of life.

4. The attachment process is important for the baby's normal development. Studies of motherless monkeys demonstrated that infant monkeys need mothers not just for food but for body contact and security. In humans, the first year is important for the development of trust, a process that requires attachment. Different kinds of attachment in infants have been demonstrated by the _____, including _____ and various kinds of insecure attachments.

*ANSWERS*

*1. Childbirth, Lamaze, attachment. 2. rooting, Babinski reflex 3. temperament 4. Strange Situations Test, secure attachments.*

# CHILDHOOD

The years between the ages of one and about twelve are exciting for both the child and the parents. Biologically, the child is growing much more slowly than during prenatal life or even during the first year. Still, the changes are remarkable, and they occur in every area of development. The child develops physically: adding weight, gaining control over major and minor muscle groups, and learning to walk, run, hop, and play ball. Socially, the child's world expands from just the parents to the family group and eventually to children and adults near home and at school. The child begins to develop morally as well. First the concepts of good and bad are associated with whatever is approved or disapproved by the parents. Later good and bad are linked to rewards and punishment. And

still later, toward the end of childhood, children acquire a sense of justice and fair play.

## Cognitive Development

Jean Piaget proposed the most influential theory of cognitive development, one that emphasized the growth of knowledge in children (Beilin, 1992). He believed that knowledge was not so much a storehouse of information but a process that included the actions a person performs. Young children have knowledge about a ball that consists of picking it up, bouncing it, pressing it between the fingers, and tossing it. As they mature, they gain more experience with this kind of direct, physical knowing, and begin to rely more on mental representations of events in the form of images and symbols. The older child's knowledge becomes increasingly mental. Young children are little physicists, doing empirical "hands-on" research. Older ones can think about the objects and use their representations to draw conclusions.

Many of Piaget's ideas about cognitive development came from direct observations of children, including his own. He presented them with problems and noted not so much whether they could solve them, but how much they understood about their own solution. Piaget noticed that at different ages children's notions about objects and events changed considerably. Even though children of different ages might be able to solve a particular problem, their cognitions about the objects and events are dramatically different. Consider the game of tiddlywinks, played on a carpet:

Experimenter: Try and get one of the pawns (her word) into the box. (She puts the small counter on the large one and then presses down on the former, with all her attention on the movement of her hand and none on the target.) Where did it go?

Flo (age 4): Onto the table.

E: How did you do it?

F: I pressed very hard.

E: Can you do it on the table?

F: (She tries.) No, because it slides.

E: Why?

F: Because the table isn't soft.

Flo was able to get the tiddlywink into the target box, but she did not understand why. She thought that the main action was simply pressing, rather than pressing the edge of the small counter on the edge of the larger one. She also could not fully grasp why the game worked on the carpet and not on the table. Older children would describe the events quite differently since they perceive the role the small counter plays (Piaget, 1976).

Based on his observations, Piaget concluded that a child's thought goes through a series of fundamental changes, such that the later ways of thinking are dependent upon, yet quite distinct from, earlier ones. Each stage is progressively more logical than the last.

The progression through these stages is brought about through two complementary processes: assimilation and accommodation. **Assimilation** *occurs when a child encounters a new experience that fits reasonably well into the knowledge structures the child already has.* For example, a child meets a St. Bernard and although she has never seen one before, she concludes that it is a dog. When the child has an experience that doesn't fit into any of her knowledge structures, one of two things can occur. She might simply fail to comprehend the experience at all and ignore it. Or she might engage in **accommodation,** *in which she would revise, refine, or add to her existing knowledge structures.* If the little girl saw a raccoon and assumed it was a dog, her parents might say, "No, that is a raccoon," and tell her a little about the differences. Then she would probably accommodate to the experience by revising her concept of dog and building a concept of a raccoon, focusing on what makes the two animals different.

Piaget proposed four stages of cognitive development: sensorimotor stage, preoperational stage, concrete operational stage, and formal operational stage (see table 9.3).

*Sensorimotor Stage*    The **sensorimotor stage** *is the earliest of Piaget's stages of cognitive development. It extends from birth to about age two. During this period, infants gradually develop the capability to coordinate their sensations and perceptions with their physical actions.*

One ability acquired during this stage is called **object permanence,** *the understanding that an object exists independent of the self and continues to exist even when it cannot be immediately perceived.* For example, when you show a toy to a five-month-old, he or she tracks it visually and may reach for it. If you hide the toy under a scarf, the baby acts as though the toy no longer exists. By the age of ten months, however, the infant will actively search for the hidden toy, demonstrating acquisition of object permanence.

The way babies of different ages respond to the unexpected appearance of a toy shows how object permanence develops. Babies of five, nine, and sixteen months were seated in an infant seat in front of a screen. A toy on a circular track moved in front of the screen, behind it, and then around in front again. After several rounds, the experimenters replaced the familiar toy with a new one, behind the screen. When the new toy came into the babies' view, the experimenters rated their facial expressions for raised brows, dropped jaws, or other signs of surprise. None of the five-month-old babies showed any surprise when the unexpected toy appeared. But all the sixteen-month-olds and some of the nine-month olds did (Gratch, 1982). The youngest infants had no sense that the first toy was permanent and continued to exist after it went behind the screen; thus, they were not surprised when a new toy appeared.

*Preoperational Stage*    The **preoperational stage,** *extending from about two years of age to seven years of age, is characterized by the acquisition of language, the growth in the use of symbols, and a limited kind of logical thinking.* Even though children are beginning to talk like adults, they are not yet thinking like adults. Their cognitive processes are different in several ways.

One such difference involves **egocentrism,** *the failure to appreciate that another person's perceptions may differ from one's own.* Preoperational children are dominated by their own visual impressions, and they think that everyone sees what they see. They might, for example, cover their eyes and claim that you can't see them. If you ask a little boy whether he has a brother, he would say "yes." But if you ask him whether his brother has a brother, the preoperational child might say "no."

Another example of the limitations of preoperational thought involves **conservation,** *the fact that basic properties of objects often remain unchanged despite superficial changes in appearance.* If you show six-year-old children two equal-sized lumps of clay and ask whether the lumps were about equal, the children would say "yes." If you then rolled one lump of clay into a snake before their eyes and asked the same question, they would probably say that the snake had more clay. Because visual impressions are so important to preoperational children, they cannot grasp that a change in shape did not affect the amount of clay present in the lump.

A remarkable and sudden change in cognitive flexibility occurs between the ages of two and a half and three,

**TABLE 9.3 Piaget's stages of cognitive development**

| Stage | General Descriptions | Age Level |
|---|---|---|
| *Sensorimotor Period* | The child progresses from instinctual reflexive action at birth to symbolic activities to the ability to separate self from object in the environment. He develops limited capabilities for anticipating the consequences of actions. | 0<br>1/2<br>1<br>1 1/2<br>2 |
| *Preoperational Period* | The child's ability to think becomes refined during this period. First, he develops what Piaget calls preconceptual thinking, in which he deals with each thing individually but is not able to group objects. The child is able to use symbols, such as words, to deal with problems. During the latter half of this period, the child develops better reasoning abilities but is still bound to the here-and-now. | 2 1/2<br>3<br>3 1/2<br>4<br>4 1/2<br>5<br>5 1/2<br>6<br>6 1/2<br>7 |
| *Concrete Operations* | At this stage, the child develops the ability to perform intellectual operations—such as reversibility; conservation; ordering of things by number, size, or class, etc. His ability to relate time and space is also matured during this period. | 7 1/2<br>8<br>8 1/2<br>9<br>9 1/2<br>10<br>10 1/2 |
| *Periods of Formal Operations* | This is the period in which the person learns hypothetical reasoning. He is able to function purely on a symbolic, abstract level. His conceptualization capacities are matured. | 11<br>11 1/2<br>12<br>12 1/2<br>13<br>13 1/2<br>14<br>14 1/2<br>15 |

From Gary S. Belkin and Jerry L. Gray, *Educational Psychology: An Introduction,* 2d ed. Copyright © 1977 Wm. C. Brown Communications, Inc., Dubuque, Iowa. Reprinted by permission of the author.

signaling the child's leap from the sensorimotor stage to the use of symbols common to preoperational thought (DeLoache, 1987). Children develop an understanding of symbolic relations. In this study, two-and-a-half-year-old and three-year-old children were shown a scale model of a room; they then saw the experimenter hide a scale model of a toy behind a piece of furniture in the miniature room. The children were then asked to find the real toy in the real room, which was hidden in the same "place." Almost none of the younger children could perform this task, but almost all of the older children could. This suggests that the older children had rather abruptly, during a period of less than six months, developed the ability to think about a symbolic object both as an object and as a symbol for another object.

*Concrete Operational Stage* The **concrete operational stage** *lasts from about age seven to age eleven and is characterized by the need to anchor thought in concrete events.* Many of the limitations of logical thought characteristic of the preoperational stage are gone, although they don't disappear all at once. Children in this stage begin to grasp the concept of conservation. If you show them two milk cartons, both the same height but one wider than the other, the child in the concrete operational stage would know that the wider carton could hold more milk. The preoperational child has much more trouble with this kind of problem because it involves an analysis of two variables at the same time (width and height). The concrete operational child would also know that the flattened clay ball was the same size as the round one because at this stage the child is able to deal with more than one dimension.

In the concrete operational stage, the child's view is less dominated by egocentrism. In addition, children in this stage can think logically; they can draw a diagram of a neighborhood and trace the route to a friend's house, organize objects by increasing size, and classify objects according to dimensions such as color or shape.

*Formal Operational Stage*     The **formal operational stage** *usually begins around puberty. It is characterized by the ability to think about both concrete and abstract events, and by the ability to formulate and test hypotheses to solve problems.* An adolescent can solve algebra problems, for example, using only abstract symbols. For Piaget, this stage was the most advanced, though others argue that advances in cognitive development come during adulthood.

The ability to use abstractions, apart from their concrete meanings, is an intriguing feature of the formal operational stage. For example, a child might be presented with the following problem:

> The garage is taller than the house, and the car is taller than the garage. Which is taller, the house or the car?

This kind of question shows the difference between the way the child in concrete operational stage thinks, and the ability of the child in the formal operational stage to use abstraction and logic, despite the apparent absurdity of the premises. A child in the formal operational stage would be able to think of the car, house, and garage as symbols, and use the relationships in the premises of the problem to give a correct answer. Children in the concrete operational stage are limited in their ability to do this.

*Evaluating Piaget's Theory*     Piaget's theories have been remarkably durable as far as psychological theories are concerned. Nevertheless, further research has produced debate about the validity of some of Piaget's theories, as well as some revisions.

One premise that needs revision involves the fact that children appear to develop certain abilities earlier than Piaget proposed. Preoperational children, for instance, are not totally egocentric; they can often describe what another person sees from that person's perspective, even when it isn't the same as their own perspective. A preoperational child who has just drawn a picture of a cat with some markings that appeared to be flowers nearby was asked what the markings were. She said they didn't have anything to do with people—they were what the cat is looking at.

Babies also seem to have a better developed sense of objects than Piaget thought. Researchers have found that infants as young as three months have some representation of an object they have seen but that is no longer visible. In one ingenious series of studies, the baby first watched a screen flap back and forth through 180 degrees. While the baby watched, the researcher placed a solid box behind the screen which should keep the screen from flipping all the way back. Again the baby watched two test events. In one case, the screen flipped back but stopped where the box should have stopped it. In the other, the screen flipped all the way back, an event that would be very puzzling to any older child who understood that the solid box should stop it. The babies looked longer at the second event, suggesting that they must have some notion of the continued existence of the box and detected strange behavior in the screen (Baillargeon, 1992).

With respect to the stages of development, it appears that they are more fluid than Piaget proposed. Children often display characteristics of more than one stage at the same time. For example, four-year-old children can arrange colors from light to dark, but they have difficulty arranging sticks in order of length. Piaget believed that the sequence of stages was invariant, but research shows that some children, particularly during a transition phase, move back and forth between stages in their cognitive approach to problems (Fischer & Silvern, 1985).

The demands of the cultural context also appear to influence the rate at which children move through the stages, at least for specific areas of knowledge. In nomadic hunting and gathering societies, children develop concrete operational reasoning on spatial tests very rapidly, apparently because they have to learn how to find their way around in large, extended territories. But in sedentary, agricultural societies, concrete operational thought develops more rapidly for quantitative concepts. For these cultures, the demands of daily life probably emphasize more numerical concepts that involve how the harvest is stored, exchanged, and sold (Dasen, 1984).

Despite the problems with Piaget's theories, his contribution was enormous and his general views continue to dominate the field. He proposed a theory of cognitive development that was comprehensive and emphasized children's active participation in the growth of their own knowledge.

# Social and Emotional Development

Human beings begin their social and emotional development from the first day of life. The attachment process is important for babies; the kind of attachment a baby develops with the primary caregiver has effects that last for at least one or two years and perhaps much longer (Matas, Arend, & Sroufe, 1978). In the years after infancy, the child's family is the most important variable in the socialization process. As the child grows older, especially after school begins, friendships play key roles in social and emotional development.

With respect to Erikson's theory, psychosocial tasks during early and middle childhood reflect how children interact first with parents and then with siblings and friends (see figure 9.1). After the trust versus mistrust conflict, children between the ages of one and a half- to three-years-old face the task of resolving **autonomy versus shame and doubt.** *During this stage, children should be developing independent and autonomous actions.* The child learns to walk, feed himself, dress, and go to the bathroom; success results in a strong sense of autonomous control and self-efficacy. It is the "me-do" age. However, the child who experiences discouragement and failure in self-control and bodily regulation may experience shame and doubt.

Children next face **initiative versus guilt,** *an Eriksonian psychosocial task of early childhood, which concerns whether children learn to initiate actions or to feel guilty if they initiate actions that are disapproved.* **Industry versus inferiority** *is the psychosocial task faced during the period of middle childhood; using neighborhood and school friends as a yardstick to measure their own competence, children will be inclined toward industriousness if they find themselves basically competent. If they feel incompetent and inferior, an unhealthy negative attitude may color their ability to attack challenging problems.*

*The Family*    The word "family" conjures up quite a variety of images across the world. In some countries in Africa, family includes just about everyone in the village who is descended from a single patriarch. The family works together to build houses and roads, and shares the chores of maintaining the economy. In the United States, the word "family" used to bring images of a nuclear family to mind, complete with a mother, father, two or three children, a dog, and a house with a picket fence. But the reality of "family" in the United States is considerably more diverse than this. Single parent homes, homes where both parents work outside, families with aging relatives, homes where the mother works and the father cares for the children, blended families with stepparents and stepchildren, and families with homosexual partners as heads of the household are all variations on the concept of "family."

The styles of interaction in families are equally diverse. Mothers, in general, have somewhat different relationships with children than do fathers. Mothers tend to spend quantitatively more time with children, and much of it is spent in care-giving activities like bathing, brushing the hair, preparing food, or cleaning the house. Fathers are more likely to engage in play or discipline.

Some parents insist on maintaining strict control over their children while others adopt a more lenient attitude. One researcher (Baumrind, 1971) found three styles of parenting that were particularly associated with social and emotional development: authoritarian, authoritative, and permissive.

The **authoritarian parent** *is restrictive and emphasizes punishment in the control of behavior.* The **authoritative parent,** *typically very warm and nurturing, encourages independence in children but still places limits and controls on their actions.* The **permissive parent** *is nonpunitive, places low demands, and allows considerable freedom.* Children of authoritarian parents tend to be anxious about social comparisons and generally ineffective in social interactions. Permissive parenting is associated with immaturity, regressive behavior, and an inability to assume leadership. The most positive qualities appear to be related to the authoritative style. Children of such parents demonstrate social competency and self-reliance.

A child grows up amidst a complex web of relationships and all of them are capable of affecting the child's development. Even before the baby is born, the parents are creating expectations about their new infant that can affect the pattern of development. In a longitudinal study conducted in Sweden, researchers found that the parents' preferences for the sex of the child before birth had effects that lasted well into adulthood. Children who did not match the parents' preference had more problems compared to children who did. This was particularly true for daughters of parents who had wanted a son. The fathers played with the daughter less, and there were more conflicts between the child and the parents. When they reached adulthood, the daughters whose parents wanted a son reported that they got along worse with their

# EXPLORING HUMAN DIVERSITY

## Multicultural Diversity in Parenting

Parenting style varies across subcultures in the United States today, but characteristics of the authoritarian, the authoritative, and the permissive parenting styles (Baumrind, 1971; Steinberg et al., 1992) are universal. In the following examples of multicultural parenting styles, try to determine which of the above universal styles can be seen in various combinations in the various subcultures.

Asian-American and Native American parenting styles are similar in that parents discipline children using conformity to group pressure, rather than physical techniques (Gibbs & Larke, 1989). Physical punishment is discouraged and infrequently used as a method of discipline. Rather, hierarchical relationships and dependence on the group are favored as means of keeping children obedient and behaved. It is no wonder, therefore, that the importance and prevalence of extended family relationships in these two cultures play a major role in the disciplining of children and in parenting styles (Dell, 1980). As one Asian-American adult recalled, "We did what our father told us, not because we were afraid of being hit, but because we didn't want to dishonor our family."

In contrast to the above American subcultures, African-Americans and Hispanic-Americans tend to use corporal punishment more readily and frequently, a fact that may be explained by the emphasis these groups place on individuality over group conformity (Slonim, 1991). Although extended families are prevalent in these subcultures as well and are multifaceted sources of strength for families, they do not function as sources of pressure to conform to group norms as do the extended families of the Native American and Asian-American cultures. When asked to compare his parents'

discipline style with that of the Asian- or Native American parents, an African-American male recalls, "I knew when I did something wrong, I would get spanked. But I was responsible for what I did. The 'group responsibility and conformity' idea wasn't part of my parents' style of discipline."

Research on parenting styles has traditionally used white, middle-class subjects, excluding examples from the many subcultures that exist in modern America. Whereas white, middle-class parents tend to embrace "scientific" methods of childrearing, changing their methods with the latest theory, parents from other American subcultures might find this style whimsical and pointless. "I read books constantly about the proper way to raise my children, believing Dr. Spock one month and Dr. Joyce Brothers the next," confessed a white, middle-class mother. "By the time I finished reading everything, I was thoroughly confused!" Therefore, unless researchers are able to include a greater variety of subjects in their studies, the image they present of parenting in the United States will become increasingly obsolete as the demographics of this country remain dynamic.

Examples of the various styles of parenting across subcultures in the United States reveal that the authoritarian, the authoritative, and the permissive styles of parenting exist to various degrees in all subcultures. Representing the "typical" American parent based on research from only one subculture, however, is no longer acceptable in modern psychology. The United States today is a complex network of subcultures, each of which needs to be studied individually if parenting styles are to be fairly compared.

---

fathers compared to daughters whose parents were neutral or who wanted a daughter (Stattin & Klackenberg-Larsson, 1991).

The presence of siblings changes the social landscape for any child. Relationships between siblings are complicated affairs consisting of warmth, closeness, and companionship on one hand and conflict, rivalry, and power on the other. Fortunately, sibling conflict generally decreases with age.

Relationships among other family members can be important to a child. For example, families in which the mother and father are happily married are more likely to be ones in which a positive relationship develops between the father and the child (Brody et al., 1986).

Disturbances in the family structure are very significant events for children. Divorce, remarriage, and death can all

cause upheaval and put tremendous strain on any family. Even in cases where the parents handle the divorce with a minimum of conflict and hostility, the children's standard of living may be reduced and they may spend less time with each parent.

Divorce is not easy for children of any age, though its effects vary with the child's age and sex. In one study (Hetherington, 1989), it was clear that the months following a divorce were an intense period of disruption for preschool children. After two years, the daughters seemed to resume more positive relationships with their mothers if they had not remarried, but the disruption in the relationship between mothers and sons continued as long as six years following the divorce. Preschoolers, with their egocentric view, tend to feel that the divorce occurred

## APPLYING PSYCHOLOGY

### Nurturing Fathers

With the entrance of so many women with young children into the labor force, the job of child rearing is increasingly shared by both mother and father. The children in such families see less of their mothers but more of their fathers as the dads take on more nurturing roles. Husbands whose wives are employed outside the home share in diapering, feeding, cuddling, comforting, and household chores.

More traditional people view these trends with surprise, although not necessarily alarm. Gail Kaufman, a working wife with a daughter now in her teens and a husband who shares child-rearing responsibilities, was out of town on a business trip when Jennifer, then two-years-old, got bronchitis. The pediatrician asked Barry, Gail's husband, if he knew how to take the child's temperature. Barry not only knew, he was quite familiar with all the other aspects of child care as well.

Psychologists who study children from such homes find that it benefits the children in important ways. Diane Ehrensaft, a psychologist from Berkeley, California, believes the children are more confident and creative than other children and are more comfortable with their own sexuality. The boys are masculine but not frantic about being macho, and the girls appear competent and feminine. Gail Kaufman believes some of the benefits lie in the fact that Jennifer always has two adults she can count on. The daughter is comfortable with both parents and trusts both men and women.

Studies of fathers show that their own psychological characteristics, as well as those of their wives, affect the quality of their nurturing. One study showed that men who were strong on affiliation and autonomy on personality tests were more supportive of their child's affiliation and autonomy. Job satisfaction was also important. Men who enjoyed work had sensitive and responsive interactions with their five-year-olds even though they generally spent less time with them (Grossman, Pollack, & Golding, 1988).

---

because of something they did. A four-year-old might think that Dad left because she left her toys on the stairs. They may idealize the departing parent, usually the father, and make up fantasies about him returning. Older children are not likely to blame themselves as much as preschoolers but they, too, have great difficulty adjusting to a divorce. Conflicts with the custodial parent increase dramatically, with more nagging, anger, withdrawal, and resistance.

Remarriage, and the possibility of blended families, are becoming realities for more and more children. Although girls generally adjust better than boys after a divorce, the reverse seems to be true for remarriage and the introduction of stepparents and stepsiblings. Stepfathers, for example, generally report better relationships with their stepsons than with their stepdaughters (Peterson & Zill, 1986). Particularly for early adolescent daughters, it is very difficult to adjust to a new stepfather.

*The Influence of Peers*    Most children have one or more siblings who contribute to their social and emotional development. In observations of forty-seven families with two or three children, the children teased, whined, yelled, talked, touched, laughed, and performed many behaviors one might expect of children. But most of the negative interactions were with one another, whereas most of the positive interactions were with parents (Baskett, 1974). Although siblings can be serious rivals, particularly with respect to parental attention, they can also have very positive effects on one another. Older siblings seem to understand many of the problems of younger children and can communicate with them about friendships, teachers, physical appearance, and sex.

The impact of peer groups becomes almost overwhelming in the adolescent years; but even in early and middle childhood, the peer group plays a critical role in social and emotional development. Peers provide developing children with a source of information about the world and give them a chance to compare their abilities and accomplishments with others their age. Infant monkeys who grow up without normal mothers show very abnormal behavior. But if they have opportunities to interact with other young monkeys, their abnormalities are very much reduced (Suomi & Harlow, 1972). The evidence that human children can be very effective "therapists" for one another is growing stronger. Some schools are even developing structured programs in which this kind of activity can take place, where children can assist one another in areas such as trust, cooperation, and leadership.

The development of friendships begins quite early. Infants as young as six months interact by smiling, touching, and vocalizing. During the second year, children's friendships revolve primarily around toys, using the objects as a focus for interaction. When the toddlers begin to use language more fluently, interactions increase in complexity.

An interesting observational study of two- to four-year-old children revealed some facets of the development of friendships in a nursery school (Corsaro, 1981). The children's behavior suggested they shared two concerns: to gain entry to ongoing interactions and to protect those interactions, once they started, by resisting the efforts of other children to join in. In the following sequence involving three-year-olds, Linda is trying to join Nancy, Barbara, and the researcher:

Barbara to Linda: You can't play!

Linda to Barbara: Yes I can. I can have some animals too.

Barbara to Linda: No, you can't. We don't like you today.

Nancy to Linda: You're not our friend.

Linda to Barbara and Nancy: I can play here too.

Barbara to Nancy: No, her can't—her can't play, right Nancy?

Nancy to Barbara: Right.

Linda to Researcher: Can I have some animals, Bill?

Researcher to Linda: You can have some of these. . . .

Linda's persistence in trying to join the group and Barbara and Nancy's equal persistence in refusing her entry demonstrate how important children consider peer interactions. They seem to be aware of their fragility and try hard to enter them and then protect them against intrusion. Children also seem to be aware of the power of friendship in social control.

What constitutes a "friend" to a child changes dramatically, and some researchers have suggested a series of stages (Selman, 1980). At first, children consider a friend to be anyone with whom they play and anyone who lives nearby, a condition that might better be called "playmate-ship." In the next stage, friendships are "one way." A person is a friend if he or she does what the child wants. In later stages, the child develops two-way friendships, in which the child appreciates cooperation and the reciprocal nature of a two-way interaction.

Rejection by peers can be particularly traumatic. There are a few lonely children in each school group who are disliked by almost everyone, and this rejection leads to adjustment problems in later life. Children who are rejected seem to fall into one of two categories. One group is composed of aggressive and disruptive children who see hostility in most interactions, and who tease and bully others. The other group includes the "easy marks," those who are socially withdrawn, avoid confrontations, and

make few but highly deferential requests. Navigating one's way through elementary and middle school is not an easy task, but it is especially difficult for the children who are rejected by their mates (Asher et al., 1990; Rubin, LaMare & Lollis, 1990).

*The Cultural Context*    The culture into which each child is born provides a developmental niche for growing, learning, and forming relationships with other people. Family and friends are a part of this, but the larger cultural context shapes the attitudes and expectations people have about each developing child. For example, the assumptions parents have about when particular behaviors should appear are largely dependent on the culture. In some cultures children are expected to be able to control their emotions and comply with parents' demands earlier than in others. When children fall short of the culturally accepted timetable, the parents believe that the child is being willfully disobedient rather than "still just a baby."

Across the world, children spend their days in an enormous variety of activities that can shape the child's development and transmit values. A weekday for a child in the United States might include six or seven hours of school and homework, one or two in caretaking activities such as bathing, eating and dressing, a half hour or less doing chores, an hour or two playing, and a couple of hours watching television. In other cultures, the profile might be very different. In a study among the Kipsigis of Kenya, a culture that practices animal husbandry and itinerant agriculture, children devoted up to sixty percent of their time to chores (Harkness & Super, 1983).

Spending so much time in activities that contribute to the group's welfare sends important signals to the children about culture values; the message is not lost on them. In studies covering several cultures, children who were expected to work more hours were more likely to offer assistance to others and make altruistic suggestions. Those who worked little made more selfish suggestions and were more likely to seek attention and assistance than to give it (Whiting & Whiting, 1975; Munroe et al., 1984).

## Moral Development

The way children come to know right from wrong, to feel guilty, to empathize with other people, and to help others when they are in distress are all components of moral development. It is a complicated process, closely related to cognitive development, that is heavily dependent on family environment, neighborhood, and culture.

*Moral Reasoning and Piaget's Stages*    One approach to the study of moral development is to investigate moral reasoning. What do children say they would do in a situation, and what are their reasons? How do children judge the actions of others?

Piaget proposed that children pass through stages of moral development. **Moral realism** *is the first stage: right and wrong are judged by the consequences of an action rather than by the intention of the actor.* For example, a child who accidentally knocked everything off a table would be judged more harshly than one who deliberately knocked over a glass of juice. **Moral autonomy** *is Piaget's second stage of moral development; in this stage, children take into account both the intentions of the actor and the consequences of the action.*

*Kohlberg's Six Stages of Moral Development*    Another theorist, Lawrence Kohlberg, elaborated on Piaget's two stages (Kohlberg, 1976; Levine, Kohlberg, & Hewer, 1985). He poses a moral dilemma to young subjects and asks them what they would do. The most famous dilemma involves a man who cannot afford to pay the exorbitant price for a drug needed by his dying wife. Should the man steal the drug? Kohlberg assesses a person's stage of moral development not by whether the person says yes or no but by a standard scoring scheme that probes the person's moral reasoning (Colby et al., 1983). For example, if the subject answers "Yes, because the drug isn't really worth that much anyway," he would be in a very low stage of moral development. If he answers, "Yes, because he should act according to his principle of preserving and respecting life," he would be in a rather advanced stage. Table 9.4 details Kohlberg's six stages.

*Evaluating Theories of Moral Development*    The notion that children pass through stages during their moral development has received some support (Kohlberg, 1984; Snarey, 1985). Their advancement appears to be particularly dependent on their cognitive development and their ability to reason about nonmoral situations. When children start to make the transition to a higher stage, they show mixtures in their judgments, but soon consolidate their reasoning and make more and more judgments consistent with the higher stage (Walker & Taylor, 1991).

Nevertheless, the stage theories, particularly Kohlberg's, have been criticized on many grounds. The subjects' answers to the stories are very difficult to score and many scientists believe the stories themselves are culturally biased

and ethnocentric. Morality in one culture may be quite different from morality in another; some of Kohlberg's work even supports this hypothesis. In one longitudinal study of adolescents living on a kibbutz in Israel, the girls and boys tended to pass progressively through the stages of moral development as expected, but they showed a greater orientation toward the welfare of the group than did American children (Snarey, Reimer, & Kohlberg, 1985).

The stories themselves seem to presuppose a world order that, though reasonable to Westerners, may not be appropriate, or even make sense, in other cultures. For example, one researcher presented the dilemma about the woman who needed the drug to a thirty-year-old male Hindu (Schweder, 1991). Here is an excerpt of his answer to the question of whether the man should steal to save his wife's life:

> "No. He is feeling desperate because his wife is going to die, and that's why he is stealing the drug. But people don't live forever, and providing her the drug does not necessarily mean she will live long. How long you live is not in our hands but in God's hands. And there are other ways to get money, like selling his landed property, or even he can sell himself to someone and can save his wife's life." (Schweder, 1991, p. 230)

Kohlberg read through the interview and said that much of the material was unscorable and did not easily fit the manual used to code responses. Nevertheless, he determined that the answers generally reflected stage 3 or 4, because the person made a judgment primarily on the basis of respect for religious law which identifies stealing as a sin. But Hindus have a different view of the world order, and it was clear from the interview that the dilemma was perceived in a rather unexpected way. For example, the Hindu was concerned for the spiritual well-being of both the husband and the wife in this life and the next, so the prolongation of this particular incarnation of his wife was of lesser importance. The Hindu also questioned the arrogance embedded in the story itself, which suggested that humans *knew* that the drug was the only way to save the woman's life.

Another significant criticism of Kohlberg's stage theory is that it places high regard on moral judgment that emphasizes fair-minded rationality, justice, and abstract principles and pays little attention to the role of emotion or human concerns (Gibbs & Schnell, 1985), important motivators for moral learning and empathy. Rationality and justice are judgments more likely to be used by men in our culture, thus creating a strong gender bias in Kohlberg's theory.

| TABLE 9.4 | Kohlberg's stages of moral development | |
|---|---|---|
| **Stage** | **Brief Description** | **Reasons for Doing Right** |
| Level I: | Preconventional | |
| 1 | Desire to avoid punishment | Avoidance of punishment and the superior power of authority; obedience for its own sake. |
| 2 | Desire to obtain rewards | Serves one's own needs and recognizes that other people have their interests, too; conforms to obtain rewards. |
| Level II: | Conventional | |
| 3 | "Good boy/Good girl" | Values the approval of others and tries to maintain mutual relationships involving trust, loyalty, respect, and gratitude; believes in the Golden Rule. |
| 4 | Respect for authority | Values society's laws and tries to uphold them; tries to keep the institution going. |
| Level III | Post-Conventional | |
| 5 | Respect for the social contract | Believes in upholding the social contract because it provides the "greatest good for the greatest number"; recognizes that a social contract is an agreement between people that benefits the public welfare. |
| 6 | Universal ethical principles | Personally committed to a set of self-chosen ethical principles, most of which may be compatible with the laws of society. When laws conflict with ethical principles, the person acts in accordance with his or her principles. |

Sources: L. Kohlberg, "The Cognitive-Developmental Approach to Socialization," *Handbook of Socialization Theory and Research,* ed. by D. A. Goslin, Rand McNally, Chicago, 1969; and L. Kohlberg, "Moral Stages and Moralization," *Moral Development and Behavior,* ed. by T. Lickona, Holt, Rinehart & Winston, New York, 1976.

Carol Gilligan (1977, 1986; Muuss, 1988) points out that Kohlberg's theory was developed from a male perspective using research data primarily from males. Any divergence from what might be considered male standards of morality is seen as a failure of moral development. In moral judgments, men are more likely than women to consider the value of abstract principles, societal goals, and justice at the expense of caring, interpersonal relationships, and emotions. Kohlberg's stages place people who use abstract principles in the high categories, so men are more likely to reach those stages. The average male reaches a moral stage of four (law and order), but the average female only reaches a stage of three (good girl/good boy) because females tend to be more sensitive to what others think and feel.

On Kohlberg's scale, people might be placed in a high stage even though they are cruel to loved ones. Gilligan contrasts the behavior of Abraham, who would have sacrificed the life of his son to demonstrate the strength of his faith, to the woman who comes before Solomon and is willing to tell a falsehood to save the life of her child. Is Abraham demonstrating a higher level of moral development than the mother because of his unswerving devotion to an abstract principle?

Gilligan and Attanucci (1988), in studies of adolescents and adults, find that most people, men and women alike, use both justice and care when they make moral judgments, but they tend to focus on one or the other. Men usually focus on justice, and women usually focus on care. Gilligan and Attanucci are not arguing that the orientation toward care is better than the orientation toward justice; they are stating that the orientation toward care is not "less advanced" as Kohlberg's six stages suggest.

The research on the stage theories relied heavily on the explanation people offered for their choices, so verbal skills were very important. It is easy to misunderstand and underestimate the moral reasoning power of young children or of people whose verbal skills are limited. Tisak and Turiel (1988) have found that even first graders make surprisingly fine distinctions, ones that show they understand much more about morality than might be expected. In one problem, children were presented with a choice of making a minor moral transgression or a rather major transgression against a social convention:

"Let's say that one day Paul and Gary were playing a game and they wanted to do something that was very different. So, they decided that whoever won the game they were playing could pick any two things they wanted the other person to do. The person who lost the game could choose one of the two things. Let's say that Paul got a real high score and won the game. Gary lost the game. He got a real low score. Now Paul tells Gary that he has to either steal an eraser from the classroom—and he could do this when no one was around so he wouldn't get caught—or else he could wear pajamas to school."

Most of the children predicted that Gary *would* steal the eraser, but most also said they thought he *should* wear pajamas to school. The children were able to tell the difference between the moral and the conventional transgressions. They also knew that they should not make the moral transgression even if they had to suffer social disapproval for doing something else.

Studies like this one, that present children with simple cases and ask what they would do, show that they have a rather complex understanding of morality. Often the criteria they use to make decisions about whether a person is responsible for harm, whether the person should be blamed, and whether the person should be punished, are very similar to the ones adults in their culture are using. For example, even children as young as six consider intentional harm as more blameworthy than unintentional harm. The intentions of the actor are an important ingredient in western judicial systems. Whenever a child causes harm, parents often hear, "But I didn't mean to do it!," clearly showing that the child believes intention should be considered.

Young children also have some notion of the role of mitigation and restitution in judging moral responsibility and assigning punishment. For example, if someone steals a toy but later apologizes and returns it, children would judge the perpetrator less harshly and assume less punishment would be in order (Darley & Shultz, 1990). Storekeepers have become very familiar with the drama of parents returning to a store with a child who has stolen something, to ensure the child apologizes and returns the item. The episode reinforces the rules by which immoral acts are judged.

## Resilience

Candida began her childhood on a farm with her large family in Nicaragua, surrounded by trees, cows, and chickens—and war. When she was nine, she was milking the cows with her parents when soldiers came and kidnapped all three of them. In the following months, separated from her parents, she was held hostage and made to steal food, fight off attempted rapes, and watch as the horrors of war unfolded. Her clothes came from a man whose throat was slit while she watched. From another hostage, she learned that her parents had been murdered. Five months after her capture, she escaped and went to live with a relative. She didn't say a word for a year and suffered from nightmares at night and anxiety during the day. Yet now, at sixteen, she plans to become a civil engineer, excels in school, and has boyfriends. She is active in politics and determined to make sure future generations will never have to go through what she did (Garbarino, Kostelny, & Dubrow, 1991).

One of the most puzzling features of human development is that so many children turn out well in a wide range of environments. Some especially resilient ones can overcome difficult and stressful family lives, child abuse, sickness, poor nutrition, trouble in school, rejection, poverty, crime, and war. Humans are amazingly resilient creatures. Many are able to endure the most difficult circumstances and go on to become well-adjusted, hardworking, and happy adults.

Psychologists are beginning to study why some children are able to overcome adversities that cripple or mentally scar others. Using interviews and case histories, researchers follow the lives of children who must cope with very difficult circumstances. Studies of the "gamins," or street urchins, in urban Columbia suggest that the successful ones have a hardy constitution, a proclivity for action, and solid support from their peers. They also are resourceful and feel as though they can exert control over their own lives. Some studies point to the importance of general intelligence as one of the factors that contribute to resilience in children. These findings emphasize the role that children themselves play in shaping their own environments. It seems the more resourceful and capable they are at this, the better they will fare and the more resistant they will be to permanent harm. One six-year-old black girl who made it through the daily violence and rejection that accompanied the desegregation of schools in the United States said that if she managed to get through these experiences, "it will be because there is more to me than I ever realized" (Dugan and Coles, 1989).

▶ **GUIDED REVIEW** *Learning Objectives 10, 11, 12 and 13*

1. Piaget's theory of cognitive development states that children go through four stages: _____, _____, _____, and _____.

2. In Erikson's theory, children face a series of psychosocial tasks affecting their social and emotional development during early and middle childhood. These include _____, _____, _____, and _____.

3. The family is an important influence in a child's social, emotional, and moral development. Three parenting styles are _____, a rigid, rule-oriented style; _____, a warm nurturing style that provides limits and rules; and _____, a laissez-faire parenting style. The authoritative style appears to promote the most desirable characteristics in children.

4. Friends play key roles in socialization and emotional development. The concept of _____ becomes more sophisticated as the child matures.

5. Cognitive approaches to moral development emphasize stages of moral reasoning that advance with cognitive development. Piaget proposed two stages: _____ and _____.

6. Kohlberg proposed a theory of _____ development that included six stages, each of which required greater cognitive abilities. The sixth stage involves adherence to universal ethical principles.

7. Kohlberg's theory has been criticized because it emphasizes logic and abstraction for the highest stages of moral development, and assumes that attention to emotion and human concerns represents a lower level of moral reasoning. Because more women than men consider human concerns in their moral reasoning, Gilligan argues that Kohlberg's theory shows _____.

8. Many children show considerable _____, meaning that they develop into happy, healthy adults despite negative environmental influences during development.

*ANSWERS*

*1. sensorimotor stage, preoperational stage, concrete operational stage, formal operational stage 2. trust versus mistrust, autonomy versus shame and doubt, initiative versus guilt, industry versus inferiority 3. authoritarian, authoritative, permissive 4. friendship 5. moral realism, moral autonomy 6. moral 7. gender bias 8. resilience*

---

# SUMMARY

I. Development refers to the patterns of forward movement or change that begin at conception and continue through the entire life span. (p. 276)

   A. Two methods of studying development are the cross-sectional study and the longitudinal study. (p. 276)

   B. Various perspectives have been used to approach the study of development, including the psychoanalytic approach, the cognitive-structural approach, and the behavioristic approach. (p. 277–278)

II. The two major forces that shape development are genes and the environment. (p. 279)

   A. Genetic forces begin their effects from conception. (p. 279)

      1. The gene, a very short length of DNA, is the basic unit of heredity; individual genes either direct the formation of specific proteins or control the activity of other genes. (p. 279)

      2. Genes can only indirectly affect behavior; the effects of genes on behavior are often investigated by use of the adoption study. (p. 280)

   B. Environmental factors influence development from conception. (p. 282)

      1. Aspects of the prenatal environment that can influence the development of the fetus include the presence or absence of hormones, the presence of drugs or alcohol, and the mother's emotional state. (p. 282)

      2. Inadequate nutrition is an environmental factor especially harmful to the growing organism if it occurs while brain cells are still dividing. (p. 282)

      3. Individuals have the power to shape their own environments by making choices and by affecting the way that others behave toward them. (p. 283)

   C. The interaction between genes and environment and their relative importance in shaping the characteristics of the developing human is often debated as part of the nature-nurture issue. The concept of critical periods demonstrates how genes and environment interact. (p. 283)

III. The first year of a baby's life is a time of very rapid development. (p. 284)

   A. Childbirth practices are undergoing many changes in the United States, including childbirth preparation classes, rooming-in, and birthing rooms. (pp. 284–285)

   B. Careful observations of newborns show that they have many abilities. (p. 286)

      1. The infant is born with several motor reflexes, such as the rooting reflex, sucking reflex, and the Babinski reflex. Motor development proceeds from the head downward. (p. 286)

**2.** Studies of the sensory abilities of newborns show they can perceive sounds, visual images, and depth; they also show preferences for the sound of their mothers' voices, for visual stimuli that resemble faces, and for faces that adults judge as attractive. (pp. 286–288)

**3.** Newborns show identifiable patterns in their vocalizations and participate in vocal "dialogues" with their mothers. (p. 288)

**C.** Emotional development begins from the first day of life. (p. 288)

    **1.** Infants show variations in temperament, a characteristic that appears to have some genetic basis but which also can change depending on environmental forces, especially on the behavior of the parents. (p. 288)

**D.** A key feature of social development in the infant is the attachment process to the primary caregiver. (p. 290)

    **1.** Studies of monkeys reared without their mothers show that they have various abnormal behavioral patterns in adulthood. (p. 290)

    **2.** The nature of the infant's early attachment appears to influence personality development. Erikson's first psychosocial task, trust vs. mistrust, emphasizes the importance of the attachment process. (p. 291)

**IV.** Childhood includes the years between the ages of one and about twelve, when puberty is beginning. (p. 293)

**A.** The most widely known theory of cognitive development was proposed by Jean Piaget. This theory suggests that children pass through four main stages, a process that relies on assimilation and accommodation. (p. 294)

    **1.** The sensorimotor stage is characterized by the development of the capability to coordinate sensations and perceptions with physical actions. (p. 294)

    **2.** The preoperational stage is characterized by the acquisition of language, the growth in the use of symbols, and the use of a limited kind of logical thinking. (p. 294–295)

    **3.** The concrete operational stage is characterized by the need to anchor thought in concrete events. (p. 295)

    **4.** The formal operational stage is characterized by the ability to think about concrete and abstract events and the ability to formulate hypotheses. (p. 296)

    **5.** Piaget's theories have endured, although recent research suggests that babies acquire some abilities earlier than he proposed, and that children show more variable patterns of movement through the stages. (p. 296)

**B.** Social and emotional development, according to Erikson, is affected by a child's ability to resolve several psychosocial conflicts including initiative vs. guilt, and industry vs. inferiority. (p. 297)

    **1.** The family is the focus of emotional and social development during early childhood. Styles of parenting that appear to affect social and emotional development include authoritarian, authoritative, and permissive. (p. 297)

    **2.** During later childhood, the influence of peers on social and emotional development grows, patterns of friendship develop, and some children experience rejection. (p. 299)

    **3.** Culture has an important impact on development; children growing up in different cultures vary widely in how they spend a typical day, and the values they later show reflect these differences. (p. 300)

**C.** Moral development refers to the process by which children learn right from wrong; it is closely related to cognitive development. (p. 300)

    **1.** Based on how children reason in situations involving moral issues, Piaget proposed two stages of moral development: moral realism and moral autonomy. (p. 301)

    **2.** Kohlberg proposed six stages of moral development; a person's stage was determined by the way he or she answered a moral dilemma. (p. 301)

    **3.** Stage theories of moral development have received some support, but Kohlberg's theory has been criticized because of its failure to appreciate gender and cultural differences in moral reasoning, and its reliance on verbal skills in assessing moral stages. (pp. 301–302)

**D.** Children can develop normally in a wide range of environments, and researchers are beginning to investigate why some children show so much resilience and develop into happy, healthy adults despite very adverse childhoods. (p. 303)

# ACTION GLOSSARY

Match the terms in the left column with the definitions in the right column.

___ 1. **Development (p. 276)**
___ 2. **Cross-sectional study (p. 276)**
___ 3. **Longitudinal study (p. 276)**
___ 4. **Autonomy versus shame and doubt (p. 297)**
___ 5. **Cognitive-structural approach (p. 278)**
___ 6. **Chromosome (p. 279)**
___ 7. **Adenine (p. 279)**

A. *A psychosocial task faced by toddlers, according to Erik Erikson, that involves the successful development of autonomous control over bodily functions. Failure to establish such control leads to shame and doubt.*
B. *Patterns of forward movement or change that begin at conception and continue through the entire life span.*
C. *A procedure for observing changes in the same group of people over time.*
D. *Long chains containing DNA, the genetic information, found in the nucleus of cells.*
E. *A procedure for comparing the characteristics of groups of people of different ages.*
F. *One of the four bases that make up DNA.*
G. *A perspective in human development that focuses on stages of intellectual development.*

___ 8. **DNA (p. 279)**
___ 9. **Cytosine (p. 279)**
___ 10. **Gene (p. 279)**
___ 11. **Heterozygous (p. 279)**
___ 12. **Homozygous (p. 279)**
___ 13. **Dominant gene (p. 280)**
___ 14. **Recessive gene (p. 280)**
___ 15. **Codominance (p. 280)**

A. *One of the four bases that make up DNA.*
B. *A gene that will be expressed regardless of which gene is on the paired chromosome.*
C. *Refers to the condition in which the two genes located on paired chromosomes and coding for the same function are identical.*
D. *A gene expressed only if it is paired with a recessive gene.*
E. *Characterizes the relationship between two genes that are both expressed on paired chromosomes in the same organism.*
F. *The basic unit of heredity. Consists of a short sequence of DNA arranged along a chromosome.*
G. *Deoxyribonucleic acid, the substance found in chromosomes that carries genetic information.*
H. *Refers to the condition in which two genes located on paired chromosomes and coding for the same function are different.*

___ 16. **Adoption study (p. 281)**
___ 17. **Thymine (p. 279)**
___ 18. **Phenylketonuria (PKU) (p. 281)**
___ 19. **Nature-nurture issue (p. 283)**
___ 20. **Rooting reflex (p. 286)**

A. *A debate involving the relative importance of genetic factors and environmental factors in human behavior and development.*
B. *The infant's response to a touch on the cheek or corner of the mouth. The infant reflexively turns his or her head in the direction of the stimulation.*
C. *A procedure in which the similarity of an adopted child and the adoptive parents is compared to the similarity between the child and the biological parents.*
D. *One of the four bases that makes up DNA.*
E. *A disease transmitted by two recessive genes that causes a lack in the enzyme required to metabolize a particular amino acid.*

___ 21. **Guanine (p. 279)**
___ 22. **Babinski reflex (p. 286)**
___ 23. **Trust versus mistrust (p. 291)**
___ 24. **Strange Situations Test (p. 291)**
___ 25. **Secure attachment (p. 291)**
___ 26. **Insecure attachments (p. 291)**
___ 27. **Sensorimotor stage (p. 294)**

A. *The earliest stage of cognitive development, according to the theory of Jean Piaget. Infants develop the capability to coordinate their sensations and perceptions with their physical actions.*
B. *A pattern of behavior in which the infant shows a healthy balance between dependency and exploration, using the mother as a secure base from which to explore a novel environment.*
C. *A response in which infants automatically curl their toes upward when the sole of their foot is stroked.*
D. *One of the four bases that makes up DNA.*
E. *A standardized procedure for measuring attachment between an infant and mother or other caregiver. The test involves a series of separations and reunions under controlled laboratory conditions.*
F. *A pattern of behavior in which the infant's behavior, in response to the mother's departure and return, includes avoidance, resistance, or ambivalent responses.*
G. *A psychosocial task faced by infants, according to Erik Erikson's theory of development. Successful resolution occurs when the baby's needs are met and he or she develops trust in the environment and his or her caregivers.*

___ 28. **Object permanence** (p. 294)

___ 29. **Preoperational stage** (p. 294)

___ 30. **Egocentrism** (p. 294)

___ 31. **Conservation** (p. 294)

___ 32. **Concrete operational stage** (p. 295)

___ 33. **Formal operational stage** (p. 296)

___ 34. **Initiative versus guilt** (p. 297)

A. *An inability to appreciate that another person's perceptions of a situation may differ from one's own.*
B. *Refers to the fact that the basic properties of objects remain unchanged despite superficial changes in appearance.*
C. *The understanding that an object exists independently of the self and continues to exist even when it cannot immediately be perceived.*
D. *The psychosocial task of early childhood, according to Erik Erikson's theory of personality development. The child is learning to initiate actions or to feel guilty about initiating ones that are disapproved.*
E. *The third stage of cognitive development, according to Jean Piaget's theory. The stage is characterized by the need to anchor logical thought in concrete events.*
F. *The second stage in the theory of cognitive development proposed by Jean Piaget, characterized by acquisition of language, growth in the use of symbols, and use of a limited kind of logical thinking.*
G. *The fourth stage of cognitive development, according to Jean Piaget's theory. The stage is characterized by the ability to think about both concrete and abstract events as well as the ability to formulate and test hypotheses to solve problems.*

___ 35. **Industry versus inferiority** (p. 297)

___ 36. **Authoritative parenting style** (p. 297)

___ 37. **Permissive parenting style** (p. 297)

___ 38. **Authoritarian parenting style** (p. 297)

___ 39. **Moral realism** (p. 301)

___ 40. **Moral autonomy** (p. 301)

___ 41. **Assimilation** (p. 294)

___ 42. **Accommodation** (p. 294)

A. *The process by which a child incorporates new experiences into the knowledge structures he or she already has.*
B. *The psychosocial task of middle childhood, according to Erik Erikson's theory. The task involves the child's comparison of his or her own abilities with those of his or her friends and schoolmates.*
C. *The first stage of moral development in Piaget's theory; children judge right and wrong by the consequences of an action rather than by the intention of the actor.*
D. *The second stage of moral development in Piaget's theory; the child can take into account the intentions of the actor and the consequences of the action.*
E. *A warm and nurturing style of parenting that encourages independence in children but still places limits and controls on their actions.*
F. *A nonpunitive style of parenting that places low demands on the child and allows considerable freedom.*
G. *A restrictive style of parenting that emphasizes punishment in the control of behavior.*
H. *The process by which a child revises, refines, or adds to her existing knowledge structures.*

*ANSWERS*

1. b, 2. e, 3. c, 4. a, 5. g, 6. d, 7. g, 8. g, 9. a, 10. f, 11. h, 12. c, 13. b, 14. d, 15. e, 16. c, 17. d, 18. e, 19. a, 20. b, 21. d, 22. c, 23. g, 24. g, 25. b, 26. f, 27. a, 28. c, 29. f, 30. a, 31. b, 32. e, 33. e, 34. d, 35. b, 36. e, 37. f, 38. g, 39. c, 40. d, 41. a, 42. h

## SELF-TEST

1. The study that tests a single group of the same people repeatedly at different ages is a _____ study.
   (a) cross-sectional
   (b) longitudinal
   (c) combined
   (d) Both a and c.
   (LO 1; p. 276)

2. The developmental perspective that focuses on personality development and emphasizes the role of the outcome of early psychosocial conflicts on later behavior patterns is the _____ perspective.
   (a) psychoanalytic
   (b) behavioristic
   (c) cognitive-structural
   (d) biological
   (LO 2; p. 278)

3. The developmental perspective that explains the development of behavior by stressing the role of reinforcement is the _____ perspective.
   (a) psychoanalytic
   (b) behavioristic
   (c) cognitive-structural
   (d) biological
   (LO 2; p. 278)

4. A human inherits how many chromosomes from the mother?
   (a) 46 pairs of chromosomes
   (b) 46 chromosomes
   (c) 23 pairs of chromosomes
   (d) 23 chromosomes
   (LO 3; p. 279)

5. One of the myths about the effects of genes on behavior is:
    (a) Genes predetermine behavioral patterns.
    (b) If genes affect a particular behavior, the expression of that behavior should be the same in all humans.
    (c) If a trait is influenced by genes, it cannot be altered.
    (d) All of the above.
    (LO 3; p. 280)

6. Which of the following is *not* an example of an environmental influence on development?
    (a) the control of protein synthesis by DNA instructions
    (b) the effects of thalidomide during prenatal life
    (c) the individual's shaping of his or her own environment
    (d) the effects of the lack of protein on brain cell division
    (LO 4; p. 282)

7. Which perspective on development is most closely aligned with the nurture side of the nature-nurture issue?
    (a) psychoanalytic
    (b) behavioristic
    (c) cognitive-structural
    (d) biological
    (LO 5; p. 283)

8. In the United States, there has been a recent trend from viewing childbirth as _____ to viewing it as _____.
    (a) a normal developmental process; a painful process
    (b) a painful process; a condition of sickness
    (c) a condition of sickness; a normal developmental process
    (d) a condition of sickness; a painful process
    (LO 6; p. 284)

9. An experiment in which newborn infants used a sucking response to control a tape recorder showed that infants
    (a) prefer to listen to their mothers' voices rather than strangers' voices.
    (b) prefer to listen to novel voices rather than their mothers' voice.
    (c) prefer to listen to their fathers' voices rather than their mothers' voices.
    (d) cannot discriminate between their mothers' voices and strangers' voices.
    (LO 7; pp. 286–287)

10. A baby who displays a difficult temperament during the first weeks of life
    (a) is likely to show more health-related problems in adulthood, such as ulcers and high blood pressure.
    (b) will tend to be rejected by schoolmates later in childhood.
    (c) may show a more agreeable temperament after several months, particularly if the parents have a happy marriage and the mother maintains harmonious relationships with the baby.
    (d) is going through a brief phase that will only last a period of about three months.
    (LO 8; pp. 289–290)

11. Research with infant monkeys who were raised with a cloth and a wire mother found that they
    (a) showed no preference.
    (b) showed a preference for the surrogate mother who fed them.
    (c) showed a preference for the wire mother when it provided the food.
    (d) showed a preference for the cloth mother whether or not it provided the food.
    (LO 9; p. 290)

12. Erikson argues that the first psychosocial task in life revolves around attachment and is termed
    (a) industry versus inferiority.
    (b) autonomy versus shame and guilt.
    (c) initiative versus guilt.
    (d) trust versus mistrust.
    (LO 9; p. 291)

13. A critical ability that develops during Piaget's sensorimotor period is
    (a) conservation.
    (b) abstract thought and reasoning.
    (c) formal operations.
    (d) object permanence.
    (LO 10; p. 294)

14. During Piaget's concrete operational period, children become capable of
    (a) appreciating the concept of conservation.
    (b) reasoning abstractly.
    (c) using language.
    (d) forming hypotheses to solve problems.
    (LO 10; p. 295)

15. A parent who places limits on a child but is also warm and loving is termed
    (a) authoritarian.
    (b) permissive-indulgent.
    (c) authoritative.
    (d) permissive-neglectful.
    (LO 11; p. 297)

**16.** For both monkeys and children who show abnormal behavior, other young of the same species can act as _____ in helping to reduce the abnormal behavior.

    **(a)** peers
    **(b)** friends
    **(c)** rivals
    **(d)** therapists
    (LO 11; p. 299)

**17.** According to Piaget, the first stage of moral development is called

    **(a)** moral autonomy.
    **(b)** moral realism.
    **(c)** preconventional.
    **(d)** conventional.
    (LO 12; p. 301)

**18.** Kohlberg's highest stage of moral development is stage six, and it emphasizes

    **(a)** human empathy.
    **(b)** the cultural relativity of moral reasoning.
    **(c)** respect for authority.
    **(d)** universal ethical principles.
    (LO 12; p. 301)

**19.** Which of the following is *not* a criticism of Kohlberg's theory of moral development?

    **(a)** Subjects' responses to the stories are difficult to score.
    **(b)** Moral reasoning has nothing to do with moral development.
    **(c)** The stories are culturally biased.
    **(d)** The role of emotion is ignored.
    (LO 12; p. 301)

**20.** Characteristics of children who show resilience in the face of adverse environments generally have

    **(a)** high intelligence and hardy constitution.
    **(b)** close association with a mentor and dependence on authority.
    **(c)** high aggressiveness and strong leadership qualities.
    **(d)** good nutrition and avoidance of drugs.
    (LO 13; p. 303)

*ANSWERS*

1. b, 2. a, 3. b, 4. d, 5. d, 6. a, 7. b, 8. c, 9. a, 10. c, 11. d, 12. d, 13. d, 14. a, 15. c, 16. d, 17. b, 18. d, 19. b, 20. a

# THINKING ABOUT PSYCHOLOGY

**1.** The "nature-nurture debate" has always occupied a prominent position in psychology. Describe the opposing sides of the debate, and explain how the forces of nature and those of nurture interact in their effects on development.

**2.** A child is shown a class photo with fifteen girls and ten boys, and asked whether there are more girls, or more boys in the photo. The child answers, "More girls." Explain this child's answer in terms of Piaget's theory of cognitive development.

**3.** Some studies have found that child abuse tends to be passed from one generation to the next. Children who are abused themselves often grow up to abuse their own children. Using what you have learned in this chapter, hypothesize on the reasons for this.

# SUGGESTED READINGS

Brenner, A. (1984). *Helping children cope with stress*. Lexington, MA: Lexington Books. A brief volume designed for human service workers; explores the nature and treatment of childhood stressors, such as parental death, divorce, and child abuse.

Caplan, N., Whitmore, J. K., and Choy, M. H. (1989) *The boat people and achievement in America: A study of family life, hard work, and cultural values*. Ann Arbor, MI: University of Michigan Press. Based on interviews and surveys of Southeast Asians who emigrated to the United States, this volume explores the impact of culture on development and success.

Damon, W. (1988). *The moral child: Nurturing children's natural moral growth*. New York: The Free Press/Macmillan. A summary of current knowledge on moral development in children.

Dugan, T. F., and Coles, R. (Eds.). (1989). *The child in our time: Studies in the development of resiliency*. New York: Brunner/Mazel. Highlights studies of children who thrive despite adversity.

Feldman, D. H. (1986). *Nature's gambit: Child prodigies and the development of human potential*. New York: Basic Books. Presents ideas on dealing with gifted children.

Flavell, J. H. (1963). *The developmental psychology of Jean Piaget*. Princeton, NJ: Van Nostrand. A classic work covering the work of Piaget.

Ginsburg, H. P., & Opper, S. (1988). *Piaget's theory of intellectual development* (3rd ed.). Englewood Cliffs, NJ: Prentice Hall. A concise introduction to Piaget's stages of cognitive development.

Hale, J. E. (1982). *Black children: Their roots, culture, and learning styles*. Provo, UT: Brigham Young University Press. A comprehensive treatment of the cognitive development of black children in America. Suggests ways of designing educational programs for disadvantaged youth.

Miller, A. B. (1990). *The day care dilemma: Concerns for American families*. New York: Plenum Press. A frank discussion of the state of day care in the United States and its potential impact on child development.

Nelson, K. (Ed.) (1989). *Narratives from the crib*. Cambridge, MA: Harvard University Press. An intriguing collection of a child's talk to herself before sleep, offering suggestions about her thought processes and development.

Rosenblith, J. F., & Sims-Knight, J. E. (1985). *In the beginning: Development in the first two years of life*. Monterey, CA: Brooks/ Cole. An introduction to research on infancy.

Schweder, R. A. (1991). *Thinking through cultures: Expeditions in cultural psychology*. Cambridge, MA: Harvard University Press. Discussions of how culture affects psychological development and personality.

White, M. (1987). *The Japanese educational challenge: A commitment to children*. New York: Free Press. An integrated discussion of Japanese culture and values and how they relate to their educational system.

# CHAPTER 10

## LIFE-SPAN DEVELOPMENT: ADOLESCENCE AND ADULTHOOD

### OUTLINE

▶ **Learning Objectives**

▶ **Adolescence**

■Biological Changes
■Sexual Development
  Sexual Differentiation
  The Adolescent's Emerging
   Sexuality
■Seeking an Identity
■Social Development

▶ **Guided Review**

▶ **Early and Middle Adulthood**

■The Early Adult Years
  Choosing a Career
  Marriage and Family
■The Middle Adult Years
  The Mid-Life Transition
  Mid-Life Changes in Women
  Beyond the Mid-Life
   Transition
■Cognitive Development in
 Adulthood

▶ **Guided Review**

▶ **Later Adulthood**

■The Aging Process
■Life Adjustments in Later
 Adulthood
  Retirement
  Family Changes
  Aging and Health
■Creativity and Productivity
■Death and Dying
  Facing Death
  The Choices of the Dying

▶ **Guided Review**

▶ **Summary**

▶ **Action Glossary**

▶ **Self-Test**

▶ **Thinking About Psychology**

▶ **Suggested Readings**

# LIFE-SPAN DEVELOPMENT: ADOLESCENCE AND ADULTHOOD
## LEARNING OBJECTIVES

**After reading this chapter, you should be able to**

▶ **1.** describe the biological factors underlying sexual development and puberty. *(pp. 314–316)*

▶ **2.** identify some patterns of sexual behavior in adolescence. *(pp. 316–319)*

▶ **3.** describe the process by which adolescents seek to establish an identity separate from their parents. *(pp. 319–321)*

▶ **4.** explain how the adolescent's social development moves from a focus on parents to a focus on peer groups. *(pp. 321–323)*

▶ **5.** describe some of the major developmental tasks and life events facing a person during the early years of adulthood. *(pp. 325–328)*

▶ **6.** describe the mid-life transition, and explain how it affects the individual during middle adulthood. *(pp. 328–329)*

▶ **7.** discuss the changes in cognitive abilities that occur during the adult years. *(p. 330)*

▶ **8.** describe the aging process. *(pp. 331–332)*

▶ **9.** identify several of the adjustments that are often necessary during later adulthood. *(pp. 332–335)*

▶ **10.** describe the role of creativity and productivity in adjustment to later adulthood. *(p. 335)*

▶ **11.** discuss the behavioral patterns people may experience when they learn they are going to die. *(pp. 336–337)*

Who is reading this paragraph? In the seventies and early eighties, we could have described most of you fairly well. You would have been in your late teens, in your freshman or sophomore year of college. You'd still be struggling with the process of separating from your parents and finding your own identity. You'd be taking an introductory psychology course partly to satisfy general education requirements, partly to learn more about yourself and your world. A few of you might be eager to go on to major in psychology and choose a career in the field.

In the 1990s, we know this description fits only a minority of our readers. Many of you are well beyond your teen years with much solid work experience under your belt. You may have a full-time job and a family, so taking college courses means considerable sacrifice. Some of you have already earned technical or business degrees and are taking this course to broaden your understanding of social sciences, humanities, and other more people-oriented subjects. Some of you are retired and enjoying the pursuit of interests you never had time for. Some of you are not taking a course at all—perhaps you're a teenager reading intriguing sections of a textbook your mother is using in *her* course.

The patterns that human lives follow from conception to puberty are relatively easy to describe. Certainly there is variation, but this early period of life involves a lot of learning and growing that is common to all normal children. With puberty, life courses begin to diverge much more dramatically. Variability has been growing, particularly in the United States as we can see just by looking at who is reading this chapter. Decades ago, the unwritten cultural script defined a college course as an appropriate task for white males who had just completed high school and were at the top of their classes. Obviously, that script no longer applies.

This chapter explores the years from the onset of puberty until death—a span of time that can cover the better part of a century. From adolescence to old age, people share many experiences but given the length of time it isn't surprising that people's lives go in different directions.

# ADOLESCENCE

The word *adolescence* comes from the Latin "adolescere," to grow up. The boy turns into a man, and the girl turns into a woman. The change is a profound one, involving much biological, social, moral, cognitive, and emotional

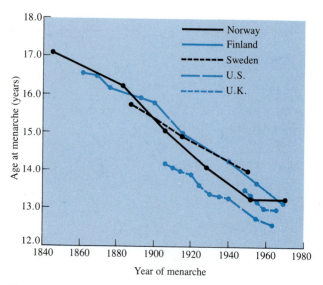

**Figure 10.1**    *The lowering age of first menses in selected northern European countries and the United States from 1845 to 1969.*

growth. It is not always an easy period of life, at least not in the United States; it can be full of conflicts, confusions, and crises. Some people weather adolescence and the transition to adulthood with little fuss, but others recall this period as one of the most stressful in their lives.

## Biological Changes

**Puberty** *marks the end of childhood and the beginning of adolescence; it is the time of sexual maturation.* The age at which this event occurs varies between boys and girls and among people of different countries. This age has been slowly declining in America and most of the other industrialized countries, partly because of improved nutrition (figure 10.1).

Although the onset of menstruation is an obvious starting point for adolescence in girls, pubertal changes actually begin much earlier. The young girl begins a growth spurt around age ten; breast development and pubic hair appear soon thereafter. The onset of menstruation, somewhere around thirteen years of age, does not necessarily mean that the girl is reproductively mature and can become pregnant. Although some girls are fertile at that age, most require several more months before their reproductive organs are able to function properly.

The growth spurt in boys begins about two years later than in girls, a biological quirk of the human species that can cause much awkwardness and embarrassment at sixth

## CLOSE UP ON RESEARCH

### The Luck of the Draw

You find an envelope in your mailbox from the lottery commission, open it with trembling hands, and read "Congratulations! You have just won $1,000,000!" This kind of chance event and many others like it are part of the reason that the patterns of change in adulthood are so variable. The human life span is long enough so that unexpected events are likely to occur to everyone and most people experience several during their lives, for better or worse (Duncan et al., 1984).

Studies of lottery winners reveal some fascinating patterns about how people cope with a very lucky event. One researcher surveyed 576 lottery winners from 12 states to learn more about their demographic characteristics, their behavior after winning, and their spending patterns. Winners were older than the general population and more often male than female. Although many people fantasize about quitting their jobs, most real winners do not. Those who did quit or retire were more likely to be the older winners or those with low educational levels. People with college educations who had about average incomes and satisfying jobs were more likely to continue.

Another myth about lottery winners is that they go on spending sprees and lose their money. In fact, most winners were much more thoughtful. Some spent more money on children and relatives, some invested it, and many gave substantial sums to charity or church. As for purchases, the most common items were a new car, a new home, or a vacation to Hawaii, Florida, or California (Kaplan, 1987).

Why are lotteries growing so rapidly, and why do people buy lottery tickets? Researchers find that ticket purchases go sky high when the jackpot gets large, and that most people prefer a lottery that has one large prize rather than several small ones. This pattern is true of lotteries in the United States as well as Canada, England, Colombia, Spain, Australia, Ghana, and West Germany. People see lotteries as a means to great wealth, something that they could never achieve otherwise. Some studies have found that the poor spend a greater proportion of their income on lotteries. In the United States, interest in lotteries has coincided with the fading of the American dream, as standards of living stagnate, jobs become less secure, and getting ahead is not as easy as it once was (Brenner & Brenner, 1990).

Unlucky chance events also happen, such as the unexpected death or sickness of a loved one, a sudden disability, a pink slip from an employer, a business bankruptcy, or an earthquake that destroys your home. People vary a great deal in how well they cope with these disasters. Some people, particularly those with a strong sense of control over their own lives and solid social support, have the resources to bounce back and begin rebuilding their lives. Others sink into feelings of hopelessness, failure, bitterness, and depression. Within the many decades of adult life, unpredictable, chance events, both good and bad, are inevitable. It's just a question of when.

and seventh grade dances. Most boys begin to show live spermatazoa in their urine by the age of twelve; this event is usually considered the onset of puberty. More obvious signals include the growth of the testes, penis, and scrotum (around age twelve), the appearance of pubic and facial hair, and the lengthening of the vocal cords, which results in a deepening of the voice.

The hormones released during puberty result in the development of primary and secondary sexual characteristics. The **primary sexual characteristics** *include those directly related to reproduction, such as the penis, the testes, the ovaries, and the fallopian tubes.* The **secondary sexual characteristics** *include those features that appear during puberty that are not directly related to reproductive functions. Examples include the change in the male voice, the growth of pubic hair and axillary hair, and muscular development in men.*

The psychological reactions adolescents have to these biological changes vary a great deal. Some express surprise and distress, others are excited and pleased about the events. Adolescents who know what to expect, and about when to expect it, tend to be more favorable about the changes. For example, girls who mature early and have no information about menstruation are more likely to report negative experiences. They feel more self-consciousness and more painful physical symptoms, and their unfavorable feelings sometimes persist into adulthood. Boys who experience their first ejaculation without knowing much about it also report more negative feelings.

Adolescents can be especially sensitive about the timing of their own developmental changes (figure 10.2). In the adolescent years, individual differences in rate of development can become points of social comparison and can affect the socialization process. Early-maturing boys, for example, seem to have more positive self-concepts and

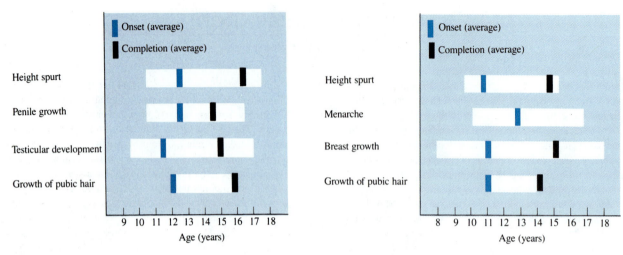

**Figure 10.2** *The sequence of pubertal events for boys and girls.* From "Growing Up" by J. M. Tanner. Copyright © 1973 by Scientific American, Inc. All rights reserved.

more successful relationships with friends. Adults also seem to respond more positively to boys whose physical maturation occurs early. One study found that the psychological characteristics associated with early maturation in boys, such as dominance and independence, were still prominent when the individuals reached their thirties (Jones & Mussen, 1958). Early maturation, however, may have some negative effects on socialization and emotional development, particularly in girls. Early-maturing girls are not as popular as their friends who mature later, nor are they considered as physically attractive, sociable, or poised. Early-maturing adolescents tend to be heavier and stockier, a physical feature that is not particularly desirable for women in the West, but is fine for men. Late-maturing girls have more time for their legs to grow so they have a better chance to match the long-legged, lithesome female ideal of beauty common in Western cultures (Mussen & Jones, 1957; Peskin, 1967; Clausen, 1975; Simmons & Blyth, 1987; Stattin & Magnusson, 1990). It appears to be the children who are most out of sync with their friends who have the most problems: early-maturing girls who are ahead of other girls and way ahead of boys, and late-maturing boys who are behind other boys and well behind all the girls.

Cultural views of puberty, and the rituals and ceremonies that sometimes accompany them, can have dramatic effects on how adolescents feel toward their changing state. In Western cultures, there are few rituals to celebrate the onset of puberty and mark it as a milestone in a person's life. (One notable exception is the bar mitzvah ceremony that marks a 13-year-old Jewish boy's attainment of the age of religious duty and responsibility.) But in many cultures, the onset of puberty has great significance, sometimes positive, sometimes negative. The Oriya Brahmans of India, for example, hold a ceremony involving bathing and seclusion that marks the first menstruation. The date, time, and place of the event has meaning and is used to make predictions about the girl's future (Schweder, 1991).

## Sexual Development

The biological changes that occur during puberty are the result of forces that begin at the moment of conception. All human beings have a total of forty-six chromosomes arranged in twenty-three pairs. The **sex chromosomes** *are one of these pairs of chromosomes; they determine the gender of the fetus. An* **X** *chromosome is present as one of the sex chromosomes in all normal people. Women have two X chromosomes; men have only one. The* **Y** *chromosome, the other, smaller, sex chromosome, is present only in men.* Because a woman has two X chromosomes, all of her egg cells contain an X. The sperm that fertilizes the egg, however, can contain either an X or a Y chromosome from the father. If the sperm contains an X chromosome, the fetus will be a girl; if it contains a Y chromosome, the fetus will be a boy.

*Sexual Differentiation*    The sex of the fetus is determined at conception, but the unfolding of those genetic directions takes considerable time. **Sexual differentiation** *is the process by which the physiological differences between males and females develop. The process has two primary components: one that involves the reproductive system of the developing organism and another that involves the organism's brain and behavior.* Androgens, *sex hormones released by the testes,* play a critical role in the process of sexual differentiation.

During the first two months of prenatal life, male and female embryos are almost indistinguishable. If the embryo contains a Y chromosome, the undifferentiated gonadal tissue develops into testes, which then begin to secrete male hormones that affect the further development of the reproductive system. Under the influence of these hormones, the cells that might have become female reproductive organs regress, and those that are to become male reproductive organs develop normally. The tissue that might have become the ovaries, uterus, vagina, or fallopian tubes regresses, and the fetus develops a penis, prostate gland, ejaculatory duct, and other male organs. If the embryo contains no Y chromosome, no testes develop, and no male hormones are released. In the absence of these male hormones, the female reproductive organs develop (Wilson, George, & Griffin, 1981).

A very unusual phenomenon demonstrates what can happen when this hormonal sequence is disrupted. A small group of children in the Caribbean who appeared to be girls at birth were reared as girls. Isabel, for example, spent her early years as a girl but then began to feel very different in late childhood. At puberty, she began adding muscle and speaking with a lower voice. What everyone thought was a clitoris became a penis. Finally, at age twelve, she put on men's clothes and became the muscular, masculine "Chi Chi" (Imperato-McGinley Guerrero, Gautier, & Peterson, 1974).

Isabel and a few others like her inherited a genetic problem that interferes with the ability to produce **dihydrotestosterone,** *the hormone released during prenatal life that is responsible for the development of the male genitals.* Although they possessed a Y chromosome and were genetically male, their testicular tissue was unable to produce dihydrotestosterone during the first months of prenatal life. In the absence of this hormone, their genitalia looked more like that of a girl, so their parents reared them as girls. They did have internal testes, however, and when they reached puberty, these internal organs began producing male hormones. The hormone

caused the development of male secondary sexual characteristics.

The process of sexual differentiation also involves the brain and behavior. The androgens released in the male during prenatal life and the absence of those hormones in the female have important effects on the developing brain. Some of the effects of these hormones are delayed and are not apparent until the organism reaches puberty.

When females reach puberty, they begin their menstrual cycle because of the cyclic release of hormones from the pituitary gland. The brains of males, however, cause those pituitary hormones to be released in fairly steady amounts from puberty onward. This difference in the way the pituitary glands of males and females direct hormonal secretion is due to differences in the neurons of the brain that control the pituitary gland (MacLusky & Naftolin, 1981). Even though the difference between the brains of males and females is not apparent until puberty, it first appears in prenatal life. The trigger for the development of differences in the brains of males and females is the hormones circulating in the embryonic male. If they are present, as they should be for a fetus with a Y chromosome, the brain is organized so that it will later direct the pituitary to release its hormones at a constant level, in the malelike fashion. If they are absent, the brain is organized so that the hormones are released cyclically after puberty, as they should be for females.

Do the hormones circulating in the prenatal brain have any influence on behavior later in life? This question has been a difficult one to answer (see chapter 2). Although it is clear that they affect behavior in small mammals, it has been a problem to determine whether they have any affect on human behavior. In the normal case, a child's chromosomes determine prenatal environment, prenatal hormonal environment determines gender, and gender influences the child's environment in very fundamental ways that depend on prevailing cultural views. One of the most basic characteristics of a person, one that influences that person's environment, choices and chances throughout life, is the person's gender. Separating all these influences is complicated.

In a few cases, the influences can be partially separated because of unusual accidents. One investigation studied girls exposed to androgens during prenatal life because their adrenal systems were functioning abnormally. These babies had masculinized genitals, even though they were genetically female. The researchers found that the girls

## APPLYING PSYCHOLOGY

### The Fine Line between Male and Female

Just before the 1985 World University Games in Kobe, Japan, Spanish hurdler Maria Patino's career was ruined. She was asked to take a routine test to determine whether she was a man or a woman; based on the results she was disqualified because she was a "man." Devastated, she faked an injury and flew home only to find she had been banned from international competitions, her scholarship had been revoked, and she was expelled from her athletic housing. Her wins were struck out from the record books.

One test used by many athletic associations checks for the second X chromosome. Normally, a person with two X chromosomes is a female—genetically, physically, and in terms of their gender identity. A person with one X and one Y is a male. But there are thousands of people whose genetic patterns are not consistent with other measures of gender. Patino, for example, has a relatively common condition called

androgen insensitivity. Although she has one X and one Y, her body does not react to the male hormone and she developed as a female, except that she lacks ovaries and fallopian tubes. Isabel and the Dominican children described in the text had another disorder that resulted in inconsistent measures of gender.

The use of genetic testing by athletic associations to determine "maleness" or "femaleness" is very controversial, and some charge that it discriminates against people with particular kinds of birth defects. Some associations are changing the test so it includes a full medical exam, including a genital inspection. Based on scientific recommendations, Patino was eventually reinstated as a female athlete. But as long as record books separate events for men and women, the debate over how to tell one from the other will continue.

preferred boys as playmates and liked trucks better than dolls. They were somewhat more active and inclined to expend more energy compared to girls who had not been exposed to the androgens. However, the study is still inconclusive because the parents may well have treated the babies more like boys because of their abnormal genitals (Ehrhardt & Meyer-Bahlburg, 1981).

Psychologists are especially interested in the role that prenatal hormones might play in a person's **gender identity,** *which refers to a person's sense of being male or female.* Does a person feel like a woman or a man because of hormones, because of the rearing and cultural environment, or because of some combination of the two? Again, clearcut answers are very difficult to obtain. In most normal people the factors contributing to gender identity can't be separated. Men and women have different hormones, and they also grow up in very different environments. From the first day of life, parents treat boys and girls differently, and they begin to act differently. Before they are out of diapers toddlers have acquired many of the behaviors their culture considers appropriate for their sex (Stern & Karraker, 1989).

A part of gender identity is sexual orientation. Do prenatal hormones have any effect on a person's preference for a male or female sexual partner? Follow-up studies conducted on the girls who were exposed to abnormally high levels of prenatal androgens found that an unusually high number (thirty-seven percent) reported

themselves as homosexual or bisexual (Money, Schwartz, & Lewis, 1984). But again, the studies are difficult to interpret. Many researchers have found that children who are born with abnormal or ambiguous genitalia generally have a sexual orientation consistent with their sex of rearing, even if it doesn't match their genetic sex.

The issue of whether the sexual orientation of homosexuals might be related to prenatal hormones is a very controversial one. Some homosexuals feel that they have always been fundamentally different and that their sexual orientation has nothing to do with choice or social environment. Others see it as an alternative life-style. Some preliminary studies (LeVay, 1991; Swaab & Hoffman, 1990) that involved autopsies have reported differences in the brains of homosexual and heterosexual men, particularly in a part of the hypothalamus that is known to be involved in sex behavior. The anatomical pattern for the homosexual men was more similar to the pattern seen in women than the one common in heterosexual men. This brain structure is known to be different in males and females because of the effects of prenatal hormones. Whether the differences in this area of the brain caused the men's homosexuality, or were even related to it, is not yet known.

*The Adolescent's Emerging Sexuality*    Around the time of puberty, when the adolescent's body undergoes so many biological changes associated with the release of pubertal hormones, there is a large increase in interest about sexual matters. The heightened attention to sexuality is caused by many factors, including the biological changes and the individual's awareness of them; the hormonal changes; and the emphasis placed on sexuality by peers, parents, and society.

Not surprisingly, the adolescent often experiences considerable inner turmoil about sexuality. Accurate information about topics such as masturbation, homosexuality, venereal disease, pregnancy, contraception, or impotence is difficult to obtain. These subjects are taboo in many homes, and most adolescents do not obtain very much information about sex from parents (see table 10.1). One woman enrolled in a class on human sexuality at a north-eastern college reported her problems of communication:

> I would like to write about my mother and the way she explained to me the facts of life. Actually, she didn't. My poor mom. Everytime I asked her anything about how babies were born, she answered so hesitantly that I almost felt sorry for her. . . . (G. L. Thornton, personal communication)

Although some adolescents are able to discuss sexual matters openly with one another, there are many topics not discussed.

Adolescents can be rather secretive about the onset of puberty. In one study, girls told far fewer friends than one might imagine. Most told only their mothers, at least until several months had passed. Boys were even more closed-mouthed about the biological changes affecting them. Most tell no one when they have their first ejaculation (Gaddis & Brooks-Gunn, 1985). Sexually active adolescents also have difficulty discussing their problems with others. One study found that although most had discussed birth control on at least one occasion, they had not discussed the matter before their first intercourse. One-fourth felt that contraception had not been adequately discussed (Polit-O'Hara & Kahn, 1985).

One of the important factors that influences a person's sexual career path in adolescence is socioeconomic status. In a study of black adolescents, the average age for the first intercourse for low socioeconomic status girls was 16.4 years; girls in middle or high scoioeconomic status were slower to become sexually active, waiting until about age 17 (Murry, 1992).

The patterns of adolescent sexual relationships have also been investigated. One earlier study (Sorensen, 1973) found that serial monogamy without marriage is a common pattern. These adolescents establish a relationship with a partner and intend to be faithful, but they are never sure how long the relationship will last. Of those in the sample who had had premarital sex, about forty percent could be

| TABLE 10.1 Adolescent sex information sources | | | |
|---|---|---|---|
| Source | Male N–392 (%) | Female N–566 (%) | Total N–958 (%) |
| Peers | 45.7 | 32.4 | 38.7 |
| Literature | 16.7 | 23.8 | 20.9 |
| School | 18.3 | 20.4 | 19.5 |
| Mother | 5.6 | 18.7 | 13.4 |
| Father | 4.1 | .7 | 2.1 |
| Experiences | 8.0 | 2.8 | 5.0 |
| Minister | 1.0 | .6 | .7 |
| Physician | .6 | .6 | .6 |
| | 100.0 | 100.0 | 100.0 |

From Herschel D. Thornburg, *Contemporary Adolescence: Readings*, 2nd ed. Copyright © 1975. Reprinted by permission of the author.

described as serial monogamists. Other surveys have found that adolescents usually do not randomly or promiscuously engage in premarital sex (Hunt, 1974). A large number of women have only one partner, whom they eventually marry. Although standards regarding premarital sex have changed considerably over the years, they have not been disregarded completely. Generally, adolescents appear to regard premarital sex as acceptable provided the two people are emotionally committed and love one another.

The concern over adolescent sexuality has become especially intense because of the risk of AIDS and other sexually transmitted diseases, and the skyrocketing rates of teen pregnancies. Unfortunately, various kinds of risky sexual behavior are correlated so an adolescent who has multiple partners is also less likely to use condoms or contraception (Metzler, Noell, & Biglan, 1992). These adolescents are often unrealistically optimistic about their risks. A study of Australians found a large group who engaged in many unsafe sexual practices but still perceived themselves to be invulnerable to the AIDS virus (Moore & Rosenthal, 1991). "It can't happen to me" is a powerful theme during this period of life.

## Seeking an Identity

How do people decide who they are? How do they decide whether to vote Republican or Democratic or whether to apply to Princeton, West Point, or air-conditioning school? How do they decide whether to go to church or whether to believe in God? Why does one person become a tax accountant, eager to make money,

## CLOSE UP ON RESEARCH

### Teen Pregnancies

Each year in the United States over one million teenagers become pregnant, with four out of five of them unmarried. About forty percent of these teens choose to have an abortion, while another thirteen percent have miscarriages. With the increasing acceptance of single mothers in this society, very few teenage mothers give up their babies for adoption. Teen mothers are more likely to be poor and to be poorly educated. If they give birth before graduating from high school, the chances for finishing are not good. They are disproportionately minority: the birth rate for black adolescents is two and a half times that for white females in the same age group. Pregnancy in adolescents tends to repeat itself from generation to generation. About one-third of girls who were teenage parents had been born to teenage mothers (Furstenberg, Brooks-Gunn, & Morgan, 1987).

Do adolescents have trouble parenting? Becoming a parent in your teens, when you are still trying to establish your own identity, have not finished school, have few prospects for employment, and are not married is, to put it mildly, a major life stressor. Studies have found that younger mothers have less knowledge about how to care for an infant, and they tend to expect children to develop faster than they really do. Teen mothers are more likely to become impatient with children and are prone to use more physical punishment. Adolescent mothers also are more likely to give birth to babies with health problems, particularly if the mother is using drugs.

Although there are exceptions, teen mothers as a group are clearly at risk for a great many problems, and so are their children.

Despite the risks and hardships, some adolescents become good mothers. One study of low-income adolescent mothers attempted to isolate the factors that contributed to problems in parenting, apart from the mother's young age. One important factor was the personal and psychological resources of the mother. Teens who had higher self-esteem, better relationships with their own mothers, and friends they could count on, were likely to have more functional attitudes about parenting. For example, they were less likely to think corporal punishment was the answer to behavior problems in children, or to unrealistically believe a child under three should be old enough to take care of himself. Teens without these personal and psychological resources were more likely to show dysfunctional parenting attitudes that might ultimately lead to child abuse or neglect (McKenry, Kotch, & Browne, 1991).

Having a baby in your teens is expected and even longed for in many cultures. In parts of sub-Saharan Africa, the social patterns welcome large families and early child rearing, partly as a means to build wealth for the group (Caldwell & Caldwell, 1990; 1992). But in industrialized countries, making the transition to parenthood in adolescence is far ahead of the culture's timetable.

another strive to solve the world hunger problem, and a third run for mayor? The answer to all of these questions involves the concept of identity, or the sense of self. Identity is who a person is and what his or her values, commitments, and beliefs are; it provides continuity to life.

The primary task of the adolescent is to establish an identity separate from his or her parents. For some, this is a painful and time-consuming task; people can take years to complete it, and a few never do. For others, the task is accomplished smoothly, and the change from adolescence to adulthood is not very difficult. The adolescent must establish a sexual identity, a vocational identity, and a social identity on the road to a stable sense of self. Adolescents must become individual people with their own principles, beliefs, friends, thoughts, and ideas. They are at a crossroad, yearning for independence but still afraid of it and still showing a great deal of dependence on their parents.

According to Erik Erikson (1972), **identity versus identity diffusion** *is the major psychosocial developmental task of adolescence. This task concerns the young person's search for a role that fits, particularly with respect to social behavior and occupational choice.* Rapid fluctuations between self-confidence and insecurity are typical of this stage. One day the adolescent may yearn for more responsibility and complain of being "treated like a baby." The next day he or she may seek comfort in dependence on parents. The adolescent is in a stage in which he or she must acquire a sense of wholeness, a feeling of continuity between childhood and adulthood.

Researchers have found that adolescents, and adults as well, fall into one of several categories with respect to their identity status. **Identity achievement,** *one category of identity status, characterizes people who have gone through a period of crisis and have developed relatively firm commitments.* **Foreclosure,** *another category of identity status, characterizes people who have never gone* *through any identity crisis but have nevertheless become committed to certain goals or values.* Most often, their commitments reflect an unexamined acceptance of the commitments of their parents, teachers, or peers.

**Moratorium,** *another type of identity status, describes people who are currently in an identity crisis.* Finally, **identity diffusion** *describes people who have never had a crisis, who are not in one now, and who have not formed any commitments or established any goals* (Marcia, 1976).

Children are only peripherally interested in questions of identity; for adolescents, the search for identity is a consuming task. Most people move from one status to another during their adolescent years, and many enter adulthood in the identity achievement status with a stable sense of self. Though the process of forming an identity begins early in adolescence, changes in identity status are especially common during late adolescence, particularly for those who attend college. Adolescents begin college in the foreclosure status or in the identity diffusion status, but many finish somewhere else. Seniors often have a much stronger sense of personal identity than freshmen do. They hold stronger commitments to and have clearer ideas about their vocational choices, their political beliefs, their feelings about sex, and their own self-worth, and their religious beliefs. (Researchers have found that college experiences seem to undermine traditional religious beliefs without helping students establish any alternative [Waterman & Goldman, 1976; Waterman, 1982]). Some interviews with adolescents show how people in these different statuses feel:

> Interviewer: Tell me how you feel about the election coming up in November.
>
> Jan: I'm not much into politics—my parents are both staunch Republicans, really conservative, you know? But I never thought about it much. It doesn't matter whether I vote or care anyway . . . . (identity diffusion)

> Interviewer: How do you feel about people who have sex before marriage?
>
> Bill: Umm . . . that's a tough one. My best friend is going to bed with his girl, I know. Sometimes I want to, and I think [my girlfriend] does too, though we don't talk about it much. I think it's not a good idea because of pregnancy, and well, you know, morals, but I'm just not sure. I'd like to know what my father did, but I'd never ask. It's confusing, but at least I think you should be in love first and not just hop in the sack with any girl. (moratorium)

> Interviewer: What are your plans for a career?

> Darien: I've got it all set to join my father's law firm . . . of course I have to finish school, but it's a good life. My parents travel a lot, and somehow, it seems like that's what I should do. (foreclosure)

> Interviewer: Have you made any decisions about what to do after college?
>
> Sean: Boy, I really sweated last year about that one. I got really scared, wondering how I was going to get a job in this economy. It's such a mess. First I took some welding classes, can you believe, in case I couldn't find a teaching job—there are so few of them, you know. But now I think I feel better about it. I did some subbing this year and loved it—teaching is what I want to do. So maybe I'll have to be a busboy on the side for awhile. Beats counting beans for Uncle Sam . . . . (identity achievement)

One of the variables related to the identity status of adolescents is their relationship with their family. Adolescents who have very close relationships with their parents are more likely to be in a foreclosure status. They view their parents as supportive and are very willing to involve family members in their life decisions. Those with very distant family relationships are more likely to be in a state of identity diffusion. They see their parents as rejecting, indifferent, detached, and lacking understanding. Adolescents in the moratorium and identity achievement statuses are more likely to be critical of their parents and to have conflict in their homes. No one knows yet whether the attitudes or behaviors of parents cause an adolescent's identity status; it could easily be the other way around. An apathetic youngster in a state of identity diffusion, showing no interest in jobs or school and having no commitments in life, is not likely to elicit enthusiastic encouragement from parents.

It is clear that the college years are important for the development of identity in adolescents. Eighteen-year-olds leave home for the first time and are exposed to an enormous array of experiences. These conditions push adolescents into questioning their beliefs and cause them to enter an identity crisis. But what happens to adolescents who do not go to college? And what happens to adults who fail to achieve a stable sense of identity during college? Later in this chapter we will see that many people still have questions about identity during adulthood.

## Social Development

During infancy, the baby's social world consists almost entirely of mother and father. Neighborhood and school friends become more important during childhood, but parents are still very significant. What mother and father consider "good" and what they say about politics or world affairs are critical influences on the child's behavior and attitudes. During adolescence, however, the social world shifts and the adolescent begins detaching from parents gaining autonomy.

From the time of pubertal maturation, closeness between parents and adolescents begins to decline and conflict increases. The onset of puberty seems to be more important than chronological age because of emotional and biological changes. Steinberg (1988) interviewed 157 adolescents twice over a one-year period and assessed both their pubertal status and their relationships with their parents. The adolescents who showed the most rapid pubertal change during the period of the study were also the ones who reported the greatest decreases in closeness with their parents, regardless of their actual age. The change in the parent-child relationships was not very large; the assumption cannot be made that every child will have stormy and stressful family relationships during puberty.

An interesting finding of Steinberg's study was that girls' rate of pubertal development during the study was faster when their relationships with their mothers were distant. This suggests that the relationship between puberty and family relations is a two-way street. A person's environment interacts with and can have affects on the biological events of puberty.

As adolescents feel more distant from their parents, the influence of friends grows dramatically. The decision to smoke or not smoke cigarettes is an example of how friends assume an important role. Two groups of children, aged eleven and fourteen, filled out questionnaires about their smoking habits and the attitudes of their parents and friends. For the eleven-year-old preadolescents, smoking habits were related to both their parents' attitudes and smoking habits and to the smoking habits of their friends. Children who did not smoke were more likely to have parents with negative attitudes toward smoking, whereas children who did smoke were more likely to have parents whose attitudes were more prosmoking. The influences on the fourteen-year-old adolescents, however, were slightly different. These children were more influenced by peers. The ones who smoked were more likely to have friends who smoked; their parents' attitudes and smoking habits were less important in their own smoking behavior (Krosnick & Judd, 1982).

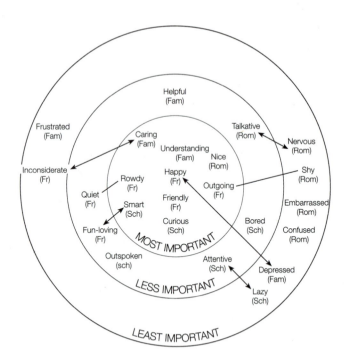

**Figure 10.3** *Prototypical self-portrait by a ninth-grade girl. (Fam = family; Rom. = romantic relationships; Fr. = friends; Sch. = school.)*

Adolescents are not just moving from parental influence to peer influence, however. They are establishing concepts of themselves that seem appropriate for each of their social roles. In one intriguing study of adolescent self-portraits, 7th, 9th, and 11th graders were all asked to describe themselves in different social roles by completing sentence stems, such as "I am _____ with my parents" (Harter & Monsour, 1992). The four roles were self with parents, self with friends, self in school, and self in romantic relationships. Each subject put the descriptive terms on some gummed labels, placed them in concentric circles based on their perceived importance, and created self-portraits like the one in figure 10.3. The subjects connected self-descriptive terms that were opposite to one another with a line, such as happy with friends-depressed with family. If the opposite pair seemed to conflict or clash, the subjects put double-pointed arrows on the line. One subject described a clash this way, "You don't want to act this way, but then something uncaring comes out in you, you try to stop it, you have to fight it all the time!"

These researchers found that the number of contradictions and conflicts in an adolescent's self-portrait were

**Figure 10.4** *The importance of the peer group for social rewards and social comparisons grows dramatically during adolescence.*

lowest in 7th grade, peaked in 9th, and began to decline again in 11th. By the 11th grade, adolescents appear better able to accept their multiple roles and understand that it is normal to behave differently and feel differently in each of them. The fact that they are outgoing with friends but shy in romantic relationships doesn't seem as conflicting as it did in middle adolescence.

The role a person plays as a member of a peer group is an important ingredient in every person's identity. But during adolescence, more than any other period of life, people are concerned with the social group, with how they behave in it, and with what peers think (figure 10.4). This change is due partly to the search for identity; adolescents need to establish themselves as individuals, separate from their parents. The dependence on their peer group seems to help them solve their identity crisis. If they uniformly adhere to the values and customs of a peer group, they are, at least temporarily, solving their identity crisis. They are adopting the identity of the group. In this way, they can avoid some of the conflicts associated with the development of a separate identity. By wearing the same kind of

jeans, buying the same makeup, using the same slang, listening to the same music, and inventing all kinds of fads that set the adolescent group apart from other groups but make up a kind of uniform for the group's members,

▶ **GUIDED REVIEW** *Learning Objectives 1, 2, 3, and 4*

1. Adolescence begins with the onset of _____, the time of sexual maturation.
2. Early maturing boys have more positive _____ and are viewed more positively by parents and teachers. However, early maturation may have negative effects as well.
3. The process of sexual development begins at conception. The newly conceived fetus either has two _____ and becomes a girl or has one X chromosome and one _____ and becomes a boy. The chromosomes then direct the process of _____, whereby the physiological differences that exist between males and females develop.
4. If the fetus is a male, it begins to release _____, which masculinize the reproductive system and the brain. If the fetus is female, no fetal hormones are released, the female reproductive system develops, and the brain will produce a cyclic release of hormones at puberty.
5. Whether the release of prenatal sex hormones influences behavior is not clear, although some scientists suggest that early androgens influence activity levels in childhood. The child's _____, however, is mainly influenced by the gender assigned at birth rather than the prenatal hormone environment.
6. All kinds of sexual behavior increase markedly after puberty. Although sexual attitudes and practices have become more permissive during the last few decades, most adolescents do not show promiscuous sexual behavior. A common behavior pattern is _____.
7. The developmental task of _____ is a major psychosocial task of adolescence. The individual must establish an identity separate from his or her parents and "tries on" many identities to see how they "fit." Identity status can fall into one of four categories: _____, _____, _____, or _____.
8. Social development in adolescence is very rapid. Individuals move from primary reliance on their _____ for social approval and support to primary reliance on their _____. The social group is an important source of comparison during the adolescent years.

*ANSWERS*

1. puberty 2. self-concepts 3. X chromosomes, Y chromosome, sexual differentiation 4. androgens 5. gender identity 6. serial monogamy without marriage 7. Identity versus identity diffusion, identity achievement, foreclosure, moratorium, identity diffusion 8. parents, peers.

adolescents can postpone their painful search for individual identity.

# EARLY AND MIDDLE ADULTHOOD

Fifteen years ago developmental psychology was almost exclusively interested in the changes that occur between conception and the end of adolescence. Changes occurring during adulthood were little understood and rarely studied. Now, however, psychologists recognize that important developmental changes may take place after adolescence.

The question of whether substantial personality changes occur during the course of adult development is an intriguing one. Some theorists maintain that personality is formed during childhood and adolescence and remains stable after that. Others argue that personality develops and changes throughout the life span. Much of the research, however, indicates a balance between these positions: some facets of personality tend to change during adulthood, particularly in conjunction with major life events and developmental tasks, whereas other facets of personality remain stable. One longitudinal study spanning twenty years found that personality traits such as a need for order, a respectful regard for others' wishes (deference), desire to help others (succorance), and endurance tended to remain stable over time. Traits such as the need for achievement, autonomy, and dominance tended to increase in many people as they grew into middle adulthood (Stevens & Truss, 1985). In later adulthood, both men and women seem to emphasize their "feminine" side, becoming more affectionate, for example (Hyde, Krajnik, & Skukdt-Niederberger, 1991).

Another issue in adult development concerns whether there are identifiable patterns. In babies, children, and adolescents, there are several rather uniform life events, such as learning to walk, acquiring language, entering school, and reaching puberty. These events occur at about the same age in all people. In adulthood, though, the course of life becomes much more variable. By the age of twenty-seven, some people have found their career niches, are married, and have two or three children. Others might still be clinging to adolescence, trying out one role after another in their search for a sense of identity. Still others might be getting divorced.

Although the study of developmental changes in early and middle adulthood is still relatively new, it seems that familiar patterns do appear in people who, on the surface,

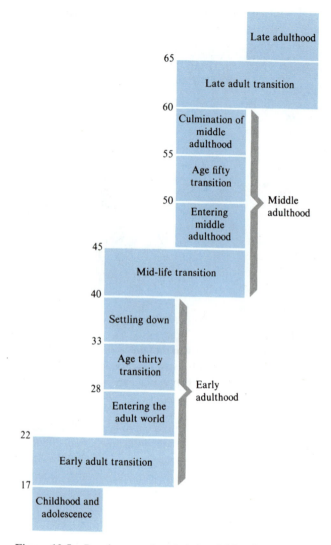

**Figure 10.5** *Developmental periods in adulthood.*

seem to be leading different lives. One study of men found that biologists, novelists, factory workers, and business executives all showed some similar trends in their adult development (Levinson, Darrow, Klein, Levinson, & McKee, 1978). This pattern, diagrammed in figure 10.5, found that similar developmental tasks face people in their early adult years (twenties, thirties, and early forties), and in middle adulthood (the forties through sixties).

One reason for some similarity in the course of adult development is that people within the same culture tend to follow similar cultural scripts about the best times for some of the most important life events. For example, in western cultures people were "expected" to marry in their twenties and have babies within a few years after marriage. If you fell back or leaped ahead of the timeline, friends, family, and even employers would have many questions and want to know why. In other cultures, the script that defines the timeline might be quite different. Women might be expected to marry much earlier and have babies long before they reached twenty. As we discussed in the beginning of this chapter, human life courses are becoming more and more variable in some cultures so the script is changing to allow more choices.

## The Early Adult Years

During the early years of adulthood, people face important developmental tasks. The first of these is to end adolescence. On the practical side, this means establishing financial independence and moving to a new residence. Psychologically, the end of adolescence can be very wrenching, and a few people avoid this task for years. Our society expects young adults in their early twenties to have a clear idea of both personal and career goals.

*Choosing a Career*    Even though some people switch careers during their adult lives, most people, men in particular, become established in a career during their twenties (Levinson et al., 1978; Super, 1980, 1985). The task of choosing a career, which occurs even earlier, is truly overwhelming because there are so many different occupations and because employment patterns are shifting so dramatically. In the late 1960s and early 1970s, many people in college chose to major in education. At the time, it seemed a wise decision because teachers were desperately needed by public school systems. However, as the baby boom subsided and the number of pupils entering schools declined, teachers became less employable. By the late seventies, individuals graduating with teaching certificates in hand found it very difficult to obtain a job. For most people, the choice of a career is only partly dictated by interests and abilities. The growth and decline of industries also affect the decision because people want to know they will be able to find a job (see table 10.2). In 1992, *U.S. News and World Report* listed twenty occupations that were on the "hot track" based on demand, industrial shifts, and salary potential. Examples were environmental accountant, network administrator, special education teacher, training manager, restaurant site selector, nurse practitioner, and toxicologist. Because of the number of large corporations downsizing, the magazine also listed outplacement consultant. But breaking into

| TABLE 10.2  To the year 2000: Fastest growing occupations |
| --- |
| Paralegals |
| Speech and hearing clinicians |
| Teacher aides and assistants |
| Physical therapists |
| School principals |
| Computer operators |
| X-ray technicians |
| Food-preparation workers |
| Preschool and elementary school teachers |
| Medical lab assistants |
| Assistant school principals |
| Sales managers |
| College and university teachers |
| Professional nurses |
| Computer specialists |

these specialties would take considerable time, and by the time an individual achieved sufficient education and experience, the career landscape may have changed again. Although the United States needs computer scientists now, there may be a glut in ten years. How do people make this difficult choice?

Most people in their late teens and early twenties have very little accurate information about occupations. What little information they do have comes from their parents, their parents' friends, the media, and perhaps some limited career education in high school. One study of twelfth-grade boys tried to determine how much they understood about the requirements for particular jobs in terms of both temperament and education. The occupations included civil engineer, physicist, psychiatrist, accountant, medical technologist, playground supervisor, credit investigator, insurance salesman, and window decorator (Nuckols & Banducci, 1974). Some of these jobs require an investigative interest and a great deal of education. Others would be appropriate for someone with a conservative or conventional personality. Sadly, the boys had very little idea about either the temperamental or educational requirements for these jobs. They were particularly ignorant of the requirements for the higher level jobs.

Most people seem to learn about the requirements for the career they have chosen after they are well along that career path. Students who enroll in nursing school are a good example:

Without exception our student nurses said that their main reason for choosing nursing as a career had been the wish to be of service to suffering people. When their freshman year began, they were disappointed upon finding that the entire first semester was devoted to academic classroom work; they had expected to learn things that were immediately useful in helping the sick. When basic nursing training began . . . , the students wanted to develop nurturant relationships with patients. They found that the faculty . . . [emphasized] specialized skills as well as proficiency in following routines and procedures . . . . During the two semesters of basic nursing, the gradual shift of interest from a humanistic concern with patients as individuals to a concern with mastery of technical repertoires was evident . . . . (Simpson, 1967)

Career counseling is becoming more available and is helping to remedy this situation. It is usually offered in high schools and colleges, and some cities offer it in the form of noncredit workshops, not just to help people choose a career in early adulthood but to help them change careers later in life.

Choosing a career is a somewhat different developmental task for men and women. Traditionally, men have been expected to enter a career or take a job and stay with it until they retire. Women have either been expected to get married and become homemakers after completing their education or to work for a few years and then become homemakers. Thus, until recently, choosing a career was not a major developmental task for women in their early adult years.

These differences between men and women are rapidly decreasing. More and more women are entering the work force because of desires to have both a family and a career and because of economic needs. According to a recent survey in Canada, professional women who take time out to marry and have children are more content than those who marry and stay childless, or those who never marry. The study surveyed professional women in medicine, law, engineering, and accounting, and except for those in medicine, the salaries of the three groups were about the same. This suggested that the career advancement of the women with children was not hindered by their choice (Roskies & Carrier, 1992).

Recent studies of occupational motivation among persons in late adolescence and early adulthood show fewer differences between the sexes (Grotevant & Thorbecke, 1982). Nevertheless, differences in attitudes toward the relationship between work and gender still exist, and these differences may affect each gender's career choices. In a survey of students in grades seven to twelve, the majority of students listed household chores such as laundry, cooking, and childcare as women's work; yardwork and car repairs were thought to be men's work

(Hansen & Darling, 1985). In addition, female adolescents tended to participate in household chores more often (Sanik & Stafford, 1985).

*Marriage and Family*     Other important developmental tasks facing young adults include adjusting to married life and raising a family. Although some people are choosing not to marry and others are choosing alternative life-styles such as cohabitation, the vast majority of men and women marry.

According to Erik Erikson (1972), **intimacy versus isolation** *is the major psychosocial developmental task faced by young adults. The focus of this task is to successfully establish relationships with other young adults and an intimate relationship with one person.* Failure to achieve this intimacy results in isolation.

The adjustments that young adults make when entering a marriage are profound. If they have not lived together before marriage, they must learn how to cope with each other's idiosyncracies. One might prefer to watch television in the evening, and the other may want to invite friends over. They both may find the financial burdens of marriage very difficult to cope with, and they are likely to feel acutely the loss of their personal freedom. Power is usually a source of controversy, particularly when both partners are working outside the home. The power equation was very much tilted toward the husband when it was the norm for the wife to stay home, but now the balance is a more equal one in many families. When both partners work and contribute to the marriage financially, who will make final decisions about what car to buy, how much to spend for a new stereo, or whether to spend the vacation in New York or Florida?

In addition to getting married, most people have children in their early adult years. Although there is a recent trend to postpone having children until the late twenties or early thirties, over ninety percent of women in the United States eventually have at least one child. The care of the children has traditionally been almost the exclusive responsibility of the mother, but this too is changing. Fathers are becoming more and more involved in childcare; many now attend Lamaze classes and play a key role in the development of their children. Scientists are discovering that the attention of fathers is important, even for infants.

They tend to provide their babies with more unpredictable physical kinds of play, whereas the mother is more likely to do the comforting and caretaking (Lamb, 1981).

# APPLYING PSYCHOLOGY

## Children of Divorce

About a third of the children in the United States will have experienced their parent's divorce before they reach the age of eighteen. The way that these millions of children adjust to this experience is an issue of national concern. The success of their adjustment depends on a great many factors, including the age and sex of the child, the amount of conflict between the divorcing parents, the custody arrangements, the availability of support services, and the socioeconomic changes that accompany the divorce.

When a husband and wife are contemplating divorce, the atmosphere in the home is often not conducive to successful child-rearing. The adults are concerned with their own problems, and they may create conflicts and stress in the child by competing for the child's loyalty. Certainly, in some cases, the children of parents who are constantly fighting may be better off if their parents divorce and they live in a single-parent home. But even when the parents have had a great deal of conflict, the year following the divorce is usually a very difficult one for the child.

If the mother is awarded custody, she may experience a sudden drop in her standard of living, particularly since only about one-third of ex-husbands contribute to child support. She may be poorly trained for employment and capable of making only a meager living. If the parents are still in conflict, visits by the noncustodial parent may be traumatic for the child. Typically, the mother's style of child-rearing becomes more restrictive and controlling, whereas the noncustodial father becomes more permissive but less available (Hetherington, Cox, & Cox, 1976). Both parents are often not consistent.

Divorce may have long-lasting effects on the behavior of children. A study of adolescent girls living with widowed mothers, divorced mothers, and with both parents revealed several differences, particularly with respect to the girls' attitudes about boys and sex. The daughters of the widowed mothers tended to be more withdrawn, passive, and inhibited, while the daughters of the divorced mothers were more aggressive and flirtatious. For example, when the girls were interviewed for the study by a man, the daughters of the widowed mothers tended to sit in the chair farthest away. In contrast, the daughters of the divorced mothers tended to sit in the closest chair (Hetherington, 1972). Follow-up studies of these daughters continue to reveal differences. The daughters of the widows were more likely to marry men with more puritanical attitudes. The daughters of both widowed and divorced mothers tended to have more sexual adjustment problems than daughters who grew up with both parents in the home (Hetherington, 1972; 1977).

Until the 1900s, children of divorcing parents were almost invariably placed into the custody of the father, since it was the father who possessed the means to support the family. The belief that both the children and the wife were the man's property also contributed to this practice. The twentieth century brought a greater concern for the welfare of the children, partly because of the influence of Freudian thinking, and mothers began gaining custody of young children. Today, courts no longer automatically award custody to the mother. Judges try to consider the welfare of the children and the home situations of each parent before they make their decisions. Preliminary psychological research suggests that children adjust better after divorce if they live with the same-sex parent (Kelly, 1987).

The age of the child is another important consideration. Preschool children are not very accurate in assessing the cause of the divorce, and many blame themselves. Children at this age are probably the most vulnerable. Although adolescents experience a great deal of conflict and stress, they are better able to assign responsibility (Wallerstein & Kelly, 1980). Nevertheless, surveys of adolescents whose parents have divorced show that they develop more negative attitudes toward their parents and themselves after the divorce (Parish & Wigle, 1985).

The divorce of a child's parents is a stressful event in almost all cases, but many stresses can be minimized. Adjustment problems seem to be fewer if the child is older, if the child's home environment remains economically stable, if the parents keep the conflict and hostility before and after the divorce low, if both parents agree about child-rearing practices and discipline, if the noncustodial parent continues to show love and interest, and if the child has the opportunity to discuss divorce-related concerns (Kurdek, 1981).

Although the effects of the father's early involvement on infant development are not clear, his involvement is very important for his own feelings of inclusion in the family.

The coming of children represents an enormous stressor in the lives of young adults. Children bring heavy financial and emotional responsibilities, even when they are planned. Because of improvements in birth control, parents can now choose when to have children and how many to have, a choice that, according to some scientists, may influence the intellectual development of children. These influences may add yet another level of responsibility to the decisions young people must make during the early adult years.

The birth of the first child represents an important event in the lives of young adults. One study of new parents found certain personality changes during those first few weeks of parenthood. Some mothers, for example, experience temporary depressions during the first few postpartum months and, as a result, feel less affectionate toward their infants and respond less to their vocalizations (Fleming, Ruble, Flett, & Shaul, 1988). One study of new parents found that the baby's behavior affects the personality of the parents. New parents who perceived their babies as "easy," in the sense that they were more cheerful, more adaptable to schedules, and less active, tended to experience more positive personality changes than did the new parents with the "difficult" babies (Sirigano & Lackman, 1985).

Young people, and especially young men, do not seem to be very well-versed in child behavior. One survey of college students found a widespread lack of knowledge about child-development patterns, particularly with regard to the age at which children are able to recognize their own wrongdoing (Shaner, Peterson, & Roscoe, 1985). This is a troubling finding because it may suggest that young people expect children to be able to control themselves and discriminate right from wrong much sooner than the children actually are able to do so.

Since the teenage years are generally ones in which individuals go through so many changes, it is not surprising that parental behavior changes as well. In an observational study of mothers ranging from ages sixteen to twenty-two, researchers found that the different age groups interacted differently with their infants. The younger mothers showed more nonverbal behavior and more efforts to control the behavior of the infants. The older mothers tended to engage in more stimulating, reciprocal interactions with their babies (Fry, 1985).

Possibly one of the most significant trends in the United States is the increase in the number of single-parent homes, both because of the increase in the number of single women having children, and the fact that families with young children are not immune to the stress of divorce. Young couples with one or two children are at least as likely to end their marriage in divorce as are childless couples. The effects of divorce on children are not clearly understood, but research suggests that children living in a single-parent household are at some disadvan-

tage. Data from a national sample demonstrate that adolescent children in single-parent homes show significantly more deviant behavior than do children living in two-parent homes (Dornbusch et al., 1985).

## The Middle Adult Years

Daniel J. Levinson and his colleagues (Levinson et al., 1978) found that men face awesome developmental tasks between the ages of forty and forty-five. They are at the peak of their careers, and they are reaching the midpoint of their lives. From age forty on, they begin to think in terms of "the number of years remaining" rather than "the number of years since birth." They begin to see signs of physical deterioration. Gray hairs, flab, failing eyesight, and slower reaction times become more troubling. Even though the aging process is a slow one and physical deterioration has been occurring in many systems since puberty, men in their forties are at a stage when these signs can create difficult adjustment problems.

At this stage of life, people begin to think about their own mortality. Although adolescents and young adults know intellectually that they are going to die, the person in mid-life begins to grasp this much more fully. His parents may have recently died, or they may be entering old age and relying on him for care. As he sees his own body age, he is confronted with his own mortality. Although there is no easily identifiable "marker" for the mid-life transition, as there is with the onset of adolescence, Levinson and others believe it is an important developmental period that repeats itself in most men at about the same age.

*The Mid-Life Transition*    The **mid-life transition** *is the period in middle adulthood when individuals change perspectives, begin to confront their mortality, and reevaluate many of the goals and values they held during early adulthood.* The way men handle this period varies considerably. Some adapt and adjust very well, and others seek to regain their lost youth by divorcing their wives, buying fast cars, and entering a series of casual sexual relationships. Some become more nurturant with their own families, finding time for things their career ambitions and eighteen-hour workdays denied them in earlier years. Still others urgently seek a purpose to which they can devote the remaining years of their lives. One of the men whom Levinson interviewed, a biologist, made this point:

The thing that's distressing to me at the moment is the absence of a goal that I consider worthwhile. I have to couch it in the framework of science, because that's the only thing I'm really trained to do. But I think the problem is perfectly general. I don't in all honesty see a goal that's worth having at the moment. . . . This is what really shakes me up . . . (Levinson et al., 1978, p. 274–275).

*Mid-Life Changes in Women*    Although most of the research on middle adulthood, particularly mid-life transitions, has focused on men, some women experience a similar kind of reevaluation period (Neugarten, 1970). Those who did not work outside the home during the years of child-rearing are in the stage when their children are beginning to leave home. Most women are very favorable toward their new freedom; they report increased happiness with their marriages and decreased strain from the children. Some, however, find the adjustment to the "empty nest" more difficult. They are faced with more free time that they must occupy with a new career or other activities. While these changes may be challenging, they also can create adjustment problems quite different from those experienced by men who have had steady employment.

In a study of white women aged 60 to 95, researchers found that having children made a significant difference in their lives. The transitions the mothers faced revolved around the lives of their children. Nonmothers' transitions had more to do with their work life. For both mothers and nonmothers, though, the bonds of their relationships were central to their lives and in that sense, their transitions had a different focus from those of men. Many of these women grew up in the Great Depression when women's roles were more confined than they are today (Mercer, Nichols, & Doyle, 1989).

While men gradually begin to notice the signs of aging, women experience an identifiable "marker"—menopause. Usually during the late forties, menses becomes irregular and eventually ceases. The ovaries degenerate, and the secretion of the female hormones, particularly estrogen, declines. This signals the end of the reproductive years. The experience of menopause can have important psychological effects, even if a woman decided long ago to have no more children. A study of the attitudes of women toward menopause revealed that the phenomenon is poorly understood (Neugarten, 1968). Many dreaded it because they believed it would affect their appearance, their ability to have sexual intercourse, or their emotional stability. About fifty-eight percent found menopause to be unpleasant, but seventy-five percent reported they were happier

and calmer after menopause. The majority also reported having better relationships with their husbands.

The physiological signs of aging may have greater impact on women because of the value many cultures place on youth and beauty. Television anchorwomen, for example, may worry that their graying hair is not attractive and will cause the network executives to move them to less prominent jobs. Gray hair in anchormen, on the contrary, may make them seem distinguished and more credible.

Since the 1950s, the number of women who continue to work outside the home during the child-rearing years has increased dramatically. The adjustment problems of these women as they approach middle age are likely to be similar to those facing men.

*Beyond the Mid-Life Transition*    The way people deal with their mid-life transitions affects their later lives. Some men and women establish closer relationships with their families based on much-improved lines of communication. After reexamining the dreams of youth, they are able to accept themselves and their limitations and find a happier and more fulfilling life. No longer tyrannized by the passions of youth and the drive to succeed, they do some of their most creative work. Relieved of the responsibility of childcare, both men and women find time to engage in other pursuits. A study of the productivity of people at various ages found that inventors showed a marked gain in creative output in their fifties (Dennis, 1966).

Other people emerge from their mid-life transition with deep scars. They find their lives lacking in meaning and excitement and their family lives in turmoil. They may be divorced and unable to establish a new intimate relationship. In their work, they may begin marking time until retirement, resenting what has become an oppressive and meaningless chore.

Erikson (1972) sees **generativity versus self-absorption** *as the major psychosocial crisis of middle adulthood. The way an individual is able to cope with the adjustments required during the forties and fifties will, in part, determine whether middle adulthood is a period of creative life effort with deeper intimacies with others and deeper commitments to worthwhile goals or one of self-absorption, self-pity, and apathy toward the outside world.* The patterns the individual established during middle adulthood affect how the person copes with the later years of life.

# Cognitive Development in Adulthood

According to Piaget's theory of cognitive development, adolescents enter the stage of formal operations around the age of eleven. They are able to engage in abstract thought and reasoning and can use deductive hypothesis testing.

Piaget proposed that there were few changes in cognitive abilities after adolescence and that adulthood was characterized by a continuation of formal operational ways of thinking. Not all psychologists agree with this point of view. Many believe that the process of cognitive development becomes more variable after childhood; some people never reach the stage of formal operations, and others develop a good deal further.

For example, during the college years and even later, there seem to be some improvements in logical reasoning, particularly in individuals who pursue specialized and abstract subjects such as physics, law, or philosophy (Neimark, 1975). Some theorists maintain that there is another stage of cognitive development after formal operations that some people do not reach. In this stage, people are capable of analyzing formal operational thought itself.

Early studies of intellectual ability through the adulthood years and beyond strongly suggested a progressive decline. Edward L. Thorndike (1931) tested people of different ages and found that twenty-two-year-olds had the best learning abilities. His data suggested a decline of about one percent for each subsequent year until about age fifty.

One problem with the early studies on cognitive change is that they relied on the cross-sectional method. In the twentieth century, the levels of educational achievement by each generation have climbed steadily. In general, older people tend to be less educated than younger people. Researchers who used longitudinal studies to investigate cognitive changes across the life span reached quite different conclusions.

In one study combining the virtues of the cross-sectional and longitudinal methods, five hundred subjects ranging in age from twenty-one to seventy were given intelligence tests. After seven years, 301 subjects were tested again (Baltes & Schaie, 1977; Schaie, 1979). These tests yielded scores on four different kinds of cognitive functioning: (1) **crystallized intelligence,** *which involves specific, practical knowledge that helps people adapt to everyday life within their culture,* (2) **cognitive flexibility,** *the ease with which the individual can shift from one way of thinking to another,* (3) **visuo-motor flexibility,** *the ability to shift from familiar to unfamiliar patterns in visuo-motor tasks,* and (4) **visualization,** *the ability to organize and process visual information.* When the researchers examined the data from a cross-sectional perspective, comparing different people in different age groups, they found a decline in all the categories of intellectual function. When they analyzed the data longitudinally, however, and noted how people changed after seven years, they found a decline only in visuo-motor flexibility.

From this and other carefully designed investigations, it has become clear that cognitive abilities do not necessarily decline with age, although older people consistently do not do as well as younger ones on tests of memory, particularly tests that involve working memory (Baltes & Kliegl, 1992; Light, 1991; Salthouse & Babcock, 1991). There may be declines in some abilities, but there may be no change or even increases in others, particularly those relating to crystallized intelligence.

Studies of cognitive development in adulthood have generally relied on measure of abilities that help children succeed in academic environments. But psychologists question the value of this approach for studying cognitive changes in adulthood. Some researchers believe that Piaget's approach, and intelligence tests in general, are far too constraining and limit our understanding of how cognitive abilities change across the life span. They emphasize that academic skills are important through adolescence, but less important as people face the challenges of adulthood. Given the measures of cognition Piaget was using, perhaps it is not surprising that his stages stopped at adolescence.

One group proposes that a major aspect of cognitive change in adulthood is (or at least can be) the development of wisdom (Dittmann-Kohli & Baltes, 1990). Wisdom is not easily measured on any test, but it has characteristics that set it apart from the abilities students need to do well in school. It involves expertise in a given area, rather than a generalized ability to do well on tasks that are content-free. It also requires a great deal of pragmatic, crystallized intelligence about the problem area. Using wisdom to attack a problem means analyzing the problem from several broad perspectives, taking into account the social consequences, moral consequences, life-span aspects, and also the fact that many elements in the problem are likely to be uncertain and ambiguous. Finally, wisdom involves a clear understanding that solutions and decisions have a strong element of relativity. There may not be one "best" answer to a problem, whose circle can be filled in with a number two pencil—the correctness of different solutions may depend on one's point of view.

---

▶ **GUIDED REVIEW** *Learning Objectives 5, 6, and 7*

1. The study of _____ is a young branch of developmental psychology. The adulthood years can be divided into early adulthood (twenties, thirties, and early forties), middle adulthood (forties, fifties, and early sixties), and later adulthood (middle sixties and older).

2. Tasks of _____ adulthood include choosing a career, establishing intimate relationships, and raising a family. Choosing a career is often a haphazard process. Adolescents know little about occupations, yet they are expected to choose a lifetime career soon after they leave high school.

3. In Erikson's view, the main developmental task of early adulthood is _____. The main task of middle adulthood is _____.

4. Middle adulthood is often characterized by a _____, in which the individual begins to confront mortality and re-examines previous goals. The period may be a difficult time of adjustment. Mid-life transitions appear to be common in men, and recent studies suggest that women may experience similar "gear shifting" in mid-life.

5. Piaget's theory of cognitive development suggests that the _____, reached in adolescence, continues through adulthood. Other theorists propose that some adults never reach formal operational thinking at all and that some bypass it to progress to even more advanced modes of thinking.

6. Longitudinal studies of changes in cognitive abilities throughout the life span reveal that some abilities decline, others stay the same, and some increase. _____ seems to suffer some decline, and _____ may increase.

*ANSWERS*

*1. adulthood 2. early 3. intimacy versus isolation, generativity versus self-absorption 4. mid-life transition 5. formal operations stage 6. Visuo-motor flexibility, crystallized intelligence*

## LATER ADULTHOOD

The stereotypes many Americans have of older adults are not flattering. Some see the old person as forgetful, cranky, dependent, senile, or lonely. Few people look forward to their later adult years; instead, they fear the aging process and death. One item in a widely used achievement test asks test-takers to fill in the blank: Youth/Beauty/Life::Age/_____/Death. The correct answer is "ugliness." The question illustrates how deeply embedded our stereotypes about later adulthood are (Schaie, 1993).

In some cultures, however, signs of aging are valued. Older adults in China are considered wise, and younger members of the society seek their counsel. It is extremely unusual for anyone in China to be named to a powerful political post before reaching the age of seventy.

Stereotypes about old age can make this a difficult period of adjustment for many people. Even though these stereotypes are filled with misconceptions, people react to older adults as though the stereotypes were true. But the aging process is not nearly as bad as many people suspect. There are a variety of physiological changes; no one can expect to be as spry as they were during their twenties; however, most people can and do lead very independent, creative, and fulfilling lives in their older adult years.

## The Aging Process

The physical changes taking place during middle adulthood continue past age sixty-five. Although the changes may not be obvious from day to day, or even from year to year, the cumulative effects of the process are unmistakable (figure 10.6). The hair turns gray or white and becomes sparse, the skin loses its natural elasticity and moisture and becomes wrinkled, the eyelids thicken, the spine begins to bow, and the person becomes shorter.

Why do people age and eventually die? Do their bodies just begin wearing out? Do the stresses and strains of life and the poisons and pollutants in the food and environment finally begin to take their toll?

One proposal, the **genetic theory of aging,** *asserts that the aging process is part of the genetic code.* The program in the code carries us through the maturational changes of infancy, childhood, adolescence, the reproductive years, and middle adulthood, and then begins to expire during later adulthood. In some animals, like flies, the code runs out of program after only a few days; in dogs, the program lasts more than a decade. In humans, the program lasts many decades. Some research on cells suggests that there may be specific genes that dictate how long a cell will continue to divide. Without these genes, a cell becomes "immortal" and may continue to divide long after its counterparts have stopped. Experiments are underway to infuse runaway tumor cells with these "mortality" genes (Erickson, 1991). Other theories point out the importance

**Figure 10.6** *Dwight Eisenhower as a young man, during middle age, and late in life.*

of stress in the aging process, the degradation of the immune system, or the buildup of toxic substances or mutations.

No one lives forever, but some people age much more slowly than others. Three groups of people are famed for their incredibly long life span: the Vilacambamba in Ecuador, the Hunza in Kashmir, and the Abkhaziain in the Soviet Republic of Georgia. These people, who often live past the age of 100, share many characteristics. Their diets consist mostly of vegetables, they eat very little fat, they stay quite thin, and they eat less than Americans.

Studies in mice have found that dietary restriction, down to almost half their usual caloric intake, resulted in longer life spans and lower incidence of cancer. The thin but apparently healthy mice received vitamin supplements and lived ten to twenty percent longer than control animals allowed to maintain their normal body weight (Weindruch & Walford, 1982). As long as it does not include malnutrition, undernutrition may decelerate the aging process.

Although the diets of the Vilacambamba, the Hunza, and the Abkhaziain may be boring by some standards, their lives are not. They maintain active sex lives, smoke or drink occasionally, stay married, and have no retirement. They also *expect* to live a long time and perceive that they have control over their own lives. Control appears to have an important influence on the adjustment process in later life (Rodin, 1986); perhaps we can learn something from the habits and attitudes of these long-lived people.

## Life Adjustments in Later Adulthood

Later adulthood, like each developmental period, brings with it its own characteristic tasks, pleasures, challenges, stresses, and conflicts. According to Erikson, **integrity versus despair** *is the major psychosocial developmental task of later adulthood. During this time, the individual who has successfully worked through earlier tasks and is able to accept the inevitability of death will experience integrity. The existence of previously unresolved conflicts and an inability to accept impending death will lead to despair.*

Later adulthood is often characterized by many changes that can have profound effects on the adjustment process. The changes might include retirement, alterations in family relationships, widowhood, illness, or a death in the family.

*Retirement*    For those who are employed outside the home, an important adjustment during later adulthood will be retirement. The success with which the individual adapts to this change in life-style can be an important factor in how satisfying later adult years will be. The change does not simply involve moving from the status of worker to nonworker. It has implications for the person's social life, personal adjustment, and self-esteem. Many people are eager to retire so they can have time to pursue goals they had no time for while they had full-time jobs. Especially if they reevaluated their life goals in middle adulthood and began to place less value on career and more on family, friends, and personal growth, retirement will offer challenging new opportunities.

## EXPLORING HUMAN DIVERSITY

### Growing Old in America: Ethnic Minority Senior Citizens

The senior citizen population among ethnic minorities in the United States is faced with the double burden of both age and culture discrimination. The extended kinship networks found among so many of these groups provided, a generation ago, a vital support network for the elderly, helping to combat the loneliness and despair often associated with old age. However, as the members of various ethnic groups have become increasingly a part of mainstream American culture, these kinship networks have deteriorated and many elderly minorities find themselves facing both economic and emotional traumas.

African-Americans tend to have better attitudes toward old age than whites, are less often institutionalized, and stay more active in family decision making (Holmes, 1983). It is this inclusion in family matters, through extended kinship networks, that can help the elderly to overcome and prevent despair. African-Americans in general have more extended networks of kin than do white Americans.

Jewish-Americans, by contrast, have assimilated into American mainstream culture more fully than African-Americans and have, therefore, adopted Anglo habits of treating the elderly (Gelfand & Olsen, 1979). Whereas in earlier years, Jewish elders played a significant role in family decisions, in modern times, the extended Jewish family is not as common, so elders do not have as many roles from which to choose. The lack of available roles for the Jewish-American elderly is not conducive to productivity and fulfillment and has been causing a great deal of stress for many Jewish families.

A study of Eastern European-American senior citizens shows that working past retirement age, pursuing traditional ethnic hobbies and crafts, and maintaining the extended family system can improve integrity in the elderly and can prevent despair (Mostwin, 1980). This study can be a valuable lesson for the elderly of all ethnic groups. Over the past several generations, extended kinship systems have become difficult for American ethnic groups to maintain because of acculturation. Studies have shown, however, that one of the best ways to prevent economic and emotional despair among the elderly is to encourage seniors to remain active past retirement, by frequent contact with family and peers in a variety of activities. It is unfortunate that the mainstream American family pattern—the nuclear family—is conducive to separation. This pattern has been responsible for much of the deterioration of the extended family among American ethnic groups.

---

Retired people have more time but less money, sometimes dramatically less. Through combined income sources, including Social Security, private pension plans, part-time work, or family contributions, retirees may live on no more than half of their pre-retirement income; many live on much less. In the early part of this century, financial planning was not so important because many people never retired at all. But now that life span is longer, many will enjoy twenty or thirty years of life in retirement. Financial planning for those years is critical.

Retirement also brings a change in friendships. Many retirees no longer try to maintain close relationships with their former colleagues and instead seek friendships with other retirees who can share their interests. The individual also must make changes in perceptions of self-worth. We live in a very work-oriented society that often judges people by their ability to make money, climb the ladder of success, and contribute to society. The retiree is not a part of this order any longer and must find new ways by which to measure self-worth.

Studies of retired men have found that most adapt to retirement very well. The National Institute of Mental Health conducted a survey of retired people and found that fifty-seven percent felt positive about retirement. Other studies have focused on individuals' adaptation styles. The largest category of retired men were well-adjusted, mature individuals who adapted very well, finding new interests and activities. Another group, "rocking-chair men," relaxed more and enjoyed the freedom of retirement. The group called "armored men" were also well-adjusted, but they developed highly organized and regimented lifestyles as a defense against feeling old. The individuals who did not adjust well to retirement were unable to face aging and blamed others for their inability to achieve their life goals. Many of these individuals became very depressed and bitter. They were unable to successfully resolve the psychosocial conflict of integrity versus despair.

Two important factors in whether a person's retirement is successful and well-adjusted appear to be whether it is

## CLOSE UP ON RESEARCH

### Another "Gender Gap": Mortality Rates

From the time of conception to old age, the mortality rate for men is higher than for women. On the average, women in industrialized countries live about four to ten years longer than men. The reasons for this are not well understood, but recent research has attempted to find clues.

Scientists estimate that at conception the sex ratio is about 115 to 100 in favor of males. Because more male fetuses die before or at birth, the sex ratio at birth is 105 to 100. The proportion of males continues to decline in infancy, child-hood, and adolescence, and by age thirty, the ratio of men to women is about equal. By age sixty-five, eighty-four percent of the women and seventy percent of the men are still alive.

Higher death rate for males during all stages of life might be explained by the sex chromosomes. Men have one Y chromosome and one X chromosome, and women have two X chromosomes. Genes on the male's X chromosome will be expressed whether they are dominant or recessive. But since the female has two X chromosomes, a recessive gene on the X chromosome will not be expressed if a normal gene is on the other X chromosome. For example, the recessive gene that causes one variety of color blindness is on the X chromosome. This condition is much more common in men than women since women would need to inherit the abnormal gene from both their mother and their father. In contrast, a man would only need to inherit the abnormal gene from the mother.

Although few genes have been identified on the Y chromosome so far, it is possible that some may limit life span. In an Amish family, many of the men inherited a Y chromosome that was missing a segment. These men outlived the women in the same family by almost five years.

Another likely candidate to explain the gender gap is hormones. After puberty, men have higher levels of androgens than women; this hormone is known to raise levels of the cholesterol associated with heart disease. Estrogen protects against heart disease by lowering the level of this cholesterol.

Behavioral risk factors do not give either men or women a clear advantage for long life. Men smoke more and may have more job stress, but women get less exercise, report more emotional stress, and feel more vulnerable to illness. Women appear to be more vulnerable to nonfatal illnesses, such as arthritis and allergies. Men, however, have a higher incidence of disorders that can be fatal, including emphysema and heart disease (Holden, 1987).

voluntary or involuntary and whether the individual plans for it. The age of sixty-five was first established as the age for mandatory retirement in late nineteenth-century Germany by Otto von Bismarck, the "Iron Chancellor." He instituted the first comprehensive social insurance program and chose sixty-five as the point when "old age" began. (Some claim he chose this age because the life expectancy then was around forty-five and he wanted to save the government money.) Other Western countries followed his lead.

The arbitrary designation of sixty-five has been criticized severely, sometimes by individuals who are actively working well into their eighties and nineties. Congress finally enacted legislation to relax rules about mandatory retirement and to prohibit age discriminatory employment practices for people between the ages of forty and seventy. It appears our society is aware that people are quite capable of working long past age sixty-five and should be allowed to do so if they wish.

*Family Changes* The later adult years are frequently characterized by changes in the structure of the family.

Children are usually well into their own careers and families and are independent. The older adult may have to depend on children, especially financially, rather than the other way around. For some individuals this represents an enormous blow to self-esteem and triggers feelings of depression and hopelessness. A particularly devastating change may be the death or serious illness of a spouse. After what might have been decades of married life, the individual loses her or his partner and must face this loss and learn to cope with widowhood.

One aspect of life that need not change much is sexual activity. It is one of the more destructive myths of aging that older adults lose interest in sex or lose their ability to have sexual relationships. Studies of sexual activity in older adults clearly show that these notions are false. One survey found that seventy percent of married couples over sixty years old were sexually active (Meyners & Wooster, 1979). A continuation of sexual activity seems to be one of the components of a successful and fulfilling older adulthood (Turner & Adams, 1988).

*Aging and Health* Reasonably good health is a key ingredient in most of the successful coping patterns of old age. A good sex life, a fulfilling social life, and an industrious and active retirement all depend to a large extent on good health. Although most older adults describe their health as reasonably good, health problems are more common in this period of life because of the aging process. The problems may also be partly due to the major life changes people over sixty-five are likely to encounter.

Aging is not necessarily the only factor that aggravates health problems in later adulthood. These years are sometimes characterized by wrenching life changes, and it appears that severe change can trigger stress reactions in the body that make an individual more vulnerable to illness. One study compared women who were anticipating the death of their husbands, women whose husbands had just died, and women whose husbands were healthy. The widowed women showed significant reductions in the activity of their natural killer cells, cells important in the body's defense against tumors and viral infections (Irwin, Daniels, Risch, & Bloom, 1988).

The **Social Readjustment Ratings Scale (SRRS)** (Holmes & Rahe, 1967) *is a short test that lists both positive and negative major life events, such as marriage, divorce, pregnancy, and retirement, and asks people to check those they have recently experienced.* Various studies have found that people who rate high on this checklist are the ones most likely to suffer physical symptoms and illnesses. Some of the most important life events are more likely to occur during later adulthood. An example is the death of one's spouse, considered the most stressful event of all. When this happens, the person must work through a lengthy period of grief to readjust to life without the loved one.

The grief process is not well understood. According to some research, it consists of eleven identifiable stages: (1) shock, (2) sobbing, (3) craziness, (4) relief, (5) physical symptoms of unresolved grief, (6) panic, (7) guilt, (8) anger, (9) limbo, (10) emerging hope, and (11) reaffirmation of reality (Tanner, 1976). These are not necessarily distinct stages; people seem to blend two or more at once and skip others. Some research, however, suggests that grief can lead to physical symptoms of illness. In a study of widowers aged fifty-five or older, 213 men died during the first six months after their wives had died, a death rate much higher than expected for married men. Most of these men died from cardiovascular disorders, which can be aggravated by stress.

## Creativity and Productivity

Michelangelo became the chief architect of St. Peter's Church in Rome at the age of seventy-two. Grandma Moses began her illustrious career as a primitive painter in her seventies. The president of a roofing supplies business says his highest sales are achieved by those over sixty. Colonel Harlan Sanders, founder of Kentucky Fried Chicken, made his first million at the age of seventy-three. At age ninety-seven, Joel Hildebrand was an active chemistry professor at the University of California, continuing to publish papers and to start new projects. Justice Oliver Wendell Holmes stayed on the Supreme Court into his nineties; his credo was "to live is to work." Creativity and productivity are not limited to the early or middle adult years. If the older adult remains reasonably healthy, he or she has much potential for creative work. Figure 10.7 describes the way a famous psychologist handled the aging process.

Creativity and productivity seem to be important factors in adjustment to later adulthood. In one of the best studies of this adjustment process, Bernice Neugarten (1971) found several patterns in the 2,000 men and women in their seventies who participated. The integrated older adults were those who were well-adjusted, open to new experiences, intact with regard to cognitive abilities, and generally high in life satisfaction. Other people in the sample showed more striving and achievement-oriented behavior and preferred to keep busy with regimented schedules. Some of the less well-adjusted individuals required considerable emotional support from family and friends, and a few showed very poor adjustment by withdrawing and engaging in almost no outside activities.

This study demonstrates that the patterns of development occurring during later adulthood are quite variable. Most people adjust to the many life changes extremely well, finding new activities and interests and seeking new ways to be creative and productive. Many very well-adjusted older adults adopt new values and motivations as well. For example, the famous psychologist D. O. Hebb noticed interesting changes as he grew older. At the age of seventy-four, he said that he would rather devote his energies to putting a ten-acre farm in shape than to solving complex psychological problems. A highly achievement-oriented individual with financial obligations might not understand this motivation, but Hebb devoted as much energy and dedication to the farm as to his work in psychology.

Intellectual Self-management in Old Age

Professor B.F. Skinner's suggestions for dealing with the "normal abnormalities" of the aging process include the following:

If you cannot read, listen to book recordings. If you do not hear well, turn up the volume on your phonograph (and wear headphones to protect your neighbors). Foods can be flavored for aging palates. Paul Tillich, the theologian, defended pornography on the ground that it extended sexuality into old age (Skinner, 1983, p. 240).

A particular problem for the aged, of course, is forgetting. Skinner has some practical advice here too. If you want to remember to take an umbrella with you when you go out because rain is in the weather forecast, hang the umbrella on the door handle so you won't forget to take it. If you think of things you must do sometime later but are afraid you will forget them, keep a notebook or a pocket tape recorder handy. If you forget the names of acquaintances you want to introduce to someone else, work out a plan with that person:

My wife and I use the following strategy: If there is any conceivable chance that she could have met the person, I simply say to her, "Of course, you remember...?" and she grasps the outstretched hand and says, "Yes, of course. How are you?" The acquaintance may not remember meeting my wife, but is not sure of his or her memory, either (Skinner, 1983, p. 240).

**Figure 10.7** *Intellectual management in old age.*

# Death and Dying

Despite the statistics, most adolescents and young adults believe that they will die suddenly, by accident or by a massive heart attack. Most people, however, do not die suddenly. They become ill, often from cardiovascular disorders or cancer, before they die. Many have ample opportunity to face their own deaths, and some have described their attitudes and fears to psychologists. A group of cancer patients reported concern over pain, disfigurement, the future, loss of work role, dependency, being a burden on others, and alienation from others (Hinton, 1973).

*Facing Death*    Some research has found that terminally ill patients anticipating their own deaths move through a series of behavioral patterns on their way to accepting the inevitable. Elizabeth Kübler-Ross (1969) interviewed more than 200 such patients and found five different stages: denial, anger, bargaining, depression, and acceptance. Some patients move through all of these stages in sequence; others showed elements of more than one attitude at the same time.

In the denial stage, the patients are stunned and refuse to believe what the doctors say, even if they have suspected the worst. Some seek exotic treatments from faith healers or untested drugs. These feelings are eventually replaced by anger, rage, envy of healthy people, and resentment. They ask "Why me?" In the bargaining stage, patients seem to accept their own death but seek to postpone it by repenting, taking their medicine regularly, going to church, or by other means.

Depression is the fourth stage in the death process, a necessary step in accepting death. This depression represents a kind of anticipatory grief as the individuals grieve for their own death before the fact. If they have enough time, the dying patients may arrive at the final stage of acceptance, in which they can openly discuss their own deaths and use their last days to arrange their affairs and say good-bye. Many express wistfulness rather than severe depression or anger at the prospect of the end of life.

*The Choices of the Dying*    Dying people often do not have too many choices about how they will die, how much pain medication they will get, whether to talk about dying with other people, or even whether they will be told they are dying.

Patients sometimes cannot discuss their attitudes and feelings about death with those around them because many people are reluctant to do so. The attendants at a geriatric hospital used one of only a few stereotyped responses every time a patient wanted to talk about death. One was reassurance: "Don't think like that—you're doing very well. . . . " Another was denial: "You don't mean that! You're going to live to 100!" The least likely response was honest and genuine discussion about death (Kastenbaum, 1967).

Our society is gradually recognizing that people want to have control over some aspects of their own deaths. Some states have legalized living wills, documents which state whether individuals want to die natural deaths or whether they want to be maintained by life-sustaining equipment for as long as possible. Surveys of older people show that most want to die a natural death and do not want to be kept alive by artificial means. Without a living will, however, or in states where such documents are not recognized, the removal of a patient from life-sustaining equipment constitutes euthanasia. Euthanasia is not legal in most places, but the Netherlands has begun allowing it. The Dutch are developing guidelines that enable patients to choose to end their own lives with the help of physicians (Horgan, 1991).

Death is the last developmental phase of life. We know almost nothing about the experience of death; however,

many people have been close enough to give us some glimpses. Such reports are often surprisingly similar. People report leaving their bodies and watching the resuscitation attempts from a distance. They also report having a sense of traveling through space very rapidly, a tunnel or passage of some kind, and the awareness of a comforting presence. Not very many feel fear, and those that do are often the healthy ones faced with sudden death. Although the methods of science can reveal fascinating information about most developmental phases, this last phase is likely to retain its mysteries.

▶ **GUIDED REVIEW** *Learning Objectives 8, 9, 10, and 11*

1. The _____ process involves graying of hair, wrinkling of skin, and other physiological changes. The _____ proposes that aging and death are programmed in our genes.
2. According to Erikson, the major developmental task of later adulthood is _____.
3. Major life adjustments in _____ adulthood include retirement, changes in family and social relationships, and changes in health. Retirement can be particularly difficult if it is accompanied by a large reduction in standard of living and if it is not voluntary. Most people adapt to retirement very well.
4. Health problems are more common during later adulthood because of the aging process and the increase in significant life changes. There is some evidence that grief can make people more vulnerable to _____.

5. Most people die from illness rather than accidents, so most can face the prospect of their own imminent deaths. Terminally ill patients may show a sequence of behavior patterns including _____, _____, _____, _____, and _____.
6. Many states recognize _____, documents that describe how an individual wishes to die, particularly whether an individual wishes to die a natural death or whether he or she wishes to be placed on life-sustaining equipment.

*ANSWERS*
*1. aging, genetic theory of aging 2. integrity versus despair 3. later 4. physical illness 5. denial, anger, bargaining, depression, acceptance 6. living wills*

## SUMMARY

**I.** The term *adolescence* comes from a Latin word meaning "to grow up." Adolescence begins at puberty. (p. 314)
  **A.** Biological changes occurring at puberty include the development of the primary and secondary sexual characteristics as a result of the release of sex hormones. (p. 315)
  **B.** A person's gender depends on his or her sex chromosomes. Women have two X chromosomes, and men have one X and one Y chromosome. (p. 316)
    **1.** Sexual differentiation, which occurs during prenatal life, is the process by which the physiological differences between males and females develop. The presence or absence of androgens affects the body, the brain, and behavior. (p. 317)

  **2.** Interest in sexuality increases greatly during adolescence. Although sexual attitudes have changed markedly in recent decades, sexual behavior is much slower to change. (pp. 318–319)
  **C.** An important developmental task of adolescence is the search for an identity separate from the parents, something Erikson referred to as identity versus identity diffusion. Categories of identity status include identity achievement, foreclosure, moratorium, and identity diffusion. (pp. 320–321)
  **D.** During adolescence, social development shifts from a focus on parents to a focus on peer groups. (p. 323)
**II.** Early and middle adulthood span the years from the end of adolescence to the early sixties, although no clear demarcations can be used to identify these periods. (p. 324)

A. The early adult years involve many developmental tasks. (p. 325)

1. Choosing a career is an important task of early adulthood. (p. 325)

2. Most people get married and start families during early adulthood. (p. 326)

B. Middle adulthood, on the surface, appears to vary for different people, but some researchers have found identifiable patterns of development. (p. 328)

1. An important stage during middle adulthood is the mid-life transition, in which the person changes perspectives, begins to confront mortality, and reevaluates earlier goals and values. (p. 328)

2. Studies of women have shown important developmental transitions during the middle adulthood period; these transitions are often associated with menopause or the "empty nest syndrome." (p. 329)

3. Erikson sees generativity versus self-absorption as the major psychosocial task of middle adulthood. (p. 329)

C. Piaget proposed that there were few changes in cognitive ability after adolescence, but recent research suggests there are improvements in logical reasoning. In middle and later adulthood, longitudinal studies have shown that some cognitive abilities improve, some decline, and many remain stable. (p. 330)

III. Stereotypes of later adulthood are usually negative, but research shows that this can be a very satisfying period for well-adjusted people. (p. 331)

A. The aging process includes a number of cumulative changes that occur gradually. Although the reason people age and die is not clear, the genetic theory of aging proposes that the aging process is genetically coded. (p. 331)

B. Later adulthood involves a number of life adjustments that can be very difficult. According to Erikson, integrity versus despair is the major psychosocial task associated with later adulthood. (p. 332)

1. Retirement involves many changes, including loss of income, change in friendships, and change in schedules. (p. 332)

2. Later adulthood is associated with more health problems, which may be due not only to the aging process but to the stresses associated with life changes. (p. 335)

C. Creativity and productivity are characteristic of many people during later adulthood, and studies have found that the majority of older adults are very satisfied with their lives. (p. 335)

D. The process of confronting death is an important feature of later adulthood. (p. 336)

1. Some research on terminally ill patients suggests that this process involves several behavioral patterns that often occur in sequence, including denial, anger, bargaining, depression, and acceptance. (p. 336)

2. The choices of the dying patient are limited because friends, family, and those in the medical profession are reluctant to share information and discuss the issue. (p. 336)

---

## ACTION GLOSSARY

Match the terms in the left column with the definitions in the right column.

___ 1. **Puberty (p. 314)**

___ 2. **Primary sexual characteristics (p. 315)**

___ 3. **Secondary sexual characteristics (p. 315)**

___ 4. **Sex chromosomes (p. 316)**

___ 5. **Sexual differentiation (p. 317)**

___ 6. **Androgens (p. 317)**

___ 7. **Dihydrotestosterone (p. 317)**

A. *A trait or organ directly concerned with reproductive function, such as the ovaries and uterus in the female and the testes in the male.*

B. *The process by which the physiological differences between males and females develop.*

C. *A hormone released during prenatal life that is responsible for the development of the male genitals.*

D. *A trait typical of one sex but not directly concerned with reproductive function, such as distribution of body fat or growth of facial hair.*

E. *The time of sexual maturation.*

F. *Sex hormones released by the fetal testes.*

G. *Chromosomes, called the X chromosome and the Y chromosome, that determine the gender of the fetus; a female has two X chromosomes, and a male has one X chromosome and one Y chromosome.*

___  8. **Gender identity (p. 318)**

___  9. **Identity versus identity diffusion (p. 320)**

___  10. **Identity achievement (p. 320)**

___  11. **Foreclosure (pp. 320–321)**

___  12. **Moratorium (p. 321)**

___  13. **Identity diffusion (p. 321)**

___  14. **Intimacy versus isolation (p. 326)**

___  15. **Mid-life transition (p. 328)**

A. *A category of identity status in which the person is actively involved in choosing an identity and seeking alternatives.*

B. *A period in middle adulthood when an individual changes perspectives, begins to confront mortality, and reevaluates many of the goals and values he or she held during early adulthood.*

C. *A category of identity status in which the individual has gone through a period of crises and has developed fairly firm commitments.*

D. *The process in which the child learns to identify with the appropriate sex; the feelings of a person about whether he or she is male or female.*

E. *A category of identity status in which a person has never had an identity crisis and has not formed any particular commitments or established any goals.*

F. *According to Erik Erikson, the major psychosocial task of adolescence.*

G. *According to Erik Erikson, the major psychosocial task faced by young adults.*

H. *A category of identity status in which the individual has never gone through any identity crisis but has become committed to goals and values, usually those of the parents.*

___  16. **Generativity versus self-absorption (p. 329)**

___  17. **Crystallized intelligence (p. 330)**

___  18. **Cognitive flexibility (p. 330)**

___  19. **Visuo-motor flexibility (p. 330)**

___  20. **Visualization (p. 330)**

___  21. **Genetic theory of aging (p. 331)**

___  22. **Integrity versus despair (p. 332)**

___  23. **Social Readjustment Rating Scale (p. 335)**

A. *A short test that asks about the number and characteristics of changes and important events in a person's life in an attempt to relate those happenings to health and illness.*

B. *Specific, practical knowledge that helps people adapt to everyday life within their culture.*

C. *The ability to shift from familiar to unfamiliar patterns in visuo-motor tasks.*

D. *The ability to organize and process visual information.*

E. *According to Erik Erikson, the major psychosocial task of later adulthood.*

F. *According to the personality theory of Erik Erikson, the major psychosocial task of middle adulthood.*

G. *The ease and flexibility with which one can shift from one mode of thinking to another.*

H. *Asserts that the aging process is programmed into the genetic code of each species.*

ANSWERS

*1. e, 2. a, 3. d, 4. g, 5. b, 6. c, 7. f, 8. d, 9. f, 10. c, 11. h, 12. a, 13. e, 14. g, 15. b, 16. f, 17. b, 18. g, 19. c, 20. d, 21. h, 22. e, 23. a*

# SELF-TEST

1. Early maturing boys generally show
   (a) more positive self-concepts and more successful relationships with friends.
   (b) more dependence on the parents compared to late maturing boys.
   (c) a reluctance to develop social relationships with girls.
   (d) behavioral disorders associated with premature sexual development.
   (LO 1; pp. 315–316)

2. The hormone(s) released during prenatal development that is (are) responsible for the development of the male genitals is (are)
   (a) estrogen.
   (b) progesterone.
   (c) dihydrotestosterone.
   (d) pituitary hormones.
   (LO 1; p. 317)

3. According to research on sexual behavior, a common pattern demonstrated by adolescents can be described as
   (a) promiscuity.
   (b) serial monogamy without marriage.
   (c) celibacy.
   (d) life-long monogamy.
   (LO 2; p. 319)

4. According to Marcia, the identity status of an adolescent who accepts an identity based on parental expectations would be
   (a) identity achieved.
   (b) identity diffused.
   (c) moratorium.
   (d) foreclosure.
   (LO 3; pp. 320–321)

5. Adolescents in the identity diffusion status are likely to
    (a) have supportive parents.
    (b) be critical of their parents and have conflict in their homes.
    (c) experience very distant family relationships.
    (d) have divorced parents.
    (LO 3; p. 321)

6. A close association with a peer group during adolescence is one way for an individual to
    (a) become an autonomous functioning individual.
    (b) hide feelings of dependence on the parents.
    (c) foreclose on an identity acceptable to the parents.
    (d) establish an identity separate from the parents.
    (LO 4; p. 322)

7. According to research, most people learn about the requirements for the career they choose
    (a) after being well along that career path.
    (b) by talking with people who are involved in that career prior to making a choice.
    (c) by reading about it prior to making any decisions.
    (d) all of the above.
    (LO 5; p. 325)

8. According to Erikson, the developmental task of early adulthood involves
    (a) establishing an identity that matches the individual's cultural script.
    (b) finding a career that suits the individual's temperament.
    (c) developing intimate relationships with other young adults.
    (d) avoiding stagnation by exploring creative outlets.
    (LO 5; p. 326)

9. According to recent research, what differences are found between the parents of babies described as "easy" and the parents of babies described as "difficult"?
    (a) Parents of easy babies become more neglectful.
    (b) Parents of difficult babies become more confident of their abilities.
    (c) Parents of easy babies show fewer vocalizations.
    (d) Parents of easy babies show more positive personality changes.
    (LO 5; p. 328)

10. The period in life when people begin to confront their own mortality and reevaluate many of the goals and values they held during early adulthood is called
    (a) generativity versus stagnation.
    (b) the mid-life transition.
    (c) menopause.
    (d) old age.
    (LO 6; p. 328)

11. According to Erikson, the psychosocial task of middle adulthood is
    (a) integrity versus despair.
    (b) identity versus identity diffusion.
    (c) intimacy versus isolation.
    (d) generativity versus self-absorption.
    (LO 6; p. 329)

12. In longitudinal research on intelligence, an intellectual decline was observed in which of the following areas?
    (a) crystallized intelligence
    (b) cognitive flexibility
    (c) visuo-motor flexibility
    (d) all of the above
    (LO 7; p. 330)

13. Cross-sectional studies of cognitive change across the life span have been criticized because
    (a) older people generally have less education than younger people.
    (b) older people do not understand the directions as well as younger people do.
    (c) older people are discriminated against because their reaction time is slower than that of younger people.
    (d) more older people drop out of the studies and therefore cannot be retested.
    (LO 7; p. 330)

14. The three groups of people who often live past the age of 100 share all of the following *except*
    (a) diets that include mostly vegetables and little fat.
    (b) abstinence from alcohol and tobacco.
    (c) an expectation that they will live a long time.
    (d) active sex lives.
    (LO 8; p. 332)

15. According to research with mice, _____ appears to be associated with longer life spans and lower incidence of cancer.
    (a) undernutrition
    (b) exercise
    (c) moderate alcohol consumption
    (d) hormone treatment
    (LO 8; p. 332)

16. Which of the following situations is not usually a change associated with old age?
    (a) retirement
    (b) widowhood
    (c) marriage
    (d) illness
    (LO 9; p. 332)

17. A survey of retired men conducted by the National Institute of Mental Health found that
    (a) a poorly adjusted group developed highly regimented and organized life-styles.
    (b) "rocking chair" men who spent most of the time relaxing became very poorly adjusted.
    (c) the largest category were well-adjusted men who had found new activities and interests.
    (d) most of the men adapted poorly to retirement because they continued to cling to former work relationships.
    (LO 9; p. 333)

18. Which of the following is one of the key criteria in most of the successful coping patterns of old age?
    (a) good health
    (b) contact with former associates at work
    (c) children
    (d) involvement in politics
    (LO 9; p. 335)

19. Neugarten's study of adjustment to later adulthood found
    (a) that most elderly adults were withdrawn from activities.
    (b) that most elderly adults required a great deal of emotional support from family and friends.
    (c) that most elderly adults were housebound and infirm.
    (d) a great deal of variability in adjustment.
    (LO 10; p. 335)

20. According to research by Kübler-Ross, a person who refuses to believe a medical diagnosis and seeks exotic treatments would probably be in
    (a) the stage of anger.
    (b) the denial stage.
    (c) the bargaining stage.
    (d) the stage of acceptance.
    (LO 11; p. 336)

ANSWERS

1. a, 2. c, 3. b, 4. d, 5. c, 6. d, 7. a, 8. c, 9. d, 10. b, 11. d, 12. c, 13. a, 14. b, 15. a, 16. c, 17. c, 18. a, 19. d, 20. b

---

## THINKING ABOUT PSYCHOLOGY

1. One of the most important tasks of adolescence is to seek an identity separate from the parents. Describe four categories into which most people fall with respect to their identity status. Which one do you feel you are in now? Think about your friends, and try to determine what identity status they are in.

2. In a relatively short period of time, family structures in the United States and many other industrialized countries have changed dramatically. Describe some of these changes, and speculate on how they affect life-span development.

3. Describe the adjustments people must make when they retire. What strategies help people make these adjustments most easily? In many cultures, the term "retirement" has little meaning because older people continue to contribute to the welfare of the group, although they may assume less physically demanding tasks. Given your understanding of how people face the process of growing old, speculate on how this adjustment would differ between cultures that have a sharply defined "retirement" and those that do not.

---

## SUGGESTED READINGS

Doyle, J. (1989). *The male experience*. (2nd ed.). Dubuque, IA: Wm. C. Brown Publishers. An interdisciplinary text on the male role in society.

Gilmore, D. D. (1990). *Manhood in the making: Cultural concepts of masculinity*. New Haven, CT: Yale University Press. Explores the concept of manhood in many cultures from a Freudian perspective.

Jackons, J. S. (Ed.) (1988). *The black American elderly: Research on physical and psychosocial health*. New York: Springer Publishing. Collection of papers examining the adaptation patterns of elderly black adults in the United States.

Keith, P. M. (1989). *The unmarried in later life*. New York: Praeger. Presents findings from a study exploring the adaptation patterns of older adults living alone.

London, M., & Mone, E. M. (1987). *Career management and survival in the workplace: Helping employees make tough career decisions, stay motivated, and reduce career stress*. San Francisco: Jossey-Bass.

Designed to help human resource professionals assist people in their careers; also useful for a person's own career.

Mercer, R. T., Nichols, E. G., & Doyle, G. C. (1989). *Transitions in a woman's life: Major life events in a developmental context*. New York: Springer Publishing. An examination of the life histories of women, showing their developmental transitions.

Pines, A., & Aronson, E. (1988). *Career burnout*. NY: The Free Press/ Macmillan. Explores the personal, organizational, and social causes of burnout.

Pleck, Joseph H. (1985). *Working wives/working husbands*. Beverly Hills, CA: Sage. An examination of the division of labor in two-earner couples.

Wellman, H. M., & Gelman, S. A. (1992). Cognitive development: Foundational theories of core domains. *Annual Review of Psychology*, 43, 337–376.

# PART IV

PERSONALITY AND ADJUSTMENT

# CHAPTER 11

## PERSONALITY
## OUTLINE

# PERSONALITY
## LEARNING OBJECTIVES

After reading this chapter, you should be able to

▶ **1.** define personality, and discuss different conceptions of personality. *(p. 346)*

▶ **2.** delineate the fundamental distinction between personality theories that define personality as a product of environmental factors (state theories) and those that see personality as the result of enduring forces within the individual (trait theories.) *(p. 346)*

▶ **3.** identify the two basic concepts of Freud's psychanalytic theory: the principle of psychic determinism and the principle of the unconscious. *(p. 347)*

▶ **4.** identify and describe the three components of the psychic apparatus: the ego, the id, and the superego. *(pp. 348–349)*

▶ **5.** list and detail the five stages of psychosexual development: the oral stage, anal stage, phallic stage, latency stage, and the genital stage. *(pp. 349–350)*

▶ **6.** describe how fixation or regression, two key mechanisms for defending the ego against attack, may come into play when difficulties are encountered at any psychosexual stage. *(p. 347)*

▶ **7.** discuss the ways in which the theories of the neo-Freudians differ from Freud's original psychoanalytic theory. *(pp. 353–355)*

▶ **8.** describe and compare learning theories of personality—classical and operant conditioning and social learning. *(pp. 355–358)*

▶ **9.** indicate how the humanistic theories of personality emphasize the unique and singular worth of the individual. *(p. 354)*

▶ **10.** discuss the similarities and the differences between psychodynamic theories, humanistic theories, and learning theories of personality. *(pp.360–361)*

▶ **11.** detail the ways in which observational methods, interviews, and projective and objective tests of personality are designed to reflect personality in its manifold forms. *(pp. 361–364)*

# PERSONALITY: WHAT IS IT?

Personality is one of those terms, like many psychological terms, that means one thing to psychologists and another to nonpsychologists. To laypeople, personality has to do with how well a person gets along with others. To psychologists, the term refers to a research area concerned with understanding and predicting behavior.

Personality psychologists themselves do not agree on how to define the term. Most agree that personality is expressed through behavior and that the goal of personality theory and research is the understanding and prediction of behavior. Many definitions of personality have been proposed through the years.

The definition the authors of this text like best was written more than fifty years ago by Gordon Allport, one of the founders of personality psychology. According to Allport (1937), **personality** *is* something and *does* something. *It is a relatively stable system of "determining tendencies" within the individual. These tendencies are aroused by "suitable stimuli" and shape the individual's specific reactions to events.*

## An Enduring Controversy: Traits and States

An enduring controversy among personality theorists is how personality and behavior develop (Bem, 1983; Funder, 1991). Is personality a set of traits within the individual? Or is it better viewed as the individual's responses to his or her environment?

Personality theories that emphasize the environment, known as **state theories,** *focus upon the cognitive and social processes of individuals in assessing and responding to their environment.* Theorists taking this position, including both behavioral and cognitive social learning theorists (such as Albert Bandura, 1986, and Walter Mischel, 1979), believe that behavior and personality can be understood best by examining the environmental context and the individual's assessment of it. These theorists study self-concept, emotions, plans, and motives, in an attempt to understand an individual's behavior.

Other personality theories emphasize the individual's unique characteristics and traits in an effort to understand behavior. These are referred to as trait or dispositional theories. **Trait theories** *discount the impact of the environment in favor of enduring attributes of the individual, such as anxiety, need for social approval, and extroversion.* Traits are thought to predict behavior and

explain personality better than momentary happenings in the individual's environment. Digman (1990), Funder (1991), McCrae (1989), and predominantly psychoanalytic theorists such as Epstein (1979), conceive personality to be the result of enduring forces within the individual that are acquired early in life.

Some behavioral theorists, including pioneering theorist/clinician Joseph Wolpe (1973, 1982), contend that classical conditioning is responsible for the bulk of human learning. Other influential behavioral and cognitive social learning theorists, including Bandura (1976), believe otherwise. The latter are convinced that the full range of learning modes, including operant conditioning, modeling, and cognitive social learning, play central roles in human behavior.

## The "Big Five" Personality Traits

One way to establish an individual's traits is through statistical analyses of psychological tests. This technique led R. B. Cattell (1965) to propose more than a dozen fundamental personality traits.

Contemporary trait theories emphasize five main personality traits, the **"big five":** *emotional stability, extroversion, openness to experience, agreeableness, and conscientiousness.* Individuals differ from one another to the extent that they differ on some or all of these traits (Cervone, 1992; Digman, 1990; McCrae & Costa, 1990). An individual can be characterized as more emotionally stable, extraverted, open to experience, agreeable to others, and conscientious than another person.

---

▶ **GUIDED REVIEW** *Learning Objectives 1 and 2*

1. Most personality theorists agree that personality is expressed through _____ and that the ultimate goal of personality theory and research is the _____ and _____ of behavior.
2. _____ theories of personality explain behavior and personality as the product of immediate environmental influences; _____ theories stress the role of enduring traits of personality on behavior.
3. Modern trait theories emphasize five primary personality traits: _____, _____, _____, _____, and _____.

*ANSWERS*

*1. behavior, understanding, prediction 2. State; trait 3. emotional stability, extraversion, openness to experience, agreeableness, conscientiousness.*

Figure 11.1   *Sigmund Freud (1856–1939).*

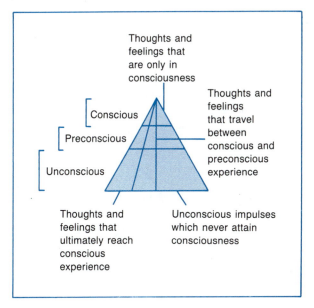

Figure 11.2   *Freud's topography of the personality*

Neither trait theorists nor state theorists agree among themselves on all issues. And neither state nor trait theories by themselves do full justice to the complexity of human behavior; a theory of personality must call upon *both* states and traits to explain the development of personality and the expression of behavior (Cantor & Kihlstrom, 1987).

## PSYCHOANALYTIC THEORIES OF PERSONALITY

The psychoanalytic theory remains one of the most comprehensive and influential theories of personality. Developed by Sigmund Freud (figure 11.1) in successive stages through his years of clinical practice at the beginning of the twentieth century, this theory has had an enormous impact on personality theory and research, not to mention art, literature, and intellectual history.

### Psychic Determinism and the Unconscious

The two basic concepts of psychoanalytic theory are the principle of psychic determinism and the unconscious. Both concepts aroused great controversy when Freud proposed them toward the end of the Victorian era. Almost one hundred years later, the same concepts continue to engender controversy between psychoanalytic theorists and clinicians and those taking a social learning position.

The principle of **psychic determinism** *states that no behavior occurs by chance.* Every human behavior—physical or psychological—occurs because of what has preceded it. Even such seemingly random events as dreaming, slips of the tongue, and forgetfulness stem from preexisting causes of which the individual is probably unaware. The source of these behaviors is the unconscious. According to Freud, the **unconscious** *is that part of the individual's mental world that cannot be brought into consciousness by effort of will.*

According to psychoanalytic theory, the **unconscious** *is composed of the person's primitive wishes, impulses, and desires.* These thoughts and feelings remain unconscious because their conscious experience would disrupt normal functioning.

Psychoanalytic theorists point to the behavior of a small child as a model of how the unconscious can affect behavior. This behavior, straight from the child's uncensored unconscious, is sometimes referred to as **primary process** because it *is primitive, immature, and unsocialized, not yet modified by society's rules and not yet altered by the child's wish to conform.* Unconscious material can also seek expression in the behavior of adults: in unconscious (Freudian) slips of the tongue, in dreams, in jokes, or during psychotherapy, a gradual process that permits the unconscious to come to consciousness (figure 11.2).

## APPLYING PSYCHOLOGY
### How to Kill a Joke

"Humor can be dissected, as a frog can, but the thing dies in the process and the innards are discouraging to any but the pure scientific mind," wrote E. B. White. In other words, nothing spoils a joke like analyzing it. And nobody analyzed jokes like Sigmund Freud.

After writing about the interpretation of dreams, it occurred to Freud that the same hidden meanings were to be found in jokes. If, as Freud believed, dreams are "the royal road to the unconscious," jokes are perhaps the back door to the unconscious.

Freud wrote *Jokes and Their Relation to the Unconscious* in 1905. An immediate non-seller, its 200 copy first printing took years to sell. You've got to say this much for Freud, he has staying power; *Jokes . . .* is still in print after 90 years. In the book Freud dissects some of his favorite jokes, like this knee-slapper:*

> A horse dealer was recommending a saddle horse to a customer. "If you take this horse and get on it at four in the morning you'll be in Pressburg at half past six in the morning."
>
> "And what would I do in Pressburg at half past six in the morning?"

William Fry (1963) offers a psychoanalytic interpretation of this story:

> A knight, sore and wounded after unsuccessful battle, is escaping through a dense and unknown forest, astride his rapidly failing horse. After several hours, the horse can go no farther. The knight, knowing that he must go on, if only to gain shelter from the approaching storm, dismounts and

struggles on alone. Soon he falters. Just as he falls, exhausted, unable to take another step, a huge shaggy dog appears, motions to the knight to get aboard him, and goes off through the forest with the knight on his back. Then the storm breaks. Lightning, thunder, hail, rain. Drenching buckets of rain. Suddenly, there is seen the twinkling of a little light far off in the forest, and the dog, with the knight still astride, runs toward the light. They discover that the light is coming from the window of a cabin. The dog raps on the door. After a few moments, an old lady hesitantly opens the door and peers out into the storm. The knight tips his visor and requests lodging. Just as the old lady is about to grant the wanderers entrance, a deep masculine voice comes from the cabin, telling her to keep them out. She immediately protests, "Husband, dear, you wouldn't keep a knight out on a dog like this."

**The Dissection:**
The joke tells a story of a knight, a dog, and an elderly couple. The knight has lost his noble virility (horse). He comes upon anxiety-ridden times (the storm), but is then supported by an amoral attitude (shaggy dog). He comes to the embrace of his mother (cabin of the old lady) and expresses his need to enter. He is cut short by the commanding voice of his father, refusing him admission. (This is the classic Oedipus solution.) Then the mother, utilizing excellent word-play, reverses the usual "dog on a night like this" and protests that this knight-dog should be allowed the comforts of the night.

Thankfully, there are also non-psychoanalytic interpretations of jokes that do not depend so heavily on speculations about unconscious wishes (McGhee & Goldstein, 1983).

*Freud's own jokes are psychoanalyzed by folklorist Elliott Oring in *The Jokes of Sigmund Freud* (1984). Philadelphia: University of Pennsylvania Press.

*Psychological Structure*    Much of the content of the unconscious is derived from what Freud (1932) called the id, one of three psychological structures that emerge. The **id** *is the reservoir of primitive drives and desires untouched and unaffected by contact with the real world and its civilizing influence.* It is the first element of the psychic structure to emerge, and it does so during earliest childhood.

Dominant in these early months of life, the id is guided by one aim, the **pleasure principle,** *the immediate gratification of impulses.* The **ego** *comes into existence as a way to adjust the id to external reality by modifying id impulses so they conform to society's moral and ethical standards and rules.* The ego enables the organism to adapt and, when necessary, to compromise. In contrast to

the id, the ego is guided by the **reality principle,** *the need to function effectively in the real world.*

The ego, the "executive" of the personality, "manages" the functioning of the person the way an executive manages the functioning of an organization. The ego mediates and arbitrates between the demands of the real world and those of the id, permitting the individual to do many things: to learn complex motor skills like driving a car; to learn to write; to sense, perceive, and then reflect on the environment; to remember, compare, and think; and to test reality. Some psychoanalysts believe the ego to be responsible for our most distinctly human social and intellectual capabilities.

The last element of the psychological apparatus to develop, the **superego** *gradually emerges when the child* *must begin to learn the rules by which society and behavior are governed; it represents internalized parents* and is at the root of an individual's conscience and morality.

Freud believed the id to be the reservoir of two basic drives: the **life instinct,** *the sexual impulses of the id,* and **death instinct,** *the aggressive drives that are also part of the id.* He also believed that the thoughts, feelings, wishes, and desires motivated by these drives are present at birth in every infant, hidden in the unconscious. It was this belief, particularly his conviction that infants and children have sexual feelings, that aroused much hostility toward Freud when he first proposed the theory of infantile sexuality. Based upon years of clinical observation, Freud concluded that very young children have some of the same sexual and aggressive urges that adults have. Prior to Freud's proposal, children were assumed to be free of such thoughts and feelings.

The ego must find socially acceptable ways, if possible, for the id to attain conscious expression. Psychoanalytic theory teaches that the artist and the sculptor may be expressing their sexual feelings in artistic creation, a process known as *sublimation,* whereas the business-person might well be competing in order to express (in disguised form) aggressive impulses.

Freud assumed the existence of the three components of psychological structure because he recognized that every healthy human being is capable of three distinct kinds of behavior: sexual and aggressive drives and wishes, the use of reason to adjust to life's varying demands, and the capacity to govern oneself according to society's rules. By describing psychological behavior in this three-part fashion, Freud could attribute the many varieties of mental disorder to problems in early life that had an impact on one or more of the components of psychological structure.

## Psychosexual Stages of Development

Freud (1960; Jones, 1953) separated personality development during childhood into several distinct phases. During these *psychosexual stages of development,* specific parts of the body, called "erogenous zones," become invested with **libido,** *the psychological energy that comes from instincts and that energizes the parts of the body involved in the successive stages of psychosexual development.* Freud believed that the interaction of the child's behavior with the environment during each psychosexual stage determined the person's psychological health later on.

*The Oral Stage*    The first stage of psychosexual development, the **oral stage,** *lasts from birth to about eighteen months. Much of the child's behavior during this time is devoted to obtaining food.* As a result, the taste and touch receptors in and around the child's mouth, lips, and tongue become especially sensitive so that they can provide the stimulation and pleasure that Freud considered to be similar to sexual pleasure. A firm believer in evolutionary theory, Freud saw evolutionary significance in the fact that psychological energy (libido) invests itself in that function of the body, food intake, that is most essential to healthy development at this time.

Central to the psychological developments that take place during the oral stage is the child's realization that she or he cannot be fed or comforted instantly. Instead, during the oral stage, *the child learns that there are important aspects of the world over which he or she can not have control.* To Freud, this intrusion of the realistic demands of the environment was most important to the developing ego and to the development of personality.

*The Anal Stage*    During the **anal stage,** *which lasts from about the ages of eighteen months to two and a half years, the young child's major focus of learning and experience is on controlling the elimination of waste products from the body.* Accordingly, the sensory receptors involved in elimination become especially sensitive during this time, ensuring that pleasurable sensations will be involved in elimination and that the sensations will motivate the child to learn to eliminate urine and feces.

Freud also believed that a child learns an important psychological lesson during these years: how to control other aspects of the environment. The child learns, for example, that he or she can exert surprising control over his or her parents, pleasing or displeasing them profoundly, simply by giving or withholding certain behaviors (love, physical affection, even feces and urine). The importance of this lesson to the child's developing sense of self-esteem and competence is immense: The parent who refuses to help the child be his or her own person and who exerts control over some of the child's behaviors prevents the child from developing the self-respect he or she needs for the rigors of what is to come in life.

*The Phallic Stage*    According to psychoanalytic theory, between the ages of three and six, the child's genital area is the major source of sensory focus and pleasure. Freud called this the phallic stage of psychosexual development. The idea of considering a five- or six-year-old capable of deriving sexual pleasure from his or her genitals still astounds many non-psychoanalysts.

It is during the phallic stage of development, Freud wrote, that the boy must deal with the "Oedipal conflict" and the girl with the "Electra conflict." The way in which these situations are resolved determines both sexual identity (the adult sexual role the person considers most appropriate for himself or herself), and later mental health or illness. The **phallic stage** *centers on concerns about the size and function of the genitals (which, at this age, are not yet capable of mature sexual functioning).* This focus leads the child into direct conflict with the same-sex parent and, at the same time, a closer relationship, one with sexual overtones, with the opposite-sex parent.

This shift in parent-child relationships culminates in a family conflict situation named for the central figure in a tragic Greek myth. In that myth, Oedipus, son of a royal Greek family, is fated to carry out a tragic prediction: that he will kill his father, the king, and marry his mother, the queen. And, true to the prediction, Oedipus ultimately does so despite his heroic efforts to avoid his fate.

Observing themes in the fantasies of five-year-old boys and girls that seemed to resemble this myth, Freud speculated that these phenomena occurred across different cultures and different eras. He observed the unconscious fantasies and wishes of five- and six-year-old children to assume the same-sex parent's place in the mind, heart, and bed of the opposite-sex parent. Freud saw little boys as wishing (unconsciously, of course) to destroy their fathers so they could become their mothers' lovers; for little girls it was just the reverse. The successful resolution of this conflict, Freud felt, was essential to healthy adult functioning. The Oedipal conflict is unconscious. Few children are aware of the aims of these fantasies.

*The Latency Period*    Following the stormy phallic period, the child enters an extended period of psychosexual quietude, the **latency period.** Freud did not think that significant developments occurred during the ages between about eight and the onset of puberty.

*The Genital Stage*    With the onset of puberty, the **genital stage** of psychosexual development begins. *During this time, the adolescent learns the perils and pleasures of adult sexuality.* How much pleasure and how much peril the adolescent experiences during this period depends on how well or how poorly he or she has progressed through the earlier stages of psychosexual development. According to Freud, the events of the oral, anal, and phallic stages largely determine both the personality and the ultimate psychological health of the adult. This proved to be a contentious issue with some of his associates, such as Erik Erikson (1968), who later wrote about the importance of childhood and adolescence in personality formation.

## Ego Defense Mechanisms

Even healthy, strong egos must adopt **defense mechanisms** *to prevent the insistent, powerful forces of the id or superego from ultimately overwhelming the "civilized" ego and seeking expression in behavior that might otherwise destroy or seriously harm the personality.* Many of these defense mechanisms are unconscious and involuntary; others are conscious or at least open to conscious recognition.

Though everyone resorts to defensive maneuvers from time to time, excessive dependence upon certain of the less adaptive defenses signals a weak or inadequate ego. According to psychoanalytic theory, this dependence results in ineffective, maladaptive, or abnormal behavior (Freud, 1914, 1924).

The most basic and important ego defense mechanism is **repression,** *the involuntary burying in the unconscious of unwanted, unacceptable, and threatening thoughts, feelings, and impulses.* Occasionally people have a vague memory of an early event that has the capacity to disquiet them; this partial memory, according to psychoanalytic theory, is probably the "tip of the iceberg" of a repressed, painful memory, too disturbing to deal with if fully remembered. Concentrating on the memory usually fails to provide any additional information about the earlier scene, though additional clues may appear in dreams, slips of the tongue, or during psychoanalysis. Such traumatic early events as the loss of a parent, an incestuous relationship, or a serious accident are the types of experiences that people are likely to repress, since remembering them and their emotional accompaniments in detail would be very painful.

Though people are not always aware of repression, they are much more familiar with **suppression,** *the deliberate decision to keep material from entering consciousness.* People employ suppression when the memory of an event involving rejection, embarrassment, or guilt is especially

## EXPLORING HUMAN DIVERSITY
### Child-Rearing Practices in Indonesia

It was once fashionable among anthropologists to explain nearly everything, from the Russian revolution to the frequency of divorce, with reference to child-rearing practices, like harsh toilet training. This view was regarded as unfashionable during the time that Nigel Barley was a graduate student in anthropology in Britain. So he was surprised to observe the clear relationship between child-rearing and adult personality in Indonesia.

"Somehow, one felt, Indonesians had read all those books (about child-rearing and personality) and believed them.

"From a very early age, children are comforted with a heavy, inert, cylindrical pillow known as a Dutch wife. If children are fractious or fretful, they are draped around such a pillow and encouraged to hug it until they fall asleep. Young men, especially, are expected to snuggle up to such chaste bedfellows until marriage. Presumably, spouses then sleep tightly intertwined as pillow substitutes. The result is that Indonesians with nothing to hug are as pipe-smokers with nothing in their mouths, restless and inattentive. On the streets, one sees them talking, and while talking they embrace lamp-posts, the corners of brick walls, the wings of their cars, each other. They are left with a definite need to hug." (Barley, 1988, p. 44)

painful. Most people have probably purposely kept from consciousness such things as the memories and emotions associated with the end of a love relationship, the automobile accident that should not have happened, or the surprisingly bad grade that should not have been received.

**Denial,** *avoiding painful experiences and thoughts by denying they exist,* is one of the earliest defense mechanisms to develop. Denying the death of a loved one and behaving as though the person were still alive is an example of denial.

**Fixation** *refers to the defense mechanism that causes a person to remain in a particular psychosexual stage because development is interfered with.* The person is unable to progress to a more advanced stage and greater psychological maturity. The child whose every desire is gratified by his mother during the oral stage may grow to adulthood believing that "the world owes me a living." Or the child neglected during the same stage may come to believe that the world will never satisfy his or her needs and that people cannot be trusted or relied upon.

**Regression** *describes the return to an earlier, less mature stage of development in the face of severe environmental stress.* Though all of us regress briefly when faced with acute stressors (crying is one of the most common forms of regression), psychologically mature persons recover quickly from ordinary stress and adapt to it satisfactorily. When regression lasts too long or when it interferes with the ability to adapt to the demands of life, then it is dysfunctional. The man who forfeits all responsibility for his family by gambling or drinking away his

resources or the woman who stops seeing her friends and spends her time watching soap operas on television because the world had gotten too complicated for her, have regressed to less complicated, less mature forms of existence in order to maintain some control over their own destinies.

Freud believed that *people replace a particularly unpleasant feeling about someone or something with the opposite feeling,* a process he called **reaction formation.** Hate is replaced by love, cruelty by kindness, and stubbornness by compliance. Psychoanalysts conclude, for example that doting, overprotective, "smothering" mothers may actually be defending against ambivalent feelings toward their children. Reaction formation takes place unconsciously; people cannot choose to make it happen.

An especially adaptive defense mechanism is **sublimation,** *the process of transferring psychological energy associated with unconscious desires and impulses into socially accepted, often creative, activities,* such as painting, composing, or hard work. The empirical data for this hypothesized process are not very substantial (Farrell, 1981; Fine, 1979). Nevertheless, there is no denying the positive value that many people derive from active, enthusiastic immersion in creative activities, especially during times of stress and conflict. The great composer Beethoven, a man whose sexual and aggressive impulses were always near conscious experience during an era when such behavior was considered especially objectionable, has been singled out as a person who dealt with these strong impulses by sublimating them in the process of creativity.

**Rationalization** *permits people to give a behavior whose motivation may be obscure, irrational, or embarrassing a rational, logical, or intellectual explanation.* Justifying the decision to attend a pornographic movie as "an educational experience" or to leave school for a year of travel through Europe "to become a more well-rounded person" are examples of rationalization.

In **displacement** *the individual attributes an unacceptable feeling or impulse to an undeserving person.* Becoming angry at a friend when the anger actually stems from conflict with a roommate, or criticizing the behavior of a child when one is actually critical of a spouse, are examples of displacement. Displacement can be troublesome when it influences behavior toward whole classes of people. For example, a woman who avoids men because she believes that all men harbor sexual designs on her as a result of early experiences with her father.

## Psychoanalytic Theory: Overview and Critique

Freudian theory traces personality development, including both normal and abnormal behavior, to the interaction of environmental events that take place during the first five or six years of life and the biologically linked stages of psychosexual development. This interaction between environmental and biological factors is what determines the relative balance and strength of the ego, the id, and the superego. In turn, the strength and balance of these three psychic elements determine, to a great extent, the person's ability to deal with the inevitable stresses and strains of adulthood.

What early events foster the development of a strong and healthy ego? According to psychoanalytic theory, those events that challenge the child to function independently, to confront age-appropriate stressors in such a way as to lead to growth in feelings of competence and self-esteem.

Situations that prevent the child from acquiring basic trust in the world or from developing the capacity to realistically view the environment are said to weaken ego function. Punishing or seductive parents are believed to foster the development of a harsh, punitive superego or a strong and uncontrollable id. Psychological health is thought to flourish when the ego is successful in mediating the demands of the sexual and aggressive impulses

(the id), the conscience (the superego), and the environment (as conveyed by the ego).

Through the years since Freud and Josef Breuer, an early collaborator, launched the psychoanalytic movement with the publication of *Studies in Hysteria* in 1895, efforts have been made to subject psychoanalytic theory to empirical study and confirmation (Farrell, 1981; Fisher & Greenberg, 1978; Kline, 1972). Two factors have interfered with these efforts. First, Freud and those who worked with and came after him were clinicians, not researchers. Accordingly, the theory was not designed for empirical validation. Second, much of psychoanalytic theory is so complex and so abstract that it defies experimental investigation. As a result, psychoanalytic theory has come to be viewed as inaccessible to controlled study. Although efforts to validate the theory empirically do continue, the basic problems associated with the scientific investigation of psychoanalytic theory remain (Liebert & Spiegler, 1990). Nevertheless, psychoanalytic theory is still around (Youngstrom, 1992). Where would we be without it?

▶ **GUIDED REVIEW** *Learning Objectives 3, 4, 5, and 6*

1. Psychoanalytic theory's two basic tenets are the principle of _____ and the _____.
2. Psychic structure includes the _____, the earliest part of the psychic apparatus to develop and the reservoir of primitive drives and impulses; the _____, the means by which the id is forced to adjust to external reality; and the _____, which functions as a conscience, or internalized set of parents.
3. During the _____, _____, _____, _____, and _____ stages of psychosexual development, successive parts of the body are invested with _____, and important psychological and interpersonal lessons associated with those bodily parts are learned.
4. Even strong egos must adopt strategies to defend against excessively strong id or superego demands. These are referred to as _____.
5. _____ is the unconscious burying of threatening events and impulses.
6. _____ is a return to earlier, more childish behavior.

*ANSWERS*

1. psychic determinism, unconscious 2. id, ego, superego 3. oral, anal, phallic, latency, genital, libido 4. ego defense mechanisms 5. Repression 6. Regression

# NEO-FREUDIAN THEORIES OF PERSONALITY

During his lifetime, some members of Freud's inner circle deviated sharply from important aspects of his theory. These men and women, including Carl Jung, Alfred Adler, and Karen Horney, developed distinct neo-Freudian psychoanalytic theories of personality. After his death, newer groups of psychoanalytic theorists continued to find areas of Freud's theory with which to disagree. While based on Freud's original work, these later theories were different enough to merit separate identities. Among the most important of these theorists are Karen Horney, Erich Fromm, and Erik Erikson, who emphasized the relationship between culture and personality.

## Defectors from the Inner Circle: Jung and Adler

Carl Jung and Alfred Adler, men Freud had worked with in developing psychoanalytic theory, found it impossible to accept all aspects of his original theory. Jung, a highly religious person, rejected Freud's theory of infantile psychosexuality. He found it impossible to believe that very young children could have sexual feelings so strong that they would wish, even unconsciously, to take the place of their same-sex parent in the arms of their opposite-sex parent.

Jung believed that people inherit a **collective unconscious**, *a depository or reservoir of their group's racial and cultural history.* The collective unconscious influences their behavior, without their knowing it, by forcing them to view their world in the light of the lengthy experience on earth of their particular racial and cultural group.

Related to this view, which has not been supported by empirical research, is Jung's concept of **archetypes,** *unconscious representations of familiar cultural figures,* such as "the wise old man," and "the loving mother." These unconscious concepts, like the collective unconscious, influence people's responses to the environment by giving them a "built-in" memory that isn't really theirs but that is, instead, a collective memory from their species' past.

Jung differentiated between extroverted and introverted personality types. **Extroverts** *are most interested in the world around them and in other people. By contrast,* **introverts** *tend to be preoccupied with their own thoughts and feelings and are less involved in the world*

**Figure 11.3**    *Karen Horney (1885–1952)*

*around them.* This fundamental personality distinction has had a continuing impact on later personality theorists' conceptions of personality. It is widely regarded as a key component of personality (Eysenck & Eysenck, 1963; Goldberg, 1990).

Alfred Adler, another member of Freud's inner circle, concluded that many emotional disorders derived from the feelings of *inferiority* all children experience *in relation to bigger, wiser, more powerful parents,* rather than from sexual conflicts, as Freud believed. The person then engages in *striving for superiority, the fundamental human motivation that attempts to compensate for feelings of inferiority. When feelings of inferiority or striving for superiority become excessive, abnormal behavior, which Adler called inferiority complex, may result.* Adler was himself a sickly child who suffered continually from accidents and illness. As a consequence, he decided early in life to become a physician in an effort to overcome his fear of death.

## The Impact of Culture on Personality: Horney, Fromm, and Erikson

During the decade of the 1930s, when most of the world struggled in the grip of depression and Europe struggled with Hitler's fascism, a second group of personality theorists modified psychoanalytic theory to emphasize the

# CLOSE UP ON RESEARCH

## Ethnic Identity

What happens when a person holds two different cultural identities, for example, one Latino, the other American? Conventional psychological theory predicts disaster. But research by California psychologist Joe Martinez predicts mild discomfort followed by a healthy blending of identities.

The question has taken on new urgency among behavioral and social scientists seeking to unravel the implications of the growing mosaic of ethnic and cultural identities in America, and, indeed, in many other nations.

Demographers and other social scientists are finding it increasingly difficult to measure or make sense of ethnic and racial identities. For example, in 1980, 350,000 "new" American Indians appeared in the United States Census. This was thirty-four percent more than demographers expected from their projections following the 1960 Census. The explanation? In the interim, researchers say, claiming an American-Indian identity became more acceptable.

The ambiguous definition of race has prompted at least one psychologist, Albert Yee of Marist College, to call on his colleagues to either develop a clear definition of race or abandon the term entirely in favor of ethnicity.

Culture identity, which can encompass race and ethnicity, has long been a topic of research both for psychologists and sociologists. In Europe, too, with its changing borders and allegiances, the study of identity has grown (Mlicki & Ellemers, 1992). Much of the psychological literature on cultural identity has its roots in the work of sociologist R. E. Park, who predicted that immigrants from other cultures would suffer a dysfunctional psychological state called "marginality," characterized by a divided sense of consciousness, feelings of inferiority, withdrawal, irrationality, and occasionally suicidal thoughts. According to this view, the route to psychological adjustment is to shed one's original cultural identity and assimilate to the host culture; biculturalism was not seen as a viable option.

Martinez disagrees. He and Francisca Azocar talked to Latino immigrants about the specific settings in which they experienced cultural conflict. This led to the Dual Cultural Identity Questionnaire, which measures different aspects of self-concept, including cultural ("I consider myself only Mexican"), personality ("I am too self-conscious"), and values ("I think only men should work"). It includes questions about choices based on cultural identity, for example, the choice of friends, residence, language used with one's children.

In their initial study of Latino immigrants, Martinez and Azocar found that while immigrants do report feeling less comfortable with newly added elements of their identity, as time passes they become increasingly comfortable with a dual identity. And the researchers found no evidence that maintaining a dual cultural identity leads to psychopathology.

Martinez and Azocar are not alone in raising questions about the traditional view that an immigrant's "success" is equated with assimilating to an American identity.

Psychologist Marta Bernal has studied the relationship between social identity and school achievement among Mexican-American high-school and junior high-school students in Arizona. She and George Knight found that, language skills being equal, immigrant students outperform native students, apparently because a strong ethnic identity often includes a belief in the value of education. Ruben Rumbaut has found a similar pattern among the children of Southeast Asian immigrants in Southern California. Sociologist Mary C. Waters has found that among the children of Jamaican immigrants in New York City, those who do the poorest in school are those who discard their ethnic identity as Jamaicans and take on the identity of black Americans. The latter identity, forged in the crucible of inner-city schools, often denigrates scholastic achievement, says Waters.

"As the population of immigrants increases, psychologists can help immigrants adjust by alerting them to the discomfort that may arise from developing a dual identity and by reassuring them that discomfort is likely to abate," concludes Martinez.

impact of culture and society on the development of personality. Chief among these theorists were Karen Horney, Erich Fromm, and Erik Erikson.

Karen Horney (figure 11.3) believed that anxiety and depression result from basic conflicts arising from contradictory trends common to humans. She summed up these trends as (1) "moving toward people," (2) "moving against people," and (3) "moving away from people."

Horney referred to the behavioral expression of these trends as "neurotic needs." Neurotic needs include the neurotic need for affection and approval, which results in trying to live up to the expectations of others, and the neurotic need for power, which results in the attempt to dominate others for its own sake.

Erich Fromm's classic work, *Escape from Freedom,* was published in 1941, at the height of the threat to the world from Nazi Germany. In it, Fromm asked whether modern men and women, in their search for maximum freedom and self-determination, might find themselves disorganized by boundless opportunities for choice in life-style and individual freedom. So great might be their discomfort at their freedom of choice that they might choose to "escape from freedom" by agreeing to a totalitarian dictatorship (like that of the Nazis, for example). The parallel that Fromm drew between what was then happening in Hitler's Germany in the late 1930s and the fundamental thesis of his book was obvious to all who read it:

> We have been compelled to recognize that millions in Germany were as eager to surrender their freedom as their fathers were to fight for it; that instead of wanting freedom, they sought for ways of escape from it; that other millions were indifferent and did not believe the defense of freedom to be worth fighting and dying for (Fromm, 1941, p. 5).

Erik Erikson's emphasis on the social and cultural factors that influence personality, and his belief that personality continues to grow and develop through the life span have struck a responsive chord in our society. Erikson's impact is shown by the number of words for key Eriksonian concepts that are now a part of our everyday vocabulary. Identity crisis, life cycle, psycho-history, and role confusion are examples.

## Neo-Freudians: An Overview

At this point, you might ask how it is that a single personality theory has been subjected to so many attempts at modification and change. Does this mean that the original theory was seriously deficient? Does it mean that new information has come to light invalidating the original

theory? Or does it mean that different personality theorists are apt to see the same thing in different ways? All these explanations are valid. Perfection in theory-building is unattainable, and men and women continue to strive to improve existing theories of personality.

## LEARNING THEORIES OF PERSONALITY

Learning theories of personality assume that most human behavior, normal and abnormal, is learned (see chapter 5).

These views of personality arose from several influences. One of the first and most important influences was the identification, during this century, of the basic modes of learning: elucidation of the principles of classical conditioning by Ivan Pavlov and John B. Watson during the first part of this century, the development of the operant conditioning model by Edward Thorndike and B. F. Skinner, and Albert Bandura's more recent discovery of the impact of modeling and vicarious reinforcement on human behavior.

However, identification of these modes of learning, while necessary before learning-based theories of personality could develop, was not sufficient for this purpose. The reaction against Freud's psychoanalytic theory was also needed. This reaction was in response to psychoanalytic theory's complexity, inaccessibility to experimental confirmation, over-emphasis on the role of childhood sexuality in personality development, and Freud's view that human behavior was a continuous struggle against inborn forces leading to emotional disorder.

### Classical Conditioning and Personality

Though Pavlov's discoveries (see chapter 5) were derived from laboratory research with animals, an enormous amount of later research has established the importance of classical conditioning so far as human beings are concerned. Scientists and clinicians have concluded that much of the autonomic learning that human beings do (learning that involves emotional reactions to people and places) obeys the principles of classical conditioning.

How are emotional responses acquired by classical conditioning? In a now famous demonstration, John B. Watson, whom many consider the father of behaviorism in this country, successfully conditioned fear of a white rat in an 18-month-old child ("Little Albert") previously unafraid of the animal. Watson and Rayner (1920) did so

---

by first exposing the child to a white rat; the child responded with interest and no fear. Then they paired the sight of the animal with a loud, frightening noise; the child responded with tears and a startled response. After Watson and Rayner had repeatedly paired the frightening noise with the rat, the child began to cry as soon as he saw the rat; a conditioned aversion to the rat, based upon fear, had been established.

Following Watson's demonstration of conditioned fear, other researchers began to study the many other emotions that can be conditioned to environmental stimuli. Their conclusions were that most emotional responses to the environment come about as the result of classical conditioning (Miller, 1984; Wilson & O'Leary, 1986).

Learning theorists believe that maladaptive emotional responses are also acquired by means of classical conditioning. The psychiatrist Joseph Wolpe, a leading spokesperson for this position, believes that learning mechanisms strikingly similar to those responsible for Little Albert's fear of the white rat are also responsible for adult fears and anxieties (Wolpe, 1973, 1982). By these mechanisms, human beings acquire inappropriate, dysfunctional fear and anxiety about people, places, and things. The practical significance of Wolpe's views on the causes of these conditions is that they are learned by means of classical conditioning. It was this conclusion that led Wolpe to develop a learning-based treatment program designed to "countercondition" neurotic anxiety and fear (see chapter 13).

## Operant Conditioning and Personality

Most learning theorists believe that much of the behavior that defines our personalities is powerfully influenced by operant conditioning mechanisms. Unlike classical conditioning, operant learning does not establish new relationships between already-existing behaviors (for example, between the frightening loud noise and the white rat to which Little Albert was exposed). Instead, operant conditioning exerts its influence on preexisting behaviors, whose frequency is increased or decreased as a function of their consequences (Dollard & Miller, 1950). As one example, consider the central role that operant conditioning plays in the development of social skills.

Social skills are important components of our personalities. Friendliness, charm, cooperativeness, and empathy are social skills that are important determinants of how successfully we interact with the world. Approval (smiles, grins, applause, verbal praise) for a particular social behavior leads to a strengthening of that behavior and an increase in the likelihood that it will be repeated. Disapproval (frowns, shakes of the head, tears, verbal criticism) leads just as quickly to reduction in the frequency of the behaviors that elicit such responses. This is how patterns of behavior are learned.

Operant conditioning also plays an important role in the development and maintenance of maladaptive behavior. Behavioral clinicians now believe that the operant model helps explain many severe and disabling conditions, including depression and alcohol and drug dependencies.

One influential operant-based theory of depression, **learned helplessness** (Seligman, 1975), states that *depression is a consequence of exposure to unavoidable events.* Learning that there are a variety of unpleasant or otherwise punishing situations from which one cannot escape, Seligman initially believed, leads some individuals to develop the enduring belief that they are not able to control the outcomes of most of their actions. These beliefs were thought to be associated with the development of depression. Originally developed from animal studies, this theory has not been well-supported in research on depression in human beings. As a result, the theory has been reformulated to describe an attributional style, a characteristic approach to life, that has important consequences on one's overall ability to function (Seligman, Abramson, Semmel, & von Baeyer, 1979). (See Close Up on Research: The Berlin Wall, the Vietnam War, the Presidential Elections, and the Pessimistic Explanatory Style, which provides some surprising historical findings concerning the pessimistic explanatory style.)

## Observational Learning and Personality

Observational learning, also called social learning, vicarious learning, or modeling (see chapter 5), was developed by Albert Bandura and his colleagues in the 1960s. Observational learning, as discussed in chapter 5, explains behavior acquired by watching others, who are referred to as "models." The most influential models are one's parents, teachers, and friends, but movie stars, cartoon characters, and sports heroes can also influence behavior (Caughey, 1985). Bandura has concluded that such behaviors as aggressiveness, the capacity to delay gratification, certain patterns of emotional responsiveness, and many forms of verbal and social interactions are acquired as a function of modeling.

## CLOSE UP ON RESEARCH

### The Berlin Wall, the Vietnam War, the Presidential Elections, and the Pessimistic Explanatory Style

Seligman's revised learned helplessness model states that the beliefs people hold about why their behavior leads to certain kinds of outcomes affect how they explain bad events. So potent are these beliefs, that they can be responsible for failure, depression, illness, disease, and even death (Zullow, Oettingen, Peterson, and Seligman, 1988). Most responsible for these bad events, these authors conclude, is a **pessimistic explanatory style,** *the tendency to see the causes of bad events as stable, global, and internal ("It's going to last forever," "It's going to undermine all that I do," and "It's me.")*

How is it that people develop pessimistic explanatory styles? Presumably the style develops when and if people repeatedly find themselves, as youngsters, in difficult situations from which they cannot figure out the means to escape. Such environmental factors as poverty and racial prejudice probably facilitate its development.

In a research program designed to investigate links between helplessness and depression, Peterson and Seligman (1984) used the Attributional Style Questionnaire (ASQ), a self-report questionnaire, to assess explanatory style. Other studies have shown explanatory style as measured by the ASQ to be an important predictor of depression following bad events (Sweeney, Anderson, & Bailey, 1986). Research following creation of the ASQ has also led to development of a technique to analyze the contents of historical documents in order to determine explanatory style (Peterson, Luborsky, & Seligman, 1983).

To test the hypothesis that explanatory style as assessed by content analysis of written or spoken materials from the past predicts behavioral outcomes, Zullow and his colleagues analyzed three sets of material: (1) ten Presidential press conference transcripts when Lyndon Johnson was President of the United States; (2) the twenty nomination acceptance speeches from 1948 to 1984 of the two major parties' Presidential nominees; (3) reports on the 1984 Winter Olympics from the sports pages of the East Berlin and West Berlin newspapers. Content analysis of these three sources of data revealed the following:

> First, shifts to a more optimistic style in Lyndon Johnson's press conferences predicted bold, risky action during the Vietnam War, whereas shifts to pessimism predicted passivity. Second, analyses of (the) presidential candidates' nomination acceptance speeches showed that candidates who were more pessimistically ruminative lost nine of the ten elections. Third, there were more behavioral signs consistent with depression among workmen in East Berlin than in West Berlin bars, (a finding that) corresponded to a comparatively more pessimistic explanatory style in East Berlin newspaper reports concerning the 1984 Winter Olympics.

Though a highly unconventional approach to research on personality, these studies are intriguing.

In his presidential address to the American Psychological Association (1974), Bandura reminded his audience that "theories that explain human behavior as the product of external rewards and punishments present a truncated image of man because people partly regulate their actions by self-produced consequences." This emphasizes Bandura's belief that operant and classical conditioning (both of which depend on external rewards and punishments) do not account for all human learning.

Bandura's statement also makes the equally important point that observational learning may take place because the observer *chooses* to model certain behaviors. Those choices involve cognitions, or thinking, which prominent social learning theorists include in the learning process (Hollon & Beck, 1986; Rosenthal, 1984).

The role of modeling in the development of maladaptive behavior has only recently begun to be explored. However, there is considerable clinical evidence that patients who complain of intense fear of new situations or of meeting people have modeled the behavior, as children, from a similarly timid, shy, and socially isolated parent. Behavioral theorists have also hypothesized that modeling may play a role in more serious psychiatric symptoms. When one family member is seriously disturbed, for example, there is an increased incidence of serious psychiatric disturbance in other family members (Ullmann & Krasner, 1976).

More recently, Bandura (1982, 1986) has focused on the cognitive aspects of social learning, particularly the concept of perceived self-efficacy. **Self-efficacy** *is an individual's belief that he or she can successfully perform the behavior necessary to produce a desired outcome.* It is an individual's perception of his or her ability to deal with a situation. People willingly and enthusiastically undertake tasks that they feel capable of managing successfully, and avoid those activities they believe are beyond them. The stronger an individual's perceived self-efficacy, the more persistent are their efforts to face obstacles and setbacks (Cervone & Peake, 1986). According to Bandura, personality change, as in psychotherapy, is effective because it strengthens a client's perceived self-efficacy.

▶ **GUIDED REVIEW** *Learning Objective 8*

1. Social learning theories assume that most of human behavior and personality is _____.
2. Social learning theorists believe that most of the emotional learning humans do is accounted for by _____ mechanisms.
3. _____ conditioning mechanisms are responsible for much of our social and interpersonal behavior. Central to this view is the fundamental assumption that behavior that is _____ will increase in frequency whereas behavior that is _____ or _____ will decrease in frequency.
4. _____ includes those aspects of our behavior acquired by watching others engage in the same behaviors.
5. _____ refers to the individual's perception that he or she has the resources to achieve a desired outcome.

*ANSWERS*

1. *learned* 2. *classical conditioning* 3. *Operant, reinforced, punished, ignored* 4. *Observational learning* 5. *Self-efficacy*

# HUMANISTIC THEORIES OF PERSONALITY

Humanistic theories of personality have had a major impact on perceptions of personality growth and development. **Humanistic theories** *emphasize the significance and uniqueness of the individual.* This approach has led to the development of behavior change techniques that help people feel better about their own individuality and uniqueness and become more willing to value their behavior, opinions, and themselves. Whereas psychoanalytic theory assumes that all of us share important experiences (those of the Oedipal period, for example), and learning theory teaches that classical and operant conditioning mechanisms are constant, humanistic theories recognize and value each person's individuality.

## Rogers' Person-Centered Theory

The psychologist Carl Rogers (figure 11.4) developed his client-centered theory from observations of troubled but essentially normal clients. Preferring the term "person" to "client or patient," Rogers' **person-centered theory** *states that personality derives from the individual's perceptions and interpretations of his or her world* rather than from

inherited potentialities (as in psychoanalytic theory) or acquired behavior patterns (as in learning theory). Because Rogers takes an optimistic view of men and women, his theory emphasizes people's potential power to effect changes in themselves and their environments to a greater extent than most other personality theories (Rogers, Gendlin, Kiesler, & Truax, 1967; Rogers, 1980).

**Figure 11.4** *Carl Rogers (1902–1987)*

Because Rogers' views of what contributes to healthy personality growth and development are based on his extensive experiences as a counselor to normal (albeit troubled) persons, they are relevant to psychologically healthy people. His views are summarized in **Applying Psychology: Carl Rogers on the Healthy Personality.**

## Maslow's Humanistic Concept of Self-Actualization

Humanistic theorist Abraham Maslow, like Carl Rogers and other humanists, based his theories on one fundamental assumption: Men and women are basically good; they can achieve their potential, or actualize themselves, if they can overcome the frustrations and anxieties that are a normal part of modern life.

Maslow wrote of a **hierarchy of needs.** *At the bottom of this hierarchy are the basic physiological needs (like food, water, and sex) necessary for survival of the individual and the species. Farther up the hierarchy are the basic social and interpersonal needs, like companion-*

**Figure 11.5** *Maslow's hierarchy of needs.*

# APPLYING PSYCHOLOGY

## Carl Rogers on the Healthy Personality

The following statements, comprising the essence of Rogers' theory of personality, bear little resemblance to either the social learning theory or the psychoanalytic theory. Thus, many theorists have concluded that Rogers' writings do not comprise a theory of personality but are instead the poetically rendered observations of a bright and sensitive human being.

These fundamental beliefs encompass both a way of life and an approach to behavioral explanation. Moreover, they have had considerable impact on the views of personality and its development. Therefore, they belong here as another example of the range of influential theories of personality.

1. In my relationships with persons I have found that it does not help, in the long run, to act as though I were something I am not.

2. I find I am more effective when I can listen acceptantly to myself and can be myself.

3. I have found it of enormous value when I can permit myself to understand another person.

4. I have found it enriching to open channels whereby others can communicate their feelings, their private perceptual worlds, to me.

5. I have found it highly rewarding when I can accept another person.

6. The more open I am to the realities in me and in the other person, the less do I find myself wishing to rush to "fix things."

7. I can trust my experiences.

8. Evaluation by others is not a guide for me . . . only one person can know whether what I am doing is honest, thorough, open, and sound, or false and defensive and unsound, and I am that person.

9. Experience is, for me, the highest authority. . . . It is to experience that I must return again and again, to discover a closer approximation to truth as it is in the process of becoming in me.

10. I enjoy the discovering of order in experience.

11. The facts are friendly . . . painful reorganizations are what is known as learning.

12. What is most personal and unique in each one of us is probably the very element which would, if it were shared or expressed, speak most deeply to others.

13. I have come to feel that the more fully the individual is understood and accepted, the more he tends to drop the false fronts with which he has been meeting life, and the more he tends to move in a direction which is forward.

14. Life, at its best, is a flowing, changing process in which nothing is fixed.

*From Carl A. Rogers,* On Becoming A Person. *Copyright © 1961 Houghton-Mifflin. Used by permission of Houghton-Mifflin.*

ship and friendship; *toward the top of the hierarchy are complex yet supremely important needs such as love, the esteem of oneself and others, and self-actualization* (see figure 11.5).

According to Maslow, normal individuals move through the hierarchy of needs as long as they live in supportive and facilitative family environments. Such environments permit them to **self-actualize**, *to strive for and achieve their greatest potential,* to reach the top of their hierarchy of needs. Self-actualized people, Maslow believed, can love and be loved, enjoy self-esteem as well as the esteem of others, and work at a job with the kind of constructive enthusiasm that leads to accomplishment.

Maslow's theory is optimistic; he believes people can be whatever they aspire to be if they find support in their environment. This is a refreshing contrast to the theories that see living as a continuous struggle against forces trying to hold us down or confront us with our darker sides.

## Existential Theory

A group of psychiatrists, including Viktor Frankl, R. D. Laing, and Rollo May, are referred to as existential theorists. Like other forms of humanistic theory, the emphasis is on the value and uniqueness of each individual. **Existential theory** *emphasizes the importance, legitimacy, and value of differences among people and the possibility of maximum human potential.*

Existentialists emphasize the significance of the individual. They believe in people's ability to determine their own lives, to question their existence, and to seek meaning in it. The goal is an understanding of the existence of a particular person at a particular moment in his life (Pervin, 1970). The existential personality theorist is concerned with *being* and with the importance of finding meaning in life. Accordingly, existential theory is particularly relevant to young people who would like to believe

| TABLE 11.1 Some characteristics of personality theories | | | | | |
|---|---|---|---|---|---|
| | **Psychoanalytic** | **Learning** | **Social Learning** | **Humanistic** | **Trait** |
| Focus on childhood | Strong | Weak | Moderate | Weak | Strong |
| Focus on normal personality | No | Yes | Yes | Yes | Yes |
| Emphasis on unconscious | Yes | No | No | No | No |
| Supportive research | Weak | Strong | Strong | Weak | Strong |

that adulthood and its responsibilities make some difference and have some meaning.

Central to existential theories of personality is the fact that human beings, unlike other animals, learn at an early age that there will be a time when they will die. Knowledge of this fundamental fact of existence confronts human beings with a range of choices. Should they value every moment of every day, live life to its fullest, constantly seek to make the very most of their strengths, and find fullest possible meaning in life? Or should they dwell on the certainty of life's end, with the result that they live with the ultimate finality of life rather than with the desire to maximize the living of every hour? Not surprisingly, the therapy derived from existential theory focuses on psychotherapeutic solutions for the problems of those who have chosen the latter course.

Viktor Frankl's version of psychotherapy, **logotherapy,** *is based on the idea that each individual must search for personal meaning in his or her life.* The importance of personal meaning became apparent to Frankl between 1942 and 1945, when he was a prisoner in a Nazi concentration camp. He observed that some prisoners were able to survive psychologically in extreme antihuman conditions because they could find some spiritual meaning in their suffering. He came to the conclusion that traditional psychology, by dealing only with the biological and psychological dimensions of human beings, omitted an equally important dimension, the spiritual.

## SIMILARITIES AND DIFFERENCES AMONG THEORIES OF PERSONALITY

The differences between the various theories of personality are apparent (table 11.1). The theories differ in their emphasis on unconscious processes, with psychoanalysis placing the most stress on them. Psychoanalytic theories emphasize early childhood more than do learning theories, and humanistic theories place little emphasis on childhood experiences. Psychoanalytic theory is a trait theory. It views personality development as a function of crucial early life experiences interacting with the stages of psychosexuality; later life experiences are of much less importance in determining behavior and personality. In contrast, social learning theory (a state theory) emphasizes learning, which continues through life, and the immediate characteristics of the environment, which powerfully affect the behavior taking place within that environment. Humanistic theories stress the immediate environment and place little emphasis on the past.

The theories also differ in complexity, accessibility to empirical validation, focus, and breadth of explanation. Social learning theory is based largely on laboratory findings, is less complex and explains less behavior than do psychoanalytic and humanistic theories. At the same time, its roots in the laboratory and the college classroom (from which subjects for many of its experiments have been drawn) mean that its explanations fit normal behavior better than they fit abnormal behavior.

▶ **GUIDED REVIEW** *Learning Objective 9*

1. Rogers' _____ theory of personality, a humanistic theory, assumes that personality derives from the individual's own _____ and _____ of the world rather than from inherited potentialities or acquired behavior patterns.
2. Maslow's _____ determines the path an individual must take to achieve self-actualization.
3. Humanistic theories of personality emphasize _____ between people, the importance, legitimacy, and value of those differences, and their _____ for enhancement of maximum human potential.

*ANSWERS*

3. *differences, potential*
1. *person-centered, perceptions, interpretations 2. hierarchy of needs*

What is less obvious than their differences are a few important similarities among theories of personality. The theories share an intent to place behavior and personality within a consistent framework, to explain the development and maintenance of both normal and abnormal behavior, and to see continuity as well as change in the lives of men and women.

Neither psychoanalytic theory, for all its breadth, depth, and history, nor humanistic theories can point to the experimental support that learning theories can claim. The validation problem remains a central one for psychoanalytic and humanistic theories. This is not to say that psychoanalytic and humanistic theories are not studied empirically (e.g., Liebert & Spiegler, 1990; Stevens, 1992). However, their concepts are not so clearly defined or easily measured as those of learning theories.

> **GUIDED REVIEW** *Learning Objective 10*

1. _____ theories place most emphasis on early childhood experiences, _____ theories the least emphasis.
2. _____ theories are based more on empirical research than _____ or _____ theories.
3. All types of personality theory have in common _____.

*ANSWERS*

*1. Psychoanalytic, humanistic 2. Learning, psychoanalytic, humanistic 3. attempts to provide a consistent framework for explaining and describing behavior*

## ASSESSMENT OF PERSONALITY

People seem always to have been interested in the behavior of their fellow human beings. Until recently, efforts to describe behavior and individual personality were unsystematic, and they were more poetic than precise.

Progress in assessing normal personality and diagnosing abnormal behavior did not begin until after the scientific revolution at the end of the nineteenth century. At that time, German psychiatrists, including Emil Kraepelin and Eugen Bleuler, offered the first comprehensive system for categorizing psychiatric patients. It included a physical examination, diagnostic interview, and systematic behavioral observation.

At the same time, Francis Galton (see chapter 7) began to develop procedures for assessing intelligence and other components of normal personality functioning. Galton's contribution to psychological assessment was a respect for psychological tests that permitted more objective examination of personality. Galton influenced Alfred Binet, a French psychologist responsible for the development of the first reliable measure of intelligence.

Building upon these early assessment efforts, psychologists now have at their disposal a vast array of personality tests and measures. With these tests and measures, clinicians can reach consensus on a diagnostic label, a treatment plan, or an expected therapeutic outcome. Personality researchers can compare personality functioning across groups or in individuals. School psychologists can identify learning disabilities in school children. Industrial psychologists can assess the qualities of potential employees and predict their contribution to the organization. Psychologists in military settings can decide which individuals ought to be sent to officers' school, to an electronics training program, or to service in the infantry.

This list of the uses for psychological assessment methods may surprise you. Psychological tests are at least as widely used for classification and assignment purposes in business, industry, education, and the military as they are with emotionally disturbed individuals.

Two personality assessment methods that involve behavioral observation, and two methods that involve the use of tests will be discussed. These methods differ in the extent to which they provide a well-defined structure for the examinee's response. In general, the more structured the assessment method, the more reliable the results of the assessment and the more easily the results can be analyzed statistically. However, highly structured methods sharply reduce the likelihood of observing spontaneous or unexpected behavior.

### Observation and Interviews

Many psychologists and psychiatrists depend almost entirely on unstructured behavioral observation and interviews to assess personality or to diagnose a psychiatric disorder.

The most useful structured observational techniques are behavior- or symptom-rating scales. The developers of these instruments based them on their own observations of behavior. Clinicians can then use the instruments to compare the behaviors of the people whom they are observing to the predetermined criteria.

# APPLYING PSYCHOLOGY

## Why Did van Gogh Cut Off His Ear?

On Sunday, December 23, 1888, Vincent van Gogh, thirty-five-years-old, cut off the lower half of his left ear and took it to a brothel, where he presented it to a prostitute named Rachel.

Over the years, more than a dozen explanations for this extraordinary act have been proposed (Lubin, 1972). They form the basis of an article by psychologist William McKinley Runyan (1981). Among the explanations considered are the following:

1. Van Gogh was frustrated by the engagement of his brother Theo, to whom he was very attached, and by his failure to establish a good relationship with Paul Gauguin. The aggressive impulses aroused by these frustrations were turned against himself.

2. The self-mutilation resulted from a conflict over homosexual impulses aroused by Gauguin. The ear was a phallic symbol (the Dutch slang word for penis, *lul*, resembles the Dutch word for ear, *lel*), and the act was a symbolic self-castration.

3. Van Gogh was influenced by bullfights he had seen, where the matador is given the ear of the bull as an award, displays his prize to the crowd, and then gives it to the lady of his choice.

4. In the months preceding the incident, there were fifteen articles in the local paper about Jack the Ripper, who mutilated the bodies of prostitutes, sometimes cutting off their ears.

5. Van Gogh's brother Theo planned to spend the holiday with his fiancee, rather than with Vincent. Van Gogh cut off his ear in an effort to force his brother to spend the holidays with him.

6. Van Gogh had great sympathy for prostitutes, identifying with their status as social outcasts. Six months before butchering his ear, he wrote "the whore is like meat in a butcher shop." He treated his own body like "meat in a butcher shop" to show his sympathy with prostitutes.

7. Van Gogh may have experienced auditory hallucinations and cut off his ear in an effort to silence the disturbing sounds.

8. In the Garden of Gethsemane scene in the Bible, Simon Peter cut off the ear of Malchus, a servant of the high priest. Van Gogh attempted to paint this scene in the summer of 1888.

What should we make of these alternative explanations? Are any of them true? Is there some other explanation that would replace all these possibilities?

Behavior is *multi-determined, it has multiple causes and meanings*. It would be surprising to find a single explanation for any human action. Events can have more than one cause, more than one meaning. But to assume that all interpretations can co-exist as equals is to abandon critical thinking. For therapeutic purposes, it may be useful to explore multiple meanings for a single event. But for scientific purposes, it is necessary to critically assess the plausibility of alternative explanations.

In science, it is not enough to propose explanations, they must be tested. Consider the hypothesis that van Gogh was influenced by newspaper articles about Jack the Ripper. This explanation assumes that van Gogh read these stories, that he noticed the ear-cutting detail (mentioned in only two of the fifteen stories), that it made a lasting impression on him, and that it influenced him the night he mutilated his own ear. "This explanation depends on a chain of assumptions, none of which has direct empirical support, which leaves this particular conjecture relatively unsubstantiated" (Runyan, 1981, p. 1073).

Consider the theory that he identified with a prostitute by treating his own body like meat in a butcher shop. The phrase "the whore is like meat in a butcher shop" occurred in a letter written six months before the ear-cutting incident. Without further supporting evidence that this image occurred to van Gogh nearer to the time of the incident, there is little reason to believe that it played a significant part in his self-mutilation.

Runyan evaluates the evidence for each claim. One explanation seems most strongly supported, the perceived loss of his brother's care. The ear-cutting incident and two other mental breakdowns coincided with learning of Theo's engagement, his marriage, and the birth of his first child. In each case, Vincent was threatened by the prospect of loss. Furthermore, van Gogh had previously injured himself in response to emotional loss. In 1881, he visited the home of a woman he loved. Her parents refused to let van Gogh see her. He thrust his hand into the flame of a lamp and said "Let me see her for as long as I can keep my hand in the flame." They blew out the lamp and sent him away. This incident makes it seem more likely that van Gogh's self-mutilation was influenced by the perceived loss of love from his brother.

Clinical and personality psychologists often use *case studies* to develop and test theories. Effective use of the case study method requires not only the formulation of explanations consistent with the evidence, but also that explanations be critically examined in light of all available evidence. Implausible alternatives will be eliminated; more than one plausible explanation may remain.

| TABLE 11.2 A portion of a structured interview on drug abuse |
| --- |

**Cardinal Question**

1. Have you ever used pot, speed, heroin, or any other drugs to make yourself feel good?

**Social Significance Questions**

2. Have drugs ever caused you problems in your life?
3. Have drugs ever interfered with your school life, your work, or your job?
4. Have drugs ever caused you problems with your family or caused your family to worry about you?
5–8. (Related social significance questions)

**Auxiliary Questions**

Did you use any of the following drugs fairly regularly for at least six months at a time:

9–15. ("Uppers," "downers," pot, narcotics, pain killers, hallucinogens, and tranquilizers are inquired about.)
16. Have you ever used two or more different street drugs fairly regularly to get high?
17. Have there been times when you stayed high or "stoned" on drugs throughout most of the day?
18. Have you ever really wanted to cut down or completely stop taking a drug but found that you couldn't?
19–24. (Additional questions about physical and psychological consequences of heavy drug use.)

**Time Profile Questions**

25. How old were you when drugs first caused you any problems?
26. How old were you when drugs last caused you any problems?
27. Have you experienced any problems because of drugs in the past month?
28. Have you experienced any problems because of drugs in the last two years?

Interviews provide information about a wide range of behaviors in a relatively short time. Interviewers may choose to provide some structure to the interview if they have some idea of what to look for in an interviewee's behavior or history. This being so, interviewers may ask specific questions designed to elicit information on some aspect of the individual's personality or behavior (the way the person handles anger, his or her reaction to frustration, or his or her history of emotional disturbance). The interviewee then responds at whatever length and in whatever way he or she chooses.

Table 11.2 lists some of the questions asked in a structured diagnostic interview widely used to elicit information about possible drug abuse.

## Projective Tests of Personality

Projective tests of personality were developed by psychoanalysts as a means of uncovering unconscious determinants of behavior. **Projective tests** *consist of ambiguous stimuli, such as drawings or inkblots, that lend themselves to many possible interpretations.* Projective tests are based on the Freudian ego defense mechanism of projection. They permit the subject to *project* his or her thoughts, fantasies, feelings, and beliefs onto the intentionally ambiguous test stimuli.

The **Rorschach Inkblot Test,** *the most widely-used projective test, consists of a series of ten cards, each of which contains a design made from inkblots.* The test was developed in 1921 by the Swiss psychiatrist Hermann Rorschach. Each card is presented to the subject, one at a time; the subject is asked to respond by telling what he thinks the blot resembles (figure 11.6).

The Thematic Apperception Test, invented by psychologists Henry Murray and Christina Morgan in 1935, is another widely used projective test (figure 11.7). As discussed in chapter 8, the **Thematic Apperception Test (TAT)** *requires the subject to tell stories about a variety of pictures of people, places, and things.*

According to those who use these tests, the subject provides the examiner with insight into unconscious or forgotten dynamics of personality. Unfortunately, both the reliability and validity of projective tests remain a problem.

## Objective Tests of Personality

Objective tests are designed to confront the troubling problems of the unreliability of observational and projective measures of personality. The administration, scoring, and interpretation of these tests are usually more reliable. Detailed instructions accompany the test; the assumption is made that clinicians who use them will follow the instructions very carefully.

Figure 11.8, the Minnesota Multiphasic Personality Inventory (MMPI), an objective test of personality developed in 1940 by psychologists Starke R. Hathaway and John C. McKinley, and revised in 1989 by James Butcher and colleagues, is probably the most widely used personality measure. The test is employed by personality psychologists who use it to provide information on the relative weightings persons give to different aspects of their behavior, and by clinical psychologists who employ it to help make diagnostic judgments about psychiatric patients.

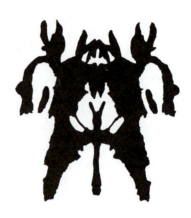

**Figure 11.6**   *The Rorschach inkblot test.*

**Figure 11.7**   *Thematic apperception test example.*

*The MMPI requires direct self-reports of beliefs, feelings, attitudes, and self-perceptions for information on past, present, and future behavior.* The person being tested completes a booklet containing 567 statements; he or she judges whether or not each statement applies to him or her. For example, "I wake up fresh and rested most mornings." The individual's pattern of responses is compared directly to response norms gathered from groups of both psychiatric patients and normal individuals. The ten clinical scales of the MMPI provide data on the extent to which a subject's behavior in ten different areas conforms to test patterns shown by the normal and psychiatric groups on whom the test was validated. Among the 10 scales of MMPI and MMPI-2 are Depression, Masculinity-Femininity, Paranoia, and Social Introversion.

The revision of the test, MMPI-2, has not been available long enough to undergo extensive evaluation. Among criticisms of the original MMPI was its use of items about religion and morality. These have been altered in MMPI-2. For the initial version of the test, the precise nature of relationships between patterns of responding and psychiatric diagnoses was uncertain (Graham & Strenger, 1988; Morey, Waugh, & Blashfield, 1985).

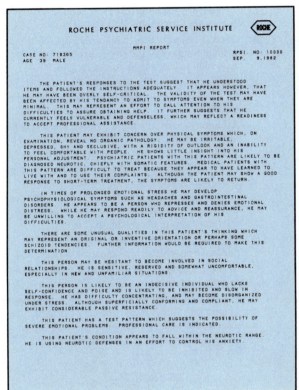
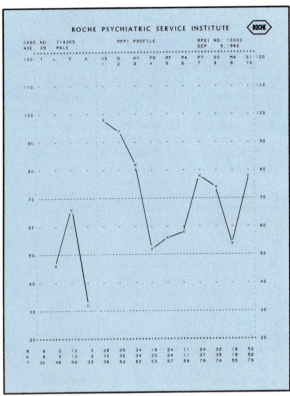

**Figure 11.8** *Sample MMPI report.*
Source: Roche Psychiatric Service Institute.

# SUMMARY

I. Personality is expressed through behavior. The ultimate goal of personality theory and research is the understanding and prediction of behavior. (p. 346)

A. State theories of personality explain behavior and personality as being the result of environmental influences. (p. 346)

B. Trait theories of personality stress the influence of enduring traits on behavior. (p. 346)

C. Five primary personality traits have been called the "big five": emotional stability, extroversion, openness to experience, agreeableness, and conscientiousness. (p. 346)

II. There are two basic tenets of psychoanalytic theory. (p. 347)

A. The principle of psychic determinism states that nothing occurs by chance in the human mind. (p. 347)

B. There are unconscious causes of behavior of which the individual is probably unaware. (p. 347)

C. The psychic structure consists of three components. (pp. 348–349)

   1. The *id,* the earliest part of the psychic apparatus to develop, is the reservoir of primitive drives and impulses. (p. 348)

   2. The *ego,* which develops later, is the part of the psychic structure that interprets external reality to the id and forces it to adjust to external reality. (p. 348)

   3. The *superego,* which develops last, functions as a conscience, or internalized set of parents who convey society's rules to the growing child. (pp. 348–349)

D. During the *oral, anal, phallic, latency,* and *genital* stages of psychosexual development, successive parts of the body are invested with libido. In the process, important psychological and interpersonal lessons associated with those bodily parts are learned. (pp. 349–350)

E. Even strong egos have to adopt strategies to defend themselves against excessive id or superego demands. Two of the most common strategies are *fixation* and *regression.* (p. 351)

III. Groups of *neo-Freudian theorists* have deviated from Freud's classical psychoanalytic theory. (pp. 353–355)

   A. Jung and Adler were members of Freud's inner circle who rejected the emphasis he placed on infantile psychosexuality. (p. 353)

   B. Another group of neo-Freudian theorists, including Horney, Fromm, and Erikson, emphasized the effects of culture and society on personality development. (pp. 353–355)

IV. *Learning theories* assume that most of human behavior and personality are learned. (p. 355)

   A. *Classical conditioning mechanisms* are thought to account for most of the emotional learning humans do, according to learning theorists. (p. 355–356)

   B. *Operant conditioning mechanisms* are responsible for much of our social and interpersonal behavior. (p. 356)

   C. According to social learning theory, *observational learning* refers to how people acquire behavior by watching others engage in the same behaviors. (p. 356)

V. *Humanistic theories of personality* emphasize the significance and uniqueness of the individual. (p. 358)

   A. *Rogers' person-centered theory* assumes that personality derives from the individual's own perceptions and interpretations of the world. (p. 358)

   B. *Maslow's hierarchy of needs* shows the path individuals must take to achieve self-actualization. (pp. 358–359)

   C. *Frankl's existential theory* focuses on the individual's search for meaning in life. (pp. 359–360)

VI. *Personality assessment procedures* include observation techniques, interviews, projective tests (including the Rorschach and the TAT), and objective tests (including the MMPI). In general, the more structured the test is, the more reliable it is. (pp. 361–364)

---

# ACTION GLOSSARY

Match the terms in the left column with the definitions in the right column.

___ 1. **Personality (p. 346)**
___ 2. **States (p. 346)**
___ 3. **Traits (p. 346)**
___ 4. **Emotional stability, openness to experience, agreeableness (p. 346)**
___ 5. **Psychic determinism (p. 347)**
___ 6. **Unconscious (p. 347)**
___ 7. **Primary process (p. 347)**
___ 8. **Id (p. 348)**

A. *A reservoir of primitive drives and desires untouched and unaffected by contact with the real world and its civilizing effects.*

B. *The principle that no behavior occurs by chance, that every psychological event is determined by events preceding it.*

C. *Immediate environmental influences.*

D. *A primitive, immature way of thinking that is not yet modified by society's rules or altered by the child's wish to conform.*

E. *The traits, values, attitudes, physical and intellectual attributes, social skills, and interpersonal experiences that distinguish one person from another, help predict his or her behavior in new settings, and give some continuity to behavior.*

F. *Among the five primary personality traits.*

G. *Enduring personal attributes like emotional stability, agreeableness, and conscientiousness.*

H. *The part of the individual's mental world that cannot be brought into consciousness by effort of will.*

___ 9. **Pleasure principle (p. 348)**
___ 10. **Reality principle (p. 348)**
___ 11. **Ego (p. 348)**
___ 12. **Superego (pp. 348–349)**
___ 13. **Life instinct (p. 349)**
___ 14. **Death instinct (p. 349)**
___ 15. **Libido (p. 349)**
___ 16. **Oral stage (p. 349)**
___ 17. **Anal stage (p. 349)**
___ 18. **Phallic stage (p. 350)**

A. *The psychological energy that comes from instincts and energizes the parts of the body involved in the successive stages of psychosexual development.*
B. *The third stage of psychosexual development. Centers on concerns about the size and function of the genitals.*
C. *That part of the psychic apparatus that helps the id adjust to external reality by modifying its impulses so they conform to society's moral and ethical rules.*
D. *The first stage of psychosexual development. Gratification is focused on activity surrounding the lips, tongue, and mouth.*
E. *The second stage of psychosexual development. Gratification is focused on controlling the eliminations of waste products from the body.*
F. *That part of the psychic apparatus that reflects parental and societal rules and expectations.*
G. *The aggressive drives and impulses that are a part of the id.*
H. *The sexual impulses and drives that reside in the id.*
I. *The aim that guides ego functioning.*
J. *The aim that guides the id to derive as much pleasure as possible from its actions.*

___ 19. **Latency period (p. 350)**
___ 20. **Genital stage (p. 350)**
___ 21. **Defense mechanisms (p. 350)**
___ 22. **Repression (p. 350)**
___ 23. **Fixation (p. 351)**
___ 24. **Regression (p. 351)**
___ 25. **Introversion-Extroversion (p. 353)**

A. *A defense mechanism by which the individual remains in a particular psychosexual stage because his/her development is interfered with.*
B. *Involuntarily burying a threatening idea in the unconscious.*
C. *A defense mechanism by which the individual returns to an earlier, less mature stage of development.*
D. *The stage of psychosexual development during which the adolescent learns about adult sexuality.*
E. *Personality trait first proposed by Jung.*
F. *Strategies that the ego uses to prevent the forces of the id and superego from seeking expression in harmful behaviors.*
G. *A stage of psychosexual development during which there is a consolidation of the psychological and social lessons learned and the behaviors acquired during earlier stages.*

___ 26. **Suppression (p. 350)**
___ 27. **Denial (p. 351)**
___ 28. **Reaction formation (p. 351)**
___ 29. **Sublimation (p. 351)**
___ 30. **Rationalization (p. 352)**
___ 31. **Displacement (p. 352)**

A. *Avoiding painful experiences and thoughts by denying they exist.*
B. *The psychoanalytic process of transferring psychological energy associated with unconscious desires and impulses into socially accepted, often creative, activities, such as painting, composing, or hard work.*
C. *An ego defense mechanism in which the individual attributes an unacceptable feeling or impulse to an undeserving person.*
D. *The deliberate decision to keep material from entering consciousness.*
E. *The ego defense mechanism that permits people to give a logical or intellectual explanation for a behavior whose motivation may be embarrassing, obscure, or irrational.*
F. *The process by which people replace a particularly unpleasant feeling about someone or something with the opposite feeling.*

___ 32. **Humanistic theory (p. 358)**
___ 33. **Hierarchy of needs (p. 358)**
___ 34. **Self-actualize (p. 359)**
___ 35. **Existential theory (p. 359)**
___ 36. **Rorschach Ink Blot Test (p. 363)**
___ 37. **Minnesota Multiphasic Personality Inventory (MMPI) (p. 364)**
___ 38. **Self-efficacy (p. 357)**

A. *A projective test of personality consisting of ten ambiguous designs made from inkblots. When shown the designs, the subject is asked to respond by telling what he or she thinks the designs resemble.*
B. *Emphasizes the significance of the individual, his or her uniqueness and singularity.*
C. *To achieve one's greatest potential; to reach the top of the hierarchy of needs.*
D. *Emphasizes the importance, legitimacy, and value of differences among people as well as their potential for enhancement of maximum human potential.*
E. *An objective test of personality functioning that requires self-reports of beliefs, feelings, attitudes, and self-perceptions.*
F. *Bandura's term for an individual's belief in the ability to perform behavior necessary to produce a desired outcome.*
G. *According to Maslow, the structure of needs leading to self-actualization.*

___ **39. Collective unconscious**
  (p. 353)

___ **40. Archetypes (p. 353)**

___ **41. Learned helplessness**
  (p. 356)

___ **42. Pessimistic explanatory**
  **style (p. 357)**

___ **43. Person-centered theory of**
  **personality (p. 358)**

___ **44. Projective tests (p. 363)**

___ **45. Thematic Apperception**
  **Test (p. 363)**

___ **46. Logotherapy (p. 360)**

A. *An operant-based theory of depression that states that depression is a consequence of exposure to unavoidable events.*
B. *A projective test that requires the subject to tell stories about a variety of pictures of people, places, and things.*
C. *Ambiguous stimuli that are subject to many possible interpretations.*
D. *Carl Rogers' belief that personality derives from the individual's perceptions and interpretations of his or her world.*
E. *Based on the idea that each individual must search for a personal meaning in life.*
F. *A depository or reservoir of people's racial and cultural history, according to Jung.*
G. *The tendency to see the causes of bad events as stable, global, and internal.*
H. *Unconscious representations of familiar cultural figures.*

*ANSWERS*

1. c, 2. c, 3. g, 4. f, 5. b, 6. h, 7. d, 8. a, 9. j, 10. i, 11. c, 12. f, 13. h, 14. g, 15. a, 16. d, 17. e, 18. b, 19. g, 20. g, 21. f, 22. b, 23. a, 24. c, 25. e, 26. d, 27. a, 28. f, 29. b, 30. e, 31. c, 32. b, 33. g, 34. c, 35. d, 36. a, 37. e, 38. f, 39. f, 40. h, 41. a, 42. g, 43. d, 44. c, 45. b, 46. e

---

# SELF-TEST

**1.** Personality is expressed through
  **(a)** thoughts.
  **(b)** feelings.
  **(c)** behavior.
  **(d)** test scores.
  (LO 1; p. 346)

**2.** The goal of personality theory and research is
  **(a)** understanding and prediction of behavior.
  **(b)** control of behavior.
  **(c)** modification of behavior.
  **(d)** description of behavior.
  (LO 1; p. 346)

**3.** Personality theories that define personality largely as a product of environmental factors are called
  **(a)** trait theories.
  **(b)** state theories.
  **(c)** environmental theories.
  **(d)** sociocultural theories.
  (LO 2; p. 346)

**4.** Trait theories of personality explain behavior as a function of
  **(a)** the environment.
  **(b)** drives and impulses within the individual.
  **(c)** enduring forces within the individual.
  **(d)** societal rules and regulations.
  (LO 2; p. 346)

**5.** Statistical analyses reveal five primary personality traits. Which of the following is *not* one of them?
  **(a)** emotional stability
  **(b)** anxiety
  **(c)** openness to experience
  **(d)** conscientiousness
  (LO 2; p. 346)

**6.** The two basic concepts of Freud's psychoanalytic theory are the principles of
  **(a)** psychic determinism and ego development.
  **(b)** psychosexual development and the unconscious.
  **(c)** fixation and regression.
  **(d)** psychic determinism and the unconscious.
  (LO 3; p. 347)

**7.** The three components of psychic structure are the
  **(a)** oral, anal, and phallic stages.
  **(b)** ego, id, and superego.
  **(c)** oral, anal, genital stages.
  **(d)** ego, superego, and libido.
  (LO 4; p. 348)

**8.** Which of the following is *not* one of the five stages of psychosexual development?
  **(a)** anal
  **(b)** phallic
  **(c)** latency
  **(d)** Oedipal
  (LO 5; pp. 349–350)

9. Fixation and regression are

    (a) syndromes of mental disorder.
    (b) signs of weak ego functioning.
    (c) derived from the superego.
    (d) ego defense mechanisms.
    (LO 6; p. 351)

10. The neo-Freudians include

    (a) Rorschach and Murray.
    (b) Frankl, Laing, and May.
    (c) Jung, Adler, and Horney.
    (d) Rogers and Maslow.
    (LO 7; p. 353)

11. The neo-Freudians objected to Freud's emphasis on

    (a) childhood aggression.
    (b) infantile psychosexuality.
    (c) the unconscious.
    (d) fixation and regression.
    (LO 7; p. 353)

12. Horney, Fromm, and Erickson emphasized the effects of

    (a) culture and society on personality development.
    (b) sex and aggression on personality development.
    (c) infantile psychological trauma on personality development.
    (d) World War II on behavior.
    (LO 7; pp. 353–354)

13. The social learning theorists assume that most human behavior is

    (a) ultimately forgotten.
    (b) learned by operant and classical mechanisms.
    (c) unconscious.
    (d) acquired by observational learning.
    (LO 8; p. 356)

14. The existential/humanistic theories of personality emphasize

    (a) our inhumanity to others.
    (b) our similarity to others.
    (c) our essential uniqueness.
    (d) our need to learn.
    (LO 9; pp. 358–359)

15. Carl Rogers' theory of personality is called the

    (a) other focused theory of personality.
    (b) humanistic theory of personality.
    (c) individualized theory of personality.
    (d) person-centered theory of personality.
    (LO 9; p. 358)

16. At the bottom of Abraham Maslow's hierarchy of needs are needs for

    (a) self-actualization.
    (b) food and water.
    (c) warmth and human understanding.
    (d) sex and aggression.
    (LO 9; p. 358)

17. Viktor Frankl's existential theory, and its psychotherapy (called logotherapy) emphasize:

    (a) the search for happiness.
    (b) the search for status.
    (c) the search for meaning.
    (d) self-actualization.
    (LO 9; p. 360)

18. Theories of personality differ in their emphases. They also differ in:

    (a) complexity.
    (b) accessibility to empirical validation.
    (c) breadth of explanation.
    (d) All of the above.
    (LO 10; p. 360)

19. The Rorschach and the TAT are

    (a) neo-Freudian theorists.
    (b) structured tests of personality.
    (c) projective tests of personality.
    (d) objective tests of personality rarely used nowadays.
    (LO 11; p. 363)

20. A reliable test

    (a) accurately predicts behavior.
    (b) is not useful for research purposes.
    (c) is likely to be unstructured.
    (d) is likely to be structured.
    (LO 11; p. 363)

*ANSWERS*

1. c, 2. a, 3. b, 4. c, 5. b, 6. d, 7. b, 8. d, 9. d, 10. c, 11. b, 12. a, 13. d, 14. c, 15. d, 16. b, 17. c, 18. d, 19. c, 20. d

# THINKING ABOUT PSYCHOLOGY

1. There is little empirical support for psychoanalytic theories. Why, then, are they still to be found in personality and clinical psychology?

2. Describe two individuals whom you know in terms of their differences on the "big five" traits of personality.

# SUGGESTED READINGS

Frankl, V. (1962). *Man's search for meaning.* Boston: Beacon. Frankl's experiences as a prisoner in a concentration camp led him to formulate a humanistic theory of personality and psychotherapy based on the individual's need to find a personal meaning in life.

Freud, S. (1966). *The psychopathology of everyday life.* New York: Norton. An entertaining book about common behavioral and memory mistakes and minor difficulties that presumably stem from unconscious impulses and conflicts.

Fromm, Erich. (1941). *Escape from freedom.* New York: Holt, Rinehart & Winston. In this classic study of the effects on behavior of the multitude of choices urban society presents modern men and women, Fromm makes a convincing case for one of its effects: the ready acceptance of the totalitarian system of government, which removes the necessity for decision making from its citizenry.

Kaminer, Wendy. (1992). *I'm dysfunctional, you're dysfunctional.* Reading, MA: Addison-Wesley. A critique of self-help programs and popular therapeutic movements.

Sayers, J. (1991). *Mothering psychoanalysis.* London: Hamish Hamilton. About the women—Helene Deutsch, Anna Freud, Karen Horney, and Melanie Klein—influential in the early development of psychoanalysis.

# CHAPTER 12

## ABNORMAL PSYCHOLOGY
### OUTLINE

# ABNORMAL PSYCHOLOGY
## LEARNING OBJECTIVES

**After reading this chapter, you should be able to**

▶ **1.** recount important events in the history of society's efforts to diagnose, treat, and prevent abnormal behavior. *(pp. 374–377)*

▶ **2.** offer alternative definitions of abnormal behavior. *(pp. 377–378)*

▶ **3.** describe "the psychoanalytic revolution." *(p. 378)*

▶ **4.** identify the most important similarities and differences between *DSM-III-R* and its predecessors. *(pp. 378–379)*

▶ **5.** recognize some limitations of *DSM-III-R.* *(p. 380)*

▶ **6.** distinguish between acute and chronic organic mental disorders, and identify some of the causes of these central nervous system dysfunctions. *(pp. 380–381)*

▶ **7.** categorize the behavioral and psychological effects of drug and alcohol abuse and dependence. *(p. 381)*

▶ **8.** list and describe the serious defects in cognitive, perceptual, and affective functioning of patients with schizophrenia. *(pp. 381–384)*

▶ **9.** discuss the relationship between depression and suicide. *(p. 386)*

▶ **10.** detail the diverse nonpsychotic disorders formerly called neuroses. *(pp. 386–388)*

▶ **11.** describe and discuss the sexual disorders. *(pp. 388–389)*

▶ **12.** discuss the deeply ingrained patterns of behavior termed the personality disorders. *(p. 389)*

▶ **13.** describe the major childhood disorders, particularly learning disabilities and childhood autism. *(p. 390)*

Joyce Brown was a forty-year-old single black woman who had been living on the streets of an affluent Manhattan neighborhood for a year and a half. On October 28, 1987, she was taken from the streets to Bellevue Hospital's emergency room and admitted to the special unit for the homeless. She refused treatment and demanded to be returned to the streets. City and hospital authorities rejected her demand, and legal hearings followed.

Was Joyce Brown homeless because she was poor or because she was mentally ill? Should we praise the efforts of the city of New York to remove her from her debased circumstances, or should we support Joyce Brown's individual rights to be free from interference by government? Lawyers for the city and their psychiatric experts argued that Miss Brown had schizophrenia, was delusional, and required hospitalization because she represented a danger to herself by virtue of self-neglect, provocative behavior, and suicidal impulses. Miss Brown's lawyers, who were members of the New York Civil Liberties Union and their psychiatric consultants asserted that Miss Brown did not have a serious mental illness, but was a "professional street person" whose difficulties on the street were a natural part of being homeless. They pointed to her ability to survive on the streets without harming herself or others. Ultimately the courts upheld Miss Brown's right to refuse medical treatment based primarily on her rational and lucid testimony (Cournos, 1989).

The case of Joyce Brown raises many questions with which this chapter is concerned, questions about the nature of abnormal behavior and mental illness, about our attitudes toward people who manifest abnormal behavior or are diagnosed as mentally ill, about appropriate treatment, and other ethical issues confronting mental health professionals.

# DEFINING ABNORMALITY

## Abnormal Behavior and "Mental Illness" Throughout History

What is considered "mental illness" has not always been considered either mental or an illness. Before science and medicine were charged with the responsibility for defining and treating mental illness, there were other quite different views (Foucault, 1965; Rosen, 1968; Szasz, 1961) (table 12.1).

## TABLE 12.1  Early events in the history of psychiatry and the treatment of mental illness

*ca. 5000 B.C. Egypt, Babylonia*

Mental illness was attributed to evil spirits. Holes were drilled into the skull to release them, a practice called "trephining."

*ca. 2600 B.C. China*

Some evidence exists that faith healing was used to treat mental illness. By 1140 B.C., institutions for the insane were established.

*ca. 500 B.C. Greece*

Pythagoras proposed that mental illness was a disease of the brain. (And you thought he was only interested in triangles.)

*4th century B.C. Greece*

Plato proposed that mental disorder was partly physical, partly moral, and partly divine.

Alexander the Great established sanitoriums for the mentally ill where exercise, work, and entertainment were provided.

*2nd century A.D. Rome*

Galen refined the "humoral theory" of bodily fluids (see text), which was to prevail for the next 1000 years.

*15th century Europe*

Vagrants and the insane were set adrift on "ships of fools."

*1547 England*

The former monastery of St. Mary of Bethlehem is converted to a mental hospital. The inhumane treatment there gave rise to the word "bedlam."

*1487 Germany*

Two Dominican monks, Jacob Sprenger and Heinrich Kraemer, receive Papal authority to write *Malleus Maleficarum (The Witches' Hammer),* which tells how to identify witches.

*1568 Spain*

The Spanish Inquisition declares the entire population of the Netherlands to be heretics and condemns it to death.

*16th–17th centuries France*

Humane treatment of mentally ill is instituted. St. Vincent de Paul argued that mental disease was in no way different from physical disease.

The belief that mental disorder is caused by supernatural forces, like devils and evil spirits, has been an influential one. It reached its peak in Europe and America in the sixteenth and seventeenth centuries. Believing that all those who suffered from mental disorder had sinned and hence "deserved" their affliction and its consequences justified widespread efforts by the church of the Middle Ages to curb mental disorder by exorcizing or otherwise destroying the evil spirits that presumably caused it. Witch-hunts were influenced particularly by *Malleus*

## TABLE 12.1 (Continued)

*1631 Germany*

Friedrich von Spee, a Jesuit priest, published *Precautions for Prisoners,* an attempt to curb witch-hunting.

*1676 France*

Louis XIII establishes a general hospital in every city in France. They were to confine "the debauched, blasphemers, libertines. . . . We leave it to medical archaeology to determine whether or not a man was sick, criminal, or insane."

*1689 United States*

Cotton Mather publishes *Memorable Providences Relating Witchcraft and Possessions,* which set the stage for the Salem witch-hunts and trials.

*1700 United States*

Robert Calef published a rebuttal to Cotton Mather. Cotton's father, the president of Harvard College, helped get the book censored.

*1716 England*

The theory that masturbation causes insanity is single-handedly initiated with the publication of *Onania, or the Heinous Sin of Self-Pollution.*

*1752 United States*

Benjamin Rush, the "father of American psychiatry," uses a medical conception of mental illness. Pennsylvania Hospital becomes the first United States institution to receive mental patients.

*1773 United States*

The Williamsburg (Virginia) Asylum is the first American institution devoted exclusively to the care of the mentally ill.

*1780 France*

Franz Anton Mesmer claims to cure disorders with magnetism.

*1793 France*

Phillipe Pinel introduces the practice of keeping case histories of mental patients and of training asylum personnel.

*1796 England*

William Tuke, with the help of the Society of Friends, established the first asylum for the mentally ill, in York. The first training program for psychiatric nurses began at York.

*1840 United States*

Dorothea Dix begins her United States campaign for humanitarian treatment of the mentally ill. As a result, many states pass laws prohibiting confinement of the insane in jails.

*1840 Germany*

Rudolf Virchow said epidemic disease was a result of social and cultural maladjustment.

Wilhelm Griesinger emphasizes the disease theory in *Pathology and Therapy of Mental Illness.*

*1840 England*

Daniel McNaghten first uses insanity as a defense against attempted murder.

*1854 United States*

The Massachusetts Commission on Lunacy states that "Insanity is a part and parcel of poverty; and wherever that involves any considerable number of persons, this disease is manifested."

*1880 Germany*

Jozef Breuer successfully treats "hysteria" using hypnosis.

*1883 Germany*

Emil Kraepelin presents a classification of mental illness in which he coins the terms "dementia praecox" (later renamed "schizophrenia" by Eugen Bleuler) and "manic-depression."

*1895 Vienna*

Breuer and Freud publish *Studies in Hysteria,* which forms the basis for psychoanalysis.

*1890–1905 France*

Important theories of hysteria and hypnosis are proposed by Jean-Martin Charcot, Hippolyte Bernheim (we are not making these up), and Pierre Janet.

*1906 United States*

Morton Prince founded the *Journal of Abnormal and Social Psychology* (which in 1965 became two journals, *Journal of Abnormal Psychology* and the *Journal of Personality and Social Psychology).* Prince believed that learning played an important role in mental illness.

*1908 United States*

Clifford Beers publishes *A Mind that Found Itself,* describing his experiences as a mental patient. The book stimulated public interest in improving conditions in mental institutions.

*1920s–1930s Europe*

Members of Freud's "Vienna Circle" split with Freud to establish their own theories of personality and psychotherapy. Among them were Alfred Adler, Erich Fromm, Karen Horney, Carl Jung, and Harry Stack Sullivan. These "neo-Freudians" emphasized social and cultural factors in personality, and minimized the role of a purely sexual libido as the sole source of psychological energy (see chapter 11).

*1939 Germany*

With the outbreak of war, Hitler orders the implementation of a "euthanasia program." The first gas chambers are built in mental hospitals and the gassing of mental patients begins.

*1950 United States*

John Dollard and Neal Miller publish *Personality and Psychotherapy,* in which learning theory is applied to psychoanalysis.

*1952 United States*

Tranquilizing drugs are introduced into psychiatric practice. These drugs lead to a new discipline, "psychopharmacology."

*United States*

Congress enacts the McCarran Act which provides that "aliens afflicted with a psychopathic personality are to be excluded from admission into the United States."

**Figure 12.1**   *Philippe Pinel freeing the insane from their chains*

*Maleficarum (The Witches' Hammer),* a book written by two Dominican brothers in 1487. The book "proved" that sin and mental disorder were linked. Between the fifteenth and seventeenth centuries, as many as 100,000 people, most of them poor old women, were executed as witches.

As the influence of the church began to wane and science ascended in public esteem, talk of witchcraft and the devil became less acceptable. Yet deviant behavior persisted. Rather than attributing it to the work of the devil, abnormal behavior was discussed in more rational terms; it was seen as the result of illness or mental disease. Poor old women were no longer thought to be witches, but wretches caught in the throes of mental disease, and were treated as other sick people in hospitals (Spanos, 1978).

*Pinel's Reforms*   The French and American revolutions toward the close of the eighteenth century coincided with a new sense of human dignity and social responsibility throughout the western world. This wave of humanism led to the establishment of mental hospitals designed to offer both refuge and humane treatment to those for whom there had previously been no safe haven. In 1793, Philippe Pinel, a French physician, was made physician-in-chief at Bicetre, a Paris hospital for psychotics. Believing that his charges deserved treatment for their disorder rather than punishment for their sins, he ordered removal of the chains with which most of the patients had been bound (figure 12.1). Later, Pinel expanded his reform efforts by requiring

attendants to provide humane treatment to their patients. Pinel's reforms in Paris gradually spread throughout Europe and America. Influenced by Pinel, Dorothea Dix humanized psychiatric hospitals in the United States in the 1840s and led a movement that ultimately prohibited imprisonment of the insane in the United States.

*The Medical Model of Mental Illness*   Some early cultures viewed abnormal behavior as the result of natural, rather than supernatural forces. As early as the seventh century B.C., Chinese physicians concluded that abnormal behavior was a natural phenomenon. An imbalance of the two essential human forces, yin and yang, resulted in physical or mental illness; yin and yang in balance assured health. This view of a proper balance mirrors that of Hippocrates, the Greek "father of medicine." Writing in the fourth century B.C., Hippocrates considered mental disorder to be the result of brain disease. Specifically, he believed it to be the product of an imbalance of the four essential fluids or "humors"—blood, phlegm, yellow bile, and black bile. Depending on the nature of the imbalance, **mania** *(extreme excitement),* **melancholia** *(depression),* or **phrenitis** *(schizophrenia)* was the result.

As more humane psychiatric hospitals followed Pinel's reforms, better records of these patients began to be kept. As a consequence, systematic efforts to classify and categorize mental disorder began. German physicians in the latter half of the nineteenth century, about sixty years after Pinel's reforms, led this effort. Three different German physicians described serious **psychoses,** *disorders typically involving hallucinations, delusions, and bizarre behaviors.* In 1883, Emil Kraepelin, concluded that these observers were all describing variations of a disorder he labeled "dementia praecox." Shortly thereafter, that disorder was renamed "schizophrenia" by the Swiss psychiatrist Eugen Bleuler. Its description as a single disorder (caused by damage to the central nervous system, according to Kraepelin) with several subtypes constituted an important diagnostic advance. Kraepelin was also centrally involved in the classification of **organic brain disorders,** *disorders of the central nervous system that* *have behavioral consequences,* and **bipolar affective disorders,** *extreme and uncontrollable mood swings.*

Today the most prevalent view of mental illness is medical. We speak of mental illness, psychiatric hospitals, symptoms, diagnoses, and treatment or therapy. This model aims to be scientific, but it is not without its critics. For example, "labeling theory" argues that mental illness or psychopathology is a socially constructed label that is applied to individuals who violate certain social norms (Scheff, 1966). Once a person is labeled mentally ill, it becomes virtually impossible to shed the social stereotype of a mentally ill person, as illustrated in a study by David Rosenhan (1973).

Rosenhan had eight normal people gain admission to nearly a dozen psychiatric facilities. (At least they were as sane as three psychologists, a psychology graduate student, a pediatrician, a psychiatrist, a painter, and a housewife tend to be.) After making an appointment at the hospital, the eight pseudopatients complained of hearing voices that said "empty," "hollow," and "thud." Beyond stating these symptoms and using a fictitious name, employer, and vocation, the pseudopatients presented factual information about themselves. All were admitted, most with a diagnosis of schizophrenia. Once admission was gained, they ceased simulating any symptoms and now tried to convince the staff that they were sane and should be released.

The length of hospitalization ranged from seven to fifty-two days, with an average of nineteen days. During their hospitalization, the eight pseudopatients were given close to 2100 pills, nearly all of which were, like much medication given to other patients, pocketed, or deposited in the toilet. Rosenhan concludes from this study that our ability to diagnose insanity and sanity is unreliable.

## Definitions of Abnormal Behavior

What does it mean to say that someone's behavior or thinking is "abnormal"? As we saw above, conceptions of mental illness and abnormal behavior change over time. There are at least five types of definition of abnormal behavior.

1. Normative: *Abnormal behavior is a violation of social norms.* When we ask how a society defines psychological abnormality, we are asking where that society draws the line between acceptable and unacceptable thought and behavior. Every human group lives by a set of **norms,** *shared definitions of desirable behavior.* Norms tell us what is "right" and "wrong."

The habitual violation of certain norms may be considered evidence of "psychopathology" or "mental illness" (Scheff, 1966; 1975). For example, an individual who talks to himself in public in a loud voice, or a woman who is more aggressive than most women, is violating unwritten social norms. These norm violations may be considered "symptoms" of an underlying mental disorder.

Once labeled "mentally ill," there is a strong social stigma, illustrated in a paper by Killian and Bloomberg (1975). One of the authors, a prominent sociologist, was admitted to a "therapeutic community."

> In spite of years of study of social psychology, all my professional sophistication vanished now. "Insane" was only the worst of the frightening words that flashed through my disordered mind. "Institutionalized," "psychiatric ward," "mentally ill," "deviant," are only a few of the others that I can remember. Not only did I know that, in terms of what we sociologists call "labeling theory," my friends would hereafter perceive me differently; I was already experiencing the pain of a new self-definition. Just the day before I had gotten my driver's license renewed. One of the questions on the application had been, "Have you ever been hospitalized for mental illness?" Never again would I be able to answer "No" to this question. The realization was devastating (pp. 42–43).

The problem with using norms as the criteria for judging psychopathology is that norms are arbitrary. They change from time to time and differ from one place to another.

2. Statistical: *Abnormal behavior is that which rarely occurs.* A second definition of abnormality is based on statistical information. Behavior is considered abnormal if it is rare. By this definition, "normal" is simply what most people do, and "abnormal behavior" is anything that very few people do.

The problem with a statistical definition of mental illness is that it does not specify which behaviors should be considered. Is Mary, whose favorite number is the highly unlikely $3^{-10}$, as mentally disturbed as Fran, who has just had the equally rare experience of seeing Elvis?

3. Subjective: *You're abnormal if you think you are.* The subjective view of mental illness assumes that if individuals are not content with their lives, if they are disturbed by their thoughts or behavior, then perhaps they require treatment. This is probably the most widely used approach in the case of the less severe psychological disorders. Most people in psychotherapy are there not because anyone has declared their behavior abnormal, but because they themselves are unsatisfied with their lives (Bootzin & Acocela, 1988).

The difficulty with the subjective view of abnormal behavior is that the same behavior pattern may cause different degrees of unhappiness in different people, or in the same people at different times. Is drinking alcoholic beverages classified as abnormal only if the drinker expresses dissatisfaction with drinking? People who see Elvis may not be unhappy, yet hallucinations and delusions may be symptoms that require attention.

4. Maladaptive: *Inability to meet the demands of life is abnormal.* If a person is unable to meet the demands of life—hold down a job, have satisfactory relationships with friends and family, deal with everyday matters—this is regarded as abnormal. Many professionals prefer this definition because it is flexible, and focuses on behavior relative to the individual's life circumstances.

   The main drawback to this definition is that, like the norm violation definition, it seems to favor individuals who conform, those who "fit in" well.

5. Ideal: *Failure to meet the criteria of an ideal personality is abnormal.* Several psychological theories describe an ideal, well-adjusted personality. Any deviation from this ideal is interpreted as abnormal to some degree. Since the ideal is difficult to achieve, most people are seen as being poorly or imperfectly adjusted.

One difficulty with this definition is that the person may have no particularly troubling psychological or behavioral symptoms, and yet be judged as in need of treatment.

So behavior may be identified as abnormal in a variety of ways, no one of which is without its difficulties. Widiger and Trull (1991) note that "The extent to which any particular person is mentally ill is only a matter of degree, type, and time of life." In practice, the judgment of abnormality, whether by professionals or by family and friends, is usually based on a combination of standards. The person's happiness, relation to social norms, and ability to cope, are all taken into account (Bootzin & Acocela, 1988).

## The Psychoanalytic Revolution

Shortly before the turn of the century, a book by two Austrian psychiatrists was about to launch the psychoanalytic revolution. It was to influence not only the treatment of psychiatric patients, but every aspect of human culture. In 1895 Jozef Breuer and Sigmund Freud published *Studies in Hysteria.* This book set forth the then-radical views that psychological factors could affect behavior in powerful ways. Furthermore, Freud and Breuer wrote that a "talking" treatment might be more effective for disordered behavior than the harsh physical treatments then in use, that behavior might be influenced by thought patterns, impulses, wishes, and desires of which the individual might be quite unaware. The basic features of psychoanalytic theories are presented in chapter 11, Personality.

▶ **GUIDED REVIEW** *Learning Objectives 1, 2, and 3*

1. Abnormal behavior has been recognized, categorized, and treated for _____.
2. Two conflicting views on the causes of mental disorder have been widely held. One saw mental disorder as the product of _____; the other believed it was caused by _____.
3. _____, published in 1487, marked the high point of the demonological, _____ view of the causes of mental disorder.
4. Shortly after the French and American revolutions, _____ humanized French psychiatric hospitals.
5. Following Pinel's reforms, the newly humane mental hospitals brought together enough patients for the first time to permit systematic efforts to _____ and _____ the mental disorders exhibited by the patients.
6. German physicians working in the latter half of the nineteenth century established the medical model of mental illness by systematizing the diagnosis of _____, setting this disorder off from what is now termed _____, and determining the physical etiology of several central nervous system (_____) disorders having behavioral consequences.
7. There are at least five ways to define abnormal behavior or mental illness. These are _____, _____, _____, _____, and _____.
8. The publication in 1895 of Breuer and Freud's _____ marked the formal beginning of the _____ movement and proceeded to revolutionize theory and research on etiology and treatment of the mental disorders.

*ANSWERS*

*1. many centuries 2. supernatural forces, natural agents 3. The Witches' Hammer, supernatural 4. Philippe Pinel 5. classify, categorize 6. schizophrenia, bipolar affective disorder, organic 7. normative, statistical, subjective, maladaptive, ideal 8. Studies in Hysteria, psychoanalytic*

# CLASSIFYING PSYCHOLOGICAL DISORDERS

## *Diagnostic and Statistical Manual of Mental Disorders: DSM-III-R and DSM-IV*

Psychiatric diagnoses in clinical settings tend to follow the system developed by the American Psychiatric Association, the *Diagnostic and Statistical Manual of Mental Disorders (DSM).* The latest version, *DSM-III-R,* was published in 1987. DSM-IV is to be published in 1993.

# APPLYING PSYCHOLOGY

## Freud's Visit to America

In October 1909 Sigmund Freud paid his only visit to the United States. The occasion was the celebration of the twentieth anniversary of Clark University in Worcester, Massachusetts. The organizer of the event, and the person who extended the invitation to Freud and his Swiss colleague Carl Jung, was Clark's president, G. Stanley Hall. Hall was the founder and first president of the American Psychological Association and the first person in America to receive a Ph.D. in psychology (from Harvard, 1878).

Freud was fifty-three when he arrived here in 1909 and was neither widely known nor highly regarded (Fowler, 1991). His book, *The Interpretation of Dreams,* was published in 1899 and sold only a few hundred copies. Freud had been denied promotion at his medical school for seventeen years and was ignored by his European colleagues. But Hall had been impressed by Freud's publications and invited him to give a series of lectures at Clark. Freud and Jung stayed at Hall's home along with another guest, the great American philosopher and psychologist William James. What dinner conversations they must have had!

According to Raymond Fowler (1991), Freud lectured brilliantly for five days to a receptive audience of United States psychologists. Jung's lectures were also well received. This marked the first international recognition of psychoanalysis and was a major victory for Freud.

---

The four versions of the *Diagnostic and Statistical Manual* evolved gradually over a period of more than eighty years, with roots extending back to Kraepelin, Bleuler, and other nineteenth century German diagnosticians. As a result, all four manuals take a decidedly medical or "disease-model" approach to mental disorder. They categorize syndromes according to symptoms and they accept the existence of a disease process for most of their entries. The major diagnostic categories are shown in table 12.2.

*DSM-III-R* includes all conditions that regularly come to the attention of mental health professionals. *DSM-III-R* contains specific criteria for diagnosis. It includes the *essential features* of the disorder, those that define it. *Diagnostic criteria* are given: a list of symptoms that *must* be present for the patient to be given this diagnosis. *Differential criteria* are also provided; they tell how to distinguish this disorder from other, similar disorders.

The descriptions also offer information on the course of the disorder, the age at onset, complications involved, predisposing factors, prevalence, and sex ratio. *DSM-III-R* requires the diagnostician to give substantial information about patients on five different "axes," or areas of functioning.

*Axis I—Clinical syndrome:* the diagnostic label for the patient's most serious psychological problem, the problem for which the person is being diagnosed.

*Axis II—Personality disorders* (adult) or *developmental disorders* (children and adolescents): any accompanying long-term disorder not covered by the Axis I diagnosis.

*Axis III—Physical disorders:* any medical problem that may be relevant to the psychological problem.

*Axis IV—Psychosocial stressors:* current sources of stress (such as divorce, retirement, pregnancy) that may have contributed to the patient's psychological problem. The diagnostician notes whether the stressor is acute or enduring, and rate its severity on a scale of 1 to 6.

*Axis V—Global assessment of functioning:* a rating, on a scale of 1 to 90, of the patient's current adjustment (at work, in social relationships) and of his or her adjustment during the past year.

Thus a hypothetical patient's diagnosis would not simply be "depression," but might be diagnosed as follows:

Axis I: Major depressive episode
Axis II: Avoidant personality disorder
Axis III: Diabetes
Axis IV: Loss of job, acute (5). Marital conflict, enduring (4)
Axis V: Current—major impairment (40). In past year, moderate difficulty (60).

*DSM-III-R* avoids suggesting the cause of a disorder unless the cause has been definitely established. This represents a change of policy. As a result, some familiar diagnoses, like "neurosis," were dropped. Furthermore, *DSM-III-R* does not recommend a particular treatment for any disorder.

*The Critics Grind a Few Axes: The Future of DSM*
Neither *DSM-III-R,* nor its successor *DSM-IV,* can unambiguously list all possible types of mental disorders, like a periodic table of elements. "It is a social document that wears many conflicting hats and must be sensitive to a variety of clinical, forensic, professional, international, and public health issues" (Widiger & Trull, 1990, p. 111; see also Wakefield, 1992). For example, caffeine dependence is not included in *DSM-III-R,* despite the fact that it shares characteristics with other substance dependencies, the development of tolerance, unsuccessful efforts to control usage, withdrawal symptoms, and continued usage despite adverse consequences (Parrott, 1991).

According to research, *DSM-III-R* is not strictly adhered to by clinicians and is not very useful in clinical practice (Jampala, Sierles, & Taylor, 1988; Morey & Ochoa, 1989; Smith & Kraft, 1989).

The process by which *DSM-IV* is being constructed is intended to be more empirically based and open to critical review, providing some safeguards against arbitrary changes (Frances, Widiger, & Pincus, 1989). Widiger and Trull (1991) anticipate that *DSM-IV* will omit all references to "organic" and "physical" disorders, to avoid the implication that mental disorders are not at least in part physical. The proposals being considered would rename "organic" mood disorders as "secondary mood disorders," and would create a new class of "cognitive disorders."

---

▶ **GUIDED REVIEW** *Learning Objectives 4 and 5*

1. The _____, the current "official" nomenclature, was published in 1987. It has been strongly influenced by the _____ or _____ model of mental disorder.
2. *DSM-III-R* does not give only a simple diagnosis, but evaluates the client on five independent _____: _____, _____, _____, _____, and _____.

*ANSWERS*

1. DSM-III-R; medical, disease 2. axes: clinical syndrome, personality disorders (adult) or developmental disorders (children and adolescents), physical disorders, psychosocial stressors, global assessment of functioning

---

# CATEGORIES OF ABNORMAL BEHAVIOR

The purpose of diagnostic categories, like the *Diagnostic and Statistical Manual (DSM),* is to allow mental health professionals to convey a great deal of information in a very few words about a person's behavior, including what it consists of, how it might have come about, and how it differs from other diagnoses. This section describes patterns of behavior that occur often enough to require special attention, understanding, and help from mental health professionals.

## Organic Brain Disorders

**Organic brain disorders** are *disorders of the brain.* Some organic mental disorders involve *temporary and reversible* (**acute**) changes in brain function while others cause *permanent and irreversible* (**chronic**) changes.

Some of the most common causes of organic mental disorders are the diseases of the brain associated with aging. These diseases include Alzheimer's disease, cerebral arteriosclerosis, senile and presenile dementia, and Parkinson's disease. These disorders generally afflict people in their sixties or older. All involve injury or destruction to portions of the brain because of changes in brain metabolism, a reduced supply of oxygenated blood to the brain, or the outright death of brain cells.

A stroke, a common cause of organic brain disorder in older people, usually involves the abrupt loss of blood supply to a portion of the brain because of a clot or a leakage from a blood vessel. Though victims of mild strokes may recover virtually all functioning relatively quickly, those who have suffered severe strokes may experience catastrophic loss of movement, sensation, and cognitive and affective abilities. They may not recover from these serious losses and may suffer permanent behavioral disabilities as a consequence.

William MacArthur was in his mid-sixties and still very energetic and very successful as senior vice president of a large insurance company. Despite persistent warnings from his doctor to cut down on travel and his twelve-hour work days, Bill persisted. One day he awoke to find that his entire right side had become paralyzed and his speech had become severely impaired. Fortunately, his thinking and remembering had been spared. Bill had suffered a cerebrovascular accident, a stroke; a small blood vessel in his brain had ruptured, allowing blood to leak into the brain and destroy some brain tissue. Through the efforts of a dedicated wife and his own hard work, Bill is back at the insurance company; however, after months of rehabilitation he must use a wheelchair and can only work for a few hours at a time.

---

**TABLE 12.2 Categories of abnormal behavior in *DSM-III-R***

Disorders usually first evident in infancy, childhood, or adolescence (forty-six diagnoses)
Organic mental disorders (sixty-three diagnoses)
Psychoactive substance use disorders (twenty-two diagnoses)
Schizophrenia (five diagnoses)
Delusional (paranoid) disorder (one diagnosis)
Psychotic disorders not classified elsewhere (five diagnoses)
Mood disorders (nine diagnoses)
Anxiety disorders (nine diagnoses)
Somatoform disorders (seven diagnoses)
Dissociative disorders (five diagnoses)
Sexual disorders (twenty diagnoses)
Sleep disorders (twelve diagnoses)
Factitious disorders (three diagnoses)
Impulse control disorders not classified elsewhere (six diagnoses)
Adjustment disorder (nine diagnoses)
Psychological factors affecting physical condition (one diagnosis)
Personality disorders (twelve diagnoses)

---

Another common cause of organic mental disorder is the chronic, heavy use of alcohol and other drugs. Simple alcohol and drug intoxication cause acute disruptions in the functioning of the brain; however, the disruptions generally resolve with no lasting effects. Delirium tremens, an alcohol withdrawal reaction, also resolves satisfactorily if treated appropriately. But chronic alcohol and drug dependence can cause a variety of permanent brain and behavior disorders. Korsakov's psychosis, one of the most serious of these disorders, is characterized by profound and permanent memory loss.

Other common sources of organic mental disorder are brain injuries, tumors, epilepsy, strokes, and infections. Untreated syphilis may infect the brain and cause a devastating chronic mental disorder called general paralysis. Before the discovery of penicillin, more psychiatric patients were hospitalized because of general paralysis than because of any other disorder.

Impairments in memory and orientation are very common symptoms of organic mental disorder. In severe, chronic cases, patients may not be able to remember where they live, what they had for breakfast, or where the bathroom is located in their home or in the hospital. They may not know where they are, what their name is, or what day or year it is. Impaired intellectual functioning and judgment are additional signs of organic mental disorder: individuals may no longer be able to think or reason as

well as before and may be willing to take risks or make hasty decisions that are both unwise and out of character.

## Psychoactive Substance Use Disorders

Many people in America drink alcoholic beverages and take prescription drugs. Most of this drinking and drug use is legal. Some of it is not. Substance abuse is considered the nation's number one public health problem. Consider the following data on some of the costs and consequences of alcohol and drug abuse:

In 1983, the 12 to 15 million alcoholics in the United States may have cost the country nearly $117 billion; of this amount, nearly $71 billion stemmed from lost employment and reduced productivity while another $15 billion went to health care costs (National Institute on Alcohol Abuse and Alcoholism, 1987). By 1990, these costs were expected to reach $150 billion. The economic costs of drug abuse among the nation's estimated 2 million drug abusers was estimated to be at least $47 billion in 1980; and $70 billion by 1988 (Harwood, 1984).

Forty-eight percent of all persons convicted of crimes in the United States in 1983 were using alcohol before they committed the crime (NIAAA, 1987).

In 1980, the last year for which these data are available, almost one hundred thousand deaths were attributable to alcohol use and abuse (NIAAA, 1987).

In the early 1960s, experience with illegal drugs was restricted to two percent or less of the United States' population. By 1982, almost one-third of the household population over the age of twelve had some experience with illegal drugs (APA Committee on Drug Abuse, 1987).

At least ten percent of violent crimes in the United States are drug-related. One-third of all federal prisoners and over one-half of all state prisoners are narcotics abusers (Goldstein, 1985).

Substance dependence is discussed further in chapter 14, Health Psychology.

## Schizophrenia

Close to one percent of the population of the United States suffers from schizophrenia. While this percentage may seem small when compared to the number of persons who suffer from substance abuse or depression, the number of schizophrenics who are incapacitated or who function at a low level is enormous. Schizophrenics are the major users of hospital beds in the United States, occupying thirty percent of all hospital beds.

# CLOSE UP ON RESEARCH

## If You Smoke and Drink, Chances Are Your Parents Do Too

When 256 California adolescents, ages thirteen through seventeen, and their parents were interviewed about their drug use, a striking relationship between adolescent drug use and parental drug use was found (Fawzy, Coombs, & Gerber, 1983). Though this finding does not prove that heavy drug use by parents always leads to heavy drug use by their children or that parents who do not smoke or drink will always have children who do not use drugs, the strong parent-child drug use relationship does cast light on two factors that may lead to youthful drug use and abuse.

The study's findings included the following:

1. Coffee consumption by parents is strongly associated with youthful substance use (defined as the use of alcohol illegally obtained, illegal drugs, and prescription drugs): Eighty-two percent of heavy coffee-drinking parents and thirty-seven percent of parents who don't drink coffee have substance-using offspring.

2. Smoking by parents is strongly associated with substance use by children: Eighty-five percent of mothers and sixty-four percent of fathers who smoke heavily have substance-using children; parents who smoke less or not at all are much less likely to have children who use drugs.

3. Seventy-two percent of fathers and seventy-seven percent of mothers who daily drink wine or beer and seventy-six percent of parents who frequently drink hard liquor have offspring who use drugs; parents who do not drink alcoholic beverages are fifty percent less likely to have substance-using children.

4. Eighty-one percent of fathers and seventy-eight percent of mothers who use marijuana or hashish have substance-using children; parents who do not use these drugs are much less likely to have substance-using children.

One interpretation of these findings emphasizes the role of youthful modeling of parental drug-use behavior in the development of the adolescents' own drug-use. Children whose parents use alcohol, drugs, or cigarettes will likely model that behavior themselves; in fact, they may "go their parents one better" by using hard drugs as well as the alcohol, coffee, and cigarettes their parents use.

The authors put forth a "deviancy/pathology" view of their findings by hypothesizing that parents who are heavy users of drugs and alcohol are more apt to be socially deviant. Their deviance, in turn, is likey to be conveyed to their children, who will then be more likely to use illegal drugs.

While studies of this kind do not prove that parental and adolescent drug use are invariably related, they do provide important information on factors that influence adolescent substance use and abuse.

Schizophrenia usually occurs before age forty-five; thirty is the median age of first admission to a hospital for the disorder. Although the same number of men and women develop schizophrenia, it occurs more often in men before they are twenty-five and more often in women after they are twenty-five (Zigler & Levine, 1981). Schizophrenia is diagnosed more often among the poor, especially those living in urban areas (Kohn, 1968).

Until the last two decades, most mental health workers believed schizophrenia was caused by social and environmental factors, especially inadequate child rearing (Bateson, Jackson, Haley, & Weakland, 1956). Although there is now agreement that these factors may influence the course of the disorder, most authorities believe that schizophrenia is caused by abnormalities in the production of one or more neurotransmitters (Gershon & Rieder, 1992; Weinberger & Kleinman, 1986). The most prevalent hypothesis is that dopamine, discussed in chapter 2, is the neurotransmitter involved in schizophrenia. These deficits in brain function may be genetically determined: having a schizophrenic parent, sibling, or other close relative markedly increases a person's chances of becoming schizophrenic (Kendler, 1986).

One theory still much debated is the diathesis-stress model, a bio-psychological model that emphasizes the interaction of individual predispositions and environmental stressors (Gottesman, 1991; Turpin, Tarrier, & Sturgeon, 1988; see also chapter 14, Health Psychology). According to this theory, an individual may inherit a predisposition for schizophrenia, but this predisposition must be combined with environmental stress for the disorder to develop. Environmental stressors can be anything from family disruption to doing poorly in school.

Although the diathesis-stress model is a considerable advance over the simpler view that everyone is equally susceptible to stress, it nevertheless has limitations (Coyne & Downey, 1991). Most important, the model is not dynamic; instead, it assumes that an individual's vulnerability is stable over time. Yet at different times in life, individuals may be more or less susceptible to stressors.

Schizophrenics suffer from a psychotic disorder: in active phases of the disorder, they lose touch with reality and act on the basis of imagined or fantasized reality.

**Thought disorder,** *a deterioration in the ability to think and use language,* is among the first and most obvious signs of schizophrenia. A disturbance in the ability to link thoughts together is a hallmark of this disorder; as a consequence, language loses much of its communication value for the schizophrenic.

Swiss psychiatrist Eugen Bleuler, an early authority on schizophrenia, cites the following short story, written by a schizophrenic and entitled "The Blossoming-Time of Horticulture," to illustrate the peculiar language of schizophrenia:

> At the time of the new moon venuses stands in the Augutsky of Egypt and lights up with its light rays the merchant-travel-harbours of Suez, Cairo and Alexandria. In this historically famous Caliphcity is the museum of Assyrian statues from Macedonia. Besides pisang, also corn, oats, clover and barley grow there. Bananas, figs, lemons, oranges and olives. Olive oil is an Arabian liqueur sauce which the Afghans, Blackamoors and Moslemites use for ostrich breeding. . . . (Bleuler, 1911)

**Delusions,** *false beliefs that are rarely altered, even in the face of conflicting facts, obvious reality, or common-sense explanations,* are another hallmark of psychosis and a common symptom of schizophrenia. While delusions of persecution are most common, schizophrenics also experience grandiose delusions (delusions of self-importance), sexual delusions, religious delusions, delusions of control (the belief that one's thoughts or actions are controlled by others), and hypochondriacal delusions (patients convince themselves that they are suffering from a serious physical disorder).

Schizophrenics also frequently experience **hallucinations,** *false perceptions by which they see, hear, smell, taste, or feel things that do not exist.* The hallucinations are associated with the delusions being experienced. Auditory hallucinations are most common (Pfohl & Andreasen, 1986). Patients typically hear voices talking to or about them. The voices may be those of God, Jesus, Satan, Elvis (usually the thin one), a long-dead parent, or long-absent friends. (In a fascinating book, *Three Christs of Ypsilanti,* Milton Rokeach brings together three schizophrenics, each claiming to be Jesus Christ.)

Many schizophrenics also suffer from **affective disorder,** *a failure in emotional responsivity.* They do not respond emotionally to events and people in their lives. Instead, they may demonstrate flat or blunted affect, *appearing withdrawn and indifferent in happy or sad situations, or* inappropriate affect, *taking pleasure in someone else's pain or experiencing obvious unhappiness in the face of another's good news.*

> Charles was in his mid-twenties when parents and friends began to notice that he had begun to lose his zest for living and his vital interest in his work and his friends. He began to spend most of his free time watching television in his small apartment. Though he would respond when someone asked him a question, he rarely volunteered an opinion about anything. One bright winter's day, after this had been going on for more than a year, Charles went over to his parents' home to tell them he knew they had been conspiring with the FBI and the Chicago police department to have him tried for treason. Asked how he knew this, he admitted that a voice he had first heard several years before had told him. Asked why he should be prosecuted, he said that he had seen and heard things about the government that no American ought to know. Ultimately diagnosed as schizophrenic and put on a regimen of phenothiazine drugs, Charles is now living in a sheltered workshop. Though his voices are still with him, they are no longer so insistent, so compelling. Charles has gone back to work and has reestablished a trusting relationship with his parents.

*Schizophrenic Subtypes*    Emil Kraepelin's great contribution was his recognition that the common psychotic syndromes that several colleagues had described and labeled in the mid-1800s (catatonia, hebephrenia, and vesania typica) were really subcategories of a single psychotic disorder. Kraepelin (1896, 1913) called the disorder "dementia praecox," meaning premature insanity. Later, Bleuler gave the disorder its present name, schizophrenia, described its signs and symptoms in detail, and identified a fourth subtype, simple schizophrenia (Bleuler, 1911).

Despite an enormous amount of research on the disorder since Kraepelin's and Bleuler's time, our diagnostic conceptions of the disorder are very much in line with their conceptions. *DSM-III-R* identifies the following subtypes of schizophrenia:

**Catatonic:** Excitement and withdrawal are two conflicting aspects of this subtype. The excited catatonic demonstrates excessive, sometimes violent, motor behavior, and the withdrawn catatonic may be negativistic, remain mute, and stuporous (barely conscious and often motionless). This subtype is rare today because the major tranquilizing drugs used to treat schizophrenia tend to prevent catatonic behavior from occurring.

**Disorganized:** These patients, labeled hebephrenic by Kraepelin, demonstrate severely disordered thinking processes and grossly inappropriate affect. Giggling, silliness, child-like behavior, poor judgment, and inadequate social skills characterize their behavior. The symptoms of schizophrenia appear early. They are least likely of all schizophrenic patients to recover from the disorder.

**Paranoid:** This subtype is the most common form of schizophrenia (Kendler & Tsuang, 1981). It is characterized most often by paranoid and persecutory delusions and hallucinations. Paranoid patients may be suspicious, hostile, and physically or verbally violent.

**Undifferentiated:** Formerly Kraepelin's simple schizophrenic label, undifferentiated schizophrenic patients do not show a clear-cut syndrome pattern. Their symptoms are drawn from more than one subtype of schizophrenia.

**Residual:** The diagnostic label of residual schizophrenia is given to patients who are not currently psychotic or schizophrenic but who were previously diagnosed. Mild or moderate symptoms of the disorder, like a moderate thought disorder or a mild affective disturbance, may remain as residuals of the schizophrenic process.

## Mood Disorders

Everyone experiences moments of great sadness and moments of great joy. When we have suffered a grievous personal loss, our sadness may be extended, just as when things are going exceptionally well, our joy may last for some time. Both sadness and happiness are common and appropriate responses to the circumstances. Likewise, all people experience feelings of anger, aggression, anxiety, and depression that accompany frustration and conflict. Most of the time, however, these feelings dissipate quickly.

When a person's emotional responses are *not* appropriate to events in the environment, mental health professionals may look for signs and symptoms of **depression** *(despondency, despair, pessimism, tearfulness, and sorrow),* as well as for disturbances in eating, sleeping,

and concentration that seem out of proportion to possible causes or that have lasted longer than seems reasonable (see Stroebe, Gergen, Gergen, & Stroebe, 1992).

**Mania** and **hypomania** are also symptoms of the mood disorders. They typically involve some combination of the following: *an exalted or grandiose view of oneself, the need to be constantly "on the move," difficulties in concentration, increased irritability, an increase in appetite and a decrease in the need for sleep, "racing thoughts," and unbridled and unrealistic optimism.*

*DSM-III-R* divides the mood disorders into two separate categories, bipolar disorders and depressive disorders.

*Bipolar Disorders*    People suffering from one of the **bipolar disorders** typically *move through periods of mania, periods of severe depression, and periods of relative normality.* It is not unusual for the periods of normality to last longer than the mania or the depression. Lithium carbonate, used to treat mania and reduce the likelihood of depression in bipolar disorder, has markedly reduced the severity of these disorders.

Nonpsychotic patients who experience *pronounced mood swings that are not as severe as those of bipolar disorder* are given the diagnosis of **cyclothymia.**

*Depressive Disorders*    Persons who experience **major depression** suffer *one or more episodes of severe depression, but do not experience mania.* Some individuals actively consider suicide. The depressive episode, which may last for weeks or months, is self-limiting unless antidepressant medication or other treatment succeeds in terminating the depression. These people are often unable to function normally and may have to spend most or all of their time at home or in a hospital because they are unable to think and act clearly and effectively enough to work or study.

**Dysthymia** (also called **depressive neurosis**), another of the depressive disorders, is characterized by *mild to moderate depression that interferes with daily functioning but is not as disabling as major depression.* These individuals are not psychotic; generally they feel sad, pessimistic, and inadequate, may have eating and sleeping difficulties, and may consider suicide. Even though their functioning is impaired, they are often able to work or study with moderate success. Psychotherapy and antidepressant medication can be helpful in treating dysthymia.

# EXPLORING HUMAN DIVERSITY

## The UFO Abduction Syndrome

A sixty-four-page booklet entitled *Unusual personal experiences: An analysis of the data from three national surveys,* by Mack et al. (1992), arrived in the mail. What sort of "unusual personal experiences?" we wondered. UFOs. It seems that nearly one in five adult Americans have had experiences consistent with being abducted by aliens. This conclusion is based on a 1991 survey conducted by the Roper Organization. Among the findings:

- Nearly one adult in five has wakened up paralyzed with the sense of a strange figure or presence in the room.

- Nearly one adult in eight has experienced a period of an hour or more in which he or she was apparently lost but could not remember why.

- Nearly one adult in ten has felt the experience of actually flying through the air without knowing why or how.

- One adult in twelve has seen unusual lights or balls of light in a room without understanding what was causing them.

- One adult in twelve has discovered puzzling scars on his or her body without remembering how or where they were acquired.

These findings suggest that "two percent of the adults in the American population have had a constellation of experiences consistent with an abduction history. Therefore, based on our sample of nearly 6,000 respondents, we believe that one out of every fifty adult Americans may have had UFO abduction experiences."

### The UFO Syndrome

Harvard psychiatrist John E. Mack writes that "mental health clinicians should learn to recognize the most common symptoms and indications in the patient or client's history that they are dealing with an abduction case." These include fear of the dark; nightmares, especially containing accounts of being taken by threatening figures inside a craft; a history of small beings or a presence around the person's bed; reports of unexplained missing time episodes; the appearance for no apparent reason of small cuts, scars or odd red spots; encounters with strange intense light. These symptoms do not fit conveniently into any of the DSM categories.

### Therapy

The authors recommend "ventilation of the experiences (i.e., talking about them), with or without the aid of hypnosis . . . . Openly discussing these memories and helping the patients deal with them will relieve much of their anxiety and allow their conscious minds to cope."

### Critique

What are we to make of these experiences and remarks? There is a surprisingly large number of people who have had "experiences consistent with a UFO abduction hypothesis." This, of course, is not proof that UFO abductions occurred. Although based on research (a survey), the document is not scientific. One hallmark of science is to provide and test alternative interpretations of the data.

What other explanations might fit the data? The authors rule out psychopathology, noting that it does not seem to be present among those who report these experiences. Psychologists and psychiatrists often look for psychopathology when confronted by deviant behavior. Yet consistent patterns of psychopathology are rarely found among behavioral deviants, whether child abusers, violent prisoners, or terrorists (Cooke & Goldstein, 1989).

We are less likely to seek explanations in the social environment. For example, it is possible to consider the "UFO Syndrome" as a form of what is sometimes called "mass hysteria." There have been many instances of imaginary events, sightings, and diseases spreading through a community or from one town to another. In one study, Kerckhoff, Back, and Miller (1965) investigated a case of hysterical contagion in which workers at a small factory were "bitten" by insects (which, in fact, did not exist). The imaginary bug first infected individuals who were on the fringes of the social groups at the factory. Only later did it spread through close circles of friends. In order better to understand such a syndrome, perhaps what we need to know about these individuals is not their level of psychopathology but the extent of their social relationships.

The periodical *The Skeptical Inquirer* contains articles that critically evaluate claims of the paranormal, mainly by providing alternative explanations that are simpler and that require less credulity of the reader.

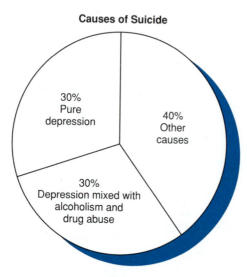

**Causes of Suicide**

30%
Pure depression

40%
Other causes

30%
Depression mixed with alcoholism and drug abuse

**Figure 12.2**  *Sixty percent of all suicides are committed by people suffering from depression.*

*Depression and Suicide*    Suicide is one of the ten leading causes of death—and is the third leading cause of death among young people in the United States. Each year some 200,000 people attempt suicide (three-fourths of them females), and 25,000 succeed (three-fourths of them males (see figure 12.2). Suicide affects people in all stations of life, apparent successes as well as failures, rogues and heroes, the famous and the infamous, urban blacks as well as suburban whites. The most common suicide is an older, white male.

Given the incidence of suicide in our society and the likelihood that it has touched many, it would be comforting to believe that only those suffering from serious mental disorders choose to end their lives at their own hands. Yet many of the people who attempt or commit suicide are not victims of serious mental illness (Schneidman, 1985).

People who are depressed, especially those who suffer from both depression and alcoholism, are most likely to commit suicide. When things are going badly for people, it is not surprising when suicide is one of the options they consider. But when people who seem to have everything going for them attempt suicide, it is much more difficult to understand their decision.

Why do people attempt suicide? Most do so to avoid continuing psychological or physical pain (56 percent) or for manipulation (13 percent) (Kovacs, Beck, & Weissman, 1975). People who believe life is no longer worth living—those who suffer from painful and/or terminal diseases, those facing criminal charges, those

convicted of a crime and facing public shame and humiliation, or those toward the end of their lives who must exist on an inadequate income without anyone to live for—attempt suicide for surcease. People sometimes attempt suicide to manipulate others—to keep a wife from leaving, to force parents to show more concern, to make a lover feel sorry that he or she has gone.

> Anne certainly seemed to have a lot going for her. Deciding to forego college for the business world (her life's ambition was to become a famous chef), she had taken an apartment with two other friends and was working long hours in a friend's small restaurant. Things seemed to be going fine, everyone thought, until, one morning, she showed up on a friend's doorstep to say she couldn't take the pressures of life anymore. Because her friend had to go to work, she couldn't do much more than tell Anne that this too would pass and that they ought to talk later that afternoon. Instead, Anne went home and, burdened by worries about some debts she had told no one about, swallowed eight of the pills she had long taken for her chronic asthma. Rushed to a hospital in critical condition, Anne survived. Now able to laugh at her dramatic response to a few hundred dollars of debt that her parents and friends were only too happy to repay, Anne still can't say whether she *really* wanted to end it all that day.

## Anxiety Disorders

The anxiety disorders share the common experience of **anxiety,** *a highly aversive state that combines physiological arousal, apprehension and fear, and a vague sense of impending disaster.* The subjective experience of anxiety, which varies from individual to individual, typically includes bodily sensations ("butterflies in the stomach," dizziness, sweating), worry, preoccupation with real or imagined problems, and a vague, overriding sense of unease. Panic disorder, agoraphobia, social phobia, simple phobia, obsessive-compulsive disorder, posttraumatic stress disorder, and anxiety disorder are all part of this group of nonpsychotic conditions. In *DSM-I* and *DSM-II,* these disorders and the somatoform disorders were termed "neuroses."

People who suffer from **panic disorder** experience *one or more attacks of terrifying, unexpected anxiety.* Their experiences are so intense they fear they are going crazy or about to die. Lasting from a few minutes to several hours, these episodes are especially frightening because they are so unpredictable. Panic disorder can be accompanied by **agoraphobia,** *the fear of being in places or situations from which escape might be difficult or embarrassing or in which help might not be available.*

# APPLYING PSYCHOLOGY

## How Anxious Are You?

Anxiety is typically measured using a series of questions, such as those below. They are a subscale of the Hospital Anxiety and Depression Scale (Zigmond & Snaith, 1983).

1. I feel tense or "wound up"
   a) most of the time
   b) a lot of the time
   c) from time to time, occasionally
   d) not at all

2. I get a sort of frightened feeling like butterflies in the stomach
   a) not at all
   b) occasionally
   c) quite often
   d) very often

3. I get a sort of frightened feeling as if something awful is about to happen
   a) very definitely and quite badly
   b) yes, but not too badly
   c) a little, but it doesn't worry me
   d) not at all

4. I feel restless as if I have to be on the move
   a) very much
   b) quite a lot
   c) not very much
   d) not at all

5. Worrying thoughts go through my mind
   a) a great deal of the time
   b) a lot of the time
   c) from time to time but not too often
   d) only occasionally

6. I get sudden feelings of panic
   a) very often
   b) quite often
   c) not very often
   d) not at all

7. I can sit at ease and feel relaxed
   a) definitely
   b) usually
   c) not often
   d) not at all

**Scoring:**
Award points as follows:

1. a) 3   b) 2   c) 1   d) 0
2. a) 0   b) 1   c) 2   d) 3
3. a) 3   b) 2   c) 1   d) 0
4. a) 3   b) 2   c) 1   d) 0
5. a) 3   b) 2   c) 1   d) 0
6. a) 3   b) 2   c) 1   d) 0
7. a) 0   b) 1   c) 2   d) 3

Add the total number of points for the seven questions. Scores of more than ten are considered higher than normal.

---

Dr. Arnold was a prominent and successful psychotherapist with such a severe case of claustrophobia (fear of enclosed spaces) that he found it immensely difficult to ride in elevators or drive through tunnels. Born, raised, and educated in New York City, an island filled with skyscrapers and separated from the mainland by tunnels and bridges, Dr. Arnold tried almost everything, including psychotherapy, behavior therapy, drugs, and meditation, to rid himself of his secret phobia. He was unable to do so and had to move to a small town in New Jersey where there were no tunnels and the tallest building in town was three stories!

Persons with **social phobia** are subject to *intense fear of social situations* and they try to avoid such situations.

Social phobias can be specific (not being able to urinate in a public toilet or eat without choking in a restaurant) or general (not being able to function in any social situation). Persons who suffer from **simple phobia** are subject to *intense fear of specific objects or situations (other than social situations) that they recognize as not being harmful or dangerous.* Common simple phobias involve animals (particularly dogs, snakes, insects, and mice); the witnessing of blood or injury; enclosed spaces; air travel; and heights. The comedian Steven Wright claims to be afraid of widths.

*Insistent, unwanted thoughts, urges, and behaviors* characterize the **obsessive-compulsive disorders. Obsessions** involve *the unavoidable, irresistible preoccupation* *with certain thoughts or ideas.* **Compulsions** are *behaviors the individual feels compelled to perform, sometimes repeatedly;* the penalty for failing to repeat a compulsive ritual is intense anxiety. Although some people are preoccupied primarily with obsessions and others are most troubled by compulsions, the two occur together in the same individual often enough to be considered two facets of the same disorder. From four to twenty percent of all neurotic patients have an obsessive-compulsive disorder (Spitzer & Williams, 1984).

Following a psychologically distressing event outside the range of usual human experience, some people develop posttraumatic stress disorder (PTSD), a delayed or continued reaction to the initial stressful event. (See the discussion of PTSD in chapter 14, Health Psychology.)

**Generalized anxiety disorder** is the diagnosis for *chronic and persistent anxiety that lasts at least six months.* People live in a state of continuous mild to intense anxiety. The anxiety is not focused on any specific object or event. Hence, these patients are said to suffer from "free-floating anxiety." Along with dysthymic disorder, this is the most common of the so-called neurotic conditions.

## Somatoform Disorders

The essential feature of **somatoform disorders** is *physical symptoms that suggest physical disorders for which there are no organic findings or physiologic mechanisms.* Additionally, *the physical symptoms seem to be associated with psychological factors or conflicts.* Another term for somatoform disorders is psychosomatic disorders.

There are psychoanalytic and behavioral explanations of somatoform disorders. For example, the psychoanalyst Franz Alexander (1935, 1962) stressed the impact of specific traumatic childhood events on the development of specific physical disorders in adulthood. According to this view, frustration of dependency needs in childhood (an unloving mother, a distant father, or punitive parents) is associated with stomach ulcers in adulthood. Other kinds of trauma in childhood lead to other somatic problems in adulthood.

Lachman (1972) believes people develop psychosomatic disorders following prolonged exposure to stressful situations. These situations, in turn, cause chronic maladaptive alterations in physiological functioning, heart rate, blood pressure, muscle tension, and gastric secretion.

These alterations in physiological functioning are responsible for development of somatic disorders.

*Conversion Disorder*    One of the most striking of the somatoform disorders is **conversion disorder,** *the experience of dramatic physical symptoms that have no organic or physical cause.* The person may awaken one morning to find that he or she has lost sensation in a hand or an arm, or cannot see from one or both eyes, or has lost control over all the voluntary muscles on one side of the body, all in the absence of physical findings to justify the condition. Another person with the same diagnosis may suffer from frequent, intense headaches or frightening heart palpitations, both without any sign of physical illness. This dramatic condition has become increasingly rare since Freud described the syndrome in several of his patients. Perhaps its increasing rarity reflects our greater sophistication with respect to both physical and psychological health and disorder.

*Hypochondriasis*    In **hypochondriasis,** *people are preoccupied with their body and health to the exclusion of any other interests.* Although not delusional, these people cannot believe that they are not seriously ill. They usually know the symptoms of an astounding array of illnesses, from cancer and heart disease to leprosy and Courvoisier's gallbladder, and are constantly anticipating the appearance of symptoms of these disorders in themselves. A slight headache may signal a stroke, and mild muscle pain may mean terminal cancer to the hypochondriac.

## Sexual Disorders

The sexual disorders include the **paraphilias,** *sexual deviations,* and **sexual dysfunctions,** *problems in sexual desire and performance.*

No longer included in the nomenclature is homosexuality. Its removal from *DSM-III-R* stems from the furor its previous inclusion aroused. It also reflects the absence of scientific evidence to support the view that persons with a homosexual orientation are more likely to be disturbed psychologically than anyone else. In deleting a diagnosis that has generated debate and been a source of stigma ever since the first edition of the *Diagnostic and Statistical Manual* was published in 1952, *DSM-III-R* marks a notable step toward ending centuries of confusion over how to consider persons whose sexual preference is for members of their own sex. Homosexuality is now regarded as a psychiatric diagnosis only when an individual expresses a desire to increase heterosexual arousal and to decrease the existence of homosexual arousal.

*Paraphilias* **Paraphiliacs** experience *repeated and intense sexual urges and fantasies that involve either nonhuman objects or the suffering or humiliation of themselves, their sexual partners, or children or other nonconsenting persons.* No one is sure why almost all persons who receive this diagnosis are men. These disorders continue to incite society's greatest disapproval.

The **exhibitionist** is *sexually aroused by exposing his genitals to an unsuspecting stranger;* the **fetishist** is *sexually aroused by using nonliving objects by themselves;* the **frotteur** is *sexually aroused by touching and rubbing against a nonconsenting person;* the **pedophile** is *sexually aroused by sexual activity with a prepubescent child or children;* the **sexual masochist** is *sexually aroused by the act of being humiliated, beaten, bound, or otherwise made to suffer;* the **sexual sadist** is *sexually aroused by acts which make the victim suffer psychologically or physically;* the **transvestic fetishist** is *a heterosexual male sexually aroused by wearing women's clothing;* and the **voyeur** is *sexually aroused by the observing of an unsuspecting naked person who is disrobing or engaging in sexual activity.*

*Sexual Dysfunctions* The **sexual dysfunctions** involve *difficulties and problems in both the desire for, as well as the ability to perform, sexual acts.*

As a result of society's increasing openness about sexual matters, during the past two decades we have begun to realize that many people suffer from sexual disorders. Contributing to this recognition are the works of pioneering sex therapists like Helen Singer Kaplan (1974) and William Masters and Virginia Johnson (1966, 1970).

The sexual dysfunctions include sexual desire disorders such as inhibited, inadequate, or deficient sexual desire; sexual arousal disorders such as the inability to respond to another person with adequate sexual arousal; orgasm disorders such as the persistent delay in or absence of orgasm following a period of normal sexual excitement or persistent premature ejaculation following minimal sexual stimulation; and sexual pain disorders, a variety of painful responses to sexual intercourse.

Current thinking hypothesizes that these disorders result from the interaction of physiological and psychological factors (Conte, 1986). Their treatment, therefore, ought to encompass a detailed assessment of both the physical and psychological factors that might be involved (Kaplan, 1979; Masters, Johnson, & Kolodny, 1985).

## Personality Disorders

Personality *traits* are deeply ingrained patterns of perceiving, relating to, and thinking about the world and people's place in it. Personality traits make each of us a separate and unique individual. ***When personality traits are inflexible and maladaptive and cause significant impairment or personal distress,*** they are considered **personality disorders.** Because the personality disorders are the most vaguely defined and diffuse of the *DSM-III-R* disorders, they are often difficult to diagnose.

The personality disorders have been grouped into three clusters in *DSM-III-R*. Cluster A includes paranoid, schizoid, and schizotypal personality disorders. People with these disorders often behave in odd or eccentric ways. Cluster B includes antisocial, borderline, histrionic, and narcissistic personality disorders. People with these disorders often behave dramatically, emotionally, or erratically. Cluster C includes avoidant, dependent, obsessive-compulsive, and passive-aggressive personality disorders. People with these disorders often show anxious or fearful behavior.

## Childhood Disorders

Some disorders are unique to childhood, for example learning disabilities, hyperactivity, and elimination disorders. Surveys in the United States and Great Britain show that about seven percent of children have moderate to severe disorders and fifteen percent, mild disorders (Knopf, 1984). The prevalence of disorders tends to increase with age and is greater among boys than among girls. Admission rates for childhood disorders increase gradually from about age six or seven, a phenomenon that may be related to a child's beginning school. After age seven, clinic admissions peak at nine to ten years of age, and again at fourteen to fifteen years of age (Rosen, Bahn, & Kramer, 1964). The latter peak probably reflects the inherent difficulties of adolescence. In every age group, clinic admission rates are higher for boys than for girls (Eme, 1979).

*DSM-III-R* lists separately **"disorders usually first evident in infancy, childhood, or adolescence."** Among these are mental retardation; pervasive developmental disorders, such as autism; and specific developmental disorders, such as language and speech disorders. A child who has no friends, who lies, steals, and bullies, and who shows no remorse over these actions is diagnosed as having a "conduct disorder, undersocialized, aggressive" (Bootzin & Acocella, 1988).

*Learning Disabilities: Specific Developmental Disorders*    A child is diagnosed as "learning disabled" if he or she has at least average intelligence and adequate schooling, but nevertheless has great trouble acquiring a certain skill. Such children lag behind other children their age in some area of intellectual functioning. Specific developmental disorders appear in reading, writing, spelling, and mathematics. In the case of reading disorder, also called *dyslexia,* children cannot identify letters or words, or their reading is distorted.

Because learning disabled children do not do well in school, they are often seen as failures by their teachers, peers, and families. There are many approaches to the treatment of learning disabilities. Some learning disabled children who are also hyperactive are treated with drugs or special diets. Instructional techniques have been devised for use in the classroom.

*Autism: A Pervasive Developmental Disability*    Autism is considered a "Pervasive Developmental Disability" because it influences all aspects of the child's functioning. **Autism *describes a range of pervasive developmental disabilities in social relationships, speech, movement, and intellect.*** About 1 in every 500 children are diagnosed as autistic.

Four common symptoms of childhood autism are disturbed social relationships, cognitive deficits, language deficits, and disturbed motor behavior. Disturbance of social relationships may take the form of total withdrawal, or an obsessive attachment to an inanimate object. The child does not relate normally to family members. Autistic children also show speech abnormalities. They may be totally mute, or their speech may be incoherent. "The most striking oddity of autistic children ... is their abnormal motor behavior. These behaviors can vary considerably, ranging from a total lack of movement (catatonia) to tics, tremors, and posturing. Most typical, however, is a limited repertoire of movements that the child repeats endlessly, with no observable goal" (Bootzin & Acocella, 1988, p. 450).

*Theories of Autism.*    No single theory of the causes of autism is agreed upon. Nor is there an accepted treatment. A review of studies on treatments for autism (Ornitz & Ritvo, 1976) found that autistic children appear to benefit most from behavior therapy and special education aimed at developing language and other skills.

*Biological Theories.* There is some evidence of a genetic component of autism (Folstein & Rutter, 1977). Many autistic children have abnormally high levels of the neurotransmitters dopamine and serotonin (Goldstein et al., 1976). "Whatever their role in the development of autism, these two neurotransmitters may play a role in its treatment. When autistic children receive stimulants such as amphetamines, which increase dopamine, their symptoms of hyperactivity, ritualistic behavior, and self-stimulation get worse (Young et al., 1982). Dopamine-inhibiting drugs such as the phenothiazines mitigate many of the symptoms of autism, including self-mutilation and repetitive motions, although they are less effective with autism than with schizophrenia. Drugs that reduce serotonin also hold promise" (Bootzin & Acocella, 1988, p. 456).

*Cognitive Theories.* Cognitive theories contend that the cognitive problems of autistic children are the cause of their social problems (e.g., Rutter, 1983). Researchers have tried to identify the fundamental cognitive defect in autism. There is some evidence that the basic problem lies in integrating input from different sources (Ritvo, 1976). Rutter (1971) argues that the autistic child's basic deficit is difficulty in understanding sounds.

*Behavioral Theories.* The focus of behavioral theories is on the treatment, rather than the origins of autism. Basic learning principles are used to influence the autistic child. Adaptive behaviors are reinforced while undesirable behaviors are either punished or simply allowed to extinguish.

*Psychodynamic Theories.* At one time it was widely accepted that unhealthy family relationships gave rise to childhood autism. Bruno Bettelheim (1967) wrote that autism is a child's response to an extreme situation in which parents reject the child during the first six months of life, when social relationships begin to form, and during the next three months, when language and locomotion begin. Because of this lack of stimulation, the child has no basis on which to form emotional attachments or to develop proper language and motor skills. Most important, because the parents are unresponsive, the child feels unable to affect the external world. Therefore, the child withdraws into fantasy. Bootzin and Acocella (1988) note that research has not supported the theory that parents of autistic children are cold and aloof (Cox et al., 1975).

In chapter 13, Psychotherapy, we discuss the many ways that have been developed to treat the symptoms and diagnoses discussed in *DSM* and in this chapter.

▶ **GUIDED REVIEW** *Learning Objectives 6, 7, 8, 9, 10, 11, 12, and 13*

1. The organic mental disorders are disorders of the _____.
2. The behavioral and psychological effects of alcohol and drug abuse and dependence are called the _____.
3. _____ is signalled by profound deficits in cognitive ability and affective functioning and by delusions and hallucinations.
4. The _____ include the bipolar affective disorders and the depressive disorders.
5. Panic disorder, agoraphobia, and posttraumatic stress disorder are all considered _____.
6. The sexual disorders include the _____ and the _____.
7. The _____ are deeply ingrained patterns of behavior that trouble the person who demonstrates them and those around him or her.
8. Disorders unique to childhood and adolescence include _____ and _____.
9. The major theoretical approaches to the study of autism are _____, _____, _____, and _____.

*ANSWERS*

*1. brain 2. psychoactive substance use disorders 3. Schizophrenia 4. mood disorders 5. anxiety disorders 6. paraphilias, sexual dysfunctions 7. personality disorders 8. learning disabilities, autism 9. biological, behavioral, cognitive, psychodynamic*

## SUMMARY

I. History of abnormal behavior (pp. 374–378)
  A. Through much of human history, two conflicting views on the causes of abnormal behavior struggled for supremacy. One position saw abnormal behavior as the product of natural forces. The other position viewed abnormal behavior as the responsibility of supernatural forces. (pp. 374–376)
  B. Pinel's reforms of the mental hospital system in France were a turning point in the history of attitudes toward the mentally ill. (p. 376)
  C. Another landmark in the history of abnormal behavior, the rise of the disease or medical model of mental illness, coincided with Kraepelin's efforts to classify what he called dementia praecox. (p. 376)
  D. Five different views of abnormal behavior are the normative, statistical, subjective, maladaptive, and ideal. (pp. 377–378)
  E. The psychoanalytic revolution altered our conceptions of mental disorder. (p. 378)

II. A current legacy of Kraepelin are the various editions of the *Diagnostic and Statistical Manual of Mental Disorders.* (p. 378)

  A. *DSM-III-R* evaluates behavior along five axes: clinical syndrome, personality disorders (adult) or developmental disorders (children and adolescents), physical disorders, psychosocial stressors, and global assessment of functioning. (p. 379)
  B. *DSM-IV* is being constructed to be more empirically based and open to critical review. (p. 380)

III. Categories of abnormal behavior. (p. 380)
  A. The organic mental disorders involve either acute or chronic dysfunctions of brain tissue. They usually involve significant impairment of behavior. (pp. 380–381)
  B. The psychoactive substance use disorders include both alcoholism and drug dependence. (p. 381)
  C. Schizophrenia is a serious psychotic condition that typically involves disturbances in cognitive, perceptual, and affective functioning. The subtypes of schizophrenia include disorganized, catatonic, paranoid, undifferentiated, and residual schizophrenia. (pp. 381–384)
  D. The mood disorders include the bipolar disorders, depressive disorders, and dysthymia. Depression is often associated with suicide. (pp. 384–386)

**E.** The anxiety and somatoform disorders include many of the conditions previously termed "neuroses." (pp. 386–388)

**F.** The sexual disorders include the paraphilias and the sexual dysfunctions. (pp. 388–389)

**G.** The personality disorders are deeply ingrained habits and patterns of behavior recognized early in life and considered a distinguishing feature of a person's behavior. (p. 389)

**H.** Disorders of childhood and adolescence include specific developmental disorders, such as language, speech, and reading disorders, and pervasive developmental disorders, including autism. (pp. 389–390)

**I.** Theories on the origins and treatment of autism stem from biological, behavioral, cognitive, and psychodynamic schools of psychology. (p. 390)

## ACTION GLOSSARY

Match the terms in the left column with the definitions in the right column.

__ **1. Melancholia** (p. 376)
__ **2. Phrenitis** (p. 376)
__ **3. Psychoses** (p. 376)
__ **4. Organic brain disorder** (pp. 376–377)
__ **5. Acute brain disorder** (p. 380)
__ **6. Chronic brain disorder** (p. 380)

*A. The temporary and reversible dysfunction of brain tissue.*
*B. The ancient Greek term for depression.*
*C. A mental disorder that typically involves hallucinations, delusions, and bizarre behaviors.*
*D. The permanent and irreversible dysfunction of brain tissue.*
*E. The ancient Greek term for schizophrenia.*
*F. Disorders of the central nervous system that have behavioral consequences.*

__ **7. Affective disorder** (p. 383)
__ **8. Depression** (p. 384)
__ **9. Mania/hypomania** (p. 384)
__ **10. Bipolar affective disorder** (p. 377)
__ **11. Dysthymia** (p. 384)
__ **12. Anxiety** (p. 386)
__ **13. Thought disorder** (p. 383)
__ **14. Agoraphobia** (p. 386)
__ **15. Social phobia** (p. 387)
__ **16. Simple phobia** (p. 387)

*A. A highly aversive state that combines physiological arousal, apprehension, and fear, and a vague sense of impending disaster.*
*B. Behavior that typically includes an exalted, grandiose view of oneself, an increase in eating, a decrease in sleeping, "racing thoughts," psychomotor hyperactivity, and difficulty in concentration.*
*C. Behavior characterized by dejection, downheartedness, a sense of decreased self-worth and self-esteem, reduced interest in the future, inability to concentrate, difficulties getting to sleep or staying asleep, and a pervasive feeling of fatigue and ennui.*
*D. The failure in emotional responsivity that typically accompanies schizophrenia.*
*E. A condition characterized by alternation among periods of mania, severe depression, and relative or complete psychological health.*
*F. Mild to moderate depression that interferes with daily functioning but is not as disabling as a major depressive disorder.*
*G. Intense fear of humiliating or embarrassing social situations.*
*H. Intense fear of non-harmful or non-dangerous objects or situations.*
*I. Fear of being in places or situations from which escape might be difficult.*
*J. Deterioration in the ability to think and use language.*

___ 17. Panic disorder (p. 386)

___ 18. Obsessive-compulsive
       disorder (p. 387)

___ 19. Obsession (p. 387)

___ 20. Compulsion (p. 388)

___ 21. Generalized anxiety
       disorder (p. 388)

___ 22. Conversion disorder
       (p. 388)

___ 23. Hypochondriasis (p. 388)

___ 24. Paraphilias (p. 388)

___ 25. Transvestic fetishist (p. 389)

A.  Unavoidable, irresistible preoccupation with certain thoughts or ideas.
B.  Preoccupation with one's body and health.
C.  A male who achieves sexual gratification by wearing female clothing.
D.  Characterized by insistent and unwanted thoughts, urges, and behaviors.
E.  Sudden and unexpected anxiety sufficient to overwhelm a person.
F.  The experience of dramatic physical symptoms that have no organic or physical cause.
G.  Gross impairment in the capacity for affectionate sexual activity between adult human partners.
H.  A behavior that an individual feels compelled to perform, sometimes repeatedly.
I.  Chronic, persistent anxiety that lasts at least six months.

___ 26. Somatoform disorders
       (p. 388)

___ 27. Frotteur (p. 389)

___ 28. Pedophile (p. 389)

___ 29. Exhibitionist (p. 389)

___ 30. Voyeur (p. 389)

___ 31. Sexual masochist (p. 389)

___ 32. Sexual sadist (p. 389)

___ 33. Sexual dysfunctions (p. 389)

___ 34. Disorders usually first
       evident in infancy,
       childhood, or adolescence
       (p. 389)

___ 35. Autism (p. 390)

A.  Problems in sexual functioning and desire.
B.  A person who gets sexual pleasure when he or she inflicts pain on a sexual partner.
C.  A person who gets sexual pleasure when pain is inflicted on him or her by a sexual partner.
D.  A person who achieves sexual gratification with children.
E.  A person sexually aroused by touching or rubbing someone else.
F.  A person who derives sexual gratification from displaying his genitals to strangers.
G.  A person who achieves sexual gratification by watching others engaged in sexual activity.
H.  Physical symptoms that suggest physical disorders for which there are no organic findings or physiologic mechanisms.
I.  A range of pervasive developmental disabilities in social relationships, speech, movement, and intellect.
J.  Mental retardation, pervasive developmental disorders, such as autism, and specific developmental disorders

*ANSWERS*

34. j, 35. i

19. a, 20. i, 21. j, 22. b, 23. b, 24. h, 25. c, 26. h, 27. e, 28. d, 29. f, 30. g, 31. o, 32. b, 33. a,

1. b, 2. e, 3. c, 4. f, 5. a, 6. d, 7. d, 8. c, 9. b, 10. e, 11. f, 12. a, 13. j, 14. i, 15. g, 16. h, 17. f, 18. e,

## SELF-TEST

1.  The two conflicting views on the causes of abnormal behavior that have struggled for supremacy through history include

    (a) the genetic and the environmental.
    (b) yin and yang.
    (c) the learning and the dynamic.
    (d) the natural and the supernatural.
        (LO 1; p. 374)

2.  The man who reformed French mental hospitals in the eighteenth century was

    (a) Pinel.
    (b) Napoleon.
    (c) Lafayette.
    (d) DeGaulle.
        (LO 1; p. 376)

3. Kraepelin coined the term
   (a) schizophrenia.
   (b) catatonia.
   (c) general paresis.
   (d) dementia praecox.
   (LO 1; p. 376)

4. Which of the following is *not* one of the bases for defining abnormal behavior?
   (a) normative
   (b) psychosis
   (c) subjective
   (d) maladaptive
   (LO 2; pp. 377–378)

5. The ideal criterion for abnormal behavior says
   (a) normal behavior cannot be achieved.
   (b) failure to meet the criteria of a healthy personality is abnormal.
   (c) behavior that rarely occurs is abnormal.
   (d) abnormal behavior is any behavior society judges unacceptable.
   (LO 2; p. 378)

6. "The psychoanalytic revolution" refers to
   (a) the influence at the turn of the century of Freud and Breuer's ideas as set forth in *Studies in Hysteria*.
   (b) the idea that unconscious psychological impulses could affect behavior in powerful ways.
   (c) the idea that a "talking" treatment might be more effective for disordered behavior than the harsh physical treatments then in use.
   (d) all of the above are features of the psychoanalytic revolution.
   (LO 3; p. 378)

7. The various versions of *DSM*
   (a) take a decidedly medical or "disease-model" approach to mental disorder.
   (b) categorize syndromes according to symptoms.
   (c) contain specific criteria for diagnosis.
   (d) all of the above are features of *DSM*.
   (LO 4; p. 379)

8. According to research, *DSM-III-R*
   (a) is strictly adhered to by clinicians.
   (b) is very useful in clinical practice.
   (c) is not as useful or research-based as it might be.
   (d) explains the causes of each disorder.
   (LO 5; p. 380)

9. Organic brain disorders
   (a) can be caused by psychological variables alone.
   (b) are inevitably severely disabling.
   (c) can be acute or chronic.
   (d) all of the above.
   (LO 6; p. 380)

10. The subtypes of schizophrenia include
    (a) catatonic, paranoid, and disorganized.
    (b) acute, chronic, and residual.
    (c) endogenous and exogenous.
    (d) process and reactive.
    (LO 8; pp. 383–384)

11. Suicide is
    (a) an inevitable consequence of serious depression.
    (b) the leading cause of death among the aged.
    (c) the third leading cause of death among young people.
    (d) a relatively uncommon event among the middle-aged.
    (LO 9; p. 386)

12. Bipolar disorders
    (a) cannot be treated successfully.
    (b) are a form of schizophrenia.
    (c) can be treated with lithium carbonate.
    (d) typically involve social withdrawal and isolation.
    (LO 9; p. 384)

13. The anxiety and somatoform disorders were formerly termed the
    (a) functional disorders.
    (b) neuroses.
    (c) nonpsychoses.
    (d) dissociative disorders.
    (LO 10; p. 386)

14. Masters and Johnson concerned themselves with
    (a) sexual dysfunctions.
    (b) transsexualism.
    (c) ego-dystonic homosexuality.
    (d) the paraphilias.
    (LO 11; p. 389)

15. Personality disorders are
    (a) responses to environmental stress.
    (b) products of impaired brain function.
    (c) deeply ingrained habits and patterns of behavior.
    (d) never disabling.
    (LO 12; p. 389)

**16.** The prevalence of disorders among children and adolescents
- **(a)** tends to increase with age.
- **(b)** is greater among boys than among girls.
- **(c)** peaks at nine to ten years of age, and again at fourteen to fifteen years of age.
- **(d)** all of the above.
(LO 13; p. 389)

**17.** Which of the following is *not* a common symptom of childhood autism?
- **(a)** disturbed social relationships
- **(b)** extraordinary ability in one area of functioning, usually memory for numbers
- **(c)** cognitive deficits
- **(d)** disturbed motor behavior
(LO 13; p. 390)

*ANSWERS*

1. d, 2. a, 3. d, 4. b, 5. b, 6. d, 7. d, 8. c, 9. c, 10. a, 11. c, 12. c, 13. b, 14. b, 15. c, 16. d, 17. b

# THINKING ABOUT PSYCHOLOGY

**1.** Abnormal behavior can be defined as behavior that differs from the norm, that is, it is different from what most people in the society do. Given this view, is it possible to consider a whole society, such as a racist culture, as "abnormal"?

**2.** Why do definitions of abnormal behavior change from time to time?

# SUGGESTED READINGS

American Psychiatric Association. (1987). *Diagnostic and statistical manual of mental disorders.* (3rd ed. revised). Washington, D.C.: American Psychiatric Association. The new nomenclature, complete with careful comparisons with preceding versions of the *DSM*.

Bleuler, E. (1950). *Dementia praecox or the group of schizophrenias.* New York: International Universities Press. Originally published more than seventy years ago, this classic text still provides some of the best descriptions of the signs and symptoms of schizophrenia.

Breuer, J., & Freud, S. (1957). Fraulein Anna O. In *Studies in hysteria.* New York: Basic Books. The case of Anna O. describes a patient who suffered from an incredible array of hysterical symptoms. The treatment she received and the theories her case and its treatment led to were important to the development of psychoanalysis.

Farberow, N. L., (Ed.). (1980). *The many faces of suicide: Indirect self-destructive behavior.* New York: McGraw-Hill. Farberow, one of the world's authorities on suicide, has edited a book bringing together informed discussions of behaviors that have not before been considered suicidal. High-risk sports, cigarette smoking, alcoholism, and failure to cooperate with medical regimens, as well as many other behaviors, are discussed as self-destructive behaviors.

Mindell, Jodi A. (1993). *Issues in clinical psychology.* Dubuque, IA: Wm. C. Brown. A collection of articles presenting alternative views on controversial topics. Includes discussions of the training of clinical psychologists, whether psychologists should be permitted to prescribe medications, sexual contact between clients and therapists, involuntary treatment and confinement, and working with homosexual clients and AIDS patients.

Styron, William. (1990). *Darkness visible: A memoir of madness.* New York: Random House. Writer William Styron suffered from suicidal depression, a disturbance also visited upon poet Randall Jarrell, author Virginia Woolf, and artist Vincent van Gogh. Styron describes his own struggle to overcome depression.

# CHAPTER 13

## PSYCHOTHERAPY
### OUTLINE

# PSYCHOTHERAPY
## LEARNING OBJECTIVES

**After reading this chapter, you should be able to**

▶ **1.** identify and describe the most important psychoanalytic techniques. *(pp. 398–399)*

▶ **2.** discuss the two crucial aspects of the psychoanalytic relationship, and explain how one aspect interferes with the therapeutic relationship while the other facilitates it. *(pp. 398–399)*

▶ **3.** describe the mechanism by which psychoanalysis helps the patient function more effectively. *(p. 399)*

▶ **4.** describe systematic desensitization, and identify those conditions for which it is appropriate. *(p. 400)*

▶ **5.** describe the roles that classical and operant conditioning methods and observational learning can play in therapy. *(pp. 401–402)*

▶ **6.** identify the foundations of cognitive behavior therapy. *(pp. 403–404)*

▶ **7.** discuss the role of behavior modification and token economies in the management of institutionalized psychotic patients. *(pp. 401–402)*

▶ **8.** summarize the assumptions and the elements comprising person-centered (also called client-centered) therapy. *(pp. 404–405)*

▶ **9.** discuss the goals, methods, and applications of group therapy procedures, including play therapy. *(pp. 405–406)*

▶ **10.** describe biomedical treatment procedures and delineate their applications. *(pp. 407–408)*

▶ **11.** summarize efforts to compare the relative effectiveness of different forms of therapy. *(pp. 408–409)*

▶ **12.** distinguish among primary, secondary, and tertiary prevention. *(pp. 410–411)*

# TREATING ABNORMAL BEHAVIOR

There is an enormous variety of psychological treatments for behavior disorders, not to mention treatment involving medications. These range from long-term psychotherapy, to family therapy, to 12-step programs like Alcoholics Anonymous (Nowinski & Baker, 1992). In most cases, the primary purpose of treatment is to return individuals to fully-functioning lives in their communities.

We can review only a sample of the most widely used therapies: psychoanalysis, behavior therapy, client-centered therapy, group and family therapy, play therapy, and drug therapies. Each one has special value in certain conditions. Yet all share the same ultimate goal: to restore the person to effective psychological and social functioning.

# PSYCHOANALYSIS

Though its greatest popularity lies in the past, classical or Freudian psychoanalysis remains attractive to many mental health professionals (Youngstrom, 1992). The psychoanalyst accepts the basic tenets of psychoanalytic theory, which include the conviction that disturbed psychological functioning is often the result of failure to adequately deal with unconscious feelings, thoughts, and impulses that originally developed in childhood but have been repressed—out of conscious awareness—since then. A psychoanalyst may be trained initially in psychology or psychiatry (a field of medicine). Psychoanalysts are further trained in theories and methods of psychoanalysis and must themselves undergo analysis as part of their training.

**Psychoanalysis** has as its aims to bring these repressed, unconscious thoughts, feelings, and wishes to consciousness so the mature adult can deal with them. The fundamental goal of psychoanalysis is to enable people to deal effectively with the world as it is. This goal is achieved when psychoanalytic patients achieve *insight* about the irrational roots of their behaviors, *awareness* that they are acting on the basis of unconscious thoughts and feelings rather than reality.

Psychoanalysis tends to be intensive (psychoanalysts typically see their patients several times a week) and expensive. More recently, **time-limited psychotherapy** *was developed to shorten the time required for significant behavior change to six months.* Time-limited psychotherapy attempts to hasten transference and overcome patient resistance (Frances, Clarkin, & Perry, 1984; Perry, 1987).

## Basic Psychoanalytic Techniques

Although there are many "schools" of psychoanalysis, the basic techniques for gaining access to unconscious early memories are similar (Horowitz, 1988). Many of these techniques have become a part of other, less intensive therapies like dynamically oriented group and family therapy.

The most important psychoanalytic technique, one of Freud's most important ideas (and about the only part of psychoanalysis that is free), is **free association,** during which *the stream of one's thoughts are unburdened or "talked out" without censorship by the patient.* Freud did not discover free association all at once. In line with the practice of the day, Freud had been hypnotizing his patients, many of them middle-class Viennese women prone to fainting spells, migraine headaches, inexplicable paralysis, and other signs of ill health. His goal was to deliver patients of the repressed memories he believed were responsible for these symptoms.

Freud was not a good hypnotist, and he was not always successful in uncovering the memories of his patients. He gradually developed the method of free association to replace hypnosis. To make the effort easier, Freud started having his patients lie on a couch (ever since, the symbol of the psychoanalyst), speak freely, and wander, without control or censorship, through the forest of available thoughts and memories.

Another important psychoanalytic technique is dream interpretation. Although generations of soothsayers, fortune-tellers, and temple priests had relied on dreams to foretell the future and explain the past and present, Freud was the first to propose specific rules for uncovering the meaning of dreams and for clarifying the extent of their behavioral influence, as discussed in chapter 3. He believed that **dreams** *were symbolic representations of unconscious conflicts stimulated by the previous day's activities and events.* The individual's *conscious memory of his or her dreams,* the **manifest content** of dreams, is less revealing than the **latent content,** *the symbolic and unconscious meaning of dreams.*

The path of psychoanalytic treatment is neither smooth nor predictable, but certain stages are recognizable. In the course of treatment, especially during the process of free association, *patients find areas in which they feel blocked: they cannot talk anymore, they find it difficult to remember crucial events from the past, and they start forgetting appointments.* These behaviors constitute aspects of **resistance.** Essentially the same phenomena

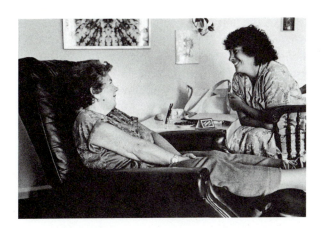

also appear during virtually every other kind of psychological counseling and therapy because they reduce the pain of exploring areas that gave pain in the past and promise to do so again in the future.

Another central component of psychoanalysis is transference. The patient's thoughts and feelings about his or her relationship with the therapist are rarely based upon a realistic assessment of the therapist's behavior during treatment. The therapist makes every effort to convey as little of himself or herself as possible in order to highlight the distortions the patient inevitably brings to his or her feelings about the analyst. These *distortions of the analyst by the patient constitute* transference, *a tendency to see in the therapist behaviors that actually belong to other important persons in the patient's life,* most often the patient's mother and father.

As a consequence of these distortions, the patient responds emotionally to the analyst in many of the same ways he or she responds to parents. It is the analyst's responsibility to help the patient experience growth-inducing insights so that the patient will be able to see the nature of the distortions and their potential for trouble. Distortions revealed during analysis reflect similar distortions occurring outside analysis, distortions presumably responsible for the patient's troubled and troubling behavior.

**Interpretation** is *the means by which transference and resistance are brought to the patient's attention.* (Transference is a form of resistance and an impediment to therapeutic progress even though it is also a means by which progress is achieved.) The therapist's interpretations are designed to confront the patient in the most non-threatening way possible with both the significance and the sources of defensive, resistant behavior.

Why should exploration of early childhood, dreams, and free associations improve the client's everyday ability to function? The key to the effectiveness of psychoanalysis is based on the ego defense mechanism of repression (see chapter 11). Psychoanalytic theory states that symptoms arise because the individual uses psychic energy to repress (that is, to keep from conscious awareness) uncomfortable thoughts, impulses, and memories. Repression is a full-time job, otherwise the threatening images would enter consciousness. The energy used to repress these threatening images deprives the ego of its full complement of energy, thus leading to impaired functioning. *If the client can discover and work through these unconscious threats, the energy is no longer needed for repression and is returned to the ego for everyday use, a process referred to as* catharsis.

## Evaluation of Psychoanalysis

There is evidence that clients in psychoanalysis feel that they gain insight into themselves (Luborsky, Crits-Christoph, & Mellon, 1986). It is generally thought that psychodynamic therapies are effective only for individuals with mild disorders, but not with psychotic patients. Because psychoanalysis is a highly verbal process, it tends to work best for those who are well-educated and articulate (Luborsky & Spence, 1978).

▶ **GUIDED REVIEW** *Learning Objectives 1, 2, and 3*

1. The most important psychoanalytic technique is _____; it permits patients to recall unconscious determinants of their behavior.
2. _____ is another way of reaching the unconscious.
3. _____ is an inevitable accompaniment of analysis and psychotherapy; it mobilizes diverse _____ designed to protect the patient from troubling memories.
4. _____, by which patients distort the psychoanalyst's thoughts, feelings, and behavior to reflect those of parents and other important figures in their lives, is central to the _____ process.
5. _____ strives to bring about total self-understanding by focusing on the unconscious determinants of behavior.
6. The symbolic and unconscious meaning of dreams is referred to by psychoanalysts as their _____.

*ANSWERS*

*1. free association 2. Dream interpretation 3. Resistance, defense mechanisms 4. Transference, psychoanalytic 5. Psychoanalysis 6. latent content*

Attempts to test theoretical aspects of psychoanalysis, for example, the validity of the latent contents of dreams, transference, and so on, suffer from the difficulties we have noted already in chapter 11, in particular. The theory is written in a way that makes it nearly impossible to test scientifically (Farrell, 1981; Fisher & Greenberg, 1978; Kline, 1972; Liebert & Spiegler, 1990).

# BEHAVIOR THERAPY

Behavior therapy, *derived from learning theories and experimental research, aims to eliminate or to modify specific maladaptive behaviors.* Unlike psychoanalysis, behavior therapy has specific goals and claims extensive experimental confirmation of theory and practice. Also unlike psychoanalytic therapies, behavior therapy does not regard abnormal behavior as a *symptom* of an underlying psychological disorder. It regards the abnormal behavior *as* the disorder.

## Historical Background

In the first decade of this century, the Russian physiologist Ivan Pavlov demonstrated that a dog will learn to salivate at the sound of a bell if that sound is first paired with food, a substance to which the dog naturally salivates (Pavlov, 1906). This form of learning is known as classical conditioning. Twenty years later, E. L. Thorndike, another of psychology's early learning theorists, discovered that an animal can also learn if the consequences of its learning are reinforcing; this form of learning is called operant conditioning (Thorndike, 1931) (see chapter 5, Learning).

Both classical and operant conditioning, as well as social learning, are now recognized as fundamental to both human and animal behavior. Psychologists knew for several decades that these learning mechanisms had the power to create and modify behavior, but it was not until the 1950s that scientists began to exploit the mechanisms' capacities to affect undesirable behavior (Dollard & Miller, 1950). Today, learning-based behavioral therapies are important elements of behavior change programs in psychiatric hospitals and in other settings where targeted behavior change is desired by both therapist and client, including detention centers, prisons, drug rehabilitation centers, mental retardation training institutions, and classrooms for the learning impaired or behaviorally disordered.

## Behavior Therapy: Systematic Desensitization

Systematic desensitization is *a widely used behavior therapy procedure designed to reduce distressing levels of anxiety.* It was developed by Joseph Wolpe (1952, 1958), a behavior therapist whose clinical work with anxious patients convinced him that anxiety is a learned behavior that can be unlearned. Wolpe's observations were influenced by an experiment by Watson and Rayner (1920), which demonstrated the role of conditioning in the acquisition of fear responses by an infant referred to as "Little Albert." (See the description of this experiment in chapter 11.)

The behavior therapist who uses systematic desensitization generally begins the process by teaching clients **deep muscle relaxation** through **progressive relaxation training.** The therapist teaches patients to contract and then relax successive muscle groups. By the fourth or fifth session, people typically report that they can achieve states of relaxation accompanied by warmth, a sense of increased inner peace, and pleasant feelings of comfort.

Systematic desensitization itself begins after client and therapist compose a list of anxiety-producing situations arranged in order of their stress-inducing potential. The situations often include parents, spouses, friends, or employers. Once the list is complete, the client is asked to concentrate on and describe in as much detail as possible the least threatening scene in the hierarchy. If the relaxed person can imagine the scene in detail for several seconds without experiencing the anxiety he or she experiences in real life, the therapist asks the client to proceed to the next scene. When the client does experience anxiety about a scene, he or she returns to the next lowest step.

Behavior therapists often ask desensitization clients to practice less anxiety-arousing situations in the real world. When they can do so with situations that arouse only modest amounts of anxiety, they may be asked to move on to more anxiety-provoking situations. The purpose is to weaken the bond between the anxiety-provoking stimuli and the anxiety response.

Another component of behavioral treatment for anxiety is **assertiveness training,** in *which client and therapist role-play situations that require assertive responses by the person.* These verbal behaviors—disagreeing with a boss, criticizing a good friend, or expressing an opinion in a group of knowledgeable people—are difficult for everyone, but they are particularly difficult when a person is anxious or fearful about the impression he or she will

# APPLYING PSYCHOLOGY

## How Assertive Are You?

How assertive are you? The following brief scenarios describe four situations in which assertiveness is necessary. How likely are you to be assertive in each situation?

1. You have had two dates with a person to whom you are very attracted. Both dates have gone very well. It is time for you to share with the other person your growing fondness for him or her.

2. You are a member of a small seminar devoted to an interesting subject outside your major. The instructor is a senior professor you respect. The problem is that the professor does not always explain the material clearly. Perhaps you ought to ask the professor to clarify the material.

3. You and some good friends are watching a political debate on television. As you watch the debate, it becomes clear that your friends do not perceive the integrity and honesty of one candidate the same way you do. You want to understand the basis for this difference in perception.

4. A good friend, notorious among those who know him for his tendency to spend money foolishly, asks you for a loan. You only have enough money to last to the end of the month. In addition, you are not sure you will be paid back or that the money will be spent for necessities. How do you respond to this request?

make. Assertive behavior will help inhibit anxiety. Can you imagine being appropriately assertive and painfully anxious at the same time?

Read Applying Psychology: How Assertive Are You? Can you imagine yourself being assertive in all of these scenes? In most of them? In any of them?

A behavioral technique also used to break the bond between fearful stimuli and anxiety is **flooding**, *the prolonged exposure to the feared stimulus.* Flooding has been used to eliminate obsessive-compulsive disorders. The clients "contaminate" themselves with whatever object they are trying to avoid. The desired result is that the clients will realize they have nothing to fear (Rachman & Hodgson, 1980). A variation on flooding is **implosive therapy**, *in which the feared stimulus is imagined instead of actually confronted.* The client is asked to imagine very anxiety-arousing scenes involving the feared object (Levis, 1985).

## Positive Reinforcement and Extinction in Behavior Therapy

Positive reinforcement involves rewarding desirable behavior, and extinction is removing reinforcers for undesirable behavior. Operant theory and research have firmly established that rewarding or reinforcing behavior increases the likelihood that the behavior will recur; while ignoring or punishing the behavior decreases that same likelihood, as discussed in chapter 5.

Positive reinforcement and extinction were among the earliest and most widely-used behavioral approaches to the modification of the behavior of psychotic people. More than three decades ago, psychologists Ayllon and Michael (1959) proposed a simple but surprisingly powerful strategy to modify the behavior of the psychotic patients in their charge at a provincial hospital in Canada. Their prescription derived from operant conditioning theory: punish unwanted psychotic behaviors to reduce their frequency and reinforce desired nonpsychotic behaviors to increase their frequency. Bizarre, psychotic verbal reports of persecution and repetitive and unnecessary visits to the nursing station by patients decreased markedly when both were ignored by ward personnel; assaultive behavior on the ward was eliminated completely when behaviors incompatible with it, like talking quietly and sensibly to nurses, were strongly reinforced; weight gain and its principal cause, stealing food, were both eliminated when patients who stole food were immediately ejected from the dining room.

Instead of using direct praise, attention, or food to modify behavior, Ayllon and Azrin (1965) developed the idea of a **token economy** as a more efficient means of encouraging behavioral change. *The use of tokens, redeemable for tangible reinforcers* like cigarettes and candy, made especially good sense for schizophrenic patients because they often experience difficulty with verbal and social reinforcers. Furthermore, giving patients the responsibility for spending their tokens provided them with a greater sense of control over their lives than many had experienced in years. (As we note in chapter 14, Health Psychology, a feeling of personal control is important to health and well-being.)

Paul and Lentz (1977) report on a six-year effort to evaluate two programs built around positive reinforcement and extinction in a large Illinois state hospital. These researchers compared the results of their token economy behavior modification program with the results of two other programs, a standard hospital program and a community program. Paul and Lentz concluded that their program's results compared favorably. The behavior modification program had generated more wanted behavior and less unwanted behavior, had more often led to release from the hospital, and had resulted in greater lengths of stay out of the hospital. These data were particularly impressive because the psychotic patients in Paul and Lentz's wards had not been given the antipsychotic drugs that patients in the two other wards had been given.

Another success story utilizing positive reinforcement and extinction is Achievement Place, a community based, family-style group home for six to eight pre-delinquent or delinquent youth under the direction of "teaching parents," couples trained to use behavioral techniques to bring about marked changes in the behavior of seriously delinquent adolescents. Based on positive reinforcement, extinction, and token economies, marked gains in academic, conversational, self-management, and conflict-negotiation skills have been reported in Achievement Place (Jones, 1979). Widely imitated, this approach to changing undesirable behaviors with serious long-term consequences has shown both short- and long-term results.

The expanded application of these techniques has promoted their use in a variety of fields. Positive reinforcement and extinction programs have been widely used in public school classrooms to accelerate learning by normal children and to motivate and increase the attention span of retarded children in special classrooms (Ollendick, 1986).

These techniques have also been used to treat several serious nonpsychotic disorders in adolescents and adults, such as anorexia nervosa, a relatively common eating disorder characterized by rapid, life-threatening weight loss caused by uncontrollable vomiting that has no apparent physical cause. Patients hospitalized for this disorder were positively reinforced for successively greater food intake, and unwanted behaviors, like vomiting and other sympathy-inducing behaviors, were ignored. Food intake increased markedly and the vomiting was eventually extinguished in most patients (Leitenberg, Rosen, Gross, Nudelman, & Vara, 1988).

Similarly, eighty-one men and women who suffered from chronic low back pain were offered an eight-session outpatient operant behavioral treatment (Turner & Clancy, 1988). The patients' spouses were instructed not to reinforce "pain behaviors" (complaints of pain, refusal to undertake an activity that might involve pain) and to reinforce "well behaviors" (participation in a wide range of vigorous physical activities). Patients set and worked toward behavioral goals in areas affected by the pain and engaged in a regular aerobic walking/jogging program. Patients provided this operant behavioral treatment showed greater pre- to post-treatment improvement, as judged by both self- and spouse-ratings, than either a waiting-list control group or another treatment group.

## Modeling and Guided Participation

**Observational learning,** a basic form of learning, involves *learning a skill or behavior by watching someone (a "model") perform it.* Clinical methods derived from observational learning, modeling, and guided participation, have been utilized very effectively.

In one of the earliest uses of these techniques in a clinical setting, Ross, Ross, and Evans (1971) successfully treated a six-year-old boy whose shyness was so severe that he had become school phobic. At the beginning of a seven-week treatment program, the therapist and the boy went to the boy's school and the boy watched the therapist interacting with the other children in the room. Next, role-playing was added to the therapeutic effect of modeling and the therapist and patient acted out social behaviors the boy could use with his classmates. Finally, guided participation was added to the therapeutic mix; the therapist and the boy both took part in play with the boy's classmates and as the boy's level of comfort rose, the therapist gradually removed himself from the play. Two months later, the boy continued to experience no fear with his peers and demonstrated markedly improved social functioning.

Mattick and Peters (1988) utilized therapist-guided exposure and cognitive restructuring to modify the severe social phobias of fifty-one men and women. Therapist-guided exposure in this study was similar to the guided participation used by Bandura, Ross, and others. Therapists joined patients in entering those business or eating establishments the patients feared the most (because they had to interact with service people); the therapists then modeled effective social behavior. The **cognitive restructuring** involved *discussing with patients the irrational* *sources of the thoughts that typically accompanied their phobic behavior.* These discussions centered on patients' concerns about the opinions of others and the omnipresent feeling that others were watching them.

## Cognitive Behavior Therapy

A relatively recent development in behavior therapy combines traditional learning theories with cognitive theory, by recognizing the impact that thoughts, beliefs, expectations, and attitudes have on behavior. **Cognitive behavior therapy** *seeks to change attitudes, beliefs, and other cognitions in order to facilitate changes in behavior.*

One of the earliest forms of cognitive behavior therapy is **rational-emotive therapy (RET)**, developed by Albert Ellis (1962, 1980). RET *helps patients identify and challenge the irrational, self-defeating beliefs behind their troubling behavior, to motivate them to take action to restore rational control over their emotions and their behavior.* Rational-emotive therapists assume that most people, especially those who are helped to do so, will substitute reason for emotion in planning and changing their behavior. RET involves learning how self-defeating it is to hold such erroneous, all-too-common underlying beliefs as, "I must be a perfect mother, wife, and daughter to be a success in life," "Everyone must love me or else I have failed," or "I must be at the top of my class or else I can't hope to do anything important in life."

Are any of the guiding beliefs in your life self-defeating? Do any of the irrational ideas listed in table 13.1 sound familiar?

Cognitive behavior therapists have focused more attention on depression than upon any other disorder. The two major cognitive-behavioral approaches for mild to moderate depression are Beck's cognitive therapy (Beck, Rush, Shaw, & Emery, 1979) and Rehm's self-control training (Rehm, 1977).

Beck assumes that depression involves a cognitive triad of negative thoughts about oneself, the situation, and the future. Depressed people consistently misinterpret facts about themselves in a negative direction, consistently focus on the most negative aspects of any situation, and consistently maintain a pessimistic attitude toward the future. Beck's cognitive therapy for depression trains depressed people to use the outcomes of their behavior to test the accuracy of their negatively skewed beliefs. Through pointed but friendly questions, patients eventually realize how unrealistic their beliefs are and, through

---

**TABLE 13.1    Common irrational ideas that cause us trouble**

Albert Ellis, founder of rational-emotive therapy, believes that many of us get into emotional difficulty because we behave according to one or more irrational ideas about life and our pursuit of it. How many of the following irrational ideas do *you* live by? If you identify one or more self-defeating ideas specific to your way of life in this list of twelve, can you ever imagine yourself living by a more rational life schema?

1. It is a *dire* necessity to be loved and approved of.
2. I *should* be *thoroughly* competent, adequate, and achieving in *all* possible respects.
3. Some people *are* bad, wicked, or vile and *should* (or *must*) be punished.
4. If things do not go (or stay) the way I very much want them to, it would be *awful, catastrophic,* or *terrible!*
5. Unhappiness is *externally* caused and I *cannot* control it (unless I control the other person).
6. One *should* remain upset or worried if faced with a dangerous or fearsome reality.
7. It is *easier* to avoid responsibility and difficulties than to face them.
8. I have a *right* to be dependent and people (or someone) *should* be strong enough to rely on (or take care of me).
9. My early childhood experiences *must* continue to *control* me and determine my emotions and behavior!
10. I *should* become upset over my and other peoples' problems or behavior.
11. There is invariably *one* right, precise, and *perfect* solution and it would be *terrible* or *catastrophic* if this perfect solution is not found.
12. The world (and especially other people) *should* be fair and justice (or mercy) *must* triumph. (From Albert Ellis's books)

From Albert Ellis (1962), Albert Ellis (1975), and Albert Ellis and Robert A. Harper (1975). Copyright by Institute for Rational-Emotive Therapy, New York, NY. Used by permission.

---

cognitive restructuring, are able to view those beliefs more realistically. Extensive empirical research comparing Beck's cognitive therapy for depression with antidepressant medication (Beck, Hollon, Young, Bedrosian, & Budenz, 1985) supports the view that Beck's treatment methods are as helpful to mildly to moderately depressed people as is medication.

Rehm's self-control therapy views depression in terms of deficits in the various stages of the self-control sequence. Treatment involves training patients in systematic self-monitoring (to heighten the accurate observation of their behavior), self-evaluation (to enhance their capacity to realistically evaluate the worth of their behavior), and self-reinforcement (to increase the likelihood that they will reward themselves when their behavior deserves reinforcement). Since depressed people are unlikely to give themselves credit for their achievements and accomplishments,

Rehm's approach focuses on the use of self-reinforcement procedures as a means of enriching the schedule of reinforcement. Like Beck's cognitive behavior therapy for depression, Rehm's self-control training has fared well in empirical tests of its comparative worth (Kornblith, Rehm, O'Hara, & Lamparski, 1983).

## Evaluation of Behavior Therapies

Undesirable behavior is not regarded by behavior therapists as a symptom of an underlying conflict, but is itself the target of treatment. This means that behavior therapists place less emphasis on the person's past than do psychoanalysts. Like humanistic therapies, behavior therapists do not believe it is so important to know where abnormal behavior came from; it is possible to deal with it in the present.

Modern behaviorism has been influenced by cognitive psychology so that nowadays few behavior therapists ignore cognitions that may give rise to or sustain undesirable behavior.

Critics sometimes argue that behavior therapy may do harm to clients by treating their symptoms in a superficial way, ignoring deeper problems. They say that *a patient might undergo "successful" treatment for a problem only to have another problem appear later because of a neglected underlying condition,* a phenomenon called **symptom substitution.** Unfortunately, there is no way to

know, if a new symptom does appear, whether it is the result of the same underlying condition or a completely independent symptom. It is possible to evaluate whether the client's general level of functioning improves after behavior therapy. On this question, research shows substantial improvement (e.g., Bandura, Grusec, & Menlove, 1967). A recent trend that will facilitate comparative studies of the effectiveness of different therapies is the creation of detailed manuals for training therapists (Beck et al., 1979; Rosengard, 1991).

Behavior therapy has a good record in treating anxiety and phobias, sexual dysfunctions, insomnia, obesity, eating disorders, alcoholism, and other problems (Kazdin & Wilson, 1978). For depression, both cognitive and traditional therapy have been shown to be effective (Berman et al., 1985).

> ▶ **GUIDED REVIEW** *Learning Objectives 4, 5, 6, and 7*
>
> 1. _____ aims at direct change of learned maladaptive behavior.
> 2. _____ stems from Joseph Wolpe's conviction that bad habits, including neuroses, can be unlearned by inhibiting the anxiety often associated with them.
> 3. Token economies substitute _____ reinforcers—tokens good for candy, cigarettes, and other reinforcers—for verbal reinforcement delivered by professional personnel.
> 4. Along with _____ and _____ conditioning, _____ learning is a principal means by which maladaptive behavior is learned and unlearned.
> 5. _____ and _____ are two behavior therapy techniques that attempt to extinguish fear responses by exposing clients to the objects of their fears.
> 6. Therapies that seek to change an individual's attitudes and beliefs, such as rational-emotive therapy, are known as _____.
>
> *ANSWERS*
>
> *1. Behavior therapy 2. Systematic desensitization 3. material 4. classical, operant, observational 5. Flooding, implosion 6. cognitive behavior therapy*

## ROGERS' PERSON-CENTERED THERAPY

Person-centered therapy (also known as client-centered therapy) was developed by Carl Rogers over a period of four decades (Rogers, 1957, 1961; Pape & Bervan, 1983). Since it appears to be most effective with people faced with normal life problems rather than those with serious psychopathology, it is mainly used by counselors to deal with students' vocational and academic problems.

According to Rogers, troubled individuals experience conflicts between their self-image and the objective facts. The function of the counselor, in his view, is to facilitate clients' (not "patients' ") resolutions of these conflicts by contributing to a warm, human relationship.

Rogers' belief that clients must take responsibility for their own treatment and his conviction that the counselor must not assume control over the course of therapy have led to *another term for person-centered therapy:* **non-directive therapy.** It is non-directive because the therapist does not attempt to "cure" the patient by giving advice, but instead sets the optimum conditions for solving life problems. Person-centered therapy is based on the premise that people can solve their own problems if they confront their fears and self-deceptions in a non-threatening setting.

Client-centered therapy is based on several core beliefs; all of them figure importantly in Rogers' theory of personality (see chapter 11).

1. *Congruence or genuineness,* an openness in which the therapist is her or his genuine, real self, being totally open, with no facade.
2. *Empathy,* accurately perceiving and responding to the feelings of the client.
3. *Unconditional positive regard,* an acceptance and valuing of the person no matter what he or she is doing or feeling. One of the counselor's prime functions is to convey genuine, empathic, and non-possessive warmth and human concern—unconditional positive regard—for clients.

By providing such a setting, Rogers believes the client is in the best position for genuine self-discovery. Therapy progresses best when the therapist and client share feelings of respect and affection for each other. The client benefits most by passing from a confrontational to an emotional sharing relationship. Significant progress is signalled when the client begins to be less self-condemning and defensive. In other words, the person-centered therapist encourages clients to talk freely about their problems and, without attempting to change their minds or to blame or criticize them, helps them to accept their feelings about themselves and others.

### Evaluation of Person-Centered Therapy

Humanistic therapies, such as Rogers' person-centered therapy, deal with the client as a whole person, rather than with fragments of behavior. They are most appropriate for the less severe disorders, and most benefit clients who are

articulate. One appeal of person-centered therapy is that it is relatively uncomplicated. Counselors do not have to interpret dreams or delve into the unconscious, nor do they have to implement highly precise treatment techniques, as in behavior therapy. What they must do is display genuineness, empathy, and unconditional positive regard. Like psychodynamic therapy, humanistic therapies have been faulted as being unscientific and even antiscientific, resisting empirical evaluation.

▶ **GUIDED REVIEW** *Learning Objective 8*

1. Rogers' _____ therapy is based on an emotional sharing relationship between client and therapist.
2. The counselor's job is to convey _____ for his/her clients, _____, and _____.

*ANSWERS*

1. client-centered 2. unconditional positive regard, empathy, genuineness

## GROUP TREATMENT

All treatment methods discussed so far have focused on one therapist working with one client. But many therapists have concluded that there is value in counseling groups of people. There are at least two reasons for the growth of group treatments. First, they are efficient. More clients can be seen by the therapist, and the cost per client is lower. Second, many psychological difficulties are interpersonal—problems in dealing with other people, particularly with parents, children, spouses, coworkers.

There are many forms of group treatment. Group therapy and family therapy emphasize the therapeutic value of groups for troubled individuals. Encounter groups are designed for healthy people who want to improve their capacity for living a full emotional life. Self-help groups, like Alcoholics Anonymous, do not involve professionals treating clients but they do have many of the same goals as professionally led group treatments. Play therapy was developed for use with children and is often used in conjunction with family therapy.

### Group Therapy

Although the "active ingredients" of group therapy are not known for certain, the loneliness and isolation of many in society are undoubtedly lessened in a group setting. In group therapy, people come closer to one another; they learn that misery loves company and that their troubles are

not unique. They also provide valuable insights. After participating in a group long enough to learn its procedures and its agreed-upon interpersonal norms, group members are often surprisingly perceptive in their observations of their peers. It is almost as though the therapist has several "co-therapists" helping each other achieve the kind of insight that takes so long to achieve in individual therapy. An additional benefit of group therapy is that it gives patients the opportunity to attempt socialization skills within an accepting, nonjudgmental framework (Kaul & Bednar, 1986).

Developed largely by Perls (1969), who was trained as a psychoanalyst, **Gestalt therapy** *is a group therapy designed to provide a group experience in attending to immediate feelings and impulses and expressing and acting upon them.* Perls emphasized the importance of living in the here-and-now rather than in the past or the future.

Gestalt therapy stems indirectly from the Gestalt psychology tradition, which teaches the necessity of attending both to a figure or foreground (the part of the environment to which we are currently attending) as well as to the background against which the figure is seen. In the Gestalt group, members try to help each other experience as fully as possible their feelings toward current problems and concerns. Gestalt therapy does not have strong empirical support.

## Family Therapy

**Family therapy** *is the technique in which an entire family is seen together in order to expose and treat destructive attitudes and patterns of interaction.* It views the family as a system of interconnected roles—mother, father, daughter, son. All their relationships influence each family member. Family therapy has grown considerably during the past decade (Gurman & Kniskern, 1981; Minuchin, Rosman, & Baker, 1978; Szapocznik et al., 1988).

Family therapy allows both the therapist and clients (the family) to observe and deal with the complex set of interactions that precipitates and maintains the child's or other family member's maladaptive behavior. For example, it does little good to help an aggressive child reduce the tendency to strike out in anger unless a parent (originally involved in or responsible for the development of that behavior) is also helped to understand how he or she may precipitate this behavior in the child (Patterson, 1985).

When the entire family sees the therapist, the gains tend to last longer and to persist beyond the walls of the consulting room. One reason family therapy is successful is that it permits all family members to rehearse new responses in the precise family setting in which they will be maintained. They can practice the new behavior in the presence of the parents, siblings, and children, in whose presence they can expect to be reinforced or punished at home.

## Play Therapy

Often when children are troubled, a therapist will wish to see the child both alone and with other members of the child's family. As we have seen above, modeling and guided participation, and various forms of behavior therapy, can be used with children as well as with their families. Some forms of psychotherapy have been developed primarily for use with children. Play therapy, first described in the classic book about childhood autism, *Dibs: In Search of Self* by Virginia Axline (1964), is one of them.

**Play therapy** *involves the use of play in a therapeutic setting to diagnose and treat children.* It is thought that children's behavior during play reveals patterns that indicate the child's emotional and social difficulties. Furthermore, the play setting is used to provide an opportunity for children to express their feelings freely, as part of a therapy program (O'Connor, 1991; D. Singer, in press).

---

▶ **GUIDED REVIEW** *Learning Objective 9*

1. _____ enables many patients to experience a lessening of the loneliness and isolation of society.
2. _____ developed from the widespread frustration of child therapists at the difficulty in translating therapeutic gains made by a troubled child in the consulting room into equivalent gains at home.
3. _____ therapy was developed for use with children both as a means of diagnosis and treatment.

*ANSWERS*

*1. Group therapy 2. Family therapy 3. Play*

# BIOMEDICAL THERAPIES

Some forms of mental disorder, particularly those involving psychosis, tend to be treated with drugs or other biomedical methods. **Biomedical therapies** *modify behavior by temporarily or permanently altering brain functions.* Sometimes these methods are used alone, but often they are used along with psychotherapy or behavior therapy.

In the 1930s and 1940s, before the discovery of the major tranquilizers, uncontrollably violent psychotic patients were often referred for psychosurgery. This surgery took several forms, but the most common, prefrontal lobotomy, involved surgical destruction of the neural pathways from portions of the frontal lobes to the rest of the brain.

Although patients receiving this surgery typically showed marked reductions in violence and anger, they also commonly suffered from serious, irreversible side effects, including memory loss, impaired intellectual abilities, and a reduction in emotional responsiveness. As a result, when the major tranquilizers were found effective in alleviating many of the symptoms of major psychiatric disorders, psychosurgery fell into disuse.

## Electroconvulsive Therapy

Psychotic patients are sometimes given **electroconvulsive therapy (ECT)**, *a brief electrical current passed across the brain.* (The technique was discussed in chapter 6 in connection with its effects on memory.) In the past, the shock was delivered with sufficient intensity to induce a grand mal seizure and unconsciousness. Today, following research indicating that a grand mal seizure is not necessary for good clinical results, the level of shock given to patients is less intense. Patients are anesthetized before the shock is administered.

Once widely used for psychotic patients, ECT is now reserved almost entirely for sufferers with affective disorders, particularly those who have become severely depressed, uncontrollably agitated, or suicidal. Empirical research shows that ECT alleviates serious depressive conditions more quickly than other treatments (Weiner, 1984). On the other hand, additional data suggest that psychotic depressions terminated by ECT are apt to recur within a shorter period of time than depressions that end on their own (Scovern & Killmann, 1980).

ECT is highly controversial. It is a radical treatment and can have irreversible side effects, including broken bones from the induced seizure and a loss in intellectual abilities

from destruction of brain tissue. ECT differs from psychosurgery in that substantial empirical data have been reported justifying its use in conditions that have failed to respond to other less drastic treatments.

## Drug Therapy

There has been a revolution in the field of mental health, beginning with the development of drugs to treat schizophrenia during the 1950s. Drug therapy has made it possible to treat acute schizophrenia and to calm other psychotic patients so they are able to benefit from other forms of therapy.

The drugs now in widest use can be placed into four distinct categories (Davis & Greenblatt, 1979; Kessler & Waletzky, 1981). A summary of these families of drugs is provided in table 13.2.

*Antipsychotics* (also known as **"major tranquilizers"**) The major tranquilizers include the large family of **phenothiazine** drugs (examples include the generic drug Chlorpromazine, trade name *Thorazine*). **The phenothiazines dramatically reduce the delusions, hallucinations, and violent behavior of many schizophrenic patients.** These drugs also permit patients to benefit from other forms of "talking" therapy, which may hasten their return to society. As a result, the chaos and bedlam of hospital "back wards" is lessened, and patients who must continue to be institutionalized have a chance for a more serene life during their hospitalization. The same drugs, unfortunately, have also been given in massive quantities to sedate patients to make caring for them easier. Some of the patients treated in this way with these drugs have suffered from serious, irreversible side effects (see table 13.2).

*Antidepressants* The antidepressant drugs are used to ease the pain and suffering of moderate and severe depression. One class of antidepressants is the Monoamine Oxidase Inhibitors (MAOIs). As the name implies, these drugs interfere with the action of the enzyme monoamine oxidase (MAO). MAO is associated with lower levels of norepinephrine and serotonin in the nervous system. Deficiencies of these neurotransmitters have been implicated in depression. By blocking MAO, the MAO inhibitors presumably correct this deficiency. Because MAO inhibitors have undesirable side effects, they have been replaced in recent years by another class of antidepressants, the *tricyclics* (e.g., Imipramine and Doxepin). They also increase the levels of norepinephrine and serotonin.

## TABLE 13.2 Drugs used to treat mental disorders

**Antipsychotics** (Also known as "major tranquilizers.") Used to treat schizophrenic patients. Decrease psychotic thinking, suspiciousness, and perplexity, normalize psychomotor behavior, and lessen the impact of hallucinations and delusions.

*Examples:* Phenothiazines: Chlorpromazine (Thorazine); perphenazine (Trilafon); haloperidol (Haldol).

*Caution:* Side effects can be formidable and irreversible.

**Antidepressants** Treatment for moderate to severe depression. Produce slight sedation, a lessening of depression, an increase in motor activity and in optimism for the future. Monoamine Oxidase Inhibitors (MAOIs).

*Examples:* Imipramine (Elavil, Tofranil); Doxepin (Sinequan); tranylcypromine (Parnate); Fluoxetine (Prozac); Trazodone (Desyrel).

*Caution:* Imipramine, doxepin and the other tricyclic antidepressants can cause dry mouth, rapid heart beat, and other autonomic effects; tranylcypromine and the other MAO inhibitors can also precipitate manic or hypomanic episodes, and in rare cases, dramatically increase blood pressure.

**Antimanic Drugs** Lithium, administered as lithium carbonate. Used to treat mania and depression in bipolar affective disorder. Reduces intensity of manic episodes in bipolar affective disorder.

*Caution:* Since the difference in a therapeutic and a toxic dose of lithium carbonate is small, careful monitoring of blood levels of lithium is necessary.

**Antianxiety Drugs** ("minor tranquilizers") Treatment for anxiety. Cause sedation, reduce anxiety, may enhance mood and increase vigor.

*Examples:* Chlordiazepoxide (Librium); diazepam (Valium); meprobamate (Equanil, Miltown); Alprazolam (Xanax); Lorazepam (Ativan); Busirone (BuSpar).

*Caution:* These drugs are dependency inducing and may cause life-threatening withdrawal symptoms.

---

Antidepressant drugs are effective in lessening the feelings of foreboding, worthlessness, and hopelessness that may overwhelm a depressed person. Seriously depressed patients are first given a trial of antidepressant drugs before ECT is considered.

*Antimanic Drugs*   Many bipolar affective disorders are responsive to lithium carbonate, a naturally occurring compound. The drug is used to terminate manic episodes and increase the interval between mania and depression in bipolar affective disorder. It appears to be very successful but also can have unfortunate side effects and can even cause death (Lydiard & Gelenberg, 1982).

*Antianxiety Drugs ("minor tranquilizers")*   The **minor tranquilizers** *enable moderately anxious patients to deal*

*more effectively with normal life stresses.* The most common minor tranquilizers are barbiturates (e.g., phenobarbital) and benzodiazepines (e.g., *Librium* and *Valium*).

The minor tranquilizers are designed for people suffering from disorders involving moderate anxiety. They are often used in conjunction with psychological treatment. Unfortunately, these drugs have been subject to abuse since they are addictive and are capable of inducing "highs." As many as one in ten adult Americans take these or other antianxiety drugs (Bootzin & Acocella, 1988).

### ▶ GUIDED REVIEW *Learning Objective 10*

1. _____, once used to treat uncontrollable psychotic behavior, is rarely used because drugs can be utilized for the same purpose.
2. _____ is a treatment for severe depression that is unresponsive to antidepressant medication.
3. The _____ tranquilizers, including the _____, are effective in reducing the delusions, hallucinations, and violent behavior of some schizophrenic patients.
4. The _____ tranquilizers, including _____ and _____, enable moderately anxious patients to deal more effectively with normal life stresses.
5. _____ drugs, including the _____ antidepressants, are effective in reducing some of the most distressing symptoms of depression.
6. _____ terminates _____ episodes and reduces the likelihood of depression in bipolar affective disorders.

*ANSWERS*

1. *Psychosurgery 2. Electroconvulsive therapy (ECT) 3. major; phenothiazines 4. minor; Librium, Valium 5. Antidepressant; tricyclic 6. Lithium carbonate; manic*

## WHAT TREATMENT FOR WHICH DISORDER?

A single answer to this all-important question is impossible because of the measurement difficulties posed by outcome research. These difficulties include diagnostic unreliability (patients in a single diagnostic group may not actually demonstrate the same symptomatology), problems of treatment standardization (patients in a single treatment group may not actually receive the same treatment to the same degree), and lack of agreement on what constitutes effective treatment (Lambert, Shapiro, & Bergin, 1986). Nonetheless, this section will review some comparative treatment outcome studies to put into perspective what is and is not known about the outcome of treatment for emotional disorders.

One of the few conclusions on which almost everyone agrees is that psychotherapy by itself is clearly less effective in modifying the behavior of schizophrenic patients than are antipsychotic drugs by themselves (Kane, 1986). Antipsychotic drugs are effective in treating symptoms, including hallucinations, delusions, and disordered thinking. Psychological treatments are effective in eliminating such symptoms as withdrawal, blunted affect, and lack of volition. Psychotherapy may help people achieve insight into some of the causes of their difficulties, but it is the phenothiazines that enable schizophrenic patients to achieve enough control over symptoms to return to greater or lesser adjustment to the world. Most clinicians also agree that electroconvulsive therapy is often the most effective treatment for severe, intractable, life-threatening depressions and that lithium carbonate is the most effective treatment for mania (Goodwin & Roy-Byrne, 1987).

What is not known is how effective psychotherapy, psychoanalysis, behavior therapy, "talking therapies," and minor tranquilizers are in treating psychological disorders that do not involve psychosis. Answers to this question would be an inestimable boon to patients and therapists alike.

Controversy over the merits of psychotherapy began in 1952 shortly after the publication of a review of the effects of psychotherapy on anxiety and moderate depression. The review, written by Hans Eysenck, was followed by similar reviews in 1960 and 1965. In all reviews, Eysenck restricted his use of the word psychotherapy to the techniques and procedures of psychoanalysis. He concluded, "There appears to be an inverse correlation between recovery and psychotherapy; the more psychotherapy, the smaller the recovery rate" (1952, p. 324). Thus, Eysenck claimed that psychotherapy makes patients worse. He bolstered his argument by citing data that the spontaneous remission rate for these disorders (the proportion of patients who rid themselves of these symptoms without therapy), is about the same as the rate for those helped by psychotherapy: roughly one out of three.

Other researchers responded to Eysenck's reviews by pointing out shortcomings in his logic, statistics, and objectivity. No one has yet been able to convincingly prove that psychotherapy or psychoanalysis has more than a moderately positive effect on the behavior of anxious

and depressed patients (Elkin, Parloff, Hadley, & Autry, 1985; Luborsky & Spence, 1978; O'Malley et al., 1988).

Controlled comparisons of psychotherapy versus drugs for the treatment of these disorders have been few. One of the best of these studies (Koegler & Brill, 1967) concluded that neither treatment is terribly effective, though the patients themselves did feel that one minor tranquilizer was most effective. Studies of drugs in combination with psychotherapy are similarly unimpressive. As a result, there is disagreement over whether either drugs or psychotherapy alone is preferable in the treatment of anxieties and depressions that do not involve psychosis.

One of the best designed, best-controlled comparative studies of psychotherapy and behavior therapy (Sloane, Staples, Cristol, Yorkston, & Whipple, 1975) suggests that behavior therapy may work faster than, and be as effective as, psychotherapy with symptoms like anxiety, phobias, and obsessive-compulsive behavior. The comparative longevity of these improvements remains in question, however.

All forms of psychotherapy have common aims. Foremost among them is to increase the ability of the client to function in the everyday world. All provide support, give information, and attempt to raise hopes.

With the recognition of common ground has come a tendency to trade ideas across perspectives. Most therapists regard themselves as "eclectic", that is, as choosing techniques and ideas that seem appropriate regardless of the source. Wachtel (1977) has suggested that therapy might involve an initial psychodynamic "working through" of the client's problem, with the goal of insight, followed by a behavioral treatment aimed at changing maladaptive cognitions and behaviors.

▶ **GUIDED REVIEW** *Learning Objective 11*

1. While _____ and _____ appear to exert a positive impact on the behavior of patients experiencing moderate but troublesome anxiety and depression, the extent and longevity of this improvement remains in question.

2. _____ seems to work as effectively and more rapidly than psychotherapy on certain symptomatic behaviors. Whether the greater speed of its effect results in greater or lesser maintenance of that effect is not yet known.

*ANSWERS*

1. psychotherapy, psychoanalysis 2. Behavior therapy

# EXPLORING HUMAN DIVERSITY

## Dutch Mental Health Effort Targets Prevention

The Netherlands has developed a network of regional institutions that attempt to prevent serious mental health problems. "The institutions, called RIAGGS—the Dutch abbreviation for Regional Institute for Out-Patient Mental Health Care—each serve about 250,000 and number 57 across the country," according to Peter Freiberg (1990), writing in the *APA Monitor*.

They can be compared to community mental health centers in the United States. But in addition to providing treatment, RIAGGS have prevention as a goal. RIAGGs are financed by national insurance. Every inhabitant of the Netherlands is entitled to free assistance from the RIAGG, although a small fee is charged for psychotherapy. Each RIAGG has its own management.

Each RIAGG has at least one prevention worker, totaling 200 nationwide, including many educational psychologists.

Prevention personnel work closely with therapists at the centers. Most of the prevention projects fall into one of these categories:

- parental education
- the school system
- sexual violence and incest
- work and unemployment
- divorce
- ethnic groups
- women
- elderly people
- suicide

A successful project in one RIAGG is transferred to other RIAGGs.

# COMMUNITY PSYCHOLOGY AND PREVENTION

In an office in Los Angeles the phone rings. "I'm going to kill myself," the voice says tensely. "I'm sitting here with a loaded gun." The person who answers the phone has heard such cries for help many times and knows the call may offer a chance to prevent a suicide attempt, but the listener cannot be sure. With a calm voice, the listener says, "Why don't you tell me what happened. Why do you want to take your life?"

As the would-be suicide pours out his troubles, fears, and utter desperation, the person listening at the other end of the line has already gestured to a colleague to trace the call. While the caller is still talking in a voice sometimes troubled, sometimes deliberate, an unmarked police car is on its way to the scene.

Suicide prevention is a dramatic example of community mobilization to abort a crisis. Ever since the end of World War II when it was discovered that mental disease affects two out of seven people in the United States, communities have directed efforts at preventive methods to diminish psychopathology. Initially, these efforts were undertaken by social workers, but in recent years, community psychologists and psychiatrists have begun to develop programs to control the biological, interpersonal, and social factors that jeopardize mental health.

Psychiatrist Gerald Caplan, considered by many to be the founder of the community mental health movement in the United States, believes that prevention operates on three levels: primary, secondary, and tertiary.

**Primary prevention** *uses the resources in a community to establish an environment more likely to nourish mental health and prevent the development of serious psychopathology.* Effective mental health consultants—specially trained psychologists, psychiatrists, social workers, and psychiatric nurses—focus on such preventive efforts as education, employment, poverty, and racism. They may advise school systems on how to facilitate race relations among students and faculty. They may help the police present a more positive image of their functions to citizens. They may consult with city government to enable it to be more responsive to the social and material needs of the people. They might help establish health education, preschool and old-age programs, and genetic counseling (to alert parents-to-be to potential birth defects) through existing community health centers.

In all cases, the intent of primary prevention is to mobilize existing community resources to create an environment that diverts problems and conflicts and stimulates constructive growth.

**Secondary prevention** *involves early detection of persons or institutions that have begun to exhibit* *preliminary signs of psychopathology.* Prevention at this level strives to minimize the harmful effects of potential psychopathology on those who demonstrate it and on those with whom they come in contact. Marital counseling, family therapy, vocational guidance, crisis intervention, and "hot lines" that bring help to youths troubled by drug abuse are examples of efforts to deal with problems before they become so disruptive of personal functioning that they cause serious difficulties in the community.

**Tertiary prevention** is the most expensive and least effective form of prevention. *It provides treatment for individuals who have developed psychopathology serious enough to cause disruption of functioning.* Psychotherapy, behavior therapy, and drug therapy are forms of intervention that aim at modifying existing disorders and

preventing their further development. The aim of community psychology and psychiatry is to reduce as much as possible the need for tertiary prevention.

▶ **GUIDED REVIEW** *Learning Objective 12*

1. _____ aims to use the community to nourish mental health and prevent development of mental illness.
2. _____ involves early detection and treatment of persons who show early signs of mental disorder.
3. _____ provides treatment for individuals who have developed mental or behavior disorders. It is the most expensive and least effective form of prevention.

*ANSWERS*

*1. Primary prevention 2. Secondary prevention 3. Tertiary prevention*

## SUMMARY

I. Psychoanalysis is the set of treatment procedures developed by Sigmund Freud. (pp. 389–399)

   A. Free association, the most important psychoanalytic technique, enables the patient to recall unconscious determinants of behavior. (p. 398)

   B. Resistance occurs during the course of psychoanalytic psychotherapy. It is caused by the erection of various defense mechanisms that protect the patient's ego from disturbing memories. (p. 398)

   C. Transference is the means by which patients distort their perception of the psychoanalyst; this distortion is frequently a function of their experience with parents and other important figures in their lives. (p. 399)

II. Behavior therapy is designed to change learned maladaptive behavior. (p. 400)

   A. Systematic desensitization, a behavior therapy technique developed by Wolpe, is designed to inhibit the anxiety often associated with bad habits. (p. 400)

   B. Learning theorists believe that classical and operant conditioning and observational learning, all basic mechanisms of learning, play a role in the development of both adaptive and maladaptive behavior. (p. 400)

   C. Systematic desensitization, flooding, and implosion are all behavior modification techniques. (pp. 400–401)

   D. Token economies involve the substitution of tangible or material reinforcers (tokens that can be exchanged for candy, cigarettes, and other rewards) for verbal reinforcement given by the mental health professional. (pp. 401–402)

   E. Observational learning, modeling, and role-playing are used to modify behavior especially phobias. (pp. 402–403)

   F. Cognitive behavior therapy seeks to change attitudes and beliefs in order to facilitate changes in behavior. (pp. 403–404)

III. Person-centered therapy is a non-analytic therapy developed by psychologist Carl Rogers. (p. 404)

   A. Person-centered therapy is based on an emotional sharing relationship between client and counselor. (p. 405)

   B. The counselor's most important tasks in person-centered therapy are to demonstrate unconditional positive regard, empathy, and genuineness. (p. 405)

IV. Group treatment methods help some clients lessen their feelings of loneliness and isolation. (pp. 405–406)

   A. Family therapy, a group treatment method, is designed to help the family understand its role in the disordered behavior of one or more of its members. (p. 406)

   B. Play therapy is used to diagnose and to treat psychological and behavioral disturbances of children. (p. 406)

V. The biomedical therapies change behavior by altering brain functioning. (pp. 407–408)

   A. Electroconvulsive therapy (ECT) is used as a method of last resort for severe depressives who do not respond to antidepressant medication. (p. 407)

   B. The major tranquilizers, consisting primarily of the phenothiazines, lessen the intensity of the hallucinations and delusions of schizophrenia. (p. 407)

   C. The tricyclic antidepressants are designed to lessen the intensity of mild to moderate depression. (p. 407)

   D. Librium and Valium enable moderately anxious people to deal more competently with normal stresses in life. (p. 408)

**E.** In bipolar affective disorder, lithium carbonate terminates manic episodes and decreases the likelihood of progression to depression. (p. 408)

**VI.** The long-term effectiveness of psychoanalysis, behavior therapy, and other forms of psychotherapy are superior to no therapy. (p. 409)

  **A.** Each type of therapy appears to be most efficient for particular symptoms and complaints. (p. 409)

**VII.** Prevention is generally considered more cost-effective than treatment. (p. 410)

**A.** Primary prevention helps communities nourish the mental health of their citizens and prevent the development of mental illness. (p. 410)

**B.** The early detection and treatment of persons showing signs of early mental disorder is called secondary prevention. (pp. 410–411)

**C.** Tertiary prevention, the least cost-effective and most expensive form of prevention, provides treatment for individual mental disorders. (p. 411)

# ACTION GLOSSARY

Match the terms in the left column with the definitions in the right column.

___ **1. Psychoanalysis** (p. 398)
___ **2. Time-limited psychotherapy** (p. 398)
___ **3. Free association** (p. 398)
___ **4. Dreams** (p. 398)
___ **5. Resistance** (p. 398)
___ **6. Transference** (p. 399)
___ **7. Behavior therapy** (p. 400)
___ **8. Catharsis** (p. 399)

**A.** *According to Freud, symbolic representations of unconscious conflicts rearoused by the previous day's activities and events consisting of manifest and latent content.*
**B.** *A term that encompasses a number of methods designed to change directly maladaptive behavior.*
**C.** *The personality theory and related therapeutic approach designed by Sigmund Freud. The therapist attempts to help the patient uncover repressed feelings so they can be faced and dealt with by the conscious mind.*
**D.** *Involves imagining the feared stimulus.*
**E.** *Prolonged exposure to the feared stimulus.*
**F.** *A phase of therapy in which patients find areas in which they feel blocked: they cannot talk anymore, they find it difficult to recollect crucial events from the past, or they start forgetting appointments.*
**G.** *Designed to produce significant behavior change within six months.*
**H.** *Energy formerly used for repression is returned to the ego for conscious use.*

___ **9. Systematic desensitization** (p. 400)
___ **10. Progressive relaxation training** (p. 400)
___ **11. Assertiveness training** (p. 400)
___ **12. Flooding** (p. 401)
___ **13. Implosive therapy** (p. 401)

**A.** *A behavior therapy technique in which the patient and the therapist role-play situations that require assertive responses.*
**B.** *A behavior therapy procedure for dealing with distressing levels of anxiety.*
**C.** *Training in relaxation that helps patients deal more effectively with anxiety.*
**D.** *The feared stimulus is imagined instead of actually confronted.*
**E.** *The prolonged exposure to the feared stimulus.*

___ 14. **Token economy** (p. 401)
___ 15. **Observational learning** (p. 402)
___ 16. **Cognitive restructuring** (pp. 402–403)
___ 17. **Cognitive behavior therapy** (p. 403)
___ 18. **Rational-emotive therapy** (RET) (p. 403)
___ 19. **Symptom substitution** (p. 404)
___ 20. **Non-directive therapy** (p. 405)
___ 21. **Gestalt therapy** (p. 406)
___ 22. **Family therapy** (p. 406)
___ 23. **Play therapy** (p. 406)

**A.** A therapeutic method developed by Albert Ellis. Helps patients identify the irrational, self-defeating beliefs behind their troublesome behavior so that they can take action to restore rational control over their emotions.

**B.** A group therapy approach, developed by Frederick Perls, designed to provide a group experience in attending to immediate feelings and impulses and expressing and acting upon them.

**C.** A behavior modification approach that uses tokens exchangeable for other reinforcers.

**D.** Discussing with patients the irrational sources of the thoughts that typically accompanied their phobic behavior.

**E.** An approach to behavior therapy through which the therapist changes the patient's attitudes and expectations in order to change the behaviors influenced by them.

**F.** Developed by psychologist Carl Rogers, this treatment is based on the premise that people can solve their own problems if they can be helped to confront their own fears and self-deceptions and come to grips with what troubles them.

**G.** A group therapy approach in which both the therapist and the patient are allowed to observe and deal with the complex set of interactions that precipitates and maintains a child's maladaptive behavior.

**H.** Learning by watching a model perform a behavior.

**I.** A symptom that appears after a previous symptom has been treated.

**J.** Uses play in the diagnosis and treatment of children.

___ 24. **Biomedical therapy** (p. 407)
___ 25. **Electroconvulsive therapy** (ECT) (p. 407)
___ 26. **Major tranquilizers** (p. 407)
___ 27. **Minor tranquilizers** (p. 408)
___ 28. **Phenothiazines** (p. 407)
___ 29. **Primary prevention** (p. 410)
___ 30. **Secondary prevention** (pp. 410–411)
___ 31. **Tertiary prevention** (p. 411)

**A.** Methods of treatment that modify behavior by physically altering brain functions.

**B.** A method of treatment in which a brief electrical current is passed across the patient's brain.

**C.** Early detection of persons or institutions that have begun to exhibit preliminary signs of psychopathology.

**D.** Drugs used to reduce the delusions, hallucinations, and violent behavior of many schizophrenic patients.

**E.** Drugs used most often to treat psychotic patients with seriously disturbed behavior.

**F.** Drugs used to treat patients suffering from disorders involving moderate anxiety.

**G.** The use of resources in the community to establish an environment more likely to nourish mental health and prevent the development of serious psychopathology.

**H.** Providing treatment for individuals who have actually developed psychopathology serious enough to cause disruption of functioning.

*ANSWERS*

1. c, 2. g, 3. d, 4. a, 5. f, 6. e, 7. b, 8. h, 9. b, 10. c, 11. a, 12. e, 13. d, 14. c, 15. h, 16. d, 17. e, 18. a, 19. i, 20. f, 21. b, 22. g, 23. j, 24. a, 25. b, 26. e, 27. f, 28. d, 29. g, 30. c, 31. h

## SELF-TEST

**1.** The most important psychoanalytic technique is
   (a) dream interpretation.
   (b) interpretation of resistance.
   (c) free association.
   (d) systematic desensitization.
   (LO 1; p. 398)

**2.** One of the most common accompaniments of psychoanalysis is
   (a) resistance.
   (b) regression.
   (c) fixation.
   (d) poverty.
   (LO 2; p. 398)

**3.** The psychoanalytic phenomenon by which patients distort reality as a function of their earlier experience with parents is called
   (a) parentification.
   (b) identification.
   (c) introjection.
   (d) transference.
   (LO 2; p. 399)

**4.** Behavior therapy aims at direct change of
   (a) all behavior.
   (b) behavior acquired by classical and operant conditioning.
   (c) all maladaptive behavior.
   (d) learned maladaptive behavior.
   (LO 4; p. 400)

5. Joseph Wolpe developed
   (a) vicarious reinforcement.
   (b) systematic desensitization.
   (c) person-centered therapy.
   (d) positive reinforcement and extinction.
   (LO 4; p. 400)

6. Which of the following is *not* one of the three principal modes of learning?
   (a) vicarious reward
   (b) classical conditioning
   (c) observational learning
   (d) operant conditioning
   (LO 5; p. 400)

7. Beck's cognitive behavior therapy assumes that depression is a result of
   (a) negative thoughts about oneself.
   (b) negative thoughts about the situation.
   (c) negative thoughts about the future.
   (d) all of the above.
   (LO 7; p. 403)

8. The counselor's principal job in person-centered therapy is to convey
   (a) thoughtful interpretations.
   (b) unconditional positive regard.
   (c) conditional positive regard.
   (d) a critical attitude toward the patient's symptomatic behavior.
   (LO 8; p. 405)

9. Family therapy
   (a) is a psychoanalytic technique based on deficiencies in superego functioning.
   (b) is used only for delinquent children.
   (c) explores the relationships of family members in order to bring about behavioral change.
   (d) is a form of Gestalt therapy.
   (LO 9; p. 406)

10. ECT is a treatment for
    (a) severe depression.
    (b) severe anxiety.
    (c) uncontrollable agitation.
    (d) psychomotor seizures.
    (LO 10; p. 407)

11. The phenothiazines reduce the hallucinations and delusions of
    (a) the manic depressive.
    (b) the severely depressed.
    (c) the schizophrenic.
    (d) all of the above.
    (LO 10; p. 407)

12. Librium and Valium are
    (a) phenothiazines.
    (b) forms of lithium carbonate.
    (c) tricyclic antidepressants.
    (d) minor tranquilizers.
    (LO 10; p. 408)

13. Lithium carbonate
    (a) terminates manic episodes.
    (b) reduces the likelihood of future depressive episodes.
    (c) is a treatment for bipolar affective disorder.
    (d) is all of the above.
    (LO 10; p. 408)

14. Psychoanalysis is
    (a) successful only in treating middle-class patients.
    (b) has influenced nearly every aspect of western culture.
    (c) well supported by empirical research.
    (d) the most cost-effective form of therapy.
    (LO 11; p. 409)

15. The least cost-effective prevention is
    (a) tertiary prevention.
    (b) secondary prevention.
    (c) initial prevention.
    (d) primary prevention.
    (LO 12; p. 411)

16. Primary prevention
    (a) attempts to nurture mental health.
    (b) attempts to prevent psychopathology.
    (c) makes use of community resources.
    (d) all of the above.
    (LO 12; p. 410)

*ANSWERS*

*1. c, 2. a, 3. d, 4. d, 5. b, 6. a, 7. d, 8. b, 9. c, 10. a, 11. c, 12. d, 13. d, 14. b, 15. a, 16. d*

# THINKING ABOUT PSYCHOLOGY

1. How might a person decide that he or she might benefit from psychotherapy? How might the person decide upon the type of therapy best suited to him or her?

2. Community psychology attempts to prevent mental illness and abnormal behavior by stemming their causes. In what areas do you think they should direct their efforts (for example, housing, education, teaching child-rearing skills, and so on)?

# SUGGESTED READINGS

Corsini, R. J. (1991). *Five therapists, one client.* Itasca IL: F. E. Peacock. How would different types of psychotherapist respond to the same patient? Corsini presents the reactions of a neo-Freudian Adlerian, a Rogerian person-centered counselor, rational-emotive-therapist, a behavior therapist, and an eclectic therapist.

Freud, S. (1959). Analysis of a phobia in a five-year-old boy. In *Collected Papers, Vol. 3.* New York: Basic Books. (Originally published 1909.) The classic psychoanalytic description of childhood phobia, this paper reveals Freud's views on the natural development of neurotic behavior and the etiological significance of the Oedipal period of psychosexual development.

Garfield, S. L., & Bergin, A. E. (Eds.). (1986). *Handbook of psychotherapy and behavior change* (3rd ed.). New York: John Wiley. The latest edition of a standard reference work containing comprehensive reviews of the major forms of psychotherapy. A data-oriented look at the comparative effectiveness of the diverse approaches to psychotherapy.

Herson, M., Kazdin, A. E., & Bellack, A. S. (Eds.). (1991). *Clinical psychology handbook.* Elmsford NY: Pergamon. A wide-ranging reference book on all facets of personality, psychopathology, and psychotherapy. Entries include child psychotherapy, group therapies, and community psychology.

Masson J. M. (1990). *Final analysis: The making and unmaking of a psychoanalyst.* Reading MA: Addison-Wesley. A controversial psychoanalyst writes of his disenchantment with the psychoanalytic establishment. Also read his *Assault on truth,* and the response to it by Janet Malcolm, *In the Freud archives.* Riveting stuff, really.

Watson, J. B., and Rayner, R. (1920). Conditioned emotional reactions. *Journal of Experimental Psychology, 3,* 1–14. The case of Little Albert demonstrated that so-called neurotic behavior could be learned, thus paving the way for more elaborate behavioral explanations of a wider variety of neurotic and psychotic behavior.

# PART V

## SOCIAL PSYCHOLOGY AND APPLICATIONS

# CHAPTER 14

## HEALTH PSYCHOLOGY
### OUTLINE

▶ **Learning Objectives**

▶ **Psychology and Medicine**
- ■ Health Psychology
- ■ Health

▶ **Guided Review**

▶ **Stress, Coping, and Illness**
- ■ Stress
  - General Adaptation Syndrome
  - Life Events and Illness
- ■ Posttraumatic Stress Disorder
- ■ Work and Stress
- ■ Alcohol and Drug Abuse as Stress Reactions
- ■ Marijuana and Cocaine

▶ **Guided Review**

▶ **Stress "Buffers"**
- ■ Cognitive Mediation of Stress
  - Perceived Control
  - Coping Styles
  - Hardiness
- ■ Social Support

▶ **Guided Review**

▶ **Heart Disease, Cancer, and AIDS**
- ■ Coronary Heart Disease
  - Risk Factors
  - Type A Behavior
- ■ Cancer, AIDS, and the Immune System
  - Stress and Cancer

▶ **Guided Review**

▶ **Compliance and Healthy Life-Styles**
- ■ Compliance
- ■ Models of Health Behavior
- ■ Physical Exercise

▶ **Guided Review**

▶ **Summary**

▶ **Action Glossary**

▶ **Self-Test**

▶ **Thinking About Psychology**

▶ **Suggested Readings**

# HEALTH PSYCHOLOGY
## LEARNING OBJECTIVES

**After reading this chapter, you should be able to identify or describe**

▶ **1.** the relationships between psychology and medicine. *(p. 420)*

▶ **2.** a definition of health psychology, its particular interests and aims. *(p. 420)*

▶ **3.** two definitions of stress and the research approaches implied by each definition. *(p. 421)*

▶ **4.** the general adaptation syndrome. *(p. 421)*

▶ **5.** how life events and daily hassles relate to illness. *(p. 422)*

▶ **6.** posttraumatic stress disorder. *(p. 422)*

▶ **7.** how both the workplace, as well as unemployment, can be stressors. *(pp. 423–424)*

▶ **8.** psychoactive substance dependence and psychoactive substance abuse. *(pp. 425–426)*

▶ **9.** the role of "buffers" in modifying the effects of stressors. *(pp. 426–427)*

▶ **10.** cognitive stress buffers, such as perceived control. *(p. 428)*

▶ **11.** how coping styles, such as hardiness, affect the response to stressors. *(p. 431)*

▶ **12.** the role of social support in health and illness. *(p. 431–432)*

▶ **13.** two types of health research: retrospective and prospective studies. *(p. 432)*

▶ **14.** psychological aspects of disease, including coronary heart disease, cancer, and AIDS. *(pp. 432–434)*

▶ **15.** four models of compliance and noncompliance with medical recommendations. *(pp. 434–437)*

▶ **16.** the effects of exercise on physical and psychological well-being. *(p. 437)*

# PSYCHOLOGY AND MEDICINE

"We are killing ourselves by a) carelessly polluting the environment, b) permitting harmful social conditions to persist, and c) our own careless habits." It was the chief medical officer of the United States, the Surgeon General, who made this remark in 1979. All three of the points he mentioned involve, not disease per se, but psychological and social elements.

At the beginning of this century the leading causes of death were infectious diseases, such as pneumonia and tuberculosis. As diseases have been controlled, illness and death resulting from human (mis)behavior have increased. Alcohol, tobacco, and drug abuse; risky sex; preventable accidents; environmental pollution; and unhealthy diet contribute increasingly to illness and premature death. Many of these behaviors are learned, and can be "un-learned."* As experts in learning and behavior, psychologists have an important role to play in medicine. The alliance of psychology and medicine is known as behavioral medicine or health psychology.

Psychology and medicine are broadly related. People's thoughts and images play a role in whether they acquire, sustain, or overcome illness. We know from chapter 7, Cognitive Psychology, that people do not always make rational decisions. This is evident in their health-related behaviors. For example, people do not always seek medical help when they think it is needed. Patients do not always take prescribed medications or follow other medical advice. For example, many diabetic patients could control their diabetes through diet and exercise, but do not (May, 1991). Despite awareness of the relation between unsafe sexual practices and AIDS, many adolescents refrain from using condoms. Even though people believe that exercise is good for them, nearly sixty percent of Americans do not exercise at all. Clearly these are issues of interest to psychologists.

All medical encounters involve a patient and one or more health professionals, each with personal needs and psychological limitations that influence their encounter. At every step in the process of dealing with disease, whether on the part of the physician or the patient, the impact of cognitive, emotional, and motivational factors is present. Under great pressure, physicians must ask the right questions, give the proper tests, and use the resulting information effectively to arrive at a correct diagnosis. Patients must also process information about their own bodies in judging whether they should seek medical assistance.

## Health Psychology

Health psychology encompasses a variety of aims. As defined by Joseph Matarazzo (1980), **health psychology** *is concerned with*

- *educational, scientific, and professional contributions of psychology*
- *the promotion and maintenance of health*
- *the prevention and treatment of illness*
- *the identification of causes and correlates of health and illness*
- *the analysis and improvement of the health care system and health policy*

Although health psychology is a "new" subdiscipline of psychology, it has been slowly gathering momentum for many years. Since ancient times people have believed that psychological factors, like emotions and personality, can affect susceptibility to disease and recovery from illness (Dubos, 1965; Goldstein, 1982). Since 1979 the American Psychological Association has had a Division of Health Psychology, and introductory psychology textbooks now devote entire chapters to the subject. In recent years, developments in the field of immunology have contributed substantially to the rapid growth of health psychology. Researchers are able to detect changes in immune system functioning that only a few years ago were almost inconceivable. It is now possible to measure the effects of psychological events, like stress and emotions, on resistance to disease (O'Leary, 1990).

## Health

There are two basic definitions of health. The first is that healthy is the absence of disease. A person is regarded as healthy if he or she suffers no illness. The second meaning of health involves more than merely the absence of illness. It is the possession of positive "healthy" traits, such as regular exercise, a healthful diet, and regular medical checkups. The World Health Organization defined health as "a state of complete physical, mental, and social well-being and . . . not merely the absence of disease or infirmity" (1946). This definition, like the Surgeon General's remarks above, suggest that people cannot be healthy without the proper social, political, and economic conditions. Definitions like this are subject to abuse. For

*You will notice that there is no entry in the Index for "unlearning"; it is really learning.

(a) An early view:

Stressor – – – – – – – – – – – – – – – –→ Stress reaction

(b) Later view:

Stressor – – – – – –→ Stress buffers – – – – –→ Stress reaction
(Perceived control,
Coping styles,
Social support)

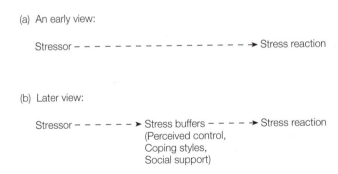

**Figure 14.1** *Two views of stress reactions.*

example, repressive governments often label their opponents as "sick" and confine them to hospitals or mental institutions (Medvedev & Medvedev, 1972). In this discussion we, like Sheridan and Radmacher (1992), view **health** as *a continuum, from optimal wellness to premature illness or death.* Given this definition, a person is not simply "healthy" or "unhealthy," but has a certain degree of healthiness, measured by symptoms, health-related behaviors, and other characteristics.

---

▶ **GUIDED REVIEW** *Learning Objectives 1 and 2*

1. The leading causes of death have changed from those caused by _____ to those resulting from _____ and _____ factors.
2. Health psychology can be considered the alliance of _____ and _____.
3. Health psychology is concerned with educational, scientific, and professional contributions of psychology to the _____, the _____, _____, and _____.
4. Health can be defined as the absence of disease, or the presence of _____.
5. The authors define health as _____.

*ANSWERS* *wellness to premature illness and death.*
*positive, healthy traits and behaviors 5. a continuum, from optimal*
*correlates of health and illness, health care system and health policy 4.*
*maintenance of health, prevention and treatment of illness, causes and*
*1. disease, behavioral, social 2. psychology, medicine 3. promotion and*

---

# STRESS, COPING, AND ILLNESS

What is stress? Is stress bad for your health? The word **"stress"** is used in two different ways. First, it *refers to something that happens to someone,* unpleasant events

and minor hassles of life, like being swamped with work, or losing your car keys. *Second, stress is used to refer to a person's reaction to a situation or event,* to the experience of unease, as in "I feel stressed today."

## Stress

*Initially medical researchers used the first meaning of stress to explore physical reactions to external "stressful" events, called* **stressors.** In this view, particular stressors cause particular kinds of stressful reaction (figure 14.1a). This was the approach of Hans Selye in his pioneering studies of reactions to stress (1956). Selye demonstrated that events, even pleasant ones, could be stressful. Nowadays, medical psychologists use the second meaning of the term. They recognize that different people react altogether differently to the same "stressful" situations. In this view, stress is a reaction to an event, rather than the event itself (figure 14.1b). Through the study of stress, psychologists have been able to make links between environmental events, personal characteristics, and illness.

*General Adaptation Syndrome* One of the most influential theories of psychosomatic disorder is by Hans Selye (1956), a Canadian physician. He formulated and studied the **General Adaptation Syndrome (GAS):** *whenever stress is imposed on a person, regardless of its precise causes, the person's body progresses through series of reactions.*

The GAS has three phases (figure 14.2). The first stage in response to stress is the **alarm reaction.** During this stage *the endocrine gland secretes a variety of hormones (ACTH, adrenaline, noradrenaline, corticosteroids) designed to deal with the stressor.* During the next GAS stage, **resistance,** *the body system best able to cope with the stress becomes most strongly activated.* If this mechanism fails to reduce the stress, **exhaustion** sets in. Harmful effects of high corticosteroid levels, such as ulcers and suppression of the immune system, become apparent, and overall resistance is decreased. If the process is allowed to continue, recovery is impossible and death is the final result.

Taking note of the fact that different persons experience different physical symptoms in the face of the same set of stressors, Selye (1977) noted, "In some people the heart, in others the nervous system or the gastrointestinal tract, may represent the weakest link. That is why people develop different types of disease under the influence of the same kind of stressors."

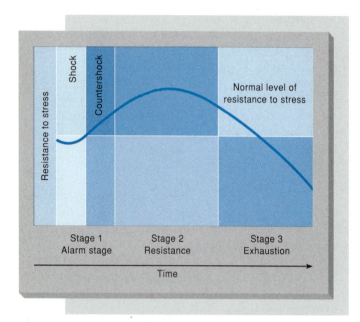

**Figure 14.2**   Selye's general adaptation syndrome. *The general adaptation syndrome (GAS) describes an individual's general response to stress. In the first stage (alarm), the body enters a temporary state of shock, a time when resistance to stress is below normal. Then a rebound called "countershock" occurs, in which resistance to stress begins to pick up. Not much later, the individual moves into the second state (resistance), during which resistance to stress is intensified in an all-out effort to combat stress. If the effort fails and stress persists, the individual moves into the third and final stage (exhaustion), when wear and tear on the body worsens, the person may collapse in a state of exhaustion, and vulnerability to disease increases.*

From Hans Selye, *The Stress of Life.* Copyright © 1976 McGraw-Hill, Inc. Reproduced by permission of McGraw-Hill, Inc., New York, NY.

Health psychology has gradually developed more sophisticated theories and methods concerning stress and health. In early research in health psychology (we are talking here only about the late 1960s and 1970s), the aim was to identify external stressors most likely to influence health and illness. Typical of this approach is the study of life events as sources of stress and illness.

*Life Events and Illness*    In 1967 Thomas Holmes and Richard Rahe developed the first widely used measure of stressful events, the Social Readjustment Rating Scale (SRRS), mentioned in chapter 10. The scale is a 43-item checklist of potentially stressful events. Following the lead of Selye, Holmes and Rahe included positive as well as negative events as sources of stress—vacations and holidays as well as divorce and debts.

The SRRS has been found consistently to correlate with heart disease (Theorell, 1982), diabetes (May, 1991), leukemia (Wold, 1968), and colds and influenza (Evans et al., 1988). Psychological illnesses such as depression have also been associated with life events (Evans, 1991). However, the correlations between the SRRS and the incidence of illness tend to be low, below .30 (Brown, 1986). Increasingly, doubts were raised about the usefulness of the SRRS (Hudgens, 1974; Suls & Mullen, 1981), and it was gradually replaced by more robust measures.

One of these was a measure of life's minor daily "hassles" and "uplifts," developed by Kanner, Coyne, Schaefer, and Lazarus (1981). They created a checklist of more than one hundred minor daily hassles, like misplacing your car keys and having too many things to do, and 100 uplifts, like completing a task and friendly encounters. In their long-term study of 100 men and women, the frequency of daily hassles was strongly correlated with undesirable symptoms. Hassles were a more powerful predictor of symptoms than life events. (See Applying Psychology: Decision Conflict as a Form of Stress.)

## Posttraumatic Stress Disorder

The effects of extremely traumatic events may occur or recur long after the events themselves. Combat veterans, victims of sexual abuse, hostages, torture victims, and holocaust survivors may be so distressed by their ordeals that they experience anxiety, depression, guilt, nightmares, sleeplessness, and flashbacks of the event months or years later. **Posttraumatic stress disorder** *is the syndrome of physical and psychological symptoms that appears as a delayed response to a distressing event.*

Natural and human-made disasters are among the forms of stress that may have long-term consequences. Rubonis and Bickman (1991) did a quantitative analysis of more than thirty published studies of the effects of disaster. They found a statistically significant relationship (r = .17) between natural disasters and post-disaster psychopathology. They estimate that there was an increase of approximately seventeen percent in the prevalence of psychopathology compared with pre-disaster rates. Greater psychopathology is apt to occur when there are many casualties, especially if the victims are females, and if the cause of the disaster is of natural as opposed to human origin. The effects of disaster on psychopathology appears to diminish with time. The effects of the eruption of Mount Saint Helen's appears to have peaked four months after

# APPLYING PSYCHOLOGY

## Decision Conflict as a Form of Stress

We are continually confronted by the need to make decisions. Most of them are insignificant; a few are monumental. Choosing what to eat for breakfast and deciding whether to wear a sweater or a jacket to class are basically unimportant decisions, the kind we must make many times a day. However, decisions that affect our future or the futures of those we love (whether to work after college or attend graduate school, or whether to marry) are much more important and much more difficult.

Conflicts are the unavoidable obstacles in life that thwart our decisions and choices. Failure to resolve some minor conflicts is normal and probably healthy. It leaves us the emotional energy to solve serious problems. But failure to resolve major conflicts is another matter. It may lead in the direction of psychopathology, toward anxiety, depression, or illness. In contrast, resolving conflicts and adjusting to them leads toward personal maturity and enhanced self-esteem.

One of the most common conflicts, the *approach-approach conflict, requires a choice between two attractive but mutually incompatible alternatives.* The best way to resolve such a conflict is to make the decision with as many of the facts at hand as possible. This is difficult when the conflicts are between equally attractive alternatives.

Cognitive dissonance theory (see chapter 15) helps us understand why people sometimes find themselves justifying their decisions again and again. When a decision has to be made between two or more alternatives that differ only in minor ways, people magnify these differences to make the option chosen seem more attractive than the one not chosen.

*Avoidance-avoidance conflicts require choices between equally disliked alternatives.* One problem with avoidance-avoidance conflicts is that moving away from one disliked alternative automatically brings you closer to an equally disliked alternative. College life is full of avoidance-avoidance conflicts. Consider the student who hates studying but who also fears his parents' displeasure over low grades. Or the senior who plans to attend graduate school, even though she hates the thought of its rigors, because the world

of work appears even more unpromising. In both cases, the choices are between unappealing alternatives.

Successful resolution of avoidance-avoidance conflict is not easy. Avoiding choice altogether by refusing both alternatives is possible only when a choice can appropriately be avoided. One of the most adaptive ways to resolve avoidance-avoidance conflicts is to scrutinize each alternative as carefully and objectively as possible to try to identify positive features.

*Approach-avoidance conflicts force you to choose to approach or avoid a single alternative having both positive and negative features.* You are confronted throughout the day with such conflicts: to eat a candy bar and gain weight; to go out with friends and be tired for the exam tomorrow; to sleep late but miss the eight o'clock chemistry lecture; all are common decisions having both attractive and aversive consequences.

People who cannot resolve approach-avoidance conflicts may choose to avoid a decision altogether. This strategy takes them away from the conflictual object, but it also deprives them of its important positive features. Or they may postpone a decision until it is too late to make it. Or, as most people who resolve approach-avoidance conflicts successfully do, they may decide that the positive features outweigh the negative ones, or vice versa.

The *double approach-avoidance conflict necessitates a choice between two or more alternatives, each of which possesses both positive and negative features.* At college, for instance, students are faced with the choice of applying themselves diligently to achieve excellent grades or working only as hard as is necessary to graduate. The former commitment requires giving up some of the unique joys of college life, but it may also enable students to go on to graduate or professional school or to feel good about their academic accomplishments. Working only hard enough to get by permits students the time to enjoy a full range of social and extracurricular activities, but it may also mean running the risk of flunking out, earning parents' ire, or having fewer options after graduation.

pouring ash on the nearby town of Othello, Washington (Adams & Adams, 1984).

## Work and Stress

There are only two sources of stress in connection with work: having a job and not having a job. Psychologists have been interested in sources of stress in connection with

work, and have also studied the effects of unemployment as a stressor.

Contrary to popular belief, it is not upper-level management and professionals who experience the greatest job-related stress. The work conditions most adverse to workers' health are found in blue-collar professions and among some health care, service, and transportation workers. In a large-scale study of workers in the United States and Sweden, the incidence of heart disease was not greater for high status management or professional occupations. Instead, the peak prevalence occurred in a subset of lower-status jobs with high psychological "work load" and low freedom to make decisions affecting the job (Levi, 1990).

Job stress is a function of two separate elements: the psychological demands of the work and the ability to make decisions about how those demands are met (Karasek & Theorell, 1990). When individuals do not have sufficient control over their work situation to be able to deal satisfactorily with the demands placed on them, strain results (Karasek et al., 1988; LaCroix & Haynes, 1987). According to Swedish stress researcher Lennart Levi (1990), the amount of decision-making freedom may turn occupational stress into either the "spice of life" or the "kiss of death."

"If a mismatch exists between the worker and the job, if the worker is (or feels) unable to control his or her work conditions, or if he or she copes ineffectively or lacks social support, then potentially pathogenic reactions may occur. These reactions can be emotional, cognitive, behavioral, and physiological" (Levi, 1990, p. 1143). Depending upon the intensity, frequency, and duration of stress, and the presence of some interacting variables, illness may result. (See Exploring Human Diversity: Gender and Minority Status in Relation to Stress.)

Employment can be stressful. So can unemployment. Increases in unemployment are associated with increases in illness and mortality. In one analysis, a fourteen percent increase in unemployment was linked to a 2.8 percent increase in death from heart disease and a 1.4 percent increase in death from cirrhosis of the liver (Brenner, 1987). (These may sound like small increases, but when speaking of millions of unemployed, they add up to many thousands of deaths.)

Although unemployment and change cannot be avoided, psychologists can show corporations how to make these events less stressful and can work with employees who must cope with these sources of stress.

There is considerable variation in people's responses to conflict and stressful events. Hans Selye believed that the individual's weakest system would be the first one to show the signs of stress. However, other factors come into play, including prior experience with stress and witnessing other people's reactions to stress. Among the many physical and behavioral reactions to stress are alcohol and drug abuse.

## Alcohol and Drug Abuse as Stress Reactions

The use of alcohol and drugs is a common behavioral reaction to stress and frustration. The drugs used vary from the nicotine in cigarettes and the caffeine in coffee to more potent and dangerous drugs like alcohol and the drugs of abuse. Other reactions to stressful events include anger, aggression, anxiety, depression, and even homelessness (*American Psychologist,* 1991).

The line between normal and abnormal use of alcohol and other drugs and normal and abnormal anger, aggression, anxiety, and depression is a difficult one to draw. Peer pressure, novelty-seeking, and modeling of parental drug use are clearly involved in many adolescents' decisions to try alcohol and other drugs.

Alcohol and drug dependence are discussed in *DSM-III-R* (the Diagnostic and Statistical Manual of the American Psychiatric Association) (see chapter 12, Abnormal Psychology). Diagnosis of dependence is based on the following criteria:

- The person takes more of the substance (alcohol, drugs, or a combination of alcohol and drugs) over a longer period of time than he or she intends.
- While recognizing that he or she uses the substance to excess, and despite trying to control consumption of the substance, the person cannot do so.
- The person spends much of his or her time obtaining, ingesting, and recovering from the effects of the substance.
- The effects of the substance, including intoxication or withdrawal, interfere with the person's ability to work, study, or meet family obligations. Important social, job-related, and recreational activities are subordinate to substance use.
- Despite experiencing substantial problems as a result of substance use, the person continues to use the substance.
- The person develops tolerance to the substance; as a result, more and more of the substance must be ingested to achieve the same feeling.
- When the person stops ingesting the substance or markedly reduces ingestion level after continued use, he or she experiences characteristic withdrawal symptoms.
- To avoid the pains of withdrawal, the person finds that he or she must continue to ingest the substance.

## EXPLORING HUMAN DIVERSITY

### Gender and Minority Status in Relation to Stress

Women are more likely than men to experience certain stressors. In particular, women may experience stressors, such as sex discrimination, sexual harassment, and comparable worth issues, more frequently than do men (Ivancevich, Matteson, Freedman, & Phillips, 1990; Ritchey, La Gory, & Mullis, 1991). "Given the growing number of women in the work force, such concerns will become even more prominent," according to Keita and Jones (1990). They add that ethnic minority workers may also be subject to unique kinds of stressors and health risks. "Current research suggests that Black Americans differ from other workers in the type and severity of environmental factors that are sources of stress (James, Strogatz, Wing, & Ramsey, 1987; Myers, 1982)" (Keita & Jones, 1990, p. 1139). Little research has been done on work-related stress and health as they pertain to ethnic minority workers.

Keita and Jones ask, "What are the effects of threatened, perceived, and actual racism and other types of discrimination on those subjected to them in the workplace?" Black women, they note, have a twenty-five percent greater chance of dying from these causes than do non-minority individuals. Hispanics are over-represented in positions in industries with the greatest number of work-related injuries. They cite data from 1980 revealing that Hispanics suffer twice the rate of severe work-related injuries as non-minority workers.

Lower socio-economic status groups (as measured by occupation, education, or income) experience greater levels of stress in terms of life events and job stress than do higher socio-economic groups. Individuals of higher SES tend to work in less dangerous jobs, not only in regard to hazards such as toxic chemicals or unsafe working conditions, but also in regard to occupational stress. Yet these higher SES groups are the most likely to receive attention through stress management and other programs (Ilgen, 1990).

---

*Persons who meet three or more of these behavioral criteria merit the diagnosis of* **psychoactive substance dependence.** *Persons who have never met these criteria but have used drugs or alcohol for a month or more despite the fact that it causes them significant problems or who use the substance in physically hazardous circumstances* (e.g., while driving a car) *merit the diagnosis of* **psychoactive substance abuse.**

Alcohol misuse is a major social problem in the United States, affecting millions of people in all walks of life. But alcoholism is only the extreme end of a continuum of alcohol misuse. Also included on the continuum is the occasional social drinker who has "one too many" one night and plows into an oncoming automobile; the heavy social drinker who invariably loses his or her composure at parties, insults hosts, embarrasses friends, and isolates himself or herself in the process; and the problem drinker, whose drinking on the job threatens to cost him or her both the job and his or her remaining self-esteem. Included as victims, too, are the family and friends of those who drink too much. They suffer directly, when their loved one hurts herself or himself or others, as well as indirectly, when they conclude that something they have or haven't done has caused their loved one to drink to excess.

A family history of alcoholism markedly increases one's risk of alcoholism because both genetic and environmental factors have been implicated in the transmission of alcoholism (Goodwin, 1985; Schuckit, 1986). In contrast, the role of genetic factors in the etiology of drug abuse is less certain (Cadoret, Troughton, O'Gorman, & Heywood, 1986; Newlin & Thomson, 1990). Drug abuse is a particular problem for the poor, less well educated, and underemployed in our society. Some believe that the excessive use of drugs serves to blunt the emptiness and despair of those struggling to survive.

## Marijuana and Cocaine

The number of Americans who use or have used drugs is staggering. Based on a 1986 survey of people twelve years of age and older, more than 18 million Americans currently use marijuana and more than 60 million have at some time used the drug (NIDA, 1986). Nearly 6 million people currently use cocaine, and more than 22 million have used it in the past. More than half of all Americans use alcohol. Although some observers believe that "hard drug" use (e.g., heroin) is now lower, others believe it has simply gone underground. Most observers agree that hallucinogen use is on the decline (Committee on Drug Abuse, APA, 1987).

One of the most dramatic and dangerous drug-related developments has been the explosive increase in the use of cocaine and its concentrated form, "crack" (see box: Cocaine in chapter 3). Cocaine is a short-acting, powerful stimulant similar in many ways to amphetamines; it is refined from the coca plant grown extensively in South America. Because it loses its effects when taken by mouth, most individuals smoke, sniff, or inject the drug. Snorting cocaine, the most popular route of administration, yields peak effects within fifteen to twenty minutes; the effects last about an hour. The drug also produces a sense of well-being and exhilaration. Once the high has passed, however, extreme depression often follows; repeated use of cocaine can result in profound physical and psychological damage to the abuser.

Washton (1985) describes "crack" as not a new drug, but a new dosage form, a new way of packaging and selling cocaine. For users of "crack," it means a more rapid, more powerful, and more destructive addiction as compared to snorting the white cocaine hydrochloride powder, the most commonly used form of the drug.

To understand the effects of alcohol and other drugs, it is important to keep in mind that we are socialized into their use, effects, and cultural meanings. The effects they have are partly determined by the user's expectations (Becker, 1953), as we mentioned in chapter 3. Alcohol is medically classified as a depressant that inhibits activity of the central nervous system. Yet in many societies alcohol is used as a stimulant and a social lubricant. How can a drug that is classified as a depressant be used as a stimulant? (Of cigarettes, one might ask the converse: How can a drug, nicotine, that arouses the autonomic nervous system, be used to relax people, which is the reason smokers often give as to why they smoke?) The answer to both questions involves our learned expectations about the effects of alcohol (or tobacco). Marlatt and his colleagues (Marlatt, Kosturn, & Lang, 1975; Marlatt & Rohsenow, 1981) compared the behavior of people who drank alcohol (vodka and tonic) with the behavior of those who only *thought* they drank alcohol (but only drank tonic). Those who believed they had been drinking vodka were more belligerent than those who had actually been drinking but did not know it. These and other studies suggest that the link between alcohol and aggression is not primarily a physiological one but a cognitive one (Brain, 1991; Critchlow, 1983; Kreutzer, Schneider, & Myatt, 1984).

▶ **GUIDED REVIEW** *Learning Objectives 3, 4, 5, 6, 7, and 8*

1. The word "stress" is used in two different ways. To refer to _____, as well as to _____.
2. The General Adaptation Syndrome involves three stages of reaction. These are _____, _____, and _____.

3. According to Hans Selye and others, stress could result from negative events, such as debt and divorce, as well as from _____.
4. Holmes and Rahe developed a checklist to measure stressful events in a person's everyday life, known as the _____.
5. Researchers of life events and daily hassles did not adequately emphasize _____.
6. The effects of extremely traumatic events may occur or recur long after the events themselves. This is referred to as _____.
7. Job stress is a function of two separate elements: _____ and _____.
8. _____ and _____ may be considered stress reactions.
9. Alcoholism is one extreme end of a continuum of alcohol misuse. Also included on the continuum are the _____, _____, and _____.
10. A family history of alcoholism markedly increases one's risk of alcoholism because both _____ and _____ factors have been implicated in the transmission of alcoholism.
11. Persons who meet three or more behavioral criteria of drug/alcohol use are diagnosed as _____.
12. Persons who do not meet the criteria for psychoactive substance abuse but who have used drugs/alcohol for at least a month despite the fact that it causes them significant problems are diagnosed as _____.
13. Personal and social _____ influence the effects of alcohol and drugs on our moods and behavior.

*ANSWERS*

1. something that happens to a person, a person's reaction to a stressor 2. alarm reaction, resistance, exhaustion 3. positive events, such as vacations and job promotions 4. Social Readjustment Rating Scale. 5. individual differences in the face of stressful events 6. posttraumatic stress disorder 7. psychological demands of work, the freedom to make decisions about how those demands are met 8. Alcoholism, drug abuse 9. the social drinker who then drives an automobile, the drinker who loses composure, the problem drinker 10. genetic, environmental 11. psychoactive substance dependence 12. psychoactive substance abuse 13. expectations

## STRESS "BUFFERS"

"No single variable, whether biological or psychological, invariably leads to disease. Psychological stress is no exception" (Baron & Graziano, 1991). Personality and cognitive factors play a role in moderating the stress-illness relationship (figure 14.1b ). Personality variables sometimes act as intervening variables or **"stress buffers"** *to moderate the effects of events that sometimes lead to unhealthy responses.* For example, it was reported in one longitudinal study that the people who coped best with life's difficulties tended to use humor, to lay problems aside when necessary, to care about others and not just themselves, and to be far-sighted about problems that

# CLOSE UP ON RESEARCH

## Laughter and Health

Jokes "promote the restoration of equilibrium and have a favorable influence upon health."—Immanuel Kant, *Critique of judgment*, 1790.

There are fads in medicine just as there are in musical taste and styles of dress. Now and then through the centuries it was fashionable to believe that humor and laughter were beneficial to physical health and psychological well-being.

*Is laughter good for you?*

According to the American physician James Walsh, "The best formula for the health of the individual is contained in the mathematical expression: Health varies as the amount of laughter" (1928). Writer/editor Norman Cousins (1979) wrote of his recovery from ankylosing spondylitis, a serious nervous system disease, with the aid of mega-doses of laughter and vitamin C.

Even Freud, who is sometimes blamed for analyzing jokes to death, designated humor as "the highest of defensive processes," a healthy adjustment to situations beyond our control (1960, p. 233). Freud believed that humor was healthy because it was a means of taking ourselves and our difficulties less seriously.*

*Is laughter bad for you?*

Ironically, it was also Freud who popularized the idea that humor and laughter might be symptoms of repression. This, apparently, is "a very bad thing." In *Jokes and their relation to the unconscious*, Freud wrote that laughter and joking were ways of releasing pent-up aggressive and sexual impulses.

Laughter is a symptom of some neurological disorders, including amyotrophic lateral sclerosis (known as "Lou Gehrig's disease") and multiple sclerosis. A change in sense of humor often accompanies Alzheimer's disease. Sufferers tend to crack silly jokes and laugh inappropriately. (However, just because you have a goofy sense of humor does not mean you have Alzheimer's.)

Given these different views, perhaps we should distinguish between two varieties of laughter: symptomatic laughter and healthy laughter. The former involves aggressive and sexual humor, including sexist, racist, and ethnic jokes. These can be indirect ways of expressing hostility and anger. Healthy laughter includes laughing at oneself and one's predicaments, laughing when "there is nothing else to do but cry." This is what Freud meant when he said that humor was "the highest of defenses."

*Humor and coping.*

In his continuing longitudinal study of Harvard University graduates, George Vaillant (1977) reported that humor is a healthy coping strategy. There is independent evidence for this.

People who use humor to cope are less depressed by stressful life events than people who use little humor (Nezu, Nezu, & Blissett, 1988; Yovetich, Dale, & Hudak, 1990). Breathing rate, heart rate, and blood pressure decline following laughter, and sensitivity to pain is reduced (Cogan, Cogan, Waltz, & McCue, 1987).

Since the work of Friedman and Rosenman (1974) on the coronary-prone Type A behavior pattern, a sense of humor has been mentioned in connection with coronary heart disease. Is the sense of humor different between Type As and Type Bs? Patients on a coronary hospital ward were given the Jenkins Activity Survey to measure the coronary-prone personality, and a variety of jokes to rate for funniness. Type Bs were found to appreciate all types of humor, but Type As appreciated only aggressive jokes (Goldstein, Mantell, Pope, & Derks, 1988).

In his book, *Anatomy of an Illness*, Norman Cousins argued that mood plays an important role in the mobilization of the person's resistance to disease. It appears he is correct. There is mounting evidence that humor is related to the functioning of the immune system. For example, the antigen secretory immunoglobulin A (S-IgA) protein is related to positive moods. After laughter, S-IgA levels increase (Dillon, Minchoff, & Baker, 1985; Martin & Dobbin, 1988; Lefcourt, Davidson-Katz, & Kueneman, 1990). As Lefcourt et al. conclude:

> Sense of humor plays a significant role in moderating the effects of stress and helps to determine certain immune-system activity that may serve to protect us from a range of potential infectious illnesses.

*For a long time psychoanalysts ignored humor (Fry & Salameh, 1987). It is curious that humor is not included among the psychoanalytic ego defense mechanisms (see chapter 11).

might come along in the future (Vaillant, 1977) (see Close Up on Research: Laughter and Health).

Many personality characteristics have weak to moderate effects on the stress-illness relationship. Among individual differences found to buffer the effects of stress on illness are an internal locus of control; self-esteem (Witmer, Rich, Barcikowski, & Mague, 1983); and optimism (or at least the absence of pessimism) (Kamen-Siegel, Rodin, Seligman, & Dwyer, 1991; Scheier, Weintraub, & Carver, 1986).

## Cognitive Mediation of Stress

Cognitive factors influence the way we perceive our environments, including events that are potentially stressful. They also influence the way we label our own physiological states (Schachter & Singer, 1962; Pennebaker, 1982). This is illustrated by the case of Susan, a woman in her late thirties, who was raised in an extremely protective family. She was made to worry about the dangers of the slightest physical exertion. Susan decided to join an aerobics class, but went into a panic during her first lesson, because her heart rate increased to alarming levels. A lengthy series of physical examinations, including an exercise stress test, failed to reveal any defect in her heart. Apparently she had so little experience of physical exertion that she was terrified by the strange sensation of having her heart speed up in response to exercise. She had never developed a framework for interpreting such cardiac responses which are so familiar to most of us (Sheridan & Radmacher, 1992).

The degree to which people perceive that they have control over events in their lives is widely regarded as having significance for health (Steptoe & Appels, 1989). Perceived control is similar to Bandura's (1986) concept of **self-efficacy**, *the belief that a person can successfully perform a behavior to produce a desired outcome.* Absence of control and low self-efficacy have predictable effects upon responses of the autonomic nervous system, endocrine, and immune systems.

*Perceived Control*     Contributions from many areas of psychology converged to highlight the importance of control, or at least the feeling that one has control, over events. In clinical psychology, Julian Rotter (1966) demonstrated the importance of "locus of control." In relation to stress, an internal (as opposed to an external) locus of control is found to buffer the stress-illness relationship (Johnson & Sarason, 1978; Krause & Stryker, 1984). In social psychology, Irving Janis (1958) studied ways to cope with the fear of surgery among hospital patients, and Stanley Schachter (1971) studied internal and external psychological factors in obesity. In experimental psychology, Martin Seligman (1975) showed the role of uncertain reinforcement schedules in feelings of helplessness and depression. In different ways, all these developments revolve around the issue of perceived control.

What makes some life events stressful appears to be their uncontrollability. Items on the Holmes and Rahe Social Readjustment Rating Scale that people felt were "uncontrollable" were correlated with the onset of illness. Items that were considered under the person's control were not related to illness (Suls & Mullen, 1981). Subsequent

research has converged to highlight the importance of control in health and illness.

**Learned helplessness** refers to *a state of the organism following prolonged exposure to uncontrollable events in which the person perceives that his or her behavior does not influence the outcome* (Seligman, 1975). Learned helplessness was first demonstrated in animals who were exposed to repeated inescapable shock. Their helplessness was so extreme that even when an avenue for escape was provided, the animal did not take it. Learned helplessness has been used to explain reactions to a variety of stressors, including unemployment (Baum, Fleming, & Reddy, 1986) and institutionalization (Langer & Rodin, 1976). Prolonged exposure to uncontrollable events results in the feeling that the individual is powerless to change the environment or to alter its effects, thus resulting in feelings of helplessness, uncontrollability, and a reduction in the sense of self-efficacy.

Perceived control is linked to stress reduction, even in rodents. Weiss (1977) paired rodents so that the aversive experience (electric shock) of one member of a pair was identical to that of the other member. When only one member of the pair can exercise control over the aversive stimulus, it is the other animal, the passive partner with no control, which develops more severe lesions. Note that the exposure to the physical "stress" is identical for both animals: when the controlling animal fails to respond, both receive shock. Thus, the two animals vary solely on the psychological dimension of being in control or not.

Even in the world of animal experimentation, however, these findings need some qualification. Controlling responses requires effort and Weiss found that effortfulness itself produces stressful reactions if it is too great. This may well explain the results of an earlier study of similar design by Brady (1958) in which monkeys were studied. Here it was the active controlling monkeys—the so-called "executive monkeys"—who suffered from ulcers. However, Brady's executive monkeys could only maintain control through highly effortful responding on a tiring time schedule, and this effortfulness was almost certainly a factor in producing Brady's results (Evans, 1991).

Physiological reactions to aversive stimuli are reduced by signals that the stressor is controllable (Glass & Singer, 1972; Thompson, 1981). For instance, people living near the damaged Three Mile Island nuclear power plant reported being less stressed and showed less chronic arousal when they also perceived the world as being

# EXPLORING HUMAN DIVERSITY

## Inequality Is Bad for Your Health

**TABLE 14.A Comparison of life expectancies and health care costs**

| Country | Life Expectancy at Birth (in years) | | Percentage of Gross Domestic Product Spent on Health Care (1986) |
|---------|------|-------|---------|
| | Men | Women | |
| Japan | 75.9 | 81.8 | 6.7 |
| Sweden | 74.8 | 80.6 | 9.1 |
| Switzerland | 74.0 | 80.9 | 8.0 |
| Netherlands | 73.7 | 79.9 | 8.3 |
| Norway | 73.3 | 79.9 | 6.8 |
| Spain | 73.1 | 79.6 | n.a. |
| Canada | 73.0 | 78.8 | 8.5 |
| Greece | 72.6 | 77.6 | 3.9 |
| Great Britain | 72.4 | 78.1 | n.a. |
| Germany* | 71.8 | 78.2 | n.a. |
| Denmark | 71.8 | 77.7 | 6.1 |
| United States | 71.4 | 78.3 | 11.1 |
| Finland | 70.7 | 78.7 | n.a. |
| Luxemburg | 70.6 | 77.9 | n.a. |
| Poland | 66.8 | 75.5 | n.a. |
| Soviet Union (CIS) | 65.0 | 73.8 | n.a. |

If health is related to income and living standards within a country, surely it should also be related to the differences in the standard of living between countries. But it is not. The United States, Luxemburg, and former West Germany are twice as rich per capita and yet have lower life expectancies than Greece or Spain. It turns out that what matters is *relative*, not absolute, income. Income distribution, or how big the differences between rich and poor are in each country, seems to be more important than absolute income as a determinant of health standards in the developed world. The smaller the gap between rich and poor, the higher the society's overall standard of health.

The contrasting experiences of Britain and Japan illustrates how close this relationship is. In the late 1960s and early 1970s, Britain and Japan were fairly similar with respect to life expectancy and income distribution: on both counts they were close to the middle of the field. But during the last 20 years Japanese life expectancy has increased very rapidly and is now the highest in the world.

Two epidemiologists who looked to see what might account for this rapid progress found no obvious explanation in terms of changes in Japanese medical care, diet, or health promotion activities. However, they did point out that Japanese income distribution had become the most egalitarian in the world.

During the 1980s income distribution widened particularly dramatically in Britain and is now the widest since good record-keeping began. The Chief Medical Officer pointed out in 1989 that death rates for British men and women throughout the fifteen to forty-five age range had actually been rising each year since 1985—a trend which he said was not the result of AIDS deaths.

Income inequality may also explain why class differences in death rates have not diminished in the post-war period—despite the unparalleled rise in prosperity. The best fit with life expectancy comes by considering the proportion of all income going to the bottom sixty or seventy percent.

What is the mechanism through which relative income influences health? According to Wilkinson (1991), it is a result of social processes. For instance, income differentials may affect health partly through the damage which inequality does to human relations, partly through an effect on self-esteem, of the difficulty of "coping," on stress and insecurity, and on the quality of the social fabric, in general.

*n.a. = not available*

*\*former West Germany*

*Note: Life expectancy figures are for most recent year available, usually 1988.*

*Sources: National Center for Health Statistics, 1989, Health, United States, 1988, Public Health Service; Statistisch Jaarboek 1992, Heerlen, The Netherlands; and Data from Richard Wilkinson, "Inequality is Bad for Your Health," The Guardian, 12 June 1991, p. 21, London.*

controllable (Davidson, Baum, & Collins, 1982). Recall that Rubonis and Bickman (1991) found that natural disasters have a stronger impact on psychopathology than disasters of human origin. Perhaps the reason for this is that natural events seem less predictable and controllable than human ones.

*Plants for Granny.*     The elderly residents of a nursing home do not have to do much for themselves. In many ways, the home is a "decision-free" environment, where all important decisions, about sleep, food, bathing, and leisure activities are decided by the staff. Having no decision-making responsibility is the same thing as having little control over day-to-day events.

Ellen Langer and Judith Rodin (1976) attempted to reverse the chain of events that lead to feelings of power-lessness. They told some residents of a Connecticut nursing home that "many of you don't realize the influence you have over your own lives here." These residents were told that they had responsibility for the arrangement of their rooms, for deciding how to spend their time, and for choosing where they would meet visitors. A comparison group was told primarily about the variety of activities in the home and the dedication of the staff to making life comfortable and pleasant for them. All residents were given a plant as a gift. The increased responsibility group was told they had to make two decisions: first, whether or not they wanted a plant at all, and second, which plant they wanted. The plants were theirs to keep and take care of as they wished. The members of the control group were also given plants, but were told that the nurses would water and care for them.

What effects did this simple emphasis on decision-making and personal control have on the elderly residents? The increased responsibility group reported being happier and more active three weeks (and also 18 months!) after this intervention (Rodin & Langer, 1977). They were rated as more alert by the interviewers, and according to the nursing staff, spent more time visiting with other patients, talking to the staff, and entertaining visitors. They also tended to assume responsibility and control over other areas of their lives.

Similar results were obtained in a field study by Schulz (1976), who had college students visit institutionalized elderly people. The residents of the retirement home were given various degrees of control over the number and timing of visits. When the visits were predictable, particularly when the residents had control over their timing,

there was a marked improvement in the health, behavior, and attitudes of the residents.

*Coping Styles*     Some people would prefer to bury their heads in the sand than to confront an impending threat, such as surgery. Others would seek additional information and opportunities to discuss it. Still others would try to control their emotional reactions to the threat, perhaps by taking a deep breath and counting to ten. These prefer-ences represent different **coping styles,** *characteristic ways of responding to stress.*

The three different coping strategies mentioned above are referred to as avoidant coping, problem-solving or attentional coping, and response-centered coping. An **avoidant coping strategy** *is one in which people turn their attention away from aspects of the stressor.* In effect, they bury their heads in the sand by deliberately distracting themselves or unconsciously denying painful aspects of impending surgery, for example.

**Attentional, or problem-centered, coping** *involves seeking information.* Here the person focuses on the source of stress by learning more about it, changing their appraisal of it, and discussing it with others. **Response-centered coping** *involves controlling one's own thoughts and emotions.* Counting to ten, literally or otherwise.

Natural disasters and accidents provide opportunities for researchers to study coping styles and illness. Eighteen months after the nuclear plant accident at Three Mile Island, nearby residents were interviewed by Baum, Fleming, and Singer (1983). A control group of people living near an undamaged nuclear plant were also inter-viewed. They were asked about strategies for coping with the threat of radiation exposure, and were administered a 90-item stress inventory. People tended to use two kinds of coping mechanisms: problem-centered and response-centered. In this study, response-centered coping was associated with significantly lower levels of stress than was problem-centered coping. More recent studies show that demographic variables like education also mediate responses to the Three Mile Island accident (Prince-Embury, 1992).

Langer, Janis, and Wolfe (1975) studied hospital patients awaiting surgery. Some patients were given information about the surgery and told about possible post-operative discomfort, but they were reassured about the quality of the hospital staff and safety of the procedures. Other patients were given "cognitive control": they were told to imagine some time in the past when they had coped successfully with pain or discomfort. People can learn to control stress by controlling attention, they were assured. Hospital staff recorded patient anxiety and requests for sedatives and tranquilizers. Results indicate that both cognitive control and information were effective devices for coping with stress. Cognitive control was significantly more effective than information control, however. In the control group of patients, ninety-three percent requested pain relievers and sedatives at least once. Seventy-three percent of those receiving information did so, and just fifty percent of those trained to cope by means of cognitive control.

Which coping strategy is most effective? Not surprisingly, it depends upon what type of stressors are involved. No strategy appears to be most effective in all situations, or for all individuals. In general, response-centered strategies tend to be superior to problem-centered/attentional strategies. Learning how to control one's emotional and cognitive reactions to potentially stressful events appears to be an important mechanism for reducing ill effects.

Suls and Fletcher (1985) compared the effectiveness of avoidant strategies and attentional (problem-centered) coping styles. In a meta-analysis, avoidant strategies appeared to be most effective under short-term conditions (meaning those measured on the same day as the stressor occurred). In studies of long-term stressors, attentional strategies tended to work better. This was confirmed by Holmes and Stevenson (1990), who found that pain patients did better with avoidant strategies in the short-term, but better with attentive strategies in the long-term.

*Hardiness*    **Hardiness** *is a disposition that moderates the negative effects of stressors.* Hardiness consists of control, commitment, and challenge (Kobasa, 1979; Kobasa et al., 1982, 1985). *Control* means that people are confident in their ability to affect their own lives, rather than seeing themselves as the powerless victims of fate. This is similar to having an "internal locus of control," to use the term from Rotter's (1966) theory. *Commitment* refers to a clear sense of personal values, as well as vigorous involvement with the environment, rather than a sense of isolation. *Challenge* means that such people see change as offering a new set of opportunities rather than as being threatening.

Hardiness differentiates individuals with the same occupations who do and do not suffer effects of stress. Neither social support nor physical exercise were as

powerful a source of resistance to illness as was hardiness (Kobasa, 1979; Kobasa, Maddi, Pucetti, & Zola, 1985). Hardiness appears to be important in keeping people healthy.

Some analyses of coping styles focus on a tendency to suppress or express anger (Gentry, Chesney, Gary, Hall, & Harburg, 1982). Anger and its expression are generally regarded as "unhealthy" behaviors (Cohen & Lazarus, 1979; Tavris, 1989). Experiencing and expressing anger are among the characteristics of the "Type A behavior pattern." Individuals who exhibit this pattern are at increased risk of heart disease. (Type A behavior is discussed later in this chapter along with Coronary Heart Disease.) However, studies of women with breast cancer point to a positive aspect of anger. Cox and MacKay (1982) found that women with breast cancer who expressed more anger had a better chance of recovering. Greer et al. (1979) reported that the greatest mortality among patients with breast cancer was shown by the group who exhibited a hopeless attitude to their illness, and the least mortality was associated with groups who showed either fighting spirit or denial styles of coping.

Since expressing anger is an active, assertive behavior, perhaps it is, once again, the sense of perceived control that is important. If the opposite of expressing anger is passivity and a sense of helplessness, then in this situation anger may be a sign of emotional strength and control.

## Social Support

It appears that the potential harmful effects of life events can be diminished if the individual is connected to a network of supportive friends, relatives, and neighbors (Brown & Harris, 1978). Even a pet can have healthful effects (Siegel, 1990). Individuals who receive support and comfort from others are less likely to die prematurely (Berkman & Syme, 1979; Cohen & Syme, 1985). Hence, in many countries, married individuals tend to live longer than single individuals (Lomans, 1992). Family support appears to be a more important factor in buffering stress for women than for men (Holahan & Moos, 1985; Wheeler & Frank, 1988). As with many stress buffers, the precise mechanisms by which social support moderates the effects of stressors is unknown (Kessler, Kendler, Heath, Neale, & Eaves, 1992).

We do not know precisely how *social support might buffer against adverse effects of stress.* A likely candidate is that social support indirectly affects the immune system. There is evidence that immune system functioning is influenced by such factors as a person's style of explaining life events (Kamen-Siegel, Rodin, Seligman, & Dwyer, 1991) and loneliness (Stein et al., 1985).

Both medical students and psychiatric patients scoring high on a measure of loneliness showed evidence of poorer immune system functioning than others. Patients hospitalized for major depressive disorders show lower counts of immune-system cells when compared with controls (Stein et al., 1985). Loneliness, which may be viewed as the absence of social support, may intensify stress.

> ▶ **GUIDED REVIEW** *Learning Objectives 9, 10, 11, and 12*
>
> 1. _____ sometimes act as intervening variables or "stress buffers" in the stress-illness relationship.
> 2. Perceived control is similar to the concept of _____, the belief that a person can successfully perform a behavior to produce a desired outcome.
> 3. Three different strategies for coping with stress are _____, _____, and _____.
> 4. An _____ coping strategy is one in which people turn their attention away from aspects of the stressor.
> 5. An _____ coping strategy is one in which people seek information about the potentially stressful situation.
> 6. _____ coping strategies involve controlling one's own thoughts and emotions.
> 7. Hardiness is one disposition that moderates the negative effects of stressors. Hardiness consists of _____, _____, and _____.
> 8. _____, or having a network of sympathetic relatives, friends, and neighbors, can act as a buffer against the effects of stressful events.
>
> *ANSWERS*
>
> *1. Personality variables 2. self-efficacy 3. avoidant coping, attentional or problem-centered coping, response-centered coping 4. avoidant 5. attentional or problem-centered 6. Response-centered 7. control, commitment, challenge 8. Social support*

# HEART DISEASE, CANCER, AND AIDS

Stress by itself may not cause disease, but it can make an individual more susceptible to contracting disease and less successful in combating disease once it is present. In this section we consider psychological factors in relation to coronary heart disease, cancer, and AIDS.

Researchers have used two strategies, prospective and retrospective, to study risk factors in illness. **Prospective studies** *begin with a healthy population and over a long period of time record which individuals develop a disease.* **Retrospective studies** *begin with patients who have a disease and work backwards in an attempt to identify causes.* Though the second method is not as desirable as the first, it is more practical and economical (Baron & Graziano, 1991).

## Coronary Heart Disease

**Coronary heart disease (CHD)** *is the nation's leading cause of death. CHD embraces two major types of coronary disorder: angina pectoris and myocardial infarction.* Both types result from coronary atherosclerosis. **Coronary atherosclerosis** *is the condition in which an accumulation of cholesterol and fatty substances form plaque on the inner walls of the coronary arteries. The coronary artery, which feeds blood to the heart, can become so narrowed that the heart is temporarily starved of oxygen. This is typically noticed following a period of exertion and constitutes an attack of* **angina.** Atherosclerosis can also lead to a more serious result. *A narrowed artery is more easily blocked by an obstruction or a blood clot. Such an event is called a* **coronary occlusion,** *and it can cut off the supply of oxygen to the heart. When this occurs, the individual suffers a* **myocardial infarction,** *a heart attack.*

*Risk Factors*    Factors that increase the risk of heart disease include age (older persons are at greater risk), sex (males are at greater risk), high levels of cholesterol in the blood, high blood pressure, smoking, diabetes (increases risk), genetics (a family history of cardiovascular disease increases risk), obesity, and lack of physical exercise. The more of these risk factors present, the greater the likelihood of coronary heart disease. However, people with many risk factors do not always develop CHD, which suggests the importance of genetic factors, whether members of one's family have had heart disease. Most of these risk factors are influenced by psychological and social processes (Booth-Kewley & Friedman, 1987). For example, smoking is initiated and maintained by a number of psychological and social forces (Leventhal & Cleary, 1980). So, too, are diet and exercise. Although the risk factors are important, when taken together they predict only about half of all new cases of CHD (Krantz, Baum, & Singer, 1983). In the search for additional risk factors, researchers have examined socio-economic status, anxiety, social support, and occupational work demands.

*Type A Behavior*    A controversial theory of CHD focuses on its relationship to a specific cluster of characteristics, the Type A behavior pattern (table 14.1). The **Type A behavior pattern** *describes hard-driving, impatient, competitive, easily angered individuals intensely interested in achievement.* These people rush to work, rush home, and rush to appointments even though there may be plenty of time available. In contrast, the Type B pattern involves greater relaxation, a lesser sense of time urgency, less competitiveness, less hostility—and less risk of CHD (Rosenman & Friedman, 1974). The Type A behavior pattern has been measured using interviews, self-reports of A-Type behavior, and questionnaires such as the Jenkins Activity Survey.

Evidence to support Type A behavior as a risk factor for CHD includes two large-scale prospective studies, in which initially healthy individuals were tracked over time. Those with Type A behavior patterns were twice as likely to suffer heart attacks or other forms of heart disease as others (Friedman & Rosenman, 1974). In the Western Collaborative Group Study (Jenkins, Rosenman, & Zyanksi, 1974), men with Type A behavior patterns were more likely to develop CHD than were Type B men.

How can something as nonspecific as a personality pattern cause blockage of coronary arteries? Although no one understands this process completely, it is clear that emotions and stress interact with other risk factors for CHD to heighten the chances of having the disease (Dembroski, MacDougall, Eliot, & Buell, 1983). Specifically, it seems that the general activation of the sympathetic nervous system during times of emotional stress may be a factor in cardiovascular disease (Roskies, 1982). The Type A person shows more intense emotions in many situations, particularly negative emotions like hostility; this may lead to increases in cholesterol levels, blood pressure, smoking, or eating.

The hypothesis that the Type A behavior pattern by itself causes CHD is too simplistic (Ragland & Brand, 1988). Recent studies of Type A behavior and heart disease have yielded inconsistent findings. Some suggest that Type A is unrelated to incidence of first heart attack. Other studies suggest that Type As may actually survive heart attacks better than do Type Bs (Ragland & Brand, 1988; Shekelle, Gale, & Norusis, 1985; Siegman & Dembrowski, 1989)—perhaps for the same reasons that women suffering from breast cancer tended to do better if they expressed anger.

| TABLE 14.1   **Type A behavior** |
|---|
| Time urgency |
| Impatience |
| Excessive drive |
| Ambition |
| Competitiveness |
| Hostility |
| Achievement-oriented behavior |
| A tendency to be ordered and well planned |
| Self-control |
| Self-confidence |
| A preference for working alone when challenged |
| Concentration on task performance even in the face of distracting events |
| Outgoingness |
| Hyperalertness |
| A tendency to be fast-paced, tense, and unrelaxed |
| Deep involvement in one's vocation |
| An inability to relax away from work |
| Denial of failure |
| Suppression of symptoms and fatigue |

From R. H. Roseman and M. A. Chesney, "The Relationship of Type A Behavior Pattern to Coronary Heart Disease" in *Activitas Nervosa Superior*, 22:1–45, 1980. Copyright © 1980 by Avicenum Czechoslavak Medical Press. Reprinted by permission.

Can Type A behavior be modified? Several large-scale programs are underway among individuals who exhibit Type A characteristics. The programs are designed primarily to teach stress-management techniques. The Montreal Type A Intervention Project examined whether a stress-management program could reduce Type A behavior and physiological reactions to stressful situations (Roskies et al., 1986). Male managers with no indications of cardiovascular disease were trained to recognize situations that arouse stress and to practice various coping skills when they encountered them. As predicted, Type A behavior decreased among these men. However, the coping skills did not decrease the men's physiological reactivity when they were placed in a stressful test situation by the researchers. As Baron and Graziano (1991, p. 643) note, perhaps these physiological reactions are caused by other factors or by more stable predispositions to stressors.

## Cancer, AIDS, and the Immune System

The general function of the immune system is to identify and eliminate **antigens,** *foreign substances that contact or enter the body.* Antigens include bacteria, viruses, and parasites. Parts of the immune system are also capable of identifying and destroying cells that have undergone alterations associated with malignancy and of attacking other foreign agents, including transplanted organs. **The immune system** *is comprised of specialized cells that originate in the bone marrow and gather in certain organs, including the thymus, the spleen, and the lymph nodes.* From these organs, these specialized cells are released into the blood stream (O'Leary, 1990).

The innate immune system uses a broad approach in attacking antigens. In contrast, **acquired immunity** *identifies the antigens and then uses complex strategies to neutralize them. With the acquired system, our bodies recognize specific antigens and take action to destroy them.*

The human immunodeficiency virus (HIV) causes acquired immunodeficiency syndrome (AIDS). HIV seropositivity (being infected with HIV) progresses to AIDS. The median period between infection with HIV and development of symptoms is 11 years (Phair, 1990). Death by AIDS and associated diseases is often slow, painful, and undignified. These diseases involve loss of control of bodily functions, and eventually impaired memory. In addition, persons with AIDS are confronted with social prejudice and rejection. AIDS patients are more than thirty-five times more likely to commit suicide than the non-AIDS population (Marzuk et al. 1988). For these patients, it is not a choice between living and dying, but between dying now or later.

Because there are currently no cures or vaccines for AIDS, its prevention is a matter for psychologists. The only protection against the disease is behavioral: not engaging in practices, such as unsafe sex or intravenous drug use, that put the individual at risk.

One relationship between psychology and medicine that we have not yet mentioned is that of helping medical personnel understand and deal with the problems of patients with particular needs, such as AIDS patients and cancer patients. Patients with AIDS may deny the realities of carrying the HIV infection. They are greatly at risk of suicide, and suffer severe depression and helplessness. Clearly HIV-positive patients require special care and sensitivity (Schmaling & DiClementi, 1992).

*Stress and Cancer*    Cancer represents more than 100 disorders involving the rapid and unrestrained growth of abnormal cells. One theory is that the immune system serves a surveillance function by detecting and destroying cells that have undergone cancerous transformation. Cancer may develop as a result of impairment of this

immune function, which, in turn, can be influenced by psychological variables. Supporting this hypothesis are animal studies in which stress is found to lead to reduced immune system functioning and enhanced tumor growth (Sklar & Anisman, 1981).

The links between stress and cancer in humans have not yet been fully established. There is no evidence that stress can make normal cells become cancerous. Although stress does not cause cancer in this sense, it does interfere with the ability of the immune system to destroy cancerous cells (Evans, 1991; Justice, 1985).

Higher cancer mortality rates for bereaved spouses have been reported (Fox 1981). In a retrospective study, Thomas, Duszynski, and Shaffer (1979) showed that male medical students who developed some form of cancer had, ten to fifteen years previously, indicated a lack of closeness to their parents (as measured by a family attitude questionnaire).

The most suggestive results of the link between depression and cancer come from a seventeen-year follow-up study of over 2000 factory workers in Cleveland, Ohio (Shekelle et al., 1981). All subjects were between forty and fifty years of age and all completed the MMPI. Among those scoring high on the Depression subscale of the MMPI, the death rate from cancer during the follow-up period was twice the expected norm. The result was not explainable in terms of such other possible explanations as age or smoking.

▶ **GUIDED REVIEW** *Learning Objectives 13 and 14*

1. Researchers have used two strategies to study risk factors in illness, _____ and _____ studies.
2. In _____ studies, a healthy population is studied over a long period of time. In _____ studies, patients who have a disease are studied in an attempt to identify causes.
3. The condition in which an accumulation of cholesterol and fatty substances form plaque on the inner walls of the coronary arteries is called _____.
4. The coronary artery can become so narrowed that the heart is temporarily starved of oxygen. This condition is known as _____.
5. When a narrowed artery is blocked by an obstruction or a blood clot, the event is called a _____.
6. When the supply of oxygen to the heart is cut off, the individual suffers a _____ or _____.
7. A person who is hard-driving, impatient, competitive, easily angered, and achievement-oriented displays a _____.

8. Type A behavior pattern has been measured using _____, _____, and _____.
9. The general function of the _____ system is to identify and eliminate _____, foreign substances that contact or enter the body.
10. The immune system is comprised of specialized cells that originate in _____ and gather in certain organs, including the _____, _____, and _____.

*ANSWERS*

*1. prospective, retrospective 2. prospective, retrospective 3. coronary atherosclerosis 4. angina 5. coronary occlusion 6. heart attack, myocardial infarction 7. Type A behavior pattern 8. interviews, self-reports, questionnaires such as the Jenkins Activity Survey 9. immune, antigens 10. bone marrow, thymus, spleen, lymph nodes*

# COMPLIANCE AND HEALTHY LIFE-STYLES

Breast cancer is the most common form of cancer in women and accounts for twenty percent of all deaths from cancer. There are three main screening methods available for detecting breast cancer: mammography, physical examination by a health practitioner, and breast self-examination. Considering the potential advantages of regular breast self-examination, relatively few women practice it. A national United States survey indicated that fewer than thirty percent of American women practice monthly breast self-examination (Pitts, 1991).

## Compliance

Patients as well as physicians often fail to follow sound medical advice and practices. Averaging results from many studies of self-administered medications, Sackett (1976) concluded that fifty percent of patients do not take prescribed medications according to instructions. Twenty to forty percent of recommended immunizations are not obtained. Scheduled medical appointments are missed twenty to fifty percent of the time. Only about one-third of those with hypertension (high blood pressure) will keep it under control (Leventhal, Zimmerman, & Guttmann, 1984). Nearly half of insulin-dependent diabetic patients do not regularly monitor their blood glucose levels (Wysocki, Green, & Huxtable, 1988).

One reason for low rates of compliance is the lack of clear and direct information given to patients by health professionals. Waitzkin and Stoeckle (1976) directly recorded the proportion of time physicians spent informing patients about their illness or treatment. The average time spent with the patients was twenty minutes, of which an average of one minute was spent informing them. When

asked to estimate how much time they had spent informing their patients, the same physicians estimated that it had been ten to fifteen minutes.

## Models of Health Behavior

Why are rates of compliance so low among patients? How can psychology help to improve healthy behaviors among both normal and patient populations? Four models of health behavior have been developed to help answer these questions.

Attempts to persuade sexually active people to use condoms are often unsuccessful. They typically involve vivid descriptions of the dangers of unsafe sex and the ravages of AIDS. The assumption of policymakers and educators seems to be that arousing fear will induce people to use condoms. According to Aronson (1992), most individuals, when contemplating having sex, do not want to think about death or disease. "If the cognitive association between death and condoms is too powerful, the thought of using condoms may be so noxious as to diminish the pleasure associated with sex" (p. 89). Under these circumstances, many individuals will block all thoughts of death, disease, and condoms out of their minds, adopting an avoidant coping strategy. Aronson recommends that the persuasive message should be designed to overcome whatever it is that sexually active people find unattractive about condoms. If they regard condoms as something that interferes with the flow of a sexual encounter, then we should find a way to change this mind-set—perhaps by discussing the putting on of the condom as a mutual event that can become an erotic aspect of lovemaking.

The **health belief model** proposes that the likelihood of a person's engaging in health-related behaviors is a function of feeling personally susceptible to a disease, feeling that the disease would have serious consequences, and that the benefits of engaging in health-related behaviors outweigh the barriers, such as pain, embarrassment, or expense. This model has been used with some success to predict the adoption of such health-related behaviors as vaccinations and screening for cancer.

The **self-regulation model** was proposed by Leventhal and Cameron (1987). It involves three stages: the cognitive representation of the health threat, including its perceived symptoms, potential causes, or possible consequences. The action plan or coping stage, in which the individual formulates and begins a plan of action. The appraisal stage in which the individual judges the success of coping actions. If it is judged unsuccessful, modifications are made in the action plan. Attractive features of this model

## APPLYING PSYCHOLOGY
### The Secrets of Successful Dieters

A notoriously difficult condition to treat, obesity has long resisted a variety of heroic efforts to induce weight loss that will be maintained over a long period of time as discussed in chapter 8. Some of the weight loss methods and personal characteristics of highly successful dieters have been identified. Colvin and Olson (1983) studied forty-one women and thirteen men who had lost at least twenty percent of their body weight and who had been able to maintain the loss for at least two years. Over half the men reported that they began to lose weight following a "critical incident," which generally involved having a physician tell them to lose weight "or else." Most women could not identify a critical incident for their decision to begin to lose weight.

Though factors that appeared to be crucial to maintaining weight loss in men could not be reliably identified, four factors crucial to maintaining weight loss in women were found. They included the following:

1. These women had lost enough weight to feel that they had attained the loss they originally felt was appropriate for them. They had reached their weight loss goal.

2. They developed diets that worked for them; they are much more aware of what they eat: they eat less sugar and fats, more fish, fowl, fruits, and green vegetables, and they no longer like feeling "full."

3. Most of the women no longer spend the day at home. Most were full-time housewives and mothers before, more than sixty percent are now business and professional women.

4. The women are much more concerned about their appearance and physical condition than before; they exercise on a regular basis, and they weigh themselves daily.

Successful maintenance of weight loss takes continued effort and vigilence. Contrary to popular opinion, it is possible to lose weight and to maintain weight loss.

---

are that it is active, stressing the individual and how that individual can operate and reflect on his or her actions (Pitts, 1991).

The **theory of reasoned action,** by Martin Fishbein and Icek Ajzen (1975), suggests that the immediate determinant of behavior is a person's intention to perform the behavior. Intentions are determined both by an individual's attitudes toward the behavior plus social norms and values. This model is widely used to predict behavior, although it is clear that factors in addition to attitudes and social norms influence behavior. As a result, Ajzen has modified the theory to emphasize the individual's sense of control in a situation as well as the impact of factors in the immediate situation.

The **stress-diathesis model** (Steptoe, 1989) emphasizes the interaction of environmental and individual (genetic and psychological) factors upon health. This type of model has been used to explain psychopathology, such as schizophrenia, as well as medical disorders such as coronary heart disease (Phillips, 1991). According to this model, psychological and physical demands threaten the individual's resources and capacity for coping which give rise to physiological reactions involving the autonomic nervous system, endocrine, and immune systems of the body. This is reminiscent of Selye's General Adaptation Syndrome.

There are several common features in these approaches to compliance. Among the factors that operate consistently to raise compliance are the patient's belief that the problem poses a real health threat. Important too is the belief that it is possible to take effective action that will reduce the threat. Knowledge of what to do also contributes to compliance. The presence of support from other people in carrying out the regimen is also a significant factor (Sheridan & Radmacher, 1992).

Psychologists and others have recently become interested in helping induce positive life-style changes in healthy persons whose life-styles have the potential to cause health problems later in life. Healthy persons who smoke heavily, overeat, and fail to exercise or follow good nutritional practices can all be helped to change their poor health practices and enhance the quality of their life now and their health later on. (See also the discussion of community psychology in chapter 13, Psychotherapy.)

Mormons in Utah have a thirty percent lower incidence of most cancers than the general population of the United States. Seventh Day Adventists have twenty-five percent fewer hospital admissions for malignancies. According to Matarazzo (1983) these statistics are evidence of the effects of a healthy style of living.

Clinical psychologist Peter Nathan (1984) was involved for several years in the implementation of the Live for Life program, a positive life-style program designed to change unhealthy life-styles among the 60,000 employees of one of the country's largest companies. A substantial number of employees stopped smoking, started exercising, and reduced excessive food intake by attending weekly "action groups" aimed at smoking cessation, weight control, exercise, and better nutritional practices. Employees were also encouraged to make use of a variety of educational activities and on-site exercise facilities.

Another feature of the Live for Life program, and a frequent component of such programs elsewhere, was stress management training designed to show highly stressed, hard-driving business people how to cope with the stressors that were an inevitable part of their jobs. Relaxation training, cognitive restructuring ("You don't have to be letter-perfect every time." "Even successful managers make a mistake once in a while."), and more flexible time-management skills were all elements designed to reduce the effects of stress on the minds and bodies of these successful business people.

## Physical Exercise

One of the things that "everyone knows" is that "physical exercise is good for you." Yet despite this widespread belief, a February 1992 survey (CNN) found that fifty-nine percent of Americans said they get "little or no exercise."

It is aerobic exercise that seems to matter. **Aerobic exercise** *is any exercise that stimulates heart and breathing activity for a period of time long enough to produce beneficial changes in the body.* Aerobic exercises use the large muscles of the body in rhythmic or dynamic movements. Aerobic exercises include brisk walking, jogging, cycling, swimming, running, and some active sports. Golf and bowling are not considered aerobic because there are frequent pauses in the activity.

Even modest levels of physical fitness are associated with reduced mortality rates. Exercise decreases the risk of heart disease, colon cancer, osteoporosis, and stroke. An adequate level of fitness can be reached through a daily thirty- to sixty-minute brisk walk (Blair et al., 1989). The American College of Sports Medicine (1978) recommends that healthy adults engage in fifteen to sixty minutes of continuous aerobic activity at sixty to ninety percent of maximum heart rate, three to five times per week. (Maximum heart rate can be obtained by subtracting an individual's age from 220.) Lower intensity exercises, like brisk walking, carried out for longer periods of time appear to be as beneficial as high intensity activities, such as racquetball, engaged in for a short time. Moderate exercise programs are in some ways superior to intense athletics. They avoid the risk of serious injuries, and it is easier to motivate people to engage in walking and calisthenic programs than in active sports.

Exercise also has psychological benefits. In a review of recent research on psychological effects of physical exercise, Thomas Plante and Judith Rodin (1990) conclude that exercise improves mood and well-being, and reduces anxiety, depression, and stress. In one study, a fifteen-minute walk produced more relaxation than a standard dose of a mild tranquilizer (DeVries & Adams, 1972).

There are many theories of how exercise produces these healthful effects. Some explanations stress biological mechanisms—for example, an increase in adrenal activity, neurotransmitters, or endorphins. Other theories emphasize psychological mechanisms, including the sense of mastery and accomplishment that accompany physical fitness and the distractions provided by intense physical activity. Plante and Rodin cite the need for further research before we are able to decide among these plausible hypotheses. Of course, they are not mutually exclusive; exercise may have multiple effects through multiple routes.

▶ **GUIDED REVIEW** *Learning Objectives 15 and 16*

1. Many studies find that both patients and physicians often fail to follow sound medical advice and practices. In other words, their rates of _____ are low.
2. Four models of health behaviors are _____, _____, _____, and _____.
3. The four models of health behavior have some common features. These include _____, _____, and _____.
4. _____ is any exercise that stimulates heart and breathing activity for a period of time long enough to produce beneficial changes in the body.
5. Even _____ levels of physical fitness are associated with reduced mortality rates.
6. Exercise decreases the risk of _____, _____, _____, and _____.

*ANSWERS*

1. compliance 2. health belief, self-regulation, reasoned action, stress-diathesis 3. the patient's belief that the problem poses a health threat, the belief that it is possible to take effective action that will reduce the threat, knowledge of what to do 4. Aerobic exercise 5. modest 6. heart disease, colon cancer, osteoporosis, stroke

# SUMMARY

I. Psychology and medicine have many common and complementary interests. Increasingly, the leading causes of death are a result of human behavior rather than disease. Medical decisions involve individual's attitudes, cognitive limitations, and habits. (p. 420)

  A. Health psychology is concerned with psychological contributions to the promotion and maintenance of health, the prevention and treatment of illness, and the analysis and improvement of the health care system and health policy. (p. 420)

  B. There are two definitions of health: the absence of disease, and the presence of positive "healthy" traits. (p. 421)

  C. The authors regard health as a continuum. Individuals may be said to be more or less healthy, rather than either healthy or ill. (p. 421)

II. The word stress is used in two different ways: to refer to something that happens to a person, and to refer to a person's response to an event. (p. 421)

  A. Events and stimuli that may cause stress or stressful responses are referred to as stressors. (p. 421)

  B. Examples of the first use of the term "stress" are Selye's General Adaptation Syndrome, and the effects of Life Events on illness. (pp. 421–422)

    1. The General Adaptation Syndrome has three phases: the alarm reaction, resistance, and exhaustion. (p. 421)

    2. According to Selye, the body system best able to cope with stress becomes most strongly activated. The weakest system will be the one most likely to show the effects of stress. (p. 421)

    3. Life Events research is an attempt to map the effects of particular stressful events, both negative, such as divorce, and positive, such as a promotion at work. Two widely used measures of life events are the Holmes and Rahe Social Readjustment Rating Scale, and a measure of "daily hassles and uplifts." (p. 422)

  C. Experiencing physical and psychological symptoms long after a stressful experience is referred to as post-traumatic stress disorder. (p. 422)

  D. Much stress is work-related. Job stress is a function of two separate elements: the psychological demands of the work and the ability to make decisions about how those demands are met. (p. 424)

  E. Among the responses to stress are the use and abuse of alcohol and other drugs. (p. 424)

    1. The effects of drugs are partly dependent upon our learned expectations. (p. 426)

III. Cognitive and personality variables moderate the effects of stressors on physical and psychological reactions. (p. 426)

  A. The importance of perceived control emerged at about the same time in different areas of psychology. (p. 428)

  B. Perceived lack of control appears to play a role in the effects of stressors on illness. The concept is useful in helping us understand people's different reactions to disasters and accidents, the effects of work-related stress, and reactions of the elderly in nursing homes. (p. 428)

  C. Coping styles refer to characteristic ways of responding to stressors. (p. 430)

    1. Avoidant coping strategies distract the individual from the stressor. (p. 430)

    2. Problem-centered or attentional coping strategies focus on gathering information about the problem and discussing it with others. (p. 430)

    3. Response-centered coping strategies involve controlling one's emotional and cognitive reactions to stressors. These include stress-management and relaxation techniques. (p. 430)

    4. No one coping style is superior in all cases. For long-term stressors, problem-centered approaches are more effective than avoidant strategies. (p. 431)

    5. Many programs designed to change eating, smoking, drinking, and drug-related behaviors employ response-centered coping strategies. (p. 431)

  D. Hardiness refers to a personality disposition that moderates the effects of stressors. Hardiness consists of a sense of personal control, commitment to values, and facing challenges. (p. 431)

  E. Social support from friends, relatives, and others appears to moderate the effects of stressors and be related to recovery from illness. (p. 431)

IV. Researchers use two different strategies to study risk factors in disease: prospective and retrospective. In a prospective study, a sample of healthy individuals is studied over a long period of time. In retrospective studies, the backgrounds of individuals suffering from a disease are explored in an attempt to identify causes. (p. 432)

  A. Coronary heart disease (CHD) consists of two types of disorder: angina pectoris and myocardial infarction. Both types result from coronary atherosclerosis. (p. 432)

    1. Coronary atherosclerosis is the build-up of cholesterol and fatty substances, which form plaque on the walls of the coronary arteries. (p. 432)

    2. When the heart is temporarily deprived of oxygen, pain may occur. This is an attack of angina. (p. 432)

    3. When an obstruction or blood clot obstructs the coronary artery (an event referred to as a coronary occlusion), the supply of oxygen to the heart may be cut off. When this happens, the individual suffers a heart attack, or myocardial infarction. (p. 432)

**B.** Risk factors for CHD include age, sex, high levels of cholesterol, high blood pressure, smoking, diabetes, a family history of heart disease, obesity, and lack of exercise. (p. 432)

   **1.** Of these risk factors, cholesterol levels, blood pressure, smoking, obesity, and exercise are all strongly influenced by psychological and behavioral events. (p. 432)

**C.** Certain behavioral patterns place the individual at increased risk of CHD. Namely, impatient, angry, competitive, hard-driving individuals appear more likely to suffer CHD. These elements comprise the Type A behavior pattern. (p. 433)

   **1.** Type A behavior by itself is not an adequate explanation for CHD. There is recent evidence that Type A individuals may survive heart attacks better than do Type Bs. (p. 433)

**D.** Cancer represents a variety of disorders involving the unrestrained growth of abnormal cells. (p. 434)

   **1.** Antigens, foreign substances that enter or contact the body, are typically identified and eliminated by the immune system. (p. 433)

   **2.** Acquired immunity is the identification and destruction of specifically recognized antigens. When this is impaired by the HIV virus, the individual is at risk of developing AIDS, acquired immunodeficiency syndrome. (p. 434)

**E.** There is as yet no convincing evidence that stress can make normal cells become cancerous. However, stress does interfere with the ability of the immune system to destroy cancerous cells. (p. 434)

**V.** Many patients fail to follow sound medical advice and procedures. Therefore, psychologists have a role to play in understanding and increasing compliance with healthy practices. (p. 434)

**A.** Four models of compliance with medical recommendations and engaging in healthy behaviors are the health belief model, the self-regulation model, the theory of reasoned action, and the stress-diathesis model. (pp. 435–436)

   **1.** These models share common features: the patient's belief that the problem is a health threat; the belief that it is possible to take effective action to reduce the threat, and knowledge of what to do. (p. 436)

**B.** Psychologists have been involved in community-wide programs to facilitate healthy life-styles. These often teach stress-management and other coping techniques. (p. 437)

**C.** Moderate aerobic exercise, like brisk walking, appears to be as effective in reducing the risk of CHD and other stress-related diseases, as more strenuous exercise. (p. 437)

---

## ACTION GLOSSARY

Match the terms in the left column with the definitions in the right column.

___ **1. Health psychology (p. 420)**
___ **2. Health (p. 421)**
___ **3. Stress (p. 421)**
___ **4. Stressor (p. 421)**
___ **5. General Adaptation Syndrome (p. 421)**
___ **6. Alarm reaction (p. 421)**
___ **7. Resistance (p. 421)**
___ **8. Exhaustion (p. 421)**

*A.* An event or stimulus that may cause stress or stressful responses.

*B.* A response to stress in which the body produces a variety of endocrine gland hormones.

*C.* Concerned with the contributions of psychology, the promotion and maintenance of health, the prevention and treatment of illness, the identification of causes and correlates of health and illness, and the analysis of improvement of the health care system and health policy.

*D.* A condition in which the body is either able to reduce the stress and eliminate the stressors, or the organism expires.

*E.* Refers either to an event that affects a person, or to a person's undesirable reaction to an event.

*F.* A continuum from optimal wellness to premature illness and death.

*G.* A response to stress in which the body system best able to cope with the stress becomes most strongly activated.

*H.* A three-phase process in reaction to stress. Includes the alarm reaction, the buildup of resistance, and gradual exhaustion.

___ 9. Posttraumatic stress disorder (p. 422)

___ 10. Psychoactive substance dependence (p. 425)

___ 11. Psychoactive substance abuse (p. 425)

A. An individual who does not meet the criteria for "psychoactive substance dependence" but who nevertheless has problems as a result of drug/alcohol use.

B. The syndrome of physical and psychological symptoms that appears as a delayed response to a distressing event.

C. An individual who meets three or more of a set of behavioral criteria regarding drug/alcohol use.

___ 12. Stress "buffers" (p. 426)

___ 13. Self-efficacy (p. 428)

___ 14. Learned helplessness (p. 428)

___ 15. Coping style (p. 430)

___ 16. Avoidant coping style (p. 430)

___ 18. Attentional, or problem-centered, coping style (p. 430)

___ 18. Response-centered coping style (p. 430)

___ 19. Hardiness (p. 431)

___ 20. Social support (p. 431)

A. The belief that a person can successfully perform a behavior to produce a desired outcome.

B. A coping style in which individuals seek information about the stressor.

C. Moderators of an individual's responses to potential stressors.

D. A coping style in which people turn their attention away from aspects of the stressor.

E. Emotional comfort and encouragement from others acts as a stress buffer.

F. A coping style in which individuals control their own reactions to stress.

G. Characteristic ways that individuals have of coping with potentially stressful events.

H. The perception that one's behavior does not influence one's outcomes. Follows prolonged exposure to uncontrollable events.

I. A personality disposition that moderates the effects of stressors. Includes control, commitment, and challenge.

___ 21. Prospective studies (p. 432)

___ 22. Retrospective studies (p. 432)

___ 23. Coronary heart disease (CHD) (p. 432)

___ 24. Coronary atherosclerosis (p. 432)

___ 25. Angina (p. 432)

___ 26. Myocardial infarction (p. 432)

___ 27. Type A behavior pattern (p. 433)

___ 28. Antigens (p. 433)

___ 29. Immune system (p. 434)

___ 30. Acquired immunity (p. 434)

A. A cut off in the supply of oxygen to the heart as a result of a coronary occlusion; a heart attack.

B. Pain as a result of a temporary reduction in oxygen supply to the heart.

C. The condition in which an accumulation of cholesterol and fatty substances form plaque on the inner walls of the coronary arteries.

D. Functions to identify and destroy antigens.

E. Studies that examine the backgrounds of patients who suffer from a disease in an effort to determine the origins of the disease.

F. Foreign substances that enter or come into contact with the body: parasites, viruses, and so on.

G. The system that recognizes and destroys specific antigens.

H. The nation's leading cause of death. Two major types are angina pectoris and myocardial infarction.

I. Behavior typically found in hard-driving, easily angered, competitive, achievement-oriented individuals.

J. Research following healthy individuals over a period of time to record which individuals develop a disease.

___ **31. Health belief model (p. 435)**

___ **32. Self-regulation model
(p. 435)**

___ **33. Theory of reasoned action
(p. 436)**

___ **34. Stress-diathesis model
(p. 436)**

___ **35. Aerobic exercise (p. 437)**

A. *Involves the three stages of the perception of the health threat, the plan of action for coping with it, and the appraisal of the coping actions.*

B. *Events present demands upon an individual's limited capacity for coping. These result in changes in the immune and other bodily systems.*

C. *The likelihood of engaging in health-related behaviors depends upon on individual's beliefs about personal susceptibility to disease, and beliefs that the benefits of engaging in a behavior outweigh the costs, such as pain, embarrassment, or expense.*

D. *Any activity that stimulates heart and breathing for a period long enough to produce beneficial changes in the body.*

E. *Suggests that health behavior is a function of the person's intention to perform the behavior.*

*ANSWERS*

29. d, 30. g, 31. c, 32. a, 33. e, 34. b, 35. d
19. i, 20. e, 21. j, 22. e, 23. h, 24. c, 25. b, 26. a, 27. i, 28. f,
1. c, 2. f, 3. e, 4. a, 5. h, 6. g, 7. b, 8. d, 9. b, 10. c, 11. a, 12. c, 13. a, 14. h, 15. g, 16. d, 17. b, 18. f,

## SELF-TEST

**1.** Health psychology is concerned with
   (a) the prevention and treatment of illness.
   (b) identifying causes and correlates of illness.
   (c) the improvement of the health care system.
   (d) all of the above.
   (LO 2; p. 420)

**2.** Health has been defined in different ways. Which of the following is *not* one of them?
   (a) the absence of illness
   (b) the presence of healthy traits and behaviors
   (c) a continuum from optimal wellness to premature illness and death
   (d) the reactions a person has to stressors and antigens
   (LO 2; p. 421)

**3.** Stress has been defined as
   (a) something unpleasant that happens to a person.
   (b) a person's undesirable reaction to an event.
   (c) the unpleasant feeling in response to an event.
   (d) all of the above.
   (LO 3; p. 421)

**4.** The General Adaptation Syndrome was first described by
   (a) Leon Festinger.
   (b) Sigmund Freud.
   (c) Hans Selye.
   (d) Charles Darwin.
   (LO 4; p. 421)

**5.** Selye's term for the series of bodily reactions a person undergoes whenever stress is present is
   (a) cognitive dissonance theory.
   (b) type A behavior pattern.
   (c) General Adaptation Syndrome.
   (d) posttraumatic stress disorder.
   (LO 4; p. 421)

**6.** In which phase of the General Adaptation Syndrome does the endocrine gland secrete hormones to deal with a stressor?
   (a) alarm reaction
   (b) resistance
   (c) exhaustion
   (d) post-traumatic
   (LO 4; p. 421)

**7.** In which phase of the General Adaptation Syndrome would the harmful physical effects of stress be apparent?
   (a) alarm reaction
   (b) resistance
   (c) exhaustion
   (d) posttraumatic
   (LO 4; p. 421)

**8.** In early stress research
   (a) the aim was to identify external stressors.
   (b) individual differences were not usually considered.
   (c) life events and daily hassles were studied in relation to health.
   (d) all of the above.
   (LO 5; p. 422)

**9.** A widely used measure of the effects of life events on illness was
   (a) Holmes and Rahe's Social Readjustment Rating Scale.
   (b) Jenkins Activity Survey.
   (c) exercise stress test.
   (d) *DSM-III-R*.
   (LO 5; p. 422)

10. Life events and daily hassles
    (a) are unrelated to illness.
    (b) are moderately correlated with various illnesses.
    (c) play no role in illness.
    (d) are the sole causes of many illnesses.
    (LO 5; p. 422)

11. An extremely stressful event that is re-experienced long afterwards is known as
    (a) schizophrenia.
    (b) posttraumatic stress disorder.
    (c) General Adaptation Syndrome.
    (d) approach-avoidance conflict.
    (LO 6; p. 422)

12. Work-related stress
    (a) is not highest among upper-level management and professionals.
    (b) is related to high work demands.
    (c) is related to lack of decision-making freedom on the job.
    (d) all of the above.
    (LO 7; pp. 423–424)

13. An individual who meets three or more of a set of behavioral criteria regarding drug/alcohol use is classified as
    (a) psychoactive substance dependent.
    (b) psychoactive substance abuser.
    (c) schizophrenic.
    (d) Type A.
    (LO 8; p. 425)

14. An individual who does not meet the criteria for "psychoactive substance dependence" but who nevertheless has problems as a result of drug/alcohol use is regarded as
    (a) psychoactive substance dependent.
    (b) psychoactive substance abuser.
    (c) schizophrenic.
    (d) Type A.
    (LO 8; p. 425)

15. Drugs often have paradoxical effects. For example, a stimulant may be used to relax a person, because
    (a) our expectations partly determine the effects of a drug.
    (b) we are socialized into the use of drugs.
    (c) we learn how and when to use drugs and what effects they are supposed to have.
    (d) all of the above.
    (LO 8; p. 426)

16. Which of the following is *not* considered a buffer or moderator of an individual's responses to stressors?
    (a) obesity
    (b) perceived control
    (c) coping style
    (d) hardiness
    (LO 9; pp. 428–430)

17. The belief that a person can successfully perform a behavior to produce the intended effect is referred to by Bandura as
    (a) learned helplessness.
    (b) hardiness.
    (c) self-efficacy.
    (d) Type A behavior.
    (LO 9; p. 428)

18. Following uncontrollable reinforcements, one may feel powerless to influence future outcomes. This is known as
    (a) self-efficacy.
    (b) hardiness.
    (c) learned helplessness.
    (d) none of the above.
    (LO 10; p. 428)

19. Elderly residents of a nursing home who were provided with a small amount of decision-making control and responsibility (choosing and caring for a plant) were
    (a) unaffected by the plants.
    (b) happier and healthier only on the day of the study.
    (c) happier and healthier for as long as 18 months afterwards.
    (d) made worse by the added responsibility of caring for the plants.
    (LO 10; p. 430)

20. Individuals have characteristic ways of coping with stressful events. Some seek information or the comfort of others; some try to distract themselves from the event. These different strategies are known as
    (a) learned helpfulness.
    (b) coping styles.
    (c) stress-diathesis.
    (d) none of the above.
    (LO 11; p. 430)

21. One coping style is to turn attention away from the stressor and try not to think about it. This is known as a(n)
    (a) avoidant coping style.
    (b) attentional, problem-centered coping style.
    (c) response-centered coping style.
    (d) foolhardiness.
    (LO 11; p. 430)

22. A coping style in which individuals seek additional information about the stressor is known as
    (a) avoidant coping style.
    (b) attentional, problem-centered coping style.
    (c) response-centered coping style.
    (d) hardiness.
    (LO 11; p. 430)

23. A coping style in which individuals try to control their own reactions to stress is referred to as
    (a) avoidant coping style.
    (b) attentional, problem-centered coping style.
    (c) response-centered coping style.
    (d) hardiness.
    (LO 11; p. 430)

24. A stress buffer involving the personality disposition that includes control, commitment, and challenge is known as
    (a) avoidant coping style.
    (b) attentional, problem-centered coping style.
    (c) response-centered coping style.
    (d) hardiness.
    (LO 11; p. 431)

25. Regarding coping styles,
    (a) no one coping style is superior in all cases.
    (b) for long-term stressors, problem-centered approaches are more effective than avoidant strategies.
    (c) for stressors of short duration, avoidant strategies are more effective than problem-centered strategies.
    (d) all of the above.
    (LO 11; p. 431)

26. A researcher has been following the medical records of a large group of individuals for many years. She is conducting a
    (a) prospective study.
    (b) retrospective study.
    (c) learned helplessness study.
    (d) meta-analysis.
    (LO 13; p. 432)

27. A researcher has been looking into the childhood illnesses and experiences of a group of cancer patients. She is conducting a
    (a) prospective study.
    (b) retrospective study.
    (c) learned helplessness study.
    (d) meta-analysis.
    (LO 13; p. 432)

28. Which of the following is *not* a risk factor in CHD?
    (a) obesity
    (b) lack of physical exercise
    (c) high blood pressure
    (d) having older siblings
    (LO 14; p. 432)

29. The Type A behavior pattern is associated with
    (a) cancer.
    (b) emphysema.
    (c) hives.
    (d) heart disease.
    (LO 14; p. 433)

30. The condition in which an accumulation of cholesterol and fatty substances form plaque on the inner walls of the coronary arteries is referred to as
    (a) coronary atherosclerosis.
    (b) angina.
    (c) coronary occlusion.
    (d) myocardial infarction.
    (LO 14; p. 432)

31. Pain may result from a temporary reduction in the supply of oxygen to the heart. This is referred to as
    (a) coronary atherosclerosis.
    (b) angina.
    (c) coronary occlusion.
    (d) myocardial infarction.
    (LO 14; p. 432)

32. A cut off in the supply of oxygen to the heart as a result of an obstruction in the coronary arteries, otherwise known as a heart attack, is called
    (a) coronary atherosclerosis.
    (b) angina.
    (c) coronary occlusion.
    (d) myocardial infarction.
    (LO 14; p. 432)

33. Foreign substances that enter or come into contact with the body, parasites, viruses, and so on, are known as
    (a) angina pectoris.
    (b) antigens.
    (c) cholesterol.
    (d) acquired immunity.
    (LO 14; p. 433)

34. HIV seropositivity (being infected with HIV) progresses to AIDS
    (a) rarely.
    (b) only in about half the cases.
    (c) in nearly all cases within eleven years.
    (d) unless treatment is begun early.
    (LO 14; p. 434)

**35.** The model that views health-related behaviors as a function of the individual's beliefs about susceptibility to disease, and the relative costs and benefits of engaging in a behavior, is the

    **(a)** health belief model.
    **(b)** self-regulation model.
    **(c)** theory of reasoned action.
    **(d)** stress-diathesis model.
    (LO 15; p. 435)

**36.** The model that views health behavior as a three stage process of perception of the health threat, the plan of action for coping with it, and the appraisal of the coping actions, is

    **(a)** health belief model.
    **(b)** self-regulation model.
    **(c)** theory of reasoned action.
    **(d)** stress-diathesis model.
    (LO 15; p. 435)

*ANSWERS*

1. d, 2. d, 3. d, 4. c, 5. c, 6. a, 7. c, 8. d, 9. a, 10. b, 11. b, 12. d, 13. a, 14. b, 15. d, 16. a, 17. c, 18. c, 19. c, 20. b, 21. a, 22. b, 23. c, 24. d, 25. d, 26. a, 27. b, 28. d, 29. d, 30. a, 31. b, 32. d, 33. b, 34. c, 35. a, 36. b

# THINKING ABOUT PSYCHOLOGY

**1.** Many people overeat, use drugs and alcohol, fail to exercise, or fail to visit physicians or to follow their advice. Why do you think people so often do things that they know are not good for them, and fail to do those things, like exercise, that they know are good for them?

**2.** How is it possible for something as abstract as cognition (such as our interpretation of a potentially stressful event) to effect something as tangible as our physical health?

# SUGGESTED READINGS

Mendelson, J. H., & Mello, N. K. (1985). *The diagnosis and treatment of alcoholism.* (2nd edition). New York: McGraw-Hill. A comprehensive summary of reviews of the etiology, diagnosis, treatment, and prevention of alcohol abuse. Written for the layperson.

Pennebaker, J. W. (1990). *Opening up: The healing power of confiding in others.* New York: Norton. A well-written summary of research on the importance of social support as a buffer of stress and illness.

Snyder, C. R., & Forsyth, D. R. (1991). *Handbook of social and clinical psychology: A health perspective.* New York: Pergamon. Articles by experts on many aspects of health and psychology.

Stone, G. C. et al., (Eds.). (1987). *Health psychology: A discipline and a profession.* Chicago: University of Chicago Press. Summarizes research findings linking important issues in the educational and training of newly prepared professionals beginning to deal with "life-style disorders."

Stroebe, W., & Stroebe, M. (1994). *The social psychology of health.* Pacific Grove CA: Brooks/Cole. A review written for the student interested in learning about the current state of health psychology.

# CHAPTER 15

## SOCIAL BEHAVIOR
OUTLINE

▶ **Learning Objectives**

▶ **Social Comparison**

▶ **Guided Review**

▶ **Social Perception and Attribution**
  ■ First Impressions
  ■ Attribution Processes

▶ **Guided Review**

▶ **Personal Attraction**
  ■ Romantic Love

▶ **Guided Review**

▶ **Social Influence**
  ■ Attitudes and Persuasion
    Cognitive Dissonance Theory
    Attitude Change: Persuasion
      and Propaganda
  ■ Prejudice and Racism
    Belief Prejudice
    Reducing Prejudice

▶ **Guided Review**

▶ **Prosocial and Antisocial Behavior**
  ■ Diffusion of Responsibility
  ■ The Just-World Phenomenon
  ■ Aggression
    Frustration-Aggression
      Theory
    Social Learning Theory and
      Aggression
    Child and Spouse Abuse
  ■ Obedience to Authority

▶ **Guided Review**

▶ **Group Processes**
  ■ Social Facilitation

▶ **Guided Review**
  ■ Attraction to Groups
    Cognitive Dissonance and
      Group Cohesion
  ■ Leadership

▶ **Guided Review**
  ■ Development of Group Norms
    Conformity
    Minority Influence

▶ **Guided Review**
  ■ Group Decisions
    Social Loafing
    Groupthink
    Collective Behavior

▶ **Guided Review**

▶ **Summary**

▶ **Action Glossary**

▶ **Self-Test**

▶ **Thinking About Psychology**

▶ **Suggested Readings**

# SOCIAL BEHAVIOR
## LEARNING OBJECTIVES

**After reading this chapter, you should be able to:**

▶ **1.** understand the functions of social comparison. *(p. 448)*

▶ **2.** know why people associate with particular individuals. *(p. 448)*

▶ **3.** recognize the differences between perceiving objects and perceiving people. *(p. 448)*

▶ **4.** discuss the nature of implicit theories of personality. *(p. 449)*

▶ **5.** distinguish between external and internal attributions. *(p. 450)*

▶ **6.** understand the bases of interpersonal attraction. *(p. 451)*

▶ **7.** understand the principal means of social influence. *(pp. 453–456)*

▶ **8.** identify the nature of attitudes and attitude change. *(p. 453)*

▶ **9.** discuss the nature of prejudice. *(p. 455)*

▶ **10.** recognize the role assumed differences play in racial prejudice. *(p. 455)*

▶ **11.** appreciate the role of situational variables in prosocial and antisocial behavior. *(pp. 456–459)*

▶ **12.** understand the concept of diffusion of responsibility. *(p. 457)*

▶ **13.** trace the development of frustration-aggression and arousal-aggression theories. *(pp. 458–459)*

▶ **14.** describe the Milgram experiments on obedience. *(pp. 460–461)*

▶ **15.** define a group. *(p. 462)*

▶ **16.** indicate how the presence of others influences learning and performance. *(p. 462)*

▶ **17.** specify the reasons people join groups and the bases for their attraction to a group. *(p. 464)*

▶ **18.** define leadership and its relation to the group's task. *(pp.464 –466)*

▶ **19.** identify how group norms develop. *(p. 466)*

▶ **20.** discuss the extent and the reasons for conformity to group norms. *(p. 467)*

▶ **21.** identify some of the obstacles that stand in the way of effective group decision-making. *(p. 469)*

▶ **22.** define collective behavior. *(p. 470)*

**Figure 15.1** *Social psychology deals with the behavior of human beings in groups*

Human beings are perhaps the most social of all animals. Who they are and what they think depend to a surprising extent on their contacts with other people(figure 15.1). Being with others helps people to define themselves and the world they live in. When people are isolated from others, they lose an important source of information and stability. Isolated prisoners and shipwrecked sailors, for example, often lose their hold on reality and even come to question their own sanity. Of course social groups are not only sources of information and support, they are also the source of much of our suffering, exemplified by ethnic and religious conflicts around the world. **Social psychology** *is the branch of psychology that examines the effects people have on one another.* It is concerned with social interaction.

## SOCIAL COMPARISON

Many of the questions people ask about themselves and about others cannot be answered objectively. There are no machines to measure how friendly or how trustworthy someone is or whether classical music is better than hard rock. Individuals arrive at answers to such questions by discussing them with other people, by listening to or reading about what others have to say, and by observing people's reactions in different situations. The answers to these questions are *socially constructed.* People engage in a process of **social comparison;** *they compare themselves and their experiences with those of other people to arrive at judgments about the social and physical world and*

*about themselves.* To some extent, people base their beliefs and opinions on the beliefs and opinions of others.

Leon Festinger's (1954) social comparison theory assumes that people have a need to evaluate their own opinions and abilities. They prefer objective evaluations, but when objective methods are unavailable, they compare themselves to people whom they expect to be somewhat similar on the trait in question. If college students wish to know how intelligent they are, they do not compare themselves to grade school children or to a physics professor; they compare themselves to other students at college.

What happens if, after comparing themselves to others, people find that their opinion or ability is strikingly different? According to the theory and supportive research (Suls & Miller, 1977; Suls & Wills, 1991), people will either change to conform to the opinion or ability of others or they will withdraw from further contact with that person or group. Social comparisons tend to be made in a way that enhances a person's self-esteem (Wheeler & Miyake, 1992). By comparing themselves with others, people arrive at socially agreed-upon ways of viewing themselves, their world, and other people (Berger & Luckmann, 1969; Gergen, 1991).

Social comparison reduces the ambiguity of uncertain events. Before undergoing surgery, patients frequently wish to talk with other patients who have undergone similar treatment (Wood, Taylor, & Lichtman, 1985). In a study of people living in an area threatened by floods, those who had no previous experience with floods engaged in social comparison. After they discussed floods with their neighbors, they were calm, more confident in their ability to cope with flooding, and more committed to taking preventive measures (Hansson, Noulles, & Bellovich, 1982).

▶ **GUIDED REVIEW** *Learning Objectives 1 and 2*

1. People often evaluate their opinions and abilities by comparing themselves with _____.
2. This process is referred to as _____.
3. People prefer to compare themselves to others they expect to be _____ to themselves.
4. Social comparison helps people to _____.

*ANSWERS*

*1. others 2. social comparison 3. similar 4. reduce uncertainty*

# EXPLORING HUMAN DIVERSITY

## The Social Animal

People are not evenly distributed across the planet. They tend to form dense clusters, mostly along bodies of water, known as cities. Within cities people go out of their way to join with others in social, religious, political, occupational, and recreational groups.

As a species, then, we are social animals. Are some of us more social than others? Curtis, Grabb, and Baer (1992) compared voluntary group membership in fifteen countries. Because many people belong to a church and to unions, the researchers also measured group membership excluding these. As can be seen from table 15.A, Americans are at or near the top in voluntary groups on nearly every measure. Seventy-three percent of Americans belong to voluntary groups. Excluding church and union membership, forty-one percent of Americans are members of voluntary groups—more than twice the proportion as in France, Italy, Japan, and Spain.

**TABLE 15.A  Percent of respondents reporting voluntary association membership in fifteen countries, 1981–1983.**

| Country | Total | Excluding church | Excluding union | Excluding church and union |
|---|---|---|---|---|
| Australia | 61 | 50 | 52 | 40 |
| Belgium | 43 | 38 | 30 | 25 |
| Canada | 58 | 44 | 53 | 37 |
| France | 27 | 25 | 22 | 20 |
| Great Britain | 53 | 44 | 43 | 31 |
| Ireland | 52 | 34 | 46 | 26 |
| Italy | 26 | 23 | 21 | 18 |
| Japan | 30 | 24 | 21 | 14 |
| N. Ireland | 67 | 37 | 61 | 28 |
| Netherlands | 63 | 49 | 59 | 44 |
| Norway | 62 | 60 | 43 | 40 |
| Spain | 31 | 21 | 27 | 17 |
| Sweden | 68 | 65 | 44 | 39 |
| United States | 73 | 47 | 70 | 41 |
| W. Germany | 49 | 43 | 38 | 32 |

# SOCIAL PERCEPTION AND ATTRIBUTION

We admire some people, love others, and fear still others. How do we arrive at these views? How and with whom do we form friendships and develop romantic attachments? In contrast to perception, which is concerned with judgments of the physical universe (see chapter 4), *social perception* deals with *judgments of other people*. Unlike our perceptions of objects, our perceptions of people take into consideration their motives, intentions, and feelings.

## First Impressions

**Impression formation** *is the study of how people form opinions of others.* In an early study of impression formation, Solomon Asch (1952) described a fictitious man to college students. The students were told that the man was intelligent, skillful, industrious, determined, practical, and cautious. Some also heard him described as "warm," whereas others heard him described as "cold." After hearing one of these two lists of adjectives, each student was asked to describe him in a brief essay. Asch found that students described the person in a complex and complete way based on a limited amount of information. Varying one adjective—"warm" or "cold"—influenced the overall impressions formed by students. A term like *intelligent* may mean one thing when it is paired with "warm" and something different when it is paired with "cold." In table 15.1, for example, a person described as "warm" is thought to be "generous" by ninety-one percent of the subjects, whereas only eight percent of those who heard him described as "cold" believed he would be generous.

Expectations about others influence our perceptions of them. People use **implicit theories of personality,** *beliefs about which traits tend to belong together.* These implicit theories are not necessarily valid. For example, many believe that someone with a good sense of humor is also intelligent. The evidence does not support this belief. Nevertheless, someone holding this implicit theory who knows only that a person has a good sense of humor will probably infer that the person is also intelligent.

**TABLE 15.1  Percent of subjects choosing each adjective**

| Adjective | Warm (%) | Cold (%) |
|---|---|---|
| Generous | 91 | 8 |
| Wise | 65 | 25 |
| Good-natured | 94 | 17 |
| Happy | 90 | 34 |
| Humorous | 77 | 13 |
| Sociable | 91 | 38 |
| Popular | 84 | 28 |
| Important | 88 | 99 |
| Humane | 86 | 31 |
| Restrained | 77 | 89 |
| Altruistic | 69 | 18 |
| Imaginative | 51 | 19 |

From Solomon E. Asch, *Social Psychology*, p. 209. Copyright © 1952 Prentice-Hall, Inc. Reprinted by permission of the author.

There is a tendency, stronger in some people than in others, to see people as either good or bad (O'Neal, 1971). For instance, if most people learned that Bob was intelligent, friendly, warm, and dishonest, they might discount, or even forget, the last characteristic when forming an impression of him. The **halo effect** refers to a *tendency to form positive impressions when only a few positive traits are known about a person.*

## Attribution Processes

People spend much of their time trying to unravel the likes and dislikes of others, attempting to find out why people do what they do. **Attribution** *is the study of how people explain the causes of behavior.*

Heider (1958) suggested that people analyze others' behavior to determine whether it is caused by some internal state, such as personality or attitudes, or by external forces, such as the demands of job or family. Attributions are based on such considerations as the actor's abilities and motivation in deciding whether the person acted as a result of internal or external factors.

If you ask your dad and your brother why mom spends so much time in the kitchen, they are apt to say that she enjoys cooking and has a talent for it. This is an internal attribution. However, if you ask your mom the same question, she might tell you that it is part of being a good mother—that her family deserves to eat well. This is an external attribution. Which explanation is correct? There is no one interpretation of someone's behavior that is completely correct. The study of attribution examines what

information is taken into account when explaining someone's behavior and what types of explanations people give (Gergen, 1991).

The attributions of mother and her family serve as examples of the **fundamental attribution bias,** *the tendency to see other people's behavior as internally caused and to see one's own behavior as externally caused* (Miller, Ashton, & Mishal, 1990). Mom explains her behavior by reference to the external situation, whereas Dad and brother interpret her behavior as internally motivated. (see box "Why did van Gogh cut off his ear?" in chapter 13).

The attributional bias is self-serving. People tend to deny being responsible for actions that have unfavorable consequences (Carver, DeGregoria, & Gillis, 1980). The coaches of winning and losing teams tend to make different attributions in explaining the outcome of a game. The winning coach believes that his decisions about plays and players were responsible for the victory. The coach of the losing team is more apt to refer to the lucky break of the opposing team, to bad officiating, or to a tiring journey to the game (Kelley, 1973; Sloan, 1989). This attribution bias is a way of avoiding personal responsibility for unfavorable outcomes and of taking credit for favorable occurrences; it enables people to feel better about themselves (Weary, 1980; see Fiske & Taylor, 1991). In one study, students at universities that had just won or lost an

▶ **GUIDED REVIEW** *Learning Objectives 3, 4, and 5*

1. The perception of people, unlike the perception of objects, must take into consideration their _____, _____, and _____.
2. People believe that certain personality traits occur together. This is referred to as _____.
3. The tendency to assume that the presence of some positive personality traits is accompanied by other positive traits is known as the _____.
4. _____ is concerned with how people explain the causes of their behavior.
5. _____ attributions explain behavior using personality, needs, wishes, and motives. _____ attributions refer to the situation in which a behavior takes place.
6. People tend to take credit for positive effects and deny responsibility for unpleasant effects, a process known as _____.

*ANSWERS*

*1. motives, needs, desires 2. implicit theory of personality 3. halo effect 4. Attribution theory 5. Internal, External 6. self-serving or fundamental attribution bias*

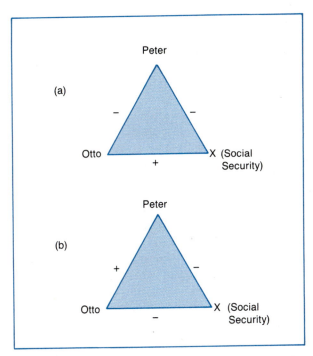

**Figure 15.2** *Heider's balance theory. (a) Peter dislikes the Social Security system; Otto likes it. Peter will probably not be attracted to Otto. (b) If both Peter and Otto hold a common attitude toward Social Security, there will be a tendency for Peter to like Otto.*

important basketball or football game were interviewed on the telephone (Cialdini et al., 1976). The students tended to refer to their school's winning team by including themselves ("We won," they said), but they distanced themselves from losing efforts ("They lost").

# PERSONAL ATTRACTION

Of the most important influences on our personalities—parents, siblings, and friends—only friends are freely chosen. Who are your closest friends, and why are they your friends? Of all the relationships a person has in a lifetime, perhaps none is more important or more carefully considered than the choice of a partner. What psychological and social forces enter into the decision to marry someone? **Interpersonal attraction** *is the area of study that looks at the social and psychological bases of friendship and love.*

The oldest and most widely recognized theory of attraction is based on the saying "Birds of a feather flock together." As early as 300 B.C., Aristotle noted, "They are

friends who have come to regard the same things as good and the same things as evil, they who are friends of the same people, and they who are the enemies of the same people. . . . We like those who resemble us, and are engaged in the same pursuits." More than 2,000 years later, Aristotle's view is still useful for understanding interpersonal attraction. Psychologists have expanded and modified this position, but similarity of attitudes and interests are still seen to lie at the core of friendship and love.

In many theories of attraction (e.g., Berscheid & Walster, 1978; Byrne, 1971; Heider, 1958; Newcomb, 1956; Smeaton, Byrne, & Murnen, 1989; Sternberg & Barnes, 1988), a person is said to be most attracted to someone with similar attitudes, behaviors, interests, or personalities. The theories differ in their views of *why* similarity leads to attraction. Heider's balance theory, presented in figure 15.2, shows that Peter, who holds an unfavorable attitude toward some object or issue such as Social Security (X), would like Otto, who holds a similar attitude toward Social Security. This would produce a tension-free or "balanced" relationship. If an unbalanced state exists, such as discovering that someone you like has an attitude different from yours, then there is a state of tension; pressure exists to change your attitude or to change your relationship with the other person.

Byrne (1971) looks at the relationship between similarity and attraction in behavioral terms. When someone holds the same attitude as you, that serves as a positive reinforcement for your position. Byrne's theory maintains that we like those people who provide us with the greatest amount of positive reinforcement. Byrne distinguishes between the *number* of similar traits that two people share and the *proportion* of similar traits they share. According to the theory, you will be most attracted to someone who shares the greatest proportion of similar traits. For example, suppose you are familiar with ten of Joe's attitudes and believe that seven of them are the same as your attitudes. You are aware of twenty of Fred's attitudes, and seven of them are the same as your's. The theory predicts you will be more attracted to Joe than to Fred because Joe's attitudes are seventy percent similar to your own, whereas Fred's are only thirty-five percent similar.

In a cross-cultural study of similarity and attraction, students in Hawaii, Japan, India, Mexico, and the continental United States were presented with attitude questionnaires presumably filled out by another student (Byrne et al., 1971). The students completed the same questionnaire; this enabled the researchers to determine the degree of

| TABLE 15.2  Attraction toward others | | | |
| --- | --- | --- | --- |
| **Proportion of Similar Responses** | | | |
| | .00–.40 | .47–.60 | .67–1.00 | Total |
| Hawaii | 7.03 | 8.27 | 8.46 | 7.92 |
| India | 7.19 | 8.34 | 9.40 | 8.31 |
| Japan | 6.27 | 6.94 | 7.53 | 6.91 |
| Mexico | 7.31 | 8.55 | 9.11 | 8.32 |
| United States | 6.00 | 7.33 | 7.38 | 6.90 |
| *Total* | 6.76 | 7.89 | 8.37 | |

Note: The higher the score, the greater the attraction.
Adapted from D. Byrne et al., "The Ubiquitous Relationship: Attitude. Similarity and Attraction. A Cross-Cultural Study," Human Relations, 24, 201–207. Copyright © 1971 by Plenum Publishing Corporation.

similarity between the two. The students were then asked to indicate how much they thought they would like the other person. The results, summarized in table 15.2, indicate that as the proportion of similar responses increased, attraction also increased. These results were obtained in each of the five groups studied.

Once a certain degree of similarity has been established, additional characteristics become important (Kerckhoff & Davis, 1962; Hendrick, Hendrick, & Adler, 1988). One person's ability to satisfy the social and psychological needs of the other has been seen as the foundation of long-lasting relationships (Winch, 1958; Pilkington, Tesser, & Stephens, 1991). *The ability of each person to satisfy the needs of the other is called* **need complementarity.** For example, if Wayne has a need to be mothered and Joan has a need to be nurturant and protective, then Wayne and Joan should be attracted to one another. There is only a minimum of empirical evidence to support this theory, in part because we do not have satisfactory ways to measure needs (Levinger & Snoek, 1972).

## Romantic Love

Love means different things to different people. There is the love of a mother for her child and of a brother for his sibling, people say they love a sport, and some profess to love humanity. Can love encompass all these things? The ancient Greeks had a separate word for each of these types of love.

Psychologists who write of love distinguish between romantic (or passionate) love, and companionate (sometimes called affectionate) love. The former is associated with strong sexual and emotional attraction. Affectionate or companionate love is a deep, committed, caring

affection for another. Love is viewed not so much as something an individual is or has, but as a *process* evolving over time (Hazan & Shaver, 1990; Shaver & Brennan, 1992; Thompson & Borrello, 1992). In Sternberg's (1988) view, there is a progression from passionate love to affectionate commitment.

Like other emotions, love has both physiological and psychological properties (see chapter 8). One theory (Schachter, 1964) states that any source of physiological arousal may be interpreted as love (or any other emotion) if the circumstances fit such an interpretation. Passionate love would be experienced when a person is aroused in the presence of someone of the opposite sex who expresses interest in the person (Berscheid & Walster, 1978; Walster & Walster, 1978). In one study (Dutton & Aron, 1974), men who had just crossed a dangerous, narrow bridge over a canyon were more likely to be attracted to a woman who spoke with them than were men who had not yet been aroused by the dangerous crossing. In other words, a slight amount of anxiety, fear, or other source of arousal may contribute to a strong emotional reaction.

How does loving a person differ from liking someone? Zick Rubin (1970) asked those in love to write descriptions of love, and others to write about friendship. Descriptions of love idealized the lover, involved sexual attraction, and a longing to be with the other. Liking involved attraction, similarity, and respect. Rubin developed a test to distinguish between liking and loving. For instance, one item that measures liking is, "I have great confidence in _____'s good judgment;" an item that measures love is, "I feel responsible for _____'s well-being." According to Rubin's analysis, loving and liking differ with respect to attitudes and behaviors.

The traditional western view of romantic love is that it is a passion. From this perspective, a person "falls" in love, as evidenced by a number of "symptoms." However, in many parts of the world, people marry for other reasons. This is true of traditional Oriental and Arab cultures where marriages are typically arranged. These marriages are frequently satisfying and stable. An examination of forty-three cultures found that romantic love was emphasized in cultures where there was most freedom to choose a partner, and where there was more contact between young men and women, through dancing and other activities (Rosenblatt & Cozby, 1972). So love may not be something that "just happens"; perhaps people fall in love when they are ready and willing to assume the role of lover (Sternberg & Barnes, 1988).

# SOCIAL INFLUENCE

Lawyers arguing a case before a jury are trying to influence the jury's attitudes and behavior. The purpose of many forms of social interaction is to influence other people's beliefs, attitudes, and actions. Here we discuss two types of social influence: persuasion and prejudice.

## Attitudes and Persuasion

It is believed that attitudes are related to behavior. Change a person's attitude, and you may also change his or her behavior. Psychologists define **attitude** as *a tendency to respond to individuals and objects in a consistently favorable or unfavorable way.* Attitudes are seen as having three components. The *cognitive* component consists of beliefs about an object; the *emotional* component is liking or disliking the object; and *behavior tendency* is the tendency to seek or avoid the object. Let us use Judy's attitude toward communism as an example. She believes communism is a stifling and unequal distribution of goods and services and that it often goes hand in hand with nondemocratic government (cognitive component). Because of these beliefs, she does not like communism (emotional component), and when the subject is raised, she speaks out against communism (behavior tendency component).

Attitudes presumably bear some relationship to an individual's behavior. However, they do not correspond perfectly to behavior (Krosnick, 1988). For instance, a person may not like strawberries, but may eat strawberries when a guest in someone's home.

In their **theory of reasoned action,** Ajzen and Fishbein (1980) state that *attitudes influence the intention to per-form a behavior, and this intention determines behavior.* The Ajzen and Fishbein model has received strong support when applied in real settings (Sheppard, Hartwick, & Warshaw, 1988). It has been used to predict behaviors as varied as donating blood (Evans, 1991) and the use of business management strategies (den Ouden, 1992).

*Cognitive Dissonance Theory*    Behavior tends to influence attitudes, and attitudes also result from behavior. This is most clearly seen in Leon Festinger's (1957) theory of cognitive dissonance. Festinger argues that people have a natural tendency to maintain consistency among their cognitions. ***When two or more cognitions are logically inconsistent with one another,*** a state of **cognitive dissonance** arises. This is a psychologically uncomfortable state that motivates people to act to reduce the dissonance. This may be done by changing a cognition or a behavior.

Suppose that someone who smokes cigarettes believes that smoking damages health. The inconsistency between belief and behavior produces cognitive dissonance that can be reduced by (1) changing a behavior (stop smoking), (2) changing a cognition (distort the extent of the health hazard by saying that smoking isn't very dangerous), or (3) adding other cognitions to reduce the extent of dissonance ("Smoking may be hazardous, but it relaxes me"). (Cooper & Fazio (1984) and Thibodeau & Aronson (1992) have offered modifications of cognitive dissonance theory.)

*Attitude Change: Persuasion and Propaganda*
Advertisers, politicians, and others interested in influencing people's behavior either wish to establish a new attitude (toward a new product or a candidate running for first-time election) or hope to change an already existing attitude (trying to get people to switch from one soft drink to another or to re-elect someone for whom they did not vote before). They attempt to persuade people to change their attitudes and their behavior.

Nearly all attempts at persuasion use some form of communication, which involves a *source* who delivers a *message* through some *medium* to an *audience.* In other words, the process of communication involves who says what to whom through which medium (Lasswell & Casey, 1946). Because much of the early work on persuasion was conducted by learning theorists, attention was focused on the source and the message. These comprise the "stimuli"

## CLOSE UP ON RESEARCH
### Subliminal Persuasion

Judging from the popularity of sensational books about advertising, from Vance Packard's *Hidden persuaders* to Wilson Bryan Key's *Subliminal seduction* and *The clam-plate orgy and other subliminal techniques for manipulating your behavior,* people seem eager to believe that advertising is subtly manipulative and highly effective. The subject of subliminal advertising offers a glimpse of the magnitude of public perceptions of the power of advertising.

Great Britain has gone so far as to prohibit subliminal advertising. In the United States, the rock band Judas Priest was placed on trial in 1990 for allegedly recording in one of their songs the subliminal message "do it." This message supposedly caused the suicides of two young avid listeners of the group's music.

Is subliminal advertising effective? According to Anthony Pratkanis, a social psychologist who testified at the Judas Priest trial, there are more than 150 popular articles on the subject of subliminal processes and more than 200 academic papers. There are also several reviews of this research (Pratkanis & Aronson, 1991; Pratkanis & Greenwald, 1988; Condry, 1989; Vokey & Read, 1985). "In none of these is there clear evidence in support of the proposition that subliminal messages influence behavior," writes Pratkanis. "Many of the studies fail to find an effect, and those that do are either fatally flawed on methodological grounds or cannot be reproduced." As cognitive psychologist Timothy Moore (1982) puts it, "There is no empirical documentation for subliminal effects, such as inducing particular behaviors or changing motivation. Moreover, such a notion is contradicted by a substantial amount of research and is incompatible with experimentally based conceptions of information processing, learning, and motivation."

Yet it would be foolish to deny that advertising affects people. Advertisers would not spend hundreds of millions of dollars annually to advertise if they themselves did not believe it was money well spent.*

*In addition to the references in this box, you may find the quarterly *Skeptical Inquirer* informative. It attempts to debunk pseudo-science, and its topics range from UFOs to ESP and channeling.

to which attitude change is the "response" (Hovland, Janis, & Kelley, 1953).

According to learning theory, people attend to and are influenced by a message stemming from a **highly credible source,** *a communicator with relevant experience who is thought to be expert and trustworthy* (Hovland & Weiss, 1951; Pratkanis, Greenwald, Leippe, & Baumgardner, 1988). If the communicator takes a stand against his own best interest (for example, a criminal arguing that judges are too lenient), then the perceived credibility of the source is increased (Eagly, Wood, & Chaiken, 1978; Walster, Aronson, & Abrahams, 1966).

The contents and structure of advertisements, for example, their use of emotional appeals, or their use of music, influence audience reactions (Pratkanis & Aronson, 1992). Some advertisements involve an emotional appeal to a product's image rather than to its quality. Other ads stress the quality of the product. Snyder and DeBono (1985) demonstrated that for individuals concerned with image or with "being the right person in the right place at the right time" (called "high self-monitoring" individuals), these image-based ads are most effective. For low self-monitors, those who do not typically mold their behavior to fit the situation, appeals to the product's quality are apt to be most effective. (See Close Up on Research: Subliminal Persuasion.)

When exposed to a persuasive message, people may think of responses that agree or disagree with the message's position. Richard Petty and John Cacioppo (1981) have shown that if the message stimulates cognitive responses that agree with it, the listener will be persuaded. If the message provokes disagreeing responses, it may produce a "boomerang effect" and lead to attitude change in the direction opposite from that advocated.

Communication must occur through some channel or medium, such as face-to-face speech, the written word, radio, television, or telephone. Because technological media are so widespread, people do not often think of face-to-face communication as particularly effective. However, personal communication is more frequent and may be more influential than mass media communications. It is often the two together that result in attitude change. Some individuals, called **opinion leaders,** *pay particular attention to the mass media.* In the **two-step flow of communications,** *opinion leaders tell their friends and colleagues in face-to-face encounters what new information they have acquired through the mass media* (Lazarsfeld, Berelson, & Gaudet, 1948; Oskamp, 1977). In this way, many people are influenced by the mass media indirectly, through opinion leaders, while personal communication has the greatest and most immediate impact on their attitudes and behavior.

## Prejudice and Racism

There are different names for the group about to be described, some of them unflattering. The Eta are not a genetically distinct group; they are not a race and they do not have any particular identifying physical characteristics. If differences between the Eta and the rest of the population exist, these differences were created by generations of segregation and inferior social status. Because the Eta are forced to spend so much of their time with one another (non-Eta will not associate with them) and because their education is minimal, they have developed distinctive speech patterns that immediately identify them as Eta.

The Eta, more properly known as Burakumin, are a sizable minority in Japan, numbering in the millions. They are scattered throughout the country and live in slums or ghettos. They are regarded as unclean and fit only for the most undesirable occupations. Intermarriage with the Eta is taboo. The average IQ of an Eta is about sixteen points lower than that of the general population (88 compared with 104). Measures of school achievement show the Eta to be considerably below others their age, with more truancy and a delinquency rate over three times as high as that found among other youth.

These differences between Eta and other groups are generally regarded as signs of innate racial inferiority and are used to justify further discrimination. Yet these differences arose as a result of centuries of discrimination, and they are cultural and historical in origin (DeVos & Wagatsuma, 1966; Klineberg, 1971). The consequences of centuries of prejudice and discrimination are strikingly similar to that found for minority groups in many countries.

Prejudice is most often regarded as an attitude. While it can refer to any irrational like or dislike, social psychologists refer to **prejudice** as *negative views and actions toward groups of people and the members of those groups* (Ashmore, 1981). **Discrimination** is *behavior that arises from prejudiced attitudes and prevents people from acting freely because of their membership in a group.*

The example of the Burakumin points out several issues. First, prejudice is a complex process involving attitudes, beliefs, and behavior. Second, prejudiced individuals are not generally open-minded about correcting their prejudices. They tend to stereotype members of

the minority; once a person is identified as a Burakumin, he is believed to be different, to be intellectually inferior, and to prefer associating with other Burakumin. A **stereotype** *is a generalization about a person or group in which all members of the group are incorrectly assumed to have some trait in common other than the one defining the group.* Once an individual holds stereotypes of particular groups, he or she selectively perceives and remembers instances that confirm the stereotype (Mullen & Johnson, 1990).

Much of what is known about prejudice was summarized in a classic book by Gordon Allport (1954). He concluded that prejudice developed in part from rigid and authoritarian parents, parents who are hostile, intolerant, and strictly adhere to middle-class morals. More recent views stress prejudice as a cultural process, focusing on stereotypes and negative portrayals of minority groups in the mass media, business, government, and the arts (Berry, 1988; Duckitt, 1992).

*Belief Prejudice* In many parts of the world, prejudice and discrimination center on issues of race. Some psychologists have proposed that racial prejudice is not primarily a result of physical differences between races but of *assumed* differences in beliefs and values (Cochrane, 1991; Rokeach, Smith, & Evans, 1960; Schwartz, et al., 1991). In the study of attraction, individuals who hold dissimilar attitudes do not like each other as much as those who hold similar attitudes. What about people who are *assumed* to be dissimilar? Whites, for example, may believe that blacks hold different values and beliefs and may have unfavorable attitudes toward them as a result. This implies that blacks who are known to hold similar beliefs and values to whites will not be viewed unfavorably, and whites known to hold dissimilar beliefs and values will be disliked.

In research testing these ideas, college students meet a person of the same or a different race who, during conversation, indicates that he or she holds beliefs that are either the same as, or different from, the subject's. These studies typically find that *both* the person's race and the person's beliefs are related to liking. If a person is known to differ in his or her views on important issues, then, regardless of race, subjects tend not to like that person. If the person holds similar beliefs on important issues, students are apt to like him or her. Although belief similarity was found to be the most important determinant of attraction, attraction is further enhanced if the other person is the same race as the subject (Insko & Robinson, 1967; Kidder & Stewart, 1975; Moe, Nacoste, & Insko, 1981).

*Reducing Prejudice*    Psychologists have helped to devise methods for the reduction and prevention of prejudice and discrimination. Increased *contact* between members of different groups reduces prejudice if the contact involves individuals acting as equals (Amir, 1976; Cook, 1985; Miller & Brewer, 1984). Barnard and Benn (1988) examined the effects of belief similarity and interracial contact on antiblack prejudice. Greater reduction in prejudice and more positive views were found when blacks expressed beliefs similar to the beliefs of the white subjects. However, interracial contact was more broadly effective than belief congruence. Even when there was disagreement in beliefs between blacks and whites, face-to-face contact reduced negative attitudes. Working on a common task also reduces stereotypic thinking and prejudicial attitudes, particularly among children (Aronson, Blaney, Sikes, Stephan, & Snapp, 1975; Eaton & Clore, 1975; Gaertner et al., 1990).

**Superordinate goals** *are tasks that require members from antagonistic groups to work together.* Muzafer Sherif and his colleagues (1961) introduced a series of superordinate goals after groups of boys had engaged in hostile and violent exchanges. Boys at a summer camp had quickly formed cohesive groups based on the location of their bunks. The boys formed friendships only within their own group. Within days, each group had staged raids on the other group's bunkhouse. At this point Sherif and colleagues introduced a task that required the cooperation of all the boys. The camp's water supply was said to be in danger, and all campers were required to work together to restore the water supply; if they cooperated, they would get to watch a movie that evening. This superordinate goal, the restoration of the water supply, forced the boys to work together to achieve the goal. The equal-status cooperation broke down animosities and stereotypes and reduced conflict between groups. Other research has supported Sherif's notion that superordinate tasks increase intergroup cooperation (Tyerman & Spencer, 1983; Blanchard, Lilly, & Vaughn, 1991).

## PROSOCIAL AND ANTISOCIAL BEHAVIOR

Among the most fascinating puzzles of human behavior is how people can be so compassionate and loving toward one another one moment and so cruel and inhumane the next. Psychologists have addressed the issues of kindness and cruelty by studying the willingness of people to help or harm others. In this section we discuss people's willingness to offer assistance to others in need (prosocial behavior), and aggression (antisocial behavior). Each section stresses the importance of the social situation in which acts of kindness or cruelty seem appropriate to the actor.

Over 300,000 charities exist in the United States, according to the American Association of Fund-Raising Council, and these charities receive much of their support from voluntary contributions and volunteer workers. In 1988, Americans contributed more than $104 billion to charitable organizations, eighty-four percent of it in the form of individual contributions. Americans, it seems, are altruistic, caring people.

Kitty Genovese was murdered on the streets of New York one night in 1964 in view of at least thirty-eight of her neighbors. Despite the fact that the slaying took about thirty minutes, not a single person tried to intervene or help in other ways. The case, a symbol of people's indifference toward others, implies that Americans are uncaring, unhelpful people.

How can people be helpful on one hand and uncharitable and reluctant to help on the other? When *The New York Times* investigated the slaying of Kitty Genovese it reported the wisdom of social scientists, philosophers, and clergymen about the unwillingness of her neighbors to offer assistance: New Yorkers are apathetic, some suggested. Everyone is alienated from society, or from God, or from their neighbors, said others. Television has turned us into passive spectators rather than actors, reported a psychiatrist. People are afraid to get involved, they have no sense of social responsibility, and they are fascinated by violence, said still others. One common element in the views reported in *The New York Times* is that the failure to help stems from some individual characteristic: apathy, fear, a feeling of isolation. As seen in our discussion of attribution, when asked to explain the causes of another person's actions, or in this instance inaction, people often refer to some characteristic of the individual's personality. However, research on this topic demonstrates that personality may have little to do with it. Instead, attention must be given to the situation in which the event occurs. Perhaps there are certain situations in which a person is more or less likely to offer help.

## Diffusion of Responsibility

Two social psychologists began a series of studies shortly after the Kitty Genovese slaying to explore why so many people failed to intervene on her behalf (Latané & Darley, 1970). New Yorkers, they found, often responded to simple requests for help, such as giving directions or change for a dollar; they were not unconcerned or apathetic about their fellow citizens.

The researchers observed that people were most likely to respond to a request for aid when they were alone. In one study, students were asked to participate in a market research survey being conducted by a young woman. They were to complete questionnaires alone or with another person while the young woman was on the other side of a sliding partition. As they worked on the questionnaires,

| TABLE 15.3  Percent of subjects helping in the emergency | |
|---|---|
| **Condition** | **Percent Offering Help** |
| Alone | 70 |
| With passive stranger | 7 |
| With another stranger | 40 |
| With friend | 70 |

From Bibb Latané and John Darley, *The Unresponsive Bystander: Why Doesn't He Help?* © 1970, pp. 60 and 62. Adapted by permission of Prentice-Hall, Inc., Englewood Cliffs, NJ.

they heard her climbing up on a chair to get a book from the top shelf of her bookcase. This was followed by a loud crash, a woman's screams, and "Oh, my God, my foot . . . I . . . I . . . can't move. . . . " This tape-recorded sequence was the "emergency" to which subjects could respond.

There were four different groups in this experiment: students alone in the testing room; two strangers in the room; two strangers in the room, one of whom was passive during the emergency; and two friends in the room. The results, shown in table 15.3, indicate that a person alone or with a friend is more likely to respond to an emergency by seeking or offering help.

Latané and Darley explain this as a **diffusion of responsibility**; *feelings of responsibility to help are spread across all individuals present.* If there is only one witness to an emergency, that person is apt to feel fully responsible for helping the victim and is most likely to help. If there are several people present, each person feels somewhat less responsible for helping the victim. After all, each of them can ask, "Why should I help when all these other people are around? Why me?"

In a study designed to examine the role of personality in helping, Latané and Darley gave students a variety of personality tests, including measures of authoritarianism, alienation, need for social approval, and social responsibility. Later in the semester, some of the students were gathered to discuss problems of college life, and one of these students (working with the researchers) stated that he was an epileptic. During the course of the discussion, the epileptic began to have a seizure. Latané and Darley correlated the students' scores on personality scales with their speed of helping. (For an explanation of correlation, see Appendix A.) The only significant correlation indicates that people who were raised in small towns responded faster to the emergency. In this research, personality is unrelated to the offer of help.

Further studies of personality and helping find that the type of emergency or request for help is important. If there are personality traits correlating with donating blood, they may not be the same ones correlated with intervening in a violent crime (Batson, 1991; Gergen, Gergen, & Meter, 1972; Hinde & Groebel, 1991).

A good mood promotes helpfulness. In a review of research on mood and helping, Carlson, Charlin, and Miller (1988) note that the following positive moods generate helpfulness: succeeding on a laboratory task, unexpectedly finding a dime in the coin return of a public telephone, listening to soothing music, being on the winning team in a football game, and being labeled a charitable person. There are many possible explanations for this effect. However, Carlson and his colleagues note that these explanations have in common something called "priming"; if one is in a good mood this evokes positive thoughts and associations and increases the willingness to help.

## The Just-World Phenomenon

Nearly everyone learns to think of events as meaningful, orderly, and caused. Every great religion teaches that God is fair and just. Events do not happen without a reason. If an emergency arises, it is assumed to have its causes. The belief in a just world motivates people to look for, and often to invent, some reason that will explain why an event occurs (Janoff-Bulman, Timko, & Carli, 1985).

Failure to offer help may occur because people distort the nature of the emergency to convince themselves that help is not really needed, that no emergency exists, or that the victims deserve their fate. Lerner (1980) has called this the "just-world phenomenon." When encountering a homeless person on the street, the belief in a just world may enable a passerby to blame the victim for his own misfortune (London, 1970).

## Aggression

Because aggression is such a troubling and complex feature of human behavior, there are studies and interpretations of aggression from nearly every conceivable position in the social and behavioral sciences. There are many summaries of this varied literature (Geen, 1991; Goldstein, 1986; Klama, 1988; Tavris, 1989).

Most psychologists define **human aggression** as *the intentional injury of another person.* This definition is not very precise because it excludes the possibility that kicking the cat is aggression and because discovering the intention of an actor's behavior is no easy task. What, for

example, is a father's intention when he spanks his child for lying? Is it his intention to injure the child? To prevent him from lying again? To teach the child how a father punishes his child? Most students of aggression agree that the motives for aggressive behavior are mixed and that aggression is usually seen by the aggressor as *instrumental,* useful in achieving some goal.

*Frustration-Aggression Theory*    The frustration-aggression theory is elegant in its simplicity (Dollard, Doob, Miller, Mowrer, & Sears, 1939). It states, "The occurrence of aggression always presupposes the existence of frustration and . . . the existence of frustration always leads to some form of aggression." Frustration is defined as any interference with ongoing behavior.

Critics quickly pointed out that interference with ongoing behavior rarely leads to aggression (Maslow, 1941). Each day people are frustrated by closed doors, waiting lines, and difficult tasks, and they are remarkably nonaggressive in the face of these persistent frustrations. Furthermore, people may be aggressive in the absence of frustration. Soldiers fighting a battle and bullies picking fights with weaker children are examples of aggression that do not stem directly from frustration (Olweus, 1992).

The original theorists conceded that many of these criticisms were valid, and they revised the theory. While frustration always leads to a *tendency* to aggress, the organism may learn other ways of responding to frustration. Furthermore, aggression may be caused by factors other than frustration (Miller, 1941). Which frustrations lead to aggression, and when will aggression occur in the absence of frustration?

Leonard Berkowitz (1969, 1978, 1989, 1993) refined frustration-aggression theory by borrowing from developments in biology. It had become increasingly obvious to students of animal behavior that animals often perform unlearned behaviors only in particular situations. The male stickleback fish will perform a complicated mating ritual only when it first sees a swollen red belly on a female stickleback (Tinbergen, 1951). Thus, the instinctive behavior of fertilizing eggs is accomplished only when a particular stimulus, the sight of a swollen red belly, triggers the behavior. Berkowitz suggested that for frustration to produce aggression, some triggering mechanism or releaser stimulus must be present. In humans this is the presence of an **aggressive cue,** *a target, situation, or object associated with aggression.* Berkowitz (1989) also added anger as an emotion that may result in aggression. If

**Figure 15.3** *According to Albert Bandura, seeing aggression performed on television may cause children to learn aggressive behaviors.*

frustration or anger occurs and there is an aggressive cue, aggressive behavior is the most likely result. In humans, unlike in stickleback fish, aggressive cues are learned. Why should just the two emotions of frustration and anger precede aggressive behavior? What is special about them? Dolf Zillmann (1979, 1983) proposes that it may not be frustration or anger that leads to aggression but the fact that these and other emotions are accompanied by physiological arousal. Perhaps what is necessary for aggression is arousal, not a particular emotion.

To test this theory, Zillmann (1971) showed groups of college men one of three films: (1) A relatively boring story that contained no aggressive or sexual scenes to arouse the students. (2) A moderately arousing and highly aggressive film. (3) A highly arousing film with explicit scenes of sexual activity. Arousal was measured by taking blood pressure readings during the experiment. The students who were most aroused (those viewing the sexually explicit film) were most aggressive, and those who were least aroused (those viewing the boring film) were least aggressive.

*Social Learning Theory and Aggression*    Children learn aggressive behaviors by being exposed to them, according to Albert Bandura (1973). Seeing aggression performed on television or by parents and siblings is sometimes sufficient for children to learn aggressive behaviors (figure 15.3). Whether or not children actually perform the learned behavior depends on whether they have been, or have seen others, rewarded or punished for aggression.

Psychoanalyst Sigmund Freud, philosopher William James, and biologist Konrad Lorenz all believed that witnessing violence in sports, in mass media, and even in war "releases" aggression, lowering the observer's own level of violence. In contrast, Bandura's social learning theory predicts that people exposed to unpunished violence learn aggression. What does the research find? It is clear from scores of studies that exposure to violence in any form—whether in the mass media, in sports, or at home—is far from a "healthy outlet" for aggression (Archer & Gaertner, 1984). There is little evidence that exposure to violence results in a "catharsis" of aggression. Whether observing aggression results in later aggressive behavior seems to depend upon characteristics of the observers (how aggressive they are to begin with), the nature of the observed violence (for example, how the violence is presented or "packaged"), the social context of viewing (alone or with family, for example), and when and how aggression is measured (Cumberbatch, 1991; Freedman, 1984; Huston et al., 1992).

*Child and Spouse Abuse*    The incidence of child abuse and spouse abuse in the United States is not known, but it is estimated that over five children per 100,000 are physically assaulted by their parents each year, and that as many as twenty-five percent of married women are physically abused by their husbands (Gelles & Edfeldt, 1986; Gil, 1970; Green, 1980; Peters, McMahon, & Quinsey, 1992).

Many studies have attempted to identify the personalities of abusive parents. So far, no consistent pattern of traits has been found (Spinetta & Rigler, 1977; Steele & Pollock, 1968). It is widely believed that abused children grow up to become abusive parents themselves. This is an oversimplification (Widom, 1989). Children who are raised in a household in which violence is used frequently tend in their later family lives to use violence (Gelles & Straus, 1979). If abusive parents and spouses do not differ in any obvious psychological way from nonabusers, perhaps the process of abuse is not different from other forms of aggressive behavior (Zimbardo, 1969).

## Obedience to Authority

A professor tells students to read chapters 5 and 6 in the textbook and they obediently do so. A captain issues

# CLOSE UP ON RESEARCH

## Sex Differences in Aggression

Everyone knows that males are more aggressive than females. Yet recent research calls this popular wisdom into question. It all hinges upon your definition of aggression.

If aggression is defined only as physical violence—hitting, shooting, stabbing—then one can safely say that men are more aggressive than women. (Of course, one would not be in a position to state *why* males are more aggressive than females, only that they are.)

Maybe males just *appear* more aggressive than females. Perhaps men and women are equally aggressive, but they express aggression in different ways. Men may express aggression in physical ways, while women use verbal means of aggression. This theory was put to rest by Maccoby and Jacklin (1974) and Frodi, Macaulay, and Thome (1977).

Frodi, Macaulay, and Thome (1977) summarized seventy-two studies of adult aggression. The widely held belief that men are more physically aggressive than women, while women display more indirect aggression was not supported. Of the seventy-two studies, sixty-one percent did not find the expected sex differences. Examining studies of physical aggression *when people are angry* yielded only a few studies where men and women were found to differ. According to Carol Tavris (1989), husbands and wives are particularly "equal" in this way. In a national sample of 2,143 American families, twelve percent of husbands and wives had attacked each other physically in the past year. In half of these violent families, both spouses attacked each other with equal frequency; in one fourth, only the husband was abusive, and in one fourth only the wife was. "But wife abuse commands medical and political attention for important reasons: male violence inflicts more injury than female violence does, largely because men tend to use fists, guns, and knives,

whereas women slap, punch, or throw something. The point here, though, is that women are not "naturally less" aggressive when they feel angry than men are, especially on home ground" (p. 207). In contrast, direct physical aggression when participants are *not* angry is primarily a male phenomenon.

The Finnish psychologists Kirsti Lagerspetz, Kaj Bjorkqvist, and their colleagues (1988) report that *verbal aggression* is displayed equally often by both 11-year-old boys and girls. Boys' aggression, whether physical or verbal, was found to be *direct,* while girls use *indirect* means, talking about people behind their backs and influencing other people to exclude the target from social groups and events.

According to Anne Campbell and colleagues (1992), one reason aggression takes different forms for males and females is that the sexes have different conceptions of aggression. Women view aggression as the loss of self-control resulting from a build-up of stress. They see it as a negative experience. Men view aggression as the exercise of control over others triggered by threats to their self-esteem or public integrity. Physical violence and fighting were often viewed by men as a positive experience.

There are other sex differences in aggression:

- Men talk about aggression and intentions to aggress more than do females.
- Sex differences are greater in public than in private settings.
- Women experience greater guilt and anxiety about aggression than do men.
- Men are more likely to aggress when not angry than are women.

For books devoted to the subject of sex differences in aggression, see Bjorkqvist and Niemela, 1992, and Campbell, 1993.

---

orders to a private who dutifully carries them out. A parent tells a child to go to bed, and the child reluctantly does so. These are all examples of obedience to authority.

Stanley Milgram (1974) wished to determine whether Germans were more obedient than other people to orders from authority figures. His intention was to gain insight into the unquestioning obedience that seemed to characterize the Nazis during World War II. This research is perhaps the most publicized of any social psychological studies, becoming the subject of a play, a television drama, films, and magazine articles. It was also the impetus for a research code of ethics (APA, 1992). The research that received all this attention was fairly simple in design and was based on no particular theory. Milgram never did

conduct his experiments in Germany; he found obedience of a surprisingly high level in the United States.

A subject entered an experimental laboratory, was introduced to another subject (actually an assistant of the experimenter), and was told that his or her job was to teach the other person a verbal task. The subject read pairs of words to the learner, such as blue box, nice day, wild duck, and in the testing sequence read the word blue, along with four other words: sky, ink, box, lamp. The learner was to state which of these four words was originally paired with the first word. Each time the learner failed to give the correct answer, the subject was to administer an electric shock to the learner. Of course, the accomplice, who was usually in an adjoining room, actually received no shock, but the subject did not know this. There were thirty switches on the shock generator, from 15 to 450 volts. Every fourth switch was labelled, from "Slight shock" to "Danger: Severe shock." The label at the extreme right end simply read "XXX."

Each time the learner made an error, the subject was to administer a shock of greater intensity than the previous shock. The learner made a prearranged number of errors on the task, and the conflict confronting the subject was whether to continue to administer increasingly painful shocks, as the experimenter requested, or to disobey the experimenter and refuse to shock the learner.

Before conducting these experiments, Milgram asked a group of psychiatrists, a class of Yale University students, and a sample of middle-class adults what they would do if they were the subjects in such an experiment. Not one of the more than one hundred people questioned said they would continue to shock the learner to the end of the shock scale. In the actual experiment, a majority of subjects administered the maximum shock.

Despite repeated protests from the learner, which began with several grunts at 75 volts and shouts of "I can't stand the pain!" at 270 volts, sixty-five percent of the subjects in the first experiment administered the maximum shock. Even when the experiment was transferred from the prestigious laboratories of Yale University to a run-down office in Bridgeport, Connecticut, nearly half the subjects continued to administer what they thought were shocks of 450 volts.

Variations on the basic procedure were made to determine the conditions that reduce obedience. The closer the subject was to the victim (learner), the less willing the subject was to administer strong shocks. Obedience was reduced to thirty percent when the subject was required to place the victim's hand on a shock plate. If two experimenters disagreed in the presence of the subject over the subject's obligation to continue administering shock, obedience completely disappeared. None of the twenty subjects receiving contradictory orders shocked the victim to the end of the shock scale.

Here is a portion of a transcript in which one subject, a thirty-two-year old industrial engineer who emigrated from the Netherlands after World War II, refused to continue in the experiment.

At 250 volts, he pushes the chair away from the shock generator and turns to the experimenter.

Subject: Oh, I can't continue this way; it's a voluntary program, if the man doesn't want to go on with it. . . .

Experimenter: Please continue.

Subject: No, I can't continue, I'm sorry.

Experimenter: The experiment requires that you go on.

Subject: The man, he seems to be getting hurt.

Experimenter: There is no permanent tissue damage.

Subject: Yes, but I know what shocks do to you. I'm an electrical engineer, and I have had shocks . . . and you get real shook up by them—especially if you know the next one is coming. I'm sorry.

Experimenter: It is absolutely essential that you continue.

Subject: Well, I won't—not with the man screaming to get out.

Experimenter: You have no other choice.

Subject: I *do* have a choice. Why don't I have a choice? I came here on my own free will. I thought I could help in a research project. But if I have to hurt somebody to do that, or if I was in his place, too, I wouldn't stay there. I can't continue. I'm very sorry. I think I've gone too far already, probably.

How can we distinguish between those people who obey the experimenter's demands to administer shock and those who refuse? Studies examining personality traits have failed to find any differences between obedient and disobedient subjects (Elms & Milgram, 1966; Kilham & Mann, 1974). Nor do there appear to be any differences in the level of obedience in different countries (Mantell, 1971). For reasons not yet clear, some people—the disobedient subjects—refuse to relinquish personal responsibility for their actions to someone else. Obedient subjects, on the other hand, appear willing to let the experimenter take responsibility for what they, the subjects, are doing. Subjects reason that the experimenter must know what he or she is doing and that they aren't responsible if they are merely acting as the experimenter's agent or assistant. Therefore, believing they are not personally responsible for what happens to the learner, obedient subjects administer what could be a lethal electrical shock (Nissani, 1990; Staub, 1989).

In many realms of social life—prosocial behavior, attraction, and prejudice, for instance—people tend to favor individuals who are similar to themselves. And there is a tendency to dislike those who are dissimilar or who belong to other groups. So potent is this tendency that even groups created at random favor in-group members over out-group members (Rabbie, 1989; Smith, in press), as we consider in Group Processes.

▶ **GUIDED REVIEW** *Learning Objectives 11, 12, 13, and 14*

1. Individuals are more likely to help a person in distress when they are alone than when they are among strangers. This is explained by the process of _____.
2. The tendency to justify a person's being a victim can be explained with Lerner's process of the _____.
3. _____ has gone through several modifications since its first appearance in 1939. A recent modification by Berkowitz states that frustration and _____ result in aggression only when an _____ is present.
4. Emotions, such as anger and frustration involve _____, which Zillmann says is necessary for aggression.
5. Exposure to violence is capable of teaching violence to observers, according to Bandura's _____.
6. According to Milgram's studies on _____, individuals may relinquish personal responsibility for their actions by following the orders of an authority figure.
7. Disobedience can be increased by bringing the subject and learner _____ and by including a second experimenter who _____ with the first experimenter.

*ANSWERS*

1. *diffusion of responsibility* 2. *just-world phenomenon* 3. *Frustration-aggression theory, anger, aggressive cue* 4. *physiological arousal* 5. *social learning theory* 6. *obedience to authority* 7. *closer together, disagrees*

# GROUP PROCESSES

Groups exert great force and may profoundly influence people's lives. Most individuals gain a sense of themselves by being members of different groups. Group membership plays an important role in answer to the question "Who am I?" "I'm Hungarian. I'm a Catholic. I play the violin. I'm an engineering major. I belong to the theater club." All people are unique in part because their group loyalties and memberships are unique (Simmel, 1955; Turner, 1985). A **group** can be defined as *two or more people who interact and are mutually aware of having something meaningful in common.*

Even groups we do not belong to may influence us, if we identify strongly with them. *Groups that a person identifies with, but does not actually belong to, are called* **reference groups.** In Philadelphia on any summer day one sees hundreds of people who are not members of the Phillies baseball team wearing Phillies caps or shirts, a sign of their identification. And when the Phillies win a game, even more people wear Phillies caps and shirts (Cialdini, Borden, Thorne, Walker, Freeman, & Sloan, 1976; Sloan, 1989). As a reference group, a sports team can be highly influential.

Individuals behave differently in groups than when acting alone (Shaw, 1976). This is clearly evident in studies of social facilitation.

## Social Facilitation

How does the mere presence of other people influence the behavior of a single individual? In one of the earliest experiments in psychology, which involved bicycle racers and, in a later study, children winding fishing reels, the subjects were observed while performing either alone or in the presence of other people (Triplett, 1897). Cyclists racing against time did not do as well as those who raced against other cyclists, and children wound fishing reels better when they were in competition than when they performed the task alone. From this and other early experiments (e.g., Dashiell, 1930), it appeared that *the presence of other people facilitated or improved performance,* a process called **social facilitation.**

However, not all studies found improved performance in the presence of others. In one study (Pessin, 1933), students learned lists of nonsense words either alone or in front of an audience. The students learned the nonsense words faster when alone than when in front of spectators. In this case, the presence of others interfered with the task.

Rats and chickens eat more in groups than when alone (Harlow, 1932; Tolman & Wilson, 1965), and ants excavate more soil in the same amount of time when other ants are working simultaneously with them (Chen, 1937). These experiments point to a facilitation of behavior when others of the same species are present. In some animal experiments, however, notably those in which animals were learning a maze or learning to make discriminations among different objects, animals did better when alone (Gates & Allee, 1933; Klopfer, 1958).

For more than sixty years, research on the effects of working alone versus working with others appeared to be contradictory. This confusion ended in 1965, when Robert Zajonc provided a clear theoretical explanation for these seemingly contradictory findings. He noted that two types of task were studied in social facilitation research: tasks that required the performance of well-learned responses and tasks that required the acquisition of new responses.

# CLOSE UP ON RESEARCH

## The Home Field Disadvantage?

Generally, playing a game at home is an important advantage to an individual athlete or team. Reasons given for this "home-team effect" include the increased motivation and arousal among athletes that is engendered by supportive fans (Edwards, 1989).

But is playing before the home crowd always beneficial?

Roy Baumeister and Andrew Steinhilber (1984) reasoned that the desire to perform well before a home crowd might increase an athlete's self-awareness and interfere with his or her athletic performance. When athletes are busy paying attention to themselves, they can't also be paying attention to the ball or concentrating on their performance. To test this hypothesis, the researchers examined the records of baseball World Series games from 1924 to 1982 and National Basketball Association championship games from 1967 to 1982. The location is determined for each of these games by a simple formula that has nothing to do with teams' won-loss records. (In alternate years, the American and National baseball leagues host the first, second, sixth, and seventh World Series games.) As it becomes more critical to win (in the last or seventh game of the World Series), self-awareness should increase, particularly among home teams, because the fans are more critical. It is in just such circumstances that performance is apt to suffer.

As can be seen in table 15.B, home teams tend to win the majority of their games early in a series. But when it is crucial to win (in the last or seventh game), home teams win only about four times out of ten.

In these circumstances, does the home team "choke" or does the visiting team excel? Baumeister and Steinhilber examined fielding errors in World Series games and found that home teams make twice as many errors in the seventh game (1.31/game) as in the first two games (.65/game). Visiting teams make fewer errors in the seventh game (.81) than in the first two games (1.04/game). Thus, there is evidence that the home team performance deteriorates at a greater rate (.65 − 1.31 = −.66) than visiting-team performance improves (1.04 − .81 = +.23).

### TABLE 15.B Outcome for home and visiting teams

**World Series Game, 1924–82**

| Games | Winners | | |
|---|---|---|---|
| | Home | Visitor | Home % |
| 1 and 2 | 59 | 39 | .602 |
| Last game | 20 | 29 | .408 |
| 7 | 10 | 16 | .385 |

**NBA Championship Games, 1967–82**

| Games | Winners | | |
|---|---|---|---|
| | Home | Visitor | Home % |
| 1–4 | 115 | 49 | .701 |
| Last game | 19 | 22 | .463 |
| 7 | 5 | 8 | .385 |

From "Paradoxical Effects of Supportive Audiences on Performance Under Pressure: The Home Field Advantage in Sports Championships" by R. Baumeister and A. Steinhibler, *Journal of Personality and Social Psychology*, 48:85–93. Copyright 1984 by the American Psychological Association. Reprinted by permission.

This is the familiar distinction made by many learning theorists between *learning* and *performance* (Bandura, 1965; Tolman, 1932).

Zajonc found that tasks requiring the subject to acquire some new response, such as learning nonsense syllables or learning to negotiate a maze, are performed better when the subject is alone. When the task requires the performance of some well-learned or instinctual response, such as riding a bicycle or eating food, performance is better when others are present.

▶ **GUIDED REVIEW** *Learning Objectives 15 and 16*

1. A group may influence people even if a person is not technically one of its members. Such groups are referred to as _____.
2. The mere presence of others may influence behavior. This area of theory and research is called _____.
3. People tend to _____ better alone and to _____ well-learned responses better in the presence of others.

*ANSWERS*

1. *reference groups* 2. *social facilitation* 3. *learn, perform*

## Attraction to Groups

Why do people join groups? What social and psychological functions do groups serve? One reason for affiliation is social comparison. People join with others to obtain information about their own abilities, opinions, and beliefs (Festinger, 1954; Suls & Miller, 1977; Suls & Wills, 1991).

Social comparison theory focuses on feedback about people's opinions and abilities. Stanley Schachter (1959) extended the theory to include feedback about people's emotional states. Schachter told college women that they were about to participate in an experiment involving either severe (or mild) electric shock. The women were then given an opportunity to wait alone or with others while the equipment was being set up. Choosing to wait with others was the measure of affiliation.

Those expecting severe shocks preferred to wait with others, whereas those expecting mild shocks preferred to wait alone or did not care whether they waited alone or with others. Schachter found that the tendency to affiliate with others was greatest for those experiencing high fear. Furthermore, subjects preferred to wait with others who were undergoing the same emotional experience. The tendency to affiliate with others was also influenced by birth order. Firstborns and only children were more likely to want to wait with others than were subjects who had older brothers or sisters (Davis, Cahan, & Bashi, 1977; Zajonc & Markus, 1975).

*Cognitive Dissonance and Group Cohesion*   In the early 1950s, publicity was given to a group that predicted the destruction of the earth by flood. Mrs. Keech, the group's leader, said she was in contact with inhabitants of the planet Clarion. She received messages telling her that she and her followers would be saved. Members of her cult gathered around her in anticipation of the arrival of a spacecraft from Clarion. Among her followers were three social psychologists interested in studying members' responses to the failure of her prophecy. What would members do if the earth was not destroyed and no spaceship appeared? There were three possibilities: the group could disband and denounce Mrs. Keech as a false prophet; they could remain intact and conclude that Mrs. Keech had gotten her messages confused; or the group could become even more cohesive in order to protect itself from ridicule. Of course, the earth was not destroyed in the 1950s and Mrs. Keech's predictions proved false. Which of the three possible responses did the group take? Her followers refused to admit that they were in error and took

credit for saving the earth from destruction! Rather than disbanding, the group began to recruit new members (Festinger, Riecken, & Schachter, 1956). Sanada and Norbeck (1975) report on a religious sect in Japan, whose leader committed suicide after his prediction of an earthquake proved to be untrue.

**Cohesiveness,** *the group's overall attractiveness to its members,* depends upon both internal and external pressures (Hogg, 1992). Members had sacrificed a great deal in preparing to leave earth. Festinger's (1957) theory of *cognitive dissonance* states that when great sacrifices are made, people tend to justify their actions because it would be inconsistent to contradict public behaviors.

An early study of the theory of cognitive dissonance concerned group loyalty. Aronson and Mills (1959) tested the hypothesis that people value a group to the extent that they make sacrifices and exert effort on its behalf. It would be inconsistent, and therefore produce dissonance, to work hard for something, such as membership in a group, and then conclude that the group was unattractive and hardly worth the effort. The researchers studied college women who had volunteered to participate in a series of group discussions about sex.

Three different "initiations" into the group were held. One-third of the women, the control group, underwent no initiation or screening. One-third of them, the mild initiation group, had to read aloud sex-related words. A third group of women, the severe initiation group, had to read obscene words and erotic passages to a male experimenter. After this "initiation," the women listened to one of the group discussions, and what they heard was a dull discussion of the sexual behavior of animals. After being allowed to join the group only to discover that it was boring, how did the three groups of women react? The women who had undergone the embarrassing severe initiation thought the group was more attractive and interesting than those who underwent a mild initiation or no initiation. Thus, attraction to a group may increase the more people suffer or sacrifice on its behalf.

## Leadership

Despite such common phrases as "a natural-born leader" or "good leadership qualities," leadership is not a characteristic that exists within a person. Instead, it defines a particular type of relationship between people. One person can sometimes force others to do something, but that is not leadership (Gibb, 1969). **Leadership** is *"the presence of a particular influence relationship between two or more* *persons"* (Hollander & Julian, 1969; Hollander, 1992). A leader needs followers as much as followers need a leader.

Much modern history is written as if historical events were shaped by the personalities of leaders (Post, 1991). Hitler, Gandhi, Churchill, and Gorbachev have all shaped the course of world events on the basis of their personal strengths and weaknesses. Many contemporary historians write psychohistorical analyses of world leaders. Whether such analyses of political leaders are capable of explaining complex international events is questionable. Instead, historians must look to the historical, social, economic, and political circumstances surrounding a leader. Note the difference in the characterizations of Gandhi and Hitler.

> There is nothing striking about Gandhi—except his whole expression of "infinite patience and infinite love. . . ." He feels at ease only in a minority, and is happiest when, in meditative solitude, he can listen to the "still small voice" within. This is the man who has stirred three hundred million people to revolt, who has shaken the foundations of the British Empire, and who has introduced into human politics the strongest religious impetus of the last two hundred years (Erikson, 1961, quoting R. Rolland).

After examining Hitler's rise to power, Hadley Cantril (1963) wrote of Hitler and the German social climate:

> When institutions and social values are disturbed and when people are disturbed they are anxious to regain mental stability. The easiest and most usual way of accomplishing this is to look for a leader, identify oneself with him, transfer one's troubles to him, and believe that he can always cope with things, that he always has another trick up his sleeve, that he can safely protect one against external dangers. . . . It is no wonder, then, that the message of Hitler, his own obvious belief in the righteousness of his program, his sincerity, and his faith in himself made an indelible impression on those who heard him. In a period of doubt and uncertainty, here was a speaker who did not argue the pros and cons of policies but who was fanatically self-confident; who did not quietly suggest that he and his program were possible solutions, but who actually shouted certainty at the top of his lungs (pp. 233–236).

Would Gandhi have become a leader in the Germany of the 1930s, or Hitler a leader in India? The **"great man theory"** *assumes that it is the personal strengths and motives of individuals that make them powerful leaders.* There do seem to be certain personality types who become charismatic leaders (House & Baetz, 1979). Yet the situation must be appropriate, and followers must be ready to accept a leader who possesses those particular traits. It is the individual and the situation confronting the individual that best explain the rise to prominence of historical figures.

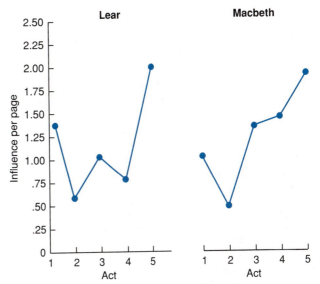

**Figure 15.4**  *Frequency of proactive influence attempts.*

The dominant view of leadership examines the interaction between leadership style and group situations (Fiedler, 1981; Fiedler, Chemers, & Mahar, 1976). Despite its poor effect on morale, a strong, focused ("task-oriented") leader is useful in times of stress and under time pressure. In these situations, a powerful, autocratic leader can impose order, set priorities and make rapid decisions. One sees this in sports: in the final moments of a close game, a successful coach cannot worry unduly about the egos of his players or take time to consider all opinions. Rather, confidence and decisiveness are necessary (Baron, Kerr, & Miller, 1992). A rigid leadership style is not always best, however. Suedfeld and Rank (1976) found that some of history's most successful revolutionary leaders varied their leadership style to fit the circumstances. In a crisis period, leaders used a rigid autocratic approach. Those who maintained power following the revolution were likely to become more flexible and less autocratic. The optimum leadership style, then, is one that suits the situation.

How do leaders influence their followers? This often depends on how powerful the leaders are. Harsh influence strategies involve threats; weak influence strategies involve verbal and material rewards; and rational tactics rely on reason and logic. To illustrate how the situation might influence the choice of tactics, David Kipnis (1984) analyzed two of Shakespeare's characters, King Lear and Macbeth. Figure 15.4 and table 15.4 show the number and type of influence tactics used in each act of each play. The number of attempts to influence others is about the same in each play, and there are many more attempts to influence others in the fifth act than in preceding acts. However, King Lear loses power as the play progresses, while Macbeth gains a kingdom. Lear's power tactics are increasingly weak as the play goes on, while Macbeth's tactics become stronger.

> **GUIDED REVIEW** *Learning Objectives 17 and 18*

1. According to the _____ theory, people join groups to receive feedback about their opinions, abilities, beliefs, and emotional states.
2. _____ are more affiliative than _____.
3. _____ is the overall attractiveness of a group to its members.
4. According to the _____, the more people sacrifice for a group, the more attractive the group becomes to them.
5. The _____ theory explains leadership in terms of the personalities of leaders.

*ANSWERS*

*1. social comparison 2. Firstborn and only children, later-born children 3. Cohesiveness 4. cognitive dissonance theory 5. great man*

## Development of Group Norms

From a family to a fraternity to a government, groups are responsible for making decisions and providing its members with support. Once individuals are assembled for the purpose of performing a task—whether it is as simple as having a good time or as complex as formulating foreign policy—norms or standards for acceptable behavior develop, and individuals influence one another in direct as well as subtle ways.

Members of a group are aware of sharing something. Often what they share, in addition to a stated interest or goal, is a set of **norms,** *standards for acting and for judging the behavior of individuals inside and outside the group.* These norms frequently emerge within the group and are taught indirectly to new members. That is why members of one fraternity may be conservative, dress well, and receive average grades, whereas another fraternity may be liberal, dress casually, and receive good grades. These standards are developed and transmitted in a group, and the group enforces conformity to them, sometimes subtly.

The behavior of people in groups is guided by the personalities of group members, by formal rules, and by a set of standards or norms that emerge within the group.

**TABLE 15.4  Strength of influence tactics used by Lear and Macbeth (in percentage)**

| Tactic | Lear | | | | | Macbeth | | | | |
|---|---|---|---|---|---|---|---|---|---|---|
| | Act 1 | Act 2 | Act 3 | Act 4 | Act 5 | Act 1 | Act 2 | Act 3 | Act 4 | Act 5 |
| Strong | 64 | 57 | 13 | 14 | 0 | 33 | 36 | 44 | 75 | 77 |
| Weak | 16 | 38 | 25 | 79 | 100 | 33 | 36 | 9 | 19 | 4 |
| Rational | 23 | 5 | 63 | 7 | 0 | 33 | 27 | 47 | 6 | 19 |

From David Kipnis, "The Use of Power in Organizations and in Interpersonal Settings" in *Applied Social Psychology Annual,* Vol. 5, ed. by Stuart Oskamp, 1984. Used by permission of the author.

The classic study of group norms was conducted by Muzafer Sherif (1936) using the **autokinetic effect,** *the apparent movement of a point of light in a dark room.*

Individual subjects were exposed to a point of light and asked to judge how far it moved. They were then tested in a group, and each subject in the group had to judge the movement of the light. In other conditions, the subjects first made their judgments as a group and were later tested individually. Sherif was interested in whether individuals would continue to use their own perceptions of distance movement once they were placed in a group and whether those who were first tested in a group would continue to use the group norm when tested alone.

Sherif found that individuals tended to see a narrow range of distances in which the light moved. Although this range differed from one person to another, each individual was fairly consistent in his or her perceptions of movement. When these individuals were then placed in a small group, the judgments of group members tended to converge, as shown in figure 15.5. For those who began their judgments in a group setting, there was evidence of convergence. As each person called out the estimate of distance moved, others modified their estimates. The final result was a narrow range of responses for all group members. The members of a group came to agree on the distance moved by the stationary light, indicating that they had formed an agreed-upon and shared social norm, a standard against which they evaluated their own perceptions. When group members were tested individually, they continued to perceive the movement of the light in terms of the group norm. The norm established in the group influenced the person's judgment even after the person was removed from the group (Jacobs & Campbell, 1961; MacNeil & Sherif, 1976).

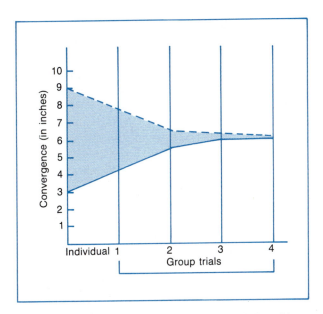

**Figure 15.5** *Distance judgments of a light made by subjects alone and in a group (autokinetic phenomenon). Subject A, dotted line; subject B, solid line.*

Research on the formation of group norms is closely allied with studies of conformity and social influence. There are occasions when group members resist social pressure and other instances when they conform to the judgments of others. To what extent does conformity occur in groups?

*Conformity*   **Conformity** *involves a change in behavior to correspond more closely to the behavior of others.* The word conformity has a bad reputation. It suggests a dependency, a loss of individuality, and mindless obedience. Yet society depends on conformity for its very existence. Without it, life would be chaotic and people unpredictable. People could not drive a car from one place to another if motorists refused to conform, more or less, to local driving customs.

It is not easy to say why any particular driver adheres to rules, but there are three general explanations (Kelman, 1958). (1) **Compliance** *is conformity that results from external rewards or punishments.* Since there are legal penalties for deviating from the speed limit, drivers may conform because of the risk of a fine or the loss of driving privileges. A sudden reduction in the speed of cars is noticeable when there is a police car ahead. People often comply with norms or customs because of penalties for noncompliance. (2) **Identification** *is conformity that results from emulating an individual or a group.* People may drive at or near the speed limit if they identify with someone who obeys the speed limit, particularly if that person is present as a passenger. (3) **Internalization** *is conformity that results from internal standards.* Some people drive at the speed limit because they have internalized the belief that laws are meaningful and beneficial. Drivers may believe that the posted speed limit is the safest or most efficient speed at which to drive. Some may believe that it is in the best interests of the society for each driver to obey the traffic laws. In these instances, the presence of a police car or the sudden change in speed of other drivers will have little effect on a person's driving speed.

One of the basic statements of Gestalt psychology (chapter 1) is that social groups influence perceptions, emotions, and behavior. Solomon Asch (1951) examined the effects of group pressure on perception. In one study, groups of from three to fifteen males were to choose which of several lines came closest to a standard line, a task shown in figure 15.6. All but one of the subjects in each group were accomplices of the experimenter. The real subject gave his judgment after hearing the judgments of the other group members. Asch arranged for the accomplices to give incorrect answers on certain trials.

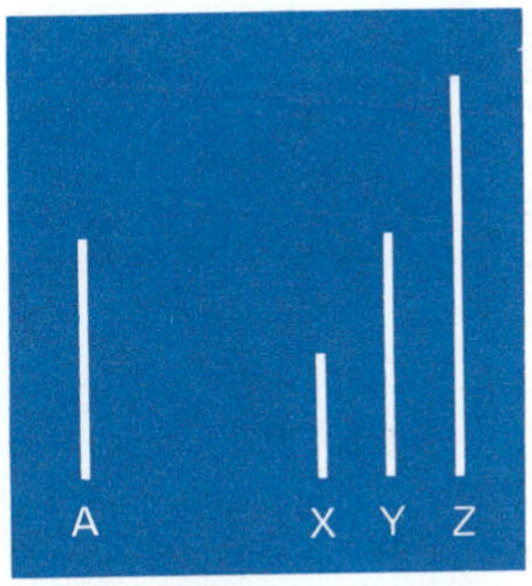

**Figure 15.6** *An experimental task utilized in the Asch conformity study.*

Regardless of group size, nearly one-third (thirty-two percent) of the subjects, when confronted with an incorrect judgment by all other group members, gave incorrect responses themselves. However, if one accomplice agreed with the real subject, the tendency to conform to the incorrect majority decreased to ten percent (see Minority Influence below).

Interviews with the subjects following this judgment task found three distinct motives for yielding to the pressure exerted by the incorrect majority: (1) wanting to appear the same as others in the group; (2) a lack of confidence and doubts about their own perceptions; and (3) an unawareness of being incorrect. In other words, some subjects perceived the incorrect response of other group members as the correct one. Conformity is not necessarily a conscious process.

*Minority Influence*    What if there is a minority of two instead of one? Researchers planted two accomplices in groups of six people. This minority of two always gave incorrect responses on a color recognition task. When the minority gave thoroughly consistent responses (saying green when the correct answer was blue), over eight percent of the true subjects said green. In a control group with no accomplices, fewer than half of one percent of the subjects said green. When the two confederates were not consistent in their position, saying green on some trials and blue on others, the true subjects were not swayed by the confederates' judgments. Thus, when the minority is not consistent, the majority is not influenced, but when the minority is consistent and persistent, and when their position is clear, a significant proportion of the majority is influenced (Maas & Clark, 1984; Moscovici, 1985; Mugny & Perez, 1991).

The studies of Sherif and Asch illustrate that individual group members are influenced by other members of the group when given ambiguous perception tasks to perform in the laboratory. Theodore Newcomb (1952, 1978; Allwin, Cohen, & Newcomb, 1991) extended research on group influence beyond the laboratory. He studied the entire student body of over 600 students at Bennington College in Vermont for a period of four years. He was particularly interested in "the manner in which the patterning of behavior and attitudes varied with different degrees of assimilation into the (college) community." Students at Bennington College came primarily from conservative, well-to-do homes, and as freshmen they entered college with the conservative attitudes of their parents. Seniors at Bennington, however, tended to be considerably more liberal than underclassmen. How does this transformation occur?

The Bennington students generally identified strongly with their college. It served as a positive reference group. There were rewards for being nonconservative. The students with the most prestige were those who were most liberal.

Seniors who remained conservative throughout their four years at Bennington tended to be those who identified strongly with "home and family." They were not well-integrated into the college community and tended to return home on weekends. For them, the college community was not a positive reference group. Those who did identify with the Bennington community found that their attitudes gradually converged toward the predominant and rewarded liberal attitudes of their peers.

When Newcomb conducted his studies at Bennington College, it was a school for women only. Do men conform to the same degree as women? There is considerable research in America that finds conformity to be more common among women than among men (Eagly & Chivala, 1986). Perhaps men tend to view conformity as a weakness, valuing independence and anti-conformity more than women. In one study, groups of male and female students stated their opinions on several issues. Their opinions were either under surveillance by other group members or were not known by others. The degree of conformity among females was unaffected by surveillance, but conformity was less among males when surveillance occurred (Eagly, Wood, & Fishbaugh, 1981). In other words, males conform less in order to maintain the appearance of independence.

▶ **GUIDED REVIEW** *Learning Objectives 19 and 20*

1. Group _____ are guidelines for behavior.
2. Sherif used the _____ to study the formation of group norms.
3. Conformity to group norms may occur for three reasons: _____, _____, and _____. Only in the case of _____ does the person conform regardless of whether others are present.
4. In Asch's experiments on conformity, about _____ percent of the naive subjects conformed to the incorrect judgments of the majority.
5. Newcomb's studies at Bennington College point to the importance of _____.

*ANSWERS*

*1. norms 2. autokinetic effect 3. compliance, identification, internalization 4. thirty-three 5. reference groups*

## Group Decisions

Imagine that the social committee has raised $10,000 for the junior class. Most of the money will be used in eight or nine months for the annual Junior Class Bash, and the committee must decide where to invest the money for the next several months. After discussing the possibilities for investment with the faculty advisor from the business department, the choices are restricted to:

**Savings account**
Pays 3 percent interest
**Blue-chip stock**
Probably won't lose money; will make about 5 percent
**Money market fund**
Variable interest, probably about 4 percent

**Mutual fund**

May lose money or make up to 10 percent with dividends and interest

**Speculative stock**

May lose money or make up to 20 percent with dividends and interest[†]

What will the committee do? Research has shown that if the individual members of the committee vote on these alternatives independently, they will suggest a more conservative investment than if the group makes a single decision after discussing the alternatives (Stoner, 1961; Dion, Baron, & Miller, 1970; Brown, 1986). This *greater risk-taking in groups, is referred to as the* **risky shift.** [This does not imply that groups *always* make riskier decisions than individuals (see Knox & Safford, 1976; Fraser, Gouge, & Billig, 1971; Isenberg, 1986).]

After many attempts to find a theoretical explanation for the risky shift, general agreement has settled upon two explanations, persuasions and social comparison. The persuasion interpretation contends that the shift results when individuals are exposed to arguments they have not previously considered, which has the effect of polarizing their initial opinions. The social comparison explanation is that people admire group members who hold extreme opinions and tend to adopt those positions. McCauley and Segal (1989) have attempted to explain such phenomena as religious cults and terrorist organizations in terms of the risky shift.

Risk-taking is influenced by many variables besides group context. One series of studies (Arkes, Herren, & Isen, 1988) found that positive feelings enhanced risk-taking. Individuals who had received free candy were willing to pay more for lottery tickets compared with individuals who had not received a gift.

*Social Loafing*    Groups often fail to achieve their maximum productivity (Stroebe, Diehl, & Abakoumkin, 1992). One reason is **social loafing,** *the reduction of individual effort when people work in groups* (Latané, Williams, & Harkins, 1979). As noted above, individuals may diffuse responsibility in an emergency when other people are present. They do something similar with regard to effort when working within a group. In a series of studies, groups of four people were found to do only about twice the work of the four individuals acting alone. Groups of six only did about two and a half times as much work as

six individuals working alone. This may be due to the fact that people are more deindividuated or less identifiable in groups. Social loafing occurs especially when each member's contributions will not be known by other group members (Brickner, Harkins, & Ostrom, 1986; Kerr & Bruun, 1981).

According to social comparison theory, there is a tendency for groups to be homogeneous. If group members tend to share the same attitudes and beliefs, it is unlikely that one member will be able to conceive of a highly original solution. Often, more effective problem solving can be achieved by a heterogeneous group. This can be seen in the phenomenon referred to as "groupthink."

*Groupthink*    Groups are often asked to make complex and difficult decisions. Presidential advisory boards and cabinets, for example, must make decisions about foreign policy that have long-lasting and irreversible consequences. Many group decisions turn out to be ill-considered and disastrous. How does this happen?

Social psychologist Irvin Janis analyzed a number of American foreign-policy decisions that were less than successful, such as the Bay of Pigs invasion in the 1960s and the escalation of the war in Vietnam (1972, 1989). He calls *the tendency of decision-makers to make irrational and uncritical decisions* **groupthink.** Groupthink is characterized by the appearance of consensus or unanimous agreement within a group. Each member believes that all members agree upon a particular decision or policy. No one expresses dissenting opinions because each person believes it would undermine the cohesion of the group and would be unpopular. Consequently, the number of alternatives considered by a cohesive group is minimal.

The quality of group decisions may be improved by strategies that encourage the voicing of all positions on an issue. Once a group decision seems reasonable, the group should analyze all the possible consequences of the decision. This can be done by role playing, by members imagining themselves acting on the basis of their decision (Janis & Mann, 1977; 't Hart, 1992; Tetlock, 1979; McCauley & Segal, 1989). The more alternatives presented and considered, the more creative and productive will be the group's decisions (Hackman & Morris, 1975).

*Collective Behavior*    Every day newspapers carry stories of strikes and riots; social, religious, and political movements; and the unfortunate consequences of panic during a fire, flood, or earthquake. Like so many seemingly

[†]If you had read the second edition of *Introduction to Psychology*, published in 1990, you would have received more interest. The corresponding figures in 1990 were 5.25 percent, 8 percent, 9 percent, 15 percent, and 50 percent.

# APPLYING PSYCHOLOGY

## Social Psychology in South African Murder Trials

When individuals commit extreme acts, from heroism to homicide, there is a tendency to explain this behavior in terms of characteristics of the actor—his bravery or psychopathology, for instance. However, much social psychological research documents the powerful influence of the social situation in such behavior. Research on attribution processes, social influence, deindividuation, obedience to authority, and group decision making all focus attention on the role played by social pressure and social definitions of the situation.

In 1987 in South Africa, eight railway workers were convicted of murdering four strike-breakers during an industrial dispute. During a gathering of strikers, the police sprayed tear gas and attacked the men with whips. On 22 April 1987, three strikers were shot dead by police. This was followed by more gatherings of strikers and further killings by the police. When a few days later the strikers learned that they had all been fired by their employer, South African Transport Services, they decided unanimously to kill five workers who had refused to join the strike. Four of the five kidnapped victims were killed, and eight of the strikers were tried for murder.

Two social psychologists, Scott Fraser from the United States and Andrew Colman, from Leicester, England, testified for the defense. The psychologists drew the court's attention to well-established social psychological phenomena that they believed influenced the defendants to varying degrees: the fundamental attribution bias, frustration-aggression, deindividuation, obedience. "We explained the group polarization effect that causes collective decisions, such as the mob decision to kill the non-strikers, to tend toward greater extremity than do the individual opinions of the group members. We discussed the research evidence on bystander apathy that helps to explain why some of the defendants stood idly by and allowed others to kill the non-strikers . . ." (Colman, 1991, p. 1074).

The court accepted conformity, obedience, group polarization, deindividuation, bystander apathy, and other well-established social psychological phenomena as extenuating factors for four of the defendants (the remaining four were sentenced to death). In a second trial, death sentences of five defendants for the killing of a young woman were reduced to twenty months imprisonment in the light of similar social psychological evidence.

In his article, Colman also discusses some of the ethical issues surrounding such psychological testimony in murder trials.

---

patternless events, these behaviors are not random or unpredictable. Collective behavior includes the study of crowds, riots, panics, fads, protest movements, rebellions, revolutions, social movements, fashion, and mass hysteria (see box, UFO Abduction Syndrome in chapter 12). **Collective behavior** *differs from other group processes in that it usually emerges spontaneously without a well-defined plan of action.*

There are important reasons to study collective behavior. For one thing, collective behavior often involves a loss of life and property, and its study may help reduce the fatalities of panics, riots, and revolutions. Furthermore, collective behavior highlights the dynamic relationship that exists between individuals and groups. A person might be a passerby on the fringe of a large crowd and decide to see what is going on. As others stop to do the same, he or she may suddenly find himself or herself no longer on the fringes of the crowd but toward its center, being pushed this way and that, caught up in the pushing and shoving so often characteristic of large numbers of people in small spaces. There are many interesting books and articles on various forms of collective behavior (Lurie, 1981; Milgram & Toch, 1969; Rudé, 1964; Turner & Killian, 1972). We examine one form, panics.

**Panic** *is a form of social disorganization in which individuals compete for access to limited resources.* Panic often results in loss of life at fires, sporting events, and rock concerts.

The classic studies of panic were conducted by Alexander Mintz (1951). He observed that it normally takes only a few minutes for patrons to file calmly out of a theater or restaurant. So deaths that occur during fires are a result of nonadaptive behavior. In Mintz's experiments, groups of people had to retrieve wooden cones from a glass bottle. Each subject was given a piece of string attached to a cone. Cooperation was required for the cones to come out since the neck of the bottle would permit only one cone to pass at a time. Mintz believed that this task was analogous to going out a theater exit that is wide enough for only one person. Subjects could win or lose money depending on how much time elapsed before they retrieved the cone. In some experiments (Mintz conducted forty-two of them!), water began to fill the bottle, and success was defined as retrieving a dry cone. In some groups, no rewards or fines were levied. In other studies, Mintz instructed accomplices to scream, swear, and behave excitedly during the task.

Results indicate that the groups that received no reward or fine had no trouble removing the cones from the bottle. Emotional excitement by some subjects had little effect on group efficiency. However, in over half of the experiments involving rewards or fines, jams developed as soon as the bottleneck was temporarily blocked. According to these studies, panics occur when people are penalized for failure to escape and when they are rewarded for successful escape. As the penalties increase for failure to escape, panic increases (Kelley, Condry, Dahlke, & Hill, 1965; Klein, 1976; Kruglanski, 1969).

▶ **GUIDED REVIEW** *Learning Objectives 21 and 22*

1. Groups often make _____ decisions than the individuals would who comprise the group.
2. Explanations for the "risky shift" include _____ and _____.
3. Groups may perform at less than their optimum level of productivity because of _____.
4. The emergence of a common focus and of common actions by a number of individuals is called _____.
5. Collective behavior includes _____, _____, _____, _____, and _____.

*ANSWERS*

1. more risky 2. persuasion, social comparison 3. social loafing 4. collective behavior 5. strikes, riots, crowds, social movements, panics

# SUMMARY

I. Social comparison is the process by which people obtain information about themselves and their world by comparing themselves with others. (p. 448)
   A. People tend to choose others for social comparison whom they expect to be similar to themselves in terms of the particular opinion or ability in question. (p. 448)
   B. Social comparison is often used to cope with stressful or ambiguous events. (p. 448)

II. Social perception refers to the process of forming judgments and impressions of other people. (p. 448)
   A. People's impressions of others are typically uniform and consistent. They form beliefs about what personality characteristics belong together. This is known as an implicit theory of personality. (p. 449)
   B. Impression formation is concerned with how people form opinions of others. First impressions are sometimes based only on simple adjective descriptions. In such situations some traits, such as "warm" or "cold," may influence how people evaluate other traits. (p. 449)
   C. Attribution is the study of how people explain the causes of behavior. People tend to judge whether a behavior is internally or externally caused, whether it is due to some characteristics of the actor or to situational pressures from the environment. There is a tendency for people to see their own behavior as internally caused when the outcome is undesirable. The opposite attributions are made when explaining someone else's behavior. This is known as the fundamental attribution bias. (p. 450)

III. Interpersonal attraction research examines the social and psychological bases of friendship and love. (p. 451)
   A. One basis for attraction is similarity of attitudes, values, beliefs, and experiences. (p. 451)
   B. Romantic love can be viewed as an emotion, with both physiological and cognitive features. (p. 452)
      1. One theory of romantic attraction states that although similarity may be important early in a relationship, complementary personality traits are important at subsequent stages. (p. 451)
      2. Love can also be seen as a learned social role. (p. 452)

IV. Social influence refers to the effects that other individuals have on people's beliefs, attitudes, and behavior. (p. 453)
   A. Attitude is a tendency to respond to a class of objects in a consistently favorable or unfavorable way. Attitudes consist of cognitive, emotional, and behavioral tendency components. (p. 453)
      1. One determinant of behavior is attitudes. Attitudes are related to behavior but do not always correspond precisely to behavior. (p. 453)
      2. Cognitive dissonance theory helps explain the relationship between attitudes and behavior. Not only do attitudes influence behavior, but behavior also influences attitudes. (p. 453)

3. Attitude change may result from persuasive communications. All communication involves a source, message, channel, and audience. If sources are high in credibility, they are generally more effective. Persuasive messages tend to be most effective when they take into account the audience's initial attitude. (pp. 453–454)

4. Mass media tend to influence attitudes indirectly among those who pay most attention to the media. These "opinion leaders" then influence their friends in face-to-face contact. (p. 454)

B. Prejudice can be viewed as an attitude in which one holds negative views about another person on the basis of that person's membership in a group. (p. 455)

1. Prejudice is usually accompanied by stereotypes, generalizations in which all members of a group are incorrectly assumed to have some trait in common other than the one defining the group. (p. 455)

2. Individuals who differ in skin pigmentation are sometimes assumed to differ in other ways. For example, people may assume that members of other races hold different beliefs and values. This is known as belief prejudice. (p. 455)

3. Prejudice can be reduced by working together toward superordinate goals. (p. 456)

V. Humans can be both altruistic and cruelly violent. Psychologists study these seemingly contradictory tendencies of prosocial and antisocial behavior. (p. 456)

A. Prosocial behavior is the extent to which people offer assistance to others. (p. 456)

1. People are more apt to help in emergencies when they are alone. This is explained by the concept of diffusion of responsibility. (p. 457)

2. Some people have a strong belief that things don't happen without a reason. This is referred to as the belief in a just world. This gives rise to the "just-world phenomenon", the tendency to blame victims for their plight. (p. 458)

B. Aggression is the intentional injury of one person by another. (p. 458)

1. Frustration-aggression theory is widely used in psychology and has been modified several times since it first appeared in 1939. (pp. 458–459)

2. Berkowitz modified the theory to include anger as well as frustration, and he added the concept of an aggressive cue as a necessary condition for aggressive behavior. (p. 458)

3. In the theory proposed by Zillmann, physiological arousal is a necessary condition for aggression. (p. 459)

4. According to social learning theory, exposure to aggression may teach observers to act aggressively. (p. 459)

5. Violence in the family, such as child abuse and spouse abuse, does not often appear to be the result of serious personality disorders. (p. 459)

6. People often obey the commands of others. This was examined in classic experiments by Stanley Milgram on obedience to authority. (pp. 460–461)

7. Obedience to authority can be reduced by bringing the teacher and learner closer together or by having a second experimenter disagree with the first experimenter in the presence of the teacher. (p. 461)

VI. A group is two or more individuals who share, and are aware of, common features or interests. (p. 462)

A. A reference group is one with which an individual identifies, even though he or she may not be an actual member of the group. (p. 462)

B. Individuals learn and perform differently when in the presence of others. This is known as social facilitation. (p. 462)

VII. Groups are attractive to individuals primarily because they provide information or feedback about individual members. (p. 464)

A. Social comparison theory states that individuals seek feedback about their opinions, abilities, and beliefs. This has been supplemented by Schachter, who suggests that individuals also seek feedback about their emotional states. For example, very fearful individuals are more likely to affiliate with others who are experiencing fear. (p. 464)

B. Cohesiveness is the attractiveness of a group to its members. (p. 464)

1. Cognitive dissonance theory states that individuals are most attracted to groups for which they have sacrificed. (p. 464)

C. Leadership is the ability of one person to influence the behavior of others. (pp. 464–465)

1. The "great man" theory of leadership argues that personality is of utmost importance. (p. 465)

2. Modern views of leadership stress the interaction of the leader's relationship with group members, the leader's power, and the type of task facing the group. (p. 465)

VIII. Groups develop norms or standards, which require a certain amount of conformity from their members. (pp. 466–467)

A. Group norms emerge when individuals face an ambiguous situation, such as the autokinetic phenomenon. Norms tend to be used by individuals even after they leave the group. Group norms are passed along from one generation of group members to another. (p. 466)

B. Three types of conformity are compliance, identification, and internalization. (p. 467)

1. In Asch's studies of conformity, about one-third of the naive subjects gave the same judgment as the (incorrect) majority of group members. (p. 467)

**2.** As demonstrated in Newcomb's studies at Bennington College, individuals gradually acquire the values or norms of their positive reference groups. (p. 468)

**3.** A minority within a group is able to influence the majority when it maintains a clear-cut position and is consistent in its view. (p. 468)

**C.** Group performance and decision making are often less than optimal. (p. 468)

    **1.** Social loafing refers to the fact that groups sometimes exert less effort than the sum of their individual members acting alone. This occurs when the contributions of each member to a task are not known by other group members. (p. 469)

    **2.** The decisions of groups are often more risky than individual decisions. This is referred to as the risky shift. Persuasion and social comparison have been offered as explanations for this phenomenon. (p. 469)

**3.** Groupthink refers to the tendency of groups to consider only a limited number of solutions to a problem and to minimize criticism within the group. (p. 469)

**D.** In response to unusual and ambiguous events, a collection of individuals may engage in collective behavior, such as a crowd, riot, panic, or revolution. (p. 470)

    **1.** Panic is a form of unorganized social behavior in which people compete for a scarce resource. Panics are greatest when there are penalties for failure to obtain the scarce resource. (pp. 470–471)

## ACTION GLOSSARY

Match the terms in the left column with the definitions in the right column.

___ **1. Social psychology (p. 448)**
___ **2. Social comparison (p. 448)**
___ **3. Implicit theory of personality (p. 449)**
___ **4. Impression formation (p. 449)**
___ **5. Halo effect (p. 450)**
___ **6. Attribution (p. 450)**
___ **7. Fundamental attribution bias (p. 450)**

*A. The tendency to see other people's behavior as internally caused and to see one's own behavior as externally caused.*
*B. A general belief that certain personality traits belong together.*
*C. The process by which individuals develop opinions of others.*
*D. The field of psychology concerned with the effects that people have on one another.*
*E. The study of how people explain the underlying causes of behavior.*
*F. The process of comparing ourselves with others in order to arrive at judgments about the social and physical world.*
*G. The tendency to form positive impressions when it is known that a person has some positive traits.*

___ **8. Interpersonal attraction (p. 451)**
___ **9. Attitude (p. 453)**
___ **10. Theory of reasoned action (p. 453)**
___ **11. Cognitive dissonance (p. 453)**
___ **12. Highly credible source (p. 454)**
___ **13. Two-step flow of communication (p. 454)**
___ **14. Opinion leaders (p. 454)**
___ **15. Prejudice (p. 455)**
___ **16. Need complementarity (p. 452)**

*A. A person who has relevant experience and is thought to be expert and trustworthy.*
*B. Negative views and actions directed toward groups or individual members of selected groups.*
*C. A tendency to respond to a class of objects in a consistently favorable or unfavorable way.*
*D. Individuals who pay particular attention to the mass media.*
*E. An uncomfortable psychological state that results when two or more cognitions are logically inconsistent.*
*F. The study of the social and psychological bases of friendship and romantic attachments.*
*G. In a relationship, the ability of each person to satisfy the other's needs.*
*H. The process by which individuals learn of mass media content from face-to-face contact with opinion leaders.*
*I. Attitudes influence the intention to perform a behavior; this intention determines behavior.*

___ 17. **Discrimination** (p. 455)
___ 18. **Stereotype** (p. 455)
___ 19. **Superordinate goal** (p. 456)
___ 20. **Diffusion of responsibility** (p. 457)
___ 21. **Human aggression** (p. 458)
___ 22. **Aggressive cue** (p. 458)

A. *A common task that requires members from antagonistic groups to work together.*
B. *A target, object, or situation associated with aggression.*
C. *Tendency to spread responsibility for acting among all potential actors.*
D. *The intentional injury of another person.*
E. *A generalization about a person or group in which all members are incorrectly assumed to have a trait in common.*
F. *Behavior that arises from prejudiced attitudes and prevents a person from acting freely because of his or her membership in a group.*

___ 23. **Group** (p. 462)
___ 24. **Reference group** (p. 462)
___ 25. **Social facilitation** (p. 462)
___ 26. **Cohesiveness** (p. 464)

A. *A group with which an individual identifies but to which he or she does not actually belong.*
B. *Two or more individuals who are aware of having something in common.*
C. *The overall attractiveness of a group to its members.*
D. *The effect that the presence of others has on learning and performance.*

___ 27. **Leadership** (p. 464)
___ 28. **Great man theory** (p. 465)
___ 29. **Autokinetic effect** (p. 466)
___ 30. **Conformity** (p. 467)
___ 31. **Compliance** (p. 467)
___ 32. **Internalization** (p. 467)
___ 33. **Identification** (p. 467)

A. *Changing one's behavior to correspond more closely to the behavior of others.*
B. *Conformity that results from external rewards or punishments.*
C. *The theory that assumes that the personal strengths and motives of individuals make them powerful leaders.*
D. *The presence of a particular influence relationship between two or more persons.*
E. *Conformity that results from emulating an individual or group whom one admires.*
F. *The tendency to perceive movement in a stationary light when there is no other reference point. Used by Sherif in studies of the development of group norms.*
G. *Conformity that results from one's internal standards.*

___ 34. **Risky shift** (p. 469)
___ 35. **Social loafing** (p. 469)
___ 36. **Collective behavior** (p. 470)
___ 37. **Panic** (p. 470)

A. *A form of social disorganization in which people compete for access to limited resources.*
B. *Behavior of individuals in a crowd that emerges spontaneously without a well-defined prior plan of action.*
C. *The reduction of individual effort when groups of people work on the same task.*
D. *The tendency for groups to take more risk when making certain decisions than would individual group members acting alone.*

*ANSWERS*

*1. d, 2. f, 3. b, 4. c, 5. h, 6. e, 7. a, 8. f, 9. c, 10. i, 11. e, 12. a, 13. h, 14. d, 15. b, 16. g, 17. f, 18. e, 19. a, 20. c, 21. d, 22. b, 23. b, 24. a, 25. d, 26. c, 27. d, 28. c, 29. f, 30. a, 31. b, 32. g, 33. e, 34. d, 35. c, 36. b, 37. a*

# SELF-TEST

1. According to Festinger's social comparison theory, people
    (a) have a need to evaluate their opinions and abilities.
    (b) prefer objective means of evaluating themselves.
    (c) compare themselves with others when objective measures of their opinions and abilities are unavailable.
    (d) all of the above.
    (e) none of the above
        (LO 1; p. 448)

2. According to social comparison theory, one reason people interact with others is to
    (a) enhance their self-esteem.
    (b) receive positive reinforcement.
    (c) receive feedback about themselves.
    (d) all of the above.
    (e) none of the above.
        (LO 1, 2; p. 448)

3. The study of social perception indicates that
   (a) object perception is just as complex as person perception.
   (b) perceiving people requires consideration of their needs and motives.
   (c) people view the causes of other's behavior objectively and accurately.
   (d) all of the above.
   (LO 3; p. 448)

4. In Asch's early study of impression formation, in which students were presented with adjectives describing a person,
   (a) the warm-cold variable was a central trait.
   (b) the warm-cold variable was a peripheral trait.
   (c) impressions were based on the sum of all the individual traits.
   (d) people were very accurate in their impressions.
   (LO 3; p. 449)

5. Otto thinks that intelligent people are also friendly. This is an example of his
   (a) perceptual constancy.
   (b) implicit theory of personality.
   (c) cognitive dissonance.
   (d) accuracy of person perception.
   (LO 4; p. 449)

6. The relationship between similarity and attraction is
   (a) widely accepted, but disagreement exists as to its best explanation.
   (b) consistent only with a cognitive approach to attraction.
   (c) consistent only with a learning approach to attraction.
   (d) not important in early stages of a relationship.
   (LO 6; p. 451)

7. According to Byrne, an individual will be most attracted to someone who is
   (a) similar on a large *number* of traits.
   (b) similar on a great *proportion* of traits.
   (c) different on some traits and similar on others.
   (d) intelligent, wealthy, and physically attractive.
   (LO 6; p. 451)

8. Need complementarity is
   (a) unrelated to attraction.
   (b) related to early stages of attraction.
   (c) important only in later stages of a relationship.
   (d) none of the above.
   (LO 6; p. 452)

9. Which of the following is not an attitude component?
   (a) cognitive
   (b) attributional
   (c) emotional
   (d) behavior tendency
   (LO 8; p. 453)

10. Attitudes
    (a) allow psychologists to predict behavior accurately.
    (b) are not always predictive of behavior.
    (c) do not concern behavior at all.
    (d) are negatively correlated with behavior.
    (LO 7, 8; p. 453)

11. The communication process includes which of the following?
    (a) source
    (b) channel
    (c) message
    (d) all of the above.
    (e) none of the above.
    (LO 8; p. 453)

12. Research indicates that reducing prejudice between two groups may occur with
    (a) any contact between the two groups.
    (b) equal-status contact between the two groups.
    (c) educational programs aimed at correcting misconceptions.
    (d) participation in competitive tasks.
    (LO 9; p. 456)

13. Conflict between groups can be reduced if the groups work together on a task for their mutual benefit. Sherif refers to this as
    (a) cognitive dissonance.
    (b) equity.
    (c) a superordinate goal.
    (d) the culture assimilator.
    (LO 9; p. 456)

14. Belief prejudice is the notion that
    (a) people prefer members of the same race who agree with them.
    (b) people prefer members of other races who disagree with them.
    (c) people prefer others who share their beliefs, regardless of race.
    (d) prejudice is a result of an authoritarian personality.
    (LO 10; p. 455)

15. According to Latané and Darley, the reason that people are unlikely to help someone in an emergency can be explained by
    (a) the personalities of the witnesses.
    (b) the tendency to devalue the victims of crime.
    (c) the number of witnesses present.
    (d) none of the above.
    (LO 11, 12; p. 457)

16. If something bad happens to a person, people may conclude that the person deserved it. This is part of which theory?
    (a) diffusion of responsibility
    (b) social learning theory
    (c) imitation and modeling
    (d) just-world phenomenon
    (LO 11; p. 458)

17. The original frustration-aggression theory by Dollard et al. states that
    (a) frustration always causes aggression.
    (b) aggression is always caused by frustration.
    (c) frustration is the interruption of ongoing behavior.
    (d) all of the above.
    (e) none of the above.
    (LO 13; p. 458)

18. Berkowitz proposed that frustration
    (a) always leads to aggression.
    (b) is not related to aggression.
    (c) leads to aggression only when an aggressive cue is present.
    (d) does not cause physiological arousal.
    (LO 13; p. 458)

19. According to Zillmann's theory, which of the following is a necessary condition for aggressive behavior?
    (a) an aggressive cue
    (b) physiological arousal
    (c) frustration
    (d) anger
    (LO 13; p. 459)

20. Milgram's research on obedience found that
    (a) only one or two percent of subjects administered the most severe shocks.
    (b) when subjects had to place the victim's hand on the shock plate, over half of the subjects administered the most intense shock.
    (c) the closer the subject was to the victim, the less likely the subject was to administer severe shock.
    (d) the more education a subject had, the less likely the subject was to obey the experimenter's demand for intense shock.
    (LO 14; p. 461)

21. Which of the following is *not* an integral part of the definition of *group*?
    (a) four or more people
    (b) interpersonal contact
    (c) meaningful interaction with others
    (d) a shared goal, attitude, or purpose
    (LO 15; p. 462)

22. A person may identify with a group he or she does not actually belong to. Such a group is called
    (a) an achieved group.
    (b) a reference group.
    (c) a socio-emotional group.
    (d) an ascribed group.
    (LO 15; p. 462)

23. The effects of the presence of other people on an individual's performance on a task is termed
    (a) the autokinetic effect.
    (b) social comparison.
    (c) social facilitation.
    (d) reference group function.
    (LO 16; p. 462)

24. Zajonc's theory of social facilitation
    (a) distinguishes between learning and performance.
    (b) is about attitude change.
    (c) states that the presence of others always increases learning.
    (d) states that the presence of others always increases performance.
    (LO 16; p. 463)

25. The overall attractiveness of a group to its members is the group's
    (a) affiliative tendency.
    (b) cohesiveness.
    (c) comparison level.
    (d) evaluative function.
    (LO 17; p. 464)

26. The text discusses leadership as a(n)
    (a) innate ability.
    (b) characteristic that some people have.
    (c) particular influence relationship between people.
    (d) all of the above.
    (e) none of the above.
    (LO 18; p. 464)

27. Sherif used the autokinetic effect to study
    (a) visual perception.
    (b) the development of social norms.
    (c) group conflict.
    (d) emergent leadership.
    (LO 19; p. 466)

28. People conform to a social norm because
    (a) there are penalties for violating social norms.
    (b) that is what other people do.
    (c) they want to.
    (d) all of the above.
    (e) none of the above.
    (LO 20; p. 467)

29. What percent of subjects in the Asch studies conformed to the incorrect judgments of the group?
    (a) 5 percent
    (b) 32 percent
    (c) 75 percent
    (d) 95 percent
    (LO 20; p. 467)

30. Newcomb's Bennington College study demonstrated that students became more liberal if
    (a) Bennington was a positive reference group for them.
    (b) they maintained strong home and family ties.
    (c) they went home every weekend.
    (d) their roommates were liberal.
    (LO 20; p. 468)

31. Groups do not always produce as much as their individual members working separately. This is referred to as
    (a) social comparison.
    (b) social learning.
    (c) social loafing.
    (d) cognitive dissonance.
    (LO 21; p. 469)

32. Panics are most apt to occur when
    (a) emotional contagion spreads through the crowd.
    (b) a sudden event occurs at an unpredictable time.
    (c) people are punished for not obtaining a scarce resource, like reaching a fire exit, or rewarded for obtaining it.
    (d) all of the above.
    (LO 22; p. 471)

ANSWERS

1. d, 2. c, 3. b, 4. a, 5. b, 6. a, 7. b, 8. c, 9. b, 10. b, 11. d, 12. b, 13. c, 14. c, 15. c,
16. d, 17. d, 18. c, 19. b, 20. c, 21. a, 22. b, 23. c, 24. a, 25. b, 26. c, 27. b, 28. d,
29. b, 30. a, 31. c, 32. c.

# THINKING ABOUT PSYCHOLOGY

1. Given what you now know about attitude change and persuasion, how effective do you think advertising is in influencing attitudes and behavior?

2. How does research on group norms help us understand how groups perpetuate their standards and beliefs over succeeding generations? How, for example, is a particular fraternity able to maintain its liberal stance on political issues despite the fact that many of the members who originally adopted these norms have long since graduated and become conservatives?

# SUGGESTED READINGS

Ajzen, I. (1988). *Attitudes, personality, and behavior.* Chicago: Dorsey.

Aronson, E. (1992). *The social animal.* (6th ed.). New York: W. H. Freeman. An overview of the major topics in social psychology, including attraction, aggression, and persuasion.

Baron, R. S., Kerr, N., and Miller, N. (1992). *Group process, group decision, group action.* Buckingham, England: Open University.

Brown, R. W. (1986). *Social psychology* (2nd ed.). New York: Macmillan. An updated classic treatment of social psychology.

Cialdini, R. B. (1993). *Influence.* (3rd ed.) New York: Harper Collins. A readable book on all forms of social influence, in politics, mass media, and interpersonal.

Mullen, B., & Geothals, G. R. (eds.) (1988). *Theories of group behavior.* New York: Springer-Verlag.

Pratkanis, A., & Aronson, E. (1991). *Age of propaganda.* New York: Freeman. Analysis of everyday persuasion and influence, from the techniques and influence of advertising to political speeches and propaganda.

Staub, E. (1990). *Roots of evil.* New York: Basic Books. Research on bystander intervention, obedience to authority, aggression, and intergroup processes is used in an analysis of war, terrorism, and genocide.

Tavris, C. (1989). *Anger: The misunderstood emotion.* (revised ed.). New York: Simon & Schuster. A social psychological view of anger, emotion, and aggression. Tavris writes that anger is a controllable, but sometimes useful, emotion.

# CHAPTER 16

## APPLYING PSYCHOLOGY
### OUTLINE

▶ **Learning Objectives**

▶ **Work and the Individual: Industrial and Organizational Psychology**

- ■ The Motivation to Work
  Herzberg's Two-Factor Theory
  Valence-Instrumentality-
  Expectancy (V-I-E) Theory
  Equity Theory
  Overcompensation and
  Intrinsic Motivation
- ■ Effects of Unemployment

▶ **Guided Review**

▶ **The Nature of Organizations**

- ■ Bureaucracy: Formal Structure
- ■ Informal Social Structure
  The Hawthorne Experiments
- ■ Communication in
  Organizations
  Informal Social
  Communication
- ■ Personnel Selection

▶ **Guided Review**

▶ **Human Factors**

- ■ Information Input
  Visual Information
  Auditory Displays
  Smell, Taste, and Touch
- ■ Motor Output
  Case Study: Three Mile Island

▶ **Guided Review**

▶ **Environmental Psychology**

- ■ Personal Space and
  Territoriality
- ■ Environmental Stressors
- ■ Energy Conservation

▶ **Guided Review**

▶ **Sports Psychology**

- ■ Enhancing Athletic
  Performance
- ■ Violence and Sports
- ■ Sports Fans

▶ **Guided Review**

▶ **Psychology and Education**

- ■ Expectancy Effects
- ■ The Cooperative Classroom:
  The Jigsaw Approach to
  Multicultural Education
- ■ Enhancing Motivation

▶ **Guided Review**

▶ **Summary**

▶ **Action Glossary**

▶ **Self-Test**

▶ **Thinking About Psychology**

▶ **Suggested Readings**

# APPLYING PSYCHOLOGY
## LEARNING OBJECTIVES

**After reading this chapter, you should be able to**

► **1.** specify five of the basic areas of applied psychology: industrial/organizational psychology, human factors, environmental psychology, sports psychology, and educational psychology. *(p. 480)*

► **2.** recognize relationships and distinctions between work and leisure. *(p. 480)*

► **3.** outline the basic theories of work motivation: valence-instrumentality-expectancy theory and equity theory. *(p. 481)*

► **4.** understand the importance of work and the effects of unemployment on the individual. *(pp. 482–483)*

► **5.** recognize that large organizations have formal structures and networks of communication and that informal social structures and communication networks exist within them. *(p. 484)*

► **6.** indicate the roles that psychology plays in industry and business. *(pp. 483–487)*

► **7.** specify some of the areas of psychology that have been applied to man-machine systems, also known as human factors. *(p. 487)*

► **8.** identify the psychological considerations in reducing accidents and increasing the efficiency of human-operated equipment. *(p. 487)*

► **9.** distinguish between personal space and territoriality. *(p. 493)*

► **10.** recognize how personal space alters with circumstances. *(p. 493)*

► **11.** understand the effects that environmental stressors, such as noise, may have on behavior. *(pp. 494–495)*

► **12.** indicate some psychological principles that help regulate energy consumption. *(pp. 496)*

► **13.** identify three areas of modern sports psychology. *(p. 496)*

► **14.** describe competing explanations for violence in sports. *(p. 497)*

► **15.** understand different motives for being a sports fan. *(p. 497)*

► **16.** identify the ways that teachers' expectations may influence their students. *(p. 498)*

► **17.** define the use of the jigsaw approach to cooperative education. *(pp. 498–499)*

► **18.** explain some of the ways in which student motivation may be increased. *(p. 499)*

Psychology is about people. It has a bearing on whatever people do. Psychology has been used to explore matters both trivial and grand, from the blink of an eye to war and global catastrophes. In this chapter we examine five distinct areas of applied psychology: business and large organizations (industrial/organizational psychology), the design and use of equipment (human factors), environmental psychology, sports psychology, and psychology and education.

# WORK AND THE INDIVIDUAL: INDUSTRIAL AND ORGANIZATIONAL PSYCHOLOGY

The marriage between psychology and industry took place near the turn of the century when F. W. Taylor (1911) launched a movement called **scientific management,** which *focused on the details of a worker's behavior, the motivation for work, and the precise measurement and description of jobs.* Since that time both psychology and industry have matured. Today, industrial and organizational psychologists perform a variety of tasks in many different work settings, as can be seen in tables 16.1 and 16.2.

**Industrial psychology** *is the application of psychological principles and findings to the world of work.* **Organizational psychology,** *the study of the behavior of, and within, large organizations,* is a branch of industrial psychology. Industrial and organizational psychologists select and train personnel, analyze jobs, develop useful research strategies for industry, and develop procedures for increasing the efficiency of decision making within organizations.

In physics, work is a force that acts against resistance and results in movement or change. In psychology, **work** *is the expenditure of energy to accomplish a task or goal,* usually in exchange for compensation. In an organization, work consists of those activities whose goals are typically set not by the individual performing the work but by the worker's employer. In contrast, **leisure** consists of *personally defined and individualistic activities* (excluding essential maintenance functions, such as shopping, cleaning, eating), *performed outside of the work context* (Kabanoff, 1983). These formal definitions, however, do not fully convey the richness of either work or leisure experiences, their social and psychological functions, their interconnectedness, and their importance for day-to-day living.

**TABLE 16.1 Principal work settings of industrial/organizational psychologists**

| | |
|---|---:|
| Universities | 31% |
| Industrial settings | 27% |
| Consulting firms | 13% |
| Government and military settings | 11% |
| Individual consulting | 8% |
| Research organizations | 5% |
| Other | 5% |

Source: American Psychological Association.

**TABLE 16.2 Principal work activities of industrial/organizational psychologists**

| | |
|---|---:|
| Management | 57% |
| Applied research | 12% |
| Teaching | 9% |
| Basic research and test development | 8% |
| Training | 7% |
| Implementing personnel programs | 5% |
| Engineering/human factors design | 2% |

Source: American Psychological Association.

## The Motivation to Work

Why do people work? Would they continue to work if they did not have to earn money to support themselves and their families? Even if people feel they must work, why are some more satisfied with their jobs than others? How can satisfaction with work be increased? These are some of the questions that industrial and organizational psychologists address. Some psychologists believe that the motivation to work comes strictly from the external environment: a person works because of the rewards that work brings. To other psychologists, work is a method of fulfilling a person's need for creativity and productivity; that is, the motivation to work arises from within the individual, from the need to feel a sense of competence and mastery. Still others see work as stemming from deep-seated unconscious motives.

This section considers the three primary explanations for work. The theories and research presented are not incompatible with one another. They should be seen as alternative perspectives, each contributing to an understanding of work.

*Herzberg's Two-Factor Theory*     Theodore Herzberg, like many personality theorists, assumes that individuals are born with different sets of needs that can be arranged in a hierarchy (Herzberg, 1966, 1976; Herzberg, Mausner, & Synderman, 1959). Closest to Herzberg's two-factor theory of work motivation is Abraham Maslow's notion of a need hierarchy (chapter 11, Personality). It is assumed that there are basic biological needs, which, once satisfied, are replaced by more abstract "higher order" needs. Herzberg proposes that *the basic needs,* which he calls **hygiene needs,** *include things such as pay, job security, relations with coworkers, general working conditions, and company policies.* The *higher order needs,* or **motivator needs,** *require people to seek challenge, creativity, stimulation, and independence.* Higher order needs are satisfied by responsible work, by being able to make independent decisions on the job, and by recognition for accomplishments.

Herzberg believes that work undertaken for motivation-seeking is preferable to work undertaken for hygiene-seeking because it yields productive activity on the part of the worker and few control problems for management (Landy & Trumbo, 1980). Motivation-seekers are people who love their work. The theory suggests that if a manager can move individuals from hygiene-seeking levels to motivation-seeking levels, the workers will be self-motivated and will not require as much supervision. In order to move individuals from a hygiene-seeking level to a motivation-seeking level, Herzberg proposes "job enrichment." This is an attempt to make work more interesting so workers will derive greater satisfaction from it (Hackman & Oldham, 1975).

*Valence-Instrumentality-Expectancy (V-I-E) Theory* Victor Vroom (1964) has proposed a cognitive model of worker motivation and satisfaction, the V-I-E theory. This examines not only the benefits of work, such as pay and fringe benefits, but also an individual's perceptions of the value and probability of receiving the benefits.

The theory focuses not merely on an individual's actual experiences on the job but on the anticipation of events that lie in the future. It refers to the expectations of what will happen as a consequence of a given action. The theory states that individuals ask themselves whether (1) the action has a high probability of leading to an outcome (expectancy); (2) that outcome will yield other outcomes (instrumentality); and (3) those other outcomes are valued (valence).

The basic model of Vroom has been modified and expanded by Lyman Porter and Edward Lawler (1968) and has become the most popular approach to motivation among industrial researchers (Locke, 1975; Lawler, 1973; Nakanishi, 1988). Research on the theory indicates that V-I-E theories are better able to predict the *effort* of individuals than their actual job *performance.*\*

*Equity Theory*     In the 1960s, J. Stacy Adams startled the business community by proposing the unthinkable: workers would be uncomfortable earning too much, as well as too little, money. He formulated **equity theory,** which *states that people attempt to make their inputs and outcomes in a situation comparable to those of their peers.* Adams (1965) represents the theory in the following manner:

$$\frac{O_p}{I_p} = \frac{O_a}{I_a}$$

where O is outcome
I is input
$_p$ is the person under discussion
$_a$ is a peer or coworker of the person.

When this outcome-input ratio is not equal, a state of inequity exists. This, like cognitive dissonance (chapter 15), is an uncomfortable psychological motivational state that causes an individual to attempt to reduce the discomfort. When inequity exists, the individual will alter either the inputs (working harder or less hard or changing the quality of the work), or the outcomes (by asking for a raise, quitting, or striking for a better contract). It suggests that overcompensating or undercompensating workers diminishes productivity and job satisfaction.

We do not need equity theory to tell us that underpayment lowers worker productivity and morale. On the other hand, the notion that overcompensation also diminishes the quantity and quality of work is surprising. In one test of equity theory (Pritchard, Dunnette, & Jorgenson, 1972), researchers hired more than 250 men to work as clerks. The men were led to believe that they were being overpaid for their work, equitably paid, or underpaid. They found that the equitably paid men were more satisfied with their jobs than were either the overpaid or the underpaid workers. Rae (1981) found that black baseball players thought that they were not paid enough in relation to white

---

\*Not everyone is good at his or her job. One reason is the well-known "Peter Principle," devised by psychologist Laurence Peter (Peter & Hull, 1969). This is the tendency for people working in organizations to be promoted for a job well done. At some point, they will be promoted to a position for which they are ill-suited, and here they will remain, performing their jobs badly.

players, although their salaries were, in fact, much higher. However, the black players were paid less than white players who performed at the same level, and hence felt inequitably compensated.

How do unfairly paid workers handle the inequity? According to equity theorists, equity may be restored in at least four ways: by altering inputs or outcomes or by psychologically distorting the perception of one's own or a coworker's inputs or outcomes (Walster, Walster, & Berscheid, 1978; Deci, 1989). For example, an underpaid worker might restore equity by (a) reducing the quantity or quality of his or her work; (b) seeking a raise; (c) empha-sizing the non-pay benefits of the work, such as medical insurance, vacation time, or the value or interest of the work; or (d) distorting the inputs or outcomes of fellow workers, such as believing they are overqualified for the job or that they find it uninteresting. Not surprisingly, the research generated by equity theory has focused on the effects of overcompensation and its effects on work.

Support for equity theory has been considerable. When workers are given an opportunity to allocate rewards for work among themselves, they tend to prefer an equitable distribution (Leventhal, Michaels, & Sanford, 1972). Workers appear to be most comfortable when they are equitably treated (Greenberg, 1987). In a field study by Greenberg (1988), support for equity theory was found: insurance company employees relocated to higher status offices raised their performance; those reassigned to lower-status offices lowered their performance levels.

*Overcompensation and Intrinsic Motivation*    Edward Deci (1975, 1980) has studied **intrinsic motivation,** *the extent to which a person wants to perform a task for its own sake.* His theory states that a task will lose some of its inherent interest if an external motivator, such as a reward, is introduced.

An interesting task will be undertaken for its own sake. That is, the motivation for performing the task is intrinsic; it lies within the individual. If the individual is paid for performing the task, it will lose some of its inherent interest. This can be seen in professional sports. Individu-als initially play a sport, say football, because it is enjoy-able and they are skilled at it. They play football because they love the game, and they will play under adverse conditions, in snow or rain, because they choose to. Once individuals are highly paid for playing football, some of the intrinsic motivation is replaced by the external condi-tion of payment. At some point, the athletes become

extrinsically motivated: they play because they are paid to play and not because they love to play.

In a study to test this hypothesis, Deci (1971) had two different campus newspaper staffs write headlines over a period of several weeks. Production records were kept for each worker. During one period, workers in one group were offered fifty cents for each headline they wrote and were told that their pay represented an effort to spend surplus funds before the end of the semester. They were told they would no longer be paid once the funds were exhausted. After this period of compensation, they returned to the no-pay system. Although there were no initial differences between the groups prior to the introduc-tion of compensation, once the compensation was with-drawn, the experimental group began to work at a signifi-cantly slower pace than the group that never received compensation.

The effects of compensation in reducing intrinsic motivation are limited to those tasks that are initially interesting to an individual, and that are undertaken for their own sake (Daniel & Esser, 1980; Harackiewicz et al., 1987; Sansone et al., 1989). If a task is not interesting, then increasing payment to perform it will not influence workers' perceptions of the task or their motivation to perform it.

Motivation to perform a task can be increased by establishing specific, moderately difficult goals, called *goal setting.* Goal setting is superior simply to asking people to "do your best" (Locke & Latham, 1990; O'Reilly, 1991). Pritchard et al. (1988) studied five intact work groups over a period of two years. They examined how goal setting, feedback, and incentives affected group productivity. Feedback increased productivity an average of fifty percent over baseline; goal setting increased productivity another twenty-five percent. Adding incen-tives increased productivity still further.

## Effects of Unemployment

Children are asked what they are going to be when they grow up. When students are asked what they are majoring in, it is usually with the aim of judging their future careers. Work is an important part of people's self-concept. The importance of work is never so clearly seen as when people are out of work. When workers are unemployed as a result of layoffs, their views of themselves may change dramatically (Kelvin & Jarrett, 1985; Warr & Jackson, 1984).

Joblessness influences not only the person without work but the person's family and the community in which the person lives. Unemployment touches nearly every aspect of family and community life and results "in higher divorce rates, increased incidence of alcoholism and drug abuse, child and spouse abuse, and juvenile delinquency," according to Senator Donald Riegle of Michigan (1982). A 1 percent rise in long-term unemployment is related to a 4.1 percent increase in suicides, a 5.7 percent increase in homicides, an almost 2 percent increase in heart disease and other stress-related disorders, and to an increased rate of psychiatric hospital admissions (Brenner, 1973, 1976). (See chapter 14, Health Psychology, for a discussion of the effects of unemployment on health.)

Two studies followed unemployed workers over long periods of time (Liem & Liem, 1979; Liem & Rayman, 1982). This afforded an opportunity to examine the effects of reemployment and long-term unemployment. Liem and Liem (1979) studied forty blue-collar families and forty white-collar families in which the husband was involuntarily without work. Each family was matched with an employed control in terms of occupation, the working status of the wife, locality, and number of children. Being without work was strongly associated with higher levels of psychiatric symptoms. Following reemployment, these symptoms diminished to a level below that of the controls. Interestingly, the researchers reported that the wives of unemployed husbands also suffered severe symptoms. They were significantly more depressed, anxious, phobic, and sensitive about their personal relationships than were the wives of working spouses.

A study called The Hartford Project examined the aircraft industry (Rayman & Bluestone, 1982). The majority of workers who experienced joblessness during any portion of a ten-year period showed signs of serious physical or emotional strain. "High blood pressure, alcoholism, increased smoking, insomnia, neurasthenia, and worry and anxiety were among the more commonly reported forms of strain. Middle-aged heads of households with young dependents experienced more intense stress effects than younger, single workers." This last finding makes it clear that the impact of joblessness depends upon age and marital and family status.

There seem to be regular, predictable reactions to job loss (Kelvin & Jarrett, 1985). When people are first unemployed, they experience shock, anger, and incomprehension. They then experience optimism, a feeling of being between jobs, a kind of vacation, although with

active job searching. Pessimism follows as job search is unsuccessful. People become worried about money and the future. Hopelessness and apathy follow, and the individual ceases to look for work.

▶ **GUIDED REVIEW** *Learning Objectives 1, 2, 3, and 4*

1. _____ is the performance of tasks in exchange for compensation.
2. _____ activities are set by the individual actor(s).
3. Three theories of worker motivation are _____, _____, and _____.
4. The _____ states that there are two innate sets of needs, _____ and _____. The former consist of external factors, such as pay and work conditions. The latter stem from within the individual and include the need for creativity and independence.
5. The _____ states that a person makes a comparison between his or her output/input ratio and the output/input ratios of others in similar positions. When these two ratios are not equal, inequity exists. This motivates the individual to attempt to restore equity (working more or less hard) or outcomes (asking for a raise, going on strike).
6. Equity can be restored by _____ or _____.
7. The equity theory leads to the interesting hypothesis that _____ creates inequity. Overcompensation may undermine the _____ to perform a task.
8. _____ influences people's emotional and physical well-being, as well as homicide, family violence, and hospital admission rates.
9. The effects of unemployment depend to some extent on _____ and _____ and _____ status.

*ANSWERS*

*1. Work 2. Leisure 3. Herzberg's two-factor theory, Vroom's valence-instrumentality-expectancy theory, equity theory 4. two-factor theory, hygiene needs, motivator needs 5. equity theory 6. altering inputs, outcomes 7. overcompensation, intrinsic motivation 8. Unemployment 9. age, marital, family*

# THE NATURE OF ORGANIZATIONS

IBM, the University of Oklahoma, the National Football League, the FBI, and the Catholic church are all formal organizations that have many features in common: an organizational structure or bureaucracy, formal and informal channels of communication, a division of labor, methods for recruiting new members and replacing old ones, goals to be accomplished and means for accomplishing them. Organizations are deliberately planned for the purpose of reaching particular objectives.

Even though many organizations discourage emotional bonds among members, for fear that emotional ties will undermine both judgment and discipline (Collins, 1983), informal social attachments nevertheless form, and friendship groups and social cliques can be found in all large organizations. Therefore, it is important when trying to understand an organization to consider its informal as well as its formal operation.

## Bureaucracy: Formal Structure

One feature of formal organizations is **bureaucracy,** *the relationships among individuals responsible for attaining the goals of the organization and for maintaining the organization itself.* Although popular usage tends to associate bureaucracy with "red tape" and inefficiency, the German sociologist Max Weber (1957) believed that modern bureaucracy was the most efficient way of organizing large numbers of people for the attainment of complex tasks. By making human activity regular, orderly, and predictable, bureaucracy exists to ensure the conditions necessary for efficient work. Whether or not this efficiency is achieved depends on factors of the informal and formal organization.

The formal bureaucratic structure of an organization, whether it is a business, an educational institution, a branch of government, or a social club, ensures that individuals have specialized jobs to perform. This *specialization of roles is known as the* **division of labor.** The work of the organization is divided into smaller tasks, and each individual becomes responsible for performing certain tasks. When each individual performs his or her job, the goals of the organization are reached.

In a small, traditional business, in contrast to the bureaucratic organization, a person would have to purchase the raw material, shape it into a new product, market the product, keep records of these transactions, and be able to maintain the facilities and equipment of the business. In the modern bureaucracy, an individual is apt to specialize in marketing, purchasing, accounting, maintenance, or personnel, and have no knowledge of the other specialties. There are obvious drawbacks to this specialization, such as monotony and inability to change jobs without retraining. On the other hand, the formal structure and explicit demands of each position enable one to train for a specific job (Argyris, 1964).

## Informal Social Structure

The formal organization specifies the requirements and tasks of its members, but there exists a parallel and often unseen informal organization that sets its own requirements and standards. Within a large organization, there are informal groups with no official structure or function. Coworkers who eat lunch together constitute such an informal social group. Probably the first recognition that informal groups exist within large organizations and exert influence on workers came from the Hawthorne experiments.

*The Hawthorne Experiments*    Beginning in the mid-1920s and continuing for ten years, a group of psychologists from Harvard University studied productivity and worker morale at the Western Electric plant in Chicago (Roethlisberger & Dickson, 1939; Mayo, 1945). In one study, the researchers examined how changes in illumination influenced worker output. Sometimes lighting in the workplace was increased; sometimes it was diminished. Each time the lighting changed, whether it became brighter or dimmer, productivity was found to increase. In other studies, women who assembled electrical relays or men who wired equipment were studied intensively over several months. Their rest periods, hours of working, days off, and pay incentives were systematically varied to determine the optimum work-rest ratios. Sometimes changes were made in worker-management relations, and worker participation in decision making. Regardless of the type of change made, productivity increased as the studies progressed.

Why would either increasing or decreasing the lighting raise productivity? Perhaps employees worked harder because they wanted to please the researchers. The researchers concluded that increased productivity was due to the fact that the workers were observed, and not the result of the other changes that were made. This is known as the **Hawthorne effect,** *the research itself is responsible for the results.*

The researchers also found that informal norms among workers set the standards for productivity. As a result, it became clear that attention must be paid to the social conditions and social relations of workers. These beliefs gave rise to the **human relations movement** in industry, *the idea that the informal social and psychological conditions of workers* (in addition to pay, benefits, and physical conditions) *influence productivity.* (See Exploring Human Diversity: The Japanese Style of Work.)

Despite the revolution in industry that resulted from the Hawthorne studies, the studies themselves and the investigators who conducted them have been critically examined

# EXPLORING HUMAN DIVERSITY

## The Japanese Style of Work

When Americans speak of international competitiveness, it is usually Japanese industry that comes to mind as its major competitor. How does the Japanese way of working differ from the traditional American way? Michael Argyle (1989) has described the Japanese style of work.

### Selection and Training

In Japan, competition for employment at the larger firms is keen because they offer good salaries, excellent social benefits, and status. Depending upon their education and examination results, people enter more or less prestigious firms at different levels. A college graduate enters at a middle management position and is slowly promoted through the hierarchy. Management trainees live for six months at a training center under "a disciplined and spartan regime," which includes team sports and martial arts training. They are also trained in leadership and interpersonal skills, as well as in technical matters (Tanaka, 1980).

### Lifetime Employment and Commitment

Employees, even those at the lowest ranks, have a feeling of sharing in the collective success of the firm. A strong feeling of identification is created, since many employees spend their whole careers with the firm and live in company houses. In some firms, the day is started by singing the company song.

Argyle notes that it has been widely reported that Japanese firms guarantee employment to age fifty-five. In fact, this is true of only about one-third of workers, those in the leading firms.

### Wages and Promotion

Wages depend primarily on age, length of service, education, and position with the firm. Managers are paid only about fifty percent more than manual workers. In addition to their pay, employees receive free meals, low-rent housing, cheap medical services, schools for their children, a pension, and other benefits. Little use is made of wage incentives. In exchange for these benefits, employees have a sense of loyalty and commitment to the firm.

### Work Groups

Japanese workers are encouraged to feel part of a team. Supervisors take an interest in the well-being of their subordinates, who, in turn, accept the supervisor's involvement with life off the job, including marriage.

### Supervision

Supervisors in Japan are expected to provide a special sort of leadership, based on the *ringi* method. This involves informal consulting prior to making a decision (Smith, 1984). Relations with subordinates are handled "with some subtlety," and much use is made of small face-saving hints (Pascale & Athos, 1982).

### Managerial Hierarchy

There are many assistant managers at every level, with overlapping authority (so there is little individual responsibility). The large number of managers is partly the result of a promotion policy based on seniority and the practice of not firing anyone. Managers are respected because they are known to have earned their position by years of service, educational qualifications, and technical expertise. On the other hand, managers eat in the same dining room, wear similar clothes, and do not earn a great deal more than their subordinates.

In Japan, there is close cooperation between industry and government. A sense of nationalism adds to the motivation of Japanese workers (Schein, 1981).

Many Japanese firms have factories in the United States and Britain. Most use a selective, watered-down version of Japanese practices which Ouchi (1981) called "Theory Z." This includes lifetime employment, slower rates of promotion, less formal leadership, concern for the whole person, less specialization, group decision-making, and responsibility to the firm.

How do these firms compare in effectiveness with American- and British-managed companies? "The evidence suggests that in the Japanese firms productivity is generally greater, and quality certainly is, while absenteeism is less; however, job satisfaction is no higher" (Argyle, 1989, p. 334; Smith, 1984).

---

(Bramel & Friend, 1981). Upon closer scrutiny, some of the studies in which increased productivity was reported did not show increased productivity at all (Franke & Kaul, 1978). In one study, the employees were required to work longer hours over a period of a few weeks. It was reported that their productivity increased, but that was true only for their total work output. If one examines output *per hour*, productivity actually decreased. Despite such criticisms, the fact remains that Mayo and his colleagues pointed to the existence and importance of informal structures, such as friendship groups, within the formal organization. Researchers now pay attention to informal social groups as well as to the formal structure of organizations.

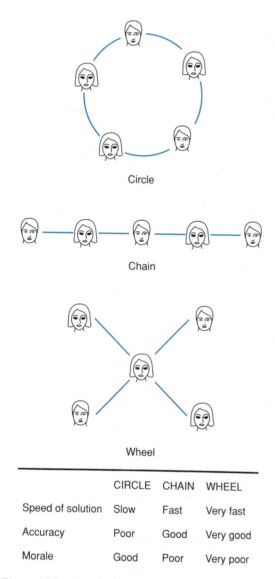

Circle

Chain

Wheel

|  | CIRCLE | CHAIN | WHEEL |
|---|---|---|---|
| Speed of solution | Slow | Fast | Very fast |
| Accuracy | Poor | Good | Very good |
| Morale | Good | Poor | Very poor |

**Figure 16.1** *Communication networks*

## Communication in Organizations

The larger an organization, the more complex and elaborate are communications between members. To facilitate communication, formal **communication networks** may be established *in which each individual is permitted to communicate only with specified other members of the organization.* Communications with the company vice-president or with someone in the marketing department may be difficult or prohibited. In the military, an official chain of command establishes who may communicate with whom. Some communication networks are shown in figure 16.1.

*Informal Social Communication*    Communications in organizations do not always follow the formal structure of the communication network. In contrast to formal communications, which tend to be about productivity and organizational problems, informal communications include "small talk," gossip, and joking.

Bales (1970) developed Interaction Process Analysis, a procedure that enables trained observers to categorize each communication that occurs during a group meeting. Bales arranged for several people to discuss a complex problem while being observed through a one-way screen. Each statement, question, or gesture (termed an *act*) was recorded. Acts were divided into task relations (those concerned with solving a problem) and socio-emotional relations (those unrelated to the task).

In a typical group session, there are between fifteen and twenty acts per minute. About half of these acts are pertinent to the problem. Typically, during the first third of the meeting, the most frequent act tends to be giving information about the problem. During the middle portion of the meeting, opinions are offered about the problem and possible solutions. Suggestions for solving the problem are most common in the last third of a session. Acts tend to alternate between socio-emotional and task-related communications. When too much emphasis is given to the problem, socio-emotional relations become strained and emphasis is placed on interpersonal relations.

There is often someone in a group who injects jokes and unrelated comments throughout the course of a meeting. Rather than being an irrelevant distraction, such people help the group move closer to its goal of solving a problem with the least amount of conflict. These "socio-emotional specialists" are an important part of an effective group; their wisecracks smooth over interpersonal relations in the group. In studies of staff conferences at psychiatric hospitals, joking occurs frequently—about once every ten minutes (Goodrich, Henry, & Goodrich, 1954). These jokes are usually directed at peers and tend to be made at the expense of a subordinate. The jokes reflect and help reinforce the structure of the group; psychiatrists joke about nurses, nurses joke about the volunteer staff, and just about everyone jokes about the patients (Chapman, 1983; Coser, 1960).

## Personnel Selection

When people apply for jobs, they have already done some preliminary assessments of the job's requirements and their ability to fulfill those requirements. There are usually more applicants for a position than there are openings, so additional screening must occur before a post is filled.

Psychologists' use of reliable and valid tests and measures for the selection, training, and assessment of personnel has improved both workers' satisfaction with their jobs and their productivity (Tornetsky & Solomon, 1982). Psychological assessment methods predict performance well enough to have practical value for an employer (Ghiselli, 1966). One study found that the use of a test with .5 validity to select computer programmers could result in greater productivity equivalent to $36,800 per year for each computer programmer (Schmidt, Hunter, McKenzie, & Muldrow, 1979).

---

▶ **GUIDED REVIEW** *Learning Objectives 5 and 6*

1. Organizations are characterized by a _____, systems of communication, division of labor, goals, and means for achieving the goals.
2. Within every large formal organization there are cliques and groups of friends. These _____ exert considerable influence on the overall functioning of the organization.
3. _____ gave rise to the focus on social relations in industry. According to Mayo and his colleagues, the mere act of studying workers was found to increase productivity. This is known as the _____.
4. Organizations may have formal _____, which differ in the _____ and _____ of each member. For simple problems, centralized networks, such as the wheel, are superior. Satisfaction is highest in networks that maximize an individual's independence.
5. _____ enhance the morale of a group, strengthen the group's structure, and enforce its norms.
6. The use of scientifically developed tests to _____ is one contribution of psychology to organizational effectiveness.

*ANSWERS*

*1. bureaucratic structure 2. informal social groups 3. The Hawthorne experiments, Hawthorne effect 4. communication networks, centrality, independence 5. Informal communications 6. select personnel*

---

# HUMAN FACTORS

The primary aim of the field known as **human factors** *is to design equipment and systems that increase the effectiveness, comfort, safety, and productivity of the people using them.* The reduction of human error through proper design is an important goal. A favorite saying among human factors researchers is, "To err is human; to

forgive, design." A large amount of human factors research is conducted after it is clear that a system has design problems (Senders & Moray, 1991).

Before equipment or complex systems that reduce human error can be designed, researchers need to know a great deal about human beings: their sensory systems, their cognitive abilities, their motor systems, and their limitations. They also need to have some understanding of people's psychological and social needs. In the past, engineers used their own abilities and inclinations as guides for the design of equipment, but this approach produced much equipment that was unsuitable for a large number of workers. A more appropriate approach is to study the capabilities and limitations of human workers and design equipment to those needs and specifications (Norman, 1988).

## Information Input

Human beings have five senses through which they can receive information. To design an effective system, such as a control panel, researchers need to know more than just the basics about the sensory systems. They must know the capacity of each system and the capability each system has to discriminate between similar stimuli. Most of the information supplied in complex systems comes through the visual and auditory channels; consequently, most human factors research concentrates on those senses.

*Visual Information*     Even though the speedometer of a car offers visual information, a designer might choose to design one with another sensory mode. The speedometer might have an auditory channel that produces a tone that varies in pitch for different speeds. When the car goes faster, the pitch becomes higher. Even without field testing this hypothetical piece of equipment, many people would be able to spot some deadly flaws. For one thing, the noise would annoy any driver and might mask honking horns, police sirens, or the music on the radio. Also, drivers would know when the speed of their car was changing, but they would not know precisely what their speed was if it was constant. A visual display of some kind is a better solution.

Figure 16.2 shows some possible speedometers. An engineer might simply arbitrarily choose one that seems "best," but a human factors researcher would test each design before making any decisions. In an actual study that tested the usefulness and readability of these different kinds of speedometers, sixty subjects read each of the five

# APPLYING PSYCHOLOGY

## Motivating Economic Achievement

Much work by industrial psychologists is limited to small-scale changes in an industry or organization. An exception to this is the work of David McClelland and David Winter (1971), who attempted to influence economic productivity in underdeveloped countries by changing people's motivations and aspirations.

McClelland and his colleagues had found that individuals with high achievement needs tend to be more enterprising, set moderately difficult goals for themselves, were interested in success for its own sake rather than for money or power, were more interested in concrete feedback on how well they perform a task, and had a greater future time perspective than those with low achievement needs. McClelland and Winter wanted to test this theory by trying to influence the achievement-motivation levels of businessmen in economically underdeveloped areas. They reasoned that an increase in the levels of need for achievement among businessmen would lead to more enterprising behavior, which would lead to the opening of more businesses and the hiring of more workers, all to the economic benefit of the community.

They gave a course designed to increase the need for achievement in Andhra Pradesh, India. The course was given to some businessmen (others in the town constituted a control group). Businessmen in a comparable town in the same state served as a second control group. Data from the experimental town of Kakinada and the control town of Rajahmundry were collected over a period of five years, beginning two years before the training commenced.

The course consisted of ten days of training in four specific types of behavior.

1. *Achievement syndrome*. The participants were trained to recognize and produce fantasies and stories related to a high need for achievement. It is through an analysis of such stories that a person's level of achievement need is measured.

2. *Self study*. The participants were given various assignments in which they had to relate the material from the classroom to their personal and business lives. As McClelland and Winter note, "The scientific implication of the research findings is inescapable. If they want to do a better entrepreneurial job, then the scientific evidence shows that the means to that end is to learn to think, talk, and act like a person with high need achievement." (p. 59)

3. *Goal setting*. Participants learned to set goals for themselves that reflected a high need for achievement—goals that were moderately difficult to attain. The goal setting included training in various types of games, such as ring-toss, in which an individual could make the task easy by standing close to the pegs or make it difficult by standing

a great distance away. Participants in the course learned to set moderately difficult goals in this and other tasks.

4. *Interpersonal supports*. The course participants quickly formed a close-knit group in which they reinforced and supported one another.

What were the effects of this ten-day training? There were two types of dependent measure in this study: individual measures of the participants' behavior and economic measures of the impact of the course on the town of Kakinada. The participants in achievement motivation courses showed significant improvement in many aspects of entrepreneurial performance, both as compared with themselves before the course and as compared with the control groups. Course participants showed more active business behavior. Participants in the training course worked longer hours, made more investments in new and fixed capital, employed more workers, and had increased gross income in their firms. About 135 new jobs were created in Kakinada. Some of the economic effects of the training are shown in table 16.A.

The effects of this brief training in need for achievement persisted for several years and had a lasting impact on the economic well-being of the town of Kakinada (McClelland & Winter, 1971). Naturally, training in achievement motivation is not a panacea for economic ills. The training was more effective for participants who were initially most dissatisfied with themselves and who believed that they might be able to solve some of their economic problems. The course provided these individuals with some of the skills and attitudes necessary to solve these problems. (Achievement motivation is explored in more detail in chapter 8.)

TABLE 16.A **Some economic effects of training in achievement motivation**

|  | Before the Course | After the Course |
| --- | --- | --- |
| *Percent Working Longer Hours* | | |
| Trained (n = 61) | 7 | 20 |
| Controls (n = 44) | 11 | 7 |
| *Percent Starting New Businesses* | | |
| Trained (n = 51) | 6 | 27 |
| Kakinada controls (n = 22) | 5 | 5 |
| Other controls (n = 35) | 9 | 14 |
| *Percent in Charge of Firm* | | |
| Trained (n = 33) | 32 | 58 |
| Kakinada controls (n = 14) | 23 | 21 |
| Other controls (n = 24) | 35 | 42 |

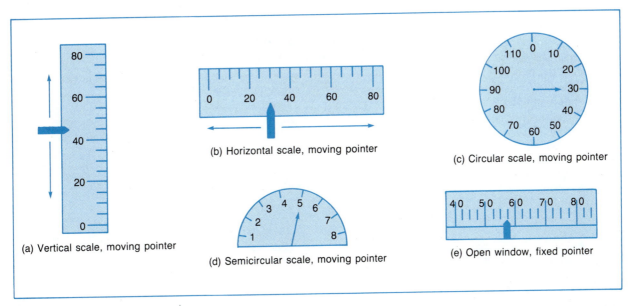

**Figure 16.2** *Possible speedometers*

types of dials seventeen times. For each reading, the subject could look at the dial for only 0.12 seconds (Sleight, 1948). Table 16.3 shows the average errors of the subjects. The open window design clearly had the advantage; subjects made far fewer errors when they read this kind of dial. (If you drive, you know that the engineers who designed your speedometer probably did not read this study.)

The error people might make in reading their car's speed would probably not be a large one and might earn them only a speeding ticket. However, the type of dial used in cockpits to display the altitude of a plane has probably been misread many times. Pilots believe it presents a dangerous hazard and should be redesigned.

Altitude is commonly displayed on a three-pointer dial. This circular display has three hands, like those of a clock. The hands represent altitudes of 10,000, 1,000, and 100 feet, much as the hands of a clock represent hours, minutes, and seconds. Studies of this dial have shown over and over again that pilots take longer to read it and make many more errors than with other types of dials (Hill & Chernikoff, 1965). Pilots have registered many complaints about these cumbersome and dangerous three-pointer altimeters, but improvements have been made very slowly.

The display of visual information has become an increasingly important issue because people who speak different languages must interact with one another frequently. Subway ticket vendors, people who design

| **TABLE 16.3  Percent errors made in trying to read various kinds of dials** | |
|---|---|
| **Type of Dial** | **Percent Error** |
| Vertical | 35.5 |
| Horizontal | 27.5 |
| Circular | 10.9 |
| Semicircular | 16.6 |
| Open window (fixed pointer) | 0.5 |

Source: R. B. Sleight, "The Effect of Instrument Dial Shape on Legibility" in *Journal of Applied Psychology*, 32:170–188, 1948. Copyright © 1948 American Psychological Association.

signs for airports, and tourist information booths, for example, must choose symbols carefully to ensure that speakers of other languages can easily understand them. Close Up On Research: Research on Symbols describes how some of these signs are developed.

*Auditory Displays*    In complex systems, auditory displays can be particularly appropriate for certain functions. They can emit warning signals to attract attention, and they can be useful when the operator is moving from one place to another. They have certain advantages over visual displays, such as their high discriminability in low lighting. They also have some disadvantages: they transmit sequential information, and because of this they cannot easily provide the operator with information that changes over time.

# CLOSE UP ON RESEARCH
## Research on Symbols

An important function of research in human factors is the assessment of the usefulness of international symbols designed to communicate information to people who speak different languages. Ideally, this research is conducted before symbols are adopted. Then when the symbols are adopted, they will communicate the correct message to the greatest number of people, and they will be uniform worldwide.

The understandability and meaning of symbols has been assessed in a variety of ways. Some experiments show subjects a series of symbols, perhaps on slides or in a booklet, and ask them to provide short definitions for each symbol. This provides insight into the kinds of misunderstandings likely to arise from each kind of symbol. Another way to assess understandability is to show subjects a variety of symbols for a specific message and ask them which one they prefer. A third approach is to let subjects choose the meanings for a particular symbol from a list.

The National Bureau of Standards conducted research on symbols that relate to fire safety (Collins & Lerner, 1982) (figure 16.A). The researchers used several approaches to assess the usefulness of various symbols, including asking subjects to write short definitions, asking them to choose the correct definition from a short list, and asking them to provide their own symbols for specific fire-safety messages such as "Fire Extinguisher," "No Smoking," "Do Not Lock," and "Fire Exit."

The results of the study demonstrated that the symbols varied considerably in understandability. Some symbols, like the one for "Do Not Block," were misunderstood by practically everyone. Others, like the symbol for "Fire Extinguisher," were understood by nearly everyone. (The percent of correct responses on the multiple-choice test is given below each of the symbols.) Studies such as this point to the importance of testing symbols for understandability *before* they are widely adopted.

**Figure 16.A** *Symbols for fire-safety alerting*

Examples of auditory displays in common use include sirens on ambulances, police cars, and fire engines; ringing noises at railroad crossings; beeping sounds made by trucks in reverse gear; and smoke-alarm signals in homes. Auditory signaling is also frequently and effectively used to transmit nonemergency information. Sonar equipment transmits high-frequency sounds underwater, and operators listen for the returning signal.

Whether the frequency of the return signal is higher, lower, or the same as the one originally transmitted depends on whether the object it intercepted is moving closer to, moving away from, or remaining the same distance from the transmitting source.

One set of studies for the Air Force suggested that auditory signals could transmit more information than most people believed (Licklider, 1961). Most Air Force warning signals were simply one repeated loud noise. The research sought to determine whether the signal could incorporate two or three pieces of information: one that signaled emergency, a second that signaled the type of emergency, and a third that signaled what action should be taken. This research found that one loud noise to attract attention and to identify the type of emergency followed by a second noise that directed action would be easily understood and would communicate more information.

*Smell, Taste, and Touch*    Studies on information input through these channels are scarce. Tactual information, in particular, is underused in complex systems. Knobs that control several different functions are often the same size and shape and differ only in their visual label. Accident reports from aircraft sometimes indicate that the pilot mistook one control, such as the landing gears, for another, such as the flaps lever. Controls can be coded by color, but a pilot or other equipment operator usually has little time for a visual search or is concentrating on visual displays elsewhere on the control panel. Errors might be reduced if frequently confused controls were given different shapes (triangles, squares) or textures (bumpy, smooth, or saw-toothed). In a nuclear power plant, for example, all the knobs that affect the coolant system could be square, and those that affect the steam generators could be oval.

Research on tactual discriminability has been conducted on blindfolded subjects in an effort to improve the design of complex control panels (Jenkins, 1947). Handles and

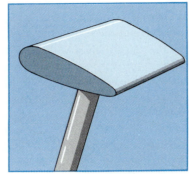

Landing flap          Landing gear

**Figure 16.3**    *Controls related in form to their function and designed to be easily distinguished by touch.*
From McCormick & Ilgen, Industrial Psychology, 7/E, © 1980, p. 353. Reprinted by permission of Prentice-Hall, Inc. Englewood Cliffs, NJ.

knobs for different levers and controls are given different shapes. Some control panels of aircraft take this concept one step further by having the control knob bear some relationship to its function. The control for the flaps is shaped like a flap, and the control for the landing gear resembles a wheel (figure 16.3). The transmission of information through the sense of touch offers the potential for correct identification without asking the operators to take their eyes away from other displays, but it does take longer than visual identification.

## Motor Output

Designing equipment and environments so that they take advantage of human motor skills and make up for human deficiencies is an important part of human factors research. Most pieces of equipment evolve through trial and error. The hammer probably began as nothing but a heavy weight on a stick. As humans used the tool, they modified it to accommodate to the average strength of ordinary humans as well as to the size and contrariness of nails.

The design of a child's schoolbag illustrates the importance of considering human motor output. An early study compared the amount of oxygen consumed by children carrying six pounds of weight in a schoolbag in one of four ways: a knapsack carried across the upper back, a bag carried across the lower back, a bag carried across the shoulder, and a bag carried by the hand. The knapsack carried across the upper back was clearly superior. Compared to carrying the knapsack, children consumed thirty-seven percent more oxygen when carrying a bag across the lower back, eighty-two percent more oxygen when carrying a shoulder bag, and one hundred forty-one percent more oxygen when carrying a schoolbag by the hand (Malhotra & Sengupta, 1965). A simple study like this could mean the difference between a child who is too tired to do homework at night and one who has enough energy to do homework, dry the dishes, and play baseball.

The design of computers also illustrates the importance of considering human motor skills. As computers enter every phase of human life, the ability to type becomes more important. The most common arrangement for letters on the keyboard is the "qwerty" style, originally designed by the Sholes brothers in 1873. Their aim was to keep frequently used keys far apart and thereby *slow down* the typist to minimize the jamming of type bars in their early typewriter design. Unlike the Sholes model, the Dvorak keyboard was designed with human factors principles in mind; the layout of keys minimizes hand and finger motion (Dvorak, 1943). One study compared the efficiency of alphabetically arranged keyboard layouts to those randomly arranged for non-typists (Norman & Fisher, 1982). After a pretest on the Sholes board to ensure they really could not type more than twenty-five words per minute, subjects were tested for ten minutes on two alphabetic keyboards and one random keyboard. The number of words typed, the number of errors, and the subjects' preferences for each keyboard were recorded. In terms of the number of words typed, the subjects performed about 10 percent better on the alphabetic keyboard arrangements than on the random keyboard.

Human beings can carry fairly heavy loads if the loads are positioned properly on the body. They can read dials and manipulate controls designed with human sensory systems and information processing abilities in mind. They can work long hours, but they must sleep. Thus, the design of equipment and jobs must take into account both human abilities and human limitations. It might seem that two people working at adjacent desks should perform equally well whether their desks are facing one another or facing away from one another. Depending on the jobs they are performing, however, these two different desk arrangements could have vastly different impacts on efficiency and productivity.

*Case Study: Three Mile Island*    The tragedy at Three Mile Island preceded the Chernobyl nuclear reactor disaster and captured worldwide attention. The incident was a sobering reminder that human beings make mistakes

and that some systems are more "accident-provocative" than others. The more complicated and the more poorly designed the systems in which humans are working, the more mistakes operators are likely to make.

Much human factors research is based on the analysis of accidents. Most complicated systems are designed by engineers, and human factors specialists are usually not consulted until humans begin making mistakes in the system. When the error costs many lives, people wonder why the system was not better designed in the first place. (The psychological impact of Three Mile Island and other catastrophic accidents is discussed in chapter 14, Health Psychology.)

The review team's evaluation of the Three Mile Island incident listed several human errors, most of which could have been prevented or reduced by appropriate system design. One major error occurred because the indicator light for a relief valve, which was actually open, showed that the valve was closed throughout the accident. The operators wrongly assumed that the valve was closed. They should have checked other indicators that would have told them the indicator light was malfunctioning.

Another important error occurred when the steam generators boiled dry. This dangerous event went unnoticed in the general confusion. The operators at Three Mile Island failed to diagnose the problem until it became a major accident. Their failure was partly due to their lack of training, particularly in nuclear power technology. At that time, operators needed only a high-school degree and minimal training to enter the control room. Instead of being trained to diagnose trouble and solve problems, they learned to follow a list of emergency procedures.

When the accident started, more than one hundred alarms went off. Under normal conditions, as many as fifty alarms might be ringing. This circumstance first created confusion, but it also might have engendered complacency in the face of constant alarms. The operators may have been legitimately confused about whether the incident was truly an emergency.

Many important control panels were mounted on the back of the consoles, facing *away* from the operators. The critical dials were not grouped together; they were scattered all over the room. An important valve in the steam cooling system had to be adjusted manually by the senior operator. This task removed him from the control room for more than forty-five minutes.

Review teams have since visited other nuclear plants and have found many design problems that make it more likely that human operators could make mistakes. In some places a red light meant that a valve was open; in others it meant that it was closed. A lever pulled down in one system closed a valve; in another system, it opened a valve.

An important development in nuclear power plant technology is the use of simulators to test equipment and operators. During simulated emergencies, operators must diagnose problems and develop solutions. This kind of simulation gives operators a chance to develop their problem-solving skills and trains them to do it under some stress, stress they would face in a real emergency.

▶ **GUIDED REVIEW** *Learning Objectives 7 and 8*

1. The field of _____ attempts to improve the efficiency, productivity, comfort, and safety of human beings operating complex man-machine systems. Its main approach to design takes the abilities and limitations of humans into account.
2. Human factors assumes that people will make mistakes, but that they will make fewer mistakes in systems that recognize the nature of the _____.
3. Aspects of _____ capabilities, such as perception, reasoning, thinking, decision making, and memory, all affect the efficiency with which humans interact with equipment.

*ANSWERS*

1. human factors 2. human operator 3. human information processing

# ENVIRONMENTAL PSYCHOLOGY

**Environmental psychology** is *the study of the relationship between behavior and the natural and constructed environment.* Environmental psychology focuses on the human use of space, the effects of environmental noise, temperature, and pollution, and environmental and energy conservation (Proshansky, Ittelson, & Rivlin, 1970; Bernard, 1991). (See Applying Psychology: Using Environmental Psychology to Catch a Rapist.)

## Personal Space and Territoriality

Although human beings tend to seek the company of others, they also require a certain amount of privacy and solitude (Altman, 1975). One way to achieve privacy while still in the presence of others is to regulate distance, both physically and psychologically.

**Personal space** is *the area individuals actively maintain around themselves* into which others cannot intrude without arousing discomfort (Hayduk, 1978). The term was popularized by the psychologist Robert Sommer (1959, 1967). Personal space may be thought of as an "invisible bubble" surrounding a person that encloses space regarded as private. The shape and size of this bubble change with the circumstances. If an individual is walking down a crowded city street, personal space may contract, thus permitting intrusions of only an inch on either side. For a person sitting in a public library, personal space may consist of several feet in all directions. Personal space also varies from one culture to another (Hall, 1966; Jones & Aiello, 1973).

Personal space is a matter of continually regulating distance. People feel uncomfortable when others intrude upon their personal space. They try to reduce this discomfort by defending or reestablishing their personal space. Territory is a fixed area that a person uses regularly and regards as his or her own (Edney, 1974). A person can leave a territory and return to it later but he or she cannot leave personal space, since it moves with the person. **Territoriality** *refers to behavior designed to preserve a particular territory,* such as one's home.

Norms about personal space are learned early, by about age ten in America (Eberts & Lepper, 1975; Guardo, 1969; Scherer, 1974). Different cultures have different standards for personal space. When people stand too close or too far away while speaking with others, they feel uncomfortable and attempt to establish a comfortable distance. Consider an informal conversation between two individuals, one British, the other American. Cultural norms impel the British person to feel most comfortable with greater distance between himself or herself and the other speaker. The American might feel that the British person, in moving away, is "aloof" or "cold." In attempting to establish a closer, more comfortable personal distance, the American may appear rude and aggressive to the Briton (Hall, 1959, 1966).

In one cross-cultural study, over 20,000 pedestrians were observed in cities in the United States, Europe, and the Middle East. Table 16.4 shows the percentage of those who were in physical contact with their companions (Berkowitz, 1971). Clearly, there is considerable variation in the extent of contact.

Circumstances sometimes force people into close contact, or prevent them from achieving a desired level of intimacy. What do people do in such circumstances?

| TABLE 16.4 Percentage of pedestrians in groups who were also in contact | |
|---|---|
| Country | Percent in Contact |
| Sweden | 18.1 |
| United States | 19.4 |
| Middle East | 15.4 |
| England | 24.1 |
| W. Germany | 26.4 |
| Italy | 29.8 |

From W. R. Berkowitz, "A Cross National Comparison of Some Social Patterns of Urban Pedestrians" in *Journal of Cross-Cultural Psychology*, 2:129–144. Copyright © 1971 by Sage Publications, Inc. Reprinted by permission.

**Equilibrium theory** *maintains that personal space or distance between individuals is a component of intimacy* (Argyle & Dean, 1965). An intimate couple will discuss personal topics, engage in frequent eye contact, and minimize personal distance. If something interferes with any of these mechanisms for expressing intimacy, there will be a tendency to compensate by changing the other mechanisms. For example, if a person is prevented from standing close to an intimate acquaintance, compensation might take the form of increased eye contact. Thus, the same level of intimacy is expressed by striking a balance between distance, eye contact, and discussion topic.

By definition, personal space is that distance whose violation by another causes feelings of discomfort. If this discomfort occurs, a person will attempt to reduce the discomfort by withdrawing or attempting to drive off the intruder. In studies conducted at a university library, people took certain defensive actions to prevent spatial invasion (Sommer, 1969). When asked where a person would sit at a rectangular table with six, eight, or ten chairs, students predicted they would sit in a location that would discourage others from sitting at the same table (figure 16.4). When the students left their chairs temporarily, they placed various kinds of "markers" such as a book or a jacket, to signal that the chairs were occupied. When such markers were used in a library, the chairs were never occupied by someone else.

Individuals feel uncomfortable not only when their personal space has been invaded by others but also when circumstances force them to violate the personal space of others (Efran & Cheyne, 1974). Imagine how you would feel if an usher told you to sit next to a stranger in an almost-empty theater.

**Figure 16.4**  *Personal space expands and contracts depending on available space.*

## Environmental Stressors

An important part of environmental psychology investigates the effects of environmental stressors, such as noise, air pollution, and extreme temperatures. Noise, in particular, cries out for attention. In the laboratory, loud noise produces a range of effects on cognitive processes, physiology, and motivation. Noise is associated with decrements in performance, decreased sensitivity to others, higher blood pressure, and increased adrenaline secretion (Broadbent, 1978; Cohen & Lezak, 1977). If the noise is unpredictable and uncontrollable, its effects on behavior and physiology are greater (Glass & Singer, 1972).

In order to make reasonable policies about allowable levels of noise ("noise pollution"), it is helpful first to know its effects. A field study examined the effects of aircraft noise on children attending elementary schools in the air corridor of Los Angeles International Airport (Cohen, Evans, Krantz, & Stokols, 1980). Planes fly overhead about every two and one-half minutes during school hours and noise levels in these areas reach peaks as high as ninety-five decibels. The behavior of the children attending these schools was compared to the behavior of children in three control schools matched for grade level, ethnic and racial distribution, and other variables.

# APPLYING PSYCHOLOGY

## Using Environmental Psychology to Catch a Rapist

In February, 1988, an English court sentenced John Duffy to serve at least thirty years in prison for five rapes and two murders. His arrest was made easier with the help of a psychological and social profile developed by psychologists at the University of Surrey in England. David Canter headed the team that developed a description of the likely assailant.

Social science research usually takes people whose occupation, age, sex, and other traits are known and predicts how they will behave. In police investigations, this procedure is reversed: the aim is to take behavior, in this case a series of rapes and murders, and formulate a prediction about the offender's age, sex, occupation, and other distinguishing characteristics (Canter, 1988).

"Broadly speaking, we have found that four different approaches to the offender have real potential for creating a profile, each drawing upon different psychological theories and methods. Possibly the most intriguing and immediately useful approach is to draw upon ideas from environmental psychology." Environmental psychologists know that people develop cognitive or mental maps of places. In the case of John Duffy, journalists recognized his preference for committing crimes near railway lines and even referred to him as "the railway rapist." "What neither they nor the police appreciated was that this characteristic was likely to be part of his way of thinking about the layout of London and so was a clue to his own particular mental map. It could, therefore, be used to see where the psychological focus of this map was and so specify the area in which he lived."

The psychologists used statistical analyses to determine the common elements in descriptions from witnesses to twenty-seven different attacks. In addition, they used psychiatric profiles of rapists developed by the FBI.

The FBI distinguishes between "sadistic attacks" and "displacement attacks." In sadistic attacks, the victim is degraded and subjected to pain. Displacement attacks are those in which the offender attempts to form some sort of relationship with the victim. Until he started murdering his victims, Duffy was not especially violent in his attacks and would often talk to the victims afterwards.

The profile prepared by the team of psychologists for the police predicted that the offender would be involved in a long-term relationship, probably marriage. This turned out to be significant. Duffy's former wife testified in court that he told her he was raping women because she rejected him. She did not believe him.

Another aspect of the psychological profile involved the notion of a "criminal career." Why would a man who had raped twenty women without being caught suddenly start to murder his victims? If he had been questioned by the police in connection with the rapes and then released, perhaps the police interest made him want to leave no witnesses behind. Duffy had once been questioned by the police in connection with a rape.

Canter raises the ethical question of whether the use of such profiles might alter criminals' behaviors so that they leave false clues to their psychological profiles. John Duffy, however, was apprehended partly on the basis of research in environmental psychology.

The children from the noisy and quiet schools differed on physiological and behavioral measures. The children from the noisy schools had higher blood pressure. On a test designed to measure distractibility, the children were asked to cross out the letter "e" each time it appeared in a two-page passage from a sixth-grade reader. Children who had been at the noisy school for only a short time did better at crossing out the letters than did children from the "quiet" school. However, those who had been at the noisy school for several years performed poorly.

Crowding may also be a source of stress. Some animal research reports that high population density has negative social and physiological effects. Animals housed for many generations in densely populated conditions display increased aggressiveness or increased passivity, a deterioration in normal social and sexual behavior, increased infant mortality, and other abnormalities (Calhoun, 1962). Is crowding also harmful to humans?

**Population density** refers to *the number of people living in a given area* (such as 100 people per square mile). **Crowding** is *the subjective feeling that there are too many people present* for comfort or freedom of movement (Schopler & Stockdale, 1977; Stokols, 1972). Short-term crowding, such as being in an elevator with many people for a few minutes, is quite different from long-term crowding, such as living in Tokyo for many years.

Freedman and his colleagues (Freedman, Klevansky, & Ehrlich, 1971; Freedman, Levy, Buchanan, & Price, 1972) examined the effects in human beings of short-term increases in population density. They found no straightforward effect of high population density on creativity, memory, performance of various tasks, or aggressiveness. High density does seem to heighten emotions (Freedman, 1975; Ross, Layton, Erickson, & Schopler, 1973). Males, who are generally more aggressive than females, become even more aggressive under densely populated conditions; females become less aggressive. Crowding does not seem to have consistent effects on everyone. It is far from clear that "density is destiny" for humans.

## Energy Conservation

Many aspects of psychology—from reinforcement principles to theories of attitude change—are applicable to energy conservation (Dennis et al., 1990; Geller, 1992; Crabb, 1992; Weyant, 1986). Pallak, Cook, and Sullivan (1980) applied social comparison theory to energy conservation. Social comparison theory posits that people have a need to evaluate themselves (see chapter 15). Pallak and his colleagues attempted to increase energy conservation by giving homeowners feedback about their energy consumption and that of comparable others. Homeowners in a control condition were sent postcards reporting how much energy they consumed, in a manner similar to their monthly utility bills. Homeowners in the comparative feedback condition learned both how much energy they consumed as well as the average amount of energy used by other homeowners in the study. As early as two weeks into the study, homeowners in the comparative feedback condition were using significantly less electricity than were those in the control condition. The effect persisted for at least six weeks after the feedback had terminated.

To run an air conditioner properly, all windows should be closed. This makes people less aware of when it cools down outside; therefore, people do not know when it would be best to turn off the air conditioner and open windows. At certain times of the day, especially early morning and evening, it is possible for the air to be cooler outside than it is inside with the air conditioner on. Becker and Seligman (1978) reasoned that people might reduce their use of air conditioning and thus save energy if they were aware of the outside temperature. They supplied people with signaling devices in their homes that alerted them when the temperature outside was below 68 degrees F (20 C). In the same housing development other homeowners who lived in identical houses were not given the signaling device and constituted the control group. Meter readings for the month following installation of the signaling device showed that when it was cool outside those homeowners who were signaled used significantly less electricity than those in the control condition. There was a 15.7 percent reduction in energy consumption in the homes with signaling devices.

▶ **GUIDED REVIEW** *Learning Objectives 9, 10, 11, and 12*

1. _____ is the study of the relationship between behavior and the environment. Topics include human spatial behavior (personal space, territoriality, and crowding), the effects of environmental stressors such as noise or pollution, and the design of environments.
2. The term _____ refers to an area around an individual into which others cannot intrude without arousing discomfort.
3. _____ theory proposes that personal space is a component of intimacy.
4. _____ behavior refers to action designed to preserve and defend a particular geographic area from intruders.
5. _____ refers to the number of individuals per unit area; _____ refers to a subjective feeling that too many others are present.
6. _____ is an environmental stressor that can have deleterious effects on behavior and physiology, particularly if it is uncontrollable and unpredictable.
7. _____ theory and _____ have been used successfully to increase energy conservation.

*ANSWERS*

*1. Environmental psychology 2. personal space 3. Equilibrium 4. Territorial 5. Density, crowding 6. Noise 7. Social comparison, feedback*

# SPORTS PSYCHOLOGY

The scientific study of sports has grown to such an extent that the American Psychological Association has added a Division of Sport Psychology. Attention is focused particularly on three areas: enhancing athletic performance, sports and aggression, and the psychology of the sports fan.

## Enhancing Athletic Performance

Teams competing at the 1992 Summer Olympic Games in Barcelona traveled not only with their coaches, trainers, and physiotherapists, but also with their sports psychologists. Aided by advances in technology, sports psychologists analyze the techniques, and motivational and emotional states of athletes in an effort to prepare them for maximum performance. One can see athletes preparing mentally for competition, relaxing before the start of a race, visualizing clearing the bar in a high jump, and pumping themselves up during competition. Sports psychologists help athletes relax during tense moments and to control and refocus their anger and anxiety.

Before athletic performance was carefully studied by psychologists, it was believed that a moderate amount of arousal or anxiety would result in optimum performance, based on the Yerkes-Dodson law (see chapter 8, Motivation and Emotion). However, the nature of the task must be considered. The Yerkes-Dodson law was developed by studying fine motor tasks, such as spotting errors in visual tasks or tracking a moving line with a pencil. In these cases, moderate arousal is related to improved performance. However, for tasks that require speed, strength, and endurance—such as track and field events—a high level of physiological arousal and anxiety will produce the best performance (Cohen, 1992).

## Violence and Sports

A fear of growing violence among athletes and sports fans has led to government hearings in the United States, Canada, Great Britain, and Germany to investigate violence in boxing, ice hockey, football, and soccer. It is widely assumed that there is more violence in sports today than formerly. Yet it is by no means clear that this is so (Guttman, 1986). Not long ago violence in sports was accepted without comment; today it is apt to result in lawsuits. Nevertheless, we do not know whether the incidence, prevalence, or severity of sports violence has changed in the past century.

There are contradictory beliefs about the effects of viewing violent or aggressive sports, such as boxing and football, and the findings from research are also inconsistent. One view, the **"catharsis"** position, is *that aggressive sports are healthy outlets for pent-up hostility, frustration, and aggression.* The overwhelming majority of sports fans do not become noticeably more violent after watching a football game or boxing match; so the catharsis view seems to describe accurately the experiences of most sports fans. The fact that fans become highly excited during a game and do *not* engage in overt aggression suggests that sports may teach self-control. There is some evidence, notably with martial arts students, that a decrease in violent behavior may result from involvement in sport (Nosanchuk, 1981).

Many studies find that fans have more hostile feelings soon after viewing an aggressive sport, compared to controls who witnessed a nonaggressive sport (Arms, Russell, & Sandilands, 1979; Goldstein & Arms, 1971). Phillips and

Hensley (1984) report that on the third day after a heavyweight championship boxing match, the number of homicides in the United States rises significantly.

Every psychologist knows that the perception of an event influences its effects. The attitudes of sports fans determine not only how the sport is perceived, but also what effects it has upon them (Hastorf & Cantril, 1954; Mann, 1974). If spectators believe that opponents in a game despise each other, they tend to *enjoy* the game more, and they perceive the game itself as more violent (Zillmann, Bryant, & Sapolsky, 1989). Harrell (1981) asked professional ice hockey fans whether they thought fighting should "be allowed to go unpenalized because it is an important part of the game." About half the fans said yes. These fans became more hostile as the hockey game progressed. Fans who were less tolerant of player aggression showed no increase in hostility.

## Sports Fans

Some televised sports, like World Cup soccer matches and heavyweight boxing matches, attract a worldwide audience of more than 100 million people. What is the attraction? The word "fan" derives from a Latin word meaning possessed by the gods or mad, and implies a certain irrationality. Research on sports fans shows them to be no less rational than anyone else.

Sports fans are motivated by basic human needs—the need for a sense of identity and self-esteem, wanting to feel part of a group, and the need to regulate emotional and physiological states (Sloan, 1989; Zillman, Bryant, & Sapolsky, 1989). Loyalty to a team fulfills belonging, self-esteem, and achievement needs (Cialdini, Borden, Throne, Walker, Freeman, & Sloane, 1976). After a victory, fans more closely identify themselves with the winning team, often wearing the team logo or colors.

▶ **GUIDED REVIEW** *Learning Objectives 13, 14, and 15*

1. Sports psychologists analyze the _____ and _____ and _____ of athletes to prepare them for maximum performance.
2. There are contradictory theories and data about the effects of _____.
3. The _____ of sports fans determine how a sport is perceived and what effects it has upon them.
4. Sports fans are motivated by basic human needs, including _____, _____, and _____.

*ANSWERS*

*1. techniques, motivational, emotional states 2. witnessing violence in sports 3. attitudes 4. self-esteem, belonging to a group, regulation of emotional and physiological states*

*Sports fans are motivated by basic human needs.*

# PSYCHOLOGY AND EDUCATION

During its early history in America, psychology was sometimes offered within colleges of education, where the focus was on processes of teaching, learning, memory, and motivation. These are still of interest to today's educational psychologists, but so, too, is the study of social processes in the classroom. We review three areas of research in psychology and education: expectancy effects, the cooperative classroom, and enhancing motivation.

## Expectancy Effects

Teachers form expectations about the performance of their students. Expectations can be formed on the basis of prior grades or the results of aptitude tests. Teachers may also form expectations based on the sex, race, religion, manner of dress, or other characteristics of their students. For example, Babad, Inbar, and Rosenthal (1982) found a very high correlation (.90) between teacher ratings of students' potential and the quality of the students' clothing!

These expectations may have profound effects on the behavior and self-concepts of students. Rosenthal and Jacobson (1968) selected a random twenty percent of pupils in an elementary school and informed their teachers that, on the basis of tests, these students would show a marked increase in IQ during the school year. By the year's end, the students classified as potential bloomers did indeed do better than their classmates, particularly in grades one through four. *Teachers' beliefs about these randomly selected pupils influenced their behavior toward them, with the result that the teachers' expectations were confirmed, a "self-fulfilling prophecy."*

Although some attempts to replicate these findings were unsuccessful (e.g., Clairborn, 1969), the teacher-expectancy effect is widely recognized as a classroom hazard (Cooper, 1979; Ross & Jackson, 1991). Teachers are now educated about expectation effects (Weyant, 1986).

## The Cooperative Classroom: The Jigsaw Approach to Multicultural Education

The controversial policy of busing children to achieve racial balance in American school systems has not done much to promote greater understanding and acceptance of members of other races. On the contrary, it seems to have led to increases in interracial prejudices and hostilities. Perhaps the reason school desegregation has not been very successful is that classrooms are structured for competition rather than for cooperation (Johnson & Johnson, 1975).

The typical American classroom has a competitive structure—students interact directly with the teacher, interaction among students is limited and usually forbidden, grades are based on individual work. Although this arrangement may motivate some students to perform well, there are also disadvantages. Competition may hinder the slower student, who sees classmates receive praise and higher grades. Competition may also create hostility among students. Calls for more cooperative classrooms are not new (Deutsch, 1949; Haines & McKeachie, 1967). Specific techniques for achieving them are.

In the 1970s, Elliot Aronson and his colleagues were contacted by officials of a local school district who were having problems with a new school busing program. To deal with the problems the **jigsaw technique** was developed (Aronson et al., 1978). *The general strategy is to*

*The jigsaw approach allows students to learn cooperatively.*

**structure the classroom so that students interact as equals pursuing common goals.** The technique involves dividing the class into small groups of five or six students. Each child in a group is given information about one part of the total lesson. For example, a lesson on Spanish and Portuguese explorers might be arranged such that one child in the group is given information about Magellan, another student receives information about Balboa, another about Ponce de Leon. The members of the group then proceed to teach their part to the group. Afterwards, the students are tested individually on the entire lesson. Just as all the pieces of a jigsaw puzzle must be put into place to get the whole picture, the only way any one student can master the entire lesson is to learn all the pieces of information from his or her peers. Equal status is attained because every student has an equally important part. The common goal is to put together the entire lesson. Slavin (1985) proposed Jigsaw II, in which all students in a team read the entire assignment. They are then assigned a particular topic on which to become an expert.

In a field study, volunteer teachers used the jigsaw technique in their fifth-grade classrooms for about forty-five minutes a day for six weeks (Blaney, Stephen, Rosenfield, Aronson, & Sikes, 1977). Anglos, blacks, and Mexican-Americans were purposely mixed together within jigsaw groups. In a control condition teachers used traditional methods of instruction. Unlike the control students, the jigsaw students showed significant increases in liking for their classmates, and in self-esteem.

When compared to traditional instruction, the cooperative classroom leads to higher achievement by minority students while not reducing the performance of majority students, more positive interracial attitudes, more positive attitudes toward school, and greater empathy for the viewpoint of others.

The jigsaw technique is applicable to a variety of situations (Aronson & Yates, 1983). One is the trend toward **mainstreaming,** *the integration of students with physical or learning disabilities into the regular classroom.* With the jigsaw technique the integration should be smoother because the handicapped and nonhandicapped would interact toward common goals on an equal-status basis. These conditions are likely to result in greater mutual attraction, empathy, and increases in self-esteem (Slavin, 1990).

## Enhancing Motivation

A common problem in school is the child who does not work to his or her potential. These underachievers have the ability to succeed, but lack the motivation to apply themselves consistently to their work. Interventions with these students aim to enhance their motivation. Dweck and Licht (1980) have shown that many school children experience learned helplessness (see chapter 11) with regard to their school work. Helpless children give up rather than persist on intellectual tasks, and they tend to attribute their failures to factors beyond their control, such as lack of ability or the difficulty of the tasks, rather than to lack of effort, which they could control. If a student believes that she is "no good at math," then she is less likely to apply herself on tasks that require mathematical skills.

*Intervention strategies attempt to change helpless students' attributions of failure from uncontrollable factors to controllable ones, namely, to lack of effort. Students are praised for making attributions regarding the need to "try harder."* After this **"re-attribution training,"** children become more persistent in attempting to read difficult sentences or solve difficult problems (Andrews & Dubus, 1978; Chapin & Dyck, 1976).

► **GUIDED REVIEW** *Learning Objectives 16, 17, and 18*

1. Teachers's expectations about their pupils may alter their behavior toward them, with the result that the teachers' expectations are confirmed. This is known as a _____.

2. The _____ involves dividing the class into small groups of five or six students. Each child in a group is given information about one part of the total lesson, and each teaches that part to the group.

3. The _____ leads to higher achievement by minority students while not reducing the performance of majority students.

4. The jigsaw technique is applicable to _____, the integration of students with physical or learning disabilities into the regular classroom.

5. Intervention strategies designed to change students' attributions of failure from uncontrollable factors to lack of effort. This sort of strategy is called _____.

ANSWERS

1. self-fulfilling prophecy 2. jigsaw strategy 3. cooperative classroom 4. mainstreaming 5. reattribution training

# SUMMARY

I. Work is such an integral part of people's lives that they often overlook its contribution to health and well-being and its relationship to nonwork activities such as recreation and leisure. (p. 480)

  A. There are different theories on the motivation to work. (p. 480)

   1. Herzberg's two-factor theory distinguishes between a person's basic needs, such as pay and job security, and higher order "motivator needs," such as the need for challenge, stimulation, and creativity. Herzberg proposes that jobs can be enriched to make them more meaningful and satisfying to workers. (p. 481)

   2. Vroom's valence-instrumentality-expectancy theory stresses people's expectations and perceptions of work and the outcomes resulting from work. (p. 481)

   3. Equity theory states that people attempt to make their inputs and outcomes comparable to those of others in similar positions. When this outcome/input ratio is not comparable to similar others, there exists a state of inequity, which a person will attempt to reduce either by altering inputs (work or the quality of work) or outcomes (asking for a raise or going on strike). (p. 481)

    Equity theory also leads to the prediction that over-compensation results in inequity because it may lower the intrinsic motivation to perform a task. (p. 481)

II. Large organizations are characterized by a division of labor, a formal structure, methods for recruiting and replacing members, and means for setting and accomplishing specific goals. (p. 483)

  A. Bureaucracy is the formal structure of relationships within an organization. A bureaucratic structure makes for predictable and orderly activity and increases the organization's efficiency by assigning specific tasks to each individual. This is known as a division of labor. (p. 484)

  B. Informal social groups form within any large bureaucratic organization. These are groups of coworkers who establish norms often at variance with those of the organization itself. (p. 484)

   1. Early psychological studies of plant productivity, known as the Hawthorne experiments, found increases in productivity with any change in lighting. It was believed that the act of studying workers itself resulted in these productivity changes; this is referred to as the "Hawthorne effect." The Hawthorne studies led to the human relations movement in industry; to a focus on the informal social structure of organizations. (p. 484)

  C. Large organizations often have formal networks of communication specifying who may communicate with whom. (p. 486)

   1. Even though organizations may have formal communication networks, informal networks usually develop. Informal communication, such as company gossip and small talk, is related to efficient group functioning. (p. 486)

III. Psychologists have developed personnel selection and training procedures and have worked with engineers to enhance equipment design. (p. 487)

  A. Personnel selection is made more efficient by the use of psychological tests and measures. (p. 487)

  B. Human factors research involves the design of equipment and systems to increase the effectiveness, comfort, safety, and productivity of the individuals who use them. (p. 487)

   1. It is important to take into account the characteristics and limitations of individuals who operate or use equipment. Research has helped in equipment design by examining each of the five sensory modalities. (p. 487)

2. Equipment designed to enhance error-free and efficient operation must consider operators' capabilities and habits. (p. 491)

3. Many design problems stemming from the failure to consider human factors were evident in the nuclear accident at Three Mile Island. (p. 492)

IV. Environmental psychology is the study of the relationship between both the natural and the constructed environment and behavior. (p. 493)

A. The area surrounding an individual that is considered private is referred to as personal space. (p. 493)

1. The size of an individual's personal space and the individual's reactions to violations of this space varies from one culture to another. (p. 493)

2. Equilibrium theory maintains that distance between individuals varies with their intimacy. As intimacy increases, interpersonal distance diminishes, eye contact increases, and topics of conversation become more personal. When one of these characteristics is restricted, individuals compensate by altering the others. (p. 494)

3. When an individual's personal space is invaded, the person attempts to reestablish it. (p. 494)

B. Territoriality is behavior designed to identify and preserve a particular geographic space, such as one's home or office. (p. 493)

C. Population density refers to the number of individuals per unit area. Crowding refers to a subjective feeling that too many others are present. (p. 495)

D. Noise and environmental pollution may be considered a source of stress. Like other stressors, noise, particularly if it is unpredictable and uncontrollable, interferes with cognitive functioning and may lead to feelings of helplessness. Noise also has physiological effects, such as increasing blood pressure. (p. 494)

E. Although many species of animal appear to suffer from overcrowding, there is little evidence that humans suffer from densely populated situations. (p. 496)

F. Many psychological theories are applicable to energy conservation. For example, social comparison theory has been used successfully to increase energy conservation. (p. 496)

V. Three areas of sports psychology are examined: enhancing athletic performance, the relationship between sports and aggression, and the psychology of the sports fan. (p. 496)

A. Psychologists help athletes control anxiety and other emotional and physiological states. (p. 496)

1. For tasks based on speed, strength, and endurance, a high level of anxiety and arousal may be optimal. (p. 497)

VI. Three topics in psychology and education are considered: expectancy effects, the cooperative classroom, and studies on enhancing motivation. (p. 498)

A. Teachers form expectations about the performance of their students, and often act in a way that will confirm their expectations. (p. 498)

1. This is an example of a self-fulfilling prophecy. (p. 498)

B. The typical classroom has a competitive structure. Cooperative education, beginning with the jigsaw technique, was developed to structure the classroom so that students interact as equals pursuing common goals. (p. 499)

1. The jigsaw technique is applicable to many situations, including mainstreaming. (p. 499)

C. One intervention strategy, re-attribution training, attempts to change students' attributions of failure from uncontrollable factors to controllable ones, namely, lack of effort. (p. 499)

# ACTION GLOSSARY

Match the terms in the left column with the definitions in the right column.

___ 1. **Scientific management** (p. 480)

___ 2. **Industrial psychology** (p. 480)

___ 3. **Organizational psychology** (p. 480)

___ 4. **Work** (p. 480)

___ 5. **Leisure** (p. 480)

___ 6. **Hygiene needs** (p. 481)

___ 7. **Motivator needs** (p. 481)

A. *Activities performed outside the work context whose goals are personally defined.*
B. *In Herzberg's theory, "higher order" needs, such as creativity and stimulation.*
C. *Focus on worker behavior, motivation for work, and precise measurement and description of jobs.*
D. *Expenditure of energy to accomplish a task or goal.*
E. *Study of behavior of and within large organizations.*
F. *Application of psychological principles and findings to work.*
G. *In Herzberg's theory, basic needs, such as pay and job security.*

___ 8. Equity theory  (p. 481)
___ 9. Intrinsic motivation
      (p. 482)
___ 10. Bureaucracy  (p. 484)
___ 11. Division of labor  (p. 484)
___ 12. Hawthorne effect  (p. 484)
___ 13. Human relations
      movement  (p. 484)
___ 14. Communication
      networks  (p. 486)

A. *Extent to which a person wants to do something for its own sake.*
B. *The finding that the act of research may alter behavior of subjects.*
C. *States that people attempt to make inputs and outcomes in a situation comparable to those of their peers.*
D. *Formal structures in which individuals may communicate only with specified others.*
E. *Specialization of roles within an organization.*
F. *The belief that informal social conditions influence worker productivity.*
G. *The recruitment of and relationships among individuals responsible for attaining the goals of an organization and for maintaining the organization itself.*

___ 15. Human factors  (p. 487)
___ 16. Environmental
      psychology  (p. 493)
___ 17. Personal space  (p. 493)
___ 18. Equilibrium theory  (p. 494)
___ 19. Territoriality  (p. 493)
___ 20. Population density  (p. 495)
___ 21. Crowding  (p. 495)

A. *The subjective feeling that too many people are present.*
B. *Behavior designed to preserve a particular geographic space, such as one's home.*
C. *The study of the relationship between behavior and the natural and constructed environment.*
D. *The field that aims to design equipment and systems that increase the effectiveness, comfort, safety, and productivity of the people using them.*
E. *States that personal distance between individuals is a component of intimacy.*
F. *The number of people living in a given area.*
G. *The area individuals actively maintain around themselves into which others cannot intrude without arousing discomfort.*

___ 22. Re-attribution training
      (p. 499)
___ 23. Jigsaw classroom
      (pp. 498–499)
___ 24. Catharsis  (p. 497)
___ 25. Mainstreaming  (p. 499)
___ 26. Self-fulfilling prophecy
      (p. 498)

A. *The idea that aggressive sports are healthy outlets for pent-up hostility, frustration, and aggression.*
B. *Acting in a way to bring about one's expectations.*
C. *Structuring tasks in such a way that students interact as equals pursuing common goals.*
D. *The integration of students with physical or learning disabilities into the regular classroom.*
E. *Learning to make attributions for failure based on lack of effort, rather than lack of ability.*

*ANSWERS*

1. c, 2. f, 3. e, 4. d, 5. a, 6. b, 7. b, 8. c, 9. a, 10. g, 11. e, 12. b, 13. f, 14. d, 15. d, 16. c, 17. g, 18. e,
19. b, 20. f, 21. a, 22. e, 23. c, 24. a, 25. d, 26. b

## SELF-TEST

1. Leisure activity differs from work primarily in that
    (a) it is more enjoyable.
    (b) its goals are personally defined.
    (c) it is unrelated to maintenance functions, such as biological needs.
    (d) it is involuntary.
    (LO 2; p. 480)

2. The fact that there are different theories of motivation to work indicates that
    (a) psychologists do not know why people work.
    (b) the motivation to work involves many different needs.
    (c) psychologists disagree among themselves about work motivation.
    (d) all of the above.
    (e) none of the above.
    (LO 2, 3; pp. 480–482)

3. Seeking a challenge in work, the need for stimulation, the need for creativity, and the desire for independence are regarded in Herzberg's two-factor theory as
   (a) basic needs.
   (b) hygiene needs.
   (c) job enrichment.
   (d) motivator needs.
   (LO 3; p. 481)

4. If a person's job outcomes, relative to his or her inputs, are not comparable to those of a coworker in the same job,
   (a) the individual experiences inequity.
   (b) the individual will alter either his or her inputs or his or her outcomes.
   (c) the individual will feel psychological discomfort.
   (d) all of the above.
   (e) none of the above.
   (LO 3; p. 481)

5. According to equity theory, being overpaid for a task may result in
   (a) lowered intrinsic motivation.
   (b) raised intrinsic motivation.
   (c) increased liking for the task.
   (d) more effort expended in completing the task.
   (LO 3; p. 482)

6. Losing one's job influences
   (a) not only the former worker but his or her family as well.
   (b) a person's physical health.
   (c) a person's emotional well-being.
   (d) all of the above.
   (LO 4; p. 483)

7. In a bureaucracy, individuals perform specialized tasks. This is referred to as
   (a) intrinsic motivation.
   (b) equity.
   (c) division of labor.
   (d) none of the above.
   (LO 5; p. 484)

8. A small group of friends who always eat lunch together at the same large company is an example of
   (a) division of labor.
   (b) bureaucracy.
   (c) a communication network.
   (d) an informal social structure.
   (LO 5; p. 484)

9. Which of the following communication networks would produce the most efficient solution to a simple problem?
   (a) One in which all members can communicate with all other members.
   (b) One in which there is a central member through whom everyone else must communicate.
   (c) One in which every member is independent.
   (d) All produce efficient solutions to simple problems.
   (e) Not enough information is given to answer the question.
   (LO 5; p. 486)

10. Human factors research is concerned with
    (a) the design of equipment and complex systems.
    (b) the comfort of workers and the safety of equipment.
    (c) interactions between humans and machines.
    (d) all of the above.
    (e) none of the above.
    (LO 6, 7, 8; p. 487)

11. The area a person maintains around himself or herself, into which others may not intrude without arousing discomfort, is
    (a) personal space.
    (b) territoriality.
    (c) a cognitive map.
    (d) human factors.
    (LO 9; p. 493)

12. Cross-cultural studies of personal space indicate that
    (a) people use space much the same way everywhere in the world.
    (b) people in the twentieth century use space in similar ways, but the use of space differed in the eighteenth and nineteenth centuries.
    (c) personal contact among pedestrians varies considerably by country.
    (d) comfortable speaking distance is the same in the Middle East as in England.
    (LO 10; p. 493)

13. Equilibrium theory concerns intimacy as a function of all but which of the following?
    (a) eye contact
    (b) conversation topic
    (c) personal distance
    (d) nationality
    (LO 10; p. 494)

14. The difference between the concepts of personal space and territoriality is that the latter
    (a) is larger.
    (b) applies only to animals.
    (c) does not move with the person or organism.
    (d) all of the above.
    (e) none of the above.
    (LO 9; p. 493)

15. The difference between population density and crowding is that the latter refers to
    (a) the number of people in a given spatial area.
    (b) physiological arousal due to the presence of too many others.
    (c) an uncomfortable feeling resulting from the presence of too many others.
    (d) the amount of resources available for a given number of people.
    (LO 11; p. 495)

16. Which psychological principle(s) have been applied to the field of energy conservation?
    (a) social comparison
    (b) feedback
    (c) reinforcement theory
    (d) all of the above
    (LO 12; p. 496)

17. Tasks that require speed, strength, and endurance, such as track and field events, will be performed better if the athlete
    (a) experiences a low level of anxiety and physiological arousal.
    (b) is familiar with the physical surroundings of the event.
    (c) experiences a high level of anxiety and physiological arousal.
    (d) has no anxiety.
    (LO 13; p. 497)

18. The effect of witnessing violence in sports
    (a) depends upon the observers' attitudes toward violence.
    (b) raises observers' level of aggression.
    (c) lowers observers' level of aggression.
    (d) none of the above.
    (LO 14; p. 497)

19. Sports fans are motivated by all but which of the following needs?
    (a) self-esteem
    (b) the need to belong to a group
    (c) the need to regulate emotional and physiological states
    (d) the need to get rid of excess aggression
    (LO 15; p. 497)

20. Compared to traditional instruction, the cooperative classroom leads to
    (a) higher achievement by minority students.
    (b) no reduction in the performance of majority students.
    (c) more positive interracial attitudes.
    (d) all of the above.
    (LO 17; p. 499)

21. Intervention strategies attempt to change helpless students' attributions of failure from uncontrollable factors to lack of effort. This is called
    (a) cognitive dissonance.
    (b) mainstreaming.
    (c) re-attribution training.
    (d) catharsis.
    (LO 18; p. 499)

ANSWERS

1. b, 2. b, 3. d, 4. d, 5. a, 6. d, 7. c, 8. d, 9. b, 10. d, 11. a, 12. c, 13. d, 14. c, 15. c, 16. d, 17. c, 18. a, 19. d, 20. d, 21. c

# THINKING ABOUT PSYCHOLOGY

1. Bureaucracy is designed to increase the efficiency of organizations. Does it? If so, why does it have a negative connotation when people speak of bureaucracies?

2. Apply additional aspects of psychology, such as personality or social learning theory, to energy conservation. What might be some methods of improving compliance with recycling regulations, for example?

# SUGGESTED READINGS

Argyle, M. (1989). *The social psychology of work.* (2nd ed.). New York: Penguin. An accessible review of research and theory on work, job performance and satisfaction, and unemployment and retirement.

Bell, P., Fisher, J., Baum, A., & Greene, T. (1990). *Environmental psychology.* (3rd ed.). New York: Holt, Rinehart and Winston. A basic introduction to the field of environmental psychology.

Dunnette, M. D. (1983). *Handbook of industrial and organizational psychology.* New York: Wiley. Thirty-seven chapters on all aspects of the application of psychology to industrial and other organizations.

Norman, D. A. (1988). *The psychology of everyday things.* New York: Basic Books. How cognitive psychology can help improve the design of ordinary objects—light switches, water faucets, control knobs, telephones, and computers.

Russell, G. (1993). *Social psychology of sport.* New York: Springer-Verlag.

Schultz, D. P., and Schultz, S. E. (1990). *Psychology and industry today* (5th ed.). New York: Macmillan. A standard textbook of industrial psychology.

Varela, J. A. (1971). *Psychological solutions to social problems.* New York: Academic Press. An engineer applies social psychology to various problems in industry, from job design to social relations among workers and management.

# APPENDIX
## STATISTICAL METHODS

A survey of the way people feel about health and illness reported some fascinating findings (Rubenstein, 1982):

Forty-two percent of the sample think about health more often than just about anything else, including love, work, and money.

Men and women whose parents were divorced feel less healthy than adults who grew up in intact families.

Four out of ten people reported avoiding salt; one-third said they did not use sugar.

Women reported an average of nine symptoms; men reported an average of seven symptoms.

Nine percent complained about being given too many drugs.

Twenty-five percent said they experienced and were bothered by a doctor's uncaring or condescending attitude.

Thirty-four percent of the men reported having trouble falling asleep; 40 percent of the women reported sleeping problems.

These findings say a great deal about how extremely health-conscious humans are. Or do they? Surveys like this one appear regularly in magazines on topics ranging from "Who has a happy sex life?" to "How do people spend their money?" They obviously help sell magazines, but do they tell us anything about human behavior?

To understand and evaluate these numerous psychological reports, it is necessary to have a basic understanding of statistics.

## DESCRIPTIVE STUDIES

One of the most valuable uses of statistics is to describe and make sense out of data. A stack of computer printouts is almost useless to people who need information unless the printouts are described and summarized. Descriptive statistics accomplishes this purpose by using frequency distributions, measures of central tendency, and measures of variation.

### Frequency Distributions

Figure A.1 lists the number of cups of coffee consumed by each member of a psychotherapy group during a session. This list becomes comprehensible when it is grouped into a frequency distribution, or a set of scores assembled

| | | | | | |
|---|---|---|---|---|---|
| Betty | 2.6 | Bob | 5.1 | Barb | 3.5 |
| Joe | 4.8 | Lisa | 2.1 | Wendell | 2.6 |
| Helga | 5.6 | Pam | 2.6 | Brian S. | 2.2 |
| Tom | 2.1 | Laura | 4.2 | Brian J. | 1.7 |
| Bill A. | 3.6 | Dennis | 4.1 | George | 3.0 |
| Bill P. | 0.7 | Wes | 2.9 | Alice | 3.4 |
| Jenny | 3.7 | Greg | 1.1 | Callie | 4.2 |
| John | 6.1 | Lou | 1.6 | | |

**Figure A.1**  *A list of the number of cups of coffee consumed by each member of a psychotherapy group*

| Interval | Frequency |
|---|---|
| 0 — 0.9 | 1 |
| 1.0 — 1.9 | 3 |
| 2.0 — 2.9 | 7 |
| 3.0 — 3.9 | 5 |
| 4.0 — 4.9 | 4 |
| 5.0 — 5.9 | 2 |
| 6.0 — 6.9 | 1 |
| 7.0 — 7.9 | 0 |

**Figure A.2**  *A frequency distribution of the data in figure A.1*

according to size and grouped into intervals (figure A.2). The numbers from figure A.1 are arranged into intervals (0–0.9, 1.0–1.9, 2.0–2.9, etc.), and the number of people who drank an amount of coffee that fell within each interval is tabulated. For example, three people drank between 1.0 and 1.9 cups of coffee.

A graph would express the data more clearly than the table. Figure A.3 shows a frequency histogram, a common means to graphically display a frequency distribution. The vertical axis is labeled *frequency,* a term that means the number of cases, and the horizontal axis is labeled number of cups of coffee. The intervals are shown across the horizontal axis, and above each interval is a bar showing the number of people who drank an amount of coffee that fell within that interval.

A frequency polygon is another common graphing technique (figure A.4). The axis labels are the same, but the frequencies are plotted with points that are connected

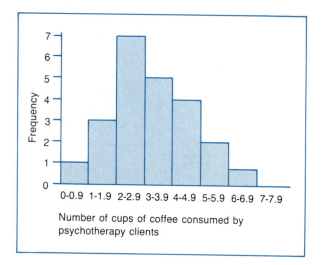

**Figure A.3**    *A frequency histogram*

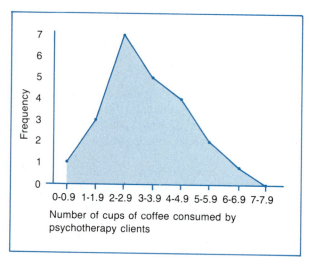

**Figure A.4**    *A frequency polygon*

with straight lines. In this example, there were only eighteen people in the psychotherapy session, so the polygon appears rather angular. If there were many more people and much smaller intervals, the frequency polygon would look more like a bell-shaped curve. When researchers measure variables in large samples and graph them on a frequency polygon, the result is much like the curve shown in figure A.5. Most scores tend to lie in the middle of the variable. When the curve is symmetrical and bell-shaped, it is called a normal distribution. If it is asymmetrical with a long "tail" on one side or the other, it is called a skewed distribution.

## Measures of Central Tendency

Another way to describe a list of figures like those in figure A.1 is to provide a single number or average of some kind. Statisticians actually use three different procedures to arrive at an average, each of which may yield a slightly different value. These three measures of central tendency are the mean, the mode, and the median.

The mean is what most people refer to when they use the word "average." It is the sum of the scores divided by the number of scores. In the psychotherapy group, the mean number of cups of coffee consumed by the clients was 3.2. The statistical symbol for mean is $\overline{X}$.

The mode is the most frequent score in a distribution. In the psychotherapy group, the mode was 2.6 cups of coffee. If a list of scores is not available, the mode can be found by looking at the frequency histogram. The highest

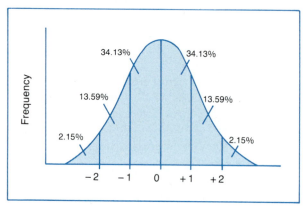

**Figure A.5**    *The normal distribution*

frequency occurs in the 2.0–2.9 interval; the mode would be the midpoint of that interval (2.5).

The median is the score below which 50 percent of the scores fall. It is the middle score; in that sense, it is like a percentile rank. The median is the score at the 50th percentile. In the example, the median is 3.0 since eleven scores fall below that and eleven fall above it.

In a normal distribution, the mean, mode, and median are all the same value. However, the three measures of central tendency diverge when the distribution is skewed. The distribution of the amount of coffee the clients drank is skewed, with most people drinking between one and four cups and a few heavy caffeine users drinking five or six cups. In this case, the mean, median, and mode are

| San Francisco | Phoenix |
|---|---|
| 32 | 65 |
| 55 | 65 |
| 61 | 67 |
| 66 | 68 |
| 78 | 73 |
| 81 | 76 |
| 84 | 76 |
| 89 | 78 |
| 94 | 84 |
| 100 | 88 |
| $\bar{x} = 74$ | $\bar{x} = 74$ |
| $s = 19.6$ | $s = 7.5$ |

**Figure A.6** *Statistics pretest scores from two different classes*

different. Of all the measures of central tendency, the mean is most affected by extreme scores. In a skewed distribution, the median usually falls between the mean and the mode.

For most distributions, the mean is the preferred measure of central tendency; however, in some highly skewed cases, the mean is very misleading. For instance, suppose a company employs ten people earning around $12,800 per year and a president earning $70,000. The mean salary at this company would be almost $18,000, a figure that would look very attractive in quarterly reports and employee newsletters. But none of the employees earn anywhere near that.

## Measures of Variation

Figure A.6 shows the scores that people in two different classes received on a statistics pretest. The test was designed to determine whether the students have the background for a course in probability. The means of the scores of the two classes are the same, but the scores of the San Francisco class are scattered much more widely. Some students did very poorly, and others did quite well. In contrast, the scores of the Phoenix group were more tightly clustered around the mean.

A teacher would certainly want to know the means of the classes, but he or she would also want to know something about variation, or scatter, around the mean. The San Francisco class will be much harder to work with because some students have so little preparation and others have so much. The two most common measures of variation are range and standard deviation.

The range is the spread between the highest and the lowest score. In the San Francisco class, the range was from 32 to 100. The range is easy to provide, but it does not tell very much about the scatter of scores.

The most useful measure of variation is the standard deviation, a statistic based on the distance of each score from the mean of the distribution. For each score, the difference between the mean and the score is squared, and then all the squared deviations are summed together. (In statistical notation, $\Sigma$ means "sum together.") The sum of the squared deviations is divided by $N$, the number of scores, to obtain an average of the squared deviations. To return to the original unsquared scale of numbers, the square root is taken. The more that the scores are scattered away from the mean, the higher the standard deviation will be. The standard deviation will be lower when the scores are tightly clustered about the mean. Notice that the standard deviation, or $s$, for the Phoenix group was 7.5. For the more widely scattered scores in the San Francisco class, the standard deviation was nearly 20.

In a normal distribution, about 34 percent of the cases fall between the mean and one standard deviation above and below the mean. About 13.59 percent of the cases fall between one and two standard deviations above or below the mean. And 2.15 percent of the cases fall more than two standard deviations away from the mean (figure A.5). This means that it is possible to approximately determine where in the distribution any particular score falls, provided the distribution is normal. If the mean on a test with normally distributed scores is 100 and the standard deviation is 10, then about 34 percent of the people scored between 100 and 110. A person who scored 110 on the test would be at the 84 percentile.

## STATISTICAL INFERENCE

Describing a set of data and drawing conclusions from it can be two very different things. A number of procedures permit researchers to draw sound conclusions from data, even when they only have a chance to observe the behavior of a small group of people. The first step is to collect data on people who are generally representative of the total group that the researchers are interested in.

## Populations and Samples

When researchers want to learn something about human behavior, they never try to observe everybody in the population of individuals with whom they are concerned; instead, they observe a small *sample* or subset of the population. For example, a researcher who is interested in the voting preferences of residents of Vermont would not try to telephone every registered voter in the state and ask questions. Instead, the researcher would obtain a list of registered voters in the state and randomly choose a small subset. If the sample is randomly chosen, each member of the population has an equal chance of being included. As long as the random sample is not too small, it should be representative of the larger population. Therefore, measures of the voting preferences of this sample should indicate fairly closely the preferences of the entire population. If 60 percent of the sample say they intend to vote for a particular candidate, one can assume that approximately 60 percent of all the registered voters in Vermont have the same preference.

In psychological research, it is not always possible to obtain a random sample. In an investigation of short-term memory processes, the population that interests the researcher probably includes all adult human beings. Getting a random sample would mean obtaining a list of all adults on earth and randomly choosing a sample of fifty of them. The sample would probably include several Chinese, Indians, Africans, and many others who do not speak English. Since this is not an option, most researchers use the *available sample,* a group that includes whomever they can get. Since psychologists are often college or university professors, the sample often includes college students who earn money or extra credit by participating in experiments. For much psychological research, the results obtained from an available sample are reasonably close to what would be obtained from a sample more representative of all adult humans. It would be very surprising to learn that the short-term memories of Chinese young adults were profoundly different from American young adults. However, probably no one would argue that a survey of the sexual practices of American college students would tell us very much about all adult Americans or adult Chinese.

The magazine surveys referred to earlier always have difficulty generalizing to all adult Americans because their samples are rarely representative of the population. It is usually limited to readers of the magazine since that is often where the survey questions appear. For the health survey in *Psychology Today,* 31 percent of the respondents were men and 68 percent were women—hardly a balance that represents what actually exists in the United States.

Furthermore, the largest proportion were never married. (In the United States, more than three-fourths of the adult population have been married.) More than half of the sample had at least a college degree and an annual family income over $25,000. Thus the survey told something about the young, well-educated readers of *Psychology Today* who have some interest in filling out a questionnaire about health. People who spare the time are often those unusually interested in the topic, making it unremarkable that the respondents seemed very health-conscious. In fact, one in five of the respondents enclosed a personal letter describing their own approach to health.

Before drawing any conclusions about the results of a study, it is important to consider the sample. Was it all men? Did it include people from all socio-economic groups? Were older and younger people included? If the sample was a narrow one, the conclusions must be very cautious; most studies will mention a caveat about the nature of the sample. The health survey stated, "These conclusions are based on a young, well-educated sample, and thus may not be applicable to all Americans." In the beginning of the report, however, the sample problem is ignored: "Our findings confirm that physical health has taken on great importance in our lives and that many of us think about it almost to the point of obsession these days."

## Significant Differences

A great deal of statistical inference is involved in determining whether differences between the means of two or more groups are significant. In statistical jargon, the word *significant* simply reflects whether it is a reliable difference that did not occur by chance. In some cases, significant differences can actually be quite small and be of little practical interest.

The health survey mentioned that women checked an average of nine symptoms and men checked an average of seven symptoms. People might hastily draw some conclusions from this finding, perhaps that women are less healthy than men, that women *think* they are less healthy than men, or that men are reluctant to talk about physical complaints. Before drawing any conclusions at all, however, they should determine whether the difference is a significant one. After all, whenever two groups of people are measured on any test, it is extremely *un*likely that the mean would be exactly the same, even if there is no difference at all between the populations from which the two samples were drawn.

Figure A.7 shows two sets of data, both of which have two groups with means of 7 and 9. In the first set the scores are tightly clustered around the means, and there is hardly any overlap between the scores of the men and the women. In the second set, there is considerable overlap. Notice that the standard deviations of the distributions in the first set are much smaller than those in the second set.

A statistical test of significance would show that the probability is extremely low that the two-point difference between the means in the first set occurred by chance. There seems little likelihood that there could accidentally be such a large difference between the means, given that the populations of men and women do not differ very much. Thus, the populations of men and women represented by the sample do indeed differ in the number of symptoms they report. In contrast, the difference between the data on men and women obtained in the second set points to the rather high probability that the two-point difference between the means occurred by chance alone.

There are many different kinds of tests of significance, each appropriate in different experimental designs. The end result of all of them is a probability figure that describes the likelihood that the difference obtained between the means of two or more groups was due to chance rather than to any real difference between the means of the populations for which the samples were drawn. It is usually abbreviated p, and it might read "$p < .05$," or "$p < .001$." This means that the probability that the difference between the means occurred by chance is less than .05 (one out of twenty), or .001 (one out of 1,000). Psychologists usually use a p of .05 as a cutoff point. If there is less than .05 chance that the difference occurred by chance, psychologists assume the difference did *not* occur by chance and that it represents a significant difference. If p is greater than .05, psychologists assume the two groups were drawn from populations that have very similar or identical means, and thus there is no significant difference between them.

In the hypothetical results from the health survey, the data in set I would have resulted in a p value less than .001. Therefore, the difference between the mean number of symptoms reported by the men and women was significant. In set II, the p value was about .2, meaning that there was a one in five chance that the difference occurred simply by chance. For psychologists, this difference is not reliable enough. The p value is too large and the difference between the means of the two groups is "nonsignificant."

| I. | | II. | |
|---|---|---|---|
| Men | Women | Men | Women |
| 6 | 8 | 1 | 3 |
| 6 | 8 | 3 | 5 |
| 7 | 9 | 5 | 7 |
| 7 | 9 | 7 | 9 |
| 7 | 9 | 9 | 11 |
| 8 | 10 | 11 | 13 |
| 8 | 10 | 13 | 15 |
| $\bar{x} = 7$ | $\bar{x} = 9$ | $\bar{x} = 7$ | $\bar{x} = 9$ |
| $s = .8$ | $s = .8$ | $s = 4.0$ | $s = 4.0$ |
| $p < .001$ | | p is about .2 | |

**Figure A.7** *Two hypothetical sets of data in which the mean number of symptoms reported by women was 9 and by men was 7. The difference between the means for set I is significant. For set II, the difference is not significant.*

(Although the survey did not actually report the p values, we guess that the difference between the mean number of reported symptoms for men and women was significant. If it were not, a responsible psychologist would not have mentioned them.)

## Graphing the Results of Experiments

The graphs used to illustrate data from experiments usually place the independent variable along the horizontal axis and the dependent variable along the vertical axis. For example, a study that explored the effects of noise on short-term memory processes might ask twenty subjects to listen to a list of words and to write down as many words as possible afterwards. The twenty subjects would be randomly divided into two groups, one that listened to the list under low-noise conditions and one that listened to the list under high-noise conditions (figure A.8). Experiments often have more complex designs using many more groups, such as the one in figure A.9. This design has *two* independent variables: amount of noise (shown across the horizontal axis) and the volume at which the word list was read to the subjects.

## CORRELATION

Correlation refers to the degree of relationship or association between two variables. It provides a method to determine whether changes in one variable are related to changes in another variable. For example, there would

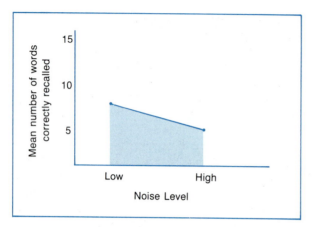

**Figure A.8**  *Graphing data from an experiment*

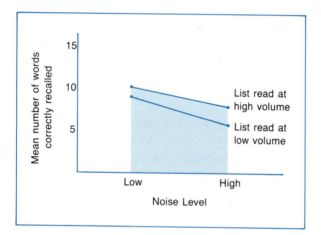

**Figure A.9**  *Graphing data from an experiment with two indepen-dent variables*

probably be a strong correlation between height and weight because tall people tend to be heavier than short people.

## The Scatter Diagram

The scatter diagram is the graph used to illustrate a correlation. The data in figure A.10 represent the number of absences of each student in a psychology class; next to each student's name is his or her grade, converted to a four-point scale. These data can be graphed by using a single point for each person (figure A.11).

In general, the more absences a person has, the lower the grade. The scatter diagram shows a general trend from the upper left to the lower right.

| Student | Number of Absences | Grade |
|---|---|---|
| Ames, S. | 2 | 3.6 |
| Barnes, C. | 5 | 2.1 |
| Bennetti, T. | 6 | 2.7 |
| Collins, D. | 1 | 2.9 |
| Davidson, B. | 7 | 1.6 |
| Eggars, K. | 6 | 3.2 |
| Frye, A. | 14 | 1.0 |
| Holland, K. | 0 | 3.6 |
| Jackson, B. | 1 | 3.9 |
| Moore, T. | 2 | 3.0 |
| Thomas, G. | 10 | 1.9 |
| Toras, J. | 3 | 3.3 |
| Wachal, N. | 8 | 2.0 |
| West, B. | 12 | 0.5 |
| Zwink, M. | 4 | 1.2 |

**Figure A.10**  *The number of absences and the corresponding grades of students in a psychology class*

## The Correlation Coefficient

A statistical measure of the direction and degree of association between two variables is obtained with the correlation coefficient. The most common coefficient is the product-moment correlation, or r, which ranges in value from −1 to +1. The direction of the relationship is shown by the sign. A minus indicates a negative correla-tion and means that as one variable increases the other decreases. The relationship between the number of absences and the student's grade is negative because as the number of absences increases, the grade decreases. A positive r means that as one variable increases, the other variable also increases. The relationship between height and weight would be positive.

The strength of the association between the two variables is indicated by the absolute value of the correla-tion coefficient. An r of .9 would indicate a very strong relationship; an r of −.95 would indicate an even stronger relationship.

The strength of the association between two variables can be computed using a formula described in any introduc-tory statistics text; it can also be estimated by looking at a scatter diagram. If the trend of the scores is from the lower left to the upper right, then the relationship is positive. If the trend of scores is from the upper left to the lower right, it is negative. If there seems to be no trend at all, r is probably close to zero. If the dots cluster tightly around an imaginary line going through the center of the scores, the correlation is

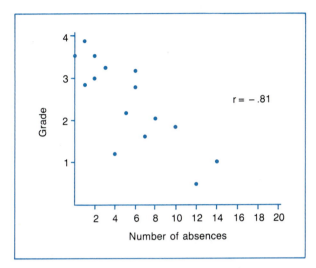

**Figure A.11**    *A scatter diagram showing the relationship between grades and number of absences*

probably very strong, and the absolute value of r is high. However, if they are scattered widely throughout the scatter diagram, r will be low. The correlation coefficient for the relationship between grade and number of absences was negative and rather strong: –.81.

## Correlation and Causation

It is a common mistake to assume that if two variables are correlated, one is probably the cause of the other. A newspaper might report that most people who commit crimes come from homes with a history of alcohol abuse.

This might lead people to suppose that a criminal's early childhood experiences with alcoholic parents led to a life of frustration, anger, and crime. Correlation, however, is not necessarily causation, and other possibilities exist. Perhaps the criminal began a life of crime early and drove the parents to drink. Or a third variable, such as poverty, could be the main cause of both the alcohol abuse in the home and the criminal behavior of the children.

One might assume at first glance that the students in the psychology class getting low grades did so because they missed so many classes, and those getting high grades did so because of good attendance. It could also be the other way around. Perhaps the students whose grades were poor began losing interest in the class and thus failed to attend.

## STATISTICS AND ANXIETY

Statistics is a course that many students approach with trepidation, perhaps because it seems remote, extremely difficult, and complicated. Some fear that it will be a grueling exercise in memorizing horrifying formulas. Skeptical students think it will be a course in learning how to conjure with figures.

The approach to statistics is very important. Students must start from the beginning and master each step before proceeding to the next one. Some sections will take two or three readings and much homework time before complete mastery. As students succeed on each level, their confidence will increase and their anxiety will eventually decrease.

# REFERENCES

Abe, K., Amatoni, M., & Oda, N. (1984). Sleep walking and recurrent sleeptalking in the children of childhood sleepwalkers. *American Journal of Psychiatry, 141,* 800–801.

Ackerman, D. (1990). A natural history of the senses. New York: Vintage Books.

Adam, B. O. (1983). Tracking . . . the instinct and dedication. *Dog World, 68*(6), 19–20.

Adams, J. S. (1965). Inequity in social exchange. In L. Berkowitz (Ed.), *Advances in social psychology* (Vol. 2). New York: Academic Press.

Adams, P. R., & Adams, G. R. (1984). Mount Saint Helens' ashfall: Evidence for a disaster stress reaction. *American Psychologist, 39,* 252–260.

Ader, R. (Ed.). (1981). *Psychoneuroimmunology.* New York: Academic Press.

Agnew, R. (1992). Foundation for a general strain theory of crime and delinquency. *Criminology, 30,* 47–87.

Ainsworth, M. D. S., & Bell, S. M. (1970). Attachment, exploration, and separation: Illustrated by the behavior of one-year-olds in a strange situation. *Child Development, 41,* 49–67.

Ainsworth, M. D. S., Blehar, M. C., Waters, E., & Wall, S. (1978). *The strange situation: Observing patterns of attachment.* Hillsdale, NJ: Lawrence Erlbaum Associates, Inc.

Ajzen, I., & Fishbein, M. (1980). *Understanding attitudes and predicting social behavior.* Englewood Cliffs, NJ: Prentice-Hall.

Akerstedt, T., & Froberg, J. E. (1976). Interindividual differences in circadian patterns of catecholamine excretion, body temperature, performance, and subjective arousal. *Biological Psychology, 4,* 277–292.

Alajouanine, T. (1963). Dostoievski's epilepsy. *Brain, 86:* 209–221.

Alexander, F. (1935). The logic of emotions and its dynamic background. *International Journal of Psychoanalysis, 16,* 339–413.

Alexander, F. (1962). The development of psychosomatic medicine. *Psychosomatic Medicine, 24,* 13–24.

Allen, L. S., & Gorski, R. A. (1991). Sexual dimorphism of the anterior commissure and massa intermedia of the human brain. *J. Comp. Neurology, 312*(1), 97–104.

Allen, L. S., Gorski, R. A., Shin, J., Barakat, N., & Hines, M. (1987). Sex differences in the corpus callosum of the living human being. *Anatomical Record, 218,* 7a (abstract).

Allen, V. L., & Wilder, D. A. (1980). Impact on group consensus and social support on stimulus meaning: Mediation of conformity by cognitive restructuring. *Journal of Personality & Social Psychology, 39,* 1116–1124.

Allport, G. W. (1937). *Pattern and growth in personality.* New York: Holt, Rinehart & Winston.

Allport, G. W. (1954). *The nature of prejudice.* Boston: Addison-Wesley.

Altman, I. (1975). *The environment and social behavior.* Monterey, CA: Brooks/Cole.

Altman, I. (1987). Centripetal and centrifugal trends in psychology. *American Psychologist, 42*(12), 1058–1069.

Alwin, D. F., Cohen, R. L., & Newcomb, T. M. (1991). *Political attitudes over the life span: The Bennington women after fifty years.*

American Psychiatric Association. (1980). *Diagnostic and statistical manual of mental disorders* (3rd ed.). Washington, DC: Author.

American Psychological Association. (1987). Resolutions approved by the National Conference on Graduate Education in Psychology. *American Psychologist, 42*(12), 1070–1084.

American Psychological Association. (1992). Code of ethics. *APA Monitor.*

Ames, F. R. (1991). Sex and the brain. *South African Medical Journal, 80*(3), 150–152.

Amir, S., Brown, Z. W., & Amir, Z. (1980). The role of endorphins in stress: Evidence and speculation. *Neuroscience and Biobehavioral Reviews, 4,* 77–86.

Amir, Y. (1976). The contact hypothesis revisited. *Psychological Bulletin.*

Anand, S., & Van Thiel, D. H. (1982). Prenatal and neonatal exposure to cimetidine results in gonadal and sexual dysfunction in adult males. *Science, 218*(4571), 493–494.

Anastasi, A. (1982). *Psychological testing.* New York: Macmillan.

Anderson, C. A., & Arnoult, L. H. (1989). An examination of perceived control, humor, irrational beliefs, and positive stress as moderators of the relation between negative stress and health. *Basic and Applied Social Psychology, 10,* 101–117.

Anderson, J. R. (1983). Retrieval of information from long-term memory. *Science, 220,* 25–30.

Anderson, J. R., & Bower, G. H. (1973). *Human associative memory.* Washington, DC: Hemisphere Press.

Anderson, M. (1992). *Intelligence and development: A cognitive theory.* Oxford: Basil Blackwell.

Andersson, B. E. (1992). Effects of day care on cognitive and socioemotional competence of thirteen-year-old Swedish schoolchildren. *Child Development, 63,* 20–36.

Andreason, N. (1988). Brain imaging: Applications in psychiatry. *Science, 239,* 1381–1388.

Andrews, G. R., & Dubus, R. L. (1978). Persistence and the causal perception of failure: Modifying cognitive attributions. *Journal of Educational Psychology, 70,* 154–166.

Andrews, I. R., & Valenzi, E. R. (1970). Overpay inequity and/or self-image as a worker: A critical examination of an experimental induction procedure. *Organizational Behavior and Human Performance, 5,* 266–276.

APA Committee on Drug Abuse. (1987). Position statement on psychoactive substance use and dependence: Update on marijuana and cocaine. *American Journal of Psychiatry, 144,* 698–701.

Archer, D., & Gartner, R. (1984). *Violence and crime in cross-national perspective.* New Haven: Yale University Press.

Argyle, M. (1975). *Bodily communication.* New York: Barnes & Noble.

Argyle, M. (1989). *The social psychology of work* (2nd ed.). London: Penguin.

Argyle, M., & Dean. J. (1965). Eye contact, distance and affiliation. *Sociometry, 28,* 289–304.

Argyle, M., & Henderson, M. *The anatomy of relationships.* London: Penguin.

Argyris, C. (1964). *Integrating the individual and the organization.* New York: Wiley.

Arkes, H. R., Herren, L. T., & Isen, A. M. (1988). The role of potential loss in the influence of affect on risk-taking behavior. *Organizational Behavior and Human Decision Processes, 42,* 181–193.

Arkin, A. M. (1978). Sleeptalking. In A. M. Arkin, J. S. Antrobus, & S. J. Ellman (Eds.), *The mind in sleep.* Hillsdale., NJ: Lawrence Erlbaum.

Arms, R. L., Russell, G. W., & Sandilands, M. L. (1979). Effects on the hostility of spectators of viewing aggressive sports. *Social Psychology Quarterly, 45,* 275–279.

Aronoff, J., Barclay, A. M., & Stevenson, L. A. (1988). The recognition of threatening facial stimuli. *Journal of Personality and Social Psychology, 54,* 647–655.

Aronson, E. (1992). *The social animal* (6th ed.). New York: Freeman.

Aronson, E., & Mills, J. (1959). The effect of severity of initiation on liking for a group. *Journal of Abnormal and Social Psychology, 59,* 177–181.

Aronson, E., & Yates, S. (1983). Cooperation in the classroom: The impact of the jigsaw method on inter-ethnic relations, classroom performance and self-esteem. In H. Blumberg, A. P., Hare, V. Kent, & M. F. Davies (Eds.), *Small groups and social interaction.* New York: Wiley.

Aronson, E., Blaney, N., Sikes, J., Stephan, C., & Snapp, M. (1975). Busing and racial tension: The jigsaw route to learning and liking. *Psychology Today, 8,* 43–50.

Aronson, E., Stephen, C., Sikes, J., Blaney, N., & Snapp, M. (1978). *The jigsaw classroom.* Beverly Hills, CA: Sage.

Asch, S. E. (1951). Effects of group pressure upon the modification and distortion of judgments. In H. Guetzkow (Ed.), *Groups, leadership, and men.* Pitsburgh: Carnegie Press.

Asch, S. E. (1952). *Social psychology.* Englewood Cliffs, NJ: Prentice-Hall.

Aschoff, J. (1981). Annual rhythms in man. In J. Aschoff (Ed.), *Handbook of Behavioral Neurobiology, 4,* 475–490. New York: Plenum.

Aserinsky, E., & Kleitman, N. (1953). Regularly occurring periods of eye motility and concomitant phenomena during sleep. *Science, 118,* 273–274.

Asher, S. R., Parkhurst, J. T., Hymel, S., & Williams, G. A. (1990). Peer rejection and loneliness in childhood. In S. R. Asher & J. D. Coie (Eds.), *Peer rejection in childhood.* New York: Cambridge University Press.

Ashmore, R. D. (1981). Prejudice. In *Encyclopedia of psychology*. Guilford, CT: DPG Reference Publishers.

Atkinson, J. W., & Feather, N. T. (1966). Review and appraisal. In J. W. Atkinson & N. T. Feather (Eds.), *A theory of achievement motivation*. New York: Wiley.

Atkinson, J. W., & Litwin, G. H. (1960). Achievement motive and test anxiety conceived as motive to approach success and motive to avoid failure. *Journal of Abnormal and Social Psychology, 60*, 52–63.

Atkinson, R. C., & Shriffrin, R. M. (1968). Human memory: A proposed system and its control processes. In K. W. Spence & J. T. Spence (Eds.), *The psychology of learning and motivation: Advances in research and theory, Vol. 2*. New York: Academic Press.

Au, T. K. (1983). Chinese and English counterfactuals: The Sapir-Whorf hypothesis revisited. *Cognition, 15*(1–3), 155–187.

Au, T. K. (1984). Counterfactuals in reply to Alfred Bloom. *Cognition, 17*(3), 289–302.

Averill, J. R. (1982). *Anger and aggression*. New York: Springer-Verlag.

Axline, V. M. (1964). *Dibs: In search of self*. New York: Norton.

Ayllon, T., & Azrin, N. H. (1965). The measurement and reinforcement of behavior of psychotics. *Journal of the Experimental Analysis of Behavior, 8*, 357–383.

Ayllon, T., & Michael, J. (1959). The psychiatric nurse as a behavioral engineer. *Journal of the Experimental Analysis of Behavior, 2*, 323–334.

Ayoub, D. Y., Greenough, W. T., & Juraska, J. M. (1983). Sex differences in dendritic structure in the preoptic area on the juvenile Macaque monkey brain. *Science, 219*, 197–198.

▼

Babad, E. Y., Inbar, J., & Rosenthal, R. (1982). Teachers' judgment of students' potential as a function of teachers' susceptibility to biasing information. *Journal of Personality and Social Psychology, 42*, 541–547.

Bachevalier, J. (1990). Ontogenetic development of habit and memory formation in primates. *Annals of the New York Academy of Sciences, 608*, 457–484.

Backman, C. W., & Secord, P. F. (1968). *A social psychological view of education*. New York: Harcourt, Brace & World.

Bailey, M., & Pillard, R. (1991, December 17). Are some people born gay? *New York Times*.

Baillargeon, R. (1992). The object concept revisited. In *Visual perception and cognition in infancy, Carnegie-Mellon Symposia on Cognition, Vol. 23*, Hillsdale, NJ: Erlbaum.

Bakan, P. (1973). Left-handedness and alcoholism. *Perceptual and Motor Skills, 36*, 514.

Bales, J. (1988). Pre-work polygraph ban signed by Reagan. *American Psychological Association Monitor, 19*(8), 5.

Bales, R. F. (1950). *Interaction process analysis*. Cambridge, MA: Addison-Wesley.

Bales, R. F. (1955). How people interact in conferences. *Scientific American, 192*(3), 31–35.

Bales, R. F. (1970). *Personality and interpersonal behavior*. New York: Holt, Rinehart & Winston.

Baltes, P. B., & Kliegl, R. (1992). Further testing of limits of cognitive plasticity: Negative age differences in a mnemonic skill are robust. *Developmental Psychology, 28*, 121–125.

Baltes, P. B., & Schaie K. W. (1977). Aging and IQ: The myth of the twilight years. In S. H. Zarit (Ed.), *Readings in aging and death: Contemporary perspectives*. New York: Harper & Row.

Bancroft, J., & Skakkebaek, N. E. (1978). Androgens and human sexual behavior. In R. Porer & J. Whelan (Eds.), *CIBA Foundation Symposium, No. 62: Sex, Hormones, and Behavior*. London: CIBA.

Bandura, A. (1965a). Influence of models' reinforcement contingencies on the acquisition of imitative responses. *Journal of Personality and Social Psychology, 1*, 589–595.

Bandura, A. (1965b). Vicarious processes: A case of no-trial learning. In L. Berkowitz (Ed.), *Advances in experimental social psychology* (Vol. 2). New York: Academic Press.

Bandura, A. (1971). Analysis of modeling processes. In A. Bandura (Ed.), *Psychological modeling*. New York: Lieber-Atherton.

Bandura, A. (1973). *Aggression: A social learning analysis*. Englewood Cliffs, NJ: Prentice-Hall.

Bandura, A. (1974). Behavior therapy and the models of man. *American Psychologist, 29*, 859–869.

Bandura, A. (1976). Effecting change through participant modeling. In J. D. Krumboltz & C. E. Thoreson (Eds.), *Counseling methods* (pp. 248–265). New York: Holt, Rinehart & Winston.

Bandura, A. (1977). *Social learning theory*. Englewood Cliffs, NJ: Prentice-Hall.

Bandura, A. (1982). Self-efficacy mechanism in human agency. *American Psychologist, 37*, 122–147.

Bandura, A. (1982). The psychology of chance encounters and life paths. *American Psychologist, 37*(7), 747–755.

Bandura, A. (1986). *Social foundations of thought and action: A social cognitive theory*. Englewood Cliffs, NJ: Prentice-Hall.

Bandura, A., Grusec, J., & Menlove, F. (1967). Vicarious extinction of avoidance behaviors. *Journal of Personality and Social Psychology, 5*, 16–23.

Bane, M. J. (1978). *HEW policy toward children, youth, and families* (Order # SA-8139-77). Cambridge, MA: Office of Assistant Secretary for Planning and Evaluation.

Banks, M., & Salapatek, P. (1981). Infant pattern vision: A new approach based on contrast sensitivity function. *Journal of Experimental Child Psychology, 31*(1), 1–45.

Banks, W. P., & Krajicek, D. (1991). Perception. *Annual Review of Psychology, 42*, 305–331.

Barahal, R. M. (1978). A comparison of parent-infant attachment and interaction patterns in day-care and non-day-care family groups (Doctoral dissertation, Cornell University, 1977). *Dissertation Abstracts International, 38*, 5639B.

Barber, T. X. (1965). The effect of "hypnosis" on learning and recall: A methodological critique. *Journal of Clinical Psychology, 21*, 19–25.

Barber, T. X. (1969). *Hypnosis: A scientific approach*. New York: Van Nostrand Reinhold Co.

Barnard, W. A., & Benn, M. S. (1988). Belief congruence and prejudice reduction in an interracial contact setting. *Journal of Social Psychology, 128*, 125–134.

Barnes, D. M. (1987). Hippocampus studied for learning mechanisms. *Science, 236*, 1628–1629.

Baron, R. M., & Graziano, W. G. (1991). *Social psychology*. Fort Worth, TX: Holt, Rinehart & Winston.

Baron, R. S., Kerr, N., & Miller, N. (1992). *Group process, group decision, group action*. Buckingham: Open University.

Barron, F., & Harrington, D. M. (1981). Creativity, intelligence, and personality. *Annual Review of Psychology, 32*, 439–476.

Barthell, C. N., & Holmes, D. S. (1968). High school yearbooks: A nonreactive measure of social isolation in graduates who later became schizophrenic. *Journal of Abnormal Psychology, 73*, 313–316.

Bartholomeus, B. (1974). Effects of task requirements of ear superiority for sung speech. *Cortex, 10*, 215–223.

Bartus, R. T., Dean, R. L., III, Beer, B., & Lippa, A. S. (1982). The cholinergic hypothesis of geriatric memory dysfunction. *Science, 217*, 408–417.

Bashore, T. R., & Rapp, P. E. (1993). Are there alternatives to traditional polygraph procedures? *Psychological Review, 113*, 3–22.

Baskett, L. (1974). *The young child's interactions with parents and siblings: A behavioral analysis*. Unpublished doctoral dissertation, University of Oregon.

Bateson, G., & Ruesch, J. (1951). *Communication: The social matrix of psychiatry*. New York: Norton.

Bateson, G., Jackson, D., Haley, J., & Weakland, J. (1956). Toward a theory of schizophrenia. *Behavioral Science, 1*, 251–264.

Batson, G. D. (1991). *The altruism question*. Hillsdale, NJ: Lawrence Erlbaum Associates.

Baum, A., Fleming, R., & Reddy, D. M. (1986). Unemployment stress: Loss of control, reactance, and learned helplessness. *Social Science and Medicine, 22*, 509–516.

Baum, A., Fleming, R., & Singer, J. E. (1983). Coping with victimization by technological disaster. *Journal of Social Issues, 39*, 117–138.

Baum, A., Harpin, R. E., & Valins, S. (1975). The role of group phenomena in the experience of crowding. *Environment and Behavior, 7*, 185–198.

Baumeister, R., & Steinhilber, A. (1984). Paradoxical effects of supportive audiences on performance under pressure: The home field advantage in sports championships. *Journal of Personality & Social Psychology, 47*, 85–93.

Baumeister, R. F., & Tice, D. M. (1984). Role of self-presentation and choice in cognitive dissonance under forced compliance: Necessary or sufficient causes? *Journal of Personality and Social Psychology, 46*, 5–13.

Baumrind, D. (1971). Current patterns of parental authority. *Developmental Psychology Monographs, 4*(1, Pt.2).

Bavelas, A. (1948). A mathematical model for group structures. *Applied Anthropology, 7*, 16–30.

Baydar, N., & Brooks-Gunn, J. (1991). Effects of maternal employment and child-care arrangements on preschoolers' cognitive and behavioral outcomes: Evidence from the children of the national longitudinal survey of youth. *Developmental Psychology, 27*, 932–945.

Beach, F. A. (1942). Effects of testosterone propionate upon the copulatory behavior of sexually inexperienced male rate. *Journal of Comparative Psychology*, 227–247a.

Bebout, J. (1974). It take one to know one: Existential-Rogerian concepts in encounter groups. In D. A. Wexler & L. N. Rice (Eds.), *Innovations in client-centered therapy*. New York: Wiley-Interscience.

Bechtel, W., & Abrahamson, A. (1991). *Connectionism and the mind: An introduction to parallel processing in networks*. Cambridge, MA: Basil Blackwell.

Beck, A. T., Hollon, S. D., Young, J., Bedrosian, R. C., & Budenz, D. (1985). Combined cognitive-pharmacotherapy versus cognitive therapy in the treatment of depressed outpatients. *Archives of General Psychiatry, 42*, 142–148.

Beck, A. T., Rush, A. J., Shaw, B. F., & Emery, G. (1979). *Cognitive therapy of depression: A treatment manual*. New York: Guilford Press.

Becker, H. S. (1953). Becoming a marijuana user. *American Journal of Sociology, 59*, 235–242.

Becker, J., & Kleinman, A. (1991). *Psychological aspects of depression*. Hillsdale, NJ: Lawrence Erlbaum Associates.

Becker, L. J., & Seligman, C. (1978). Reducing air conditioning waste by signaling it is cool outside. *Personality and Social Psychology Bulletin, 4*, 412–415

Becker, P. T., & Thoman, E. B. (1981). Rapid eye movement storms in infants: Rate of occurrence at 6 months predicts mental development at 1 year. *Science, 212*, 1415–1416.

Begleiter, H., & Porjesz, B. (1975). Evoked brain potentials as indicators of decision making. *Science, 187*, 754–755.

Beilin, H. (1992). Piaget's enduring contribution to developmental psychology. *Developmental Psychology, 28*, 191–204.

Bell, P. A., Fisher, J. D., & Loomis, R. J. (1978). *Environmental psychology*. Philadelphia: Saunders.

Belsky, J., & Rovine, M. J. (1988). Nonmaternal care in the first year of life and the security of the infant-parent attachment. *Child Development, 59*, 157–167.

Belsky, J., Fish, M., & Isabella, R. (1991). Continuity and discontinuity in infant negative and positive emotionality: Family antecedents and attachment consequences. *Developmental Psychology, 27*(3), 421–431.

Bem, D. J. (1983). Constructing a theory of the triple typology: Some (second) thoughts on nomothetic and idiographic approaches to personality. *Journal of Personality, 51*, 566–577.

Benbow, C. (1985). The left hand of math and verbal talent. Paper presented at the Conference on Neurobiology of Intellectual Giftedness, New York. Reported by Bower, B. *Science News, 127*, 263.

Benderly, B. L. (1980). *Dancing without music: Deafness in America*. New York: Anchor Press.

Bennett, B. M., Hoffman, D. D., & Prakash, C. (1989). *Observer Mechanics: A formal theory of perception*. New York: Academic Press.

Bennett, E. L., Diamond, M. D., Krech, D., & Rosenzweig, M. R. (1964). Chemical and anatomical plasticity of brain. *Science, 146*, 610–619.

Bennett, W., & Gurin, J. (1982, March). Do diets really work? *Science, 82*, 42–50.

Benton, A. L. (1980). The neuropsychology of facial recognition. *American Psychologist, 35*(2), 176–186.

Berger, P. L., & Luckmann, T. (1969). *Social construction of reality*. Garden City, NY: Doubleday.

Berger, R. J. (1969). Oculomotor control: A possible function of REM sleep. *Psychological Review, 76*, 144–164.

Berk, R. A., & Aldrich, H. E. (1972). Patterns of vandalism during civil disorders as an indicator of selection of targets. *American Sociological Review, 37*, 533–547.

Berkman, L. F., & Syme, S. L. (1979). Social networks, host resistance, and mortality: A nine-year follow-up study of Alameda County residents. *American Journal of Epidemiology, 109*, 186–204.

Berkowitz, L. (1969). *Roots of aggression: A re-examination of the frustration-aggression hypothesis*. New York: Atherton.

Berkowitz, L. (1978). Whatever happened to the frustration-aggression hypothesis? *American Behavioral Scientist, 21*, 691–708.

Berkowitz, L. (1983). Aversively stimulated aggression: Some parallels and differences in research with animals and humans. *American Psychologist, 11*, 1135–1144.

Berkowitz, L. (1989). Frustration-aggression hypothesis: Examination and reformulation. *Psychological Bulletin, 106*, 59–73.

Berkowitz, L. (1993). *Aggression*. New York: McGraw-Hill.

Berkowitz, W. R. (1971). A cross-national comparison of some social patterns of urban pedestrians. *Journal of Cross-Cultural Psychology, 2*, 129–144.

Berkun, M. M. (1964). Performance decrement under psychological stress. *Human Factors, 6*, 21–30.

Berkun, M. M., Bialek, H. M., Kern, R. P., & Yagi, K. (1962). Experimental studies of psychological stress in man. *Psychological Monographs, 76*(15, Whole No. 534).

Berlin, B., & Kay, P. (1969). *Basic color terms: Their universality and evolution*. Berkeley, University of California Press.

Berman, J. S., Miller, C., & Massman, P. J. (1985). Cognitive therapy versus systematic desensitization: Is one treatment superior? *Psychological Bulletin, 97*, 451–461.

Bernard, Y. (1991). Environmental psychology in France. *Journal of Environmental Psychology, 11*, 277–285.

Berscheid, E. (1966). Opinion change and communicator-communicatee similarity and dissimilarity. *Journal of Personality and Social Psychology, 4*, 670–680.

Berscheid, E., & Walster, E. H. (1978). *Interpersonal attraction* (2nd ed.). Reading, MA: Addison-Wesley.

Bettelheim, B. (1967). *The empty fortress*. New York: Free Press.

Bevan, W. (1982). A sermon of sorts in three plus parts. *American Psychologist, 37*, 1303–1322.

Bickman, L. (1987). Graduate education in psychology. *American Psychologist, 42*(12), 1041–1047.

Birnholz, J. C. (1981). The development of human fetal eye movement patterns. *Science, 213*, 679–681.

Bjerner, B., Holm, A., & Swensson, A. (1955). Diurnal variation in mental performance: A study of three-shift workers. *British Journal of Industrial Medicine, 12*, 103–110.

Bjorkqvist, K., & Niemela, P. (1992). *Of mice and women: Aspects of female aggression*. San Diego, CA: Academic Press.

Bjorkqvist, K., Lagerspetz, K. M. J., & Kaukiainen, A. (1992). Do girls manipulate and boys fight? Developmental trends in regard to direct and indirect aggression. *Aggressive Behavior, 18*, 117–127.

Black, I. B., Adler, J. E., Dreyfus, C. F., Friedman, W. F., LaGamma, E. F., & Roach, A. H. (1987). Biochemistry of information storage in the nervous system. *Science, 236*, 1263–1268.

Blackmore, S. (1991). Lucid dreaming: Awake in your sleep? *Skeptical Inquirer, 15*, 362–370.

Blair, S. N., Kohl, H. W., Paffenbarger, R. S., Jr., Clark, D. G., Cooper, K. H., & Gibbons, L. W. (1989). Physical fitness and all-cause mortality: A prospective study of healthy men and women. *Journal of the American Medical Association, 262*, 2395–2401.

Blanchard, F. A., Lilly, T., & Vaughn, L. A. (1991). Reducing the expression of racial prejudice. *Psychological Science, 2*, 101–105.

Blanchard, R. J., & Blanchard, D. C. (Eds.). (1984). *Advances in the study of aggression*. Orlando, FL: Academic Press.

Bland, J. (1982, January). The junk-food syndrome. *Psychology Today*, 92.

Blaney, N., Stephan, C., Rosenfield, D., Aronson, E., & Sikes, J. (1977). Interdependence in the classroom: A field study. *Journal of Educational Psychology, 69*, 121–128.

Bleier, R., Houston, L., & Byne, W. (1986). Can the corpus callosum predict gender, age, handedness, or cognitive differences? *Trends in Neurosciences, 9*, 391–394.

Bleuler, E. (1950). *Dementia praecox or the group of schizophrenias*. New York: International Universities Press. (Original work published 1911) (J-Zinkin, transl.).

Blonder, L. X., Burns, A. F., Bowers, D., Moore, R. W., & Heilman, K. M. (1993). Right hemisphere facial expressivity during natural conversation. *Brain and Cognition, 21*, 44–56.

Bloom, F. (1985) Paper presented at the meeting of American Association for the Advancement of Science, Los Angeles.

Bochner, S., & Insko, C. A. (1966). Communicator discrepancy, source credibility, and opinion change. *Journal of Personality and Social Psychology, 4*, 614–621.

Boden, M. (1977). *Artificial intelligence and natural man*. New York: Basic Books.

Bogen, J. E. (1969). The other side of the brain: An oppositional mind. *Bulletin of the Los Angeles Neurological Societies, 34*(3), 135–162.

Bolles, R. C., & Fanselow, M. S. (1982). Endorphins and behavior. Annual Review of Psychology, 33, 87–101.

Bolos, A. M., Dean, M., & Ransburg, M. (1990). Population and pedigree studies reveal a lack of association between the dopamine D2 receptor gene and alcoholism. *Journal of the American Medical Association, 264,* 3156.

Bond, C. F., & Titus, L. J. (1983). Social facilitation: A meta-analysis of 241 studies. *Psychological Bulletin, 94,* 265–292.

Booth-Kewley, S., & Friedman, H. S. (1987). Psychological predictors of heart disease: A quantitative review. *Psychological Bulletin, 101,* 343–362.

Bootzin, R. R., & Acocella, J. R. (1988). Abnormal psychology: Current perspectives (5th ed.). New York: Random House.

Borgatta, E. F., Couch, A. S., & Bales, R. F. (1954). Some findings relevant to the great man theory of leadership. *American Sociological Review, 19,* 755–759.

Borgens, R. B., Blight, A. R., & McGinnis, M. E. (1987). Behavioral recovery induced by applied electric fields after spinal cord hemisection in guinea pig. *Science, 238,* 366–369.

Bossard, J. H. S. (1945). Law of family interaction. *American Journal of Sociology, 50,* 292–294.

Bouchard, T., & McGue, M. (1981). Familial studies of intelligence: A review. *Science, 212,* 1055–1059.

Bouton, M. E., & Swartzentruber, D. (1991). Sources of relapse after extinction in Pavlovian and instrumental conditioning. *Clinical Psychology Review, 11,* 123–140.

Bower, G. H. (1981). Mood and memory. *American Psychologist, 36*(2), 129–148.

Bowerman, M. (1973). Structural relationships in children's utterances: Syntactic or semantic? In T. Moore (Ed.), *Cognitive development and the acquisition of language.* New York: Academic Press.

Boynton, R. M. (1988). Color vision. *Annual Review of Psychology, 39,* 69–100.

Brackbill, Y., & Nichols, P. L. (1982). A test of the confluence model of intellectual development. *Developmental Psychology, 18*(2), 192–198.

Bradshaw, J. L. (1989). *Hemispheric specialization and psychological function.* New York: Wiley.

Brady, J. V. (1958). Ulcers in "executive monkeys." *Scientific American, 199,* 95–100.

Brain, P. F. (1991). Alcohol and violence: A personal view. *Bulletin of the International Society for Research on Aggression, 13*(1), 3–6.

Bramel, D., & Friend, R. (1981). Hawthorne, the myth of the docile worker, and class bias in psychology. *American Psychologist, 36,* 867–878.

Bransford, J. D., & Johnson, M. K. (1973). Considerations of some problems of comprehension. In W. G. Chase (Ed.), *Visual information processing.* New York: Academic Press.

Braungart, J. M., Plomin, R., DeFries, J. C., & Fulker, D. W. (1992). Genetic influences on tester-rated infant temperament as assessed by Bayley's infant behavior record: Nonadoptive and adoptive siblings and twins. *Developmental Psychology, 28,* 40–47.

Breland, K., & Breland, M. (1966). *Animal behavior.* New York: Macmillan.

Brenner, M. H. (1973). *Mental illness and the economy.* Cambridge, MA: Harvard University Press.

Brenner, M. H. (1976). *Estimating the social costs of national economic policy.* Washington, DC: Joint Economic Committee of Congress. (In Liem & Rayman, 1982)

Brenner, M. H. (1987). Economic change, alcohol consumption and heart disease mortality in nine industrialized countries. *Social Science and Medicine, 25,* 119–132.

Brenner, R., & Brenner, G. A. (1990). *Gambling and speculation: A theory, history, and a future of some human decisions.* Cambridge, MA: Cambridge University Press.

Brickner, M. A., Harkins, S., & Ostrom, T. M. (1986). Personal involvement: Thought provoking implications for social loafing. *Journal of Personality and Social Psychology, 51,* 763–769.

Broadbent, D. E. (1978). *Decision and uncertainty.* Cambridge: Cambridge University Press.

Brobeck, J. R., Tepperman, J., & Long, C. N. H. (1943). Experimental hypothalamic hyperphagia in the albino rat. *Yale Journal of Biology and Medicine, 15,* 831–853.

Brody, G., Pillegrini, A., & Sigel, I. (1986). Marital quality and mother-child and father-child interactions with school-aged children. *Developmental Psychology, 22,* 291–296.

Brooks-Gunn, J., Warren, M. P., Samelson, M., & Fox, R. (1986). Physical similarity of the disclosure of menarcheal status to friends: Effects of grade and pubertal status. *Journal of Early Adolescence, 6,* 3–14.

Brower, K. J., Catlin, D. H., Blow, F. C., Eliopulos, G. A., & Beresford, T. P. (1991). Clinical assessment and urine testing for anabolic-androgenic steroid abuse and dependence. *American Journal of Drug and Alcohol Abuse, 17*(2), 161–171.

Brown, D. E. (1991). *Human Universals.* Philadelphia: Temple University Press.

Brown, G. W., & Harris, T. O. (1978). *Social origins of depression: A study of psychiatric disorder in women.* London: Tavistock.

Brown, J. (1958). Some tests of the decay theory of immediate memory. *Quarterly Journal of Experimental Psychology, 10,* 12–21.

Brown, J. D. (1991). Staying fit and staying well: Physical fitness as a moderator of life stress. *Journal of Personality and Social Psychology, 60,* 555–561.

Brown, J. D., & McGill, K. L. (1989). The cost of good fortune: When positive life events produce negative health consequences. *Journal of Personality and Social Psychology, 57,* 1103–1110.

Brown, N. R., Rips, L. J., & Shevell, S. K. (1985). The subjective dates of natural events in very-long-term memory. *Cognitive Psychology, 17,* 139–177.

Brown, R. (1986). *Social psychology* (2nd ed.). New York: Macmillan.

Brown, R. T. (1968). Early experience and problem-solving ability. *Journal of Comparative and Physiological Psychology, 65,* 433–440.

Brown, R. W. (1973). *A first language: The early stages.* Cambridge: Harvard University Press.

Bruner, J. S. (1977). Early social interaction and language acquisition. In H. R. Schaffer (Ed.), *Studies in mother-infant interaction.* London: Academic Press.

Bruner, J. S., Goodnow, J., & Austin, G. A. (1956). *A study of thinking.* New York: Wiley.

Bryden, M. P. (1982). *Laterality: Functional asymmetry in the intact brain.* New York: Academic Press.

Buck, R. (1980). Nonverbal behavior and the theory of emotion: The facial feedback hypothesis. *Journal of Personality and Social Psychology, 38,* 811–824.

Buck, R. (1984). *The communication of emotion.* New York: Guilford Press.

Buckley, W. E., Yesalis, C. E., & Friedl, K. E. (1988). Estimated prevalence of anabolic steroid use among male high school seniors. *Journal of the American Medical Association, 260,* 3441–3445.

Buss, D. (1990). Paper presented at American Psychological Association. Boston.

Byrne, D. (1971). *The attraction paradigm.* New York: Academic Press.

Byrne, D., Gouaux, C., Griffitt, W., Lamberth, J., Murakawa, N., Prasad, M. B., Prasad, A., & Ramirez, M., III. (1971). The ubiquitous relationship: Attitude similarity and attraction. A cross-cultural study. *Human Relations, 24,* 201–207.

Cacioppo, J. T., Rourke, P., Tassinary, L., Marshall-Goodall, B., & Baron, R. S. (1990). Rudimentary physiological effects of mere observation. *Psychophysiology, 27,* 177–186.

Cacioppo, J. T., Uchino, B. N., Crites, S. L., Snydersmith, M. A., Smith, G., Bernston, G. G., & Lang, P. J. (1992). Relationship between facial expressiveness and sympathetic activation in emotion: A critical review, with emphasis on modeling underlying mechanisms and individual differences. *Journal of Personality and Social Psychology, 62*(1), 110–128.

Cadoret, R. J., Troughton, E., O'Gorman, T. W., & Heywood, E. (1986). An adoption study of genetic and environmental factors in drug abuse. *Archives of General Psychiatry, 43,* 1131–1136.

Calder, B. J., Ross, M., & Insko, C. A. (1973). Attitude change and attitude attribution: Effects of incentive, choice, and consequences. *Journal of Personality and Social Psychology, 25,* 84–99.

Caldwell, J. C., & Caldwell, P. (1990, May). High fertility in sub-Saharan Africa. *Scientific American,* 118–125.

Caldwell, J. C., & Caldwell, P. (1992). What does the Matlab fertility experience really show? *Studies in Family Planning, 23,* 292.

Calhoun, J. B. (1962). Population density and social pathology. *Scientific American, 206,* 139–148.

Callaway, M. R., Marriott, R. G., & Esser, J. K. (1985). Effects of dominance on group decision making: Toward a stress-reduction explanation of groupthink. *Journal of Personality and Social Psychology, 49,* 949–952.

Calvin, W. H. (1991). *The throwing madonna: Essays on the brain.* New York: Bantam Books.

Campbell, A. (1983). *Men, women, and aggression.* New York: Bask Books.

Campbell, A., Muncer, S., & Coyle, E. (1992). Social representation of aggression as an example of gender differences: A preliminary study. *Aggressive Behavior, 18,* 95–108.

Campbell, D. T., Naroll, R. (1972). The mutual methodological relevance of anthropology and psychology. In F. L. K. Hsu (Ed.), *Psychological anthropology* (rev. ed.). Cambridge, MA: Schenkman.

Canter, D. (1988). To catch a rapist. *New Society, 4* (March), 14–15.

Cantor, N., & Kihlstrom, J. F. (1987). *Personality and social intelligence*. Englewood Cliffs, NJ: Prentice-Hall.

Cantril, H. (1963). *The psychology of social movements*. New York: Wiley. (Original work published 1941)

Caplan, N., Choy, M. H., & Whitemore, J. K. (1992, February). Indochinese refugee families and academic achievement. *Scientific American, 266,* 18–24.

Cardé, R. T. (1984). Chemo-orientation in flying insects. In W. J. Bell and R. T. Cardé (Eds.), *Chemical ecology of insects*. Sunderland, MA: Sinauer Associates, Inc.

Cardé, R. T. & Hagaman, T. E. (1979). Behavioral responses of the gypsy moth in a wind tunnel to air-borne enantiomers of disparlure. *Environmental Entomology, 8,* 475–484.

Carlson, M., Charlin, V., & Miller, N. (1988). Positive mood and helping behavior: A test of six hypotheses. *Journal of Personality and Social Psychology, 55,* 211–229.

Carter-Saltzman, L. (1980). Biological and sociocultural effects on handedness: Comparison between biological and adoptive families. *Science, 209,* 1263–1265.

Cartwright, R. (1977) *A primer on sleep and dreaming*. Reading, MA: Addison-Wesley.

Carver, C. S., DeGregoria, E., & Gillis, R. (1980). Field study of an ego-defensive bias in attribution among two categories of observers. *Personality and Social Psychology Bulletin, 6,* 44–50.

Cattell, R. B. (1965). *The scientific analysis of personality*. Baltimore: Penguin.

Caughey, J. (1985). *Imaginary social worlds*. Lincoln, NE: University of Nebraska Press.

Cazden, C. (1972). *Child language and education*. New York: Holt, Rinehart & Winston.

Cervone, D. (1992). The two disciplines of personality psychology. Review of L. A. Pervin (Ed.), "Handbook of personality: Theory and research." *Psychological Science, 2,* 371–377.

Cervone, D., & Peake, P. K. (1986). Anchoring, efficacy, and action: The influence of judgmental heuristics on self-efficacy judgments and behavior. *Journal of Personality and Social Psychology, 50,* 492–501.

Chamberlain, H. D. (1928). The inheritance of left-handedness. *Journal of Heredity, 19,* 557–559.

Champion, D. J. (1990). *Criminal justice in the United States*. Columbus, OH: Merrill.

Chapin, M., & Dyck, D. G. (1976). Persistence in children's reading behavior as a function of N length and attribution retraining. *Journal of Abnormal Psychology, 85,* 511–515.

Chapman, A. J. (1983). Humor and laughter in social interaction and some implications for humor research. In P. E. McGhee & J. H. Goldstein (Eds.), *Handbook of humor research, Vol. 1: Basic issues* (pp. 135–157). New York: Springer-Verlag.

Charney, D. S., Heninger, G. R., & Jatlow, P. I. (1985). Increased angiogenic effects of caffeine in panic disorders. *Archives of General Psychiatry, 42,* 233–243.

Chen, S. C. (1937). The leaders and followers among the ants in nest building. *Physiological Zoology, 10,* 437–455.

Cheng, P., & Casida, L. E. (1949). Effects of testosterone propionate upon sexual libido and the production of semen and sperm in the rabbit. *Endocrinology, 44,* 38–48.

Chermol B. H. (1983, July). Psychiatric casualties. *Military Review,* 27–32.

Cherry, E. C. (1953). Some experiments on the recognition of speech, with one or with two ears. *Journal of the Acoustical Society of America, 25,* 975–979.

Chiesa, M. (1992). Radical behaviorism and scientific frameworks. *American Psychologist, 47,* 1287–1299.

Chomsky, N. (1959). Review of "Verbal behavior" by B. F. Skinner. *Language, 35,* 26–58.

Chomsky, N. (1972.) *Language and mind*. New York: Harcourt, Brace & World.

Chomsky, N. (1979). Species of intelligence. Encounter, a dialogue with Noam Chomsky and David Premack. *The Sciences, 19,* 6–11, 23.

Christman, S. (1989). Perceptual characteristics in visual laterality. *Brain and Cognition, 11,* 238.

Christman, S., Kitterle, F. L., & Hellige, J. (1991). Hemispheric asymmetry in the processing of relative spatial frequency. *Brain and Cognition, 16,* 62.

Christopher, F. S. (1988). An initial investigation into a continuum of premarital sexual pressure. *The Journal of Sex Research, 25,* 255–266.

Cialdini, R. B. (1985). *Influence: Science and Practice*. Glenview, IL: Scott Foresman.

Cialdini, R. B., Borden, R. J., Thorne, A., Walker, M. R., Freeman, S., & Sloan, L. R. (1976). Basking in reflected glory: Three (football) field studies. *Journal of Personality and Social Psychology, 34,* 366–375.

Cimmerman, A. (1981). The Fay case. *Criminal Defense, 8,* 7.

Clairborn, W. L. (1969). Expectancy effects in the classroom: A failure to replicate. *Journal of Educational Psychology, 60,* 377–383.

Clark, H. H., & Clark, E. V. (1977). *Psychology and language*. New York: Harcourt Brace Jovanovich.

Clark, W. C., & Clark, S. B. (1980). Pain responses in Nepalese porters. *Science, 209,* 410–412.

Clarke, P. G. H., & Whitteridge, D. (1978). A comparison of stereoscopic mechanisms in cortical visual areas V1 and V2 of the cat. *Journal of Physiology, London, 275,* 92–93.

Clausen, J. A. (1975). The social meaning of differential physical and sexual maturation. In S. E. Dragastin & G. E. Elder (Eds.), *Adolescence in the life cycle: Psychological change and the social context*. New York: Halsted.

Cloward, R. A., & Ohlin, L. E. (1960). *Delinquency and opportunity*. New York: Free Press.

Cochrane, R. (1991). Racial prejudice. In R. Cochrane & D. Carroll (Eds.), *Psychology and social issues*. London: Falmer Press.

Code, C. (1987). *Language, aphasia, and the right hemisphere*. Chichester, England: John Wiley & Sons.

Cogan, R., Cogan, D., Waltz, W., & McCue, M. (1987). Effects of laughter and relaxation on discomfort thresholds. *Journal of Behavioral Medicine, 10,* 139–143.

Cohen, D. (1992, July 25). Zen and the art of dealing with stress. *New Scientist, 135,* 28–31.

Cohen, D. J., Bruun, R. D., & Leckman, J. F. (Eds.). (1988). *Tourette's syndrome and tic disorders*. New York: John Wiley & Sons.

Cohen, F., & Lazarus, R. S. (1979). Coping with the stresses of illness. In G. C. Stone, F. Cohen, & N. Adler (Eds.), *Health psychology: A handbook* (pp. 217–254). San Francisco: Jossey-Bass.

Cohen, S., & Lezak, A. (1977). Noise and inattentiveness to social cues. *Environment and Behavior, 9,* 559–572.

Cohen, S., & Syme, S. L. (1985), *Social support and health*. New York: Academic Press.

Cohen, S., & Wills, T. A. (1985). Stress, social support, and the buffering hypothesis. *Psychological Bulletin, 98,* 310–357.

Cohen, S., Evans, G. W., Krantz, D. S., & Stokols, D. (1980). Physiological, motivational, and cognitive effects of aircraft noise on children. *American Psychologist, 35*(3), 231–243.

Colby, A., Kohlberg, L., Gibbs, J., Candee, D., Speicher-Dubin, B., Hewer, A., & Power, C. (1983). *The measurement of moral development: Standard issue scoring manual*. New York: Cambridge University Press.

Cole, M., & Scribner, S. (1974). *Culture and thought: A psychological introduction*. New York: John Wiley & Sons.

Cole, M., & Scribner, S. (1977). Cross-cultural studies of memory and cognition. In R. V. Kail & J. H. Hagen (Eds.), *Perspectives on the development of memory & cognition*. Hillsdale, NJ: LEA.

Colen, John L., & McNeely, R. L. (1983). *Aging in minority groups*. Beverly Hills: Sage Publications.

Coles, M. G., Gale, A., & Kline, P. (1971). Personality and habituation of the orienting reaction: Tonic and response measures of electrodermal activity. *Psychophysiology, 8,* 54–63.

Collins, A. M., & Quillian, M. R. (1969). Retrieval time from semantic memory. *Journal of Verbal Learning and Verbal Behavior, 8,* 240–247.

Collins, E. (1983, September). Managers and love. *Harvard Business Review, 5,* 142–153.

Collins, W. A., & Gunnar M. R. (1990). Social and personality development. *Annual Review of Psychology, 41,* 387–416.

Colman, A. M. (1991). Crowd psychology in South African murder trials. *American Psychologist, 46,* 1071–1079.

Colvin, R. H., & Olson, S. B. (1983). A descriptive analysis of men and women who have lost significant weight and are highly successful at maintaining the loss. *Addictive Behaviors, 8,* 287–296.

Condry, J. (1977). Enemies of exploration: Self-initiated versus other-initiated learning. *Journal of Personality and Social Psychology, 35,* 459–477.

Condry, J. (1989). *The psychology of television*. Hillsdale, NJ: Lawrence Erlbaum.

Conte, G., Vita, A., & Sacchetti, E. (1988). Interepisode reliability of urinary MHPG excretion in major depression. *Biological Psychiatry, 24,* 240–243.

Conte, H. R. (1986). Multivariate assessment of sexual dysfunction. *Journal of Consulting and Clinical Psychology, 54,* 149–157.

Cook, M., & Mineka, S. (1987). Second-order conditioning and overshadowing in the observational conditioning of fear in monkeys. *Behavior Research and Therapy, 25*(5), 349–364.

Cook, S. W. (1985). Experimenting on social issues: The case of school desegregation. *American Psychologist, 40,* 452–460.

Cooke, M., & Goldstein, J. H. (1989). Social isolation and violent behavior. *Forensic Reports, 2,* 287–294.

Cooley, C. H. (1909). *Social organization.* New York: Scribner's.

Cooper, H. M. (1979). Pygmalion grows up: A model for teacher expectation, communication, and performance influence. *Review of Educational Research, 49,* 389–410.

Cooper, J., & Fazio, R. H. (1984). A new look at dissonance theory. In L. Berkowitz (Ed.), *Advances in experimental social psychology.* Vol. 17. Orlando, FL: Academic Press.

Corballis, M. C., & Beale, I. L. (1976). *The psychology of left and right.* Hillsdale, NJ: Lawrence Erlbaum Associates.

Coren, S., Porac, C., & Ward, L. M. (1979). *Sensation and perception.* New York: Academic Press.

Corsaro, W. A. (1981). Friendship in the nursery school: Social organization in a peer environment. In S. R. Asher & J. M. Gottman (Eds.), *The development of children's friendships.* Cambridge: Cambridge University Press.

Corsini, R. J. (1991). *Five therapists and one client.* Itasca, IL: F. E. Peacock.

Coser, R. L. (1960). Laughter among colleagues. *Psychiatry, 23,* 81–95.

Cottrell, N. B. (1968). Performance in the presence of other human beings. In E. Simmel, R. Hoppe, & G. Milton (Eds.), *Social facilitation and imitative behavior.* Boston: Allyn and Bacon.

Coulter, J. (1973). *Approaches to insanity.* London: Robertson.

Cournos, F. (1989). Involuntary medication and the case of Joyce Brown. *Hospital and Community Psychiatry, 40,* 736–740.

Cousins, N. (1979). *Anatomy of an illness.* New York: Norton.

Cousins, S. D. (1989). Culture and self-perception in Japan and the United States. *Journal of Personality and Social Psychology, 56,* 124–131.

Cox, A., Rutter, M., Newman, S., & Bartak, L. (1975). A comparative study of infantile autism and specific developmental language disorders: II. Parental characteristics. *British Journal of Psychiatry, 126,* 146–159.

Cox, T., & MacKay, C. (1982). Psychosocial factors and psychophysiological mechanisms in the aetiology and development of cancer. *Social Science and Medicine,* 381–396.

Coyne, J. C., & Downey, G. (1991). Social factors and psychopathology: Stress, social support, and coping processes. *Annual Review of Psychology, 42,* 401–425.

Crabb, P. B. (1992). Effective control of energy-depleting behavior. *American Psychologist, 47,* 815–816.

Craik, F. I. M., & Lockhart, R. S. (1972). Levels of processing: A framework for memory research. *Journal of Verbal Learning and Verbal Behavior, 11,* 671–684.

Cramer, D. (1991). *Personality and psychotherapy.* London: Open University.

Crick, F., & Koch, C. (1992, September). The problem of consciousness. *Scientific American, 267,* 110–117.

Critchlow, B. (1983). Blaming the booze: The attribution of responsibility for drunken behavior. *Personality and Social Psychology Bulletin, 9,* 451–473.

Cross, T. G. (1978). Mothers' speech and its association with rate of syntactic acquisition in young children. In N. Waterson & C. Snow (Eds.), *The development of communication.* New York: Wiley.

Crowell, J. A., & Feldman, S. S. (1991). Mothers' working models of attachment relationships and mother and child behavior during separation and reunion. *Developmental Psychology, 27,* 597–605.

Cumberbatch, G. (1991). Is television violence harmful? In R. Cochrane & D. Carroll (Eds.), *Psychology and social issues.* London: Falmer.

Curry, F. K. W. (1967). A comparison of left-handed and right-handed subjects on verbal and non-verbal dichotic listening tasks. *Cortex, 3,* 343–352.

Curtis, J. E., Grabb, E. G., & Baer, D. E. (1992). Voluntary association membership in fifteen countries: A comparative analysis. *American Sociological Review, 57,* 139–152.

Curtiss, S. (1977). *Genie: A psycholinguistic study of a modern-day "wild child."* New York: Academic Press.

Czeisler, C. A., Moore-Ede, M. C., & Coleman, R. M. (1985). Rotating shift work schedules that disrupt sleep are improved by applying circadian principles. *Science, 217,* 460–463.

▼

Dahlberg, C., & Jaffe, J. (1977). *Stroke.* New York: Norton.

Dainoff, M. J., Happ, A., & Crane, P. (1981). Visual fatigue and occupational stress in VDT operators. *Human Factors, 23*(4), 421–438.

Daniel, T. L., & Esser, J. K. (1980). Intrinsic motivation as influenced by rewards, task interest, and task structure. *Journal of Applied Psychology, 65,* 566–573.

Darley, J. M., & Schultz, T. R. (1990). Moral rules: Their content and acquisition. *Annual Review of Psychology, 41,* 525–556.

Darwin, C. J., Turvey, M. T., & Crowder, R. G. (1972). An auditory analogue of the Sperling partial-report procedure: Evidence for brief auditory storage. *Cognitive Psychology, 3,* 255–267.

Dasen, P. R. (1984). The cross-cultural study of intelligence: Piaget and the Baoulé. *International Journal of Psychology, 19,* 407–434.

Dashiell, J. S. (1930). An experimental analysis of some group effects. *Journal of Abnormal and Social Psychology, 25,* 190–199.

Davenport, W. H. (1977). Sex in cross-cultural perspective. In F. A. Beach (Ed.), *Human sexuality in four perspectives.* Baltimore: Johns Hopkins University Press.

Davidson, J. M. (1966). Characteristics of sex behavior in male rats following castration. *Animal Behaviour, 14* 266–272.

Davidson, L. M., Baum, A., & Collins, D. L. (1982). Stress and control-related problems at Three Mile Island. *Journal of Applied Social Psychology, 12,* 349–359.

Davidson, R. J. (1984). Affect, cognition, and hemispheric specialization. In C. E. Izard, J. Kagan, & R. B. Zajonc (Eds.), *Emotions, cognition, and behavior.* Cambridge, England: Cambridge University Press.

Davis, D., Cahan, S., & Bashi, J. (1977). Birth order and intellectual development: The confluence model in the light of cross-cultural evidence. *Science, 196,* 1470–1471.

Davis, J. M., & Greenblatt, D. (1979). *Psychopharmacology update.* New York: Grune & Stratton.

De Koninck, J., & Brunette, R. (1991). Presleep suggestion related to a phobic object: Successful manipulation of reported dream affect. *The Journal of General Psychology, 118*(3), 185–199.

de Lacoste, M. C., Horvath, D. S., & Woodward, D. J. (1991). Possible sex differences in the developing human fetal brain. *Journal of Clinical and Experimental Neuropsychology, 13*(6), 831–846.

Deaux, K. (1985). Sex and gender. *Annual Review of Psychology, 36,* 49–81.

DeCasper, A. J., & Fifer, W. P. (1980). Of human bonding: Newborns prefer their mothers' voices. *Science, 208,* 1174–1176.

Deci, E. (1980). *The psychology of self-determination.* Lexington, MA: D. C. Heath.

Deci, E. L. (1971). Effects of externally mediated rewards on intrinsic motivation. *Journal of Personality and Social Psychology, 18,* 105–115.

Deci, E. L. (1975). *Intrinsic motivation.* New York: Plenum.

Dee, H. L. (1971). Auditory asymmetry and strength of manual preference. *Cortex, 7,* 236–245.

Deikman, A. J. (1971). Bimodal consciousness. *Archives of General Psychiatry, 25,* 481–489.

Dell, P. F. (1980). The Hopi family therapist and the Aristotelian parents. *Journal of Marital and Family Therapy, 6,* 123–130.

DeLoache, J. S. (1987). Rapid change in the symbolic functioning of very young children. *Science, 238,* 1556–1557.

Dembroski, T. M., MacDougall, J. M., Eliot, R. S., & Buell, J. C. (1983). Stress, emotions, behavior, and cardiovascular disease. In L. Temoshok, C. Van Dyke, & L. S. Zegans (Eds.), *Emotions in health and illness: Theoretical and research foundation.* New York: Grune & Stratton.

Dembroski, T. M. MacDougall, J. M., Williams, R. B., Haney, T. L., & Blumenthal, J. A. (1985). Components of Type A, hostility, and anger-in: Relationship to angiographic findings. *Psychosomatic Medicine, 47,* 219–233.

Dennis, M. I., Soderstrom, E. J., Koncinski, W. S., Jr., & Cavanaugh, B. (1990). Effective dissemination of energy-related information: Applying social psychological and evaluation research. *American Psychologist, 45,* 1109–1117.

Dennis, W. (1966). Creative productivity between the ages of 20 and 80 years. *Journal of Gerontology, 21,* 1–8.

Descartes, R. (1960). *Discourse on method and meditations* (L. Lafleur, Trans.). Indianapolis: Bobbs-Merrill. (Original work published 1637.)

Desor, J. A. (1972). Toward a psychological theory of crowding. *Journal of Personality and Social Psychology, 21,* 79–83.

Deutsch, D. (1980). Handedness and memory for tonal pitch. In J. Herron (Ed.), *Neuropsychology of left-handedness.* New York: Academic Press.

Deutsch, J. A., & Deutsch, D. (1963). Attention: Some theoretical considerations. *Psychological Review, 70,* 80–90.

Deutsch, M. (1949). An experimental study of the effects of cooperation and competition upon group process. *Human Relations, 2,* 199–231.

DeValois, R. L., Abramov, I., & Jacobs, G. H. (1966). Analysis of response patterns in LGN cells. *Journal of the Optical Society of America, 56,* 966–977.

DeValois, R. L., & DeValois, K. K. (1980). Spatial vision. *Annual Review of Psychology, 31,* 309–341.

DeVos, G., & Wagatsuma, H. (1966). *Japan's invisible race.* Berkeley: University of California Press.

DeVries, H. A., & Adams, G. M. (1972). Electromyographic comparison of single doses of exercise and meprobamate as to effects on muscular relaxation. *American Journal of Physical Medicine, 51,* 130–141.

Dichter, M. A., & Ayala, G. F. (1987). Cellular mechanisms of epilepsy: A status report. *Science, 237* 157–163.

Dienstbier, R. A., & Munter, P. O. (1971). Cheating as a function of the labeling of natural arousal. *Journal of Personality and Social Psychology, 17,* 208–213.

Digman, J. M. (1990). Personality structure: Emergence of the five-factor model. *Annual Review of Psychology, 41,* 417–440.

Dillon, K. M., Minchoff, B., & Baker, K. H. (1985). Positive emotional states and enhancement of the immune system. *International Journal of Psychiatry in Medicine, 15,* 13–18.

Dimberg, U. (1990). Facial electromyography and emotional reactions. *Psychophysiology, 27,* 481–494.

Dimond, E. G. (1971). Acupuncture anaesthesia: Western medicine and Chinese traditional medicine. *J. Amer. Med. Assoc. 218,* 1558–1563.

Dion, K. L., Baron, R. S., & Miller, N. (1970). Why do groups make riskier decisions than individuals? In L. Berkowitz (Ed.), *Advances in experimental social psychology* (Vol. 5). New York: Academic Press.

Dittmann-Köhli, F., & Baltes, P. B. (1990). Toward a neofunctionalist conception of adult intellectual development: Wisdom as a prototypical case of intellectual growth. In C. N. Alexander and E. J. Langer (Eds.), *Higher stages of human development: Perspectives on adult growth.* New York: Oxford University Press.

Doise, W. (1969). Intergroup relations and polarization of individual and collective judgments. *Journal of Personality and Social Psychology, 12,* 136–143.

Dollard, J., & Miller, N. E. (1950). *Personality and psychotherapy.* New York: McGraw-Hill.

Dollard, J., Doob, L., Miller, N. E., Mowrer, O. H., & Sears, R. R. (1939). *Frustration and aggression.* New Haven, CT: Yale University Press.

Domjan, M. (1987). Animal learning comes of age. *American Psychologist, 42*(6), 556–564.

Dornbusch, S. M., et al. (1985). Single parents, extended households, and the control of adolescence. *Child Development, 56*(2), 326–341.

Drickamer, L. C. (1988). Acceleration and delay of sexual maturation in female house mice (Mus domesticus) by urinary chemosignals: Mixing urine sources in unequal proportions. *Journal of Comparative Psychology, 102*(3), 215–221.

Drucko, P. N. (1991). Biofeedback in the management of headache: II *Headache Quarterly,2*(1), 17–22.

Dubinsky, J. M., Rothman, S. M., & Gottlieb, D. I. (1988). Localization of GAD to presynaptic sites corresponds to the onset of inhibitory synaptic transmission in-vitro. *Soc. Neuroscience Abstract, 14*(1), 515.

Dubos, R. (1965). *Man adapting.* New Haven: Yale University Press.

Duckitt, J. (1992). Psychology and prejudice: A historical analysis and integrative framework. *American Psychologist, 47,* 1182–1193.

Dugan, T. F., & Coles, R. (Eds). (1989). *The child in our times: Studies in the development of resiliency.* New York: Brunner/Mazel.

Dumaret, A. (1985). IQ scholastic performance and behavior of sibs raised in contrasting environments. *Journal of Child Psychology and Psychiatry, 26,* 553–580.

Duncan, C. P. (1949). The retroactive effect of electroshock on learning. *Journal of Comparative and Physiological Psychology, 42,* 32–44.

Duncan, G. J., Coe, R. D., Corcoran, M. E., Hill, M. S., Hoffman, S. D., & Morgan, J. N. (1984). *Years of poverty, years of plenty: The changing economic fortunes of American workers and families.* Ann Arbor, MI: Institute for Social Research.

Dunn, A. J., & Bondy, S. C. (1974). *Functional chemistry of the brain.* New York: Spectrum Publications.

Dutton, D. G., & Aron, A. P. (1974). Some evidence for heightened sexual attraction under conditions of high anxiety. *Journal of Personality and Social Psychology, 30,* 510–517.

Duyme, M. (1985). Scholastic achievement as a function of parental social class: An adoption study. In C. J. Brainero & V. F. Reyna (Eds.), *Developmental psychology.* Amsterdam: Elsevier Science.

Dvorak, A. (1943). There is a better typewriter keyboard. *National Business Education Quarterly, 11,* 58–66.

Dweck, C. S. (1992). The study of goals in psychology. *Psychological Science, 3,* 165.

Dweck, C. S., & Licht, B. G. (1980). Learned helplessness and intellectual achievement. In J. Garber & M. E. P. Seligman (Eds.), *Human helplessness: Theory and application.* New York: Academic Press.

Eagly, A. H. (1987). *Sex differences in social behavior.* Hillsdale, NJ: Lawrence Erlbaum Associates.

Eagly, A. H., & Chivala, C. (1986). Sex differences in conformity: Status and gender-role interpretations. *Psychology of Women Quarterly, 10,* 203–220.

Eagly, A. H., & Steffen, V. J. (1986). Gender and aggressive behavior: A meta-analytic review of the social psychological literature. *Psychological Bulletin, 100,* 309–330.

Eagly, A. H., Wood, W., & Chaiken, S. (1978). Causal inferences about communicators and their effect on opinion change. *Journal of Personality and Social Psychology, 3,* 424–435.

Eagly, A. H., Wood, W., & Fishbaugh, L. (1981). Sex differences in conformity: Surveillance by the group as a determinant of male nonconformity. *Journal of Personality and Social Psychology, 40,* 384–394.

Eaton, W. O., & Clore, G. L. (1975). Interracial imitation at a summer camp. *Journal of Personality and Social Psychology, 32,* 1099–1105.

Ebbinghaus, H. (1964). *Memory* (H. A. Ruger & C. E. Bussenius, Trans.). New York: Dover. (Original work published 1885)

Eberts, E. H., & Lepper, M. R. (1975). Individual consistency in the proxemic behavior of preschool children. *Journal of Personality and Social Psychology, 32,* 841–849.

Edney, J. J. (1974). Human territoriality. *Psychological Bulletin, 81,* 959–975.

Edwards, G., Arif, A., & Hodgson, R. (1981). Nomenclature and classification of the drug- and alcohol-related problems: A WHO memorandum. *Bulletin of the World Health Organization, 59,* 225–242.

Edwards, G., Gross, M. M., Keller, M., & Moser, J. (1976). Alcohol-related problems in the disability perspective. *Journal of Studies on Alcohol, 37,* 1360–1382.

Edwards, J. D. (1989). The home-field advantage. In J. H. Goldstein (Ed.), *Sports, games, and play* (2nd ed.). Hillsdale, NJ: Lawrence Erlbaum Associates (Wiley).

Efran, M. G., & Cheyne, J. A. (1974). Affective concomitants of the invasion of shared space: Behavioral, physiological, and verbal indicators. *Journal of Personality and Social Psychology, 29,* 219–226.

Efron, R. (1990). *The decline and fall of hemispheric specialization.* Hillsdale, NJ: Lawrence Erlbaum Associates.

Egan, J. P. (1975) *Signal detection theory and ROC analysis.* New York: Academic Press.

Ehrhardt, A. A., & Meyer-Bahlburg, H. F. L. (1981). Effects of prenatal sex hormones on gender-related behavior. *Science, 211,* 1312–1317.

Ekman, P. (1982). *Emotion in the human face* (2nd ed.). New York: Cambridge University Press.

Ekman, P., & Friesen, W. V. (1975). *Unmasking the face.* Englewood Cliffs, NJ: Prentice-Hall.

Ekman, P., & Friesen, W. V. (1982). Felt, false, and miserable smiles. *Journal of Nonverbal Behavior, 6,* 218–252.

Ekman, P., & Friesen, W. V. (1986). A new pan-cultural facial expression of emotion. *Motivation and Emotion, 10,* 159–168.

Ekman, P., & Friesen, W. V. (1988). Who knows what about contempt: A reply to Izard and Haynes. *Motivation and Emotion, 12,* 17–22.

Ekman, P., O'Sullivan, M., Friesen, W. V., & Scherer, K. R. (1991). Invited article: Face, voice, and body in detecting deceit. *Journal of Nonverbal Behavior, 15*(2), 125–135.

Ekstrom, R. B., French, J. W., Harman, H. H., & Derman, D. (1976). *Manual for kit of factor-referenced cognitive tests.* Princeton, NJ: Educational Testing Service.

Elkin, I. E., Parloff, M. B., Hadley, S. W., & Autry, A. H. (1985). NIMH Treatment of Depression Collaborative Research Program: Background and research plan. *Archives of General Psychiatry, 42,* 305–316.

Elkins, R. L. (1991). An appraisal of chemical aversion (emetic therapy) approaches to alcoholism treatment. *Behavioral Research and Therapy, 29*(5), 387–413.

Ellis, A. (1962). *Reason and emotion in psycho-therapy.* New York: Lyle Stuart.

Ellis, A. (1980). Rational-emotive therapy and cognitive behavior therapy: Similarities and differences. *Cognitive Therapy and Research, 4,* 325–340.

Ellis, H. C., Thomas, R. L., McFarland, A. D., & Lane, J. W. (1985). Emotional mood and retrieval in episodic memory. *Journal of Experimental Psychology, 11*(2), 363–370.

Elms, A. C., & Milgram, S. (1966). Personality characteristics associated with obedience and defiance toward authoritative command. *Journal of Experimental Research in Personality, 2,* 282–289.

Emde, R. N. (1985). Adult judgments in infant emotions: Replication studies within and across laboratories. *Infant Behavior and Development, 8*(1), 79–88.

Eme, R. F. (1979). Sex differences in childhood psychopathology: A review. *Psychological Bulletin, 86,* 574–595.

Epstein, S. (1979). Explorations in personality today and tomorrow: A tribute to Henry A. Murray. *American Psychologist, 34,* 649–653.

Epstein, S. M. (1967). Toward a unified theory of anxiety. In B. A. Maher (Ed.), *Progress in experimental personality research* (Vol. 4). New York: Academic Press.

Erickson, D. (1991, April). Seeking senescence. *Scientific American,* 18.

Ericsson, K. A., & Simon, H. A. (1984). *Protocol analysis: Verbal reports as data.* Cambridge, MA: MIT Press.

Ericsson, K. A., Chase, W. G., & Faloon, S. (1980). Acquisition of a memory skill. *Science, 208,* 1181–1182.

Erikson, E. H. (1961). *Ghandi's truth.* New York: Norton.

Erikson, E. H. (1968). *Identity: Youth and crisis.* New York: Norton.

Erikson, E. H. (1972). Eight stages of man. In C. S. Lavatelli & F. Stendler (Eds.), *Readings in child behavior and child development.* New York: Harcourt Brace Jovanovich.

Eron, L. D. (1982). Parent-child interaction, television violence, and aggression of children. *American Psychologist, 37*(2), 197–211.

Etaugh, C. (1980). Effects of nonmaternal care on children: Research evidence and popular views. *American Psychologist, 35,* 309–319.

Evans, G. W., Palsane, M. N., Carrere, S. (1987). Type A behavior and occupational stress: A cross-cultural study of blue-collar workers. *Journal of Personality and Social Psychology, 52,* 1002–1007.

Evans, M. G. (1991). The problem of analyzing multiplicative composites. *American Psychologist, 46,* 6–15.

Evans, P. (1991). Stress and coping. In M. Pitts & K. Phillips, (Eds.), *The psychology of health* (pp. 30–48). New York & London: Routledge.

Evans, P. D., Pitts, M. K., & Smith, K. (1988). Minor infection, minor life events and the four day desirability dip. *Journal of Psychosomatic Research, 32,* 533–539.

Eysenck, H. (1952). The effects of psychotherapy: An evaluation. *Journal of Consulting Psychology, 16,* 319–324.

Eysenck, H. J. (1959). *The Maudsley Personality Inventory.* London: University of London Press.

Eysenck, H. J. (1967). *The biological basis of personality.* Springfield, IL: Thomas.

Eysenck, S. B. G., & Eysenck, H. J. (1963). The validity of questionnaire and rating assessments of extraversion and neuroticism, and their factorial stability. *British Journal of Psychology, 54,* 51–62.

Fabes, R. A., Eisenberg, N., Nyman, M., & Michealieu, Q. (1991). Young children's appraisals of others' spontaneous emotional reactions. *Developmental Psychology, 27*(5), 858–866.

Fagot, B. I. (1974). Sex differences in toddlers' behavior and parental reaction. *Developmental Psychology, 10,* 554–558.

Fallows, D. (1985). *A mother's work.* Boston: Houghton Mifflin Company.

Faludi, G., Magyar, I., Tekes, K., Tothfalusi, L., & Magyar, K. (1988). Measurement of 3H-serotonin uptake in blood platelets in major depressive episodes. *Biological Psychiatry, 23,* 829–833.

Fancher, R. E. (1979). *Pioneers of psychology.* New York: W. W. Norton.

Fantz, R. L. (1961). The origin of form perception. *Scientific American, 204,* 66–72.

Fantz, R. L., Fagan, J. F., & Miranda, S. B. (1975). Early visual acuity. In L. B. Cohen & P. Salapatek (Eds.), *Infant perception: From sensation to cognition* (Vol. 2). New York: Academic Press.

Frantz, R. L., Fagan, J. F., & Miranda, S. B. (1975b). Early visual selectivity. In L. B. Cohen & P. Salapatek (Eds.), *Infant perception: From sensation to congition* (Vol. 1). New York: Academic Press.

Farley, J., & Alkon, D. L. (1985). Cellular mechanisms of learning, memory, and information storage. *Ann. Rev. Psychology, 36,* 419–494.

Farrell, B. A. (1981). *The standing of psychoanalysis.* Oxford: Oxford University Press.

Fawl, C. L. (1963). Disturbances experienced by children in their natural habitats. In R. G. Barker (Ed.), *The stream of behavior.* New York: Appleton.

Fawzy, F. I., Coombs, R. H., & Gerber, B. (1983). Generational continuity in the use of substances: The impact of parental substance use on adolescent substance use. *Addictive Behaviors, 8,* 109–114.

Feather, N. T. (1962). The study of persistence. *Psychological Bulletin, 59,* 94–115.

Fedorchak, P. M., & Bolles, R. C. (1988). Nutritive expectancies mediate cholecystokinin's suppression-of-intake effect. *Behavioral Neuroscience, 102,* 151–455.

Feierabend, I. K., & Feierabend, R. L. (1966). Aggressive behavior within polities, 1948–1962: A cross-national study. *Journal of Conflict Resolution, 10,* 249–271.

Feierabend, I. K., & Feierabend, R. L. (1972). Systematic conditions of political aggression: An implication of frustration-aggression theory. In I. K. Feierabend, R. L. Feierabend, & T. R. Gurr (Eds.), *Anger, violence, and politics: Theory and research.* Englewood Cliffs, NJ: Prentice-Hall.

Feierabend, I. K., Feierabend, R. L., & Scanland, F. (1972). The relation between sources of systematic frustration, international conflict, and political instability. Study 5. In I. K. Feierabend, R. L. Feierabend, & T. R. Gurr (Eds.), *Anger, violence, and politics: Theory and research.* Englewood Cliffs, NJ: Prentice-Hall.

Feinberg, I., Fein, G., Walker, J. M., Price, L. J., Floyd, T. C., & March, J. D. (1977). Flurazepam effects of slow-wave sleep: Stage 4 suppressed but number of delta waves constant. *Science, 198,* 847–848.

Feldman, H., Goldin-Meadow, S., & Gleitman, L. R. (1978). Beyond Herodotus: The creation of language by linguistically deprived children. In A. Lock (Ed.), *Action, gesture, and symbol: The emergence of language.* London: Academic Press.

Ferguson, C. A., & Slobin, D. I. (Eds.). (1971). *Studies of child language development.* New York: Holt, Rinehart & Winston.

Festinger, L. (1954). Theory of social comparison processes. *Human Relations, 7,* 117–140.

Festinger, L., Pepitone, A., & Newcomb, T. M. (1952). Some consequences of deindividuation in a group. *Journal of Abnormal and Social Psychology, 47,* 382–389.

Festinger, L., Riecken, H. W., & Schachter S. (1956). *When prophecy fails: A social and psychological study of a modern group that predicted the destruction of the world.* Minneapolis: University of Minnesota Press.

Festinger, L., Schachter, S., & Back, K. (1950). *Social pressures in informal groups: A study of human factors in housing.* New York: Harper.

Fiedler, F. E. (1981). Leadership effectiveness. *American Behavioral Scientist, 24,* 619–632.

Fiedler, F. E., Chemers, M. M., & Mahar, L. (1976). *Improving leadership effectiveness.* New York: Wiley.

Field, T. M., Woodson, R., Greenberg, R., & Cohen, D. (1982). Discrimination and imitation of facial expressions by neonates. *Science, 218,* 179–181.

Fine, A. (1986). Transplantation in the central nervous system. *Scientific American, 255,* 52–58B.

Fine, R. (1979). *A history of psychoanalysis.* New York: Columbia University Press.

Fischer, K. W., & Silvern, L. (1985). Stages and individual differences in cognitive development. *Annual Review of Psychology, 36,* 613–648.

Fishbein, M., & Ajzen, I. (1975). *Belief, attitude, intention, and behavior.* Reading, MA: Addison-Wesley.

Fisher, S., & Greenberg, R. P. (1978). *The scientific evaluation of Freud's theories and therapy.* New York: Basic Books.

Fishman, J. A. (1982). Whorfianism of the third kind: Ethnolinguistic diversity as a worldwide societal asset (The Whorfian Hypothesis: Varieties of validation, confirmation, and disconfirmation II). *Language & Society, 11,* 1–14.

Fiske, S. T., & Taylor, S. E. (1991). *Social cognition* (2nd ed.). New York: McGraw-Hill.

Fitzsimons, J. T. (1961). Drinking by rats depleted of body fluid without increase in osmotic pressure. *Journal of Physiology* (London), *159,* 297–309.

Fitzsimons, J. T. (1972). Thirst. *Physiological Reviews, 52,* 468–561.

Fleming, A. S., Ruble, D. N., Flett, G. L., & Shaul, D. L. (1988). Postpartum adjustment in first-time mothers: Relations between mood, maternal attitudes, and mother-infant interactions. *Developmental Psychology, 24,* 71–81.

Flowers, M. L. (1977). A laboratory test of some implications of Janis' groupthink hypothesis. *Journal of Personality and Social Psychology, 35,* 888–896.

Fodor, J. A., Bever, T. G., & Garrett, M. F. (1974). *The psychology of language.* New York: McGraw-Hill.

Folkins, C. H., & Sime, W. E. (1981). Physical fitness and mental health. *American Psychologist, 36,* 373–389.

Folstein, S., & Rutter, M. (1977). Genetic influences and infantile autism. *Nature, 265,* 726–728.

Ford, C. S., & Beach, F. A. (1951). *Patterns of sexual behavior.* New York: Harper.

Foucault, M. (1965). *Madness and civilization.* (R. Howard, transl.). New York: Random House.

Fowler, R. D. (1991, November). Some thoughts on Freud's 1909 visit with U.S. psychologists. *APA Monitor, 22,* 3.

Fox, B. H. (1981). Psychosocial factors and the immune system in human cancer. In R. Ader (Ed.), *Psychoneuroimmunology.* New York: Academic Press.

Fox, N., & Fein, G. G. (Eds.). (1990). *Infant day care: The current debate.* Norwood, NJ: Ablex.

Fox, R. (1988). The Seville declaration: Anthropology's auto-da-fe. *Academic Questions, 1,* 35–47.

Frances, A. Widiger, T., Pincus, H. (1989). The development of DSM-IV. *Archives of General Psychiatry, 46,* 373–375.

Frances, A. J., Clarkin, J., & Perry, S. W. (1984). *Differential therapeutics in psychiatry: The art and science of treatment selection.* New York: Brunner/Mazel.

Franco, L., Sperry, R. W. (1977). Hemispheric lateralization for cognitive processing of geometry. *Neuropsychologia, 15,* 107–114.

Franke, R. H., & Kaul, J. D. (1978). The Hawthorne experiments: First statistical interpretation. *American Sociological Review, 43,* 623–643.

Frankl, V. (1962). *Man's search for meaning.* Boston: Beacon.

Fraser, S., Gouge, C., & Billig, M. (1971). Risky shifts, cautious shifts and group polarization. *European Journal of Social Psychology, 1,* 7–29.

Frederiksen, N. (1986). Toward a broader conception of human intelligence. *American Psychologist, 41,* 445–452.

Freedman, J. L. (1964) Involvement, discrepancy, and change. *Journal of Abnormal and Social Psychology, 69,* 209–295.

Freedman, J. L. (1975). *Crowding and behavior.* San Francisco: Freeman.

Freedman, J. L. (1984). Effects of television violence on aggression. *Psychological Bulletin, 96,* 227–246.

Freedman, J. L., Heshka, S., & Levy, A. (1975). Population density and pathology: Is there a relationship? *Journal of Experimental Social Psychology, 11,* 539–552.

Freedman, J. L., Klevansky, S., & Ehrlich, P. R. (1971). The effect of crowding on human task performance. *Journal of Experimental Social Psychology, 1,* 7–25.

Freedman, J. L., Levy, A., Buchanan, R. W., & Price, J. (1972). Crowding and human aggressiveness. *Journal of Experimental Social Psychology, 8,* 528–548.

Freeman, W. J. (1991, February). The physiology of perception. *Scientific American,* 78–85.

Freiberg, P. (1990, October). Dutch mental health effort targets prevention. *APA Monitor,* 34.

Freud, A. (1936). *The ego and the mechanisms of defense.* New York: International Universities Press.

Freud, S. (1914). *Further reflections on the technique of psychoanalysis, recollection, repetition and working through.* In *Collected papers.* Vol. 2. New York: Basic Books, 1959.

Freud, S. (1924). *Neurosis and psychosis. In Collected papers.* Vol. 2. New York: Basic Books, 1959.

Freud, S. (1945). *Group psychology and the analysis of the ego.* London: Hogarth. (original work published 1921)

Freud, S. (1949). *Three essays on the theory of sexuality.* In *Standard edition* (Vol. 7). London: Hogarth. (Original work published 1905)

Freud, S. (1950). *The ego and the id.* In *Standard edition* (Vol. 19). London: Hogarth. (Original work published 1932)

Freud, S. (1950). *Further reflections on the technique of psychoanalysis, recollection, repetition and working through.* In *Collected papers* (Vol. 2). New York: Basic Books. (Original work published 1914)

Freud, S. (1959). *Neurosis and psychosis. In Collected papers* (Vol. 2). New York: Basic Books. (Original work published 1924)

Freud, S. (1960). *Jokes and their relation to the unconscious.* (James Strachey, Trans.). New York: Norton. (Original work published 1905)

Friedman, H. S. (1991). *Hostility, coping, and health.* Washington, DC: American Psychological Association.

Friedman, H. S., & Miller-Herringer, T. (1991). Nonverbal display of emotion in public and in private: Self-monitoring, personality, and expressive cues. *Journal of Personality and Social Psychology, 61*(5), 766–775.

Friedman, L. (1981). How affiliation affects stress in fear and anxiety situations. *Journal of Personality and Social Psychology, 40,* 1102–1117.

Friedman, M., & Rosenman, R. H. (1974). *Type A behavior and your heart.* New York: Knopf.

Frijda, N. (1988). *The emotions.* Cambridge: Cambridge University Press.

Frisch, R. E. (1988). Fatness and fertility. *Scientific American, 258,* 88–95.

Frodi, A., Macaulay, J., & Thome P. R. (1977). Are women always less aggressive than men? A review of the experimental literature. *Psychological Bulletin, 84,* 634–660.

Fromm, E. (1941). *Escape from freedom.* New York: Rinehart & Co.

Fromm, E. (1970). Age regression with unexpected reappearance of a repressed childhood language. *International Journal of Clinical and Experimental Hypnosis, 18,* 79–88.

Fry, P. S. (1985). Relations between teenagers' age, knowledge, expectations and maternal behaviour. *British Journal of Developmental Psychology, 3*(1), 47–55.

Fry, W. F., Jr. (1963). *Sweet madness: A study of humor.* Palo Alto, CA: Pacific Books.

Fry, W. F., Jr., & Salameh, W. A. (Eds.). (1987). *Handbook of humor and psychotherapy.* Sarasota, FL: Professional Resource Exchange.

Funder, D. C. (1991). Global traits: A neo-Allportian approach to personality. *Psychological Science, 2,* 31–39.

Furstenberg, F. F., Jr., Brooks-Gunn, J., & Morgan, S. P. (1987). *Adolescent mothers in later life.* New York: Cambridge University Press.

Gackenbach, J. (1991). Frameworks for understanding lucid dreaming: A review. *Dreaming: Journal of the Association for the Study of Dreams, 1,* 109–128.

Gackenbach, J., & LaBerge, S. (Eds.). (1988). *Conscious mind, sleeping brain.* New York: Plenum.

Gaddis, A., & Brooks-Gunn, J. (1985). The male experience of pubertal change. *Journal of Youth and Adolescence, 14,* 62.

Gaertner, S. L., Dovidio, J. F., Mann, J. A., Murrell, A. J., & Pomare, M. (1990). How does cooperation reduce intergroup bias? *Journal of Personality and Social Psychology, 59,* 692–704.

Gage, D. F., & Safer, M. A. (1985). Hemispheric differences in the mood state-dependent effect for recognition of emotional faces. *Journal of Experimental Psychology: Learning, Memory, and Cognition, 11*(4), 752–763.

Galbraith, R. C. (1982). Just one look was all it took: Reply to Berbaum, Markus, and Zajonc. *Developmental Psychology, 18*(2), 181–191.

Garbarino, J., Kostelny, K., & Dubrow, N. (1991). What children can tell us about living in danger. *American Psychologist, 46,* 376.

Garcia, J., & Koelling, R. A. (1966). Relation of cue to consequence in avoidance learning. *Psychonomic Science, 4,* 123–124.

Garcia, J., Rusiniak, K. W., & Brett, L. P. (1977). Conditioned food illness aversion in wild animals: Caveant canonici. In H. Davis & H. M. B. Hurwitz (Eds.), *Operant-Pavlovian interactions.* Hillsdale, NJ: Lawrence Erlbaum Associates, Inc.

Gardner, B. T., & Gardner, R. A. (1971). Two-way communication with an infant chimpanzee. In A. M. Schrier & F. Stollnitz (Eds.), *Behavior of nonhuman primates* (Vol. 4). New York: Academic Press.

Gardner, H. (1987). *The mind's new science.* New York: Basic Books.

Gaston, S., & Menaker, M. (1968). Pineal function: The biological clock in the sparrow? *Science, 160*, 1125–1127.

Gates, M. J., & Allee, W. C. (1933). Conditional behavior of isolated and grouped cockroaches on a simple maze. *Journal of Comparative Psychology, 15*, 331–358.

Gazzaniga, M. S. (1967). The split brain in man. *Scientific American, 217*, 24–29.

Geen, R. G. (1991). *Human aggression*. London, England: Open University.

Geen, R. G., & Donnerstein, E. I. (1983). *Aggression* (Vols. 1–2). New York: Academic Press.

Gelfand, Donald E., & Kutzik, Alfred J. (Eds.). (1979). *Ethnicity and aging: Theory, research and policy*. New York: Springer Publishing Co.

Geller, E. S. (1992). It takes more than information to save energy. *American Psychologist, 47*, 814–815.

Gelles, R. J., & Edfeldt, A. W. (1986). Violence towards children in the United States and Sweden. *Child Abuse and Neglect, 10*, 501–510.

Gelles, R. J., & Straus, M. A. (1979). Determinants of violence in the family: Toward a theoretical integration. In W. R. Burr, R. Hill, F. I. Nye, & I. L. Reiss (Eds.), *Contemporary theories about the family*. New York: Free Press.

Gentry, W. D., Chesney, A. P., Hall, R. P., & Harburg, E. (1981). Effect of habitual anger-coping pattern of blood pressure in black/white, high/low stress area respondents. *Psychosomatic Medicine, 43*, 88–93.

Gentry, W. D., Chesney, M. A., Gary, H. E., Hall, R. P., & Harburg, E. (1982). Habitual anger-coping styles. Effect on mean blood pressure and risk for essential hypertension. *Psychosomatic Medicine, 44*, 195–202.

George, W. C., Cohn, S. J., & Stanley, J. C. (Eds.). (1979). *Educating the gifted*. Baltimore: Johns Hopkins University Press.

Gergen, K. J. (1991). *The saturated self*. New York: Basic Books.

Gergen, K. J., Gergen, M. M., & Meter, K. (1972). Individual orientations to prosocial behavior. *Journal of Social Issues, 28*, 105–130.

Gershon, E. S., & Rieder, R. O. (1992, September). Major disorders of mind and brain. *Scientific American, 267*, 89–95.

Geschwind, N., & Galaburda, A. (1987). *Cerebral lateralization: Biological mechanisms, associations, and pathology*. Cambridge, MA: MIT Press.

Getzels, J. W. (1975). Problem finding and inventiveness of solutions. *Journal of Creative Behavior, 9*, 12–18.

Ghiselli, E. E. (1966). *The validity of occupational aptitude tests*. New York: Wiley.

Gibb, C. A. (Ed.). (1969). *Leadership*. Baltimore: Penguin.

Gibbs, J. C., & Schnell, S. V. (1985). Moral development "versus" socialization: A critique. *American Psychologist, 40*, 1071–1080.

Gibbs, J. T., & Larke, N. H. (1989). *Children of color: Psychological intervention with minority youth*. San Francisco: Jossey-Bass.

Gibson, H. B. (1977). *Hypnosis: Its nature and therapeutic uses*. New York: Taplinger Publishing Co.

Giel, R., & Ormel, J. (1977). Crowding and subjective health in the Netherlands. *Social Psychiatry, 12*, 37–42.

Gil, D. (1970). *Violence against children*. Cambridge, MA: Harvard University Press.

Gilligan, C. (1977). In a different voice: Women's conception of the self and morality. *Harvard Educational Review, 47*, 481–517.

Gilligan, C. (1986). In a different voice: An interdisciplinary forum: Reply. *Signs, 11*, 324–333.

Gilligan, C., & Attanucci, J. (1988). Two moral orientations: Gender differences and similarities. *Merrill-Palmer Quarterly, 34*(3), 223–237.

Gillum, R., Leon, G. R., Kamp, J., & Becerra-Aldama, J. (1980). Predictions of cardiovascular and other disease onset and mortality from 30-year longitudinal MMPI data. *Journal of Consulting and Clinical Psychology, 48*, 405–406.

Gilovich, T. (1991). *How we know what isn't so: The fallibility of human reasoning in everyday life*. New York: Free Press.

Glaser, R. (1981). The future of testing: A research agenda for cognitive psychology and psychometrics. *American Psychologist, 36*, 923–936.

Glass, A. L., Holyoak, K. J., & Santa, J. L. (1979). *Cognition*. Reading, MA: Addison-Wesley.

Glass, D. C., & Singer, J. E. (1972). *Urban stress: Experiments on noise and social stressors*. New York: Academic Press.

Glick, P. C. (1979). Children of divorced parents in demographic perspective. *Journal of Social Issues, 35*(4), 170–182.

Glucksberg, S., & Cowen, G. N., Jr. (1970). Memory for nonattended auditory material. *Cognitive Psychology, 1*, 149–156.

Goethals, G., & Darley, J. (1977). Social comparison theory: An attributional approach. In J. M. Suls (Ed.), *Social comparison processes*. Hillsdale, NJ: Lawrence Erlbaum Associates.

Goffman, E. (1959). *The presentation of self in everyday life*. New York: Doubleday.

Gold, P. E., & van Buskirk, R. (1975). Enhancement of time-dependent memory processes with post-trial epinephrine injections. *Behavioral Biology, 13*, 145–153.

Gold, P. E., & van Buskirk, R. (1978). Effects of alpha and beta adrenergic receptor antagonists on post-trial epinephrine modulation of memory: Relationship to posttraining brain norepinephrine concentrations. *Behavioral Biology, 24*, 168–184.

Gold, P. E., Macri, J., & McGaugh J. L. (1973). Retrograde amnesia gradients: Effects of direct cortical stimulation. *Science, 179*, 1343–1345.

Goldberg, L. R. (1990). An alternative description of personality: The big-five factor structure. *Journal of Personality and Social Psychology, 59*, 1216–1229.

Golden, W. L., et al. (1991). *Psychological treatment of cancer patients: A cognitive/behavioral approach*. Elmsford, NY: Pergamon.

Goldstein, A. P., & Rosenbaum, A. (1982). *Aggress-less: How to turn anger and aggression into positive action*. Englewood Cliffs, NJ: Prentice-Hall.

Goldstein, J. H. (Ed.). (1989). *Sports, games, and play*. (2nd ed.) Hillsdale, NJ: Lawrence Erlbaum Associates.

Goldstein, J. H. (1982). A laugh a day: Can mirth keep disease at bay? *The Sciences, 22*(6), 21–25.

Goldstein, J. H. (1986a). *Aggression and crimes of violence* (2nd ed.). New York: Oxford University Press.

Goldstein, J. H. (1986b). *Reporting science: The case of aggression*. Hillsdale, NJ: Lawrence Erlbaum Associates.

Goldstein, J. H. (1987). Therapeutic effects of laughter. In W. F. Fry, Jr., & W. A. Salameh (Eds.), *Handbook of humor and psychotherapy* (pp. 1–20). Sarasota, FL: Professional Resource Exchange.

Goldstein, J. H., & Arms, R. L. (1971). Effects of observing athletic contests on hostility. *Sociometry, 34*, 83–90.

Goldstein, J. H., Davis, R. W., & Herman, D. (1975). Escalation of aggression: Experimental studies. *Journal of Personality and Social Psychology, 31*, 162–170.

Goldstein, J. H., Mantell, M., Pope, B., & Derks, P. (1988). Humor and the coronary-prone behavior pattern. *Current Psychology, 7*, 115–121.

Goldstein, M., Mahanand, D., & Lee, J. et al. (1976). Dopamine-best-hydroxylase and endogenous total 5-hydroxindole levels in autistic patients and controls. In M. Coleman (Ed.), *The autistic syndrome*. Amsterdam: North Holland.

Goldstein, P. J. (1985). The drugs/violence nexus: A tripartite conceptual framework. *Journal of Drug Issues, 15*, 493–506.

Gomersall, E. A., & Myers, M. S. (1966). Breakthrough in on-the-job training. *Harvard Business Review, 44*(4), 62–72.

Goodall, J. (1963). My life among the wild chimpanzees. *National Geographic, 124*, 272–308.

Goodrich, A. J., Henry, J., & Goodrich, D. W. (1954). Laughter in psychiatric staff conferences: A sociopsychiatric analysis. *American Journal of Orthopsychiatry, 24*, 175–184.

Goodwin, D. W. (1979). Alcoholism and heredity. *Archives of General Psychiatry, 36*, 57–61.

Goodwin, D. W. (1985). Genetic determinants of alcoholism. In J. H. Mendelson & N. K. Mello (Eds.), *The diagnosis and treatment of alcoholism* (pp. 65–87). New York: McGraw-Hill.

Goodwin, F. K., & Roy-Byrne, P. (1987). Treatment of bipolar disorders. In R. E. Hales & A. J. Frances (Eds.), *American Psychiatric Association Annual Review* (Vol. 6, pp. 81–107). Washington, DC: American Psychiatric Press.

Gordon, H. W. (1980). Degree of ear asymmetries for perception of dichotic chords and for illusory chord localization in musicians of different levels of competence. *Journal of Experimental Psychology: Human Perception and Performance, 6*, 516–527.

Gordon, H. W., & Kravetz, S. (1991). The influence of gender, handedness, and performance level on specialized cognitive functioning. *Brain and Cognition, 15*(1), 37.

Gorman, A. N. (1961). Recognition memory for names as a function of abstractness and frequency. *Journal of Experimental Psychology, 61*, 23–29.

Gottesman, I. I. (1991). *Schizophrenia genesis: The origins of madness*. San Francisco: Freeman.

Gottlieb, D. I. (1988). GABAergic neurons. *Scientific American, 258*(2), 82–89.

Gould, S. J. (1981). *The mismeasure of man*. New York: Norton.

Graen, G., Orris, J., & Alvares, K. (1971). The contingency model of leadership effectiveness: Some experimental results. *Journal of Applied Psychology, 55*, 196–201.

Graham, J. R., & Strenger, V. E. (1988). MMPI characteristics of alcoholics: A review. *Journal of Consulting and Clinical Psychology, 56*, 197–205.

Graham, S. (1992). "Most of the subjects were white and middle class": Trends in published research on African Americans in Selected APA Journals, 1970–1989. *American Psychologist, 47*, 629–639.

Gratch, G. (1982). Responses to hidden persons and things by 5-, 9-, and 16-month-old infants is a visual tracking situation. *Developmental Psychology, 18*(2), 232–237.

Gray, J. A., & McNaughton, N. (1983). Comparison between the behavioural effects of septal and hippocampal lesions: A review. *Neuroscience and Biobehavioral Reviews, 7*, 119–188.

Green, M. R. (1980). *Violence and the family.* Boulder, CO: Westview.

Greenberg, J. (1987). Reactions to procedural injustice in payment distributions: Do the means justify the ends? *Journal of Applied Psychology, 72*, 55–61.

Greenberg, J. (1988). Equity and workplace status: A field experiment. *Journal of Applied Psychology, 73*, 606–613.

Greenough W. T. (1975). Experimental modification of the developing brain. *American Scientist, 63*, 37–46.

Greenwald, A. G., & Ronis, D. L. (1978). Twenty years of cognitive dissonance: Case study of the evolution of a theory. *Psychological Review, 85*, 53–57.

Greer, H. S., Morris, T., & Pettingale, K. W. (1979). Psychological response to breast cancer: Effect on outcome. *Lancet*, ii, 785–787.

Gregory, R. L. (1966). *Eye and brain.* New York: McGraw-Hill.

Grieser, D. L., & Kuhl, P. K. (1988). Maternal speech to infants in a tonal language: Support for universal prosodic features in motherese. *Developmental Psychology, 24*, 14–20.

Griffin, G. R. (1980). Hypnosis: Towards a logical approach in using hypnosis in law enforcement agencies. *Journal of Police Science and Administration,8*(4), 385–389.

Grisham, J. C. (1987, June). Hypnotically refreshed testimony. *The American Psychological Association Monitor.*

Grossman, F. K., Pollack, W. S., & Golding, E. (1988). Fathers and children: Predicting the quality and quantity of fathering. *Developmental Psychology, 24*, 82–91.

Grotevant, H. D., & Thorbecke, W. L. (1982). Sex differences in styles of occupational identity formation in late adolescence. *Developmental Psychology, 18*(3), 396–405.

Guardo, C. J. (1969). Personal space in children. *Child Development, 40*, 143–151.

Guilford, J. P. (1967). *The nature of human intelligence.* New York: McGraw-Hill.

Guilford, J. P. (1984). Humanistic psychology. In R. J. Corsini (Ed.), *Encyclopedia of psychology* (Vol. 2). New York: Wiley.

Guilford, J. P., & Hoepfner, R. (1971). *The analysis of intelligence.* New York: McGraw-Hill.

Gurman, A., & Kniskern, D. (Ed.). (1981). *Handbook of family therapy.* New York: Brunner/Mazel.

Guttman, A. (1986). *Sports spectators.* New York: Columbia University Press.

Haber, R. (1974). Eidetic images. In R. Held (Ed.), *Image, object, and illusion.* San Francisco: Freeman.

Habib, M., Gayraud, D., Oliva, A., Regis, J., Salamon, G., & Khalil, R. (1991). Effects of handedness and sex on the morphology of the corpus callosum: A study with brain magnetic resonance imaging. *Brain and Cognition, 16*, 41–61.

Hackman, J. R., & Morris, C. G. (1975). Group tasks, group interaction process, and group performance effectiveness: A review and proposed integration. In L. Berkowitz (Ed.), *Advances in experimental social psychology* (Vol. 8). New York: Academic Press.

Hackman, J.R., & Oldham, G. R. (1980). *Work redesign.* Reading, MA: Addison-Wesley.

Haines, D. B., & McKeachie, W. J. (1967). Cooperative versus competitive discussion methods in teaching introductory psychology. *Journal of Educational Psychology, 58*, 386–390.

Hall, D. T., & Nougaim, K. E. (1968). An examination of Maslow's need hierarchy in an organizational setting. *Organizational Behavior and Human Performance, 3*, 12–35.

Hall, E. T. (1959). *The silent language.* Garden City, NY: Doubleday.

Hall, E. T. (1966). *The hidden dimension.* Garden City, NY: Doubleday.

Hamilton, J. O. (1974). Motivation and risk-taking behavior: A test of Atkinson's theory. *Journal of Personality and Social Psychology, 29*, 856–864.

Hansel, C. E. M. (1980). *ESP and parapsychology: A critical re-evaluation.* Buffalo, NY: Prometheus Press.

Hansen, S. L., & Darling, C. A. (1985). Attitudes of adolescents toward division of labor in the home. *Adolescence 20*(77), 61–72.

Hansson, R. O., Noulles, D., & Bellovich, S. J. (1982). Social comparison and urban-environmental stress. *Personality and Social Psychology Bulletin, 8*, 68–73.

Harackeiwicz, J. M., Abrahams, S., & Wageman, R. (1987). Performance evaluation and intrinsic motivation: The effects of evaluative focus, rewards, and achievement orientation. *Journal of Personality and Social Psychology, 53*, 1015–1023.

Hardin, G. (1968). The tragedy of the commons. *Science, 162*, 1243–1248.

Hardyck, C., & Petrinovitch, L. F. (1977). Left-handedness. *Psychological Bulletin, 84*, 385–404.

Hardyck, C., Petrinovitch, L.F., & Goldman, B. D. (1976). Left-handedness and cognitive deficit. *Cortex, 12*, 266–280.

Hardyck, J. A., & Braden, M. (1962). Prophecy fails again: A report of a failure to replicate. *Journal of Abnormal and Social Psychology, 65*, 136–141.

Harkness, S., & Super C. M. (1983). The cultural construction of child development. *Ethos, 11*, 221–231.

Harlow, H. F. (1932). Social facilitation of feeding in the albino rat. *Journal of Genetic Psychology, 43*, 211–221.

Harlow, H. F. (1962). The heterosexual affectional system in monkeys. *American Psychology, 17*, 1–9.

Harlow, J. M. (1848). Passage of an iron rod through the head. *Boston Medical and Surgical Journal, 39*, 389–393.

Harlow, J. M. (1868). Recovery from passage of an iron bar through the head. *Massachusetts Medical Society, 2*, 327–346.

Harrell, W. S. (1981). Verbal aggressiveness in spectators at professional hockey games: The effects of tolerance of violence and amount of exposure to hockey. *Human Relations, 34*, 643–655.

Harris, M. (1974). *Cows, pigs, wars, and witches.* New York: Vintage Books.

Hart, P. 't (1991). Irving L. Janis' victims of groupthink. *Political Psychology, 12*, 247–278.

Hart, R. D. A. (1960). Monthly rhythm of libido in married women. *British Medical Journal, 1*, 1023–1024.

Harter, S., & Monsour, A. (1992). Developmental analysis of conflict caused by opposing attributes in the adolescent self-portrait. *Developmental Psychology, 28*, 251–260.

Harwood, H. J. (1984). *Economic cost to society of alcohol and drug abuse and mental illness: 1980.* Washington, DC: Alcohol, Drug, and Mental Health Administration.

Haskell, W. L. (1984). Overview: Health benefits of exercise. In J. D. Matarazzo, S. M. Weiss, J. A. Herd, N. E. Miller, & S. M. Weiss (Eds.), *Behavioral health: A handbook of health enhancement and disease prevention* (pp. 409–423). New York: Wiley.

Hastorf, A., & Cantril, H. (1954). They saw a game: A case study. *Journal of Abnormal and Social Psychology, 49*, 129–134.

Hauser, W. A., & Hesdorffer, D. C. (1990). *Epilepsy: Frequency, causes, and consequences.* New York: Demos Publications.

Haviland, J., & Lelwica, M. (1987). The induced affect response: 10-week-old infants' responses to three emotional expressions. *Developmental Psychology, 23*, 97–104.

Hawkins, C., & Williams, T. I. (1992). Nightmares, life events, and behavior problems in preschool children. *Child: Care, Health and Development, 18*(2), 117–128.

Hayden, A. H., & Haring, N. G. (1985). The acceleration and maintenance of developmental gains in school-aged Down's syndrome children. In R. I. Jahiel, J, Byrne, R. Lubin, & J. Gorelick (Eds.), *Handbook of prevention of mental retardation and developmental disabilities.* New York: Van Nostrand Reinhold.

Hayduk, L. A. (1978). Personal space: An evaluative and orienting overview. *Psychological Bulletin, 85*, 117–134.

Hayes, K. J., & Hayes, C. (1951). The intellectual development of a home-raised chimpanzee. *Proceedings of the American Philosophical Society, 95*, 105–109.

Hazan, C., & Shaver, P. R. (1990). Love and work: An attachment-theoretical perspective. *Journal of Personality and Social Psychology, 59*, 270–280.

Heath, R. G. (1964). Pleasure response of human subjects to direct stimulation of the brain: Physiologic and psychodynamic considerations. In R. G. Heath, (Ed.), *The role of pleasure in behavior.* New York: Harper & Row.

Hebb, D. O. (1949). *The organization of behavior.* New York: Wiley.

Hecaen, H., & Ajuriaguerra, J. (1964). *Left-handedness: Manual superiority and cerebral dominance.* New York: Grune and Stratton.

Heider, F. (1958). *The psychology of interpersonal relations.* New York: Wiley.

Helgeson, V. S., & Sharpsteen, D. J. (1987). Perceptions of danger in achievement and affiliation situations: An extension of the Pollak and Gilligan versus Benton et al. debate. *Journal of Personality and Social Psychology, 53,* 727–733.

Hellige, J. B. (1990). Hemispheric asymmetry. *Annual Review of Psychology, 41,* 55–80.

Hendrick, C. (Ed.). (1987). *Group processes.* Beverly Hills, CA: Sage.

Hendrick, S., & Hendrick, C. (1987). Multidimensionality of sexual attitudes. *The Journal of Sex Research, 23,* 502–526.

Hendrick, S. S., Hendrick, C., & Adler, N. (1988). Romantic relationships: Love, satisfaction, and staying together. *Journal of Personality and Social Psychology, 54,* 980–988.

Henley, N. M. (1977). *Body politics: Power, sex, and nonverbal communication.* Englewood Cliffs, NJ: Prentice-Hall.

Hepworth, J. T., & West, S. G. (1988). Lynchings and the economy: A time-series reanalysis of Hovland and Sears (1940). *Journal of Personality and Social Psychology, 54,* 239–247.

Herd, J. A., & Hartley, L. H. (1984). Hypertension and exercise: The role of physical conditioning in treatment and prevention. In J. D. Matarazzo, S. M. Weiss, J. A. Herd, N. E. Miller, & S. M. Weiss (Eds.), *Behavioral health* (pp. 836–845). New York: Wiley.

Herron, J. (Ed.). (1980). *Neuropsychology of left-handedness.* New York: Academic Press.

Herson, M., Kazdin, A. E., & Bellack, A. S. (1991). *Clinical psychology handbook* (2nd ed.). Elmsford, NY: Pergamon.

Herzberg, T. (1966). *Work and the nature of man.* Cleveland: World.

Herzberg, T. (1976). *The managerial choice.* Homewood, IL: Dow-Jones/Irwin.

Herzberg, T., Mausner, B., & Snyderman, B. (1959). *The motivation to work.* New York: Wiley.

Hetherington, E. M. (1972). Effects of father absence on personality development in adolescent daughters. *Developmental Psychology, 7,* 313–326.

Hetherington, E. M. (1977). *My heart belongs to daddy: A study of the remarriages of daughters of divorcees and widows.* Unpublished manuscript, University of Virginia.

Hethrington, E. M. (1989). Coping with family transitions: Winners, losers, and survivors. *Child Development, 60,* 1–14.

Hetherington, E. M., Cox, M., & Cox, R. (1976). Divorced fathers. *Family Coordinator, 25,* 417–428.

Hewstone, M., Stroebe, W., Codol, J. P., & Stephenson, G. M. (Eds.). (1988). *Introduction to social psychology: A European perspective.* Oxford, England: Basil Blackwell.

Heyman, G. D., & Dweck, C. S. (1992). Achievement goals and intrinsic motivation: Their relation and their role in adaptive motivation. *Motivation and Emotion, 16,* 231.

Higgins, E. A., Chiles, W. D., McKenzie, J. M., Iampietro, P. F., Winget, C. M., Funkhauser, G. E., Burr, M. J., Vaughan, J. A., & Jennings, A. E. (1975, October). *The effects of a 12 hour shift in the wake-sleep cycle of physiological and biochemical responses and on multiple task performance* (FAA-AM-75-10). Washington, DC: U.S. Dept. of Transportation, Federal Aviation Administration.

Hilgard, E. R. (1977). *Divided consciousness: Multiple controls in human thought and action.* New York: Wiley.

Hilgard, E. R. (1980). Consciousness in contemporary psychology. *Annual Review of Psychology, 31,* 1–26.

Hilgard, E. R., & Hilgard, J. R. (1975). *Hypnosis in the relief of pain.* Los Altos, CA: William Kaufmann, Inc.

Hill, J. H., & Chernikoff, R. (1965, January 26). *Altimeter display evaluations: Final report* (USN, NEL Report 6242).

Hinde, R. (1987, June). Reply to Manson and Wrangham. *Human Ethology Newsletter, 5,* 5.

Hinde, R. A., & Groebel, J. (1991). *Cooperation and prosocial behavior.* Cambridge, England: Cambridge University Press.

Hinton, J. (1973). Bearing cancer. *British Journal of Medical Psychology, 46,* 105–113.

Hintzman, D. L. (1990). Human learning and memory: Connections and dissociations. *Annual Review of Psychology, 41,* 109–139.

Hirsch, E. D. (1987). *Cultural literacy.* New York: Houghton Mifflin.

Hirsch, H. V. B., & Spinelli D. N. (1971). Modification of the distribution of receptive field orientation in cats by selective visual exposure during development. *Experimental Brain Research, 13,* 509–527.

Hirsch-Pasek, K., Kemler Nelson, D. G. Juscyzk, P. W., Cassidy, K. W., Druss, B., & Kennedy, L. (in press). Clauses are perceptual units for young infants.

Hitchcock, P. F., & Hickey T. L. (1980). Ocular dominance columns: Evidence for their presence in humans. *Brain Research, 182,* 176–179.

Hobfoll, S. E., Lomranz, J., Eyal, N., Bridges, A., & Tzemach, M. (1989). Pulse of a nation: Depressive mood reactions of Israelis to the Israel-Lebanon war. *Journal of Personality and Social Psychology, 56,* 1002–1012.

Hodgkin, A. L. (1964). *The conduction of the nervous impulse.* Springfield, IL: Thomas.

Hodgkin, A. L, & Katz, B. (1949). The effect of sodium ions in the electrical activity of the giant axon of the squid. *Journal of Physiology, 108,* 37–77.

Hoffman, L. R. (1965). Group problem solving. In L. Berkowitz (Ed.), *Advances in experimental social psychology* (Vol. 2). New York: Academic Press.

Hoffman, L. R., & Maier, N. R. F. (1964). Valence in the adoption of solutions by problem-solving groups: Concept, method, and results. *Journal of Abnormal and Social Psychology, 69,* 264–271.

Hogan, J. (1989). Personality correlates of physical fitness. *Journal of Personality and Social Psychology, 56,* 284–288.

Hogan, R. A. (1968). The implosive technique. *Behavior Research and Therapy, 6,* 423–431.

Hogg, M. A. (1992). *Social psychology of group cohesiveness.* London, England: Simon & Schuster.

Holahan, C., & Moos, R. (1985). Personality, coping, and family resources in stress resistance: A longitudinal analysis. *Journal of Personality and Social Psychology, 51,* 381–395.

Holden, C. (1980). Twins reunited. *Science, 80*(1), 54–59.

Holden, C. (1982). NAS backs cautious use of ability tests. *Science, 215,* 950.

Holden, C. (1987). Why do women live longer than men? *Science, 238,* 158–160.

Hollander, E. P. (1985). Leadership and power. In G. Lindzey & E. Aronson (Eds.), *Handbook of social psychology* (Vol. 1). New York: Random House.

Hollander, E. P. (1992). The essential interdependence of leadership and followership. *Current Directions in Psychological Science, 1,* 71–75.

Hollander, E. P., & Julian, J. W. (1969). Leadership. In E. F. Borgatta (Ed.), *Social psychology: Readings and perspectives.* Chicago: Rand McNally.

Hollis, K. (1984). The biological function of Pavlovian conditioning: The best defense is a good offense. *Journal of Experimental Psychology: Animal Behavior Process,10*(4), 413–425.

Hollon, S., & Beck, A. T. (1986). Research on cognitive therapies. In S. L. Garfield & A. E. Bergin (Eds.), *Handbook of psychotherapy and behavior change* (pp. 443–482). New York: Wiley.

Holloway, M. (1991, March). Rx for addiction. *Scientific American,* 1991.

Holmes, J. A., & Stevenson, C. A. Z. (1990). Differential effects of avoidant and attentional coping strategies on adaptation to chronic and recent-onset pain. *Health Psychology, 5,* 577–584.

Holmes, L. D. (1983). *Other cultures, elder years.* Minneapolis: Burgess.

Holmes, T. H., & Rahe, R. H. (1967). The social readjustment rating scale. *Journal of Psychosomatic Research, 11,* 213–218.

Honzik, M. P., MacFarlane, J. W., & Allen, I. (1948). The stability of mental test performance between two and eighteen years. *Journal of Experimental Education, 17,* 309–324.

Horgan, J. (1991, March). Death with dignity. *Scientific American,* 17–18.

Horgan, J. (1992, February). The Mephistopheles of neurobiology: Profile of Francis H. C. Crick. *Scientific American,* 16–17.

Horne, J. A., & Ostberg, O. (1977). Individual differences in human circadian rhythms. *Biological Psychology, 5,* 179–190.

Horney, K. (1942). *Self-analysis.* New York: Norton.

Horowitz, M. J. (1988). *Introduction to psychodynamics.* New York: Basic Books.

Hosobuchi, Y., Adams, J. E., & Linchitz, R. (1977). Pain relief by electrical stimulation of the central grey matter in humans and its reversal by naloxone. *Science, 197,* 183–186.

House, R. J., & Baetz, M. L. (1979). Leadership: Some empirical generalizations and new research directions. *Research in Organizational Behavior, 1,* 399–401.

Hovland, C. I., & Sears, R. R. (1940). Minor studies of aggression. VI. Correlations of lynchings with economic indices. *Journal of Psychology, 9,* 301–310.

Hovland, C. I., & Weiss, W. (1951). The influence of source credibility on communication effectiveness. *Public Opinion Quarterly, 15,* 635–650.

Hovland, C. I., Janis, I. L., & Kelley, H. H. (1953). *Communication and persuasion.* New Haven, CT: Yale University Press.

Howard, A., Pion, G. M., Gottfredson, G. D., Flattau, P. E., Oskamp, S. Pfafflin, S. M. Bray, D. W., & Burstein, A. G. (1986). The changing face of American psychology: A report from the committee on employment and human resources. *American Psychologist, 41*(12), 1311–1327.

Howes, C. (1988). Relations between early child care and schooling. *Developmental Psychology, 24,* 53–57.

Hrushesky, W. J. M. (1985). Circadian timing of cancer chemotherapy. *Science, 228,* 73–75.

Hubel, D. H., & Wiesel, T. N. (1959). Receptive fields of single neurons in the cat's striate cortex. *Journal of Physiology, 148,* 574–591.

Hubel, D. H., & Wiesel, T. N. (1962). Receptive fields, binocular interaction and functional architecture in the cat's visual cortex. *Journal of Physiology, 160,* 106–154.

Hubel, D. H., & Wiesel, T. N. (1965). Receptive fields and functional architecture in two nonstriate visual areas (18 and 19) of the cat. *Journal of Neurophysiology, 28,* 229–289.

Hubel, D. H., & Wiesel, T. N. (1979, September). Brain mechanisms of vision. *Scientific American,* 150–162.

Hubel, D. H., Wiesel, T. N., & Stryker, M. P. (1978). Anatomical demonstration of orientation columns in macaque monkeys. *Journal of Comparative Neurology, 177,* 361–380.

Hudgens, R. W. (1974). Personal catastrophe and depression: A consideration of the subject with respect to medically ill adolescents, and a requiem for life-event studies. In B. S. Dohrenwend & B. P. Dohrenwend (Eds.), *Stressful life events: Their nature and effects.* New York: Wiley.

Hugdahl, K. (Ed.). (1988). *Handbook of dichotic listening: Theory, methods, and research.* Chichester, England: Wiley.

Hughes, J., Smith, T. W., Kosterlitz, H. W., Fothergill, L. A., Morgan, B. A., & Morris, H. R. (1975). Identification of two related pentapeptides from the brain with potent opiate agonist activity. *Nature* (London), *258,* 577–579.

Hull, C. I. (1943). *Principles of behavior: An introduction to behavior theory.* New York: Appleton-Century-Crofts.

Hull, C. I. (1952). *A behavior system: An introduction to behavior theory concerning the individual organism.* New Haven, CT: Yale University Press.

Hunt, M. (1974). *Sexual behavior in the 1970's.* Chicago: Playboy Press.

Hurvich, I. M., & Jameson, D. (1974). Opponent processes as a model of neural organization. *American Psychologist, 29,* 88–102.

Huston, A. C., Donnerstein, E., Fairchild, H., Feshbach, N. D., Katz, P. A., Murray, J. P., Rubinstein, E. A., Wilcox, B. L., & Zuckerman, D. (1992). *Big world, small screen: The role of television in American society.* Lincoln: University of Nebraska Press. (The APA Task Force on Television and Society.)

Hyde, J. S. (1984). How large are gender differences in aggression? A developmental meta-analysis. *Developmental Psychology, 20,* 724–736.

Hyde, J. S., Krajnik, M., & Skuldt-Niederberger, K. (1991). Androgyny across the life span: A replication and longitudinal follow-up. *Developmental Psychology, 27,* 516–519.

Ilgen, D. R. (1990). Health issues at work: Opportunities for industrial/organizational psychology. *American Psychologist, 45,* 273–283.

Imperato-McGinley, J., Guerrero, L., Gautier, T., & Peterson, R. E. (1974). Steroid 5 alpha reductase deficiency in man: An inherited form of male pseudohermaphroditism. *Science, 186,* 1213–1215.

Innes, J. M., & Ahrens, C. R. (1990). Beliefs about testing for the prevention of the spread of AIDS: Self-monitoring and identifiability in response to televised information. *Basic & Applied Social Psychology, 11,* 165–177.

Insko, C. A., & Robinson, J. E. (1967). Belief similarity versus race as determinants of reactions to Negroes by southern white adolescents: A further test of Rokeach's theory. *Journal of Personality and Social Psychology, 7,* 216–221.

Irwin, M., Daniels, M., Risch, S. C., & Bloom E. (1988). Plasma cortisol and natural killer cell activity during bereavement. *Biological Psychiatry, 24,* 173–178.

Isacson, R. L., & Pribram, K. H. (Eds.). (1975). *The hippocampus* (Vol. 2.). New York: Plenum Press.

Isenberg, D. J. (1986). Group polarization: A critical review and meta-analysis. *Journal of Personality and Social Psychology, 50,* 1141–1151.

Ivancevich, J. M., Matteson, M. T., Freedman, S. M., & Phillips, J. S. (1990). Work stress management interventions. *American Psychologist, 45,* 252–261.

Izard, C. E., & Haynes, D. M. (1988). On the form and universality of the contempt expression: A challenge to Ekman and Freisen's claim of discovery. *Motivation and Emotion, 12* 1–16.

Jacobs, R. C., & Campbell, D. T. (1961). The perpetuation of an arbitrary tradition through several generations of a laboratory microculture. *Journal of Abnormal and Social Psychology, 62,* 649–658.

James, W. (1894/1950). *The principles of psychology.* New York: Dover. (Original work published 1890)

James, W. H. (1971). The distribution of coitus within the human intermenstrum. *Journal of Biosocial Science, 3,* 159–171.

James. S. A., Strogats, D. S., Wing, S. B., & Ramsey, D. L. (1987). Socioeconomic status, John Henryism, and hypertension in Blacks and Whites. *American Journal of Epidemiology, 126,* 664–673.

Jampala, V., Sierles, F., & Taylor, M. (1988). The use of DSM-III in the United States: A case of not going by the book. *Comparative Psychiatry, 29,* 39–47.

Janis, I. L. (1958). *Psychological stress: Psychoanalytic and behavioral studies of surgical patients.* New York: Wiley.

Janis, I. L. (1972). *Victims of groupthink: A psychological study of foreign-policy decisions and fiascoes.* Boston: Houghton Mifflin.

Janis, I. L. (1982). *Groupthink.* Boston: Houghton Mifflin.

Janis, I. L. (1989). *Crucial decisions: Leadership in policy-making and crisis management.* New York: Free Press.

Janis, I. L., & Mann, L. (1977). *Decision making: A psychological analysis of conflict, choice and commitment.* New York: Free Press.

Janoff-Bulman, R., Timko, C., & Carli, L. L. (1985). Cognitive biases in blaming the victim. *Journal of Experimental Social Psychology, 21,* 161–177.

Jemmott, J. B., III., & Magliore, K. (1988). Academic stress, social support, and secretory immunoglobulin A. *Journal of Personality and Social Psychology, 55,* 803–810.

Jenkins, C. D., Rosenman, R. H., & Zyanski, S. J. (1974). Prediction of clinical coronary heart disease by a test for the coronary-prone behavior pattern. *New England Journal of Medicine, 23,* 1271–1275.

Jenkins, W. O. (1947). The tactual discrimination of shapes for coding aircraft-type control. In P. M. Fitts (Ed.), *Psychological research in equipment design* (Research Report 19). Army Air Force, Aviation Psychology Program.

Jensen, A. R. (1968). How much can we boost IQ and scholastic achievement? *Harvard Educational Review, 39,* 1–123.

Jessor, R., & Jessor, S. L. (1976). *Problem behavior and psychosocial development: A longitudinal study of youth.* New York: Academic Press.

John, E. R., Prichep, L. S., Fridman, J., & Easton, P. (1988). Neurometrics: Computer-assisted differential diagnosis of brain dysfunctions. *Science, 239,* 162–169.

Johnson, D. W. (1970). *Social psychology of education.* New York: Holt, Rinehart and Winston.

Johnson, D. W., & Johnson, R. T. (1975). *Learning together and alone.* Englewood Cliffs, NJ: Prentice-Hall.

Johnson, E. S. (1971). Objective identification of strategy on a selection concept learning task. *Journal of Experimental Psychology Monograph, 90*(1), 167–196.

Johnson, E. S. (1978). Validation of concept-learning strategies. *Journal of Experimental Psychology: General, 107,* 237–266.

Johnson, J., & Sarason, I. (1978). Life stress, depression and anxiety: Internal-external control as a moderator variable. *Journal of Psychological Research, 22,* 205–208.

Johnson-Laird, P. N. (1983). *Mental models: Towards a cognitive science of language, inference, and consciousness.* Cambridge, MA: Harvard University Press.

Jones, E. (1953). *The life and work of Sigmund Freud* (Vols. 1–3). New York: Basic Books.

Jones, J. M., Levine, I. S., & Rosenberg, A. A. (1991). Homelessness. (Special issue.) *American Psychologist, 46*(11).

Jones, M. C., & Mussen, P. H. (1958). Self-conceptions, motivations, and impersonal attitudes of early- and late-maturing girls. *Child Development, 29,* 491–501.

Jones, R. (1979, September). *Therapeutic effects of the teaching family group home model*. Paper presented at the meeting of the American Psychological Association, New York.

Jones, S. E., & Aiello, J. R. (1973). Proxemic behavior of black and white first-, third-, and fifth-grade children. *Journal of Personality and Social Psychology, 25*, 21–27.

Justice, A. (1985). Review of the effects of stress on cancer in laboratory animals. *Psychological Bulletin, 98*, 108–138.

▼

Kübler-Ross, E. (1969). *On death and dying*. New York: Macmillan.

Kabanoff, B. (1983). Work and non-work: A review of models, methods, and findings. *Psychological Bulletin*.

Kahn, R. S., van Praag, H. M., Wetzler, S., Asnis, G. M., & Bar, G. (1988). Serotonin and anxiety revisited. *Biological Psychiatry, 23*, 189–208.

Kahneman, D., Slovic, P., & Tversky, A. (1982). *Judgment under uncertainty: Heuristics and biases*. Hillsdale, NJ: Lawrence Erlbaum Associates.

Kahnenam, D. (1991). Judgment and decision making: A personal view. *Psychological Science, 2*, 142–145.

Kaitz, M., Meschulach-Sarfaty, O., Auerbach, J., & Eidelman, A. (1988). A reexamination of newborn's ability to imitate facial expressions. *Developmental Psychology, 24*, 3–7.

Kales, A., & Kales, J. D. (1984). *Evaluation and treatment of insomnia*. New York: Oxford University Press.

Kamarck, T., & Jennings, J. R. (1991). Biobehavioral factors in sudden cardiac death. *Psychological Bulletin, 109*, 42–75.

Kamen-Siegel, L., Rodin, J., Seligman, M. E. P., & Dwyer, J. (1991). Explanatory style and cell-mediated immunity in elderly men and women. *Health Psychology, 10*, 229–235.

Kandel, E. R. (1976). *The cellular basis of behavior*. San Francisco: W. H. Freeman.

Kane, J. M. (1986). Somatic therapy. In A. J. Frances & R. E. Hales (Eds.), *American Psychiatric Association Annual Review* (Vol. 5, pp. 78–95). Washington, DC: American Psychiatric Press.

Kanner, A. D., Coyne, J. C., Schaeffer, C., & Lazarus, R. S. (1981). Comparison of two modes of stress measurement: Daily hassles and uplifts versus major life events. *Journal of Behavioral Medicine, 4*, 1–39.

Kantner, J. F., & Zelnik, M. (1973). Contraception and pregnancy: Experience of young unmarried women in the United States. *Family Planning Perspectives, 5*, 21–35.

Kantowitz, B. H. (1984). Information-processing theory. In R. J. Corsini (Ed.), *Encyclopedia of psychology*. New York: Wiley.

Kaplan, B. (1973). *EEG biofeedback and epilepsy*. Paper presented at the meeting of the American Psychological Association, Montreal.

Kaplan, H. R. (1987). Lottery winners: The myth and reality. *Journal of Gambling Behavior, 3*, 168–178.

Kaplan, H. S. (1974). *The new sex therapy: Active treatment of sexual dysfunctions*. New York: Brunner/Mazel.

Kaplan, H. S. (1979). *Disorders of sexual desire*. New York: Brunner/Mazel.

Kaplan, R. M. (1982). Nader's raid on the testing industry: Is it in the best interest of the consumer? *American Psychologist, 37*, 15–23.

Karasek, R. A., & Theorell, T. (1960). *Healthy work*. New York: Basic Books.

Karasek, R. A., et al. (1988). Job characteristics in relation to the prevalence of myocardial infarction in the U.S. Health Examination Survey and the Health and Nutrition Examination Survey. *American Journal of Public Health, 78*, 910–916.

Kasper, S., Rosenthal, N. E., Barberi, S., & Williams, A. (1991). Immunological correlates of seasonal fluctuations in mood and behavior and their relationship to phototherapy. *Psychiatry Research, 36*(3), 253–264.

Kastenbaum, R. (1967). Multiple perspectives on a geriatric "Death Valley." *Community Mental Health Journal, 3*, 21–29.

Kaul, T. J., & Bednar, R. L. (1986). Research on group and related therapies. In S. L. Garfield & A. E. Bergin (Eds.), *Handbook of psychotherapy and behavior change* (pp. 671–714). New York: Wiley.

Kaye, D. B., Sternberg, R. J., & Fonseca, L. (1987). Verbal comprehension: The lexical decomposition strategy to define unfamiliar words. *Intelligence, 11*(1), 1–20.

Kazdin, A. E., & Wilson, G. T. (1978). *Evaluation of behavior therapy*. Cambridge, MA: Ballinger.

Keita, G. P., & Jones, J. M. (1990). Reducing adverse reaction to stress in the workplace: Psychology's expanding role. *American Psychologist, 45*, 1137–1141.

Kelley, H. H. (1973). The processes of causal attribution. *American Psychologist, 28*, 107–128.

Kelley, H. H., Condry, J. C., Dahlke, A. E., & Hill, A. H. (1965). Collective behavior in a simulated panic situation. *Journal of Experimental Social Psychology, 1*, 20–54.

Kellogg, W. N., & Kellogg, L. A. (1933). *The ape and the child*. New York: Whittlesey.

Kelly, C. (1990). Social identity and intergroup perceptions in minority-majority contexts. *Human Relations, 43*, 583–599.

Kelly, J. (1987). Invited address. American Psychological Association Convention.

Kelman, H. C. (1958). Compliance, identification, and internalization: Three processes of attitude change. *Journal of Conflict Resolution, 2*, 51–60.

Kelvin, P., & Jarrett, J. (1985). *The social psychological effects of unemployment*. Cambridge, England: Cambridge University Press.

Kendler, K. S. (1986). Genetics of schizophrenia. In A. J. Frances & R. E. Haled (Eds.), *American Psychiatric Association Annual Review* (Vol. 5, pp. 25–41). Washington, DC: American Psychiatric Press.

Kendler, K. S., & Tsuang, M. T. (1981). Nosology of paranoid schizophrenia and other paranoid psychoses. *Schizophrenia Bulletin, 7*, 594–610.

Kerckhoff, A. C., & Davis, K. E. (1962). Value consensus and need complementarity in mate selection. *American Sociological Review, 27*, 295–303.

Kerckhoff, A. C., Back, K. W., & Miller, N. (1965). Sociometric patterns in hysterical contagion. *Sociometry, 28*, 2–15.

Kerr, N. L., & Bruun, S. (1981). Ringlemann revisited: Alternative explanations for the social loafing effect. *Journal of Experimental Social Psychology, 7*, 224–231.

Kertesz A., Lau, W. K., & Polk, M. (1993). The structural determinants of recovery in Wernicke's aphasia. *Brain and Language, 44*, 153–164.

Kessler, K. A., & Waletzky, J. P. (1981). Clinical use of the antipsychotics. *American Journal of Psychiatry, 138*, 202–209.

Kessler, R. C., Kendler, K. S., Heath, A., Neale, M. C., & Eaves, L. J. (1992). Social support, depressed mood, and adjustment to stress: A genetic epidemiologic investigation. *Journal of Personality and Social Psychology, 62*, 257–272.

Key, W. B. (1973). *Subliminal seduction*. Englewood Cliffs, NJ: Prentice-Hall.

Kidder, L. H., & Stewart, V. M. (1975). *The psychology of intergroup relations: Conflict and consciousness*. New York: McGraw-Hill.

Kilham, W., & Mann, L. (1974). Level of destructive obedience as a function of transmitter and executant roles in the Milgram obedience paradigm. *Journal of Personality and Social Psychology, 29*, 696–702.

Killian, L. M., & Bloomberg, S. (1975). Rebirth in a therapeutic community: A case study. *Psychiatry, 38*, 39–54.

Kimura, D. (1961). Cerebral dominance and the perception of verbal stimuli. *Canadian Journal of Psychology, 15*, 166–171.

Kimura, D. (1991). Paper presented at the Society for Neuroscience.

King, F. L., & Kimura, D. (1972). Left-ear superiority in dichotic perception of vocal nonverbal sounds. *Canadian Journal of Psychology, 26*, 11–116.

King, M. B. (1990). Sneezing as a fetishistic stimulus. *Sexual and Marital Therapy, 5*(1), 69–72.

Kinsey, A. C., Pomeroy, W. B., Martin, O. E., & Gebhard, P. H. (1953). *Sexual behavior in the human female*. Philadelphia: Saunders.

Kintsch, W. (1977). *Memory and cognition* (2nd ed.). New York: John Wiley.

Kintsch, W., & Keenan, J. M. (1973). Reading rate as a function of the number of propositions in the base structure of sentences. *Cognitive Psychology, 5*, 257–274.

Kinzel, A. F. (1971, January 28). Body-buffer zones in violent prisoners. *New Society*, 149–150.

Kipnis, D. (1984). The use of power in organizations and in interpersonal setting. In S. Oskamp (Ed.), *Applied social psychology annual 5*. Beverly Hills, CA: Sage.

Kipnis, D. (1991). The technological perspective. *Psychological Science, 2*, 62–69.

Kipnis, D., & Schmidt, S. (1983). An influence perspective on bargaining. In M. Bazerman & R. Lewicki (Eds.), *Negotiating in organizations*. Beverly Hills, CA: Sage.

Kircher, J. C., & Raskin, D. C. (1988). Human versus computerized evaluations of polygraph data in a laboratory setting. *Journal of Applied Psychology, 73*(2), 291–302.

Kirk-Smith, M., Booth, D. A., Carroll, D., & Davies, P. (1978). Human social attitudes affected by androstenol. *Research Communications in Psychology, Psychiatry, and Behavior, 3*(4), 379–384.

Kissel, S. (1965). Stress-reducing properties of social stimuli. *Journal of Personality and Social Psychology, 2,* 378–384.

Klama, J. (1988). *Aggression: Conflict in animals and humans reconsidered.* London, England: Longman.

Klawans, H. L. (1990). *Newton's madness: Further tales of clinical neurology.* New York: Harper and Row Publishers.

Klein, A. L. (1976). Changes in leadership appraisal as a function of the stress of a simulated panic situation. *Journal of Personality and Social Psychology, 34,* 1143–1154.

Kleinmuntz, B., & Szucko, J. J. (1984a). A field study of the fallibility of polygraphic lie detection. *Nature, 308,* 449–450.

Kleinmuntz, G., & Szucko, J. J. (1984b). Lie detection in ancient and modern times. *American Psychologist, 39*(7), 766–776.

Kline, P. (1972). *Fact and fantasy in Freudian theory.* London: Methuen.

Klineberg, O. (1938). Emotional expression in Chinese literature. *Journal of Abnormal and Social Psychology, 33,* 517–520.

Klineberg, O. (1971). Black and white in international perspective. *American Psychologist, 26,* 119–128.

Klopfer, P. H. (1958). Influence of social interaction on learning rates in birds. *Science, 128,* 903–904.

Knopf, I. J. (1984). *Childhood psychopathology: A developmental approach.* Englewood Cliffs, NJ: Prentice-Hall.

Knowles, E. S., & Sibicky, M. E. (1990). Continuity and diversity in the stream of selves: Metaphorical resolutions of William James' one-in-many selves paradox. *Personality & Social Psychology Bulletin, 16,* 676–687.

Knox, R. E., & Safford, R. K. (1976). Group caution at the racetrack. *Journal of Experimental Social Psychology, 12,* 317–324.

Knudsen, E. I. (1981, December). The hearing of the barn owl. *Scientific American, 245,* 112–125.

Kobasa, S. C. (1979). Stressful life events, personality, and health: An inquiry into hardiness. *Journal of Personality and Social Psychology, 37,* 1–10.

Kobasa, S. C., Maddi, S. R., & Kahn, S. (1982). Hardiness and health: A prospective study. *Journal of Personality and Social Psychology, 42,* 168–177.

Kobasa, S. C. Maddi, S. R., Pucetti, M., & Zola, M. (1985). Effectiveness of hardiness, exercise, and social support as resources against illness. *Journal of Psychosomatic Research, 29,* 525–533.

Koegler, R. R., & Brill, N. Q. (1967). *Treatment of psychiatric outpatients.* New York: Appleton-Century-Crofts.

Kohlberg, L. (1976). Moral stages and moralization. The cognitive-developmental approach. In T. Lickona (Ed.), *Moral development and behavior.* New York: Holt, Rinehart & Winston.

Kohlberg, L., Ricks, D., & Snarey, J. (1984). Childhood development as a predictor of adaptation in adulthood. *Genetic Psychology Monographs, 110*(1), 91–172.

Köhler, W. (1925). *The mentality of apes.* New York: Harcourt, Brace.

Kohn, M. L. (1968). Social class and schizophrenia: A critical review. In D. Rosenthal & S. S. Kety (Eds.), *The transmission of schizophrenia.* Elmsford, NY: Pergamon Press.

Kohn, P. M., Lafreniere, K., & Gurevich, M. (1991). Hassles, health, and personality. *Journal of Personality and Social Psychology, 61,* 478–482.

Kolligian, J., & Sternberg, R. G. (1987a). Intelligence, information processing, and specific learning disabilities: A triarchic synthesis. *Journal of Learning Disabilities, 20*(1), 8–17.

Kolligian, J., & Sternberg, R. J. (1987b). Another look at intelligence and learning disabilities: A reply to Reynolds' "rap." *Journal of Learning Disabilities, 20*(6), 325–326.

Koob, G. F., & Bloom F. E. (1983). Behavioural effects of opioid peptides. *British Medical Bulletin, 39,* 89–94.

Kornblith, S. J., Rehm, L.P., O'Hara, M. W., & Lamparski, D. M. (1983). The contribution of self-reinforcement training and behavioral assignments to the efficacy of self-control therapy for depression. *Cognitive Therapy and Research, 7,* 499–528.

Kornhauser, R. R. (1978). *Social sources of delinquency.* Chicago: University of Chicago Press.

Kosslyn, S., & Hatfield, G. (1984). Representation without symbol systems. *Social Research, 51,* 1019–1045.

Kovacs, M., Beck, A. T., & Weissman, M. M. (1975). The use of suicidal motives in the psychotherapy of attempted suicides. *American Journal of Psychotherapy, 29,* 363–368.

Kraepelin, E. (1896). *Dementia praecox and paraphrenia.* Edinburgh: Livingston.

Kraepelin, E. (1913). *Psychiatrie* (Vol. 3, Part 2) 8th ed. (Translated in 1919 as *Dementia praecox and paraphrenia.*) Edinburgh: Livingston.

Krantz, D. S., Baum, A., & Singer, J. E. *Handbook of psychology and stress.* Vol 3. *Cardiovascular disorders and behavior.* Hillsdale, NJ: Lawrence Erlbaum.

Krantz, D. S., Grunberg, N. E., & Baum A. (1985). Health psychology. In M. R. Rosenzweig & L. W. Porter (Eds.), *Annual review of psychology* (pp. 349–384.) Palo Alto, CA: Annual Reviews.

Krause, N., & Stryker, S. (1984). Stress and well-being: The buffering roles of locus of control beliefs. *Social Science and Medicine, 18,* 783–790.

Kreutzer, J. S., Schneider, H. G., & Myatt, C. R. (1984). Alcohol, aggression, and assertiveness in men: Dosage and expectancy effects. *Journal of Studies on Alcohol, 45,* 275–278.

Krosnick, J. A. (1988). The role of attitude importance in social evaluation: A study of policy preferences, presidential candidate evaluations, and voting behavior. *Journal of Personality and Social Psychology, 55,* 196–210.

Krosnick, J. A., & Judd, C. M. (1982). Transitions in social influence at adolescence: Who induces cigarette smoking? *Developmental Psychology, 18*(3), 359–368.

Kruglanski, A. W. (1969). Incentives in interdependent escape as affecting the degree of group incoordination. *Journal of Experimental Social Psychology, 5,* 454–466.

Kuffler, S. W. (1953). Discharge patterns and functional organization of mammalian retina. *Journal of Neurophysiology, 16,* 37–68.

Kunzendorf, R. G. (1989). After-images of eidetic images: A developmental study. *Journal of Mental Imagery, 13,* 55–62.

Kurdek, L. A. (1981). An integrative perspective on children's divorce adjustment. *American Psychologist, 36*(8), 856–866.

La Croix, A. Z., & Haynes, S. G. (1987). Gender differences in the stressfulness of workplace roles: A focus on work and health. In R. Barnett, G. Baruch, & L. Biener (Eds.), *Gender and stress.* New York: Free Press.

LaBerge, S. (1985). *Lucid dreaming.* Los Angeles: Tarcher.

Lacey, J. I. (1959). Psychophysiological approaches to the evaluation of psychotherapeutic process and outcome. In E. A. Rubinstein & M. B. Parloff (Eds.), *Psychophysiological approaches to the evaluation of psychotherapeutic process and outcomes in research and psychotherapy.* Washington, DC: American Psychological Association.

Lachman, S. J. (1972). *Psychosomatic disorders: A behavioristic interpretation.* New York: Wiley.

Ladd, G. T. (1887). *Elements of physiological psychology.* New York: Scribner.

LaFreniere, P. J., & Sroufe, L. A. (1985). Profiles of peer competence in the preschool: Interrelations between measures, influence of social ecology, and relation to attachment history. *Developmental Psychology, 21*(1), 56–69.

Lagercrantz, H., & Slotkin, T. A. (1986). The "stress" of being born. *Scientific American, 245*(4), 100–107.

Lagerspetz, K. M. J., Bjorkqvist, K., & Peltonen, T. (1988). Is indirect aggression typical of females? Gender differences in aggressiveness in 11- to 12-year-old children. *Aggressive Behavior, 14,* 403–414.

Lakoff, G. (1972). Hedges: A study in meaning criteria and the logic of fuzzy concepts. *Papers from the eighth regional meeting, Chicago Linguistics Society.* Chicago: University of Chicago Linguistics Department.

Lalonde, R. N. (1992). The dynamics of group differentiation in the face of defeat. *Personality and Social Psychology Bulletin, 18,* 336–342.

Lamb, M. E. (1981). The development of father-infant relationships. In M. E. Lamb (Ed.), *The role of the father in child development* (rev. ed.). New York: Wiley.

Lambert, M. J., Shapiro, D. A., & Bergin, A. E. (1986). The effectiveness of psychotherapy. In S. L. Garfield & A. E. Bergin (Eds.), *Handbook of psychotherapy and behavior change* (3rd ed., pp. 157–212). New York: Wiley.

Lambert, N. M. (1981). Psychological evidence in *Larry P. v. Wilson Riles:* An evaluation by a witness for the defense. *American Psychologist, 36,* 937–952.

Landy, F. J., & Trumbo, D. A. (1980). *Psychology of work behavior.* Homewood, IL: Dorsey.

Langer, E. J., Rodin, J. (1976). The effects of choice and enhanced personal responsibility for the aged: A field study in an institutional setting. *Journal of Personality and Social Psychology, 34,* 191–198.

Langer, E. J., Janis, I. L., & Wolfer, J. A. (1975). Reduction of psychological stress in surgical patients. *Journal of Experimental Social Psychology, 11,* 155–165.

Langlois, J. H., Ritter, J. M., Roggman, L. A., & Vaughn, L. S. (1991) Facial diversity and infant preferences for attractive faces. *Developmental Psychology, 27*, 79–84.

Lasswell, H. D., & Casey, R. D. (1946). *Propaganda communication and public opinion.* Princeton: Princeton University Press.

Latané, B., & Darley, J. (1970). *The unresponsive bystander: Why doesn't he help?* New York: Appleton.

Latané, B., Williams, K., & Harkins, S. (1979). Many hands make light the work: The causes and consequences of social loafing. *Journal of Personality and Social Psychology, 37*, 822–832.

Laudenslager, M., Ryan, S., Drugan, R., Hyson, R., & Maier, S. (1983). Coping and immunosuppression: Inescapable but not escapable shock suppresses lymphocyte proliferation. *Science, 221*, 568–570.

Laughlin, P. R., & Earley, P. C. (1982). Social combination models, persuasive arguments theory, social comparison theory, and choice shift. *Journal of Personality and Social Psychology, 42*, 273–280.

Laughlin, P. R., Lange, R., & Adamopoulos, J. (1982). Selection strategies for "Mastermind" problems. *Journal of Experimental Psychology: Learning, Memory and Cognition, 8*, 475–483.

Lawler, E. E. (1973). *Motivation in work organizations.* Monterey, CA: Brooks/Cole.

Lawler, E. E., & Suttle, J. L. (1972). A causal correlational test of the need hierarchy concept. *Organizational Behavior and Human Performance, 7*, 265–287.

Lazarsfeld, P. F., Berelson, B., & Gaudet, H. (1948). *The people's choice.* New York: Columbia University Press.

Lazarus, R. S. (1984). On the primacy of cognition. *American Psychologist, 39*(2), 117–123.

Le, A. D., Poulos, C. X., & Cappell, H. (1979). Conditioned tolerance to the hypothermic effect of ethyl alcohol. *Science, 206*(4422), 1109–1110.

Leahy, T. H. (1991). *A history of modern psychology.* Englewood Cliffs, NJ: Prentice-Hall.

LeBon, G. (1896). *The crowd.* London: Benn.

Lebra, T. S. (1979). *Japanese patterns of behavior.* Honolulu: University of Hawaii Press.

Lefcourt, H. M., & Martin R. A. (1986). *Humor and life stress.* New York: Springer-Verlag.

Lefcourt, H. M., Davidson-Katz, K., & Kueneman, K. (1990). Humor and immune-system functioning. *Humor, 3*, 305–321.

Leitenberg, H., Rosen, J. C., Gross, J., Nudelman, S., & Vara, L. S. (1988). Exposure plus response-prevention treatment of bulimia nervosa. *Journal of Consulting and Clinical Psychology, 56*, 535–541.

Lenneberg, E. H. (1967). *Biological foundations of language.* New York: Wiley.

Leon, G. R., & Roth, L. (1977). Obesity: Psychological causes, correlations, and speculations. *Psychological Bulletin, 84*, 117–139.

Leonard, C. M., Rolls, E. T., Wilson, F. A. W., & Baylis, G. C. (1985). Neurons in the amygdala of the monkey with response selective for faces. *Behavioral Brain Research, 15*, 159–176.

Leonard, C. M., Voeller, K. K. S., & Kuldau, J. M. (1991). When's a smile a smile? Or how to detect a message by digitizing the signal. *Psychological Science, 2*, 166–172.

Lerner, M. J. (1980). *The belief in a just world: A fundamental delusion.* New York: Plenum.

Lesser, G. S., Krawitz, R. N., & Packard, R. (1963). Experimental arousal of achievement motivation in adolescent girls. *Journal of Abnormal and Social Psychology, 66*, 59–66.

Leventhal, G. S., Michaels, J. W., & Sanford, C. (1972). Inequity and interpersonal conflict: Reward allocation and secrecy about reward as methods of preventing conflict. *Journal of Personality and Social Psychology, 23*, 88–102.

Leventhal, H. (1970). Findings and theory in the study of fear communications. In L. Berkowitz (Ed.), *Advances in experimental social psychology* (Vol. 5). New York: Academic Press.

Leventhal, H., & Cameron, L. (1987). Behavioral theories and the problem of compliance. *Patient Education and Counseling, 10*, 117–138.

Leventhal, H., & Cleary, P. D. (1980). The smoking problem: A review of research and theory in behavioral risk modification. *Psychological Bulletin, 88*, 370–405.

Leventhal, H., Zimmerman, R., & Guttman, M. (1984). Compliance: A self-regulation perspective. In W. D. Gentry (Ed.), *Handbook of behavioral medicine* (pp. 395–436). New York: Guilford Press.

Levanthal, H. (1980). Toward a comprehensive theory of emotion. In L. Berkowitz (Ed.), *Advances in experimental social psychology* (Vol. 13). New York: Academic Press.

LeVay, S. (1991, December). *Archives of General Psychiatry.*

LeVay, S. (1991). A difference in hypothalamic structure between heterosexual and homosexual men. *Science, 253*, 1034–1037.

Levi, L. (1990). Occupational stress: Spice of life or kiss of death? *American Psychologist, 45*, 1142–1145.

Levine, C., Kohlberg, L., & Hewer, A. (1985). The current formulation of Kohlberg's theory and a response to critics. *Human Development, 28*(2), 94–100.

Levine, J. D., & Gordon, N. C. (1984). Influence of the method of drug administration on analgesic response. *Nature, 312*, 755–756.

Levinger, G., & Rausch, H. L. (1977) *Close relationships.* Amherst: University of Massachusetts Press.

Levinger, G., & Snock, J. D. (1972). *Attraction in relationship: A new look at interpersonal attraction.* New York: General Learning Press.

Levinson, D. J., Darrow, C. N., Klein, E. B., Levinson, M. H., & KcKee, B. (1978). *The seasons of a man's life.* New York: Alfred A. Knopf.

Levis, D. J. (1985). Implosive therapy: A comprehensive extension of conditioning theory of fear/anxiety to psychology. In S. Reiss & R. Bootzin (Eds.), *Theoretical issues in behavior therapy.* New York: Academic Press.

Lewicki, P., Hill, T., & Czyzewska, M. (1992). Nonconscious acquisition of information. *American Psychologist, 47*, 796–801.

Lewin, R. (1987). Brain grafts benefit Parkinson's patients. *Science, 236*, 149.

Lewin, R. (1988). Brain graft puzzles. *Science, 240*, 879.

Lewis, E. R., & Narens, P. M. (1985). Do frogs communicate with seismic signals? *Science, 227*, 187–189.

Lewis, S. A., Sloan, J. P., & Jones, S. K. (1978). Paradoxical sleep and depth perception. *Biological Psychology, 6*, 17–25.

Lewy, A. J., Sack, R. L., Singer, C. M., White, D. M., & Hoban, T. M. (1988). Winter depression and the phase-shift hypothesis for bright light's therapeutic effects: History, theory, and experimental evidence. *Journal of Biological Rhythms, 3*, 121–134.

Licklider, J. C. R. (1959) Three auditory theories. In I. S. Koch (Ed.), Psychology: *A study of a science* (Vol. 1). New York: McGraw-Hill.

Licklider, J. C. R. (1961, March). *Audio warning signals for Air Force weapon systems.* USAF, WADD, TR 60–814.

Lieberson, S., & Silverman, A. R. (1965). The precipitants and underlying conditions of race riots. *American Sociological Review, 30*, 887–898.

Liebert, R. M., & Spiegler, M. D. (1990). *Personality: Strategies and issues* (6th ed.). Pacific Grove CA: Brooks/Cole.

Liebeskind, J. C., & Paul, L. A. (1977). Psychological and physiological mechanisms of pain. *Annual Review of Psychology, 28*, 41–60.

Liem. R., & Liem, J. (1979). Social support and stress: Some general issues and their application to the problem of unemployment. In L. Ferman & J. Gordus (Eds.), *Mental health and the economy.* Kalamazoo, MI: Upjohn Institute.

Liem, R., & Rayman, P. (1982). Health and social costs of unemployment: Research and policy considerations. *American Psychologist, 37*, 1116–1123.

Light, L. L. (1991). Memory and aging: Four hypotheses in search of data. *Annual Review of Psychology, 42*, 333–376.

Linder, D. E., Cooper, J., & Jones, E. E. (1967). Decision freedom as a determinant of the role of incentive magnitude in attitude change. *Journal of Personality and Social Psychology, 6*, 245–254.

Lindheim, R. (1970). Factors which determine hospital design. In H. M. Proshansky, W. H. Ittelson, & L. G. Rivlin (Eds.), *Environmental psychology: Man and his physical setting.* New York: Holt, Rinehart & Winston.

Linn, R. L. (1982). Admissions testing on trial. *American Psychologist, 37*, 279–291.

Lisk, R. D., Pretlow, R. A., & Friedman, S. (1969). Hormonal stimulation necessary for elicitation of maternal nest building in the mouse (*Mus musculus*). *Animal Behavior, 17*, 730–737.

Livingstone, M. S. (1988). Art, illusion, and the visual system. *Scientific American, 258*(1), 78–85.

Livingstone, M. S., & Hubel, D. H. (1984). Anatomy and physiology of a color system in the primate visual cortex. *Journal of Neuroscience, 4*, 309–356.

Locke, E. A. (1975). Personnel attitudes and motivation. *Annual Review of Psychology, 26*, 457–480.

Locke, E. A., & Latham G. P. (1990). *A theory of goal setting and task performance.* Englewood Cliffs, NJ: Prentice-Hall.

Loehlin, J. C., Willerman, L., Horn, J. M. (1988). Human behavior genetics. *Annual Review of Psychology, 30*, 101–133.

Loftus, E., & Ketcham, K. (1991). *Witness for the Defense.* New York: St. Martin's Press.

Loftus, E. F., & Greene, E. (1980). Warning: Even memory for faces may be contagious. *Laws & Human Behavior, 4*(4), 323–334.

Loftus, E. F., & Loftus, G. R. (1980). On the permanence of stored information in the human brain. *American Psychologist, 35*(5), 409–420.

Loftus, E. F., Miller, D. G., & Burns, H. J. (1978). Semantic integration of verbal information into a visual memory. *Journal of Experimental Psychology: Human Learning & Memory, 4*(1), 19–31.

Lomans, P. (1992, April 17). Gezondheidsrisico's voor alleenstaanden. (Health risks for single individuals.) *Intermediair, 28*, 37–38.

London, M., & Bray, D. W. (1980). Ethical issues in testing and evolution for personnel decisions. *American Psychologist, 35*, 890–901.

London, P. (1970). The rescuers: Motivational hypotheses about Christians who saved Jews from the Nazis. In J. Macaulay & L. Berkowitz (Eds.), *Altruism and helping behavior.* New York: Academic Press.

Lord, C. G. (1982). Predicting behavioral consistency from an individual's perception of situational similarities. *Journal of Personality and Social Psychology, 42*, 1076–1088.

Lothstein, L. M. (1971). *Personal space in assault-prone male adolescent prisoners.* Doctoral dissertation, Duke University.

Lubin, A. J. (1972). *Stranger on the earth: A psychological biography of Vincent van Gogh.* New York: Holt, Rinehart & Winston.

Luborsky, L., Crits-Christoph, P., & Mellon, J. (1986). Advent of objective measures of the transference concept. *Journal of Consulting and Clinical Psychology, 54*, 39–47.

Luborsky, L., Singer, G., & Luborsky, L. (1975). Comparative studies of psychotherapies: Is it true that everyone has won and all must have prizes? *Archives of General Psychiatry, 32*, 995–1008.

Luborsky, L., & Spence, D. P. (1978). Quantitative research on psychoanalytic therapy. In *Handbook of psychotherapy and behavior change* (2nd ed.). New York: Wiley.

Luce, G. G. (1970). *Biological rhythms in psychiatry and medicine.* Public Health Service Report, National Institute of Health.

Luchins, A. S. (1942). Mechanization in problem-solving: The effect of *Einstellung. Psychological Monographs, 54*(6, Whole No. 248).

Ludel, J. (1978). *Introduction to sensory processes.* San Francisco: Freeman.

Ludwig, A. M., Brandsma, J. M., Wilbur, C. B., Bendfeldt, F., & Jameson, D. H. (1972). The objective study of a multiple personality. *Archives of General Psychiatry, 26*, 298–310.

Lundin, R. W. (1987). Structuralism. In R. J. Corsini (Ed.), *Concise encyclopedia of psychology.* New York: John Wiley & Sons.

Lupker, S. J., Harbluk, J. L., & Patrick, A. S. (1991). Memory for things forgotten. *Journal of Experimental Psychology: Learning, Memory, and Cognition, 17*(5), 897–907.

Lydiard, R. B., & Gelenberg, A. J. (1982). Hazards and adverse effects of lithium. *Annual Review of Medicine, 33*, 327–344.

Lykken, D. T., McGue, M., Tellagen, A., & Bourchard, T. J. (1992). Emergencies: Genetic traits that may not run in families. *American Psychologist, 12*, 1565–1577.

Lynn, S. J., & Rhue, J. W. (1988). Fantasy proneness: Hypnosis, developmental antecedents, and psychopathology. *American Psychologist, 43*, 35–44.

Lynn, S. J., Weekes, J. R., Neufield, V., Zivney, O., Brentar, J., & Weiss, F. (1991). Interpersonal climate and hypnotizability level: Effects on hypnotic performance, rapport, and archaic involvement. *Journal of Personality and Social Psychology, 60*, 739–743.

Lyons, M. J., Faust, I. M., Hemmes, R. B., Buskirk, D. R., Hirsch, J., & Zabriskie, J. B. (1982). A virally induced obesity syndrome in mice. *Science, 216*, 82–85.

▼

Maas, A., & Clark, R. D. III. (1984). Hidden impact of minorities: 15 years of minority influence research. *Psychological Bulletin, 95*, 428–450.

Maas, J., Bowden, C., Koslow, S., Katz, M., Davis, J., & Frazer, A. A new catecholamine hypothesis (abstract). *Biological Psychiatry, 25*(71), 2A.

Maas, J. W. (Ed.). (1983). *MHPG: Basic mechanisms and psychopathology.* Orlando, FL: Academic Press.

Maccoby, E. E., & Jacklin, C. N. (1974). *The psychology of sex differences.* Stanford, CA: Stanford University Press.

Machungwa, P. D., & Schmitt, N. (1983). Motivation in country. *APPCW, 68*, 31–47.

Mack, J. E., Hopkins, B., Jacobs, D. M., Westrum, R., & Bigelow, R. (1992). *Unusual personal experiences: An analysis of the data from three national surveys.* Las Vegas, NV: Bigelow.

MacLusky, N. J., & Naftolin, F. (1981). Sexual differentiation of the central nervous system. *Science, 211*, 1294–1302.

MacNeil, M. K., & Sherif, M. (1976). Norm change over subject generations as a function of arbitrariness of prescribed norms. *Journal of Personality and Social Psychology, 34*, 762–773.

Maehr, M. L. (1974). Culture and achievement motivation. *American Psychologist, 29*, 887–896.

Maehr, M. L., & Kleiber, D. A. (1981). The graying of achievement motivation. *American Psychologist, 36*, 787–793.

Maehr, M. L. & Nicholls, J. G. (1980). Culture and achievement motivation: A second look. In N. Warren (Ed.), *Studies in cross-cultural psychology* (Vol. 3). New York: Academic Press.

Malamuth, N., Feshbach, S., & Jaffe, Y. (1977). Sexual arousal and aggression: Recent experiments and theoretical issues. *Journal of Social Issues, 33*(2), 110–133.

Malamuth, N. M., Donnerstein, E. I. (1984). *Pornography and aggression.* Orlando, FL: Academic Press.

Malhotra, M. S., & Sengupta, J. (1965). Carrying of school bags by children. *Ergonomics, 8*(1), 55–60.

Malinowski, B. (1927). *Sex and repression in savage society.* London: Humanities Press.

Malpass, R. S., & Devine, P. G. (1981). Eyewitness identification: Lineup instructions and the absence of the offender. *Journal of Applied Psychology, 66*, 482–489.

Mandler, G. (1985). *Cognitive psychology: As essay in cognitive science.* Hillsdale, NJ: Lawrence Erlbaum Associates.

Mandler, J. M. (1979). Categorical and schematic organization in memory. In C. R. Puff, (Ed.), *Memory organization and structure,* New York: Academic Press.

Mandler, J. M. (1990). Recall of events by preverbal children. In A. Diamond, (Ed.). *The development and neural bases of higher cognitive functions.* New York: New York Academy of Sciences.

Mann, L. (1974). On being a sore loser: How fans react to their team's failure. *Australian Journal of Psychology, 26*, 37–47.

Mann, L., Newton, J. W., & Innes, J. M. (1982). A test between deindividuation and emergent norm theories of crowd aggression. *Journal of Personality and Social Psychology, 42*, 260–272.

Mantell, D. M. (1971). The potential for violence in Germany. *Journal of Social Issues, 27*(4), 101–112.

Marcia, J. E. (1976). Identity six years later: A follow-up study. *Journal of Youth and Adolescence, 5*, 145–160.

Marcus, E. A., & Carew, T. J. (1990). Ontogenetic analysis of learning in a simple system. In A. Diamond, (Ed.), *The development and neural bases of higher cognitive functions.* New York: New York Academy of Sciences.

Marks, D., & Kammann, R. (1980). *The psychology of the psychic.* Buffalo, NY: Prometheus Books.

Marks, W. B., Dobelle, W. H., & MacNichol, E. F. (1964). Visual pigments of single primate cones. *Science, 143*, 1181–1183.

Marlatt, G. A., & Baer, J. S. (1988). Addictive behaviors: Etiology and treatment. *Annual Review of Psychology, 39*, 223–252.

Marlatt, G. A., & Rohsenow, D. J. (1981, December). The think-drink effect. *Psychology Today*, 60–69, 93.

Marlatt, G. A., Kosturn, C., & Lang, A. (1975). Provocation to anger and opportunity for retaliation as determinants of alcohol consumption in social drinkers. *Journal of Abnormal Psychology, 84*, 652–659.

Marler, P., & Hamilton, W. (1966). *Mechanisms of animal behavior.* New York: Wiley.

Marshall, G. N. (1991). Levels of analysis and personality: Lessons from the person-situation debate? *Psychological Science, 2*, 427–428.

Marshall, J. E., & Heslin, R. (1975). Boys and girls together: Sexual composition and the effect of density and group size on cohesiveness. *Journal of Personality and Social Psychology, 31*, 952–961.

Martin, G. B., & Clark, R. D. (1982). Distress crying in neonates: Species and peer specificity. *Developmental Psychology, 18*(1), 3–9.

Martin, P. R. (1991). *Handbook of behavior therapy and psychological science.* Oxford/New York: Pergamon.

Martin, R. A., & Dobbin, J. P. (1988). Sense of humor, hassles, and immunoglobulin A: Evidence for a stress-moderating effect of humor. *International Journal of Psychiatry in Medicine, 18*, 93–105.

Martinez, J. L., Jr., Weinberger, S. B., & Schultees, G. (1988). Enkephalins and learning and memory: A review of evidence for a site of action outside the blood-brain barrier. *Behavior and Neural Biology, 49*, 192–221.

Marzuk, P. M., Tierney, H., Tardiff, K., Gross, E. M., Morgan, E. B., Hsu, M., & Mann, J. J. (1988). Increased risk of suicide in persons with AIDS. *Journal of the American Medical Association, 259*, 1333–1337.

Maslow, A. H. (1941). Deprivation, threat, and frustration. *Psychological Review, 48,* 364–366.

Maslow, A. H. (1954). *Motivation and personality.* New York: Harper & Row.

Masson, J. M. (1990). *Final analysis: The making and unmaking of a psychoanalyst* Reading, MA: Addison-Wesley.

Masters, W., & Johnson, V. (1970). *Human sexual inadequacy.* Boston: Little, Brown.

Masters, W. H., & Johnson, V. E. (1966). *Human sexual response.* Boston: Little, Brown.

Masters, W. H., Johnson, V. E., & Kolodny, R. C. (1985). *Human sexuality* (2nd ed.). Boston: Little, Brown.

Masterson, J. F., et al. (1991). *Comparing psychoanalytic psychotherapies.* NY: Brunner/Mazel.

Matarazzo, J. (1983). Computerized psychological testing. *Science, 221,* 323.

Matarazzo, J. D. (1980). Behavioral health and behavioral medicine: Frontiers for a new health psychology. *American Psychologist, 35,* 807–817.

Matarazzo, J. D. (1983). Behavioral immunogens and pathogens in health and illness. In B. L. Hammond & C. J. Scheier (Eds.), *Psychology and health.* Washington, DC: American Psychological Association.

Matas, L., Arend, R. A., & Sroufe, L. A. (1978). Continuity in adaptation: Quality of attachment and later competence. *Child Development, 49,* 547–556.

Matsuoka, K., Onizawa, T., Hatakeyama, T., & Yamaguchi, H. (1987). Incidence of young adult eidetikers, and two kinds of eidetic imagery. *Tohoku Psychologica Folia, 46,* 62–74.

Mattick, R. P., & Peters, L. (1988). Treatment of severe social phobia: Effects of guided exposure with and without cognitive restructuring. *Journal of Consulting and Clinical Psychology, 56,* 251–260.

Maurer, D., & Salapatek, P. (1976). Developmental changes in the scanning of faces by young infants. *Child Development, 47,* 523–527.

Mauro, R., Sata, K., & Tucker, J. (1992). The role of appraisal in human emotions: A cross-cultural study. *Journal of Personality and Social Psychology, 62*(2), 301–317.

Mausner, B. (1954). The effect of prior reinforcement on the interaction of observer pairs. *Journal of Abnormal and Social Psychology, 49,* 65–68.

May, B. (1991). Diabetes. In M. Pitts & K. Phillips (Eds.), *The psychology of health* (pp. 214–230). London: Routledge.

Mayo, E. (1945). *The social problems of an industrial civilization.* Cambridge, MA: Harvard University, School of Business Administration.

McCall, R. B. (1985). The confluence model and theory. *Child Development, 56,* 217–218.

McCann, T., & Sheehan, P. W. (1988). Hypnotically induced pseudomemories—sampling their conditions among hypnotizable subjects. *Journal of Personality and Social Psychology, 54,* 339–346.

McCauley, C. R. (1989). The nature of social influence in groupthink: Compliance and internalization. *Journal of Personality and Social Psychology, 57,* 250–260.

McCauley, C. R., & Segal, M. E. (1989). Terrorist individuals and terrorist groups: The normal psychology of extreme behavior. In J. Groebel & J. H. Goldstein (Eds.), *Terrorism: Psychological perspectives.* Seville, Spain: University of Seville Press.

McClelland, D. C., & Kirschnit, C. (1988). The effect of motivational arousal through films on salivary immunoglobin A. *Psychology and Health, 2,* 31–52.

McClelland, D. C., & Winter, D. (1969). *Motivating economic achievement.* New York: Free Press.

McClelland, D. C., Atkinson, J. W., Clark, R. A., & Lowell, E. I. (1953). *The achievement motive.* New York: Appleton-Century-Crofts.

McCrae, R. R. (1989). Why I advocate the five-factor model: Joint factor analyses of the NEO-PI with other instruments. In D. M. Buss & N. Cantor (Eds.), *Personality psychology: Recent trends and emerging directions* (pp. 237–245). New York: Springer-Verlag.

McCrae, R. R., & Costa, P. T., Jr. (1990). *Personality in adulthood.* New York: Guilford.

McGhee, P. E., & Goldstein, J. H. (1983). *Handbook of humor research.* 2 Vols. New York: Springer-Verlag.

McGinty, D., & Szymusiak, R. (1988). Neuronal unit activity patterns on behaving animals: Brainstem and limbic system. *Annual Review of Psychology, 39,* 135–168.

McGuire, W. J. (1969). The nature of attitudes and attitude change. In G. Lindzey & E. Aronson (Eds.), *Handbook of social psychology.* Reading, MA: Addison-Wesley.

McKenna, R. J. (1972). Some effects of anxiety level and food cues on the eating behavior of obese and normal subjects: A comparison of the Schachterian and psychosomatic conceptions. *Journal of Personality and Social Psychology, 22,* 311–319.

McKenry, P. C., Kotch. J. B., & Browne, D. H. (1991). Correlates of dysfunctional parenting attitudes among low-income adolescent mothers. *Journal of Adolescent Research, 6,* 212–234.

McKenzie, R. E., Ehrisman, W. J., Montgomery, P. S., & Barnes, R. H. (1974). The treatment of headache by means of electroencephalographic biofeedback. *Headache, 13,* 164–172.

McLin, W. M. (1992). Introduction to issues in psychology and epilepsy. *American Psychologist, 47,* 1124–1125.

McNeill, D. (1970). The development of language. In P. H. Mussen (Ed.), *Carmichael's manual of child psychology* (3rd ed.). New York: Wiley.

McNemar, Q. (1942). Revision of the Stanford-Binet Test. Stanford, CA: Stanford University Press.

Mebert, C. J., & Michel, G. F. (1980). Handedness in artists. In J. Herron (Ed.), *Neuropsychology of left-handedness.* New York: Academic Press.

Medvedev, Z., & Medvedev, R. A. (1972). *A question of madness.* New York: Random House.

Meehl, P. E. (1950). On the circularity of the law of effect. *Psychological Bulletin, 47,* 52–75.

Melzack, R. (1990). The tragedy of needless pain. *Scientific American, 262,* 2, 27–33.

Melzack, R., & Wall, P. D. (1965). Pain mechanisms: A new theory. *Science, 150,* 971–979.

Menzel, E. W. (1973). Chimpanzee spatial memory organization. *Science, 182,* 943–945.

Menzel, E. W. (1978). Cognitive mapping in chimpanzees. In S. H. Hulse, H. Fowler, & W. K. Honig (Eds.), *Cognitive processes in animal behavior.* Hillsdale, NJ: Lawrence Erlbaum Associates.

Mercer, R. T., Nichols, E. G., & Doyle, G. C. (1989). *Transitions in a woman's life: Major life events in a developmental context.* New York: Springer.

Merikle, P. M. (1992). Perception without awareness. *American Psychologist, 47,* 792–795.

Messick, D. M., & Mackie, D. M. (1989). Intergroup relations. *Annual Review of Psychology, 40,* 45–81.

Messick, S. (1980). Test validity and the ethics of assessment. *American Psychologist, 35,* 1012–1027.

Metzler, C. W., Noell, J., & Biglan, A. (1992). The validation of a construct of high-risk sexual behavior in heterosexual adolescents. *Journal of Adolescent Research, 7,* 233–249.

Meyners, R., & Wooster, C. (1979). *Sexual style: Facing and making choices about sex.* New York: Harcourt Brace Jovanovich.

Mickelson, R. A. (1990). The attitude-achievement paradox among Black adolescents. *Sociology of Education, 63,* 44–61.

Middlebrooks, J. C., & Green, D. M. (1991). Sound localization by human listeners. *Annual Review of Psychology, 42,* 135–160.

Milgram, S. (1961). Nationality and conformity. *Scientific American, 205*(6), 45–51.

Milgram, S. (1974). *Obedience to authority.* New York: Harper.

Milgram, S., & Toch, H. (1969). Collective behavior: Crowds and social movements. In G. Lindzey & E. Aronson (Eds.), *Handbook of social psychology* (Vol. 4). Reading, MA: Addison-Wesley.

Miller, A. G., Ashton, W., & Mishal, M. (1990). Beliefs concerning the features of constrained behavior: A basis for the fundamental attribution error. *Journal of Personality and Social Psychology, 59,* 635–650.

Miller, G. A. (1956). The magical number seven, plus or minus two: Some limits on out capacity to process information. *Psychological Review, 63,* 81–97.

Miller, J. S., & Spear, N. E. (1989). Ontogenetic differences in short-term retention of Pavlovian conditioning. *Developmental Psychobiology, 22*(4), 377–387.

Miller, N., & Brewer, M. (Eds.). (1984). *Groups in contact: The psychology of desegregation.* New York: Academic Press.

Miller, N. E. (1941). The frustration-aggression hypothesis. *Psychological Review, 38,* 337–342.

Miller, N. E. (1984). Learning: Some facts and needed research relevant to maintaining health. In J. D. Matarazzo, S. M. Weiss, J. A. Herd, N. E. Miller, & S. M. Weiss (Eds.), *Behavioral health* (pp. 199–208). New York: Wiley.

Miller, R. R., & Springer, A. D. (1973). Amnesia consolidation and retrieval. *Psychological Review, 80,* 69–70.

Miller, S., & Peacock, R. (1982). Evidence for the uniqueness of eidetic imagery. *Perceptual and Motor Skills, 55,* 1219–1233.

Miller, S. M., & Mangan, C. E. (1983). Interacting effects of information and coping style in adapting to gynecologic stress: Should the doctor tell all? *Journal of Personality and Social Psychology, 45,* 223–236.

Milner, B. (1970). Memory and the temporal regions of the brain. In K. H. Pribram & D. E. Broadbent (Eds.), *Biology of memory*. New York: Academic Press.

Minami, M., & McCabe A. (1991). *Haiku* as a discourse regulation device: A stanza analysis of Japanese children's personal narratives. *Language in Society, 20*, 577–599.

Mindell, J. (1992). *Issues in clinical psychology*. Dubuque, IA: Wm. C. Brown Communications, Inc.

Mineka, S. (1985). The frightful complexity of the origins of fears. In F. R. Brush & J. B. Overmier (Eds.), *Affect, conditioning, and cognition*. Hillsdale, NJ: Lawrence Erlbaum Associates.

Mineka, S., & Snowdon, C. T. (1978). Inconsistency and possible habituation of CCK induced satiety. *Physiology and Behavior, 21*, 65–72.

Mintz, A. (1951). Non-adaptive group behavior. *Journal of Abnormal and Social Psychology, 46*, 150–159.

Minuchin, S., Rosman, B., & Baker, L. (1978). *Psychosomatic families: Anorexia nervosa in context*. Cambridge, MA: Harvard University Press.

Mischel, W. (1979). On the interface of cognition and personality: Beyond the person-situation debate. *American Psychologist, 34*, 740–754.

Mlicki, P. & Ellemers, N. (in press). Being different or being better? National and European identities of Polish and Dutch students. *European Journal of Social Psychology*.

Moe, J. L., Nacoste, R. W., & Insko, C. A. (1981). Belief versus race as determinants of discrimination: A study of southern adolescents in 1966 and 1979. *Journal of Personality and Social Psychology, 41*, 1031–1050.

Moltz, H., Lubin, M., Leon, M., & Numan, M. (1970). Hormonal induction of maternal behavior in the ovariectomized nulliparous rat. *Physiology and Behavior, 5*, 1373–1377.

Money, J., & Ehrhardt, A. A. (1972). *Man and woman, boy and girl*. Baltimore: Johns Hopkins Press.

Money, J., Schwartz, M., & Lewis, V. G. (1984). Adult herotosexual status and fetal hormonal masculinization and demasculinization: 46, XX congenital virilizing adrenal hyperplasia and 46, XY androgen-insensitivity syndrome compared. *Psychoneuroendocrinology, 9*, 405–414.

Moore, C. L. (1985). Another psychobiological view of sexual differentiation. *Developmental Review, 5*(1), 18–55.

Moore, S., & Rosenthal, D. (1991). Adolescent invulnerability and perceptions of AIDS risk. *Journal of Adolescent Research, 6*, 164–180.

Moore, T. E. (1982). Subliminal advertising: What you see is what you get. *Journal of Marketing, 46*, 38–47.

Moore, T. W. (1975). Exclusive early mothering and its alternatives: The outcomes to adolescence. *Scandinavian Journal of Psychology, 16*, 255–272.

Moran, J., & Desimone, R. (1985). Selective attention gates visual processing in the extrastriate cortex. *Science, 229*, 782–784.

Moray, N. (1959). Attention in dichotic listening: Affective cues and the influence of instructions. *Quarterly Journal of Experimental Psychology, 11*, 56–60.

Morey, N., Bates, A., & Barnett, I. (1965). Experiments on the four-eared man. *Journal of the Acoustical Society of America, 38*, 196–201.

Morell, P., & Norton, W. T. (1980, May). Myelin. *Scientific American*, 74–89.

Morey, L., & Ochoa, E. (1989). An investigation of adherence to diagnostic criteria: Clinical diagnosis of the DSM-III personality disorders. *Journal of Personality Disorders, 3*, 180–192.

Morey, L. C., Waugh, M. H., & Blashfield, R. K. (1985). MMPI scales for DSM-III personality disorders: Their derivation and correlates. *Journal of Personality Assessment, 49*, 245–251.

Morley, J. E., & Blundell, J. E. (1988). The neurobiological basis of eating disorders: Some formulation. *Biological Psychiatry, 23*, 53–78.

Morris, W. N., Worchel, S., Bois, J. L., Pearson, J. A., Rountree, C. A., Samaha, G. M., Wachtler, J., & Wright, S. L. (1976). Collective coping with stress: Group reactions to fear, anxiety, and ambiguity. *Journal of Personality and Social Psychology, 33*, 674–679.

Moscovici, S. (1985). Social influence and conformity. In G. Lindzey & E. Aronson (Eds.), *Handbook of social psychology* (3rd ed., Vol. 2). New York: Random House.

Moscovici, S., Lage, E., & Naffrechoux, M. (1969). Influence of a consistent minority on the responses of a majority in a color perception task. *Sociometry, 32*, 365–380.

Mostwin, D. (1980). *Social dimension of family treatment*. Washington, DC: National Association of Social Workers.

Moyer, K. E. (1976). *The psychobiology of aggression*. New York: Harper & Row,

Muehlenhard, C., & Cook, S. (1988). Men's self-reports of unwanted sexual activity. *The Journal of Sex Research, 24*, 58–72.

Mugny, G., & Perez, J. A. (1991). *The social psychology of minority influence*. Cambridge, England: Cambridge University Press.

Mullen, G., & Johnson, C. (1990). Distinctiveness based illusory correlations and stereotyping: A meta-analytic integration. *British Journal of Social Psychology, 29*, 11–27.

Mummendey, A., & Mummendey, H. D. (1983). Aggressive behavior of soccer players as social interaction. In J. H. Goldstein (Ed.), *Sports violence*. New York: Springer-Verlag.

Munroe, R. H., Munroe, R. L., & Shimmin, H. S. (1984). Children's work in four cultures: Determinants and consequences. *American Anthropologist, 86*, 369–379.

Munroe, R. L., & Munroe, R. H. (1972). Population density and affective relationships in three East African societies. *Journal of Social Psychology, 88*, 15–120.

Murnane, K., & Shiffrin, R. M. (1991). Interference and the representation of events in memory. *Journal of Experimental Psychology, 17*(5), 855–874.

Murray, H. A. (1938). *Explorations in personality*. New York: Oxford.

Murray, J. B. (1991). Psychophysiological aspects of nightmares, night terrors, and sleepwalking. *The Journal of General Psychology, 118*(2), 113–127.

Murry, V. M. (1992). Sexual career paths of Black adolescent females: A study of socioeconomic status and other life experiences. *Journal of Adolescent Research, 7*, 4–27.

Mussen, P. H., & Jones, M. C. (1957). Self-conceptions, motivations, and interpersonal attitudes of late- and early-maturing boys. *Child Development, 28*, 243–256.

Musto, D. F. (1991, July). Opium, cocaine, and marijuana in American history. *Scientific American*, 40–47.

Muuss, R. E. (1988). Carol Gilligan's theory of sex differences in the development of moral reasoning during adolescence. *Adolescence, 23*, 229–243.

Myers, H. F. (1982). Stress, ethnicity, and social class: A model for research with Black populations. In E. E. Jones & S. Korchin (Eds.), *Minority mental health* (pp. 118–148). New York: Praeger.

Nahemow, L., & Lawton, M. P. (1975). Similarity and propinquity in friendship formation. *Journal of Personality and Social Psychology, 32*, 205–213.

Nakanishi, M. (1988). Group motivation and group task performance: The expectancy-valence theory approach. *Small Group Behavior, 19*, 35–55.

Nathan, P. E. (1984). The worksite as a setting for health promotion and positive life-style change. In N. E. Miller, J. D. Matarazzo, J. A. Herd, & S. M. Weiss (Eds.), *Behavioral health: A handbook of health enhancement and disease prevention*. New York: Wiley.

Nathans, J. Thomas, D., & Hogness, D. S. (1986). Molecular genetics of human color vision: The genes encoding the blue, green, and red pigments. *Science, 232*, 193–202.

National Coalition on Television Violence. (1983). *NCTV Newsletter*.

National Institute on Alcohol Abuse and Alcoholism. (1981). *Fourth special report to the U.S. Congress on alcohol and health*. Washington, DC: U.S. Government Printing Office.

National Institute on Alcohol Abuse and Alcoholism. (1987). *Sixth special report to the U.S. Congress on alcohol and health*. Washington DC: NIAAA.

National Institute on Drug Abuse. (1986). *National household survey on drug abuse, 1985*. Rockville, MD: National Institutes of Health.

Neary, R. S., & Zuckerman, M. (1976). Sensation seeking: Trait and state anxiety and the electrodermal orienting response. *Psychophysiology, 13*, 205–211.

Neimark, E. D. (1975). Intellectual development during adolescence. In F. D. Horowitz (Ed.), *Review of child development research* (Vol. 4). Chicago: University of Chicago Press.

Nelson, K. E. (1978). *Children's language* (Vol. 1). New York: Gardner Press.

Nelson, R. J., Badura, L. L. & Goodman, B. D. (1990). Mechanisms of seasonal cycles of behavior. *Annual Review of Psychology, 41*, 81–108.

Neugarten, B. L. (1968). *Middle age and aging*. Chicago: University of Chicago Press.

Neugarten, B. L. (1970). Dynamics of transition from middle age to old age: Adaptation and the life cycle. *Journal of Geriatric Psychiatry, 4*, 71–87.

Neugarten, B. L. (1971, December). Grow old along with me! The best is yet to be. *Psychology Today*, 45–48.

Newcomb, T. M. (1952). Attitude development as a function of reference groups: The Bennington study. In G. Swanson, T. Newcomb, & E. Hartley (Eds.), *Readings in social psychology*. New York: Holt, Rinehart & Winston.

Newcomb, T. M. (1956). Prediction of interpersonal attraction. *American Psychologist, 11,* 575–586.

Newcomb, T. M. (1978). The acquaintance process: Looking mainly backward. *Journal of Personality and Social Psychology, 36,* 1075–1083.

Newell, A., & Simon, H. A. (1972). *Human problem solving.* Englewood Cliffs, NJ: Prentice-Hall.

Newlin, D. B., & Thomson, J. B. (1990). Alcohol challenge with sons of alcoholics: A critical review and analysis. *Psychological Bulletin, 108,* 383–402.

Newman, E., & Hartline, P. (1982). The infrared "vision" of snakes. *Scientific American, 246*(3), 116–127.

Nezu, A. M., Nezu, C. M., & Blissett, S. E. (1988). Sense of humor as a moderator of the relation between stressful events and psychological distress: A prospective analysis. *Journal of Personality and Social Psychology, 54,* 520–525.

Niccum, N., & Speaks, C. (1991). Interpretation of outcome on dichotic listening tests following stroke. *Journal of Clinical and Experimental Neuropsychology, 13,* 614.

Nicklaus, L. K., Cassel, J. F., Carlson, R. B., & Gustavson, C. R. (1983). Taste-aversion conditioning of crows to control predation on eggs. *Science, 220,* 212–214.

Nicoll, R. A. (1988). The coupling of neurotransmitter receptors to ion channels in the brain. *Science, 241,* 545–551.

Nissani, M. (1990). A cognitive reinterpretation of Stanley Miltran's observations on obedience to authority. *American Psychologist, 45,* 1384–1385.

Norman, D. A. (1968). Toward a theory of memory and attention. *Psychological Review, 75,* 522–536.

Norman, D. A. (1969). Memory while shadowing. *Quarterly Journal of Experimental Psychology, 21,* 85–93.

Norman, D. A. (1988). *The psychology of everyday things.* New York: Basic Books.

Norman, D. A., & Fisher, D. (1982). Why alphabetic keyboards are not easy to use: Keyboard layout doesn't much matter. *Human Factors, 24*(5), 509–519.

Nosanchuk, T. A. (1981). The way of the warrior: The effects of traditional martial arts training on aggressiveness. *Human Relations, 34,* 435–444.

Novaco, R. (1975). *Anger control.* Beverly Hills: Sage.

Nowinski, J., & Baker S. (1992). *The twelve-step facilitation handbook: A systematic approach to early recovery from alcoholism and addiction.* New York: Lexington Books.

Nuckols, T. E., & Banducci, R. (1974). Knowledge of occupations—is it important in occupational choice? *Journal of Counseling Psychology, 21,* 191–195.

O'Connor, K. J. (1991). *The play therapy primer.* New York: Wiley.

O'Keefe, J. (1979). A review of the hippocampal place cells. *Progress in Neurobiology, 13* 419–439.

O'Leary, A. (1990). Stress, emotion, and human immune functioning. *Psychological Bulletin, 108,* 363–382.

O'Leary, K. D., & Smith, D. A. (1991). Marital interactions. *Annual Review of Psychology, 42,* 191–212.

O'Malley, S. S., Foley, S. H., Rounsaville, B. J., Watkins, J. T., Imber, S. D., Sotsky, S. M., & Elkin, I. (1988). Therapist competence and patient outcome in interpersonal psychotherapy of depression. *Journal of Consulting and Clinical Psychology, 56,* 496–501.

O'Neal, E. C. (1971). Influence of future choice importance and arousal upon the halo effect. *Journal of Personality and Social Psychology, 19,* 334–340.

O'Reilly, C. A., III. (1991). Organizational behavior: Where we've been, where we're going. *Annual Review of Psychology, 42,* 427–458.

Oatley, K., & Jenkins, J. M. (1992). Human emotions: Function and dysfunction. *Annual Review of Psychology, 43,* 55–85.

Oldham, G. R. (1988). Effects of changes in workspace partitions and spatial density on employee reaction.: A quasi-experiment. *Journal of Applied Psychology, 73,* 253–258.

Olds, J. (1958). Self-stimulation of the brain. *Science, 127,* 315–323.

Olds, J., & Milner, P. (1954). Positive reinforcement produced by electrical stimulation of septal area and other regions of rat brain. *Journal of Comparative and Physiological Psychology, 47,* 419–427.

Olds, M. E., & Fobes, J. L. (1981). The central basis of motivation: Intracranial self-stimulation studies. *Annual Review of Psychology, 32,* 523–574.

Ollendick, T. H. (1986). Behavior therapy with children and adolescents. In S. L. Garfield & A. E. Bergin (Eds.), *Handbook of psychotherapy and behavior change* (3rd ed., pp. 525–564). New York: Wiley.

Olton, D. S., & Noonberg, A. R. (1980). *Biofeedback: Clinical applications in behavioral medicine.* Englewood Cliffs, NJ: Prentice-Hall.

Olweus, D. (1992). Bullying among schoolchildren: Intervention and prevention. In R. Peters, R. McMahon, & V. Quinsey (Eds.), *Aggression and violence through the life span.* Newbury Park, CA: Sage.

Oring, E. (1984). *The jokes of Sigmund Freud.* Philadelphia: University of Pennsylvania Press.

Orive, R. (1988). Social projection and social comparison of opinions. *Journal of Personality and Social Psychology, 54,* 953–964.

Ornitz, E. M., & Ritvo, E. R. (1976). The syndrome of autism: A critical review. *American Journal of Psychology, 133,* 27–65.

Oskamp, S. (1977). *Attitudes and opinions.* Englewood Cliffs, NJ: Prentice-Hall.

Osterberg, G. (1935). Topography of the layer of rods and cones in the human retina. *Acta Ophthalmologica,* Supplement.

Ouchi, W. (1981). *Theory Z.* Reading, MA: Addison-Wesley.

Ouden, M. den. (1992). *Transfer na bedrijfsopleidingen.* [Transfer after corporate education.] Doctoral dissertation. University of Utrecht. The Netherlands.

Over, R. (1982a). Collaborative research and publication in psychology. *American Psychologist, 37*(9), 996–1001.

Over, R. (1982b). Research productivity and impact of male and female psychologists. *American Psychologist, 37*(1), 24–31.

Overton, D. (1964). State-dependent or "dissociated" learning produced with pentobarbital. *Journal of Comparative and Physiological Psychology, 57,* 3–12.

Pallack, M. S., Cook, D. A., & Sullivan, J. J. (1980). Commitment and energy conservation. In L. Bickman (Ed.), *Applied Social Annual, 1,* 235–253.

Paller, K. A., Mayes, A. R., & Thompson, K. M. (1992). Priming of face matching in amnesia. *Brain and Cognition, 18,* 46–59.

Pape, D. A., & Bervan, N. (1983). Effects of training on interviewing skills in rehabilitation counseling. *Rehabilitation Counseling Bulletin, 26,* 164–173.

Parish, T. S., & Wigle, S. E. (1985). A longitudinal study of the impact of parental divorce on adolescents' evaluations of self and parents. *Adolescence, 20*(77), 239–244.

Parrott, A. (1991). Social drugs: The effects upon health. In M. Pitts & K. Phillips (Eds.), *Psychology of health.* London: Routledge.

Pascale, R. T., & Athos, A. G. (1982). *The art of Japanese management.* Harmondsworth, United Kingdom: Penguin.

Pashler, H. (1984). Processing stages in overlapping tasks: Evidence for a central bottleneck. *Journal of Experimental Psychology: Human Perception and Performance, 10*(3), 358–377.

Patel, C. (1984). A relaxation-centered behavioral package for reducing hypertension. In J. D. Matarazzo, J. A. Herd, N. E. Miller, & S. M. Weiss (Eds.), *Behavioral health* (pp. 846–861). New York: Wiley.

Patterson, G. R. (1985). A microsocial analysis of anger and irritable behavior. In M. Chesney & R. Rosenman (Eds.), *Anger and hostility in cardiovascular and behavioral disorders.* Washington, DC: Hemisphere.

Paul, G. L., & Lentz, R. J. (1977). *Psychosocial treatment of chronic mental patients: Milieu vs. social-learning programs.* Cambridge, MA: Harvard University Press.

Paul, S. M., Hulihan-Giblin, B., & Skolnick, P. (1982). (+)-Amphetamine binding to rat hypothalamus: Relation to anorexic potency of phenylethylamines. *Science, 218,* 487–490.

Pavlov, I. P. (1906). The scientific investigation of the psychical faculties or processes in the higher animals. *Science, 24,* 613–619.

Pavlov, I. P. (1927). *Conditioned reflexes.* London: Clarendon Press.

Pellegrino, J. W. (1984). Inductive reasoning ability. In R. J. Sternberg (Ed.), *Human abilities: An information processing approach.* San Francisco: Freeman.

Penfield, W. (1975). *The mystery of the mind.* Princeton, NJ: Princeton University Press.

Pennebaker, J. W. (1982). *The psychology of physical symptoms.* New York: Springer-Verlag.

Pennebaker, J. W. (1990). *Opening up: The healing power of confiding in others.* New York: Norton.

Perlman, D., & Cozby, P. C. (1983). *Social psychology.* New York: Holt, Rinehart & Winston.

Perls, F. S. (1969). *Gestalt therapy verbatim.* Lafayette, CA: Real People Press.

Perry, S. W. (1987). The choice of duration and frequency for outpatient psychotherapy. In R. E. Hales & A. J. Frances (Eds.), *American Psychiatric Association Annual Review* (Vol. 6, pp. 398–414. Washington DC: American Psychiatric Press.

Persky, V. W., Kempthorne-Rowe, J., & Shekelle, R. B. (1987). Personality and risk of cancer: 20-year follow-up of the Western electricity study. *Psychosomatic Medicine, 49,* 435–449.

Pervin, L. A. (1970). *Personality: Theory, assessment, and research.* New York: Wiley.

Pervin, L. A. (1990). *Handbook of personality: Theory and research.* New York: Guilford.

Peskin, H. (1967). Pubertal onset and ego functioning. *Journal of Abnormal Psychology, 72,* 1–15.

Pessin, J. (1933). The comparative effects of social and mechanical stimulation on memorizing. *American Journal of Psychology, 45,* 263–270.

Peter, L. J., & Hull, R. (1969). *The Peter principle.* New York: Morrow.

Peters, L., Hartke, D. D., & Pohlmann, J. (1985). Fiedler's contingency theory of leadership: An application of the meta-analysis procedures of Schmidt & Hunter. *Psychological Bulletin, 97,* 247–285.

Peters, R. McMahon, R., & Quinsey, V. (1992). *Aggression and violence through the life span.* Newbury Park, CA: Sage.

Peterson, C., & Seligman, M. E. P. (1984). Causal explanations as a risk factor for depression: Theory and evidence. *Psychological Review, 91,* 347–374.

Peterson, C., Luborsky, L., & Seligman, M. E. P. (1983). Attributions and depressive mood shifts: A case study using the symptom-context method. *Journal of Abnormal Psychology, 92,* 96–103.

Peterson, J. L., & Zill, N. (1986). Marital disruption, parent-child relationship, and behavior problems in children. *Journal of Marriage and Family, 48,* 295–307.

Peterson, L. R., & Peterson, M. J. (1959). Short-term retention of individual verbal items. *Journal of Experimental Psychology, 58,* 193–198.

Petty, R. E., & Cacioppo, J. T. (1981). *Attitudes and persuasion.* Dubuque, IA: Wm. C. Brown Publishers.

Pfaff, D. W. (Ed.). (1985). *Taste, olfaction, and the central nervous system.* New York: Rockefeller University Press.

Pfaffman, C. (1955). Gustatory nerve impulses in rat, cat, and rabbit. *Journal of Neurophysiology, 18,* 429–440.

Pfohl, B., & Andreasen, N. C. (1986). Schizophrenia: Diagnosis and classification. In A. J. Frances & R. E. Hales (Eds.), *American Psychiatric Association Annual Review* (Vol. 5, pp. 7–24). Washington, DC: American Psychiatric Press.

Phair, J. P. (1990). Natural history of HIV infection. In M. A. Sande & P. A. Volberding (Eds.), *The medical management of AIDS* (2nd ed.). Philadelphia: Saunders.

Phillips, D. P., & Hensley, J. E. (1984). When violence is rewarded or punished: The impact of mass media stories on homicide. *Journal of Communication, 34,* 101–116.

Piaget, J. (1976). *The child and reality: Problems of genetic psychology.* New York: Penguin Books.

Pilkington, C. J., Tesser, A., & Stephens, D. (1991). Complementarity in romantic relationships: A self-evaluation maintenance perspective. *Journal of Social & Personal Relationships, 8,* 481–504.

Pimental, P. A., & Kingsbury, N. A. (1989). *Neuropsychological aspects of right brain injury.* Austin, TX: Pro-ed.

Pine, C. J. (1985). Anxiety and eating behavior in obese and nonobese American Indians and white Americans. *Journal of Personality and Social Psychology, 49*(3), 774–780.

Pitts, M. (1991). An introduction to health psychology. In M. Pitts & K. Phillips, (Eds.), *The psychology of health.* New York & London: Routledge.

Pitts, M. & Phillips, K. (Eds.). (1991). *The psychology of health.* New York & London: Routledge.

Plante, T. G., & Rodin, J. (1990). Physical fitness and enhanced psychological health. *Current Psychology, 9,* 3–24.

Plomin, R., Loehlin, J. C., & DeFries, J. C. (1985). Genetic and environmental components of "environmental" influences. *Developmental Psychology, 21,* 391–402.

Plotkin, W. B. (1979). The alpha experience revisited. *Psychological Bulletin, 86,* 1132–1148.

Polit-O'Hara, D., & Kahn, J. R. (1985). Communication and contraceptive practices in adolescent couples. *Adolescence, 20,* 33–43.

Pope, K. S., & Vetter, V. A. (1992). Ethical dilemmas encountered by members of the American Psychological Association: A national survey. *American Psychologist, 47,* 397–411.

Pope, K. S., Tabachnick, B. G., & Keith-Spiegel, P. (1987). Ethics of practice: The beliefs and behaviors of psychologists as therapists. *American Psychologist, 42*(11), 993–1006.

Porter, L. W. (1961). A study of perceived need satisfactions in bottom and middle management jobs. *Journal of Applied Psychology, 45,* 1–10.

Porter, L. W., & Lawler, E. E. (1968). *Managerial attitudes and performance.* Homewood, IL: Irwin.

Post, J. M. (1991). Saddam Hussein in Iraq: A political psychology profile. *Political Psychology, 12,* 291–308.

Powley, T. L. (1977). The ventromedial hypothalamus syndrome, satiety, and a cephalic phase hypothesis. *Psychological Review, 84,* 89–126.

Pratkanis, A., & Aronson, E. (1992). *Age of propaganda: The everyday use and abuse of persuasion.* New York: Freeman.

Pratkanis, A. R., Greenwald, A. G., Leippe, M. R., & Baumgardner, M. (1988). In search of reliable persuasion effects: III. The sleeper effect is dead. Long live the sleeper effect. *Journal of Personality and Social Psychology, 54,* 203–218.

Pratt, J. G. (1973). *ESP research today: A study of developments in parapsychology since 1960.* Metuchen, NJ: Scarecrow Press.

Premack, A. J., & Premack, D. (1982). Teaching language to an ape. In W. S. Y. Wang (Ed.), *Human communication: Language & its psychobiological bases.* San Francisco: Freeman.

Premack, D. (1959). Toward empirical behavioral laws: I. Positive reinforcement. *Psychological Review, 66,* 219–233.

Premack, D. (1965). Reinforcement theory. In M. R. Jones (Ed.), *Nebraska symposium on motivation: 1965.* Lincoln: University of Nebraska Press.

Premack, D. (1971). Language in chimpanzee? *Science, 172,* 808–872.

Pribram, K. H. (1982). Localization and distribution of function in the brain. In J. Orbach (Ed.), *Neuropsychology after Lashley.* Hillsdale, NJ: Lawrence Erlbaum Associates.

Prince-Embury, S. (1992). Psychological symptoms as related to cognitive appraisals and demographic differences among information seekers in the aftermath of technological disaster at Three Mile Island. *Journal of Applied Social Psychology, 22,* 38–54.

Pritchard, R. D., Dunnette, M. D., & Jorgenson, D. O. (1972). Effects of perceptions of equity and inequity on worker performance and satisfaction. *Journal of Applied Psychology Monograph, 56,* 75–94.

Pritchard, R. D., Jones, S. D., Roth, P. L., Stuebing, K. K. & Ekeberg, S. E. (1988). Effects of group feedback, goal setting, and incentives on organizational productivity. *Journal of Applied Psychology, 73,* 337–358.

Proshansky, H. M., Ittleson, W. H., & Rivlin, L. G. (Eds.). (1970). *Environmental psychology: Man and his physical setting.* New York: Holt, Rinehart & Winston.

Rabbie, J. M. (1989). Group processes as stimulants of aggression. In J. Groebel & R. A. Hinde (Eds.), *Aggression and War: Their biological and social bases.* Cambridge, England: Cambridge University Press.

Rachman, S., & Arntz, A. (1991). The overprediction and underprediction of pain. *Clinical Psychology Review, 11,* 339–355.

Rachman, S., & Hodgson, R. J. (1968). Experimentally-induced "sexual fetishism": Replication and development. *Psychological Record, 18,* 25–27.

Rachman, S. J., & Hodgson, R. J. (1980). *Obsessions and compulsions.* Englewood Cliffs, NJ: Prentice-Hall.

Rae, D. (1981). *Equalities.* Cambridge, MA: Harvard University Press.

Ragland, D. R., & Brand, R. J. (1988). Type A behavior and mortality from coronary heart disease. *The New England Journal of Medicine, 318,* 65–69.

Ray, W. J., & Cole, H. W. (1985). EEG alpha activity reflects attentional demands, and beta activity reflects emotional and cognitive processes. *Science, 228,* 750–752.

Rayman, P., & Bluestone, B. (1982). *Private and social response to job loss.* Rockville, MD: National Institute of Mental Health. Center for Work and Mental Health.

Raymond, C. (1992). The complexity of ethnic identity. *American Psychological Society Observer, 5*(3), 9, 12.

Raynor, J. O. (1982). Future orientation, self-evaluation, and achievement motivation: Use of an expectancy x value theory of personality functioning and change. In N. T. Feather (Ed.), *Expectations and actions: Expectancy-value models in psychology.* Hillsdale, NJ: Lawrence Erlbaum Associates.

Razran, G. H. S. (1939). A quantitative study of meaning by a conditioned salivary technique (semantic conditioning). *Science, 90*, 89–90.

Recipe concocted to ward off bears. (July 14, 1989). *Associated Press.*

Reed, T. E. (1985). Ethnic differences in alcohol use, abuse, and sensitivity: A review with genetic interpretation. *Social Biology, 32*, 195–209.

Rees, H. D., Brogan, L. L., Entingh, D. J., Dunn, A., Shinkman, P. G., Damstra-Entingh, T., Wilson, J. E., & Glassman, E. (1974). Effect of sensory stimulation on the uptake and incorporation of radioactive lysine into protein of mouse brain and liver. *Brain Research, 68*, 143–156.

Rehm, L. P. (1977). A self-control model of depression. *Behavior Therapy, 8*, 787–804.

Reid, J. E., & Inbau, F. E. (1977). *Truth and deception: The polygraph ("lie detection") technique* (2nd ed.). Baltimore: Williams and Wilkins.

Reissland, N. (1988). Neonatal imitation in the first hour of life: Observations in rural Nepal. *Developmental Psychology, 24*, 464–469.

Reitman, J. S. (1971). Mechanisms of forgetting in short-term memory. *Cognitive Psychology, 2*, 185–195.

Rescorla, R. A. (1988). Pavlovian conditioning: It's not what you think it is. *American Psychologist, 43*, 151–160.

Rescorla, R. A., & Holland, P. C. (1982). Behavioral studies of associative learning in animals. *Annual Review of Psychology, 33*, 265–308.

Resnick, S. M. (1993). Sex differences in mental rotations: An effect of time limits? *Brain and Cognition, 21*, 71–79.

Richards, R., Kinney, D. K., Benet, M., & Merzel, A. P. C. (1988). Assessing everyday creativity: Characteristics of the Lifetime Creativity Scales and validation with three large samples. *Journal of Personality and Social Psychology, 54* 476–485.

Richards, R. A. (1976). A comparison of selected Guiford and Wallach-Kogan creative thinking tests in conjunction with measures of intelligence. *Journal of Creative Behavior, 10*, 151–164.

Riegel, D. W. Jr. (1982). The psychological and social effects of unemployment. *American Psychologist, 37*, 1113–1115.

Rife, D. C. (1940). Handedness, with special reference to twins. *Genetics, 25*, 178–186.

Ritchey, F. J., La Gory, M., & Mullis, J. (1991). Gender differences in health risks and physical symptoms among the homeless. *Journal of Health and Social Behavior, 32*, 33–48.

Ritvo, E. R. (1976). *Autism: Diagnosis, current research, and management.* New York: Spectrum.

Robbins, M. J., & Meyer, D. R. (1970). Motivational control of retrograde amnesia. *Journal of Experimental Psychology, 84*, 220–225.

Robertson, L. C., & Lamb, M. R. (1991). Neuropsychological contributions to theories of part/whole organization. *Cognitive Psychology, 23*, 299–330.

Rodieck, R. W., & Stone, J. (1965). Response of cat retinal ganglion cells to moving visual patterns. *Journal of Neurophysiology, 28*, 819–832.

Rodin, J. (1981). Current status of the internal-external hypotheses for obesity: What went wrong? *American Psychologist, 36*(4), 361–372.

Rodin, J. (1986). Aging and health: Effects of the sense of control. *Science, 233*, 1271.

Rodin, J., & Langer, E. J. (1977). Long-term effects of a control-relevant intervention with institutionalized aged. *Journal of Personality and Social Psychology, 35*, 897–902.

Rodin, J., & Plante, T. G. (1989). The psychological effects of exercise. In R. S. Williams & A. Wallace (Eds.), *Biological effects of physical activity.* Champaign, IL: Human Kinetics.

Rodin, J., & Slowchower, J. (1976). Externality in the nonobese: The effects of environmental responsiveness on weight. *Journal of Personality and Social Psychology, 29*, 557–565.

Roethlisberger, F. J., & Dickson, W. J. (1939). *Management and the worker.* Cambridge, MA: Harvard University Press.

Roffwarg, H. P., Muzio, J. N., & Dement, W. C. (1966). The ontogenetic development of the sleep-dream cycle in the human. *Science, 152*, 604–619.

Rogers, C. R. (1957). The necessary and sufficient conditions of therapeutic personality change. *Journal of Consulting Psychology, 21*, 95–103.

Rogers, C. R. (1961). *On becoming a person.* Boston: Houghton Mifflin.

Rogers, C. R. (1980). *A way of being.* Boston: Houghton Mifflin.

Rogers, C. R., Gendlin, E. T., Kiesler, D. J., & Rruax, C. B. (1967). *The therapeutic relationship and its impact: A study of psychotherapy with schizophrenics.* Madison, WI: University of Wisconsin Press.

Rogers, R. W. (1975). A protection motivation theory of fear appeals and attitude change. *Journal of Psychology, 91*, 93–114.

Rogler, L. H., Cortes, D. E., & Malgady, R. G. (1991). Acculturation and mental health status among Hispanics. *American Psychologist, 46*, 585–597.

Rokeach, M., Smith, P. W., & Evans, R. I. (1960). Two kinds of prejudice or one? In M. Rokeach (Ed.), *The open and closed mind.* New York: Basic Books.

Rosch, E. H. (1973). On the internal structure of perceptual and semantic categories. In T. E. Moore (Ed.), *Cognitive development and the acquisition of language.* New York: Academic Press.

Rosch, E. H. (1975). Cognitive representations and semantic categories. *Journal of Experimental Psychology, 104*, 192–233.

Rose, D. F., Smith, P. D., & Sato, S. (1987). Magnetoencephalography and epilepsy research. *Science, 238*, 329–335.

Rose, R. M., Bernstein, I. S., & Gordon, T. P. (1975). Consequences of social conflict on plasma testosterone levels in Rhesus monkeys. *Psychosomatic Medicine, 37*, 50–61.

Rose, R. M., Bourne, P. G., Poe, R. O., Mougey, E. H., Collins, D. R., & Mason, J. W. (1969). Androgen responses to stress: II. Excretion of testosterone, epitestosterone, androsterone, and etiocholanolone during basic combat training and under attack. *Psychosomatic Medicine, 31*, 418–436.

Rosen, B. M., Bahn, S. K., & Kramer, M. (1964). Demographic and diagnostic characteristics of psychiatric patients in the U.S.A., 1961. *American Journal of Orthopsychiatry, 24*, 455–467.

Rosenblatt, A., & Greenberg, J. (1988) Depression and interpersonal attraction: The role of perceived similarity. *Journal of Personality and Social Psychology, 55*, 112–119.

Rosenblatt, P. C., & Cozby, P. C. (1972). Courtship patterns associated with freedom of choice of spouse. *Journal of Marriage and the Family, 34*, 689–695.

Rosengard, Pamela. (1991). *A comparative analysis of four psychotherapy manuals and a proposed model for psychotherapy manuals.* Frankfurt: Peter Lang.

Rosenhan, D. L. (1973). On being sane in insane places. *Science, 179*, 250–258.

Rosenman, R., & Friedman, M. (1974). The role of behavior patterns and neurogenic factors in the pathogenesis of coronary heart disease. In R. Elliot (Ed.), *Stress and the heart.* New York: Futura.

Rosenthal, M. K. (1973). The study of infant-environment interaction: Some comments on trends and methodology. *Journal of Child Psychology and Psychiatry, 14*, 301–317.

Rosenthal, N. E. (1985). Seasonal affective disorder and phototherapy. *Annals of the New York Academy of Sciences, 453*, 260–269.

Rosenthal, N. E., Sack, D. A., Skwerer, R. G., Jacobsen, F. M., & Wehr, T. A. (1988). Phototherapy for seasonal affective disorder. *Journal of Biological Rhythms, 3*, 101–120.

Rosenthal, R., & Jacobson, L. (1968). *Pygmalion in the classroom.* New York: Holt, Rinehart & Winston.

Rosenthal, T. L. (1982). Social learning theory. In G. T. Wilson & C. M. Franks (Eds.), *Contemporary behavior therapy.* New York: Guilford.

Rosenthal, T. L. (1984). Cognitive social learning theory. In N. S. Endler & J. McV. Hunt (Eds.), *Personality and the behavior disorders* (pp. 113–146). New York: Wiley.

Rosenzweig, M. R. (1984). Experience, memory, and the brain. *American Psychologist, 39*(4), 365–376.

Rosenzweig, M. R. (1992). Psychological science around the world. *American Psychologist, 47*, 718–722.

Roskies, E. (1982). Type A intervention: Finding the disease to fit the cures. In R. S. Surwit, R. B. Williams, A. Steptoe, & R. Biersner (Eds.), *Behavioral treatment of disease* (pp. 71–85). New York: Plenum Press.

Roskies, E., & Carrier, S. (1992, November 21). Paper presented at American Psychological Association/National Institute for Occupational Safety and Health Conference, Washington, DC.

Roskies, E., Seraganian, P., Oseasohn, R. Hanley, J. A., Collu, R., Martin, N., & Smilga, C. (1986). The Montreal Type A intervention project: Major findings. *Health Psychology, 5*, 45–70.

Rosnow, R. L., & Fine G. A. (1977). *Rumor and gossip.* New York: Elsevier.

Ross, D. M., Ross, S. A., & Evans, T. A. (1971). The modification of extreme social withdrawal by modeling with guides participation. *Journal of Behavior Therapy and Experimental Psychiatry, 2*, 273–280.

Ross, L., & Nisbett, R. (1991). *The person and the situation.* New York: McGraw-Hill.

Ross, M. H. (1991). The role of evolution in ethnocentric conflict and its management. *Journal of Social Issues, 47*, 167–185.

Ross, M., Layton, B., Erickson, B., & Schopler, J. (1973). Affect, facial regard, and reactions to crowding. *Journal of Personality and Social Psychology, 28,* 69–76.

Ross, P. E. (1992, February). New whoof in Whorf. *Scientific American,* 11–12.

Ross, R. T., & Randich, A. (1984). Unconditioned stress-induced analgesia following exposure to brief footshock. *Journal Experimental Psychology: Animal Behavior Processes, 10*(2), 127–137.

Ross, S. I., & Jackson, J. M. (1991). Teachers' expectations for black males' and black females' academic achievement. *Personality and Social Psychology Bulletin, 17,* 78–82.

Rothbart, M. K. (1991). Temperament: A developmental framework. In J. Strelau, & A. Angleitner, *Explorations in temperament: International perspectives on theory and measurement.* London: Plenum Press.

Rotter, J. B. (1966). Generalized expectancies for internal versus external control of reinforcement. *Psychological Monographs, 80,* 1–28.

Routtenberg, A., & Lindy, J. (1965). Effects of the availability of rewarding septal and hypothalamic stimulation on barpressing for food under conditions of deprivation. *Journal of Comparative and Physiological Psychology, 60,* 158–161.

Rowe, J. W., & Kahn, R. L. (1987). Human aging: Usual and successful. *Science, 237,* 143–149.

Rowland, N. E., & Antelman, S. M. (1976). Stress-induced hyperphagia and obesity in rats: A possible model for understanding human obesity. *Science, 191,* 310–312.

Rubin, K. H., LeMare, L. J., & Lollis, S. (1990). Social withdrawal in childhood: Developmental pathways to peer rejection. In S. R. Asher & J. D. Coie (Eds.), *Peer rejection in childhood.* New York: Cambridge University Press.

Rubin, R. T., Reinisch, J. M., & Haskett, R. F. (1981). Postnatal gonadal steroid effects on human behavior. *Science, 211*(4488), 1318–1324.

Rubin, Z. (1970). Measurement of romantic love. *Journal of Personality and Social Psychology, 16,* 265–273.

Rubonis, A. B., & Bickman, L. (1991). Psychological impairment in the wake of disaster: The disaster-psychopathology relationship. *Psychological Bulletin, 109,* 384–399.

Rudé, G. (1964). *The crowd in history.* New York: Wiley.

Rumbaugh, D. M., Gill, T. V., & VonGlasersfeld, E. C. (1973). Reading and sentence completion by a chimpanzee. *Science, 182,* 1468–1472.

Runyan, W. M. (1981). Why did van Gogh cut off his ear? The problem of alternative explanations in psychobiography. *Journal of Personality and Social Psychology, 40,* 1070–1077.

Russek, M. (1975). Current hypotheses in the control of feeding behaviour. In G. J. Morgenson & F. R. Calaresu (Eds.), *Neural integration of physiological mechanisms and behaviour.* Toronto: University of Toronto Press.

Russell, J. A. (1980). A circumplex model of affect. *Journal of Personality and Social Psychology, 39,* 1161–1178.

Rutter, M. (1971). The description and classification of infantile autism. In D. W. Churchill, G. D. Alpern, & M. K. DeMyer (Eds.), *Infantile autism.* Springfield, IL: Charles C. Thomas.

Rutter, M. (1983). Cognitive deficits in the pathogenesis of autism. *Journal of Child Psychology and Psychiatry, 24,* 513–531.

Sachar, E. J., & Baron, M. (1979). The biology of affective disorders. *Annual Review of Neuroscience, 2,* 505–518.

Sackett, D. L. (1976). The magnitude of compliance and noncompliance. In D. L. Sackett & R. B. Haynes (Eds.), *Compliance with therapeutic regimens.* Baltimore: Johns Hopkins University Press.

Sacks, O. (1985). *The man who mistook his wife for a hat.* London: Ducksworth and Co.

Sagan, C. (1977). *The dragons of Eden: Speculations on the evolution of human intelligence.* New York: Ballantine.

Sagi, A., & Hoffman, M. L. (1976). Empathetic distress in the newborn. *Developmental Psychology, 12,* 175–176.

Sagi, A., Van Ijzendoorn, M. H., & Koren-Karie, N. (1991). Primary appraisal of the strange situation: A cross-cultural analysis of preseparation episodes. *Developmental Psychology, 27*(4), 587–596.

Salapatek, P. (1975). Pattern perception in early infancy. In L. B. Cohen & P. Salapatek (Eds.), *Infant perception: From sensation to cognition* (Vol. 1). New York: Academic Press.

Salmon, V. J., & Geist, S. H. (1943). The effect of androgen upon libido in women. *Journal of Clinical Endocrinology and Metabolism, 3,* 275–288.

Salthouse, T. A., & Babcock, R. L. (1991). Decomposing adult age differences in working memory. *Developmental Psychology, 27,* 763–776.

Samuel, A. L. (1963). Some studies in machine learning using the game of checkers. In E. A. Fiegenbaum & J. Feldman (Eds.), *Computers and thought.* New York: McGraw-Hill.

Sanada, T., & Norbeck, E. (1975). Prophecy continues to fail: A Japanese sect. *Journal of Cross-Cultural Psychology, 6,* 331–345.

Sanders, G. S., & Simmons, W. L. (1983). Use of hypnosis to enhance eyewitness accuracy: Does it work? *Journal of Applied Psychology, 68,* 70–77.

Sanik, M. M., & Stafford, K. (1985). Adolescent's contribution to household production: Male and female differences. *Adolescence, 20*(77), 207–215.

Sanna, L. J. (1992). Self-efficacy theory: Implications for social facilitation and social loafing. *Journal of Personality and Social Psychology, 62,* 774–786.

Sansome, C., Sachau, D. A., & Weir, C. (1989). Effects of instruction on intrinsic interest: The importance of context. *Journal of Personality and Social Psychology, 57,* 819–829.

Satz, P. (1972). Pathological left-handedness: An explanatory model. *Cortex, 8,* 121–135.

Satz, P. (1980). Incidence of aphasia in left-handers: A test of some hypothetical models of cerebral speech organization. In J. Herron (Ed.), *Neuropsychology of left-handedness.* New York: Academic Press.

Sayers, J. (1991). *Mothering psychoanalysis.* London: Hamish Hamilton.

Scarr, S. S. (1992). Developmental theories for the 1990s: Development and individual differences. *Child Development, 63,* 1–19.

Schachter, D. L. (1987). Implicit memory: History and current status. *Journal of Experimental Psychology: Learning, Memory, and Cognition, 13,* 501–518.

Schachter, D. L. (1990). Perceptual representation systems and implicit memory: Toward a resolution of the multiple memory systems debate. In A. Diamond, (Ed.), *The development and neural bases of higher cognitive functions.* New York: New York Academy of Sciences.

Schachter, S. (1959). *The psychology of affiliation.* Stanford, CA: Stanford University Press.

Schachter, S. (1964). The interaction of cognitive and physiological determinants of emotional state. In L. Berkowitz (Ed.), *Advances in experimental social psychology* (Vol. 1). New York: Academic Press.

Schachter, S. (1971). *Emotion, obesity, and crime.* New York: Academic Press.

Schachter, S. (1982). Recidivism and the self-cure of smoking and obesity. *American Psychologist, 37,* 436–444.

Schachter, S., & Gross, L. (1968). Manipulated time and eating behavior. *Journal of Personality and Social Psychology, 10,* 98–106.

Schachter, S., & Singer, J. E. (1962). Cognitive, social, and physiological determinants of emotional state. *Psychological Review, 69,* 379–399.

Schaeffer, C., et al. (1991). *Play diagnosis and assessment.* New York: Wiley.

Schaie, K. W. (1979). The primary mental abilities in adulthood: An exploration in the development of psychometric intelligence. In P. B. Baltes & O. G. Brim, Jr. (Eds.), *Life span development and behavior.* New York: Academic Press.

Schaie, K. W. (1993). Ageist language in psychological research. *American Psychologist, 48,* 49–51.

Schanberg, S., & Field, T. (1987, December). Paper presented at the American College of Neuropsychopharmacology meeting.

Schanberg, S., Bartolome, J., & Kuhn, C. (1987, December). Paper presented at the American College of Neuropsychopharmacology meeting.

Scheff, T. J. (1966). *Being mentally ill: A sociological theory.* Chicago: Aldine.

Scheibel, M. E., & Scheibel, A. B. (1975). Structural changes in the aging brain. In H. Brody, D. Harman, & J. M. Ordy (Eds.), *Aging* (Vol. 1). New York: Raven Press.

Scheier, M., Weintraub, J., & Carver, C. S. (1986). Coping with stress: Divergent strategies of optimists and pessimists. *Journal of Personality and Social Psychology, 51,* 1257–1264.

Schein, E. H. (1981). Does Japanese management style have a message for American managers? *Sloan Management Review,* 55–68.

Scherer, K. (1984). On the nature and function of emotion: A component-process approach. In K. Scherer & P. Ekman (Eds.), *Approaches to emotion.* Hillsdale, NJ: Erlbaum.

Scherer, K., Wallbott, H., & Summerfield, A. (1986). *Experiencing emotions: A cross-cultural study.* New York: Cambridge University Press.

Scherer, S. E. (1974). Proxemic behavior of primary school children as a function of their socioeconomic class and subculture. *Journal of Personality and Social Psychology, 29,* 800–805.

Schifter, D. E., & Ajzen, I. (1985). Intention, perceived control, and weight loss: An application of the theory of planned behavior. *Journal of Personality and Social Psychology, 49,* 843–851.

Schildkraut, J. J. (1974). Biogenic amines and affective disorders. *Annual Review of Medicine, 25,* 333–348.

Schildkraut, J. J. (1978). Current status of the catecholamine hypothesis of affective disorders. In M. A. Lipton, A. Di Mascio, & K. F. Killiam (Eds.), *Psychopharmacology: A generation of progress.* New York: Raven Press.

Schmaling, K. B., & DiClementi, J. D. (1992). Cognitive therapy with the HIV seropositive patient. In J. Mindell (Ed.), *Issues in clinical psychology.* Dubuque, IA: Wm. C. Brown Communications, Inc.

Schmidt, F. L., Hunter, J. E., McKenzie, R. C., & Muldrow, T. W. (1979). Impact of valid selection procedures on work-force productivity. *Journal of Applied Psychology, 64,* 609–626.

Schmitt, F. O., Dev, P., & Smith, B. H. (1976). Electronic processing of information by brain cells. *Science, 193,* 114–120.

Schnapf, J. L., Kraft, T. W., & Baylor, D. A. (1987). Spectral sensitivity of human cone photoreceptors. *Nature, 324,* 439–441.

Schneider, W., & Shiffrin, R. M. (1977). Controlled and automatic human information processing: I. Detection, search, and attention. *Psychological Review, 84,* 1–66.

Schneider-Rosen, K., Braunwald, K. G., Carlson, V., & Cicchetti, D. (1985). Current perspectives in attachment theory: Illustration from the study of maltreated infants. In I. Bretherton & E. Waters (Eds.), *Growing points of attachment theory and research.* Monographs of the Society for Research on Child Development *50:* No. 209, pp. 194–210.

Schneidman, E. (1985). *Definition of suicide.* New York: John Wiley & Sons.

Schopler, J., & Stockdale, J. E. (1977). An interference analysis of crowding. *Environmental Psychology and Nonverbal Behavior, I,* 81–88.

Schroeder, D. H., & Costa, P. T., Jr. (1984). Influence of life event stress on physical illness: Substantive effects or methodological flaws? *Journal of Personality and Social Psychology, 46,* 853–863.

Schuckit, M. A. (1986). Genetic and clinical implications of alcoholism and affective disorder. *American Journal of Psychiatry, 143,* 140–146.

Schuckit, M. A., Gold, E., & Risch, C. (1987). Plasma cortisol levels following ethanol in sons of alcoholics and controls. *Archives of General Psychiatry, 44*(11), 942–945.

Schuckit, M. A., Gold, E., & Risch, C. (1987). Serum prolactin levels in sons of alcoholics and control subjects. *American Journal of Psychiatry, 144*(7), 854–859.

Schultes, R. E., & Hoffman, A. (1973). *The botany and chemistry of hallucinogens.* Springfield, IL.: Charles C. Thomas.

Schultz, R. (1976). Effects of control and predictability on the physical well-being of the institutionalized aged. *Journal of Personality and Social Psychology, 33,* 563–573.

Schwalbe, C. P., & Mastro, V. C. (1988). Gypsy moth mating disruption: Dosage effects. *J. Chem Ecology, 14*(2), 581–588.

Schwartz, G. M., Izard, C. E., & Ansul, S. E. (1985). The 5 month-old's ability to discriminate facial expressions of emotion. *Infant Behavior and Development, 8,* 65–77.

Schwartz, S., Link, B. G., Dohrenwend, B. P., Naveh, G., Levav, I., & Shrout, P. (1991). Separating class and ethnic prejudice: A study of North African and European Jews in Israel. *Social Psychology Quarterly, 57.*

Schweder, R. A. (1991). *Thinking through cultures: Expeditions in cultural psychology.* Cambridge, MA: Harvard University Press.

Scovern, A. W., & Kilman, P. R. (1980). Status of electroconvulsive therapy: Review of the outcome literature. *Psychological Bulletin, 87,* 260–303.

Scribner, S., & Cole, M. (1978). Unpackaging literacy. *Social Science Information, 17*(1), 19–40.

Searle, J. (1980). Minds, brains, and programs. *Behavioral & Brain Sciences, 3,* 417–457.

Sears, R. R. (1977). Sources of life satisfactions of the Terman gifted men. *American Psychologist, 32,* 119–128.

Segall, M. H., Campbell, D. T., & Herskovitz, M. J. (1966). *The influence of culture on visual perception.* Indianapolis: Bobbs-Merrill.

Segall, M. H., Dasen, P. R., Berry, J. W., & Poortinga, Y. H. (1990). *Human behavior in global perspective: An introduction to cross-cultural psychology.* New York: Pergamon.

Seidenberg, M., & Berent, S. (1992). Childhood epilepsy and the role of psychology. *American Psychologist, 47,* 1130–1133.

Seligman, M. E. P. (1975). *Helplessness: On depression, development, and death.* San Francisco: Freeman.

Seligman, M. E. P., Abramson, L. Y., Semmel, A., & von Baeyer, C. (1979). Depressive attributional style. *Journal of Abnormal Psychology, 88,* 242–247.

Selman, R. L. (1980). *The growth of interpersonal understanding: Developmental and clinical analyses.* New York: Academic Press.

Selye, H. (1956). *The stress of life.* New York: McGraw-Hill.

Selye, H. (1977). *The stress of my life.* Toronto: McClelland & Stewart.

Senders, J. W., & Moray, N. P. (1991). *Human errors: Their causes, prediction and reduction.* Hillsdale, NJ: Lawrence Erlbaum.

Shaner, J. M., Peterson, K. L., & Roscoe, B. (1985). Older adolescent females knowledge of child development norms. *Adolescence, 20*(77), 53–59.

Shapiro, A. K., Shapiro, E. S., Young, J. G., & Feinberg, T. E. (Eds.) (1988). *Gilles de la Tourette syndrome* (2nd ed.). New York: Raven Press.

Shapiro, D. A., & Shapiro, D. (1982). Meta-analysis of comparative therapy outcome studies: A replication and refinement. *Psychological Bulletin, 92,* 581–604.

Shaver, P. R., & Brennan, K. A. (1992). Attachment styles and the "big five" personality traits: Their connections with each other and with romantic relationship outcomes. *Personality and Social Psychology Bulletin, 18,* 536–545.

Shaw, M. E. (1964). Communication networks. In L. Berkowitz (Ed.), *Advances in experimental social psychology* (Vol. 1). New York: Academic Press.

Shaw, M. E. (1976). An overview of small group behavior. In J. W. Thibaut, J. T. Spence, & R. C. Carson (Eds.), *Contemporary topics in social psychology.* Morristown, NJ: General Learning Press.

Shekelle, R. B., Gale, M., & Norusis, M. (1985). Type A score (Jenkins Activity Survey) and risk of recurrent coronary heart disease in the Aspirin Myocardial Infarction Study. *American Journal of Cardiology, 56,* 221–225.

Shekelle, R. B., Gale, M., Ostfield, A.M., & Paul, O. (1983). Hostility, risk of coronary heart disease and mortality. *Psychosomatic Medicine, 45,* 109–114.

Shekelle, R. B., Rayner, W. J., Ostfield, A. M., Garron, D. C., Bieliauskas, L. A., Liu, S. C., Maliza, C., & Paul, O. (1981). Psychological depression and 17 year risk and death from cancer. *Psychosomatic Medicine, 43,* 117–125.

Shepard, R. N. (1967), Recognition memory for words, sentences, and pictures. *Journal of Verbal Learning and Verbal Behavior, 6,* 156–163.

Sheppard, B. H., Hartwick, J., & Warshaw, P. R. (1988). The theory of reasoned action: A meta-analysis of past research with recommendations for modifications and future research. *Journal of Consumer Research, 15,* 325–343.

Sheridan, C. L., & Radmacher, S. A. (1992). *Health psychology.* New York: Wiley.

Sherif, M. (1936). *The psychology of social norms.* New York: Harper.

Sherif, M., Harvey, O. J., White, B. J., Hood, W. R., & Sherif, C. W. (1961). *Intergroup conflict and cooperation: The Robber's Cave experiment.* Norman: University of Oklahoma Press.

Shiffrin, R. M. (1970). Forgetting: Trace erosion or retrieval failure? *Science, 168,* 1601–1603.

Shotland, R. L., & Heinold, W. D. (1985). Bystander response to arterial bleeding: Helping skills, the decision-making process, and differentiating the helping response. *Journal of Personality and Social Psychology, 49,* 347–356.

Siddle, D. A., Morrish, R. B., White, K. D. & Mangen, G. L. (1969). Relation of visual sensitivity to extraversion. *Journal of Experimental Research in Personality, 3,* 264–267.

Sidtis, J. J. (1984). Music, pitch perception, and the mechanisms of cortical hearing. In M. S. Gazzaniga (Ed.), *Handbook of cognitive neuroscience.* New York: Plenum Press.

Siegel, J. M. (1990). Stressful life events and use of physician services among the elderly: The moderating role of pet ownership. *Journal of Personality and Social Psychology, 58,* 1081–1086.

Siegel, S. (1975). Evidence from rats that morphine tolerance is a learned response. *Journal of Comparative and Physiological Psychology, 89,* 498–506.

Siegel, S. (1988). State dependent learning and morphine tolerance. *Behavioral Neuroscience, 102*, 228–232.

Siegel, S., Hinson, R. E., Krank, M. D., & McCully, J. (1982). Heroin "overdose" death: Contribution of drug-associated environmental cues. *Science, 216*, 436–437.

Siegman, A. W., & Dembrowski, T. (1989). *In search of coronary-prone behavior.* Hillsdale, NJ: Lawrence Erlbaum Associates.

Sigvardsson, S., Cloninger, C. R., Bohman, M., & von Knorring, A. L. (1985). Prevention and treatment of alcohol abuse: Uses and limitations of the high risk paradigm. *Social Biology, 32*, 185–194.

Silveira, J. (1971). *Incubation: The effect of interruption timing and length on problem solution and quality of problem processing.* Unpublished doctoral dissertation, University of Oregon.

Simmel, G. (1955). *Conflict and the web of group affiliations.* Glencoe, IL: Free Press.

Simmons, R. G., & Blyth, D. A. (1987). *Moving into adolescence.* New York: Aldine DeGruyter.

Simner, M. L. (1971). Newborn's response to the cry of another infant. *Developmental Psychology, 5*, 136–150.

Simpson, I. H. (1967). Patterns of socialization into professions: The case of student nurses. *Sociological Inquiry, 37*, 47–53.

Singer, D. G. (in press). Play as healing. In J. H. Goldstein (Ed.), *Toys, Play and Child Development.* New York: Cambridge University Press.

Sirigano, S. W., & Lackman, M. E. (1985). Personality change during the transition to parenthood: The role of perceived infant temperament. *Developmental Psychology, 21*, 558–567.

Sitaram, N., Weingartner, H., & Gillin, J. C. (1978). Human serial learning: Enhancement with arecholine and choline and impairment with scopolamine. *Science, 201*, 274–276.

Skinner, B. F. (1938). *The behavior of organisms.* New York: Appleton-Century-Crofts.

Skinner, B. F. (1948). Superstition in the pigeon. *J. Experimental Psychology, 38*, 168–172.

Skinner, B. F. (1953). *Science and human behavior.* New York: Macmillan.

Skinner, B. F. (1957). *Verbal behavior.* New York: Appleton-Century-Crofts.

Skinner, B. F. (1974). *About behaviorism.* New York: Knopf.

Skinner, B. F. (1984). Representations and misrepresentations. *The Behavioral and Brain Sciences, 7*, 655–667.

Skinner, B. F. (1987). Whatever happened to psychology as the science of behavior? *American Psychologist, 42*(8), 780–786.

Sklar, L. S., & Anisman, H. (1981). Stress and cancer. *Psychological Bulletin, 89*, 369–406.

Skowronski, J. J., Betz, A. L., Thompson, C. P., & Shannon, L. (1991). Social memory in everyday life: Recall of self-events and other-events. *Journal of Personality and Social Psychology, 60*(6), 831–843.

Slavin, R. E. (1983). *Cooperative learning.* New York: Longmans.

Slavin, R. E. (1985). An introduction to cooperative learning research. In R. E. Slavin, S. Sharan, S. Kagan, R. Hertz Lazarowitz, C. Webb, & R. Schmuck (Eds.), *Learning to cooperate, cooperating to learn.* New York: Plenum.

Slavin, R. E. (1990). *Cooperative learning: Theory, research, and practice.* Englewood Cliffs, NJ: Prentice-Hall.

Sleight, R. B. (1948). The effect of instrument dial shape on legibility. *Journal of Applied Psychology, 32*, 170–188.

Sloan, L. R. (1989). The motives of sports fans. In J. H. Goldstein (Ed.), *Sports, games, and play.* (2nd ed.). Hillsdale, NJ: Lawrence Erlbaum Associates.

Sloane, M., & Blake, R. (1984). Selective adaptation of monocular and binocular neurons in human vision. *Journal of Experimental Psychology: Human Perception and Performance, 10*(3), 406–412.

Sloane, R. B., Staples, F. R., Cristol, A. H., Yorkston, N. J., & Whipple K. (1975). *Psychoanalysis versus behavior therapy.* Cambridge, MA: Harvard University Press.

Slobin, D. I. (1971, May). *Cognitive prerequisites for the development of grammar.* Paper presented at the meeting of the Southeastern Conference on Linguistics, University of Maryland.

Slobin, D. I. (1979). *Psycholinguistics* (2nd ed.). Glenview, IL: Scott, Foresman & Co.

Slonim, M. B. (1991). *Children, culture & ethnicity: Evaluating and understanding the impact.* New York: Garland Publishers.

Smeaton, G., Byrne, D., & Murnen, S. K. (1989). The repulsion hypothesis revisited: Similarity irrelevance or dissimilarity bias? *Journal of Personality and Social Psychology, 56*, 54–59.

Smith, C., & Ellsworth, P. (1985). Patterns of cognitive appraisal in emotion. *Journal of Personality and Social Psychology, 48*, 813–848.

Smith, C. R., Williams, L., & Willis, R. H. (1967) Race, sex, and belief as determinants of friendship acceptance. *Journal of Personality and Social Psychology, 5*, 127–137.

Smith, D., & Kraft, W. (1989). Attitudes of psychiatrists toward diagnostic options and issues. *Psychiatry, 52*, 66–77.

Smith, E. E., Shoben, E. J., & Rips, L. J. (1974). Structure and process in semantic memory: A featural model for semantic decisions. *Psychological Review, 81*, 214–241.

Smith, G. P., & Gibbs, J. (1976). Cholescystokinin and satiety: Theoretic and therapeutic implications. In D. Novin, W. Wyrwicka, & G. Bray (Eds.), *Hunger: Basic mechanisms and clinical implications.* New York: Raven.

Smith, M. B. (in press). Nationalism, ethnocentrism, and the new world order. *Journal of Humanistic Psychology.*

Smith, M. L., Glass, G. V., & Miller, T. J. (1980). *The benefits of psychotherapy.* Baltimore: Johns Hopkins University Press.

Smith, M. M., Morris, P. E., Levy, P., & Ellis, A. W. (1987). *Cognition in action.* London: Lawrence Erlbaum Associates.

Smith, P. B. (1984). The effectiveness of Japanese styles of management: A review and critique. *Journal of Occupational Psychology, 57*, 121–136.

Smyth, M. M., Morris, P. E., Levy, P., & Ellis, A. W. (1987). *Cognition in action.* London: Lawrence Erlbaum Associates.

Snarey, J. R. (1985). Cross-cultural universality of social-moral development: A critical review of Kohlbergian research. *Psychological Bulletin, 97*(2), 202–232.

Snarey, J. R., Reimer, J., & Kohlberg, L. (1985). Development of social-moral reasoning among kibbutz adolescents: A longitudinal cross-cultural study. *Developmental Psychology, 21*, 3–17.

Snyder, C. R., & Forsyth, D. R. (Eds.) (1991). *Handbook of social and clinical psychology: A health perspective.* New York: Pergamon.

Snyder, M., & DeBono, K. G. (1985). Appeals to image and claims about quality: Understanding the psychology of advertising. *Journal of Personality and Social Psychology, 49*, 586–597.

Snyderman, M., & Rothman, S. (1987). Survey of expert opinion on intelligence and aptitude testing. *American Psychologist, 42*, 137–144.

*Society today.* (1971). Del Mar, CA: CRM Books.

Solomon, R. L. (1980). The opponent process theory of acquired motivation. *American Psychologist, 35*, 691–712.

Solomon R. L., & Corbit, J. D. (1974). An opponent process theory of motivation: I. Temporal dynamics of affect. *Psychological Review, 81*, 119–145.

Solomon, Z. (1990). Does the war end when the shooting stops? The psychological toll of war. *Journal of Applied Social Psychology, 20.*

Sommer, R. (1959). Studies in personal space. *Sociometry, 22*, 247–260.

Sommer, R. (1969). Small group ecology. *Psychological Bulletin, 67*, 145–152.

Sonderegger, T. B. (1970). Intracranial stimulation and maternal behavior. *Proceedings of the Annual Convention of the American Psychological Association, 5*(Pt. 1), 245–246.

Sorce, J. F., Emde, R. N., Campos, J. J., & Klinnert, M. D. (1985). Maternal emotional signaling: Its effect on the visual cliff behavior of 1 year olds. *Developmental Psychology, 21*, 195–200.

Sorenson, R. C. (1973). *Adolescent sexuality in contemporary America.* New York: World Publishing Co.

Spanos, N. P. (1978). Witchcraft in histories of psychiatry. *Psychological Bulletin, 85*, 417–439.

Spear, N. E. (1979). Experimental analysis of infantile amnesia. In J. F. Kihlstrom & F. J. Evans (Eds.), *Functional disorders of memory.* Hillsdale, NJ: Lawrence Erlbaum Associates.

Spear, N. E., Miller, J. S., & Jagielo, J. A. (1990). Animal memory and learning. *Annual Review of Psychology, 41*, 169–212.

Spence, J. T. (1985). Achievement American style: The rewards and costs of individualism. *American Psychologist, 40*, 1285–1295.

Spence, K. W. (1956). *Behavior theory and conditioning.* New Haven, CT: Yale University Press.

Sperling, G. (1960). The information available in brief visual presentation. *Psychological Monographs, 74*, 1–29.

Sperry, R. W. (1974). Lateral specialization in the surgically separated hemispheres. In F. O. Schmitt & F. G. Worden (Eds.), *The neurosciences: Third study program.* Cambridge, MA: MIT Press.

Sperry, R. W. (1982). Some effects of disconnecting the cerebral hemispheres. *Science, 217,* 1223–1226.

Spinetta, J. J., & Rigler, D. (1977). The child-abusing parent: A psychological review. In R. Kalmar (Ed.), *Child abuse: Perspectives on diagnosis, treatment and prevention.* Dubuque, IA: Kendall/Hunt.

Spiro, M. (1982). *Oedipus in the Trobriands.* Chicago: University of Chicago Press.

Spitz, C. J., Gold, A. R., & Adams, D. B. (1975). Cognitive and hormonal factors affecting coital frequency. *Archives of Sexual Behavior, 4,* 249–264.

Spitzer, R. L., & Williams, J. B. W. (1984). Diagnostic issues in the DSM-III classification of the anxiety disorders. In L. Grinspoon (Ed.), *American Psychiatric Association Annual Review* (Vol. 3, pp. 392–402). Washington, DC: American Psychiatric Press, Inc.

Squire, L. R., & McKee, R. (1992). Influence of prior events on cognitive judgments in amnesia. *Journal of Experimental Psychology: Learning, Memory, and Cognition, 18*(1), 106–115.

Sroufe, L. A. (1985). Attachment classification from the perspective of infant care-giver relationships and infant temperament. *Child Development, 56*(1), 1–14.

Staats, A. W. (1971). Linguistic-mentalistic theory versus an explanatory S-R learning theory of language development. In D. Slobin (Ed.), *The ontogenesis of grammar.* New York: Academic Press.

Stacks, J. F. (1983). Plain vanilla, but very good. *Time, 122*(2), 44–45.

Stanley, J. C. (1976). Identifying and nurturing the intellectually gifted. *Gifted Child Quarterly, 20*(1), 66–75.

Stapp, J., Tucker, A. M., & VandenBos, G. R. (1985). Census of psychological personnel: 1983. *American Psychologist, 40,* 1317–1351.

Stattin, L., & Klackenberg-Larsson, I. (1991). The short- and long-term implications for parent-child relations of parents' prenatal preferences for their child's gender. *Developmental Psychology, 27,* 141–147.

Stattin H., & Magnusson, D. (1990). *Pubertal maturation in female development.* Hillsdale, NJ: Lawrence Erlbaum.

Staub, E. (1989). *Roots of evil.* Cambridge, MA: Cambridge University Press.

Ste-Marie, D. E., & Lee, T. D. (1991). Prior processing effects on gymnastic judging. *Journal of Experimental Psychology, 17,* 126–136.

Steele, B. F., & Pollock, C. B. (1968). A psychiatric study of parents who abuse infants and small children. In R. E. Helfer & C. H. Kempe (Eds.), *The battered child.* Chicago: University of Chicago Press.

Stein, M., Keller, S. E., & Schliefer, S. J. (1985). Stress and immunomodulation: The role of depression and neuroendocrine. *Journal of Immunology, 135,* 827–833.

Steinberg, L. (1988). Reciprocal relations between parent-child distance and pubertal maturation. *Developmental Psychology, 24,* 122–128.

Steinberg, L., Dornbusch, S. M., & Brown, B. B. (1992). Ethnic differences in adolescent achievement: An ecological perspective. *American Psychologist, 47,* 723–729.

Steiner, I. D. (1972). *Group process and productivity.* New York: Academic Press.

Stelmack, R. M., & Campbell, K. B. (1974). Extraversion and auditory sensitivity to high and low frequency. *Perceptual and Motor Skills, 38,* 875–879.

Steptoe, A. (1989). Psychophysiological interventions in behavioral medicine. In G. Turpin (Ed.), *Handbook of clinical psychophysiology.* New York: Wiley.

Steptoe, A., & Appels, A. (Eds.). (1989). *Stress, personal control and health.* New York: Wiley.

Steptoe, A., Patel, C., Marmot, M., & Hunt, B. (1987). Frequency of relaxation practice, blood pressure reduction, and the general effects of relaxation following a controlled trial of behavior modification for reducing coronary risks. *Stress Medicine, 3,* 101–107.

Stern, M., & Karraker, K. H. (1989). Sex stereotyping of infants: A review of gender labeling studies. *Sex Roles, 20,* 501.

Stern, P. C. (1976). Effect of incentives and education on resource conservation decisions in a simulated commons dilemma. *Journal of Personality and Social Psychology, 34,* 1285–1292.

Sternberg, R. J. (1980). Sketch of a componential subtheory of intelligence. *Behavioral and Brain Sciences, 3,* 573–614.

Sternberg, R. J. (1985). Implicit theories of intelligence, creativity, and wisdom. *Journal of Personality and Social Psychology, 49*(3), 607–627.

Sternberg, R. J. (1988). *The triangle of love.* New York: Basic Books.

Sternberg, R. J., & Barnes, M. L. (Eds.). (1988). *The psychology of love.* New Haven: Yale University Press.

Sternberg, R. J., & Grajek, S. (1984). The nature of love. *Journal of Personality and Social Psychology, 47,* 312–329.

Sternberg, S. (1966). High-speed scanning in human memory. *Science, 153,* 652–654.

Sternberg, S. (1967). Two operations in character-recognition: Some evidence from reaction-time measurements. *Perception and Psychophysics, 2,* 45–53.

Sternberg, S. (1969). Mental processes revealed by reaction-time experiments. *American Scientist, 57,* 421–457.

Stevens, D. P., & Truss, C. V. (1985). Stability and change in adult personality over 12 and 20 years. *Developmental Psychology, 21,* 568–584.

Stevens, M. J. (1992). Predictors of existential openness. *Journal of Research in Personality, 26,* 32–43.

Steward, V. M. (1973). Tests of the "carpentered world" hypothesis by race and environment in American and Zambia. *International Journal of Psychology, 8,* 83–94.

Stogdill, R. M. (1948). Personal factors associated with leadership: A survey of the literature. *Journal of Psychology, 25,* 35–71.

Stokols, D. (1972). On the distinction between density and crowding: Some implications for future research. *Psychological Review, 79,* 275–277.

Stone, A. A., Cox, D. S., Valdimarsdottir, H., & Jandorf, L. (1987). Evidence that secretory IgA antibody is associated with daily mood. *Journal of Personality and Social Psychology, 52,* 988–993.

Stoner, J. A. F. (1961). *A comparison of individual and group decisions involving risk.* Unpublished master's thesis, Massachusetts Institute of Technology.

Straus, M., Gelles, R., & Steinmetz, S. (1980). *Behind closed doors: Violence in the American family.* Garden City, NY: Doubleday.

Streissguth, A. P., Landesman-Dwyer, S., Martin, J. C., & Smith, D. W. (1980). Teratogenic effects of alcohol in humans and laboratory animals. *Science, 209,* 353–361.

Stricker, E. M. (1981). Thirst and sodium appetite after colloid treatment in rate. *Journal of Comparative and Physiological Psychology, 95,* 1–25.

Strickland, B. R. (1987). On the threshold of a second century of psychology. *American Psychologist, 42*(12), 1055–1056.

Stroebe, M., Gergen, M. M., Gergen, K. J., & Stroebe, W. (1992). Broken hearts or broken bonds: Love and death in historical perspective. *American Psychologist, 47,* 1205–1212.

Stroebe, W., & Stroebe, M. (1992). *Health psychology.* London: Open University.

Stroebe, W., Diehl, M., & Abakoumkin, G. (1992). The illusion of group effectivity. *Personality and Social Psychology Bulletin, 18,* 643–650.

Strohmeyer, C. F. (1970, December). Eidetikers. *Psychology Today,* 76–80.

Strube, M. J., Miles, M. E., & Finch, W. H. (1981). The social facilitation of a simple task: Field tests of alternative explanations. *Personality and Social Psychology Bulletin, 7,* 701–707.

Styron, William. (1990). *Darkness visible: A memoir of madness.* New York: Random House.

Suedfeld, P., & Rank, A. D. (1976). Revolutionary leaders: Long-term success as a function of changes in conceptual complexity. *Journal of Personality and Social Psychology, 34,* 169–178.

Sullivan, M. W., & Lewis, M. (1989). Emotion and cognition in infancy: Facial expressions during contingency learning. *International Journal of Behavioral Development, 12,* 221–237.

Sullivan, M. W., Lewis, M., & Alessandri, S. M. (1992). Cross-age stability in emotional expressions during learning and extinction. *Developmental Psychology, 28*(1), 58–63.

Suls, J., & Wills, T. A. (Eds.). (1991). *Social comparison: Contemporary theory and research.* Hillsdale, NJ: LEA.

Suls, J. M., & Fletcher, E. (1985). The relative efficacy of avoidant and nonavoidant coping strategies: A meta-analysis. *Health Psychology, 4,* 249–288.

Suls, J. M., & Miller, R. L. (1977). *Social comparison processes.* New York: Wiley.

Suls, J. M., & Mullen, B. (1981). Life events, perceived control, and illness: The role of uncertainty. *Journal of Human Stress, 7,* 30–34.

Suls, J. M., & Wan, C. K. (1989). Effects of sensory and procedural information on coping with stressful medical procedures and pain: A meta-analysis. *Journal of Consulting and Clinical Psychology, 57,* 372–379.

Suomi, S. J., & Harlow, H. F. (1972). Social rehabilitation of isolate-reared monkeys. *Developmental Psychology, 6,* 487–496.

Super, D. E. (1980). A life-span, life-space, approach to career development. *Journal of Vocational Behavior, 13,* 282–298.

Super, D. E. (1985). Coming of age in Middletown. *American Psychologist, 40*(4), 405–414.

Swaab, D. F., & Hoffman, M. A. (1990). An enlarged suprachiasmatic nucleus in homosexual men. *Brain Research, 537,* 141.

Swain, R. A., Shinkman, P. G., Nordholm, A. F., & Thompson, R. F. (1992). Cerebellar stimulation as an unconditioned stimulus in classical conditioning. *Behavioral Neuroscience, 106,* 739–750.

Swanson, J. M., & Kinsbourne, M. (1976). Stimulant-related state-dependent learning in hyperactive children. *Science, 192,* 1354–1357.

Sweeney, P. D., Anderson, K., & Bailey, S. (1986). Attributional style in depression: A meta-analytic review. *Journal of Personality and Social Psychology, 50,* 974–998.

Szapocznik, J., Perez-Vidal, A., Brickman, A. L., Foote, F. H., Santisteban, D., Hervis, O., & Kurtines, W. M. (1988). Engaging adolescent drug abusers and their families in treatment: A strategic structural systems approach. *Journal of Consulting and Clinical Psychology, 56,* 552–557.

Szasz, T. S. (1961). *The myth of mental illness.* New York: Harper & Row.

Tajfel, H., & Turner, J. C. (1986). The social identity theory of intergroup behavior. In S. Worchel & W. G. Austin (Eds.), *Psychology of intergroup relations.* Chicago: Nelson-Hall.

Takahashi, J. S., & Zatz, M. (1982). Regulation of circadian rhythmicity. *Science, 217,* 1104–1111.

Talbot, J. D., Marrett, S., Evans, A. C., Meyer, E., Bushnell, M. C., & Duncan, G. H. (1991). Multiple representations of pain in human cerebral cortex. *Science, 251,* 1355–1358.

Tanaka, H. (1980). The Japanese method of preparing today's graduate to become tomorrow's manager. *Personnel Journal, 59,* 109–112.

Tannen, D. (1990). *You just don't understand: Men and women in conversation.* New York: Morrow.

Tanner, I. (1976). *The gift of grief.* New York: Hawthorne Books.

Targ, R., & Puthoff, H. (1977). *Mind-reach.* New York: Delacorte Press.

Tavris, C. (1989). *Anger: The misunderstood emotion* (rev. ed.). New York: Simon & Schuster.

Taylor, F. W. (1911). *Scientific management.* New York: Harper.

Taylor, S. E. (1991). *Health psychology* (2nd ed.) New York: McGraw-Hill.

Terborg, J. R., Castore, C., & DeNinno, J. A. (1976). A longitudinal field investigation of the impact of group composition on group performance and cohesion. *Journal of Personality and Social Psychology, 34,* 782–790.

Terman, L. M. (1925). *Genetic studies of genius: Mental and physical traits of a thousand gifted children* (Vol. 1). Stanford, CA: Stanford University Press.

Terman, M. (1988). On the question of mechanism in phototherapy for seasonal affective disorder: Considerations for clinical efficacy and epidemiology. *Journal of Biological Rhythms, 3,* 155–172.

Terrace, H. S. (1985). In the beginning was the "name." *American Psychologist, 40*(9), 1011–1028.

Terrace, H. S., Petitto, L. A., Sanders, D. L., & Bever, T. G. (1979). Can an ape create a sentence? *Science, 206,* 891–902.

Tetlock, P. E. (1979). Identifying victims of groupthink from public statements of decision makers. *Journal of Personality and Social Psychology, 37,* 1314–1324.

Theorell, T. (1982). Review of research on life events and cardiovascular illness. *Advances in Cardiology, 29,* 140–147.

Thibaut, J. W., & Kelley, H. H. (1959). *The social psychology of groups.* New York: Wiley.

Thibaut, J. W., & Kelley, H. H. (1978). *Interpersonal relations.* New York: Wiley.

Thibodeau, R., & Aronson, E. (1992). Taking a closer look: Reasserting the role of the self-concept in dissonance theory. *Personality and Social Psychology Bulletin, 18,* 591–602.

Tholey, P. (1983). Techniques for controlling and manipulating lucid dreams. *Perceptual and Motor Skills, 57,* 79–90.

Thomas, C. B., Duszynski, K. R., & Shaffer, J. W. (1979). Family attitudes reported in youth as potential predictors of cancer. *Psychosomatic Medicine, 41,* 287–301.

Thomas, L. (1974). *Lives of a cell: Notes of a biology watcher.* New York: Viking Press.

Thomas, R. M. (Ed.). (1988). *Oriental theories of human development.* New York: Peter Lang.

Thompson, B., & Borrello, G. M. (1992). Different views of love: Deductive and inductive lines of inquiry. *Correct Directions in Psychological Science, 1,* 154–156.

Thompson, L. A., Detterman, D. K., & Plomin, R. (1991). Associations between cognitive abilities and scholastic achievement: Genetic overlap but environmental differences. *Psychological Science, 2,* 158–165.

Thompson, R. (1986). The neurobiology of learning and memory. *Science, 233,* 941–947.

Thompson, R. (1987). The cerebellum and memory storage: Response to James R. Bloedel. *Science, 238,* 1729–1730.

Thompson, R. F., Patterson, M. M., & Berger, T. W. (1978). Associative learning in the mammalian nervous system. In T. J. Teyler (Ed.), *Brain and learning.* Stamford, CT: Greylock Publishers.

Thompson, S. C. (1981). Will it hurt less if I can control it? A complex answer to a simple question. *Psychological Bulletin, 90,* 89–101.

Thorndike, E. L. (1931). *Human learning.* New York: Century.

Thorndike, E. L., et al. (1928). *Adult learning.* New York: Macmillan.

Thornton, G. C., III, & Zorich, S. (1980). Training to improve observer accuracy. *Journal of Applied Psychology, 65,* 351–354.

Thurstone, L. L. (1938). Primary mental abilities. *Psychometric Monographs,* No. 1.

Tilley, A. J., & Empson, J. A. C. (1978). REM sleep and memory consolidation. *Biological Psychology, 6,* 293–233.

Tinbergen, N. (1951). *The study of instinct.* Oxford: Oxford University Press.

Tisak, M. S., & Turiel, E. (1988). Variation in seriousness of transgressions and children's moral and conventional concepts. *Developmental Psychology, 24*(3), 352–357.

Tizard, B. (1975). *Early childhood education—A review discussion of current research in Britain.* Windsor, England: NFER.

Tizard, B., & Rees, J. (1975). The effect of early institutional rearing on the behaviour problems and affectional relationships of four-year-old children. *Journal of Child Psychology and Psychiatry & Allied Disciplines 16*(1), 61–73.

Tolman, C. W., & Wilson, G. T. (1965). Social feeding in domestic chicks. *Animal Behavior, 13,* 134–142.

Tolman, E. C. (1932). *Purposive behavior in animals and men.* New York: University of California Publications in Psychology.

Tolman, E. C., & Honzik, C. H. (1930). Insight in rats. *University of California Publ. Psychology, 4,* 215–232.

Tomkins, S. S. (1981a). The role of facial response in the experience of emotion: A reply to Tourangeau and Ellsworth. *Journal of Personality and Social Psychology, 40,* 355–357.

Tomkins, S. S. (1981b). The quest for primary motives: Biography and autobiography of an idea. *Journal of Personality and Social Psychology, 41,* 306–329.

Tonry, M. (1991). The politics and processes of sentencing commissions. *Crime and Delinquency, 37,* 309.

Tonry, M., Ohlin, L. E., & Farrington, D. P. (1991). *Human development and criminal behavior.* New York: Springer-Verlag.

Torentzky, L. G., & Solomon, T. (with T. Bikson, R. Cole, L. Friedman, J. Hage, C. A. Kiesler, O. Larsen, D. Menzel, S. D. Nelson, L. Sechrest, D. Stokes, & G. Zaltman). (1982). Contributions of social science to innovation and productivity. *American Psychologist, 37,* 737–746.

Tourangeau, R., & Ellsworth, P. C. (1979). The role of facial response in the experience of emotion. *Journal of Personality and Social Psychology, 37,* 1519–1531.

Trad, P. (1992). *Interventions with infants and parents: The theory and practice of previewing.* New York: Wiley.

Trick, R. W. (1985). Communicating emotions: The role of prosodic features. *Psychological Bulletin, 97*(3), 412–429.

Triplett, N., (1897). The dynamogenic factors in peacemaking and competition. *American Journal of Psychology, 9,* 507–533.

True, R. M. (1949). Experimental control in hypnotic age regression. *Science, 110,* 583–584.

Tucker, D. M. (1989). Asymmetries of neural architecture and the structure of emotional experience. In R. Johnson & W. Roth (Eds.), *Eighth event-related potentials international conference.* New York: Oxford University Press.

Tucker, J., & Friedman, S. T. (1972). Population density and group size. *American Journal of Sociology, 77,* 742–749.

Tulving, E. (1972). Episodic and semantic memory. In E. Tulving & W. Donaldson (Eds.), *Organization of memory.* New York: Academic Press.

Tulving, E., & Pearlstone, Z. (1966). Availability versus accessibility of information in memory for words. *Journal of Verbal Learning and Verbal Behavior, 5,* 381–391.

Turnbull, C. (1961). Some observations regarding the experiences and behavior of the Bambuti pygmies. *American Journal of Psychology, 74,* 304–308.

Turner, B. F., & Adams, C. G. (1988). Reported change in preferred sexual activity over the adult years. *Journal of Sex Research, 25*, 289–303.

Turner, J. A., & Clancy, S. (1988). Comparison of operant behavioral and cognitive-behavioral group treatment for chronic low back pain. *Journal of Consulting and Clinical Psychology, 56*, 261–266.

Turner, J. C. (1985). Social categorization and the self-concept: A social cognitive theory of group behavior. In E. J. Lawler (Ed.), *Advances in group processes: Theory and research*. Vol. 12. Greenwich, CT: JAI Press.

Turner, R. H., & Killian, L. M. (1972). *Collective behavior* (3rd ed.). Englewood Cliffs, NJ: Prentice-Hall.

Turpin, G., Tarrier, N., & Sturgeon, D. (1988). Social psychophysiology and the study of biopsychosocial models of schizophrenia. In H. L. Wagner (Ed.), *Social psychophysiology and emotions: Theory and clinical applications*. New York: Wiley.

Tversky, B. (1973). Encoding processes in recognition and recall. *Cognitive Psychology, 5*, 275–287.

Tyerman, A., & Spencer, C. (1983). A critical test of the Sherifs' Robber's Cave experiments: Intergroup competition and cooperation between groups of well-acquainted individuals. *Small Group Behavior, 14*, 515–531.

Udry, J. R. & Morris, N. M. (1968). Distribution of coitus in the menstrual cycle. *Mature, 220*, 593–596.

Ullmann, L., & Krasner, L. (1976). *A psychological approach to abnormal behavior*. (2nd ed.). Englewood Cliffs, NJ: Prentice-Hall.

Vaillant, G. E. (1977). *Adaptation to life*. Boston: Little, Brown.

Vallone, R. P., Ross, L., & Lepper, M. R. (1985). The hostile media phenomenon: Biases perception and perceptions of media bias in coverage of the Beirut massacre. *Journal of Personality and Social Psychology, 49*, 557–569.

Van Lancker, D. (1987). Old familiar voices. *Psychology Today, 21*(11), 12–13.

Van Raalte, J. L., Brewer, B. W., Nemeroff, C. J., & Linder, D. E. (1991). Chance orientation and superstitious behavior on the putting green. *Journal of Sport Behavior, 14*(1), 41–50.

Vandell, D. L., & Corasaniti, M. A. (1990). Child care and family: Complex contributors to child development. In K. McCartney (Ed.), *New directions in child development*. San Francisco: Jossey-Bass.

Vandell, D. L., & Ramanan, J. (1991). Children in the national longitudinal survey of youth: Choices in after-school care and child development. *Developmental Psychology, 27*, 637–643.

VanDyke, C., & Byck, R. (1982). Cocaine. *Scientific American, 246*(3), 108–119.

Veroff, J., Atkinson, J. W., Feld, S. C., & Gurin, G. (1960). The use of thematic apperception to assess motivation in a nationwide interview study. *Psychological Monographs, 74*(12, Whole No. 499).

Visintainer, M., Volpicelli, J., & Seligman, M. (1982). Tumor rejection in rats after inescapable or escapable shock. *Science, 216*, 437–439.

Vokey, J. R., & Read, J. D. (1985). Subliminal messages: Between the devil and the media. *American Psychologist, 40*, 1231–1239.

von Békésy, G. (1949). The vibration of the cochlear partition in anatomical preparations in the models of the inner ear. *Journal of the Acoustical Society of America, 21*, 235–245.

Votey, H. L. (1991). Employment, age, race and crime: A theoretic investigation. *Journal of Quantitative Criminology, 7*, 123–153.

Vrij, A., & Winkel, F. W. (1991). Cultural patterns in Dutch and Surinam nonverbal behavior: An analysis of simulated police/citizen encounters. *Journal of Nonverbal Behavior, 15*, 169.

Vroom, V. H. (1964). *Work and motivation*. New York: Wiley.

Wachtel, P. (1977). *Psychoanalysis and behavior therapy: Toward an integration*. New York: Basic Books.

Wagner, R. K., Sternberg, R. J. (1985). Practical intelligence in real-world pursuits: The role of tacit knowledge. *Journal of Personality and Social Psychology, 49*(2), 436–458.

Wagner, R. V. (1992). Psychologists in pursuit of a Division of Peace Psychology: A history. *Peace Psychology Bulletin, 1*(1), 9–12.

Wahba, M. A., & Bridwell, L. B. (1976). Maslow reconsidered: A review of research on the need hierarchy theory. *Organizational Behavior and Human Performance, 15*, 212–240.

Waitzkin, H., & Stoeckle, J. B. (1976). Information control and the micropolitics of health care. *Social Science and Medicine, 10*, 263–276.

Wakefield, J. C. (1992). Disorder as harmful dysfunctioning: A conceptual critique of DSM-III-R's definition of mental disorder. *Psychological Review, 99*, 232–247.

Wald, G. (1968). The molecular basis of visual excitation. *Nature 219*, 800–807.

Waldfogel, S. (1948). The frequency and affective character of childhood memories. *Psychological Monographs, 62*(Whole No. 291).

Waldrop, M. M. (1987). The workings of working memory. *Science, 237*, 1564–1567.

Walk, R. D., & Gibson, E. J. A. (1961). Comparative and analytic study of visual depth perception. *Psychological Monographs, 75*(15, Whole No. 519).

Walker, L. J., & Taylor, J. H. (1991). Stage transitions in moral reasoning: A longitudinal study of developmental processes. *Developmental Psychology, 27*, 330–337.

Wallace, P. (1977). Individual discrimination of humans by odor. *Physiology and Behavior, 19*, 577–579.

Wallach, H., Newman, E. G., & Rosenzweig, M. R. (1949). The precedence effect in sound localization. *American Journal of Psychology, 62*, 315–336.

Wallach, M. A., Kogan, N., & Bem, D. J. (1964). Diffusion of responsibility and level of risk taking in groups. *Journal of Abnormal and Social Psychology, 68*, 263–274.

Wallerstein, J. S., & Kelley, J. B. (1980). *Surviving the break-up: How children and parents cope with divorce*. New York: Basic Books.

Walsh, J. (1928). *Laughter and health*. New York: Appleton.

Walster, E., & Walster, G. W. (1978). *A new look at love*. Reading, MA: Addison-Wesley.

Walster, E., Aronson, E., & Abrahams, D. (1966). On increasing the persuasiveness of a low prestige communicator. *Journal of Experimental Social Psychology, 2*, 325–342.

Walster, E., Walster, G. W., & Berscheid, E. (1978). *Equity: Theory and research*. Boston: Allyn & Bacon.

Warr, P. B., & Jackson, P. R. (1984). Men without jobs: Some correlations of age and length of unemployment. *Journal of Occupational Psychology, 57*, 77–85.

Washton, A. M. (1985, December) The cocaine epidemic: Special dangers of "CRACK." *U.S. Journal of Drug and Alcohol Dependence, 9*, 17.

Waterman, A. S., & Goodman, J. A. (1976). A longitudinal study of ego identity development at a liberal arts college. *Journal of Youth and Adolescence, 5*, 361–369.

Waterman, W. S. (1982). Identity development from adolescence to adulthood: An extension of theory and a review of research. *Developmental Psychology, 18*(3), 341–358.

Watson, J. B. (1913). Psychology as the behaviorist views it. *Psychological Review, 20*, 158–177.

Watson, J. B., & Rayner, R. (1920). Conditioned emotional reactions. *Journal of Experimental Psychology, 3*, 1–14.

Weary, G. (1980). Examination of affect and egotism as mediators of bias in causal attributions. *Journal of Personality and Social Psychology, 38*, 348–357.

Webb, W. B. (1975). *Sleep: The gentle tyrant*. Englewood Cliffs, NJ: Prentice-Hall.

Webb, W. B., & Cartwright, R. D. (1978). Sleep and dreams. *Annual Review of Psychology, 29*, 223–252.

Weber, M. (1957). *The theory of social and economic organizations* (A. M. Henderson & T. Parsons, Trans.). New York: Free Press.

Wechsler, D. (1939). *The measurement of adult intelligence*. Baltimore: Williams and Wilkins.

Weick, K. E. Bougon, M. G., & Maruyama, G. (1976). The equity context. *Organizational Behavior and Human Performance, 15*, 32–65.

Weidner, G., & Chesney, M. A. (1985). Stress, Type A behavior, and coronary heart disease. In W. E. Connor & J. D. Bristow (Eds.), *Coronary heart disease: Prevention, complications and treatment* (pp. 157–172). Philadelphia: Lippincott.

Weinberger, D. R., & Kleinman, J. E. (1986). Observations on the brain in schizophrenia. In A. J. Frances & R. E. Hales (Eds.), *American Psychiatric Association Annual Review* (Vol. 5, pp. 42–67). Washington, DC: American Psychiatric Press.

Weindruch, R., & Walford, R. L. (1982). Dietary restriction in mice beginning at 1 year of age: Effect on life-span and spontaneous cancer incidence. *Science, 215*, 1415–1418.

Weiner, R. D. (1984). Does ECT cause brain damage? *Behavioral and Brain Sciences, 7*, 1–53.

Weinstein, C. S. (1991). The classroom as a social context for learning. *Annual Review of Psychology, 42*, 493–526.

Weiss, B. (1981). Food colors and behavior. *Science, 212*, 578–579.

Weiss, J. M. (1977). Psychological and behavioral influences on gastrointestinal lesions in animal models. In J. D. Maser & M. E. P. Seligman (Eds.), *Psychopathology: Experimental models.* San Francisco: Freeman.

Weisz, D. J., & LoTurco, J. J. (1988). Reflex facilitation of the nictitating membrane response remains after cerebellar lesions. *Behavioral Neuroscience, 102*(2), 203–209.

Welgan, P. R. (1974). Learned control of gastric acid secretions in ulcer patients. *Psychosomatic Medicine, 36*, 411–419.

Weyant, J. M. (1986). *Applied social psychology.* New York: Oxford University Press.

Wheeler, L., & Miyake, K. (1992). Social comparison in everyday life. *Journal of Personality and Social Psychology, 62*, 760–773.

Wheeler, R. J., & Frank, M. S. (1988). Identification of stress buffers. *Behavioral Medicine, 14,*(2), 78–89.

White, B. C., Lincoln, C. A., Pearce, N. W., Reeb, R., & Vaida, C. (1980). Anxiety and muscle tension as consequences of caffeine withdrawal. *Science, 209*, 1547–1548.

White, D. G., Phillips, K. C., Clifford, B. R., Davies, M. M., Elliott, J. R., & Pitts, M. K. (1989). AIDS and intimate relationships: Adolescents' knowledge and attitudes. *Current Psychology, 8*, 130–143.

White, L. T. (1990). Social psychology, European style. (Review of Hewstone, Stroebe, Codol, and Stephenson. *Introduction to social psychology: A European perspective.*) *Contemporary Psychology, 35*, 1153–1154.

White, S. H., & Pillemer, D. B. (1979). Childhood amnesia and the development of socially accessible memory systems. In J. F. Kihlstrom & F. J. Evans (Eds.), *Functional disorders of memory.* Hillsdale, NJ: Lawrence Erlbaum Associates.

Whiting, B. B., & Whiting, J. W. M. (1975). *Children of six cultures: A psycho-cultural analysis.* Cambridge, MA: Harvard University Press.

Whitten, W. K., & Bronson, F. H. (1970). The role of pheromones in mammalian reproduction. In J. W. Johnston, D. G. Moulton, & A. Turk (Eds.), *Advances in chemoreception* (Vol. 1). New York: Appleton-Century-Crofts.

Whorf, B. L. (1956). *Language, thought and reality* (J. B. Carroll, Ed.). Cambridge, MIT Press.

Widiger, T. A., & Trull, T. J. (1991). Diagnosis and clinical assessment. *Annual Review of Psychology, 42*, 109–133.

Widom, C. S. (1989). Does violence beget violence? A critical examination of the literature. *Psychological Bulletin, 106*, 3–28.

Wiebe, D. J., & McCallum, D. M. (1986). Health practices and hardiness as mediators in the stress-illness relationship. *Health Psychology, 5*, 425–438.

Wilkinson, R. (1991, June 12). Inequality is bad for your health. *The Guardian.*

Williams, M. D. (1976). *Retrieval from very long-term memory.* Unpublished doctoral dissertation, University of California, San Diego.

Williams, R. B., Jr., Haney, T. L., Lee, K. L., Kong, Y. H., Blumenthal, J. A., & Whalen, R. E. (1980). Type A behavior, hostility, and coronary atherosclerosis. *Psychosomatic Medicine, 42*, 539–549.

Wilson, G. T., & O'Leary, G. D. (1986). *Behavior therapy* (2nd ed.). Englewood Cliffs, NJ: Prentice-Hall.

Wilson, J. D., George, F. W., & Griffin, J. E. (1981). The hormonal control of sexual development. *Science, 211*(4488), 1278–1284.

Winch, R. F. (1958). *Mate selection.* New York: Harper.

Winick, M., & Rosso, P. (1975). Malnutrition and central nervous system development. In J. W. Prescott, M. S. Read, & D. B. Coursin (Eds.), *Brain function and malnutrition.* New York: Wiley.

Witelson, S. F. (1985). The brain connection: The corpus callosum is larger in left-handers. *Science, 229*, 665–668.

Witelson, S. F. (1987). Neurobiological aspects of language in children. *Child Development, 52*, 653–688.

Witelson, S. F. (1989). Hand and sex differences in the isthmus and genu of the human corpus callosum: A postmortem morphological study. *Brain, 112*, 799.

Witmer, J., Rich, C., Barcikowski, R., & Mague, J. (1983). Psychosocial characteristics mediating the stress response: An exploratory study. *Personnel and Guidance Journal, 62*, 73–77.

Wold, D. A. (1968). The adjustment of siblings to childhood leukemia. Unpublished manuscript, University of Washington, Seattle.

Wolkowitz, O. M., Doran, A. R., Cohen, M. R., Cohen, R. M., Wise, T. N., & Picker, D. (1988). Single dose naloxone acutely reduces eating in obese humans: Behavioral and biochemical effects. *Biological Psychiatry, 24*, 483–487.

Wolpe, J. (1952). Experimental neuroses as learning behavior. *British Journal of Psychiatry, 43*, 243–268.

Wolpe, J. (1958). *Psychotherapy by reciprocal inhibition.* Stanford, CA: Stanford University Press.

Wolpe, J. (1973). *The practice of behavior therapy* (2nd ed.). New York: Pergamon Press.

Wolpe, J. (1982). *The practice of behavior therapy* (3rd ed.). New York: Pergamon Press.

Wood, J. V., Taylor, S. E., & Lichtman, R. R. (1985). Social comparison in adjustment to breast cancer. *Journal of Personality and Social Psychology, 49*, 1169–1183.

Woods, P. J., & Burns, J. (1984). Type A behavior and illness in general. *Journal of Behavioral Medicine, 7*, 411–415.

Wright, L. (1988). The Type A behavior pattern and coronary artery disease: Quest for the active ingredients and the elusive mechanism. *American Psychologist, 43*, 2–14.

Wundt, W. (1900–1920). Volkerspsychologie. [Psychology of societies.] (10 vols.). Leipzig: Englemann.

Wurtman, R. J., & Wurtman, J. J. (1989). Carbohydrates and depression. *Scientific American, 262*, 68–75.

Wysocki, T., Green, L., & Huxtable, K. (1988). Behavioral application of reflectance meters with memory in juvenile diabetics. *Diabetes, 37*, Suppl. 1, 18A.

Yang, R. K., Zweig, A. R., Douthitt, T. C., & Federman, E. J. (1976). Successive relationships between maternal attitudes during pregnancy, analgesic medication during labor and delivery, and newborn behavior. *Developmental Psychology, 12*, 6–14.

Yerkes, R. M., & Dodson, J. D. (1908). The relations of strength of stimulus to rapidity of habit-formation. *Journal of Comparative Neurology, 28*, 459–482.

Young, J. G., Kavanagh, M. E., Anderson, G. M., Shaywitz, B. A., & Cohen, D. J. (1982). Clinical neurochemistry of autism and associated disorders. *Journal of Autism and Developmental Disorders, 12*, 147–165.

Youngstrom, N. (1992, April 24–25). Field of psychoanalysis undergoes resurgence. *APA Monitor.*

Yovetich, N. A., Dale, J. A., & Hudak, M. A. (1990). Benefits of humor in reduction of threat-induced anxiety. *Psychological Reports, 66*, 51–58.

Zaidel, E. (1975). A technique for presenting lateralized visual input with prolonged exposure. *Vision Research, 15*, 283–289.

Zajonc, R. B. (1976). Family configuration and intelligence. *Science, 192*, 227–236.

Zajonc, R. B. (1980). Feeling and thinking: Preferences need not inferences. *American Psychologist, 35*, 151–175.

Zajonc, R. B. (1984). On the primacy of affect. *American Psychologist, 39* (2), 117–123.

Zajonc, R. B. (1986). The decline and rise of Scholastic Aptitude Scores: A prediction derived from the confluence model. *American Psychologist, 41*, 862–867.

Zajonc, R. B., & Markus, G. B. (1975). Birth order and intellectual development. *Psychological Review, 82*, 74–88.

Zaleska, M. (1978). Some experimental results: Majority influence on group decisions. In H. Brandstatter, J. H. Davis, & H. Schuler. (Eds.), *Dynamics of group decisions.* Beverly Hills, CA: Sage.

Zeki, S. (1983). Color coding in the cerebral cortex: The responses of wavelength-selective and colour coded cells in monkey visual cortex to changes in wavelength composition. *Neuro-science, 9*, 767–781.

Zigler, E., & Levine, J. (1981). Age on first hospitalization of schizophrenics: A developmental approach. *Journal of Abnormal Psychology, 90*, 459–467.

Zillman, D. (1971). Excitation transfer in communication-mediated aggressive behavior. *Journal of Experimental Social Psychology, 7*, 419–434.

Zillmann, D. (1979). *Hostility and aggression.* New York: Halsted Press.

Zillmann, D. (1983). Arousal and aggression. In R. Geen & E. Donnerstein (Eds.), *Aggression: Theoretical and empirical reviews* (Vol. 1). Orlando, FL: Academic Press.

Zillmann, D. (1984). *Connections between sex and aggression.* Hillsdale, NJ: Lawrence Erlbaum.

Zillman, D., Bryant, J, & Sapolsky, B. S. (1989). Enjoyment from sports spectatorship. In J. H. Goldstein (Ed.), *Sports, games, and play* (2nd ed.). Hillsdale, NJ: Lawrence Erlbaum Associates.

Zimbardo, P. G. (1969). The human choice: Individuation, reason, and order versus deindividuation, impulse and chaos. In W. J. Arnold & D. Levine (Eds.), *Nebraska symposium on motivation* (Vol. 17). Lincoln, NE: University of Nebraska Press.

Zimbardo, P. G., Andersen, S. M., & Kabat, L. G. (1981). Induced hearing deficit generates experimental paranoia. *Science, 212,* 1529–1531.

Zimmerman, B., & Smith, D. (1978). *Careers in health: The professionals give you the inside picture about their jobs.* Boston: Beacon Press.

Zizek, S. (1991). *For they know not what they do: Enjoyment as a political factor.* London: Verso.

Zola-Morgan, S., & Squire, L. R. (1990). The neuropsychology of memory: Parallel findings in humans and nonhuman primates. In A. Diamond (Ed.), *The development and neural bases of higher cognitive functions.* New York: New York Academy of Sciences.

Zola-Morgan, S., Squire, L. R., & Amaral, D. G. (1986). Human amnesia and the medial temporal region: Enduring memory impairment following a bilateral lesion limited to field CAI of the hippocampus. *Journal of Neuroscience, 6,* 2950–2967.

Zucker, I., Rusak, B., & King, R. G. (1976). Neural bases for circadian rhythms in rodent behavior. In A. H. Riesen & R. F. Thompson (Eds.), *Advances in psychobiology* (Vol. 3). New York: Wiley.

Zuckerman, M. (1979). *Sensation seeking: Beyond the optimal level of arousal.* Hillsdale, NJ: Lawrence Erlbaum Associates.

Zuckerman, M., Klorman, R., Larrance, D. T., & Spiegel, N. H. (1981). Facial, autonomic, and subjective components of emotion: The facial feedback hypothesis vs. the externalizer-internalizer distinction. *Journal of Personality and Social Psychology, 41,* 929–944.

Zullow, H. M., Oettingen, G., Peterson, C., & Seligman, M. E. P. (1988). Pessimistic explanatory style in the historical record. *American Psychologist, 43,* 673–682.

# CREDITS

## Illustrations and Text

**Plate 8B** From G. Wald and P. K. Brown, "Human Color Vision and Color Blindness" in *Cold Spring Harbor Laboratory Symposia on Quantitative Biology* 30:351. Copyright © 1965 Cold Spring Harbor Laboratory Press. Used by permission.
**Plate 12B** From John W. Santrock, *Children.* Copyright © 1988 Wm. C. Brown Communications, Inc., Dubuque, Iowa. All Rights Reserved. Reprinted by permission.

### Chapter 2

**Figure 2.3** From Philip M. Groves and Kurt Schlesinger, *Introduction to Biological Psychology,* 2d ed. Copyright © 1982 Wm. C. Brown Communications, Inc., Dubuque, Iowa. All Rights Reserved. Reprinted by permission.
**Figure 2.4** From Leland G. Johnson, *Biology,* 2d ed. Copyright © 1987 Wm. C. Brown Communications, Inc., Dubuque, Iowa. All Rights Reserved. Reprinted by permission.
**Figure 2.5** From Kurt Schlesinger and Philip M. Groves, *Psychology: A Dynamic Science.* Copyright © 1976 Wm. C. Brown Communications, Inc., Dubuque, Iowa. All Rights Reserved. Reprinted by permission.
**Figure 2.7** From John W. Hole, Jr., *Human Anatomy and Physiology,* 3d ed. Copyright © 1984 Wm. C. Brown Communications, Inc., Dubuque, Iowa. All Rights Reserved. Reprinted by permission.
**Figure 2.10A** From John W. Hole, Jr., *Human Anatomy,* 4th ed. Copyright © 1987 Wm. C. Brown Communications, Inc., Dubuque, Iowa. All Rights Reserved. Reprinted by permission.
**Figure 2.10B** From Leland G. Johnson, *Biology,* 2d ed. Copyright © 1987 Wm. C. Brown Communications, Inc., Dubuque, Iowa. All Rights Reserved. Reprinted by permission.
**Figure 2.12** Reprinted with the permission of Macmillan Publishing Company from *The Cerebral Cortex of Man* by Wilder Penfield and Theodore Rasmussen. Copyright 1950 Macmillan Publishing Company; copyright renewed © 1978 Theodore Rasmussen.
**Figure 2.13** From Benjamin B. Lahey, *Psychology: An Introduction,* 3d ed. Copyright © 1989 Wm. C. Brown Communications, Inc., Dubuque, Iowa. All Rights Reserved. Reprinted by permission.
**Figure 2.14** From John W. Hole, Jr., *Human Anatomy,* 3d ed. Copyright © 1984 Wm. C. Brown Communications, Inc., Dubuque, Iowa. All Rights Reserved. Reprinted by permission.
**Figure 2.15** From John W. Hole, Jr., *Human Anatomy,* 3d ed. Copyright © 1984 Wm. C. Brown Communications, Inc., Dubuque, Iowa. All Rights Reserved. Reprinted by permission.
**Figure 2.17** From Benjamin B. Lahey, *Psychology: An Introduction,* 2d ed. Copyright © 1986 Wm. C. Brown Communications, Inc., Dubuque, Iowa. All Rights Reserved. Reprinted by permission.

**Figure 2.18** From L. Dodge Fernald and Peter Fernald, *Introduction to Psychology,* 5th ed. Copyright © 1985 Wm. C. Brown Communications, Inc., Dubuque, Iowa. All Rights Reserved. Reprinted by permission.

### Chapter 3

**Figure 3.5** From R. J. Berger, "The Sleep and Dream Cycles" in *Sleep: Physiology and Pathology,* ed. by A. Kales. Copyright © 1969 J. B. Lippincott Co. Reprinted by permission.

### Chapter 4

**Figure 4.1** From Stuart Ira Fox, *Human Physiology,* 1st ed. Copyright © 1984 Wm. C. Brown Communications, Inc., Dubuque, Iowa. All Rights Reserved. Reprinted by permission.
**Figure 4.2** From L. Dodge Fernald and Peter Fernald, *Introduction to Psychology,* 5th ed. Copyright © 1985 Wm. C. Brown Communications, Inc., Dubuque, Iowa. All Rights Reserved. Reprinted by permission.
**Figure 4.3** From Leland G. Johnson, *Biology,* 2d ed. Copyright © 1987 Wm. C. Brown Communications, Inc., Dubuque, Iowa. All Rights Reserved. Reprinted by permission.
**Figure 4.5** From Leland G. Johnson, *Biology,* 2d ed. Copyright © 1987 Wm. C. Brown Communications, Inc., Dubuque, Iowa. All Rights Reserved. Reprinted by permission.
**Figure 4.6** From Leland G. Johnson, *Biology,* 2d ed. Copyright © 1987 Wm. C. Brown Communications, Inc., Dubuque, Iowa. All Rights Reserved. Reprinted by permission.
**Figure 4.8** From Benjamin B. Lahey, *Psychology: An Introduction,* 3d ed. Copyright © 1989 Wm. C. Brown Communications, Inc., Dubuque, Iowa. All Rights Reserved. Reprinted by permission.
**Figure 4.13a&b** From L. Dodge Fernald and Peter Fernald, *Introduction to Psychology,* 5th ed. Copyright © 1985 Wm. C. Brown Communications, Inc., Dubuque, Iowa. All Rights Reserved. Reprinted by permission.
**Figure 4.15** From Benjamin B. Lahey, *Psychology: An Introduction,* 1st ed. Copyright © 1983 Wm. C. Brown Communications, Inc., Dubuque, Iowa. All Rights Reserved. Reprinted by permission.

### Chapter 5

**Figure 5.3** From Benjamin B. Lahey, *Psychology: An Introduction,* 3d ed. Copyright © 1989 Wm. C. Brown Communications, Inc., Dubuque, Iowa. All Rights Reserved. Reprinted by permission.
**Figure 5.4** From Benjamin B. Lahey, *Psychology: An Introduction,* 3d ed. Copyright © 1989 Wm. C. Brown Communications, Inc., Dubuque, Iowa. All Rights Reserved. Reprinted by permission.
**Figure 5.8** From *Learning and Behavior* by Paul Chance. © 1979 by Wadsworth Publishing Company, Inc. Reprinted by permission of the publisher.

**Figure 5.7** From Lee C. Drickamer and Stephen H. Vessey, *Animal Behavior: Mechanisms, Ecology, and Evolution,* 3d ed. Copyright © 1992 Wm. C. Brown Communications, Inc., Dubuque, Iowa. All Rights Reserved. Reprinted by permission.

### Chapter 6

**Figure 6.7** From J. D. Bransford and M. K. Johnson, "Watching a Peace March from the 40th Floor" in *Visual Information Processing,* ed. by W. G. Chase. Copyright © 1973 Academic Press, Orlando, FL. Reprinted by permission.
**Figure 6.8** From A. M. Collins and M. R. Quillian, "Retrieval Time from Semantic Memory" in *Journal of Verbal Learning and Learning Behavior* 8:240–248. Copyright © 1969 Academic Press, Orlando, FL. Reprinted by permission.

### Chapter 7

**Figure 7.3** From "The Recognition of Threatening Facial Stimuli" by J. Aronoff, A. M. Barclay and L. A. Stevenson, 1988, *Journal of Personality and Social Psychology,* 54, pp. 647–655. Copyright 1988 by the American Psychological Association. Adapted by permission.
**Figure 7.6** Figure on page 37 showing connections among the cognitive sciences from *The Mind's New Science* by Howard Gardner. Copyright © 1985 by Howard Gardner. Reprinted by permission of Basic Books, Inc., a division of HarperCollins, Publishers, Inc.
**Figure 7.8** From *An Introduction to Cognitive Psychology* by Danny R. Moates. © 1980 Wadsworth, Inc. Reprinted by permission of the publisher.
**Figure 7A** Reprinted with permission from Scholastic Testing Service, Inc., Bensenville, Illinois.

### Chapter 8

**Figure 8.1** From Benjamin B. Lahey, *Psychology: An Introduction,* 3d ed. Copyright © 1989 Wm. C. Brown Communications, Inc., Dubuque, Iowa. All Rights Reserved. Reprinted by permission.
**Figure 8.2** From "An Opponent-process Theory of Motivation. II. Cigarette Addiction" in *Journal of Abnormal Psychology,* 81:158–171. Copyright 1973 by the American Psychological Association. Reprinted by permission.
**Figure 8.6** From "A Circocomplex Model of Affect" by James A. Russell in *Journal of Personality and Social Psychology* 39:1161–1178. Copyright 1980 by the American Psychological Association. Reprinted by permission.

### Chapter 9

**Figure 9.1** Reprinted from *Childhood and Society,* 2d Edition, by Erik H. Erikson, by permission of W. W. Norton & Company, Inc. Copyright 1950, © 1963 by W. W. Norton & Company, Inc. Copyright renewed 1978 by Erik H. Erikson.

**Figure 9.3** From John W. Hole, Jr., *Human Anatomy,* 3d ed. Copyright © 1984 Wm. C. Brown Communications, Inc., Dubuque, Iowa. All Rights Reserved. Reprinted by permission.
**Figure 9.5** From P. Salapatek, "Pattern Perception in Early Infancy" in *Infant Perception: From Sensation to Cognition,* 1, 1975, ed. by L. B. Cohen and P. Salapatek. Copyright © 1975 Academic Press, Orlando, FL. Reprinted by permission.

*Chapter 10*
**Figure 10.1** From A. F. Roche, "Secular Trends in Stature, Weight, and Maturation" in *Monographs of the Society for Research in Child Development,* 1977, 44, Serial No. 179. © The Society for Research in Child Development, Inc. Used by permission.
**Figure 10.3** From "Developmental Analysis of Conflict Caused by Opposing Attributes in the Adolescent Self-Portrait" by S. Harter and A. Monsour, 1992, *Developmental Psychology* 28(2):251–260. Copyright 1992 by the American Psychological Association.
**Figure 10.5** Reprinted by permission of the publishers from *Themes of Work and Love in Adulthood* edited by Neil J. Smelser and Erik H. Erikson, Cambridge, Mass.: Harvard University Press, Copyright © 1980 by the President and Fellows of Harvard College.
**Text box 10.1** From C. Holden, "Why Do Women Live Longer than Men?" in *Science* 238:158–160, 1987. Copyright 1987 by the AAAS. Reprinted by permission.

*Chapter 11*
**Figure 11.2** From Peter E. Nathan and S. L. Harris, *Psychopathology and Society,* p. 91. Copyright © 1975 McGraw-Hill Book Company. Reprinted by permission.
**Figure 11.7** Reprinted by permission of the publishers from Henry A. Murray, *Thematic Apperception Test,* Cambridge, Mass.: Harvard University Press, Copyright © 1943 by the President and Fellows of Harvard College, © 1971 by Henry A. Murray.

*Chapter 15*
**Table 15.2** From Donn E. Byrne, et al., "The Ubiquitous Relationship: Attitude Similarity and Attraction. A Cross-cultural Study," *Human Relations* 24:201–207, 1971. Copyright © 1971 Plenum Publishing Corporation. Used by permission.
**Figure 15.4** From David Kipnis, "The Use of Power in Organizations and in Interpersonal Settings" in *Applied Social Psychology Annual,* Vol. 5, ed. by Stuart Oskamp, 1984. Used by permission of the author.
**Figure 15.5** Adaptation of 2 figures (showing distance judgments made by subjects alone and in a group) from *The Psychology of Social Norms* by Muzafer Sherif. Copyright 1936 by Harper & Row, Publishers, Inc. Reprinted by permission of HarperCollins, Publishers, Inc.

**Figure 15.6** From Benjamin B. Lahey, *Psychology: An Introduction,* 4th ed. Copyright © 1992 Wm. C. Brown Communications, Inc., Dubuque, Iowa. All Rights Reserved. Reprinted by permission.

*Chapter 16*
**Figure 16A** From B. L. Collins and N. D. Lerner, "Assessment of Fire-Safety Symbols," *Human Factors,* 1982, Vol. 24 (1), fig. 1, p. 78. Copyright 1982 by the Human Factors Society, Inc. and reproduced by permission.
**Figure 16.3** From Ernest J. McCormick/Daniel Ilgen, *Industrial Psychology,* Seventh Edition, © 1980, p. 353. Reprinted by permission of Prentice-Hall, Inc., Englewood Cliffs, New Jersey.

## Photos

*Part Openers*
**Part 1:** © Richard Hutchings/Photo Edit; **Part 2, 3, 4:** © James Shaffer; **Part 5:** © Leo de Wys

*Color Plates*
**Plate 1A:** © Dr. Colin Chumbley/Photo Researchers; **Plate 1B:** © Dr. Christopher Frederickson; **Plate 3A:** Courtesy of American Medical Assoc.; **Plate 3B:** From Phelps and Mazziotta (1985). *Science,:*799–809 © 1985 by the AAAS.; **Plate 4A:** Dan McCoy/Rainbow; **Plate 5B:** © Helmut Gritscher; **Plate 5C:** © Douglas B. Nelson; **Plate 5D, E:** © Fritz Goro, Life Magazine Time, Inc.; **Plate 6A-1:** Courtesy of Munsell Color, Baltimore, MD; **Plate 6B:** © Morris Karol; **Plates 7A, 9A, 9B, 9C, 10A, 10B:** © Lennart Nilsson; **Plates 10C, 11B, 11C:** © Erika Stone; **Plate 11D:** © Nancy Dawe Communications; **Plate 11E:** © Erika Stone; **Plate 11F:** © Nancy Dawe Communications; **Plate 11G:** © Erika Stone; **Plate 12A:** © J. Pavlousky/Sygma

*Chapter 1*
**Figure 1.2:** © James Shaffer; **Figure 1.4:** Courtesy National Library of Medicine; **Figure 1.5:** Courtesy National Library of Medicine; **Figure 1.6:** © The Bettmann Archive; **Figure 1.7:** © Christopher Johnson/Stock Boston; **Figure 1.8:** © The Bettmann Archive

*Chapter 2*
**Figure 2.1:** Courtesy National Library of Medicine; **Figure 2.2:** © Ed Reschke; **Figure 2.9:** © Leo de Wys

*Chapter 3*
**Figure 3.3:** © Leo de Wys; **Figure 3.6:** © The Bettmann Archive; **Figure 3.7:** Courtesy Dr. Anne Pytkowitz Strussguth/University of Washington

*Chapter 4*
**Figure 4.7:** © David Young Wolff/Photo Edit; **Figure 4.9:** © Michael Newman/Photo Edit; **Figure 4.12:** © Bob Coyle; **Figure 4.17:** © Joe Sohm/Stock Market

*Chapter 5*
**Figure 5.1:** © National Anthropological Archive, Smithsonian Institute; **Figure 5.10A:** Courtesy B. F. Skinner; **Figure 5.10B:** Courtesy Gerbrands, Corp.; **Figure 5.11:** Courtesy of Albert Bandura

*Chapter 6*
**Figure 6.11:** © James Shaffer

*Chapter 7*
**Figure 7.4:** © Leo de Wys; **Figure 7.5:** Courtesy Susan Kuklin; **Figure 7.15:** © Culver Pictures, Inc.

*Chapter 8*
**Figure 8.4:** Courtesy Phillip Teitelbaum; **Figure 8.7A:** © Steve Takatsuno; **Figure 8.7B:** © Bob Coyle; **Figure 8.7C:** © Richard Good; **Figure 8.7D:** © James Shaffer; **Figure 8.7E:** © Ron Byers

*Chapter 9*
**Figure 9.4A:** © Landrum Shettles; **Figure 9.4B:** © Landrum Shettles; **Figure 9.4C:** © Steve Takatsuno; **Figure 9.4D:** © Steve Takatsuno; **Figure 9.6:** Courtesy William Vandivert and Scientific American, April 1960; **Figure 9.7:** Courtesy Harlow Primate Lab

*Chapter 10*
**Figure 10.4:** © James Shaffer; **Figure 10.6A, B, C:** © Culver Pictures, Inc.

*Chapter 11*
**Figure 11.1, 3:** © Bettmann Archives; **Figure 11.4:** Courtesy National Library of Medicine; **Figure 11.7:** © Harvard University Press

*Chapter 12*
**Figure 12.1:** © Bettmann Archives

*Chapter 13*
**Page 394:** © Mark Anton/Image Works; **Page 400:** © James Shaffer; **Page 402:** © Zefa/Stock Market

*Chapter 15*
**Figure 15.1:** © James Shaffer; **Figure 15.3:** © Mary Kate Denny/Photo Edit

*Chapter 16*
**Figure 16.4:** © Jean Claude Lejeune; **Page 493:** © James Shaffer; **Page 495:** © James Shaffer

# NAME INDEX

▼

Abakoumkin, G., 469
Abe, K., 81
Abrahams, D., 454
Abrahams, S., 482
Abrahamson, A., 213
Abramson, L. Y., 356
Ackerman, D., 120
Acocella, J. R., 377, 378, 390, 391, 408
Adamopoulos, J., 220
Adams, C. G., 334
Adams, D. B., 251
Adams, G. M., 437
Adams, G. R., 423
Adams, J. E., 118
Adams, J. S., 481
Adams, P. R., 423
Adler, J. E., 189
Adler, N., 452
Aiello, J. R., 493
Ainsworth, M. D. S., 291, 292
Ajzen, I., 250, 436, 453
Akerstedt, T., 78
Alessandri, S. M., 277
Alexander, F., 388
Alkon, D. L., 187
Allee, W. C., 462
Allen, I., 232
Allen, L. S., 48
Allport, G. W., 346, 455
Altman, I., 493
Alwin, D. R., 468
Amaral, D. G., 45, 178, 179
Amatoni, M., 81
American Psychiatric Association, 460, 480
American Psychological Association, 17, 357
*American Psychologist,* 424
Ames, F. R., 48
Amir, Y., 456
Andersen, S. M., 113
Anderson, G. M., 390
Anderson, J. R., 204
Anderson, K., 357
Anderson, M., 223, 225

Andersson, B. E., 289
Andreason, N., 44
Andreason, N. C., 383
Andrews, G. R., 499
Anisman, H., 434
Antelman, S. M., 249
Anzul, S. E., 258
APA Comittee on Drug Abuse, 381
Appels, A., 428
Archer, D., 459
Arend, R. A., 297
Argyle, M., 208, 485, 494
Argyris, C., 484
Arkin, A. M., 81
Arms, R. L., 497
Arntz, A., 124
Aron, A. P., 452
Aronoff, J., 208
Aronson, E., 435, 453, 454, 456, 464, 499
Asch, S. E., 450, 467, 499
Aschoff, J., 79
Aserinsky, E., 82
Ashmore, R. D., 455
Ashton, W., 450
Athos, A. G., 485
Atkinson, J. W., 254, 255
Atkinson, R. C., 172
Attanucci, J., 302
Au, T. K., 214
Autry, A. H., 409
Axline, V. M., 406
Ayala, G. F., 56
Ayllon, T., 401
Azrin, N. J., 401

▼

Babad, E. Y., 498
Babcock, R. L., 330
Bachevalier, J., 180
Back, K. W., 385
Badura, L. L., 79
Baer, D. E., 449
Baer, J. S., 94
Baetz, M. L., 465
Bahn, S. K., 389

Bailey, S., 357
Baillargeon, R., 296
Baker, K. H., 427
Baker, L., 406
Baker, S., 398
Bales, R. F., 486
Baltes, P. B., 330
Bancroft, J., 251
Banducci, R., 325
Bandura, A., 158, 159, 205, 346, 356, 357, 402, 404, 428, 459, 463
Banks, M., 287
Barakat, N., 48
Barber, T. X., 86, 194
Barberi, S., 79
Barcikowski, R., 427
Barclay, A. M., 208
Barnard, W. A., 456
Barnes, M. L., 451, 453
Barnett, I., 173
Baron, F., 226
Baron, R. M., 426, 432, 433
Baron, R. S., 465, 469
Bartak, L., 391
Bartholomeus, B., 62
Bartolome, J., 290
Bartus, R. T., 191
Bashi, J., 464
Bashore, T. R., 261
Baskett, L., 299
Bates, A., 173
Bateson, G., 208, 382, 458
Batson, G. D., 458
Baum, A., 428, 430, 432
Baumeister, R., 463
Baumgardner, M., 454
Baumrind, D., 297, 298
Baydar, N., 289
Baylor, D. A., 107
Beach, F. A., 250, 252
Bechtel, W., 213
Beck, A. T., 357, 386, 403, 404
Becker, H. S., 426
Becker, P. T., 276
Bednar, R. L., 406
Bedrosian, R. C., 403

# SUBJECT INDEX